BRITISH ATHLETICS 2018

Compiled by the
National Union of Track Statisticians

Editors: Tony Miller, Rob Whittingham & Peter Matthews

Publications Administrator	Stuart Mazdon 77 Forest Approach Woodford Green Essex IG8 9BU
Published by	Lulu.com Check website for details of this annual British Athletics 2017 at http://www.lulu.com/content/paperback-book/british-athletics-2017/20683043
Copyright	Umbra Athletics Limited/National Union of Track Statisticians All rights reserved ISBN 9780904612264
Front Cover:	The British 4x100 metres team World Champions
Photos:	Photograph provided by Mark Shearman MBE - Athletics Images 22, Grovelands Road, Purley, Surrey, CR8 4LA Tel: 020 8660 0156 email mark@athleticimages.com His help is greatly appreciated

CONTENTS

NATIONAL UNION OF TRACK STATISTICIANS AND COMPILERS

President: Peter Radford

President Emeritus: Sir Eddie Kulukundis

Vice Presidents: Patrick E Brian   Les Crouch Stanley Greenberg Shirley Hitchcock
Andrew Huxtable Richard Hymans Martin H James Tim G Lynch-Staunton
Tony O'Neill Mel Watman   Rob Whittingham Alf Wilkins Colin Young

Honorary Members: Roberto L Quercetani

Executive Committee: Peter J Matthews (Chairman)   Stuart Mazdon (Hon Sec)
Don Turner (Treasurer)   Elizabeth Sissons (Membership Secretary)

	Stanley Greenberg	Melvyn F Watman	Shirley Hitchcock
	Colin Young	Jack Miller	Mike Fleet
Alf Wilkins (ex officio)	Les Crouch (ex officio)	Bob Phillips (ex officio)	Rob Whittingham (ex officio)

Annual

General Editors - Rob Whittingham, Peter Matthews, Tony Miller

Relays - Keith Morbey   Multi-Events - Alan Lindop   Walks - John Powell

Also acknowledgements for specific help to Arnold Black (Scotland),
Marian Williams (Wales)
John Glover (Northern Ireland) and various other NUTS members.

Editor, Track Stats: Bob Phillips
Webmaster: Stuart Mazdon
Secretary Historical Group: Ian Tempest

ABBREVIATIONS & NOTES

A	-	mark set at altitude over 1000m	q	-	quarter final
a	-	automatic timing only known	r	-	race number
		to one tenth of a second	s	-	semi final
B	-	walk not held under IAAF regulations	t	-	track
D	-	performance made in a Decathlon	u	-	unofficial time
dh	-	downhill	un	-	unconfirmed performance
e	-	estimated time	w	-	wind assisted (> 2.0 m/sec)
et	-	extra trial	W	-	wind assisted (over 4m/sec in
ex	-	exhibition			decathlon/heptathlon)
h	-	heat	x	-	relay team may include outside
H	-	performance made in a Heptathlon			age-group members
hc	-	handicap race	+	-	intermediate time
i	-	indoor	*	-	legal performance where best is
m	-	position in race when intermediate			wind assisted
		time taken	"	-	photo electric cell time
mx	-	performance in mixed race	#	-	Unratified (may not be ratifiable)
O	-	performance made in an Octathlon	&	-	as yet unratified
o	-	over age	§	-	now competes for another nation
P	-	performance made in a Pentathlon	¶	-	drugs ban (as per IAAF)
Q	-	qualifying round			

AGE GROUP DESIGNATIONS for 2017

U13 - Under 13	(born 1.9.04 or later)	U15 - Under 15	(born 1.9.02 to 31.8.04)
U17 - Under 17	(born 1.9.99 to 31.8.02)	U20 - Under 20	(born 1.1.98 to 31.12.00)
Vxx - Veteran	(age 40 or over Men)	Vxx - Veteran	(age 35 or over Women)

Care must be taken with very young age groups for athletes with an unknown date of birth from Northern Ireland since their age groups differ slightly.

Italics indicates the athlete competes for a British club or university but is not eligible to represent Britain.

MULTI - EVENTS
Pentathlon, Heptathlon and Decathlon lists show the complete breakdown of individual performances in the following order:

Pentathlon (women) - U17: 80mH, SP, HJ, LJ, 800m; U15: 75mH, SP, HJ, LJ, 800m
Heptathlon (women) - 100mH, HJ, SP, 200m (1st day); LJ, JT, 800m (2nd day) (80mH - Inters)
Decathlon (men)   - 100m, LJ, SP, HJ, 400m (1st day); 110mH, DT, PV, JT, 1500m (2nd day)

Totals which include performances made with following winds in excess of 4 m/s are denoted by W. The date shown is the second day of competition.

RANKING LISTS:
These show the best performances in each event recorded during the 2017 season.
For each performance the following details are shown:

Performance; wind reading (where appropriate);   name (with, where appropriate, age-group category); date of birth (DDMMYY);   position in competition;   venue;   date.

The following numbers are used, although strength of performance or lack of information may vary the guidelines -

50 perfomances   100 athletes for each standard event

Age Groups - 40 Under 20, 30 Under 17, 20 Under 15, 10 Under 13

In the junior men, athletes are shown in older age groups if their performances merit this, except U15 are not shown in U17 lists. For junior women, athletes are shown in their age group as per womens rules, although juniors of any age will be shown in the main list on merit.

INDEX
Club details and previous personal bests, where better than those recorded in 2017, are shown in the index for all athletes in the main lists.

VENUES

A list of London tracks for clarification

LONDON (O)	Olympic Stadium
LONDON (BP)	Millenium Arena, Battersea Park
LONDON (Cat)	Ladywell Arena, Silvermere Road, Catford (6L, 8S)
LONDON (Col)	Metropolitan Police (Hendon) Track, Hendon Police Training Coll, Colindale (7L, 7S)
LONDON (CP)	Crystal Palace National Sports Centre, Ledrington Road
LONDON (Cr)	Croydon Sports Arena, Albert Road
LONDON (Coul)	Track Coulsdon, Woodcote High School, Meadow Hill, Coulsdon
LONDON (Elt)	Sutcliffe Park, Eltham Road (6L, 8S)
LONDON (FP)	Finsbury Park, Endymion Road (6L, 10S)
LONDON (Ha)	New River Sports Centre, White Hart Lane, Wood Green, Haringey
LONDON (He)	Allianz Park Stadium, Greenlands Lane, Hendon
LONDON (LV)	Lee Valley Athletics centre, Meridian Way, Picketts Lock
LONDON (ME)	Mile End Stadium, Rhodeswell Road
LONDON (Nh)	Terence McMillan Stadium, Newham Leisure Centre, Plaistow
LONDON (Pa)	Paddington Recreation Ground, Randolph Avenue (6L, 6S)
LONDON (PH)	Parliament Hill Fields, Highgate Road, Hampstead
LONDON (SP)	Southwark Park, Hawkstone Road, Surrey Quays (7L, 7S)
LONDON (TB)	Tooting Bec Athletics Track, Tooting Bec Road
LONDON (WF)	Waltham Forest Track, Chingford Road, Walthamstow
LONDON (Wil)	Willesden Sports Stadium, Donnington Road (6L, 8S)
LONDON (WL)	Linford Christie Stadium, Du Cane Road, West London
LONDON (WP)	Wimbledon Park, Home Park Road (6L, 8S)

ATHLETICS ADDRESSES

British Athletics
Athletics House
Alexander Stadium
Walsall Road
Perry Barr
Birmingham
B42 2BE
Tel: 0121 713 8400
lbirchall@britishathletics.org.uk
www.uka.org.uk

SCOTLAND
Scottish Athletics Ltd
Caledonia House, South Gyle
Edinburgh   EH12 9DQ
Tel: 0131 539 7320

admin@scottishathletics.org.uk
www.scottishathletics.org.uk

NORTHERN IRELAND
Athletics Northern Ireland
Athletics House
Old Coach Road
Belfast   BT9 5PR
Tel: 028 906 02707
info@athleticsni.org
www.athleticsni.org

Northern Athletics
7a Wellington Road East
Dewsbury
West Yorkshire   WF13 1HF
Tel: 01924 457922
northernath@btconnect.com
www.northernathletics.org.uk

British Athletics Supporters Club
Chairman: Philip Andrew OBE
philip@basclub.org.uk
www.basclub.org.uk

National Union of Track Statisticians
Secretary: Stuart Mazdon
77 Forest Approach
Woodford Green
Essex IG8 9BU
Tel: 020 8491 6155
stuart@mazdon.com
www.nuts.org.uk

England Athletics
Athletics House
Alexander Stadium
Walsall Road
Perry Barr
Birmingham
B42 2BE
Tel: 0121 347 6543
enquiries@englandathletics.org
www.englandathletics.org

WALES
Welsh Athletics Limited
Cardiff International Sports Stadium
Leckwith Road
Cardiff   CF11 8AZ
Tel: 029 2064 4870
office@welshathletics.org
www.welshathletics.org

Midland Counties A.A.
Alexander Stadium
Walsall Road
Perry Barr
Birmingham   B42 2LR
Tel: 0121 344 4201
administration@mcaa.org.uk
www.midlandathletics.org.uk

South of England A.A.
Crystal Palace National Sports Centre
Ledrington Road
London   SE19 2BB
Tel: 020 8778 7167
competitions@seaa.org.uk
www.seaa.org.uk

British Statistics
www.topsinathletics.org

Scottish Statistics
www.scotstats.net

Welsh Statistics
athleticsstatswales.webeden.co.uk

The NUTS website at www.nuts.org.uk gives details of NUTS publications and has various interesting stats features, such as a complete list of medallists at the AAC, AAA, WAAA and UK Championships, and sample articles from Track Stats (now of 64 A5 pages each quarter), a subscription to which gives NUTS membership at £25 per annum in the UK.
There are also scanned copies of almost all editions of NUTS Notes, the fore-runner of Track Stats and previously unpublished photo times from the 60s and 70s.

FOREWORD - by Peter Matthews

We organise top sporting events brilliantly in Britain, and the 2017 World Athletics Championships in the London Stadium were no exception. There was terrific crowd support for the athletes – especially, but far from exclusively, for the British competitors and it was marvellous to have capacity crowds, up to the 56,000 maximum figure for the morning sessions, in marked contrast to all too many major events around the world. Britain won six medals and in the more revealing placing table, Britain was third behind the USA and Kenya. Our 105 points was the best ever, although 104 at Helsinki 1983 was achieved with slightly fewer events on the programme. This compared to 92.5 at the 2016 Olympics and 94 at the 2015 Worlds, so on this measure our elite level is in good shape. However, while medals in all the relays was marvellous Mo Farah was the only individual medallist and we will surely miss his huge contributions (on the track) following those of Jessica Ennis-Hill with her retirement the previous year.

Looking to future hopes at the top level Britain headed the points table at the European U20 Championships with 19 medals (5 gold, 6 silver and 8 bronze) but the tally at the European U23s was somewhat disappointing with ten medals including four gold. Overall these tallies pretty much maintained the standard set at recent global and European events but one must remember that European standards continue to decline against the rest of the world. I should also mention continuing success by Britain at the European Cross-Country Championships. Records at global or national level are broken much less often than was the case when the sport was developing fast from the 1950s through to the 1980s. In 2017 UK national records were set at just two standard events outdoors – that superb men's 4x100m run at the Worlds and three women's pole vault marks by Holly Bleasdale. Indoors there were new marks at three men's and six women's events across all events, with Laura Muir starring with records at 1000m, 1500m, 3000m and 5000m. Muir and Farah led the way by each ranking in the Athletics International world merit rankings in two events – and in all 17 top ten positions taken by British athletes equalled the number achieved in 2016.

As usual I like to check on British lists for all standard events. The 10th best male athlete was better in 2017 than 2016 in 13 events to 8 and at 50th best level (at which walks are not included as there are insufficient numbers competing – or steeplechase for women) 2016 and 2017 were level 10-10, so, as in other recent years, not too much change. But for the women 2017 beat 2016 by 14-6 (1 tie) for 10th best and by 13-4 (2 ties) for 50th best. We have also improved a little with the number of places taken by British athletes in world top 100s at standard events – for men 73 in 2016 and 81 in 2017 and for women 79 in 2016 and 87 in 2017.

A more disturbing picture is that of the declining standard of competitions in Britain after the top televised events and, as can be seen by the figures at the end of this book, the number of active athletes in the 20-35 age group in track and field continues to decline as our governing body concentrates on the super-elite and those deemed of 'podium potential'. The sport's authorities seem to remain substantially in denial of such trends. Our marvellous volunteers do a terrific job as officials but increasingly they are working at meetings for kids rather than seniors.

The sport owes a huge debt of gratitude to all involved in the production of this Annual, especially, for many years now, the dedicated work of Tony Miller and Rob Whittingham. But both have indicated that they may not be able to continue. While detailed statistics for British athletes are available on the Power of Ten web site, as well as on the topsinathletics.info site run by Rob and Tony, we believe that it is essential to have a comprehensive annual reference book each year and, in these days of instant access on the internet, it would be tragic if such a definitive record as is presented here were to be jeopardised. Under the brilliant editorship of Bob Phillips the NUTS quarterly Track Stats continues to flourish with excellent research and good reading and the NUTS will celebrate our 60th anniversary this year with several of the founding members still going strong but we have an elderly membership and desperately need younger people to help in our role of documenting the sport – a job that we have taken pride in despite considerable apathy for much of the time by our governing bodies.

MAJOR OUTDOOR FIXTURES IN 2018

MARCH

1-4	IAAF World Indoor Championships	Birmingham
10-11	European Throwing Cup	Leira, POR
24	IAAF World Half Marathon Championships	Valencia, ESP

APRIL

| 8-14 | Commonwealth Games | Gold Coast, AUS |
| 22 | Virgin Money London Marathon | London |

MAY

5-6	IAAF World Race Walking Team Championships	Taicang, CHN
5-7	BUCS Championships	Bedford
12-13	County Championships	various
19	European Cup/Highgate Night of 10ks	Parliament Hill
20	Loughborough International	Loughborough
26-27	England Combined Events Championships	Bedford
26-27	European Champion Clubs Senior	Birmingham
26-27	IAU 24 Hour European Championships	Timisoara, ROM

JUNE

9	Northern Ireland Championships	Belfast
9-10	England Area Championships	various
16-17	England Athletics U23 & U20 Championships & Trials	Bedford
30-1Jul	British Athletics Championships & European Trials	Birmingham

JULY

5-8	European Youth Championships	Gyor, HUN
10-15	IAAF World U20 Championships	Tampere, FIN
13-14	English Schools Championships	Birmingham
13-14	Welsh Championships	Cardiff
14	The Meet (GBR v USA)	London (O)
21	Schools Home International	Grangemouth
21-22	Muller Aniversary Games & GP Diamond League	London (O)
28-29	England & CAU Championships	Bedford

AUGUST

7-12	European Championships	Berlin, GER
11-12	Scottish Championships	Grangemouth
15	Manchester International	Manchester (SC)
20	IAAF Diamond League/Muller Grand Prix	Birmingham
25-26	England Athletics U17 & U15 Championships	Bedford

SEPTEMBER

8	IAU 100k World Championships	Sveti Martin na Muri, CRO
8-9	IAAF Continental Cup	Ostrava, CZE
9	BUPA Great North Run	Tyneside

OCTOBER

| 11-17 | Youth Olympic Games | Buenos Aires, ARG |

DECEMBER

| 9 | European Cross Country Championships | Tilburg, NED |

RECORDS - MEN
as at 31 December 2017

W = World, E = European, C = Commonwealth, A = UK All-Comers, N = UK, J = Junior

Event		Time		Name	Nat	Date			Place
100m	W,C	9.58		Usain Bolt	JAM	16	Aug	09	Berlin
	A	9.63		Usain Bolt	JAM	5	Aug	12	London (O)
	E	9.86		Francis Obikwelu	POR	22	Aug	04	Athens
		9.86		Jimmy Vicaut	FRA	4	Jul	15	Saint-Denis
		9.86		Jimmy Vicaut	FRA	7	Jun	16	Montreuil
	N	9.87		Linford Christie		15	Aug	93	Stuttgart
	WJ	9.97		Trayvon Bromell	USA	13	Jun	14	Eugene
	EJ	10.04		Christophe Lemaitre	FRA	24	Jul	09	Novi Sad
	NJ	10.05		Adam Gemili		11	Jul	12	Barcelona
200m	W,C	19.19		Usain Bolt	JAM	20	Aug	09	Berlin
	A	19.32		Usain Bolt	JAM	9	Aug	12	London (O)
	E	19.72	A	Pietro Mennea	ITA	12	Sep	79	Mexico City
	N	19.87	A#	John Regis		31	Jul	94	Sestriere
		19.94		John Regis		20	Aug	93	Stuttgart
	WJ	19.93		Usain Bolt	JAM	11	Apr	04	Hamilton, BER
	EJ	20.04		Ramil Guliyev	AZE	10	Jul	07	Belgrade
	NJ	20.29		Christian Malcolm		19	Sep	98	Kuala Lumpur
300m	W, C	30.81		Wayde van Niekerk	RSA	28	Jun	17	Ostrava
	E,A,N	31.56		Doug Walker		19	Jul	98	Gateshead
	WJ	31.61		Clarence Munyai	RSA	28	Jun	17	Ostrava
	EJ,NJ	32.53		Mark Richardson		14	Jul	91	London (Ha)
400m	W,C	43.03		Wayde van Niekerk	RSA	14	Aug	16	Rio de Janeiro
	A	43.89		Steven Gardiner	BAH	6	Aug	17	London (O)
	E	44.33		Thomas Schönlebe	GER	3	Sep	87	Rome
	N	44.36		Iwan Thomas		13	Jul	97	Birmingham
	WJ	43.87		Steve Lewis	USA	28	Sep	88	Seoul
	EJ	45.01		Thomas Schönlebe	GER	15	Jul	84	Berlin
	NJ	45.35		Martin Rooney		21	Mar	06	Melbourne
600m	W	1:12.81		Johnny Gray	USA	24	May	86	Santa Monica
	C,A	1:13.10		David Rudisha	KEN	5	Jun	16	Birmingham
	E	1:13.21		Pierre-Ambroise Bosse	FRA	5	Jun	16	Birmingham
	N	1:14.95		Steve Heard		14	Jul	91	London (Ha)
	WJ	1:14.8	A	Mark Winzenreid	USA	31	Aug	68	Echo Summit
	NJ	1:16.79		Andrew Lill		24	Jul	90	Mansfield
800m	W,C,A	1:40.91		David Rudisha	KEN	9	Aug	12	London (O)
	E	1:41.11		Wilson Kipketer	DEN	24	Aug	97	Cologne
	N	1:41.73	"	Sebastian Coe		10	Jun	81	Florence
	WJ	1:41.73		Nijel Amos	BOT	9	Aug	12	London (O)
	EJ	1:44.33		Yuriy Borzakovskiy	RUS	25	Sep	00	Sydney
	NJ	1:45.64		David Sharpe		5	Sep	86	Brussels
1000m	W,C	2:11.96		Noah Ngeny	KEN	5	Sep	99	Rieti
	E,N	2:12.18		Sebastian Coe		11	Jul	81	Oslo
	A	2:12.88		Steve Cram		9	Aug	85	Gateshead
	WJ	2:13.93	#	Abubaker Kaki	SUD	22	Jul	08	Stockholm
		2:15.00		Benjamin Kipkurui	KEN	17	Jul	99	Nice
	EJ	2:17.40		Yuriy Borzakovskiy	RUS	8	Jul	00	Nice
	NJ	2:18.98		David Sharpe		19	Aug	86	Birmingham
1500m	W	3:26.00		Hicham El Guerrouj	MAR	14	Jul	98	Rome
	C	3:26.34		Bernard Lagat	KEN	24	Aug	01	Brussels
	E,N	3:28.81		Mo Farah		19	Jul	13	Monaco
	A	3:29.33		Asbel Kiprop	KEN	5	Jun	16	Birmingham
	WJ	3:28.81		Ronald Kwemoi	KEN	18	Jul	14	Monaco
	EJ	3:35.51		Reyes Estévez	SPA	16	Aug	95	Zürich
	NJ	3:36.6		Graham Williamson		17	Jul	79	Oslo

1 Mile	W	3:43.13		Hicham El Guerrouj	MAR	7 Jul 99	Rome
	E,N	3:46.32		Steve Cram		27 Jul 85	Oslo
	C	3:43.40		Noah Ngeny	KEN	7 Jul 99	Rome
	A	3:45.96		Hicham El Guerrouj	MAR	5 Aug 00	London (CP)
	WJ	3:49.29		William Biwott Tanui	KEN	3 Jul 09	Oslo
	EJ,NJ	3:53.15		Graham Williamson		17 Jul 79	Oslo
2000m	W	4:44.79		Hicham El Guerrouj	MAR	7 Sep 99	Berlin
	E,N	4:51.39		Steve Cram		4 Aug 85	Budapest
	C	4:48.74		John Kibowen	KEN	1 Aug 98	Hechtel
	A	4:48.36		Hicham El Guerrouj	MAR	19 Jul 98	Gateshead
	WJ	4:56.25		Tesfaye Cheru	ETH	5 Jul 11	Reims
	EJ	5:04.4		Harald Hudak	GER	30 Jun 76	Oslo
	NJ	5:06.56		Jon Richards		7 Jul 82	Oslo
3000m	W,C	7:20.67		Daniel Komen	KEN	1 Sep 96	Rieti
	E	7:26.62		Mohammed Mourhit	BEL	18 Aug 00	Monaco
	A	7:26.69		Kenenisa Bekele	ETH	15 Jul 07	Sheffield
	N	7:32.62		Mo Farah		5 Jun 16	Birmingham
	WJ	7:28.19		Yomif Kejelcha	ETH	27 Aug 16	Saint-Denis
	EJ	7:43.20		Ari Paunonen	FIN	22 Jun 77	Cologne
	NJ	7:48.28		Jon Richards		9 Jul 83	Oslo
2 Miles	W,C	7:58.61		Daniel Komen	KEN	19 Jul 97	Hechtel
	E,N	8:03.40	i	Mo Farah		21 Feb 15	Birmingham
		8:07.85		Mo Farah		24 Aug 14	Birmingham
	A	8:01.72		Haile Gebrselassie	ETH	7 Aug 99	London (CP)
	WJ	8:13.47		Richard Limo	KEN	30 May 99	Hengelo
	EJ,NJ	8:28.31		Steve Binns		31 Aug 79	London (CP)
5000m	W	12:37.35		Kenenisa Bekele	ETH	31 May 04	Hengelo
	E	12:49.71		Mohammed Mourhit	BEL	25 Aug 00	Brussels
	C	12:39.74		Daniel Komen	KEN	22 Aug 97	Brussels
	A	12:49.60	i#	Kenenisa Bekele	ETH	20 Feb 04	Birmingham
		12:55.51		Haile Gebrselassie	ETH	30 Jul 04	London (CP)
	N	12:53.11		Mo Farah		22 Jul 11	Monaco
	WJ	12:47.53		Hagos Gebrhiwet	ETH	6 Jul 12	Saint-Denis
	EJ,NJ	13:27.04		Steve Binns		14 Sep 79	London (CP)
10000m	W	26:17.53		Kenenisa Bekele	ETH	26 Aug 05	Brussels
	E,N	26:46.57		Mo Farah		3 Jun 11	Eugene
	C	26:27.85		Paul Tergat	KEN	22 Aug 97	Brussels
	A	26:49.51		Mo Farah		4 Aug 17	London (O)
	WJ	26:41.75		Samuel Wanjiru	KEN	26 Aug 05	Brussels
	EJ	28:22.48		Christian Leuprecht	ITA	4 Sep 90	Koblenz
	NJ	29:21.9		Jon Brown		21 Apr 90	Walnut
10k Road	W,C	26:44		Leonard Komen	KEN	26 Sep 10	Utrecht
	A	27:21		Micah Kogo	KEN	20 May 07	Manchester
	E,N	27:34		Nick Rose		1 Apr 84	New Orleans
	WJ	27:11		Mathew Kimeli	KEN	9 Sep 17	Prague
	NJ	29:35		Jon Gascoyne		24 Nov 91	Basingstoke
15k Road	W,C	41:13		Leonard Komen	KEN	21 Nov 10	Nijmegen
	E,N	42:03	+	Mo Farah		26 Mar 16	Cardiff
20000m	W	56:26.0	+	Haile Gebrselassie	ETH	27 Jun 07	Ostrava
	E	57:18.4	+	Dionisio Castro	POR	31 Mar 90	La Flèche
	C,N	57:28.7	+	Carl Thackery	Eng	31 Mar 90	La Flèche
	A	58:39.0	+	Ron Hill		9 Nov 68	Leicester

20k Road	W	55:21	+	Zersenay Tadese	ERI	21	Mar	10	Lisbon
		55:48		Haile Gebrselassie	ETH	15	Jan	06	Phoenix
	C	55:31	+	Samuel Wanjiru	KEN	17	Mar	07	The Gague
	E,N	56:27	+	Mo Farah		22	Mar	15	Lisbon
1 Hour	W	21,285 m		Haile Gebrselassie	ETH	27	Jun	07	Ostrava
	E	20,944 m		Jos Hermens	HOL	1	May	76	Papendal
	C,N	20,855 m		Carl Thackery	Eng	31	Mar	90	La Flèche
	A	20,472 m		Ron Hill		9	Nov	68	Leicester
	NJ	18,221 m		Eddie Twohig		16	Jun	81	Leamington
Half	W	58:23		Zersenay Tadese	ERI	21	Mar	10	Lisbon
Marathon	C	58:33		Samuel Wanjiru	KEN	17	Mar	07	The Hague
	E,N	59:22	#	Mo Farah		13	Sep	15	South Shields
		59:32		Mo Farah		22	Mar	15	Lisbon
	A	58:56	#	Martin Mathathi	KEN	18	Sep	11	South Shields
	WJ	59:16		Samuel Wanjiru	KEN	11	Sep	05	Rotterdam
	NJ	66:41		Stuart Jones		12	Jun	88	Weaverham
25000m	W,C	1:12:25.4	+	Moses Mosop	KEN	3	Jun	11	Eugene
	E	1:13:57.6		Stéphane Franke	GER	30	Mar	99	Walnut
	A,N	1:15:22.6		Ron Hill		21	Jul	65	Bolton
25k Road	W,C	1:11:18		Dennis Kimetto	KEN	6	May	12	Berlin
	E,N	1:13:30	+	Steve Jones		20	Oct	85	Chicago
30000m	W,C	1:26:47.4		Moses Mosop	KEN	3	Jun	11	Eugene
	E,A,N	1:31:30.4		Jim Alder		5	Sep	70	London (CP)
30k Road	W,C,A	1:27:13	+	Eluid Kipchoge	KEN	24	Apr	16	London
	W,C,A	1:27:13	+	Stanley Biwott	KEN	24	Apr	16	London
	E,N	1:28:40	+	Steve Jones	POR	20	Oct	85	Chicago
Marathon	W,C	2:02:57		Dennis Kimetto	KEN	28	Sep	14	Berlin
	A	2:03:05		Eluid Kipchoge	KEN	24	Apr	16	London
	E	2:05:48		Sondre Nordstad Moen	NOR	3	Dec	17	Fukuoka
	N	2:07:13		Steve Jones		20	Oct	85	Chicago
	WJ	2:04:32		Tsegaye Mekonnen	ETH	24	Jan	14	Dubai
	NJ	2:23:28		Eddie Twohig		28	Mar	82	Wolverhampton
100k Road	W	6:13:33		Takahiro Sunada	JPN	21	Jun	98	Tokoro
	E	6:15:30		Jean-Paul Praet	BEL	24	Jun	89	Torhout
	C,N	6:24:05		Simon Pride	Eng	15	May	99	Chavagnes
2000m SC	W,E	5:10.68		Mahiedine Mekhissi-Benabbab	FRA	30	Jun	10	Reims
	C	5:14.43		Julius Kariuki	KEN	21	Aug	90	Rovereto
	A	5:19.68		Samson Obwocha	KEN	19	Jul	86	Birmingham
	N	5:19.86		Mark Rowland		28	Aug	88	London (CP)
	WJ	5:19.99		Meresa Kahsay	ETH	12	Jul	13	Donetsk
	EJ	5:25.01		Arsenios Tsiminos	GRE	2	Oct	80	Athens
	NJ	5:29.61		Colin Reitz		18	Aug	79	Bydgoszcz
3000m SC	W	7:53.63		Saif Saeed Shaheen	QAT	3	Sep	04	Brussels
	E	8:00.09		Mahiedine Mekhissi-Benabbad	FRA	6	Jul	13	Saint-Denis
	C	7:53.64		Brimin Kipruto	KEN	22	Jul	11	Monaco
	A	8:00.12		Conseslus Kipruto	KEN	5	Jun	16	Birmingham
	N	8:07.96		Mark Rowland		30	Sep	88	Seoul
	WJ	7:58.66		Stephen Cherono	KEN	24	Aug	01	Brussels
	EJ	8:26.81		Jakob Ingebrigtsen	NOR	8	Jul	17	Kortrijk
	NJ	8:29.85		Paul Davies-Hale		31	Aug	81	London (CP)

110m H	W	12.80		Aries Merritt	USA	7 Sep 12	Brussels
	C	12.90		Omar McLeod	JAM	24 Jun 17	Kingston
	E,N	12.91		Colin Jackson	Wal	20 Aug 93	Stuttgart
	A	12.92		Aries Merritt	USA	8 Aug 12	London (O)
	WJ	13.12		Liu Xiang	CHN	2 Jul 02	Lausanne
	EJ,NJ	13.44		Colin Jackson		19 Jul 86	Athens
99cm	WJ,EJ	12.99		Wilhem Belocian	FRA	24 Jul 14	Eugene
	NJ	13.17		David Omoregie		22 Jun 14	Bedford
400m H	W	46.78		Kevin Young	USA	6 Aug 92	Barcelona
	E	47.37		Stéphane Diagana	FRA	5 Jul 95	Lausanne
	C	47.10		Samuel Matete	ZAM	7 Aug 91	Zürich
	A	47.63		Félix Sánchez	DOM	6 Aug 12	London (O)
	N	47.82		Kriss Akabusi		6 Aug 92	Barcelona
	WJ	48.02		Danny Harris	· USA	17 Jun 84	Los Angeles
	EJ	48.74		Vladimir Budko	RUS	18 Aug 84	Moscow
	NJ	50.20		Richard Davenport		15 Jul 04	Grosseto
High	W	2.45		Javier Sotomayor	CUB	27 Jul 93	Salamanca
Jump	E	2.42		Patrik Sjöberg	SWE	30 Jun 87	Stockholm
		2.42	i#	Carlo Thränhardt	GER	26 Feb 88	Berlin
		2.42	i	Ivan Ukhov	RUS	25 Feb 14	Prague
		2.42		Bohdan Bondarenko	UKR	14 Jun 14	New York
	A	2.41		Javier Sotomayor	CUB	15 Jul 94	London (CP)
	C	2.40		Derek Drouin	CAN	25 Apr 14	Des Moines
	N	2.38	i#	Steve Smith		4 Feb 94	Wuppertal
	N,WJ,EJ,NJ	2.37		Steve Smith		20 Sep 92	Seoul
	N	2.37		Steve Smith		22 Aug 93	Stuttgart
	N	2.37		Robbie Grabarz		23 Aug 12	Lausanne
	WJ,EJ	2.37		Dragutin Topic	YUG	12 Aug 90	Plovdiv
Pole	W,E	6.16	i	Renaud Lavillenie	FRA	15 Feb 14	Donetsk
Vault	C	6.05		Dmitriy Markov	AUS	9 Aug 01	Edmonton
	A	6.05		Sergey Bubka	UKR	10 Sep 93	London (CP)
	N	5.83	i	Luke Cutts		25 Jan 14	Rouen
		5.82		Steve Lewis		21 Jul 12	Szczecin
	WJ,EJ	5.90		Armand Duplantis	SWE	1 Apr 17	Austin
	NJ	5.60		Adam Hague		28 Mar 15	Austin
Long	W	8.95		Mike Powell	USA	30 Aug 91	Tokyo
Jump	E	8.86	A	Robert Emmiyan	ARM	22 May 87	Tsakhkadzor
	C	8.62		James Beckford	JAM	5 Apr 97	Orlando
	A	8.54		Mike Powell	USA	10 Sep 93	London (CP)
	N	8.51		Greg Rutherford		24 Apr 14	Chula Vista
	WJ,EJ	8.35		Sergey Morgunov	RUS	19 Jun 12	Cheboksary
	NJ	8.14		Greg Rutherford		22 Jul 05	Kaunas
Triple	W,E,C,N	18.29		Jonathan Edwards	Eng	7 Aug 95	Gothenburg
Jump	A	18.00		Jonathan Edwards		27 Aug 95	London (CP)
	WJ,EJ	17.50		Volker Mai	GER	23 Jun 85	Erfurt
	NJ	16.58		Tosi Fasinro		15 Jun 91	Espoo
Shot	W	23.12		Randy Barnes	USA	20 May 90	Los Angeles (Ww)
	E	23.06		Ulf Timmermann	GER	22 May 88	Hania
	C	22.21		Dylan Armstrong	CAN	25 Jun 11	Calgary
		22.21		Tom Walsh	NZL	5 Sep 16	Zagreb
	A	22.45		Christian Cantwell	USA	11 Jun 06	Gateshead
	N	21.92		Carl Myerscough		13 Jun 03	Sacramento
	WJ,EJ	21.14		Konrad Bukowiecki	POL	9 Jun 16	Oslo
	NJ	19.46		Carl Myerscough		6 Sep 98	Blackpool
6kg	WJ,EJ	23.34		Konrad Bukowiecki	POL	19 Jul 16	Bydgoszcz
	NJ	21.03		Carl Myerscough		13 May 98	Street

Event	Cat	Mark		Name	Country	Date	Place
Discus	W,E	74.08		Jürgen Schult	GER	6 Jun 86	Neubrandenburg
	C	70.32		Frantz Kruger	RSA	26 May 02	Salon-de-Provence
	A	69.83		Piotr Malachowski	POL	10 Jul 10	Gateshead
	N	68.24		Lawrence Okoye		19 May 12	Halle
	WJ	65.62	#	Werner Reiterer	AUS	15 Dec 87	Melbourne
	WJ,EJ	65.31		Mykyta Nesterenko	UKR	3 Jun 08	Tallinn
	NJ	60.97		Emeka Udechuku		5 Jul 98	Bedford
1.75 kg	WJ,EJ	70.13		Mykyta Nesterenko	UKR	24 May 08	Halle
	NJ	64.35		Emeka Udechuku		21 Jun 98	Bedford
Hammer	W,E	86.74		Yuriy Sedykh	UKR/RUS	30 Aug 86	Stuttgart
	C	80.63		Chris Harmse	RSA	15 Apr 05	Durban
	A	85.60		Yuriy Sedykh	UKR/RUS	13 Jul 84	London (CP)
	N	77.55		Nick Miller		22 Jul 15	Karlstad
	WJ,EJ	78.33		Olli-Pekka Karjalainen	FIN	5 Aug 99	Seinäjoki
	NJ	69.39		Taylor Campbell		4 May 15	Bedford
6kg	WJ	85.57		Ashraf Amgad El-Seify	QAT	14 Jul 12	Barcelona
	EJ	82.97		Javier Cienfuegos	ESP	17 Jun 09	Madrid
	NJ	78.74		Taylor Campbell		20 Jun 15	Bedford
Javelin	W,E	98.48		Jan Zelezny	CZE	25 May 96	Jena
	C	92.72		Julius Yego	KEN	26 Aug 15	Beijing
	N	91.46		Steve Backley		25 Jan 92	Auckland (NS)
	A	95.66		Jan Zelezny	CZE	29 Aug 93	Sheffield
	WJ,	86.48		Neeraj Chopra	IND	23 Jul 16	Bydgoszcz
	EJ	84.69		Zigismunds Sirmais	LAT	22 Jun 11	Bauska
	NJ	79.50		Steve Backley		5 Jun 88	Derby
Decathlon	W	9045		Ashton Eaton	USA	29 Aug 15	Beijing
	E	9026		Roman Sebrle	CZE	27 May 01	Götzis
	C,N	8847		Daley Thompson	Eng	9 Aug 84	Los Angeles
	A	8869		Ashton Eaton	USA	9 Aug 12	London (O)
	WJ,EJ	8435		Niklas Kaul	GER	23 Jul 17	Grosseto
	NJ	8082		Daley Thompson		31 Jul 77	Sittard
(with 1986 Javelin)							
	C,N	8811	#	Daley Thompson	Eng	28 Aug 86	Stuttgart
	NJ	7727		David Guest		6 Jun 10	Bedford
4x100m	W,C,A	36.84		Jamaica		11 Aug 12	London (O)
	E,N	37.47		UK National Team		12 Aug 17	London (O)
	WJ	38.66		United States		18 Jul 04	Grosseto
	EJ,NJ	39.05		UK National Team		22 Oct 00	Santiago
4x200m	W,C	1:18.63		Jamaica		24 May 14	Nassau
	E	1:20.66		France		24 May 14	Nassau
	A	1:20.85		USA		11 Jun 89	Portsmouth
	N	1:21.29		UK National Team		23 Jun 89	Birmingham
	NJ	1:25.40	i#	UK National Team		2 Mar 96	Liévin
		1:27.6		Borough of Enfield Harriers		13 Jun 82	London (He)
4x400m	W	2:54.29		United States		22 Aug 93	Stuttgart
	E,N	2:56.60		UK National Team		3 Aug 96	Atlanta
	C,A	2:56.72		Bahamas		10 Aug 12	London (O)
	WJ	3:00.33		United States		23 Jul 17	Trujillo
	EJ,NJ	3:03.80		UK National Team		12 Aug 90	Plovdiv
4x800m	W,C	7:02.43		Kenya		25 Aug 06	Brussels
	E,A,N	7:03.89		UK National Team		30 Aug 82	London (CP)
	NJ	7:26.2		BMC Junior Squad		2 Sep 95	Oxford
4x1500m	W,C	14:22.22		Kenya		25 May 14	Nassau
	E	14:38.8		West Germany		17 Aug 77	Cologne
	A	15:04.7		Italy		5 Jun 92	Sheffield
	N	14:54.57		England		4 Sep 09	Brussels
	NJ	15:52.0		BMC Junior Squad		30 Apr 97	Watford

4x1Mile	W,E	15:49.08		Irish Republic		17	Aug	85	Dublin (B)
	C	15:59.57		New Zealand		1	Mar	83	Auckland
	A	16:21.1		BMC National Squad		10	Jul	93	Oxford
	N	16:17.4		Bristol A.C./Western Kentucky U		25	Apr	75	Des Moines
	NJ	16:56.8		BMC Junior Squad		10	Jul	93	Oxford

Ekiden	W,C	1:57:06		Kenya		23	Nov	05	Chiba
Road Relay	E,N	1:59:41		UK National Team		10	Nov	91	Potsdam

Track Walking

3000m	W,E	10:47.11		Giovanni DeBenedictis	ITA	19	May	90	S. G. Valdarno
	C	10:56.22		Andrew Jachno	AUS	7	Feb	91	Melbourne
	A,N	10:58.21	i#	Tom Bosworth		28	Feb	16	Sheffield
	A,N	11:15.26	+	Tom Bosworth		2	Jul	17	Birmingham
	WJ,EJ	11:13.2		Jozef Pribilinec	SVK	28	Mar	79	Banská Bystrica
	NJ	11:36.2		Callum Wilkinson		15	May	16	Bury St Edmonds

5000m	W	18:05.49		Hatem Ghoula	TUN	1	May	97	Tunis
	E	18:07.08	i#	Mikhail Shchennikov	RUS	14	Feb	95	Moscow
		18:17.22		Robert Korzeniowski	POL	3	Jul	92	Reims
	C	18:41.83		Jared Tallent	AUS	28	Feb	09	Sydney
	A	18:38.79	i#	Robert Korzeniowski	POL	15	Feb	04	Belfast
	N	18:39.71	i#	Tom Bosworth		12	Feb	17	Sheffield
	A,N	18:43.28		Tom Bosworth		2	Jul	17	Birmingham
	WJ,EJ	19:03.16		Diego Garcia	ESP	24	Jun	15	Plasencia
	NJ	19:35.4		Callum Wilkinson		2	Jul	16	Tamworth

10000m	W,E	37:53.09		Francisco Fernandez	ESP	27	Jul	08	Santa Cruz
	C	38:06.6		Dave Smith	AUS	25	Sep	86	Sydney
	A	39:26.02		Guillaume Leblanc	CAN	29	Jun	90	Gateshead
	N	40:06.65		Ian McCombie		4	Jun	89	Jarrow
	WJ,EJ	38:46.4		Viktor Burayev	RUS	20	May	00	Moscow
	NJ	40:41.62		Callum Wilkinson		23	Jul	16	Bydgoszcz
(Road)	W(J),E(J)	36:16		Vladimir Kanaykin	RUS	19	Jun	04	Saransk
	NJ	40:30		Callum Wilkinson		7	May	16	Rome

20000m	W	1:17:25.6		Bernardo Segura	MEX	7	May	94	Fana
	E	1:18:35.2		Stefan Johansson	SWE	15	May	92	Fana
	C	1:19:48.1		Nathan Deakes	AUS	4	Sep	01	Brisbane
	A	1:23:20.86		Lebogang Shange	RSA	21	Jun	15	Bedford
	N	1:23:26.5		Ian McCombie		26	May	90	Fana
	WJ	1:20:11.72		Li Gaobo	CHN	2	Nov	07	Wuhan
	EJ	1:21:29.2	#	Victor Burayev	RUS	4	Sep	01	Brisbane
		1:22:42		Andrey Perlov	RUS	6	Sep	80	Hefei
	NJ	1:31:34.4		Gordon Vale		28	Jun	81	Brighton

30000m	W,E	2:01:44.1		Maurizio Damilano	ITA	4	Oct	92	Cuneo
	C	2:04:55.7		Guillaume Leblanc	CAN	16	Jun	90	Sept Îles
	A,N	2:11:54	#	Chris Maddocks		31	Dec	89	Plymouth
	A	2:17:26.4		Jorge Llopart	ESP	28	Jun	81	Brighton
	N	2:19:18		Chris Maddocks		22	Sep	84	Birmingham

50000m	W,E	3:35:27.2		Yohan Diniz	FRA	12	Mar	11	Reims
	C	3:43:50.0		Simon Baker	AUS	9	Sep	90	Melbourne
	A	4:03:52		Gerhard Weidner	GER	1	Jun	75	Woodford
	N	4:05:44.6		Paul Blagg		26	May	90	Fana

Road Walking - Fastest Recorded Times

20km	W	1:16:36		Yusuke Suzuki	JPN	15	Mar	15	Nomi
	E	1:16:43	#	Sergey Morozov	RUS	8	Jun	08	Saransk
		1:17:02		Yohann Diniz	FRA	8	Mar	15	Arles
	C	1:17:33		Nathan Deakes	AUS	23	Apr	05	Cixi
	A	1:18:46		Chen Ding	CHN	4	Aug	12	London
	N	1:20:13		Tom Bosworth		12	Aug	16	Rio de Janeiro
	WJ,EJ	1:18:06		Viktor Burayev	RUS	4	Mar	01	Adler
	NJ	1:26:13		Tim Berrett §		25	Feb	84	Dartford
30km	W,E	2:01:44.1	t	Maurizio Damilano	ITA	4	Oct	92	Cuneo
	C	2:04:55.7	t	Guillaume Leblanc	CAN	16	Jun	90	Sept Îles
	A	2:07:47		Simon Baker	AUS	31	Jul	86	Edinburgh
	N	2:07:56		Ian McCombie		27	Apr	86	Edinburgh
	WJ,EJ	2:02:27	+	Vladimir Kanaykin	RUS	8	Feb	04	Adler
	NJ	2:30:46		Phil Vesty		31	Jul	82	London (VP)
50km	W,E	3:32:33		Yohann Diniz	FRA	15	Aug	14	Zürich
	C	3:35:47		Nathan Deakes	AUS	2	Dec	06	Geelong
	A	3:33:12		Yohann Diniz	FRA	13	Aug	17	London
	N	3:51:37		Chris Maddocks		28	Oct	90	Burrator
	WJ	3:41:10		Zhao Jianguo	CHN	16	Apr	06	Wajima
	EJ	4:07:23		Aleksandr Volgin	RUS	27	Sep	86	Zhytomyr
	NJ	4:18:18		Gordon Vale		24	Oct	81	Lassing

RECORDS set in 2017

300m	W,C	30.81		Wayde van Niekerk	RSA	28	Jun	17	Ostrava
300m	WJ	31.61		Clarence Munyai	RSA	28	Jun	17	Ostrava
400m	A	43.89		Steven Gardiner	BAH	6	Aug	17	London (O)
10000m	A	26:49.51		Mo Farah		4	Aug	17	London (O)
10kR	WJ	27:11		Mathew Kimeli	KEN	9	Sep	17	Prague
3000mSC	EJ	8:26.81		Jakob Ingebrigtsen	NOR	8	Jul	17	Kortrijk
110H	C	12.90		Omar McLeod	JAM	24	Jun	17	Kingston
PV	WJ,EJ	5.90		Armand Duplantis	SWE	1	Apr	17	Austin
Decathlon	WJ,EJ	8435		Niklas Paul	GER	23	Jul	17	Grosseto
3000 W	A,N	11:15.26	+	Tom Bosworth		2	Jul	17	Birmingham
5000 W	N	18:39.47	i	Tom Bosworth		12	Feb	17	Sheffield
	N	18:43.28		Tom Bosworth		2	Jul	17	Birmingham
50k W	A	3:33:12		Yohann Diniz	FRA	13	Aug	17	London
4x100	E,N	37.47		UK National Team		12	Aug	17	London (O)
4x400	WJ	3:00.33		United States		23	Jul	17	Trujillo

Women continued from page 21

400H	WJ	53.82	Sydney McLaughlin	USA	25	Jun	17	Sacramento
Pole Vault	C	4.82	Eliza McCartney	NZL	26	Feb	17	Auckland
Pole Vault	N	4.72	Holly Bradshaw		26	May	17	Manchester
	N	4.80	Holly Bradshaw		26	May	17	Manchester
	N	4.81	Holly Bradshaw		15	Jul	17	Rottach-Egern
Discus	C	69.64	Dani Stevens	AUS	13	Aug	17	London (O)
Hammer	A	77.90	Anita Wlodarczyk	POL	7	Aug	17	London (O)
4x100	WJ,EJ	43.27	Germany		23	Jul	17	Grosseto
4x200	C	1:29:04	Jamaica		22	Apr	17	Nassau
50kW	W,E,A	4:05:56	Inês Henriques	POL	13	Aug	17	London

RECORDS - WOMEN
as at 31 December 2017

100m	W	10.49		Florence Griffith Joyner	USA	16	Jul	88	Indianapolis
	E	10.73		Christine Arron	FRA	19	Aug	98	Budapest
	C	10.70		Shelly-Ann Fraser-Pryce	JAM	29	Jun	12	Kingston
		10.70		Elaine Thompson	JAM	1	Jul	16	Kingston
	A	10.75		Shelly-Ann Fraser-Pryce	JAM	4	Aug	12	London (O)
	N	10.99		Dina Asher-Smith		25	Jul	15	London (O)
	WJ,EJ	10.88		Marlies Oelsner/Göhr	GER	1	Jul	77	Dresden
	NJ	11.14		Dina Asher-Smith		5	Jul	14	Mannheim
200m	W	21.34		Florence Griffith Joyner	USA	29	Sep	88	Seoul
	E	21.63		Dafne Schippers	NED	28	Aug	15	Beijing
	C	21.64		Merlene Ottey	JAM	13	Sep	91	Brussels
	A	21.88		Allyson Felix	USA	8	Aug	12	London (O)
	N	22.07		Dina Asher-Smith		28	Aug	15	Beijing
	WJ	22.11	A#	Allyson Felix	USA	3	May	03	Mexico City
		22.18		Allyson Felix	USA	25	Aug	04	Athens
	EJ	22.19		Natalya Bochina	RUS	30	Jul	80	Moscow
	NJ	22.61		Dina Asher-Smith		14	Aug	14	Zürich
300m	W	35.30	A	Ana Guevara	MEX	3	May	03	Mexico City
	W,E	35.00	+	Marie-José Pérec	FRA	27	Aug	91	Tokyo
		34.1	+	Marita Koch	GER	6	Oct	85	Canberra
	C,A,N	35.46		Kathy Cook	Eng	18	Aug	84	London (CP)
	A	35.46		Chandra Cheeseborough	USA	18	Aug	84	London (CP)
	WJ,EJ	36.24	+	Grit Breuer	GER	29	Aug	90	Split
		35.4	+	Christina Brehmer/Lathan	GER	29	Jul	76	Montréal
	NJ	36.46		Linsey Macdonald		13	Jul	80	London (CP)
		36.2		Donna Murray/Hartley		7	Aug	74	London (CP)
400m	W,E	47.60		Marita Koch	GER	6	Oct	85	Canberra
	C	48.63		Cathy Freeman	AUS	29	Jul	96	Atlanta
	A	49.05		Sanya Richards	USA	28	Jul	06	London (CP)
	N	49.41		Christine Ohuruogu		12	Aug	13	Moscow
	WJ,EJ	49.42		Grit Breuer	GER	27	Aug	91	Tokyo
	NJ	51.16		Linsey Macdonald		15	Jun	80	London (CP)
600m	W,C	1:21.77		Caster Semenya	RSA	27	Aug	17	Berlin
	E	1:23.5		Doina Melinte	ROU	27	Jul	86	Poiana Brasov
	N	1:24.36		Marilyn Okoro		5	Jul	12	Liège (NX)
	A	1:25.90		Delisa Walton-Floyd	USA	28	Aug	88	London (CP)
	WJ,EJ	1:25.2		Vera Nikolic	YUG		Jun	67	Belgrade
	NJ	1:27.33		Lorraine Baker		13	Jul	80	London (CP)
800m	W,E	1:53.28		Jarmila Kratochvílová	CZE	26	Jul	83	Munich
	C,WJ	1:54.01		Pamela Jelimo	KEN	29	Aug	08	Zurich
	A	1:55.16		Caster Semenya	RSA	13	Aug	17	London (O)
	N	1:56.21		Kelly Holmes		9	Sep	95	Monaco
	EJ	1:57.45	#	Hildegard Ullrich	GER	31	Aug	78	Prague
		1:59.17		Birte Bruhns	GER	20	Jul	88	Berlin
	NJ	1:59.75		Charlotte Moore		29	Jul	02	Manchester (C)
1000m	W,E	2:28.98		Svetlana Masterkova	RUS	23	Aug	96	Brussels
	C	2:29.66		Maria Lurdes Mutola	MOZ	23	Aug	96	Brussels
	A,N	2:31.93	i#	Laura Muir		18	Feb	17	Birmingham
	A,N	2:32.55		Kelly Holmes		15	Jun	97	Leeds
	WJ,EJ	2:35.4	a	Irina Nikitina	RUS	5	Aug	79	Podolsk
		2:35.4		Kathrin Wühn	GER	12	Jul	84	Potsdam
	NJ	2:38.58		Jo White		9	Sep	77	London (CP)

1500m	W	3:50.07		Genzebe Dibaba	ETH	17 Jul 15	Monaco
	E	3:52.47		Tatyana Kazankina	RUS	13 Aug 80	Zürich
	C,N	3:55.22		Laura Muir	Sco	27 Aug 16	Saint-Denis
	A	3:57.49		Laura Muir		22 Jul 16	London (O)
	WJ	3:51.34		Lang Yinglai	CHN	18 Oct 97	Shanghai
	EJ,NJ	3:59.96		Zola Budd		30 Aug 85	Brussels
1 Mile	W,E	4:12.56		Svetlana Masterkova	RUS	14 Aug 96	Zürich
	C,A	4:16.56		Hellen Obiri	KEN	9 Jul 17	London (O)
	N,WJ,EJ,NJ	4:17.57		Zola Budd		21 Aug 85	Zürich
2000m	W	5:23.75	i#	Genzebe Dibaba	ETH	7 Feb 17	Sabadell
	W,E,A	5:25.36		Sonia O'Sullivan	IRL	8 Jul 94	Edinburgh
	C,N	5:26.93		Yvonne Murray	Sco	8 Jul 94	Edinburgh
	WJ,EJ,NJ	5:33.15		Zola Budd		13 Jul 84	London (CP)
3000m	W	8:06.11		Wang Junxia	CHN	13 Sep 93	Beijing
	E	8:21.42		Gabriela Szabo	ROU	19 Jul 02	Monaco
	A	8:21.64		Sonia O'Sullivan	IRL	15 Jul 94	London (CP)
	C	8:20.68		Hellen Obiri	KEN	9 May 14	Doha
	N	8:22.20		Paula Radcliffe		19 Jul 02	Monaco
	WJ,EJ,NJ	8:28.83		Zola Budd		7 Sep 85	Rome
2 Miles	W	8:58.58		Meseret Defar	ETH	14 Sep 07	Brussels
	C,A	9:11.49		Mercy Cherono	KEN	24 Aug 14	Birmingham
	E,N	9:17.4	+e	Paula Radcliffe		20 Jun 04	Bydgoszcz
	E	9:19.56		Sonia O'Sullivan	IRL	27 Jun 98	Cork
	N	9:32.07		Paula Radcliffe		23 May 99	Loughborough
	NJ	9:29.6	+e	Zola Budd		26 Aug 85	London (CP)
		10:35.10		Jane Potter		23 May 99	Loughborough
5000m	W	14:11.15		Tirunesh Dibaba	ETH	6 Jun 08	Oslo
	E	14:23.75		Liliya Shobukhova	RUS	19 Jul 08	Kazan
	C	14:18.37		Hellen Obiri	KEN	8 Jun 17	Rome
	N	14:29.11		Paula Radcliffe		20 Jun 04	Bydgoszcz
	A	14:31.42		Paula Radcliffe		28 Jul 02	Manchester (SC)
	WJ	14:30.88		Tirunesh Dibaba	ETH	11 Jun 04	Fana
	EJ,NJ	14:48.07		Zola Budd		26 Aug 85	London (CP)
10000m	W	29:17.45		Almaz Ayana	ETH	12 Aug 16	Rio de Janeiro
	C	29:32.53		Vivian Cheruiyot	KEN	12 Aug 16	Rio de Janeiro
	E	29:56.34		Evlan Abeylegesse	TUR	15 Aug 08	Beijing
	N	30:01.09		Paula Radcliffe		6 Aug 02	Munich
	A	29:59.20		Meseret Defar	ETH	11 Jul 09	Birmingham
	WJ	30:26.50		Linet Masai	KEN	15 Aug 08	Beijing
	EJ	31:40.42		Annemari Sandell	FIN	27 Jul 96	Atlanta
	NJ	32:35.75		Charlotte Purdue		4 Aug 10	Tipton
10k Road	W,C	29:43		Joycilene Jepkosgei	KEN	9 Sep 17	Prague
	E,N	30:21		Paula Radcliffe		23 Feb 03	San Juan
	A	30:38		Paula Radcliffe		22 Sep 03	London (RP)
	WJ	31:27		Sally Barsosio	KEN	21 Apr 96	Vancouver
	NJ	32:20		Zola Budd		2 Mar 85	Phoenix
15k Road	W,C	45:37	+	Joycilene Jepkosgei	KEN	1 Apr 17	Prague
	E	46:59	+	Lornah Kiplagat	NED	14 Oct 07	Udine
	N	46:41	+#	Paula Radcliffe		21 Sep 03	South Shields
	N	47:43		Liz McColgan		13 Feb 88	Tampa
1 Hour	W	18,517 m		Dire Tune	ETH	12 Jun 08	Ostrava
	C	18,393 m	#	Tegla Loroupe	KEN	3 Sep 00	Borgholzhausen
	C	18,340 m		Tegla Loroupe	KEN	7 Aug 98	Borgholzhausen
	E	18,084 m		Silvana Cruciata	ITA	4 May 81	Rome
	A,N	16,460 m	i#	Bronwen Cardy-Wise		8 Mar 92	Birmingham
	N	16,495 m	#	Michaela McCallum		2 Apr 00	Asti
	A,N	16,364 m		Alison Fletcher		3 Sep 97	Bromley
	NJ	14,580 m		Paula Simpson		20 Oct 93	Bebington

20000m	W,C	1:05:26.6		Tegla Loroupe	KEN	3 Sep 00	Borgholzhausen
	E	1:06:55.5	#	Rosa Mota	POR	14 May 83	Lisbon
	A,N	1:15:46	+	Caroline Hunter-Rowe		6 Mar 94	Barry
20k Road	W,C	61:25	+	Joycilene Jepkosgei	KEN	1 Apr 17	Prague
	E,A,N	62:21	+#	Paula Radcliffe		22 Sep 03	South Shields
	E	62:57	+	Lorna Kiplagat	NED	14 Oct 07	Udine
	A,N	63:26	+	Paula Radcliffe		6 Oct 01	Bristol
Half	W,C	64:51		Joycilene Jepkosgei	KEN	22 Oct 17	Valencia
Marathon	A	65:39	#	Mary Keitany	KEN	7 Sep 14	South Shields
	E,N	65:40	#	Paula Radcliffe		22 Sep 03	South Shields
	E	66:25		Lorna Kiplagat	NED	14 Oct 07	Udine
	A	66:36		Mary Keitany	KEN	11 Oct 09	Birmingham
	WJ	67:57		Abebu Gelan	ETH	20 Feb 09	Ra's al-Khaymah
	NJ	77:52		Kathy Williams		28 Mar 82	Barry
25000m	W,C	1:27:05.84		Tegla Loroupe	KEN	21 Sep 02	Mengerskirchen
	E	1:28:22.6		Helena Javornik	SLO	19 Jul 06	Maribor
	A,N	1:35:16	+	Caroline Hunter-Rowe		6 Mar 94	Barry
25k Road	W,C,A	1:19:43	+	Mary Keitany	KEN	23 Apr 17	London
	(E,A,N)	1:20:36	#+	Paula Radcliffe		13 Apr 03	London
	E	1:21:31	#+	Constantina Tomescu	ROU	22 Oct 06	Chicago
	N	1:22:47	+	Paula Radcliffe		14 Aug 05	Helsinki
30000m	W,C	1:45:50.0		Tegla Loroupe	KEN	7 Jun 03	Warstein
	E	1:47:05.6		Karolina Szabó	HUN	22 Apr 88	Budapest
	A,N	1:55:03		Caroline Hunter-Rowe		6 Mar 94	Barry
30k Road	(W,C,A)	1:36:05	#+	Mary Keitany	KEN	23 Apr 17	London
	(E,N)	1:36:36	#+	Paula Radcliffe	Eng	13 Apr 03	London
	W,C	1:38:19		Valary Aiyabei	KEN	7 May 17	Prague
	E	1:38:23	#+	Liliya Shobukhova	RUS	9 Oct 11	Chicago
	E	1:38:30		Constantina Tomescu	ROU	22 Oct 06	Chicago
	E,N	1:39:22	+	Paula Radcliffe	Eng	14 Aug 05	Helsinki
Marathon	WECAN	2:15:25		Paula Radcliffe	Eng	13 Apr 03	London
	WJ	2:20:59		Shure Demise	ETH	23 Jan 15	Dubai
	NJ	2:50:09		Siobhan Quenby		16 Oct 83	Milan
100k Road	W	6:33:11		Tomoe Abe	JPN	25 Jun 00	Yubetsu
	E	7:10:32		Tatyana Zhyrkova	RUS	11 Sep 04	Winschoten
	C,N	7:27:19	#	Carolyn Hunter-Rowe	Eng	8 Aug 93	Torhout
	C,N	7:28:56		Elizabeth Hawker	Eng	8 Oct 06	Misari
2000m SC	W,C	6:02.16		Virginia Nyambura	KEN	6 Sep 15	Berlin
	E	6:03.38		Wioletta Janowska	POL	15 Jul 06	Gdansk
	A	6:19.00		Irene Limika	KEN	20 May 01	Loughborough
	N	6:21.31		Lennie Waite		1 Jun 17	Houston
	WJ,EJ	6:19.55		Oona Kettunen	FIN	13 Jul 13	Kotka
	NJ	6:32.45		Louise Webb		14 Jul 07	Ostrava
3000m SC	W	8:52:78		Ruth Jebet	BRN	27 Aug 16	Saint-Denis
	E	8:58.81		Gulnara Galkina	RUS	17 Aug 08	Beijing
	C, WJ	8:58.78		Celliphine Chespol	KEN	26 May 17	Eugene
	A	9:02.58		Emma Coburn	USA	11 Aug 17	London (O)
	N	9:24.24		Barbara Parker		2 Jun 12	Eugene
	EJ	9:32.68		Anna Emilie Moller	DEN	13 Aug 16	Rio de Janeiro
	NJ	10:06.12		Emily Pidgeon		3 Jul 05	Bedford
100m H	W,A	12.20		Kendra Harrison	USA	22 Jul 16	London (O)
	E	12.21		Yordanka Donkova	BUL	20 Aug 88	Stara Zagora
	C	12.28		Sally Pearson	AUS	3 Sep 11	Daegu
	N	12.51		Tiffany Porter		14 Sep 14	Marrakech
	WJ	12.74		Dior Hall	USA	13 Jun 15	Eugene
	EJ	12.85		Elvira Herman	BLR	24 Jul 16	Bydgoszcz
	NJ	13.07		Alicia Barrett		18 Jun 17	Bedford

400m H	W,E	52.34	Yuliya Pechonkina	RUS	8	Aug	03	Tula	
	C	52.42	Melaine Walker	JAM	20	Aug	09	Berlin	
	A	52.70	Natalya Antyukh	RUS	8	Aug	12	London (O)	
	N	52.74	Sally Gunnell		19	Aug	93	Stuttgart	
	WJ	53.82	Sydney McLaughlin	USA	25	Jun	17	Sacramento	
	EJ	55.26	Ionela Tîrlea	ROU	12	Jul	95	Nice	
	NJ	56.16	Shona Richards		26	Jul	14	Eugene	
High	W,E	2.09	Stefka Kostadinova	BUL	30	Aug	87	Rome	
Jump	C	2.06	Hestrie Cloete	RSA	31	Aug	03	Saint-Denis	
	A	2.05	Kajsa Bergqvist	SWE	28	Jul	06	London (CP)	
		2.05	Anna Chicherova	RUS	11	Aug	12	London (O)	
	N	1.98	Katarina Johnson-Thompson		12	Aug	16	Rio de Janeiro	
	WJ,EJ	2.01	Olga Turchak	KZK/UKR	7	Jul	86	Moscow	
		2.01	Heike Balck	GER	18	Jun	89	Chemnitz	
	NJ	1.94	Morgan Lake		22	Jul	14	Eugene	
		1.94	i	Morgan Lake		14	Feb	15	Sheffield
		1.94		Morgan Lake		21	Jun	15	Bedford
		1.94		Morgan Lake		1	Aug	15	Eberstadt
		1.94		Morgan Lake		18	Aug	16	Rio de Janeiro
Pole	W,E	5.06	Yelena Isinbayeva	RUS	28	Aug	09	Zurich	
Vault	A	5.00	Yelena Isinbayeva	RUS	22	Jul	05	London (CP)	
	C	4.82	Eliza McCartney	NZL	26	Feb	17	Auckland	
	C,N	4.87	i#	Holly Bleasdale/Bradshaw		21	Jan	12	Villeurbanne
	N	4.81		Holly Bradshaw		15	Jul	17	Rottach-Egern
	WJ,EJ	4.71	i#	Wilma Murto	FIN	31	Jan	16	Zweibrucken
	WJ	4.64		Eliza McCartney	NZL	19	Dec	15	Auckland
	EJ	4.61		Alyona Lutkovskaya	RUS	21	May	15	Irkutsk
	NJ	4.52	i#	Katie Byres		18	Feb	12	Nevers
		4.40		Lucy Bryan		29	Jun	13	Mannheim
Long	W,E	7.52	Galina Chistyakova	RUS	11	Jun	88	St. Petersburg	
Jump	C	7.16	A	Elva Goulbourne	JAM	22	May	04	Mexico City
	A	7.14		Galina Chistyakova	RUS	24	Jun	89	Birmingham
	N	7.07		Shara Proctor		28	Aug	15	Beijing
	WJ,EJ	7.14		Heike Daute/Drechsler	GER	4	Jun	83	Bratislava
	NJ	6.90		Beverly Kinch		14	Aug	83	Helsinki
Triple	W,E	15.50	Inessa Kravets	UKR	10	Aug	95	Gothenburg	
Jump	C	15.39	Françoise Mbango	CMR	17	Aug	08	Beijing	
	A	15.27	Yamilé Aldama	CUB	8	Aug	03	London (CP)	
	N	15.16	i#	Ashia Hansen		28	Feb	98	Valencia
		15.15		Ashia Hansen		13	Sep	97	Fukuoka
	WJ,EJ	14.62		Tereza Marinova	BUL	25	Aug	96	Sydney
	NJ	13.75		Laura Samuel		22	Jul	10	Moncton
Shot	W,E	22.63	Natalya Lisovskaya	RUS	7	Jun	87	Moscow	
	C	21.24	Valerie Adams	NZL	29	Aug	11	Daegu	
	A	21.95	Natalya Lisovskaya	RUS	29	Jul	88	Edinburgh	
	N	19.36	Judy Oakes		14	Aug	88	Gateshead	
	WJ,EJ	20.54	Astrid Kumbernuss	GER	1	Jul	89	Orimattila	
	NJ	17.12	Sophie McKinna		25	May	13	Halle	
Discus	W,E	76.80	Gabriele Reinsch	GER	9	Jul	88	Neubrandenburg	
	C	69.64	Dani Stevens	AUS	13	Aug	17	London (O)	
	A	73.04	Ilke Wyludda	GER	5	Aug	89	Gateshead	
	N	67.48	Meg Ritchie		26	Apr	81	Walnut	
	WJ,EJ	74.40	Ilke Wyludda	GER	13	Sep	88	Berlin	
	NJ	55.28	Eden Francis		2	Sep	07	London (He)	
Hammer	W,E	82.98	Anita Wlodarczyk	POL	28	Aug	16	Warsaw	
	C	75.73	Sultana Frizell	CAN	22	May	14	Tucson	
	A	77.90	Anita Wlodarczyk	POL	7	Aug	17	London (O)	
	N	74.54	Sophie Hitchon		15	Aug	16	Rio de Janeiro	
	WJ	73.24	Zhang Wenxiu	CHN	24	Jun	05	Changsha	
	EJ	71.71	Kamila Skolimowska	POL	9	Sep	01	Melbourne	
	NJ	66.01	Sophie Hitchon		24	Jul	10	Moncton	

Javelin	W,E	72.28	Barbora Spotakova	CZE	13 Sep 08	Stuttgart
	C	69.35	Sunette Viljoen	RSA	9 Jun 12	New York
	A	69.55	Barbora Spotakova	CZE	9 Aug 12	London (O)
	N	66.17	Goldie Sayers		14 Jul 12	London (CP)
	WJ	63.86	Yulenmis Aguilar	CUB	2 Aug 15	Edmonton
	EJ	63.01	Vira Rebryk	UKR	10 Jul 08	Bydgoszcz
	NJ	55.40	Goldie Sayers		22 Jul 01	Grossetto

Decathlon	W,E	8358	Austra Skujyte	LTU	15 Apr 05	Columbia, MO
	C	6915	Margaret Simpson	GHA	19 Apr 07	Reduit
	N	6878	Jessica Taylor		13 Sep 15	Erith

Heptathlon	W	7291	Jackie Joyner-Kersee	USA	24 Sep 88	Seoul
	E	7032	Carolina Klüft	SWE	26 Aug 07	Osaka
	C,A,N	6955	Jessica Ennis	Eng	4 Aug 12	London (O)
	WJ,EJ	6542	Carolina Klüft	SWE	10 Aug 02	Munich
	NJ	6267	Katarina Johnson-Thompson		4 Aug 12	London (O)

4x100m	W,A	40.82	United States		10 Aug 12	London (O)
	E	41.37	East Germany		6 Oct 85	Canberra
	C	41.07	Jamaica		29 Aug 15	Beijing
	N	41.77	UK National Team		19 Aug 16	Rio de Janeiro
	WJ.EJ	43.27	Germany		23 Jul 17	Grosseto
	NJ	43.81	UK National Team		21 Jul 13	Rieti

4x200m	W	1:27.46	United States		29 Apr 00	Philadelphia
	E	1:28.15	East Germany		9 Aug 80	Jena
	C	1:29.04	Jamaica		22 Apr 17	Nassau
	N	1:29.61	UK National Team		25 May 14	Nassau
	A	1:31.49	Russia		5 Jun 93	Portsmouth
	NJ	1:38.34 i#	UK National Team		2 Mar 96	Liévin
		1:42.2	London Olympiades AC		19 Aug 72	Bracknell

4x400m	W,E	3:15.17	U.S.S.R.		1 Oct 88	Seoul
	A	3:16.87	United States		11 Aug 12	London (O)
	C	3:18.71	Jamaica		3 Sep 11	Daegu
	N	3:20.04	UK National Team		2 Sep 07	Osaka
	WJ	3:27.60	United States		18 Jul 04	Grosseto
	EJ	3:28.39	East Germany		31 Jul 88	Sudbury
	NJ	3:30.46	UK National Team		21 Jul 02	Kingston, JAM

4x800m	W,E	7:50.17	U.S.S.R.		5 Aug 84	Moscow
	C	8:04.28	Kenya		25 May 14	Nassau
	A	7:57.08	Russia		5 Jun 93	Portsmouth
	N	8:13.46	UK National Team		27 Apr 13	Philadelphia
	NJ	8:38.22	Kelly's Camp		7 Jun 06	Twickenham

4x1500m	W,C	16:33.28	Kenya		24 May 14	Nassau
	A	17:09.75	Australia		25 Jun 00	London (BP)
	E	17:19.09	Irish Republic		25 Jun 00	London (BP)
	N	17:34.58	Scotland		17 Aug 06	Grangemouth
	NJ	18:17.40	BMC Junior Squad		17 Aug 06	Grangemouth

4x1Mile	W	18:39.58	University of Oregon		3 May 85	Eugene
	ECAN	19:17.3	BMC National Squad	Eng	10 Jul 93	Oxford
	NJ	20:16.2	BMC Junior Squad		11 Jun 97	Watford

Ekiden	W	2:11:41	China		28 Feb 98	Beijing
Road Relay	C	2:13:35	Kenya		23 Nov 06	Chiba
	E	2:14:51	Russia		23 Nov 06	Chiba
	N	2:17:31	UK National Team		23 Feb 92	Yokahama

Track Walking

3000m	W,E,A	11:35.34 i#	Gillian O'Sullivan	IRL	15 Feb 03	Belfast
	W.E	11:48.24	Ileana Salvador	ITA	29 Aug 93	Padua
	C	11:51.26	Kerry Saxby-Junna	AUS	7 Feb 91	Melbourne
	A	12:32.37	Yelena Nikolayeva	RUS	19 Jun 88	Portsmouth
	N	12:22.62 +	Jo Jackson		14 Feb 09	Sydney

3000m	WJ	12:10.31	#	Chen Zhou	CHN	28	Aug	05	Zhengzhou
	EJ	12:24.47		Claudia Iovan	ROU	24	Jul	97	Ljubljana
	NJ	13:03.4		Vicky Lupton/White		18	May	91	Sheffield
5000m	W,E	20:01.80		Eleonora Giorgi	ITA	18	May	14	Misterbianco
	C	20:13.26		Kerry Saxby-Junna	AUS	25	Feb	96	Hobart
	A	21:08.65		Yelena Nikolayeva	RUS	19	Jun	88	Portsmouth
	N	20:46.58		Jo Jackson		14	Feb	09	Sydney
	WJ,EJ	20:28.05		Tatyana Kalmykova	RUS	12	Jul	07	Ostrava
	NJ	22:36.81		Vicky Lupton/White		15	Jun	91	Espoo
5k(Road)	WJ,EJ	20:24		Lyudmila Yefimkina	RUS	28	May	00	Saransk
10000m	W	41:37.9	#	Gao Hongmiao	CHN	7	Apr	94	Beijing
	W,E	41:56.23		Nadezhda Ryashkina	RUS	24	Jul	90	Seattle
	C	41:57.22		Kerry Saxby-Junna	AUS	24	Jul	90	Seattle
	A,N	45:09.57		Lisa Kehler		13	Aug	00	Birmingham
	WJ,EJ	42:47.25		Anezka Drahotová	CZE	23	Jul	14	Eugene
	NJ	47:04		Vicky Lupton		30	Mar	91	Sheffield (W)
20000m	W,E	1:26:52.3		Olimpiada Ivanova	RUS	6	Sep	01	Brisbane
	C	1:33:40.2		Kerry Saxby-Junna	AUS	6	Sep	01	Brisbane
	A,N	1:36:39.70		Bethan Davies		21	Jun	15	Bedford
	WJ	1:29:32.4	#	Song Hongjuan	CHN	24	Oct	03	Changsha
		1:37:33.9		Gao Kelian	CHN	18	Sep	99	Xian
	EJ	1:39:20.5		Vera Santos	POR	4	Aug	00	Almada

Road Walking - Fastest Recorded Times

10km	W,E	41:04		Yelena Nikolayeva	RUS	20	Apr	96	Sochi
	C	41:30		Kerry Saxby-Junna	AUS	27	Aug	88	Canberra
	A	43:39		Kjersti Tysse Plätzer	NOR	14	Sep	02	Leamington
	N	43:52		Jo Jackson		14	Mar	10	Coventry
	WJ,EJ	41:52		Tatyana Mineeva	RUS	5	Sep	09	Penza
	NJ	47:04 t		Vicky Lupton/White		30	Mar	91	Sheffield (W)
20km	W	1:24:38		Hong Liu	CHN	6	Jun	15	La Coruña
	E	1:24:47		Elmira Alembekova	RUS	27	Feb	15	Sochi
	A	1:25:02		Yelena Lashmanova	RUS	11	Aug	12	London
	C	1:27:44		Jane Saville	AUS	2	May	04	Naumburg
	N	1:30:41		Jo Jackson		19	Jun	10	La Coruna
	WJ,EJ	1:25:30		Anisya Kirdyakpina	RUS	23	Feb	09	Adler
	NJ	1:43:26		Emma Achurch		2	Oct	16	Hayes
50km	W,E,A	4:05:56		Inês Henriques	POR	13	Aug	17	London

RECORDS set in 2017

600m	**W,C**	1:21.77		Caster Semenya	RSA	27	Aug	17	Berlin
800m	**A**	1:55.16		Caster Semenya	RSA	13	Aug	17	London (O)
1000m	N	2:31.93 i#		Laura Muir		18	Feb	17	Birmingham
1 Mile	C,A	4:16.56		Hellen Obiri	KEN	9	Jul	17	London (O)
2000m	W	5:23.75 i#		Genzebe Dibaba	ETH	7	Feb	17	Sabadell
5000m	C	14:18.37		Hellen Obiri	KEN	8	Jun	17	Rome
10k Road	W,C	29:43		Joycilene Jepkosgei	KEN	9	Sep	17	Prague
15k Road	W,C	45:37 +		Joycilene Jepkosgei	KEN	1	Sep	17	Prague
20k Road	W,C	61:25		Joycilene Jepkosgei	KEN	1	Sep	17	Prague
HMarathon	W,C	64:52		Joycilene Jepkosgei	KEN	1	Sep	17	Prague
HMarathon	W,C	64:51		Joycilene Jepkosgei	KEN	22	Oct	17	Valencia
25k Road	W,C,A	1:19:43 +		Mary Keitany	KEN	23	Apr	17	London
30k Road	W,C,A	1:36:05 +		Mary Keitany	KEN	23	Apr	17	London
	W,C	1:38:19		Valary Aiyabei		7	May	17	Prague
2000SC	N	6:21.31		Lennie Waite		1	Jun	17	Houston
3000SC	C,WJ	8:58:78		Celiphine Chespol	BRN	26	May	17	Eugene
	A	9:02.58		Emma Coburn	USA	11	Aug	17	London (O)
100H	N	13.07		Alicia Barrett		18	Jun	17	Bedford (heat)
	N	13.07		Alicia Barrett		18	Jun	17	Bedford (final)

continued on page 15

21

NATIONAL RECORDS OF THE UK - MEN
as at 31 December 2017
These are the best authentic performances for the four home countries of the U.K.
E = England S = Scotland W = Wales NI = Northern Ireland

100m	E	9.87	Linford Christie	15	Aug 93	Stuttgart, GER
	S	10.11	Allan Wells	24	Jul 80	Moscow, RUS
	W	10.11	Christian Malcolm	5	Aug 01	Edmonton, CAN
	NI	10.22	Jason Smyth (IRL per IAAF)	21	May 11	Clermont
200m	E	19.87 A#	John Regis	31	Jul 94	Sestriere, ITA
		19.94	John Regis	20	Aug 93	Stuttgart, GER
	W	20.08	Christian Malcolm	8	Aug 01	Edmonton, CAN
	S	20.21	Allan Wells	28	Jul 80	Moscow, RUS
	NI	20.38	Leon Reid	2	Jul 17	Birmingham
300m	S	31.56	Dougie Walker	19	Jul 98	Gateshead
	E	31.67	John Regis	17	Jul 92	Gateshead
	W	32.06	Jamie Baulch	31	May 97	Cardiff
	NI	33.33	Paul McKee (IRL)	12	Jun 08	Ostrava, CZE
400m	W	44.36	Iwan Thomas	13	Jul 97	Birmingham
	E	44.37	Roger Black	3	Jul 96	Lausanne, SUI
		44.37	Mark Richardson	9	Jul 98	Oslo, NOR
		44.37	Mark Richardson	8	Aug 98	Monaco, MON
	S	44.93	David Jenkins	21	Jun 75	Eugene, USA
	NI	45.58	Paul McKee (IRL)	14	Jul 02	Dublin (S), IRL
600m	E	1:14.95	Steve Heard	14	Jul 91	London (Ha)
	S	1:15.4	Tom McKean	21	Jul 91	Grangemouth
	NI	1:16.52 A	James McIlroy	24	Jan 05	Potchefstroon
	W	1:17.8 i	Bob Adams	20	Dec 69	Cosford
		1:18.02	Glen Grant	2	Aug 78	Edmonton, CAN
800m	E	1:41.73 "	Sebastian Coe	10	Jun 81	Florence, ITA
	S	1:43.88	Tom McKean	28	Jul 89	London (CP)
	W	1:44.98	Gareth Warburton	7	Jun 12	Oslo, NOR
	NI	1:44.65	James McIlroy	28	Aug 05	Rieti, ITA
1000m	E	2:12.18	Sebastian Coe	11	Jul 81	Oslo, NOR
	S	2:16.82	Graham Williamson	17	Jul 84	Edinburgh
	W	2:17.36	Neil Horsfield	9	Aug 91	Gateshead
	NI	2:15.57	James McIlroy (IRL)	5	Sep 99	Rieti, ITA
1500m	E	3:28.81	Mo Farah	19	Jul 13	Monaco, MON
	S	3:33.61	Chris O'Hare	21	Jul 17	Monaco, MON
	NI	3:34.76	Gary Lough	9	Sep 95	Monaco, MON
	W	3:35.08	Neil Horsfield	10	Aug 90	Brussels, BEL
1 Mile	E	3:46.32	Steve Cram	27	Jul 85	Oslo, NOR
	S	3:50.64	Graham Williamson	13	Jul 82	Cork, IRL
	W	3:54.39	Neil Horsfield	8	Jul 86	Cork, IRL
	NI	3:55.0	Jim McGuinness	11	Jul 77	Dublin (B), IRL
2000m	E	4:51.39	Steve Cram	4	Aug 85	Budapest, HUN
	S	4:58.38	Graham Williamson	29	Aug 83	London (CP)
	NI	5:02.61	Steve Martin	9	Jun 84	Belfast
	W	5:05.32	Tony Simmons	4	Jul 75	London (CP)
3000m	E	7:32.62	Mo Farah	5	Jun 16	Birmingham
	S	7:37.56	Andrew Butchart	9	Jul 17	London (O)
	W	7:46.40	Ian Hamer	20	Jan 90	Auckland, NZL
	NI	7:49.1	Paul Lawther	27	Jun 78	Oslo, NOR

2 Miles	E	8:03.40 i	Mo Farah	21 Feb 15	Birmingham
		8:07.85	Mo Farah	24 Aug 14	Birmingham
	S	8:12.63 i	Andrew Butchart	11 Feb 17	New York (Armory), USA
		8:19.37	Nat Muir	27 Jun 80	London (CP)
	W	8:20.28	David James	27 Jun 80	London (CP)
	NI	8:30.6	Paul Lawther	28 May 77	Belfast
5000m	E	12:53.11	Mo Farah	22 Jul 11	Monaco
	W	13:08.61	Andrew Burchart	20 Aug 16	Rio de Janeiro, BRA
	S	13:17.9	Nat Muir	15 Jul 80	Oslo, NOR
	NI	13:27.63	Dermot Donnelly	1 Aug 98	Hechtel, BEL
10000m	E	26:46.57	Mo Farah	3 Jun 11	Eugene, USA
	W	27:39.14	Steve Jones	9 Jul 83	Oslo, NOR
	S	27:43.03	Ian Stewart	9 Sep 77	London (CP)
	NI	28:32.15	Dermot Donnelly (IRL)	10 Apr 99	Barakaldo, ESP
20000m	E	57:28.7	Carl Thackery	31 Mar 90	La Flèche, FRA
	S	59:24.0	Jim Alder	9 Nov 68	Leicester
	W	62:23.0	Bernie Plain	1 Dec 73	Bristol
	NI	77:16.0	Ian Anderson	5 Mar 00	Barry
1 Hour	E	20,855 m	Carl Thackery	31 Mar 90	La Flèche, FRA
	S	20,201 m	Jim Alder	9 Nov 68	Leicester
	W	18,898 m	Mike Rowland	7 Aug 73	Stockholm, SWE
	NI	18,354 m	Dave Smyth	19 Sep 65	Bristol (?)
25000m	E	1:15:22.6	Ron Hill	21 Jul 65	Bolton
	S	1:15:34.4	Jim Alder	5 Sep 70	London (CP)
	W	1:18:50.0	Bernie Plain	1 Dec 73	Bristol
	NI	1:37:18.0 e	Ian Anderson	5 Mar 00	Barry
30000m	S	1:31:30.4	Jim Alder	5 Sep 70	London (CP)
	E	1:31:56.4	Tim Johnston	5 Sep 70	London (CP)
	W	1:33:49.0	Bernie Plain	1 Dec 73	Bristol
	NI	1:57:30.0	Ian Anderson	5 Mar 00	Barry
Half Marathon	E	59:22	Mo Farah	13 Sep 15	South Shields
	S	60:00	Callum Hawkins	5 Feb 17	Marugame, (JPN)
	W	60:59	Steve Jones	8 Jun 86	South Shields
	NI	62:09	Paul Pollock (IRL)	29 Mar 14	Copenhagen, DEN
Marathon	W	2:07:13	Steve Jones	20 Oct 85	Chicago, USA
	E	2:08:21	Mo Farah	13 Apr 14	London
	S	2:09:16	Allister Hutton	21 Apr 85	London
	NI	2:13:06	Greg Hannon	13 May 79	Coventry
2000m SC	E	5:19.86	Mark Rowland	28 Aug 88	London (CP)
	S	5:21.77	Tom Hanlon	11 Jun 92	Caserta, ITA
	W	5:23.6	Roger Hackney	10 Jun 82	Birmingham
	NI	5:31.09	Peter McColgan	5 Aug 86	Gateshead
3000m SC	E	8:07.96	Mark Rowland	30 Sep 88	Seoul, KOR
	S	8:12.58	Tom Hanlon	3 Aug 91	Monaco, MON
	W	8:18.91	Roger Hackney	30 Jul 88	Hechtel, BEL
	NI	8:27.93	Peter McColgan	25 Jun 91	Hengelo, HOL
110m H	W	12.91	Colin Jackson	20 Aug 93	Stuttgart, GER
	E	13.00	Tony Jarrett	20 Aug 93	Stuttgart, GER
	S	13.44	Chris Baillie	21 Mar 06	Melbourne, AUS
	NI	13.48	Ben Reynolds (IRL)	1 Aug 15	Bedford
200m H	W	22.63	Colin Jackson	1 Jun 91	Cardiff
	E	22.79	John Regis	1 Jun 91	Cardiff
	S	23.76	Angus McKenzie	22 Aug 81	Edinburgh
	NI	24.81	Terry Price	31 Aug 92	Belfast

400m H	E	47.82		Kriss Akabusi	6	Aug 92	Barcelona, ESP
	W	47.84		Dai Greene	6	Jul 12	Saint Denis, FRA
	NI	49.60		Phil Beattie	28	Jul 86	Edinburgh
	S	50.24		Charles Robertson-Adams	4	Jul 01	Loughborough
High	E	2.38	i	Steve Smith	4	Feb 94	Wuppertal, GER
Jump		2.37		Steve Smith	20	Sep 92	Seoul, KOR
		2.37		Steve Smith	22	Aug 93	Lausanne, SUI
		2.37		Robbie Grabarz	23	Aug 12	Stuttgart, GER
	S	2.31		Geoff Parsons	26	Aug 94	Victoria, CAN
	W	2.25		Robert Mitchell	28	Jul 01	Bedford
	NI	2.20		Floyd Manderson	14	Jul 85	London (CP)
		2.20		Floyd Manderson	21	Jun 86	London (CP)
		2.20		Floyd Manderson	16	Aug 86	Leiden, HOL
Pole	E	5.83	i	Luke Cutts	25	Jan 14	Rouen, FRA
Vault		5.82		Steve Lewis	21	Jul 12	Szczecin, POL
	S	5.65		Jax Thoirs	16	May 15	Los Angeles, USA
		5.65	i	Jax Thoirs	1	Jul 15	Grangemouth
	W	5.60		Neil Winter	19	Aug 95	Enfield
	NI	5.25		Mike Bull	22	Sep 73	London (CP)
Long	E	8.51		Greg Rutherford	24	Apr 14	Chula Vista, USA
Jump	W	8.23		Lynn Davies	30	Jun 68	Berne, SUI
	NI	8.14		Mark Forsythe	7	Jul 91	Rhede, GER
	S	8.01		Darren Ritchie	16	Jun 04	Guadalajara, ESP
Triple	E	18.29		Jonathan Edwards	7	Aug 95	Gothenburg, SWE
Jump	W	16.71		Steven Shalders	3	Aug 05	Manchester
	S	16.17		John Mackenzie	17	Sep 94	Bedford
	NI	15.78		Michael McDonald	31	Jul 94	Corby
Shot	E	21.92		Carl Myerscough	13	Jun 03	Sacramento
	W	20.45		Shaun Pickering	17	Aug 97	London (CP)
	S	18.93		Paul Buxton	13	May 77	Los Angeles(Ww), USA
	NI	17.61		Iain McMullan	13	Jul 02	Dublin (S), IRL
Discus	E	68.24		Lawrence Okoye	19	May 12	Halle, GER
	W	66.84		Brett Morse	30	Jun 13	Cardiff
	S	63.38		Nicholas Percy	22	Jul 16	Helsingborg, SWE
	NI	51.76		John Moreland	1	Jul 95	Antrim
Hammer	E	77.55		Nick Miller	22	Jul 15	Karlstad, GER
	NI	77.54		Martin Girvan	12	May 84	Wolverhampton
	S	76.93		Mark Dry	17	May 15	Loughborough
	W	70.00		Osain Jones	29	Jul 17	Leiria, POR
Javelin	E	91.46		Steve Backley	25	Jan 92	Auckland(NS), NZL
	W	81.70		Nigel Bevan	28	Jun 92	Birmingham
	S	80.38		James Campbell	18	Jul 10	Dunfermline
	NI	79.55		Michael Allen	10	Jun 06	Belfast
Dec.	E	8847		Daley Thompson	9	Aug 84	Los Angeles, USA
	S	7885	#h	Brad McStravick	6	May 84	Birmingham
		7856	#	Brad McStravick	28	May 84	Cwmbrân
	NI	7874		Colin Boreham	23	May 82	Götzis, AUT
	W	7882		Ben Gregory	14	Apr 16	Azusa, USA
(with 1986 Javelin)							
	E	8811	#	Daley Thompson	28	Aug 86	Stuttgart, GER
	S	7739		Jamie Quarry	30	May 99	Arles, FRA
	NI	7510		Peter Glass	14	Jul 13	Grangemouth

4x100m	E	37.37	C. Ujah, A. Gemili (UK)			
			D. Talbot, N. Mitchell-Blake	12 Aug 17	London (O)
	W	38.73	K. Williams, D. Turner,			
			C. Malcolm, J. Henthorn	21 Sep 98	Kuala Lumpur, MAS
	S	39.24	D. Jenkins, A. Wells,			
			C. Sharp, A. McMaster	12 Aug 78	Edmonton, CAN
	NI	40.71	J. Smyth, L. Reid,			
			D. Adams, C. Robinson	9 Jul 17	London (O)
4x400m	E	2:57.53	R. Black, D. Redmond, (UK)			
			J. Regis, K. Akabusi	1 Sep 91	Tokyo, JAP
	W	3:00.41	T. Benjamin, I. Thomas,			
			J. Baulch, M. Elias	31 Jul 02	Manchester (C)
	S	3:03.94	K. Robertson, J. Bowie,			
			G. Louden, G. Plenderleith	1 Aug 14	Glasgow (HP)
	NI	3:07.27	B. Forbes, M. Douglas,			
			E. King, P. McBurney	21 Sep 98	Kuala Lumpur, MAS

Track Walking

3000m	E	10:58.21	i	Tom Bosworth	28 Feb 16	Sheffield
		11:15.26	+	Tom Bosworth	2 Jul 17	Birmingham
	W	11:45.77		Steve Johnson	20 Jun 87	Cwmbrân
	S	11:53.3	#	Martin Bell	9 Aug 95	Birmingham
		11:59.47		Martin Bell	25 May 98	Bedford
	NI	13:15.0		David Smyth	5 Sep 70	Plymouth
5000m	E	18:39.47	i	Tom Bosworth	12 Feb 17	Sheffield
		18:43.28		Tom Bosworth	2 Jul 17	Birmingham
	W	20:08.04	i	Steve Barry	5 Mar 83	Budapest, HUN
		20:22.0		Steve Barry	20 Mar 82	London (WL)
	S	20:13.0		Martin Bell	2 May 92	Enfield
	NI	23:50.0		Jimmy Todd	28 Aug 68	Ballyclare
10000m	E	40:06.65		Ian McCombie	4 Jun 89	Jarrow
	W	41:13.62		Steve Barry	19 Jun 82	London (CP)
	S	41:13.65		Martin Bell	22 Jul 95	Cardiff
	NI	47:37.6		David Smyth	26 Apr 70	Bournemouth
1 Hour	E	14,324 m	#	Ian McCombie	7 Jul 85	London (SP)
		14,158 m		Mark Easton	12 Sep 87	Woodford
	W	13,987 m		Steve Barry	28 Jun 81	Brighton
	S	13,393 m		Bill Sutherland	27 Sep 69	London (He)
	NI	12,690 m	#	David Smyth	26 Apr 70	Bournemouth
		12,646 m		David Smyth	23 Sep 67	London (PH)
20000m	E	1:23:26.5		Ian McCombie	26 May 90	Fana, NOR
	W	1:26:22.0		Steve Barry	28 Jun 81	Brighton
	S	1:38:53.6		Alan Buchanan	6 Jul 75	Brighton
2 Hours	E	27,262 m	#	Chris Maddocks	31 Dec 89	Plymouth
		26,037 m		Ron Wallwork	31 Jul 71	Blackburn

Road Walking

10km	E	39:36		Tom Bosworth	1 Mar 15	Coventry
	W	40:35		Steve Barry	14 May 83	Southport
	S	41:28		Martin Bell	24 Apr 99	Sheffield
	NI	44:49	#	David Smyth	20 Jun 70	Clevedon
		51:53		Arthur Agnew	6 Aug 80	Helsinki, FIN
		51:53		G. Smyth	6 Aug 80	Helsinki, FIN
20km	E	1:20:13		Tom Bosworth	12 Aug 16	Rio de Janeiro, BRA
	W	1:22:51		Steve Barry	26 Feb 83	Douglas, I of M
	S	1:25:42		Martin Bell	9 May 92	Lancaster
	NI	1:39:01		David Smyth	Jul 67	Cardiff
30km	E	2:07:56		Ian McCombie	27 Apr 86	Edinburgh
	W	2:10:16		Steve Barry	7 Oct 82	Brisbane, AUS
	S	2:22:21		Martin Bell	8 May 94	Cardiff
	NI	2:41:15		David Smyth	26 Apr 69	Winterbourne

50km	E	3:51:37		Chris Maddocks	28	Oct	90	Burrator
	W	4:11:59		Bob Dobson	22	Oct	81	Lassing, AUT
	S	4:13:18		Graham White	27	Jun	98	Stockport
	NI	4:45:48		David Smyth	3	May	69	Bristol

NATIONAL RECORDS OF THE UK - WOMEN
as at 31 December 2017

100m	E	10.99		Dina Asher-Smith	25	Jul	15	London (O)
	W	11.39		Sallyanne Short	12	Jul	92	Cwmbrân
		11.39		Elaine O'Neill	4	Jul	10	La Chaux de Fonds, SUI
		11.39	A	Hannah Brier	16	Jul	15	Cali, COL
		11.39		Hannah Brier	21	Jul	16	Bydgoszcz, POL
	S	11.40		Helen Golden/Hogarth	20	Jul	74	London (CP)
	NI	11.40		Amy Foster (IRL)	10	May	14	Clermont, USA
200m	E	22.07		Dina Asher-Smith	28	Aug	15	Beijing, CHN
	W	22.80		Michelle Scutt	12	Jun	82	Antrim
	S	22.98		Sandra Whittaker	8	Aug	84	Los Angeles, USA
	NI	23.53		Amy Foster (IRL)	18	Aug	11	Shenzhen, CHN
300m	E	35.46		Kathy Cook	18	Aug	84	London (CP)
	W	36.01		Michelle Probert/Scutt	13	Jul	80	London (CP)
	S	36.46		Linsey Macdonald	13	Jul	80	London (CP)
	NI	38.20		Linda McCurry	2	Aug	78	Edmonton, CAN
400m	E	49.41		Christine Ohuruogu	12	Aug	13	Moscow, RUS
	W	50.63		Michelle Scutt	31	May	82	Cwmbrân
	S	50.71		Allison Curbishley	18	Sep	98	Kuala Lumpur, MAS
	NI	52.54		Stephanie Llewellyn	9	Jul	95	Cwmbrân
		52.4		Stephanie Llewellyn	1	Jul	95	London (He)
600m	E	1:24.36		Marilyn Okoro	5	Jul	12	Liège (NX), BEL
	W	1:26.5		Kirsty McDermott/Wade	21	Aug	85	Zürich, SUI
	S	1:27.4	i	Linsey Macdonald	12	Dec	81	Cosford
		1:27.51	+	Lynsey Sharp	16	Aug	14	Zürich, SUI
	NI	1:29.46		Jo Latimer	19	May	93	Birmingham
800m	E	1:56.21		Kelly Holmes	9	Sep	95	Monaco, MON
	W	1:57.42		Kirsty McDermott/Wade	24	Jun	85	Belfast
	S	1:57.69		Lynsey Sharp	20	Aug	16	Rio de Janeiro, BRA
	NI	2:00.79		Ciara Mageean (IRL)	22	Jul	16	Dublin, IRL
1000m	S	2:31.93	i	Laura Muir	18	Feb	17	Birmingham
		2:37.05		Christine Whittingham	27	Jun	86	Gateshead
	E	2:32.55		Kelly Holmes	15	Jun	97	Leeds
	W	2:33.70		Kirsty McDermott/Wade	9	Aug	85	Gateshead
	NI	2:48.59		Jane Ewing	26	Jun	90	Antrim
1500m	S	3:55.22		Laura Muir	27	Aug	16	Saint-Denis, FRA
	E	3:57.90		Kelly Holmes	28	Aug	04	Athens, GRE
	W	3:59.95		Hayley Tullett	31	Aug	03	Saint-Denis, FRA
	NI	4:01.46		Ciara Mageean (IRL)	27	Aug	16	Saint-Denis, FRA
1 Mile	E	4:17.57		Zola Budd	21	Aug	85	Zürich, SUI
	S	4:18.03		Laura Muir	9	Jul	17	London (O)
	W	4:19.41		Kirsty McDermott/Wade	27	Jul	85	Oslo, NOR
	NI	4:22.40		Ciara Mageean (IRL)	9	Jul	17	London (O)
2000m	S	5:26.93		Yvonne Murray	8	Jul	94	Edinburgh
	E	5:30.19		Zola Budd	11	Jul	86	London (CP)
	W	5:45.81	i	Kirsty Wade	13	Mar	87	Cosford
		5:50.17		Susan Tooby/Wightman	13	Jul	84	London (CP)
	NI	5:57.24		Ursula McKee/McGloin	25	Jun	90	Antrim

3000m	E	8:22.20	Paula Radcliffe	19 Jul 02	Monaco, MON
	S	8:26.41 i	Laura Muir	4 Feb 17	Karlsruhe, GER
		8:29.02	Yvonne Murray	25 Sep 88	Seoul, SKO
	W	8:43.72 #mx	Melissa Courtney	6 Sep 17	Watford
		8:45.36 i	Hayley Tullett	10 Mar 01	Lisbon, POR
		8:45.39	Hayley Tullett	15 Jul 00	Gateshead
	NI	8:55.09 i	Ciara Mageean (IRL)	14 Feb 15	New York, USA
		9:07.47	Ciara Mageean (IRL)	7 May 16	Belfast
2 Miles	E	9:17.4 +e	Paula Radcliffe	20 Jun 04	Bydgoszcz, POL
		9:32.00 i	Joanne Pavey	17 Feb 07	Birmingham
		9:32.07	Paula Radcliffe	23 May 99	Loughborough
	S	9:36.85 i	Yvonne Murray	15 Mar 87	Cosford
		9:49.75	Laura Whittle	24 Aug 14	Birmingham
	W	9:49.73	Hayley Tullett	23 May 99	Loughborough
5000m	E	14:29.11	Paula Radcliffe	20 Jun 04	Bydgoszcz, POL
	S	14:48.49	Eilish McColgan	1 Sep 17	Brussels, BEL
	W	15:13.22	Angela Tooby	5 Aug 87	Oslo, NOR
	NI	15:50.55	Emma Mitchell (IRL)	13 May 17	Solihull
10000m	E	30:01.09	Paula Radcliffe	6 Aug 02	Munich, GER
	S	30:57.07	Liz McColgan	25 Jun 91	Hengelo, HOL
	W	31:55.30	Angela Tooby	4 Sep 87	Rome, ITA
	NI	32:51.78	Emma Mitchell (IRL)	20 May 17	London (PH)
1 Hour	E	16,495 m #	Michaela McCallum	2 Apr 00	Asti
		16,364 m	Alison Fletcher	3 Sep 97	Bromley
	W	16,460 m i#	Bronwen Cardy-Wise	8 Mar 92	Birmingham
		14,400 m	Ann Franklin	5 Mar 89	Barry
	S	12,800 m	Leslie Watson	12 Mar 83	London (He)
20000m	E	1:15:46	Carolyn Hunter-Rowe	6 Mar 94	Barry
	W	1:23:56	Ann Franklin	9 Mar 86	Barry
25000m	E	1:35:16 e	Carolyn Hunter-Rowe	6 Mar 94	Barry
	W	1:44:58 e	Ann Franklin	9 Mar 86	Barry
	S	1:54:55	Leslie Watson	12 Mar 83	London (He)
30000m	E	1:55:03	Carolyn Hunter-Rowe	6 Mar 94	Barry
	W	2:05:59	Ann Franklin	9 Mar 86	Barry
	S	2:16:44	Leslie Watson	12 Mar 83	London (He)
Half Marathon	E	65:40	Paula Radcliffe	22 Sep 03	South Shields
	S	67:11	Liz McColgan	26 Jan 92	Tokyo, JPN
	W	69:56	Susan Tooby/Wightman	24 Jul 88	South Shields
	NI	72:57	Teresa Duffy (IRL)	1 Apr 01	Berlin, GER
Marathon	E	2:15:25	Paula Radcliffe	13 Apr 03	London
	S	2:26:52	Liz McColgan	13 Apr 97	London
	W	2:31:33	Susan Tooby/Wightman	23 Sep 88	Seoul, KOR
	NI	2:35:27	Teresa Duffy (IRL)	22 Apr 01	London
2000mSC	S	6:21.31	Lenny Waite	1 Jun 17	Houston, USA
	E	6:26.08	Louise Webb	16 Apr 16	Milton Keynes
	NI	6:37.50	Kerry Harty	6 Jul 13	Manchester (SC)
	W	6:38.76	Jade Williams	13 May 17	Solihull
3000mSC	E	9:24.24	Barbara Parker	2 Jun 12	Eugene, USA
	S	9:35.82	Eilish McColgan	10 Aug 13	Moscow, RUS
	NI	9:42.61	Kerry O'Flaherty (IRL)	10 Jul 15	Letterkenney, IRL
	W	10:25.03	Jade Williams	21 May 17	Loughborough

Event		Mark		Athlete	Date		Venue
100m H	E	12.51		Tiffany Porter	14	Sep 14	Marrakech, MAR
	W	12.91		Kay Morley-Brown	2	Feb 90	Auckland, NZL
	NI	13.29		Mary Peters	2	Sep 72	Munich, GER
	S	13.35		Pat Rollo	30	Jul 83	London (CP)
400m H	E	52.74		Sally Gunnell	19	Aug 93	Stuttgart, GER
	S	54.09		Eilidh Doyle	15	Jul 16	Monaco, MON
	NI	55.91		Elaine McLaughlin	26	Sep 88	Seoul, KOR
	W	56.43		Alyson Layzell	16	Jun 96	Birmingham
High Jump	E	1.98		Katarina Johnson-Thompson	12	Aug 16	Rio de Janeiro, BRA
	NI	1.92		Janet Boyle	29	Sep 88	Seoul, KOR
	S	1.91		Jayne Barnetson	7	Jul 89	Edinburgh
	W	1.90	i	Julie Crane	28	Feb 04	Otterberg, GER
		1.89		Julie Crane	15	Aug 04	Glasgow (S)
Pole Vault	E	4.87	i#	Holly Bleasdale/Bradshaw	21	Jan 12	Villerbanne, FRA
		4.81		Holly Bradshaw	15	Jul 17	Rottach-Egern, GER
	S	4.35		Henrietta Paxton	26	Jun 10	Birmingham
	NI	4.45		Zoe Brown (IRL)	15	Jul 14	Cardiff
	W	4.42	i	Sally Peake	18	Feb 12	Nevers, FRA
		4.40		Sally Peake	12	Jul 14	Glasgow (HP)
		4.40		Sally Peake	21	Apr 16	Chula Vista, USA
Long Jump	E	7.07		Shara Proctor	28	Aug 15	Beijing, CHN
	W	6.54		Rebecca Chapman	2	Jul 17	Birmingham
	S	6.47		Jade Nimmo	14	Apr 12	Bowling Green,USA
	NI	6.13		Linzi Herron	2	Jul 13	Cork, IRL
Triple Jump	E	15.16	i	Ashia Hansen	28	Feb 98	Valencia, SPA
		15.15		Ashia Hansen	13	Sep 97	Fukuoka, JPN
	S	13.62		Nony Mordi	5	Jul 08	Machester (SC)
	W	12.95		Hannah Frankson	9	Jun 13	Alphen, NED
	NI	12.10		Mary Devlin	26	Apr 03	Marsa, MLT
Shot	E	19.36		Judy Oakes	14	Aug 88	Gateshead
	S	18.99		Meg Ritchie	7	May 83	Tucson, USA
	W	19.06	i	Venissa Head	7	Apr 84	St. Athan
		18.93		Venissa Head	13	May 84	Haverfordwest
	NI	16.63		Eva Massey	20	May 07	Loughborough
Discus	S	67.48		Meg Ritchie	26	Apr 81	Walnut, USA
	E	65.10		Jade Lally	27	Feb 16	Sydney, AUS
	W	64.68		Venissa Head	18	Jul 83	Athens, GRE
	NI	60.72		Jackie McKernan	18	Jul 93	Buffalo, USA
Hammer	E	74.54		Sophie Hitchon	15	Aug 16	Rio de Janeiro, BRA
	S	67.58		Shirley Webb	16	Jul 05	Loughborough
	W	66.80		Carys Parry	15	Jul 14	Cardiff
	NI	59.57		Hayley Murray	18	Jul 17	Cork, IRL
Javelin	E	66.17		Goldie Sayers	14	Aug 12	London (CP)
	S	57.19		Lorna Jackson	9	Jul 00	Peterborough
	W	52.78		Tesni Ward	29	May 11	Bedford
	NI	49.23		Laura Kerr	20	Aug 05	Belfast
Hept.	E	6955		Jessica Ennis	4	Aug 12	London (O)
	S	5803		Jayne Barnetson	20	Aug 89	Kiyev, UKR
	NI	5759		Kate O'Connor	21	Jul 17	Grosseto, ITA
	W	5642		Sarah Rowe	23	Aug 81	Utrecht, HOL
(with 1999 Javelin)							
	S	5552		Laura Redmond	8	Jun 03	Arles, FRA
	W	5430		Katia Lennon	23	Jul 06	Berne, SUI

4x100m	E	41.77	A. Philip, D. Henry, (UK)			
			D. Asher-Smith, D. Neita	19 Aug 16	Rio de Janeiro, BRA
	W	44.51	H. Brier, H. Thomas			
			M. Moore, R. Johncock	2 Aug 14	Glasgow (HP)
	S	45.37	J. Booth, K. Hogg,			
			J. Neilson, S. Whittaker	8 Jun 86	Lloret de Mar,ESP
		45.2	A. MacRitchie, S. Pringle, (ESH)			
			H. Hogarth, E. Sutherland	27 Jun 70	London (CP)
	NI	46.36	K. Graham, H. Gourlay,			
			J. Robinson, R. Gaylor	31 Aug 85	Tel Aviv, ISR
4x400m	E	3:22.01	L. Hanson, P. Smith, (UK)			
			S. Gunnell, L. Staines	1 Sep 91	Tokyo, JPN
	S	3:30.91	G Nicol, E Child,			
			K Evans, L. McConnell	12 Oct 10	Dehli, IND
	W	3:35.60	C. Smart, K. Wade,			
			D. Fryar, M. Scutt	4 Jul 82	Dublin (S), IRL
	NI	3:40.12	Z. Arnold, V. Jamison,			
			J. Latimer, S. Llewellyn	22 Jun 96	Belfast

Track Walking

3000m	E	12:22.62	Jo Jackson	14 Feb 09	Sydney, AUS
	W	12:24.70	Bethan Davies	11 Jun 16	Cardiff
	S	13:16.23	Verity Snook	27 May 96	Bedford
5000m	E	20:46.58	Jo Jackson	14 Feb 09	Sydney, AUS
	W	21:21.52	Bethan Davies	2 Jul 17	Birmingham
	S	23:22.52	Verity Snook	19 Jun 94	Horsham
10000m	E	45:09.57	Lisa Kehler	13 Aug 00	Birmingham
	W	47:05.97	Bethan Davies	29 Jan 17	Canberra, AUS
	S	47:10.07	Verity Larby/Snook	19 Jun 93	Horsham
1 Hour	E	11,590 m	Lisa Langford/Kehler	13 Sep 86	Woodford
20000m	W	1:36:39.70	Bethan Davies	21 Jun 15	Bedford
	E	1:56:59.7	Cath Reader	21 Oct 95	Loughborough
2 Hours	E	20,502 m	Cath Reader	21 Oct 95	Loughborough

Road Walking

5km	E	21:36	Vicky Lupton/White	18 Jul 92	Sheffield
	W	22:28 +	Bethan Davies	6 Mar 16	Coventry
	S	22:45	Verity Snook	25 Aug 94	Victoria, CAN
10km	E	43:52	Jo Jackson	14 Mar 10	Covenrty
	W	44:59	Bethan Davies	6 Mar 16	Coventry
	S	46:06	Verity Snook	25 Aug 94	Victoria, CAN
20km	E	1:30:41	Jo Jackson	19 Jun 10	La Coruna, ESP
	S	1:36:40	Sara Cattermole	4 Mar 00	Perth, AUS
	W	1:33:04	Bethan Davies	25 Jun 17	Leeds
50km	E	4:50:51	Sandra Brown	13 Jul 91	Basildon

UK INDOOR RECORDS
as at 31 Dec 2017

MEN

50m	5.61 +	Jason Gardener	16 Feb 00	Madrid, ESP
60m	6.42	Dwain Chambers	7 Mar 09	Turin, ITA
200m	20.25	Linford Christie	19 Feb 95	Liévin, FRA
400m	45.39	Jamie Baulch	9 Feb 97	Birmingham
800m	1:44.91	Sebastian Coe	12 Mar 83	Cosford
1000m	2:17.86	Matthew Yates	22 Feb 92	Birmingham
1500m	3:34.20	Peter Elliott	27 Feb 90	Seville, ESP
1 Mile	3:52.02	Peter Elliott	9 Feb 90	East Rutherford, USA
2000m	4:57.09	John Mayock	25 Feb 01	Liévin, FRA
3000m	7:33.1 +	Mo Farah	21 Feb 15	Birmingham
	7:34.47	Mo Farah	21 Feb 09	Birmingham
5000m	13:09.16	Mo Farah	18 Feb 17	Birmingham
50m Hurdles	6.40	Colin Jackson	5 Feb 99	Budapest, HUN
60m Hurdles	7.30	Colin Jackson	6 Mar 94	Sindelfingen, GER
High Jump	2.38	Steve Smith	4 Feb 94	Wuppertal, GER
Pole Vault	5.83	Luke Cutts	25 Jan 14	Rouen, FRA
Long Jump	8.26A	Greg Rutherford	5 Feb 16	Albuquerque, USA
Triple Jump	17.75	Phillips Idowu	9 Mar 08	Valencia, ESP
Shot	21.49	Carl Myerscough	15 Mar 03	Fayetteville, USA
Heptathlon	6165	Tim Duckworth	11 Mar 17	College Station, USA

(6.77, 7.77, 13.09, 2.16, 8.10, 5.26, 3:04.24)

5000m Walk	18:39.47	Tom Bosworth	12 Feb 17	Sheffield
4 x 200m Relay	1:22.11	UK National Team	3 Mar 91	Glasgow

(Linford Christie, Darren Braithwaite, Ade Mafe, John Regis)

4 x 400m Relay	3:03.20	UK National Team	7 Mar 99	Maebashi, JPN

(Allyn Condon, Solomon Wariso, Adrian Patrick, Jamie Baulch)

WOMEN

50m	6.21	Wendy Hoyte	22 Feb 81	Grenoble, FRA
60m	7.06	Asha Philip	5 Mar 17	Belgrade, SRB
200m	22.83	Katharine Merry	14 Feb 99	Birmingham
400m	50.02	Nicola Sanders	3 Mar 07	Birmingham
800m	1:58.43	Jenny Meadows	14 Mar 10	Doha, QAT
1000m	2:31.93	Laura Muir	18 Feb 17	Birmingham
1500m	4:02.39	Laura Muir	4 Mar 17	Belgrade, SRB
1 Mile	4:23.86	Kirsty Wade	5 Feb 88	New York, USA
2000m	5:40.86	Yvonne Murray	20 Feb 93	Birmingham
3000m	8:26.41	Laura Muir	4 Feb 17	Karlsruhe, GER
5000m	14:49.12	Laura Muir	4 Jan 17	Glasgow
50m Hurdles	6.83	Tiffany Ofili/Porter	28 Jan 12	New York, USA
60m Hurdles	7.80	Tiffany Ofili/Porter	4 Mar 11	Paris, FRA
High Jump	1.97	Katarina Johnson-Thompson	14 Feb 15	Sheffield
Pole Vault	4.87	Holly Bleasdale	21 Jan 12	Villeurbanne, FRA
Long Jump	6.97	Lorriane Ugen	5 Mar 17	Belgrade, SRB
Triple Jump	15.16	Ashia Hansen	28 Feb 98	Valencia, ESP
Shot	19.06	Venissa Head	7 Apr 84	St. Athan
Pentathlon	5000	Katarina Johnson-Thompson	6 Mar 15	Prague, CZE

(8.18, 1.95, 12.32, 6.89, 2:12.78)

3000m Walk	12:44.99	Bethan Davies	28 Feb 16	Sheffield
4 x 200m Relay	1:33.96	UK National Team	23 Feb 90	Glasgow

(Paula Thomas, Jenni Stoute, Linda Staines, Sally Gunnell)

4 x 400m Relay	3:27.56	UK National Team	3 Mar 13	Gothenburg, SWE

(Eilidh Child, Shana Cox, Christine Ohuruogu, Perri Shakes-Drayton)

UK ALL TIME LISTS - MEN
as at 31 December 2017

100 Metres

9.87	Linford Christie ¶	15	Aug	93
9.91	Christie	23	Aug	94
9.91	James Dasaolu	13	Jul	13
9.92	Christie	25	Aug	91
9.96	Christie	1	Aug	92
9.96	Chijindu Ujah	8	Jun	14
9.96	Ujah	24	Jul	15
9.96	Joel Fearon	30	Jul	16
9.97	Christie	24	Sep	88
9.97	Christie	15	Aug	93
9.97 A	Christie	23	Sep	95
9.97	Dwain Chambers ¶	22	Aug	99
9.97	Dasaolu	11	Aug	13
9.97	Adam Gemili	7	Jun	15
9.97	Ujah	24	Aug	17
9.98	Jason Gardener	2	Jul	99
9.99	Nethaneel Mitchell-Blake	13	May	17
10.01	Richard Kilty	16	Jul	16
10.03	Simeon Williamson	12	Jul	08
10.03	Reece Prescod	4	Aug	17
10.04	Darren Campbell	19	Aug	98
10.04	Mark Lewis-Francis	5	Jul	02
10.04	James Ellington	7	Jul	16
10.06	Marlon Devonish	10	Jul	07
10.06	Tyrone Edgar	31	May	08
10.08	Harry Aikines-Aryeetey	13	Jul	13
10.09	Jason Livingston ¶	13	Jun	92
10.10	Andy Robertson	23	Aug	14
10.10	Zharnel Hughes	16	Apr	16
10.11	Allan Wells	24	Jul	80
10.11	Christian Malcolm	5	Aug	01
10.12	Darren Braithwaite	15	Jul	95
10.12	Ojie Edoburun	17	Jun	17
10.14	Craig Pickering	13	Jul	07
10.14	Danny Talbot	31	May	14
10.14	Sean Safo-Antwi	7	Jun	14
10.15	Michael Rosswess	15	Sep	91
10.15	John Regis	29	May	93
10.16	Rikki Fifton	28	Sep	07
10.17	Ian Mackie	25	Aug	96
10.18	Deji Tobais	7	Jun	14
10.18	Kieran Daly	21	Jun	14
10.18	Reuben Arthur	17	Jun	17
10.20	Cameron Sharp	24	Aug	83
10.20	Elliot Bunney	14	Jun	86
10.20	Ryan Scott	17	Jul	08
10.20	Josh Swaray (now SEN)	13	Jul	13
10.21 A	Ainsley Bennett	8	Sep	79
10.21	Jamie Henderson	6	Aug	87
10.21	Allyn Condon	14	Aug	99
10.21	Luke Fagan	15	Sep	11
10.21	Samuel Osewa	2	Jun	17
10.21	Kyle De Escofet	2	Jun	17
10.21	Romell Glave	17	Jun	17
10.22	Mike McFarlane	20	Jun	86
10.22	Tim Abeyie	22	Jun	06
10.22	Leevan Yearwood	17	Jul	08
10.22	James Alaka	13	May	12
10.23	Marcus Adam	26	Jul	91
10.23	Jason John	15	Jul	94
10.23	Terry Williams	22	Aug	94
10.23	Theo Etienne	20	Jul	16
10.23	Adam Thomas	22	Jul	17

wind assisted

9.90	Christie	24	Aug	91
9.90	Harry Aikines-Aryeetey	15	Apr	17
9.91	Christie	11	Jun	94
9.92	Richard Kilty	29	May	16
9.93	Christie	28	Jan	90
9.93	Dasalaolu	25	Jun	16
9.93	Ojie Edoburun	15	Apr	17
9.95	Christie	22	Jun	90
9.95	Ujah	27	May	17
9.96	James Ellington	25	Jun	16
9.97 †	Mark Lewis-Francis	4	Aug	01
10.00	Ian Mackie	18	Jul	98
10.01	Doug Walker ¶	18	Jul	98
10.02	Allan Wells	4	Oct	82
10.03	Kieran Showler-Davis	3	Aug	16
10.04 A	Tyrone Edgar	10	May	03
10.04	Deji Tobais	23	Aug	14
10.07	Cameron Sharp	4	Oct	82
10.07	John Regis	28	Aug	90
10.07	Toby Box	11	Jun	94
10.07	Michael Rosswess	11	Jun	94
10.07	Sean Safo-Antwi	23	Aug	14
10.08	Mike McFarlane	27	May	84
10.08	Jason John	11	Jun	94
10.08	Craig Pickering	17	Jun	09
10.08	Zharnel Hughes	15	Apr	17
10.09 †	Christian Malcolm	4	Aug	01
10.10	Donovan Reid	26	Jun	83
10.10	Leevan Yearwood	3	Jul	09
10.11	Drew McMaster	26	Jun	83
10.12	Buster Watson	27	May	84
10.13	Jonathan Barbour	30	Jun	01
10.13	Danny Talbot	21	May	17
10.14	Ernest Obeng	20	Jun	87
10.14	Marcus Adam	28	Jan	90
10.14	Theo Etienne	20	Jul	16
10.16	Daniel Money	21	Jun	97
10.16	Roy Ejiakuekwu	25	May	17
10.17	Terry Williams	23	Aug	94
10.17	Owusu Dako	5	Jul	98

† wind gauge faulty - probably windy

hand timing

10.1	David Jenkins	20	May	72
10.1	Brian Green	3	Jun	72

hand timing - wind assisted

10.0	Allan Wells	16	Jun	79
10.0	Drew McMaster	1	Jun	80
10.1	Dave Roberts	17	Jul	82

200 Metres

	19.87 A	John Regis	31	Jul	94
	19.94	Regis	20	Aug	93
	19.95	Nethaneel Mitchell-Blake	14	May	16
	19.97	Adam Gemili	9	Sep	16
	19.98	Gemili	16	Aug	13
	19.98	Gemili	15	Aug	14
	20.01	Regis	2	Aug	94
	20.02	Zharnel Hughes	27	Aug	15
	20.04	Mitchell-Blake	27	May	17
	20.05	Hughes	24	Jul	15
	20.08	Christian Malcolm	8	Aug	01
	20.09	Linford Christie ¶	28	Sep	88
	20.13	Darren Campbell	27	Sep	00
	20.16	Danny Talbot	7	Aug	17
	20.18	Julian Golding	19	Sep	98
10	20.19	Marlon Devonish	29	Jul	02
	20.21	Allan Wells	28	Jul	80
	20.22	Chris Clarke	25	Aug	13
	20.31	Dwain Chambers ¶	22	Jul	01
	20.31	James Ellington	30	Apr	16
	20.34	Chris Lambert	20	Jul	03
	20.34	Richard Kilty	7	Jul	13
	20.35	Doug Walker ¶	26	Jul	98
	20.36	Todd Bennett	28	May	84
	20.37	Toby Sandeman	18	Jul	09
20	20.37	Thomas Somers	24	Jul	14
	20.38	Jeffrey Lawal-Balogun	28	Jun	09
	20.38	Reece Prescod	25	Aug	16
	20.38	Leon Reid	2	Jul	17
	20.39	Chijindu Ujah	8	Apr	17
	20.40	Delano Williams	16	May	15
	20.41	Marcus Adam	13	Jun	92
	20.42 A	Ainsley Bennett	12	Sep	79
	20.43	Mike McFarlane	7	Oct	82
	20.43	Doug Turner	9	Jun	96
30	20.43	Leon Baptiste	10	Oct	10
	20.44	Miguel Francis	15	Apr	17
	20.45	James Alaka	13	May	12
	20.46	Rikki Fifton	6	Jun	09
	20.46	Harry Aikines-Aryeetey	3	Jul	11
	20.47	Cameron Sharp	9	Sep	82
	20.47	Darren Braithwaite	13	May	95
	20.49	Alex Nelson	5	Jul	08
	20.50	Terry Williams	24	Aug	94
	20.50	Tony Jarrett	16	Jul	95
40	20.50	Solomon Wariso	16	Jul	95
	20.51	Michael Rosswess	28	Sep	88
	20.53 i	Allyn Condon	8	Feb	98
	20.54	Ade Mafe	25	Aug	85
	20.56	Roger Black	4	May	96
	20.57	Owusu Dako	16	Jul	95
	20.57	Tim Abeyie	5	Jul	08
	20.58	Dwayne Grant	10	Aug	03
	20.60	Luke Fagan	13	Aug	11
	20.60	David Bolarinwa	8	Jun	13
50	20.60 i	Sam Watts	13	Feb	16
	20.61	Deji Tobais	7	Jul	12
	20.62	Buster Watson	5	Jun	83
	20.62	Donovan Reid	28	May	84
	20.62	Mark Richardson	24	Aug	97
	20.62 i	Daniel Caines	1	Mar	02

wind assisted

19.86	Danny Talbot	15	Apr	17
19.96	Mitchell-Blake	28	May	16
20.10	Marcus Adam	1	Feb	90
20.11	Allan Wells	20	Jun	80
20.18	Marlon Devonish	14	Jul	02
20.26	Ade Mafe	1	Feb	90
20.36	Doug Turner	27	Jul	97
20.38	Dwayne Grant	23	Aug	03
20.40	Ojie Edoburun	28	Apr	17
20.48	Michael Rosswess	9	Sep	90
20.50	Sam Watts	21	Mar	14
20.51	Jason John	2	Jul	93
20.52	Edmond Amaning	7	Jun	17
20.55	Buster Watson	10	Aug	85
20.55	Roy Ejiakuekwu	27	May	17
20.56	Greg Cackett	7	Jul	13
20.56	Toby Harries	9	Sep	15
20.57	Tyrone Edgar	10	May	03
20.57	Tommy Ramdhan	18	Jul	15
20.59	Allyn Condon	25	Jul	99
20.60	Tim Benjamin	7	Aug	99

hand timing (* 220 yards time less 0.1)

20.3	David Jenkins	19	Aug	72
20.4 *	Peter Radford	28	May	60
20.6	Donovan Reid	1	Jul	84

hand timing - wind assisted

20.4	Buster Watson	11	Aug	85
20.5	Roger Black	6	Jul	96
20.6	Ainsley Bennett	22	Jun	74
20.6	Mark Richardson	6	Jul	96

300 Metres

31.56	Doug Walker ¶	19	Jul	98
31.67	John Regis	17	Jul	92
31.87	Mark Richardson	19	Jul	98
31.98	Regis	19	Jun	93
31.99	Regis	21	Jun	91
32.06	Jamie Baulch	31	May	97
32.08	Roger Black	8	Aug	86
32.14	Todd Bennett	18	Aug	84
32.14	Delano Williams	7	Jun	15
32.23	Solomon Wariso	19	Jul	98
32.26	Mark Hylton	19	Jul	98
32.29	Chris Clarke	13	Sep	15
32.31	Rabah Yousif Bkheit	7	Sep	14
32.32	Derek Redmond	16	Jul	88

during 400m

32.06 +	Roger Black	29	Aug	91
32.08 +	Iwan Thomas	5	Aug	97
32.26 +	Derek Redmond	1	Sep	87
32.35 +	David Grindley	26	Jun	93

400 Metres

44.36	Iwan Thomas	13	Jul	97
44.37	Roger Black	3	Jul	96
44.37	Mark Richardson	9	Jul	98
44.37	Richardson	8	Aug	98
44.38	Thomas	8	Aug	98
44.39	Black	16	Jun	96
44.41	Black	29	Jul	96
44.45	Martyn Rooney	23	Aug	15
44.46	Thomas	2	Jul	97
44.47	David Grindley	3	Aug	92
44.47	Richardson	5	Aug	97
44.47	Richardson	24	Aug	99
44.48	Matthew Hudson-Smith	13	Aug	16
44.50	Derek Redmond	1	Sep	87
44.54	Rabah Yousif Bkheit	24	Aug	15
44.56	Tim Benjamin	9	Sep	05
44.57	Jamie Baulch	3	Jul	96
44.66	Du'aine Ladejo	16	Jun	96
44.68	Solomon Wariso	26	Jul	98
44.74	Michael Bingham	19	Aug	09
44.93	David Jenkins	21	Jun	75
44.93	Kriss Akabusi	7	Aug	88
44.94	Andrew Steele	18	Aug	08
44.98	Daniel Caines	27	Jul	02
45.01	Robert Tobin	11	Jun	05
45.06	Conrad Williams	6	Jun	15
45.09	Jarryd Dunn	20	Jun	15
45.11	Nigel Levine	7	Jun	12
45.20	Sean Baldock	12	Aug	00
45.22	Brian Whittle	25	Sep	88
45.23	Luke Lennon-Ford	2	Jun	12
45.24	Mark Hylton	12	Aug	98
45.26	Phil Brown	26	May	85
45.27	Todd Bennett	7	Aug	88
45.30	Ade Mafe	23	Jul	93
45.33	Paul Sanders	15	Jun	91
45.34	Dwayne Cowan	20	Aug	17
45.42	Delano Williams	9	May	15
45.45	George Caddick	26	May	17
45.47	David McKenzie	12	Jun	94
45.48	John Regis	17	Apr	93
45.48	Richard Strachan	7	Jul	13
45.49	Glen Cohen	21	May	78
45.57	Jared Deacon	16	Jun	02
45.58	Ian Mackie	13	Jul	03
45.59	Chris Clarke	24	Jul	09
45.60	Malachi Davis	24	Jul	05
45.61	Richard Buck	2	Jun	12
45.63	Adrian Patrick	5	Jul	95
45.64	Paul Harmsworth	7	Aug	88
45.64	Cameron Chalmers	18	Jun	17
45.65	Alan Bell	14	Jun	80
45.67	Roger Hunter	19	May	85
45.74	Steve Heard	26	May	85
45.75	Robbie Brightwell	19	Oct	64
45.76	Guy Bullock	16	Jun	96
45.77	Louis Persent	2	Jun	12
45.81	Terry Whitehead	14	Jun	80
45.82	Dai Greene	31	Jul	11

hand timing (* 440 yards time less 0.3)

45.6 *	Robbie Brightwell	14	Jul	62
45.7	Adrian Metcalfe	2	Sep	61

600 Metres

1:14.95	Steve Heard	14	Jul	91
1:15.0 +	Sebastian Coe	10	Jun	81
1:15.4	Garry Cook	30	Jul	84
1:15.4	Tom McKean	21	Jul	91
1:15.6	David Jenkins	3	Aug	74
1:15.87	Michael Rimmer	5	Jun	16

800 Metres (* 880 yards time less 0.60)

1:41.73"	Sebastian Coe	10	Jun	81
1:42.33	Coe	5	Jul	79
1:42.88	Steve Cram	21	Aug	85
1:42.97	Peter Elliott	30	May	90
1:43.07	Coe	25	Aug	85
1:43.19	Cram	7	Sep	86
1:43.22	Cram	31	Jul	86
1:43.38	Coe	29	Aug	89
1:43.41	Elliott	1	Sep	87
1:43.42	Cram	17	Aug	88
1:43.77	Andrew Osagie	9	Aug	12
1:43.84	Martin Steele	10	Jul	93
1:43.88	Tom McKean	28	Jul	89
1:43.89	Michael Rimmer	29	Aug	10
1:43.98	David Sharpe	19	Aug	92
1:44.09	Steve Ovett	31	Aug	78
1:44.55	Garry Cook	29	Aug	84
1:44.59	Tony Morrell	2	Jul	88
1:44.65	Ikem Billy	21	Jul	84
1:44.65	Steve Heard	26	Aug	92
1:44.65	James McIlroy	28	Aug	05
1:44.92	Curtis Robb	15	Aug	93
1:44.98	Gareth Warburton	7	Jun	12
1:44.99	Elliot Giles	9	Jul	17
1:45.05	Matthew Yates	26	Aug	92
1:45.10	Richard Hill	10	Jun	06
1:45.10	Guy Learmouth	29	Aug	17
1:45.12	Andy Carter	14	Jul	73
1:45.14	Chris McGeorge	28	Jun	83
1:45.14	John Gladwin	22	Jul	86
1:45.25	Kyle Langford	8	Aug	17
1:45.31	Rob Harrison	21	Jul	84
1:45.35	Kevin McKay	16	Aug	92
1:45.42	Jake Wightman	9	Jul	17
1:45.44	Neil Horsfield	28	Jul	90
1:45.47	Brian Whittle	20	Jul	90
1:45.53	Charlie Grice	22	Jul	16
1:45.6	Graham Williamson	12	Jun	83
1:45.64	Paul Herbert	5	Jun	88
1:45.66	Paul Forbes	8	Jun	83
1:45.67	Sam Ellis	10	Jun	06
1:45.67	Mukhtar Mohammed	26	Jul	13
1:45.68	Mark Sesay	7	Aug	99
1:45.69	Steve Crabb	17	Aug	88
1:45.69	Craig Winrow	21	Jun	96
1:45.70	Ricky Soos	25	Aug	04

33

40	1:45.71	Andy Hart	19	Sep	98		3:32.37	Michael East	2	Jul	04
	1:45.74	Darren St.Clair	13	Aug	10		3:32.69	Peter Elliott	16	Sep	90
	1:45.76	Frank Clement	10	Jul	76		3:33.34	Steve Crabb	4	Jul	87
	1:45.76	Tom Lancashire	13	May	06		3:33.60	Charlie Grice	15	Jul	16 [10]
	1:45.81	David Strang	12	Jul	96		3:33.61	Chris O'Hare	21	Jul	17
	1:45.81	Anthony Whiteman	5	Aug	00		3:33.79	Dave Moorcroft	27	Jul	82
	1:45.81 A	Neal Speaight	8	Apr	03		3:33.83	John Robson	4	Sep	79
	1:45.82	Jason Lobo	7	Aug	99		3:33.96	Tom Lancashire	27	Aug	10
	1:45.96	James Bowness	23	Jul	16		3:34.00	Matthew Yates	13	Sep	91
	1:46.10	Gary Marlow	10	Jul	87		3:34.01	Graham Williamson	28	Jun	83
50	1:46.1	Colin Campbell	26	Jul	72		3:34.1 +	Tony Morrell	14	Jul	90
	1:46.16	Gareth Brown	2	Jul	84		3:34.17	Jake Wightman	15	Jun	17
	1:46.20	David Warren	29	Jun	80		3:34.36 +	Andrew Baddeley	6	Jun	08
	1:46.20	Joe Thomas	26	Jul	08		3:34.50	Adrian Passey	4	Jul	87 [20]
	1:46.21	Pete Browne	14	Jul	73		3:34.53	Mark Rowland	27	Jul	88
	1:46.26	Phil Lewis	27	Jan	74		3:34.59	Kevin McKay	24	Aug	97
	1:46.27	Michael East	31	Jul	04		3:34.76	Gary Lough	9	Sep	95
							3:34.76	Ross Murray	27	May	12
	1000 Metres						3:35.08	Neil Horsfield	10	Aug	90
	2:12.18	Sebastian Coe	11	Jul	81		3:35.26	John Gladwin	5	Sep	86
	2:12.88	Steve Cram	9	Aug	85		3:35.28	Jack Buckner	1	Jul	86
	2:13.40	Coe	1	Jul	80		3:35.53	Andrew Graffin	6	Sep	02
	2:14.90	Coe	16	Jul	86		3:35.66	Frank Clement	12	Aug	78
	2:15.57	James McIlroy	5	Sep	99		3:35.66 i	Lee Emanuel	21	Feb	15 [30]
	2:15.91	Steve Ovett	6	Sep	79		3:36.29		16	May	16
	2:16.30	Peter Elliott	17	Jan	90		3:35.74	Rob Harrison	26	May	86
	2:16.34	Matthew Yates	6	Jul	90		3:35.74	Nick McCormick	22	Jul	05
	2:16.82	Graham Williamson	17	Jul	84		3:35.94	Paul Larkins	10	Jul	87
	2:16.99	Tony Morrell	28	Aug	88		3:35.99	Josh Kerr	14	Apr	17
	2:16.99	Andy Baddeley	7	Aug	07		3:36.22	James Shane	31	Jul	11
10	2:17.13	Michael Rimmer	20	Aug	12		3:36.53	David Strang	15	Jul	94
	2:17.14	John Gladwin	6	Jul	90		3:36.81	Mike Kearns	26	Jul	77
	2:17.20	Rob Harrison	18	Aug	84		3:36.97	Robbie Fitzgibbon	2	Jun	17
	2:17.36	Neil Horsfield	9	Aug	91		3:37.06	James Thie	4	Jul	04
	2:17.43	Gareth Brown	18	Aug	84		3:37.06	Colin McCourt	10	Jul	10 [40]
	2:17.45	Chris McGeorge	20	Aug	84		3:37.17	James Brewer	14	Aug	09
	2:17.63	Kevin McKay	14	Jul	89		3:37.36	Chris Mulvaney	22	Jul	05
	2:17.63	Tom Lancashire	31	Jul	09		3:37.45	Tom Marshall	9	Jul	17
	2:17.75	Steve Crabb	5	Aug	87		3:37.51	David Bishop	29	Apr	12
	2:17.79	David Sharpe	31	Aug	92		3:37.55	Colin Reitz	27	Jun	85
20	2:17.95	Mark Scruton	17	Jul	84		3:37.58 i+	Andrew Butchart	4	Feb	17
	2:17.96	Ikem Billy	14	Jul	89		3:37.64	Brendan Foster	2	Feb	74
	2:18.18	Mal Edwards	11	Jul	86		3:37.67	Richard Peters	27	Jul	13
	2:18.2	John Boulter	6	Sep	69		3:37.75	Jon McCallum	1	Aug	00
	2:18.28	Garry Cook	23	Aug	81		3:37.88	Jason Dullforce	17	Jul	92 [50]
	2:18.31 i	David Strang	30	Jan	93		3:37.90	Tom Farrell	12	Jul	14
							3:37.97	Rod Finch	30	Jul	93
	1500 Metres (+ during 1 mile)						3:37.99	Rob Denmark	5	Jun	95
	3:28.81	Mo Farah	19	Jul	13		3:38.05	Glen Grant	12	Aug	78
	3:28.93	Farah	17	Jul	15		3:38.06	Tim Hutchings	31	Aug	84
	3:29.67	Steve Cram	16	Jul	85		3:38.08	Tom Hanlon	28	Jun	92
	3:29.77	Sebastian Coe	7	Sep	86		3:38.1	Jim McGuinness	1	Aug	77
	3:30.15	Cram	5	Sep	86		3:38.12	Rowan Axe	14	Jun	17
	3:30.77	Steve Ovett	4	Sep	83		3:38.18	Tom Mayo	29	Jun	03
	3:30.95	Cram	19	Aug	88		3:38.2 a	James Espir	11	Jul	80 [60]
	3:31.34	Cram	27	Jun	85		3:38.22	Peter Stewart	15	Jul	72
	3:31.36	Ovett	27	Aug	80		3:38.27	Steve Mitchell	5	Jul	14
	3:31.43	Cram	19	Aug	87		3:38.31	Matt Barnes	23	Jul	93
	3:31.86	John Mayock	22	Aug	97		3:38.33	Neil Speaight	15	Jul	07
	3:32.34	Anthony Whiteman	16	Aug	97		3:38.35	Adam Clarke	2	Jun	17

1 Mile

	Time	Name	Date	
	3:46.32	Steve Cram	27 Jul 85	
	3:47.33	Sebastian Coe	28 Aug 81	
	3:48.31	Cram	5 Jul 86	
	3:48.40	Steve Ovett	26 Aug 81	
	3:48.53	Coe	19 Aug 81	
	3:48.8	Ovett	1 Jul 80	
	3:48.85	Cram	2 Jul 88	
	3:48.95	Coe	17 Jul 79	
	3:49.20	Peter Elliott	2 Jul 88	
	3:49.22	Coe	27 Jul 85	
	3:49.34	Dave Moorcroft	26 Jun 82	
	3:49.38	Andrew Baddeley	6 Jun 08	
	3:50.32	John Mayock	5 Jul 96	
	3:50.64	Graham Williamson	13 Jul 82	
	3:51.02	John Gladwin	19 Aug 87	
10	3:51.31	Tony Morrell	14 Jul 90	
	3:51.57	Jack Buckner	29 Aug 84	
	3:51.76hc	Steve Crabb	14 Aug 87	
	3:52.20		1 Jul 89	
	3:51.90	Anthony Whiteman	16 Jul 98	
	3:52.02	Nick McCormick	29 Jul 05	
	3:52.44	John Robson	11 Jul 81	
	3:52.50	Michael East	21 Aug 05	
	3:52.64	Charlie Grice	28 May 16	
	3:52.75	Matthew Yates	10 Jul 93	
	3:52.77	Ross Murray	14 Jul 12	
20	3:52.91 i	Chris O'Hare	20 Feb 16	
	3:53.34		27 May 17	
	3:52.99	Mark Rowland	10 Sep 86	
	3:53.20	Ian Stewart II	25 Aug 82	
	3:53.39	Tom Lancashire	14 Aug 10	
	3:53.64	Kevin McKay	22 Jul 94	
	3:53.82	Gary Staines	12 Aug 90	
	3:53.85	Rob Harrison	15 Jul 86	
	3:54.20	Jake Wightman	22 Jul 16	
	3:54.2	Frank Clement	27 Jun 78	
	3:54.23 i	Andrew Butchart	4 Feb 17	
30	3:54.30	David Strang	22 Jul 94	
	3:54.30 i	Lee Emanuel	25 Jan 14	
	3:54.75		27 Jul 13	
	3:54.39	Neil Horsfield	8 Jul 86	
	3:54.53	Tim Hutchings	31 Jul 82	
	3:54.70	Andrew Graffin	23 Aug 02	
	3:54.80	James Brewer	25 Jul 09	
	3:54.9	Adrian Passey	20 Aug 89	
	3:55.0	Jim McGuinness	11 Jul 77	
	3:55.3	Peter Stewart	10 Jun 72	
40	3:55.37	Tom Mayo	8 Aug 03	
	3:55.38	Rob Denmark	12 Aug 90	
	3:55.41	Colin Reitz	31 Jul 82	
	3:55.68	Alan Simpson	30 Aug 65	
	3:55.8	Geoff Smith	15 Aug 81	
	3:55.84	Neil Caddy	25 Aug 96	
	3:55.9	Brendan Foster	10 Jun 72	
	3:55.91	Gary Lough	27 Aug 95	
	3:55.96	David Lewis	23 Aug 83	
	3:56.0	Jim Douglas	10 Jun 72	
50	3:56.04	Mike Downes	25 Aug 82	
	3:56.04 i	Richard Peters	14 Feb 13	

2000 Metres

Time	Name	Date	
4:51.39	Steve Cram	4 Aug 85	
4:52.82	Peter Elliott	15 Sep 87	
4:53.06	Jack Buckner	15 Sep 87	
4:53.69	Gary Staines	15 Sep 87	
4:55.20	Cram	28 Aug 88	
4:55.72	Elliott	28 Aug 88	
4:56.75	John Mayock	30 Jul 99	
4:57.09 i	Mayock	25 Feb 01	
4:57.39	Nick McCormick	9 Mar 06	
4:57.71	Steve Ovett	7 Jul 82	
4:58.38	Graham Williamson	29 Aug 83	
4:58.84	Sebastian Coe	5 Jun 82	
4:59.57	Nick Rose	3 Jun 78	10
5:00.37	Tim Hutchings	29 Aug 83	
5:01.09	Eamonn Martin	19 Jun 84	
5:01.28	Andrew Graffin	25 Jun 00	
5:01.48	Paul Larkins	5 Jun 88	
5:02.01	Lee Emanuel	28 Jun 13	
5:02.1+	Mo Farah	5 Jun 16	
5:02.35	Sean Cahill	4 Aug 85	
5:02.61	Steve Martin	19 Jun 84	
5:02.8 a	Frank Clement	10 Sep 78	
5:02.86	David Moorcroft	19 Jul 86	20
5:02.90	Allen Graffin	25 Jun 00	
5:02.93	Brendan Foster	4 Jul 75	
5:02.98	Ian Stewart I	4 Jul 75	
5:02.98	Gary Lough	11 Aug 96	
5:02.99	Neil Caddy	11 Aug 96	

3000 Metres (+ during 2 Miles)

7:32.62	Mo Farah	5 Jun 16	
7:32.79	Dave Moorcroft	17 Jul 82	
7:33.1 i+	Farah	21 Feb 15	
7:34.47 i	Farah	21 Feb 09	
7:34.66	Farah	24 Jul 15	
7:35.1	Brendan Foster	3 Aug 74	
7:36.40	John Nuttall	10 Jul 96	
7:37.56	Andrew Butchart	9 Jul 17	
7:39.55	Rob Denmark	1 Aug 93	
7:39.86	Andy Baddeley	25 May 12	
7:40.4	Nick Rose	27 Jun 78	
7:40.43	Jack Buckner	5 Jul 86	
7:40.94	Eamonn Martin	9 Jul 83	10
7:41.09 i	John Mayock	6 Feb 02	
7:47.28		23 Jul 95	
7:41.3	Steve Ovett	23 Sep 77	
7:41.79	Gary Staines	14 Jul 90	
7:42.22	Nick Goolab	9 Jul 17	
7:42.26	Graeme Fell	9 Jul 83	
7:42.47	David Lewis	9 Jul 83	
7:42.47 i	Tom Farrell	5 Feb 16	
7:42.77	Billy Dee	18 Jul 92	
7:43.03	Tim Hutchings	14 Jul 89	
7:43.1 +	Steve Cram	29 Aug 83	20
7:43.34	Chris Thompson	13 Aug 10	
7:43.37	Marc Scott	9 Jul 17	
7:43.61	Anthony Whiteman	27 Jun 98	
7:43.90	Ian Stewart II	26 Jun 82	
7:44.48 i	Lee Emanuel	7 Mar 15	
7:44.40	Colin Reitz	9 Jul 83	

	7:44.76	Paul Davies-Hale	20	Jul	85
	7:45.2 +	Geoff Turnbull	12	Sep	86
	7:45.29	Dennis Coates	9	Sep	77
	7:45.41	Jon Brown	1	Aug	98
30	7:45.49 i	Andy Vernon	7	Mar	14
	7:45.75		17	Jul	13
	7:45.81	John Robson	13	Jul	84
	7:46.22 i	Mark Rowland	27	Feb	90
	7:46.39	Adrian Royle	28	Jun	83
	7:46.40	Ian Hamer	20	Jan	90
	7:46.4	David Bedford	21	Jun	72
	7:46.6 +	Dave Black	14	Sep	73
	7:46.73 i	Jonathan Mellor	15	Feb	14
	7:46.83	Ian Stewart I	26	May	76
40	7:46.85 i	Ricky Wilde	15	Mar	70
	7:46.95	David James	26	May	80
	7:47.12	Simon Mugglestone	27	Jun	88
	7:47.54	Paul Larkins	14	Jul	89
	7:47.56	Dick Callan	15	Jul	83
	7:47.6	Dick Taylor	6	Sep	69
	7:48.00	Richard Nerurkar	15	Jul	92
	7:48.09	Adrian Passey	28	Jul	89
	7:48.18	Mike McLeod	9	Jul	78
	7:48.28	Jon Richards	9	Jul	83
50	7:48.28	Ian Gillespie	25	May	97
	7:48.6 +	Nat Muir	27	Jun	80
	7:48.66	Julian Goater	26	May	80
	7:48.76	Neil Caddy	2	Aug	98

2 Miles

	8:03.40 i	Mo Farah	21	Feb	15
	8:07.85		24	Aug	14
	8:08.07 i	Farah	18	Feb	12
	8:12.63 i	Andrew Butchart	11	Feb	17
	8:13.51	Steve Ovett	15	Sep	78
	8:13.68	Brendan Foster	27	Aug	73
	8:14.93	Steve Cram	29	Aug	83
	8:15.53	Tim Hutchings	12	Sep	86
	8:15.98	Geoff Turnbull	12	Sep	86
	8:16.75	Dave Moorcroft	20	Aug	82
	8:16.94	Foster	17	Jul	79
	8:17.06 i	John Mayock	17	Feb	02
10	8:17.12	Jack Buckner	12	Sep	86
	8:18.4 i	Nick Rose	17	Feb	78
	8:22.41		15	Sep	78
	8:18.98	Eamonn Martin	16	Jul	88
	8:19.37	Nat Muir	27	Jun	80
	8:20.28	David James	27	Jun	80
	8:20.66	David Lewis	7	Sep	84
	8:21.09	Barry Smith	27	Jun	80
	8:21.24 i	Lee Emanuel	31	Jan	15
	8:21.86	David Black	14	Sep	73
	8:21.97	Rob Denmark	9	Aug	91
20	8:22.0	Ian Stewart I	14	Aug	72
	8:22.65	Ian Hamer	17	Jul	92
	8:22.7 i	Graeme Fell	19	Feb	82
	8:22.98	Geoff Smith	27	Jun	80
	8:23.16	Gary Staines	9	Aug	91
	8:23.80	Billy Dee	9	Aug	91

5000 Metres

12:53.11	Mo Farah	22	Jul	11	
12:56.98	Farah	2	Jun	12	
12:57.94	Farah	19	Aug	10	
12:59.29	Farah	23	Jul	16	
13:00.41	Dave Moorcroft	7	Jul	82	
13:00.70	Farah	27	May	17	
13:03.30	Farah	20	Aug	16	
13:05.66	Farah	10	Jul	10	
13:05.88	Farah	1	Jun	13	
13:06.04	Farah	13	Jul	12	
13:08.61	Andrew Butchart	20	Aug	16	
13:09.80	Ian Hamer	9	Jun	92	
13:10.15	Jack Buckner	31	Aug	86	
13:10.24	Rob Denmark	9	Jun	92	
13:10.48	Tom Farrell	18	Jul	15	
13:11.50	Tim Hutchings	11	Aug	84	
13:11.50	Andy Vernon	4	May	14	
13:11.51	Chris Thompson	10	Jul	10	10
13:14.28	Gary Staines	15	Aug	90	
13:14.6 a	Brendan Foster	29	Jan	74	
13:15.59	Julian Goater	11	Sep	81	
13:16.70	John Nuttall	8	Jun	95	
13:17.21	Dave Bedford	14	Jul	72	
13:17.21	Keith Cullen	19	Jul	97	
13:17.84	Eamonn Martin	14	Jul	89	
13:17.9	Nat Muir	15	Jul	80	
13:18.06	Ian Gillespie	19	Jul	97	
13:18.6	Steve Jones	10	Jun	82	20
13:18.81	Nick McCormick	7	Jun	12	
13:18.91	Nick Rose	28	Jun	84	
13:19.03	Jon Brown	5	Aug	98	
13:19.43	John Mayock	31	Jul	02	
13:19.45	Sam Haughian	31	Jul	02	
13:19.66	Ian McCafferty	14	Jul	72	
13:20.06	Steve Ovett	30	Jun	86	
13:20.09	Adrian Passey	19	Jul	97	
13:20.30	Karl Keska	20	Jul	02	
13:20.85	Andy Baddeley	4	Mar	10	30
13:21.13	David Lewis	4	Jul	85	
13:21.14	Barry Smith	7	Jun	81	
13:21.2	Tony Simmons	23	May	76	
13:21.60	Paul Davies-Hale	8	Jul	88	
13:21.73	Geoff Turnbull	5	Sep	86	
13:21.83	Mark Rowland	1	Jun	88	
13:22.17 i	Geoff Smith	12	Feb	82	
13:22.37	Marc Scott	22	Jul	17	
13:22.39	Jon Solly	7	Jul	86	
13:22.54	Dave Clarke	28	Jun	83	40
13:22.85	Ian Stewart I	25	Jul	70	
13:23.26	Mike McLeod	24	Jun	80	
13:23.36	Richard Nerurkar	10	Aug	90	
13:23.48	John Doherty	1	Jun	85	
13:23.52	Dave Black	29	Jan	74	
13:23.71	Steve Binns	1	Jun	88	
13:23.94	Jonathan Davies	28	May	16	
13:24.07	Rory Fraser	19	Apr	13	
13:24.44	Mike Openshaw	14	Jul	01	
13:25.38	Paul Evans	28	Jun	95	50
13:26.0	Bernie Ford	30	Jul	77	

10000 Metres

26:46.57	Mo Farah	3	Jun	11
26:49.51	Farah	4	Aug	17
26:50.97	Farah	29	May	15
26:53.71	Farah	27	May	16
27:01.13	Farah	22	Aug	15
27:05.17	Farah	13	Aug	16
27:12.09	Farah	28	Jun	17
27:14.07	Farah	28	Aug	11
27:18.14	Jon Brown	28	Aug	98
27:21.71	Farah	10	Aug	13
27:23.06	Eamonn Martin	2	Jul	88
27:27.36	Chris Thompson	1	May	11
27:30.3	Brendan Foster	23	Jun	78
27:30.80	Dave Bedford	13	Jul	73
27:31.19	Nick Rose	9	Jul	83
27:34.58	Julian Goater	26	Jun	82
[10] 27:36.27	David Black	29	Aug	78
27:39.14	Steve Jones	9	Jul	83
27:39.76	Mike McLeod	4	Sep	79
27:40.03	Richard Nerurkar	10	Jul	93
27:42.62	Andy Vernon	2	May	15
27:43.03	Ian Stewart I	9	Sep	77
27:43.59	Tony Simmons	30	Jun	77
27:43.74	Bernie Ford	9	Sep	77
27:43.76	Geoff Smith	13	Jun	81
27:44.09	Karl Keska	25	Sep	00
[20] 27:47.16	Adrian Royle	10	Apr	82
27:47.79	Paul Evans	5	Jul	93
27:48.73	Gary Staines	6	Jul	91
27:50.33	Keith Cullen	10	Apr	99
27:51.76	Jon Solly	20	Jun	86
27:55.06	Ross Millington	11	Jun	16
27:55.66	Steve Binns	9	Jul	83
27:55.77	Dave Clarke	25	May	82
27:57.23	Andrew Lemoncello	24	Apr	09
27:57.77	Ian Hamer	13	Sep	91
[30] 27:59.12	Allister Hutton	30	May	86
27:59.24	Carl Thackery	16	Jul	87
27:59.33	Steve Harris	22	Jul	86
28:00.50	Andres Jones	22	Jul	00
28:00.62	Jim Brown	1	Aug	75
28:00.64	Billy Dee	13	Sep	91
28:03.31	Rob Denmark	22	Jul	00
28:04.04	Andy Bristow	17	Aug	90
28:04.2	Ian Robinson	20	Apr	96
28:04.48	Mark Steinle	22	Jul	00
[40] 28:05.2	Dave Murphy	10	Apr	81
28:06.13	Barry Smith	7	Aug	81
28:06.6	Dick Taylor	22	Jun	69
28:07.43	John Nuttall	25	Aug	95
28:07.57	Tim Hutchings	7	Jul	90
28:07.97	Marc Scott	5	May	17
28:08.12	Charlie Spedding	23	Jul	83
28:08.44	David Lewis	5	Jun	88
28:09.39	Mark Dalloway	5	Jun	88
28:11.07	Karl Harrison	20	Jun	86
[50] 28:11.72	Lachie Stewart	18	Jul	70
28:11.85	Lawrie Spence	29	May	83
28:13.04	Gerry Helme	29	May	83

10 Kilometres Road

27:34	Nick Rose	1	Apr	84
27:44	Mo Farah	31	May	10
27:53	Mike O'Reilly	19	Oct	86
27:55	Mark Scrutton	5	Mar	84
27:56	Steve Harris	4	Dec	83
27:56	John Doherty	4	Jul	86
27:59	Steve Jones	28	Apr	84
28:00	Roger Hackney	4	Dec	83
28:01	Barry Smith	4	Dec	83
28:02	Steve Binns	15	Apr	89 [10]
28:03	Jon Solly	5	Apr	86
28:03	Jack Buckner	28	Feb	87
28:05	Jon Brown	17	Oct	93
28:06	Geoff Smith	2	Mar	85
28:07	Colin Reitz	28	Apr	84
28:07	Peter Whitehead	4	Jul	96
28:09	Dave Moorcroft	16	May	82
28:10	Adrian Leek	10	Mar	84
28:10	Dave Clarke	5	May	85
28:11	Jon Richards	5	May	85 [20]

course measurement uncertain

28:01	Steve Kenyon	21	Sep	86
28:04	Dave Bedford	27	Mar	77
28:08	Kevin Forster	15	Jul	84
28:08	Dave Clarke	15	Jul	84

downhill

27:20	Jon Brown	24	Sep	95
27:57	Malcolm East	25	Sep	82

short (50m)

27:50	Mark Scrutton	6	Dec	81

10 Miles Road

45:13	Ian Stewart I	8	May	77
46:02	Richard Nerurkar	17	Oct	93
46:11	Gary Staines	10	Oct	93
46:19	Nerurkar	23	Jul	95
46:25	Mo Farah	25	Oct	09
46:26	Carl Thackery	7	Apr	91
46:35	Paul Evans	21	Sep	97
46:41	Roger Hackney	6	Apr	86
46:42	Dave Murphy	28	Apr	84
46:43	Steve Kenyon	21	Aug	82
46:43	Nick Rose	25	Apr	87 [10]
46:47	Martyn Brewer	25	Apr	87
46:49	Steve Jones	2	Apr	89
47:00	Paul Davies-Hale	10	Oct	93

intermediate times

46:10 +	Paul Evans	14	Sep	97
46:21 +	Nigel Adams	15	Sep	91
46:21 +	Carl Thackery	15	Sep	91

estimated times

45:15 +	Mo Farah	26	Mar	16
46:02 +	Steve Jones	8	Jun	86

course measurement uncertain

45:37	Barry Smith	22	Mar	81
45:44	Mike McLeod	9	Apr	78
46:03	Colin Moore	29	Aug	83
46:08	Nick Rose	26	Apr	81
46:11	Steve Kenyon	20	Jun	81
46:14	Charlie Spedding	12	Oct	86
46:17	Brendan Foster	9	Apr	78

downhill

46:05	Allister Hutton	3	Apr	82

Half Marathon

	59:22	Mo Farah	13	Sep	15
	59:32	Farah	22	Mar	15
	59:59	Farah	26	Mar	16
	60:00	Farah	7	Sep	14
	60:00	Callum Hawkins	5	Feb	17
	60:59	Steve Jones	8	Jun	86
	61:00	Chris Thompson	16	Sep	12
	61:03	Nick Rose	15	Sep	85
	61:04	Carl Thackery	12	Apr	87
	61:06	Richard Nerurkar	14	Apr	96
	61:17	David Lewis	20	Sep	92
	61:18	Paul Evans	14	Sep	97
10	61:25	Scott Overall	18	Mar	12
	61:28	Steve Brooks	23	Mar	97
	61:31	Steve Kenyon	8	Jun	86
	61:33	Dewi Griffiths	1	Oct	17
	61:39	Geoff Smith	25	Sep	83
	61:39	Paul Davies-Hale	15	Sep	91
	61:49	Jon Brown	14	Sep	97
	61:53	Nigel Adams	15	Sep	91
	61:56	Mark Flint	22	Aug	93
	61:57	Gary Staines	14	Sep	97
20	62:07	Kevin Forster	5	Apr	87
	62:07	Martyn Brewer	20	Sep	87
	62:07	Andrew Pearson	14	Sep	97
	62:08	Steve Harris	20	Oct	85
	62:11	Dave Clarke	5	Apr	92
	62:11	Keith Cullen	20	Aug	00
	62:15	Dave Murphy	16	Sep	84
	62:16	Jim Haughey	20	Sep	87
	62:19	Dave Long I	11	Dec	81
	62:22	Colin Moore	26	May	85
30	62:23	Mark Steinle	10	Oct	99
	62:23	Jonathon Mellor	19	Mar	17
	62:24	Jimmy Ashworth	8	Jun	86
	62:25	Barry Royden	18	Sep	94
	62:28	Terry Greene	12	Apr	86
	62:28	Allister Hutton	21	Jun	87
	62:28	Andy Coleman	22	Oct	00
	62:30	Tony Milovsorov	21	Jun	87
	62:33	Steve Brace	15	Sep	91
	62:33	Billy Dee	4	Apr	93
40	62:33	Peter Whitehead	5	May	95

course measurement uncertain

61:47	Dave Long II	17	Mar	91
62:08	Ray Smedley	28	Mar	82
62:19	Mike Carroll	3	Jun	90

short

60:09	Paul Evans (80m)	15	Jan	95

Marathon

2:07:13		Steve Jones	20	Oct	85	
2:08:05		Jones	21	Oct	84	
2:08:16		Jones	21	Apr	85	
2:08:20		Jones	6	Nov	88	
2:08:21		Mo Farah	13	Apr	14	
2:08:33		Charlie Spedding	21	Apr	85	
2:08:36		Richard Nerurkar	13	Apr	97	
2:08:52		Paul Evans	20	Oct	96	
2:09:08		Geoff Smith	23	Oct	83	
2:09:12		Ian Thompson	31	Jan	74	
2:09:16		Allister Hutton	21	Apr	85	
2:09:17		Mark Steinle	14	Apr	02	
2:09:24		Hugh Jones	9	May	82	10
2:09:28		Ron Hill	23	Jul	70	
2:09:28		John Graham	23	May	81	
2:09:31		Jon Brown	17	Apr	05	
2:09:43		Mike Gratton	17	Apr	83	
2:09:49		Dewi Griffiths	29	Oct	17	
2:09:54		Tony Milovsorov	23	Apr	89	
2:10:12		Gerry Helme	17	Apr	83	
2:10:17		Callum Hawkins	6	Aug	17	
2:10:30		Dave Long II	21	Apr	91	
2:10:35		Steve Brace	21	Jan	96	20
2:10:37		Tomas Abyu	29	Oct	07	
2:10:39		Mike O'Reilly	5	Dec	93	
2:10:48		Bill Adcocks	8	Dec	68	
2:10:50		Eamonn Martin	18	Apr	93	
2:10:51		Bernie Ford	2	Dec	79	
2:10:52		Kevin Forster	17	Apr	88	
2:10:55	dh	Chris Bunyan	18	Apr	83	
2:10:55		Scott Overall	25	Sep	11	
2:11:06		Dave Buzza	31	Oct	93	
2:11:18		Dave Murphy	12	Jun	83	30
2:11:19		Chris Thompson	13	Apr	14	
2:11:22		Dave Cannon	6	Sep	80	
2:11:25		Paul Davies-Hale	29	Oct	89	
2:11:25		Gary Staines	20	Oct	96	
2:11:36		Malcolm East	20	Apr	81	
2:11:36		Kenny Stuart	15	Jan	89	
2:11:40		Steve Kenyon	13	Jun	82	
2:11:43		Jimmy Ashworth	29	Sep	85	
2:11:44		Jim Dingwall	17	Apr	83	
2:11:50		Fraser Clyne	2	Dec	84	40
2:11:54		Martin McCarthy	17	Apr	83	
2:11:58		Mark Hudspith	2	Apr	95	
2:12:04		Jim Alder	23	Jul	70	
2:12:07		Jon Solly	14	Oct	90	
2:12:07		Mark Flint	17	Apr	94	
2:12:12		Dennis Fowles	13	May	84	
2:12:12		Andy Green	25	Apr	93	
2:12:13		John Wheway	17	Apr	88	
2:12:14		Dan Robinson	18	Oct	09	
2:12:17		Dave Long I	16	Jan	82	50
2:12:19		Don Faircloth	23	Jul	70	
2:12:20		Matt O'Dowd	3	Nov	02	
2:12:23		Peter Whitehead	2	Apr	95	
2:12:23		Tsegai Teweide	24	Apr	16	

short (148m)

2:11:10	Nick Brawn	25	Oct	81

2000 Metres Steeplechase

5:19.86	Mark Rowland	28	Aug	88
5:20.56	Rowland	17	Aug	90
5:21.77	Tom Hanlon	11	Jun	92
5:22.37	Rowland	16	Sep	90
5:22.96	Hanlon	16	Sep	90
5:23.56	Tom Buckner	17	Jul	92
5:23.6	Roger Hackney	10	Jun	82
5:23.71	Colin Walker	28	Aug	88
5:23.87	Colin Reitz	28	Jun	84
5:24.91	Eddie Wedderburn	19	Aug	86
5:26.24	Paul Davies-Hale	26	Aug	85
5:26.64	Nick Peach	19	Aug	86
5:26.82 "	David Lewis	12	Jun	83
5:30.6	Dennis Coates	23	Apr	78
5:30.86	Tony Staynings	26	May	76
5:31.04	John Hartigan	17	Aug	90
5:31.09	Peter McColgan	5	Aug	86
5:31.43	John Bicourt	26	May	76
5:31.59	Mick Hawkins	20	Jan	90
5:32.45	Neil Smart	17	Aug	90
5:33.09	Spencer Duval	17	Jul	92
5:33.59	Mark Sinclair	19	Aug	86
5:33.76	Graeme Fell	9	Sep	79

3000 Metres Steeplechase

	8:07.96	Mark Rowland	30	Sep	88
	8:12.11	Colin Reitz	5	Sep	86
	8:12.58	Tom Hanlon	3	Aug	91
	8:13.27	Rowland	30	Aug	90
	8:13.50	Reitz	4	Aug	85
	8:13.65	Hanlon	4	Jul	92
	8:13.78	Reitz	21	Jul	84
	8:14.73	Hanlon	15	Jul	92
	8:14.95	Reitz	27	Jul	85
	8:15.16	Graeme Fell	17	Aug	83
	8:18.32	Eddie Wedderburn	5	Jul	88
	8:18.91	Roger Hackney	30	Jul	88
	8:18.95	Dennis Coates	25	Jul	76
	8:20.83	Paul Davies-Hale	10	Jun	84
	8:22.42	Rob Mullett	20	May	16
10	8:22.48	John Davies II	13	Sep	74
	8:22.76	James Wilkinson	12	Jun	14
	8:22.82	John Bicourt	8	Jun	76
	8:22.95	Andrew Lemoncello	18	Jul	08
	8:23.66	Stuart Stokes	16	Jun	08
	8:23.90	Justin Chaston	18	Jul	94
	8:24.64	Spencer Duval	16	Jul	95
	8:25.15	Colin Walker	28	Jun	92
	8:25.37	Christian Stephenson	19	Aug	00
	8:25.50	Tom Buckner	28	Aug	92
20	8:26.05	Keith Cullen	21	Aug	95
	8:26.33	Rob Hough	6	Jul	96
	8:26.4	Andy Holden	15	Sep	72
	8:26.6	Gordon Rimmer	4	Jun	80
	8:27.21	Tony Staynings	15	Jun	80
	8:27.8	Steve Hollings	5	Aug	73
	8:27.93	Peter McColgan	25	Jun	91
	8:28.43	Adam Bowden	22	Jul	06
	8:28.48	Luke Gunn	28	Jun	08

8:28.6	Dave Bedford	10	Sep	71	
8:29.46	Julian Marsay	14	Jul	79	30
8:29.72	David Lewis	29	May	83	
8:30.17	Zak Seddon	31	Mar	17	
8:30.41	Jermaine Mays	13	Jun	07	
8:30.6 a	Peter Griffiths	17	Jul	77	
8:30.8	Gerry Stevens	1	Sep	69	
8:31.09	Ian Gilmour	16	Jul	78	
8:31.22	Dave Lee	19	Jun	92	
8:31.40	Frank Tickner	13	Jun	07	
8:32.00	Steve Jones	8	Aug	80	
8:32.06	David Camp	10	Aug	74	40
8:32.13	Barry Knight	25	Jul	82	
8:32.4 a	Maurice Herriott	17	Oct	64	
8:32.68	Ben Whitby	15	Jul	01	
8:33.0	John Jackson	13	Aug	69	
8:33.59	Ieuan Thomas	27	May	17	
8:33.0	William Gray	27	May	17	
8:33.8 a	Gareth Bryan-Jones	23	Jul	70	
8:33.8	Peter Morris	4	Aug	73	
8:33.83	Richard Charleston	24	May	80	
8:33.89	Nick Peach	21	Jun	86	50

110 Metres Hurdles

12.91	Colin Jackson	20	Aug	93	
12.97 A	Jackson	28	Jul	93	
12.98	Jackson	15	Sep	94	
12.99	Jackson	3	Sep	93	
12.99	Jackson	6	Sep	94	
13.00	Tony Jarrett	20	Aug	93	
13.02	Jackson	30	Aug	94	
13.02	Jackson (sf)	22	Aug	98	
13.02	Jackson (final)	22	Aug	98	
13.03	Jackson	4	Sep	94	
13.04	Jackson	16	Aug	92	
13.04	Jackson	12	Aug	94	
13.04	Jarrett	12	Aug	95	
13.04	Jackson	25	Aug	99	
13.14	Andy Pozzi	1	Jul	17	
13.16	William Sharman	14	Aug	14	
13.22	Andy Turner	30	Jun	11	
13.24	David Omoregie	3	Sep	16	
13.29	Jon Ridgeon	15	Jul	87	
13.31	Lawrence Clarke	8	Aug	12	
13.36	Robert Newton	31	Jul	03	
13.42	David Nelson	27	Aug	91	10
13.43	Mark Holtom	4	Oct	82	
13.44	Hugh Teape	14	Aug	92	
13.44	Chris Baillie	21	Mar	06	
13.48	David King	2	Jun	17	
13.49	Andy Tulloch	30	Jun	99	
13.51	Nigel Walker	3	Aug	90	
13.53	Paul Gray	22	Aug	94	
13.53	Allan Scott	17	Jul	08	
13.54	Damien Greaves	13	Jul	02	
13.54	Gianni Frankis	26	Jun	13	20
13.54	Alex Al-Ameen	26	Apr	14	
13.56	Callum Priestley ¶	29	Jul	09	
13.57	David Hughes	23	Jul	06	
13.59	Khai Riley-La Borde	21	May	17	

Time	Name	Date		Time	Name	Date
13.60	Wilbert Greaves	21 Aug 85		13.96	Mike Robbins	28 Mar 98
13.60	Neil Owen	28 Jun 95		13.97	Brett St Louis	30 Jul 88
13.64	Richard Alleyne	2 Jun 12		13.99	Bob Danville	14 Aug 76
13.64	Joseph Hylton	24 Jun 12		13.99	Edward Dunford	9 Sep 07
13.64	Gabriel Odujobi	14 May 16				

hand timing

13.66	Ross Baillie	20 Feb 99		13.4	David King	6 Jun 16
13.68	Jake Porter	26 Jul 17		13.5	Berwyn Price	1 Jul 73
13.69	Berwyn Price	18 Aug 73		13.6	David Hemery	5 Jul 69
13.69	James Weaver	29 Jul 17		13.7	Alan Pascoe	5 Jul 69
13.71	James Gladman	30 Jun 13		13.7	C. J. Kirkpatrick	29 Jun 74
13.72	David Hemery	1 Aug 70		13.7	Mensah Elliott	2 Sep 00
13.72	Nick Gayle	29 Jun 13		13.8	Martin Nicholson	25 Jun 94
13.74	Julien Adeniran	11 Aug 11		13.9	Mike Parker	2 Oct 63
13.75	Lloyd Cowan	17 Jul 94		13.9	David Wilson	29 Jun 74
13.75	Ben Reynolds	29 Jun 11		13.9	Brian Taylor	8 May 93
13.76	Duncan Malins	15 Aug 04				
13.77	Edirin Okoro	29 Jun 14				

hand timing - wind assisted

13.78	Dominic Girdler	5 Jul 03		12.8	Colin Jackson	10 Jan 90
13.79	Alan Pascoe	17 Jun 72		13.0	Jarrett	2 Jun 96
13.79	Mohammed Sillah-Freckleton	31 Jul 03		13.4	Berwyn Price	7 Jul 76
13.82	Mensah Elliott	30 Jul 00		13.5	Neil Owen	2 Jun 96
13.83	Dominic Bradley	14 Jul 01		13.7	Lloyd Cowan	27 Apr 95
13.86	Ken Campbell	23 Aug 94				
13.86	Matt Hudson	27 Jun 10				

400 Metres Hurdles

13.87	Yannick Budd	18 May 14		47.82	Kriss Akabusi	6 Aug 92
13.89	David Feeney	31 May 15		47.84	Dai Greene	6 Jul 12
13.93	Tristan Anthony	30 May 04		47.86	Akabusi	27 Aug 91
13.94	David Guest	5 May 13		47.88	Greene	4 Sep 10
13.96	Steve Buckeridge	31 May 86		47.91	Akabusi	26 Aug 91
13.97	Daniel Davis	4 Sep 10		47.92	Akabusi	29 Aug 90
13.97	Jack Meredith	7 May 12		48.01	Akabusi	5 Aug 92
13.98	Matthew Butler	16 Jul 05		48.10	Greene	13 Jul 12
14.00	Matt Douglas	23 May 99		48.12 A	David Hemery	15 Oct 68
				48.52		2 Sep 72

wind assisted

12.94 A	Jackson	31 Jul 94		48.12	Greene	31 Jul 10
12.95	Jackson	10 Sep 89		48.14	Chris Rawlinson	11 Aug 99
12.99	Jackson	23 Jun 89		48.54	Matt Douglas	28 Aug 03
13.01	Jackson	2 Jul 93		48.59	Alan Pascoe	30 Jun 75
13.14	Lawrence Clarke	7 Jul 12		48.60	Jack Green	13 Jul 12
13.38	Gabriel Odujobi	15 Apr 17		48.71	Nathan Woodward	3 Jul 11
13.41	Allan Scott	17 Jul 08		48.73	Jon Ridgeon	6 Sep 92
13.49	Nigel Walker	3 Jun 89		48.80	Niall Flannery	17 Jun 14 [10]
13.50	Damien Greaves	17 Jul 04		48.84	Rhys Williams	17 Jul 13
13.53	Gianni Frankis	7 Jul 13		48.90	Anthony Borsumato	14 Jul 02
13.56	David Hughes	17 Jul 05		49.03 A	John Sherwood	15 Oct 68
13.64	Mohammed Sillah-Freckleton	30 May 04		49.88		13 Aug 69
13.65	Berwyn Price	25 Aug 75		49.06	Rick Yates	26 Jul 08
13.66	David Hemery	18 Jul 70		49.07	Gary Cadogan ¶	22 Jul 94
13.68	Duncan Malins	21 Aug 04		49.11	Gary Oakes	26 Jul 80
13.69	Mensah Elliott	19 Aug 00		49.11	Matt Elias	28 Jul 02
13.69	Yannick Budd	29 Jun 14		49.16	Paul Gray	18 Aug 98
13.72	Matt Hudson	30 May 10		49.19	Seb Rodger	13 Jul 13
13.72	Julian Adeniran	22 May 11		49.25	Max Robertson	28 Aug 90 [20]
13.84	Daniel Davis	30 May 10		49.26	Peter Crampton	8 Aug 94
13.85	Tristan Anthony	17 Jul 04		49.29	Du'aine Thorne-Ladejo	9 Jun 01
13.90	Oliver McNeillis	22 Jun 08		49.36	Tom Burton	6 Jun 15
13.91 A	Tim Reetz	3 May 02		49.49	Mark Holtom	20 Jul 85
	13.93	24 May 02		49.49	Jacob Paul	9 Jul 17
13.92	Ben Kelk	18 Jul 12		49.54	Dale Garland	15 Aug 09

	49.57	Ben Sumner	26 May 12	
	49.58	David Hughes	8 Aug 10	
	49.60	Phil Beattie	28 Jul 86	
30	49.62	Lloyd Gumbs	18 Jul 09	
	49.65	Bill Hartley	2 Aug 75	
	49.76	Richard Davenport	30 Jul 11	
	49.78	Thomas Phillips	26 Jun 11	
	49.82	Martin Gillingham	14 Aug 87	
	49.82	Gary Jennings	27 Jun 95	
	49.86	Martin Briggs	6 Jun 84	
	49.95	Steve Sole	24 Jul 83	
	49.96	Tony Williams	24 Jul 99	
	50.01	Phil Harries	5 Jun 88	
40	50.05	Lawrence Lynch	15 Jun 96	
	50.1 a	John Cooper	16 Oct 64	
	50.12	Ryan Dinham	2 Jul 06	
	50.12	Steve Green	2 Aug 08	
	50.16	Paul Thompson	17 May 96	
	50.16	Steve Surety	16 Jun 02	
	50.19	Steve Coupland	12 Jun 94	
	50.23	Toby Ulm	30 May 09	
	50.24	Charles Robertson-Adams	4 Jul 01	
	50.25	Jack Lawrie	18 Jun 17	
50	50.27	Jack Houghton	8 Aug 15	
	50.28	Ben Carne	9 Jun 07	
	50.29	Nick Stewart	22 Jul 05	
	50.30	Liam Collins	14 Jul 02	
	50.37	Bob Danville	27 Jul 82	
	50.38	Andy Todd	18 Sep 69	
	50.40	James Hillier	1 Jul 01	
	50.41	James Forman	27 Jun 11	

hand timing

49.9	Andy Todd	9 Oct 69	

High Jump

	2.38 i	Steve Smith	4 Feb 94		2.30 i	Martyn Bernard	3 Mar 07	
	2.37		20 Sep 92		2.30		29 Jun 08	
	2.37 i	Smith	14 Mar 93		2.30	Tom Gale	29 Jul 17	
	2.37	Smith	22 Aug 93		2.29 i	Allan Smith	15 Feb 15	
	2.37 i	Dalton Grant	13 Mar 94		2.26		14 Jul 13	
	2.36		1 Sep 91		2.28 i	John Holman	28 Jan 89	
	2.37	Robbie Grabarz	23 Aug 12		2.24		27 May 89	
	2.36 i	Smith	5 Feb 93		2.28	Ray Bobrownicki	13 Jul 14	
	2.36 i	Smith	24 Feb 94		2.26	James Brierley	3 Aug 96	
	2.36 i	Smith	10 Feb 96		2.26	Matt Roberts	21 Aug 10	
	2.36 i	Smith	8 Feb 98		2.26 i	Chris Kandu	21 Feb 15	
	2.36	Smith	27 Jun 99		2.25		17 Jun 17	
	2.36	Grabarz	9 Jun 12		2.26 i	David Smith	21 Feb 15	
	2.36 i	Chris Baker	13 Feb 16		2.25		24 May 14	
	2.29		10 Jul 16		2.25	Floyd Manderson	20 Aug 88	20
	2.34	Germaine Mason	19 Aug 08		2.25	Robert Mitchell	28 Jul 01	
	2.32 i	Brendan Reilly	24 Feb 94		2.25	Adam Scarr	11 Jun 06	
	2.31		17 Jul 92		2.25	Mike Edwards	19 Jul 15	
	2.31	Geoff Parsons	26 Aug 94		2.24	Mark Naylor	28 Jun 80	
	2.31 i	Samson Oni	4 Mar 10		2.24	John Hill	23 Aug 85	
	2.30		8 Jun 08		2.24	Phil McDonnell	26 Aug 85	
	2.31 i	Tom Parsons	13 Feb 11		2.23	Mark Lakey	29 Aug 82	
	2.30		13 Jul 08		2.23 i	David Abrahams	12 Mar 83	
10	2.30	Ben Challenger	13 Jul 99		2.19		7 Oct 82	
					2.22	Danny Graham	20 May 00	
					2.22 i	Luke Crawley	1 Mar 03	30
					2.21	Fayyaz Ahmed	29 Jun 86	
					2.21	Steve Chapman	30 Jul 89	
					2.21 i	Martin Lloyd	28 Jan 07	
					2.20		4 Aug 07	
					2.21	Brian Hall	25 Aug 07	
					2.21	Alan McKie	1 Jun 08	
					2.20	Brian Burgess	11 Jun 78	
					2.20	Trevor Llewelyn	15 Jul 83	
					2.20	Byron Morrison	14 Jul 84	
					2.20 i	Henderson Pierre	10 Jan 87	
					2.18		16 Aug 86	
					2.20	Alex Kruger	18 Jun 88	40
					2.20	Ossie Cham	21 May 89	
					2.20 i	Warren Caswell	10 Mar 90	
					2.18		2 Sep 90	
					2.20	Colin Bent	16 Jun 96	
					2.20 i	Stuart Ohrland	1 Feb 97	
					2.18		28 Aug 99	
					2.20	Stuart Smith	13 Apr 97	
					2.20	David Barnetson	3 Aug 97	
					2.20	Dan Turner	28 May 01	
					2.20	Darryl Stone	10 Jul 05	
					2.20	Nick Stanisavljevic	8 Jul 06	
					2.19 i	Mike Robbins	3 Feb 96	50
					2.19	Jamie Russell	18 May 02	
					2.18	Tim Foulger	23 Sep 79	
					2.18	Rupert Charles	25 Jul 82	
					2.18	Steve Ritchie	15 Jul 89	
					2.18	Hopeton Lindo	23 Jul 89	
					2.18	Andrew Lynch	9 Jul 95	
					2.18 i	Tony Gilhooly	9 Mar 97	
					2.18		12 Sep 99	
					2.18	Chuka Enih-Snell	21 Apr 01	
					2.18	Andrew Penk	17 Jul 04	
					2.18 i	Martin Aram	29 Jan 06	60

41

Pole Vault					Long Jump				
5.83 i	Luke Cutts	25	Jan	14	8.51	Greg Rutherford	24	Apr	14
5.70		27	Jul	13	8.41	Rutherford	25	Aug	15
5.82	Steve Lewis	21	Jul	12	8.35	Chris Tomlinson	8	Jul	11
5.81 i	Nick Buckfield	8	Feb	02	8.35	Rutherford	3	May	12
5.80		27	May	98	8.35	Rutherford	7	Jun	15
5.80	Lewis	23	Aug	12	8.34	Rutherford	30	Jul	15
5.77 i	Lewis	2	Mar	12	8.32	Rutherford	31	May	12
5.75	Buckfield	7	Sep	97	8.32	Rutherford	3	Sep	15
5.75 A	Buckfield	14	Apr	01	8.31	Rutherford	4	Aug	12
5.75 i	Lewis	17	Jan	09	8.31	Rutherford	2	Jun	16
5.75	Lewis	10	Aug	12	8.26	Nathan Morgan	20	Jul	03
5.65	Keith Stock	7	Jul	81	8.23	Lynn Davies	30	Jun	68
5.65	Jax Thoirs	16	May	15	8.21	Daniel Bramble	18	Apr	15
5.64 i	Max Eaves	5	Mar	16	8.16	Bradley Pickup	2	Aug	14
5.62		19	Jul	14	8.15	Stewart Faulkner	16	Jul	90
5.61	Kevin Hughes	28	Jul	99	8.14	Mark Forsythe	7	Jul	91
5.60	Neil Winter	19	Aug	95	8.11	JJ Jegede	13	Jul	12
5.60	Adam Hague	28	Mar	15	8.10	Fred Salle	9	Sep	94 [10]
5.59 [10]	Brian Hooper	6	Sep	80	8.08	Roy Mitchell	27	Sep	80
5.55	Paul Williamson	13	May	00	8.08	Julian Reid	25	Jun	11
5.55	Tim Thomas	6	Jun	04	8.05 i	Barrington Williams	11	Feb	89
5.55 i	Andrew Sutcliffe	11	Feb	12	8.01		17	Jun	89
5.46		11	Aug	12	8.03	Steve Phillips	5	Aug	98
5.52	Mike Edwards	13	May	93	8.03	Jonathan Moore	18	May	02
5.51	Joel Leon Benitez	12	Jul	17	8.01	Daley Thompson	8	Aug	84
5.50 i	Ashley Swain	8	Feb	04	8.01	Darren Ritchie	16	Jun	01
5.41		27	Jul	03	8.00	Derrick Brown	7	Aug	85
5.47 i	Keith Higham	4	Feb	06	7.98	Alan Lerwill	29	Jun	74
5.40		25	Jun	05	7.96	Daniel Gardiner	31	Jul	16 [20]
5.45 i	Andy Ashurst	16	Feb	92	7.96	Jacob Fincham-Dukes	25	May	17
5.40		19	Jun	88	7.94 i	Paul Johnson	10	Mar	89
5.45	Mike Barber	27	Jul	97	7.85		3	Jun	89
5.45 i [20]	Paul Walker	2	Mar	14	7.94 i	Matthew Burton	9	Feb	13
5.40		23	Jun	07	7.87		9	Jun	14
5.45	Gregor MacLean	10	May	14	7.93	Chris Kirk	12	Jul	08
5.45	Charlie Myers	10	Jun	17	7.91	John King	26	Sep	87
5.42 i	Scott Simpson	10	Mar	07	7.90	Ian Simpson	3	Jun	89
5.41		27	Aug	06	7.90	Chris Davidson	19	Jun	99
5.42	Nick Cruchley	3	Jul	11	7.89	George Audu	12	Aug	00
5.42	Harry Coppell	6	Jun	15	7.89	Feron Sayers	2	Jul	17
5.40 A	Jeff Gutteridge ¶	23	Apr	80	7.88	Allan Hamilton	15	Apr	16 [30]
5.40		5	Jun	83	7.87	Keith Fleming	7	Jun	87
5.40 i	Matt Belsham	10	Feb	96	7.87	Timothy Duckworth	8	Apr	17
5.35		26	Jun	93	7.86	James McLachlan	19	Apr	13
5.40	Ben Flint	25	Jul	99	7.86	Elliot Safo	19	Jul	13
5.40	Joe Ive	23	Jun	07	7.84	Wayne Griffith	25	Aug	89
5.40 i [30]	Daniel Gardner	22	Feb	14	7.83	Phillips Idowu	25	Jul	00
5.35	Ian Tullett	26	Jul	98	7.80	Nick Newman	4	Feb	12
5.35	Mark Beharrell	29	Jun	03	7.80	Feron Sayers	30	Jun	13
5.35 i	Matt Devereux	17	Feb	13	7.79	John Morbey	11	Jul	64
5.34		27	May	12	7.79	Geoff Hignett	31	May	71
5.30	Dean Mellor	17	Jun	95	7.79	Don Porter	13	Jul	75 [40]
5.30	Christian North	25	Jul	99	7.79	Paul Ogun	31	Jul	16
5.30	Andrew Marsh	26	Jun	11	7.79 i	Ashley Bryant	28	Jan	17
5.26	Mark Johnson	31	Aug	91	7.78	Oliver Newport	14	May	16
5.26 i	Timothy Duckworth	11	Mar	17	7.77	Len Tyson	25	Jul	82
5.26	Scot Huggins	13	May	17	7.77	Dean Macey	27	Sep	00
					7.77	John Carr	14	Jul	12
					7.77 i	James Groocock	8	Dec	12

7.77	Felix Maisey-Curtis	6	Jul	14
7.76	Carl Howard	31	Jul	93

wind assisted

8.36	Rutherford	14	May	16
8.32	Rutherford	4	Jun	11
8.17	Mark Forsythe	11	Jun	89
8.16	Roy Mitchell	26	Jun	76
8.15	Alan Lerwill	29	May	72
8.12	Derrick Brown	14	Jun	86
8.12	Jonathan Moore	16	Aug	08
8.11	Daley Thompson	7	Aug	78
8.08	Darren Ritchie	29	Jun	03
8.07	Steve Phillips	11	Jul	99
8.04	Ian Simpson	3	Jun	89
8.02	Jacob Fincham-Dukes	15	Apr	17
7.96	Colin Jackson	17	May	86
7.95	Feron Sayers	2	Jul	17
7.94	John Herbert	25	Jul	82
7.94	John King	20	Jun	86
7.94	Chris Davidson	21	Jun	97
7.93	David Burgess	15	Jun	86
7.91	Steve Ingram	18	Jun	94
7.89	John Shepherd	20	Jun	86
7.87	Paul Johnson	15	May	88
7.85	Efe Uwaifo	6	May	17
7.84	Darren Thompson	16	Jun	01
7.84	Leigh Smith	3	Sep	05
7.82	Peter Reed	20	Jul	68
7.82	Femi Abejide	20	Jun	86
7.82	Kevin Liddington	25	Jun	89

Triple Jump

18.29	Jonathan Edwards	7	Aug	95
18.01	Edwards	9	Jul	98
18.00	Edwards	27	Aug	95
17.99	Edwards	23	Aug	98
17.98	Edwards	18	Jul	95
17.92	Edwards	6	Aug	01
17.88	Edwards	27	Jul	96
17.86	Edwards	28	Jul	02
17.82	Edwards	25	Jun	96
17.81	Phillips Idowu	29	Jul	10
17.64	Nathan Douglas	10	Jul	05
17.57 A	Keith Connor	5	Jun	82
	17.31 i	13	Mar	81
	17.30	9	Jun	82
17.41	John Herbert	2	Sep	85
17.30	Larry Achike	23	Sep	00
17.21	Tosi Fasinro	27	Jul	93
17.18	Francis Agyepong	7	Jul	95
17.06	Julian Golley	10	Sep	94
17.01	Eric McCalla	3	Aug	84
16.95	Julian Reid	4	Jul	15
16.87	Mike Makin	2	Aug	86
16.86	Aston Moore	16	Aug	81
16.86	Tosin Oke	3	Aug	07
16.81	Nathan Fox	13	May	17
16.75	Vernon Samuels	7	Aug	88
16.74	Ben Williams	12	Jun	15
16.71	Steven Shalders	3	Sep	05

16.63 A	Femi Akinsanya	10	Apr	99
	16.58	15	Jun	96
16.61	Kola Adedoyin	26	Apr	14
16.49 i	Nick Thomas	11	Feb	06
	16.44	22	Jul	00
16.46	Fred Alsop	16	Oct	64
16.45	Nonso Okolo	13	May	17
16.43	Jonathan Moore	22	Jul	01
16.43 i	Michael Puplampu	9	Feb	13
	16.20	8	Jun	13
16.38	Sam Trigg	27	May	17
16.33	Gary White	15	Jul	07
16.32	Tayo Erogbogbo	21	Aug	95
16.31 i	Daniel Lewis	8	Feb	14
	16.26	21	Jun	14
16.30	Femi Abejide	26	Jul	03
16.29 i	David Johnson	1	Mar	78
	16.18	22	Jun	75
16.26	Joe Sweeney	3	Aug	91
16.22	Derek Boosey	15	Jun	68
16.20	Rez Cameron	5	Jun	88
16.18	Tony Wadhams	6	Jul	69
16.17	John Mackenzie	17	Sep	94
16.16	Conroy Brown	19	Sep	81
16.16	Elliot O'Neill	4	Aug	07
16.15	Wayne Green	10	Jul	88
16.15	Michael Brown	23	Jul	89
16.15 i	Montel Nevers	21	Feb	16
	16.14	6	Aug	16
16.13	Steven Anderson	11	Jun	83
16.10	Alan Lerwill	28	Aug	71
16.09	Courtney Charles	17	Jun	90
16.08	Craig Duncan	21	Jun	86
16.07 i	Tunde Amosu	28	Feb	15
16.06	Mike McKernan	29	Jul	07
16.06	Jonathan Ilori	11	Jun	17
16.02	Peter Akwaboah	15	Jun	89
16.01	Lawrence Davis	19	Feb	17

wind assisted

18.43	Jonathan Edwards	25	Jun	95
18.08	Edwards	23	Jul	95
18.03	Edwards	2	Jul	95
17.81	Keith Connor	9	Oct	82
17.31	Larry Achike	15	Jul	00
17.30	Tosi Fasinro	12	Jun	93
17.29 A	Francis Agyepong	29	Jul	95
	17.24	2	Jul	95
17.02	Aston Moore	14	Jun	81
17.00	Steven Shalders	10	Jul	05
16.96	Julien Reid	28	May	16
16.82	Vernon Samuels	24	Jun	89
16.65	Fred Alsop	13	Aug	65
16.59	Michael Puplampu	10	Jun	12
16.49	Tony Wadhams	16	Sep	69
16.44	Tayo Erogbogbo	31	May	97
16.38	Femi Abejide	10	Jun	89
16.38	Courtney Charles	22	Jul	90
16.33	Dave Johnson	28	May	78
16.32	Craig Duncan	20	Jun	87
16.32	Rez Cameron	21	May	89
16.21	Alan Lerwill	28	Aug	71

Shot

	Mark	Name	Date		
	21.92	Carl Myerscough ¶	13	Jun	03
	21.68	Geoff Capes	18	May	80
	21.55	Capes	28	May	76
	21.55	Myerscough	27	Jul	03
	21.50	Capes	24	May	80
	21.50	Myerscough	8	Aug	03
	21.49 i	Myerscough	15	Mar	03
	21.37	Capes	10	Aug	74
	21.36	Capes	19	Jun	76
	21.35	Capes	5	Jun	80
	20.88	Mark Edwards ¶	7	Jun	08
	20.85 i	Mark Proctor	25	Jan	98
	20.40		7	Jul	99
	20.45	Shaun Pickering	17	Aug	97
	20.43	Mike Winch	22	May	74
	20.33	Paul Edwards ¶	9	Jul	91
	19.59	Scott Lincoln	28	May	16
	19.56	Arthur Rowe	7	Aug	61
10	19.49	Matt Simson	28	Aug	94
	19.44 i	Simon Williams	28	Jan	89
	19.17		18	May	91
	19.43	Bill Tancred	18	May	74
	19.42	Zane Duquemin	27	Jul	13
	19.18	Jeff Teale ¶	7	Aug	68
	19.02 i	Kieren Kelly ¶	21	Feb	09
	18.83		12	Jul	09
	19.01	Billy Cole	21	Jun	86
	18.97	Scott Rider	4	Jun	05
	18.97	Emeka Udechuku	24	Jun	06
	18.94	Bob Dale	12	Jun	76
20	18.93	Paul Buxton	13	May	77
	18.85	Lee Newman	2	Jun	96
	18.79	Steph Hayward	6	Sep	00
	18.66 i	Ryan Spencer-Jones	15	Dec	13
	18.32		18	May	14
	18.62	Martyn Lucking	2	Oct	62
	18.59 i	Alan Carter	11	Apr	65
	18.26		1	May	65
	18.59 i	Greg Beard	13	Jan	13
	18.29		14	Jul	13
	18.50	Mike Lindsay	2	Jul	63
	18.46	Roger Kennedy	22	May	77
	18.46 i	Simon Rodhouse	20	Feb	82
	18.20		25	Jul	82
30	18.35	Peter Tancred	9	Jul	74
	18.34	Richard Slaney	3	Jul	83
	18.34	Youcef Zatat	21	May	17
	18.29 i	Jamie Williamson	13	Jan	13
	18.17		28	Jul	12
	18.14 i	Neal Brunning ¶	26	Jan	92
	18.07	Gareth Winter	23	May	15
	18.05	John Watts	19	Aug	72
	18.04	Andy Vince	30	Apr	83
	17.96	Nigel Spratley	28	Aug	94
	17.95	Graham Savory	4	Jun	88
40	17.92	Nick Tabor	9	Apr	83
	17.90	Chris Gearing	26	May	07
	17.90	Carl Fletcher ¶	18	Aug	09
	17.87	Bill Fuller	15	Jul	72
	17.87 i	Ian Lindley	15	Mar	81
	17.87 i	Antony Zaidman	22	Jan	83
	17.85	Gary Sollitt	4	Jun	82
	17.85	Jamie Stevenson	28	Jun	09
	17.79	John Alderson	31	Jul	74
	17.78	Steve Whyte	11	Feb	89
	17.71	Sam Westlake-Cann	11	Aug	07	50

Discus

	Mark	Name	Date			
	68.24	Lawrence Okoye	19	May	12	
	67.63	Okoye	9	Jul	11	
	67.25	Okoye	4	Sep	12	
	66.84	Brett Morse	30	Jun	13	
	66.67	Okoye	20	Apr	12	
	66.64	Perriss Wilkins ¶	6	Jun	98	
	66.25	Okoye	26	Apr	12	
	66.06	Morse	27	Jul	11	
	65.44	Abdul Buhari	9	Jul	11	
	65.30	Morse	13	Aug	11	
	65.24	Carl Myerscough ¶	9	Jun	12	
	65.16	Richard Slaney	1	Jul	85	
	65.11	Glen Smith	18	Jul	99	
	65.08	Robert Weir	19	Aug	00	
	64.94	Bill Tancred	21	Jul	74	
	64.93	Emeka Udechuku	17	Jul	04	10
	63.46	Zane Duquemin	30	Jun	12	
	63.38	Nicholas Percy	22	Jul	16	
	63.00	Chris Scott	9	Jul	11	
	62.36	Peter Tancred	8	May	80	
	61.86	Paul Mardle	13	Jun	84	
	61.62	Peter Gordon ¶	15	Jun	91	
	61.14	Simon Williams	18	Apr	92	
	61.10	Kevin Brown	30	Aug	97	
	61.00	Allan Seatory	6	Oct	74	
	60.92	Graham Savory	10	May	86	20
	60.48	Lee Newman	10	May	97	
	60.42	Mike Cushion	16	Aug	75	
	60.28	Gregory Thompson	5	May	17	
	60.08	Abi Ekoku	16	May	90	
	59.98	Tom Norman	18	Jun	11	
	59.84	Colin Sutherland ¶	10	Jun	78	
	59.76	John Hillier	27	Jul	74	
	59.70	John Watts	14	Jul	72	
	59.58	Jamie Williamson	30	Jun	12	
	59.33	Alan Toward	26	Feb	17	30
	58.84	Simon Cooke	16	Jun	12	
	58.77	Angus McInroy	10	Jul	10	
	58.69	Marcus Gouldbourne	25	Jul	06	
	58.64	Steve Casey	19	May	91	
	58.58	Darrin Morris	22	Jun	91	
	58.36	Paul Reed	11	Jul	99	
	58.34	Geoff Capes	29	Sep	73	
	58.08	Mike Winch	7	Sep	75	
	57.58	Arthur McKenzie	17	Aug	69	
	57.14	Mark Proctor	24	Jun	00	40
	57.12	Paul Edwards ¶	10	Aug	88	
	57.10	Dennis Roscoe	3	May	80	
	57.09	Leslie Richards	21	Aug	10	
	57.07	Curtis Griffith-Parker	19	Jun	10	
	57.00	Gerry Carr	17	Jul	65	
	56.97	Matt Brown	26	Apr	08	
	56.79	Alex Parkinson	11	Feb	17	
	56.77	George Armstrong	17	Jun	17	
	56.71	Roy Hollingsworth	14	Sep	63	
	56.66	Gary Herrington	15	Jun	96	50

Hammer

	Mark	Name	Date		
	77.55	Nick Miller	22	Jul	15
	77.54	Martin Girvan	12	May	84
	77.51	Miller	21	Apr	17
	77.42	Miller	22	Aug	15
	77.31	Miller	11	Aug	17
	77.30	Dave Smith I	13	Jul	85
	77.16	Girvan	13	Jul	84
	77.04	Smith I	25	May	85
	77.02	Matt Mileham	11	May	84
	76.97	Miller	2	May	15
	76.93	Mark Dry	17	May	15
	76.45	Chris Bennett	18	Jun	16
	76.43	Mick Jones	2	Jun	01
	75.63	Alex Smith	3	Mar	12
	75.40	Chris Black	23	Jul	83
10	75.10	Dave Smith II	27	May	96
	75.08	Robert Weir	3	Oct	82
	74.02	Paul Head	30	Aug	90
	73.86	Barry Williams	1	Jul	76
	73.80	Jason Byrne	19	Sep	92
	73.40	Taylor Campbell	30	Apr	17
	73.20	Paul Dickenson	22	May	76
	72.79	Bill Beauchamp	25	Aug	03
	72.79	Andy Frost	22	May	11
	72.45	Mike Floyd	20	Aug	11
20	71.75	Peter Smith	15	Apr	12
	71.70	Matt Lambley	23	May	10
	71.60	Shane Peacock	24	Jun	90
	71.28	Peter Vivian	25	Jun	95
	71.01	Amir Williamson	21	Jul	13
	71.00	Ian Chipchase	17	Aug	74
	70.98	Joseph Ellis	12	May	17
	70.90	Michael Bomba	6	Apr	13
	70.88	Howard Payne	29	Jun	74
	70.82	James Bedford	19	May	13
30	70.33	John Pearson	30	Jul	00
	70.30	Stewart Rogerson	14	Aug	88
	70.28	Paul Buxton	19	May	79
	70.18	Chris Shorthouse	8	Aug	15
	70.00	Osian Jones	29	Jul	17
	69.79	Craig Murch	22	May	16
	69.74	Iain Park	7	Sep	03
	69.52	Jim Whitehead	23	Sep	79
	69.13	Callum Brown	30	Jul	17
	68.86	Jake Norris	1	Apr	17
40	68.69	Simon Bown	6	Sep	09
	68.64	Shaun Pickering	7	Apr	84
	68.18	Ron James	2	Jun	82
	67.85	Nicholas Percy	7	May	16
	67.82	Steve Whyte	15	Apr	89
	67.45	Steve Pearson	27	Jun	98
	67.32	Gareth Cook	1	Jun	91
	66.97	Chris Howe	6	Jun	98
	66.95 A	Karim Chester	23	Apr	05
	66.84	Michael Painter	8	Apr	17
50	66.53	Russell Devine	15	Feb	01
	66.28	Jonathan Edwards	31	May	14
	66.07	Sam Coe	8	Aug	10
	65.88	Jac Lloyd Palmer	18	Jun	17

Javelin

Mark	Name	Date			
91.46	Steve Backley	25	Jan	92	
90.81	Backley	22	Jul	01	
89.89	Backley	19	Jul	98	
89.85	Backley	23	Sep	00	
89.72	Backley	23	Aug	98	
89.58	Backley	2	Jul	90	
89.22	Backley	11	Jun	98	
89.02	Backley	30	May	97	
88.80	Backley	2	Aug	98	
88.71 A	Backley	13	Sep	98	
86.94	Mick Hill	13	Jun	93	
85.67	Mark Roberson	19	Jul	98	
85.09	Nick Nieland	13	Aug	00	
83.84	Roald Bradstock	2	May	87	
83.52	Mervyn Luckwell	25	Sep	11	
82.38	Colin Mackenzie	7	Aug	93	
81.70	Nigel Bevan	28	Jun	92	
80.98	Dave Ottley	24	Sep	88	
80.38	James Campbell	18	Jul	10	10
79.72	Lee Doran	23	Jun	12	
79.55	Michael Allen	10	Jun	06	
78.54	Gary Jenson	17	Sep	89	
78.33 A	David Parker	24	Mar	01	
77.84	Peter Yates	21	Feb	87	
77.47	Matti Mortimore	31	Mar	17	
77.03	James Whiteaker	6	May	17	
76.92	Chris Hughff	4	May	09	
76.81	Harry Hughes	1	May	17	
76.77	Matthew Hunt	1	May	11	20
76.66 i	Stuart Faben	3	Mar	96	
76.17		30	May	02	
76.13	Joe Dunderdale	18	May	14	
76.10	Keith Beard	18	May	91	
75.89	Dan Pembroke	12	Jun	11	
75.71	Joe Harris	29	Jul	17	
75.52	Marcus Humphries	25	Jul	87	
75.32	Steve Harrison	9	Jul	95	
75.28	Nigel Stainton	5	Aug	89	
74.92	Neil McLellan	22	Jun	07	
74.90	Daryl Brand	27	Jun	86	30
74.72	Chris Crutchley	13	Jul	86	
74.71	Benji Pearson	26	Apr	14	
74.70	Myles Cottrell	16	May	92	
74.64	Bonne Buwembo	24	Aug	14	
74.62 A	Alex van der Merwe	29	Mar	08	
73.56	Dan Carter	16	Sep	00	
73.41	Neil Crossley	6	May	13	
73.26	David Messom	25	Apr	87	
72.92	Stefan Baldwin	8	May	93	
72.73	Freddie Curtis	7	Jun	15	40
72.52	Richard Shuttleworth	25	Sep	11	
72.41	Steven Turnock	15	Apr	17	
72.35	Anthony Lovett	24	Jul	04	
72.26	Felix Hatton	2	Jul	11	
71.86	Tony Hatton	3	May	93	
71.83	Brett Byrd	20	Jun	10	
71.79	Phill Sharpe	27	Aug	00	
71.60	Stuart Harvey	22	Jun	08	
71.15	Greg Millar	24	May	17	
71.00	Mike Tarran	30	Jun	02	50

Decathlon (1985 Tables)

	8847	Daley Thompson	9	Aug	84
	8811	Thompson	28	Aug	86
	8774	Thompson	8	Sep	82
	8730	Thompson	23	May	82
	8714	Thompson	13	Aug	83
	8667	Thompson	18	May	86
	8663	Thompson	28	Jul	86
	8648	Thompson	18	May	80
	8603	Dean Macey	7	Aug	01
	8567	Macey	28	Sep	00
	8163	Ashley Bryant	28	May	17
	8131	Alex Kruger	2	Jul	95
	8102	Daniel Awde	27	May	12
	7980	Simon Shirley	24	Aug	94
	7973	Timothy Duckworth	9	Apr	17
	7965	John Lane	13	Apr	17
	7922 w	Brad McStravick	28	May	84
	7885		6	May	84
10	7904	David Bigham	28	Jun	92
	7901 h	Peter Gabbett	22	May	72
	7889	Eugene Gilkes	18	May	86
	7882	Ben Gregory	14	Apr	16
	7874	Colin Boreham	23	May	82
	7861	Tony Brannen	30	Apr	95
	7857	Liam Ramsay	19	Jul	15
	7787	Brian Taylor	30	May	93
	7766	Barry Thomas	2	Sep	95
	7748	Eric Hollingsworth	30	May	93
20	7740	Greg Richards	7	Jun	87
	7739	Jamie Quarry	30	May	99
	7734	Edward Dunford	9	May	07
	7727	David Guest	6	Jun	10
	7726	Ben Hazell	28	Jun	09
	7713	Jim Stevenson	5	Jun	93
	7712	Martin Brockman	8	Oct	10
	7708	Fidelis Obikwu	28	May	84
	7663	Rafer Joseph	24	Aug	94
	7651	David Hall	13	Jun	15
30	7643 w	Tom Leeson	8	Sep	85
	7565		11	Aug	85
	7635 w	Du'aine Ladejo	24	May	98
	7633		18	May	98
	7597	Osman Muskwe	30	Aug	15
	7596	Mike Corden	27	Jun	76
	7594	Mark Bishop	3	Sep	89
	7579	Mark Luscombe	8	May	88
	7571	Alexis Sharp	17	Apr	98
	7571	Kevin Sempers	8	Oct	10
	7535	Duncan Mathieson	24	Jun	90
	7515	Ken Hayford	9	Jun	85
40	7510 w	John Heanley	6	Jun	04
	7443		16	May	04
	7510	Peter Glass	14	Jul	13
	7500	Barry King	22	May	72
	7500	Pan Zeniou	2	Aug	81
	7500	Curtis Mathews	17	Sep	17
	7472	Anthony Sawyer	30	May	04
	7469	Louis Evling-Jones	13	Jul	08
	7457	Roger Skedd	12	Apr	13

7440	Oliver McNeillis	27	Jul	08	
7439	Kevan Lobb	19	Aug	84	
7435 w	Paul Field	21	May	95	50

3000 Metres Track Walk

10:58.21 i	Tom Bosworth	28	Feb	16	
11:15.26 +		2	Jul	17	
11:43.44		31	May	10	
11:13.09	Callum Wilkinson	12	Jun	17	
11:19.10	Cameron Corbishley	12	Jun	17	
11:23.99 i	Alex Wright	27	Jan	13	
11:38.16		31	May	10	
11:24.4	Mark Easton	10	May	89	
11:28.4	Phil Vesty	9	May	84	
11:29.6 i	Tim Berrett	21	Jan	90	
11:31.0	Andi Drake	22	Jul	90	
11:32.2	Ian McCombie	20	Jul	88	
11:33.4	Steve Partington	12	Jul	95	10
11:34.62	Daniel King	30	May	05	
11:35.5	Andy Penn	10	May	97	
11:39.0 i+	Martin Rush	8	Feb	92	
11:44.68	Roger Mills	7	Aug	81	
11:45.1	Chris Maddocks	9	Aug	87	
11:45.77	Steve Johnson	20	Jun	87	
11:47.12 i	Philip King	26	Feb	95	

5000 Metres Track Walk

18:39.47 i	Tom Bosworth	12	Feb	17	
18:43.28		2	Jul	17	
18:56.96	Callum Wilkinson	2	Jul	17	
19:22.29 i	Martin Rush	8	Feb	92	
19:27.39	Alex Wright	14	Jun	13	
19:28.20 i	Andi Drake	13	Feb	91	
19:35.0	Darrell Stone	16	May	89	
19:42.90 i	Tim Berrett	23	Feb	90	
19:55.8 +	Ian McCombie	4	Jun	89	
19:57.91	Dominic King	24	Jul	04	

10000 Metres Track Walk

40:06.65	Ian McCombie	4	Jun	89	
40:39.77	McCombie	5	Jun	88	
40:41.62	Callum Wilkinson	23	Jul	16	
40:42.53	McCombie	28	Aug	89	
40:53.60	Phil Vesty	28	May	84	
40:55.6	Martin Rush	14	Sep	91	
41:06.57	Chris Maddocks	20	Jun	87	
41:10.11	Darrell Stone	16	Jul	95	
41:13.62	Steve Barry	19	Jun	82	
41:13.65	Martin Bell	22	Jul	95	
41:14.3	Mark Easton	5	Feb	89	
41:14.61	Steve Partington	16	Jul	95	10
41:18.64	Andi Drake	5	Jun	88	
41:34.9 +	Tom Bosworth	21	Jun	15	
41:37.44	Cameron Corbishley	18	Jun	17	
41:49.06	Sean Martindale	26	Jun	90	
41:55.5	Phil Embleton	14	Apr	71	
41:59.10	Andy Penn	27	Jul	91	

track short

40:54.7	Steve Barry	19	Mar	83

20 Kilometres Road Walk

1:20:13	Tom Bosworth	12	Aug	16
1:20:41	Bosworth	19	Mar	16
1:20:58	Bosworth	1	Apr	17
1:21:21	Bosworth	21	May	17
1:21:53	Bosworth	19	Mar	17
1:22:03	Ian McCombie	23	Sep	88
1:22:12	Chris Maddocks	3	May	92
1:22:17	Callum Wilkinson	21	May	17
1:22:20	Bosworth	12	Apr	14
1:22:33	Bosworth	5	Jul	15
1:22:51	Steve Barry	26	Feb	83
1:23:05	Alex Wright	17	Mar	13
1:23:34	Andy Penn	29	Feb	92
1:23:34	Martin Rush	29	Feb	92
1:23:58	Darrell Stone	24	Feb	96
1:24:04	Mark Easton	25	Feb	89
1:24:04.0t	Andi Drake	26	May	90
1:24:07.6t	Phil Vesty	1	Dec	84
1:24:09	Steve Partington	24	Sep	94
1:24:25	Tim Berrett	21	Apr	90
1:24:50	Paul Nihill	30	Jul	72
1:25:42	Martin Bell	9	May	92
1:25:53.6t	Sean Martindale	28	Apr	89
1:26:00	Cameron Corbishley	8	Apr	17
1:26:02	Jamie Higgins	12	Apr	14
1:26:08	Dominic King	25	Jun	17
1:26:14	Dan King	28	Feb	04
1:26:53	Chris Cheeseman	21	Mar	99
1:27:00	Roger Mills	30	Jun	80
1:27:05	Mike Parker	5	Apr	86
1:27:16	Les Morton	25	Feb	89
1:27:30	Ben Wears	15	May	10
1:27:35	Olly Flynn	3	Oct	76
1:27:43	Luke Finch	20	Jun	10
1:27:46	Brian Adams	11	Oct	75
1:27:59	Phil Embleton	3	Apr	71
1:28:02	Paul Blagg	27	Feb	82
1:28:15	Ken Matthews	23	Jul	60
1:28:26	Chris Harvey	29	Sep	79
1:28:30	Allan King	11	May	85
1:28:34	Chris Smith	11	May	85
1:28:34	Steve Hollier	19	Jun	99
1:28:37	Dave Jarman	30	Jun	80
1:28:38	Guy Thomas	3	Jun	17
1:28:40	Matt Hales	21	Apr	01
1:28:46	Jimmy Ball	4	Apr	87
1:28:46	Steve Taylor	20	Dec	92
1:28:46	Jamie O'Rawe	21	Mar	99
1:28:50	Amos Seddon	3	Aug	74
1:29:07	Philip King	20	Aug	95
1:29:19	Stuart Phillips	31	May	92
1:29:24	George Nibre	6	Apr	80
1:29:27	Graham White	19	Apr	97
1:29:29 +	Steve Johnson	16	Apr	89
1:29:37	John Warhurst	28	Jul	73
1:29:42	Dennis Jackson	10	May	86

no judges

1:27:04.0t	Steve Hollier	9	Jan	00

50 Kilometres Road Walk

3:51:37	Chris Maddocks	28	Oct	90
3:53:14	Maddocks	25	Nov	95
3:55:48	Dominic King	8	Oct	16
3:57:10	Maddocks	12	Mar	00
3:57:48	Les Morton	30	Apr	89
3:58:25	Morton	20	Mar	88
3:58:36	Morton	11	Oct	92
3:59:22	King	10	Oct	15
3:59:30	Morton	30	Sep	88
3:59:55	Paul Blagg	5	Sep	87
4:03:08	Dennis Jackson	16	Mar	86
4:03:53	Mark Easton	25	Apr	98
4:04:49	Dan King	29	Mar	08
4:06:14	Barry Graham	20	Apr	85
4:07:18	Steve Hollier	18	Jun	00
4:07:23	Bob Dobson	21	Oct	79
4:07:49	Chris Cheesman	2	May	99
4:07:57	Ian Richards	20	Apr	80
4:08:41	Adrian James	12	Apr	80
4:09:15un	Don Thompson	10	Oct	65
4:12:19		20	Jun	59
4:09:22	Mike Smith	27	Mar	89
4:10:23	Darrell Stone	6	May	90
4:10:42	Amos Seddon	9	Mar	80
4:11:32	Paul Nihill	18	Oct	64
4:12:00	Sean Martindale	16	Oct	93
4:12:02	Martin Rush	28	Jul	91
4:12:37	John Warhurst	27	May	72
4:12:50	Darren Thorn	6	May	90
4:13:18	Graham White	27	Jun	98
4:13:25	Allan King	16	Apr	83
4:14:03	Tom Misson	20	Jun	59
4:14:25	Dave Cotton	15	Jul	78
4:15:14	Shaun Lightman	13	Oct	73
4:15:22	Brian Adams	17	Sep	78
4:15:52	Ray Middleton	27	May	72
4:16:30	Karl Atton	20	Apr	97
4:16:45	Gareth Brown	21	Apr	02
4:16:47	George Nibre	9	Mar	80
4:17:24	Andi Drake	18	Oct	87
4:17:34	Gordon Vale	9	Oct	83
4:17:40	Steve Partington	26	Jun	05
4:17:52	Stuart Elms	17	Apr	76
4:18:30	Peter Ryan	10	Apr	82
4:19:00	Carl Lawton	17	Jul	71
4:19:13	Bryan Eley	19	Jul	69
4:19:26	Roger Mills	9	Apr	83
4:19:55	Mick Holmes	4	Aug	73
4:19:57	Barry Ingarfield	21	Oct	79
4:20:05	George Chaplin	27	May	72
4:20:22	Scott Davis	13	Sep	09
4:20:43	Tim Watt	8	Oct	95
4:20:48	Andrew Trigg	1	May	88
4:20:51	Murray Lambden	18	Jul	82
4:21:02	Ron Wallwork	17	Jul	71
4:22:05	Mel McCann	14	Sep	86
4:22:41.0t	Charley Fogg	1	Jun	75
4:23:12	Peter Hodkinson	21	Jul	79
4:23:22	Chris Berwick	12	Jul	86

4 x 100 Metres Relay

37.47	Great Britain & NI	12	Aug	17

Ujah, Gemili, Talbot, Mitchell-Blake

37.73	Great Britain & NI	29	Aug	99

Gardener, Campbell, Devonish, Chambers ¶

37.76	Great Britain & NI	12	Aug	17

Ujah, Gemili, Talbot, Mitchell-Blake

37.77	Great Britain & NI	22	Aug	93

Jackson, Jarrett, Regis, Christie ¶

37.78	Great Britain & NI	23	Jul	16

Dasaolu, Gemili, Ellington, Ujah

37.81	Great Britain & NI "B"	23	Jul	16

Kilty, Aikines-Aryeetey, Talbot, Edoburun

37.90	Great Britain & NI	1	Sep	07

Malcolm, Pickering, Devonish, Lewis-Francis

37.93	Great Britain & NI	25	May	14

Kilty, Aikines-Aryeetey, Ellington, Talbot

37.93	Great Britain & NI	17	Aug	14

Ellington, Aikines-Aryeetey, Kilty, Talbot

10   37.98   Great Britain & NI   1 Sep 90

Braithwaite, Regis, Adam, Christie ¶

37.98   Great Britain & NI   19 Aug 16

Kilty, Aikines-Aryeetey, Ellington, Gemili

38.02   Great Britain & NI   22 Aug 09

Williamson, Edgar, Devonish, Aikines-Aryeetey

38.02   England   2 Aug 14

Gemili, Aikines-Aryeetey, Kilty, Talbot

38.05   Great Britain & NI   21 Aug 93

John, Jarrett, Braithwaite, Christie ¶

38.06   Great Britain & NI   18 Aug 16

Kilty, Aikines-Aryeetey, Ellington, Ujah

38.07   Great Britain & NI   28 Aug 04

Gardener, Campbell, Devonish, Lewis-Francis

38.08   Great Britain & NI   8 Aug 92

Adam, Jarrett, Regis, Christie ¶

38.08   Great Britain & NI   24 Jun 17

Ujah, Hughes, Talbot, Aikines-Aryeetey

38.09   Great Britain & NI   1 Sep 91

Jarrett, Regis, Braithwaite, Christie ¶

20   38.09 A   Great Britain & NI   12 Sep 98

Condon, Devonish, Golding, Chambers ¶

38.11   Great Britain & NI   21 Aug 09

Williamson, Edgar, Devonish, Aikines-Aryeetey

38.12   Great Britain & NI   18 Aug 13

Kilty, Aikines-Aryeetey, Ellington, Chambers ¶

38.12   Great Britain & NI   9 Jul 16

Dasaolu, Gemili, Ellington, Ujah

38.14   Great Britain & NI   10 Aug 97

Braithwaite, Campbell, Walker, Golding

38.16   Great Britain & NI   19 Jun 99

Gardener, Campbell, Devonish, Golding

38.17   Great Britain & NI 'A'   7 Aug 99

Gardener, Campbell, Devonish,Golding

38.17   Great Britain & NI   10 Jul 16

Dasaolu, Gemili, Ellington, Ujah

38.19   Great Britain & NI   25 May 14

Kilty, Aikines-Aryeetey, Ellington,Talbot

38.20   England   21 Sep 98

Chambers ¶, Devonish, Golding, Campbell

30   38.20   Great Britain & NI   29 Aug 15

Kilty, Aikines-Aryeetey, Ellington,Talbot

4 x 400 Metres Relay

2:56.60   Great Britain & NI   3 Aug 96

Thomas, Baulch, Richardson, Black

2:56.65   Great Britain & NI   10 Aug 97

Thomas, Black, Baulch, Richardson

2:57.53   Great Britain & NI   1 Sep 91

Black, Redmond, Regis, Akabusi

2:58.22   Great Britain & NI   1 Sep 90

Sanders, Akabusi, Regis, Black

2:58.51   Great Britain & NI   30 Aug 15

Yousif, Williams, Dunn, Rooney

2:58.68   Great Britain & NI   23 Aug 98

Hylton, Baulch, Thomas, Richardson

2:58.79   Great Britain & NI   17 Aug 14

Williams, Hudson-Smith, Bingham, Rooney

2:58.81   Great Britain & NI   23 Aug 08

Steele, Tobin, Bingham, Rooney

2:58.82   Great Britain & NI   14 Aug 05

Benjamin, Rooney, Tobin, Davis

2:58.86   Great Britain & NI   6 Sep 87 10

Redmond, Akabusi, Black, Brown

2:59.00   Great Britain & NI   13 Aug 17

Hudson-Smith, Cowan, Yousif, Rooney

2:59.05   Great Britain & NI   29 Aug 15

Yousif, Williams, Dunn, Rooney

2:59.13   Great Britain & NI   11 Aug 84

Akabusi, Cook, T Bennett, Brown

2:59.13   Great Britain & NI   14 Aug 94

McKenzie, Whittle, Black, Ladejo

2:59.33   Great Britain & NI   22 Aug 08

Steele, Tobin, Bingham, Rooney

2:59.46   Great Britain & NI   22 Jun 97

Black, Baulch, Thomas, Richardson

2:59.49   Great Britain & NI   31 Aug 91

Mafe, Redmond, Richardson, Akabusi

2:59.53   Great Britain & NI   10 Aug 12

Williams, Green, Greene, Rooney

2:59.71 A Great Britain & NI   13 Sep 98

Hylton, Baulch, Baldock, Thomas

2:59.73   Great Britain & NI   8 Aug 92 20

Black, Grindley, Akabusi, Regis

2:59.84   Great Britain & NI   31 Aug 86

Redmond, Akabusi, Whittle, Black

2:59.85   Great Britain & NI   19 Aug 96

Baulch, Hylton, Richardson, Black

3:00.10   Great Britain & NI   12 Aug 17

Yousif, Cowan, Green, Rooney

3:00.19   Great Britain & NI   9 Aug 97

Hylton, Black, Baulch, Thomas

3:00.25   Great Britain & NI   27 Jun 93

Ladejo, Akabusi, Regis, Grindley

3:00.32   Great Britain & NI   25 May 14

Bingham, Williams, Levine, Rooney

3:00.34   Great Britain & NI   25 Jun 95

Thomas, Patrick, Richardson, Black

3:00.38   Great Britain & NI   1 Sep 11

Strachan, Levine, Clarke, Rooney

3:00.38   Great Britain & NI   9 Aug 12

Levine, Williams, Green, Rooney

3:00.40   England   31 Jul 02 30

Deacon, Baldock, Rawlinson, Caines

UNDER 23

100 Metres

9.96	Chijindu Ujah	8	Jun	14
9.97	Adam Gemili	7	Jun	15
9.97	Dwain Chambers ¶	22	Aug	99
10.03	Simeon Williamson	12	Jul	08
10.03	Reece Prescod	4	Aug	17
10.04	Mark Lewis-Francis	5	Jul	02
10.09	Jason Livingston ¶	13	Jun	92
10.09	James Dasaolu	6	Jun	09
10.09	Nethaneel Mitchell-Blake	16	Apr	16
10.10	Harry Aikines-Aryeetey	7	Sep	08
10.10	Zharnel Hughes	16	Apr	16

wind assisted

9.93	Ojie Edoborun	15	Apr	17
9.97	Mark Lewis-Francis	30	Jun	02
10.04	Tyrone Edgar	10	May	03
10.07	Toby Box	11	Jun	94
10.08	Zharnel Hughes	15	Apr	17
10.09 †	Christian Malcolm	4	Aug	01
10.10	Donovan Reid	26	Jun	83
10.10	Leevan Yearwood	3	Jul	09

hand timing

10.1	David Jenkins	20	May	72

wind assisted

10.1	Drew McMaster	16	Jun	79

200 Metres

19.95	Nethaneel Mitchell-Blake	14	May	16
19.98	Adam Gemili	16	Aug	13
20.02	Zharnel Hughes	27	Aug	15
20.08	Christian Malcolm	8	Aug	01
20.18	John Regis	3	Sep	87
20.34	Chris Lambert	20	Jul	03
20.36	Todd Bennett	28	May	84
20.37	Toby Sandeman	18	Jul	09
20.38	Julian Golding	24	Aug	97
20.38	Reece Prescod	25	Aug	16

wind assisted

20.10	Marcus Adam	1	Feb	90
20.38	Dwayne Grant	23	Aug	03

hand timing

20.3	David Jenkins	19	Aug	72

400 Metres

44.47	David Grindley	3	Aug	92
44.48	Matthew Hudson-Smith	13	Aug	16
44.50	Derek Redmond	1	Sep	87
44.59	Roger Black	29	Aug	86
44.60	Martyn Rooney	19	Aug	08
44.66 A	Iwan Thomas	14	Apr	96
44.69		16	Jun	96
45.01	Robert Tobin	11	Jun	05
45.04	Tim Benjamin	30	Jul	04
45.09	Mark Richardson	10	Jul	92
45.14	Jamie Baulch	23	Aug	95

800 Metres

1:43.97	Sebastian Coe	15	Sep	78
1:43.98	Peter Elliott	23	Aug	83
1:44.45	Steve Cram	17	Jul	82
1:44.65	Ikem Billy	21	Jul	84
1:44.68	Michael Rimmer	29	Jul	08
1:44.92	Curtis Robb	15	Aug	93
1:45.10	Richard Hill	10	Jun	06
1:45.14	Chris McGeorge	28	Jun	83
1:45.25	Kyle Langford	8	Aug	17
1:45.32	James McIlroy (IRL)	16	Jul	98
1:45.44	Steve Ovett	25	Jul	76

1000 Metres

2:15.12	Steve Cram	17	Sep	82
2:16.34	Matthew Yates	6	Jul	90

1500 Metres

3:33.66	Steve Cram	18	Aug	82
3:33.83	John Robson	4	Sep	79
3:34.00	Matthew Yates	13	Sep	91
3:34.45	Steve Ovett	3	Sep	77
3:34.76	Ross Murray	27	May	12
3:35.16	Steve Crabb	28	Jun	84
3:35.29	Charlie Grice	18	Jul	15
3:35.49	Jake Wightman	12	Jul	14
3:35.72	Graham Williamson	15	Jul	80
3:35.99	Josh Kerr	14	Apr	17

1 Mile

3:49.90	Steve Cram	13	Jul	82
3:50.64	Graham Williamson	13	Jul	82
3:52.74	John Robson	17	Jul	79
3:52.77	Ross Murray	14	Jul	12
3:53.20	Ian Stewart II	25	Aug	82
3:53.44	Jack Buckner	13	Jul	82
3:54.20	Jake Wightman	22	Jul	16
3:54.36	Steve Crabb	21	Jul	84
3:54.39	Neil Horsfield	8	Jul	86
3:54.61	Charlie Grice	27	Jul	13

2000 Metres

5:01.90	Jack Buckner	29	Aug	83
5:02.67	Gary Staines	4	Aug	85
5:02.99	Neil Caddy	11	Aug	96

3000 Metres

7:41.3	Steve Ovett	23	Sep	77
7:42.47	David Lewis	9	Jul	83
7:43.90	Ian Stewart II	26	Jun	82
7:45.45	Paul Davies-Hale	13	Jul	84
7:46.6+	David Black	14	Sep	73
7:47.12	Simon Mugglestone	27	Jun	88
7:47.82	Steve Cram	26	Jul	81
7:48.47 i	John Mayock	1	Mar	92
7:48.6+	Nat Muir	27	Jun	80
7:49.45	Paul Lawther	9	Sep	77

2 Miles

8:19.37	Nat Muir	27	Jun	80

5000 Metres

13:15.31	Tom Farrell	29	Apr	12
13:17.9	Nat Muir	15	Jul	80
13:19.78	Jon Brown	2	Jul	93
13:22.2	Dave Bedford	12	Jun	71
13:22.85	Ian Stewart I	25	Jul	70
13:23.52	David Black	29	Jan	74
13:23.94	Jonathan Davies	28	May	16
13:24.59	Paul Davies-Hale	1	Jun	84
13:25.0	Steve Ovett	30	Jul	77
13:26.97	John Mayock	9	Jun	92

10000 Metres

27:47.0	Dave Bedford	10	Jul	71
27:48.49	David Black	25	Jan	74
28:09.95	Bernie Ford	6	Oct	73
28:12.42	Dave Murphy	13	Jul	79
28:14.08	Jon Richards	20	Jun	86
28:18.8	Nicky Lees	7	May	79
28:19.6	Jon Brown	17	Apr	92
28:20.71	Jim Brown	12	Jul	74
28:20.76	Steve Binns	27	Aug	82
28:24.01	Jack Lane	10	Aug	71

Marathon

2:12:19	Don Faircloth	23	Jul	70
2:16:04	Ian Ray	27	Oct	79
2:16:21	Norman Wilson	10	Sep	77
2:16:47	Ieuan Ellis	19	Sep	82
2:17:13	Brent Jones	13	May	84

3000 Metres Steeplechase

8:16.52	Tom Hanlon	23	Aug	89
8:18.80	Colin Reitz	6	Jul	82
8:20.83	Paul Davies-Hale	10	Jun	84
8:22.48	John Davies	13	Sep	74
8:28.6	Dave Bedford	10	Sep	71
8:29.72	David Lewis	29	May	83
8:29.86	Tony Staynings	2	Aug	75
8:30.64	Dennis Coates	2	Aug	75
8:31.72	Keith Cullen	28	Jun	92
8:31.80	Graeme Fell	8	Aug	81

110 Metres Hurdles

13.11 A	Colin Jackson	11	Aug	88
13.11		14	Jul	89
13.21	Tony Jarrett	31	Aug	90
13.24	David Omoregie	3	Sep	16
13.29	Jon Ridgeon	15	Jul	87
13.31	Lawrence Clarke	8	Aug	12
13.34	Andrew Pozzi	13	Jul	12
13.36	Rob Newton	31	Jul	03
13.49	William Sharman	23	Jul	06
13.54	David King	22	May	16
13.56	Callum Priestley	29	Jul	09

wind assisted

12.95	Colin Jackson	10	Sep	89
13.14	Lawrence Clarke	7	Jul	12
13.45	William Sharman	15	Jul	06

hand timing

13.4	David King	6	Jun	16

400 Metres Hurdles

48.60	Jack Green	13	Jul	12
48.71	Nathan Woodward	3	Jul	11
49.06	Rick Yates	26	Jul	08
49.09	Rhys Williams	23	Mar	06
49.11	Gary Oakes	26	Jul	80
49.19	Seb Rodger	13	Jul	13
49.49	Jacob Paul	9	Jul	17
49.53	Dai Greene	10	Sep	08
49.57	Matt Elias	14	Jul	01
49.62	Lloyd Gumbs	18	Jul	09
49.62	Niall Flannery	30	Jun	13

High Jump

2.38 i	Steve Smith	4	Feb	94
2.37		22	Aug	93
2.32 i	Brendan Reilly	24	Feb	94
2.31		17	Jul	92
2.31	Dalton Grant	25	Sep	88
2.30 i	Geoff Parsons	25	Jan	86
2.28		18	May	86
2.30	Ben Challenger	13	Jul	99
2.28 i	John Holman	28	Jan	89
2.27	Martyn Bernard	31	May	04
2.27	Robbie Grabarz	1	Jun	08
2.26	Allan Smith	14	Jul	13
2.26 i	Chris Kandu	21	Feb	15

Pole Vault

5.71 i	Steven Lewis	14	Mar	08
5.71		1	Jul	08
5.70	Nick Buckfield	23	Jul	95
5.65	Jax Thoirs	16	May	15
5.62 i	Luke Cutts	18	Jan	09
5.60		19	Jul	09
5.60	Neil Winter	19	Aug	95
5.55 i	Andrew Sutcliffe	11	Feb	12
5.46		11	Aug	12
5.50	Paul Williamson	6	Jul	96
5.50 i	Adam Hague	8	Jan	17
5.50		7	Feb	17
5.47 i	Keith Higham	4	Feb	06
5.40		25	Jun	05
5.45	Charlie Myers	10	Jun	17

Long Jump

8.27	Chris Tomlinson	13	Apr	02
8.26	Greg Rutherford	15	Jul	06
8.15	Stewart Faulkner	16	Jul	90
8.11	Nathan Morgan	24	Jul	98
8.07	Lynn Davies	18	Oct	64
8.04	Roy Mitchell	25	Jun	77
8.00	Daley Thompson	25	Jul	80
8.00	Derrick Brown	7	Aug	85
7.97	Fred Salle	13	Jul	86
7.96	Jacob Fincham-Dukes	10	Mar	89

wind assisted

8.16	Roy Mitchell	26	Jun	76
8.11	Daley Thompson	7	Aug	78

Triple Jump

17.21	Tosi Fasinro	27	Jul	93
17.12	Phillips Idowu	23	Sep	00
17.05	John Herbert	8	Jul	83
16.95	Julian Golley	10	Jul	92
16.95	Nathan Douglas	11	Jul	04
16.76	Keith Connor	12	Aug	78
16.74	Jonathan Edwards	23	Jul	88
16.71	Vernon Samuels	18	May	86
16.69	Aston Moore	12	Aug	78
16.65	Tosin Oke	28	Jul	02
16.54	Eric McCalla	17	Sep	82
16.50 i	Kola Adedoyin	9	Feb	13

wind assisted

17.30	Tosi Fasinro	12	Jun	93
17.21	Keith Connor	12	Aug	78
16.76	Aston Moore	25	Sep	78

Shot

19.48	Geoff Capes	21	Aug	71
19.42	Zane Duquemin	27	Jul	13
19.44 i	Simon Williams	28	Jan	89
18.93		23	Jul	89
19.23	Matt Simson	23	May	91
19.01	Billy Cole	21	Jun	86
18.93	Paul Buxton	13	May	77
18.63 i	Carl Myerscough ¶	6	Feb	99
18.59 i	Alan Carter	11	Apr	65
18.54	Scott Lincoln	5	Jul	15
18.46	Lee Newman	9	Jul	95

Discus

68.24	Lawrence Okoye	19	May	12
66.06	Brett Morse	27	Jul	11
63.46	Zane Duquemin	30	Jun	12
63.38	Nicholas Percy	22	Jul	16
62.07	Emeka Udechuku	19	Aug	00
61.86	Paul Mardle	13	Jun	84
60.48	Robert Weir	13	May	83
59.90	Chris Scott	19	Jun	10
59.78	Glen Smith	5	Jun	94
59.22	Gregory Thompson	10	Jul	16
58.99	Carl Myerscough ¶	2	Jul	99

Hammer

77.55	Nick Miller	22	Jul	15
75.10	Dave Smith II	27	May	96
75.08	Robert Weir	3	Oct	82
74.62	David Smith I	15	Jul	84
74.18	Martin Girvan	31	May	82
73.80	Jason Byrne	19	Sep	92
73.40	Taylor Campbell	30	Apr	17
72.95	Alex Smith	8	Oct	10
71.75	Peter Smith	15	Apr	12
71.08	Paul Head	1	Sep	85
71.00	Ian Chipchase	17	Aug	74
70.98	Joseph Ellis	12	May	17

Javelin (1986 Model)

89.58	Steve Backley	2	Jul	90
80.92	Mark Roberson	12	Jun	88
80.38	James Campbell	18	Jul	10
79.70	Nigel Bevan	3	Feb	90
78.56	Mick Hill	2	Aug	86
78.54	Gary Jenson	17	Sep	89
78.33 A	David Parker	24	Mar	01
76.81	Harry Hughes	1	May	17
76.77	Matthew Hunt	1	May	11
76.66 i	Stuart Faben	3	Mar	96
76.28	Nick Nieland	9	Jul	94
76.13	Joe Dunderdale	18	May	14

Decathlon (1985 Tables)

8648	Daley Thompson	18	May	80
8556	Dean Macey	25	Aug	99
8070	Ashley Bryant	12	Jul	13
7973	Timothy Duckworth	9	Apr	17
7904	David Bigham	28	Jun	92
7822	Liam Ramsay	31	Aug	14
7751	Daniel Awde	29	Jun	08
7723 w	Eugene Gilkes	8	Jul	84
7660		8	Jul	84
7713	Jim Stevenson	5	Jun	93
7668	Fidelis Obikwu	5	Oct	82
7651	David Hall	13	Jun	15
7643 w	Tom Leeson	8	Sep	85
7616	Barry Thomas	23	Aug	92

3000 Metres Track Walk

11:13.09	Callum Wilkinson	12	Jun	17

10000 Metres Track Walk

40:53.60	Phil Vesty	28	May	84
41:24.7	Martin Rush	6	Jul	86
41:37.44	Cameron Corbishley	18	Jun	17
41:51.55	Andi Drake	25	May	87
41:55.6	Darrell Stone	7	Feb	88
42:07.11	Tom Bosworth	6	Aug	11
42:24.61	Ian McCombie	29	May	83
42:28.0	Philip King	17	May	95
43:00.67	Sean Martindale	5	Jun	88
43:08.59	Daniel King	30	Aug	03

20 Kilometres Road Walk

1:22:17	Callum Wilkinson	21	May	17
1:24:07.6t	Phil Vesty	1	Dec	84
1:24:49	Tom Bosworth	9	Jun	12
1:24:53	Andi Drake	27	Jun	87
1:25:46	Alex Wright	20	Jun	10
1:26:00	Cameron Corbishley	8	Apr	17
1:26:02	Jamie Higgins	12	Apr	14
1:26:14	Darrell Stone	27	Mar	89
1:26:18 +	Martin Rush	27	Apr	86
1:26:21	Ian McCombie	8	Aug	82

50 Kilometres Road Walk

4:10:23	Darrell Stone		6	May	90

UNDER 20

100 Metres

10.05	Adam Gemili	11	Jul	12
10.06	Dwain Chambers	25	Jul	97
10.10	Mark Lewis-Francis	5	Aug	00
10.12	Christian Malcolm	29	Jul	98
10.16	Ojie Edoburun	23	Aug	14
10.21	Jamie Henderson	6	Aug	87
10.21	Romell Glave	17	Jun	17
10.22	Craig Pickering	22	May	05
10.24	Simeon Williamson	2	Jul	05
[10] 10.25	Jason Livingston ¶	9	Aug	90
10.25	Jason Gardener	21	Jul	94
10.26	Leevan Yearwood	26	Aug	07
10.26	Chijindu Ujah	25	Aug	12
10.29	Peter Radford (10.31?)	13	Sep	58
10.29	David Bolarinwa	29	May	11
10.30	Deji Tobais	3	Jul	10
10.31	Chris Lambert	21	Aug	99
10.31	Alex Nelson	18	Jun	05
10.31	Oliver Bromby	17	Jun	17
[20] 10.32	Mike McFarlane	6	Aug	78

wind assisted

9.97 †	Mark Lewis-Francis	4	Aug	01
10.10	Christian Malcolm	18	Jul	98
10.15	Ojie Edoburun	23	Aug	14
10.17	Tyrone Edgar	30	Jun	01
10.20	Wade Bennett-Jackson	28	Aug	05
10.20	Joseph Dewar	19	Aug	15
10.22	Lincoln Asquith	26	Jun	83
10.22	Dwayne Grant	30	Jun	01
10.22	Simeon Williamson	21	Aug	05

200 Metres

20.29	Christian Malcolm	19	Sep	98
20.37	Thomas Somers	24	Jul	14
20.38	Adam Gemili	9	Sep	12
20.54	Ade Mafe	25	Aug	85
20.62	Leon Reid	20	Jul	13
20.62	Nathaneel Mitchell-Blake	20	Jul	13
20.63	Chris Lambert	21	Aug	99
20.64	Dwayne Grant	16	Jun	01
20.67	David Jenkins	4	Sep	71
[10] 20.67	Tim Benjamin	17	Jun	01
20.68	Elliot Powell	28	Jun	15
20.69	Alex Nelson	30	Jul	05
20.69	David Bolarinwa	2	Jun	12
20.70	Reece Prescod	6	Jun	15
20.71	Cameron Tindle	21	Jul	16
20.73 A	Ralph Banthorpe	15	Oct	68
20.75	Kieran Showler-Davis	20	Jun	10
20.78	John Regis	29	Sep	85
20.79	Jamahl Alert-Khan	7	Sep	03
[20] 20.80	Mike McFarlane	1	Jul	79

wind assisted

20.56	Toby Harries (U17)	9	Sep	15
20.57	Tommy Ramdhan	18	Jul	15
20.60	Tim Benjamin	7	Aug	99
20.61	Darren Campbell	11	Aug	91

20.73	Julian Golding	17	Sep	94
20.80	Ben Lewis	11	Jul	99
20.80	Rio Mitcham	11	Jun	17

hand timing

20.6	David Jenkins	19	Sep	71

hand timing - wind assisted

20.4	Dwayne Grant	1	Jul	01
20.7	Lincoln Asquith	2	Jul	83

300 Metres

32.53	Mark Richardson	14	Jul	91
32.85	Ade Mafe	18	Aug	84

400 Metres

45.35	Martyn Rooney	21	Mar	06
45.36	Roger Black	24	Aug	85
45.41	David Grindley	10	Aug	91
45.45	David Jenkins	13	Aug	71
45.53	Mark Richardson	10	Aug	91
45.59	Chris Clarke	24	Jul	09
45.83	Mark Hylton	16	Jul	95
46.03	Peter Crampton	8	Aug	87
46.10	Tim Benjamin	25	Aug	01
46.13	Guy Bullock	31	Jul	93 [10]
46.22	Wayne McDonald	17	Jun	89
46.31	Nigel Levine	10	Jun	07
46.32	Derek Redmond	9	Sep	84
46.35	Jack Crosby	23	Jul	14
46.39	Elliott Rutter	22	Jun	14
46.46	Adrian Metcalfe	19	Sep	61
46.47	Richard Buck	21	Aug	05
46.48	Roger Hunter	20	May	84
46.49	Owen Richardson	22	Jul	17
46.51	Cameron Chalmers	21	Jul	16 [20]

hand timing

45.7	Adrian Metcalfe	2	Sep	61

800 Metres (* 880 yards time less 0.60)

1:45.64	David Sharpe	5	Sep	86
1:45.77	Steve Ovett	4	Sep	74
1:45.78	Kyle Langford	25	Jul	15
1:46.46	John Gladwin	7	Jul	82
1:46.63	Curtis Robb	6	Jul	91
1:46.80*	John Davies I	3	Jun	68
1:46.97	Markhim Lonsdale	27	May	17
1:47.0	Ikem Billy	12	Jun	83
1:47.02	Chris McGeorge	8	Aug	81
1:47.02	Niall Brooks	25	Jul	10 [10]
1:47.18	Rick Soos	14	Aug	02
1:47.22	Kevin McKay	5	Jun	88
1:47.26	James Brewer	10	Aug	07
1:47.27	Tom Lerwill	22	Jul	96
1:47.33	Charlie Grice	21	Jul	12
1:47.34	Andrew Osagie	20	May	07
1:47.35	Peter Elliott	23	Aug	81
1:47.53	Graham Williamson	1	Aug	79
1:47.6	Julian Spooner	24	Apr	79
1:47.69	Simon Lees	5	Sep	98 [20]

1000 Metres

2:18.98	David Sharpe	19	Aug	86
2:19.92	Graham Williamson	8	Jul	79
2:20.0	Steve Ovett	17	Aug	73
2:20.02	Darryl Taylor	18	Aug	84
2:20.37	Johan Boakes	17	Jun	84
2:21.17	Curtis Robb	16	Sep	90
2:21.41	Stuart Paton	17	Sep	82
2:21.7 A	David Strang (GBR?)	26	Jan	87
2:21.71	Kevin Glastonbury	18	Jun	77

1500 Metres

3:36.6 +	Graham Williamson	17	Jul	79	
3:38.62	Niall Brooks	10	Jul	10	
3:40.09	Steve Cram	27	Aug	78	
3:40.68	Brian Treacy	24	Jul	90	
3:40.72	Gary Taylor	8	Jul	81	
3:40.90	David Robertson	28	Jul	92	
3:40.95 +	Charlie Grice	14	Jul	12	
3:41.08	Josh Kerr	8	Jun	16	
3:41.33	Adam Cotton	11	Jun	11	
3:41.43 [10]	Shaun Wyllie	7	Jun	14	
3:41.59	Chris Sly	22	Jul	77	
3:41.6	David Forrester	14	Jun	08	
3:41.77	Simon Horsfield	15	Aug	09	
3:42.12	Jake Heyward	29	Jul	17	
3:42.2	Paul Wynn	9	Aug	83	
3:42.48	Tom Lancashire	13	Jul	04	
3:42.5	Colin Reitz	8	Aug	79	
3:42.51	James Gormley	24	Jun	17	
3:42.67	Matthew Hibberd	28	Jul	92	
3:42.7 [20]	David Sharpe	17	Oct	85	

1 Mile

3:53.15	Graham Williamson	17	Jul	79
3:57.03	Steve Cram	14	Sep	79
3:57.90	Charlie Grice	14	Jul	12
3:58.68	Steve Flint	26	May	80
3:59.4	Steve Ovett	17	Jul	74
4:00.31	Johan Boakes	5	Aug	86
4:00.6	Simon Mugglestone	16	Sep	87
4:00.62	Jake Wightman	27	Jul	13

2000 Metres

5:06.56	Jon Richards	7	Jul	82

3000 Metres

7:48.28	Jon Richards	9	Jul	83
7:51.84	Steve Binns	8	Sep	79
7:56.28	John Doherty	13	Jul	80
7:58.68 i	Tom Farrell	13	Feb	10
7:59.55	Paul Davies-Hale	8	Aug	81
8:00.1 a	Micky Morton	11	Jul	78
8:00.7	Graham Williamson	29	Jul	78
8:00.73	David Black	24	Jul	71
8:00.8	Steve Anders	1	Aug	78
8:00.88 [10]	Paul Taylor	12	Jun	85
8:01.2	Ian Stewart I	7	Sep	68
8:01.26	Darius Burrows	21	Aug	94
8:01.43	Nat Muir	28	Aug	77

5000 Metres

13:27.04	Steve Binns	14	Sep	79	
13:35.95	Paul Davies-Hale	11	Sep	81	
13:37.4	David Black	10	Sep	71	
13:37.60	Alexander Yee	27	May	17	
13:43.82	Simon Mugglestone	24	May	87	
13:44.64	Julian Goater	14	Jul	72	
13:48.74	Jon Richards	28	May	83	
13:48.84	John Doherty	8	Aug	80	
13:49.1 a	Nat Muir	21	Aug	77	
13:53.30	Ian Stewart I	3	Aug	68	[10]
13:53.3 a	Nicky Lees	21	Aug	77	
13:54.2	Mick Morton	1	Jul	78	
13:54.52	Keith Cullen	8	Jun	91	
13:56.31	Mo Farah	23	Jun	01	
13:57.16	Jonathan Hay	28	May	11	
14:00.7	Peter Tootell	19	Jun	82	
14:00.7	Mike Chorlton	19	Jun	82	
14:00.85	Paul Taylor	15	Sep	84	
14:03.0	Steve Anders	1	Jul	78	
14:03.09	Jon Brown	11	Aug	90	[20]

10000 Metres

29:21.9	Jon Brown	21	Apr	90
29:38.6	Ray Crabb	18	Apr	73
29:44.0	Richard Green	27	Sep	75
29:44.8	Jack Lane	23	Sep	69

2000 Metres Steeplechase

5:29.61	Colin Reitz	18	Aug	79	
5:31.12	Paul Davies-Hale	22	Aug	81	
5:32.84	Tom Hanlon	20	Jul	86	
5:34.76	Micky Morris	24	Aug	75	
5:36.37	Zac Seddon	19	Jun	13	
5:38.01	Ken Baker	1	Aug	82	
5:38.2	Spencer Duval	8	Jul	89	
5:39.3 a	Graeme Fell	11	Jul	78	
5:39.93	Eddie Wedderburn	9	Sep	79	
5:40.2	Paul Campbell	31	Jul	77	[10]
5:40.2	John Hartigan	27	Jun	84	

3000 Metres Steeplechase

8:29.85	Paul Davies-Hale	31	Aug	81	
8:34.42	Zak Seddon	28	Apr	13	
8:42.75	Colin Reitz	6	Jun	79	
8:43.21	Kevin Nash	2	Jun	96	
8:44.68	Alastair O'Connor	12	Aug	90	
8:44.91	Ken Baker	30	May	82	
8:45.65	Spencer Duval	17	Jun	89	
8:47.49	Tom Hanlon	8	Jun	86	
8:47.8	Stephen Murphy	16	Jun	02	
8:48.43	Graeme Fell	16	Jul	78	[10]
8:50.14	Dave Long I	13	Jul	73	
8:51.02	Tony Staynings	14	Jul	72	
8:51.48	Matthew Graham	1	May	10	
8:51.54	James Wilkinson	26	Jul	09	
8:51.93	Mark Buckingham	12	Jun	04	
8:52.79	Jack Partridge	7	May	12	
8:54.15	Stuart Kefford	18	Sep	92	
8:54.56	Luke Gunn	12	Jun	04	
8:54.6	Micky Morris	7	Sep	75	
8:54.92	Mark Wortley	4	Jun	88	[20]

110 Metres Hurdles (99cm)

	13.17	David Omoregie	22 Jun	14
	13.29	Andy Pozzi	3 Jul	11
	13.30	James Gladman	23 Jun	12
	13.32	Jack Meredith	4 Jun	10
	13.33	James Weaver	25 Jun	16
	13.37	Lawrence Clarke	25 Jul	09
	13.47	Gianni Frankis	22 Jul	07
	13.48	Matthew Treston	19 Jun	16
	13.48	Robert Sakala	22 Jul	17
10	13.57	Chris Baillie	21 Aug	99
	13.62	Callum Priestley	22 Jul	07
	13.62	Khai Riley-La Borde	18 May	14
	13.62	Jack Hatton	27 Jun	15
	13.64	David King	16 Jun	13
	13.64	Jason Nicholson	21 May	17
	13.65	Euan Dickson-Earle	18 May	14
	13.69	Cameron Fillery	21 May	17

wind assisted

13.34	James Weaver	25 Jun	16
13.36	Lawrence Clarke	3 Jul	09
13.55	Jack Hatton	21 Jun	15
13.68	Jack Kirby	21 Jun	15

110 Metres Hurdles (106.7cm)

	13.44	Colin Jackson	19 Jul	86
	13.46	Jon Ridgeon	23 Aug	85
	13.53	David Omoregie	26 Jul	14
	13.72	Tony Jarrett	24 May	87
	13.73	Andy Pozzi	11 Aug	11
	13.84	Chris Baillie	27 Aug	00
	13.91	David Nelson	21 Jun	86
	13.91	Lawrence Clarke	29 Jul	09
	13.95	Robert Newton	27 Aug	00
10	13.95	Gianni Frankis	11 Aug	07
	13.97	Paul Gray	30 Jul	88
	14.01	Ross Baillie	25 Aug	96
	14.03	Brett St Louis	27 Jun	87
	14.04	Damien Greaves	25 Aug	96

wind assisted

13.42	Colin Jackson	27 Jul	86
13.66	Andy Pozzi	11 Aug	11
13.82	David Nelson	5 Jul	86
13.82	Lawrence Clarke	3 May	09
13.89	Callum Priestley	17 Jul	08
13.93	Robert Newton	7 Aug	99

400 Metres Hurdles

	50.20	Richard Davenport	15 Jul	04
	50.22	Martin Briggs	28 Aug	83
	50.49	Jack Green	23 Jul	10
	50.70	Noel Levy	8 Jul	94
	50.71	Jacob Paul	21 Jul	13
	50.96	Steven Green	6 Jul	02
	50.99	Toby Ulm	21 Jul	07
	51.07	Philip Beattie	20 Aug	82
	51.07	Niall Flannery	28 Jun	09
10	51.14	Dai Greene	23 Jul	05
	51.15 A	Andy Todd	18 Oct	67
	51.15	Rhys Williams	26 Jul	03

51.31	Gary Oakes	9 Sep	77	
51.39	Richard McDonald	19 Jun	99	
51.48	Bob Brown	19 Jun	88	
51.50	Nathan Woodward	20 May	07	
51.51	Max Robertson	24 Jul	82	
51.52	Jack Lawrie	8 Aug	15	
51.55	Mark Whitby	26 Aug	83	
51.62	Ryan Dinham	27 Jun	04	20

hand timing

51.0	Richard McDonald	24 Jul	99
51.4	Rupert Gardner	29 Jun	03

High Jump

2.37	Steve Smith	20 Sep	92	
2.30	Tom Gale	29 Jul	17	
2.27	Brendan Reilly	27 May	90	
2.26	James Brierley	3 Aug	96	
2.25	Geoff Parsons	9 Jul	83	
2.24	John Hill	23 Aug	85	
2.24	Chris Kandu	22 Jun	14	
2.23	Mark Lakey (U17)	29 Aug	82	
2.23 i	Ben Challenger	1 Mar	97	
2.21		24 Aug	96	
2.22	Dalton Grant	3 Jul	85	10
2.22	Robbie Grabarz	19 Jun	05	
2.21	Martyn Bernard	6 Jul	02	
2.20	Byron Morrison	14 Jul	84	
2.20	Alan McKie	2 Sep	07	
2.18	Ossie Cham	14 Jun	80	
2.18	Alex Kruger	26 Jun	82	
2.18	Steve Ritchie	15 Jul	89	
2.18	Hopeton Lindo	23 Jul	89	
2.18	Chuka Enih-Snell	21 Apr	01	
2.18	Tom Parsons	4 May	03	20

Pole Vault

5.60	Adam Hague	28 Mar	15	
5.51	Joel Leon Benitez	12 Jul	17	
5.50	Neil Winter	9 Aug	92	
5.42	Harry Coppell	6 Jun	15	
5.40 i	Luke Cutts	24 Feb	07	
5.30		19 Aug	06	
5.36 i	Andrew Sutcliffe	14 Feb	10	
5.35		22 Jul	10	
5.35	Steven Lewis	21 Aug	05	
5.30	Matt Belsham	16 Sep	90	
5.30	Charlie Myers	16 Aug	15	
5.25	Matt Deveraux	4 Jul	10	10
5.25	Rowan May	20 Jul	13	
5.21	Andy Ashurst	2 Sep	84	
5.21 i	Christian Linskey	20 Feb	99	
5.20		24 May	98	
5.20	Billy Davey	5 Jun	83	
5.20	Warren Siley	4 Aug	90	
5.20	Nick Buckfield	31 May	92	
5.20	Ben Flint	2 Aug	97	
5.20	Andrew Marsh	14 Jun	08	
5.20 i	Jax Thoirs	4 Jul	12	
5.20 i	Daniel Gardner	15 May	13	20
5.20		13 Jul	13	

Long Jump

8.14	Greg Rutherford	22	Jul	05
8.03	Jonathan Moore	18	May	02
7.98	Stewart Faulkner	6	Aug	88
7.91	Steve Phillips	10	Aug	91
7.90	Nathan Morgan	25	Jul	97
7.86	Elliot Safo	19	Jul	13
7.84	Wayne Griffith	25	Aug	89
7.80	Feron Sayers	30	Jun	13
7.76	Carl Howard	31	Jul	93
10 7.75	Jacob Fincham-Dukes	17	Jul	15
7.73	Jason Canning	20	Apr	88
7.72	Daley Thompson	21	May	77
7.70	Kevin Liddington	27	Aug	88
7.70	Oliver Newport	2	Jun	12
7.70	Alexander Farquharson	28	May	16
7.66	Barry Nevison	7	Jul	85
7.64	Chris Kirk	28	Jun	03
7.63	James McLachlan	7	May	11
7.62	Colin Mitchell	11	Jul	78
20 7.62	Chris Tomlinson	21	Oct	00
7.62	Bernard Yeboah	21	Aug	04

wind assisted

8.04	Stewart Faulkner	20	Aug	88
7.97	Nathan Morgan	13	Jul	96
7.96	Colin Jackson	17	May	86
7.82	Kevin Liddington	25	Jun	89
7.72	John Herbert	15	Jun	80
7.70	Andrew Staniland	30	May	05

Triple Jump

16.58	Tosi Fasinro	15	Jun	91
16.57	Tosin Oke	8	Aug	99
16.53	Larry Achike	24	Jul	94
16.43	Jonathan Moore	22	Jul	01
16.24	Aston Moore	11	Jun	75
16.22	Mike Makin	17	May	81
16.13	Steven Anderson	11	Jun	83
16.09	Ben Williams	26	Aug	09
16.03	John Herbert	23	Jun	81
10 15.99	Steven Shalders	20	Oct	00
15.95	Keith Connor	30	Aug	76
15.94	Vernon Samuels	27	Jun	82
15.93	Tayo Erogbogbo	17	Sep	94
15.93	Kola Adedoyin	23	May	10
15.92	Lawrence Lynch	13	Jul	85
15.88	Julian Golley	28	Jul	90
15.87	Stewart Faulkner	22	Aug	87
15.86	Phillips Idowu	5	Jul	97
15.84	Francis Agyepong	29	Sep	84
20 15.83	Montel Nevers	21	Jun	15

wind assisted

16.81	Tosi Fasinro	15	Jun	91
16.67	Larry Achike	24	Jul	94
16.43	Mike Makin	14	Jun	81
16.34	Phillips Idowu	27	Jul	97
16.31	Aston Moore	9	Aug	75
16.07	Vernon Samuels	14	Aug	82
16.01	Julian Golley	22	Jul	90

Shot (7.26kg)

19.46	Carl Myerscough ¶	6	Sep	98
18.21 i	Matt Simson	3	Feb	89
	18.11	27	Aug	89
17.78 i	Billy Cole	10	Mar	84
	17.72	2	Jun	84
17.38	Chris Gearing	3	Sep	05
17.36 i	Chris Ellis	8	Dec	84
	17.10	7	Jul	85
17.28 i	Jamie Williamson	4	Feb	06
	17.09	21	May	06
17.26 i	Geoff Capes	16	Nov	68
	16.80	30	Jul	68
17.25	Emeka Udechuku	20	Sep	97
17.22	Antony Zaidman	4	Jul	81
16.97	Curtis Griffith-Parker	17	May	09 10
16.78	Kieren Kelly	9	Jul	05
16.78	Jamie Stevenson	18	May	08
16.69	Greg Beard	30	Sep	00
16.61	Simon Williams	10	Aug	86
16.60	Alan Carter	11	May	63
16.48	Martyn Lucking	24	Aug	57
16.47	Paul Buxton	25	May	75
16.38	Zane Duquemin	11	Sep	10

Shot (6kg) (E 6.25kg)

21.03 E	Carl Myerscough ¶	13	May	98
19.47 E	Matt Simson	20	May	89
19.30	Curtis Griffith-Parker	31	May	09
19.15 E	Billy Cole	19	May	84
18.98	Chris Gearing	4	Sep	05
18.73	Jamie Williamson	4	Sep	05
18.68	Anthony Oshodi	13	Jun	10
18.66 iE	Simon Williams	15	Nov	86
	18.52 E	11	Jul	86
18.59 i	Jamie Stevenson	10	Feb	08
	18.55	11	May	08
18.42	Zane Duquemin	15	Aug	10 10
18.26	Gregory Thompson	1	Jun	13
18.20 iE	Chris Ellis	16	Feb	85
	18.13 E	14	Jul	84
18.11	Kai Jones	18	May	14
18.06 E	Greg Beard	2	Sep	01
18.05	George Evans	18	Jun	16
17.96	Kieren Kelly	3	Jul	05

Discus (2kg)

60.97	Emeka Udechuku	5	Jul	98
60.19	Carl Myerscough ¶	8	Aug	98
56.87	Brett Morse	18	May	08
56.44	Nicholas Percy	26	Aug	13
55.95	Curtis Griffith-Parker	17	May	09
55.10	Glen Smith	31	Aug	91
53.42	Paul Mardle	25	Jul	81
53.40	Robert Weir	10	Aug	80
53.32	Paul Buxton	9	Aug	75
53.02	Simon Williams	16	Aug	86 10
53.00	Gregory Thompson	29	Apr	13
52.94	Lee Newman	29	Aug	92
52.91	Zane Duquemin	12	Sep	09
52.90	Simon Cooke	13	Jun	04

52.84	Jamie Murphy	14	Jun	92
52.14	Robert Russell	4	Jul	93
51.70	Richard Slaney	27	Jul	75

Discus (1.75kg)

64.35	Emeka Udechuku	21	Jun	98
63.92	Lawrence Okaye	20	Jun	10
62.79	Nicholas Percy	23	Jun	13
62.34	Curtis Griffith-Parker	25	May	08
61.81	Carl Myerscough ¶	18	Aug	98
60.76	Glen Smith	26	May	91
60.46	Brett Morse	24	May	08
60.37	George Evans	15	Apr	17
59.21	Gregory Thompson	28	Apr	13
[10] 59.11	Zane Duquemin	15	Aug	10
58.80	George Armstrong	25	Jun	16
57.93	Simon Cooke	27	Jun	04
56.71	Louis Mascarenhas	16	May	15
56.64	Jamie Murphy	19	May	90
56.10	Lee Newman	5	Jul	92
56.00	Simon Williams	17	May	86

Hammer (7.26kg)

69.39	Taylor Campbell	4	May	15
68.86	Jake Norris	1	Apr	17
67.56	Nick Miller	1	Jul	12
67.48	Paul Head	16	Sep	84
67.10	Jason Byrne	6	Aug	89
66.38	Peter Smith	15	Aug	09
66.14	Martin Girvan	21	Jul	79
65.86	Robert Weir	6	Sep	80
65.30	Karl Andrews	2	Jul	94
[10] 64.89	Alex Smith	21	May	06
64.14	Ian Chipchase	25	Sep	71
63.84	Andrew Tolputt	7	Sep	86
63.72	Gareth Cook	10	Jul	88
63.25	Jac Palmer	4	May	15
62.82	Mick Jones	29	Aug	82
62.63	Michael Painter	20	Apr	13

Hammer (6kg) (E 6.25kg)

78.74	Taylor Campbell	20	Jun	15
78.09	Jake Norris	21	May	17
76.67	Peter Smith	10	Jul	09
74.92 E	Jason Byrne	17	Dec	89
73.81	Alex Smith	25	Jun	06
73.76	Nick Miller	30	Jun	12
73.34	Michael Painter	10	Jun	12
73.28 E	Robert Weir	14	Sep	80
73.09	Callum Brown	23	Jun	12
[10] 72.66 E	Paul Head	2	Sep	84
71.84 E	Gareth Cook	28	May	88
70.88	Jac Palmer	18	Apr	15
70.82	James Bedford	17	Jun	07
70.36 E	Andrew Tolputt	21	Sep	86
69.53	Nicholas Percy	28	Jul	13
69.33	Bayley Campbell	10	Jun	17
69.10 E	Karl Andrews	3	Aug	94
69.10	Andrew Elkins	29	Apr	12
68.97	Amir Williamson	18	Jun	06

Javelin

79.50	Steve Backley	5	Jun	88
77.48	David Parker	14	Aug	99
77.03	James Whiteaker	6	May	17
75.46	Harry Hughes	21	May	16
74.54	Gary Jenson	19	Sep	86
74.24	Mark Roberson	18	Jul	86
73.76	Nigel Bevan	29	Aug	87
73.18	James Campbell	16	Aug	06
72.55	Joe Dunderdale	25	Jun	11
72.54	Dan Pembroke	12	Jun	10 [10]
72.52	Richard Shuttleworth	25	Sep	11
71.90	Matthew Hunt	17	May	09
71.83	Freddie Curtis	5	Jul	14
71.79	Phill Sharpe	27	Aug	00
71.76	Benji Pearson	18	Aug	13
71.74	Myles Cottrell	29	Jul	89
71.14	Dan Carter	11	Jul	98
70.80	Bonne Buwembo	13	Sep	08
70.60	Matti Mortimore	11	Sep	10
69.62	Stefan Baldwin	8	Jul	89 [20]

Decathlon (1985 Tables)

8082	Daley Thompson	31	Jul	77
7727	David Guest	6	Jun	10
7488	David Bigham	9	Aug	90
7480	Dean Macey	22	Aug	96
7299	Eugene Gilkes	24	May	81
7274	Jim Stevenson	24	Jun	90
7247	Brian Taylor	7	May	89
7194	Ashley Bryant	15	Aug	10
7169	Barry Thomas	5	Aug	90
7156	Timothy Duckworth	15	May	15 [10]
7126	Fidelis Obikwu	16	Sep	79
7115	Liam Ramsay	4	Sep	11
7112	Gavin Sunshine	30	Jul	93
7018	Jamie Quarry	30	Jun	91
6958	Roy Mitchell	29	Sep	74
6936	Anthony Brannen	24	May	87
6925	Roger Hunter	4	Jun	95
6843	Ed Coats	30	May	99
6839	Mark Bushell	30	Apr	95

IAAF Junior E - 6.25kg SP

7691	David Guest	21	Jul	10
7567	Daniel Gardiner	14	Jun	09
7440	David Hall	23	Jul	14
7381	Daniel Awde	23	Jul	06
7377	Sam Talbot	30	Apr	17
7342	Ashley Bryant	6	Jun	10
7320	Jack Andrew	6	Jun	10
7308 w	Liam Ramsay	18	Sep	11
7233		26	Jun	11
7232	Guy Stroud	9	Sep	07
7200	Seb Rodger	16	May	10 [10]
7160	Timothy Duckworth	26	Jun	14
7147	Ben Gregory	14	Jun	09
7134 E	Dean Macey	17	Sep	95
7128	Nicholas Hunt	29	Jun	14
7056	Lewis Church	20	Sep	15

3000 Metres Track Walk

11:36.2	Callum Wilkinson	15	May	16
11:39.75 i	Cameron Corbishley	11	Dec	16
11:53.08		15	May	16
11:50.34 i	Guy Thomas	11	Dec	16
11:50.55	Nick Ball	29	May	06
11:54.23	Tim Berrett	23	Jun	84
12:00.99 i	Dominic King	2	Feb	02

5000 Metres Track Walk

19:35.4	Callum Wilkinson	2	Jul	16
20:16.40	Philip King	26	Jun	93
20:33.4 +	Darrell Stone	7	Aug	87

10000 Metres Track Walk

40:41.62	Callum Wilkinson	23	Jul	16
41:52.13	Darrell Stone	7	Aug	87
42:06.35	Gordon Vale	2	Aug	81
42:17.1	Dominic King	4	May	02
42:18.94	Cameron Corbishley	19	Jun	16
42:25.06	Jamie Higgins	20	Jul	13
42:28.20	Guy Thomas	19	Jun	16
42:46.3	Phil Vesty	20	Mar	82
42:47.7	Philip King	2	May	92
43:04.09	Tim Berrett	25	Aug	83
43:09.82	Lloyd Finch	18	May	02
43:42.75	Martin Rush	29	May	83
43:50.94	Nick Ball	23	Jul	06
43:54.25	Gareth Brown	7	Aug	87
44:06.6	Daniel King	4	May	02
44:22.12	Gareth Holloway	5	Jun	88
44:22.4	Jon Vincent	1	Apr	89
44:30.0	Andy Penn	15	Mar	86
44:38.0	Ian McCombie	29	Mar	80
44:42.0	Luke Finch	23	May	04

10k Road - where superior to track time

40:30	Callum Wilkinson	7	May	16
41:47	Darrell Stone	26	Sep	87
41:57	Ben Wears	4	Apr	09
42:29	Steve Hollier	10	Dec	95
42:39	Martin Rush	7	May	83
42:40	Tim Berrett	18	Feb	84
42:55	Guy Thomas	7	May	16
43:02	Luke Finch	1	Dec	02

20 Kilometres Road Walk

1:26:13	Tim Berrett	25	Feb	84
1:29:10	Phil Vesty	18	Jul	82
1:29:48	Dominic King	15	Jun	02
1:30:17	Guy Thomas	4	Sep	16
1:30:55	Martin Rush	10	Sep	83
1:31:34.4t	Gordon Vale	28	Jun	81
1:32:38	Ben Wears	1	Mar	08
1:32:46	Graham Morris	26	Feb	77

50 Kilometres Road Walk

4:18:18	Gordon Vale	24	Oct	81

UNDER 17

100 Metres

10.31	Mark Lewis-Francis	21	Aug	99	
10.39	David Bolarinwa	4	Aug	10	
10.45	Jordan Huggins	23	Jun	07	
10.49	Wade Bennett-Jackson	28	Jul	03	
10.49	Olufunmi Sobodu	5	Aug	06	
10.53	Craig Pickering	11	Jul	03	
10.56	Rikki Fifton	29	Jul	01	
10.57	Owin Sinclair	5	Jul	14	
10.57	Dom Ashwell	31	May	15	
10.57	Toby Harries	20	Jun	15	10
10.58	Deji Tobais	19	Jul	08	
10.58	Ronnie Wells	18	Aug	12	
10.59	Harry Aikines-Aryeetey	22	Aug	04	
10.59	Jona Efoloko	27	Aug	16	
10.60	Tyrone Edgar	16	Aug	98	
10.60	Antonio Infantino	11	Aug	07	
10.60	Andy Robertson	11	Aug	07	
10.60	Kieran Showler-Davis	7	Sep	08	

wind assisted

10.26	Mark Lewis-Francis	5	Aug	99
10.38	Kevin Mark	3	Jul	93
10.42	Shaun Pearce	31	Aug	13
10.44	Luke Davis	13	Jul	96
10.47	Owin Sinclair	5	Jul	14
10.51	Tim Benjamin	4	Jul	98
10.52	Dom Ashwell	31	May	15
10.52	Toby Harries	31	May	15
10.54	Rechmial Miller	30	Aug	14
10.55	Antonio Infantino	11	Aug	07
10.55	Daniel Afolabi	17	Jun	17

200 Metres

20.79	Jamahl Alert-Khan	7	Sep	03	
20.84	Thomas Somers	14	Jul	13	
20.92	Ade Mafe	27	Aug	83	
20.92	Toby Harries	19	Jul	15	
21.12	Jona Efoloko	30	Aug	15	
21.14	Kieran Showler-Davis	10	May	08	
21.16	Chris Clarke	28	Jul	06	
21.17	David Bolarinwa	20	Jun	10	
21.19	Tim Benjamin	31	Jul	98	
21.24	Peter Little	21	Aug	77	10
21.25	Mark Richardson	24	Jul	88	
21.35	Andrew Watkins	12	Jul	03	
21.36	Joseph Massimo	7	May	16	
21.37	Jermaine Hamilton	9	May	12	

wind assisted

20.56	Toby Harries	9	Sep	15
20.98	Tim Benjamin	18	Jul	98
21.17	Mark Richardson	20	Aug	88
21.25	Trevor Cameron	25	Sep	93
21.28	Antonio Infantino	12	Aug	07
21.31	Monu Miah	15	Jul	00
21.32	Graham Beasley	9	Jul	94
21.33	Ryan Gorman	17	Aug	14

hand timing - wind assisted

21.0	Peter Little	30	Jul	77

400 Metres

46.43	Mark Richardson	28	Jul	88
46.74	Guy Bullock	17	Sep	92
46.74	Clovis Asong	25	Jul	11
47.08	Kris Robertson	15	Aug	04
47.18	Chris Clarke	8	Jul	06
47.29	Richard Davenport	25	May	02
47.47	Ellis Greatrex	18	Jun	16
47.71	Richard Buck	17	Aug	03
47.81	Mark Hylton	17	Jul	93
10 47.82	Ethan Brown	27	Aug	17
47.85	Bruce Tasker	15	Aug	04
47.86	Kris Stewart	13	Jul	96
47.90	Thomas Evans	18	Jun	17
47.92	Benjamin Snaith	19	Aug	12
47.96	Joshua Street	10	Jul	10
47.99	Ben Sturgess	30	Aug	08
48.03	Greg Louden	13	Sep	09

hand timing

47.6	Kris Stewart	3	Aug	96

800 Metres

1:48.24	Sean Molloy	9	Jun	12
1:49.42	Max Burgin	27	Jun	17
1:49.9	Mark Sesay	18	Jul	89
1:50.38	Grant Baker	17	Jul	04
1:50.42	Ben Greenwood	9	Sep	15
1:50.48	James Brewer	17	Jul	04
1:50.55	Michael Rimmer	6	Aug	02
1:50.55	George Mills	17	Jun	15
1:50.58	Markhim Lonsdale	22	Aug	15
10 1:50.61	Charlie Grice	21	Jul	10
1:50.7	Peter Elliott	16	Sep	79
1:50.90	Craig Winrow	21	Aug	88
1:50.90	Mark Mitchell	15	Aug	04
1:51.0	Chris McGeorge	1	Jul	78
1:51.05	Mal Edwards	20	Sep	74
1:51.06	Rikki Letch	3	Jun	09
1:51.06	Matthew McLaughlin	7	Sep	11

1000 Metres

2:20.37	Johan Boakes	17	Jun	84

1500 Metres

3:44.11	Matthew Shirling	7	Aug	12
3:46.51	James McMurray	10	Jul	11
3:47.20	Jack Crabtree	6	Aug	13
3:47.7	Steve Cram	14	May	77
3:48.49	Johan Boakes	28	Jun	84
3:48.70	Charlie Grice	30	Jun	10
3:48.83	Harvey Dixon	30	Jun	10
3:48.92	Markhim Lonsdale	30	May	15
3:48.97	Archie Davis	30	May	15
10 3:49.40	Anthony Moran	23	Jul	02
3:49.70	Luke Duffy	20	Jul	17
3:49.9	Kelvin Newton	20	Jun	79
3:49.92	Scott Halstead	19	Aug	12
3:50.01	Ross Millington	8	Aug	06
3:50.10	Liam Dee	25	Jul	12

1 Mile

4:06.7	Barrie Williams	22	Apr	72

2000 Metres

5:28.2 +	Kevin Steere	10	Jul	71

3000 Metres

8:13.42	Barrie Moss	15	Jul	72
8:15.34	Kevin Steere	30	Aug	71
8:16.18	Mo Farah	21	Aug	99
8:18.26	Simon Horsfield	27	Jun	06
8:19.08	Darren Mead	26	Aug	85
8:19.38	Johan Boakes	24	Jun	84
8:21.01	Ben Dijkstra	1	Jul	15
8:21.39	Gus Cockle	29	May	13
8:22.46	Jack Crabtree	1	May	13
8:22.71	Matthew Shirling	26	Aug	12 10
8:22.82	Jamie Dee	10	Sep	14
8:24.2	Simon Goodwin	16	Jul	80
8:24.2	Jason Lobo	13	Aug	86
8:24.42	Gordon Benson	14	Aug	10
8:24.87	Thomas Keen	6	Sep	17
8:24.93	Luke van Oudtshoorn	31	May	17

5000 Metres

14:41.8	Nicky Lees	24	Aug	74

1500 Metres Steeplechase

4:11.2	Steve Evans	15	Jul	74
4:12.3	Chris Sly	15	Jul	74
4:13.1	John Crowley	15	Jul	74
4:13.2	David Lewis	1	Jul	78
4:13.66	Zak Seddon	9	Jul	10
4:13.7	Danny Fleming	31	Jul	77
4:13.9	Eddie Wedderburn	31	Jul	77
4:14.0	Dave Robertson	8	Jul	89
4:14.4	Stephen Arnold	7	Sep	85
4:15.0	David Caton	9	Jun	84 10
4:15.0	Spencer Duval	12	Jul	86
4:15.2	Garrie Richardson	8	Jul	89
4:15.3	John Wilson	26	Jul	75
4:15.38	William Battershill	5	Sep	14
4:16.6	Adrian Green	9	Jun	84

2000 Metres Steeplechase

5:52.06	Noel Collins	23	Jul	07
5:52.13	Zak Seddon	23	Aug	10
5:55.0	John Wilson	23	Aug	75
5:55.0	David Lewis	20	Aug	78

3000 Metres Steeplechase

9:16.6	Colin Reitz	19	Sep	76

100 Metres Hurdles (91.4cm)

12.60	Tristan Anthony	14	Aug	99
12.68	Matthew Clements	8	Aug	93
12.70	Jack Meredith	12	Jul	08
12.70	Mayowa Osunsami	28	Aug	16
12.75	James McLean	14	Jul	07
12.76	Jordan Auburn	21	Aug	11
12.76	Sam Bennett	27	Aug	17
12.84	Tre Thomas	17	Apr	16
12.85	Jack Kirby	1	Sep	13

[10] 12.85 Jack Sumners 14 May 17

12.85	Jack Sumners	14 May	17
12.88	Julian Adeniran	8 Jul	05
12.90	Steve Markham	17 Aug	91
12.91	Allan Scott	14 Aug	99
12.93	Themba Luhana	11 Jul	09
12.93	Jason Nicholson	30 Aug	15
12.93	Jushua Zeller	8 Jul	17

wind assisted

12.47	Matthew Clements	9 Jul	94
12.70	Damien Greaves	9 Jul	94
12.70	Rory Dwyer	31 Aug	14
12.74	Jack Kirby	1 Sep	13
12.75	Kertis Beswick	19 Aug	12
12.88	Nick Csemiczky	13 Jul	91
12.90	Ricky Glover	13 Jul	91
12.90	Ben Warmington	8 Jul	95

hand timing

12.8	Brett St Louis	28 Jul	85
12.8	Richard Dunn	29 Jun	91
12.8	Jack Kirby	12 May	13
12.8	Tre Thomas	1 May	16
12.8	Jack Sumners	3 Jun	17

hand timing - wind assisted

12.6	Brett St Louis	20 Jul	85

110 Metres Hurdles (91.4cm)

13.51	Jack Sumners	27 May	17
13.60	Sam Bennett	27 May	17
13.71	Matthew Clements	19 May	94
13.79	Sam Talbot	16 Jul	15
13.82	James McLean	23 Jul	07
13.95	Matthew Treston	21 Jun	15

hand timing

13.6	Jon Ridgeon	16 Jul	83

110 Metres Hurdles (99cm)

14.18	Andy Pozzi	15 Jun	08
14.19	Rory Dwyer	1 Jun	14

wind assisted

13.92	Matthew Clements	27 Aug	94

110 Metres Hurdles (106.7cm)

14.89	Tristan Anthony	4 Jul	99

400 Metres Hurdles (84cm)

52.15	Nathan Woodward	10 Sep	06
52.20	Tristan Anthony	18 Jul	99
52.57	Niall Flannery	26 Aug	07
52.69	Jeffrey Christie	18 Jul	99
52.70	Mike Baker	15 Jul	06
52.72	Jacob Paul	16 Jul	11
52.81	Richard McDonald	10 Aug	96
52.86	Alistair Chalmers	14 May	16
52.88	Joe Fuggle	30 Aug	15
[10] 52.98	Jack Green	24 May	08
52.98	Ben Lloyd	27 Aug	17
53.01	Lloyd Gumbs	17 Jul	04
53.08	Richard Davenport	11 Aug	02
53.11	David Martin	14 Aug	05
53.14	Martin Briggs	2 Aug	80
53.21	Karl Johnson	27 Aug	17

400 Metres Hurdles (91cm)

53.06	Phil Beattie	2 Aug	80

High Jump

2.23	Mark Lakey	29 Aug	82
2.16	Rory Dwyer	22 Jun	14
2.15	Ossie Cham	14 Jul	79
2.15	Brendan Reilly	7 May	89
2.15	Stanley Osuide	1 Sep	91
2.15	Chuka Enih-Snell	10 Sep	00
2.12	Femi Abejide	11 Jul	81
2.11	Leroy Lucas	6 Aug	83
2.11 i	Ken McKeown	12 Jul	98
2.11		18 Jul	98
2.10	Dalton Grant	18 Sep	82 [10]
2.10	Tim Blakeway	29 Aug	87
2.10	James Brierley	16 May	93
2.10	Martin Lloyd	28 Sep	96
2.10	Martin Aram	23 Jul	00
2.10	Sam Bailey	27 Sep	08
2.10	Joel Khan	27 Aug	16

Pole Vault

5.20	Neil Winter	2 Sep	90
5.15	Christian Linskey	23 Aug	96
5.00	Adam Hague	21 Apr	13
4.93	Harry Coppell	21 Jul	12
4.92	Rowan May	6 Aug	11
4.92 i	Frankie Johnson	5 Feb	17
4.86		7 Jul	17
4.90	Warren Siley	8 Sep	89
4.90	Andrew Marsh	3 Sep	06
4.82 i	Joel Leon Benitez	1 Mar	14
4.71		11 Jul	14
4.80	Billy Davey	14 Sep	80 [10]
4.80	Keith Higham	25 May	02
4.76	Nick Buckfield	11 Jun	89
4.72	Ian Lewis	24 Aug	85
4.71	Chris Tremayne	27 Aug	01
4.70	Richard Smith	7 Jun	97
4.70	Mark Christie	25 Aug	01
4.70	Luke Cutts	5 Sep	04
4.70	Ethan Walsh	5 Jun	13
4.70	Nikko Hunt	24 Aug	14

Long Jump

7.53	Brian Robinson	21 Jul	97
7.50	Oliver McNeillis	17 Jul	04
7.47	Bernard Yeboah	13 Jul	02
7.46	Jonathan Moore	30 Jul	00
7.46	Onen Eyong	9 Sep	01
7.36	Toby Adeniyi	5 Jul	13
7.35	Kadeem Greenidge-Smith	26 Aug	07
7.33	Patrick Sylla	24 May	15
7.32	Kevin Liddington	16 May	87
7.25	Alan Slack	12 Jun	76 [10]
7.25	Feron Sayers	25 Jun	11
7.24	Elliot Safo	11 Apr	10
7.22	Dominic Ogbechie	1 Sep	17
7.21	Hugh Teape	17 May	80
7.21	Jordan Lau	8 Jul	00

wind assisted

7.60	Brian Robinson	21	Jul	97
7.47	Onen Eyong	2	Sep	01
7.40	Matthew John	10	May	86
7.33	Dominic Ogbechie	15	Jul	17
7.31	Elliot Safo	29	May	10
7.31	Feron Sayers	25	Jun	11

Triple Jump

16.02	Jonathan Moore	13	Aug	00
15.72	Ben Williams	11	Jul	08
15.65	Vernon Samuels	18	Jul	81
15.50	Junior Campbell	18	May	86
15.45	Steven Anderson	2	Aug	81
15.32	Wesley Matsuka-Williams	16	Jul	16
15.28	Larry Achike	22	Jun	91

note resident but not British citizen at this time

15.22	Tunde Amosu	31	Aug	08
15.22	Efe Uwaifo	3	Sep	11
10 15.14	Marvin Bramble	8	Aug	93
15.14	Steven Shalders	18	Jul	98
15.11	Nathan Fox	24	Jul	07
15.11	Teepee Princewill	2	Sep	16
15.08	Kola Adedoyin	27	May	06
15.02	Lanri Ali-Balogun	17	Jul	04

wind assisted

15.78	Ben Williams	19	Jul	08
15.43	Wesley Matsuka-Williams	16	Jul	16
15.40	Steven Shalders	18	Jul	98
15.26	Tunde Amosu	19	Jul	08
15.25	Marvin Bramble	3	Jul	93
15.08	Lawrence Lynch	29	Apr	84
15.06	Craig Duncan	7	Aug	82

Shot (7.26kg)

17.30	Carl Myerscough ¶	3	Aug	96

Shot (6.25kg)

16.88	Greg Beard	29	Aug	99

Shot (6kg)

18.07	Kai Jones	1	May	13

Shot (5kg)

21.20	Carl Myerscough ¶	22	Sep	96
19.57	Curtis Griffith-Parker	10	Jun	07
19.45	Kai Jones	27	Apr	13
19.22	Chris Ellis	4	Jun	82
19.07 i	Michael Wheeler	15	Dec	07
18.86		31	Aug	08
18.91	Greg Beard	19	Sep	99
18.90	Neal Brunning ¶	6	Sep	87
18.82	Anthony Oshodi	16	Sep	08
18.70	Chris Gearing	10	Jul	03
10 18.59	Daniel Cartwright	9	Sep	15
18.44	Matt Simson	27	Jul	86
18.43	Emeka Udechuku	28	May	95
18.25	Billy Cole	1	Aug	81
18.08	Jay Thomas	2	Jul	05
17.99	Reece Thomas	19	Jul	08

Discus (2kg)

50.60	Carl Myerscough ¶	28	Jul	96
48.96	Emeka Udechuku	19	Aug	95

Discus (1.75kg)

54.70	Emeka Udechuku	18	Jun	95
52.50	Paul Mardle	7	Jul	79

Discus (1.5kg)

62.96	Nicolas Percy	10	Sep	11
62.22	Emeka Udechuku	10	Jul	95
60.62	George Armstrong	30	Aug	14
59.76	Matthew Blandford	18	Aug	12
59.13	James Tomlinson	31	Jul	16
58.25	Curtis Griffith-Parker	13	Jul	07
58.14	Carl Myerscough ¶	12	May	96
56.70	Sam Herrington	18	May	03
56.64	Alfie Scopes	24	Jul	16
56.16	Matthew Baptiste	2	Sep	07 10
56.14	Chris Symonds	6	Sep	87
55.94	Simon Williams I	9	Sep	84
55.90	Guy Litherland	14	Sep	85
55.72	Keith Homer	27	Jun	82
55.52	Glen Smith	14	May	88
55.36	Neal Brunning ¶	7	Jun	87

Hammer (7.26kg)

59.94	Andrew Tolputt	30	Sep	84
59.07	Alex Smith	8	Aug	04

Hammer (6.25kg)

66.70	Andrew Tolputt	2	Sep	84
64.00	Matthew Sutton	22	Aug	98

Hammer (6kg)

66.85	Alex Smith	8	Aug	04

Hammer (5kg)

76.52	Alex Smith	17	Jul	04
76.28	Andrew Tolputt	11	Aug	84
75.02	Peter Smith	5	Aug	06
74.17	Jake Norris	25	Apr	15
73.90	Paul Head	29	Aug	81
73.76	Matthew Sutton	14	Jun	98
73.00	Nick Steinmetz	17	Jul	93
71.97	Ben Hawkes	13	May	17
71.34	Tony Kenneally	7	Sep	80
70.85	Michael Painter	28	Jul	11 10
70.82	Jason Byrne	20	Jun	87
69.84	Bayley Campbell	24	Jul	16
69.47	Taylor Campbell	7	Jun	12
69.28	Andrew Jordon	7	Sep	08
68.62	Peter Vivian	16	May	87
68.43	Jacob Richards	2	Sep	16
68.42	George Marvell	10	Jul	15

Javelin (800g -1986 model)

68.26	David Parker	19	May	96
62.63	Huw Bevan	17	Apr	11
62.30	Harry Hughes	7	Sep	13
62.21	Thomas Peters	16	Jun	12

Javelin (800g Original model)

72.78	Gary Jenson	10	Sep	83
69.84	Colin Mackenzie	12	May	79
66.14	David Messom	14	May	81
65.32	Marcus Humphries	26	Aug	78
64.80	Paul Bushnell	1	Sep	85
64.34	Steve Backley	1	Sep	85
63.44	Michael Williams	16	Sep	79

Javelin (700g)

77.12	James Whiteaker	12	Jul	14
74.06	Tom Hewson	5	Aug	17
73.56	David Parker	20	Jul	96
72.77	Harry Hughes	4	Aug	13
72.48	Gary Jenson	3	Jul	83
71.68	Dan Pembroke	22	Apr	07
70.30	Colin Mackenzie	6	Jul	79
70.07	George Davies	19	Jul	14
69.60	Huw Bevan	21	Aug	11
68.88	Phill Sharpe	19	Jul	97
68.88	Matti Mortimore	7	Jun	09
68.34	James Campbell	29	Aug	04
68.26	Ian Marsh	30	Jul	77
68.18	James Hurrion	3	Jun	90
67.31	Lee Doran	21	Jul	01
66.93	Sam Taylor-Outridge	6	Sep	09
66.88	David Messom	4	Jul	81

Decathlon (Senior Implements)

6484	David Bigham	27	Sep	87
6299	Tom Leeson	21	Sep	80

Decathlon (Junior Implements)

6554	Jim Stevenson	25	Sep	88
6316	Jack Andrew	27	Aug	08
6093	Robert Hughes	28	May	89

Decathlon (U17 Implements)

6860w	David Guest	9	Sep	07
6858	Edward Dunford	2	Sep	01
6781	Joel McFarlane	1	Jul	17
6706	David Bigham	28	Jun	87

Octathlon (D during decathlon)

5800 D	Edward Dunford	2	Sep	01
5741		17	Jun	01
5786	Nicholas Hunt	1	Jul	12
5690	Oliver McNeillis	19	Sep	04
5626	Ashley Bryant	20	May	07
5550	Dominic Girdler	20	Sep	98
5494	Kristian Brown	20	Sep	15
5468	Ben Gibb	24	Jun	07
5426	John Holtby	20	Sep	98
5425	Andrae Davis	22	Sep	02
5423	Leo Barker	17	Sep	95
5423	Ben Gregory	16	Sep	07
5409 D	Joel McFarlane	1	Jul	17
5392 D	David Bigham	28	Jun	87
5380	David Guest	30	Sep	07
5378	Matthew Lewis	20	Sep	92

5330	James Lelliott	20	Sep	09
5311	Dean Macey	18	Sep	94
5311	Adam Akehurst	19	Sep	04

with 100m

5531	Jim Stevenson	18	Sep	88

3000 Metres Track Walk

12:04.9	Philip King	18	May	91
12:25.1	Nick Ball	15	May	04
12:29.90	Andy Parker	2	Jul	00
12:30.14	Luke Finch	1	Sep	02
12:34.98	Lloyd Finch	17	Jul	99
12:35.94	David Hucks	30	Aug	82
12:45.38	Ben Wears	28	May	06
12:50.67 i	Stuart Monk	18	Feb	95
12:52.9		12	Jul	95
12:50.9	Jon Vincent	8	Jul	87
12:53.1	Chris Snook	14	May	16

5000 Metres Track Walk

20:46.5	Philip King	29	Sep	91
21:28.26	Nick Ball	11	Jul	04
21:49.66	Ben Wears	16	Sep	06
21:52.7	Stuart Monk	22	Jul	95
21:58.8	Luke Finch	22	Sep	01
22:17.5	Russell Hutchings	27	Sep	86
22:19.11	Lloyd Finch	18	Sep	99
22:31.62	Chistopher Snook	17	Sep	16
22:32.5	Gareth Holloway	27	Sep	86
22:35.0	Ian Ashforth	6	Jun	84
22:36.02	Cameron Corbishly	14	Jul	13
22:37.0	Jon Bott	27	Sep	86
22:42.0	Martin Young	20	Aug	88
22:42.19	Jon Vincent	6	Jun	86
22:48.91	Andy Parker	30	Jul	00
22:50.51	Dom King	18	Sep	99
22:53.7	Tim Berrett	28	Jun	81
22:53.8	David Hucks	10	Mar	82

5k Road - where superior to track time

21:33	Jon Vincent	1	Nov	86
21:47	Lloyd Finch	20	Jun	99
22:04	Gareth Holloway	14	Sep	86
22:05	Karl Atton	19	Mar	88
22:30	Gordon Vale	15	Oct	77
22:31	Jon Bott	3	May	86
22:39	Matthew Hales	23	Jun	96
22:41	Thomas Taylor	26	Apr	97

10000 Metres Track Walk

43:56.5	Philip King	2	Feb	91
45:47.0	Ian Ashforth	12	Sep	84
45:52.39	Lloyd Finch	4	Jul	99
46:11.0	Jon Vincent	20	May	87

10k Road - where superior to track time

43:38 hc	Lloyd Finch	20	Nov	99
44:21		13	Nov	99
43:49	Philip King	29	Jun	91
45:19	Luke Finch	31	Aug	02

UNDER 15

100 Metres

10.83	Kesi Oludoyi	31	Jul	13
10.89	Jona Efoloko	17	May	14
10.90	Kaie Chambers-Brown	30	Aug	14
10.91	Tyrese Johnson-Fisher	12	Jul	14
10.92	Owin Sinclair	7	Jul	12
10.93	Mark Lewis-Francis	12	Jul	97
10.94	Graig Anya Joseph	26	Aug	17
10.97	Jaleel Roper	26	Aug	17
10.98	Alex Kiwomya	21	Aug	10
10.98	Kyle Reynolds-Warmington	27	Aug	16
10.99	Andrew Watkins	20	Jul	02
10.99	Deji Tobais	26	Aug	06

wind assisted

10.77	Kesi Oludoyi	31	Jul	13
10.80	Camron Lyttle	31	Aug	13
10.83	Owin Sinclair	18	Aug	12
10.91	Deji Tobias	28	Aug	05
10.92	Joshua Oshunrinde	3	Sep	16
10.93	Ryan Gorman	18	Aug	12
10.96	Dijon Archer	7	Jul	06
10.97	Rueben Arthur	27	Aug	11
10.97	Michael Olsen	31	Aug	13
10.98	Tom Mosley	7	Jul	06

hand timing

10.9	Tommy Ramdhan	18	Jun	11
10.9	Owin Sinclair	12	May	12

200 Metres

22.13	Andrew Watkins	6	Jul	02
22.13	Jaleel Roper	27	Aug	17
22.14	Jona Efoloko	18	May	14
22.19 i	Alex Kiwomya	28	Feb	10
22.36		10	Jul	10
22.20	Owin Sinclair	19	Aug	12
22.21	Rhion Samuel	6	Aug	06
22.25	Deji Tobais	6	Aug	06
22.28	Cameron Sprague	11	Jul	15
22.30	Jamie Nixon	29	Sep	84
22.31	Mike Williams II	10	Aug	86
22.35	Tristan Anthony	12	Jul	97
22.35	Chris Clarke	10	Jul	04
22.36	Tony Corrigan	9	Jul	05

wind assisted

22.03	Julian Thomas	7	Jul	01
22.14	Owin Sinclair	21	Apr	12
22.19	Joseph Massimo	31	Aug	14
22.26	Steven Daly	9	Jul	94
22.26	Simon Farenden	8	Jul	00
22.28	Jamahl Alert-Khan	7	Jul	01
22.32	Kaie Chambers-Brown	31	Aug	14

hand timing

22.2	Mike Williams II	12	Jul	86

hand timing - wind assisted

21.9	Tony Cairns	21	Jun	86

300 Metres

35.21	Joseph Massimo	12	Jul	14
35.41	Ben Pattison	27	Aug	16
35.58	Chenna Okoh Mason	31	Aug	14
35.69	Tom Evans	11	Jul	15
35.70	Joe Milton	6	Jul	13
35.74	Matthew Pagan	19	Aug	12
35.79	George Sudderick	27	Aug	17
35.84	Channah Okoh	6	Jul	13
35.84	Evan Blackman	27	Aug	16

hand timing

35.8	Evan Blackman	13	Sep	16

during 400m

35.7 +	Richard Davenport	23	Aug	00

400 Metres

48.86	Clovis Asong	11	Jul	09
49.74	Richard Davenport	23	Aug	00
49.79	Daniel Gray	2	Jul	11
49.96	Craig Erskine	18	Jul	98
49.97	David McKenzie	23	Jun	85
49.97	Stanley Livingstone	21	Aug	11
49.98	Ryan Preddy	11	Jul	98
49.99	Aaron Pitt	22	Aug	10
50.05	Will Grist	12	Jul	08
50.07	Matthew Webster	6	Aug	06

hand timing

49.0	Alex Kiwomya	27	Jun	10
49.8	Mark Tyler	25	Aug	82
49.9	David McKenzie	11	Aug	85
50.0	Simon Heaton	7	Jul	79

600 Metres

1:23.6	Chris Davies	26	Jul	00

800 Metres

1:53.1	Max Burgin	25	Jul	16
1:54.52	Ben Pattison	2	May	16
1:54.72	Jordon West	23	Jul	03
1:55.36	Oliver Carvell	26	Jul	16
1:55.56	Michael Rimmer	25	Jul	00
1:55.70	Luke Carroll	2	Aug	08
1:55.8	Markhim Lonsdale	3	Jun	13
1:55.89	Rikki Letch	27	Jun	07
1:55.98	Jordan Bransberg	29	Jul	09
1:56.04	Daniel Joyce	27	Aug	17
1:56.1	Craig Winrow	12	Jul	86
1:56.54	Joshua Hulse	11	Jul	15
1:56.6	Paul Burgess	13	Jul	85
1:56.71	James Senior	8	Jul	06

1000 Metres

2:35.4	Alex Felce	25	Jul	01

1500 Metres

3:59.20	Ben Greenwood	21	Jun	13
4:00.13	Jack Crabtree	27	Jul	11
4:00.20	Ethan Hussey	19	Aug	17
4:01.0	Luke Carroll	9	Sep	08
4:03.0	Glen Stewart	28	Aug	85
4:03.0	Scott West	28	Aug	90

4:03.29	Canaan Soloman	26	Jun	13
4:03.52	Mike Isherwood	17	Sep	82
4:03.54	Tom Purnell	2	Aug	08
4:03.56	Richard Youngs	17	Sep	82
4:03.6	Doug Stones	7	Jul	79
4:03.7	David Gerard	31	Jul	83

1 Mile

4:21.9	Glen Stewart	11	Sep	85

2000 Metres

5:45.8	Richard Slater	16	Jun	74

3000 Metres

8:44.61	Mohamed Sharif Ali	22	Jul	17
8:46.24	Jack Crabtree	24	Aug	11
8:47.0	Ben Mabon	16	Jul	85
8:47.48	Mohammed Farah	5	Jul	97
8:48.8	Dale Smith	14	Aug	85
8:49.59	Tommy Dawson	26	Jun	17
8:51.1	Mark Slowikowski	4	Jun	80
8:53.0	Ben Dijkstra	16	Jul	13
8:53.17	Archie Parkinson	6	Sep	17
8:53.66	Tom Snow	7	Jun	00
8:53.66	Luke van Oudtshoorn	29	Jun	16
8:54.6	Gary Taylor	14	Sep	77
8:54.6	David Bean	22	Jul	79

80 Metres Hurdles (84cm)

10.50	Joseph Harding	8	Jul	17
10.71	Matthew Clements	15	Aug	92
10.75	Daniel Davis	13	Jul	02
10.81	Adeyinka Adeniran	31	Aug	14
10.82	Richard Alexis-Smith	12	Aug	01
10.87	Daniel Maynard	11	Aug	02
10.91	James McLean	14	Aug	05
10.95	Chris Musa	7	Jul	01
10.95	Onatade Ojora	11	Jul	14
10.98	Max Price	1	Sep	13
10.98	Daniel Knight	28	Aug	16
10.99	Edward Dunford	14	Aug	99
10.99	Sam Bennett	10	Jul	15

wind assisted

10.68	Richard Alexis-Smith	12	Aug	01
10.73	Chris Musa	7	Jul	01
10.88	James McLean	28	Aug	05
10.99	Tom Stimson	7	Jul	01

100 Metres Hurdles (91cm)

13.3	Matthew Clements	23	Aug	92

400 Metres Hurdles (76.2cm)

56.59	Stanley Livingstone	26	May	11

High Jump

2.04	Ross Hepburn	22	Aug	76
2.01	Ken McKeown	10	Aug	96
2.00	Samuel Brereton	17	Jun	17
1.97	Andrew Lynch	29	Aug	88
1.97	Wayne Gray	3	Sep	95

1.97	Richard Byers	4	Sep	05
1.97	Miles Keller-Jenkins	17	Jun	12
1.96	Chuka Enih-Snell	29	Aug	98
1.96	Dominic Ogbechie	28	Aug	16
1.95	Mark Lakey	14	Sep	80
1.95	Mark Bidwell	26	Sep	99
1.95	Feron Sayers	20	Jun	09
1.94	Brian Hall	16	Aug	97

Pole Vault

4.32	Frankie Johnson	21	Jun	15
4.31	Richard Smith	28	Aug	95
4.30	Neil Winter	2	Jul	88
4.30	Christian Linskey	18	Jun	94
4.20	Tony Hillier	18	Sep	05
4.20	Adam Hague	11	Sep	11
4.18	Ian Lewis	24	May	83
4.02 i	Tom Gibson	10	Mar	07
4.00	Jimmy Lewis	9	Sep	79
4.00	Andrew Marsh	4	Sep	04
3.95 i	Mark Mellor	1	Sep	16
3.91	Glen Quayle	27	Aug	16

Long Jump

7.03	Feron Sayers	19	Sep	09
6.93	Rowan Powell	17	Aug	13
6.88	Patrick Sylla	14	Apr	13
6.81	Dominic Ogbechie	5	Jun	16
6.79	Oni Onuorah	17	Sep	88
6.78	Brandon McCarthy	7	Jul	13
6.77	Barry Nevison	30	Aug	81
6.76	Joseph Harding	13	May	17
6.74	Kevin Hibbins	17	Jun	95
6.71	Mark Awanah	17	Aug	97
6.69	Luke Thomas	14	Jun	03
6.68	Onew Eyong	9	Jul	99
6.67	Gary Wilson	27	Aug	00

wind assisted

7.12	Oni Onuorah	17	Sep	88
6.89	James Dunford	30	Jul	00
6.87	Joseph Harding	16	Sep	17

downhill

6.77	Eric Wood	25	Aug	58

Triple Jump

14.11	Nathan Fox	14	Aug	05
13.86	Jamie Quarry	10	Jul	87
13.79	Paul Dundas	11	Jun	88
13.77	Eugene Hechevarria	16	Sep	78
13.71	Larry Achike	10	Jun	89

note resident but not British citizen at this time

13.69	Vernon Samuels	25	Aug	79
13.67	Dwyte Smith	6	Aug	06
13.64	Jimi Tele	11	Jul	08
13.63	Miraj Ahmed	28	Aug	16
13.61	Patrick Sylla	26	May	13
13.60	Steven Anderson	9	Jun	79
13.60	Steve Folkard	11	Jul	80
13.59	Kevin Metzger	19	Aug	12

wind assisted

13.92	Eugene Hechevarria	7	Jul	78
13.87	Vernon Samuels	20	Sep	79
13.83	Chris Tomlinson	12	Jul	96
13.73	Donovan Fraser	6	Jul	79
13.69	Kevin O'Shaughnessy	7	Jul	78
13.60	Dean Taylor	12	Jul	96

Shot (5kg)

16.62	Michael Wheeler	29	Jul	06

Shot (4kg)

19.71	Curtis Griffith-Parker	28	Aug	05
19.28	Michael Wheeler	3	Sep	06
18.71	Chris Ellis	14	Jun	80
18.03	Anthony Oshodi	5	Aug	06
18.02	Jay Thomas	24	Aug	03
18.01	Kai Jones	21	Aug	11
17.36	Mathew Evans	16	Aug	03
16.86	Reece Thomas	9	Sep	06
16.59	William Adeyeye	19	Sep	15
16.54	Geoff Hodgson	7	Jul	72
16.50	Carl Saggers	14	Jul	98
16.47	Josh Newman	10	Aug	08
16.40	Shane Birch	11	Sep	02

Discus (1.5kg)

51.55	Curtis Griffith-Parker	14	Aug	05

Discus (1.25kg)

55.39	Curtis Griffith-Parker	13	Aug	05
53.08	Emeka Udechuku	5	Sep	93
52.54	Alfie Scopes	15	Jun	14
52.43	Sam Herrington	1	Sep	01
50.85	Shane Birch	12	Jul	02
50.80	Paul Mardle	3	Sep	77
50.50	James Tomlinson	27	Sep	14
50.48	Anthony Oshodi	26	Aug	06
50.32	Chris Symonds	23	Jul	85
50.24	Liam Biddlecombe	16	Sep	07
50.11	Matthew Williams	10	Sep	11
50.04	Keith Homer	11	Jul	80
49.98	George Armstrong	7	Jul	12

Hammer (5kg)

60.10	Andrew Tolputt	5	Sep	82

Hammer (4kg)

70.78	Andrew Tolputt	9	Jul	82
68.15	Jake Norris	14	Sep	13
67.24	Peter Vivian	22	Sep	85
66.48	Ashley Gilder	5	Sep	09
65.42	Matthew Sutton	29	Sep	96
64.77	Ciaran Wright	27	Aug	11
64.70	Matt Lambley	3	Jul	02
64.66	George Marvell	17	Aug	13
64.28	Jason Byrne	22	Sep	85
64.16	Andrew Jordon	8	Jul	06
63.68	Paul Binley	29	Sep	85
63.60	Richard Fedder	26	Aug	79
63.57	Michael Painter	15	Aug	09

Javelin (700g)

61.81	Matti Mortimore	8	Sep	07

Javelin (600g 1999 Model)

65.87	Oliver Bradfield	12	Jun	10
65.16	Max Law	24	Sep	16
64.74	Thomas Peters	21	Aug	10
63.68	Matti Mortimore	26	Aug	07
60.38	Matthew Blandford	21	Aug	10
59.97	Harry Hughes	13	May	12
59.23	James Whiteaker	17	Jul	13
58.36	George Davies	14	Jul	12
58.27	Mark Lindsay	30	Aug	99
58.09	Pedro Gleadall	27	Aug	16
57.91	Sam Allan	14	Jun	03

Javelin (600g pre 1999 Model)

62.70	Paul Godwin	21	May	89
60.56	David Messom	6	Jul	79
60.56	Clifton Green	3	Jul	94
60.34	Richard Lainson	18	Aug	96

Decathlon (Under 15 implements)

5341	Jamie Quarry	28	Jun	87

Octathlon (Under 15 implements)

4364	Joel McFarlane	9	Aug	15

Pentathlon (80H,SP,LJ,HJ,800)

3403	Edward Dunford	22	Aug	99
3298	Reuben Esien	15	Sep	12
3297	David Guest	23	Sep	06
3293	Gregor Simey	9	Aug	03
3281	Andrae Davis	16	Sep	00
3272	Chris Dack	20	Sep	97
3260	Joseph Connolly	19	Sep	15
3258	Joseph Harding	16	Sep	17
3253	Harry Sutherland	15	Sep	12
3208	Dominic Ogbechie	17	Sep	16
3187	Marc Newton	27	Aug	94
3184	Theo Adesina	17	Sep	16

(100,SP,LJ,HJ,800)

3199	Onochie Onuorah	17	Sep	88

3000 Metres Track Walk

12:44.64	Lloyd Finch	24	May	98
13:19.57	Philip King	29	May	89
13:35.0	Russell Hutchings	7	Sep	85
13:45.0	John Murphy	14	May	95
13:45.05	Cameron Corbishley	21	Aug	11
13:51.0	Robert Mecham	12	May	92
13:57.06	James Davis	29	Aug	99
13:58.0	Jon Vincent	7	Sep	85
14:03.0	Neil Simpson	1	Apr	89

3k Road - where superior to track time

13:20	Jonathan Deakin	18	Sep	88
13:29	Robert Mecham	20	Apr	92
13:32	Russell Hutchings	10	Nov	84
13:34	Nick Ball	30	Jun	02
13:39	Neil Simpson	6	May	89

5000 Metres Track Walk

22:54.0	Lloyd Finch	15	Jul	98

UNDER 13

100 Metres
11.63	Jaleel Roper	2	Sep	15
11.71	Owin Sinclair	1	Aug	10
11.86	Chris Julien	3	Sep	00
11.89	Kareem Jerome	9	Aug	15
11.91	Nathanael Thomas	2	Sep	12
11.94	Graig Anya Joseph	31	Jul	16
11.98	Kenny Konrad	21	Jun	09
12.00	Remi Jokosenumi	31	Aug	16

wind assisted
11.85	Kareem Jerome	6	Sep	15

hand timing
11.6	Owin Sinclair	12	Jun	10
11.6	William Andoh	17	Jun	14
11.6	Jaleel Roper	16	Jun	15
11.7	Kareem Jerome	2	Aug	15

200 Metres
23.35	Jaleel Roper	2	Sep	15
23.60	Nathanael Thomas	2	Sep	12
23.92	Owin Sinclair	30	Aug	10
24.16	Jona Efoloko	2	Sep	12
24.29	Charles Hagan	27	Jul	14
24.46	Kenny Konrad	26	Jul	09
24.49	Jairzinho Morris	27	Jul	14
24.53	Tony Corrigan	31	Aug	03

wind assisted
24.28	Chris Julien	3	Sep	00

hand timing
23.4	Owin Sinclair	13	May	10
24.0	Stephen Buttler	26	Jul	87
24.0	Alex Kiwomya	25	Aug	08
24.1	Tristan Anthony	30	Jul	95
24.2	Kareem Jerome	2	Aug	15
24.2	Remi Jokosenumi	18	Sep	16

300 Metres
41.8	Dominic Jones	5	Jul	97

400 Metres
57.30	Samuel Higgins	13	May	06

hand timing
55.1	Cephas Howard	2	Jul	89
56.5	Craig Erskine	22	Sep	96
56.5	Matthew Lumm	1	Jul	03

800 Metres
2:04.1	Ben Mabon	8	Jul	83
2:05.4	Eric Kimani	28	Jul	79
2:06.35	Jaden Kennedy	10	Aug	16
2:07.48	Ben Pattison	16	Jul	14
2:07.74	Sidnie Ward	15	Jul	15
2:09.1	Max Kaye	9	Jul	06
2:09.40	Tom Kendrick	11	Jun	12
2:09.6	Rory Howorth	23	Aug	14
2:09.78	James Fradley	13	Aug	11
2:09.81	Harley Norman	24	May	15
2:10.21	Markhim Lonsdale	24	Jul	11

1500 Metres
4:18.4	Eric Kimani	26	Sep	79
4:20.5	Ben Mabon	18	Jun	83
4:20.62	Rowan Fuss	26	Aug	15
4:21.61	Jaden Kennedy	3	Aug	16
4:22.3	David Gerard	12	Aug	81
4:22.74	Rory Howorth	27	Aug	14
4:23.34	Tom Kendrick	25	Jul	12
4:23.9	Mark Slowikowski	12	Jul	78
4:28.0	Ciaran Murphy	16	Jun	84
4:28.08	Hugo Milner	30	Aug	11

1 Mile
4:52.0	Tom Quinn	20	Jul	69

3000 Metres
9:31.4	Ben Mabon	24	Jul	83
9:41.4	Mark Slowikowski	21	May	78
9:47.99	Robert Pickering	25	Jun	00
9:49.5	John Tilley	9	Jul	86
9:50.45	Adam Hickey	30	Aug	00

75 Metres Hurdles (76.2cm)
11.43	Karl Johnson	28	Jul	13
11.48	Samuel Ball	29	Jul	17
11.5	Stanley Livingstone	13	Sep	09
11.66		26	Jul	09
11.6	James McLean	14	Jun	03
11.65	William Adeyeye	29	Sep	13
11.69	Cameron Goodall	26	Aug	06
11.7	Stephen Cotterill	16	Jul	78
11.7	Sean Ashton	12	Sep	98
11.7	Luke Webber	9	Jun	04
11.73	Joseph Ellis	31	Jul	11

80 Metres Hurdles (76.2cm)
11.9	Matthew Clements	27	Aug	90
12.1	Sean Ashton	27	May	98
12.4	Jon Crawshaw	14	Aug	94

80 Metres Hurdles (84cm)
12.92	Sam Allen	18	Aug	91

hand timing
12.4	Stanley Livingstone	12	Sep	09
12.6	James Dunford	27	Sep	98

High Jump
1.73	Max Price	14	Aug	11
1.70	Adrian Pettigrew	22	Jun	99
1.69	Patrick O'Connor	7	Sep	08
1.68	Sam Allen	22	Sep	91
1.68	James Dunford	29	Sep	98
1.67	Glen Carpenter	3	Jul	83
1.67	Jamie Dalton	28	Jun	92
1.67	Alex Cox	17	Sep	06
1.67	Adam Robinson	11	Sep	16
1.67	Kehinde Ashaolu	5	Jul	17
1.66	Tim Greenwood	23	Jul	95
1.66	Derek Colquhoun	27	Aug	08
1.66	Tom Bosher	16	Aug	09

Pole Vault

3.40	Neil Winter	27	Jul	86
3.20	Ian Lewis	8	Sep	81
3.01	Frankie Johnson	4	Aug	13
3.01 i	Jack Harris	29	Sep	13

Long Jump

5.86	Owin Sinclair	13	May	10
5.82	William Adeyeye	29	Sep	13
5.80	Joseph Harding	23	May	15
5.72	Samuel Ball	28	Aug	17
5.71	Kieran Showler-Davis	25	Jul	04
5.65	Sam Allen	14	Sep	91
5.65	Deji Ogunnowo/Tobias	1	Aug	04
5.64	Kevin Hibbins	18	Jul	93
5.62	Paul Twidale	31	Jul	99
5.61	Robert Creese	23	Jun	90
5.61	Clovis Asong	22	Jul	07

wind assisted

5.88	Ian Tobin	4	Aug	02
5.76	Seamas Cassidy	5	Sep	99
5.74	Edward Dunford	21	Sep	97

Triple Jump

12.57	Rigsby Agoreyo	9	Aug	69
11.78	Edward Dunford	27	Sep	97
11.75	Alain Kacon	15	Sep	01

Shot (4kg)

12.65	Matthew Evans	12	Aug	01

Shot (3kg)

14.64	Sebastian Dickens	10	Sep	14
14.48	Luke Bowen-Price	26	Jun	12
14.47	Matthew Evans	22	Jul	01
14.22	Khaul Njoya	9	Sep	06
13.94	Michael Wheeler	21	Aug	04
13.93	Jack Halpin	11	Sep	16
13.92	Harry Sutherland	4	Sep	10
13.56	Reece Thomas	11	Sep	04
13.48	Max Price	11	Aug	11
13.36	Chris Hughes	21	Aug	91
13.11	Tony Quinn	28	Aug	93

Discus (1.25kg)

36.98	Sam Herrington	5	Sep	99

Discus (1kg)

42.94	Luke Bowen-Price	31	Jul	12
42.50	Sam Herrington	12	Sep	99
42.38	Ben Barnes	1	Sep	91
40.18	Alfred Mawdsley	25	Aug	13
38.92	Chris Hughes	28	Jul	91
38.58	Carl Saggers	15	Sep	96
38.39	Harry Sutherland	4	Sep	10
38.30	Liam Walsh	13	Aug	94
38.20	James Anderson	15	Sep	12
36.56	Sam Mace	7	Aug	13
36.55	Nicholas Hunt	23	Aug	08

Discus (750g)

43.70	Sam Herrington	8	Jul	99

Hammer (4kg)

41.64	Michael Painter	24	Jun	07

Hammer (3.25kg)

48.18	Kieran Phillips	20	Sep	09
46.52	Sam Foster	7	Sep	06
45.60	Ciaran Wright	8	Sep	09
44.86	Michael Painter	5	Aug	07
44.38	Ross Thompson	4	Sep	94

Javelin (600g 1999 Model)

47.86	Oliver Bradfield	28	Sep	08

Javelin (400g)

57.55	Oliver Bradfield	17	Aug	08
50.35	Benjamin East	24	Sep	16
49.84	Max Law	14	Sep	14
48.28	Archie Goodliff	18	Jul	15
48.16	Thomas Peters	23	Aug	08
46.20	Jonah McCafferty	26	Sep	15
45.22	Matthew Blandford	28	Sep	08
45.12	James Yun-Stevens	29	Aug	11
44.98	Harri Mortimore	27	Jul	08
44.87	Jack Halpin	14	Sep	16

Pentathlon (80H,SP,LJ,HJ,800 U15)

2444	James Dunford	27	Sep	98

Pentathlon (75H,SP,LJ,HJ,800)

2562	Edward Dunford	28	Sep	97

1000 Metres Track Walk

4:46.0	Luke Finch	15	Jul	98

1k Road - where superior to track time

4:34	Luke Finch	27	Sep	97

2000 Metres Track Walk

9:40.0	Luke Finch	12	Nov	97
9:40.3	Thomas Taylor	19	Jun	93
9:51.0	Lloyd Finch	11	Aug	96
9:57.0	Jamie Nunn	7	Feb	88
10:06.0	Grant Ringshaw	23	Jul	78
10:10.0hc	Dom King	23	Mar	95

2k Road - where superior to track time

9:16	Lloyd Finch	28	Sep	96
9:38	Luke Finch	12	Sep	98
9:52	Matthew Halliday	6	Mar	04
9:55 hc	Nick Ball	5	Sep	00
9:56	Grant Ringshaw	27	Oct	79

3000 Metres Track Walk

15:02.62	Lloyd Finch	21	Sep	96
15:15.5	Robert Mecham	25	Jul	89

3k Road - where superior to track time

14:44	Martin Young	22	Sep	84

66

UK ALL TIME LISTS - WOMEN

100 Metres

Time	Name	Day	Month	Year
10.99	Dina Asher-Smith	25	Jul	15
11.02	Asher-Smith	24	May	15
11.05	Montell Douglas	17	Jul	08
11.06	Asher-Smith	25	Jul	15
11.06	Desiree Henry	15	Apr	16
11.07	Henry	5	Jun	16
11.07	Asher-Smith	23	Jul	16
11.08	Asher-Smith	5	Jul	15
11.08	Asher-Smith	5	Jun	16
11.08	Henry	23	Jul	16
11.08	Henry	12	Aug	16
11.10	Kathy Cook	5	Sep	81
11.10	Asha Philip	24	May	15
11.11	Laura Turner	4	Jul	10
11.14	Jeanette Kwakye	17	Aug	08
11.14	Daryll Neita	9	Jul	17
11.15	Paula Thomas	23	Aug	94
11.16	Andrea Lynch	11	Jun	75
11.17	Abi Oyepitan	25	Jul	04
11.17	Bianca Williams	14	Jun	14
11.17	Imani Lansiquot	20	Jul	16
11.18	Anyika Onuora	29	May	11
11.18	Jodie Williams	22	Jul	11
11.19	Ashleigh Nelson	12	Aug	14
11.20	Sonia Lannaman	25	Jul	80
11.20	Heather Oakes	26	Sep	80
11.21	Emma Ania	6	Jun	08
11.22 A	Bev Callender	8	Sep	79
11.35		22	Jul	81
11.23	Joice Maduaka	15	Jul	06
11.27	Stephi Douglas	26	Jul	91
11.27	Sophie Papps	30	Jul	16
11.28	Margaret Adeoye	14	Jun	14
11.29	Bev Kinch	6	Jul	90
11.31	Wendy Hoyte	4	Oct	82
11.31	Shirley Thomas	3	Jul	83
11.31	Simmone Jacobs	24	Sep	88
11.31	Hayley Jones	22	Jun	13
11.32	Joan Baptiste	24	Aug	83
11.32	Christine Bloomfield	3	Jul	99
11.33	Emily Freeman	14	Jun	09
11.34	Katharine Merry	25	Jun	94
11.34	Shani Anderson	26	Aug	00
11.34	Amanda Forrester	27	Jul	02
11.35	Sharon Danville	20	Aug	77
11.35	Marcia Richardson	4	Jun	00
11.35	Christine Ohuruogu	4	May	08
11.36 A	Della Pascoe	14	Oct	68
11.36	Annabelle Lewis	12	Jul	13
11.39 A	Val Peat	14	Oct	68
11.39	Sallyanne Short	12	Jul	92
11.39 +	Jessica Ennis	16	May	10
11.39	Elaine O'Neill	4	Jul	10
11.39	Cindy Ofili	11	Jun	15
11.39 A	Hannah Brier	16	Jul	15
11.39	Corinne Humphreys	15	Jun	17
11.40	Helen Hogarth	20	Jul	74
11.40	Vernicha James	11	Jun	02
11.41	Jayne Andrews	27	May	84
11.41	Kadi-Ann Thomas	17	Jul	08
11.41	Lorraine Ugen	16	Jul	17

wind assisted

Time	Name	Day	Month	Year
10.93	Sonia Lannaman	17	Jul	77
10.95	Montell Douglas	17	Jul	08
11.01	Heather Oakes	21	May	80
11.03	Asher-Smith	5	Jul	14
11.04	Desiree Henry	26	Apr	14
11.06	Lannaman	21	May	80
11.08	Oakes	27	May	84
11.08	Kathy Cook	24	Aug	83
11.09	Laura Turner	7	Jul	07
11.13	Bev Kinch	6	Jul	83
11.13	Shirley Thomas	27	May	84
11.13	Paula Thomas	20	Aug	88
11.13	Jodie Williams	26	Apr	14
11.15	Ashleigh Nelson	29	Jun	14
11.18	Wendy Hoyte	4	Oct	82
11.18	Simmone Jacobs	11	Jun	97
11.19	Bev Callender	21	May	80
11.19	Joice Maduaka	10	Jun	07
11.23	Joan Baptiste	24	Aug	83
11.23	Jayne Andrews	17	Jul	84
11.24	Sarah Wilhelmy	9	Jun	01
11.27	Katharine Merry	11	Jun	94
11.29	Marcia Richardson	29	May	00
11.30	Hayley Jones	7	Jul	13
11.30	Katarina Johnson-Thompson	21	Jun	14
11.31	Lorraine Ugen	15	Apr	17
11.32	Donna Fraser	25	Apr	97
11.32	Shani Anderson	6	Jul	02
11.34	Sandra Whittaker	22	May	83
11.35	Amarachi Pipi	13	May	17
11.36	Sallyanne Short	26	Aug	89
11.37	Val Peat	17	Jul	70
11.37	Kaye Scott	22	May	83
11.37	Helen Burkart	11	Sep	83
11.37	Hannah Brier	31	May	15
11.37	Rachel Johncock	30	Jul	16

hand timing

Time	Name	Day	Month	Year
10.9	Andrea Lynch	28	May	77
11.1	Sonia Lannaman	29	Jun	80
11.1	Heather Oakes	29	Jun	80
11.1	Joan Baptiste	16	Jul	85
11.2	Helen Golden	29	Jun	74
11.2	Sharon Danville	25	Jun	77
11.2	Bev Kinch	14	Jul	84
11.2	Geraldine McLeod	21	May	94

hand timing - wind assisted

Time	Name	Day	Month	Year
10.8	Sonia Lannaman	22	May	76
11.1	Sharon Danville	22	May	76
11.1	Bev Kinch	9	May	87
11.2	Margaret Williams	15	May	76
11.2	Donna Fraser	31	Jan	98

200 Metres

22.07	Dina Asher-Smith	28	Aug	15
22.10	Kathy Cook	9	Aug	84
22.12	Asher-Smith	27	Aug	15
22.13	Cook	9	Sep	82
22.21	Cook	20	Aug	84
22.22	Asher-Smith	26	Aug	15
22.22	Asher-Smith	11	Aug	17
22.25	Cook	22	Aug	84
22.26	Cook	24	Aug	83
22.30	Asher-Smith	7	Jun	15
22.46	Jodie Williams	15	Aug	14
22.46	Desiree Henry	27	Aug	16
22.50	Abi Oyepitan	23	Aug	04
22.58	Sonia Lannaman	18	May	80
22.58	Bianca Williams	31	Jul	14
22.64	Emily Freeman	20	Aug	09
22.64	Anyika Onuora	31	Jul	14
10 22.69	Paula Thomas	26	Aug	94
22.72	Bev Callender	30	Jul	80
22.73	Jenni Stoute	3	Aug	92
22.75	Donna Hartley	17	Jun	78
22.76	Katharine Merry	25	Jul	00
22.79	Katarina Johnson-Thompson	28	May	16
22.80	Michelle Scutt	12	Jun	82
22.83	Joice Maduaka	25	Jul	99
22.83	Jessica Ennis	3	Aug	12
22.85	Christine Bloomfield	25	Jul	99
20 22.85	Christine Ohuruogu	1	Jun	09
22.86	Joan Baptiste	9	Aug	84
22.86	Finette Agyapong	15	Jul	17
22.88	Margaret Adeoye	8	Sep	13
22.92	Heather Oakes	28	Aug	86
22.93	Vernicha James	21	Jul	01
22.94	Shannon Hylton	17	May	15
22.95	Simmone Jacobs	25	Apr	96
22.95	Amarachi Pipi	22	Apr	17
22.96 i	Donna Fraser	23	Feb	97
23.05		2	May	04
30 22.96	Shani Anderson	6	Jul	02
22.96	Ashleigh Nelson	23	Apr	16
22.98	Sandra Whittaker	8	Aug	84
23.04	Maya Bruney	22	Jul	17
23.06	Sam Davies	28	Aug	00
23.09	Charlotte McLennaghan	10	May	15
23.10	Diane Smith	11	Aug	90
23.11	Jeanette Kwakye	14	Jul	07
23.14	Helen Hogarth	7	Sep	73
23.14	Helen Burkart	17	Jul	82
40 23.15	Andrea Lynch	25	Aug	75
23.16	Lee McConnell	31	May	08
23.17	Stephi Douglas	12	Jun	94
23.18	Joslyn Hoyte-Smith	9	Jun	82
23.20	Sarah Reilly	21	Jun	97
23.20 i	Amy Spencer	2	Mar	03
23.20	Helen Pryer	22	Jul	09
23.23	Sarah Wilhelmy	13	Jun	98
23.23	Cheriece Hylton	10	Jun	17
23.24	Sallyanne Short	28	Jun	92
50 23.25	Emma Ania	18	Jul	08

wind assisted

22.21	Cook	7	Oct	82
22.48	Michelle Scutt	4	Jul	82
22.69	Bev Callender	24	Jun	81
22.73	Shannon Hylton	18	Jul	15
22.80	Donna Fraser	3	Sep	05
22.83	Amarachi Pipi	14	May	17
22.84	Sarah Wilhelmy	10	Jun	01
22.90	Andrea Lynch	11	Jun	75
22.90	Allison Curbishley	17	Jul	98
22.97	Helen Hogarth	26	Jul	74
23.00	Joslyn Hoyte-Smith	13	Jun	82
23.07	Asha Phillip	14	Jul	13
23.11	Linsey Macdonald	5	Jul	80
23.12	Alisha Rees	3	Jun	17
23.14	Shirley Thomas	28	May	84
23.14	Zoey Clarke	3	Jun	17
23.15	Margaret Williams	22	Jul	70
23.15	Cheriece Hylton	17	May	15
23.19	Sallyanne Short	29	Jan	90
23.22	Kadi-Ann Thomas	17	Jul	08
23.22	Hayley Jones	17	Jun	12
23.23	Sinead Dudgeon	29	Jul	00

hand timing

22.9	Heather Oakes	3	May	80
22.9	Helen Burkart	6	Aug	83
23.0	Helen Golden	30	Jun	74
23.1	Andrea Lynch	21	May	77
23.1	Linda Keough	5	Jul	89
23.1	Lee McConnell	7	Jun	08
23.2	Dorothy Hyman	3	Oct	63
23.2	Margaret Williams	2	Aug	70

hand timing - wind assisted

23.1	Margaret Williams	14	Jul	74
23.1	Sharon Danville	17	Sep	77
23.1	Linda McCurry	2	Jul	78

300 Metres

35.46	Kathy Cook	18	Aug	84
35.51	Cook	9	Sep	83
35.71	Donna Fraser	28	Aug	00
36.00	Katharine Merry	28	Aug	00
36.01	Michelle Scutt	13	Jul	80
36.44	Sally Gunnell	30	Jul	93
36.45	Joslyn Hoyte-Smith	5	Jul	80
36.46	Linsey Macdonald	13	Jul	80
36.64	Nicola Sanders	3	Jun	07
36.65	Joan Baptiste	18	Aug	84
36.69	Helen Burkart	9	Sep	83

hand timing

36.2	Donna Hartley	7	Aug	74

during 400m

36.0 i+	Nicola Sanders	3	Mar	07
	36.17 +	29	Aug	07
35.7 +	Christine Ohuruogu	27	Jul	13
	36.13 +	29	Aug	07

68

400 Metres

	Time	Name	Date		
	49.41	Christine Ohuruogu	12	Aug	13
	49.43	Kathy Cook	6	Aug	84
	49.59	Katharine Merry	11	Jun	01
	49.61	Ohuruogu	29	Aug	07
	49.62	Ohuruogu	19	Aug	08
	49.65	Nicola Sanders	29	Aug	07
	49.70	Ohuruogu	5	Aug	12
	49.72	Merry	25	Sep	00
	49.75	Ohuruogu	11	Aug	13
	49.77	Sanders	27	Aug	07
	49.79	Donna Fraser	25	Sep	00
	50.40	Phylis Smith	3	Aug	92
	50.50	Perri Shakes-Drayton	22	Jun	13
	50.63	Michelle Scutt	31	May	82
	50.71	Allison Curbishley	18	Sep	98
10	50.75	Joslyn Hoyte-Smith	18	Jun	82
	50.82	Lee McConnell	20	Sep	02
	50.87	Anyika Onuora	25	Aug	15
	50.93	Lorraine Hanson	26	Aug	91
	50.98	Linda Staines	26	Aug	91
	51.04	Sally Gunnell	20	Jul	94
	51.12	Shana Cox	27	Jul	13
	51.16	Linsey Macdonald	15	Jun	80
	51.18	Melanie Neef	6	Aug	95
	51.23	Emily Diamond	4	Jun	16
20	51.26	Seren Bundy-Davies	11	Jun	16
	51.28	Donna Hartley	12	Jul	75
	51.36	Catherine Murphy	27	Jul	02
	51.41	Sandra Douglas	2	Aug	92
	51.45 i	Eilidh Doyle	3	Mar	13
	51.83		27	Jul	13
	51.53	Jenni Stoute	12	Aug	89
	51.70	Verona Elder	10	Jun	78
	51.78	Helen Karagounis	19	Jul	03
	51.81	Zoey Clark	7	Aug	17
	51.90 i	Laviai Nielsen	18	Feb	17
	52.25		27	May	15
30	51.93	Janine MacGregor	28	Aug	81
	51.93	Margaret Adeoye	13	Jul	13
	51.96	Kelly Massey	24	Aug	14
	51.97	Linda Forsyth	31	May	82
	52.02	Marilyn Okoro	8	Aug	06
	52.05	Sinead Dudgeon	3	Jul	99
	52.12 A	Lillian Board	16	Oct	68
	52.13	Helen Burkart	28	Jun	84
	52.13	Kirsty McAslan	9	Jul	15
	52.15 i	Lesley Owusu	9	Mar	01
	52.27		15	Jul	01
40	52.19	Kelly Sotherton	31	Aug	08
	52.20	Ann Packer	17	Oct	64
	52.20	Kim Wall	11	Jun	05
	52.21	Montenae Speight	18	Apr	15
	52.25 A	Catherine Reid	17	Jul	15
	52.26	Pat Beckford	14	Aug	88
	52.26	Nadine Okyere	6	Aug	11
	52.27	Desiree Henry	31	Mar	16
	52.32 i	Laura Maddox	21	Feb	15
	52.40	Helen Frost	17	Sep	00
50	52.40	Vicky Barr	4	Jul	10

hand timing

Time	Name	Date		
51.2	Donna Hartley	28	Jul	78
51.4	Verona Elder	22	May	76
52.2	Liz Barnes	22	May	76
52.4	Stephanie Llewellyn	1	Jul	95

600 Metres

Time	Name	Date		
1:24.36	Marilyn Okoro	5	Jul	12
1:25.41	Kelly Holmes	2	Sep	03
1:25.81 i	Jenny Meadows	7	Jan	07

800 Metres

Time	Name	Date			
1:56.21	Kelly Holmes	9	Sep	95	
1:56.38	Holmes	23	Aug	04	
1:56.80	Holmes	25	Sep	00	
1:56.95	Holmes	13	Aug	95	
1:57.14	Holmes	7	Jul	97	
1:57.42	Kirsty Wade	24	Jun	85	
1:57.45	Wade	21	Aug	85	
1:57.48	Wade	17	Aug	85	
1:57.56	Holmes	16	Jul	95	
1:57.69	Lynsey Sharp	20	Aug	16	
1:57.93	Jenny Meadows	19	Aug	09	
1:58.20	Rebecca Lyne	11	Jun	06	
1:58.45	Marilyn Okoro	26	Jul	08	
1:58.65	Diane Modahl	14	Jul	90	
1:58.69	Laura Muir	6	Jul	17	
1:58.74	Jemma Simpson	22	Jul	10	
1:58.86	Shelayna Oskan-Clarke	27	Aug	15	10
1:58.97	Shireen Bailey	15	Sep	87	
1:59.02	Susan Scott	24	Mar	06	
1:59.05	Christina Boxer	4	Aug	79	
1:59.37	Emma Jackson	11	May	12	
1:59.50 i	Jo Fenn	7	Mar	04	
1:59.86		29	Jul	02	
1:59.66	Hannah England	20	Aug	12	
1:59.67	Lorraine Baker	15	Aug	86	
1:59.74	Amanda Pritchard	28	Jul	06	
1:59.75	Charlotte Moore	29	Jul	02	
1:59.76	Paula Fryer	17	Jul	91	20
1:59.77	Jessica Judd	11	Jun	14	
1:59.81	Ann Griffiths	10	Aug	94	
2:00.04 mx	Adele Tracey	7	Sep	16	
2:00.26		11	Aug	17	
2:00.08	Alison Leonard	12	Jul	14	
2:00.10	Tanya Blake	31	May	98	
2:00.14	Lisa Dobriskey	14	Aug	10	
2:00.15	Rosemary Wright	3	Sep	72	
2:00.20	Anne Purvis	7	Jul	82	
2:00.30	Cherry Hanson	25	Jul	81	
2:00.39	Bev Hartigan	28	Aug	88	30
2:00.49	Hayley Tullett	19	Jul	03	
2:00.49	Vicky Griffiths	31	May	08	
2:00.53 i	Karen Harewood	27	Jan	06	
2:00.53	Alexandra Bell	22	Jul	16	
2:00.55 mx	Zola Budd	21	Jun	86	
2:00.6 a	Jane Finch	9	Jul	77	
2:00.80	Yvonne Murray	10	Jul	87	
2:00.92 mx	Katie Snowden	14	Aug	17	
2:01.10	Sarah McDonald	23	Jul	16	

40	2:01.1 a	Ann Packer	20	Oct	64
	2:01.11	Lynne MacDougall	18	Aug	84
	2:01.16	Celia Taylor	13	Aug	10
	2:01.2	Joan Allison	1	Jul	73
	2:01.2	Christine Whittingham	26	Aug	78
	2:01.24	Chris Benning	28	Jul	79
	2:01.34	Claire Gibson	15	Aug	09
	2:01.35	Liz Barnes	10	Jul	76
	2:01.35	Laura Finucane	13	Jun	07
	2:01.36	Gillian Dainty	31	Aug	83
50	2:01.40	Janet Bell	10	Jul	87

1000 Metres

	2:31.93 i	Laura Muir	18	Feb	17
	2:32.55	Kelly Holmes	15	Jun	97
	2:32.82	Holmes	23	Jul	95
	2:32.96 i	Holmes	20	Feb	04
	2:33.70	Kirsty Wade	9	Aug	85
	2:34.73 i	Jo Fenn	20	Feb	04
	2:34.92	Christina Boxer	9	Aug	85
	2:35.32	Shireen Bailey	19	Jul	86
	2:35.51	Lorraine Baker	19	Jul	86
	2:35.86	Diane Modahl	29	Aug	93
	2:36.13	Jenny Meadows	24	May	15
	2:37.05	Christine Whittingham	27	Jun	86
10	2:37.29	Yvonne Murray	14	Jul	89
	2:37.61	Bev Hartigan	14	Jul	89
	2:37.82	Gillian Dainty	11	Sep	81
	2:38.44	Evelyn McMeekin	23	Aug	78
	2:38.49	Laura Weightman	6	Sep	13
	2:38.49	Sarah McDonald	11	Jul	17
	2:38.58	Jo White	9	Sep	77
	2:38.67	Lynne MacDougall	19	Jul	86
	2:38.83	Lynn Gibson	29	Aug	93

1500 Metres

	3:55.22	Laura Muir	27	Aug	16
	3:57.49	Muir	22	Jul	16
	3:57.85	Muir	1	Sep	16
	3:57.90	Kelly Holmes	28	Aug	04
	3:58.07	Holmes	29	Jun	97
	3:58.66	Muir	17	Jul	15
	3:59.50	Lisa Dobriskey	28	Aug	09
	3:59.95	Hayley Tullett	31	Aug	03
	3:59.96	Zola Budd	30	Aug	85
	4:00.07	Muir	5	Jul	14
	4:00.17	Laura Weightman	5	Jul	14
	4:00.57	Christina Boxer	6	Jul	84
	4:00.73	Kirsty Wade	26	Jul	87
	4:01.10	Helen Clitheroe	19	Jul	02
10	4:01.20	Yvonne Murray	4	Jul	87
	4:01.38	Liz McColgan	4	Jul	87
	4:01.53	Chris Benning	15	Aug	79
	4:01.60	Eilish McColgan	27	Aug	17
	4:01.79	Jo Pavey	13	Sep	03
	4:01.89	Hannah England	22	Jul	11
	4:02.32	Shireen Bailey	1	Oct	88
	4:02.54	Stephanie Twell	19	Aug	10
	4:03.17	Alison Wyeth	7	Aug	93
	4:03.73	Jessica Judd	4	Aug	17

4:03.74 mx	Charlene Thomas	4	Sep	13	20
4:05.06		7	Jun	16	
4:04.14	Wendy Sly	14	Aug	83	
4:04.81	Sheila Carey	9	Sep	72	
4:05.29	Katie Snowden	14	Jun	17	
4:05.37	Paula Radcliffe	1	Jul	01	
4:05.48	Sarah McDonald	4	Aug	17	
4:05.66	Bev Hartigan	20	Jul	90	
4:05.75	Lynn Gibson	20	Jul	94	
4:05.82 +	Melissa Courtney	9	Jul	17	
4:06.00		11	Jun	17	
4:05.83 mx	Emma Jackson	4	Sep	13	
4:05.96	Lynne MacDougall	20	Aug	84	30
4:06.0	Mary Cotton	24	Jun	78	
4:06.24	Christine Whittingham	5	Jul	86	
4:06.39	Jemma Simpson	22	May	10	
4:06.69 mx	Katrina Wootton	12	Aug	09	
4:07.94		13	Jun	09	
4:06.81	Stacey Smith	10	Jul	11	
4:06.85	Rebecca Lyne	6	Jul	06	
4:07.00	Susan Scott	27	Jun	08	
4:07.11	Janet Marlow	18	Aug	82	
4:07.59	Ann Griffiths	9	Jun	92	
4:07.69	Teena Colebrook	19	Aug	90	40
4:07.90	Gillian Dainty	16	Jun	84	
4:08.74	Abby Westley	20	May	07	
4:08.96 mx	Alison Leonard	9	Aug	16	
4:09.16 mx	Laura Whittle	18	Aug	09	
4:09.26	Lisa York	13	Jun	92	
4:09.29	Angela Newport	20	Jul	94	
4:09.37	Joyce Smith	7	Sep	72	
4:09.46	Karen Hargrave	4	Sep	89	
4:09.5	Penny Forse	6	Aug	80	
4:09.54	Jo Fenn	2	Jul	04	50

1 Mile

4:17.57	Zola Budd	21	Aug	85	
4:18.03	Laura Muir	9	Jul	17	
4:19.12		9	Jun	16	
4:19.41	Kirsty Wade	27	Jul	85	
4:20.35	Lisa Dobriskey	7	Sep	08	
4:20.88	Laura Weightman	9	Jul	17	
4:22.64	Christina Boxer	7	Sep	84	
4:22.64	Yvonne Murray	22	Jul	94	
4:23.15	Melissa Courtney	9	Jul	17	
4:24.57	Chris Benning	7	Sep	84	
4:24.87	Alison Wyeth	6	Jul	91	10
4:24.94	Paula Radcliffe	14	Aug	96	
4:25.39	Stephanie Twell	9	Jul	17	
4:25.89	Kate Snowden	9	Jul	17	
4:26.11	Liz McColgan	10	Jul	87	
4:26.16	Teena Colebrook	14	Jul	90	
4:26.50 i	Hayley Tullett	6	Feb	00	
4:26.52	Bev Hartigan	14	Aug	92	
4:27.80	Lisa York	14	Aug	92	
4:27.95	Charlene Thomas	14	Sep	07	
4:28.04	Kelly Holmes	30	Aug	98	20
4:28.07	Wendy Sly	18	Aug	84	
4:28.59	Jessica Judd	9	Jul	17	
4:28.8	Karen Hargrave	20	Aug	89	

2000 Metres

5:26.93	Yvonne Murray	8	Jul	94
5:29.58	Murray	11	Jul	86
5:30.19	Zola Budd	11	Jul	86
5:33.85	Christina Boxer	13	Jul	84
5:37.00	Chris Benning	13	Jul	84
5:37.01 +	Paula Radcliffe	19	Jul	02
5:38.50	Alison Wyeth	29	Aug	93
5:40.24	Liz McColgan	22	Aug	87
5:41.2 i+	Jo Pavey	3	Feb	07
5:41.5 i+e	Laura Muir	4	Feb	17
10 5:42.15	Wendy Sly	17	Sep	82

3000 Metres

8:22.20	Paula Radcliffe	19	Jul	02
8:26.41 i	Laura Muir	4	Feb	17
8:30.64		21	Jul	17
8:26.97	Radcliffe	29	Jun	01
8:27.40	Radcliffe	11	Aug	99
8:28.07	Radcliffe	17	Aug	01
8:28.83	Zola Budd	7	Sep	85
8:29.02	Yvonne Murray	25	Sep	88
8:31.00	Eilish McColgan	20	Aug	17
8:31.27	Jo Pavey	30	Aug	02
8:34.80 i	Liz McColgan	4	Mar	89
8:38.23		15	Jul	91
8:37.06	Wendy Sly	10	Aug	83
8:38.42	Alison Wyeth	16	Aug	93
10 8:39.81 i	Helen Clitheroe	19	Feb	11
8:51.82		29	Aug	10
8:40.97	Kathy Butler	24	Aug	01
8:40.98	Stephanie Twell	15	Jul	16
8:43.24 mx	Jessica Judd	6	Sep	17
8:43.46 mx	Laura Weightman	14	May	13
8:43.72 mx	Melissa Courtney	6	Sep	17
8:44.46	Chris Benning	22	Aug	84
8:45.36 i	Hayley Tullett	10	Mar	01
8:45.39		15	Jul	00
8:45.69	Jane Shields	10	Aug	83
8:46.38	Julia Bleasdale	26	Aug	12
20 8:47.25 i	Lisa Dobriskey	4	Mar	07
8:54.12		20	May	07
8:47.36	Jill Hunter	17	Aug	88
8:47.59	Angela Tooby	5	Jul	88
8:47.7	Kirsty Wade	5	Aug	87
8:47.71	Lisa York	31	Jul	92
8:48.72	Karen Hargrave	28	Jan	90
8:48.74	Paula Fudge	29	Aug	78
8:49.89	Christina Boxer	20	Jul	85
8:50.37	Laura Whittle	13	Sep	09
8:50.52	Debbie Peel	7	Aug	82
30 8:50.69 i	Katrina Wootton	16	Feb	08
8:51.02	Rosie Clarke	20	Aug	17
8:51.33	Sonia McGeorge	29	Aug	90
8:51.40	Ruth Partridge	7	Aug	82
8:52.00 i	Lauren Howarth	16	Feb	13
8:52.79	Ann Ford	28	Aug	77
8:52.90 i	Barbara Parker	6	Feb	10
8:53.12 i	Kate Avery	14	Feb	15
8:53.52 i	Nicky Morris	4	Mar	89
8:53.94 i	Beth Potter	27	Jul	16

5000 Metres

14:29.11	Paula Radcliffe	20	Jun	04
14:31.42	Radcliffe	28	Jul	02
14:32.44	Radcliffe	31	Aug	01
14:39.96	Jo Pavey	25	Aug	06
14:40.71	Pavey	8	Jul	05
14:43.54	Radcliffe	7	Aug	99
14:44.21	Radcliffe	22	Jul	01
14:44.36	Radcliffe	5	Aug	00
14:45.51	Radcliffe	22	Aug	97
14:46.76	Radcliffe	16	Aug	96
14:48.07	Zola Budd	26	Aug	85
14:48.49	Eilish McColgan	1	Sep	17
14:49.12 i	Laura Muir	4	Jan	17
14:52.07		13	Aug	17
14:54.08	Stephanie Twell	27	Aug	10
14:56.94	Yvonne Murray	7	Jul	95
14:59.56	Liz McColgan	22	Jul	95
15:00.37	Alison Wyeth	7	Jul	95
15:02.00	Julia Bleasdale	7	Aug	12 10
15:05.51	Kathy Butler	3	Sep	04
15:06.75	Helen Clitheroe	6	Aug	11
15:07.45	Emelia Gorecka	4	May	14
15:08.24	Laura Weightman	18	May	17
15:08.58	Laura Whittle	1	May	16
15:09.98	Jill Hunter	18	Jul	92
15:12.81	Barbara Parker	7	Aug	12
15:13.22	Angela Tooby	5	Aug	87
15:14.08	Natalie Harvey	31	Jul	04
15:14.51	Paula Fudge	13	Sep	81 20
15:16.44	Hayley Yelling	23	Jul	05
15:19.78	Catherine Berry	31	Jul	04
15:21.45	Wendy Sly	5	Aug	87
15:23.4	Charlotte Purdue	28	Aug	10
15:24.02	Jessica Andrews	16	Jul	16
15:25.23	Kate Avery	3	Apr	15
15:26.5	Freya Ross	28	Aug	10
15:27.60	Rhona Auckland	25	Jul	15
15:27.6 mx	Katrina Wootton	25	Aug	17
15:30.82		18	May	13
15:28.32	Beth Potter	1	May	16 30
15:28.58	Mara Yamauchi	24	Jun	06
15:28.63	Andrea Wallace	2	Jul	92
15:28.95	Melissa Courtney	5	May	17
15:29.04	Sonia McGeorge	27	May	96
15:29.07	Charlotte Taylor	5	May	17
15:29.10	Kate Reed	25	Jul	07
15:29.26	Lauren Howarth	5	May	17
15:29.50	Jessica Coulson	25	Jul	15
15:29.94	Katie Brough	4	Apr	14
15:31.78	Julie Holland	18	Jul	90 40
15:32.19	Susan Tooby	26	May	85
15:32.27	Emily Pidgeon	12	Jun	10
15:32.34	Jane Shields	5	Jun	88
15:32.62	Andrea Whitcombe	25	Jun	00
15:34.16	Jill Harrison	26	May	85
15:34.40	Lucy Elliott	2	Jun	97
15:34.82	Jessica Judd	27	May	17
15:35.27	Emma Pallant	9	Jun	12
15:36.35	Birhan Dagne	5	Aug	00
15:37.3	Caryl Jones	21	Jul	12 50

10000 Metres

	30:01.09	Paula Radcliffe	6 Aug	02
	30:17.15	Radcliffe	27 Jun	04
	30:26.97	Radcliffe	30 Sep	00
	30:27.13	Radcliffe	26 Aug	99
	30:40.70	Radcliffe	10 Apr	99
	30:42.75	Radcliffe	6 Aug	05
	30:48:58	Radcliffe	4 Apr	98
	30:53.20	Jo Pavey	3 Aug	12
	30:55.63	Julia Bleasdale	3 Aug	12
	30:55.80	Radcliffe	7 Apr	01
	30:57.07	Liz McColgan	25 Jun	91
	31:07.88	Jill Hunter	30 Jun	91
	31:35.77	Kate Reed	4 May	08
	31:35.92	Jessica Andrews	12 Aug	16
	31:36.90	Kathy Butler	12 Jun	04
	31:41.44	Kate Avery	2 May	15
10	31:45.14	Hayley Yelling	12 Jun	04
	31:45.63mx	Katrina Wootton	3 Sep	17
	32:27.47		20 May	17
	31:49.40	Mara Yamauchi	21 Mar	06
	31:53.36	Wendy Sly	8 Oct	88
	31:55.30	Angela Tooby	4 Sep	87
	31:56.97	Yvonne Murray	24 Aug	94
	31:58.39	Liz Yelling	30 Jul	02
	32:03.45	Beth Potter	1 Apr	16
	32:03.55	Charlotte Purdue	29 Apr	12
	32:10.59	Eilish McColgan	31 Mar	17
20	32:11.29	Helen Clitheroe	4 Jun	11
	32:11.80	Charlotte Taylor	31 Mar	17
	32:14.01	Natalie Harvey	12 Jun	04
	32:16.23	Stephanie Twell	20 May	17
	32:17.05	Elinor Kirk	4 Apr	14
	32:20.77	Lily Partridge	11 Apr	15
	32:20.95	Susan Tooby	2 Jul	88
	32:21.61	Andrea Wallace	6 Jun	92
	32:22.79	Rhona Auckland	10 Jul	15
	32:23.44	Freya Ross	5 Jun	10
30	32:24.63	Sue Crehan	4 Jul	87
	32:29.28	Alice Wright	5 May	17
	32:30.4	Birhan Dagne	22 Jul	00
	32:32.42	Vikki McPherson	15 Jul	93
	32:34.7	Sarah Wilkinson	22 Jul	00
	32:34.81	Gemma Steel	3 Jun	12
	32:36.07	Sarah Waldron	6 Apr	12
	32:36.09	Helen Titterington	29 Aug	89
	32:37.52	Charlotte Arter	19 Aug	17
	32:39.36	Sonia Samuels	4 May	14
40	32:41.17	Vicky Gill	30 Apr	04
	32:41.29	Jenny Clague	20 Jun	93
	32:41.59	Jessica Coulson	16 May	15
	32:42.0	Jane Shields	24 Aug	88
	32:42.84	Angie Hulley	6 Aug	89
	32:44.06	Suzanne Rigg	27 Jun	93
	32:45.94	Aine Hoban	31 Mar	07
	32:47.78	Julie Holland	31 Aug	90
	32:47.96	Hayley Haining	30 Jun	07
	32:51.38	Claire Duck	20 May	17
50	32:52.53	Caryl Jones	23 Jun	12
	32:52.60	Charlotte Dale	12 Apr	03

10 Kilometres Road

30:21	Paula Radcliffe	23 Feb	03	
30:38	Radcliffe	22 Sep	02	
30:39	Liz McColgan	11 Mar	89	
30:43	Radcliffe	17 Feb	02	
30:45	Radcliffe	29 Jun	04	
30:45	Radcliffe	26 Mar	05	
31:27	Gemma Steel	2 Aug	14	
31:29	Wendy Sly	27 Mar	83	
31:42	Jill Hunter	21 Jan	89	
31:43	Mara Yamauchi	19 Feb	06	
31:45	Helen Clitheroe	15 May	11	
31:47	Jo Pavey	20 May	07	
31:47	Katrina Wootton	18 Dec	16	
31:56	Andrea Wallace	4 Aug	91	10
32:01	Eilish McColgan	13 Jan	17	
32:07	Kate Reed	7 Oct	07	
32:10	Charlotte Purdue	15 Apr	12	
32:13	Charlotte Dale	6 Feb	05	
32:14	Priscilla Welch	23 Mar	85	
32:15	Angela Tooby	31 Mar	84	
32:17	Alyson Dixon	6 Sep	15	
32:20	Zola Budd	2 Mar	85	
32:24	Yvonne Murray	2 Nov	97	
32:24	Kathy Butler	4 Jul	05	20
32:24	Michelle Ross-Cope	24 Feb	08	
32:24	Hayley Haining	27 Jul	08	
32:27	Ruth Partridge	11 Mar	89	
32:28	Freya Ross	6 Sep	09	
32:30	Stephanie Twell	16 Nov	14	
32:31	Heather Knight	6 Nov	94	
32:31	Hayley Yelling	5 Feb	06	
32:31	Caryl Jones	9 Sep	12	
32:31	Laura Weightman	31 Dec	17	
32:33	Lauren Howarth	22 Apr	11	30
32:35	Suzanne Rigg	15 Aug	92	
32:35	Elinor Kirk	11 Dec	16	

intermediate times

31:40 +	Mara Yamauchi	8 Jul	07
32:03 +	Freya Ross	24 Oct	10
32:26 +	Stephanie Twell	24 Oct	10

course measurement uncertain

31:43	Zola Budd	6 May	84
31:58	Sandra Branney	10 May	89
32:03	Paula Fudge	29 Aug	82
32:29	Yvonne Danson	13 Nov	94

10 Miles Road

51:11	Paula Radcliffe	26 Oct	08
51:41	Jill Hunter	20 Apr	91
51:51	Angie Hulley	18 Nov	89
51:57	Hunter	7 Apr	91
52:00	Liz McColgan	5 Oct	97
52:15	Marian Sutton	5 Oct	97
52:27	Freya Ross	24 Oct	10
52:42	Gemma Steel	26 Oct	14
52:44	Jo Pavey	25 Oct	15
52:53	Jessica Coulson	16 Oct	11
53:03	Hayley Yelling	9 Oct	05

intermediate times

50:01 +	Paula Radcliffe	21	Sep	03
52:00 +e	Gemma Steel	7	Sep	14
52:20 +	Jo Pavey	5	Oct	08
52:30 +	Liz Yelling	25	Mar	07
52:45 +	Mara Yamauchi	21	Mar	10

Half Marathon

	65:40	Paula Radcliffe	21	Sep	03
	66:47	Radcliffe	7	Oct	01
	67:07	Radcliffe	22	Oct	00
	67:11	Liz McColgan	26	Jan	92
	67:35	Radcliffe	4	Oct	03
	68:13	Gemma Steel	7	Sep	14
	68:29	Mara Yamauchi	1	Feb	09
	68:53	Jo Pavey	5	Oct	08
	69:28	Liz Yelling	25	Mar	07
	69:39	Andrea Wallace	21	Mar	93
	69:41	Marian Sutton	14	Sep	97
	69:56	Susan Tooby	24	Jul	88
10	70:32	Susan Partridge	3	Mar	13
	70:32	Lily Partridge	22	Mar	15
	70:38	Alyson Dixon	29	Mar	14
	70.47	Louise Damen	25	Mar	07
	70:53	Hayley Haining	5	Oct	08
	70:54	Alison Wyeth	29	Mar	98
	70:57	Helen Clitheroe	18	Sep	11
	71:05	Kathy Butler	17	Sep	06
	71:17	Véronique Marot	21	Jun	87
	71:18	Caryl Jones	16	Sep	12
20	71:29	Charlotte Purdue	23	Dec	17
	71:33	Vikki McPherson	14	Sep	97
	71:36	Ann Ford	30	Jun	85
	71:36	Jessica Coulson	4	Oct	15
	71:37	Paula Fudge	24	Jul	88
	71:38	Sally Ellis	20	Mar	88
	71:44	Jill Harrison	29	Mar	87
	71:44	Lorna Irving	6	Sep	87
	71:47	Charlotte Dale	26	Sep	04
	71:50	Hannah Walker	30	Sep	12

intermediate times

71:44 +	Sally-Ann Hales	21	Apr	85

course measurement uncertain

71:44	Karen Macleod	15	Jan	95

Marathon

2:15:25	Paula Radcliffe	13	Apr	03
2:17:18	Radcliffe	13	Oct	02
2:17:42	Radcliffe	17	Apr	05
2:18:56	Radcliffe	14	Apr	02
2:20:57	Radcliffe	14	Aug	05
2:23:09	Radcliffe	4	Nov	07
2:23:10	Radcliffe	7	Nov	04
2:23:12	Mara Yamauchi	26	Apr	09
2:23:46	Radcliffe	25	Sep	11
2:23:56	Radcliffe	2	Nov	08
2:25:56	Véronique Marot	23	Apr	89
2:26:51	Priscilla Welch	10	May	87
2:26:52	Liz McColgan	13	Apr	97

2:27:44		Claire Hallissey	22	Apr	12
2:28:04		Sonia Samuels	27	Sep	15
2:28:06		Sarah Rowell	21	Apr	85
2:28:10		Freya Ross	22	Apr	12
2:28:24		Jo Pavey	17	Apr	11
2:28:33		Liz Yelling	13	Apr	08
2:28:38		Sally-Ann Hales	21	Apr	85
2:28:39		Kathy Butler	22	Oct	06
2:28:42		Marian Sutton	24	Oct	99
2:29:06		Alyson Dixon	23	Apr	17
2:29:18		Hayley Haining	13	Apr	08
2:29:23		Charlotte Purdue	23	Apr	17
2:29:29	dh	Sally Eastall	8	Dec	91
2:29:43		Joyce Smith	9	May	82
2:29:47		Paula Fudge	30	Oct	88
2:30:00		Louise Damen	17	Apr	11
2:30:38		Ann Ford	17	Apr	88
2:30:42		Tracy Barlow	23	Apr	17
2:30:46		Susan Partridge	21	Apr	13
2:30:51		Angie Hulley	23	Sep	88
2:30:53	dh	Yvonne Danson	17	Apr	95
2:31:33		Susan Tooby	23	Sep	88
2:31:33		Andrea Wallace	12	Apr	92
2:31:45		Lynn Harding	23	Apr	89
2:32:10		Lily Partridge	19	Feb	17
2:32:40		Emma Stepto	26	Oct	14
2:32:53		Gillian Castka	2	Dec	84
2:33:04		Sheila Catford	23	Apr	89
2:33:07		Nicky McCracken	22	Apr	90
2:33:13		Tracey Morris	19	Mar	06
2:33:16		Karen Macleod	27	Aug	94
2:33:22		Carolyn Naisby	6	Dec	87
2:33:24		Sally Ellis	23	Apr	89
2:33:38		Lynda Bain	21	Apr	85
2:33:41		Sue Reinsford	16	Apr	00
2:33:44		Amy Whitehead	22	Apr	12
2:33:56		Tish Jones	23	Apr	17
2:34:11		Sally Goldsmith	3	Mar	96
2:34:11		Helen Davies	22	Apr	12
2:34:17		Jo Lodge	29	Sep	02
2:34:19		Jill Harrison	23	Apr	89
2:34:21		Suzanne Rigg	24	Sep	95
2:34:26		Heather MacDuff	16	Oct	88
2:34:43		Beth Allott	2	Dec	01
2:34:45		Birhan Dagne	18	Apr	04
2:35:03		Sandra Branney	23	Apr	89

2000 Metres Steeplechase

6:21.31	Lennie Waite	1	Jun	17
6:26.08	Louise Webb	16	Apr	16
6:26.79	Racheal Bamford	25	Aug	15
6:28.07	Tara Krzywicki	26	Jul	03
6:29.53	Rosie Clarke	19	Mar	16
6:29.58	Emma Raven	16	May	10
6:30.8	Hattie Dean	12	May	07
6:32.55	Sarah Hopkinson	14	Jul	07
6:34.12	Charlotte Taylor-Green	6	May	17
6:35.07	Emily Moyes	1	May	17
6:35.50	Claire Entwistle	30	May	05
6:35.50	Charlotte Green	9	Aug	15

3000 Metres Steeplechase (s short water jump)

	Time	Name	Date		
	9:24.24	Barbara Parker	2	Jun	12
	9:29.14	Helen Clitheroe	15	Aug	08
	9:29.22	Parker	14	Jul	12
	9:30.19	Hatti Dean	30	Jul	10
	9:32.07	Parker	4	Aug	12
	9:32.10	Rosie Clarke	29	Aug	17
	9:34.66	Parker	25	Jul	09
	9:35.17	Parker	3	Jul	10
	9:35.82	Eilish McColgan	10	Aug	13
	9:35.91	Lennie Waite	12	Jun	16
	9:39.03	Iona Lake	29	Aug	17
	9:43.88	Jo Ankier	31	May	08
	9:45.51	Racheal Bamford	30	Jul	14
10	9:47.97	Pippa Woolven	30	Jul	14
	9:48.08	Tina Brown	14	Aug	10
	9:48.51	Lizzie Hall	10	Jun	06
	9:51.42	Emily Stewart	27	Jul	13
	9:52.71 s	Tara Krzywicki	1	Jul	01
	9:54.76	Elizabeth Bird	29	May	15
	9:57.18	Louise Webb	26	Jun	16
	9:58.85	Charlotte Taylor-Green	14	Jun	17
	9:59.86	Aimee Pratt	14	Jun	17
	10:00.25	Claire Entwistle	13	Jun	08
20	10:00.74	Sarah Benson	18	Apr	14
	10:02.34	Katie Ingle	2	Jul	17
	10:05.92	Emma Raven	21	Jul	10
	10:06.12	Emily Pidgeon	3	Jul	05
	10:09.14	Ruth Senior	1	May	10

100 Metres Hurdles

	Time	Name	Date		
	12.51	Tiffany Porter	14	Sep	14
	12.54	Jessica Ennis	3	Aug	12
	12.55	Porter	17	Aug	13
	12.56	Porter	3	Sep	11
	12.56	Porter	18	Apr	15
	12.60	Porter	22	Jul	11
	12.60	Cindy Ofili	13	Jun	15
	12.62	Porter	28	Aug	15
	12.63	Porter	3	Sep	11
	12.63	Porter	17	Aug	13
	12.63	Porter	12	Aug	14
	12.63	Ofili	17	Aug	16
	12.80	Angie Thorp	31	Jul	96
	12.81	Sarah Claxton	17	Jul	08
	12.82	Sally Gunnell	17	Aug	88
	12.84	Lucy Hatton	18	Apr	15
	12.87	Shirley Strong	24	Aug	83
	12.87	Serita Solomon	7	Jul	15
10	12.90	Jacqui Agyepong	25	Jun	95
	12.91	Kay Morley-Brown	2	Feb	90
	12.92	Diane Allahgreen	29	Jul	02
	12.95	Keri Maddox	25	Aug	99
	12.96	Natasha Danvers	7	Jun	03
	13.02	Gemma Bennett	17	Jul	08
	13.03	Lesley-Ann Skeete	3	Aug	90
	13.04	Clova Court	9	Aug	94
	13.05	Judy Simpson	29	Aug	86
	13.07	Lorna Boothe	7	Oct	82
20	13.07	Rachel King	8	Jun	03
	13.07	Alicia Barrett	18	Jun	17
	13.08	Sam Farquharson	4	Jul	94
	13.08	Julie Pratt	29	Jul	02
	13.11	Sharon Danville	22	Jun	76
	13.12	Melani Wilkins	4	Jun	02
	13.13	Denise Lewis	29	Jul	00
	13.13	Yasmin Miller	27	Jul	14
	13.16	Wendy Jeal	27	Aug	86
	13.18	Kelly Sotherton	15	Aug	08
30	13.18	Angie Broadbelt-Blake	11	Jun	11
	13.20	Sara McGreavy	26	Jul	06
	13.21	Meghan Beesley	18	Jul	15
	13.24	Kim Hagger	31	Aug	87
	13.24	Louise Hazel	29	Aug	11
	13.24	Louise Wood	5	May	12
	13.26	Michelle Campbell	3	Aug	90
	13.28	Ashley Helsby	10	Jul	11
	13.28	Mollie Courtney	22	Jul	16
	13.29	Mary Peters	2	Sep	72
40	13.29	Katarina Johnson-Thompson	27	May	17
	13.32	Sam Baker	29	Aug	93
	13.34	Judy Vernon	7	Sep	73
	13.35	Pat Rollo	30	Jul	83
	13.36	Louise Fraser	17	Aug	91
	13.36	Holly Pattie-Belleli	15	May	16
	13.36	Karla Drew	22	May	16
	13.37	Gemma Werrett	20	Jul	08
	13.37	Zara Hohn	28	Jun	09
	13.42	Jessica Hunter	18	Jun	17
	13.43	Liz Fairs	30	May	04
50	13.44	Judith Robinson	1	Jul	89

wind assisted

Time	Name	Date		
12.47	Tiffany Porter	21	Apr	12
12.61	Porter	21	Apr	12
12.62	Porter	23	Jun	13
12.78	Shirley Strong	8	Oct	82
12.80	Sally Gunnell	29	Jul	88
12.84 A	Kay Morley-Brown	8	Aug	90
12.90	Lorna Boothe	8	Oct	82
13.01	Lesley-Ann Skeete	1	Feb	90
13.06	Sharon Danville	14	Jul	84
13.07	Angie Broadbelt-Blake	16	Apr	11
13.08	Michelle Campbell	26	May	95
13.08	Melani Wilkins	1	Jul	01
13.12	Pat Rollo	27	May	84
13.13	Ashley Helsby	3	Jul	11
13.20	Louise Hazel	3	Jun	06
13.22	Heather Ross	27	May	84
13.25	Zara Hohn	10	Jul	10
13.27	Holly Pattie-Belleli	14	May	16
13.31	Sophie Yorke	11	Jun	17
13.32	Gemma Werrett	22	Jun	08
13.32	Karla Drew	12	Apr	14

hand timing

Time	Name	Date		
13.0	Judy Vernon	29	Jun	74
13.0	Blondelle Caines	29	Jun	74
13.1	Melanie Wilkins	2	Jul	95
13.2	Pat Rollo	11	Jun	83

74

hand timing - wind assisted

12.7	Kay Morley-Brown	10 Jan 90
12.8	Natasha Danvers	3 Apr 99
12.9	Judy Vernon	18 May 74
13.1	Mary Peters	19 Aug 72
13.2	Ann Simmonds	19 Aug 72
13.2	Liz Sutherland	8 May 76

400 Metres Hurdles

52.74	Sally Gunnell	19 Aug 93
53.16	Gunnell	29 Aug 91
53.23	Gunnell	5 Aug 92
53.33	Gunnell	12 Aug 94
53.51	Gunnell	24 Jul 94
53.52	Gunnell	4 Aug 93
53.62	Gunnell	7 Aug 91
53.67	Perri Shakes-Drayton	26 Jul 13
53.73	Gunnell	26 Jun 93
53.77	Shakes-Drayton	13 Jul 12
53.84	Natasha Danvers	20 Aug 08
54.09	Eilidh Doyle	15 Jul 16
54.52	Meghan Beesley	23 Aug 15
54.63	Gowry Retchakan	3 Aug 92
55.22	Keri Maddox	12 Aug 00
55.24	Sinead Dudgeon	24 Jul 99
55.25	Lee McConnell	23 Mar 06
55.32	Nicola Sanders	23 Mar 06	[10]
55.70	Emma Duck	28 Jul 06
55.91	Elaine McLaughlin	26 Sep 88
56.04	Sue Chick	10 Aug 83
56.05	Wendy Cearns	13 Aug 89
56.05	Shona Richards	12 Jul 15
56.06	Christine Warden	28 Jul 79
56.08	Jessica Turner	16 Jul 17
56.15	Jacqui Parker	27 Jul 91
56.26	Louise Fraser	7 Jun 92
56.42	Vicki Jamison	20 Jun 98	[20]
56.42	Sian Scott	18 Aug 05
56.43	Alyson Layzell	16 Jun 96
56.43	Hayley McLean	29 Jun 14
56.46	Yvette Wray-Luker	11 Jul 81
56.53	Tracey Duncan	16 Jun 02
56.59	Caryl Granville	22 Jul 17
56.61	Louise Brunning	16 Jun 96
56.65	Liz Fairs	18 Jun 05
56.67	Ese Okoro	11 Jun 14
56.69	Shante Little	11 Apr 15	[30]
56.70	Lorraine Hanson	13 Aug 89
56.72	Gladys Taylor	6 Aug 84
57.00	Simone Gandy	6 Aug 88
57.07	Verona Elder	15 Jul 83
57.13	Nusrat Ceesay	11 Jul 09
57.17	Laura Wake	29 May 14
57.26	Aisha Naibe-Wey	25 May 15
57.29	Katie Jones	3 Jul 05
57.31	Kirsten McAslan	30 Jul 17
57.38	Sarah Dean	27 Jul 91	[40]
57.41	Jennie Mathews	6 Aug 88
57.43	Liz Sutherland	6 Jul 78
57.49	Maureen Prendergast	16 Jun 84
57.50	Hannah Douglas	11 Jul 09
57.51	Justine Kinney	6 Jun 09
57.52	Clare Sugden	3 Jun 90
57.52	Abigayle Fitzpatrick	14 Jul 13
57.55	Sharon Danville	8 May 81
57.70	Bethany Close	26 Jun 16
57.76	Aileen Mills	5 Aug 86	[50]
57.79	Susan Cluney	15 Jun 80

hand timing

57.5	Vicky Lee	28 Jun 86

High Jump

1.98	Katarina Johnson-Thompson	12 Aug 16
1.97 i	Johnson-Thompson	14 Feb 15
1.97	Isobel Pooley	4 Jul 15
1.96 i	Johnson-Thompson	8 Feb 14
1.96	Pooley	24 Aug 14
1.96	Morgan Lake	1 Jul 17
1.95	Diana Davies	26 Jun 82
1.95 i	Debbi Marti	23 Feb 97
1.94		9 Jun 96
1.95	Susan Jones	24 Jun 01
1.95	Jessica Ennis	5 May 07
1.95 i	Johnson-Thompson	6 Mar 15
1.95	Johnson-Thompson	22 Jul 16
1.95	Johnson-Thompson	27 May 17
1.95	Lake	12 Aug 17
1.94	Louise Gittens	25 May 80
1.94 i	Jo Jennings	13 Mar 93
1.91		20 Sep 98
1.93	Michelle Dunkley	2 Sep 00	[10]
1.92	Barbara Simmonds	31 Jul 82
1.92	Judy Simpson	8 Aug 83
1.92	Janet Boyle	29 Sep 88
1.92 i	Julia Bennett	10 Mar 90
1.89		11 Jun 94
1.92	Lea Haggett	15 Jun 96
1.92 i	Vicki Hubbard	21 Feb 10
1.88		7 Jul 06
1.91	Ann-Marie Cording	19 Sep 81
1.91	Gillian Evans	30 Apr 83
1.91	Jayne Barnetson	7 Jul 89
1.90	Kim Hagger	17 May 86	[20]
1.90	Sharon Hutchings	1 Aug 86
1.90 i	Julie Crane	28 Feb 04
1.89		15 Aug 04
1.90	Stephanie Pywell	20 May 07
1.89 i	Emma Perkins	11 Feb 12
1.89 i	Abby Ward	7 Feb 16
1.86		22 May 16
1.89	Niamh Emerson	22 May 16
1.89 i	Bethan Partridge	11 Feb 17
1.87		12 Jul 15
1.88 i	Debbie McDowell	17 Jan 88
1.88 i	Kerry Roberts	16 Feb 92
1.86		6 Jun 92
1.88 i	Kelly Thirkle	16 Feb 92	[30]
1.88	Lee McConnell	19 Aug 00
1.88	Rebecca Jones	1 Jun 02
1.88	Natalie Clark	6 Jun 04
1.88 i	Kelly Sotherton	2 Mar 07
1.87		7 Jul 07

75

1.88 i	Emma Nuttall	8	Mar	14
1.87		13	Jul	13
1.87	Barbara Lawton	22	Sep	73
1.87	Moira Maguire	11	May	80
1.87	Louise Manning	6	May	84
1.87	Rachael Forrest	7	Jul	95
40 1.87	Denise Lewis	21	Aug	99
1.87	Aileen Wilson	15	Jul	01
1.87 i	Jayne Nisbet	8	Feb	14
1.86		10	Jul	11
1.86	Claire Summerfield	7	Aug	82
1.86	Jennifer Farrell	11	May	86
1.86	Catherine Scott	8	May	87
1.86	Michele Marsella	31	May	87
1.86 i	Dalia Mikneviciute	16	Jan	00
1.86		4	Jun	00
1.86	Jessica Leach	21	Jun	09
1.86 i	Kay Humberstone	31	Jan	10
50 1.86	Nikki Manson	30	Jul	17

Pole Vault

4.87 i	Holly Bleasdale	21	Jan	12
4.81		15	Jul	17
4.80	Bleasdale	26	May	17
4.77 i	Bleasdale	9	Feb	13
4.76 i	Bleasdale	31	Aug	16
4.75 i	Bleasdale	3	Feb	13
4.73 i	Bleasdale	8	Feb	14
4.72 i	Bleasdale	23	Feb	12
4.71	Bleasdale	24	Jun	12
4.71 i	Bleasdale	10	Dec	11
4.71 i	Bleasdale	31	Jan	14
4.71 i	Bleasdale	15	Feb	14
4.61	Kate Dennison	22	Jul	11
4.52 i	Katie Byres	18	Feb	12
4.36		17	Jun	12
4.47	Janine Whitlock ¶	22	Jul	05
4.42 i	Sally Peake	18	Feb	12
4.40		12	Jul	14
4.40	Lucy Bryan	29	Jun	13
4.36 i	Jade Ive	19	Feb	17
4.20		16	Jul	17
4.35	Henrietta Paxton	26	Jun	10
4.35	Molly Caudrey	22	Jul	17
10 4.31 i	Emma Lyons	21	Feb	09
4.25		7	Aug	10
4.26 i	Zoe Brown	21	Feb	04
4.20		17	Jul	05
4.26 i	Ellie Spain	30	Jan	07
4.21		16	Jul	06
4.21	Louise Butterworth	6	Jun	08
4.20	Irie Hill	6	Aug	00
4.20 i	Rhian Clarke	10	Mar	01
4.15		7	Apr	00
4.20	Sally Scott	19	Jun	10
4.16	Liz Hughes	6	Jul	02
4.16	Bryony Raine	9	Jul	11
4.15	Tracey Grant	26	Jul	03
20 4.15 i	Kirsty Maguire	24	Feb	07
4.05		10	Jun	00
4.15	Sian Morgan	22	May	15

4.13 i	Maria Seager	2	Feb	10	
4.05		13	Jun	09	
4.13	Rachel Gibbens	7	Feb	16	
4.05		29	Aug	15	
4.10	Fiona Harrison	29	Jul	07	
4.10	Sophie Upton	9	Jun	10	
4.08	Abigail Roberts	29	Aug	15	
4.06	Claire Maurer	10	Aug	17	
4.05	Sonia Lawrence	19	Jul	03	
4.05	Caroline Adams	10	Aug	13	
4.05 i	Olivia Curran	19	Jul	14	30
4.05	Jessica Robinson	11	Jun	16	
4.04	Lucy Webber	15	Jul	00	
4.02 i	Kim Skinner	30	Dec	09	
4.02 i	Jessica Abraham	15	Jan	11	
4.00		3	Jul	10	
4.02	Sophie Cook	5	Jul	14	
4.02 i	Courtney MacGuire	31	Jan	15	
4.00		15	Jul	14	
4.00	Alison Davies	12	Aug	00	
4.00	Abigail Haywood	26	Jun	11	
4.00	Katie James	15	Jul	14	
4.00 i	Anna Gordon	27	Feb	16	40
4.00	Jessica Swannack	8	Jul	17	
4.00	Clare Blunt	16	Jul	17	
3.95 A	Allie Jessee	25	Jun	99	
3.95 i	Jennifer Graham	21	May	06	
3.95		29	Jul	07	
3.95 i	Sarah McKeever	28	May	16	
3.91	Emma Hornby	27	Jun	98	
3.91	Emily Taylor	23	Jul	11	
3.91 i	Sophie Dowson	28	Jan	17	

Long Jump

7.07	Shara Proctor	28	Aug	15	
6.98	Proctor	25	Jul	15	
6.97 i	Lorraine Ugen	5	Mar	17	
6.95	Proctor	24	Jun	12	
6.95	Proctor	15	May	15	
6.93 i	Katarina Johnson-Thompson	21	Feb	15	
6.93 i	Ugen	18	Mar	16	
6.92	Proctor	4	Jul	13	
6.92	Johnson-Thompson	11	Jul	14	
6.92	Ugen	15	May	15	
6.90	Bev Kinch	14	Aug	83	
6.88	Fiona May	18	Jul	90	
6.83	Sue Hearnshaw	6	May	84	
6.81	Jade Johnson	22	Jun	08	
6.80	Abigail Irozuru	9	Jun	12	
6.79	Kelly Sotherton	25	Jul	08	
6.76	Mary Rand	14	Oct	64	10
6.76	Jo Wise	2	Aug	99	
6.75	Joyce Hepher	14	Sep	85	
6.75	Jazmin Sawyers	26	Jun	16	
6.73	Sheila Sherwood	23	Jul	70	
6.73	Yinka Idowu	7	Aug	93	
6.70	Kim Hagger	30	Aug	86	
6.69	Sue Reeve	10	Jun	79	
6.69	Denise Lewis	30	Jul	00	
6.63	Mary Agyepong	17	Jun	89	
6.63	Jessica Ennis-Hill	26	Jun	16	20

6.56	Sarah Claxton	23	May	99
6.55	Ann Simmonds	22	Jul	70
6.54	Dominique Blaize	19	May	13
6.54	Rebecca Chapman	2	Jul	17
6.52	Gill Regan	29	Aug	82
6.52	Georgina Oladapo	16	Jun	84
6.51 i	Ruth Howell	23	Feb	74
6.49		16	Jun	72
6.51	Julie Hollman	3	Sep	00
6.47 A	Ashia Hansen	26	Jan	96
30 6.47 i	Amy Harris	11	Feb	07
6.43		20	Apr	12
6.47	Phyllis Agbo	31	May	09
6.47	Jade Nimmo	14	Apr	12
6.45	Carol Zeniou	12	May	82
6.45	Margaret Cheetham	18	Aug	84
6.44	Sharon Danville	15	Jun	77
6.44	Barbara Clarke	13	Sep	81
6.44	Louise Hazel	9	Oct	10
6.43	Myra Nimmo	27	May	73
6.43 i	Gillian Cooke	3	Feb	08
6.39		13	May	07
40 6.42	Sarah Warnock	29	Jun	14
6.40	Judy Simpson	26	Aug	84
6.40	Sharon Bowie	28	Jun	86
6.40 i	Amy Woodman	14	Feb	09
6.37		31	May	09
6.39	Moira Maguire	22	Jul	70
6.39	Maureen Chitty	28	Jun	72
6.39	Sue Longden	12	Sep	76
6.39	Tracy Joseph	27	Jun	98
6.39 i	Jahisha Thomas	10	Feb	17
6.38	Ann Danson	16	Jun	02
50 6.37	Kelly Wenlock	24	Apr	82

wind unconfirmed

6.43	Moira Maguire	18	Sep	70

wind assisted

7.00	Sue Hearnshaw	27	May	84
6.98	Fiona May	4	Jun	89
6.96	Lorraine Ugen	28	Mar	15
6.93	Bev Kinch	14	Aug	83
6.86	Jazmin Sawyers	8	Jul	16
6.84	Sue Reeve	25	Jun	77
6.80	Joyce Hepher	22	Jun	85
6.77	Denise Lewis	1	Jun	97
6.65	Mary Agyepong	4	Jun	89
6.57	Ann Simmonds	22	Aug	70
6.56	Judy Simpson	30	Aug	86
6.56	Dominique Blaize	27	May	13
6.54	Ruth Howell	16	Jun	72
6.54	Myra Nimmo	19	Jun	76
6.49	Margaret Cheetham	4	Sep	83
6.48	Moira Maguire	17	May	70
6.48	Amy Harris	3	Jul	11
6.45	Donita Benjamin	23	Jul	00
6.44	Tracy Joseph	21	Jun	97
6.41	Allison Manley	28	Jul	79
6.41	Amy Woodman	12	Jun	11
6.40	Barbara-Anne Barrett	17	Jul	71
6.40	Gillian Cooke	12	Mar	06

Triple Jump

15.16 i	Ashia Hansen	28	Feb	98	
15.15		13	Sep	97	
15.02 i	Hansen	7	Mar	99	
15.01 i	Hansen	15	Mar	03	
14.96	Hansen	11	Sep	99	
14.94	Hansen	29	Jun	97	
14.86	Hansen	31	Jul	02	
14.85 i	Hansen	15	Feb	98	
14.82 i	Yamilé Aldama	10	Mar	12	
14.65		31	May	12	
14.81 i	Hansen	21	Feb	99	
14.09	Laura Samuel	29	Jul	14	
14.08	Michelle Griffith	11	Jun	94	
13.95	Connie Henry	27	Jun	98	
13.85 A	Yasmine Regis	18	May	08	
13.76		5	Aug	11	
13.82	Shara Proctor	14	Apr	17	
13.77	Nadia Williams	12	Jun	11	
13.70	Sineade Gutzmore	20	Jul	16	
13.64	Rachel Kirby	7	Aug	94	10
13.64	Naomi Ogbeta	1	Jul	17	
13.62	Nony Mordi	5	Jul	08	
13.56	Mary Agyepong	5	Jun	92	
13.53	Chioma Matthews	17	May	15	
13.46	Evette Finikin	26	Jul	91	
13.44	Hannah Frankson	26	Jun	11	
13.43	Angela Barrett	16	Aug	17	
13.31	Karlene Turner	28	May	06	
13.30	Shakira Whight	24	Jun	12	
13.27	Zainab Ceesay	5	Jul	08	20
13.27 i	Alex Russell	12	Feb	17	
13.05		4	Jul	15	
13.25	Gillian Kerr	30	Jun	07	
13.25	Jahisha Thomas	1	Jul	17	
13.24	Stephanie Aneto	18	Jul	10	
13.23 i	Rebecca White	27	Jan	06	
13.17		27	Jul	07	
13.11	Jade Johnson	19	Aug	01	
13.09	Debbie Rowe	26	Aug	06	
13.08	Denae Matthew	30	Jun	07	
13.03	Shani Anderson	4	May	96	
13.03	Kate Evans	26	Apr	97	30
13.03	Lisa James	21	Jun	15	
13.03	Naomi Reed	31	Jun	16	
13.03	Emily Gargan	21	May	17	
13.02 i	Emily Parker	12	Feb	05	
12.97		3	May	04	
13.01	Jayne Nisbet	22	Apr	07	
13.01	Emma Pringle	26	May	13	
13.00 i	Zara Asante	15	Feb	15	
12.99		15	Jun	13	
12.98	Danielle Freeman	13	Jul	02	
12.97	Claire Linskill	20	Jun	09	
12.96	Laura Zialor	28	May	16	40
12.96 i	Simi Fajemisin	26	Feb	17	
12.96		27	May	17	
12.94	Lorna Turner	9	Jul	94	
12.92	Liz Patrick	5	Aug	00	
12.90 i	Leandra Polius	12	Feb	05	

12.89	Karen Skeggs	17	May	92
12.89	Kelly Hilton	17	Jul	11
12.88	Ahtollah Rose	1	Jul	11
12.87	Shanara Hibbert	15	Apr	17
12.86 i	Sandra Alaneme	9	Feb	08
50 12.84	Anna-Maria Thorpe	23	May	99

wind assisted

15.00	Hansen	10	Aug	02
14.14	Michelle Griffith	25	Jul	00
13.94	Nadia Williams	17	Jul	11
13.82	Yasmine Regis	13	Jun	09
13.76	Nony Mordi	10	May	08
13.68	Naomi Ogbeta	21	Jul	17
13.51	Rebecca White	3	Sep	05
13.42	Gillian Kerr	30	Jun	07
13.40	Alex Russell	31	Jul	16
13.35	Katarina Johnson-Thompson	6	Jul	14
13.22	Lisa James	21	Jun	15
13.14	Debbie Rowe	22	Jul	00
13.06	Alison McAllister	11	Jul	03
13.04	Kate Evans	23	Jul	00
12.93	Karen Skeggs	13	Jun	92

Shot

19.36	Judy Oakes	14	Aug	88
19.33	Oakes	3	Sep	88
19.26	Oakes	29	Jul	88
19.13	Oakes	20	Aug	88
19.06 i	Venissa Head	7	Apr	84
18.93		13	May	84
19.05	Oakes	16	Jul	88
19.03	Myrtle Augee	2	Jun	90
19.01	Oakes	17	Sep	88
19.01	Oakes	11	Jun	89
19.01	Oakes	11	May	96
18.99	Meg Ritchie	7	May	83
17.53	Angela Littlewood	24	Jul	80
17.53	Rachel Wallader	4	Jun	16
17.45	Yvonne Hanson-Nortey	28	Jul	89
17.24	Eden Francis	20	May	12
17.14	Sophie McKinna	9	Jul	16
10 17.13	Jo Duncan	13	Aug	06
17.13	Amelia Strickler	27	Aug	17
16.76	Rebecca Peake	15	Aug	10
16.64	Divine Oladipo	22	Apr	17
16.63	Eva Massey	29	Jul	07
16.57	Maggie Lynes	20	Jul	94
16.42	Kirsty Yates	30	Jul	14
16.40 i	Mary Peters	28	Feb	70
16.31		1	Jun	66
16.40	Julie Dunkley	12	Aug	00
16.39	Shanaugh Brown	19	May	13
20 16.34	Adele Nicoll	2	Jul	16
16.29	Brenda Bedford	26	May	76
16.17	Eleanor Gatrell	18	Jul	10
16.12	Denise Lewis	21	Aug	99
16.09 i	Alison Rodger	21	Feb	10
15.88		28	Jun	08
16.05	Janis Kerr	15	May	76
15.95 i	Philippa Roles	6	Feb	99
15.62		1	Jun	03

15.88 i	Ade Oshinowo	7	Feb	04
15.78		11	Jul	04
15.85 i	Alison Grey	12	Feb	94
15.69		11	Jun	94
15.81	Tracy Axten	19	Jul	98
15.80	Sharon Andrews	30	Jul	93 30
15.75 i	Caroline Savory	23	Feb	83
15.50		19	Jun	83
15.60 i	Justine Buttle	27	Feb	88
15.45		25	Aug	88
15.55	Christina Bennett	13	Jun	99
15.48	Mary Anderson	8	Sep	85
15.46	Vanessa Redford	14	Jun	80
15.45	Susan King	27	Mar	83
15.44	Vickie Foster	14	May	00
15.41	Fatima Whitbread	29	Apr	84
15.32 i	Helen Hounsell	13	Feb	82
15.28	Amy Hill	31	May	09 40
15.23	Judy Simpson	18	Jun	88
15.21	Uju Efobi	23	Apr	94
15.21 i	Kara Nwidobie	12	Feb	06
15.18	Suzanne Allday	18	May	64
15.18 i	Lana Newton		Jan	79
15.09		6	Sep	78
15.09	Jayne Berry	22	Jul	93
15.09	Nicola Gautier	1	Jul	00
15.08	Janet Kane	3	Jun	79
15.08	Susan Tudor	30	May	82
14.98 i	Sandra Smith	21	Dec	85 50
14.95		18	Aug	85

Discus

67.48	Meg Ritchie	26	Apr	81
67.44	Ritchie	14	Jul	83
66.04	Ritchie	15	May	82
65.96	Ritchie	19	Jul	80
65.78	Ritchie	17	Jul	81
65.34	Ritchie	24	Apr	83
65.18	Ritchie	17	May	81
65.10	Jade Lally	27	Feb	16
65.08	Ritchie	26	Apr	80
65.02	Ritchie	5	May	84
64.68	Venissa Head	18	Jul	83
62.89	Philippa Roles	8	Jun	03
61.22	Shelley Newman	8	Jun	03
60.72	Jackie McKernan	18	Jul	93
59.78	Eden Francis	6	Aug	11
58.56	Debbie Callaway	19	May	96
58.18	Tracy Axten	31	May	97
58.02	Rosemary Payne	3	Jun	72 10
57.79	Kirsty Law	26	Aug	12
57.75	Emma Merry	9	Aug	99
57.32	Lynda Wright	16	Jun	84
57.27	Kara Nwidobie	18	Jun	05
57.26	Emma Carpenter	12	Jul	08
56.73	Claire Smithson	29	Jul	06
56.25	Rebecca Roles	6	Jun	04
56.24	Sharon Andrews	12	Jun	94
56.06	Kathryn Farr	27	Jun	87
55.52	Jane Aucott	17	Jan	90 20
55.42	Lesley Bryant	12	Sep	80

	Mark	Name	Date		Mark	Name	Date
	55.06	Janet Kane	17 Jun 78		61.77	Kimberley Reed	3 May 14
	55.04	Lorraine Shaw	14 May 94		61.48	Suzanne Roberts	17 Jul 04
	54.72	Karen Pugh	27 Jul 86		60.88	Rachael Beverley	23 May 99
	54.68	Emma Beales	10 Jun 95		60.75	Abbi Carter	12 Jul 12
	54.46	Ellen Mulvihill	14 May 86		59.76	Phillipa Wingate	2 Jul 17
	54.46	Janette Picton	17 Aug 90		59.57	Hayley Murray	18 Jul 17
	54.27	Amy Holder	29 May 17		59.38	Kayleigh Presswell	7 Oct 17
	54.24	Nicola Talbot	15 May 93		59.14	Amy Herrington	21 Apr 17
30	53.96	Julia Avis	27 Apr 86		58.97	Diana Holden	4 Jun 02
	53.66	Rosanne Lister	22 Jun 91		58.94	Annabelle Palmer	11 Sep 16 30
	53.44	Judy Oakes	20 Aug 88		58.59	Rebecca Keating	25 May 17
	53.44	Navdeep Dhaliwal	5 Sep 10		58.48	Joanne John	2 Jul 08
	53.44	Shadine Duquemin	11 May 14		58.47	Mhairi Walters	12 May 02
	53.16	Sarah Winckless	18 Jun 94		58.27	Katie Lambert	21 May 17
	53.13	Divine Oladipo	26 May 17		57.96	Olivia Stevenson	10 Jun 17
	52.84	Sarah Henton	7 Jul 13		57.63	Nicola Dudman	16 Jun 02
	52.52	Alison Grey	18 Jun 94		57.43	Anna Purchase	30 Apr 17
	52.46	Vanessa Redford	4 Jul 82		57.40	Sarah Moore	29 Apr 01
40	52.31	Lauren Keightley	18 Jul 98		57.16	Hannah Evenden	7 Apr 12
	51.87	Phoebe Dowson	21 May 17		57.08	Monique Buchanan	28 Aug 06 40
	51.82	Catherine Bradley	20 Jul 85		56.78	Victoria Thomas	22 Jul 06
	51.77	Shaunagh Brown	1 Jun 14		56.76	Esther Augee	15 May 93
	51.60	Dorothy Chipchase	20 Jul 73		56.74	Rachel Blackie	17 Jun 06
	51.43	Claire Griss	30 May 05		56.69	Philippa Davenall	11 Jun 17
	51.18	Angela Sellars	12 Aug 90		56.67	Danielle Brown	10 Jun 17
	51.12	Joanne Brand	26 May 86		56.43	Amber Simpson	10 Jun 17
	51.07	Samantha Milner	19 May 13		56.40	Sara Bobash	8 May 16
	50.64	Kathryn Woodcock	6 May 17		56.23	Steph Hendy	18 May 14
50	50.57	Brenda Bedford	24 Aug 68		56.03	Alice Barnsdale	29 Jul 17
					55.81	Toni Wells	3 Mar 12 50

Hammer

	74.54	Sophie Hitchon	15 Aug 16
	73.97	Hitchon	21 May 17
	73.86	Hitchon	27 Aug 15
	73.68	Hitchon	27 Jun 17
	73.05	Hitchon	5 Aug 17
	72.97	Hitchon	23 Jun 13
	72.42	Hitchon	28 Aug 16
	72.32	Hitchon	7 Aug 17
	72.23	Hitchon	9 Aug 15
	72.02	Hitchon	15 Aug 17
	68.97	Sarah Holt	25 Jul 15
	68.93	Lorraine Shaw	8 Jun 03
	68.63	Zoe Derham	17 Jul 08
	67.58	Shirley Webb	16 Jul 05
	66.85	Shaunagh Brown	14 Jun 14
	66.80	Carys Parry	15 Jul 14
	66.46	Rachel Hunter	26 Feb 17
	65.03	Susan McKelvie	20 Aug 11
10	64.74	Laura Douglas	8 Aug 10
	63.98	Christina Jones	25 Apr 15
	63.96	Lyn Sprules	20 Aug 00
	63.61	Liz Pidgeon	27 May 00
	63.11	Myra Perkins	18 May 14
	63.05	Lesley Brannan	19 Feb 06
	63.05	Jessica Mayho	22 Apr 17
	62.96	Samantha Hynes	19 May 12
	62.74	Lucy Marshall	10 Jun 17
	62.66	Rachel Wilcockson	20 Aug 11
20	62.30	Louisa James	29 Jun 14

Javelin (1999 Model)

	Mark	Name	Date
	66.17	Goldie Sayers	14 Jul 12
	65.75	Sayers	21 Aug 08
	65.05	Sayers	20 May 07
	64.87	Kelly Morgan	14 Jul 02
	64.73	Sayers	31 May 12
	64.46	Sayers	18 Jun 11
	63.96	Sayers	6 Jun 08
	63.82	Sayers	26 Jul 08
	63.66	Sayers	12 Jun 08
	63.65	Sayers	15 Mar 08
	60.68	Laura Whittingham	15 Aug 10
	59.50	Karen Martin	14 Jul 99
	58.63	Izzy Jeffs	26 Apr 14
	57.48	Shelley Holroyd	10 Jul 04
	57.44	Jo Blair	26 Jun 16
	57.19	Lorna Jackson	9 Jul 00
	55.91	Kirsty Morrison	23 May 99
	55.36	Freya Jones	12 Apr 14 10
	54.71	Kike Oniwinde	14 Jun 14
	54.62	Chloe Cozens	3 Aug 03
	52.86	Linda Gray	10 Jun 01
	52.78	Tesni Ward	29 May 11
	52.76	Jenny Kemp	23 Jun 01
	52.68	Lianne Clarke	25 Aug 07
	52.41	Katy Watts	31 May 09
	52.34	Jade Dodd	2 Sep 07
	52.32	Eloise Meakins	9 Sep 12
	52.27	Emma Hamplett	14 May 16 20

	Mark	Name	Date	
	52.09	Lauren Therin	5 May 07	
	51.57	Hannah Johnson	21 May 17	
	51.48	Denise Lewis	10 Jul 04	
	51.13	Becky Bartlett	15 May 04	
	50.85	Sharon Gibson	18 Jul 99	
	50.43	Rosie Semenytsh	22 Jun 13	
	50.21	Louise Watton	10 Jun 07	
	50.19	Sam Cullinane	17 Jun 12	
	49.96	Hayley Thomas	19 Jun 11	
30	49.66	Jo Chapman	22 Aug 04	
	49.56	Bethan Rees	2 Jul 17	
	49.56	Kelly Bramhald	30 Jul 17	
	49.25	Nicola Gautier	1 Jul 01	
	49.24	Louise Lacy	30 Jul 17	
	49.23	Laura Kerr	20 Aug 05	
	49.17	Sarah Roberts	29 May 11	
	49.13	Laurensa Britane	16 Aug 17	
	48.73	Suzanne Finnis	23 Mar 03	
	48.39	Katie Amos	1 Jun 02	
40	48.35	Natasha Wilson	23 Apr 16	
	48.33	Jessica Ennis	23 Jul 13	
	48.31	Eloise Manger	4 Jul 09	
	48.24	Tammie Francis	29 Apr 00	
	48.18	Amber Burdett	19 Sep 10	
	48.13	Christine Lawrence	17 May 09	
	47.74	Joanne Bruce	7 Sep 02	
	47.73	Helen Mounteney	12 Jul 02	
	47.72	Alison Moffitt	21 Aug 99	
	47.66	Samantha Redd	29 Jun 02	
50	47.57	Amy Harvey	7 Oct 00	

Javelin (pre 1999)

77.44	Fatima Whitbread	28 Aug 86
76.64	Whitbread	6 Sep 87
76.34	Whitbread	4 Jul 87
76.32	Whitbread	29 Aug 86
75.62	Whitbread	25 May 87
74.74	Whitbread	26 Aug 87
73.58	Tessa Sanderson	26 Jun 83
73.32	Whitbread	20 Jun 87
62.32	Sharon Gibson	16 May 87
62.22	Diane Royle	18 May 85
60.12	Shelley Holroyd	16 Jun 96
60.00	Julie Abel	24 May 87
59.40	Karen Hough	28 Aug 86
59.36	Kirsty Morrison	4 Sep 93
58.60	Jeanette Rose	30 May 82
58.39	Lorna Jackson	6 Jun 98
57.90	Anna Heaver	1 Jul 87
57.84	Mandy Liverton	3 Jun 90
57.82	Karen Martin	19 Sep 98
56.96	Nicky Emblem	1 Feb 90
56.50	Caroline White	8 Jun 91
56.50	Denise Lewis	11 Aug 96

Heptathlon (1985 Tables)

6955	Jessica Ennis	4 Aug 12
6906	Ennis	27 May 12
6831	Denise Lewis	30 Jul 00
6823	Ennis	31 Jul 10
6790	Ennis	29 May 11
6775	Ennis	13 Aug 16

Mark	Name	Date	
6751	Ennis	30 Aug 11	
6736	Lewis	1 Jun 97	
6733	Ennis	26 Jun 16	
6731	Ennis	16 Aug 09	
6691	Katarina Johnson-Thompson	28 May 17	
6623	Judy Simpson	30 Aug 86	
6547	Kelly Sotherton	29 May 05	
6259	Kim Hagger	18 May 86	
6166 w	Louise Hazel	17 Jul 11	
6156		9 Oct 10	
6148	Morgan Lake	23 Jul 14	
6135	Julie Hollman	2 Jun 02	
6125	Tessa Sanderson	12 Jul 81	10
6094 h	Joanne Mulliner	7 Jun 87	
6022	Clova Court	27 Aug 91	
6013	Niamh Emerson	21 Jul 17	
6011 w	Fiona Harrison	18 Jul 04	
5754		3 Jul 05	
6005 w	Kerry Jury	24 May 98	
5908		1 Aug 99	
5952	Phyllis Agbo	31 May 09	
5913	Jess Taylor	15 May 16	
5873	Katie Stainton	18 Jun 17	
5826	Jenny Kelly	3 Jul 94	
5819	Grace Clements	9 Oct 10	20
5803	Jayne Barnetson	20 Aug 89	
5798	Ros Gonse	26 Aug 07	
5784	Nicola Gautier	1 Jul 01	
5776	Kathy Warren	12 Jul 81	
5770	Jessica Tappin	1 Jun 14	
5747 w	Julia Bennett	5 May 96	
5538		4 Jun 00	
5702	Yinka Idowu	21 May 95	
5702	Jo Rowland	2 Jun 13	
5700	Vikki Schofield	5 May 96	
5691 w	Pauline Richards	24 May 98	30
5563		5 Jul 98	
5687	Holly McArthur	21 Jul 17	
5671	Domique Blaize	6 Jun 10	
5644	Danielle Freeman	4 Jun 00	
5642	Sarah Rowe	23 Aug 81	
5633	Marcia Marriott	18 May 86	
5632	Emma Beales	1 Aug 93	
5618 w	Sarah Damm	5 May 96	
5605	Lucy Boggis	26 Jul 09	
5601 w	Jade Surman	3 Jun 07	
5538		19 Aug 06	
5594	Gillian Evans	22 May 83	40
5577	Katherine Livesey	18 May 02	
5557	Kate Cowley	20 Jul 03	
5556 w	Louise Wood	8 May 11	
5502		8 May 11	
5555 w	Diana Bennett	24 May 98	
5550		1 Jun 97	
5548	Val Walsh	18 May 86	
5535	Karla Drew	30 Jun 13	
5529	Catherine Holdsworth	27 Jul 08	
5495	Charmaine Johnson	24 May 92	
5493	Sally Gunnell	28 May 84	
5455	Claire Phythian	19 May 95	50

3000 Metres Track Walk

12:22.62 +	Jo Jackson	14	Feb	09	
12:24.70	Bethan Davies	11	Jun	16	
12:40.98	Jackson	26	May	08	
12:49.16	Betty Sworowski	28	Jul	90	
12:50.61	Lisa Kehler	29	Jul	00	
12:59.3	Vicky Lupton	13	May	95	
12:59.75	Gemma Bridge	12	Jun	17	
13:07.04	Heather Lewis	11	Jun	16	
13:08.64imx	Niobe Menendez	2	Feb	02	
13:14.73		11	Aug	01	
13:12.01 i	Julie Drake	12	Mar	93	

5000 Metres Track Walk

20:46.58	Jo Jackson	14	Feb	09	
21:01.24	Jackson	7	Feb	09	
21:21.52	Bethan Davies	2	Jul	17	
21:21.67	Jackson	12	Jul	09	
21:30.75	Jackson	13	Jul	08	
21:42.51	Lisa Kehler	13	Jul	02	
21:52.38	Vicky Lupton	9	Aug	95	
22:02.06	Betty Sworowski	28	Aug	89	
22:09.87	Heather Lewis	29	Jun	14	
22:37.47	Julie Drake	17	Jul	93	
22:41.19	Cal Partington	16	Jul	95	
22:51.23	Helen Elleker	25	Jun	90	
10 23:11.2	Carol Tyson	30	Jun	79	
23:11.7	Catherine Charnock	19	Jun	99	
23:15.04	Bev Allen	25	May	87	
23:19.2	Marion Fawkes	30	Jun	79	
23:20.00	Ginney Birch	25	May	85	
23:20.19	Erica Kelly	2	Jul	17	
23:22.52	Verity Snook	19	Jun	94	
23:34.43	Sylvia Black	5	Jul	92	
23:35.54	Nicky Jackson	25	May	87	
23:37.55	Sophie Lewis Ward	14	Jul	16	
20 23:38.3	Irene Bateman	28	Jun	81	
23:40.75	Ellie Dooley	29	Jun	14	
23:46.30	Niobe Menendez	14	Jul	01	

5k Road - where superior to track time

21:36	Vicky Lupton	18	Jul	92	
21:50	Betty Sworowski	6	May	90	
22:45 +	Verity Snook	25	Aug	94	
22:51	Marion Fawkes	29	Sep	79	
22:52 +	Gemma Bridge	25	Jun	17	
22:59	Carol Tyson	29	Sep	79	
23:00 +	Bev Allen	1	Sep	87	
23:00 +e	Heather Lewis	5	May	17	
23:09	Catherine Charnock	5	Jun	99	
23:13	Sylvia Black	13	Feb	93	
23:24	Melanie Wright	9	Apr	95	
23:25	Irene Bateman	29	Sep	79	

10000 Metres Track Walk

45:09.57	Lisa Kehler	13	Aug	00	
45:18.8	Vicky Lupton	2	Sep	95	
45:53.9	Julie Drake	26	May	90	
46:23.08	Betty Sworowski	4	Aug	91	
46:25.2	Helen Elleker	26	May	90	

47:05.97	Bethan Davies	5	Jan	17	
47:10.07	Verity Snook	19	Jun	93	
47:56.3	Ginney Birch	15	Jun	85	
47:58.3	Bev Allen	21	Jun	86	
48:11.4	Marion Fawkes	8	Jul	79	10
48:20.0	Cal Partington	7	May	94	
48:34.5	Carol Tyson	22	Aug	81	
48:35.8	Melanie Wright	2	Sep	95	
48:56.5	Sarah Brown	18	Apr	91	
48:57.6	Irene Bateman	20	Mar	82	
49:06.83	Heather Lewis	22	Jun	14	
49:27.0	Sylvia Black	22	Apr	95	
49:39.0	Karen Ratcliffe	22	May	91	
49:41.0	Elaine Callinan	22	Apr	95	
49:51.6	Sara-Jane Cattermole	7	Feb	01	20

track short

48:52.5	Irene Bateman	19	Mar	83

10k Road - where superior to track time

43:52	Jo Jackson	6	Mar	10	
44:59	Bethan Davies	6	Mar	16	
45:03	Lisa Kehler	19	Sep	98	
45:52 +	Gemma Bridge	25	Jun	17	
45:59	Betty Sworowski	24	Aug	91	
46:06	Verity Snook	25	Aug	94	
46:26	Cal Partington	1	Jul	95	
46:38	Niobe Menendez	15	Jun	02	
46:59	Heather Lewis	1	Mar	14	
47:05	Sara-Jane Cattermole	15	Jul	01	
47:49	Emma Achurch	15	Mar	15	
47:51	Catherine Charnock	5	Sep	99	
47:58	Nicky Jackson	27	Jun	87	

20 Kilometres Road Walk

1:30.41	Jo Jackson	19	Jun	10	
1:32:33	Gemma Bridge	25	Jun	17	
1:33:04	Bethan Davies	25	Jun	17	
1:33:57	Lisa Kehler	17	Jun	00	
1:36:40	Sara Cattermole	4	Mar	00	
1:37:39	Heather Lewis	19	Mar	17	
1:37:44	Vicky Lupton	27	Jun	99	
1:38:29	Catherine Charnock	11	Sep	99	
1:39:59	Niobe Menendez	21	Apr	02	
1:40:45	Irene Bateman	9	Apr	83	10
1:41:27	Erika Kelly	25	Jun	17	
1:42:02 hc	Lillian Millen	9	Apr	83	
1:44:42		2	Apr	83	
1:43:26	Emma Achurch	2	Oct	16	
1:43:29	Sharon Tonks	3	Mar	02	
1:43:50	Betty Sworowski	22	Feb	88	
1:43:52	Sylvia Black	14	Jun	97	
1:44:19	Katie Stones	25	Feb	06	
1:44:29	Kim Braznell	21	Mar	99	
1:44:30	Wendy Bennett	26	Apr	03	
1:44:54	Cal Partington	23	Mar	02	20

50 Kilometres Road Walk

4:50:51	Sandra Brown	13	Jul	91
5:01:52	Lillian Millen	16	Apr	83

4 x 100 Metres Relay

41.77 Great Britain & NI 19 Aug 16
Philip, Henry, Asher-Smith, Neita
41.81 Great Britain & NI 22 Jul 16
Philip, Henry, Asher-Smith, Neita
41.86 Great Britain & NI 24 Aug 17
Philip, Henry, Asher-Smith, Neita
41.93 Great Britain & NI 18 Aug 16
Philip, Henry, Asher-Smith, Neita
41.93 Great Britain & NI 12 Aug 17
Philip, Henry, Asher-Smith, Neita
42.10 Great Britain & NI 29 Aug 15
Philip, Asher-Smith, J Williams, Henry
42.12 Great Britain & NI 12 Aug 17
Philip, Henry, Asher-Smith, Neita
42.21 Great Britain & NI 28 Aug 14
Philip, Nelson, Onuora, Henry
42.24 Great Britain & NI 17 Aug 14
Philip, Nelson, J Williams, Henry
10 42.43 Great Britain & NI 1 Aug 80
Oakes, Cook, Callender, Lannaman
42.45 Great Britain & NI 10 Jul 16
Philip, Asher-Smith, B Williams, Neita
42.48 Great Britain & NI 29 Aug 15
Philip, J Williams, B Williams, Henry
42.59 Great Britain & NI 9 Jul 16
Philip, Asher-Smith, B Williams, Neita
42.60 Great Britain & NI 11 Aug 01
Richardson, Wilhelmy, James, Oyepitan
42.62 Great Britain & NI 28 Aug 14
Philip, Nelson, Onuora, Henry
42.66 Great Britain & NI 11 Sep 82
Hoyte, Cook, Callender, S.Thomas
42.69 Great Britain & NI 26 Jul 13
Asher-Smith,Onuora, Lewis, Nelson
42.71 Great Britain & NI 10 Aug 83
Baptiste, Cook, Callender, S.Thomas
42.72 Great Britain & NI 3 Sep 78
Callender, Cook, Danville, Lannaman
20 42.74 Great Britain & NI 11 Jul 14
Philip, Nelson, J Williams, Henry
42.75 Great Britain & NI 18 Aug 13
Asher-Smith, Nelson, Lewis, H Jones
42.75 Great Britain & NI 24 May 14
Philip, B Williams, J Williams, Henry
42.80 Great Britain & NI 24 Jul 15
Asher-Smith, B Williams, J Williams, Henry
42.82 Great Britain & NI 1 Sep 07
Turner, Douglas, Freeman, Maduaka
42.84 England 31 Jul 02
Maduaka, Anderson, James, Oyepitan
42.84 Great Britain & NI 3 May 15
Philip, Nelson, B Williams, Adeoye
42.87 Great Britain & NI 1 Sep 07
Turner, Douglas, Freeman, Maduaka
42.87 Great Britain & N.I. 18 Aug 13
Asher-Smith, Nelson, Lewis, H Jones
42.91 Great Britain & NI 19 Apr 14
Papps, Onuora, J Williams, Henry
30 42.95 Great Britain & NI 21 Jun 08
Onuora, Douglas, Kwakye, Ania

4 x 400 Metres Relay

3:20.04 Great Britain & NI 2 Sep 07
Ohurougu, Okoro, McConnell, Sanders
3:22.01 Great Britain & NI 1 Sep 91
Hanson, Smith, Gunnell, Keough
3:22.61 Great Britain & NI 17 Aug 13
Child, Cox, Adeoye, Ohuruogu
3:22.68 Great Britain & NI 23 Aug 08
Ohuruogu, Sotherton, Okoro, Sanders
3:22.68 Great Britain & NI 27 Apr 13
Child, Cox, Ohuruogu, Shakes-Drayton
3:23.05 Great Britain & NI 2 Sep 11
Ohuruogu, Sanders, McConnell, Shakes-Drayton
3:23.41 Great Britain & NI 22 Aug 93
Keough, Smith, Joseph, Gunnell
3:23.62 Great Britain & NI 30 Aug 15
Ohuruogu, Onuora, Child, Bundy-Davies
3:23.63 Great Britain & NI 3 Sep 11
Shakes-Drayton, Sanders, Ohuruogu, McConnell
3:23.89 Great Britain & NI 31 Aug 91 10
Smith, Hanson, Keough, Gunnell
3:23.90 Great Britain & NI 29 Aug 15
Child, Onuora, McAslan, Bundy-Davies
3:24.14 Great Britain & NI 14 Aug 94
Neef, Keough, Smith, Gunnell
3:24.23 Great Britain & NI 8 Aug 92
Smith, Douglas, Stoute, Gunnell
3:24.25 Great Britain & NI 30 Jun 91
Gunnell, Hanson, Stoute, Keough
3:24.32 Great Britain & NI 1 Aug 10
Sanders, Okoro, McConnell, Shakes-Drayton
3:24.34 Great Britain & N.I. 17 Aug 14
Child, Massey, Cox, Adeoye
3:24.36 Great Britain & NI 5 Jun 93
Smith, Joseph, Stoute, Gunnell
3:24.44 Great Britain & NI 14 Aug 05
McConnell, Fraser, Sanders, Ohuruogu
3:24.74 Great Britain & NI 12 Aug 17
Clark, Lav Nielsen, Shakes-Drayton, Diamond
3:24.76 Great Britain & NI 11 Aug 12 20
Cox, McConnell, Shakes-Drayton, Ohuruogu
3:24.78 Great Britain & NI 1 Sep 90
Gunnell, Stoute, Beckford, Keough
3:24.81 Great Britain & NI 19 Aug 16
Diamond, Onuora, Massey, Ohuruogu
3:25.00 Great Britain & NI 13 Aug 17
Clark, Lav Nielsen, Doyle, Diamond
3:25.05 Great Britain & NI 10 Aug 12
Cox, McConnell, Child, Ohuruogu
3:25.05 Great Britain & NI 10 Jul 16
Diamond, Onuora, Doyle, Bundy-Davies
3:25.12 Great Britain & NI 28 Aug 04
Fraser, Murphy, Ohuruogu, McConnell
3:25.16 Great Britain & NI 23 Aug 09
McConnell, Ohuruogu, Barr, Sanders
3:25.20 Great Britain & NI 7 Aug 92
Douglas, Smith, Stoute, Gunnell
3:25.23 Great Britain & NI 22 Aug 09
Sanders, Barr, Meadows, McConnell
3:25.28 Great Britain & N.I. 29 Sep 00 30
Frost, D.Fraser, Curbishley, Merry

UNDER 23

100 Metres
10.99	Dina Asher-Smith	25	Jul	15
11.05	Montell Douglas	17	Jul	08
11.06	Desiree Henry	15	Apr	16
11.10	Kathy Smallwood	5	Sep	81
11.14	Daryll Neita	9	Jul	17
11.17	Bianca Williams	14	Jun	14
11.20	Heather Hunte	26	Sep	80
11.20	Jodie Williams	19	Apr	14
11.22	Sonia Lannaman	13	Aug	77
11.25	Paula Dunn	27	Aug	86

wind assisted
10.93	Sonia Lannaman	17	Jul	77
10.95	Montell Douglas	17	Jul	08
11.01	Heather Hunte	21	May	80
11.13	Shirley Thomas	27	May	84
11.13	Jodie Williams	26	Apr	14
11.14	Paula Dunn	27	Jul	86
11.17	Abi Oyepitan	30	Jun	01
11.23	Jayne Andrews	17	Jul	84
11.24	Sarah Wilhelmy	9	Jun	01

hand timing
11.1	Andrea Lynch	29	Jun	74
11.1	Heather Hunte	29	Jun	80

hand timing - wind assisted
10.8	Sonia Lannaman	22	May	76
10.9	Andrea Lynch	18	May	74
11.1	Sharon Colyear	22	May	76

200 Metres
22.07	Dina Asher-Smith	28	Aug	15
22.13	Kathy Smallwood	9	Sep	82
22.46	Jodie Williams	15	Aug	14
22.46	Desiree Henry	27	Aug	16
22.58	Bianca Williams	31	Jul	14
22.80	Michelle Scutt	12	Jun	82
22.81	Sonia Lannaman	2	May	76
22.85	Katharine Merry	12	Jun	94
22.86	Finette Agyapong	15	Jul	17
22.89	Katarina Johnson-Thompson	31	May	14
22.94	Shannon Hylton	2	Jul	17

wind assisted
22.48	Michelle Scutt	4	Jul	82
22.69	Sonia Lannaman	10	Jul	77
22.83	Amarachi Pipi	14	May	17
22.84	Sarah Wilhelmy	10	Jun	01
22.90	Allison Curbishley	17	Jul	98

hand timing
22.9	Heather Hunte	3	May	80

hand timing - wind assisted
22.6	Sonia Lannaman	23	May	76

300 Metres
36.01	Michelle Scutt	13	Jul	80

during 400m
35.8+	Kathy Smallwood	17	Sep	82

400 Metres
50.28	Christine Ohuruogu	21	Mar	06
50.46	Kathy Smallwood	17	Sep	82
50.63	Michelle Scutt	31	May	82
50.71	Allison Curbishley	18	Sep	98
51.26	Seren Bundy-Davies	11	Jun	16
51.28	Donna Murray	12	Jul	75
51.48	Perri Shakes-Drayton	14	Aug	10
51.77 i	Sally Gunnell	6	Mar	88
51.78	Helen Karagounis	19	Jul	03
51.90 i	Laviai Nielsen	18	Feb	17

600 Metres
1:26.18	Diane Edwards	22	Aug	87

800 Metres
1:59.05	Christina Boxer	4	Aug	79
1:59.30	Diane Edwards	4	Jul	87
1:59.67	Lorraine Baker	15	Aug	86
1:59.75	Marilyn Okoro	28	Jul	06
1:59.76	Paula Fryer	17	Jul	91
1:59.94	Hannah England	20	Jun	09
1:59.99	Jemma Simpson	22	Jul	06
2:00.39	Bev Nicholson	28	Aug	88
2:00.42	Laura Muir	7	Jun	15
2:00.46	Emma Jackson	11	Oct	10

1000 Metres
2:35.51	Lorraine Baker	19	Jul	86

1500 Metres
3:58.66	Laura Muir	17	Jul	15
4:01.93	Zola Budd	7	Jun	86
4:02.54	Stephanie Twell	19	Aug	10
4:02.99	Laura Weightman	8	Aug	12
4:03.73	Jessica Judd	4	Aug	17
4:04.29	Hannah England	28	Jul	09
4:05.42 mx	Lisa Dobriskey	30	Aug	05
4:05.76	Yvonne Murray	5	Jul	86
4:06.0	Mary Stewart	24	Jun	78
4:06.81	Stacey Smith	10	Jul	11
4:06.84	Paula Radcliffe	2	Jul	95

1 Mile
4:23.08	Yvonne Murray	5	Sep	86

2000 Metres
5:29.58	Yvonne Murray	11	Jul	86
5:30.19	Zola Budd	11	Jul	86

3000 Metres
8:34.43	Zola Budd	30	Jun	86
8:37.15	Yvonne Murray	28	Aug	86
8:38.47	Laura Muir	24	May	15
8:40.40	Paula Radcliffe	16	Aug	93
8:42.75 mx	Stephanie Twell	8	Sep	10
8:43.24 mx	Jessica Judd	6	Sep	17
8:43.46 mx	Laura Weightman	14	May	13
8:46.53	Liz Lynch	18	Jul	86
8:47.36	Jill Hunter	17	Aug	88
8:47.71	Lisa York	31	Jul	92

5000 Metres

14:49.27	Paula Radcliffe	7	Jul	95
14:54.08	Stephanie Twell	27	Aug	10
15:07.45	Emilia Gorecka	4	May	14
15:17.77	Jill Hunter	26	Aug	88
15:27.60	Rhona Auckland	25	Jul	15
15:32.27	Emily Pidgeon	12	Jun	10
15:34.82	Jessica Judd	27	May	17
15:34.92	Jane Furniss	26	Jun	82
15:35.12	Kate Avery	9	Jun	12
15:36.35	Birhan Dagne	5	Aug	00

10000 Metres

31:41.42	Liz Lynch	28	Jul	86
32:03.55	Charlotte Purdue	29	Apr	12
32:22.79	Rhona Auckland	10	Jul	15
32:30.4	Birhan Dagne	22	Jul	00
32:32.42	Vikki McPherson	15	Jul	93
32:36.09	Helen Titterington	29	Aug	89
32:36.11	Alice Wright	1	May	16
32:41.29	Jenny Clague	20	Jun	93
32:57.17	Kath Binns	15	Aug	80
32:59.52	Jenny Nesbitt	20	May	17

2000 Metres Steeplechase

6:36.45	Emily Stewart	6	May	13
6:36.50	Barbara Parker	26	Jul	03

3000 Metres Steeplechase

9:38.45	Eilish McColgan	7	Jun	12
9:47.97	Pippa Woolven	30	Jul	14
9:48.51	Lizzie Hall	10	Jun	06
9:51.42	Emily Stewart	27	Jul	13

100 Metres Hurdles

12.60	Cindy Ofili	13	Jun	15
12.82	Sally Gunnell	17	Aug	88
12.84	Lucy Hatton	18	Apr	15
12.97	Jessica Ennis	25	Aug	07
13.03	Diane Allahgreen	11	Jul	97
13.06	Shirley Strong	11	Jul	80
13.07	Lesley-Ann Skeete	14	Aug	87
13.11	Sharon Colyear	22	Jun	76
13.17	Jacqui Agyepong	3	Aug	90
13.17	Gemma Bennett	26	Jul	06

wind assisted

12.80	Sally Gunnell	29	Jul	88

hand timing

13.0	Blondelle Thompson	29	Jun	74

hand timing - wind assisted

12.8	Natasha Danvers	3	Apr	99

400 Metres Hurdles

54.03	Sally Gunnell	28	Sep	88
54.18	Perri Shakes-Drayton	30	Jul	10
55.32	Eilidh Child	18	Jul	09
55.69	Natasha Danvers	19	Jul	98
55.69	Meghan Beesley	16	Jul	11
56.05	Shona Richards	12	Jul	15
56.08	Jessica Turner	16	Jul	17
56.26	Louise Fraser	7	Jun	92
56.42	Vicki Jamison	20	Jun	98
56.42	Sian Scott	18	Aug	05

High Jump

1.97 i	Katarina Johnson-Thompson	14	Feb	15
1.96	Isobel Pooley	24	Aug	14
1.96	Morgan Lake	1	Jul	17
1.95	Diana Elliott	26	Jun	82
1.95	Jessica Ennis	5	May	07
1.94	Louise Miller	25	May	80
1.93	Susan Jones	2	Sep	00
1.93	Michelle Dunkley	2	Sep	00
1.92	Barbara Simmonds	31	Jul	82
1.92 i	Julia Bennett	10	Mar	90
1.92 i	Vikki Hubbard	21	Feb	10

Pole Vault

4.87 i	Holly Bleasdale	21	Jan	12
4.71		24	Jun	12
4.40 i	Lucy Bryan	10	Mar	17
4.40		15	Jul	17
4.35	Kate Dennison	28	Jul	06
4.35 i	Katie Byres	16	Feb	13
4.20		12	Jul	13
4.31 i	Emma Lyons	21	Feb	09
4.12		12	Jul	08
4.26 i	Zoe Brown	21	Feb	04
4.20		17	Jul	05
4.16 i	Sally Scott	13	Feb	11
4.15	Louise Butterworth	4	Aug	07
4.13 i	Maria Seager	2	Feb	10
4.10	Sophie Upton	9	Jun	10

Long Jump

6.93 i	Katarina Johnson-Thompson	21	Feb	15
6.92		11	Jul	14
6.88	Fiona May	18	Jul	90
6.80	Abigail Irozuru	9	Jun	12
6.79	Bev Kinch	7	Jul	84
6.77	Lorraine Ugen	5	Jun	13
6.75	Joyce Oladapo	14	Sep	85
6.75	Jazmin Sawyers	26	Jun	16
6.73	Yinka Idowu	7	Aug	93
6.73	Jade Johnson	7	Aug	02
6.58	Mary Berkeley	14	Sep	85

wind assisted

6.98	Fiona May	4	Jun	89
6.86	Jazmin Sawyers	8	Jul	16
6.83	Lorraine Ugen	16	Mar	12
6.80	Joyce Oladapo	22	Jun	85

Triple Jump

13.85 A	Yasmine Regis	18	May	08
13.52		31	May	08
13.75	Michelle Griffith	18	Jul	93
13.75	Laura Samuel	17	Jun	12
13.62	Nony Mordi	5	Jul	08
13.48 i	Ashia Hansen	13	Feb	93
13.31		18	Jul	92
13.44	Hannah Frankson	26	Jun	11
13.31	Connie Henry	9	Jul	94
13.31	Karlene Turner	28	May	06
13.16	Rachel Kirby	26	Jul	91
13.11	Jade Johnson	19	Aug	01

wind assisted

13.93	Michelle Griffith	2	Jul	93
13.77	Laura Samuel	17	Jul	11
13.76	Nony Mordi	10	May	08
13.75	Yasmine Regis	27	May	06

Shot

18.19	Myrtle Augee	14	Aug	87
17.20	Judy Oakes	8	Aug	80
17.14	Sophie McKinna	9	Jul	16
16.91	Amelia Strickler	13	Feb	15
16.72		2	May	15
16.55	Yvonne Hanson-Nortey	15	Jun	86
16.53	Eden Francis	31	May	09
16.42	Kirsty Yates	30	Jul	14
16.40	Julie Dunkley	12	Aug	00
16.34	Adele Nicoll	2	Jul	16
16.31	Shaunagh Brown	17	Jun	12
16.28	Rachel Wallader	17	Jul	11

Discus

60.00	Philippa Roles	9	May	99
59.27	Eden Francis	31	May	09
57.32	Lynda Whiteley	16	Jun	84
56.63	Emma Carpenter	16	Jun	02
56.06	Kathryn Farr	27	Jun	87
55.93	Claire Smithson	20	Aug	05
55.70	Shelley Drew	25	Jun	95
55.52	Jane Aucott	17	Jan	90
54.72	Karen Pugh	27	Jul	86
54.47	Jade Nicholls	1	Aug	09
54.46	Ellen Mulvihill	14	May	86

Hammer

72.97	Sophie Hitchon	23	Jun	13
66.30	Rachel Hunter	18	May	14
65.33	Sarah Holt	24	May	09
63.35	Shirley Webb	29	Jun	03
63.11	Myra Perkins	18	May	14
62.30	Louisa James	29	Jun	14
62.27	Zoe Derham	16	Jun	02
62.03	Susan McKelvie	27	Aug	06
61.75	Laura Douglas	10	Jul	05
61.70	Lyn Sprules	12	Jul	97
61.13	Shaunagh Brown	18	Jul	12

Javelin (1999 Model)

64.87	Kelly Morgan	14	Jul	02
60.85	Goldie Sayers	10	Jul	04
58.63	Izzy Jeffs	26	Apr	14
55.36	Freya Jones	12	Apr	14
54.71	Kike Oniwide	14	Jun	14
52.88	Laura Whittingham	28	Jul	07
52.84	Jo Blair	9	Jul	06
52.78	Tesni Ward	29	May	11
52.76	Jenny Kemp	23	Jun	01
52.68	Lianne Clarke	25	Aug	07
52.09	Lauren Therin	5	May	07

Javelin (pre 1999 Model)

69.54	Fatima Whitbread	3	Jul	83
67.20	Tessa Sanderson	17	Jul	77
60.10	Shelley Holroyd	16	Jul	93
60.00	Julie Abel	24	May	87
59.88	Sharon Gibson	3	Jul	83
58.20	Lorna Jackson	16	Jun	96
57.82	Mandy Liverton	21	Jun	92

Heptathlon (1985 Tables)

6682	Katarina Johnson-Thompson	1	Jun	14
6469	Jessica Ennis	26	Aug	07
6325	Denise Lewis	23	Aug	94
6259	Judy Livermore	10	Sep	82
6094	Joanne Mulliner	7	Jun	87
5894	Louise Hazel	8	Aug	06
5873	Katie Stainton	18	Jun	17
5816 w	Julie Hollman	24	May	98
5803	Jayne Barnetson	20	Aug	89
5765	Kim Hagger	17	Jul	83
5765	Jenny Kelly	5	Aug	90
5760	Nicola Gautier	23	May	99

3000 Metres Track Walk

13:10.60+	Johanna Jackson	29	Jul	07
13:11.80 i	Heather Lewis	16	Feb	14
13:15.16+	Vicky Lupton	28	Jun	92

5000 Metres Track Walk

22:03.65	Johanna Jackson	29	Jul	07
22:09.87	Heather Lewis	29	Jun	14
22:12.21	Vicky Lupton	28	Jun	92

5k Road - where superior to track time

21:36	Vicky Lupton	18	Jul	92
22:09	Lisa Langford	8	Apr	89

10000 Metres Track Walk

45:53.9	Julie Drake	26	May	90
46:30.0	Vicky Lupton	14	Sep	94
49:06.83	Heather Lewis	22	Jun	14

10k Road - where superior to track time

45:42	Lisa Langford	3	May	87
45:48	Vicky Lupton	25	Aug	94
46:59	Heather Lewis	1	Mar	14

20 Kilometres Road Walk

1:36:28	Johanna Jackson	13	Jul	07
1:38:25	Sara Cattermole	31	Oct	99
1:39:03	Heather Lewis	15	Mar	15
1:44:19	Katie Stones	25	Feb	06
1:44:48	Vicky Lupton	3	Sep	94
1:47:21	Debbie Wallen	17	Apr	99
1:49:12	Nikki Huckerby	26	Sep	99
1:49:18	Helen Sharratt	16	Oct	93
1:49:32	Nicola Phillips	26	Apr	03
1:50:16	Sophie Hales	10	Mar	07
1:52:37	Sally Warren	23	Apr	00

UNDER 20

100 Metres

11.14	Dina Asher-Smith	5	Jul	14
11.17	Imani Lansiquot	20	Jul	16
11.18	Jodie Williams	22	Jul	11
11.21	Desiree Henry	12	Aug	14
11.27 A	Kathy Smallwood	9	Sep	79
11.42		11	Aug	79
11.30	Bev Kinch	5	Jul	83
11.36 A	Della James	14	Oct	68
11.36	Ashleigh Nelson	14	Jun	09
11.37	Asha Philip (U17)	23	Jun	07
11.39 A	Hannah Brier	16	Jul	15
11.40	Vernicha James	11	Jun	02
11.40	Daryll Neita	20	Jun	15
11.43	Shirley Thomas	7	Aug	82
11.45	Sonia Lannaman (U17)	1	Sep	72
11.45	Simmone Jacobs	6	Jul	84
11.46	Shaunna Thompson	14	Oct	08
11.47	Bianca Williams	20	Apr	12
11.47	Sophie Papps	16	Jun	12

10 (margin)

wind assisted

11.03	Dina Asher-Smith	5	Jul	14
11.04	Desiree Henry	26	Apr	14
11.13	Bev Kinch	6	Jul	83
11.25	Shirley Thomas	20	Aug	81
11.26	Simmone Jacobs	27	May	84
11.37	Hannah Brier	31	May	15
11.39	Vernicha James	29	Jun	02
11.39 mx	Sophie Papps	8	May	13
11.40	Katharine Merry	3	Jul	93
11.42	Annie Tagoe	25	Jun	11
11.43	Dorothy Hyman	2	Sep	60
11.45	Stephi Douglas	25	Jun	88
11.45	Rebecca White	4	Jul	98
11.45	Abi Oyepitan	4	Jul	98

hand timing

11.3	Sonia Lannaman	9	Jun	74
11.3	Heather Hunte	15	Jul	78
11.4	Della James	2	Aug	67

hand timing - wind assisted

11.2	Wendy Clarke	22	May	76
11.3	Helen Golden	30	May	70
11.3	Linsey Macdonald (U17)	3	May	80
11.4	Anita Neil	30	Jun	68
11.4	Helen Barnett	16	May	76
11.4	Jane Parry (U17)	5	Jul	80

downhill

11.3 w	Denise Ramsden	28	Jun	69

200 Metres

22.61	Dina Asher-Smith	14	Aug	14
22.70 A	Kathy Smallwood	12	Sep	79
22.84		5	Aug	79
22.79	Jodie Williams (U17)	23	May	10
22.93	Vernicha James	21	Jul	01
22.94	Shannon Hylton	17	May	15

23.04	Maya Bruney	22	Jul	17
23.09	Charlotte McLennaghan	10	May	15
23.10	Diane Smith (U17)	11	Aug	90
23.20	Katharine Merry	13	Jun	93
23.20 i	Amy Spencer	2	Mar	03 10
23.45 (U17)		15	Jul	01
23.23	Sonia Lannaman	25	Aug	75
23.23	Sarah Wilhelmy	13	Jun	98
23.24	Sandra Whittaker	12	Jun	82
23.25	Desiree Henry (U17)	10	Jul	11
23.28	Simmone Jacobs (U17)	28	Aug	83
23.32	Alisha Rees	16	Aug	17
23.33	Linsey Macdonald	9	Jun	82
23.35	Donna Murray	26	May	74
23.37	Hayley Jones	21	Jul	07

wind assisted

22.73	Shannon Hylton	18	Jul	15
23.01	Simmone Jacobs	28	May	84
23.11	Linsey Macdonald (U17)	5	Jul	80
23.12	Alisha Rees	3	Jun	17
23.15	Cheriece Hylton	17	May	15
23.16	Donna Murray	27	Jul	74
23.16	Desiree Henry	31	May	14
23.20	Sarah Wilhelmy	18	Jul	98

hand timing

23.1	Sonia Lannaman	7	Jun	75
23.3	Donna Murray	9	Jun	74
23.3	Sharon Colyear	30	Jun	74
23.3	Linsey Macdonald	8	May	82

hand timing - wind assisted

22.9	Donna Murray	14	Jul	74
23.2	Debbie Bunn (U17)	2	Jul	78

300 Metres

36.46	Linsey Macdonald (U17)	13	Jul	80

hand timing

36.2	Donna Murray	7	Aug	74

400 Metres

51.16	Linsey Macdonald (U17)	15	Jun	80
51.77	Donna Murray	30	Jul	74
52.25	Laviai Nielsen	27	May	15
52.25 A	Catherine Reid	17	Jul	15
53.34		31	May	15
52.54	Donna Fraser	10	Aug	91
52.55	Hannah Williams	22	Jul	17
52.65	Jane Parry	11	Jun	83
52.77	Sabrina Bakare	12	Jul	13
52.80	Sian Morris	18	Jun	83
52.98	Karen Williams	6	Aug	78 10
52.99	Angela Bridgeman	24	Jul	82
53.01 i	Marilyn Neufville	14	Mar	70
53.08	Loreen Hall (U17)	29	Jul	84
53.14	Michelle Probert	28	Jul	79
53.16	Cheriece Hylton	17	Jul	15
53.17	Maya Bruney	29	Jul	17
53.18	Lisa Miller	16	Jun	02
53.20	Verona Bernard	8	Jul	72
53.23	Laura Finucane	3	Jul	04

86

hand timing

52.6	Marilyn Neufville	20	Jun	70
52.8	Lillian Board	9	Jul	67
52.9	Verona Bernard	15	Sep	72

600 Metres

1:27.33	Lorraine Baker (U17)	13	Jul	80

800 Metres

1:59.75	Charlotte Moore	29	Jul	02
1:59.77	Jessica Judd	11	Jun	14
2:01.11	Lynne MacDougall	18	Aug	84
2:01.66	Lorraine Baker	26	Jun	82
2:01.95	Emma Jackson	9	Jun	07
2:02.00	Diane Edwards	14	Sep	85
2:02.0	Jo White (U17)	13	Aug	77
2:02.15	Alison Leonard	11	Jul	08
2:02.18	Lynne Robinson	18	Jul	86
2:02.32	Emily Dudgeon	11	Jul	12
2:02.8 a	Lesley Kiernan	2	Sep	74
2:02.88 i	Kirsty McDermott	22	Feb	81
2:02.89	Sarah Kelly	21	Jul	10
2:03.11	Janet Prictoe	19	Aug	78
2:03.18	Paula Newnham	17	Jun	78
2:03.18 mx	Laura Weightman	24	Aug	10
2:03.18	Adelle Tracey	21	Jul	12
2:03.32	Molly Long	30	May	15
2:03.42	Jemma Simpson	26	Jul	03
2:03.43	Rowena Cole	23	Jul	11

1000 Metres

2:38.58	Jo White (U17)	9	Sep	77

1500 Metres

3:59.96	Zola Budd	30	Aug	85
4:05.83	Stephanie Twell	18	Jul	08
4:05.96	Lynne MacDougall	20	Aug	84
4:09.60 mx	Laura Weightman	21	Aug	10
4:12.82		28	Aug	10
4:09.93	Jessica Judd	15	Jul	12
4:10.61	Bobby Clay	5	Jun	16
4:11.12	Bridget Smyth	26	May	85
4:11.22	Emma Pallant	19	Jul	08
4:12.28	Jemma Reekie	2	Jul	17
4:12.96	Jennifer Walsh	15	Jul	12
4:13.00	Charlotte Moore	8	Aug	03
4:13.38	Emma Ward	7	May	01
4:13.40	Wendy Smith	19	Aug	78
4:13.59 mx	Harriet Knowles-Jones	15	Aug	17
4:14.15 mx	Sarah Kelly	10	Aug	10
4:14.22 mx	Emelia Gorecka	27	Jun	12
4:14.40	Janet Lawrence	20	Aug	77
4:14.40	Georgia Peel	13	Apr	13
4:14.50	Wendy Wright	20	Jun	87
4:14.52 mx	Laura Muir	3	Aug	12
4:14.56	Andrea Whitcombe	22	Aug	90

1 Mile

4:17.57	Zola Budd	21	Aug	85

2000 Metres

5:33.15	Zola Budd	13	Jul	84

3000 Metres

8:28.83	Zola Budd	7	Sep	85	
8:50.89	Stephanie Twell	14	Sep	08	
8:51.78	Paula Radcliffe	20	Sep	92	
8:55.11	Emelia Gorecka	26	Aug	12	
8:56.08 mx	Harriet Knowles-Jones	3	May	17	
8:59.12 mx	Bobby Clay	9	Sep	15	
9:00.06 i	Jessica Judd	16	Feb	13	
9:08.5 mx	(U17)	6	Apr	11	
9:03.35	Philippa Mason	19	Jul	86	
9:04.14	Yvonne Murray	28	May	83	
9:06.16	Helen Titterington	19	Jun	88	10
9:06.87	Emily Pidgeon	7	Jun	06	
9:07.02	Carol Haigh	24	Jun	85	
9:07.28	Emma Pallant	4	Jun	08	
9:09.14	Lisa York	19	Jul	89	
9:10.34 mx	Charlotte Purdue	8	Sep	10	
9:10.67	Sian Edwards	8	Jul	06	
9:10.9	Julie Holland	7	Apr	84	
9:11.20 mx	Jemma Reekie	25	Apr	17	
9:12.28	Hayley Haining	20	Jul	91	
9:12.80	Laura Muir	6	May	12	20

5000 Metres

14:48.07	Zola Budd	26	Aug	85	
15:23.4	Charlotte Purdue	28	Aug	10	
15:34.21	Emelia Gorecka	9	Jun	12	
15:41.00	Emily Pidgeon	24	Jun	06	
15:42.48	Sian Edwards	23	Jul	06	
15:47.53	Stephanie Twell	7	Aug	07	
15:51.62	Carol Haigh	26	May	85	
15:52.55	Yvonne Murray	29	May	83	
15:53.27	Annabel Gummow	28	May	11	
15:58.8 mx	Charlotte Dale	12	May	02	10
15:59.97	Rebecca Weston	1	Jun	13	
16:04.60	Kate Avery	13	Jun	09	
16:06.41 mx	Rebecca Straw	24	Aug	13	
16:11.03	Louise Small	13	Jun	09	
16:11.61 i	Jenny Clague	22	Feb	92	
16:13.93	Lauren Howarth	31	May	08	
16:15.36	Louise Kelly	31	Jul	98	
16:16.39	Collette Fagan	20	Jul	01	
16:16.77 i	Paula Radcliffe	22	Feb	92	
16:19.66	Grace Baker	30	May	15	20

10000 Metres

32:36.75	Charlotte Purdue	14	Aug	10

2000 Metres Steeplechase

6:32.45	Louise Webb (U17)	14	Jul	07
6:32.55	Sarah Hopkinson (U17)	14	Jul	07
6:35.07	Emily Moyes	1	May	17

3000 Metres Steeplechase

10:06.12	Emily Pidgeon (U17)	3	Jul	05
10:10.34	Louise Webb	25	Jul	09
10:11.86	Pippa Woolven	9	Jun	12
10:12.50	Ruth Senior	15	Aug	06

100 Metres Hurdles

	Mark	Name	Date		
	13.07	Alicia Barrett	18	Jun	17
	13.13	Yasmin Miller	27	Jul	14
	13.25	Diane Allahgreen	21	Jul	94
	13.26	Jessica Ennis	9	Jul	05
	13.28	Mollie Courtney	22	Jul	16
	13.30	Sally Gunnell	16	Jun	84
	13.32	Keri Maddox	21	Jul	91
	13.45	Natasha Danvers	6	Aug	95
	13.46	Nathalie Byer	26	Aug	83
10	13.47	Sam Baker	30	Jun	91
	13.47	Sophie Yorke	18	Jun	17
	13.48	Katarina Johnson-Thompson	13	Jul	12
	13.49	Angie Thorp	30	Jun	91
	13.50	Lesley-Ann Skeete	6	Jun	86
	13.52	Julie Pratt	5	Jul	98
	13.53	Symone Belle	25	Jul	03
	13.56	Wendy McDonnell	3	Jun	79
	13.57	Bethan Edwards	29	Aug	92
	13.58	Lauraine Cameron	19	Jun	90

wind assisted

	Mark	Name	Date		
	13.24	Lesley-Ann Skeete	7	Jun	86
	13.28	Sarah Claxton	5	Jul	98
	13.31	Sophie Yorke	11	Jun	17
	13.39	Lauraine Cameron	1	Jul	90
	13.45	Louise Fraser	30	Jul	89
	13.45	Sam Baker	30	Jun	91
	13.46	Wendy McDonnell	30	Jun	79
	13.48	Julie Pratt	5	Jul	98
	13.54	Heather Jones	7	Jun	05
	13.55	Shirley Strong	10	Jul	77
	13.56	Ann Girvan	15	Jul	84

hand timing

Mark	Name	Date		
13.5	Christine Perera	19	Jul	68

hand timing - wind assisted

Mark	Name	Date		
13.1	Sally Gunnell	7	Jul	84
13.3	Keri Maddox	14	Jul	90
13.4	Judy Livermore	27	May	79
13.4	Sam Baker	14	Jul	90

400 Metres Hurdles

	Mark	Name	Date		
	56.16	Shona Richards	26	Jul	14
	56.46	Perri Shakes-Drayton	21	Jul	07
	57.08	Meghan Beesley	11	Jul	08
	57.26	Hayley McLean	21	Jul	13
	57.27	Vicki Jamison	28	Jul	96
	58.02	Vyv Rhodes	28	Jun	92
	58.36	Sian Scott	29	Jun	03
	58.37	Alyson Evans	1	Sep	85
	58.38	Abigayle Fitzpatrick	23	Jul	11
10	58.44	Jessica Turner	5	Jul	14
	58.68	Kay Simpson	15	Jul	83
	58.68	Chelsea Walker	12	Jun	16
	58.72	Lauren Bouchard	14	Jun	09
	58.74	Ellen Howarth-Brown	18	Jun	06
	58.76	Simone Gandy	28	May	84
	58.91	Rachael Kay	6	Aug	99
	58.96	Nicola Sanders	17	Jul	99
	59.00	Diane Heath	19	Jul	75
	59.01	Sara Elson	24	Aug	89
	59.04	Allison Curbishley	31	Jul	93 [20]

hand timing

Mark	Name	Date		
58.3	Simone Gandy	14	Jul	84
58.7	Sara Elson	18	Jun	89
59.0	Tracy Allen	9	Jul	88

High Jump

	Mark	Name	Date		
	1.94	Morgan Lake	22	Jul	14
	1.91	Lea Haggett	2	Jun	91
	1.91	Susan Jones	31	Aug	97
	1.90	Jo Jennings	29	Sep	88
	1.89	Debbi Marti (U17)	2	Jun	84
	1.89 i	Michelle Dunkley	16	Feb	97
	1.87		7	Jul	95
	1.89	Katarina Johnson-Thompson	3	Aug	12
	1.89 i	Abby Ward	7	Feb	16
	1.86		22	May	16
	1.89	Niamh Emerson	22	May	16
	1.88	Jayne Barnetson	3	Aug	85 [10]
	1.88	Rebecca Jones	1	Jun	02
	1.88	Vikki Hubbard	7	Jul	06
	1.87	Louise Manning	6	May	84
	1.87	Rachael Forrest	7	Jul	95
	1.87	Aileen Wilson	15	Jul	01
	1.87	Jessica Ennis	15	Aug	05
	1.86	Barbara Simmonds	9	Sep	79
	1.86	Claire Summerfield	7	Aug	82
	1.86	Michele Wheeler	31	May	87
	1.86	Stephanie Pywell	11	Jun	06 [20]
	1.86 i	Isobel Pooley	27	Feb	11

Pole Vault

	Mark	Name	Date		
	4.52 i	Katie Byres	18	Feb	12
	4.36		17	Jun	12
	4.40	Lucy Bryan	29	Jun	13
	4.35	Holly Bleasdale	26	Jun	10
	4.35	Molly Caudery	22	Jul	17
	4.20	Sally Scott	19	Jun	10
	4.08	Abigail Roberts	29	Aug	15
	4.05	Jade Ive	14	Oct	08
	4.05	Maria Seager	13	Jun	09
	4.05	Jessica Robinson	11	Jun	16
	4.00	Kate Dennison	18	Jul	02 [10]
	4.00	Zoe Brown	28	Jul	02
	4.00 i	Anna Gordon	27	Feb	16
	3.85		21	Jun	14
	4.00	Jessica Swannack	8	Jul	17
	3.95	Abigail Haywood	27	Jun	09
	3.91 i	Sophie Dowson	28	Jan	17
	3.90	Ellie Spain	6	May	00
	3.90	Hannah Olson (U17)	13	Jun	04
	3.90	Natalie Olson	8	Aug	04
	3.90 i	Kim Skinner	6	Feb	05
	3.80		30	May	05
	3.90	Emma Lyons	3	Sep	06 [20]
	3.90	Ellie Gooding (U17)	5	Jul	13
	3.90	Olivia Connor	2	Aug	15
	3.83 i	Felicia Miloro	24	Sep	17

Long Jump

6.90	Bev Kinch	14	Aug	83
6.82	Fiona May	30	Jul	88
6.68	Sue Hearnshaw	22	Sep	79
6.67	Jazmin Sawyers	13	Jul	12
6.63	Yinka Idowu	21	May	89
6.55	Joyce Oladapo	30	Jul	83
6.52	Georgina Oladapo	16	Jun	84
6.52	Sarah Claxton	31	Jul	98
6.52	Jade Johnson	23	May	99
10 6.51	Katarina Johnson-Thompson	12	Jul	12
6.47	Jo Wise	30	Jul	88
6.45	Margaret Cheetham (U17)	18	Aug	84
6.43	Myra Nimmo	27	May	73
6.39	Moira Walls	22	Jul	70
6.38	Amy Harris	8	Jul	06
6.35	Sharon Bowie	1	Jun	85
6.35	Lorraine Ugen	4	Jul	10
6.34	Ann Wilson	3	Aug	68
6.33	Jo Dear	19	May	93
20 6.32	Morgan Lake	29	Jun	14

wind unconfirmed

6.43	Moira Walls	18	Sep	70

wind assisted

6.93	Bev Kinch	14	Aug	83
6.88	Fiona May	30	Jul	88
6.81	Katarina Johnson-Thompson	13	Jul	12
6.71	Yinka Idowu	15	Jun	91
6.69	Jo Wise	30	Jul	88
6.53	Sarah Claxton	12	Jul	97
6.49	Margaret Cheetham (U15)	4	Sep	83

Triple Jump

13.75	Laura Samuel	22	Jul	10
13.64	Naomi Ogbeta	1	Jul	17
13.13	Yasmine Regis	2	Jul	05
13.05	Michelle Griffith	16	Jun	90
13.03	Emily Gargan	21	May	17
13.01	Jayne Nisbet	22	Apr	07
12.96	Laura Zialor	28	May	16
12.88	Nony Mordi	10	Sep	06
12.88	Ahtollah Rose	1	Jul	11
10 12.82	Denae Matthew	23	Jul	06
12.79	Naomi Reid	1	Jul	11
12.76	Shakira Whight	12	Jul	08
12.73	Melissa Carr	11	Jul	08
12.72	Claire Linskill	3	Sep	06
12.71	Lia Stephenson	15	Jun	14
12.68	Rachel Brenton	16	May	04
12.60	Emily Parker	8	Jun	03
12.59 i	Nikita Campbell-Smith	2	Mar	14
12.58	Alison McAllister	5	Jul	03
20 12.56 i	Katarina Johnson-Thompson	15	Jan	12

wind assisted

13.68	Naomi Ogbeta	21	Jul	17
13.06	Alison McAllister	11	Jul	03
12.78	Claire Linskill	3	Sep	06
12.77	Kerri Davidson	10	Jul	15
12.67	Emily Parker	8	Jun	03

Shot

17.12	Sophie McKinna	25	May	13
17.10	Myrtle Augee	16	Jun	84
16.64	Divine Oladipo	22	Apr	17
16.24 i	Judy Oakes	26	Feb	77
	16.05	26	Aug	77
15.82	Eden Francis	1	Jul	07
15.72 i	Alison Grey	29	Feb	92
	15.26	13	Jul	91
15.60 i	Justine Buttle	27	Feb	88
	15.45	25	Aug	88
15.55	Adele Nicoll	18	Jul	15
15.48	Mary Anderson	8	Sep	85
15.45	Susan King	27	Mar	83 10
15.27	Julie Dunkley	21	Jun	98
15.22	Kirsty Yates	16	Jun	12
14.85	Morgan Lake	31	May	14
14.75 i	Cynthia Gregory	12	Dec	81
	14.70	29	Aug	81
14.72	Sally Hinds	3	Jul	05
14.71 i	Nicola Gautier	26	Jan	97
14.68	Claire Smithson	26	May	01
14.66 i	Terri Salt	7	Jan	84
14.60	Philippa Roles	4	Sep	96

Discus

55.28	Eden Francis	2	Sep	07
55.03	Claire Smithson	30	Jul	02
54.78	Lynda Whiteley	4	Oct	82
53.13	Divine Oladipo	26	May	17
53.12	Emma Carpenter	1	Sep	01
53.10	Kathryn Farr	19	Jul	86
52.58	Emma Merry	22	Aug	93
52.31	Lauren Keightley	18	Jul	98
51.89	Amy Holder	18	Apr	15
51.82	Catherine Bradley	20	Jul	85 10
51.60	Philippa Roles	24	Jul	97
51.48	Shadine Duquemin	19	May	13
51.24	Jane Aucott	11	Jun	86
51.18	Shaunagh Brown	12	May	07
51.12	Janette Picton	6	Jun	82
50.44	Karen Pugh	8	Jul	83
50.34	Angela Sellars	27	Jul	86
50.30	Julia Avis	19	Sep	82
49.74	Shelley Drew	10	May	92
49.60	Fiona Condon	3	Jun	79 20

Hammer

66.01	Sophie Hitchon	24	Jul	10
61.94	Myra Perkins	1	May	11
61.77	Kimberley Reed	3	May	14
60.83	Louisa James	26	May	13
60.75	Abbi Carter	12	Jul	12
59.14	Amy Herrington	21	Apr	17
58.34	Rebecca Keating	26	Jun	16
58.27	Katie Lambert	21	May	17
57.97	Rachael Beverley	25	Jul	98
57.96	Olivia Stephenson	10	Jun	17 10
57.63	Nicola Dudman	16	Jun	02
57.45	Sarah Holt	29	Jun	06

57.43	Anna Purchase	30	Apr	17
56.78	Victoria Thomas	22	Jul	06
56.74	Rachel Blackie	17	Jun	06
56.69	Philippa Davenhall	11	Jun	17
56.67	Danielle Broom	10	Jun	17
56.43	Amber Simpson	10	Jun	17
56.24	Samantha Hynes	4	May	05
20 56.03	Alice Barnsdale	29	Jul	17

Javelin (1999 Model)

55.40	Goldie Sayers	22	Jul	01
54.89	Izzy Jeffs	15	Aug	10
54.61	Kelly Morgan	4	Sep	99
52.82	Freya Jones	29	May	11
52.54	Jenny Kemp	3	Jul	99
52.34	Jade Dodd	2	Sep	07
52.32	Eloise Meakins	9	Sep	12
52.27	Emma Hamplett	14	May	16
51.23	Jo Blair	24	Apr	05
10 51.13	Becky Bartlett	15	May	04
50.95	Lianne Clarke	7	Aug	04
50.57	Laura Whittingham	3	Sep	05
49.83	Hayley Thomas (U17)	24	May	03
49.66	Jo Chapman	22	Aug	04
49.56	Bethan Rees	2	Jul	17
49.35	Kike Oniwinde	16	Apr	11
49.17	Sarah Roberts	29	May	11
48.87	Tesni Ward	19	Jun	10
48.79	Kelly Bramhald	10	Jun	12
20 48.18	Amber Burdett	19	Sep	10

Javelin (pre 1999 Model)

60.14	Fatima Whitbread	7	May	80
59.40	Karen Hough	28	Aug	86
59.36	Kirsty Morrison	4	Sep	93

Heptathlon (1985 Tables)

6267	Katarina Johnson-Thompson	4	Aug	12
6148	Morgan Lake	23	Jul	14
6013	Niamh Emerson	21	Jul	17
5910	Jessica Ennis	16	Aug	05
5833	Joanne Mulliner	11	Aug	85
5687	Holly McArthur	21	Jul	17
5642	Sarah Rowe	23	Aug	81
5601 w	Jade Surman	3	Jun	07
5538		19	Aug	06
5496	Yinka Idowu	3	Sep	89
10 5493	Sally Gunnell	28	May	84
5484	Denise Lewis	30	Jun	91
5459	Jenny Kelly	30	Jul	88
5444	Zoe Hughes	13	Apr	17
5442	Jade O'Dowda	17	Sep	17
5405	Dominique Blaize	23	Jul	06
5391 w	Jackie Kinsella	22	Jun	86
5331		19	Jul	86
5383	Emma Buckett	13	Jul	12
5377	Uju Efobi	18	Jul	93
5358 w	Chloe Cozens	24	May	98
20 5356	Katie Stainton	15	Jun	14
5311	Nicola Gautier	21	Sep	97

3000 Metres Track Walk

13:03.4	Vicky Lupton	18	May	91
13:29.19 i	Emma Achurch	15	Feb	15
13:29.46 i	Ellie Dooley	16	Feb	14
13:36.42 i	Sophie Hales	29	Feb	04
13:38.05 i	Katie Stones	29	Feb	04

5000 Metres Track Walk

22:36.81	Vicky Lupton	15	Jun	91
23:31.67	Lisa Langford	23	Aug	85
23:37:55	Sophie Lewis Ward	14	Jul	16
23:40.75	Ellie Dooley	29	Jun	14
23:55.27	Susan Ashforth (U17)	25	May	85
23:56.9	Julie Drake	24	May	88
24:02.13	Heather Lewis	24	Jun	12
24:02.15	Nicky Jackson	27	May	84
24:06.6	Rebecca Mersh (U17)	23	Apr	05
24:08.4	Jill Barrett	28	May	83
24:14.96	Emma Achurch	29	Jun	14

5k Road - where superior to track time

23:05	Lisa Langford	2	Nov	85
23:18	Julie Drake	27	Feb	88
23:29	Emma Achurch	1	Mar	15
23:30 +	Johanna Jackson	28	Nov	04
23:35	Lisa Simpson	31	Oct	87
23:36	Sophie Lewis Ward	9	Apr	16

10000 Metres Track Walk

47:04.0	Vicky Lupton	30	Mar	91
48:34.0	Lisa Langford	15	Mar	86
49:48.7	Julie Drake	7	Feb	88
50:22.2	Emma Achurch	7	Dec	14
50:25.0	Lisa Simpson	1	Apr	87
51:00.0	Karen Nipper (U17)	21	Feb	81
51:31.2	Helen Ringshaw	17	Mar	84
51:57.20	Heather Lewis	17	Jun	12
52:07.36	Ellie Dooley	16	Jun	13
52:09.0	Elaine Cox	8	Apr	78
52:10.4	Sarah Brown	20	Mar	82

short

50:11.2	Jill Barrett	19	Mar	83

10k Road - where superior to track time

47:49	Emma Achurch	15	Mar	15
49:10	Vicky Lawrence	14	Mar	87
49:14	Carolyn Brown	29	Mar	92
49:26	Julie Drake	21	May	88
49:26	Ellie Dooley	1	Mar	14
49:33	Lisa Simpson	14	Mar	87
49:40	Sophie Hales	6	Mar	04
49:47	Jill Barrett	24	Sep	83
49:51	Heather Lewis	14	Apr	12
50:02	Johanna Jackson	28	Nov	44
50:29	Katie Stones	1	May	04
50:39	Rebecca Mersh	12	Mar	06

Note: LJ, Hep. Although Idowu competed for UK Juniors, she was a Nigerian citizen at the time.

UNDER 17

100 Metres

11.24	Jodie Williams	31	May	10
11.37	Asha Philip	23	Jun	07
11.45	Sonia Lannaman	1	Sep	72
11.54	Dina Asher-Smith	16	Jun	12
11.56	Ashleigh Nelson	10	Jun	07
11.57	Hannah Brier	31	May	14
11.59	Simmone Jacobs	25	Aug	83
11.60	Katharine Merry	28	Jul	90
11.60	Imani Lansiquot	30	Aug	14
10 11.61	Diane Smith	9	Aug	90
11.61	Annie Tagoe	8	Aug	09
11.63	Daryl Neita	7	Jul	12
11.64	Shaunna Thompson	9	Aug	08
11.64	Shannon Hylton	25	May	13

wind assisted

11.47	Katharine Merry (U15)	17	Jun	89
11.50	Rebecca Drummond	9	Jul	94
11.51	Amy Spencer	29	Jun	02
11.51	Desiree Henry	25	Jun	11
11.53	Sophie Papps	9	Sep	11
11.53	Amy Hunt	7	May	17

hand timing

11.6	Denise Ramsden	19	Jul	68
11.6	Linsey Macdonald	25	May	80
11.6	Jane Parry	2	Aug	80

hand timing - wind assisted

11.3	Linsey Macdonald	3	May	80
11.4	Sonia Lannaman	3	Jun	72
11.4	Jane Parry	5	Jul	80
11.5	Sharon Dolby	20	Jul	85

200 Metres

22.79	Jodie Williams	23	May	10
23.10	Diane Smith	11	Aug	90
23.25	Desiree Henry	10	Jul	11
23.28	Simmone Jacobs	28	Aug	83
23.42	Debbie Bunn	17	Jun	78
23.42	Shaunna Thompson	31	Aug	08
23.43	Linsey Macdonald	20	Aug	80
23.44 i	Amy Spencer	27	Jan	02
23.45		15	Jul	01
23.49 i	Vernicha James	30	Jan	00
23.62		8	Jul	00
10 23.49	Dina Asher-Smith	9	Sep	12
23.49	Cheriece Hylton	10	Aug	13
23.50	Katharine Merry	20	Jul	91
23.54	Shannon Hylton	19	May	13
23.59	Carley Wenham	11	Jul	03
23.60	Michelle Probert	12	Sep	76
23.63	Hannah Brier	1	Jun	14

wind assisted

23.11	Linsey Macdonald	5	Jul	80
23.41	Katharine Merry	15	Jun	91
23.48	Vernicha James	21	Aug	99
23.54	Hannah Brier	1	Jun	14

hand timing - wind assisted

23.2	Debbie Bunn	2	Jul	78
23.3	Amy Spencer	1	Jul	01
23.4	Hayley Clements	10	Aug	85

300 Metres

36.46	Linsey Macdonald	13	Jul	80
37.59	Cheriece Hylton	25	May	13
37.72 i	Amy Spencer	24	Feb	02
37.79	Amber Anning	1	Sep	17
37.79	Eleanor Caney	22	Jul	00
38.21	Lesley Owusu	27	Aug	95
38.43	Hayley Jones	9	Jul	05
38.43	Sabrina Bakare	9	May	12
38.47	Carmen Gedling	15	Jul	06
38.49	Kim Wall	24	May	98 10
38.49	Gemma Nicol	3	Aug	02
38.52	Rachel Dickens	2	Jul	11
38.55	Katie Kirk	5	Jun	10
38.56 i	Katarina Johnson-Thompson	24	Feb	08
38.60	Karlene Palmer	12	Jul	97
38.65	Ella Barrett	12	Jul	14
38.66	Kelsey Stewart	20	Jul	13

hand timing

38.2	Marilyn Neufville	6	Sep	69
38.3	Joey Duck	1	Aug	04
38.4	Kim Wall	10	May	98

400 Metres

51.16	Linsey Macdonald	15	Jun	80
53.08	Loreen Hall	29	Jul	84
53.68	Amber Anning	21	Jul	17
53.75	Linda Keough	8	Aug	80
54.01	Angela Bridgeman	16	Aug	80
54.25	Emma Langston	19	Jun	88

hand timing

53.7	Linda Keough	2	Aug	80

600 Metres

1:27.33	Lorraine Baker	13	Jul	80

800 Metres

2:02.0	Jo White	13	Aug	77
2:02.70	Jessica Judd	15	Jun	11
2:03.66	Lesley Kiernan	26	Aug	73
2:03.72	Lorraine Baker	15	Jun	80
2:04.59	Loren Bleaken	31	Jul	12
2:04.85	Louise Parker	28	Jul	79
2:05.03	Katy-Ann McDonald	17	Aug	16
2:05.68	Isobelle Boffey	28	Aug	16
2:05.7 mx	Katie Snowden	23	Jun	10
2:05.86	Charlotte Moore	31	Jul	01 10
2:05.87	Katrina Wootton	14	Aug	02
2:06.18	Nikki Hamblin	12	Jun	04
2:06.20	Georgia Peel	29	Jul	09
2:06.22	Tilly Simpson (U15)	11	Jul	15
2:06.23	Anna Burt	31	May	16

1000 Metres

2:38.58	Jo White	9	Sep	77

1500 Metres

4:14.21	Jessica Judd	28	May	11
4:15.20	Bridget Smyth	29	Jul	84
4:15.32 mx	Rosie Johnson	1	Jul	14
	4:19.90	12	Jul	14
4:15.55	Sandra Arthurton	29	Jul	78
4:15.61	Ella McNiven	24	Jun	17
4:16.24	Georgia Peel	11	Jul	09
4:16.41	Bobby Clay	13	Jul	13
4:16.79	Emelia Gorecka	12	Jun	10
4:16.8	Jo White	30	Jul	77
10 4:17.83	Emily Pidgeon	25	Jun	05
4:17.99	Anna Smith	20	Jul	17
4:18.45 mx	Nikki Hamblin	8	Aug	04
4:19.09	Sarah Kelly	30	May	09
4:19.52	Sabrina Sinha	12	Jul	14
4:19.93	Katrina Wootton	15	Jun	02
4:20.29 mx	Emily Williams	31	May	17

1 Mile

4:43.67	Amy-Eloise Neale	11	Jun	11

3000 Metres

9:08.5 mx	Jessica Judd	6	Apr	11
9:13.93 mx	Emilia Gorecka	8	Sep	10
	9:18.38	9	May	10
9:17.9	Emily Pidgeon	21	Aug	05
9:19.51	Sian Edwards	13	Jul	05
9:20.2 mx	Katrina Wootton	28	Aug	02
9:22.84	Non Stanford	30	Jul	04
9:23.41 mx	Georgia Peel	12	Aug	09
9:23.76	Harriet Knowles-Jones	22	Jun	14
9:24.38 mx	Rachel Nathan	20	Aug	02
10 9:24.40 mx	Danni Barnes	6	May	02
9:24.44 mx	Charlotte Purdue	20	Sep	06
9:24.50 mx	Ella McNiven	13	Jun	17
9:24.61	Jess Coulson	28	Jul	06
9:24.99 +	Bobby Clay	1	Jun	13
9:25.61 mx	Agnes McTighe (U15)	5	Aug	15

5000 Metres

15:56.87	Emilia Gorecka	29	May	10
16:04.46	Emily Pidgeon	21	May	05
16:09.44	Charlotte Purdue	25	Aug	07

1500 Metres Steeplechase

4:50.3	Sarah Hopkinson	23	May	07
4:50.9	Louise Webb	23	May	07
4:53.94	Holly Page	16	Jul	16

80 Metres Hurdles (76.2cm)

10.94	Pippa Earley	1	Sep	17
11.01	Alicia Barrett	1	Sep	13
11.02	Helen Worsey	15	Aug	98
11.02	Yasmin Miller	22	Aug	10
11.04	Marcia Sey	1	Sep	17
11.07	Amanda Parker	7	Jun	86
11.10	Serita Solomon	9	Jul	05
11.12	Sam Farquharson	7	Jun	86
11.12	Georgia Atkins	11	Jul	09
10 11.13	Claire St. John	2	Jun	79
11.13	Kylie Robilliard	30	May	04

11.15	Victoria Johnson	8	Jul	17
11.16	Ann Girvan	4	Jul	81
11.16	Stephi Douglas	27	Jul	85

wind assisted

10.87	Alicia Barrett	31	Aug	14
10.96	Helen Worsey	11	Jul	98
11.00	Sharon Davidge	11	Jul	98

hand timing

11.0	Wendy McDonnell	2	Jul	77

hand timing - wind assisted

10.9	Ann Wilson	16	Jul	66
10.9	Wendy McDonnell	9	Jul	77
10.9	Sam Farquharson	20	Jul	85

100 Metres Hurdles (76.2cm)

13.61	Pippa Earley	18	Jun	17
13.64	Yasmin Miller	4	Jun	11
13.66	Ann Girvan	25	Jul	81
13.66	Moesha Howard	11	Jul	13
13.66	Amber-Leigh Hall	21	Jun	15

wind assisted

13.30	Yasmin Miller	10	Sep	11

100 Metres Hurdles (83.8cm)

13.72	Megan Marrs	25	May	14
13.73	Ann Girvan	7	Aug	82
13.88	Natasha Danvers	28	Aug	93
13.90	Yasmin Miller	11	Aug	11
13.94	Phyllis Agbo	30	Jun	02
13.98	Claire St. John	11	Aug	79

wind assisted

13.67	Ann Girvan	4	Jul	82
13.76	Natasha Danvers	27	Aug	94

hand timing

13.7	Ann Girvan	29	Aug	81

hand timing - wind assisted

13.7	Nathalie Byer	4	Sep	82

300 Metres Hurdles

41.41	Meghan Beesley	6	Aug	06
41.48	Perri Shakes-Drayton	9	Jul	05
41.84	Shona Richards	19	Aug	12
41.96	Amy Pye	27	Aug	17
41.97	Eilidh Child	17	Aug	03
41.98	Rachael Kay	3	Aug	97
41.99	Natasha Danvers	10	Jul	93
42.50	Justine Roach	21	Jul	01
42.52	Lauren Williams	30	Aug	15
42.54	Chelsea Walker	6	Jul	13 10
42.55	Jasmine Jolly	8	Jul	17
42.57	Ellen Howarth-Brown	19	Jul	03
42.57	Chloe Esegbona	30	Aug	15
42.58	Syreeta Williams	12	Jul	97
42.63	Hayley McLean	21	Aug	11
42.64	Claire Triggs	15	Aug	17

hand timing

41.8	Rachael Kay	17	Aug	97
42.4	Keri Maddox	8	May	88
42.4	Syreeta Williams	17	Aug	97
42.5	Louise Brunning	8	May	88

400 Metres Hurdles

58.74	Hayley McLean	7	Jul	11
60.06	Faye Harding	13	Jul	01
60.18	Meghan Beesley	18	Jun	06
60.23	Holly McArthur	19	Jun	16
60.73	Katie Purves	8	Sep	13
60.75	Laura Burke	22	Jul	09
60.87	Karin Hendrickse	31	Jul	82

hand timing

59.7	Keri Maddox	9	Jul	88
59.8 mx	Eildith Child	27	Jul	03

High Jump

1.90	Morgan Lake	12	Jul	13
1.89	Debbi Marti	2	Jun	84
1.85	Louise Manning	11	Sep	82
1.85	Jayne Barnetson	21	Jul	84
1.84	Ursula Fay	6	Aug	83
1.83	Jo Jennings	26	Jul	85
1.83	Tracey Clarke	2	Aug	87
1.83	Aileen Wilson	8	Jul	00
1.82	Elaine Hickey	9	Aug	80
10 1.82	Kerry Roberts	16	Jul	83
1.82	Susan Jones	20	May	94
1.82	Vicki Hubbard	15	May	05
1.82 i	Katarina Johnson-Thompson	8	Mar	09
1.82		10	Jul	09
1.82	Niamh Emerson	29	Aug	15

Pole Vault

4.10	Lucy Bryan	9	Jul	11
4.06	Molly Caudery	24	Jul	16
4.05	Katie Byres	1	Aug	10
4.00 i	Jade Ive	24	Feb	08
3.95		15	Jun	08
3.90	Hannah Olson	13	Jun	04
3.90	Ellie Gooding	5	Jul	13
3.83 i	Felicia Miloro	24	Sep	17
3.81		27	Aug	17
3.82	Natasha Purchas	28	Aug	17
3.80	Sophie Upton	16	Jun	07
10 3.80	Sally Scott	23	Jun	07
3.80	Abigail Roberts	22	Jun	13
3.80 i	Victoria Barlow	29	Jan	17

Long Jump

6.45	Margaret Cheetham	18	Aug	84
6.32	Georgina Oladapo	23	Jul	83
6.31	Katarina Johnson-Thompson	11	Jul	09
6.30	Fiona May (U15)	7	Jul	84
6.29	Holly Mills	16	Aug	15
6.26	Jo Wise	31	May	87
6.25	Sue Hearnshaw	9	Jul	77
6.24	Sarah Claxton	15	Jun	96
6.23	Sue Scott	27	Jul	68
10 6.22	Ann Wilson	18	Sep	66
6.22	Michelle Stone	28	Apr	84
6.19	Morgan Lake	18	Aug	12
6.18	Sheila Parkin	4	Aug	62
6.15	Zainab Ceesay	20	Aug	00

wind assisted

6.49	Margaret Cheetham (U15)	4	Sep	83
6.49		23	Sep	84
6.47	Fiona May	28	Jun	86
6.41	Sue Hearnshaw	9	Jul	77
6.34	Sarah Claxton	12	Jul	96
6.33	Sue Scott	27	Aug	68
6.28	Bev Kinch	6	Sep	80
6.24	Jade Johnson	28	May	95

Triple Jump

12.61	Naomi Ogbeta	31	Aug	14
12.37	Claudimira Landim	28	Aug	16
12.35	Morgan Lake	8	Sep	13
12.32	Kerri Davidson	15	Sep	13
12.26	Emily Gargan	13	Jun	15
12.25	Jade Oni	27	Aug	17
12.24	Hannah Frankson	18	Sep	05
12.23	Naomi Reid	22	Aug	10
12.22	Amy Williams	6	Jul	13
12.21	Jazz Sears	27	Aug	17 10
12.19	Rebekah Passley	17	Aug	03
12.19	Eloise Harvey	19	Aug	17
12.18	Mary Fasipe	21	Aug	11
12.16	Hannah Francis-Smithson	16	Jul	05
12.16	Simi Fajemisin	16	Aug	14

wind assisted

12.45	Naomi Reid	17	Jul	10
12.45	Morgan Lake	11	Aug	13
12.37	Kayley Alcorn	12	Aug	06
12.33	Hanna Hewitson	12	Aug	06
12.27	Rachel Brenton	21	Jul	01
12.27	Rebekah Passley	19	Jul	03

Shot (4kg)

15.14	Sophie McKinna	22	Aug	10
15.08	Justine Buttle	16	Aug	86
14.87	Eden Francis	3	Sep	05
14.40	Susan King	17	May	81
14.33	Adele Nicoll	14	Sep	13
14.04	Mary Anderson	6	May	84
14.03 i	Terri Salt	19	Mar	83
13.77		17	Sep	83
13.94	Jenny Bloss	13	May	67
13.89 i	Alison Grey	11	Feb	89
13.83		20	May	89

Shot (3kg)

16.00	Adele Nicoll	1	Jun	13
15.83	Sarah Omoregie	19	Jun	16
15.65	Serena Vincent	18	Nov	17
15.64	Rhea Southcott	26	Aug	17
15.37	Divine Oladipo	20	Jun	15
15.33	Hannah Molyneaux	26	Aug	17
15.01	Tony Buckingham	16	Aug	14
15.00	Gaia Osborne	25	Sep	16
14.95	Amaya Scott	26	Jun	17
14.77	Ada'ora Chigbo	18	Apr	15 10
14.70	Morgan Lake	1	Jun	13

Discus

51.60	Emma Merry	27	Jun	90
49.56	Jane Aucott	3	Aug	85
49.36	Claire Smithson	10	Jul	99
49.25	Shadine Duquemin	9	Sep	11
48.88	Philippa Roles	13	Aug	94
48.84	Karen Pugh	7	Aug	82
47.58	Catherine Bradley	14	Jul	84
47.54	Lauren Keightley	12	Jul	95
47.50	Sarah Symonds	16	May	90
10 47.35	Sophie Mace	16	Aug	15
47.24	Amanda Barnes	3	Aug	85
47.04	Georgie Taylor	31	Aug	13
47.00	Eden Francis	4	Sep	05
46.76	Fiona Condon	6	Aug	77
46.55	Emma Carpenter	5	Sep	98

Hammer (4kg)

55.98	Kimberley Reed	10	Jun	11
55.44	Abbi Carter	8	Aug	10
54.87	Louisa James	26	Jun	10
54.56	Sophie Hitchon	26	Aug	07
52.62	Katie Head	27	Sep	15
52.56	Rebecca Keating	4	Sep	13

Hammer (3kg)

65.06	Katie Head	9	Jul	16
63.40	Olivia Stevenson	14	May	16
63.23	Tara Simpson-Sullivan	10	Sep	17
63.08	Katie Lambert	4	Sep	15
60.53	Carlotte Williams	9	Apr	16
60.51	Anna Purchase	17	Jul	16
59.63	Molly Walsh	25	Sep	16
59.55	Rebecca Keating	27	Apr	13
59.25	Myra Perkins	5	Jul	08
10 59.21	Phoebe Baggott	25	Jun	17
59.09	Jade Williams	4	Jun	16
59.09	Charlotte Payne	19	Aug	17

Javelin 600gm (1999 Model)

51.28	Freya Jones	30	May	10
49.83	Hayley Thomas	24	May	03
48.77	Emma Hamplett	13	Sep	14
47.72	Izzy Jeffs	30	Aug	08
47.52	Laura McDonald	7	Aug	10
46.94	Louise Watton	12	Jul	02
46.80	Natasha Wilson	16	Jun	12
46.80	Bethan Rees	23	Jul	16
45.60	Kike Oniwinde	9	Aug	09
10 45.55	Lianne Clarke	3	Aug	03

Javelin 600 gm (pre 1999 Model)

56.02	Mandy Liverton	11	Jun	89
53.42	Karen Hough	15	Jul	84
53.22	Kirsty Morrison	15	Aug	92

Javelin 500gm

57.14	Emma Hamplett	1	Jun	14
50.64	Bethan Rees	24	Jul	16
50.34	Emma Howe	1	Sep	17
48.84	Bethany Moule (U15)	16	Jul	16
47.70	Laurie Dawkins	12	Sep	15
47.01	Paula Holguin	12	Sep	15

Heptathlon (1985 Tables) Senior

5481	Katarina Johnson-Thompson	14	Jun	09
5251	Jade Surman	29	May	05
5208	Michelle Stone	30	Sep	84
5194	Jessica Ennis	4	Aug	02
5184	Claire Phythian	20	Aug	89
4969	Kaneesha Johnson	27	Jul	08
4910	Becky Curtis-Harris	6	Jun	10
4901	Phyllis Agbo	28	Apr	02

Heptathlon (1985 Tables) with 80mH

5474	Morgan Lake	4	Aug	13
5146	Katarina Johnson-Thompson	21	Sep	08
5037	Michelle Stone	1	Jul	84
5031	Yinka Idowu	18	Sep	88
4945	Phyllis Agbo	24	Jun	01

with 100mH (2'6")

5750	Katarina Johnson-Thompson	11	Jul	09
5241	Jade Surman	16	Jul	05
5071	Debbie Marti	5	Jun	83

IAAF U18 2013 (100H 2'6", SP 3kg, JT 500g)

5725	Morgan Lake	4	Aug	13

with 80H 2'6", SP 3kg, JT 500g

5226	Jade O'Dowda	18	Sep	16
5214	Emily Race	17	Sep	17
5140	Anna Rowe	21	Sep	14
5123	Pippa Earley	17	Sep	17
5114	Olivia Dobson	17	Sep	17
5051	Holly McArthur	3	Jul	16

3000 Metres Track Walk

13:50.52	Rebecca Mersh	31	May	04
14:04.1	Susan Ashforth	19	May	85
14:05.8	Tasha Webster	31	May	12
14:09.81	Amy Hales	19	Sep	98
14:17.96 i	Katie Ford	28	Feb	98

5000 Metres Track Walk

23:55.27	Susan Ashforth	25	May	85
24:06.6	Rebecca Mersh	23	Apr	05
24:22.3	Vicky Lawrence	21	Jun	86
24:34.6	Tracy Devlin	17	Sep	89
24:45.4	Karen Eden	9	Jul	78
24:56.34	Jenny Gagg	15	Aug	04
24:57.5	Angela Hodd	24	Jun	86
24:58.8	Ana Garcia (U15)	10	May	14
25:11.46	Nicola Phillips	21	Aug	99

5k Road - where superior to track time

23:57	Sarah Brown	6	Dec	80
24:17	Sophie Lewis Ward	11	Apr	15
24:20	Karen Eden	3	Dec	78

10000 Metres Track Walk

51:00.0	Karen Nipper	21	Feb	81
53:13.8	Rebecca Mersh	14	Oct	03

10k Road - where superior to track time

50:45	Rebecca Mersh	6	Mar	04

UNDER 15

100 Metres

11.56	Jodie Williams	9	Aug	08
11.58	Ashleigh Nelson	9	Jul	05
11.67	Katharine Merry	13	May	89
11.79	Joey Duck	24	May	03
11.83	Asha Phillip	9	Jul	05
11.86	Hayley Clements	2	Jul	83
11.89	Joanne Gardner	20	Aug	77
11.89	Shaunna Thompson	5	Aug	06
11.92	Jane Parry (U13)	20	Aug	77
11.95	Tatum Nelson	7	Aug	93

false start (athlete ran 100 metres)

11.85	Maya Bruney	18	Aug	12

wind assisted

11.47	Katharine Merry	17	Jun	89
11.67	Tatum Nelson	10	Jul	93
11.78	Jane Parry	8	Aug	78
11.81	Hannah Brier	2	Jun	12
11.82	Maya Bruney	18	Aug	12

hand timing

11.8	Janis Walsh	7	Jul	74
11.8	Joanne Gardner	2	Jul	77
11.9	Sonia Lannaman	9	Aug	69
11.9	Linsey Macdonald	26	Aug	78
11.9	Jane Parry	22	Apr	79
11.9	Etta Kessebeh	11	Jul	80
11.9	Carley Wenham	21	Jul	02
11.9	Emma Jackson	20	May	07

hand timing - wind assisted

11.7	Diane Smith	30	Jul	89
11.8	Sonia Lannaman	30	May	70
11.8	Debbie Bunn (U13)	28	Jun	75
11.8	Delmena Doyley	6	Jul	79

200 Metres

23.72	Katharine Merry	17	Jun	89
23.90	Diane Smith	3	Sep	89
24.05	Jane Parry	16	Jul	78
24.06	Joey Duck	12	Jul	03
24.14	Jodie Williams	19	Apr	08
24.18	Desiree Henry	6	Sep	09
24.22	Ashleigh Nelson	4	Sep	05
24.23	Shaunna Thompson	9	Jul	05
24.31	Amy Spencer	8	Jul	00
24.36	Chinedu Monye	5	Sep	04
24.36	Alicia Regis	28	Aug	16

wind assisted

23.54	Katharine Merry	30	Jul	89
23.99	Sarah Wilhelmy	9	Jul	94
24.09	Charlotte McLennaghan	6	Jul	12
24.24	Amy Spencer	8	Jul	00
24.25	Vernicha James	11	Jul	98

hand timing

23.8	Janis Walsh	23	Jun	74
24.1	Sonia Lannaman	29	Aug	70

hand timing - wind assisted

23.6	Jane Parry (U13)	9	Jul	77
23.8	Diane Smith	9	Sep	89

300 Metres

38.73	Amber Anning	30	Aug	15
39.16 mx	Dina Asher-Smith	4	Aug	09
39.7	Hannah Brier	24	Jun	12
40.15	Holly Mpassy	2	Sep	17
40.18	Jade Hutchison	7	Sep	16

400 Metres

56.4	Katie Snowden	21	Jun	08
56.7	Jane Colebrook	25	Jun	72

800 Metres

2:06.22	Tilly Simpson	11	Jul	15
2:06.47	Katy-Ann McDonald	20	Aug	14
2:06.5	Rachel Hughes	19	Jul	82
2:07.26 mx	Jessica Judd	1	Jul	09
2:08.89		26	Aug	09
2:07.84	Molly Canham	28	May	16
2:08.21 mx	Saskia Millard	28	Jun	14
2:08.7	Emma Langston	12	Jul	86
2:08.72 mx	Khahisa Mhlanga	10	Sep	14
2:08.85		20	Aug	14
2:08.75	Bobby Clay	21	Aug	11
2:08.81	Georgia Bell	19	Jul	08

1500 Metres

4:21.03 mx	Jessica Judd	15	Jul	09
4:23.02		24	May	09
4:23.45	Isabel Linaker	7	Jul	90
4:23.72 mx	Katy-Ann McDonald	2	Jul	14
4:27.14		17	May	14
4:24.62	Sabrina Sinha	6	Jul	13
4:24.95	Emelia Gorecka	5	May	08
4:25.5	Tilly Simpson	13	Sep	15
4:26.06	Sarah Hopkinson	11	Jun	05
4:26.40	Olivia Mason	7	Sep	16
4:27.67 mx	Kathleen Faes	24	Jun	15
4:27.70	Emily Pidgeon	12	Jul	03
4:27.9	Joanne Davis	9	Jul	88

1 Mile

4:46.87	Emelia Gorecka	28	Jun	08

3000 Metres

9:22.80 mx	Emelia Gorecka	13	Aug	08
9:25.61 mx	Agnes McTighe	15	Aug	15

75 Metres Hurdles (76cm)

10.85	Shirin Irving	2	Jul	11
10.86	Heather Jones	17	Jun	01
10.86	Pippa Earley	20	Sep	15
10.88	Amber Hornbuckle	20	Sep	15
10.91	Helen van Kempen	14	Aug	05
10.93	Rachel Halstead-Peel	27	Jul	85
10.93	Marcia Sey	28	Aug	16
10.99	Danielle Rooney	9	Jul	05
11.00	Louise Fraser	27	Jul	85
11.00	Danielle Selley	20	Jun	98
11.00	Moesha Howard	21	Aug	11
11.00	Victoria Johnson	28	Aug	16

wind assisted

10.95	Symone Belle	9	Jul	99

hand timing
10.8	Symone Belle	29	Aug	99

hand timing - wind assisted
10.7	Orla Bermingham	14	Jul	90

80 Metres Hurdles (76.2cm) U17
11.29	Shirin Irving	21	Aug	11

High Jump
1.83	Ursula Fay	5	Jun	82
1.81	Debbi Marti	18	Sep	82
1.81	Lea Haggett	6	Jun	86
1.80	Jo Jennings	12	Aug	84
1.80	Katarina Thompson	26	Aug	07
1.79 i	Julia Charlton	24	Feb	80
1.78		13	Jul	80
1.79	Aileen Wilson	4	Jul	98
1.78	Claire Summerfield	28	Jul	79
1.78	Dominique Blaize	30	Jun	02
1.76	Morgan Lake	4	Sep	11
1.76	Rebecca Hawkins	21	Jun	14

Pole Vault
3.80	Hannah Olson	8	Jun	02
3.61 i	Katie Byres	16	Mar	08
3.61 i	Jade Spencer-Smith	13	Feb	16
3.46		27	Aug	16
3.56	Sophie Ashurst	26	Aug	17
3.53	Molly Caudery	27	Sep	14
3.51	Natalie Hooper	15	Jul	12
3.50	Fiona Harrison	24	Aug	96
3.50 i	Kim Skinner	22	Dec	01
3.48	Lucy Bryan	8	Aug	09
3.46	Gemma Tutton (U13)	12	Jun	17
3.46	Lucy Allen	26	Aug	17
3.46	Jasmine Carey	26	Aug	17

Long Jump
6.34	Margaret Cheetham	14	Aug	83
6.30	Fiona May	7	Jul	84
6.07	Georgina Oladapo	21	Jun	81
6.07	Amy Williams	7	Jul	12
5.98	Sandy French	22	Jul	78
5.96	Jade Surman	1	Jun	03
5.96	Morgan Lake	11	Sep	11
5.93	Jackie Harris	10	Jul	87
5.93	Simi Fajemisin	7	Jul	12
5.91	Symone Belle	29	Aug	99
5.88	Sue Scott	11	Aug	66

wind assisted
6.49	Margaret Cheetham	4	Sep	83
6.07	Jade Surman	4	May	03
6.05	Katharine Merry	18	Sep	88
6.02	Michelle Stone	10	Jul	82
6.01	Morgan Lake	7	Aug	11

Triple Jump
12.02	Yasmine Opre-Fisher	2	Aug	08
11.65	Amber Anning	16	Aug	15
11.62	Kerri Davidson	3	Jul	10
11.58	Morgan Lake	11	Sep	11
11.48 i	Amy Williams	26	Feb	12

Shot (4kg)
12.76	Adele Nicoll	16	Jul	11

Shot (3.25kg)
14.38	Sophie Merritt	16	Sep	12
14.27	Susan King	19	May	79
14.23	Adele Nicoll	27	Aug	11
13.98	Morgan Lake	26	Jun	11
13.88 i	Chloe Edwards	21	Apr	01
13.79	Eden Francis	14	Sep	03
13.77	Liz Millward	6	Sep	03

Shot (3kg)
14.59	Bekki Roche	10	Jun	17
14.34	Hannah Molyneaux	16	Aug	15
14.33	Nana Gyedu	14	Aug	17

Discus
44.12	Philippa Roles	30	Aug	92
42.06	Sophie Mace	7	Aug	13
41.92	Catherine Garden	12	Sep	93
41.06	Katie Wickman	18	Sep	05
40.92	Sandra McDonald	24	Jun	78
40.84	Natalie Kerr	24	Jul	94
40.54	Claire Smithson	25	May	97
40.51	Sophie Merritt	26	Aug	12
40.44	Catherine MacIntyre	12	Sep	82
40.36	Shadine Duquemin	12	Sep	09
40.34	Natalie Hart	23	Mar	86

Hammer (4kg)
47.61	Abbi Carter	18	May	08

Hammer (3kg)
58.01	Phoebe Baggott	9	Jul	16
57.83	Kirsty Costello	5	Aug	17
57.74	Tara Simpson-Sullivan	9	Aug	15
57.10	Charlotte Williams	24	Sep	16
56.89	Katie Head	17	Aug	14
55.41	Charlotte Payne	21	Aug	16
55.37	Abbi Carter	6	Sep	08
54.59	Lucy Koenigsberger	27	Aug	16
54.26	Olivia Stevenson	27	Sep	14
54.26	Bekki Roche	10	Sep	17
54.00	Jade Williams	15	Jul	15

Javelin 600gm(1999 Model)
44.23	Freya Jones	12	Jul	08
43.13	Laura McDonald	11	Jul	09
42.44	Emma Hamplett	8	Sep	12
41.44	Louise Watton	8	Sep	01
40.98	Sophie Merritt	8	Sep	12
40.78	Hayley Thomas	11	Aug	01
40.57	Natasha Wilson	9	Jul	10

Javelin (pre 1999 Model)
48.40	Mandy Liverton	31	Aug	87

Javelin 500gm
48.84	Bethany Moule	16	Jul	16
47.56	Bethan Rees	13	Sep	14
44.81	Rebekah Walton	30	Aug	14
44.38	Kate O'Connor	18	Jul	15
43.70	Kirsty Costello	26	Aug	17

Pentathlon (with 800m & 75m hdls)

3755	Morgan Lake	30	Jul	11
3626	Katarina Thompson	16	Sep	07
3532	Kierra Barker	1	Jul	12
3518	Katharine Merry	18	Sep	88
3512	Kate O'Connor	27	Jun	15
3509	Aileen Wilson	20	Sep	98
3467	Jade Surman	21	Sep	03
3467	Jazmin Sawyers	21	Sep	08
3462w	Rhea Southcott	28	Jun	15
3342		20	Sep	15
3462	Pippa Earley	20	Sep	15
3447	Anna Rowe	22	Sep	13
3350 +	Abigail Pawlett	13	Aug	17
3348 w	Shirin Irving	26	Jun	11
3333	Jackie Harris	27	Jun	87
3321	Ebony Wake	26	Jun	11
3314	Iris Oliarnyk	18	Sep	16

with 80mH

3444	Jane Shepherd	16	Jul	83
3350	Claire Smith	3	Jul	82

2000 Metres Track Walk

9:20.3	Ana Garcia (U13)	19	Sep	13

2500 Metres Track Walk

11:50.0	Susan Ashforth	12	Sep	84

3000 Metres Track Walk

14:17.3	Rebecca Mersh	10	May	03
14:34.2	Ana Garcia	13	Sep	15
14:56.4	Sarah Bennett	26	Sep	93
15:00.0	Susan Ashforth	19	Jun	84
15:00.6	Sally Wish	16	Sep	72
15:03.7	Heather Butcher	24	Mar	12
15:06.69	Kelly Mann	30	May	98
15:10.06	Sophie Lewis Ward	21	Sep	13
15:10.28	Jenny Gagg	21	Sep	02
15:12.7	Sarah Foster	20	Sep	03
15:14.6	Amy Hales	31	Aug	96

3k Road - where superior to track time

14:47	Amy Hales	23	Jun	96
14:48	Nikola Ellis	16	Sep	84
14:55	Lisa Langford	6	Dec	80
14:58	Carolyn Brown	19	Aug	87
14:59	Julie Snead	16	Sep	84
15:07	Stephanie Cooper	10	Dec	83
15:07	Kathryn Granger	23	Apr	05
15:09	Angela Hodd	29	Jul	84
15:09	Lauren Whelan	28	Jan	07

5000 Metres Track Walk

24:58.8	Ana Garcia	10	May	14
25:41.9	Rebecca Mersh	27	Sep	03
26:10.8	Sarah Foster	27	Sep	03
26:52.0	Nina Howley	14	Sep	92

5k Road - where superior to track time

24:01	Ana Garcia	2	May	14
26:20	Tracy Devlin	14	Feb	87
26:37	Vicky Morgan	9	Dec	06

UNDER 13

75 Metres

9.54	Hannah Brier	1	Aug	10
9.65	Success Eduan	1	May	17
9.67	Yasmin Miller	27	Aug	07
9.67	Tyra Khambai-Annan	18	Jun	17
9.70	Trezeguet Taylor	29	May	17
9.71	Charlotte McLennaghan	1	Aug	10
9.78	Kitan Eleyae	16	May	04
9.80	Marian Owusuwaah	16	Jul	16
9.83	Amy Spencer	6	Sep	98
9.86	Simone Ager	1	Aug	10

hand timing

9.5	Lukesha Morris	13	Apr	08
9.5	Kenisha Allen	31	May	09
9.5	Hannah Brier	18	Jul	10

100 Metres

11.92	Jane Parry	20	Aug	77
12.21	Trezeguet Taylor	26	Aug	17
12.32	Katharine Merry	24	Jul	87

hand timing

12.1	Katharine Merry	26	Sep	87
12.3	Joanne Gardner	24	Aug	75
12.3	Debbie Bunn	30	Aug	75
12.3	Omolola Ogunnowo	31	Aug	13
12.4	Lorraine Broxup	13	Jun	76
12.4	Sarah Claxton	31	Aug	92
12.4	Yasmin Miller	20	Jun	07

hand timing - wind assisted

11.8	Debbie Bunn	28	Jun	75

150 Metres

18.80	Hannah Brier	1	Aug	10
18.81	Success Eduan	29	May	17
19.12	Trezeguet Taylor	29	May	17
19.19	Uzoma Nwachukwu	2	Sep	07
19.28	Dina Asher-Smith	7	Sep	08
19.28	Tyla Beckles	5	Sep	10
19.29	Charlotte McLennaghan	4	Sep	10
19.29	Imaan Denis	18	Jul	15
19.30	Alyson Bell	22	May	16
19.31	Maya Bruney	1	Aug	10

wind assisted

19.03	Jayda Regis	17	May	14

hand timing

18.7	Alicia Regis	19	Jul	14
19.0	Uzoma Nwachukwu	3	Jun	07
19.0	Omolola Ogunnowo	4	May	13
19.0	Ore Adamson	19	Jul	14
19.1	Emma Ania	7	Sep	91
19.1	Emma Heath	18	Jul	99
19.1	Torema Dorsett	2	Jun	02
19.1	Charlotte Richardson	30	May	15

200 Metres

24.49	Jane Parry	20	Aug	77
25.83	Ayomide Cole	27	Aug	17
25.87	Amy Spencer	2	Aug	98
25.88	Myra McShannon	4	Sep	88
25.95	Sandy French	20	Aug	76

hand timing

24.2	Jane Parry	28	May	77
25.3	Emma Ania	28	Jun	92
25.4	Katharine Merry	21	Jun	87
25.4	Myra McShannon	8	May	88
25.6	Debbie Bunn	5	Jul	75
25.6	Joanne Gardner	24	Aug	75
25.6	Jane Riley	30	Jun	85

wind assisted

23.6	Jane Parry	9	Jul	77

600 Metres

1:37.3	Lisa Lanini	19	Mar	00
1:37.5	Hannah Wood	17	Jul	94

800 Metres

2:13.87	Ruby Simpson	20	Aug	17
2:14.17	Molly Canham	29	Jul	14
2:14.19 mx	Jessica Hicks	17	Jul	04
	2:16.1	12	Jun	04
2:14.8	Janet Lawrence	10	Jul	71
2:15.05	Rachel Hughes	11	Sep	81
2:15.46	Olivia Mason	16	Aug	14
2:15.74 mx	Khahisa Mhlanga	22	Aug	12
2:15.93	Emma Shipley	20	Aug	17
2:16.1	Lisa Lanini	5	Aug	00
2:16.2	Sarah Hopkinson	5	Jul	03

1000 Metres

3:00.1	Charlotte Moore	25	Aug	97
3:04.0 +mx	Jessica Hicks	29	Sep	04

1200 Metres

3:41.83	Rosa Yates	18	Jul	10
3:43.2	Keely Hodgkinson	19	Jul	14
3:43.4 +mx	Jessica Hicks	29	Sep	04
3:43.7	Emma Shipley	15	Jul	17
3:44.43	Megan Warner	15	Sep	12
3:44.5 +	Sarah Hopkinson	14	Jun	03
3:44.8	Hope Goddard	10	Apr	11
3:44.9	Kathleen Faes	1	Jun	13
3:44.96	Eleanor Twite	4	Jun	12

1500 Metres

4:36.9	Rachel Hughes	20	Jul	81
4:38.94 mx	Jessica Hicks	29	Sep	04
	4:41.67	21	Jul	04
4:39.3	Charlotte Moore	2	Aug	97
4:39.84	Sarah Hopkinson	14	Jun	03
4:40.63 mx	Khahisa Mhlanga	25	Jul	12
4:41.7 mx	Olivia Mason	7	Jul	14
4:42.1	Stacey Washington	18	Jul	84
4:42.14 mx	Sarah Coutts	2	Sep	15
4:43.0	Julie Adkin	18	Jul	84
4:43.47 mx	Jessica Judd	19	Sep	07

1 Mile

5:14.1	Sarah Hopkinson	30	Jul	03

70 Metres Hurdles (68.5cm)

11.05	Marcia Sey	27	Jul	14
11.12	Megan Corker	28	Aug	17
11.15	Lauren Beales	25	May	13
11.15	Christa Hetherington	27	Jul	14
11.17	Anne-Marie Massey	3	Sep	95
11.18	Olivia Gauntlett	8	Aug	10
11.18	Iona Irvine	1	Apr	17
11.18	Grace Colmer	2	Sep	17
11.19	Carys Poole	5	Jun	16

wind assisted

11.01	Carys Poole	3	Sep	16
11.02	Nafalya Francis	27	Aug	01
11.09	Yasmin Miller	9	Sep	07

hand timing

10.9	Charlotte Maxwell	31	Aug	04
11.0	Katharine Merry	20	Sep	87
11.0	Justine Roach	13	Sep	97
11.0	Amy Wakeham	31	Aug	04
11.0	Megan Corker	18	Jun	17

wind assisted

10.8	Charlotte Maxwell	30	Aug	04

75 Metres Hurdles (76cm)

11.78	Caroline Pearce	7	Aug	93

hand timing

11.3	Katharine Merry	26	Sep	87

High Jump

1.69	Katharine Merry	26	Sep	87
1.68	Julia Charlton	6	Aug	78
1.65	Debbie Marti	20	Sep	80
1.65	Jane Falconer	20	Sep	87
1.65	Emma Buckett	4	Sep	05
1.63	Lindsey Marriott	11	Aug	79
1.63	Paula Davidge	13	Sep	81
1.63	Ashleigh Bailey	31	Aug	13
1.63	Isabel Pinder	17	Jul	16

Pole Vault

3.46	Gemma Tutton	12	Jun	17
3.12 i	Jade Spencer-Smith	21	Sep	14
3.00		17	Aug	14
3.10	Hannah Olson	9	Sep	00
2.92 i	Molly Caudrey	23	Sep	12
2.91	Olivia Connor	26	Sep	10

Long Jump

5.71	Sandy French	20	Aug	76
5.45	Sarah Wilhelmy	31	Aug	92
5.43	Margaret Cheetham	19	Sep	81
5.42	Katharine Merry	7	Jun	87
5.40	Kerry Gray	1	Sep	84
5.40	Amy Williams	23	Jun	10
5.38	Toyin Campbell	6	Aug	77
5.35	Debbie Bunn	7	Sep	75
5.34	Fiona May	12	Jun	82
5.34 i	Julia Winogrodzka	4	Mar	17

wind assisted

5.55	Katharine Merry	10	Jul	87

Triple Jump

10.24	Karina Harris	12	Aug	13

Shot (3.25kg)

12.20	Susan King	3	Sep	77
11.52	Adele Nicoll	9	Aug	09
11.21	Sophie Merritt	14	Jul	10

Shot (2.72kg)

12.80	Sophie Merritt	11	Jul	10
12.12	Erin Lobley	13	Aug	17
12.07	Becki Hall	14	Aug	01
11.91	Meghan Porterfield	19	Aug	17
11.81	Adele Nicoll	31	Aug	09
11.78	Morgan Lake	12	Jul	09
11.59	Eden Francis	8	Sep	01
11.53	Finesse Thompson	30	Jun	02
11.51	Kirsty Finlay	27	Sep	14
11.50	Nimi Iniekio	5	Sep	99

Discus (1kg)

34.22	Catherine Garden	25	Aug	91
33.71	Sophie Merritt	22	Aug	10
33.61	Sophie Mace	4	Aug	11

Discus (750g)

40.31	Sophie Merritt	17	Jul	10
39.44	Catherine Garden	8	Sep	91
38.20	Sophie Mace	18	Sep	11
37.64	Sandra Biddlecombe	4	Jul	90
36.90	Samantha Callaway	24	Aug	14
35.21	Shadine Duquemin	8	Sep	07
35.15	Charlotte Payne	21	Sep	14
34.80	Rebecca Saunders	28	Aug	00
34.61	Becki Hall	27	Aug	01
33.89	Samaia Dhir	3	Sep	17

Hammer (3kg)

47.10	Lily Murray	12	Jun	17
43.04	Kirsty Costello	6	Jun	15
40.85	Katie Gibson	30	Sep	17

Javelin (600g 1999 model)

32.18	Alisha Levy	8	Sep	12
31.16	Laura Carr	1	Sep	01

Javelin (500g)

35.86	Lucinda White	1	Aug	17

Javelin (400g)

38.37	Hannah Lewington	28	Oct	17
38.18	Lucinda White	23	Sep	17
38.11	Alisha Levy	8	Sep	12
38.07	Louise Watton	12	Sep	99
37.96	Emily Green	6	Jun	10
37.73	Ellie Vernon	15	Jul	13
37.49	Jemma Tewkesbury	30	Sep	03
37.38	Bethan Rees	8	Sep	12
37.37	Anouska Fairhurst	19	Jun	16
37.02	Natalie Whisken	13	Jul	08

Pentathlon (Under 15 implements)

2607	Jane Shepherd	6	Jun	81
2604	Alison Kerboas	19	Sep	93
2541 ?	Jane Falconer	23	Aug	87

Pentathlon

3114	Erin Lobley	16	Sep	17
3046	Morgan Lake	27	Sep	09
2811	Katharine Merry	20	Sep	87
2787	Jessica Hicks	26	Sep	04
2718	Julia Winogrodzka	2	Jul	17
2692	Holly McArthur	23	Sep	12
2664	Amy Wakeham	26	Sep	04
2645	Maisie Jeger	29	Aug	16
2641	Amy Williams	15	Aug	10
2624	Emma Dawson	21	May	06

1000 Metres Track Walk

4:26.77	Ana Garcia	7	Sep	13
4:47.63	Kathryn Granger	25	Aug	03
4:53.4	Fiona McGorum	9	Sep	01
4:56.93	Evie Butcher	7	Sep	13

1k Road - where superior to track time

4:42	Kelly Mann	23	Sep	95
4:43	Natalie Watson	23	Sep	95

2000 Metres Track Walk

9:20.3	Ana Garcia	29	Sep	13
10:09.0	Kelly Mann	10	Sep	95
10:15.4	Kathryn Granger	28	Jun	03
10:17.0	Sarah Bennett	27	Sep	92
10:19.0	Joanne Ashforth	7	Sep	85
10:19.3	Lauren Gimson	14	Jun	03
10:19.8	Fiona McGorum	29	Sep	01

2k Road - where superior to track time

10:03	Kelly Mann	23	Jun	96
10:15	Fiona McGorum	5	May	01

2500 Metres Track Walk

12:48.9	Claire Walker	20	Jul	85
12:50.5	Vicky Lawrence	4	Jul	82
12:53.3	Kelly Mann	11	May	96

2.5k Road - where superior to track time

12:39	Amy Hales	16	Oct	93
12:41	Stephanie Cooper	1	May	82

3000 Metres Track Walk

15:02.0	Ana Garcia	24	Jun	13
15:41.0	Kelly Mann	30	Jul	95

3k Road - where superior to track time

14:23	Ana Garcia	10	May	13
15:25	Nicola Greenfield	21	Mar	87

UK CLUB RELAY RECORDS

MEN

Seniors

4 x 100m	39.37	Newham &EB	30	May	09
4 x 200m	1:23.5	Team Solent	19	Jul	87
4 x 400m	3:04.48	Team Solent	29	Jun	90
1600m Medley	3:20.8	Wolverhampton & Bilston	1	Jun	75
4 x 800m	7:24.4*	North Staffs and Stone	27	Jul	65
4 x 1500m	15:12.6	Bristol	5	Aug	75

* = 4 x 880y time less 2.8sec

Under 20

4 x 100m	40.83	Enfield & Har	15	Sep	07
4 x 200m	1:27.6	Enfield	13	Jun	82
4 x 400m	3:15.3	Enfield	5	Sep	82
1600m Medley	3:31.6	Cardiff	14	Aug	71
4 x 800m	7:35.3	Liverpool H	14	Aug	90
4 x 1500m	16:04.3	Blackburn	15	Sep	79
4 x 110H	1:04.8	Oundle Sch	19	May	79

Under 17

4 x 100m	41.92	Enfield & Har	2	Sep	07
4 x 200m	1:31.2	Herc Wimb	12	Jul	78
4 x 400m	3:19.8	Sale	17	Jul	11
1600m Medley	3:36.1	Thurrock	13	Jun	84
4 x 800m	7:52.1	Clydebank	29	Aug	87
4 x 1500m	16:27.0	Liverpool H	14	Sep	88

Under 15

4 x 100m	44.2	Herne Hill	30	Jul	11
4 x 200m	1:36.6	Whitgift Sch	30	Apr	14
4 x 300m	2:33.4	Sale Harriers	18	Jul	17
4 x 400m	3:31.5o?	Ayr Seaforth	5	Sep	82
	3:31.6	Shaftesbury B	26	Jul	88
1600m Medley	3:48.4	Blackheath	28	Sep	86
4 x 800m	8:13.28o?	Clydebank	2	Sep	89
	8:16.8	Shaftesbury	14	Sep	88
4 x 1500m	17:52.4 o	Stretford	22	Oct	85
	18:18.4	Tonbridge	6	Jul	80

Under 13

4 x 100m	49.2	Trafford	4	Jun	16
	49.81	Team Hounslow	24	Jul	15
4 x 200m	1:40.4	Herne Hill	5	Aug	07
4 x 400m	4:04.5	Blackheath	12	Sep	93
1600m Medley	4:13.7	Blackheath	28	Sep	86
4 x 800m	9:29.8	Sale	28	Jun	88

WOMEN

Seniors

4 x 100m	43.79	Hounslow	18	Sep	82
4 x 200m	1:35.15	Stretford	14	Jul	91
4 x 400m	3:31.62	Essex Ladies	31	May	92
1600m Medley	3:50.6	Coventry Godiva	5	May	84
3 x 800m	6:32.4	Cambridge H	29	Jun	74
4 x 800m	8:41.0	Cambridge H	26	May	75

Under 20

4 x 100m	45.75	Guildford & G	9	Jul	17
4 x 200m	1:42.2	London Oly	19	Aug	72
4 x 400m	3:46.39	Blackheath & B	8	Sep	02
3 x 800m	6:39.8	Havering	13	Sep	78

Under 17

4 x 100m	46.35	Blackheath & B	9	Sep	12
4 x 200m	1:42.2	London Oly.	19	Aug	72
4 x 300m	2:43.1	WSE&H	21	Jul	09
4 x 400m	3:52.1	City of Hull	3	Jul	82
1600m Medley	4:07.8	Warrington	14	Aug	75
3 x 800m	6:46.5	Haslemere	15	Sep	79
	6:46.5	Bromley L	1	Jul	84
4 x 800m	8:53.1	Havering	24	May	80

Under 15

4 x 100m	48.12	Croydon	9	Jul	17
4 x 200m	1:44.0	Bristol	15	Sep	79
4 x 300m	2:49.13	Blackheath & B	15	Jul	17
3 x 800m	6:39.8	Havering	13	Sep	78
4 x 800m	9:21.4	Sale	5	Aug	78

Under 13

4 x 100m	51.6	Swansea	22	May	11
	52.02	Herne Hill	12	Sep	15
4 x 200m	1:51.1	Blackheath & B	10	Sep	17
3 x 800m	7:18.0	Mid Hants	14	Sep	83
4 x 800m	10:02.4	Warrington	16	Sep	75

o overage by current rules

GB & NI v CZE v FRA v ESP v POL Combined Events Indoors
Prague, CZE 28 - 29 January 2017

MEN – Heptathlon
1	Jorge Ureña	ESP	6249
2	**Ashley Bryant**		**5975**
5	**Ben Gregory**		**5770**
8	**Liam Ramsay**		**5618**
11	**Aiden Davies**		**5512**

U20 MEN – Heptathlon
1	Ondrej Kopecký	CZE	5741
10	**Howard Bell**		**5068**
12	**Joseph Hobson**		**4893**
14	**Dylan Carlsson-Smith**		**4411**

MEN – Team Score
1	Spain	17,383
2	**Great Britain & NI**	**17.363**

U20 MEN – Team Score
1	Czech Republic	11,100
5	**Great Britain & NI**	**9.961**

WOMEN – Pentathlon (29 Jan)
1	Laura Arteil	FRA	4263
3	**Jessica Taylor-Jemmett**		**4155**
5	**Katie Stainton**		**4147**
11	**Elise Lovell**		**3892**
14	**Danielle McGifford**		**3834**

U20 WOMEN – Pentathlon (29 Jan)
1	Jana Novotná	CZE	4098
4	**Holly McArthur**		**3859**
10	**Grace Bower**		**3713**
14	**Ada'ora Chigbo**		**3620**

WOMEN – Team Score
1	Poland	12,308
2	**Great Britain & NI**	**12,194**

U20 WOMEN – Team Score
1	Poland	7,937
5	**Great Britain & NI**	**7,572**

BRITISH ATHLETICS INDOOR CHAMPIONSHIPS
Sheffield 11 - 12 February 2017

MEN

60 Metres (11 Feb)
1	Andrew Robertson	6.57
2	Theo Etienne	6.59
3	Dwain Chambers	6.62

200 Metres (12 Feb)
1	Antonio Infantino	ITA	21.05
2	Connor Wood	1UK	21.19
3	Christopher Stone		21.47

400 Metres (12 Feb)
1	Jarryd Dunn	46.97
2	Cameron Chalmers	47.31
3	Lee Thompson	47.87

800 Metres (12 Feb)
1	Guy Learmonth	1:48.19
2	Markhim Lonsdale	1:49.05
3	Spencer Thomas	1:49.12

1500 Metres (28 Feb)
1	Elliot Giles	3:45.59
2	Tom Lancashire	3:46.45
3	James West	3:47.36

3000 Metres (12 Feb)
1	Lee Emanuel	7:55.91
2	Andrew Heyes	7:57.00
3	Nick Goolab	7:58.13

60 Metres Hurdles (11 Feb)
1	Andy Pozzi	7.51
2	David King	7.76
3	Jake Porter	7.86

High Jump (12 Feb)
1	Allan Smith	2.25
2	Robbie Grabarz	2.25
3	Chris Kandu	2.25

Pole Vault (12 Feb)
1	Luke Cutts	5.43
2	Max Eaves	5.43
3	Harry Coppell	5.32

Long Jump (11 Feb)
1	Daniel Bramble	7.80
2	Ashley Bryant	7.71
3	Daniel Gardiner	7.70

Triple Jump (11 Feb)
1	Nathan Fox		16.53
2	Tosin Oke	NGR	16.40
3	Julian Reid		16.30

Shot (12 Feb)
1	Scott Lincoln	18.76
2	Youcef Zatat	18.22
3	Joseph Watson	17.16

5000m Walk (12 Feb)
1	Tom Bosworth		18:39.47
2	Callum Wilkinson		19:49.23
3	Fredrik Vaeng Røtnes	NOR	20:51.15

Heptathlon (Sheffield 7/8 Jan)
1	Liam Ramsay	5832
2	John Lane	5712
3	Aiden Davies	5401

WOMEN

60 Metres (11 Feb)
1	Asha Philip	7.19
2	Shannon Hylton	7.38
3	Rachel Miller	7.47

200 Metres (12 Feb)
1	Finette Agyapong	23.78
2	Amy Allcock	23.89
3	Maya Bruney	24.00

400 Metres (12 Feb)
1	Eilidh Doyle	52.63
2	Laviai Nielsen	52.86
3	Lina Nielsen	52.89

800 Metres (11 Feb)
1	Shelayna Oskan-Clarke	2:03.54
2	Adelle Tracey	2:04.04
3	Mhairi Hendry	2:05.22

1500 Metres (12 Feb)
1	Sarah McDonald	4:19.41
2	Eilish McColgan	4:19.99
3	Revee Walcott-Nolan	4:21.73

3000 Metres (11 Feb)
1	Eilish McColgan		9:05.07
2	Stephanie Twell		9:05.30
3	Giulia Viola	ITA	9:08.16

60 Metres Hurdles (12 Feb)
1	Mollie Courtney	8.32
2	Emma Nwofor	8.43
3	Sophie Yorke	8.46

High Jump (11 Feb)
1=	Morgan Lake		1.89
1=	Bethan Partridge		1.89
3	Pippa Rogan	IRL	1.82

Pole Vault (11 Feb)
1	Jade Ive	4.35
2	Sally Peake	4.16
3	Courtney MacGuire	3.94

Long Jump (12 Feb)
1	Lorraine Ugen	6.72
2	Katarina Johnson-Thompson	6.69
3	Jazmin Sawyers	6.54

Triple Jump (12 Feb)
1	Alex Russell		13.27
2	Saragh Buggy	IRL	13.08
3	Emily Gargan		12.47

Shot 11 Feb)
1	Rachel Wallader	17.43
2	Sophie McKinna	16.74
3	Adele Nicoll	15.93

3000m Walk (12 Feb)
1 Gemma Bridge   13:23.59
2 Emma Achurch   13:48.83
3 Tatyana Gabellone ITA   13:49.49

Pentathlon (Sheffield 8 Jan)
1 Jessica Taylor-Jemmett   4090
2 Elise Lovell   3778
3 Danielle McGifford   3765

ENGLISH NATIONAL
XC CHAMPIONSHIPS
Wollaton Park 25 February 2017

MEN (12k)
1 Ben Connor   39:35
2 Alex Teuten   39:49
3 Sam Stabler   39:59

U20 MEN (10k)
1 Ellis Cross   32:25
2 Ben Dijkstra   32:29
3 Paulos Surafel   32:41

U17 MEN (6k)
1 James Puxty   20:28

U15 MEN (4.5k)
1 Kristian Imroth   14:23

U13 MEN (3k)
1 Jaden Kennedy   12:00

WOMEN (8k)
1 Jessica Judd   29:07
2 Louise Small   29:10
3 Claire Duck   29:21

U20 WOMEN (6k)
1 Harriet Knowles-Jones   22:03
2 Gemma Holloway   22:48
3 Philippa Stone   23:04

U17 WOMEN (5k)
1 Amelia Quirk   18:35

U15 WOMEN (4k)
1 Olivia Mason   15:47

U13 WOMEN (3k)
1 Maisy Luke   12:53

ENGLAND ATHLETICS INDOOR JUNIOR CHAMPIONSHIPS
Sheffield 25 - 26 February 2017

MEN	Under 20		Under 17		Under 15	
60	Dom Ashwell	6.78	Raphael Bouju	6.88	Jaleel Roper	7.09
200	Rio Mitcham	21.42	Adam Clayton	22.22	Jaleel Roper	22.62
300					George Sudderick	37.76
400	Owen Richardson	47.61	Ben Higgins	48.99		
800	Markhim Lonsdale	1:48.71	Joshua Hulse	1:56.74	Gabriel Gisborne	2:02.35
1500	Benjamin Davies	3:51.82	Luke Duffy	4:03.42		
60H	Tre Thomas	7.80	Jack Sumners	7.99	Joseph Harding	8.32
HJ	Tom Gale	2.13	Dominic Ogbechie	2.04	Samuel Brereton	1.90
PV	Joel Leon Benitez	5.40	Frankie Johnson	4.50	Reuben Nairne	3.27
LJ	Sam Talbot	7.48	Jack Sumners	6.63	Joseph Harding	6.36
TJ	Jude Bright-Davies	15.29	Josh Woods	13.00		
SP	Daniel Cartwright	17.70	George Hyde	15.80	Michael Burfoot	13.34
Hept	Joseph Hobson	5109	Joel McFarlane	4948	Joseph Harding	3132
	Hept Sheffield 7/8 Jan		Hept Sheffield 11/12 Mar		Pen Sheffield 12 Mar	

WOMEN	Under 20		Under 17		Under 15	
60	Hannah Brier	7.36	Amy Hunt	7.43	Leah Duncan	7.78
200	Alisha Rees	23.79	Alicia Regis	24.72	Acacia Williams-Hewitt	25.10
300			Sophie Porter	39.99		
400	Jill Cherry	55.65				
800	Isabelle Boffey	2:07.57	Molly Canham	2:11.95	Daisy Worthington	2:16.41
1500	Jemma Reekie	4:27.97	Kiara Frizelle	4:35.00		
60H	Alicia Barrett	8.25	Pippa Earley	8.47	Abigail Pawlett	8.85
HJ	Sommer Lecky IRL	1.79	Ashleigh West	1.76	Lucy-Jane Matthews	1.55
PV	Molly Caudery	4.05	Victoria Barlow	3.80	Lucy Allen	3.21
LJ	Holly Mills	6.15	Ore Adamson	5.89	Molly Palmer	5.56
TJ	Abazz Shayaam-Smith	11.79	Eloise Harvey	12.02		
SP	Gaia Osborne	12.81	Serena Vincent	14.51	Millie Noyce	12.47
Pen	Holly McArthur	3804	Pippa Earley	3952	Lucy-Jane Matthews	3649
	Pen Sheffield 7 January		Pen Sheffield 11 Mar		Pen Sheffield 12 Mar	

34th EUROPEAN INDOOR CHAMPIONSHIPS
Belgrade, SRB 3 - 5 March 2017

MEN

60 Metres (4 Mar)
1	**Richard Kilty**		**6.54**
	(1h2 6.61, 1s1 6.58)		
2	Ján Volko	SVK	6.58
3	Austin Hamilton	SWE	6.63
5	**Theo Etienne**		**6.67**
	(1h3 6.62, 1s2 6.59)		
	Andrew Robertson		**dq**
	(1h4 6.66, 3s2 6.63)		

400 Metres (4 Mar)
1	Pavel Maslák	CZE	45.77
2	Rafal Omelko	POL	46.08
3	Liemarvin Bonevacia	NED	46.26

800 Metres (5 Mar)
1	Adam Kszczot	POL	1:48.87
2	Andreas Bube	DEN	1:49.32
3	Álvaro de Arriba	ESP	1:49.68
4s1	**Kyle Langford**		**1:49.23**
	(1h3 1:49.93)		
5h4	**Guy Learmonth**		**1:48.73**

1500 Metres (4 Mar)
1	Marcin Lewandowski	POL	3:44.82
2	Kalle Berglund	SWE	3:45.56
3	Filip Sasínek	CZE	3:45.89
5	**Tom Lancashire**		**3:46.57**
	(1h1 3:47.37)		

3000 Metres (5 Mar)
1	Adel Mechaal	ESP	8:00.50
2	Henrik Ingebrigtsen	NOR	8:00.93
3	Richard Ringer	GER	8:01.01
6h2	**Nick Goolab**		**8:02.49**

60 Metres Hurdles (3 Mar)
1	**Andy Pozzi**		**7.51**
	(1h1 7.52)		
2	Pascal Martinot-Lagarde	FRA	7.52
3	Petr Svoboda	CZE	7.53
6h2	**David King**		**7.70**
3h3	**David Omoregie**		**7.71**

High Jump (3 Mar)
1	Sylwester Bednarek	POL	2.32
2	**Robbie Grabarz**		**2.30**
	(Q 2.25)		
3	Pavel Seliverstov	BLR	2.27
8	**Allan Smith**		**2.18**
	(Q 2.25)		
10Q	**Chris Kandu**		**2.25**

Pole Vault (3 Mar)
1	Piotr Lisek	POL	5.85
2	Konstadínos Filippídis	GRE	5.85
3	Pawel Wojciechowski	POL	5.85

Long Jump (4 Mar)
1	Izmir Smajlaj	ALB	8.08
2	Michel Tornéus	SWE	8.08
3	Serhiy Nykyforov	UKR	8.07
12Q	**Daniel Bramble**		**7.64**

Triple Jump (5 Mar)
1	Nelson Évora	POR	17.20
2	Fabrizio Donato	ITA	17.13
3	Max Hess	GER	17.12

Shot (4 Mar)
1	Konrad Bukowiecki	POL	21.97
2	Tomás Stanek	CZE	21.43
3	David Storl	GER	21.30

Heptathlon (5 Mar)
1	Kevin Mayer	FRA	6479
2	Jorge Ureña	ESP	6227
3	Adam Helcelet	GER	6110
9	**Ashley Bryant**		**5945**
13	**Liam Ramsay**		**5622**

4 x 400 Metres (5 Mar)
1	Poland	3:06.99
2	Belgium	3:07.80
3	Czech Republic	3:08.60

WOMEN

60 Metres (5 Mar)
1	**Asha Philip**		**7.06**
	(1h5 7.25, 1s2 7.20)		
2	Olesya Povh	UKR	7.10
3	Ewa Swoboda	POL	7.10

400 Metres (4 Mar)
1	Florei Guei	FRA	51.90
2	Zuzana Hejnová	CZE	52.42
3	Justyna Swiety	POL	52.52
4	**Laviai Nielsen**		**52.79**
	(1h4 53.74, 2s3 52.31)		
3s1	**Eilidh Doyle**		**52.81**
	(1h3 53.28)		

800 Metres (5 Mar)
1	Selina Büchel	SUI	2:00.38
2	**Shelayna Oskan-Clarke**		**2:00.39**
	(1h1 2:06.02, 1s2 2:03.09)		
3	Anita Hinriksdóttir	ISL	2:01.25

1500 Metres (4 Mar)
1	**Laura Muir**	**4:02.39**
	(1h1 4:10.28)	
2	Konstanze Klosterhalfen GER	4:04.45
3	Sofia Ennaoui POL	4:06.59
6	**Sarah McDonald**	**4:13.67**
	(2h2 4:12.50)	

3000 Metres (5 Mar)
1	**Laura Muir**		**8:35.67**
	(5h2 8:55.56)		
2	Yasemin Can	TUR	8:43.46
3	**Eilish McColgan**		**8:47.43**
	(2h1 8:57.85)		
5	**Stephanie Twell**		**8:50.40**
	(2h2 8:55.02)		

60 Metres Hurdles (3 Mar)
1	Cindy Roleder	GER	7.88
2	Alina Talay	BLR	7.92
3	Pamela Dutkiewicz	GER	7.95

High Jump (4 Mar)
1	Airine Palsyte	LTU	2.01
2	Ruth Beitia	ESP	1.94
3	Yuliya Levchenko	POL	1.94
8	**Morgan Lake**		**1.85**
	(Q 1.90)		

Pole Vault (4 Mar)
1	Ekaterini Stefanidi	GRE	4.85
2	Lisa Ryzih	GER	4.75
3=	Angelica Bengtsson	SWE	4.55
3=	Maryna Kylypko	UKR	4.55

Long Jump (5 Mar)
1	Ivana Španović	SRB	7.24
2	**Lorraine Ugen**		**6.97**
	(Q 6.80)		
3	Claudia Salman-Rath	GER	6.94
6	**Jazmin Sawyers**		**6.67**
	(Q 6.64)		

Triple Jump (4 Mar)
1	Kristin Gierisch	GER	14.37
2	Patricia Mamona	POL	14.32
3	Paraskevi Papahristou	GRE	14.24

Shot (3 Mar)
1	Anita Márton	HUN	19.28
2	Radoslava Mavrodieva	BUL	18.36
3	Yuliya Leontyuk	BLR	18.32
10Q	**Rachel Wallader**		**17.35**

Pentathlon (3 Mar)
1	Nafissatou Thiam	BEL	4870
2	Ivona Dadic	AUT	4767
3	Györgyi Zsivoczky-Farkas	HUN	4723

4 x 400 Metres (5 Mar)
1	Poland	3:29.94
2	**Great Britain & NI**	**3:31.05**
	(Doyle, Lowe, Iheke, Lav Nielsen)	
3	Ukraine	3:32.10

INTERCOUNTIES XC
Loughborough 11 March 2017

MEN (12k)

1	Andy Vernon	37:50
2	Alexander Teuten	38:14
3	Andy Maud	38:19

WOMEN (8k)

1	Jessica Judd	29:54
2	Claire Duck	30:07
3	Gemma Steel	30:13

U20 MEN (8k)

1	Jonathan Shields	27:13
2	Scott Beattie	27:15
3	Luke Prior	27:17

U20 WOMEN (6k)

1	Anna MacFadyen	22:12
2	Gillian Black	22:17
3	Victoria Weir	22:24

REGIONAL CROSS COUNTRY CHAMPIONSHIPS

Scotland
Falkirk 25 February 2017

MEN (10k)

1	Callum Hawkins	33:34

WOMEN (10k)

1	Morag MacLarty	38:32

Wales
Swansea 25 February 2017

MEN (10.1k)

1	Dewi Griffiths	33:40

WOMEN (6.42k)

1	Beth Kidger	23:52

Northern Ireland
Lurgan 4 March 2017

MEN (12k)

1	Aaron Doherty	39:08

WOMEN (6k)

1	Jessica Craig	23:07

17th EUROPEAN THROWING CUP
Las Palmas de Gran Canaria/Vecindario, ESP 11 - 12 March 2017

MEN

Shot

5B	Scott Lincoln	19.00
8B	Youcef Zatat	17.08

Discus

5B	Zane Duquemin	58.44
7B	Alan Toward	55.16

Hammer

9	Chris Bennett	70.65
6B	Chris Shorthouse	67.22
4U23	Taylor Campbell	67.51

Javelin

4U23	Harry Hughes	76.59

WOMEN

Shot

4	Rachel Wallader	17.47
5	Sophie McKinna	17.03
3U23	Adele Nicoll	16.21

Discus

7U23	Amy Holder	52.94

Hammer

5B	Rachel Hunter	64.21

Senior Events
Las Palmas de Gran Canaria
U23 Events
Vecindario

RWA CHAMPIONSHIPS

Leeds 25 June 2017
MEN 20k

1	Tom Bosworth	1:24:59

WOMEN 20k

1	Gemma Bridge	1:32:33

JUNIOR MEN 10k

1	Tom Partington	45:10

JUNIOR WOMEN 10k

1	Ana Garcia	51:53

Coventry 29 April 2017
MEN 10k

1	Callum Wilkinson	41:03

WOMEN 10k

1	Erika Kelly	48:54

Douglas IOM 3 September 2017
MEN 50k

1	David Walker	5:29:12

WOMEN 50k

1	Jayne Farquhar	6:01:31

EUROPEAN CUP 10,000 METRES
Minsk, BLR 10 June 2017

MEN

12	Matthew Leach	30:02.36
13	Graham Rush	30:03.97
	Kristian Jones	dnf

Team Result

4	Great Britain & NI	dnf

WOMEN

11	Katrina Wootton	33:49.74
12	Claire Duck	34:08.72
16	Louise Small	34:29.54

Team Result

4	Great Britain & NI	1:42:28.00

IAAF WORLD RELAY CHAMPIONSHIPS
Nassau, BER 22-23 April 2017

MEN

4x100 Metres (22 Apr)

	Great Britain & NI	dnf
	(Ujah, Hughes, Talbot, Edoburun)	
1h3		38.32
	(Ujah, Hughes, Gemili, Talbot)	

MEN

4x400 Metres (23 Apr)

6	Great Britain & NI	3:05.63
	(Hudson-Smith, D Williams, Dunn Campbell)	
2h1		3:05.19

WOMEN

4x400 Metres (23 Apr)

4	Great Britain & NI	3:28.72
	(Diamond, Lav Nielsen, Doyle, Ohuruogu)	
2h2		3:33.00
	(Doyle, Diamond, Onuora, Massey)	

IAAF WORLD CROSS COUNTRY CHAMPIONSHIPS
Kampala, UGA 26 March 2017

SENIOR MEN (9.858k)

1	Geoffrey Kamworor	KEN	28:24
2	Leonard Barsoton	KEN	28:36
3	Abadi Hadis	ETH	28:43
4	Jemal Yimer	ETH	28:46
5	Aron Kifle	ERI	28:49

Team Result

1	Ethiopia	21
2	Kenya	22
3	Uganda	72

JUNIOR MEN (7.858k)

1	Jacob Kiplimo	UGA	22:40
2	Amdework Walelegn	ETH	22:43
3	Richard Yator	KEN	22:52
44	Sam Stevens		25:52
48	Scott Beattie		26:01
61	Jonathan Shields		26:35
70	Hugo Milner		26:58
81	Luke Prior		27:24
89	Benjamin Davies		28:01

Team Result

1	Ethiopia	10
2	Kenya	28
3	Eritrea	55
10	Great Britain & NI	223

SENIOR WOMEN (9.858k)

1	Irene Cheptai	KEN	31:57
2	Alice Aprot Nawowuna	KEN	32:01
3	Lilian Rengeruk	KEN	32:11
4	Hyvin Jepkemoi	KEN	32:32
5	Agnes Tirop	KEN	32:32
38	Louise Small		35:51
42	Rebecca Murray		36:04
62	Claire Duck		37:12
89	Emily Hosker-Thornhill		41:51

Team Result

1	Kenya	10
2	Ethiopia	45
3	Bahrain	59
14	Great Britain & NI	231

JUNIOR WOMEN (5.858k)

1	Letesenbet Gidey	ETH	18:34
2	Hawi Feysa	ETH	18:57
3	Celliphine Chespol	KEN	19:02
40	Victoria Weir		21:43
46	Gillian Black		21:59
48	Anna MacFadyen		22:04
57	Phoebe Barker		22:19
64	Cari Hughes		22:29
	Amelia Quirk		dnf

Team Result

1	Ethiopia	19
2	Kenya	20
3	Uganda	63
9	Great Britain & NI	191

Mixed 4x2k Relay

1	Kenya	22:22
2	Ethiopia	22:30
3	Turkey	22:37

LONDON MARATHON
23 April 2017

MEN

1	Daniel Wanjiru	KEN	2:05:48
2	Kenenisa Bekele	ETH	2:05:57
3	Bedan Karoki	KEN	2:07:41
4	Abel Kirui	KEN	2:07:45
5	Alphonce Felix Simbu	TAN	2:09:10
14	Joshua Griffiths	1UK	2:14:53
16	Robbie Simpson	2UK	2:15:04
17	Andrew Davies	3UK1Eng	2:15:11
21	Scott Overall	2Eng	2:16:54
23	Matthew Sharp	3Eng	2:17:48

WOMEN

1W	Mary Keitany	KEN	2:17:01
2W	Tirunesh Dibaba	ETH	2:17:56
3W	Aselefech Mergia	ETH	2:23:08
4W	Vivian Cheruiyot	KEN	2:23:50
5W	Lisa Weightman	AUS	2:25:15
14W	Alyson Dixon	1UK1Eng	2:29:06
15W	Charlotte Purdue	2UK2Eng	2:29:23
16W	Tracy Barlow	3UK3Eng	2:30:42
18W	Tish Jones		2:33:56
21W	Susan Partridge		2:37:51
1	Anna Boniface		2:37:17

EUROPEAN RACE WALKING CUP
Podebrady, CZE
21 May 2017

MEN - 20Km

4	Tom Bosworth	1:21:21
10	Callum Wilkinson	1:22:17
36	Cameron Corbishley	1:27:26
47	Dominic King	1:29:28

Team Result

4	Great Britain & NI	50

UNDER 20 MEN - 10Km

19	Christopher Snook	44:23

WOMEN - 20Km

14	Gemma Bridge	1:34:24
22	Bethan Davies	1:36:04
39	Heather Lewis	1:44:41

Team Result

6	Great Britain & NI	75

UNDER 20 WOMEN - 10Km

31	Molly Jade Davey	54:02

IAU 24 Hour WORLD CHAMPIONSHIPS
Belfast
1/2 July 2017

MEN

23	Steven Holyoak	245.492k
28	Pat Robbins	242.114k
38	Daniel Lawson	231.280k
60	Marco Consani	218.557k
118	James Stewart	178.416k

Team Result

8	Great Britain & NI	715.582k

MEN

6	Jess Baker	238.713k
25	Alison Young	217.875k
41	Debbie Martin-Consani	204.118k
68	Sharon Law	182.642k
77	Beth Pascall	172.730k

Team Result

6	Great Britain & NI	657.402k

7th EUROPEAN TEAM CHAMPIONSHIPS - Super League
Villeneuve d'Ascq, FRA 23 - 25 June 2017

MEN

100 Metres wind -0.7 (24 Jun)
1 Harry Aikenes-Aryeetey   **10.21**
   (1h1 10.33)
2 Julian Reus   GER   10.27
3 Churandy Martina   NED   10.30

200 Metres wind 0.4 (25 Jun)
1 Serhiy Smelyk   UKR   20.53
2 Mickaël-Méba Zeze   FRA   20.57
3 Likoúrgos-Stéfanos Tsákonas   GRE   20.59
5 Samuel Miller   **20.79**
   (3h1 20.88)

400 Metres (24 Jun)
1 Dwayne Cowan   **45.46**
   (1h1 46.04)
2 Rafal Omelko   POL   45.53
3 Davide Re   ITA   45.56

800 Metres (25 Jun)
1 Thijmen Kupers   NED   1:47.18
2 Giordano Benedetti   ITA   1:47.94
3 James Bowness   **1:48.19**

1500 Metres (24 Jun)
1 Marcin Lewandowski   POL   3:53.40
2 Jake Wightman   **3:53.72**
3 Timo Benitz   GER   3:54.28

3000 Metres (25 Jun)
1 Jakub Holuša   CZE   7:57.60
2 Marc Scott   **7:58.52**
3 Carlos Mayo   ESP   7:58.97

5000 Metres (24 Jun)
1 Antonio Abadía   ESP   13:59.40
2 Nick Goolab   **13:59.72**
3 Amanal Petros   GER   13:59.83

WOMEN

100 Metres wind 0.4 (24 Jun)
1 Carole Zahi   FRA   11.19
2 Gina Lückenkemper   GER   11.35
3 Corinne Humphreys   **11.50**
   (2h2 11.53)

200 Metres wind 0.4 (25 Jun)
1 Maria Belibasáki   GRE   22.6
2 Anna Kielbasinska   POL   22.8
3 Rebekka Hasse   GER   22.8
4 Finette Agyapong   **23.0**
   (4h1 23.31)

400 Metres (24 Jun)
1 Lisanne de Witte   NED   51.71
2 Olha Zemlyak   UKR   51.88
3 Laura Müller   GER   52.09
6 Mary Iheke   **52.60**
   (5h2 52.92)

3000 Metres Steeplechase (25 Jun)
1 Mahiedine Mekhissi-Benabbad   FRA   8:26.71
2 Sebastián Martos   ESP   8:27.46
3 Krystian Zalewski   POL   8:33.02
4 Rob Mullett   **8:33.99**

110 Metres Hurdles wind 0.2 (25 Jun)
1 Orlando Ortega   ESP   13.20
2 Aurel Manga   FRA   13.25
3 David Omoregie   **13.36**
   (1h1 13.34)

400 Metres Hurdles (24 Jun)
1 Jack Green   **49.47**
   (1h1 49.96)
2 Sérgio Fernández   ESP   49.72
3 Patryk Dobek   POL   49.79

High Jump (24 Jun)
1 Mickaël Hanany   FRA   2.26
2 Marco Fassinotti   ITA   2.22
3 Eike Onnen   GER   2.22
8= Chris Baker   **2.12**

Pole Vault (25 Jun)
1 Renaud Lavillenie   FRA   5.80
2= Hendrik Gruber   GER   5.55
2= Igor Bychov   ESP   5.55
8 Luke Cutts   **5.30**

Long Jump (24 Jun)
1 Daniel Bramble   **8.00**
2 Eusebio Cáceres   ESP   7.96
3 Radek Juska   CZE   7.86

Triple Jump (25 Jun)
1 Max Hess   GER   17.02
2 Ben Williams   **16.73**
3 Pablo Torrijos   ESP   16.71

800 Metres (24 Jun)
1 Olha Lyakhova   UKR   2:03.09
2 Yusneysi Santiusti   ITA   2:03.56
3 Esther Guerrero   ESP   2:03.70
9 Katie Snowden   **2:05.19**

1500 Metres (25 Jun)
1 Konstanze Klosterhalfen   GER   4:09.57
2 Angelika Cichocka   POL   4:12.16
3 Nataliya Pryshchepa   UKR   4:13.51
9 Rhianwedd Price   **4:17.60**

3000 Metres (24 Jun)
1 Sofia Ennaoui   POL   9:01.24
2 Hanna Klein   GER   9:01.64
3 Simona Vrzalová   CZE   9:02.77
9 Harriet Knowles-Jones   **9:14.86**

Shot (24 Jun)
1 Tomás Stanek   CZE   21.63
2 David Storl   GER   21.23
3 Konrad Bukowiecki   POL   20.83
10 Scott Lincoln   **17.96**

Discus (25 Jun)
1 Robert Harting   GER   66.30
2 Robert Urbanek   POL   66.25
3 Lolassonn Djouhan   FRA   64.35
5 Zane Duquemin   **61.23**

Hammer (25 Jun)
1 Pawel Fajdek   POL   78.29
2 Pavel Boreysha   BLR   77.52
3 Nick Miller   **76.65**

Javelin (24 Jun)
1 Jakub Vadlejch   CZE   87.95
2 Ioánnis Kiriazís   GRE   86.33
3 Thomas Röhler   GER   84.22
8 Matti Mortimore   **72.42**

4x100 Metres Relay (24 Jun)
1 Great Britain & NI   **38.08**
(Ujah, Hughes, Talbot, Aikines-Aryeetey)
2 Germany   38.30
3 France   38.68

4x400 Metres Relay (24 Jun)
1 Spain   3:02.32
2 Netherlands   3:02.37
3 Czech Republic   3:03.31
6B Great Britain & NI (9)   **3:07.49**
(Yousif, Dunn, Chalmers, Miller)

5000 Metres (25 Jun)
1 Ana Lozano   ESP   15:18.40
2 Yuliya Shmatenko   UKR   15:30.36
3 Alina Reh   GER   15:32.50
6 Calli Thackery   **16:12.16**

3000 Metres Steeplechase (24 Jun)
1 Gesa-Felicitas Krause   GER   9:27.02
2 Lennie Waite   **9:43.33**
3 Irene Sánchez   ESP   9:43.51

100 Metres Hurdles wind 0.4 (25 Jun)
1 Pamela Dutkiewicz   GER   12.62
2 Alina Talay   BLR   12.91
3 Hanna Plotitsyna   UKR   13.05
6 Alicia Barrett   **13.27**
   (3h2 13.32)

400 Metres Hurdles (24 Jun)

1	Eilidh Doyle		54.60
	(1h1 55.76)		
2	Yadisleidy Pedroso	ITA	55.39
3	Olena Kolesnychenko	UKR	55.51

High Jump (25 Jun)

1	Kamila Lićwinko	POL	1.97
2	Marie-Laurence Jungfleisch	GER	1.97
3=	Michaela Hrubá	CZE	1.94
3=	Alessia Trost	ITA	1.94
7=	**Morgan Lake**		**1.85**

Pole Vault (24 Jul)

1	Ekateríni Stefanidi	GRE	4.70
2	Iryna Zhuk	BLR	4.60
3	Ninon Guillon-Romarin	FRA	4.45
6	**Sally Peake**		**4.35**

Long Jump (25 Jun)

1	Claudia Salman-Rath	GER	6.66
2	Rogul Sow	FRA	6.45
3	Maryna Bekh	UKR	6.43
4	**Jazmin Sawyers**		**6.42**

Triple Jump (24 Jun)

1	Paraskevi Papahristou	GRE	14.24
2	Kristin Gierisch	GER	14.13

3	Jeanine Assani Issouf	FRA	14.00
9	**Shara Proctor**		**13.39**

Shot (25 Jun)

1	Alyona Dubitskaya	BLR	18.39
2	Melissa Boekelman	NED	17.72
3	Paulina Guba	POL	17.67
10	**Amelia Strickler**		**15.40**

Discus (24 Jun)

1	Mélina Robert-Michon	FRA	62.62
2	Nadine Müller	GER	62.57
3	Hrisoula Anagnostopoúlou	GER	59.28
10	**Jade Lally**		**54.01**

Hammer (24 Jun)

1	Hanna Malyshik	BLR	74.56
2	Malwina Kopron	POL	73.06
3	Alyona Shamotina	UKR	70.02
5	**Sophie Hitchon**		**69.30**

Javelin (25 Jun)

1	Barbora Spotáková	CZE	65.14
2	Tatyana Kholodovich	BLR	64.60
3	Marcelina Witek	POL	60.98
9	**Jo Blair**		**50.61**

4x100 Metres Relay (24 Jun)

1	Germany	42.47
2	Poland	43.07
3	Ukraine	43.09
	Great Britain & NI	**dnf**
	(Philip, S Hylton, Henry, Neita)	

4x400 Metres Relay (25 Jun)

1	Poland	3:27.60
2	Ukraine	3:28.02
3	Germany	3:28.47
4	**Great Britain & NI**	**3:28.96**
	(Diamond, Lav Nielsen, McAslan, Onuora)	

Team

1	Germany	321.5
2	Poland	295
3	France	270
4	**Great Britain & NI**	**269**
5	Spain	242.5
6	Ukraine	236.5
7	Italy	220
8	Czech Rebublic	213.5
9	Greece	196.5
10	Belarus	188.5
11	Netherlands	175

EUROPEAN CUP COMBINED EVENTS - Super League
Tallinn, EST 1 - 2 July 2017

MEN

Decathlon

1	Janek Oiglane	EST	8170
10	**Ben Gregory**		**7530**
11	**John Lane**		**7348**
15	**Andrew Murphy**		**7084**
	James Finney		**dnf**

WOMEN

Heptathlon

1	Alina Shukh	UKR	6208
6	**Jessica Taylor-Jemmett**		**5702**
10	**Jo Rowland**		**5518**
18	**Lucy Turner**		**5199**
	Zoe Hughes		**dnf**

Team

1	Ukraine	40,085
2	Estonia	39,779
3	France	39,771
4	**Great Britain & NI**	**38,381**

BRITISH ATHLETICS CHAMPIONSHIPS & WORLD TRIALS
Birmingham 1 - 2 July 2017

MEN

100 Metres wind .0 (1 Jul)

1	Reece Prescod	10.09
2	James Dasaolu	10.11
3	Harry Aikines-Aryeetey	10.20
4	Ojie Edoburun	10.21
5	Joel Fearon	10.26
6	Reuben Arthur	10.31
7	Samuel Osewa	10.38
	Chijindu Ujah	dns

200 Metres wind 0.8 (2 Jul)

1	Nethaneel Mitchell-Blake	20.18
2	Danny Talbot	20.20
3	Leon Reid	20.38
4	Zharnel Hughes	20.42
5	Samuel Miller	20.90
6	Adam Gemili	20.97
7	Roy Ejiakuekwu	21.15

400 Metres (2 Jul)

1	Matthew Hudson-Smith	44.99
2	Rabah Yousif	45.82
3	Cameron Chalmers	46.11
4	Dwayne Cowan	46.12
5	Martyn Rooney	46.13
6	George Caddick	46.62
7	Theo Campbell	47.29
8	Jamal Rhoden-Stevens	47.61

800 Metres (2 Jul)

1	Elliot Giles	1:49.52
2	Guy Learmouth	1:49.89
3	Kyle Langford	1:50.13
4	Daniel Rowden	1:50.27
5	Andrew Osagie	1:50.54
6	James Bowness	1:50.93
7	John Bird	1:51.15
8	Jamie Webb	1:51.47

1500 Metres (2 Jul)

1	Chris O'Hare	3:47.28
2	Josh Kerr	3:47.71
3	Jake Wightman	3:47.74
4	Neil Gourley	3:48.45
5	Charlie Grice	3:48.84
6	James West	3:49.19
7	Josh Carr	3:49.46
8	Rowan Axe	3:50.34

5000 Metres (1 Jul)

1	Andrew Butchart	13:50.56
2	Andy Vernon	13:54.63
3	Ben Connor	13:56.71
4	Marc Scott	14:06.93
5	Luke Traynor	14:09.25
6	Chris Thompson	14:09.61
7	Graham Rush	14:15.96
8	Andrew Heyes	14:17.33

10000 Metres (20 May London(PH))

1	Andy Vernon		28:21.15
2	Dewi Griffiths		28:31.88
3	Samuel Barata	POR	28:40.19
4	Ricardo Serrano	ESP	28:46.38
5	Ben Connor	3 UK	28:46.45
6	Bart van Nunen	NED	28:57.73
7	Abel Tsegay	ERI	28:59.63
8	Ellis Cross		29:00.49

3000 Metres Steeplechase (1 Jul)

1	Rob Mullett	8:41.43
2	Zak Seddon	8:43.14
3	Ieuan Thomas	8:43.77
4	Douglas Musson	8:44.33
5	William Gray	8:44.57
6	Adam Kirk-Smith	8:45.37
7	Ryan Driscoll	8:53.00
8	Luke Gunn	8:54.94

110 Metres Hurdles wind 2.1 (2 Jul)

1	David King	13.55w
2	Khai Riley-La Borde	13.71w
3	Jake Porter	13.79w
4	James Weaver	13.88w
5	David Omoregie	13.93w
6	Edirin Okoro	13.99w
7	Miguel Perera	14.34w
	David Feeney	dns

400 Metres Hurdles (2 Jul)

1	Jack Green	49.34
2	Jacob Paul	49.66
3	Seb Rodger	50.23
4	Tom Burton	50.36
5	Jack Lawrie	50.65
6	Niall Flannery	50.75
7	James Forman	51.16
8	Chris McAlister	51.83

High Jump (2 Jul)

1	Robbie Grabarz	2.26
2=	Chris Baker	2.20
2=	David Smith	2.20
2=	Mike Edwards	2.20
5	Matt Roberts	2.16
6	Allan Smith	2.16
7	Ryan Webb	2.12
8	Jonathan Broom-Edwards	2.12

WOMEN

100 Metres wind -1.3 (1 Jul)

1	Asha Philip	11.21
2	Daryll Neita	11.25
3	Ashleigh Nelson	11.28
4	Bianca Williams	11.47
5	Corinne Humphreys	11.50
6	Dina Asher-Smith	11.53
7	Finette Agyepong	11.56
8	Rachel Miller	11.58

Pole Vault (2 Jul)

1	Luke Cutts	5.45
2	Jax Thoirs	5.40
3=	Harry Coppell	5.30
3=	Max Eaves	5.30
5	Charlie Myers	5.30
6	Scott Huggins	5.15
7	Rhys Searles	5.00
8=	Nick Cruchley	5.00
8=	Jack Phipps	5.00
8=	Rowan May	5.00

Long Jump (2 Jul)

1	Daniel Bramble	8.02
2	Feron Sayers	7.95w
3	Jacob Fincham-Dukes	7.90
4	Timothy Duckworth	7.84w
5	Allan Hamilton	7.60
6	Daniel Gardiner	7.45
7	Scott Hall	7.44
8	Tom French	7.36

Triple Jump (1 Jul)

1	Ben Williams	16.71
2	Nathan Fox	16.42w
3	Nonso Okolo	16.29
4	Nathan Douglas	16.27
5	Jonathan Ilori	15.74
6	Julian Reid	15.73
7	Jonathan Sawyers	15.49
8	Chukwudi Onyia	15.40

Shot (1 Jul)

1	Scott Lincoln	17.82
2	Gareth Winter	17.35
3	Youcef Zatat	16.68
4	Daniel Cartwright	15.98
5	Craig Sturrock	14.86
6	Matthew Baptiste	14.79
7	Michael Wheeler	14.78
8	Martin Tinkler	14.28

Discus (1 Jul)

1	Nicholas Percy	60.78
2	Zane Duquemin	60.36
3	Brett Morse	60.12
4	Alan Toward	56.30
5	Gregory Thompson	55.57
6	Matthew Blandford	53.82
7	George Armstrong	53.25
8	Mark Plowman	52.61

200 Metres wind 0.0 (2 Jul)

1	Shannon Hylton	22.94
2	Bianca Williams	23.05
3	Desiree Henry	23.14
4	Kimbely Baptiste	23.36
5	Jodie Williams	23.41
6	Beth Dobbin	23.42
7	Amarachi Pipi	23.60
8	Louise Bloor	23.76

Hammer (2 Jul)

1	Nick Miller	74.98
2	Taylor Campbell	72.87
3	Mark Dry	70.51
4	Chris Bennett	70.50
5	Joseph Ellis	68.05
6	Craig Murch	67.92
7	Chris Shorthouse	66.96
8	Jake Norris	66.93

Javelin (1 Jul)

1	Joe Dunderdale	73.58
2	Matti Mortimore	72.19
3	Joe Harris	70.50
4	Steve Turnock	70.31
5	Neil McLellan	67.70
6	Harry Hughes	66.61
7	Jack Swain	66.56
8	Greg Millar	64.87

5000 Metres Walk (2 Jul)

1	Tom Bosworth		18:43.28
2	Callum Wilkinson		18:56.96
g	Damian Blocki	POL	19:43.39
g	Cian McManamon	IRL	20:24.37
3	Christopher Snook		21:39.09
4	Tom Partington		22:04.01
5	Luc Legon		22:53.81
6	Francisco Reis	POR	23:52.75

Decathlon (Bedford 27-28 May)

1	James Finney		7263
2	Peter Moreno	NGR	7252
3	Andrew Murphy		7170
4	Jack Andrew		7048
5	Mick Bowler	IRL	6768
6	Curtis Mathews		6736
7	Harry Kendall		6625
8	Charlie Roe		6523

400 Metres (2 Jul)

1	Zoey Clark	52.30
2	Emily Diamond	52.34
3	Anyika Onuora	52.82
4	Cheriece Hylton	52.98
5	Amy Allcock	53.40
6	Perri Shakes-Drayton	53.52
7	Kirsten McAslan	54.14
8	Margaret Adeoye	54.81

800 Metres (2 Jul)
1	Shelayna Oskan-Clarke	2:01.54
2	Adelle Tracey	2:01.80
3	Lynsey Sharp	2:01.81
4	Alexandra Bell	2:02.79
5	Mhairi Hendry	2:03.37
6	Marilyn Okoro	2:03.81
7	Hannah Segrave	2:04.39
8	Ellie Baker	2:04.81

1500 Metres (2 Jul)
1	Laura Weightman	4:06.49
2	Jessica Judd	4:07.09
3	Sarah McDonald	4:08.14
4	Katie Snowden	4:09.70
5	Melissa Courtney	4:10.16
6	Charlene Thomas	4:11.25
7	Jemma Reekie	4:12.28
8	Hannah England	4:13.15

5000 Metres (2 Jul)
1	Stephanie Twell	15:35.50
2	Eilish McColgan	15:38.57
3	Charlotte Arter	15:43.46
4	Verity Ockenden	15:46.11
5	Jessica Judd	15:49.05
6	Emelia Gorecka	15:51.93
7	Louise Small	16:02.75
8	Holly Rees	16:04.24

10000 Metres (20 May London (PH))
1	Beth Potter		32:04.63
2	Stephanie Twell		32:16.23
3	Katrina Wootton		32:27.47
4	Jo Pavey		32:42.93
5	Claire Duck		32:51.38
6	Charlotte Arter		32:51.72
7	Emma Mitchell	IRL	32:51.78
8	Iwona Bernardelli	POL	32:55.06

3000 Metres Steeplechase (2 Jul)
1	Iona Lake	9:57.53
2	Charlotte Taylor-Green	9:59.58
3	Katie Ingle	10:02.34
4	Lennie Waite	10:13.81
5	Stacie Taylor	10:23.23
6	Laura Riches	10:27.03
7	Melanie Wilkins	10:37.50
8	Aimee Pratt	10:45.36

100 Metres Hurdles wind -1.4 (1 Jul)
1	Alicia Barrett	13.26
2	Yasmin Miller	13.29
3	Jessica Hunter	13.45
4	Mollie Courtney	13.58
5	Megan Marrs	13.71
6	Heather Paton	13.84
7	Sophie Yorke	13.99
8	Gemma Bennett	13.99

400 Metres Hurdles (2 Jul)
1	Eilidh Doyle	55.59
2	Meghan Beesley	56.68
3	Jessica Turner	56.79
4	Caryl Granville	57.46
5	Ese Okoro	57.62
6	Jessie Knight	58.00
7	Lauren Thompson	58.62
8	Nisha Desai	58.80

High Jump (1 Jul)
1	Morgan Lake	1.96
2	Emma Nuttall	1.83
3	Nikki Manson	1.79
4=	Niamh Emerson	1.79
4=	Bethan Partridge	1.79
6	Kate Anson	1.75
7	Emily Borthwick	1.75
8=	Rebecca Hawkins	1.71
8=	Natasha Smith	1.71

Pole Vault (1 Jul)
1	Holly Bradshaw	4.45
2	Lucy Bryan	4.35
3	Sally Peake	4.25
4	Henrietta Paxton	4.15
5	Abigail Roberts	4.00
6	Claire Maurer	3.85
7=	Courtney MacGuire	3.85
7=	Jessica Swannack	3.85

Long Jump (2 Jul)
1	Lorraine Ugen	6.59
2	Rebecca Chapman	6.54
3	Holly Mills	6.31
4	Jahisha Thomas	6.28
5	Sarah Warnock	6.16
6	Eleanor Broome	6.16
7	Niamh Ermerson	6.03
8	Katie Stainton	6.01

Triple Jump (1 Jul)
1	Naomi Ogbeta	13.64
2	Sineade Gutzmore	13.44
3	Jahisha Thomas	13.25
4	Angela Barrett	13.05
5	Chioma Matthews	13.00
6	Allison Wilder	12.45
7	Montana Jackson	12.44
8	Shanara Hibbert	12.18

Shot (2 Jul)
1	Rachel Wallader	16.70
2	Amelia Strickler	16.59
3	Sophie McKinna	16.23
4	Eden Francis	16.02
5	Adele Nicoll	15.52
6	Sarah Omoregie	14.12
7	Sophie Merritt	13.80
8	Sophie Littlemore	13.61

Discus (2 Jul)
1	Jade Lally	58.14
2	Kirsty Law	52.73
3	Shadine Duquemin	51.31
4	Phoebe Dowson	51.04
5	Amy Holder	50.90
6	Kathryn Woodcock	47.60
7	Jemma Ibbetson	44.46
8	Sophie Mace	44.08

Hammer (1 Jul)
1	Sophie Hitchon	67.58
2	Rachel Hunter	63.27
3	Sarah Holt	61.53
4	Myra Perkins	61.27
5	Lucy Marshall	61.03
6	Kayleigh Presswell	57.78
7	Phillipa Wingate	57.11
8	Hayley Murray	57.02

Javelin (2 Jul)
1	Laura Whittingham	52.07
2	Jo Blair	51.31
3	Emma Hamplett	51.02
4	Bethan Rees	49.56
5	Natasha Wilson	47.68
6	Laurensa Britane	47.59
7	Hannah Johnson	46.51
8	Eloise Meakins	44.73

5000 Metres Walk (2 Jul)
1	Bethan Davies		21:21.52
g	Alana Barber	NZL	21:59.41
g	Elisa Neuvonen	FIN	22:46.85
2	Erika Kelly		23:20.19
g	Kate Veale	IRL	23:53.98
3	Sophie Lewis Ward		24:57.51
g	Natalie le Roux	RSA	25:02.99
g	Ester Montaner	ESP	25:47.85

Heptathlon (Bedford 28-28 May)
1	Niamh Emerson		5801
2	Jessica Taylor-Jemmett		5674
3	Lucy Turner		5436
4	Elise Lovell		5330
5	Jessica Tappin		5301
6	Laura Voss	GER	5165
7	Katie Garland		5076
8	Lucy Chappell		4634

11th EUROPEAN Under 23 CHAMPIONSHIPS
Bydgoszcz, POL 13 - 16 July 2017

MEN

100 Metres wind 0.0 (14 Jul)
1 Ojie Edoburun 10.14
(1h4 10.37, 1s2 10.26)
2 Ján Volko SVK 10.18
3 Jonathan Quarcoo NOR 10.29
5 Reuben Arthur 10.39
(1h5 10.51, 3s3 10.35)
3s1 Joseph Dewar 10.45
(1h2 10.48)

200 Metres wind 1.6 (15 Jul)
1 Ján Volko SVK 20.33
2 Gautier Dautremer FRA 20.66
3 Roger Gurski GER 20.70

400 Metres (15 Jul)
1 Luka Janežič SLO 45.33
2 Karsten Warholm NOR 45.75
3 Benjamin Lobo Vedel DEN 46.08
4 Cameron Chalmers 46.29
(2h2 47.25, 3s1 46.32)

800 Metres (16 Jul)
1 Andreas Kramer SWE 1:48.15
2 Daniel Rowden 1:48.16
(1h1 1:47.51)
3 Marc Reuther GER 1:48.66

1500 Metres (15 Jul)
1 Marius Probst GER 3:49.06
2 Filip Sasinek CZE 3:49.23
3 Michal Rozmys POL 3:49.30
4 Neil Gourley 3:49.53
(3h1 3:43.99)
8 Robbie Fitzgibbon 3:50.07
(4h2 3:43.47)
8h2 James West 3:44.72

5000 Metres (15 Jul)
1 Yemaneberhan Crippa ITA 14:14.28
2 Simon Debognies BEL 14:14.71
3 Carlos Mayo ESP 14:15.07
Alex George dnf

10000 Metres (13 Jul)
1 Carlos Mayo ESP 29:28.06
2 Amanal Petros GER 29:34.94
3 Emmanuel Roudolff Lévisse FRA 29:42.85
5 Ellis Cross 29:53.64

3000 Metres Steeplechase (16 Jul)
1 Yohanes Chiappinelli ITA 8:34.33
2 Ahmed Abdelwahed ITA 8:37.02
3 Jamaine Coleman 8:40.44
(1h2 8:50.15)
12 Daniel Jarvis 9:03.07
(7h1 8:52.65)

110 Metres Hurdles wind 0.8 (15 Jul)
1 Ludovic Payen FRA 13.49
2 Khai Riley-La Borde 13.65
(1h1 14.01)
3 Dylan Caty FRA 13.66
4 James Weaver 13.75
(1h3 13.85)

400 Metres Hurdles (16 Jul)
1 Karsten Warholm NOR 48.37
2 Dany Brand SUI 49.14
3 Ludvy Vaillant FRA 49.31
5 Jacob Paul 49.98
(2h4 51.04, 2s1 49.85)
7 Jack Lawrie 50.60
(2h1 50.40, 4s2 50.46)

High Jump (15 Jul)
1 Dmitriy Nabokov BLR 2.24
2 Christian Falocchi ITA 2.24
3 Viktor Lonskyy UKR 2.24
Chris Kandu nh
(Q 2.18)

Pole Vault (16 Jul)
1 Ben Broeders BEL 5.60
2 Axel Chapelle FRA 5.60
3 Adrián Valles ESP 5.50
11= Charlie Myers 5.20
(Q 5.25)

Long Jump (14 Jul)
1 Vladyslav Mazur UKR 8.04
2 Filippo Randazzo ITA 7.98w
3 Thobias Nilsson Montler SWE 7.96
4 Jacob Fincham-Dukes 7.83w
(Q 7.67)

Triple Jump (16 Jul)
1 Nazim Babayev AZE 17.18
2 Simo Lipsanen FIN 17.14
3 Max Hess GER 16.68

Shot (14 Jul)
1 Konrad Bukowiecki POL 21.59
2 Denzel Comenentia NED 19.86
3 Sebastiano Bianchetti ITA 19.69

Discus (16 Jul)
1 Sven Martin Skagestad NOR 61.00
2 Alin Firfirica ROU 60.17
3 Clemens Prüfer GER 60.08

Hammer (14 Jul)
1 Bence Halász HUN 73.30
2 Bence Pásztor HUN 71.51
3 Alexej Mikhailov GER 70.60
4 Taylor Campbell 70.59
(Q 67.43)

Javelin (15 Jul)
1 Norbert Rivasz-Tóth HUN 83.08
2 Ioánnis Kiriazis GRE 81.04
3 Andrian Mardare MDA 78.76

Decathlon (15-16 Jul)
1 Jiri Sykora CZE 8084
2 Fredrik Samuelsson SWE 8010
3 Elmo Savola FIN 7956
Timothy Duckworth dnf

20 Kilometres Walk (16 Jul)
1 Diego Garcia ESP 1:22:29
2 Karl Junghannss GER 1:22:52
3 Gabriel Bordier FRA 1:23:03

4x100 Metres Relay (16 Jul)
1 Germany 39.11
2 Great Britain & NI 39.11
(Etienne, de Escofet, Arthur, Edoburun)
(1h1 39.45)
3 Finland 39.70

4x400 Metres Relay (16 Jul)
1 Great Britain & NI 3:03.65
(Thompson, Snaith, Hazel, Chalmers)
(2h1 3:06.20)
(Thompson, Snaith, Hazel, Somers)
2 Poland 3:04.22
3 France 3:05.24

WOMEN

100 Metres wind -0.6 (14 Jul)
1 Ewa Swoboda POL 11.42
2 Kristina Tsimanovskaya BLR 11.54
3 Sina Mayer GER 11.58
4 Imani Lansiquot 11.58
(2h1 11.72, 2s2 11.47)

200 Metres wind 1.3 (15 Jul)
1 Finette Agyapong 22.87
(2h4 23.04, 1s1 22.86)
2 Sarah Atcho SUI 22.90
3 Yana Kachur UKR 23.20
5 Amarachi Pipi 23.41
(2h1 23.37, 2s2 23.26)

400 Metres (15 Jul)
1 Gunta Latiseva-Cudare LAT 52.00
2 Laura Müller GER 52.42
3 Laura de Witte NED 52.51
5 Laviai Nielsen 53.18
(1h2 52.80)

800 Metres (15 Jul)
1 Renée Eykens BEL 2:04.73
2 Anita Hinriksdóttir ISL 2:05.02
3 **Hannah Segrave** 2:05.53
   (1h3 2:05.54)

1500 Metres (16 Jul)
1 Konstanze Klosterhalfen GER 4:10.30
2 Sofia Ennaoui POL 4:13.54
3 Martyna Galant POL 4:17.91
5 **Amy Griffiths** 4:19.16
   (2h1 4:17.11)

5000 Metres (16 Jul)
1 Yasemin Can TUR 15:01.67
2 Alina Reh GER 15:10.57
3 Sarah Lahti SWE 15:14.17

10000 Metres (14 Jul)
1 Yasemin Can TUR 31:39.80
2 Sarah Lahti SWE 32:46.91
3 Büsra Nur Koku TUR 33:33.22
4 **Phoebe Law** 33:40.75
6 **Jenny Nesbitt** 33:50.37
8 **Philippa Bowden** 34:04.57

3000 Metres Steeplechase (15 Jul)
1 Anna Emilie Møller DEN 9:43.05
2 Nataliya Strebkova UKR 9:44.52
3 Emma Oudiou FRA 9:50.30
14 **Aimee Pratt** 10:28.64
   (2h2 10:10.15)

100 Metres Hurdles wind 2.3 (15 Jul)
1 Nadine Visser NED 12.92w
2 Elvira Herman BLR 12.95w
3 Luca Kozák HUN 13.06w
4 **Yasmin Miller** 13.32w
   (2h4 13.48, 3s2 13.40)

400 Metres Hurdles (16 Jul)
1 Ayomide Folorunso ITA 55.82
2 **Jessica Turner** **56.08**
   (2h2 58.54, 3s2 57.32)
3 Arna Gudmundsdóttir ISL 56.37

High Jump (16 Jul)
1 Yuliya Levchenko UKR 1.96
2 Iryna Herashchenko UKR 1.92
3 Erika Furlani ITA 1.86

Pole Vault (15 Jul)
1 Angelica Moser SUI 4.55
2 Maryna Kylypko UKR 4.45
3 **Lucy Bryan** 4.40
   (Q 4.20)

Long Jump (16 Jul)
1 Yanis David FRA 6.56
2 Anna Bühler GER 6.50
3 Maryna Bekh UKR 6.48

Triple Jump (14 Jul)
1 Elena Panturoiu ROU 14.27
2 Ana Peleteiro ESP 14.19
3 Rouguy Diallo FRA 13.99w

Shot (15 Jul)
1 Fanny Roos SWE 18.14
2 Klaudia Kardasz POL 17.67
3 Alina Kenzel GER 17.46

Discus (14 Jul)
1 Claudine Vita GER 61.79
2 Daria Zabawska POL 59.08
3 Veronika Domjan SLO 58.48
9 **Amy Holder** 51.81
   (Q 51.37)

Hammer (15 Jul)
1 Alyona Shamotina UKR 67.46
2 Camille Sainte-Luce FRA 66.98
3 Beatrice Nedberge Llano NOR 66.74

Javelin (16 Jul)
1 Sara Kolak CRO 65.12
2 Anete Kocina LAT 64.47
3 Marcelina Witek POL 63.03

Heptathlon (13-14 Jul)
1 Caroline Agnou SUI 6330
2 Verena Preiner AUT 6232
3 Celina Leffler GER 6070
7 **Katie Stainton** 5836

20 Kilometres Walk (16 Jul)
1 Klavdiya Afanasyeva RUS 1:31:15
2 Mária Pérez ESP 1:31:29
3 Ziviklé Vaiciukeviciuté LTU 1:32:21

4x100 Relay (16 Jul)
1 Spain 43.96
2 France 44.06
3 Switzerland 44.07
h2 **Great Britain & NI** **dnf**
   (Walker, Agyepong, Pipi, Stephenson)

4x400 Relay (16 Jul)
1 Poland 3:29.66
2 Germany 3:30.18
3 Ukraine 3:30.22
4 **Great Britain & NI** **3:30.74**
   (Lina Nielsen, Lav Nielsen, Turner, C.Hylton)

24th EUROPEAN Under 20 CHAMPIONSHIPS
Grosseto, ITA 20 - 23 July 2017

MEN

100 Metres wind -4.3 (21 Jul)
1 Filippo Tortu ITA 10.73
2 Samuel Purola FIN 10.79
3 **Oliver Bromby** 10.88
   (2h5 10.70, 1s3 10.54)
8s1 **Rechmial Miller** 10.94
   (1h2 10.55)
3s2 **Dom Ashwell** 10.67
   (1h3 10.52)

200 Metres wind -0.9 (22 Jul)
1 **Toby Harries** 20.81
   (1h3 21.20, 1s3 20.89)
2 Jona Efoloko 20.92
   (1h1 21.26, 2s1 21.20)
3 Samuel Purola FIN 21.00
4s2 **Nick Stewart** 21.52
   (3h5 21.36)

400 Metres (22 Jul)
1 Vladimir Aceti ITA 45.92
2 Tymoteusz Zimny POL 46.04
3 Jonathan Sacoor BEL 46.23
5 **Owen Richardson** 46.49
   (1h5 46.70, 4s2 46.85)

800 Metres (23 Jul)
1 Marino Bloudek CRO 1:48.70
2 **Markhim Lonsdale** 1:48.82
   (1h1 1:53.92, 1s3 1:48.24)
3 John Fitzsimons IRL 1:49.15
4 **Ben Greenwood** 1:49.37
   (2h3 1:51.57, 1s1 1:49.32)
4s2 Canaan Solomon 1:49.42
   (3h4 1:52.11)

1500 Metres (22 Jul)
1 **Jake Heyward** 3:56.73
   (4h2 3:46.64)
2 Dries De Smet BEL 3:56.98
3 Adrian Ben ESP 3:57.32
5 **Archie Davis** 3:57.65
   (4h1 3:48.35)
12h2 **James Gormley** 3:53.76

5000 Metres (22 Jul)
1 Jacob Ingebrigtsen NOR 14:41.67
2 Tariku Novales ESP 14:44.66
3 Dorin Andrei Rusu ROU 14:46.07
12 **Tom Mortimer** 16:00.54

10000 Metres (20 Jul)
1 Dorin Andrei Rusu ROU 31:08.86
2 Sergiy Polikarpenko ITA 31:10.85
3 Sezgin Atac TUR 31:12.18

3000 Metres Steeplechase (23 Jul)

1	Jacob Ingebrigtsen	NOR	8:50.00
2	Alexis Phelut	FRA	8:53.73
3	Louis Gilavert	FRA	8:57.12
	William Battershill		**dnf**
	(3h1 9:07.97)		

110 Metres Hurdles 99cm wind 0.0 (22 Jul)

1	Jason Joseph	SUI	13.41
2	**Robert Sakala**		**13.48**
	(2h1 13.62, 3s3 13.88)		
3	Luis Salort	ESP	13.48
3s1	**Jason Nicholson**		**14.09**
	(5h5 14.25)		
3s2	**Cameron Fillery**		**14.11**
	(3h2 14.17)		

400 Metres Hurdles (23 Jul)

1	Wilfried Happio	ITA	49.93
2	Alessandro Sibilio	ITA	50.34
3	David José Pineda	ITA	50.41
h1	**Alex Knibbs**		**dq**

High Jump (22 Jul)

1	Maksim Nedasekov	BLR	2.33
2	Dmytro Nikitin	UKR	2.28
3	**Tom Gale**		**2.28**
	(Q 2.12)		
18Q	**Joel Khan**		**2.09**
22=Q	**Thomas Hewes**		**2.00**

WOMEN

100 Metres wind -1.4 (21 Jul)

1	Gina Akpe-Moses	IRL	11.71
2	Keshia Beverly Kwadwo	GER	11.75
3	Ingvild Meinseth	NOR	11.77
4	**Olivia Okoli**		**11.86**
	(1h2 11.65, 2s2 11.78)		

200 Metres wind -1.0 (22 Jul)

1	**Maya Bruney**		**23.04**
	(1h3 23.47, 1s1 23.07)		
2	Sophia Junk	GER	23.45
3	Katrim Fehm	GER	23.49
4	**Alisha Rees**		**23.54**
	(2h4 24.06, 2s3 23.65)		

400 Metres (22 Jul)

1	Anastasiya Bryzhina	UKR	52.01
2	Andrea Miklos	ROU	52.31
3	**Hannah Williams**		**52.55**
	(2h3 53.08, 2s1 53.61)		
5	**Lauren Russell**		**53.87**
	(3h1 53.71, 5s2 54.14)		

800 Metres (22 Jul)

1	**Khahisa Mhlanga**		**2:06.96**
	(1h2 2:08.47)		
2	**Ellie Baker**		**2:07.01**
	(1h1 2:08.90)		
3	Gabriele Gajanová	SVK	2:07.15

Pole Vault (23 Jul)

1	Armand Duplantis	SWE	5.65
2	Bo Kanda Lita Baehre	GER	5.45
3	Romain Gavillon	FRA	5.35
	Joel Leon Benitez		**nm**
	(Q 5.10)		

Long Jump (21 Jul)

1	Miltiádis Tentóglou	GRE	8.07
2	Jakub Andrzejczak	POL	8.02
3	Héctor Santos	ESP	7.96

Triple Jump (23 Jul)

1	Martin Lamou	FRA	16.97
2	Andrea Dallavalle	ITA	16.87
3	Melvin Raffin	FRA	16.82

Shot 6kg (21 Jul)

1	Marcus Thomsen	NOR	21.36
2	Szymon Mazur	POL	20.70
3	Odisséas Mouzenídis	GRE	20.67

Discus 1.75kg (24 Jul)

1	Oskar Stachnik	POL	62.01
2	Hleb Zhuk	BLR	60.16
3	**George Evans**		**59.05**
	(Q 56.91)		

Hammer 6kg (21 Jul)

1	Hlib Piskunov	UKR	81.75
2	Aliaksandr Shymanovich	BLR	77.74
3	Dániel Rába	HUN	75.95
7	**Jake Norris**		**72.68**
	(Q 76.62)		

1500 Metres (23 Jul)

1	**Jemma Reekie**		**4:13.25**
	(2h2 4:19.57)		
2	Liliana Georgieva	BUL	4:16.73
3	**Harriet Knowles-Jones**		**4:17.53**
	(2h1 4:21.14)		
4	**Amelia Quirk**		**4:19.23**
	(5h2 4:19.75)		

3000 Metres (22 Jul)

1	Delia Sclabas	SUI	9:10.13
2	Mathilde Senechal	FRA	9:20.05
3	Nadia Battocletti	ITA	9:24.01
4	**Jemma Reekie**		**9:24.81**

5000 Metres (23 Jul)

1	Jasmijn Lau	NED	16:38.85
2	Miriam Dattke	GER	16:39.81
3	Floor Doornwaard	NED	16:41.71

3000 Metres Steeplechase (22 Jul)

1	Lisa Oed	GER	10:00.79
2	Tatyana Shabonova	BLR	10:03.32
3	Gülnaz Uskun	TUR	10:19.44
11	**Emily Moyes**		**10:39.05**
	(7h1 10:27.16)		

Javelin (22 Jul)

1	Cyprian Mrzyglod	POL	80.52
2	Aliaksei Katkavets	BLR	76.91
3	Lukas Moutarde	FRA	74.22
16Q	**James Whiteaker**		**66.34**

Decathlon Junior implements (22-23 Jul)

1	Niklas Kaul	GER	8435
2	Johannes Erm	EST	8141
3	Karel Tilga	EST	8002
	Sam Talbot		**dnf**

10000 metres Walk (22 Jul)

1	Sergey Shirobokov	RUS	43:21.29
2	José Manuel Pérez	ESP	44:17:23
3	Eduard Zabuzhenko	UKR	44:22.16

4x100 Metres Relay (23 Jul)

1	Germany	39.48
2	Italy	39.50
3	Spain	39.59
4	**Great Britain & NI**	**39.67**
	(Ashwell, Bromby, K.Jones, E Davis)	
	(1h1 39.84)	

4x400 Metres Relay (23 Jul)

1	Italy	3:08.68
2	France	3:09.04
3	Poland	3:09.32

100 Metres Hurdles wind 0.1 (22 Jul)

1	Solene Ndama	FRA	13.15
2	**Alicia Barrett**		**13.28**
	(1h3 13.37, 1s3 13.41)		
3	Klaudia Siciarz	POL	13.33
5	**Sophie Yorke**		**13.51**
	(2h5 13.58, 3s2 13.75)		

400 Metres Hurdles (23 Jul)

1	Yasmin Giger	SUI	55.90
2	Agata Zupin	SLO	55.96
3	Viivi Lehikoinen	FIN	56.49
7s1	**Orla Brothers**		**59.59**
	(4h2 59.81)		

High Jump (23 Jul)

1	Michaela Hrubá	CZE	1.93
2	Karina Taranda	BLR	1.87
3	Maja Nilsson	SWE	1.85

Pole Vault (22 Jul)

1	Lisa Gunnarsson	SWE	4.40
2	**Molly Caudery**		**4.35**
	(Q 4.05)		
3	Wilma Murto	FIN	4.15

Long Jump (23 Jul)
1 Milica Gardasevic SRB 6.46
2 Tabea Christ GER 6.41
3 Kaiza Karlén SWE 6.32

Triple Jump (21 Jul)
1 Violetta Skvartsova BLR 14.21w
2 Ilionis Guillaume FRA 13.97w
3 **Naomi Ogbeta** **13.68w**
   (Q 13.25)
14Q **Emily Gargan** 12.46

Shot (22 Jul)
1 Julia Ritter GER 17.24
2 Jorinde van Klinken NED 16.89
3 Anna Niedbala POL 16.32
4 **Divine Oladipo** **16.03**
   (Q 14.60)

Discus (21 Jul)
1 Alexandra Emilianov MDA 56.38
2 Karolina Urban POL 53.88
3 Kristina Rakocevic MNE 53.56
17Q **Divine Oladipo** **46.11**

Hammer (22 Jul)
1 Katerina Skypalová CZE 64.78
2 Eva Mustafic CRO 63.09
3 Michaela Walsh IRL 61.27

Javelin (21 Jul)
1 Nikol Tabacková CZE 55.10
2 Carolina Visca ITA 53.65
3 Elina Kinnunen FIN 52.94

Heptathlon (20-21 Jul)
1 Alina Shukh UKR 6381
2 Géraldine Ruckstuhl SUI 6357
3 Sarah Lagger AUT 6083
4 **Niamh Emerson** **6013**
11 **Holly McArthur** **5687**

10000 metres Walk (20 Jul)
1 Yana Smerdova RUS 47:19.69
2 Teresa Zurek GER 47:33.20
3 Meryem Bekmez TUR 48:33.88

4x100 Relay (23 Jul)
1 Germany 43.44
2 France 44.03
3 **Great Britain & NI** **44.17**
   (Carr, Rees, Bruney, Okoli)
   (1h2 44.50)
   (Brier, Rees, Crawford, Okoli)

4x400 Relay (23 Jul)
1 Ukraine 3:32.82
2 Germany 3:33.08
3 **Great Britain & NI** **3:33.68**
   (M Edwards, Bruney, E Barrett, H Williams)
   (2h2 3:40.62)
   (Cherry, M Edwards, E Barrett, McArthur)

ENGLAND/CAU CHAMPIONSHIPS
Bedford 29 - 30 July 2017

MEN

100 Metres wind -0.1 (29 Jul)
1 Ojie Edoburun 10.26

200 Metres wind 0.3 (30 Jul)
1 Antonio Infantino ITA 21.14
2 Christopher Stone 1-Eng 21.14

400 Metres (30 Jul)
1 Sadam Koumi SUD 46.14
2 Benjamin Snaith 1-Eng 46.21

800 Metres (29 Jul)
1 James McMurray 1:50.41

1 Mile (30 Jul)
1 Jonathan Davies 4:00.58

5000 Metres (30 Jul)
1 Alexander Teuten 14:54.56

3000 Metres Steeplechase (29 Jul)
1 Douglas Musson 8:43.34

110 Metres Hurdles wind 0.0 (29 Jul)
1 James Weaver 13.73

400 Metres Hurdles (30 Jul)
1 James Forman 50.72

High Jump (29 Jul)
1 Tom Gale 2.30

Pole Vault (29 Jul)
1 Joel Leon Benitez 5.25

Long Jump (30 Jul)
1 Jack Roach 7.43w

Triple Jump (29 Jul)
1 Nathan Douglas 16.40w

Shot (30 Jul)
1 Scott Lincoln 18.54

Discus (30 Jul)
1 Alan Toward 57.59

Hammer (30 Jul)
1 Callum Brown 69.13

Javelin (29 Jul)
1 Joe Harris 75.71

3000 metres Walk (30 Jul)
1 Christopher Snook 12:42.73

WOMEN

100 Metres wind -0.5 (29 Jul)
1 Diani Walker 11.45

200 Metres wind 0.7 (30 Jul)
1 Kimbely Baptiste 23.54

400 Metres (30 Jul)
1 Margaret Adeoye 53.14

800 Metres (29 Jul)
1 Hannah England 2:06.68

1500 Metres (30 Jul)
1 Hannah England 4:17.84

5000 Metres (30 Jul)
1 Verity Ockenden 16:36.91

3000 Metres Steeplechase (29 Jul)
1 Iona Lake 9:50.61

100 Metres Hurdles wind -0.2 (29 Jul)
1 Yasmin Miller 13.32

400 Metres Hurdles (30 Jul)
1 Kirsten McAslan 57.31

High Jump (30 Jul)
1 Emma Nuttall 1.86
2 Emily Borthwick 1-Eng 1.76

Pole Vault (30 Jul)
1 Jade Ive 4.05

Long Jump (29 Jul)
1 Katie Stainton 6.07

Triple Jump (30 Jul)
1 Angela Barrett 13.15

Shot (29 Jul)
1 Amelia Strickler 16.79

Discus (29 Jul)
1 Amy Holder 50.84

Hammer (29 Jul)
1 Susan McKelvie 61.80
2 Sarah Holt 1-Eng 61.31

Javelin (30 Jul)
1 Laura Whittingham 54.88

3000 metres Walk (30 Jul)
1 Erika Kelly 13:50.72
2 Emily Ghose 1-Eng 15:34.69

18th IAAF WORLD CHAMPIONSHIPS
London 4-13 August 2017

MEN

100 Metres wind -0.8 (5 Aug)

1	Justin Gatlin	USA	9.92
2	Christian Coleman	USA	9.94
3	Usain Bolt	JAM	9.95
4	Yohan Blake	JAM	9.99
5	Akani Simbini	RSA	10.01
6	Jimmy Vicaut	FRA	10.08
7	**Reece Prescod**		**10.17**

(3h3 10.03, 2s2 10.05)

8	Su Bingtian	CHN	10.27
5s1	**James Dasaolu**		**10.22**

(2h6 10.13)

4s3	**Chijindu Ujah**	**10.12**

(2h4 10.07)

200 Metres wind -0.1 (10 Aug)

1	Ramil Guliyev	TUR	20.09
2	Wayde van Niekerk	RSA	20.11
3	Jereem Richards	TTO	20.11
4	**Nethaneel Mitchell-Blake**		**20.24**

(1h7 20.08, 3s1 20.19w)

5	Ameer Webb	USA	20.26
6	Isaac Makwala	BOT	20.44
7	Abdul Sani Brown	JPN	20.63
8	Isiah Young	USA	20.64
7s2	**Zharnel Hughes**		**20.85**

(4h6 20.43)

5s3	**Danny Talbot**	**20.38**

(2h3 20.16)

400 Metres (8 Aug)

1	Wayde van Niekerk	RSA	43.98
2	Steven Gardiner	BAH	44.41
3	Abdalelah Haroun	QAT	44.48
4	Baboloki Thebe	BOT	44.66
5	Nathon Allen	JAM	44.88
6	Demish Gaye	JAM	45.04
7	Fred Kerley	USA	45.23
	Isaac Makwala	BOT	dns
8s1	**Dwayne Cowan**		**45.96**

(3h3 45.39)

4s2	**Matthew Hudson-Smith**	**44.74**

(5h1 45.31)

6h5	**Martyn Rooney**	**45.75**

800 Metres (8 Aug)

1	Pierre-Ambroise Bosse	FRA	1:44.67
2	Adam Kszczot	POL	1:44.95
3	Kipyegon Bett	KEN	1:45.21
4	**Kyle Langford**		**1:45.25**

(5h2 1:46.38, 2s2 1:45.81)

5	Nijel Amos	BOT	1:45.83
6	Mohammed Aman	ETH	1:46.06
7	Thiago André	BRA	1:46.30
8	Brandon McBride	CAN	1:47.09
5s1	**Guy Learmouth**		**1:46.75**

(3h6 1:45.90)

6s1	**Elliot Giles**	**1:46.95**

(3h3 1:45.86)

1500 Metres (13 Aug)

1	Elijah Manangoi	KEN	3:33.61
2	Timothy Cheruiyot	KEN	3:33.99
3	Filip Ingebrigtsen	NOR	3:34.53
4	Adel Mechaal	ESP	3:34.71
5	Jakub Holuša	CZE	3:34.89
6	Sadik Mikhou	BRN	3:35.81
7	Marcin Lewandowski	POL	3:36.02
8	Nick Willis	NZL	3:36.82
12	**Chris O'Hare**		**3:38.28**

(3h2 3:42.53 4s2 3:38.59)

8s1	**Jake Wightman**	**3:41.79**

(4h3 3:38.50)

11h1	**Josh Kerr**	**3:47.30**

5000 Metres (12 Aug)

1	Muktar Edris	ETH	13:32.79
2	**Mo Farah**		**13:33.22**

(2h1 13:30.18)

3	Paul Chelimo	USA	13:33.30
4	Yomif Kejelcha	ETH	13:33.51
5	Selemon Barega	ETH	13:35.34
6	Mohammed Ahmed	CAN	13:35.43
7	Aron Kifle	ERI	13:36.91
8	**Andrew Butchart**		**13:38.73**

(7h2 13:24.78)

18h2	**Marc Scott**	**13:58.11**

10000 Metres (4 Aug)

1	**Mo Farah**		**26:49.51**
2	Joshua Cheptegei	UGA	26:49.94
3	Paul Tanui	KEN	26:50.60
4	Bedan Karoki	KEN	26:52.12
5	Jemal Yimer	ETH	26:56.11
6	Geoffrey Kamworor	KEN	26:57.77
7	Abadi Hadis	ETH	26:59.19
8	Mohamed Ahmed	CAN	27:02.35

Marathon (6 Aug)

1	Geoffrey Kirui	KEN	2:08:27
2	Tamirat Tola	ETH	2:09:49
3	Alphonce Felix Simbu	TAN	2:09:51
4	**Callum Hawkins**		**2:10:17**
5	Gideon Kipketer	KEN	2:10:56
6	Daniele Meucci	ITA	2:10:56
7	Yohanes Ghebregergis	ERI	2:12:07
8	Daniel Wanjiru	KEN	2:12:16
31	**Andrew Davies**		**2:17:59**
39	**Joshua Griffiths**		**2:20:06**

3000 Metres Steeplechase (8 Aug)

1	Conseslus Kipruto	KEN	8:14.12
2	Soufiane El-Bakkali	MAR	8:14.49
3	Evan Jager	USA	8:15.53
4	Mahiedine Mekhissi-Benabbad	FRA	8:15.80
5	Stanley Kebenei	USA	8:21.09
6	Matthew Hughes	CAN	8:21.84
7	Tesfaye Deriba	ETH	8:22.12
8	Tafese Seboka	ETH	8:23.02

10h1	**Zak Seddon**	**8:32.84**
15h2	**Ieuan Thomas**	**8:52.96**
15h3	**Rob Mullett**	**8:47.99**

110 Metres Hurdles wind 0.0 (7 Aug)

1	Omar McLeod	JAM	13.04
2	Sergey Shubenkov	RUS	13.14
3	Balázs Baji	HUN	13.28
4	Garfield Darien	FRA	13.30
5	Aries Merritt	USA	13.31
6	Shane Braithwaite	BAR	13.32
7	Orlando Ortega	ESP	13.37
8	Hansle Parchment	JAM	13.37
4s2	**Andy Pozzi**		**13.28**

(1h4 13.28)

6h1	**David Omoregie**	**13.59**
8h2	**David King**	**13.67**

400 Metres Hurdles (9 Aug)

1	Karsten Warholm	NOR	48.35
2	Yasmani Copello	TUR	48.49
3	Kerron Clement	USA	48.52
4	Kemar Mowatt	JAM	48.99
5	TJ Holmes	USA	49.00
6	Juander Santos	DOM	49.04
7	Abderrahaman Samba	QAT	49.74
8	Kariem Hussien	SUI	50.07
4s2	**Jack Green**		**49.93**

(5h5 49.55)

High Jump (13 Aug)

1	Mutaz Essa Barshim	QAT	2.35
2	Danil Lysenko	RUS	2.32
3	Majed El Dein Ghazal	SYR	2.29
4	Edgar Rivera	MEX	2.29
5	Mateusz Przybylko	GER	2.29
6=	**Robbie Grabarz**		**2.25**

(Q 2.31)

6=	Ilya Ivanyuk	RUS	2.25
8	Bryan McBride	USA	2.25

Pole Vault (8 Aug)

1	Sam Kendricks	USA	5.95
2	Piotr Lisek	POL	5.89
3	Renaud Lavillenie	FRA	5.89
4	Xue Changrui	CHN	5.82
5	Pawel Wojciechowski	POL	5.75
6	Axel Chappelle	FRA	5.65
7	Kurtis Marschall	AUS	5.65
8	Shawnacy Barber	CAN	5.65

Long Jump (5 Aug)

1	Luvo Manyonga	RSA	8.48
2	Jarrion Lawson	USA	8.44
3	Rushwahl Samaai	RSA	8.32
4	Aleksandr Menkov	RUS	8.27
5	Maykel Masso	CUB	8.26
6	Shi Yuhao	CHN	8.23
7	Wang Jianan	CHN	8.23
8	Michel Tornéus	SWE	8.18

Triple Jump (10 Aug)

1	Christian Taylor	USA	17.68
2	Will Claye	USA	17.63
3	Nelson Évora	POR	17.19
4	Cristian Nápoles	CUB	17.16
5	Alexis Copello	AZE	17.16
6	Chris Benard	USA	17.16
7	Andy Diaz	CUB	17.13
8	Jean-Marc Pontvianne	FRA	16.68
19Q	**Nathan Fox**		**16.49**

Shot (6 Aug)

1	Tomas Walsh	NZL	22.03
2	Joe Kovacs	USA	21.66
3	Stipe Žunic	CRO	21.46
4	Tomás Stanek	CZE	21.41
5	Michal Haratyk	POL	21.41
6	Ryan Crouser	USA	21.20
7	Ryan Whiting	USA	21.09
8	Konrad Bukowiecki	POL	20.89

Discus (5 Aug)

1	Andrius Gudzius	LTU	69.21
2	Daniel Ståhl	SWE	69.19
3	Mason Finley	USA	68.03
4	Fedrick Dacres	JAM	65.83
5	Piotr Malachowski	POL	65.24
6	Robert Harting	GER	65.10
7	Robert Urbanek	POL	64.15
8	Traves Smikle	JAM	64.04
29Q	**Nicholas Percy**		**56.93**

Hammer (19 Aug)

1	Pawel Fajdek	POL	79.81
2	Valeriy Pronkin	RUS	78.16
3	Wojciech Nowicki	POL	78.03
4	Quentin Bigot	FRA	77.67

WOMEN

100 Metres wind 0.1 (6 Aug)

1	Tori Bowie	USA	10.85
2	Marie-Josée Ta Lou	CIV	10.86
3	Dafne Schippers	NED	10.96
4	Murielle Ahouré	CIV	10.98
5	Elaine Thompson	JAM	10.98
6	Michelle-Lee Ahye	TTO	11.01
7	Rosângela Santos	BRA	11.06
8	Kelly-Ann Baptiste	TTO	11.09
4s1	Daryll Neita		11.16
	(1h6 11.15)		
5s2	**Desiree Henry**		**11.24**
	(4h3 11.32)		
7s3	**Asha Philip**		**11.19**
	(4h1 11.14)		

200 Metres wind 0.8 (11 Aug)

1	Dafne Schippers	NED	22.05
2	Marie-Josée Ta Lou	CIV	22.08
3	Shaunae Miller-Uibo	BAH	22.15
4	**Dina Asher-Smith**		**22.22**
	(1h5 22.73, 2s3 22.73)		

5	Aleksey Sokirskiy	RUS	77.50
6	**Nick Miller**		**77.31**
	(Q 75.52)		
7	Dilshod Nazarov	TJK	77.22
8	Serghei Marghiev	MDA	75.87
21Q	**Chris Bennett**		**72.05**

Javelin (12 Aug)

1	Johannes Vetter	GER	89.89
2	Jakub Vadlejch	CZE	89.73
3	Petr Frydrych	CZE	88.32
4	Thomas Röhler	GER	88.26
5	Tero Pitkämäki	FIN	86.94
6	Ioánnis Kiriazís	GRE	84.52
7	Keshorn Walcott	TTO	84.48
8	Andreas Hofmann	GER	83.98

Decathlon (11-12 Aug)

1	Kevin Mayer	FRA	8768
2	Rico Freimuth	GER	8564
3	Kai Kazmirek	GER	8488
4	Janek Oiglane	EST	8371
5	Damian Warner	CAN	8309
6	Oleksiy Kasyanov	UKR	8234
7	Kurt Felix	GRN	8227
8	Adam Sebastian Helcelet	CZE	8222
11	**Ashley Bryant**		**8049**

20 Kilometres Walk (13 Aug)

1	Eider Arévalo	COL	1:18:53
2	Sergey Shirobokov	RUS	1:18:55
3	Caio Bonfim	BRA	1:19:04
4	Lebogang Shange	RSA	1:19:18
5	Christopher Linke	GER	1:19:21
6	Dane Bird-Smith	AUS	1:19:28
7	Wang Kaihua	CHN	1:19:30
8	Alvaro Martin	ESP	1:19:41
41	**Callum Wilkinson**		**1:23:54**
	Tom Bosworth		**dq**

5	Deajah Stevens	USA	22.44
6	Kimberlyn Duncan	USA	22.59
7	Crystal Emmanuel	CAN	22.60
8	Tynia Gaither	BAH	23.07
6s2	**Bianca Williams**		**23.40**
	(4h1 23.30)		
4h3	**Shannon Hylton**		**23.39**

400 Metres (9 Aug)

1	Phyllis Francis	USA	49.92
2	Salwa Eid Naser	BRN	50.06
3	Allyson Felix	USA	50.08
4	Shaunae Miller-Uibo	BAH	50.49
5	Shericka Jackson	JAM	50.76
6	Stephanie Ann McPherson	JAM	50.86
7	Kabange Mupopo	ZAM	51.15
8	Novlene Williams-Mills	JAM	51.48
7s3	**Zoey Clark**		**51.81**
	(3h5 51.88)		
5h2	**Emily Diamond**		**52.20**
7h6	**Anyika Onuora**		**52.58**

50 Kilometres Walk (13 Aug)

1	Yohann Diniz	FRA	3:33:12
2	Hirooki Arai	JPN	3:41:17
2	Kai Kobayashi	JPN	3:41:19
4	Igor Hlavan	UKR	3:41:42
5	Satoshi Maruo	JPN	3:43:03
6	Maté Helebrandt	HUN	3:43:56
7	Rafal Augustyn	POL	3:44:18
8	Robert Heffernan	IRL	3:44:41
	Dominic King		**dq**

4 x 100 Metres (12 Aug)

1	**Great Britain & NI**	**37.47**
	(Ujah, Gemili, Talbot, Mitchell-Blake)	
	(2h1 37.76)	
2	United States	37.52
3	Japan	38.04
4	China	38.34
5	France	38.48
6	Canada	38.59
7	Turkey	38.73
	Jamaica	dnf

4 x 400 Metres (13 Aug)

1	Trinidad & Tobago	2:58.12
2	United States	2:58.61
3	**Great Britain & NI**	**2:59.00**
	(Hudson-Smith, Cowan, Yousif, Rooney)	
	(4h2 3:00.10)	
	(Yousif, Cowan, Green, Rooney)	
4	Belgium	3:00.04
5	Spain	3:00.65
6	Cuba	3:01.10
7	Poland	3:01.59
8	France	3:02.00

800 Metres (13 Aug)

1	Caster Semenya	RSA	1:55.16
2	Francine Niyonsaba	BDI	1:55.92
3	Ajee' Wilson	USA	1:56.65
4	Margaret Wambui	KEN	1:57.54
5	Melissa Bishop	CAN	1:57.68
6	Angelika Cichocka	POL	1:58.41
7	Charlene Lipsey	USA	1:58.73
8	**Lynsey Sharp**		**1:58.98**
	(2h4 2:01.04, 4s2 1:59.47)		
6s1	**Adelle Tracey**		**2:00.26**
	(4h6 2:00.28)		
6s3	**Shelayna Oskan-Clarke**		**2:02.26**
	(3h2 2:01.30)		

1500 Metres (7 Aug)

1	Faith Kipyegon	KEN	4:02.59
2	Jennifer Simpson	USA	4:02.76
3	Caster Semenya	RSA	4:02.90
4	**Laura Muir**		**4:02.97**
	(4h2 4:08.97, 2s1 4:03.64)		

5	Sifan Hassan	NED	4:03.34
6	**Laura Weightman**		**4:04.11**
	(4h3 4:03.50, 4s2 4:05.63)		
7	Angelika Cichocka	POL	4:04.16
8	Rabab Arrafi	MAR	4:04.35
10s1	**Jessica Judd**		**4:10.14**
	(6h1 4:03.73)		
9s2	**Sarah McDonald**		**4:06.73**
	(9h3 4:05.48)		

5000 Metres (13 Aug)

1	Hellen Obiri	KEN	14:34.86
2	Almaz Ayana	ETH	14:40.35
3	Sifan Hassan	NED	14:42.73
4	Senbere Teferi	ETH	14:47.45
5	Margaret Chelimo	KEN	14:48.74
6	**Laura Muir**		**14:52.07**
	(7h1 14:59.34)		
7	Sheila Kiprotich	KEN	14:54.05
8	Susan Krumins	NED	14:58.33
10	**Eilish McColgan**		**15:00.43**
	(4h2 15:00.38)		
15h2	**Stephanie Twell**		**15:41.29**

10000 Metres (5 Aug)

1	Almaz Ayana	ETH	30:16.32
2	Tirunesh Dibaba	ETH	31:02.69
3	Agnes Tirop	KEN	31:03.50
4	Alice Nawowuna	KEN	31:11.86
5	Susan Krumins	NED	31:20.24
6	Emily Infield	USA	31:20.45
7	Irene Cheptai	KEN	31:21.11
8	Molly Huddle	USA	31:24.78
21	**Beth Potter**		**32:15.88**
27	**Charlotte Taylor**		**32:51.33**
	Jessica Martin		**dnf**

Marathon (6 Aug)

1	Rose Chelimo	BRN	2:27:11
2	Edna Kiplagat	KEN	2:27:18
3	Amy Cragg	USA	2:27:18
4	Flomena Cheyech	KEN	2:27:21
5	Shure Demise	ETH	2:27:28
6	Eunice Jepkirui	BRN	2:28:17
7	Helah Kiprop	KEN	2:28:19
8	Mare Dibaba	ETH	2:28:49
13	**Charlotte Purdue**		**2:29:48**
18	**Alyson Dixon**		**2:31:36**
43	**Tracy Barlow**		**2:41:03**

3000 Metres Steeplechase (11 Aug)

1	Emma Coburn	USA	9:02.58
2	Courtney Frerichs	USA	9:03.77
3	Hyvin Jepkemoi	KEN	9:04:03
4	Beatrice Chepkoech	KEN	9:10.45
5	Ruth Jebet	BRN	9:13.96
6	Celliphine Chespol	KEN	9:15.04
7	Etenesh Diro	ETH	9:22.46
8	Winfred Yavi	BRN	9:22.67
10h1	**Lennie Waite**		**9:54.97**
9h3	**Rosie Clarke**		**9:49.36**

100 Metres Hurdles wind 0.1 (12 Aug)

1	Sally Pearson	AUS	12.59
2	Dawn Harper-Nelson	USA	12.63
3	Pamela Dutkiewicz	GER	12.72
4	Kendra Harrison	USA	12.74
5	Christina Manning	USA	12.74
6	Alina Talay	BLR	12.81
7	Nadine Visser	NED	12.83
8	Nia Ali	USA	13.04
8h1	**Alicia Barrett**		**13.42**
6h2	**Tiffany Porter**		**13.18**

400 Metres Hurdles (10 Aug)

1	Kori Carter	USA	53.07
2	Dalilah Muhammad	USA	53.50
3	Ristananna Tracey	JAM	53.74
4	Zuzana Hejnová	CZE	54.20
5	Léa Sprunger	SUI	54.59
6	Sage Watson	CAN	54.92
7	Cassandra Tate	USA	55.43
8	**Eilidh Doyle**		**55.71**
	(3h4 55.49, 3s3 55.33)		
6s2	**Meghan Beesley**		**56.61**
	(6h5 56.41)		
6h2	**Jessica Turner**		**56.98**

High Jump (12 Aug)

1	Mariya Lasitskené	RUS	2.03
2	Yuliya Levchenko	UKR	2.01
3	Kamila Lićwinko	POL	1.99
4	Marie-Laurence Jungfleisch	GER	1.95
5	**Katarina Johnson-Thompson**		**1.95**
	(Q 1.92)		
6	**Morgan Lake**		**1.95**
	(Q 1.92)		
7=	Mirela Demireva	BUL	1.92
7=	Airine Palšytė	LTU	1.92

Pole Vault (6 Aug)

1	Ekateríni Stefanídi	GRE	4.91
2	Sandi Morris	USA	4.75
3=	Robeilys Peinado	VEN	4.65
3=	Yarisley Silva	CUB	4.65
5	Lisa Ryzih	GER	4.65
6	**Holly Bradshaw**		**4.65**
	(Q 4.50)		
7	Alysha Newman	CAN	4.65
8	Olga Mullina	RUS	4.55

Long Jump (11 Aug)

1	Brittney Reese	USA	7.02
2	Darya Klishina	RUS	7.00
3	Tianna Bartoletta	USA	6.97
4	Ivana Španović	SRB	6.96
5	**Lorraine Ugen**		**6.72**
	(Q 6.63)		
6	Brooke Stratton	AUS	6.67
7	Chantel Malone	IVB	6.57
8	Blessing Okagbare	NGR	6.55
13Q	**Shara Proctor**		**6.45**
20Q	**Jazmin Sawyers**		**6.34**

Triple Jump (7 Aug)

1	Yulimar Rojas	VEN	14.91
2	Caterine Ibargüen	COL	14.89
3	Olga Rypakova	KAZ	14.77
4	Hanna Minenko	ISR	14.42
5	Kristin Gierisch	GER	14.33
6	Anna Jagaciak Michalska	POL	14.25
7	Ana Peleteiro	ESP	14.23
8	Shanieka Ricketts	JAM	14.13

Shot (9 Aug)

1	Gong Lijiao	CHN	19.94
2	Anita Márton	HUN	19.49
3	Michelle Carter	USA	19.14
4	Danniel Thomas-Dodd	JAM	18.91
5	Gao Yang	CHN	18.25
6	Brittany Crew	CAN	18.21
7	Yuliya Leontyuk	BLR	18.12
8	Yaniuvis Lopez	CUB	18.03
23Q	**Rachel Wallader**		**16.81**

Discus (13 Aug)

1	Sandra Perkovic	CRO	70.31
2	Dani Stevens	AUS	69.64
3	Mélina Robert-Michon	FRA	66.21
4	Yaime Perez	CUB	64.82
5	Denia Caballero	CUB	64.37
6	Nadine Müller	GER	64.13
7	Su Xinyue	CHN	63.37
8	Feng Bin	CHN	61.56
19Q	**Jade Lally**		**57.71**

Hammer (7 Aug)

1	Anita Wlodarczyk	POL	77.90
2	Wang Zheng	CHN	75.98
3	Malwina Kopron	POL	74.76
4	Zhang Wenxiu	CHN	74.53
5	Hanna Skydan	AZE	73.38
6	Joanna Fiodorow	POL	73.04
7	**Sophie Hitchon**		**72.32**
	(Q 73.05)		
8	Katerina Safránková	CZE	71.34

Javelin (8 Aug)

1	Barbora Spotáková	CZE	66.76
2	Li Lingwei	CHN	66.25
3	Lu Huihui	CHN	65.26
4	Sara Kolak	CRO	64.95
5	Eda Tugsuz	TUR	64.52
6	Tatyana Kholodovich	BLR	64.05
7	Katharina Molitor	GER	63.75
8	Liu Shiying	CHN	62.84

Heptathlon (5-6 Aug)

1	Nafissatou Thiam	BEL	6784
2	Carolin Schäfer	GER	6696
3	Anouk Vetter	NED	6636
4	Yorgelis Rodriguez	CUB	6594
5	Katarina Johnson-Thompson		6558
6	Ivona Dadic	AUT	6417
7	Nadine Visser	NED	6370
8	Claudia Salman-Rath	GER	6362

20 Kilometres Walk (13 Aug)

1	Yang Jiayu	CHN	1:26:18
2	Maria Guadalupe González	MEX	1:26:19
3	Antonella Palmisano	ITA	1:26:36
4	Erica de Sena	BRA	1:26:59
5	Sandra Arenas	COL	1:28:10
6	Ana Cabecinha	POR	1:28:57
7	Kimberly Garcia	PER	1:29:13
8	Wang Na	CHN	1:29:26
29	**Bethan Davies**		**1:33:10**
40	**Gemma Bridge**		**1:36:04**

50 Kilometres Walk (13 Aug)

1	Inês Henriques	POR	4:05:56
2	Yin Hang	CHN	4:08:58
3	Yang Shuquig	CHN	4:20:49
4	Kathleen Burnett	USA	4:21:51

4 x 100 Metres (12 Aug)

1	United States	41.82
2	**Great Britain & NI**	**42.12**
	(Philip, Henry, Asher-Smith,Neita)	
	(2h1 41.93)	
3	Jamaica	42.19
4	Germany	42.36
5	Switzerland	42.51
6	Trinidad & Tobago	42.62
7	Brazil	42.63
8	Netherlands	43.07

4 x 400 Metres (13 Aug)

1	United States	3:19.02
2	**Great Britain & NI**	**3:25.00**
	(Clark, Lav Nielsen, Doyle, Diamond)	
	(2h1 3:24.74)	
	(Clark, Lav Nielsen, Shakes-Drayton, Diamond)	
3	Poland	3:25.41
4	France	3:26.56
5	Nigeria	3:26.72
6	Germany	3:27.45
7	Botswana	3:28.00
	Jamaica	dnf

29th WORLD UNIVERSITY GAMES
Taipei, TPE 23-28 August 2017

MEN

100 Metres wind -0.9 (24 Aug)

1	Yang Chun-Han	TPE	10.22
5s1	**Samuel Osewa**		**10.42**
	(3h10 10.49, 4q3 10.48)		

200 Metres wind -3.8 (26 Aug)

1	Jeffrey John	FRA	20.93

400 Metres (25 Aug)

1	Luguelín Santos	DOM	45.24

800 Metres (28 Aug)

1	Jesus López	MEX	1:46.06
4s3	**James Bowness**		**1:48.78**
	(1h1 1:50.49)		

1500 Metres (25 Aug)

1	Timo Benitz	GER	3:43.35
3	**Jonathan Davies**		**3:43.99**
	(3h1 3:43.95)		

5000 Metres (28 Aug)

1	François Barrer	FRA	14:00.86
2	**Jonathan Davies**		**14:02.46**
	(4h2 14:25.43)		

10000 Metres (24 Aug)

1	Sadiq Bahati	UGA	29:08.68

WOMEN

100 Metres wind -0.3 (24 Aug)

1	Shashalee Forbes	JAM	11.18
4=	**Corrinne Humphreys**		**11.49**
	(2h7 11.48, 3q4 11.52, 3s2 11.71)		

200 Metres wind -1.4 (26 Aug)

1	Irene Siragusa	ITA	22.96

400 Metres (25 Aug)

1	Malgorzata Holub	POL	51.76

800 Metres (25 Aug)

1	Rose Mary Almanza	CUB	2:02.21
5	**Adelle Tracey**		**2:03.72**
	(1h4 2:05.78, 3s1 2:03.30)		

Half Marathon (27 Aug)

1	Kei Katanishi	JPN	66:09

3000 Metres Steeplechase (27 Aug)

1	Krystian Zalewski	POL	8:35.88
6	**Zak Seddon**		**8:39.30**

110 Metres Hurdles wind -0.5 (27 Aug)

1	Bálazs Baji	HUN	13.35

400 Metres Hurdles (26 Aug)

1	Juander Santos	DOM	48.65
3s3	**Jacob Paul**		**50.37**
	(1h4 51.38)		

High Jump (25 Aug)

1	Falk Wendrich	GER	2.29
4	**Allan Smith**		**2.23**
	(Q 2.15)		

Pole Vault (27 Aug)

1	Diogo Ferreira	POR	5.55

Long Jump (28 Aug)

1	Radek Juska	CZE	8.02
14Q	**Daniel Gardiner**		**7.59**

1500 Metres (28 Aug)

1	Amela Terzic	SRB	4:19.18
5	**Melissa Courtney**		**4:21.14**
	(2h2 4:18.68)		

5000 Metres (27 Aug)

1	Hanna Klein	GER	15:45.28
3	**Jessica Judd**		**15:51.19**
4	**Louise Small**		**15:55.55**

10000 Metres (23 Aug)

1	Darya Maslova	KGZ	33:19.27
5	**Jenny Nesbitt**		**34:01.34**
10	**Louise Small**		**35:03.93**

Triple Jump (25 Aug)

1	Nazim Babayev	AZE	17.01
12	**Sam Trigg**		**14.94**
	(Q 15.61)		

Shot (23 Aug)

1	Francisco Belo	POR	20.86

Discus (28 Aug)

1	Reginald Jagers	USA	61.24
8	**Gregory Thompson**		**57.52**
	(Q 57.94)		

Hammer (24 Aug)

1	Pawel Fajdek	POL	79.16

Javelin (26 Aug)

1	Cheng Tsao-Tsun	TPE	91.36

Decathlon (24/5 Aug)

1	Kyle Cranston	AUS	7687
	John Lane		**dnf**

20 Kilometres Walk (26 Aug)

1	Toshikazu Yamanishi	JPN	1:27:30

4x100 Metres Relay (28 Aug)

1	Japan	38.65

4x400 Metres Relay (28 Aug)

1	Dominican Republic	3:04.34

Half Marathon (27 Aug)

1	Yuki Munehisa	JPN	73:48

3000 Metres Steeplechase (26 Aug)

1	Tugba Güvenc	TUR	9:51.27

100 Metres Hurdles wind -1.3 (26 Aug)

1	Nadine Visser	NED	12.98
5s2	**Alicia Barrett**		**13.75**
	(3h3 13.75)		

400 Metres Hurdles (25 Aug)

1	Ayomide Folorunso	ITA	55.63
5	**Jessica Turner**		**57.45**
	(2h1 57.73)		

High Jump (28 Aug)
1   Oksana Okuneva   UKR   1.97

Pole Vault (26 Aug)
1   Iryna Zhuk   BLR   4.40

Long Jump (24 Aug)
1   Alina Rotaru   ROU   6.65

Triple Jump (27 Aug)
1   Neele Eckhardt   GER   13.91

Shot (27 Aug)
1   Brittany Crew   CAN   18.34
6   **Amelia Strickler**   **17.13**
    (Q 16.38)

Discus (24 Aug)
1   Kristen Pudenz   GER   59.09

Hammer (26 Aug)
1   Malwina Kopron   POL   76.85

Javelin (25 Aug)
1   Marcelina Witek   POL   63.31

Heptathlon (26/7 Aug)
1   Verena Preiner   AUT   6224

20 Kilometres Walk (26 Aug)
1   Inna Kashyna   UKR   1:39:44

4x100 Metres Relay (28 Aug)
1   Switzerland   43.81

4x400 Metres Relay (28 Aug)
1   Poland   3:26.75

6th COMMONWEALTH YOUTH GAMES
Nassau, BAH 20-23 Jul 2017

MEN

100 Metres wind 0.0 (20 Jul)
1   Adell Colthrust   TTO   10.55
4s1 Adam Clayton   10.93
    (1h2 10.93)

200 Metres wind -1.6 (23 Jul)
1   Aaron Sexton   NI   21.57
    (1h3 21.93, 1s2 21.83)
3   Chad Miller   Eng   21.65
    (2h4 21.76, 3s1 21.76)
7   Fraser Angus   Sco   21.92
    (4h2 21.84, 4s1 22.09)

400 Metres (21 Jul)
1   Kennedy Luchembe   ZAM   47.63

800 Metres (22 Jul)
1   **Alex Botterill**   Eng   **1:52.22**
    (1h1 1:54.86)
3   Joshua Allen   Eng   1:53.09
    (3h2 1:56.60)
7   William Brown   Jer   1:57.24
    (4h2 1:58.27)
5h1 Isaac du Val   Jer   1:59.74

1500 Metres (20 Jul)
1   John Mwangi Waweru   KEN   3:48.86
2   **Joshua Lay**   Eng   **3:49.35**
3   **Luke Duffy**   Eng   **3:49.70**
8   David Mullarkey   IoM   3:57.61
9   Adam Scott   Sco   4:01.60
10 William Brown   Jer   4:10.99
    Isaac du Val   Jer   dnf

3000 Metres (22 Jul)
1   Edwin Kiplagat Bett   KEN   8:23.96
5   Adam Scott   Sco   9:04.69

110 Metres Hurdles 91.4cm wind -0.4 (22 Jul)
1   **Samuel Bennett**   Eng   **13.71**
2   **Jack Sumners**   Eng   **13.85**

400 Metres Hurdles 84cm (23 Jul)
1   Alastair Chalmers   Gue   51.22
    (1h2 52.78)
2   Seamus Derbyshire   Eng   52.00
    (2h1 52.25)
    Joshua Faulds   Eng   dq
    (3h2 53.13)

High Jump (22 Jul)
1   Sean Szalek   AUS   2.11

Long Jump (21 Jul)
1   Sheldon Noble   ANT   7.64
4   **Alessandro Schenini**   Sco   **6.87**
    Callum Henderson   Sco   **nj**

Shot 5kg (21 Jul)
1   Alexander Kolesnikoff   AUS   19.76

Discus 1.5kg (20 Jul)
1   Connor Bell   NZL   63.17
2   **James Tomlinson**   Wal   **60.11**

Javelin 700gm (23 Jul)
1   Neil Janse Van Rensburg   RSA   74.19
7   **Don Baker**   Eng   **60.63**

WOMEN

100 Metres wind -0.3 (20 Jul)
1   Julien Alfred   LCA   11.56
5= **Vera Chinedu**   Eng   **12.04**
    (2h3 12.20, 3s2 12.14)
7s2 Madeleine Silcock   Sco   12.75
    (6h4 12.85)
5h5 Abigail Galpin   Gue   13.05

200 Metres wind -0.3 (23 Jul)
1   Riley Day   AUS   23.42
4   **Georgina Adam**   Eng   **24.30**
    (1h4 24.51, 2s2 24.74)
7s1 Lauren Greig   Sco   25.54
    (3h4 25.31)
5h1 Abigail Galpin   Gue   26.65
5h2 Eleanor Gallagher   Gue   26.28

400 Metres (21 Jul)
1   Bendere Opamo Oboya   AUS   52.69
3   **Amber Anning**   Eng   **53.68**
    (2h1 54.42)
6   **Emma Alderson**   Eng   **54.90**
    (1h3 54.61)
8   Davicia Patterson   NI   55.86
    (2h3 55.54)
4h1 Eleanor Gallagher   Gue   56.34
5h2 Sophie Porter   Gue   56.76
6h2 Olivia Vareille   Sco   57.22
8h2 Olivia Allbut   Jer   58.82

800 Metres (22 Jul)
1   Carley Thomas   AUS   2:05.04
2   **Anna Burt**   Eng   **2:05.31**
    (1h2 2:10.37)
4   **Isabelle Boffey**   Eng   **2:06.67**
    (3h1 2:12.86)
6   Erin Wallace   Sco   2:08.30
    (3h2 2:10.52)
4h1 Naomi Reid   Wal   2:13.00

1500 Metres (20 Jul)
1   Erin Wallace   Sco   4:16.61
4   Anna Smith   Eng   4:17.99
12 Olivia Mason   Eng   4:30.88

3000 Metres (22 Jul)
1   Emmaculate Chepkirui   KEN   9:25.20
7   Claudia Lance-Jones   Eng   9:58.76
10 Naomi Lang   Sco   10:11.34

100 Metres Hurdles 76.2cm wind -1.3 (22 Jul)

1	Shanette Allison	JAM	13.26
4	**Pippa Earley**	Eng	13.72
	(1h1 13.73)		
6h1	Bethany McAndrew	Sco	14.63
5h2	**Anna McCauley**	NI	14.26
6h2	**Lauren Evans**	Wal	14.70

400 Metres Hurdles (23 Jul)

1	Johnelle Thomas	JAM	59.40
7	**Olivia Allbut**		65.16
	(5h2 67.51)		

High Jump (23 Jul)

1	**Sommer Lecky**	NI	1.83

Long Jump (20 Jul)

1	**Holly Mills**	Eng	6.19
3	**Lucy Hadaway**	Eng	5.90

Shot 3kg (20 Jul)

1	Trinity Tutti	CAN	17.82
2	**Sarah Omoregie**	Wal	16.74
6	**Gaia Osborne**	Eng	14.91
9	**Serena Vincent**	Eng	13.41

Discus (21 Jul)

1	Trinity Tutti	CAN	49.57

Javelin 500gm (22 Jul)

1	Josephine Lalam	UGA	51.89
3	**Emma Howe**	Eng	47.04
6	**Bethany Moule**	Wal	43.27

Mixed 4x100 Metres Relay (23 Jul)

1	Australia	43.19

Mixed 4x200 Metres Relay (23 Jul)

1	Bahamas	1:31.50
2	**England**	1:31.77
(V. Chinedu, G. Adam, C. Miller, S. Bennett)		
4	**Scotland**	1:36.35
(O. Vareille, A. Schenini, B. McAndrew, C. Henderson)		

Mixed 4x400 Metres Relay (23 Jul)

1	Australia	3:25.08
2	**England**	3:25.45
(E. Alderson, A. Anning, A. Botterill, J. Faulds)		

24th EUROPEAN CROSS COUNTRY CHAMPIONSHIPS
Šamorín, SVK 10 December 2017

SENIOR MEN (10.18k)

1	Kaan Kigen Özbilen	TUR	29:45
3	**Andrew Butchart**		30:00
6	**Ben Connor**		30:08
26	**Tom Lancashire**		30:54
38	**Alex Teuten**		31:20
45	**Sam Stabler**		31:31
	Dewi Griffiths		dnf

Team

1	Turkey	17
3	**Great Britain & NI**	35

SENIOR WOMEN (8.23k)

1	Yasemin Can	TUR	26:48
6	**Charlotte Taylor**		27:23
8	**Emilia Gorecka**		27:34
9	**Gemma Steel**		27:41
10	**Steph Twell**		27:43
15	**Lily Partridge**		27:55
48	**Elle Vernon**		28:53

Team

1	**Great Britain & NI**	23

U23 MEN (8.23k)

1	Jimmy Gressier	FRA	24:35
12	**Mahamed Mahamed**		24:50
13	**Chris Olley**		24:52
16	**Patrick Dever**		25:02
25	**Joe Steward**		25:13
31	**Jack Rowe**		25:25
42	**Daniel Jarvis**		25:34

Team

1	France	7
3	**Great Britain & NI**	41

U23 WOMEN (6.28k)

1	Alina Reh	GER	20:22
3	**Jessica Judd**		20:45
4	**Amy-Eloise Neale**		20:59
5	**Amy Griffiths**		21:02
9	**Mhairi MacLennan**		21:26
10	**Phoebe Law**		22:16
13	**Phillipa Bowden**		21:29

Team

1	**Great Britain & NI**	12

Mixed Relay (6.28k)

1	**Great Britain & NI**	18:24
(M Courtney, C Boyek, S McDonald, T Marshall)		

JUNIOR MEN (6.28k)

1	Jakob Ingebrigtsen	NOR	18:39
14	**Matthew Willis**		18:57
17	**Ben Dijkstra**		19:01
25	**William Richardson**		19:10
27	**Scott Beattie**		19:14
30	**Jake Heyward**		19:23
60	**Lachlan Wellington**		19:49

Team

1	Spain	20
6	**Great Britain & NI**	56

JUNIOR WOMEN (4.18k)

1	**Harriet Knowles-Jones**	13:48
9	**Cari Hughes**	14:15
11	**Khahisa Mhlanga**	14:16
12	**Niamh Brown**	14:17
43	**Phoebe Barker**	14:49
52	**Victoria Weir**	14:57

Team

1	**Great Britain & NI**	21

REGIONAL CHAMPIONSHIPS

SCOTLAND
Grangemouth 26-27 August

WALES
Cardiff 9-10 June

NORTHERN IRELAND
Belfast 10 June

MEN

Event	Scotland		Wales		Northern Ireland		
100	Cameron Tindle	10.68	Samuel Gordon	10.32	Leon Reid		10.59
200	Krishawn Aiken	21.65	Thomas Williams	20.97	Leon Reid		21.12
400	Krishawn Aiken	48.11	Owen Smith	47.41	Craig Newell	IRL	47.31
800	Patrick Taylor	1:53.90	Alex Coomber	1:50.75	Mark Hoy	IRL	1:57.80
1500	Dale Colley	3:56.85	Rowan Axe	3:47.46	Daniel Mooney	IRL	3:44.40
3000			Michael Ward	9:03.32			
5000	Grant Sheldon	14:22.34	Dewi Griffiths	13:50.35	James Edgar	IRL	14:54.81
10000	Kristian Jones	29:16.39	Glyn Fletcher	33:56.4	Eoghan Totten		31:29.23
3kSt	Michael Deason USA	9:26.07			Ciaran Doherty	IRL	9:39.28
110H	Calum Innes	15.09	Glen Elsdon	14.93	Ben Reynolds	IRL	13.99
400H	Jack Lawrie	51.69	Paul Bennett	54.49	Jason Harvey	IRL	51.42
HJ	David Smith	2.21	William Edwards	2.00			
PV	Jax Thoirs	5.32	Max Eaves	5.25	David Donegan	IRL	4.60
LJ	David John Martin	7.53w	Simeon Clarence	7.06	Adam McMullan	IRL	7.64w
TJ	Chukwudi Onyia	15.63	Osaze Aghedo	14.98	Caolan O'Callaghan	IRL	13.10
SP	Scott Lincoln	18.80	Gareth Winter	16.98	John Kelly	IRL	16.11
DT	Angus McInroy	51.13	Brett Morse	59.76	Marco Pons	IRL	50.31
HT	Andy Frost	59.10	Osian Jones	66.90			
JT	Greg Millar	62.58	Jason Copsey	64.77	Jack Magee		60.28
Dec	Curtis Mathews	6245	Curtis Mathews	6736	Shane Aston	IRL	6522
3kW			Jordan Price	15:59.18			

10000 Glasgow 28 April
Dec Grangemouth 1-2 July

10000 Cardiff 12 August
3000 Cardiff 20 July
Dec Bedford 27-28 May

10000 Belfast 8 July
Dec Belfast 2-3 September

WOMEN

Event	Scotland		Wales		Northern Ireland		
100	Katy Wyper	11.63	Mica Moore	11.69	Lauren Roy		12.40
200	Alisha Rees	23.38w	Hannah Thomas	24.67	Amy Foster	IRL	24.13
400	Kelsey Stewart	54.27	Rachel Donnison	55.87	Catherine McManus	IRL	54.36
800	Jemma Reekie	2:08.39	Rachel McClay	2:11.29	Ciara Mageean	IRL	2:07.49
1500	Stephanie Pennycook	4:25.34	Cari Hughes	4:25.56	Emma Mitchell	IRL	4:24.18
3000			Lauren Cooper	10:37.13			
5000	Naomi Lang	16:45.09	Bronwen Owen	16:36.50	Sinead Sweeney	IRL	17:39.91
10000	Annabel Simpson	35:33.46	Alaw Beynon-Thomas	35:49.1	Marina Murphy		38:27.68
3kSt	Lauren Stoddart	10:51.42	Katie Ingle	10:22.89			
100H	Megan Mars	13.66w	Caryl Granville	13.91	Mollie Courtney		13.61
400H	Nisha Desai	59.05	Caryl Granville	58.79	Kate McGowan	IRL	62.57
HJ	Nikki Manson	1.81	Belen Simarro ESP	1.57	Sommer Lecky	IRL	1.70
PV	Hannah Lawler	3.30	Lucy Bryan	4.25	Sarah McKeever	IRL	3.90
LJ	Jade Nimmo	5.98w	Rebecca Chapman	6.31	Lydia Mills		5.63
TJ	Chioma Matthews	12.45	Sian Swanson	12.08w	Saragh Buggy	IRL	13.18w
SP	Kirsty Yates	14.00	Adele Nicoll	15.64	Laura Frey		10.67
DT	Kirsty Law	54.54	Awen Rosser	40.96	Niamh Fogarty	IRL	45.86
HT	Myra Perkins	61.48	Carys Parry	65.32	Hayley Murray		59.49
JT	Aileen Rennie	41.54	Bethan Rees	46.01	Kate O'Connor	IRL	41.06
Hep	Ellen Barber	5082			Moe Sasegbon	NGR	5367
3kW			Bethan Davies	12:26.45			
5kW					Rebecca Collins		28:53.32

10000 Glasgow 28 April
Hep Grangemouth 1-2 July

10000 Cardiff 12 August
Hep Bedford 27-28 May
3000 Cardiff 20 July

10k Belfast 8 July
Hep Belfast 2-3 September

AREA CHAMPIONSHIPS

	SOUTH			MIDLAND			NORTH	
	Crystal Palace 10-11 June			Nuneaton 11 June			Manchester (SC) 10-11 June	

MEN — SOUTH

100	Confidence Lawson	10.58
200	Leroy Cain	21.63
400	Jamal Rhoden-Stevens	47.89
800	Sean Molloy	1:54.38
1500	Phil Norman	3:50.40
5000	Shaun Antell	15:00.41
10000	Nathan Pask	33:27.08
3kSt	James Senior	9:23.05
110H	Miguel Perera	14.78
400H	Lennox Thompson	53.15
HJ	Ryan Bonifas	2.11
PV	Scott Huggins	5.20
LJ	James Lelliott	7.65
TJ	Jonathan Ilori	16.06
SP	Matthew Baptiste	15.72
DT	Louis Mascarenhas	48.47
HT	Taylor Campbell	70.33
JT	Neil McLennan	66.28
Dec	Harry Kendall	6691
Dec	Oxford (H) 22-23 July	
10000	Aylesbury 20 September	

MEN — MIDLAND

100	Dan Putnam	10.35w
200	Dan Putnam	20.65w
400	Christian Byron	47.43
800	Adam Wright	1:56.52
1500	Daniel Owen	4:12.01
3000	Daniel Owen	8:31.34
	Jack Bancroft	15:04.19
	Daniel Owen	31:41.4
	Daniel Owen	9:46.75
	Travis Christie	56.29
	Damien Chambefort FRA	1.95
	Callum Court	4.40
	Charlie Roe	6.93w
	Fraser Kesteven	13.45w
	William Knight	13.74
	Najee Fox	53.84
	Craig Murch	67.32
	Emmish Prosper LCA	59.61
	Charlie Roe	6523
Dec	Bedford 27-28 May	
3000	Coventry 13 August	
10000	Tipton 26 August	

MEN — NORTH

100	Jona Efoloko	10.53w
200	James Gladman	21.02w
400	Lee Thompson	47.72
800	Matthew Wigelsworth	1:57.01
1500	Matthew Wigelsworth	3:55.54
	Jack Morris	14:39.98
	Ollie Lockley	29:27.18
	Daniel Eckersley	9:22.13
	David Feeney	14.11w
	James Webster	52.95
	Christopher Mann	1.98
	Harry Lord	3.70
	Michael Causer	7.29w
	Kevin Metzger	14.89w
	Craig Sturrock	15.80
	Daniel Fleming	47.47
	Michael Bomba	62.74
	Alexander Ingham	52.35
	James Finney	7263
Dec	Bedford 27-28 May	
10000	Manchester (Str) 19 August	

WOMEN — SOUTH

100	Rachel Miller	11.78
200	Risqat Fabunmi-Alade	24.63
400	Victoria Ohuruogu	53.98
800	Hollie Parker	2:09.30
1500	Tamara Armoush JOR	4:25.80
3000	Chloe Tighe AUS	9:29.05
3kSt	Claire Bentley	11:29.64
100H	Jessica Hunter	13.89
400H	Jessie Knight	59.18
HJ	Pippa Rogan IRL	1.76
PV	Caroline Parkinson	3.05
LJ	Kitan Eleyae	5.85
TJ	Zara Asante	12.57
SP	Sophie McKinna	15.96
DT	Jade Lally	57.56
HT	Phillipa Wingate	58.60
JT	Jo Blair	50.63
Hep	Moe Sasegbon NGR	5254
Hep	Oxford (H) 22-23 July	

WOMEN — MIDLAND

100	Dionne Samuels	11.94w
200	Nardhia Kidd-Walker	24.53w
400	Kate Anderson	57.71
800	Amy Griffiths	2:12.13
1500	Sarah Mackness	4:47.19
	Jenny Nesbitt	9:29.17
5000	Ellie Stevens	17:54.11
10000	Lucy Holt	39:23.8
2kSt	Sian Davies	7:41.80
	Gabriella Burton	13.90w
	Natalie Ainge	64.17
	Emma Lowry	1.60
	Elizabeth Edden	3.70
	Heidi Jarosinski	5.72
	Anna Bates	12.04
	Georgina Page	8.60
	Eden Francis	57.53
	Lucy Marshall	61.29
	Laura Whittingham	51.27
Hep	Bedford 27-28 May	
3000	Coventry 13 August	
10000	Tipton 26 August	

WOMEN — NORTH

100	Louise Bloor	11.65w
200	Louise Bloor	23.80
400	Georgia Yearby	55.98
800	Rochelle Harrison	2:14.72
1500	Jenna Hill	4:33.00
	Rebecca Rigby	16:22.31
	Charlotte Arter	32:37.52
2kSt	Jacqueline Etherington	7:56.72
	Chelsea Walker	13.98w
	Nisha Desai	58.85
	Emily Borthwick	1.75
	Clare Blunt	3.70
	Katherine James	4.94
	Amy Lupton	11.35w
	Christina Nick GER	13.39
	Jemma Ibbetson	46.85
	Maggie Okul	51.89
	Natasha Wilson	45.14
	Niamh Emerson	5801
Hep	Bedford 27-28 May	
10000	Manchester (Str) 19 August	

AGE CHAMPIONSHIPS

U23
Bedford 17-18 June

MEN

100	Ojie Edoburun	10.12
200	Leroy Cain	20.94
400	Cameron Chalmers	45.64
800	Daniel Rowden	1:48.15
1500	Neil Gourley	3:44.25
5000	Philip Crout	14:39.55
3kSt	Daniel Jarvis	8:59.64
110H	Khai Riley-La Borde	13.73
400H	Jacob Paul	50.07
HJ	Chris Kandu	2.25
PV	Charlie Myers	5.35
LJ	Jacob Fincham-Dukes	7.56
TJ	Efe Uwaifo	15.91
SP	John Kelly IRL	16.95
DT	George Armstrong	56.67
HT	Jac Lloyd Palmer	65.88
JT	Jack Swain	66.68
10kW	Cameron Corbishley	41:37.44

U20
Bedford 17-18 June

MEN

100	Romell Glave	10.21
200	Romell Glave	21.08
400	Owen Richardson	47.24
800	Markhim Lonsdale	1:50.57
1500	Jake Heyward	3:57.97
3000	Ben Dijkstra	8:27.56
	William Battershill	9:13.57
	Robert Sakala	13.83
	Alistair Chalmers	52.06
	Tom Gale	2.18
	Joel Leon Benitez	5.20
	Ben Fisher	7.36w
	Teepee Princewill	15.19
	George Evans	16.39
	George Evans	55.26
	Jake Norris	77.67
	James Whiteaker	74.64
	Christopher Snook	46:18.98
Dec	Caius Joseph	6469

Dec/Hep 27-28 May Bedford

U17
Bedford 26-27 August

MEN

100	Jeremiah Azu	10.65
200	Dominic Ogbechie	21.52
400	Ethan Brown	47.82
800	Max Burgin	1:50.26
1500	Oliver Dustin	3:53.62
	Thomas Keen	8:32.28
1500St	Remi Adebiyi	4:21.43
100H	Sam Bennett	12.76
	Ben Lloyd	52.98
	Kaya Walker	2.04
	Frankie Johnson	4.31
	Callum Orange	6.89w
	Joel Townley	13.99
	George Hyde	17.42
	Jay Morse	55.28
	Ben Hawkes	71.91
	Max Law	62.24
5kW	Oisin Lane IRL	24:07.58
Dec	Joel McFarlane	6594

Dec/Hept 12-13 August Bedford

WOMEN (U23)

100	Daryll Neita	11.20
200	Shannon Hylton	23.20
400	Kelsey Stewart	53.63
800	Mhairi Hendry	2:05.65
1500	Jessica Judd	4:21.78
5000	Hannah Viner	17:05.96
3kSt	Aimee Pratt	10:08.64
100H	Yasmin Miller	13.23
400H	Jessica Turner	57.68
HJ	Morgan Lake	1.94
PV	Lucy Bryan	4.20
LJ	Sarah McCarthy IRL	6.21w
TJ	Simi Fajemisin	12.39
SP	Adele Nicoll	16.24
DT	Amy Holder	52.84
HT	Michaela Walsh IRL	62.71
JT	Natasha Wilson	46.19

WOMEN (U20)

100	Kristal Awuah	11.61
200	Alisha Rees	23.52
400	Hannah Williams	53.66
800	Isabelle Boffey	2:05.87
1500	Jemma Reekie	4:18.38
3000	Jemma Reekie	9:37.22
	Emily Moyes	10:31.81
	Alicia Barrett	13.07
	Orla Brothers	59.46
	Rebecca Hawkins	1.76
	Molly Caudery	3.90
	Holly Mills	6.19
	Naomi Ogbeta	13.36w
	Michaela Walsh IRL	16.13
	Divine Oladipo	50.50
	Michaela Walsh IRL	62.62
	Emma Hamplett	49.19
Hep	Holly McArthur	5332

WOMEN (U17)

100	Amy Hunt	11.72
200	Amber Anning	23.76
300	Hannah Foster	39.10
800	Keely Hodgkinson	2:06.85
1500	Kiara Frizelle	4:32.31
3000	Charlotte Alexander	9:49.92
1.5kSt	Elowen Penfold	5:17.11
80H	Pippa Earley	10.97
300H	Amy Pye	41.96
	Emily Race	1.75
	Felicia Miloro	3.81
	Funminiyi Olajide	5.83
	Jade Oni	12.25
	Hannah Molyneux	15.33
	Heather Cubbage	44.94
	Jade Williams	59.77
	Ellie Vernon	46.03
5kW	Sarah Glennon IRL	26:02.66
	Jessica Hopkins	4850

U15 Bedford 26-27 August

MEN (U15)

100	Jaleel Roper	11.01
200	Jaleel Roper	22.13
300	George Sudderick	35.79
800	Daniel Joyce	1:56.04
1500	Ethan Hussey	4:10.95
3000	Mohamed Ali	8:58.93

80H	Elliott Harris	11.13
HJ	Samuel Brereton	1.97
PV	George Hopkins	3.51
LJ	Archie Yeo	6.34
TJ	Oyare Aneju	13.31
SP	Jack Halpin	14.11

DT	Ben Copley	47.18
HT	Kenneth Ikeji	61.92
JT	Ben Copley	55.74
Oct	Ben Hillman	4336
3kW	Alex MacHeath	16:43.64

Oct/Hex 12-13 August Bedford

WOMEN (U15)

100	Abigail Pawlett	12.04
200	Precious Adu	24.58
300	Tia Anderson	40.35
800	Emma Horsey	2:15.74

1500	Sian Heslop	4:33.76
75H	Ruby Bridger	11.07
HJ	Molly Hole	1.65
PV	Sophie Ashurst	3.56
LJ	Caitlyn Mapps	5.45
TJ	Eleanor Brown	11.16

SP	Bekki Roche	14.34
DT	Zara Obamakinwa	37.89
HT	Kirsty Costello	57.11
JT	Kirsty Costello	43.70
Hex	Abigail Pawlett	3750
3kW	Hannah Hopper	18:01.77

UK MERIT RANKINGS 2017 by Peter Matthews

My annual merit rankings of British athletes (of which this is the 50th successive year!) are an assessment of form and achievements during the outdoor season. The major factors by which the rankings are determined are win-loss record, performances in major meetings, and sequence of marks. Unlike the AI World Rankings here I consider both indoor and outdoor results. Outdoor marks are still listed first and any variances in the rankings on outdoor form only are shown at the end of the lists for the event.

I endeavour to be as objective as possible in assessing what actually happened in 2017, but form can often provide conflicting evidence, or perhaps an athlete may not have shown good enough to justify a ranking that his or her ability might otherwise warrant. I can only rank athletes on what they have actually achieved. Much depends on having appropriate opportunities and perhaps getting invitations for the prestige meetings. This year the major targets for top athletes were the World Championships and for younger athletes the European Junior and U23 Championships. Difficulties arise when athletes reach peak form at different parts of the season or, through injury, miss significant competition. Also, as noted every year, many of our top track athletes compete only rarely in Britain, choosing (or being sent to) overseas meetings instead of British ones, which makes comparisons of form difficult and severely weakens the sport in this country, where the number of good class domestic meetings continues to decline very worryingly.

For each event the top 12 are ranked (except in those events where are insufficient British athletes producing adequate performances). On the first line is shown the athlete's name, then their date of birth followed, in brackets, by the number of years ranked in the top 12 (including 2017) and their ranking last year (2016), and finally, their best mark prior to 2017. The following lines include their best performances of the year (generally six), followed, for completeness, by significant indoor marks indicated by 'i'. Then follow placings at major meetings, providing a summary of the athlete's year at the event.

Abbreviations include

Anniv	Anniversary Games (DL) at London (Olympic Stadium)
BIG	Bedford Jumps and Throws Fest (BIGish)
BL	British League/UK Womens' League
B'ham DL	Diamond League at Birmingham
B.Univs	British Universities at Bedford
CAU	Inter-Counties/England Champs at Bedford
Comm-Y	Commonwealth Youth Games
EI	European Indoor Championships at Belgrade
EJ	European Junior Championships at Grosseto
E.Clubs	European Clubs Cup
E.Sch	English Schools at Birmingham
Eng-J	England Under-20 Championships
Eng-23	England Under-23 Championships
ET	European Team Championships at Villeneuve d'Ascq
EU23	European U23 Championships at Bydgoszcz
GNC	Great North City Games - Gateshead/Newcastle
LEAP	Loughborough European Athletics Permit Meeting
LI	Loughborough International
MCG	Manchester City Games
MI	Manchester International
Sch.G	Schools Games at Loughbororough
UK ·	UK Championships at Birmingham
UKi	UK Indoor Championships at Sheffield
WCh	World Championships in London
WI	World Indoor Championships at Portland
WInt	Welsh International at Cardiff
WL	UK Women's League
WUG	World University Games at Taipei
YDL	Youth Development League Final

100 METRES

1 **Chijindu Ujah** 5.03.94 (5y, 3) 9.96 '14   9.97, 9.98, 10.02, 10.02, 10.02, 10.02; 9.95w, 9.98w
   1B Tempe, 2 Mt.SAC, 3 Eugene, 1 Rome, 2 Oslo, 1s1/dns UK, 1 Anniv, 1 Rabat, 4 Monaco, 4s3 WCh, 1 B'ham DL, 1 Zürich
2 **Reece Prescod** 29.2.96 (1y, -) 10.04 '16   10.03, 10.05, 10.09, 10.09, 10.11, 10.17; 10.15w
   1 Newham 7/5, 1 Gavardo, 7 Oslo, 1 UK, 7 WCh
3 **James Dasaolu** 5.09.87 (10y, 4) 9.91 '13   10.06, 10.11, 10.11, 10.12, 10.12, 10.13
   3r1 G'ville, 2 Basel, 1 MCG, 3 Marseille, 1A Geneva, 2 UK, 5 Lausanne, 2 Anniv, 5s1 WCh, 2 B'ham DL, 4 Rovereto, 6 Brussels
4 **Nethaneel Mitchell-Blake** 2.4.94 (2y, 9) 10.09 '16   9.99, 10.03, 10.07, 10.17, 10.18, 10.26
   4 Mt SAC, 2 SEC, 2q1 NCAA-E, 6 NCAA, 3 Rabat
5 **Adam Gemili** 6.10.93 (6y, 2) 9.97 '15   10.08, 10.10, 10.13, 10.13, 10.18, 10.21; 10.03w
   1 Azusa, 7 Eugene, 4 Oslo, 1 Mannheim, dq fs B'ham DL, 8 Zürich, 3 ISTAF, 4 Zagreb
6 **Harry Aikines-Aryeetey** 29.8.88 (11y, 8) 10.08 '13   10.13, 10.13, 10.15, 10.16, 10.18, 10.19; 9.90w, 9.97w, 10.16w
   1 Clermont, 1r2 G'ville, 3 LI, 5 Prague, 5 Turku, 1 ET, 3 UK, 4 Anniv, 8 Luzern, 1 LEAP, 4 B'ham DL, 5 ISTAF, 7 Brussels
7 **Ojie Edoburun** 2.6.96 (3y, 7) 10.16, 10.15w '14   10.12, 10.14, 10.15, 10.20, 10.21, 10.22; 9.93w, 9.99w, 10.06w, 10.07w
   2 Clermont, 3r2 G'ville, 1 LI, 4 Gavardo, 1 Eng-23, 4 UK, 1 EU23, 1 CAU, 5 B'ham DL
8 **Zharnel Hughes** 13.7.95 (1y, -) 10.10 '16   10.12, 10.13, 10.08w
   1rB K'ston 11/3, 1 K'ston 15/4, 3 B'ham DL
9 **Joel Fearon** 11.10.88 (4y, 7) 9.96 '16   10.21, 10.24, 10.25, 10.26, 10.26, 10.27; 10.20w, 10.23w
   4 LI, 2 MCG, 3 Bilbao, 5 UK, dq fs Anniv, 2B/2C Luzern, 1 BLP (3), 2 LEAP
10 **Richard Kilty** 2.9.89 (5y, 6) 10.01 '16   10.18, 10.20, 10.23, 10.27, 10.28, 10.37
   3 Gavardo, 4 Turku, 7 Anniv, 2 n/s BLP (3)
11 **Reuben Arthur** 12.10.96 (1y, -) 10.30 '16   10.18, 10.20, 10.31, 10.33, 10.34, 10.35; 10.20w, 10.29w
   1 B.Univs, 3h1 Newham 7/5, 5 LI, 1/2 Newham 29/5, 1B Geneva, 2 Eng-23, 6 UK, 5 EU23, 3 CAU
12 **Andrew Robertson** 17.12.90 (5y, 10) 10.10 '14   10.23, 10.23, 10.24, 10.27, 10.30, 10.31; 10.15w, 10.18w, 10.26w
   2 Newham 7/5, 3A LI, 3 MCG, 1 R'burg, 1 Leiden, 5s1 UK, 2 CAU, 1 MI, 6 B'ham DL, 1 LV 30/8
– **Kyle de Escofet** 4.10.96 (0y, -) 10.45 '15   10.21, 10.22, 10.22, 10.27, 10.29, 10.31
   1 BLP (1), 1A LI, 1 Aarhus, 2A Geneva, 3s3/dns Eng-23, 4s3 UK, 2 La Roche, 6 LEAP, 3 Castres, 7 B'ham DL
– **Samuel Osewa** 17.04.91 (1y, 12) 10.19 '16   10.21, 10.24, 10.29, 10.31, 10.33, 10.38; 10.20w, 10.29w, 10.29w
   2 B.Univs, 2A LI, 2 P'frugel, 3 Bydgoszcz, 2 Dessau, 7 UK, 4 LEAP, 5s1 WUG

Despite not running in the UK final or making the World Championship final, Ujah was the clear number one for the second time, and his win in the DL final at Zurich was the best by a Briton on the global stage since Linford Christie. Prescod followed up his fast time at the 2016 Inter-Counties with a real breakthrough to win the UK title and make the World final. Mitchell-Blake became the seventh British man to break 10 seconds although focusing mostly on the 200m, but ranks below Dasoulu who had the better big meeting record. HAA and Edoburun headed Hughes due to much deeper seasons, even though Hughes was 1-0 against them both. HAA was slower than Edoburun but beat him 4-1. In the definite drop off behind Hughes 9th to 12th was especially tight with Osewa and Kyle de Escofet unlucky to miss out. 50th best of 10.53 was another new record for the fourth successive year. Top sprint performance of the year was, of course, the brilliant run, the best ever by a British quartet, to win the World 4x100m title.

200 METRES

1 **Nethaneel Mitchell-Blake** 2.4.94 (4y, 2) 19.95 '16   20.04, 20.08, 20.09, 20.15, 20.18, 20.24; 20.19w
   1 Baton Rouge. 2 SEC, 2 NCAA, 1 UK, 4 Anniv, 4 WCh, 5 B'ham DL, 7 Brussels
2 **Danny Talbot** 1.5.91 (7y, 3) 20.27 '15   20.16, 20.20, 20.31, 20.33, 20.36, 20.38; 19.86w
   1 Clermont, 1 Gavardo, 1 Hengelo, 2 UK, 6 Anniv, 5s3 WCh, 6 B'ham DL
3 **Zharnel Hughes** 13.7.95 (3y, 6) 20.02 '15   20.22, 20.22, 20.27, 20.29, 20.33, 20.42
   3/4 Kingston, 4 Boston, 4 UK, 5 Anniv, 3 Rabat, 7s2 WCh, 6 Brussels
4 **Leon Reid** 26.7.94 (4y, 9) 20.62 '13   20.38, 20.57, 20.59, 20.78, 20.79, 20.81
   1 Waterford, 1A LI, 1 NI, 3 UK, 1 Belfast, 5 Luzern, 3 Cork, BLP: -,1,1,2
5 **Adam Gemili** 6.10.93 (5y, 1) 19.97 '16   20.35, 20.64, 20.79, 20.97   3 Shanghai, 3 Hengelo, 6 UK
6 **Richard Kilty** 2.9.89 (6y, -) 20.34 '13   20.51, 20.76, 20.86   1 LI, 3 Gavardo, 1 Gothenburg
7 **Samuel Miller** 2.9.93 (1y, -) -0-   20.79, 20.80, 20.83, 20.85, 20.88, 20.90; 20.84w
   3A LI, 1 Budapest, 5 ET, 5 UK, 1 LEAP, dns CAU
8 **Roy Ejiakuekwu** 2.2.95 (1y, -) 20.93, 20.78w '15   20.65, 20.82, 20.88, 20.93, 21.15; 20.55w, 20.63w, 20.86w; 21.03i
   2 & 5 F'ville, 5h5 SEC, 6s3 NCAA, 7 UK
9 **Edmond Amaning** 27.10.93 (1y, -) 21.07 '13   20.86, 20.95, 21.06, 21.11, 21.14, 21.26; 20.52w, 20.78w, 21.05w; 2118i
   2r4 Clermont, 1 LV 7/6. 3h2 UK, 3 CAU, BLP: -,2,2,1; Ind: dq UKi
10 **Elliott Powell** 5.3.96 (2y, -) 20.68 '15   20.94, 21.00, 21.03, 21.14, 21.17, 21.21; 20.73w, 20.82w, 20.90w, 20.91w
   4A LI, 2 Mid, dq Eng-23, 3h4 UK, 4 CAU, 1 MI, BLP: 2,1B,1B,1B
11 **Toby Harries** 30.9.98 (1y, -) 20.92A, 20.56w '15   20.81, 20.89, 20.90, 21.11, 21.18, 21.20   2 Eng-J, dnf UK, 1 EJ
12 **James Dasaolu** 5.09.87 (1y, -) 21.9 '07   20.73, 20.62w; 2r5 Clermont, 7A Geneva
– **Chijindu Ujah** 5.3.94 (2y, 7) 20.47 '15   20.39; 1 Tempe
– **Miguel Francis** 28.3.95 (0y, -) 19.88 '16   20.44, 20.46; 4 & 6 Kingston
nr **Antonio Infantino** ITA 22.3.91 (as UK 2y, -) 20.53 '16   20.59, 20.70, 20.74, 20.84, 20.90, 20.94; 20.45w, 20.51w, 20.74w
   3 Clermont, 1 Newham 7/5, 2 LV 7/6, 4A Geneva, 5h2 ET, 2 ITA Ch. 1 Eng Ch; Ind: 1 UKi

Mitchell-Blake and Talbot moved up a place to take the top two rankings and both were highly ranked in the world, with Hughes close behind. Unfortunately injury restricted the four-time no.1 Gemili to just three meetings. Miller made a fine start to his career at 200m.

400 METRES

1   **Matthew Hudson-Smith** 26.10.94 (4y, 1) 44.48 '16   44.74, 44.99, 45.16, 45.31, 45.52, 46.08
   1 G'ville, 7 Eugene, 2 Oslo, 1 UK, dnf Anniv, 4s2 WCh
2   **Dwayne Cowan** 1.1.85 (2y, 7) 46.02 '16   45.34, 45.36, 45.39, 45.46, 45.63, 45.75
   3 Clermont, 3 G'ville, 1T'hassee, 3 LI, 5 Aarhus, 3= Geneva, 4 Turku, 1 ET, 4 UK, 3 Anniv, 8s1 WCh, 1 B'ham DL, 1 Rovereto
3   **Rabah Yousif** 11.12.86 (4y, 2) 44.54 '15   45.58, 45.74, 45.76, 45.81, 45.81, 45.82
   2 Marseille, 2 Szczecin, 1 Turku, 6 Stockholm, 2 UK, 5 Anniv, 1 G'burg, 1 BLP (3), 2 Heusden, 3 B'ham DL, 4 Zagreb, 2 Brussels
4   **Cameron Chalmers** 6.2.97 (2y, 12) 46.51 '16   45.64, 45.71, 45.93, 46.11, 46.29, 46.32
   1 B.Univs, 1 LI, 1 Eng-23, 3 UK, 4 EU23; Ind: 1 Scot, 2 UKi1 B.Univs
5   **Martyn Rooney** 3.4.87 (13y, 3) 44.45 '15   45.65, 45.75, 45.99, 46.13, 46.18, 46.28
   2B St George's, 2r2 Z'roda, 1 UK, 6 Anniv, 6 Madrid, 6h5 WCh, 7 B'ham DL, 7 Zagreb, 3 Brussels
6   **George Caddick** 29.7.94 (3y, 10) 45.90 '15   45.45, 45.76, 45.80, 45.89, 46.10, 46.13
   2/4 Waco, 2 Big 12, 7s2 NCAA, 6 UK; Ind: 1/1 Coll.Stn, 3h1 F'ville, 1 Big 12, 4h2 NCAA
7   **Delano Williams** 23.12.93 (3y, 6) 45.42 '15   45.85, 45.92, 46.23, 46.67, 47.40, 47.87
   1/2/3/1/5 Kingston, 2 C'hagen, 8 Anniv
8   **Owen Richardson** 5.9.98 (1y, -) 47.22 '16   46.49, 46.70, 46.85, 47.24, 47.54, 47.64; 47.50i
   4 LI, 1 Eng-J, 3 Mannheim, 5 EJ; Ind: 1 South-J, 4s2 UKi, 1 Eng-Ji
9   **Benjamin Snaith** 17.9.95 (1y, -) 46.89 '14   46.21, 47.04, 47.24, 47.26, 47.28, 47.44
   2 CAU, 1 MI, BL2: 1,1,-; Ind: 4 London
10   **Edmond Amaning** 27.10.93 (1y, -) 49.31 '09   46.49, 46.77, 46.78, 47.09, 47.12, 47.25
   3C G'ville, 1B BLP (1), 1A LI, 3 CAU, 2 MI
11   **Conrad Williams** 20.3.82 (13y, 9) 45.08 '12   46.54, 46.78, 46.97, 47.10, 47.21, 47.43
   7 G'ville, 1B Z'roda, 6 Geneva, 3 C'hagen, 2h4 UK, 3 Dublin, dns CAU
12   **Owen Smith** 7.11.94 (1y, -) 46.23 '16   46.91, 46.93, 46.94, 47.36, 47.40, 47.41
   5 LI, 2B Oordegem, 3 Munich, 1 Welsh, 3h2 UK, 1 Hilversum, 4 CAU, 4 MI, BL1: 1,-,1,
−   **Theo Campbell** 14.7.91 (1y, 8) 46.02 '16 46.81, 46.87, 47.03, 47.29, 47.60   2 Munich, 8 Geneva, 1 Lisbon, 7 UK
−   **Sebastian Rodger** 29.6.91 (0y, -) 46.48i, 46.68 '16   46.57i, 46.86i, 46.98i; 1 Vienna, 1 Athlone, 5 B'ham
nr   **Sadam Koumi** 6.4.94 SUD 45.67 '16   46.00, 46.12, 46.14, 46.28, 46.46, 46.51
   2 Clermont, 2 LI, 7 Turku, 1 C'hagen, 2 LEAP, 1 CAU/Eng, BLP: -.1,2,-

Hudson-Smith raced lightly but broke 45 secs twice, including his year's best at the Worlds. Cowan maintained his remarkable breakthrough and at the age of 32 reduced his pb by 0.68 and Yousif had a solid season for third ranking. Top junior Chalmers made another major advance. Rooney ties the event record (with David Jenkins and Roger Black and, with this year, Conrad Williams) of 13 years ranked, but his 5th place ties his lowest ever position that he had in his first in 2005. Overall standards slipped so that 10th best was the worst since 2008 and 111 at 49.0 or better was the lowest since 2007.

800 METRES

1   **Kyle Langford** 2.2.96 (5y, 7) 1:45.78 '15   1:45.25, 1:45.45, 1:45.69, 1:45.81, 1:45.91, 1:46.38
   2 Eagle Rock. 8 Oordegem, 1 Brighton, 3 Hengelo, 6 Samorin, 3 UK, 8 Anniv, 1 Dublin, 4 WCh, 6 B'ham DL; Ind: 5 UKi, 3 B'ham, 4s1 EI
2   **Elliot Giles** 26.5.94 (3y, 2) 1:45.54 '16   1:44.99, 1:45.44, 1:45.86, 1:46.10, 1:46.38, 1:46.95
   2 Brighton, 7 Hengelo, 2 Dessau, 1 Bilbao, 1 UK, 5 Anniv, 9 Monaco, 6s1 WCh, 5 B'ham DL, 7 Brussels
3   **Guy Learmonth** 20.4.92 (6y, 5) 1:46.65 '15   1:45.10, 1:45.77, 1:45.90, 1:46.07, 1:46.28, 1:46.75
   3 Montgeron, 1 Manchester, 2 Bydgoszcz, 4 Dessau, 2 UK, 10 Anniv, 4 B'zona, 5s1 WCh, 8 B'ham DL, 4 Rovereto; Ind: 1 Vienna, 3 Karlsruhe, 1 UKi, 5 B'ham, 5h4 EI
4   **Andrew Osagie** 19.2.88 (8y, -) 1:43.77 '12   1:45.54, 1:45.73, 1:45.75, 1:45.75, 1:46.05, 1:46.36
   3 Eagle Rock, 3 Andújar, 3 Belfort, 2 Huelva, 5 UK, 9 Anniv, 6 B'zona, 3 Karlstad, 6 Rovereto; Ind: 6 B'ham, 4 Madrid
5   **Jake Wightman** 11.7.94 (5y, 8) 1:47.13 '16   1:45.42, 1:45.82, 1:46.07, 1:46.36; 1:50.22i
   1 Solihull, 5 Somerville, 1 Gothenburg, 7 Anniv
6   **Daniel Rowden** 9.9.97 (2y, 9) 1:48.13 '16   1:46.64, 1:46.86, 1:47.51, 1:47.51, 1:47.79, 1:48.15
   2 Solihull, 5 Oordegem, 1 Eng-23, 4 UK, 2 EU23, 5 Karlstad, 5 Sopot, BLP: 1,-,-,1
7   **Michael Rimmer** 3.2.86 (13y, 1) 1:43.89 '10   1:46.72, 1:46.89, 1:47.56, 1:47.91, 1:47.98, 1:48.29
   7 Eagle Rock, 4 Kawasaki, 8 Andújar, 9 Huelva, 3h1 UK, dnf Kortrijk, 5 Luzern, 4 Cork, 1 Stretford 15/8
8   **James Bowness** 26.11.91 (4y, 6) 1:45.86 '16   1:46.40, 1:47.43, 1:48.19, 1:48.78, 1:49.3, 1:49.95
   1B Stret 16/5, 7/3 Oordegem, 3 ET, 6 UK, 4s3 WUG
9   **Markhim Lonsdale** 9.1.99 (1y, -) 1:49.07 '16   1:46.97, 1:47.07, 1:47.63, 1:48.24, 148.78, 1:48.82; 1:48.77i
   1 Manchester, 1 Dublin, 1 Eng-J, 3h4 UK, 1 Lough 8/7, 2 EJ, 2 MI, 1 Stret 19/8; Ind: 1 North-J, 2 UKi, 1 Eng-Ji
10   **Spencer Thomas** 26.8.97 (2y, 11) 1:48.24 '16   1:47.83, 1:47.84, 1:48.18, 1:48.35, 1:48.48, 1:48.71; 1:49.52i
   4 Irvine, 2 Castiglione, 2 LI, 2C Oordegem, 3 Brighton, 4 Gothenburg, 3 Eng-23, 4 Watford 12/7, 4 CAU; Ind: 3B Vienna, 3 UKi
11   **John Bird** 17.5.92 (1y, -) 1:49.74 '15   1:47.79, 1:48.84, 1:48.90, 1:49.68, 1:50.2
   3B Stret 16/5, 1B Manchester, 2 Watford 14/6 & 24/6, 7 UK

12   **Sean Molloy** 18.9.95 (1y, -) 1:48.24 '14   1:47.76, 1:48.33, 1:48.66, 1:48.99, 1:49.32, 1:49.48
     1/1 Eltham, 3B Manchester, 4 Brighton, 1 Watford 14/6, 2 Eng-23, 5 Watford 24/6, 4h2 UK, 5B Karlstad, 6 Watford 9/8
In a fine year for British 800m running Rimmer, who had been in the top three for eleven years, slips to 7th and is succeeded as number one by Langford due to his splendid Worlds 4th place, although he was beaten 3-2 by Giles. Learmonth had a splendidly consistent year and it was good to welcome back Osagie, top each year 2011-14, for his first ranking since then, although he has no wins. Rowden and Lonsdale won European U23/U20 silver medals. 50th best of 1:50.07 was the best since 1992 and third best ever.

1500 METRES – 1 MILE
1   **Chris O'Hare** 23.11.90 (7y, 3) 3:34.83 '15, 3:52.91Mi '16, 3:56.35 '15   3:33.61, 3:34.35, 3:34.75, 3:53.34M/3:38.14, 3:55.01M, 3:38.28
     2 Stanford, 3 Eagle Rock, 2B Eugene, 1 Somerville, 1 UK, 1 Anniv, 7 Monaco, 12 WCh, 2 B'ham DL, 1 Huntington
2   **Jake Wightman** 11.7.94 (4y, 4) 3:35.49 '14, 3:54.20M '16   3:34.17, 3:35.25, 3:35.93, 3:54.92M/3:40.80, 3:38.50, 3:41.79; 3:57.24Mi
     1 Oordegem, 1 Oslo, 2 ET, 3 UK, 8s1 WCh, 1 B'ham DL, 7 Zürich
3   **Charlie Grice** 7.11.93 (5y, 2) 3:33.60, 3:52.64M '16 3:35.72, 3:36.29, 3:53.62M/3:37.37, 3:37.78, 3:39.52, 3:41.28
     10 Eugene, 7 Prague, 6 Oslo, 4 Bilbao, 5 UK, 5 Anniv, 12 Heusden
4   **Mohamed Farah** 23.3.83 (9y, 1) 3:28.81 '13   2 Eagle Rock 3:34.19
5   **Josh Kerr** 8.10.97 (2y, 7) 3:41.08 '16   3:35.99, 3:43.03, 3:43.46, 3:44.60, 3:47.30, 3:47.71; 3:59.90Mi, 4:03.22Mi
     1 Azusa, 1 MWC, 1 NCAA, 2 UK, 11h1 WCh; Ind: 1 MWCi, 1 NCAAi
6   **Neil Gourley** 7.2.95 (3y, 12) 3:39.92, 3:59.58Mi '16   3:40.52, 3:42.82, 3:43.99, 3:44.14, 3:44.25, 3:44.39; 4:00.10Mi, 4:01.14Mi
     2 Knoxville, 5 C'ville, 1 ACC, 5 NCAA, 1 Eng-23, 4 UK, 4 EU23; Ind: 1 B'burg, 2 Ames
7   **Tom Marshall** 12.6.89 (3y, 9) 3:39.41 '16, 4:00.74Mi '11, 4:01.04M '13   3:37.45, 3:37.62, 3:39.27, 3:58.31M, 3:45.79, 3:46.25; 3:59.84Mi
     8 Solihull, 9 Oordegem, 1 Watford, 12 UK, 11 Anniv, 8 Dublin, 13B Heusden; Ind: 3 Athlone
8   **Jonathan Davies** 28.10.94 (1y, -) 3:43.15 '16   3:39.00, 4:00.58M, 3:43.48, 3:43.95, 3:48.13
     1 B.Univs, 3 Watford, 1 CAU, 2 Watford 9/8, 1 MI, 3 WUG
9   **Robbie Fitzgibbon** 23.3.96 (2y, 10) 3:44.34 '15, 4:00.18M '16   3:36.97, 3:37.74, 3:38.00, 3:40.38, 3:40.42, 4:00.63M
     3 Stanford, 2 Tübingen, 4 Nijmegen, 9 Huelva, 3 Eng-23, 9 UK, 13 Anniv, 8 EU23, 12 B'ham DL; Ind: 6 Mondeville, 6 UKi
10   **Andrew Butchart** 14.10.91 (1y, -) 3:44.57 '15, 4:05.40 '13   3:39.61, 3:47.61; 3:54.23M/3:37.58i
     4 Watford, 5h3 UK; Ind: 1 New York
11   **Adam Clarke** 3.4.91 (1y, -) 3:40.29 '15   3:38.35, 3:39.66, 3:41.63, 3:41.72, 3:42.77, 3:43.18
     3 Castiglione, 9 Nijmegen, 9 Padua, 6B Heusden, 3 Sopot, 8 Brussels
12   **Tom Lancashire** 2.7.85 (11y, 6) 3:33.96, 3:53.39M '10   3:38.85, 3:41.10, 3:43.07, 3:47.45; 3:38.52i, 3:39.96i, 3:46.45i
     8B Eagle Rock, 10 Nijmegen, 16 Prague, 14 Stretford 19/8; Ind: 7 Karlsruhe, 2 UKi, 5 EI
–   **James West** 30.1.96 (1y, 11) 3:40.0 '16   3:39.65, 3:43.92, 3:43.95, 3:44.32, 3:44.34, 3:44.72; 3:42.81i, 3:43.33i
     1 Watford 3/5, 1 Solihull, 4 LI, 5 Watford, 2 Eng-23, 6 UK, 8h2 EU23, 3 Watford 9/8; Ind: 2 Vienna, 3 UKi, 9 B'ham
–   **Rowan Axe** 17.5.91 (0y, -) 3:44.99 '16   3:38.12, 3:42.30, 3:43.94, 3:44.24, 3:47.36, 3:50.34
     10C Oordegem, 1 Welsh, 2 Watford, 8 UK, 8B Heusden
     Outdoors only: 10 Clarke, 11 West, 12 Axe
O'Hare and Wightman move up two places from 2016, so world finalist O'Hare regains the top ranking he had in 2014. They met twice: O'Hare winning the UK title and Wightman winning in Birmingham (a second DL win in 2016 with Oslo as well). Farah again had just one race at the event but this was not in a major race although he finished ahead of O'Hare. Kerr continued his exciting progress and won NCAA titles indoors and out, but failed to advance from his heat at the Worlds. Fitzgibbon and Marshall went 1-1, but although Gourley had much slower times, he excelled in major races and beat Fitzgibbon 3-0. Note also Jake Heyward, who won the European Junior title. 10th best of 3:38.35 was, as in 2016, the best since 1992.

5000 METRES
1   **Mohamed Farah** 23.3.83 (14y, 1) 12:53.11 '11   1 Eugene 13:00.70, 1 Zürich 13:06.05, 13:25.53+ Ostrava,
     2 WCh 13:33.22 (13:30.18 ht), 13:36.20+; 1 B'ham 13:09.16i
2   **Andrew Butchart** 14.10.91 (3y, 2) 13:08.61 '16
     8 Eugene 13:11.45, 4 Berlin 13:12.73, 8 WCh 13:38.73 (13:24.78 ht), 1 UK 13:50.56
3   **Marc Scott** 21.12.93 (3y, 10) 13:36.81 '15   4B Heusden 13:22.37, 1 Mt.SAC 13:37.45, 18h2 WCh 13:58.11,
     2 AAC 14:27.87, 4 NCAA 14:36.57; 2 NCAA 13:43.83i
4   **Andrew Vernon** 7.1.86 (11y, 4) 13:11.50 '11   15 Heusden 13:22.65, 2 UK 13:54.63
5   **Ben Connor** 17.10.92 (1y, -) 13:53.74 '16   3 Dublin 13:29.90, 2 Nijmegen 13:42.89, 3 UK 13:56.71, 14:09+
6   **Dewi Griffiths** 9.8.91 (1y, -) 13:53.85 '15   5 Dublin 13:33.60, 1 Welsh 13:50.35, 1 BL1 (2) 13:50.83, 1 BL1 (4) 13:57.41
7   **Jonathan Davies** 28.10.94 (3y, 5) 13:23.94 '16   11 Carquefou 13:37.13, 25 Oordegem 13:51.40,
     2 WUG 14:02.46 (14:25.43 ht); dnf UK 14:01.19; 8 B'ham 13:58.04i
8   **Nicholas Goolab** 30.1.90 (1y, -) 14:39.6 '13   13 Oordegem 13:33.48, 2 ET 13:59.72, dnf Heusden
9   **Sam Stabler** 17.5.92 (2y, -) 13:30.15 '15   10B Heusden 13:37.30, 6B Oordegem 13:38.09, 1 Watford 13:59.12
10   **Alexander Yee** 18.2.98 (2y, 12) 13:52.01 '16   2B Oordegem 13:37.60
11   **Adam Clarke** 3.4.91 (1y, -) 13:44.47 '16   20 Oordegem 13:39.21, 15B Stanford 14:09.14
12   **Alex George** 6.2.96 (1y, -) 13:49.46 '16   5 Stanford 31/3 13:40.66, 2 SEC 13:53.83, dnf EU23
The great Farah ranks top for the 13th year (again increasing the event record) and Butchart maintained his presence amongst the world's best. 10th best of 13:37.60 is a further improvement and is the best since 1992 as is 11 men under 13:40 and 50th best at 14:11.33.

10,000 METRES
1 **Mohamed Farah** 23.3.83 (8y, 1) 26:46.57 '11   1 WCh 26:49.51, 1 Ostrava 27:12.09
2 **Andrew Vernon** 7.1.86 (7y, 4) 27:53.65 '12   9 Stanford 27:58.69, 1 UK 28:21.15, 15 Hengelo 28:33.65
3 **Dewi Griffiths** 9.8.91 (4y, 3) 28:28.55 '16   14 Stanford 28:16.07, 7 Leiden 28:24.71, 2 UK 28:31.88
4 **Marc Scott** 21.12.93 (2y, -) 28:30.33 '15   12 Stanford 28:07.97, 1 NCAA 29:01.54, 1h NCAA-W 29:50.49
5 **Ben Connor** 17.10.92 (2y, 6) 29:18.62 '14   6 Leiden 28:23.58, 5 (3) UK 28:46.45
6 **Chris Thompson** 17.4.81 (6y, -) 27:27.36 '11   1 ENG 28:40.40
7 **Ellis Cross** 22.9.96 (1y, -) -0-   8 UK 29:00.49, 5 EU23 29:53.64
8 **Luke Caldwell** 2.8.91 (4y, 5) 28:29.61 '15   9 UK 29:01.76
9 **Sam Stabler** 17.5.92 (1y, -) 31:23.18 '15   2 ENG 29:03.64
10 **Luke Traynor** 6.7.93 (2y, 7) 29:10.19 '16   3 ENG 29:08.52, 8 NCAA 29:10.58, 12 Mt.SAC 29:15.44, 4 NCAA-W 29:54.31
11 **Matthew Leach** 25.9.93 (2y, 10) 29:14.36 '16   13 Stanford 31/3 28:45.48, 16 UK 29:29.79
12 **Alex Short** 7.1.94 (2y, 11) 29:19.55 '16   15 Stanford 31/3 28:46.83, 12 ECp 30:02.36
Farah added two wins to his career tally and had to run his fastest ever time in a championships to win at the Worlds. He bows out on his track career with his event record ninth top ranking (in ten years). The Parliament Hill races, which incorporated the UK Champs. again proved a huge success and 34 of the 79 British men to better 31 minutes set their bests at this meeting. This helped to raise overall standards so that 10th best at 29:01.76 was the fastest since 2002 and 50th at 30:23.08 and 80 under 31 minutes the best since 1992

10 MILES - HALF MARATHON (First ranked 1999)
1 **Mohamed Farah** 23.3.83 (8y, 1) 59:22 '15   1 GNR (ENG) 60:06
2 **Callum Hawkins** 22.6.92 (4y, 2) 60:24 '16   1 Marugame 60:00 (15k 42:37), 2 New York 60:08 (15k 42:52),
2 Gt.Scot 63:18, dnf Olomouc   15k: 10 Nijmegen 44:45
3 **Dewi Griffiths** 9.8.91 (3y, 5) 63:27 '16
4 Cardiff 61:33 (15k 43:25, 20k 58:25), 7 GNR 62:53, 63:49+ Frankfurt, 3 Reading 63:54, 1 Swansea 64:49
4 **Chris Thompson** 17.4.81 (6y, 3) 61:00 '12
1 Gt.Scot 62:44, 13 GNR (2 ENG) 65:28, 2 Reading 63:39, 1 Nottingham 64:58   10M: 1 Gt. South (1 ENG) 48:32
5 **Tsegai Tewelde** 8.12.89 (1y, -) 63:34 '15   9 GNR 63:14, 3 Gt.Scot 63:18
6 **Andrew Vernon** 19.9.89 (5y, 5) 62:46 '14   1 Reading 63:49, 1 Chertsey 65:28
7 **Jonathan Mellor** 27.12.96 (5y, 7) 62:59 '12   10 New York 62:23, 1 Lake Vymwy 64:57   15k: 14 Nijmegen 44:53
8 **Ross Millington** 19.9.89 (3y, -) 0   11 New York 62:40
9 **Luke Traynor** 6.7.93 (1y, -) -0-   1 Manchester 64:10   15k: 5 's-Heerenberg 43:47
10 **Matthew Sharp** 25.4.89 (2y, 8) 62:23 '16   13 Reading 67:39, 1 Isle of Wight 71:38   10M: 2 Gt. South (2 ENG) 48:35
11 **Ben Connor** 17.10.92 (2y, 9)   10M: 3 Gt. South (3 ENG) 48:36
12= **Matthew Leach** 25.9.93 (1y, -) -0-   4 San Jose 64:22
12= **Mohamud Aadan** 11.1.90 (1y, -) -0-   11 GNR 64:26
Farah, with his fourth successive win of the Great North Run, is top for the seventh year at these distances. Hawkins started the year splendidly to take second place and Griffiths made terrific progress, following a pb in the GNR with a 1:20 improvement in Cardiff.

MARATHON
1 **Callum Hawkins** 22.6.92 (3y, 1) 2:12:17 '15   4 WCh 2:10:17
2 **Dewi Griffiths** 9.8.91 (1y, -) -0-   5 Frankfurt 2:09:49
3 **Jonathan Mellor** 27.12.96 (2y, -) 2:16:52 '15   10 Berlin 2:12:57, 23 Elite/29 London 2:18:48
4 **Joshua Griffiths** 3.11.93 (1y, -) -0-   1M/14 London 2:14:53, 39 WCh 2:20:06
5 **Robbie Simpson** 14.11.91 (2y, 6) 2:15:38 '16   16 London 2:15:04
6 **Andrew Davies** 30.10.79 (4y, 9) 2:16:55 '15   17 London 2:15:11, 31 WCh 2:17:59
7 **Tsegai Tewelde** 8.12.89 (2y, -) 2:12:23 '16   6 Beirut 2:14:45
8 **Matthew Sharp** 25.4.89 (1y, -) 2:29:25 '15   20 Berlin 2:16:02, 23 London (2 ENG) 2:17:48
9 **Scott Overall** 9.2.83 (6y, 10) 2:10:55 '11   21 London (1 ENG) 2:16:54
10 **Paul Martelletti** 1.8.79 (3y, 7) 2:16:49 '11   24 Berlin 2:17:10
11 **Nicholas Torry** 19.2.77 (4y, -) 2:15:08 '13   20 Frankfurt 2:17:37
12 **Aaron Scott** 11.4.87 (2y, 11) 2:19:22 '16   24 London (3 ENG) 2:17:50
Prospects continue to look up, as Callum Hawkins excelled with 4th at the Worlds, and Dewi Griffiths made a splendid debut at Frankfurt. Josh Griiffiths ran splendidly in the mass field in London to make the World team. Although of course well short of standards set in the 1980s, 17 men broke 2:20 and 43 men broke 2:25 (best since 1995), up from 15 and 38 in 2016. 10th best of 2:17:10 was the best since 1997.

3000 METRES STEEPLECHASE
1 **Rob Mullett** 31.7.87 (8y, 1) 8:22.42 '16   8:30.06, 8:33.99, 8:41.43, 8:47.99
3 Eagle Rock 18/3, 4 ET, 1 UK, 15h3 WCh
2 **Zak Seddon** 28.6.94 (6y, 2) 8:33.09 '16   8:30.17, 8:32.84, 8:38.00, 8:39.30, 8:41.11
1 Florida R, 1 J'ville, 2 Copenhagen, 2 UK, 10h1 WCh, 6 WUG

3   **Ieuan Thomas** 17.7.89 (3y, -) 8:40.64 '14   8:33.59, 8:33.68, 8:34.93, 8:43.77, 8:52.96
    2 Stanford 31/3, 7 Oordegem, 2 Leiden, 3 UK, 1 BL2 (3), 15h2 WCh
4   **William Gray** 24.1.93 (3y, 6) 8:45.82 '16   8:33.68, 8:44.57, 8:46.18, 8:54.48. 8:55.85
    9 Castiglione, 8rA Oordegem, 11 Belfort, 5 UK, 12 Letterkenny
5   **Jonathan Hopkins** 3.6.92 (4y, 5) 8:37.43 '16   8:34.03, 8:36.96, 8:39.42, 8:42.39, 8:49.25
    1 B.Univs, 9 Oordegem, 3 Bydgoszcz, 3 Leiden, 9 UK, 1 MI
6   **Douglas Musson** 8.4.94 (3y, 7) 8:51.16 '16   8:38.54, 8:41.17, 8:43.34, 8:44.33, 8:53.56
    1 Manchester, 3 Gothenburg, 4 UK, 5 L'kenny, 1 CAU, 3 MI
7   **Adam Kirk-Smith** 30.1.91 (1y, -) 9:02.73 '16   8:37.41, 8:37.62, 8:45.37, 8:46.26, 8:47.06
    1 BLP (1), 3 LI, 15 Oordegem, 19 Huelva, 6 UK, 4 L'kenny, 1 Irish
8   **Jamaine Coleman** 22.9.95 (2y, 9) 8:53.72 '16   8:34.19, 8:40.44, 8:42.82, 8:43.85, 8:48.56
    1B Stanford 31/3, 1 C'ville, 1 Ohio Valley, 2h2 NCAA-E, 6s1 NCAA, 10 UK, 3 EU23
9   **Luke Gunn** 22.3.85 (13y, 4) 8:28.48 '08   8:38.69, 8:54.94, 8:59.05
    16 Oordegem, dnf Leiden, 8 UK, 4 CAU
10   **Phil Norman** 20.10.89 (1y, -) 9:08.57 '16   8:42.89, 8:46.18, 8:50.53, 8:53.17, 9:05.23
    1 LI, 13 UK, 2 CAU, 2 MI, BLP: 2,-,-,1
11   **Daniel Jarvis** 21.10.95 (1y, -) 9:05.55 '16   8:43.09, 8:52.65, 8:59.64, 9:01.35, 9:03.07
    1 Yeovil, 3 B.Univs, 2 LI, 1 Eng-23, dnf UK, 12 EU23
12   **Ryan Driscoll** 25.1.94 (2y, -) 8:56.77 '16   8:50.87, 8:53.00, 8:56.99, 9:03.23
    4C Stanford, 4 Eagle Rock 6/5, 6h2 NCAA-W, 7 UK
–   **Tommy Horton** 7.11.93 (2y, 11) 8:58.57 '16   8:48.26, 8:49.71, 8:56.79, 9:00.37, 9:02.51
    9B Oordegem, 11 UK, 9 L'kenny, 3 CAU, 4 MI
—   **Adam Visokay** 11.3.94 (2y, 10) 8:43.60 '15   8:47.34, 8:50.51, 8:51.44, 8:52.55, 8:57.25

Although no athlete broke 8:30 and 34 under 9:20 was a drop compared to the last three years, there was a remarkable growth in top-level depth with nine men under 8:40 (just 2 in 2015 and 5 in 2016) and a 10th best of 8:42.89 the fastest since 1994. Nonetheless the standard in greater depth was poor (50th was 9:32.76). Mullett narrowly retains his top spot of the last two years from an improving Seddon (2nd for the 3rd year running) while Thomas made a successful return to the rankings and also made the World Champs. Training partners Kirk-Smith and Norman are the top newcomers, dropping their previous bests by 25 seconds each. Very little between those ranked 4th to 8th and between those 10th to 14th.

110 METRES HURDLES

1   **Andrew Pozzi** 15.5.92 (5y, 1) 13.19 '16   13.14, 13.19, 13.24, 13.24, 13.24, 13.28; 13.13w, 13.17w
    1 Clermont, 2 Drake R, 1/1 LI, 5 Eugene, 4 Rome, dq fs Stockholm, 2 Paris, 4s2 WCh, 6 B'ham DL, 5 Zagreb
2   **David Omoregie** 1.11.95 (4y, 2) 13.24 '16   13.34, 13.36, 13.43, 13.47, 13.51, 13.59
    2/2 LI, 9 Hengelo, 3 ET, 5 UK, 8 Anniv, 5 Madrid, 6h1 WCh
3   **David King** 13.6.94 (4y, 4) 13.54, 13.4h '16   13.48, 13.49, 13.51, 13.56, 13.57, 13.57; 13.55w
    2 Montgeron, 4/3 LI, 3 MCG, 2 Bydgoszcz, 5 Hengelo, 1 UK, 6h2 Anniv, 8h2 WCh, 7 B'ham DL, 6 Zagreb
4   **Khai Riley-LaBorde** 8.11.95 (3y, 6) 13.60 '16   13.59, 13.65, 13.66, 13.67, 13.73, 13.73; 13.71w
    3 LI, 1 Linz, 3 Aarhus, 1 Eng-23, 2 UK, 2 EU23, 5 Liège, 2 MI, BL1: 1,1,1,1
5   **James Weaver** 25.7.97 (1y, -) -0-   13.69, 13.73, 13.75, 13.77, 13.85, 14.01; 13.78w
    6/3 LI, 5 Aarhus, 3= Geneva, 2 Eng-23, 4 UK, 4 EU23, 1 CAU
6   **Jake Porter** 13.11.93 (3y, 9) 13.91, 13.78w '15   13.68, 13.79, 13.81, 13.84, 13.85, 13.86; 13.79w, 13.79w
    2 B.Univs, 5 LI, 3 Linz, 4 Aarhus, 6 Hérouville, 3 UK, 7h1 Anniv, 1 Castres, 2 CAU, 1 MI, 4 Rovereto, 4 GNC, BLP: 2,1,1,1
7   **Gabriel Odujobi** 15.7.87 (2y, 7) 13.64, 13.57w '16   13.65, 13.68, 13.71, 13.84, 13.85, 13.85; 13.38w, 13.51w
    2 Melbourne, 2 Orlando, 3 C.Gables, 2 & 1 Clermont, 8 G'ville, 2 Linz
8   **Edirin Okoro** 4.4.89 (8y, -) 13.77 '14   13.77, 13.88, 13.94, 13.94, 13.95, 13.99
    5/2 LI, 1B Bydgoszcz, 6 C'hagen, 6 UK, 2 Belfast, 3 LEAP, 3 CAU, 4 Warsaw, BLP: -,-,1B,1B
9   **William Sharman** 12.9.84 (14y, 5) 13.16 '14, 12.9w '10   13.72, 13.74, 13.91, 14.10, 14.24
    4h G'ville, 1 Hérouville, 1 Sheffield
10   **David Feeney** 17.10.87 (5y, 10) 13.89 '15   14.09, 14.10, 14.11, 14.15, 14.17, 14.19; 14.11w
    6/7 LI, 1 Budapest, 1 North, dns UK, 4 CAU, 4 MI
11   **Miguel Perera** 30.9.96 (1y, -) 14.66 '16   14.09, 14.31, 14.34, 14.35, 14.3, 14.39; 14.25w
    6 B.Univs, 1B LI, 3 Bydgoszcz, 2 Lough 7/6, 1 South, 4 Eng-23, 7 UK, dnf LEAP. 5 CAU; BL1: -.-,1,1
12   **Cameron Fillery** 2.11.98 (1y, -) 15.1 '16   14.22, 14.23, 14.35, 14.56   7 LI, 6 CAU; BL1
nr   **Alex Al-Ameen** NGR 2.3.89 (4y pre NGR) 13.54 '14   13.93, 13.93, 13.94, 13.94, 14.05, 14.06
    6 C.Gables, 5B Clermont, 1 BLP (1), 7 Montgeron, 4/1 LI, 5 Forbach, 2B Montverde, 8 C'hagen, 1h NGR Ch, 5 LEAP
nr   **Ben Reynolds** 26.9.90 IRL (2y pre IRL) 13.48 '15   13.60, 13.67, 13.69, 13.82, 13.87, 13.92
    4r3 Clermont, 1 Aarhus, 1 NI, 4 Huelva, 4 Dessau, dq h1 ET-1, 1 Belfast

Pozzi retained top ranking and had his best year yet, on the edge of the world top ten. He is followed by Omoregie, who did not quite capture top form, and was 2-2 v King who completed a British trio at the Worlds. Lawrence Clarke did not compete after seven years in the top seven. 49 men under 15.30 was the worst since 2003 and 60 men to 15.59 (or 15.4 hand) was the lowest figure for 40 years.

400 METRES HURDLES
1   **Jack Green** 6.10.91 (6y, 2) 48.60 '12   48.77, 49.10, 49.27, 49.29, 49.34, 49.41
    1 BL2 (1), 1 Kent, 1 LI, 2 Bydgoszcz, 2 Prague, 1 Turku, 4 Stockholm, 1 ET, 1 UK, 6 Anniv, 4s2 WCh, 6 Zürich, 5 Zagreb
2   **Jacob Paul** 6.2.95 (5y, 5) 50.17 '16   49.49, 49.60, 49.66, 49.85, 49.98, 50.06
    1 BL1 (1), 2A LI, 1B Geneva, 1 Eng-23, 2 UK, 5 EU23, 8 Anniv, 3 LEAP, 3s3 WUG
3   **Sebastian Rodger** 29.6.91 (6y, 2) 49.19 '13   49.58, 49.78, 49.82, 49.86, 49.97, 50.10
    1 Oordegem 1/5 & 22/8, 1 BLP (1), 2 LI, 4A Geneva, 2 Samorín, 3 C'hagen, 3 UK, 3B Luzern, 5 Padua. 2 LEAP, 1 MI
4   **Tom Burton** 29.10.88 (7y, 4) 49.36 '15   49.95, 49.95, 50.07, 50.36, 50.36, 50.84
    6 Kawasaki, 1 Aarhus, 6A Geneva, 4 UK, 1=B Madrid
5   **Niall Flannery** 26.4.91 (8y, 7) 48.80 '14   49.74, 50.28, 50.35, 50.48, 50.57, 50.64
    1 Tampa, 4 LI, 2B Geneva, 1 Samorín, 4 Tarare, 6 UK, 2 C.Ligure, 4 Cork, 1 LEAP, 5 MI, 2 Guernsey, BLP: 2,-,1,1
6   **Jack Lawrie** 21.2.96 (2y, 11) 50.85 '16   50.25, 50.34, 50.40, 50.46, 50.55, 50.60
    3 LI, 6B Geneva, 2 Eng-23, 5 UK, 7 EU23, 4 LEAP, 3 CAU, 2 MI, 1 Scot, BLP: 3,1,-,-
7   **James Forman** 12.12.91 (7y, 10) 50.41 '11   50.72, 50.73, 51.16, 51.40, 51.50, 51.52
    2 BLP (2), 1 & 1 Hendon, 7 UK, 1 CAU, 3 MI, 1 Guernsey
8   **Matthew Sumner** 17.3.92 (2y, -) 51.26 '12   51.21, 52.24, 52.40, 52.49, 52.56, 52.57
    6 LI, 3h3 UK, 2 Belfast, 2 CAU, 4 MI, 5 Guernsey, BL1: -,2,1,1
9   **Christopher McAlister** 3.12.95 (2y, 12) 50.88 '16   51.82, 51.83, 51.83, 52.05, 52.11, 52.48
    3 T'molinos, 4 B.Univs, 6B Oordegem, 5C Geneva, 3 Eng-23, 8 UK, 6 Dublin, BLP: -,4,5,-
10 **Paul Bennett** 11.12.92 (2y, -) 51.55 '14   51.71, 51.97, 52.32, 52.61, 52.74, 52.76
    8 LI, 1 Welsh, 2h2 UK, 1 WInt, 5 Cork, 7 MI, BL1: 2,1,2,3
11 **Martin Lipton** 14.1.89 (1y, -) 51.41 '16   51.33, 52.14, 52.15, 52.55, 52.61, 53.17
    1 Scot-W, 3A LI, 6C Geneva, 3h2 UK, BLP: 4,3,3,2
12 **Alistair Chalmers** 31.3.00 (1y, -) -0-   52.06, 52.21, 52.73, 52.82, 53.14, 54.58
    1 Eng-J, 1 Island G, 2 E.Sch, 1 Comm-Y (51.22 yth hurdles), 3 Guernsey
–   **James Webster** 27.2.95 (0y, -) 52.81 '13 '16   52.21, 52.44, 52.67, 52.70, 52.74, 52.75
    3 B.Univs, 7A LI, 1 North, 4 Eng-23, 4h1 UK, 3 Belfast, 1 Brussels, 6 CAU, 2 Scot, BLP: 1B,1B,1B,1B

Jack Green, unbeaten by a British athlete, retains his top ranking. Rodger's times were slightly worse than in 2016 and he is narrowly overtaken by Paul, who ran seven times inside his pre-season best and beat Rodger at the UKs, although they were 1-1 in the year. Burton was again 4th at the UKs and retains that ranking place. Flannery had slightly better times than Lawrie, with whom he was 3-3. 17 year-old Chalmers showed promise for the future, but the standard in depth was well down with 10th best of 51.71 the worst since 1991 (apart from equal to 2008) and 50th best of 55.39 the worst since 1975.

HIGH JUMP
1   **Robbie Grabarz** 3.10.87 (13y, 1) 2.37 '12   2.31, 2.31, 2.27, 2.26, 2.25, 2.25; 2.30i, 2.28i
    7= Shanghai, 7 Oslo, 6= Paris, 1 UK, 2= Rabat, 6= WCh, 7= B'ham DL, 4 Zürich, 7= Eberstadt; Ind: 2 UKi, 2 EI
2   **Tom Gale** 18.12.98 (2y, 9) 2.18 '16   2.30, 2.28, 2.24, 2.23, 2.22, 2.22
    1 BL2 (1), 3= LI, 2 BIG, 1 Eng-J, 9= UK, 1 E.Sch, 1 WInt, 3 EJ, 1 CAU, 1 MI, 3 B'ham DL, 8 Zürich, 1 Klaverblad;
    Ind: 2 Cardiff, 9 Cologne, 1 Welsh, 1B Hustopece, 8 UKi, Eng-UJi, 1 WInt
3   **Chris Baker** 2.2.91 (7y, 2) 2.36i, 2.29 '16   2.28, 2.27, 2.26, 2.22, 2.21, 2.20; 2.21i
    7 Doha, 2 Montgeron, 2= Zeulenroda, 1 Geneva, 5 Samorín, 8= ET, 2= UK, 1 BL1 (3), 1 Cork, 2 LEAP, 2 CAU;
    Ind: 1 Cardiff, 6= Hirson, 6= Cologne
4   **Allan Smith** 6.11.92 (7y, 3) 2.26 '13   2.24, 2.23, 2.22, 2.20, 2.20, 2.16; 2.26i, 2.25i, 2.25i, 2.25i
    1 Oordegem, 1= LI, 3 BLP (2), 3 Geneva, 6 Samorín, 6 UK, 7 Cologne, 3 MI, 4 WUG; Ind: 2 Hirson,
    2 Cologne, 4= Hustopece, 1 UKi, 4 B'ham, 8 EI
5   **Chris Kandu** 10.9.95 (5y, 4) 2.24 '14   2.25, 2.22, 2.22, 2.19, 2.18, 2.08; 2.26i, 2.25i, 2.25i
    1 BIG, 1 Eng-23, 9= UK, nh EU23, 3 LEAP , 3 Klaverblad; Ind: 3 Hustopece, 3 UKi, 7 B'ham, dnq 10 EI
6   **Mike Edwards** 11.7.90 (9y, 5) 2.25 '15   2.23, 2.22, 2.22, 2.21, 2.21, 2.20
    1/1 Atlanta, 1 Columbia, 1 J'ville, 1 Clermont, 7 Drake R, 1= LI, 1 Lund, 2= UK, 2 Cork, 5 Liège, 1 LEAP, 2 MI,
    BLP: -,2,-,1; Ind: 7 B'ham 14/1, 2 Scot, 8 Hustopece, 4= UKi, 2 Athlone, 2 Istanbul
7   **David Smith** 14.7.91 (8y, 6) 2.25 '14   2.21, 2.21, 2.20, 2.19, 2.18, 2.16; 2.21i
    6 LI, 1 BLP (2), 10 UK, 2 Lund, 4 Lisbon, 2= UK, 6 Liège, 1 Scot, 2 Klaverblad; Ind: 3 B'ham 14/1, 1 Scot, 6 UKi
8   **Matt Roberts** 22.12.84 (10y, 7) 2.26 '10   2.22, 2.16, 2.15, 2.14; 2.20i, 2.16i, 2.16i, 2.16i
    1 BLP (1), 3= LI, 2 P'frugell, 5 UK; Ind: 2 B'ham 14/1, 1 Lough, 9 Hustopece, 7 UKi
9   **Joel Khan** 30.9.99 (1y, -) 2.10 '16   2.16, 2.16, 2.15, 2.13, 2.13, 2.11   7 LI, 4 BIG, 2 Eng-J, 12= UK, 2 E.Sch,
    dnq 18 EJ, 3 CAU, 4 MI, BLP: 5,4,-,-; UK Ind: 6 B'ham 14/1, 1J Hustopece, 10 UKi, 2 Eng-Ji
10 **Tim Duckworth** 18.6.96 (1y, -) 2.13 '16   2.13, 2.11, 2.10, 2.10, 2.05; 2.16i, 2.16i, 2.15i, 2.14i
    7 SEC, dnq 22 NCAA-E, 2D NCAA; Ind: 2 Lexington, 4= SEC, 1H NCAAi
11 **Ryan Webb** 19.10.97 (1y, -) 2.14 '16   2.13, 2.12, 2.11, 2.10, 2.10, 2.09; 2.13i, 2.12i
    5 BIG, 5 Eng-23, 7 UK, 4 LEAP, 5 MI, BLP: 6,7,1,3; Ind: 2 Lough, 7B Hustopece, 9 UKi
12 **Thomas Hewes** 15.9.99 (1y, -) 2.05 '15   2.15, 2.12, 2.10, 2.07, 2.06, 2.03
    1B BIG, 1 South-J, 3= Eng-J, nh UK, 3 E.Sch, 2 WInt, dnq 22= EJ, 13= CAU, BL3: -,1-,1; Ind: 2 South-J
Outdoors only: 5 Edwards, 6 Kandu, 7 D Smith, 8 Roberts, 9 Khan, 10 Webb, 11 Hewes, 12 Duckworth

Grabarz, ranked first for the fifth time, maintained his place in the world top ten, but was still well short of the 2.37 he cleared in 2012. The seven men who all jumped 2.22 or more in 2016 were joined in the top eight, who were clear of the rest, by the immensely promising 18 year-old Gale, who has improved from 2.05i in 2015 and 2.18 in 2016 to 2.30. A year younger at 17 were Khan and Hewes, who also competed at the European Juniors. Baker was 3-0 v A Smith outdoors, but 0-2 indoors. Like Smith, Kandu was at his best indoors.

POLE VAULT
1   **Luke Cutts** 13.2.88 (12y, 2) 5.83i '14, 5.70 '13   5.50, 5.45, 5.40, 5.30, 5.30, 5.15; 5.43i, 5.40i, 5.35i 1 Innsbruck,
    1 Geneva, 3 C'hagen, 8 ET, 1 UK, 3 Dublin, 2 BLP (3), 5 GNC; Ind: 2= Manch, 1 UKi, 1 B'ham G, 1= Welsh Int, 2 Manch 19/3
2   **Adam Hague** 29.8.97 (4y, 4) 5.60 '15   5.50, 5.35, 5.35, 5.30, 5.20, 5.20; 5.50i, 5.50i, 5.41i, 5.40i 3=/1/2= Melbourne,
    1 B.Univs, 3= LI; Ind: 1 Manch 8/1, 1 Manch, 2 UKi, 1= Welsh Int, 1 Cardiff, 1 Gateshead, 1 Manch 19/3
3   **Joel Leon Benitez** 31.8.98 (3y, 9) 5.25i '16, 5.10 '15   5.51, 5.50, 5.38, 5.37, 5.30, 5.30; 5.40i, 5.33i
    1 BL3 (1), 1 LI, 3 Welsh, 1 Eng-J, 3 Mannheim, 1 WInt, nh EJ, 2 (1) CAU/Eng, 2 So'ton, 1 MI, 5/1/2 Berlin;
    Ind: 1/3/2 Cardiff, 1 B'ham G, 1 Eng-Ji, 3 Welsh Int
4   **Jax Thoirs** 7.4.93 (7y, 5) 5.65 '15   5.40, 5.40, 5.33, 5.32, 5.20, 4.83; 5.52i, 5.31i
    6 LI, 2 UK, 2 MI, 1 Scot BL1: 4,1,-, 1; Ind: 1 Scot, 2= Manch, 6 Tsaotun
5   **Max Eaves** 31.5.88 (11y, 3) 5.62 '14   5.30, 5.25, 5.20, 5.03, 4.95; 5.43i, 5.33i, 5.31i, 5.31i
    3= LI, 1 Welsh, 4 Cardiff, 3= UK, BLP: 7,2,-,-; Ind: 3 North, 2= Manch, 2 Sheffield, 2 London, 2 UKi, 3 Welsh Int, 3 Cardiff
6   **Charlie Myers** 12.6.97 (3y, 7) 5.30 '15   5.45, 5.40, 5.35, 5.35, 5.31, 5.30; 5.40i, 5.32i
    2 B.Univs, 2 LI, 1 Budapest, 2 Geneva, 1 Eng-23, 2 C'hagen, 5 UK, 11= Eur23, 1 So'ton, 6 GNC;
    Ind: 2 North, 6 Manch, 1 Scot, 4 UKi, 1 B.Uns I, 5 Cardiff, 1/1/2 Gateshead
7   **Harry Coppell** 11.7.96 (5y, 8) 5.40 '14   5.40, 5.40, 5.30, 5.25, 5.23, 5.20; 5.32i   3 B.Univs, 7 LI, 3 Geneva,
    2 Eng-23, 1 C'hagen, 3= UK, 4 MI, BLP: 3,1,3,1; Ind: 2 Manch 8/1, 5 North, 2 Sutton, 3 UKi, 4 Cardiff
8   **Daniel Gardner** 26.3.94 (5y, -) 5.40i '14, 5.210 '13   5.32i, 5.31i, 5.16i, 5.12i, 5.10i, 5.10i
    Ind: 1 South, 5 Manch, 3= London, 2 Cardiff 5/2, 5 UKi
9   **Nick Cruchley** 1.1.90 (8y, -) 5.42 '11   5.20, 5.20, 5.05, 5.00, 4.85; 5.32i, 5.30i, 5.25i, 5.21i   8 LI, 11 Rehlingen,
    1 Cardiff, 8= UK, 3 WInt, 6 BLP (3); Ind: 14 Orleans, 8= Manch, 1 Welsh, 6 UKi, 3 B.Uns I, 4 Welsh Int
10 **Jack Phipps** 2.4.94 (3y, 10) 5.20 '15   5.10, 5.10, 5.10, 5.05, 5.00, 4.95; 5.25i, 5.22i, 5.20i, 5.18i, 5.13i
    4 B.Univs, 2 South, 8= UK, 2 Dublin, 4 (3) CAU, 5 MI, BLP: 2,4,1,-; Ind: 7 Manch, 1 Brunel. 7 UKi, 4 B.Uns-I, 6 Cardiff
11 **Scott Huggins** 24.7.89 (3y, -) 5.23i '16, 5.10 '08   5.26, 5.20, 5.20, 5.15, 5.10, 5.05; 5.16i
    3= LI, 1 South, 6 UK, 3 (2) CAU, 6 So'ton, BL1: 1,-,1,-; Ind: 2 South, 3 London
12 **Timothy Duckworth** 18.6.96 (2y, -) 5.00 '14, 2H NCAA   5.07, 5.07, 5.01, 4.97; 5.26i, 5.20i, 5.12i, 5.03i
    5 Florida R, 6= SEC, 2D NCAA; Ind: 7 Lexington, 6 SEC
–   **Euan Bryden** 17.5.94 (0y, -) 4.80i, 4.65 '16   5.15, 5.11, 5.00, 5.00, 4.95, 4.93; 5.12i, 5.03i   2 Welsh, 3 Cardiff,
    11 UK, 2 WInt, 7 So'ton, 3 ScotBL1: 2,-,2,2; Ind: 5 London, 4 Cardiff 5/2, 2 B'ham G, 1 Brunel, 7 Cardiff
Outdoors only: 2 Leon Benitez, 3 Hague, 4 Thoirs, 5 Myers, 6 Coppell, 7 Eaves 8 Huggins, 9 Cruchley,10 Phipps,
11 Bryden, 12 Duckworth
There was little between the top seven men, but Cutts was UK champion indoors and out and retains top ranking. Hague was the best indoors, but his outdoor season ended in May. Eaves beat Myers 3-1 indoors and they were 1-1 outdoors. Leon Benitez continued to progress and his 5.51 was the best British outdoor mark of the year (the lowest such since 2006) just making the world top 100. Gardner only competed indoors. Steve Lewis misses out after 14 years in the rankings. As with so many events standards in depth continue to decline – 103 men at 4.10 or higher is the lowest since 2007.

LONG JUMP
1   **Daniel Bramble** 14.10.90 (7y, 2) 8.21 '15   8.02, 8.01, 8.00, 8.00, 7.95, 7.91w
    1 Clermont, 1 LI, 2 Marseille, 1 ET, 1 UK, 5 Anniv, 2 Padua, 3 Sestriere, 1 MI, 6 B'ham DL; Ind: 1 Brunel, 1 UKi, dnq 12 EI
2   **Greg Rutherford** 17.11.86 (12y, 1) 8.51 '14   8.18, 7.95; 1 Manchester, 1 Gavardo
3   **Jacob Fincham-Dukes** 12.1.97 (3y, 12) 7.75 '15   8.02w, 7.96, 7.90, 7.87w, 7.83w/7.70, 7.67; 7.86Ai
    1 Stanford 31/3, 5 Fort Worth, 1 Big 12, 9 NCAA, 1 Eng-23, 3 UK, 4 EU23; Ind: 4 F'ville, 2 A'que, 2 Big12-I, 10 NCAA-i
4   **Timothy Duckworth** 18.6.96 (1y, -) 7.64 '16   7.87, 7.84w (7.60), 7.64; 7.80i, 7.77i, 7.72i
    3 Florida R, 1 D Athens GA, 4 UK; Ind: 5 Lexington, 4 SEC, 2H NCCC-i
5   **Feron Sayers** 15.10.94 (2y, -) 7.80 '13   7.95w/7.89, 7.59, 7.54, 7.54, 7.49w, 7.45
    6 LI, 3 BIG, 1 Lomza, 2 UK,2 Liège, 2 Heusden. 2 Karlstad, 7 MI, BLP: 2,2,1,-
6   **Daniel Gardiner** 25.6.90 (5y, 3) 7.96 '16   7.83, 7.69, 7.69w, 7.65, 7.59, 7.58; 7.76i, 7.74i, 7.70i   1 B.Univs, 2 LI,
    4 Manchester, 1 BIG, 1 Geneva, 3 Bilbao, 6 UK, 2 BLP (3), dnq 14 WUG; Ind: 1 North, 1 Vienna, 1 Reykjavik, 3 UKi, 8 B'ham
7   **Ashley Bryant** 17.5.91 (3y, 11) 7.67i '14, 7.58 '16   7.49w, 7.44, 7.42, 7.30, 7.22; 7.79i, 7.71i, 7.66i, 7.57i
    4 LI, 3D Götzis, 2 BL1 (3), 9 Anniv, 13D WCh; Ind: 1H Prague, 2 UKi, 6 Bham
8   **Allan Hamilton** 14.7.92 (4y, 4) 7.88 '16   7.71, 7.60, 7.49w, 7.41, 7.30, 7.25; 7.42i
    4 P'frugell, 7 Copenhagen, 2 Scot-E, 7 Geneva, 5 UK, 1 Cork, BL1 : -,-,1,2; Ind: 3 Scot-i
9   **Oliver Newport** 7.1.95 (2y, 7) 7.78 '16   7.77w, 7.60, 7.43, 7.40, 7.40, 7.35; 7.50i
    1 T'loosa, 1/1 Louisville, dnq 14 NCAA-E, 2 South, 3 Eng-23; Ind: 4 Lexington, 4/2/4 N.Dame
10 **James Lelliott** 11.2.93 (2y, 9) 7.53/7.61w '16   7.70w, 7.65, 7.40, 7.32, 7.25, 7.22w
    1 South, 11 UK, 5 CAU, 1 B'n'mth, BL2: 2,1,-,-

11 **Julian Reid** 23.9.88 (5y, -) 8.08 '11, 8.18w '09   7.73i, 7.52i, 7.50i, 7.44i   Ind: 1 B'ham, 2 Vienna, 4 UKi
12 **Jack Roach** 8.1.95 (1y, -) 7.25 '15   7.58, 7.43w, 7.41w/7.27, 7.41w/7.26, 7.30, 7.27
   3 B.Uns, 8 LI, 5 Eng-23, 1 CAU, 2 B'n'mth, 5 MI, 4 Scot; Ind: 6 B.Uns-i
– **Michael Causer** 27.5.95 (1y, -) 7.52i '14, 7.50 '12   7.52, 7.43, 7.40, 7.29w/7.20, 7.20, 7.07   1 North, 2 CAU
– **Efe Uwaifo** 15.5.95 (0y, -) 7.26 '12   7.85w, 7.35w/7.15; 6.72i; 1 Heps
nr **Adam McMullen** IRL 5.7.90 7.84 '16, 7.89w '15   7.94w/7.80, 7.85, 7.75w, 7.74, 7.64, 7.64w   6 G'ville,
   1 Clermont, 1 NI, 4 ET-1, 3 Chaux-de-Fonds, 1 Belfast, 2 Cork, 1 IRL, 2 MI; Ind: 2 Jablonec, 5 UKi.1 IRL-i
nr **Che Richards** TTO 8.5.97 7.53 '16   7.80, 7.63, 7.63w, 7.53, 7.52w, 7.22; 7.64i, 7.53i
   1 Scot Un, 2 B.Uns, 1 TTO Ch, BP: 4,1,-,-; Ind: 1 Scot-I, 9 UKi, 1 B.Uns, 2 Scot Un

Outdoors only: 11 Roach, 12 Causer

Rutherford only competed twice, so although he won both those competitions and had the year's best mark (for the tenth time by a UK athlete), it was not really enough to sustain his top ranking after eight years in that position. Daniel Bramble takes over with five marks at 8.00 or more. The 2015 European Junior champion Fincham-Dukes made excellent progress at college in the USA to rank third. ahead of another US-based athlete Duckworth. Sayers beat them both at the UKs, but did not otherwise approach their marks, although he beat Gardiner 2-1. There was a small improvement in 50th best – at 7.15 – with 86 men at 6.95 or better (wind-legal) these were the best since 1987 and 1989.

TRIPLE JUMP
1 **Ben Williams** 25.1.92 (8y, 3) 16.74 '15   16.73, 16.71, 16.46, 16.45, 16.43, 16.18
   1 LI, 1 BIG, 4 Geneva, 2 ET, 1 UK, 1 LEAP
2 **Nathan Fox** 21.10.90 (10y, 4) 16.69 '14   16.81, 16.49, 16.42w/16.40, 16.33, 15.99, 15.91; 16.53i, 16.45i, 16.39i
   1 T'hassee, 1 Clermont, 2 BIG, 9 Lisbon, 2 UK, 5 G'burg, 4 LEAP, dnq 19 WCh, 2 BLP (4), 4 L'ranta Ind: 1 B'ham, 2 Chemnitz, 1 UKi
3 **Nathan Douglas** 4.12.82 (16y, 2) 17.64 '05   16.80, 16.53, 16.40w, 16.39, 16.35, 16.27
   3 Clermont, 9 Drake R, 3 Geneva, 4 UK, 2 Hilversum, 2 LEAP, 1 CAU, 1 MI
4 **Nonso Okolo** 7.12.89 (3y, 5) 16.06 '14, 16.28w '16   16.45, 16.29, 16.25, 16.21, 16.07, 15.92
   5 Clermont, 5 Lisbon, 3 UK, 3 LEAP, BLP: 4,1,2,-
5 **Julian Reid** 23.9.88 (7y, 1) 16.98, 17.10w '09   16.01, 16.01, 15.73; 16.30i   2 LI, 3 BIG, 6 UK; Ind: 3 UKi
6 **Montel Nevers** 22.5.96 (3y, 6) 16.15i, 16.14 '16   16.05w/15.55, 15.99, 15.86w, 15.75, 15.51, 15.33; 15.90i, 15.88i
   4/3 T'hasssee, 2 Stanford 21/4, 2 ACC, 6 NCAA, 3 Eng-23, 10 UK, 1 BL3 (3); Ind: 1 B.Uns-i, 4 UKi
7 **Sam Trigg** 1.11.93 (3y, 8) 15.74 '15, 15.77w '16   16.38, 16.12w/16.05, 15.97w/15.75, 15.78w, 15.61,
   15.50w/15.48I; 15.87Ai 15.76Ai   4 Tempe, 3 Azusa, 1 Austin, 2 MWC, 8 NCAA, 3 CAU, 12 WUG
8 **Jonathan Ilori** 14.8.93 (5y, 11) 15.89, 16.10w '14   16.06, 15.89, 15.74, 15.69, 15.44, 15.30; 15.44i
   2 Ellwangen, 4 BIG, 1 South, 5 UK, 2 CAU, 2 MI, BL1: -,1,1,-; Ind: 2 South, 7 UKi
9 **Efe Uwaifo** 15.5.95 (4y, 7) 15.98 '16   16.18w/15.73, 15.91, 15.68w/15.57, 15.65w/15.65, 15.36, 14.88; 15.82i, 15.43i
   3 Stanford 21/4, 1 Heps, 15 NCAA, 2 South, 1 Eng-23, 11 UK; Ind: 1 Heps-i
10 **Lawrence Davis** 31.5.95 (1y, -) 15.71 '15   15.43, 15.41, 15.35w/15.21w, 15.31, 15.27w, 15.20; 16.01i, 15.40i
   2 B.Uns, 4 LI, 5 BIG, 2 South, 2 Eng-23, 12 UK, 5 CAU; Ind: 1 B.Uns
11 **Jude Bright-Davies** 27.3.99 (1y, -) 15.40 '16   15.71, 15.35w/15.08, 14.43; 15.56i, 15.46i, 15.44i, 15.42i
   1 Middx, 3 LI, 6 Eng-J; Ind: 1 Sth-J, 4 Vienna, 5 UKi, 1 Eng-J, 1 W.Int
12 **Chukwudi Onyia** 28.2.88 (2y, 10) 15.57 '16   15.63, 15.43, 15.40, 15.23, 14.94, 14.56; 15.54i
   5 LI, 9 UK, 1 Scot, BL2: 1,1,1,1; Ind: 1 Scot-I
– **Jonathon Sawyers** 24.8.92 (4y, -) 15.64 '13   15.57, 15.49, 15.25, 15.18   2 Linz, 7 UK, 2 BL1 (3)
nr **Tosin Oke** NGR 1.10.80 (ranked for 10 years 1999-2008 as GBR) 17.23 '13   16.70, 16.67, 16.34, 16.33, 16.27,
   16.17; 16.40i, 16.40i   2 Clermont, 2 Brazil GP, 4 Kingston, 3 Lisbon, BP: -,-,1,1; Ind: 2 B'ham, 3 Chemnitz, 2 UKi

Outdoors only: 11 Onyia, 12 Sawyers

Williams moved up from 3rd to take his first top ranking; on the year list he was third behind Fox and Douglas, but beat them 3-0 and 2-1. Fox beat Douglas 2-1 (and 1-0 indoors). Nevers and Uwaifo were 2-2, while Okolo and Trigg made significant improvement.

SHOT
1 **Scott Lincoln** 7.5.93 (6y, 1) 19.59 '16   19.00, 18.91, 18.85, 18.80, 18.79, 18.73; 18.87i   5B E.Throws, 7 Halle,
   1 LI, 1 Oordegem, 1 BLP (2), 10 ET, 1 UK, 1 L'kenny, 3 Cork, 2 (1) CAU, 1 MI, 11 B'ham DL, 1 Scot; Ind: 1 North, 1 Vienna, 1 UKi
2 **Youcef Zatat** 13.4.94 (4y, 5) 18.01 '16   18.34, 17.82, 17.78, 17.63, 17.41, 17.38; 18.22i, 17.58i
   1 B.Univs, 2 LI, 1 Geneva, 5 Halluin, 3 UK, 5 G'burg, 4 Cork, 2 CAU, BLP: 1,-,1,-; Ind: 3 Vienna, 2 UKi
3 **Gareth Winter** 19.3.92 (5y, 3) 18.07 '15   17.42, 17.35, 17.34, 17.29, 17.07, 16.98
   3 LI, 1 Welsh, 2 UK, 5 Cork, BLP: 3,4,3,1
4 **Joseph Watson** 23.9.95 (3y, 6) 17.42 '16   16.05; 17.16i, 16.81i, 16.75i, 16.63i, 16.47i   2 B.Univs; Ind: 1 South, 3 UKi
5 **Samuel Heawood** 25.9.90 (1y, -) 15.13 '16   15.54, 15.10, 14.99, 16.23i, 16.19i, 16.07i, 15.83i, 15.34i
   4 B.Univs; Ind: 2 South, 4 UKi
6 **Daniel Cartwright** 14.11.98 (2y, 11) 15.51 '15   16.14, 16.10. 15.98, 15.48, 15.45, 15.04, 15.04; 15.84i
   4 UK, 4 CAU, BLP: 6,6,5,6; Ind: 5 UKi
7 **Craig Sturrock** 7.1.85 (7y, -) 16.87i '13, 16.72 '14   15.87, 15.80, 15.55, 15.11, 15.03, 14.91; 15.52i, 15.14i
   1 N.East, 1 North, 5 UK, 5 CAU, 1 MI, 2 Scot, BLP: 5,1,6,-; Ind: 1 Scot
8 **Matthew Baptiste** 28.10.90 (1y, -) 14.44 '16   15.72, 15.64, 15.52, 15.44, 15.34, 15.23
   2 BIG, 1 South, 6 UK, 6 CAU, BLP: -,-,4,4

9 **Kai Jones** 14.12.96 (2y, 10) 16.36i, 16.00 '16   16.04, 15.27, 14.61; 14.89i, 14.70i
   3 B.Univs, BLP: 10,7,-,-; Ind: 1 B.Uns-i, 6 UKi
10 **Nicholas Percy** 5.12.94 (2y, 8) 15.65 '15   14.35, 16.56i, 15.59i
11 **Michael Wheeler** 23.9.91 (3y, 9) 17.08 '12   15.73, 15.36, 15.28, 14.91, 14.83, 14.78   1 Surrey, 7 UK, BL2: 2,2,1,1
12 **Greg Thompson** 5.5.94 (1y, -) 15.61 '16   15.75, 15.74, 14.82   9 UK, 7 BLP (3), 6 CAU
Outdoors only: 4 Cartwright, 5 Sturrock, 6 Baptiste, 7 Watson, 8 Jones, 9 Wheeler,10 Thompson, 11 Heawood
Lincoln was a class apart in this third year at the top, but his marks were well down on 2016. Zatat improved to 18.34, but Lincoln had 20 meetings better than this. As in 2016 there were just 8 men at 16m or more, but only three men were regularly over this outdoors. Watson and Heawood did not compete outdoors after the British Universities at the end of April. The standard in depth was again depressing, 10th best at 15.75 was little higher than in 2016 but otherwise the worst since 1966, while 50th best of 13.78 was the worst since 1963 (peak 14.74 in 1990).

DISCUS
1 **Nicholas Percy** 5.12.94 (5y, 3) 63.38 '16   62.91, 62.38, 61.27, 61.27, 60.78, 60.61   1 Tempe, 2 Lincoln,
   1 Columbia, 1 Norman, 1 Lubbock,1 Big 10, 14 NCAA, 2/3 Växjö, 5 Malmö, 1 UK, 4 H'borg, 7 G;burg, dnq 29 WCh
2 **Zane Duquemin** 23.9.91 (7y, 2) 63.46 '12   62.68, 62.30, 61.99, 61.34, 61.23, 60.80   1 Lough-w, 5B E.Throws,
   1 Leiria 22/4, 4B Halle, 2 LI, 1 BIG, 2/6 G'burg, 5 ET, 2 UK, 9 Anniv, 6/5 Leiria, 2 Guernsey, BLP: 1,1,1,-
3 **Brett Morse** 11.2.89 (11y, 1) 66.84 '13   61.15, 60.97, 60.82, 60.12, 59.76, 59.63
   nt Lough-w, 1 LI, 1 Welsh, 3 UK, 2 MI, 1 Guernsey, BL1: 1,1,1,1
4 **Alan Toward** 31.10.92 (4y, 4) 58.81 '16   59.33, 59.00, 57.87, 57.59, 56.86, 56.30
   2 Lough-w, 7B E.Throws, 1 N.East, 4 LI, 2 Welsh, 4 UK, 1 CAU, 4 MI, BLP: 2,3,-,4
5 **Greg Thompson** 5.5.94 (4y, 5) 59.22 '16   60.28, 59.75, 59.33, 58.70, 57.94, 57.84
   4 Florida R, 5 Penn R, 4 Big 10, 15 NCAA, 5 UK, 1 Sth IC, 4 BLP (3), 1 LIC 57.37, 3 CAU, 1 MI, 8 WUG
6 **George Armstrong** 8.12.97 (1y, -) -0-   56.77, 55.95, 55.54, 54.87, 54.53, 54.24
   1 B.Univs, 3 LI, 2 BIG, 1 Eng-23, 7 UK, 2 CAU, BLP: 4,2,2,3
7 **Matthew Blandford** 21.10.95 (3y, 10) 55.68 '16   55.60, 55.06, 54.72, 53.86, 53.82, 53.68
   2 B.Univs, 6 LI, 2 Eng-23, 6 UK, 5 CAU
8 **Chris Scott** 21.3.88 (7y, -) 63.00 '11   56.51, 55.48, 54.25, 53.94, 53.93, 53.88
   2 Leiria 22/4, 1 B.Univs, 10 UK, 2 SthIC, 2 LIC 29/7, 4 CAU, 4 Guernsey, BLP: 3,-,3,-
9 **Mark Plowman** 26.3.87 (5y, 11) 56.04 '14   54.68, 53.38, 53.27, 53.15, 52.69, 52.60   8 UK, 1 IS, 6 CAU, 1 BL3 (4)
10 **Angus McInroy** 13.2.87 (10y, 9) 58.77 '10   55.29, 53.25, 53,20, 53.18, 52.68, 52.68
   4 Lough-w, 3 Leiria 22/4, 5 LI, 3 BIG, 11 UK, 3 LIC 52.60, 8 CAU, 5 MI, 1 Scot, BLP: 5,4,-,2
11 **Najee Fox** 1.12.92 (3y, -) 53.00 '14   54.79, 53.84, 52.57, 52.21, 52.21, 52.11
   3 Lough-w, 4 BIG, 1 Mid, 9 UK, 9 CAU, 6 MI, BLP: 7,5,5,6
12 **Louis Mascarenhas** 5.12.96 (1y, -) 47.87 '15   51.24, 50.34, 47.47, 48.35, 48.30, 47.30   1 South, 5 Eng-23, BL1: 2,-,-,3
The top three were closely matched and are ranked in the order they finished in the UKs. The champion Percy just shades Duquemin, who beat Morse 3-1. Toward beat Thompson 2-1, so although the latter had a better set of marks, they stay in that order. Armstrong had a good first year as a senior and comes in at 6th, with Scott, returning after last ranking in 2013. Alex Parkinson (best of 56.79) stayed in New Zealand (he has dual citizenship) and does not rank this year.

HAMMER
1 **Nick Miller** 1.5.93 (6y, 3) 77.55 '15   77.51, 77.31, 76.81, 76.65, 76.25. 76.18
   1 Stanford 1/4, 1 Salinas, 3 Halle, 2 Forbach, 4 Montreuil, 3 Szczecin, 1 Huelva, 5 Samorín, 3 ET, 6 Ostrava,
   1 UK, 5, Sz'vár, 4 Madrid, 1 LEAP, 6 WCh, 2 B'ham DL, 1 Tallinn, 1 Kohila
2 **Chris Bennett** 17.12.89 (7y, 1) 76.45 '16   75.72, 72.68, 72.05, 71.72, 70.65, 70.50
   9 E.Throws, 2 LI, 1 Fr-Crumbach, 4 UK, 2 LEAP, dnq 21 WCh
3 **Taylor Campbell** 30.6.96 (3y, 4) 72.70 '16   73.40, 72.89, 72.87, 71.96, 70.59, 70.33
   4 E.Throws U23, 1 B.Univs, 1 Halle U23, 5 Forbach, 1 South, 2 Eng-23, 2 UK, 4 EU23, 5 LEAP. 4 CAU
4 **Mark Dry** 11.10.87 (10y, 2) 76.93 '15   71.73, 71.69, 70.81, 70.51, 70.26, 70.19
   1 LI, 8 Fr-Crumbach, 2 Nikíti, 3 UK, 1 BLP (3), 3 LEAP, 1 MI
5 **Joseph Ellis** 10.4.96 (2y, 12) 68.25 '16   70.98, 70.33, 69.30, 68.05, 68.00, 67.07
   1 Durham, 1/1 Austin, 1 Big 10, 8 NCAA, 5 UK
6 **Craig Murch** 27.6.93 (3y, 5) 69.79 '16   68.83, 68.54, 68.52, 68.48, 68.31, 68.29
   4 LI, 1 BIG, 1 Mid, 6 UK, 1 WInt, 4 LEAP, 2 CAU, 5 MI, 1 Liverpool, BL3: 1,1,1,1
7 **Chris Shorthouse** 23.6.88 (7y, 6) 70.18 '15   69.80, 68.02, 67.91, 67.77, 67.46, 67.42
   1 Lough-w, 6B E.Throws, 1 Lough 9/4, 3 LI, 3 BIG, 2 Mid, 7 UK, 7 LEAP, 3 CAU, 2 Liverpool, BLP: 2,2,3,1
8 **Callum Brown** 20.7.94 (3y, 7) 67.31 '14   69.13, 68.62, 67.51, 67.18, 67.05, 66.69
   5 LI, 2 BIG, nt UK, 1 BL1 (3), 1 CAU, 2 MI
9 **Osian Jones** 23.6.93 (3y, -) 67.96 '16   70.00, 69.20, 67.89, 66.90, 66.52, 65.77
   3 Lough-w, 2 Lough 9/4, 5 BLP (2), 1 Welsh, 1 Belfast, 2 WInt, 6 LEAP, 3/2 Leiria
10 **Jake Norris** 30.6.99 (1y, -) 61.70 '16   68.86, 67.73, 67.65, 66.93   1 BL1 (1), 8 UK

11   **Michael Bomba** 10.10.86 (9y, -) 70.90 '13   69.15, 67.05, 65.23, 64.81, 64.79, 64.69
      2 Lough-w, 1 North, 4 Belfast, 5 CAU, BLP: 3,-, -,3
12   **Nicholas Percy** 5.12.94 (2y,10) 67.85 '16   67.72, 67.16, 66.70, 66.01, 65.81
      1 Tempe, 1 Columbia, 1 Norman, 1 Lubbock, 3 Big 10
Miller returned to the top ranking he had in 2014-15 with a splendidly consistent season that meant he was the only British thrower in world top ten rankings. He had a UK record 13 performances over 75m and all 19 at 71.69 or better. Murch beat Shorthouse 6-3 and Brown made a breakthrough at the CAU Champs, but did not have the depth of performances of those men. Jake Norris had a terrific season with the 6kg hammer, but his four competitions with senior hammer also showed his immense potential. In contrast to other throwing events, hammer throwing thrives with a record level for 10th best of 68.86 (previous best 68.35 in 2013) although the 100th best was better each year 1984-2001.

JAVELIN
1   **Matti Mortimore** 16.5.93 (6y, 2) 75.79 '16   77.47, 77.15, 77.08, 76.82, 74.79, 74.33
      1 Tempe,1 Stanford 31/3, 1 Lincoln, 2 Long Beach, 5 NCAA, 8 ET, 2 UK
2   **Harry Hughes** 26.9.97 (3y, 1) 75.46 '16   76.81, 76.59, 74.69, 72.80, 72.03, 71.66
      1 Lough-w, 4 E.Throws U23, 1 B.Univs, 2 LI, 4 Halle, 6 UK, BLP: 1,-,1
3   **Joe Dunderdale** 4.9.92 (7y, 3) 76.13 '14   74.88, 73.58, 73.41, 73.38, 72.50, 70.63
      5/2 Melbourne, 1 BLP (1), 1 UK, 1 L'kenny, 2 CAU, 2 MI, BLP: 2,-,2,-
4   **Joe Harris** 23.5.97 (2y, 11) 67.70 '16   75.71, 71.46, 70.50, 69.00, 68.57, 67.64
      3 Lough-w, 2 Eng-23, 2 Island G, 3 UK, 2 L'kenny, 1 LEAP, 1 CAU
5   **James Whiteaker** 8.10.98 (1y, 4) 72.51 '16   77.03, 74.64, 73.40, 69.55, 66.34   1 BL1 (1), 1 Eng-J, dnq 16 EJ
6   **Steven Turnock** 7.11.92 (4y, 7) 70.78 '16   72.41, 71.84, 70.82, 70.31, 70.02, 70.01
      3 B.Univs, 1 LI, 1 Carnival, 4 UK, 2 LEAP, 3 CAU, 1 MI, BLP: 3,1,2,3
7   **Greg Millar** 19.12.92 (5y, 5) 71.12 '16   71.15, 69.77, 69.70, 69.34, 67.54, 65.88
      2 B.Univs, 3 LI, 2 Carnival, 8 UK, 3 L'kenny, 5 CAU, 3 MI, 1 Socot, 1 Guernsey, BLP: 6,3,-,4
8   **Gavin Johnson-Assoon** 19.12.82 (4y, 8) 69.36 '16   69.69, 67.04, 66.43, 65.99, 65.46, 65.20
      4 Carnival, 3 South, 10 UK, 5 LEAP, 4 CAU, 4 MI, 2 Guernsey BLP: 5,2,5,2
9   **Neil McLellan** 10.9.78 (11y, 1) 74.92 '07   67.70, 66.28, 62.61, 62.61, 59.94, 59.73   1 South, 5 UK
10   **Jack Swain** 27.2.95 (1y, -) 62.96 '16   67.10, 66.68, 66.56, 62.87, 62.85, 61.03
      3 Carnival, 1 Eng-23, 7 UK, 7 CAU, BLP: 8,4,-,-
11   **Ashley Bryant** 17.5.91 (2y, 12) 70.44 '13   67.97, 67.54, 67.04, 63.55   3D WCh
12   **George Davies** 27.1.98 (1y, -) 66.12 '16   65.11, 64.38, 63.76, 63.57, 62.94, 62.64   4 LI, 2J Carnival, 9 UK, BLP: 4,-,3,-
–   **Craig Lacy** 17.7.91 (1y, -) 68.46 '11   67.71, 65.84, 64.94, 63.77, 63.00, 62.46
      5 Carnival, 2 South, 11 UK, 8 CAU, BLP: 9,5,4,1
Eight men over 70m was at least better than seven in 2015 and the four men over 75m all set pbs. Hughes was not able to sustain a promising start, so Mortimore takes his first top ranking after two years in second place although his best marks came in the USA. Dunderdale won the UK title, but did not have as good a set of performances. Harris made the greatest improvement, but Whiteaker was restricted by injury. Johnson-Assoon and Miller were 4-4, but the latter had better marks. Former number one Bonne Buwembo dropped out after eight years ranked, but McLellan ranks for the first time since 2010. Neil Crossley had just one competition (2 Lough-w 70.31). 55 year-old Roald Bradstock is 14th on the year list, 37 years after he was first ranked.

DECATHLON
1   **Ashley Bryant** 17.5.91 (7y, 1) 8141 '14   10 Götzis 8163, 11 W.Ch 8049, 11 Talence 7635
2   **Ben Gregory** 21.11.90 (7y, 2) 7882 '16   1 ESP Ch 7799, 5 Mt.SAC 7769, 9 Talence 7667, 10 Eur Cup 7530, dnf Arona
3   **John Lane** 29.1.89 (6y, -) 7922 '14
      2 Mt.SAC 7965, 2 AUS Ch 7362, 11 Eur Cup 7348, 23 Götzis 7162 (dnf 1500m), dnf, WUG
4   **Timothy Duckworth** 18.6.96 (3y, 3) 7709 '16   2 Athens GA 7973, 19 NCAA 7026 (nj LJ), dnf EU23
5   **Curtis Mathews** 22.1.92 (2y, -) 7422 '14
      1 Kent 7500, 1 South 7170, 6 ENG 6736, 1 Scot 6245 (dnf 1500m), 1 Sheffield 6240 (dnf 400m)
6   **Andrew Murphy** 26.12.94 (1y, -) 6440 '14   3 Woerden 7248, 3 ENG 7170, 15 Eur Cup 7084, 7 events at Hexham (4813)
7   **James Finney** 7.4.96 (1y, -) 5552 '14   1 ENG 7263, dnf Eur Cup
8   **Jack Andrew** 12.10.91 (3y, -) 7170 '15   4 ENG 7048, 1 Dilbeek 7028
9   **Peter Glass** 1.5.88 (5y, -) 7510 '13   7 Arona 7120, dnf Street
10   **Harry Maslen** 2.9.96 (2y, 9) 6770 '16   4 NCAA II 7065, 2 Lone Star 7010w
11   **Lewis Church** 27.9.96 (2y, 8) 6889 '16   2 Kent 7068
12   **David Hall** 25.4.95 (2y, -) 7651 '15   9 Arona 7038, 4 South 6601
nr   **Peter Moreno** 30.12.90 NGR 6920 '15   2 ENG 7252, 2 South 6671
Ashley Bryant is top for the fourth time while Duckworth continued his rapid progress, but then did not complete two decathlons and ranks behind the consistent Gregory and Lane, who did not complete his two most important decathlons. Once again there is disappointing depth.

20 KILOMETRES WALK
1   **Tom Bosworth** 17.1.90 (8y, 1) 1:20:13 '16
    2 Rio Maior 1:20:58, 4 Eur Cup 1:21:21, 2 Lugano 1:21:53, 1 Leeds (RWA) 1:24:59, 20 Lake Taihu 1:27:48; dq WCh
2   **Callum Wilkinson** 14.3.97 (1y, -) 0   10 Eur Cup 1:22:17, 8 Lugano 1:23:47, 41 WCh 1:23:54, 2 Leeds (RWA) 1:24:59
3   **Cameron Corbishley** 31.3.97 (2y, 5) 1:33:00 16   11 Podébrady1:26:00, 36 Eur Cup 1:27:26, 18 Lugano 1:31:20
4   **Dominic King** 30.5.83 (13y, 3) 1:27:52 '04
    4 Leeds (3 RWA) 1:26:09, 34 La Coruña 1:27:20, 47 Eur Cup 1:29:28, 1 Douglas 1:29:36, 1:32:57+, 1:33:19+
5   **Guy Thomas** 1.7.97 (2y, 4) 1:30:17 16   37 La Coruña 1:28:38, dq Podébrady, Leeds and Douglas
6   **Daniel King** 30.5.83 (12y, 2) 1:26:14 '04   39 La Coruña 1:29:10, dq Leeds, dq Douglas
Bosworth is top for the fifth time, and started the year well before his dq at the Worlds. The 20 year-olds Wilkinson, Corbishley Guy Thomas continued to progress and enabled six men to be ranked, the most since 2011. With Wilkinson joining Bosworth, for the first time since 1992 Britain has two men in the world top 100.

50 KILOMETRES WALK
1   **Dominic King** 30.5.83 (6y, 1) 3:55:48 '16   13 Dudince 4:04:16, dq WCh, dq Gleina
Dominic King is top for the fifth time, maintaining a British presence in the event just about on his own, as the second best British man at the event recorded 5:15:09.

WOMEN

100 METRES
1   **Asha Philip** 25.10.90 (9y, 3) 11.10 '15   11.14, 11.18, 11.19, 11.19, 11.19, 11.20
    1 Manchester, 3 Marseille, 1 UK, 6 Anniv, 7s3 WCh, 6h2 B'ham DL, 5 Zürich, 2 GNC
2   **Daryll Neita** 29.8.96 (3y, 4) 11.23 '16   11.14, 11.15, 11.16, 11.16, 11.20, 11.22
    1 LV 24/5, 1 Newham 29/5, 1 Gavardo, 1 Eng-23, 2 UK, 7 Anniv, 6 Rabat, 4s1 WCh
3   **Dina Asher-Smith** 4.12.95 (5y, 1) 10.99 '15   11.13, 11.21, 11.22+, 11.23, 11.41, 11.41
    6 UK, 5 Lignano, 5 B'ham DL, 2 Zagreb, 1 in 150m GNC
4   **Desiree Henry** 26.8.95 (5y, 2) 11.06 '16, 11.04w '14   11.09, 11.23, 11.24, 11.26, 11.32, 11.32
    1B Azusa, 3 Manchester, 3 Boston, 6 Rome, 6 Hengelo, 5s2 WCh, 8h2 B'ham DL, 3B Berlin, 4 Zagreb, 1 GNC
5   **Ashleigh Nelson** 20.2.91 (12y, 6) 11.19/11.14w '14   11.27, 11.28, 11.30   1 LV 21/6, 3 UK, 8h1 Anniv
6   **Bianca Williams** 18.12.93 (4y, -) 11.17 '14   11.30, 11.40, 11.41+, 11.47, 11.51, 11.59; 11.18w, 11.20w, 11.24w
    4 Clermont. 1B Gainesville, 4 Manchester, 3h1 Geneva, 4 UK, 7h1 B'ham DL, 1B Zürich, 2 in 150m GNC
7   **Imani Lansiquot** 17.12.97 (3y, 5) 11.17 '16   11.34, 11.35, 11.39, 11.41, 11.43, 11.47; 11.39w
    5B Clermont, 1 LI, 2/1 Newham 29/5, 3 Gavardo, dns Eng-23, 4 EU23
8   **Corinne Humphreys** 7.11.91 (1y, -) 11.71 '14, 11.59w '16   11.39, 11.42, 11.48, 11.49, 11.50; 11.41w
    1 B.Univs, 1 WLP (1), 2 LI, dnf H'ville, 3 ET, 5 UK, 4= WUG
9   **Finette Agyapong** 1.2.97 (1y, -) 11.76, 11.71w '16   11.49, 11.56, 11.56, 11.70, 11.74, 11.76; 11.58w
    1 Tergnier, 2B Geneva, 7 UK
10   **Rachel Miller** 29.1.90 (2y, 11) 11.46, 11.45w '16   11.45, 11.45, 11.53, 11.54, 11.54, 11.58
    2A LI, 2 LV 24/5, 1 WLP (2), 1 South, 1 Bilbao, 8 UK, 6 Cork, 3 CAU
11   **Diani Walker** 14.7.95 (1y, -) 11.74, 11.53w '16   11.45, 11.51, 11.56, 11.63, 11.64, 11.65; 11.44w, 11.49w
    3B Clermont, 3 B.Univs, 5 Newham 7/5, 1B LI, 5 Oordegem, 1C Geneva, 2 AAA-23, 5s2 UK, 4 LEAP, 1 CAU, 1 MI
12   **Lorraine Ugen** 22.8.91 (1y, -) 11.42 '15, 11.34w '12   11.41, 11.47; 11.31w   2 Arlington, 3 Fort Worth, 1 WLP (3)
The closely-matched top women did best when they combined as a relay team. Philip retained the UK title and regained the top ranking that she had in 2013 and 2015, just holding off Neita. Nelson was 3rd behind them at the UKs, but injury restricted her to three meetings. Henry ran the fastest time, but did not have the depth of performance of 2016. The 50th best of 11.94 was a new record as was 59 women beating 12 secs on auto timing and 107 at 12.19 (or 12.0 hand timing) or better.

200 METRES
1   **Dina Asher-Smith** 4.12.95 (6y, 1) 22.07 '15   22.22, 22.41, 22.73, 22.73, 22.89, 23.15
    3 Padua, 3 Monaco, 4 WCh, 1 Berlin (ISTAF)
2   **Bianca Williams** 18.12.93 (5y, 6) 22.58 '14   22.83, 22.89, 22.94, 23.05, 23.19, 23.30
    5 Gainesville, 1 Regensburg, 5 Oslo, 1 Lisbon, 2 UK. 7 Lausanne, 6s2 WCh,
3   **Finette Agyapong** 1.2.97 (2y, 9) 23.55 '16   22.86, 22.87, 23.04, 23.22, 23.23, 23.24, 23.0h
    3 B.Univs, 1 Tergnier, 2 Eng-23, 4 ET, 1 EU23, 5 Monaco; Ind: 1 South, 1 UKi, 1 B.Univs-i
4   **Shannon Hylton** 19.12.96 (5y, 11) 22.94, 22.73w '15   22.94, 23.05, 23.09, 23.20, 23.39, 23.61
    2 Geneva, 1 Eng-23. 1 UK, 6 Luzern, 4h3 WCh
5   **Katarina Johnson-Thompson** 9.1.93 (3y, 5) 22.79 '64   22.81, 22.86, 23.43; 23.25w; 1 Nice, 1H Götzis, 1H WCh
6   **Desiree Henry** 26.8.95 (7y, 2) 22.46 '16   22.69, 23.08, 23.14, 23.22   2 Azusa, 7 Doha, 3 UK
7   **Amarachi Pipi** 26.11.95 (2y, 4) 23.20 '16   22.95, 22.98, 23.15, 23.26, 23.37, 23.41; 22.83w, 22.89w, 22.99w; 23.19i, 23.21i
    2 Westwood, 1 Norman, 2 Big 12, 8s1 NCAA, 7 UK, 5 EU23; Ind: 1 New York, 4 F'ville, 1 Big 12, sh3 NCAA
8   **Maya Bruney** 24.2.98 (1y, -) 24.23, 24.04w '16   23.04, 23.07, 23.47, 23.51, 23.57, 23.70
    1 B.Univs, 3A LI, 2 Mannheim, 1 EJ, 1 MI, 1 Scot-J, 1 Scot; WLP: 1,1,2; Ind: 3 UKi, 3 Eng-Ji
9   **Alisha Rees** 16.4.99 (2y, 10) 23.57 '16   23.32, 23.52, 23.54, 23.61, 23.65, 23.66; 23.12w, 23.38w, 23.54w
    1 Scot-E, 1A LI, 1 Eng-J, 2 Mannheim, 4 EJ, 1 MI, 1 Scot-J, 1 Scot; WLP: 1,1,2; Ind: 1 Scot-Ji, 1 Eng-Ji

10   **Chereice Hylton** 19.12.96 (1y, -) 23.49 '13, 23.15w '15   23.23, 23.32, 23.44, 23.63   1 LI, 4 Geneva, 3 Eng-23
11   **Kimbely Baptiste** 27.12.92 (1y, -) 23.86, 23.66w '16   23.34, 23.36, 23.43, 23.54, 23.69, 23.88; 23.81w
     5A LI, 4 UK, 4 Cork, 1 CAU; WL2: 1,1,1
12   **Zoey Clark** 25.10.94 (1y, -) 24.15, 23.97i, 23.62w '16   23.36; 23.14w; WLP: -,2,1
–   **Beth Dobbin** 7.6.94 (0y, -) 23.94, 23.74w '16   23.31, 23.42, 23.50, 23.61, 23.63, 23.72
     4A LI, 4 P'frugell, 2 Nivelles, 6 UK, 2 LEAP, 2 CAU, 2 MI, 2 Scot; WLP: 1B,1B,-
–   **Jodie Williams** 28.9.93 (7y, 3) 22.46 '14   23.27, 23.41, 23.53, 23.63, 23.75   4 Claremont, 5 UK, 2 Cork, 3 LEAP
Asher-Smith made a terrific return from injury to retain her top ranking and remain in the world élite. Great breakthroughs were made by Agyapong who won the European U23 title and Maya Bruney who ran pbs in each round of the European Juniors, 23.04 to win the title after a pre-meet best of 23.51. New records were set for 10th best of 23.27 (previous record of 23.31 in 2013), 50th of 24.40 and 100th of 24.89.

400 METRES
1   **Zoey Clark** 25.10.94 (2y, 9) 52.58 '17   51.81, 51.84, 51.88, 52.30, 52.33, 52.64
     1 B.Univs , 1 LI, 1 Geneva, 1 UK, 7s3 WCh, 8 B'ham DL, WLP: 1,1,-
2   **Emily Diamond** 11.6.91 (4y, 2) 51.23 '16   51.67, 51.85, 52.20 52.34, 52.35
     2 Gainesville, dnf Hengelo, 2 UK, 7 Anniv, 5h2 WCh
3   **Anyika Onuora** 28.10.84 (3y, 2) 50.87 '15   51.81, 51.92, 52.48, 52.52, 52.82, 53.10
     1 Azusa, 3 Gainesville, 9 Shanghai, 2 Leiden, 3 UK, 3 Sotteville, 3 Madrid, 7h6 WCh, 5 Rovereto
4   **Eilidh Doyle** 20.2.87 (5y, -) 51.45i, 51.83 '13   52.36; 51.86i, 52.33i, 52.47i, 52.63i, 52.75i
     2 Huelva; Ind: 1 South, 1 Vienna, 1B Mondeville, 1 UKi, 4 B'ham, 3s1 EI
5   **Laviai Nielsen** 13.3.96 (3y, 5) 52.25 '15   52.60, 52.80, 52.80, 53.18, 53.47, 53.77; 51.90i, 52.31i, 52.58i, 52.68i
     4 Oordegem, 5 Somerville, 2h3 UK, 5 EU23, 2B Rovereto; Ind: 2 Vienna, 2 UKi, 4 EI
6   **Perri Shakes-Drayton** 21.12.88 (8y, 8) 51.26 '12   52.19, 52.37, 52.72, 53.02, 53.16, 53.49
     2 Newham, 6 Marseille, 6 UK, 2 Sotteville, 1 Novo Mesto, 2 Rovereto
7   **Margaret Adeoye** 22.4.85 (5y, 7) 51.93 '13   52.32, 52.46, 52.56, 52.70, 53.09, 53.14
     8 UK, 1 Brussels, 2 LEAP, 1 CAU, 1 MI, 1 Kessel-Lo, 1B Rovereto, 1 Treviglio, 1 Domazlice
8   **Chereice Hylton** 19.12.96 (1y, -) 53.16 '15   52.68mx, 52.88, 52.98, 53.16, 53.60, 54.31
     2A LI, 1 Newham, 8 Geneva, 4 UK, 5 LEAP, 1 L'ranta
9   **Mary Iheke** 19.11.90 (4y, 8) 52.81 '15   52.60, 52.92, 52.99, 53.47, 53.79, 54.20; 53.58i, 53.73i
     2 LI, 1 WLP (2), 6 ET, 2h2 UK, 3 Brussels, 4 LEAP, 3 Willesden; Ind: 5 UKi
10   **Hannah Williams** 23.4.98 (1y, -) 52.60 '16   52.55, 53.08, 53.39, 53.61, 53.66, 54.03
     4B Gainesville, 4 LI, 7 Geneva, 1 Eng-J, 3 EJ; Ind: 2 South
11   **Lina Nielsen** 13.3.96 (1y, -) 52.97 '16   53.72; 52.89i, 52.94i, 53.32i, 53.78i   5h1 UK; Ind: 1 LV, 3 UKi, 5 B'ham
12   **Amy Allcock** 20.8.93 (2y, -) 52.83 '14   52.85, 53.40, 53.60mx, 53.95; 5 UK, 6 Brussels
–   **Kirsten McAslan** 1.9.93 (3y, -) 52.13 '15   52.90, 53.10, 53.19, 53.38, 54.14; 54.63i
     1C Oordegem, 6 Bydgoszcz, 1B Geneva, 7 UK; Ind: 5s2 UKi
Outdoors only: 4 Shakes-Drayton, 5 Adeoye, 6 La. Nielsen, 7 Hylton, 8 Iheke, 9 Williams, 10 Allcock, 11 McAslan, 12 Doyle
It is the end of an era, as Christine Ohuruogu drops out after 13 years in the rankings. She is succeeded at top of the lists by Clark, who made a significant breakthrough and takes top ranking, winning the UKs from Diamond, who only completed five 400m races There is actually little between most of the top women with mixed form, Adeoye, for instance, making a late start to the season. Nielsen did not fare as well outdoors as indoors, except in the World Champs relays. Another to drop out, one hopes only temporarily, was Seren Bundy-Davies. New records were set for 50th best 54.94, 100th best 56.45 and 126 women under 57 secs.

800 METRES
1   **Lynsey Sharp** 11.7.90 (7y, 1) 1:57.69 '16   1:58.01, 1:58.35, 1:58.80, 1:58.98, 1:59.33mx, 1:59.47
     dnf Eagle Rock, 8 Eugene, 4 Somerville, 8 Oslo, 8 Stockholm, 3 UK, 7 Lausanne, 4 Anniv, 6 Monaco, 8 WCh, 2 B'ham DL, 3 Zagreb
2   **Shelayna Oskan-Clarke** 20.1.90 (5y, 2) 1:58.86 '15   1:59.82, 2:00.17, 2:00.73, 2:01.30, 2:01.54, 2:02.26; 2:00.39i
     1 Oordegem, 1 Montreuil, 1 UK, 2 Anniv, 6s3 WCh
3   **Laura Muir** 9.5.93 (5y, 4) 2:00.42 '15   5 Lausanne 1:58.69; 2:00.56+i
4   **Adelle Tracey** 27.5.93 (4y, 5) 2:00.04mx 16, 2:01.10 '16   2:00.26, 2:00.28, 2:00.34, 2:00.35, 2:01.53, 2:01.80
     1B Stanford, 2 Eagle Rock, 6 Oordegem, 1 Samorín, 2 UK, 6 Anniv, 1 Dublin, 6s1 WCh, 5 WUG; Ind: 2 Vienna, 2 UKi, 6 B;ham
5   **Alexandra Bell** 4.11.92 (3y, 6) 2:00.53 '16   2:00.62, 2:00.69, 2:01.87mx, 2:02.20, 2:02.30, 2:02.39
     1 Solihull, 1 LI, 5 Montreuil, 4 Prague, 4 Turku, 4 UK, 8 Anniv, 5 Dublin, 1 Stretford, 7 B'ham DL
6   **Sarah McDonald** 2.8.93 (2y, 8) 2:01.10 '16   2:01.2, 2:01.25, 2:02.47, 2:02.5, 2:04.90
     2 Solihull, 4 Samorín, 1/1 Tipton. 7 Zagreb
7   **Laura Weightman** 1.7.91 (1y, 2:02.52 '12   2:01.87, 2:02.67mx; 2 Stretford
8   **Hannah England** 6.3.87 (8y, 9) 1:59.66 '12   2:01.23, 2:02.15, 2:03.34, 2:04.40, 2:04.62, 2:05.88mx
     4 Watford 24/6, 6 Cork, 4 Stretford, 1 CAU, 1 Watford 9/8, 2 MI, 1 Stretford 19/8, 6 Zagreb
9   **Katie Snowden** 9.3.94 (3y, 12) 2:01.77 '15   2:00.92mx, 2:02.09mx, 2:03.91, 2:05.19   9 ET, 1 Watford 9/8
10   **Jessica Judd** 7.1.95 (6y, -) 1:59.77 '14   2:02.14mx, 2:02.67mx, 2:02.84mx, 2:05.52, 2:08.65   1 B.Univs
11   **Mhairi Hendry** 31.3.96 (1y, -) 2:04.69 '16   2:03.37, 2:04.10, 2:04.11, 2:04.75, 2:04.84, 2:05.09
     2 B.Univs, 3 LI, 1 Glasgow, 1 Eng-23, 5 UK, 3 Lough 8/7, 1 Watford 12/7, 7 Cork, 4 MI, 2 Scot

12   **Marilyn Okoro** 23.9.84 (12y, -) 1:58.45 '08   2:02.50, 2:03.44, 2:03.81, 2:04.07, 2:04.94, 2:05.52; 2:03.26i
1 Florida R, 7 M.SAC, 5 Kingston, 4 Lisbon, 6 UK; Ind: 1 Nashville
–   **Revee Walcott-Nolan** 6.3.95 (1y, 10) 2:02.32 '16   2:03.20, 2:03.64, 2:03.93, 2:04.00mx, 2:04.21, 2:04.22
5 Tübingen, 7 Montreuil, dnf Turku, 2 Eng-23, 1 Watford 24/6, 2h4 UK, 2 Lough 8/7, 8 Padua, 2 Watford 9/8, 2 Stretford 19/8
Sharp is top for the fourth successive year, once again in top world class with eight sub-2 min times (from her last 11 800m races). Oskan-Clarke only broke 2 minutes once, but had a splendid competitive record, while Muir had just one race at 800m, but that was in a major DL meeting with a fast time. Tracey has still to break 2 mins, but got so close so often and Bell had a splendidly consistent season, running between 2:00.62 and 2:03.44 in all her 12 races. 140 women to 2:12.0 ties the all-time record set in 2016.

1500 METRES
1   **Laura Muir** 9.5.93 (5y, 5) 3:58.66 '16, 4:19.12M '16   4:18.03M/4:00.35. 4:00.47, 4:02.97, 4:03.64, 4:05.01, 4:08.97; 4:02.39i   3 Eugene, 2 Anniv, 1 Padua, 4 WCh; Ind: 1 EI
2   **Laura Weightman** 1.7.91 (8y, 2) 4:00.17 '14   4:00.71, 4:20.88M/4:03.23, 4:01.95, 4:03.07, 4:03.50, 4:04.11
13 Eugene, 4 Hengelo, 1 UK, 4 Rabat, 6 Anniv, 6 WCh, 8 B'ham, 7 Brussels
3   **Jessica Judd** 7.1.95 (5y, 12) 4:09.56 '15, 4:39.49M '16   4:03.73, 4:05.20, 4:07.09, 4:28.59M/4:08.23, 4:10.14, 4:11.15   1 Watford 3/5 & 14/6, 1 Solihull, 1 Eng-23, 2 UK, 14 Anniv, 10s1 WCh
4   **Sarah McDonald** 2.8.93 (2y, 4) 4:07.18 '16   4:05.48, 4:05.83, 4:06.73, 4:08.14, 4:08.21, 4:09.70   5 Stanford, 2 Tübingen, 8 Hengelo, 3 UK, dnf Padua, 9s2 WCh, 13 B'ham DL; Ind: 1 Cardiff, 3 New York, 1 UKi, 3 Athlone, 6 EI
5   **Melissa Courtney** 30.8.93 (4y, 8) 4:07.55 '16   4:23.15M/4:05.82, 4:06.00, 4:07.02, 4:08.42, 4:08.42mx, 4:10.16
4 Oordegem, 9 Hengelo, 5 UK, 8 Anniv, 2 Dublin, 5 WUG; Ind: 1 B.Uns-i
6   **Katie Snowden** 9.3.94 (1y, -) 4:13.06mx '16, 4:17.29 '15   4:05.29, 4:25.89M/4:06.39, 4:09.32, 4:09.70, 4:10.97, 4:12.21   1B Stanford, 2B Oordegem, 1 Gothenburg, 2 Watford 14/6, 4 UK, 13 Anniv, 14 B'ham DL
7   **Eilish McColgan** 25.11.90 (4y, 7) 4:03.74 '16   2 Berlin 4:01.60, Ind: 2 UKi 4:19.99, 4:29.37i
8   **Stephanie Twell** 17.8.89 (10y, 9) 4:02.54 '10, 4:28.16M '07   1 Anniv 4:25.39M/4:06.92, 4:07.39mx
9   **Charlene Thomas** 6.5.82 (10y, 3) 4:03.74mp '13, 4:05.06 '09   4:09.32, 4:11.25, 4:12.11, 4:13.27, 4:13.35, 4:14.38
2 Melbourne, 7 Tübingen, 4 Bydgoszcz, 1 Watford 24/6, 6 UK, 5 Dublin, 2 MI
10   **Hannah England** 6.3.87 (10y, 5) 4:01.89 '11, 4:30.29Mi '09, 4:47.42M '05   4:09.52, 4:09.84, 4:13.15, 4:14.47, 4:15.61, 4:17.84   1 LI, 1 Lahti, 9 Huelva. 8 UK, 13 Padua, 1 CAU, 1 Watford 9/8
11   **Jemma Reekie** 6.3.98 (1y, -) 44:24.22 '16   4:12.28, 4:13.25, 4:14.27, 4:15.09, 4:15.48mx, 4:15.90
5 Manchester, 7 Gothenburg, 1 Eng-J, 7 UK, 2J Lausanne, 1 EJ, 1 MI, 2 Stretford 19/8
12   **Amy-Eloise Neale** 5.8.95 (1y, -) 4:14.93 '16   4:11.00, 4:11.02, 4:13.81, 4:14.89, 4:18.82, 4:22.65; 4:34.15Mi, 4:35.12Mi   5 Mt.SAC, 2 Eugene 5/5, 6 Pac-12, 8 NCAA; Ind: 7/8/2/3 Seattle, 9 NCAAi
–   **Rhianwedd Price** 11.8.94 (2y, -) 4:09.56 '15   4:12.07, 4:13.84, 4:15.07, 4:15.35, 4:16.40, 4:17.03
1 Florida R, 7 Mt.SAC, 4 SEC, 9 NCAA, 13 Portland, 9 ET, 12 UK; Ind: 3 SECi
Muir retained her top ranking, and World 4th was terrific bearing in mind her interrupted preparation through injury that meant she could not quite recapture her brilliant indoor form. Weightman continued to show her steady world-class form and Judd recaptured hers – splendid front-running led to the fastest ever heat in women's 1500m World Championship history. Behind her McDonald, Snowden and Courtney, 3-4-5 in the UKs, all made significant improvement. It was close at the foot of the rankings with Amy Griffiths and Harriet Knowles-Jones also in contention. 50th best of 4:20.66 was a new record.

5000 METRES
1   **Laura Muir** 9.5.93 (1y, -) -0-   6 WCh 14:52.07 (14:59.34 ht); 1 Glasgow ind 14:49.12
2   **Eilish McColgan** 25.11.90 (4y, 1) 15:05.00 '16
8 Brussels 14:48.49, 10 WCh 15:00.43 (15:00.38 ht), 6 Eugene 15:07.43, 5 Stanford 15:22.12, 2 UK 15:38.57
3   **Stephanie Twell** 17.8.89 (8y, 2) 14:54.08 '10   1 Watford 15:16.65, 16 Rome 15:24.05, 1 UK 15:35.50, 15h2 WCh 15:41.29
4   **Laura Weightman** 1.7.91 (1y, -) -0-   1 Eagle Rock 15:08.24
5   **Jessica Judd** 7.1.95 (1y, -) -0-   1 Manchester 15:34.82, 5 UK 15:49.05, 3 WUG 15:51.19, 1B B.Univs 15:55.40
6   **Charlotte Arter** 18.6.91 (1y, -) 16:00.44 '15   2 Watford 15:40.15, 3 UK 15:43.46, 15:56.0mx, 13 Andújar 16:20.84
7   **Katrina Wootton** 2.9.85 (8y, 9) 15:30.82 '13   1 Nottingham 15:27.6mx, 2 Solihull 15:49.48
8   **Melissa Courtney** 30.8.93 (1y, -) 16:13.45 '15   4B Stanford 15:28.95
9   **Lauren Howarth** 21.4.90 (3y, 12) 15:44.28 '16   5B Stanford 15:29.26
10   **Calli Thackery** 9.1.93 (2y, -) 15:37.44 '16   3 Portland 15:37.90, 9B Stanford 15:39.44, 6 ET 16:12.16, dnf UK
11   **Verity Ockenden** 31.8.91 (1y, -) 16:14.81 '16   4 UK 15:46.11, 1 CAU/ENG 16:36.91
12   **Emelia Gorecka** 26.1.94 (1y, -) 15:47.45 '14   10B Stanford 15:44.34, 6 UK 15:51.93, 11 Andújar 16:02.92
–   **Louise Small** 27.3.92 (2y,10-) 15:41.91 '16
1 Catford 15:40.5mx, 1 Solihull 15:42.27, 4 WUG 15:55.55, 4 Watford 16:02.08, 7 UK 16:02.75
–   **Charlotte Taylor** 17.1.94 (1y, -) 16:05.88 '16
13 Stanford 5/5 15:29.07, 7h1 NCAA-W 16:46.70; Ind: 12 Seattle 16:08.98i
Muir excelled in her first season of 5000m running, with Scottish records both indoors and out, before McColgan beat the latter. McColgan continued to improve despite hanging back for too long far too much in her races. She was beaten by Twell at the UKs, but Twell disappointed at the Worlds. Last year's 3rd to 8th in the rankings drop out this year. 10th best of 15:37.90 and 50th of 16:41.95 are new records.

10,000 METRES
1   **Beth Potter** 27.12.91 (3y, 3) 32:03.45 '16   1 UK 32:04.63, 21 WCh 32:15.88
2   **Katrina Wootton** 2.9.85 (2y, 9) 33:07.93 '16   1mx Catford 31:45.63, 3 UK 32:27.47, 11 Eur Cup 33:49.74
3   **Charlotte Taylor** 17.1.94 (1y, -) 32:46.57 '15
     4 Stanford 31/3 32:11.80, 1 NCAA 32:38.57, 27 WCh 32:51.33, 4h NCAA-W 34:16.97
4   **Eilish McColgan** 25.11.90 (1y, -) -0-   3 Stanford 31/3 32:10.59
5   **Stephanie Twell** 17.8.89 (1y, -) -0-   2 UK 32:16.23
6   **Alice Wright** 3.11.94 (3y, 5) 32:36.11 '16   16 Stanford 32:29.28, 2 NCAA 32:42.64, 1h NCAA-W 34:06.78
7   **Charlotte Arter** 18.6.91 (1y, -) 34:26.42 '16   1 ENG 32:37.51, 6 UK 32:51.72
8   **Jo Pavey** 20.9.73 (8y, 1) 30:53.20 '12   4 UK 32:42.93
9   **Claire Duck** 29.8.85 (1y, -) 33:40.73 '16   5 UK 32:51.38, 12 Eur Cup 34:08.72
10   **Jennifer Nesbitt** 24.1.95 (3y, 10) 33:43.19 '16   10 UK 32:59.52, 6 EU23 33:50.37; 5 WUG 34:01.34
11   **Sonia Samuels** 16.5.79 (6y, -) 32:39.46 '14   20 Stanford 5/5 32:41.19, 12 UK 33:00.74, 6 Huelva 33:20.61
12   **Louise Small** 27.3.92 (3y, -) 33:50.63 '14   9 UK 32:56.11, 16 Eur Cup 34:29.54; 10 WUG 35:03.93
–   **Jessica Martin** 1.10.92 (1y, 2) 31:35.92   11 UK 33:00.24, 9 Huelva 33:55.24, dnf WCh
UK champion Beth Potter takes over top ranking and was joined on the World Champs team by Taylor, who became a rare UK winner of an NCAA title. The UK championship race at Parliament Hill was again a huge success and 18 of the top 50 women set their bests at this meeting. Wootton smashed her best in this race in 3rd place and went on to run the UK season's fastest in a mixed race, while Twell and McColgan made good debuts at the event. Jessica Martin's career proved to be short one in world class as after ranking 2nd in 2016 she just misses the top 12 and retired to help her husband's top cycling career. New records were set for 10th 32:51.38 and 50th 37:02.39.

10 MILES - 20Km - HALF MARATHON (First ranked 1999)
1   **Charlotte Purdue** 10.6.91 (6y, 4) 71:43 '14   13 Okayama 71:29, 1 Reading 72:15, 2 Gt.Scot 72:18,
     5 Hamburg 72:39   10M: 3 Gt.South (3 ENG) 55:43
2   **Gemma Steel** 12.11.85 (7y, 2) 68:13 '14   6 GNR 71:32, 2 Granollers 72:47, 2 Reading 73:37, 1 Bermuda 74:28
     10M: 1 Gt.South (1 ENG) 55:25
3   **Lily Partridge** 9.3.91 (3y, 31 70:32 '15   7 GNR 72:10, 3 Santa Pola 72:12 (15k 51:00), 12 Gifu 78:14
     10M: 2 Gt.South (2 ENG) 55:37
4   **Alyson Dixon** 24.9.78 (8y, 3) 70:38 '14   8 GNR 72:29, 73:21+ London, 1 Redcar 77:30
5   **Jennifer Nesbitt** 24.1.95 (2y, 7) 72:54 '16   5 Cardiff 73:23 (15k 51:39, 20k 69:37), 4 Reading 74:26
6   **Tracy Barlow** 18.6.85 (1y, -) 74:24 '16   10 Barcelona 72:48 (20k 69:09), 1 Paddock Wood 74:07, 1 Cambridge 76:23
7   **Sarah Inglis** 28.9.91 (1y, -) 82:04'13   5 Monterrey 73:36, 1 Victoria BC 74:21, 15 Lisbon 74:51
8   **Emma Pallant** 4.1.80 (1y, -) 75:42 '11   1 Lanzarote 73:43   10M: 2 Twickenham 54:53
9   **Jenny Spink** 7.8.81(3y, -) 73:02 '15   12 Barcelona 73:36 (20k 69:50)
10   **Kate Reed** 28.9.82 (1y, -) -0-   1 Tallahassee 73:44
11   **Sonia Samuels** 16.5.79 (4y, -) 72:36 »'13   74:03+ Berlin, 9 Olomouc 74:39
12   **Caryl Jones** 24.4.87 (2y, -) 71:18 '12   9 GNR 74:22, 6 Cardiff 75:24, 3 Swansea 77:53
–   **Katrina Wootton** 2.9.85 (2y, 11) 73:36 '16   3 Reading 74:18
–   **Hannah Walker** 9.8.91 (1y, -) 71:50 '12   1 Lillebælt 74:25, 5 Reading 74:36
The top four are the same as in 2016, although in a different order, and it is close at the top. Purdue's top mark of the year came in Japan on December 23 and that gave her the best set of times and just gave her the edge over Steel and Partridge.

MARATHON
1   **Charlotte Purdue** 10.6.91 (2y, 2) 2:30:04 '16   15 London (2 ENG) 2:29:23, 13 WCh 2:29:48, 4 Seitama 2:30:34
2   **Alyson Dixon** 24.9.78 (6y, 1) 2:29:30 '15   14 London (1 ENG) 2:29:06, 18 WCh 2:31:36
3   **Sonia Samuels** 16.5.79 (5y, 2) 2:28:04 '15   7 Berlin 2:29:34
4   **Tracy Barlow** 18.6.85 (3y, 4) 2:32:05 '16   16 London (3 ENG) 2:30:42, 43 WCh 2:41:03
5   **Lily Partridge** 9.3.91 (1y, -) -0-   4 Seville 2:32:10, dnf Berlin
6   **Tish Jones** 7.9.85 (2y, 7) 2:36:13 '17   18 London 2:33:56, dnf Toronto
7   **Caryl Jones** 4.4.87 (1y,-) -0-   11 Amsterdam 2:34:16
8   **Elinor Kirk** 26.4.89 (1y, -) -0-   4 Florence 2:36:22
9   **Georgie Bruinvels** 20.10.88 (3y, 9) 2:37:21 '15   1 Manchester 2:37:03
10   **Anna Boniface** 27.4.91 (1y, -) 2:45:53 '16   1M London 2:37:17, dnf Toronto
11   **Susan Partridge** 4.1.80 (12y, -) 2:30:46 '13   21 London 2:37:51
12   **Jenny Spink** 7.8.81 (3y, -) 2:36:00 '15   22 London 2:38:11
nr   **Laura Graham** IRL 5.3.86 2:41:54 '16   4 Berlin 2:37:05, 4 Dublin (IRL Ch) 2:39:07, 1 Belfast 2:41:46, 24 London 2:42:38
In her second year of marathon running Purdue moves to top ranking, breaking 2:30 twice and being just outside that despite strong winds in Japan. Just behind Dixon in London, she came out on top at the Worlds. Samuels, in Berlin, became the third British woman to break 2:30 in 2017. There were new records for 50th best 2:50:55, 100th 2:57:08 and 141 under 3 hours.

2000/3000 METRES STEEPLECHASE (First ranked 2001)
1   **Rosie Clarke** 17.11.91 (2y, 2) 9:51.97 '16   9:32.10, 9:36.75, 9:38.85, 9:49.36
     1 Stanford 5/3, 9h3 W.Ch, 9 Berlin, 7 Zagreb   2000mSt: 1 P.Hill 6:29.53
2   **Lennie Waite** 4.2.86 (10y, 2) 9:35.91 '16   9:37.94, 9:43,33, 9:43.87, 9:48.44, 9:54.97
     1/14 Eagle Rock, 7 Portland, 2 ET, 4 UK, 2 L'kenny, 3 G'burg, 6 Lapinlahti, 10h1 WCh   2000mSt: 1 Houston 6:21.31u
3   **Iona Lake** 15.1.93 (5y, 5) 9:56.64 '15   9:39.03, 9:48.87, 9:50.61, 9:57.53, 9:58.05
     1 UK, 4 L'kenny, 1 CAU (ENG), 1 MI, 8 Zagreb   2000mSt: 6:46.0
4   **Charlotte Taylor-Green** 2.4.85 (3y, 4) 10:15.26 '19   9:58.85, 9:59.58, 10:01.05, 10:07.86, 10:11.12
     5 Stanford 31/3, 21 Oordegem, 8 Huelva, 2 UK, 8 L'kenny, 2 (1) CAU   2000mSt: 1 BL1 (1) 6:34.12
5   **Aimee Pratt** 3.10.97 (2y, 9) 10:19.08 '16   9:59.86, 10:08.64, 10:10.15, 10:19.70, 10:28.64
     25 Oordegem, 9 Huelva, 1 Eng-23, 8 UK, 13 EU23   2000mSt: 2 MI 6:39.54
6   **Kate Ingle** 4.3.95 (4y, -) 10:13.99 '14   10:02.34, 10:10.73, 10:20.51, 10:22.89, 10:43.35
     5 LI, 1 Welsh, 4 Eng-23, 3 UK, 3 CAU   2000mSt: 2 Solihull 6:44.34
7   **Elizabeth Bird** 4.10.94 (4y, 6) 9:54.76 '15   10:09.04, 10:14.34, 10:17.15   2 Princeton, 1 Heps, 7h1 NCAA-E
8   **Philippa Bowden** 29.3.95 (1y, -) 10:44.16 '16   10:14.26   2 Eng-23
9   **Stacie Taylor** 12.10.95 (2y, 8) 10:13.23 '16   10:16.07, 10:23.23, 10:29.13, 10:33.07, 10:40.87
     1 F'ville, 14 Mt.SAC, 3 AAC, 8h2 NCAA-W, 3 Eng-23, 5 UK
10   **Emily Moyes** 314.6.98 (1y, -) 11:15.81 '1   10:25.23, 10:27.15, 10:27.16, 10:31.81, 10:39.05
     2 LI, 1 Eng-J, 11 EJ, 3 MI   2000mSt: 1 B.Univs 6:35.07
11   **Jade Williams** 7.9.92 (1y, -) -0-   10:25.03; 1 LI, dnf UK; 2000mSt: 6:38.76, 1 Solihull
12   **Laura Riches** 7.8.93 (3y, 12) 9:54.76 '15   10:27.03, 10:30.08, 10:31.43, 10:40.63
     3 LI, 6 UK, 4 CAU, 4 MI   2000mSt: 3 B.Univs 6:45.41, 1 BLP1 (3) 6:46.99, 3 Solihull 6:48.19
nr   **Kerry O'Flaherty** IRL 15.7.81 9:42.61 '15   9:50.75, 9:54.40, 9:57.47, 9:59.46, 10:00.85   11 Belfast, 1 Huelva,
     7 ET I, 11 Szék'vár, 5 L'kenny, 8 G'burg, 3 Ninove,1 IRL Ch, 4 Karlstad, 2 MI, 13 Berlin 2000mSt: 1 BLP (2) 6:52.98
In her second year at the event Clarke took over top ranking from Waite. Lake made notable progress with three big pbs
in her last three steeplechases.

100 METRES HURDLES
1   **Tiffany Porter** 13.11.87 (7y, 2) 12.51 '14, 12.47w '12   12.75, 12.87, 12.89, 12.93, 12.99, 13.00
     2 Greensboro, 8 Drake R, 2 Kawasaki, 3 Manchester, 5 Boston, 1 Monteverde, 5 Oslo, 2 Bellinzona, 6h2 WCh
2   **Cindy Ofili** 5.8.94 (3y, 1) 12.60 '15   12.92, 13.07, 13.08, 13.09, 13.42, 13.76
     3 Greensboro, 6 Drake R, 7 Doha, 3 Kawasaki, 4 Manchester, dnf ht Boston
3   **Alicia Barrett** 25.3.98 (2y, 5) 13.15 '16   13.07, 13.07, 13.22, 13.23, 13.26, 13.27; 13.18w
     dns B.Uns, 2 LI, 3 Oordegem, 4 Geneva, 1 Eng-J, 6 ET, 1 UK, 2 EJ, 8h1 WCh, 5s2 WUG
4   **Yasmin Miller** 24.5.95 (5y, 10) 13.13 '14   13.23, 13.23, 13.27, 13.29, 13.32, 13.33; 13.16w, 13.23w, 13.23w
     1 B.Univs, 3 LI, 5 Oordegem, 5 Bydgoszcz, 3 Hérouville, 1 Eng-23, 2 UK, 6h2 Anniv, 4 EU23, 2 LEAP, 1 CAU
5   **Katarina Johnson-Thompson** 9.1.93 (6y, 12) 13.37 '15   13.29, 13.33, 13.45, 13.57
     1 Montpelier, 1H Götzis, 8h1 Anniv, 5H WCh
6   **Jessica Hunter** 4.12.96 (2y, -) 13.66 '15   13.42, 13.43, 13.45, 13.51, 13.52, 13.53; 13.42w
     2 Lough 10/5, 1A LI, 1 Oordegem, 1 South, 2 Eng-23, 3 UK, 1 Karlstad, 2 CAU, 5 MI
7   **Mollie Courtney** 2.7.97 (2y, 6) 13.28 '16   13.44, 13.48, 13.49, 13.50, 13.51, 13.51; 13.40w, 13.46w
     2 B.Uns, 4 LI, 1 NI, 3 Eng-23, 4 UK, 2/1 Belfast, 3 LEAP, 3 CAU, 1 MI, WLP: 2,1,1
8   **Sophie Yorke** 7.7.98 (1y, -) 14.47 '15   13.47, 13.51, 13.58, 13.63, 13.74, 13.6h; 13.31w, 13.55w, 13.57w
     3A LI, 1 Mid-J, 2 Eng-J, 7 UK, 1 W.Int, 5 EJ, 3 MI
9   **Megan Marrs** 25.9.97 (1y, -) 13.72 '14   13.51, 13.54, 13.58, 13.59, 13.62, 13.67; 13.56w
     7 B.Uns, 6 LI, 2 NI, 5 Eng-23, 5 UK, 1/3 Belfast, 5 LEAP, 4 CAU, 5 Warsaw, 1 Scot, 1 Guernsey, WLP: -,4,3
10   **Caryl Granville** 24.9.89 (1y, -) 13.77 '12   13.48, 13.55, 13.57, 13.65, 13.71, 13.83; 13.46w, 13.63w
     1 Aarhus, 1 Welsh, 1 Nivelles, 2 Lokoren, 3 Celle L, 2 MI, 1 Welsh I-R, WLP: 1B,-,1B
11   **Angelita Broadbelt-Blake** 12.9.85 (8y, 8) 13.18, 13.07w '11   13.58, 13.66, 13.69, 13.70, 13.76, 13.80; 13.67w
     5 LI, 2 South, 3h2 UK, 2 Celle L, 5 CAU, dq MI, WLP: -,2,2
12   **Heather Paton** 9.4.96 (1y, -) 14.06 '15   13.47, 13.55, 13.57, 13.61, 13.62, 13.66; 13.59w, 13.61w
     7 LI, 1 NI, 2 Lough 7/6, 6 Eng-23, 6 UK, 3/2 Belfast, 6 CAU, 4 MI, 2 Scot, 2 Guernsey, WLP: 1,3,4
-    **Lucy Hatton** 8.11.94 (5y, 4) 12.84 '15   13.41, 13.51; 1 Lough 7/6, 7 Geneva
Last year's no. 1 Ofili was unable to compete after the beginning of June through injury, and while her sister Porter regained
the top ranking, she was not able to be near her best at the Worlds. Barrett continued her progress and set UK junior
records in heat and final of the national U20 championships and another junior Yorke made major improvement and joined
Barrett in the European Junior final. 50th best at 14.38 was a new record

400 METRES HURDLES
1   **Eilidh Doyle** 20.2.87 (13y, 1) 54.09 '16   54.36, 54.60, 54.75, 54.82, 54.89, 54.92
     1 Lisse, 9 Rome, 2 Huelva, 1 ET, 1 UK, 3 Lausanne, 4 Anniv, 3 Rabat, 8 WCh, 4 B'ham DL, 5 Zürich, 4 Brussels
2   **Meghan Beesley** 15.11.89 (11y, 2) 54.52 '15   56.14, 56.41, 56.61, 56.63, 56.68, 56.88
     6A Geneva, 6 Copenhagen, 2 UK, 1 L'kenney, 1 WLP (3), 2 LEAP, 6s2 WCh
3   **Jessica Turner** 8.8.95 (4y, 3) 57.00 '16   56.08, 56.68, 56.76, 56.79, 56.98, 57.07
     1 Lough 10/5, 1 LI, 1B Oordegem, 2 Aarhus, 5 Geneva, 1 Eng-23, 3 UK, 2 EU23, 6h2 WCh, 5 WUG

4 **Caryl Granville** 24.9.89 (6y, 4) 57.19 '13   56.59, 57.17, 57.42, 57.46, 57.62, 57.62
  1 Lough 22/4, 3 LI, 2C Oordegem, 5 Aarhus, 1 Welsh, 2 Leiden, 1 Nivelles, 2 Lokoren, 4 UK, 5 LEAP, 1 MI, WLP: 1,-,2
5 **Ese Okoro** 4.7.90 (8y, 9) 56.67 '14   57.62, 57.81, 57.87, 58.03, 58.13, 58.25
  2 LI, 4 Aarhus, 3 Copenhagen, 5 UK, 1B WLP (3), 7 LEAP, dns CAU
6 **Lina Nielsen** 13.3.96 (1y, -) 58.99 '16   57.87, 57.94, 58.47, 58.87, 59.08, 59.12
  2 WLP (2), 1D Geneva, 2 Eng-23, 1B LEAP, 2 CAU
7 **Jessie Knight** 15.6.94 (1y, -) 59.06 '16   58.00, 58.43, 58.50, 59.18, 59.21, 59.81
  5A LI, 7C Geneva, 1 South, 6 UK, 4B LEAP, 4 CAU, WLP: 1B,3,-
8 **Nisha Desai** 5.8.84 (8y, 11) 58.21 '13   58.3, 58.38, 58.80, 58.83, 58.84, 58.85
  3 Lough 22.4, 3A LI, 1 North, 8 UK, 2B LEAP, 3 CAU, 2 MI, 1 Scot, WL1: 1,1,1
9 **Kirsten McAslan** 1.9.93 (1y, -) -0-   57.31, 58.10, 58.97, 59.11   1B WL2 (3), 1 CAU, 3 MI
10 **Hayley McLean** 9.9.94 (7y, 8) 56.43 '14   58.33, 58.83, 58.85, 58.99, 59.20, 59.33
  2A LI, 6A Oordegem, 6B Geneva, 3 Nivelles, 4 Lokoren, 3h3 UK, 5 L'kenney, 3B LEAP, dq CAU
11 **Jessica Tappin** 17.5.90 (3y, -) 58.13 '15 58.34, 58.9, 59.05, 59.1, 59.25, 59.52   3h1 UK, 2B WLP (3), 5B LEAP, 5 CAU, 4 MI
12 **Bethany Close** 30.12.95 (3y, 5) 57.70 '16   58.38, 58.80, 59.50, 59.50, 60.02, 61.80
  3 G'ville, 7 LI, 7C Geneva, 6 Eng-23, 4h3 UK, 3B WLP (3)
nr **Christine McMahon** IRL 6.7.92 56.06 '16   58.08, 58.15, 58.30, 58.31, 59.00, 59.59
  4A LI, 5A Oordegem, 5 Marseille, 6 Prague, 4h2 ET1, 1 Belfast, 2 L'kenney, 5B Rabat
Doyle was again clearly our number one for the fourth time, but was a little below her best. Beesley just held on to second place against Turner, who continued to improve with excellent international results. Last year's number four Philippa Lowe concentrated on 400m flat in 2017 and was replaced by Granville, who had her best ever year after two years out of the rankings. McAslan had an excellent debut season at the event, but did not run it often enough to rank higher. 50th best at 63.26 was the best since 1995.

HIGH JUMP
1 **Morgan Lake** 12.5.97 (6y, 2) 1.94 '14   1.96, 1.95, 1.94, 1.93, 1.92, 1.91; 1.92i
  1H Florence, 1 LI, 1H Eng, 4= Rome, 4= Hengelo, 1 Eng-23, 7= ET, 1 UK, 4 Lausanne, 7 Anniv, 6 WCh,
  4 Eberstadt, 5 Zagreb, 8= Brussels; Ind: 1 Hustopece,1= UKi, 8 EI
2 **Katarina Johnson-Thompson** 9.1.93 (11y, 1) 1.98 '16   1.95, 1.95, 1.93, 1.92, 1.88, 1.80   2H Götzis, 7H WCh, 5 WCh
3 **Bethan Partridge** 11.7.90 (7y, 3) 1.87 '15   1.85, 1.83, 1.83, 1.82, 1.80, 1.80; 1.89i, 1.88i, 1.86i, 1.86i, 1.84i
  2 WLP (1), 2 LI, 6 Lund, 2 Carquefou, 4= UK, 4= Sotteville, 4 Marseille, 6= Heusden; Ind: 1 B'ham,
  2 Nantes, 5= Hustopece, 1= UKi
4 **Emma Nuttall** 23.4.92 (6y, 4) 1.88i '14, 1.87 '13   1.86, 1.86, 1.83, 1.83, 1.80, 1.80
  4= LI, 5 Lund, 4= Velenje, 2 UK, 4= Sotteville, 1= Cork, 1 CAU, 1 MI, 2 L'pool; Ind: 3 B'ham
5 **Nikki Manson** 15.10.94 (3y, 10) 1.81 '16   1.86, 1.85, 1.81, 1.81, 1.81, 1.80; 1.84i   4 Texas R, 2 Athens GA,
  2 MAC, 5 NCAA, 3 UK, 4 Cork, 5 Karlstad, 2 CAU, 4 MI, 1 Scot, 1 L'pool; Ind: 1 Univ Pk, 1 MAC, 10 NCAA
6 **Emily Borthwick** 2.9.97 (3y, 8) 1.80 '15   1.83, 1.81, 1.81, 1.80, 1.77, 1.76; 1.83i, 1.82i   3 B.Uns, 4= LI, 1 North,
  3 Eng-23, 7 UK, 4 Belfast; 1= Cork, 3 CAU, 3 MI, WL2: 1,3,-; Ind: 2 B'ham, 1 North, 1B Hustopece, 4 UKi, 4 B.Uns
7 **Niamh Emerson** 22.4.99 (3y, 5) 1.89 '16   1.83, 1.82, 1.81, 1.79, 1.74   3 LI, 2H Eng, 4= UK, 5H EJ
8 **Kate Anson** 14.3.95 (1y, -) 1.78 '10   1.80, 1.78, 1.77, 1.77, 1.75, 1.75
  1 B.Uns, 1 WL3 (1), 6 LI, 1 BIG, 2 Eng-23, 6 UK; Ind: 3 North, 9 B.Uns
9 **Rebecca Hawkins** 27.9.99 (2y, 12) 1.77 '17   1.77, 1.77, 1.76, 1.75, 1.75, 1.74; 1.80i, 1.78i, 1.76i   9 LI, 2 BIG,
  1 Sth-J, 1 Eng-J, 8= UK, 3 E.Sch, 1 WInt, 6 CAU, 7 MI, 2 EJ Clubs, WLP: 3=,3,1; Ind: 1 Sth-17i, 1 Eng-17i
10 **Temi Ojora** 24.1.02 (3y, 9) 1.69 '15   1.77, 1.76, 1.74, 1.74, 1.73, 1.72   2 Eng-J, 1 E.Sch-I, 1 Sch Int
11 **Laura Armorgie** 5.12.97 (1y, -) 1.78 '16   1.71, 1.70. 1.66; 1.82i, 1.80i
  7= LI, 10= UK, WL2: 4=,1=,-; Ind: 1 London, 5 UKi
12 **Ada'ora Chigbo** 2.1.99 (3y, 9) 1.83 '16   1.75, 1.74, 1.72, 1.70; 1.80i, 1.74i, 1.73i
  1 West, 5 BIG, 4 Eng-J, 2 E.Sch, 1 BL1 (3); Ind: 1J Hustopece, 7 UKi
nr **Philippa Rogan** 4.2.94 IRL 1.80 '16   1.78, 1.76, 1.75, 1.75, 1.73, 1.72; 1.82i, 1.80i, 1.78i, 1.78i
  5 B.Univs, 1 South, 1 P'gell, 1 IRL Ch, WLP: 3=,4,2; Ind: 1 South, 2 London, 3 UKi, 1 B.Uns-i
Outdoors only: 3 Manson, 4 Nuttall, 5 Partridge,... 11 Chigbo, 12 Poppy Lake
Lake concentrated on the event, improved her best to 1.96 and was rewarded with a fine 6th place at the Worlds. This was a place behind, although with the same height, as Johnson-Thompson, who had a much thinner season at the event and thus Lake took the top ranking. After two years out of the rankings Nuttall returned with a fine season in the close battle for rankings 3-5. Emerson concentrated on the heptathlon and did not reach her 2016 heights.

POLE VAULT
1 **Holly Bradshaw** 2.11.91 (6y, 1) 4.87i, 4.71 '12   4.81, 4.80, 4.70, 4.65, 4.62i, 4.61
  4 Doha, 1 Manchester, 7= Rome, I UK, 6 Anniv, 1 Rottach-E, 6 WCh, 2 B'ham DL, 4= Zürich, 4 Beckum. 6 Brussels
2 **Lucy Bryan** 22.5.95 (7y, 3) 4.40 '13   4.40, 4.35, 4.25, 4.20, 4.15; 4.40i, 4.33i, 4.30i, 4.28i
  2= Akron, 1 Welsh, 1 Eng-23, 3 Cardiff, 2 UK, 3 EU23; Ind: 1 Lexington, 1/2/1 Akron, 3 Univ Pk, 2 Mid-Am, 4 NCAA
3 **Sally Peake** 8.2.86 (7y, 2) 4.42i '12, 4.40 '14   4.35, 4.35, 4.25, 4.15, 4.01, 4.00; 4.26i, 4.23i, 4.16i
  2 LI, 2= MCG, 3 Rehlingen, 6 ET, 3 UK, 8 Sotteville; Ind: 8= Orleans, 1 Welsh, 2 UKi, 7 B'ham, 2 W.Int. 1 Cardiff

4 **Jade Ive** 22.1.92 (8y, 4) 4.15 '15   4.20, 4.15, 4.10, 4.10, 4.06, 4.05; 4.36i, 4.35i, 4.26i, 4.20i
   1 Surrey, 1 LI, nh South, 1 WLP (3), 2 CAU (1 ENG), 2 So'ton, 2 MI; Ind: 1 South-i, 1 V.London, 1 UKi, 8 B'ham, 1 W.Int
5 **Molly Caudery** 17.3.00 (3y, 9) 4.06 '16   4.35, 4.25, 4.20, 4.15, 4.05, 4.05; 4.10i   3 LI, 1 WLP (2), 1 Eng-J,
   2 Cardiff, 4 Mannheim, 1 E.Sch, 2 EJ, 1 MI; Ind: 4 Welsh, 1B V.London, 1 Eng-Ji, 3= W.Int, 3 Cardiff
6 **Henrietta Paxton** 19.9.83 (8y, 6) 4.35 '10   4.25, 4.15, 4.15, 4.05, 3.90, 3.80; 4.10i, 4.01i
   5= LI, 1 Welsh, 1 Cardiff, 4 UK; WLP: 1,2=,-; Ind: 2 South, 2 Manchester
7 **Abigail Roberts** 9.7.97 (5y, 12) 4.08 '15   4.05, 4.00, 4.00, 3.90, 3.90, 3.85; 4.01i, 3.95i, 3.95i
   3=/2 Melbourne, 1 Yorks, 3 Geneva, 2 Eng-23, 5 UK, WL3: 1,1,-; Ind: 1 North, 1 Manchester, 4 Cardiff
8 **Rachel Gibbens** 31.1.86 (9y, 5) 4.13i '16, 4.05 '15   4.05, 4.00, 4.00, 4.00, 3.90, 3.85
   2=MCG, 9= UK, 4 MI, WL2: 1,1,1
9 **Clare Maurer** 10.6.91 (1y, -) 3.71i, 3.70 '15   4.06, 4.00, 3.95, 3.92, 3.90, 3.90   1 B.Univs, 2 Surrey, 5= LI,
   3 Welsh, 6 UK, 3= So'ton, 6 MI, WL2: 2,5,2; Ind: 8 South, 1B Manchester, 8B London, 3 B.Univs
10 **Courtney MacGuire** 30.4.90 (2y, -) 4.02i '15, 4.00 '14   4.00, 3.90, 3.85, 3.85, 3.80, 3.80; 3.94i, 3.90i
   8 LI, 2 Welsh, 7= UK, 1 W.Int, nh So'ton. WLP: 3,4,3; Ind: 9 Manchester, 4B London, 3 UKi, 5 W.Int, 6 Cardiff
11 **Clare Blunt** 28.9.87 (1y, -) 3.85 '15   4.00, 3.93, 3.92, 3.85, 3.80, 3.70; 3.92i, 3.81i
   2 Yorks, 1 North, 14 UK, 3 CAU,7 MI, WL1: 2,-,1; Ind: 2B London, 5 UKi
12 **Jessica Swannack** 26.9.98 (2y, -) 3.90 '16   4.00, 3.85, 3.75, 3.60, 3.60, 3.50; 3.91i, 3.83i, 3.75i
   1 North-J, 4 Eng-J, 7= UK, 2 E.Sch; Ind: 1 North-Ji, 10 Manchester, 1 B'ham G, 3 Eng=J, 3= W,Int, 5 Cardiff
nr **Sarah McKeever** IRL 11.8.95 (1y, 8) 3.95i, 3.90 '16   3.95, 3.90, 3.85, 3.80, 3.80, 3.80; 4.13i, 4.00i, 3.96i, 3.94i, 3.91i
   2 B.Univs, 1 NI, 5= LI, 3 Eng-23, 12 ET-1, 1 IRL U23, dnq 20 EU23, 5 MI
Outdoors only: 4 Caudery, 5 Ive
The top three women are the same for the fifth year. Bradshaw is clearly top for the seventh successive year (overtaking Janine Whitlock) with three UK outdoor records and her highest ever world ranking, but then Peake and Bryan swap for 2nd and 3rd. Ive remains 4th, but had a nice improvement of 21cm in her eighth year in the rankings and the top four are then followed by 17 year-old Caudery, who won the European Junior silver medal with two years remaining as a junior. Five juniors (two 16 year-olds) appear in these rankings. 50th best at 3.50 tied the record set in 2016.

LONG JUMP
1 **Lorraine Ugen** 22.8.91 (8y, 2) 6.92, 6.96w '15   6.78, 6.76, 6.72, 6.65, 6.63, 6.61; 6.97i, 6.80i, 6.76i
   1 Drake R, 2 Baie Mahault, 3 Eugene, 6 Oslo, 1 UK, 5 Lausanne, 6 Anniv, 5 WCh, 7 Berlin, 2 Brussels,
   1 Berlin 2/9, 1 GNC; Ind: 1 UKi, 1 Athlone, 1 B'ham, 2 EI
2 **Shara Proctor** 16.9.88 (7y, 5) 6.95 '12   6.73, 6.65, 6.63, 6.62, 6.53, 6.50
   2 Kawasaki, 8 Eugene, 1 Somerville, 4 Oslo, nj Lausanne, dnq 13 WCh, 3 Berlin, 4 GNC
3 **Katarina Johnson-Thompson** 9.1.93 (8y, 4) 6.93i '15, 6.92 '14   6.75, 6.63, 6.56, 6.53; 6.69i
   1 Montpelier, 6H Götzis, 4 Anniv, 2H WCh; Ind: 2 UKi
4 **Jazmin Sawyers** 21.5.94 (7y, 2) 6.75, 6.86w '16   6.55w/6.49, 6.53, 6.48, 6.46, 6.44, 6.42; 6.71i, 6.67i, 6.54i, 6.54i
   1 BIG, 2 Montreuil, 10 Oslo, 4 ET, nj UK, 9 Anniv, 4 G'burg, 7 B'zona, dnq 20 WCh, 2 Kosice, 3 GNC; Ind: 3 UKi, 2 B'ham, 6 EI
5 **Rebecca Chapman** 27.9.92 (3y, -) 6.23i '15, 6.17 '14   6.54, 6.42w/6.19, 6.32, 6.31, 6.23. 6.16
   1 LI, 1 Welsh, 2 C'hagen, 2 UK, 1 W.Int, WL1: 1,1,1, 4 Karlstad, 4 Rome; Ind: 1 Welsh
6 **Jahisha Thomas** 22.11.94 (2y, 10) 6.21i '16, 6.17 '15   6.35w, 6.32, 6.28, 6.15; 6.39i, 6.23i, 6.20i
   4 MtSAC, 2 Big Ten, 16 NCAA, 4 UK; Ind: 1/1 Iowa City, 3 F'ville, 3 Big 10
7 **Holly Mills** 15.4.00 (3y, 6) 6.29 '15   6.31, 6.22, 6.19, 6.19, 6.18, 6.02; 6.16i
   7 LI, 1 South-J, 1 Eng-J, 3 UK, 1 Comm-Y, 2 YDL, WLP: 1,2,-; Ind: 1 South-J, 1 Vienna, 1 Eng-J, 1 W.Int
8 **Sarah Warnock** 5.6.91 (5y, 11) 6.42 '14   6.16, 6.12, 5.99, 5.98, 5.96w, 5.81
   3 LI, 2 BIG, 5 UK, 9 Liège, WLP: -,3,3; Ind: 1 Scot-I, 3 UKi
9 **Eleanor Broome** 6.2.99 (2y, 7) 6.26 '16   6.16, 6.13, 6.10, 6.10, 6.08, 6.06; 6.10i
   5 LI, 3 BIG, 2 Eng-J, 6 UK, 1 E.Sch, 2 (1) CAU, 1 YDL, WL3: 1,1,-; Ind: 2 Eng-Ji
10 **Katie Stainton** 8.1.95 (2y, 9) 6.18, 6.23w '16   6.12w, 6.11w, 6.10, 6.07, 6.07, 6.01; 6.06i
   2 WL2 (2), 8 UK, 6H EU23, 1 CAU, 1 MI; Ind: 4 UKi, 6 B'ham
11 **Danielle McGifford** 11.4.95 (1y, -) 6.06 '13   6.16, 6.08, 6.01, 6.01, 5.94, 5.87; 6.10i
   1 WL2 (1), 2 LI, 2 Eng-23, 9 UK; Ind: 1 North
12 **Simi Fajemisin** 15.8.97 (1y, -) 6.13A '14, 5.98 '13   6.15, 6.14, 5.96, 5.91, 5.91, 5.90; 6.09i
   3 Houston, 6 C.Gables, 4 Florida R, 4 MtSAC, 3 Stanford 21/4, 2 Heps, dnq 35 NCAA-E, 3 Eng-23; Ind: 2 Heps
Ugen peaked with 2nd in the European Indoors, but also had a solid outdoor season to rank 5th in the World. The rest of our world class jumpers slipped a little from previous standards, but Proctor was on the edge of the world elite. Chapman had her best ever year, while Thomas progressed in the USA and 17 year-old Mills had another fine season, topped by Commonwealth Youth gold. Although Broome had better marks, she was beaten 3-0 by Warnock. Standards in depth improved a little as there were a record 111 women at 5.55 or more.

TRIPLE JUMP
1 **Naomi Ogbeta** 18.4.98 (3y, 6) 12.98 '15   13.68w/13.50, 13.64, 13.47, 13.36w/13.07, 13.25, 13.25w
   1 B.Uns, 5 LI, 3 BIG, 1 North-J, 1 Eng-J, 1 UK, 3 EJ, 2 MI; Ind: 3 B'lava, 1 B.Uns
2 **Shara Proctor** 16.9.88 (1y, -) 13.88i '10, 13.74 '09   13.82, 13.39; 1 Azusa, 9 ET
3 **Laura Samuel** 19.2.91 (9y, 1) 14.09 '14   13.60, 13.51w/13.36, 13.26, 12.97
   2 Clermont, 1 MI, 10 B'ham DL, 2 Lappeenranta

4   **Sineade Gutzmore** 9.10.86 (9y, 2) 13.70 '16   13.44, 13.39w/13.32, 13.16, 13.03, 13.00w
1 WLP (1), 2 LI, 1 BIG, 2 Copenhagen, 2 UK
5   **Angela Barrett** 25.12.85 (9y, 5) 13.19 '16   13.43, 13.23, 13.23, 13.15, 13.05, 13.02w
5 Clermont, 4 UK, 1 CAU, 3 MI, 1 Bellinzona, WLP: 2,2,1
6   **Jaheisha Thomas** 22.11.94 (1y, -) 12.72, 12.89w '16   13.25, 13.05w/12.66, 12.91w/12.09, 12.86, 12.58; 13.00i, 12.66i
8 Florida R, 5 Big10, dnq 15 NCAA-W, 3 UK; Ind: 7 Big10
7   **Alexandra Russell** 27.3.90 (3y, 7) 13.05 '15, 13.40w '17   13.27i, 13.10i, 13.07i, 12.94i Ind: 1 North, 1 B'lava, 1 UK
8   **Chioma Matthews** 12.3.81 (7y, 3) 13.53 '15   13.00, 13.00, 12.92, 12.78, 12.78, 12.77
4 LI, 2 BIG, 3 Carquefou, 5 UK, 4 Castres, 4 MI, 1 Scot; WLP: -,1,4
9   **Simi Fajemisin** 15.9.97 (1y, -) 12.16 '14   12.96, 12.78, 12.74w/12.66, 12.67, 12.39; 12.96i, 12.55i
6 Florida R, 6 Mt.SAC, 1 Heps, dnq 13 NCAA-E, 1 Eng-23; Ind: 2 Heps
10   **Emily Gargan** 29.12.98 (3y, -) 12.36 '16   13.03, 12.68, 12.68, 12.64, 12.62, 12.46, 12.47i
1 N.East, 3 LI, 2 Eng-J, 3 Mannheim, dnq 14 EJ; Ind: 2 North, 3 UKi
11   **Alison Wilder** 30.10.88 (1y, -) 13.22 '11   12.55w/12.47, 12.50, 12.50w/12.32, 12.45; 12.37i, 12.37i
6 UK, 2 CAU, Ind: 5 UKi
12   **Montana Jackson** 2.12.93 (2y, 12) 12.69, 12.72w '16   12.44, 12.41, 12.22w, 12.12; 12.66i, 12.44i, 12.38i, 12.25i
2 South, 7 UK, WLP: -,3,3; Ind: 1 London, 4 UKi, 2 B.Univs
–   **Zara Asante** 7.7.82 (4y, -) 13.00i, 12.99 '13   12.57, 12.44, 12.30w, 12.22, 12.17, 12.17w
2 Middx, 6 LI, 4 BIG, 1 South. 9 UK, 4 CAU, WLP: -,4,2
–   **Shanara Hibbert** 22.3.93 (2y, 12) 12.51 '16   12.87, 12.45, 12.31, 12.18, 12.16, 12.16; 12.23i
1 East, 8 UK, 5 CAU; Ind: 2 South, 2 London, 7 UKi
Outdoors only : 7 Matthews, 8 Fajemisin, 9 Gargan, 10 Wilder, 11 Asante, 12 Jackson
For the first time since 2010 no British woman exceeded 14m and there was rather thin competition at the top: the 2016 no. 1 Samuel competed only four times, the no. 2 Gutzmore only five times, and while Proctor had the top mark of the year, 13.82, she only had two TJ competitions in 2017. The most prolific competitors were Barrett and Ogbeta, who respectively added 24cm and 66cm to their pb, the latter taking the UK title and with European Junior bronze also securing top ranking. Russell won the UK indoor title but did not compete outdoors. New (wind-legal) records were set for 50th at 11.62 and 129 women over 11m.

SHOT

1   **Rachel Wallader** 1.9.89 (9y, 1) 17.53 '16   17.47, 17.08, 16.90, 16.87, 16.81, 16.70; 17.43i, 17.35i, 17.25i; 17.18i
4 Eur Throws, 1 LI, 1 UK, dnq 23 WCh, WLP: 1,-,1; Ind: 1 Vienna, 1 UKi, 3 B'ham GP. dnq 10 EI
2   **Amelia Strickler** 24.1.94 (2y, 5) 16.91i, 16.72 '15   17.13, 16.94, 16.85, 16.79, 16.72, 16.61; 17.12i, 17.03i.
3 T'loosa, 2 All Ohio, 2 Mid American, dnq 17= NCAA-E, 10 ET, 2 UK, 2 WLP (3), 1 CAU, 1 MI, 6 WUG; Ind: 2 Mid-Ami, 10 NCAAi
3   **Sophie McKinna** 31.8.94 (8y, 2) 17.14 '16   17.03, 16.62, 16.61, 16.27, 16.23, 16.10; 16.74i, 16.73i
5 E.Throws, 2 LI, 2 WLP (2), 1 South, 3 UK, 2 MI; Ind: 1 South, 2 UKi, 5 B'ham, 1 Capes
4   **Eden Francis** 19.10.88 (14y, 4) 17.24 '12   16.52, 16.29, 16.22, 16.19, 16.02, 15.88
1 BIG, 4 UK, 2 CAU, 4 MI, WLP: 2,1,3
5   **Adele Nicoll** 28.9.96 (6y, 3) 16.34 '16   16.27, 16.25, 16.24, 16.21, 15.90, 15.85; 16.09i, 15.93i
3 Eur U23 Throws, 1 B.Univs, 8 Halle, 3 LI, 1 Welsh, 1 Eng-23, 5 UK, 6 Székes, 3 CAU, 3 MI, WLP: -,3,4; Ind: 3 UKi, 1 WInti
6   **Divine Oladipo** 5.10.98 (2y, 10) 14.05 '16   16.64, 16.03, 16.00, 15.92, 15.82, 15.73; 16.41i
11 Florida R, 6 Penn R, 2 AAC, dnq 21= NCAA-E, 2 Eng-J, 3 Mannheim, 5 WLP (3), 4 EJ; Ind: 1 AAC, 1 ECAC
7   **Sophie Merritt** 9.4.98 (2y, 9) 14.10 '16   14.59, 14.56, 14.41, 14.40, 14.26, 14.15; 14.55i
5 OVC, 5 LI, 3 BIG, 2 South-J, 3 Eng-J, 7 UK, 1 WInt, 5 MI, WL1: -,1,1; Ind: 3 OVC
8   **Danielle Opara** 22.6.95 (6y, 7) 14.62 '15   13.42, 13.29, 13.28, 13.26, 12.96; 14.47i, 14.17i, 13.89i
4 B.Univs, 6 LI, 3 Eng-23, 5 UK, 1 CAU, 9 UK, WLP: 4,9,10; Ind: 2 South-i, 5 B.Uns-i, 5 UKi
9   **Sarah Omoregie** 2.4.00 (1y, -) 12.29i '16   14.12, 13.90, 13.81, 13.53, 13.47, 13.40; 13.85i
2 Welsh, 4 Eng-J, 6 UK, 1 WL1 (1): (3kg: 2 Comm-Y 16.74, 1 LI 16.28)
10   **Kirsty Yates** 14.5.93 (7y, 6) 16.42 '14   14.00, 13.71, 13.60   1 Scot, WLP: -,6,9
11   **Michella Obijiaku** 6.11.97 (1y, -) 13.69 '16   14.08, 13.38, 13.38, 13.27, 12.82; 13.12i, 12.95i 3 Sun Belt; Ind: 18 Sun Belt i
12   **Jo Rowland** 29.12.89 (2y, -) 13.71i '14,13.47 '13   13.64, 13.49, 13.39, 13.31, 13.18, 13.15; 13.47i, 13.20i
1 Scot, WL2: 1.-.1; 6 UKi
Outdoors only : 7 Omoregie, 8 Yates, 9 Obijiaku, 10 Opara
Wallader is top for the fourth successive year. Strickler's fine form, capped by WUG 6th, takes her to second ahead of, McKinna. Francis beat Nicoll 4-1. The top six (all in the top 50 in Europe) are well clear of the rest, led by the prolific Merritt.

DISCUS

1   **Jade Lally** 30.3.87 (11y, 1) 65.10 '16   62.15, 59.87, 58.70, 58.24, 58.19, 58.14   1/2 Sydney, 2 Canberra,
11 Halle, 1 LI, 1 South, 10 ET, 1 UK, 6 Gothenburg, 1 Dublin, nt CAU, dnq 19 WCh, 9 B'ham DL; WLP: -,1,1
2   **Kirsty Law** 11.10.86 (12y, 3) 57.79 '12   54.91, 54.71, 54.54, 54.27, 54.19, 53.92
2 LI, 2 BIG, 1 2 UK, 6/6 Leiria, 1 MI, 1 Scot, 1 Guernsey, WL2: 1,1,1
3   **Eden Francis** 19.10.88 (13y, 2) 59.78 '11   57.53, 57.44, 54.88, 54.17, 52.15, 51.73
4 BIG, 1 Mid, nt UK, 2 CAU, 4 MI; WLP: 1,4,3
4   **Amy Holder** 4.8.96 (4y, 4) 53.43 '16   54.27, 53.05, 52.94, 52.84, 52.47, 52.36
1 Lough-w, 7 E.Throws-23, 3 LI, 1 BIG, 4 South, 1 Eng-23, 2 LIC 24/6, 5 UK, 9 EU23, 1 CAU, 5 MI, WLP: 3,3,-
5   **Shadine Duquemin** 4.11.94 (7y, 6) 53.44 '14   51.79, 51.67, 51.31, 51.25, 50.85, 50.09
4 LI, 3 BIG, 2 South, 3 LIC 24/6, 3 UK, 8/8 Leiria, 3 MI, 2 Guernsey, WLP: 4,5,5

6   **Phoebe Dowson** 17.4.94 (7y, 5) 51.12 '14   51.87, 51.80, 51.47, 51.04, 50.47, 49.96
      2 Lough-w, 3 South, 4 UK, 3 Dublin, 3 CAU, WL1: 2,2,1
7   **Divine Oladipo** 5.10.98 (2y, 7) 48.11 '16   53.13, 51.59, 50.63, 50.50, 50.30, 49.44
      11 Florida R, 2 Penn R, 3 AAC, dnq 13 NCAA-E, 1 Eng-J, 3 Mannheim, 4 WLP (3), dnq 17 EJ
8   **Kathryn Woodcock** 29.4.97 (2y, 9) 47.45 '16   50.64, 50.63, 50.50, 49.78, 49.62, 48.97
      5 Lough-w, 1 B.Univs, 5 LI, 2 Eng-23, 6 CAU, WL1: 1,1,-
9   **Sophie Mace** 7.10.98 (3y, 10) 47.35 '15   45.76, 45.47, 44.85, 44.84, 44.65, 44.41
      4 Lough-w, 5 BIG, 8 UK, 1 E.Sch, 1 Sth IC-J, WLP: 8,7,7
10   **Samantha Milner** 28.12.92 (4y, -) 51.07 '13   48.35, 46.42, 45.09, 44.95, 44.71, 44.50
      6 B.Univs, 5 South, 5 CAU, WLP: 12,14,6
11   **Tara Park** 4.4.95 (1y, -) 48.09 '16   47.22A, 45.45, 44.67, 44.49, 43.45, 43.36
      22 Mt.SAC, 9 MWC, 9 UK, 2 Scot
12   **Luisa Chantler-Edmond** 7.6.99 (1y, -) 45.25 '16   46.48, 45.80, 45.72, 44.55, 44.27, 43.80
      3 Lough-w, 6 LI, 1 South-J, 3 Eng-J, 4 E.Sch-I, 10 UK, 8 MI
-    **Jemma Ibbetson** 3.9.97 (2y, 9) 40.66 '16   46.85, 44.46, 44.13, 43.81, 43.01, 42.50
      2 Yorks, 1 North, 4 Eng-23, 7 UK, 7 CAU

Lally is clearly top for the seventh successive year, but it was disappointing that her only 60m plus competition was her first., in Australia in February. Francis had the better top marks, but was beaten 3-0 by Law, so they swap positions. The top three have each had over a decade in the rankings (with Francis tenth successive top three ranking, Lally ninth and Law seventh) and Holder retains fourth place. Oladipo, now at the University of Connecticut, made the biggest advance, adding 5.02m to her pb, but her overall level was not quite enough to move her ahead of Duquemin and Dowson. There is a big gap after Woodcock in 8th, but 50 women over 40m is the most since 1997.

HAMMER
1   **Sophie Hitchon** 11.7.91 (11y, 1) 74.54 '16   73.97, 73.68, 73.05, 72.32, 72.02, 70.96
      2 Kawasaki, 4 Prague, 6 Szczecin, 5 ET, 4 Ostrava 1 UK, 7 WCh, 4 Warsaw, 2 B'ham DL
2   **Rachel Hunter** 30.8.93 (5y, 4) 66.30 '14   66.46, 64.74, 64.21, 63.67, 63.27, 61.45
      1 Lough-w, 5B E.Throws, 1 Scot-W, 3 LI, 2 UK, 1 LEAP
3   **Carys Parry** 24.7.81 (17y, 3) 66.80 '14   65.32, 65.01, 64.25, 63.52, 63.24, 62.72
      4 Budapest, 1 Welsh, 1 WInt, 2 LEAP, 2/1Leiria
4   **Sarah Holt** 17.4.87 (13y, 2) 68.97 '15   63.41, 63.40, 61.53, 61.31, 59.38, 55.38
      1 LI, 3 UK, 3 W.Int, 3 LEAP, 2 CAU, 4 MI
5   **Myra Perkins** 21.1.92 (8y, 9) 63.11 '14   62.97, 62.54, 62.10, 61.90, 61.48, 61.46
      1 Lough 9/4, 2 LI, 2 Lough 24/5, 5 Budapest, 4 UK, 2 WInt, 4 LEAP, 3 CAU, 1 MI, 1 Scot, 1/1 H.Circle, WLP: 2,-,1
6   **Susan McKelvie** 15.6.85 (14y, 5) 65.03 '11   62.07, 61.80, 61.75, 61.59, 61.08, 60.36
      5 Lough 9/4, 4 LI, 2 NI, 5 LEAP, 1 CAU, 2 MI, 2 Scot, WLP: 1,1,2
7   **Lucy Marshall** 28.11.81 (5y, 7) 62.12 '16   62.74, 62.32, 61.35, 61.32, 61.29, 61.11
      3 Lough-w, 2 Lough 9/4, 1 Lough 24/5, 3 BIG, 2 Welsh, 1 Mid, 1 B.Masters-35, 5 UK, 6 LEAP, 5 CAU, WLP: 4,2,3
8   **Christina Jones** 5.4.90 (5y, 6) 63.98 '15   62.96, 60.91, 60.18, 60.13, 59.86, 59.62
      4 Lough-w, 4 Lough 9/4, 1 West, 3 Welsh, 4 WInt, 7 LEAP, 6 CAU, WL1: -,1,1
9   **Jessica Mayho** 14.6.93 (3y, 10) 61.02 '16   63.05, 61.62, 61.00, 60.54, 60.53, 60.43
      5 Lough-w, 3 Lough 9/4, 1 Yorks, 5 LI, 2 Cork, WLP: 3,-,4
10   **Philippa Wingate** 12.5.93 (2y, 11) 59.14 '16   59.76, 59.46, 59.06, 58.77, 58.61, 58.60
      1 South, 7 UK, 1 Sth IC, 4 CAU, WLP: 5,9,5
11   **Kayleigh Presswell** 14.3.95 (1y, -) 57.09 '16   59.38, 59.18, 58.82, 58.60, 58.39, 58.30
      5 BIG, 2 South, 2 Eng-23, 6 UK, 9 CAU, 2/2 H.Circle, WL2: 1,-,1
12   **Hayley Murray** 13.9.89 (5y, -) 58.39 '13   59.57, 59.49, 57.67, 57.66, 57.19, 57.11
      8 Lough 9/4, 2 BIG, 1 NI, 2 Mid, 8 UK, 3 Cork, 8 CAU, 3 MI, 3 Scot, WL3: 1,1,1

Hitchon, the one British woman thrower in world class, is top for the seventh successive year. All her ten competitions were over 67.5m, thus well ahead of the rest. Holt had a limited season and slips from her 2nd of 2015-16, overtaken by Parry and Hunter. Parry now has event records of 17 years and a 18-year ranking span. Perkins and McKelvie make it three Scots in the top six. There is a bit of a gap after the nine 60m plus women. Murray is 12th, as in her previous four years in the rankings!

JAVELIN
1   **Laura Whittingham** 6.6.86 (12y, 3) 60.68 '10   55.74, 54.88, 53.64, 53.30, 53.01, 52.07
      1 LI, 2 Carnival, 1 Mid, 1 UK, 1 WInt, 1 CAU, 2 MI, 3 Rovereto, 1 Guernsey, WLP: -,1,1
2   **Joanna Blair** 1.3.86 (14y, 2) 57.44 '16   53.52, 52.63, 52.47, 51.74, 51.31, 50.63
      1 Carnival, 1 South, 9 ET, 2 UK, WLP: -,1,1
3   **Hannah Johnson** 14.6.94 (2y, 8) 49.82 '16   51.57, 49.74, 49.34, 47.93, 47.92, 46.51
      1 B.Univs, 2 WLP (1), 2 LI, 6 Carnival, 3 South, 7 UK, 3 CAU
4   **Emma Hamplett** 27.7.98 (5y, 4) 52.27 '16   51.02, 49.47, 49.43, 49.35, 49.25, 49.19
      5 LI, 5 & 1J Carnival, 2 WLP (2), 1 Mid-J, 1 Eng-J, 3 UK, 2 Brussels, 5 CAU, 5 MI
5   **Kike Oniwinde** 6.10.92 (6y, 5) 54.71 '14   50.45, 49.86, 49.45, 48.70, 48.02, 44.66
      3 LI, 4 Carnival, 6 Jena, WL1: 1,1,-

6   **Laurensa Britane** 18.5.87 (2y, - ex LAT) 48.29 '14   49.13, 49.01, 48.30, 48.00, 47.59, 47.46
     1 Lough-w, 7 Carnival, 4 South, 6 UK, 6 CAU, 4 MI, WLP: 1,3,2
7   **Bethan Rees** 27.9.99 (2y, 12) 46.80 '16   49.56, 48.80, 48.60, 48.00, 47.61, 46.43
     2J Lough-w, 4 LI, 2J Carnival. 1 Welsh, 2 Mid-J, 2 Eng-J, 4 UK, 1 E.Sch, 2 WInt, 3B/4 Leiria, 6 MI, 1 Welsh-J, WLP: 3,4,-
8   **Natasha Wilson** 5.11.95 (4y, 9) 47.90 '13   47.68, 46.19, 45.40, 45.14, 45.14
     9 Carnival, 1 North, 1 Eng-23, 5 UK
9   **Eloise Meakins** 26.1.93 (5y, 10) 52.32 '12   46.70, 46.40, 45.45, 44.92, 44.73, 43.95
     2 South, 8 UK, 7 CAU, WL2: 3,2,3
10   **Louise Lacy** 28.4.89 (2y, -) 48.87 '15   49.24, 47.39, 46.33, 45.62, 43.71, 43.06
     2 WL2 (1), 1 Essex, 8 Carnival, 5 South, 11 UK, 4 CAU
11   **Kelly Bramhald** 10.6.94 (2y, -) 48.79 '12   49.56, 45.00, 43.03, 42.86, 42.74, 42.01
     10 Carnival, 2 CAU, 7 MI, WLP: 8,-,4
12   **Rebekah Walton** 20.9.99 (1y, -) 44.81 '14   46.59, 45.48, 44.62, 43.12, 42.88, 42.31
     5 WLP (1), 6J Carnival, 3 Mid-J, 3 Eng-J, 2 E.Sch, 1 YDL. 3 EJ Clubs
There was a new number one after the 13 years at the top by Goldie Sayers – Whittingham, who had previously ranked 2nd four times (2008-11) and 3rd four times, had a lead of over 2m in the ranking lists in 2017 and overtakes Blair, whose ranking is subject to a possible drugs suspension. Johnson beat Hamplett 2-1, Britane 3-1 v Rees. Rosie Semenytsh narrowly missed a ranking after eleven years in the top ten. Freya Jones threw 47.67 in her one competition.

HEPTATHLON
1   **Katarina Johnson-Thompson** 9.1.93 (9y, 2) 6682 '14   4 Götzis 6691, 5 WCh 6558, dnf FRA Ch
2   **Niamh Emerson** 22.4.99 (1y, -) -0-   4 EJ 6013, 1 ENG 5801
3   **Katie Stainton** 8.1.95 (4y, 5) 5777(w), 5763 '16   7 Kladno 5873, 7 EU23 5836, 5 Florence 5766, 2 Woerden 5664, dnf ENG
4   **Jessica Taylor-Jemmett** 27.6.88 (7y, 3) 5913(w) '16
     7 Talence 5767, 6 Eur Cup 5702, 2 ENG 5674, 6 Woerden 4841 (dnf 800m), dnf ESP Ch
5   **Joanne Rowland** 29.12.89 (7y, 6) 5702 '13
     13 Florence 5614, 3 Arona 5573, 10 Eur Cup 5518, 1 Hexham 5512, 1 Yorks 5421
6   **Holly McArthur** 20.12.99 (1y, -) -0-   11 EJ 5687, 5 Arona 5478, 1J ENG 5332, dnf Scot
7   **Lucy Turner** 14.2.97 (1y, -) 4958 '16   3 ENG 5436, 2 Hexham 5398,18 Eur Cup 5199
8   **Zoe Hughes** 1.2.98 (1y, -) 4971 '16   6 Mt.SAC 5444,1 Heps 5332w, dnf Eur Cup
9   **Jade O'Dowda** 9.9.99 (1y, -) -0-   1 E.Sch 5442, 1 ES-Mid 5120, 1J Woerden 5070
10   **Ellen Barber** 5.12.97 (1y, -) 5014 '16   4 Woerden 5344, 4 Hexham 5088, 1 Scot 5082w
11   **Elise Lovell** 9.5.92 (4y, 7) 5284 '16   4 ENG 5330, dnf South
12   **Jessica Tappin** 17.5.90 (5y, -) 5770 '14   5 ENG 5301
–   **Olivia Montez Brown** 22.5.96 (2y, 9) 5254w/5187 '16   4 NCAA II 5251, 1 Mankato 5140, 16 Mt.SAC 4937
nr   **Moe Sasegbon** 16.9.91 (1y, -) NGR 5582 '16   1 NI 5367, 1 South 5254, 5 Woerden 5244
Johnson-Thompson is top for the third time (after 2013-14). It was disappointing that she missed a World medal through her high jumping in London, but while she has yet to reach her potential, she nonetheless ranks fifth in the world. Emerson continued her brilliant progress and became Britain's 15th 6000 point heptathlete with 4th in the European Juniors and another year in junior ranks. Another brilliant prospect is McArthur, who set three Scottish U20 records and O'Dowda makes it three girls born in 1999 in the rankings. Much promise then, but only 18 women over 5000 points is disappointing, although 10th best at 5344 is the best since 1998.

WALKS
Priority is given to form at the standard international distance of 20 kilometres, although performances at 10km are also considered.
1   **Bethan Davies** 7.11.90 (6y, 6) 44:59 16, 1:33:48 '16
     10km: 45:53+, 46:04+, 1 Coventry 46:07 , 46:31+, 46:36+, 47:05+, 6 Canberra 47:05.97t/49:40.95t
     20km: 3 Leeds (2 RWA) 1:33:04, 29 WCh 1:33:10, 6 Adelaide 1:35:47, 22 Eur Cup 1:36:04, dq Lugano
2   **Gemma Bridge** 17.5.93 (2y, 4) 50:33 '16
     10km: 45:52+, 46:42+, 2 Coventry (1 ENG) 47:07, 47:09+, 47:21+, 47:49+
     20km: 1 Leeds (RWA) 1:32:33, 14 Eur Cup 1:34:24, 10 Podébrady 1:35:03; 40 WCh 1:36:04, 8 Lugano 1:37:36
3   **Heather Lewis** 25.10.93 (7y, 2) 46:59 '14, 1:38:22 '16   10km: 6 Coventry 47:17, 47:51+, 1 Hillingdon 49:17, 50:27+
     20km: 9 Lugano 1:37:39, 2 Gleina 1:40:06, 5 Leeds (RWA) 1:42:29, 39 Podébrady 1:44:41
4   **Erika Kelly** 6.12.92 (1y, 8) 52:39 '16, 1:59:27 '16   10km: 1 RWA 48:54, 6 Coventry 52:17
     20km: 4 Leeds (RWA) 1:41:27, 2 Douglas 1:41:52/1:47:35
5   **Hannah Hunter** 7.10.82 (x, 8) 51:37 '16, 1:53:47 '16   10km: 1 Isle of Man 51:45
     20km: 1 Douglas 1:47:17, 8 Leeds (RWA) 1:47:29, 1 Coventry 1:52:44
nr   **Tatyana Gabellone** ITA 20.10.84 46:24 '15, 1:34:42 '15   10km: 5 Coventry 47:10, 1 Acquaviva 47:41.49t
     20km: 4 ITA Ch 1:39:02
All those ranked set pbs, with Bridge making a splendid start at the 20k distance. She beat Davies 3-1, but the latter was well ahead at the Worlds, so maintains her top ranking. Erika Kelly made a major advance to rank for the first time, but the depth sadly fell so that only five were ranked compared to eight in 2016.

2017 LISTS - MEN

60 Metres - Indoors

6.54	Richard Kilty			2.09.89	1	Belgrade, SRB	4	Mar
6.57					1	Stockholm, SWE	28	Jan
6.58					3	Birmingham	18	Feb
6.58					1s1	Belgrade, SRB	4	Mar
6.60					2	Val-de-Reuil, FRA	6	Feb
6.61					1h2	Belgrade, SRB	4	Mar
6.62					1s2	Sheffield	11	Feb
6.62					2h2	Birmingham	18	Feb
6.56	Chijindu Ujah			5.03.94	2	Torun, POL	10	Feb
6.61					2h2	Torun, POL	10	Feb
6.62					3h2	Birmingham	18	Feb
6.64					6	Birmingham	18	Feb
6.57	James Dasaolu			5.09.87	1	Berlin, GER	10	Feb
6.60					1h2	Berlin, GER	10	Feb
6.63					5	Düsseldorf, GER	1	Feb
6.63					4h1	Birmingham	18	Feb
6.65					1h2	Düsseldorf, GER	1	Feb
6.65					7	Birmingham	18	Feb
6.57	Andrew Robertson			17.12.90	1	Sheffield	11	Feb
6.60					1A2	London (LV)	29	Jan
6.63					1A1	London (LV)	29	Jan
6.63					3s2	Belgrade, SRB	4	Mar
6.64					1A2	Loughborough	14	Jan
6.64					1s1	Sheffield	11	Feb
6.58	Joseph Dewar	U23		27.01.96	1A1	Eton	5	Mar
6.59	Kyle de Escofet	U23		4.10.96	2h1	Mondeville, FRA	4	Feb
6.61					1	Nantes, FRA	21	Jan
6.61					4	Mondeville, FRA	4	Feb
6.64					1A2	Birmingham	15	Jan
6.65					4	Sheffield	11	Feb
6.65					4h2	Birmingham	18	Feb
6.59	Theo Etienne	U23		3.09.96	2	Sheffield	11	Feb
6.59					1s2	Belgrade, SRB	4	Mar
6.62					1h3	Belgrade, SRB	4	Mar
6.63					2A2	London (LV)	29	Jan
6.64					1A1	London (Nh)	25	Jan
6.64					2A1	London (LV)	29	Jan
6.65					1s3	Sheffield	11	Feb
6.62	Reece Prescod	U23		29.02.96	5	Torun, POL	10	Feb
6.62	Dwain Chambers	V35		5.04.78	3	Sheffield	11	Feb
6.64					1A2	London (LV)	1	Jan
6.64A					2	Tignes, FRA	5	Jan
6.65					4	Val-de-Reuil, FRA	6	Feb
6.65A	Nethaneel Mitchell-Blake			2.04.94	1	Albuquerque, USA	4	Feb
6.65					2h2	Nashville, USA	24	Feb
(10)								
6.65	John Otugade	U23		24.01.95	2s2	Sheffield	11	Feb
	46 performances to 6.65 by 11 athletes							
6.66	Harry Aikines-Aryeetey			29.08.88	1	Boston (R), USA	28	Jan
6.67	Emmanuel Stephens			13.03.93	1q1	London (LV)	14	Jan
6.68	Samuel Osewa			17.04.91	4A2	London (LV)	29	Jan
6.68	Imran Rahman			5.07.93	6	Sheffield	11	Feb
6.69	Danny Talbot			1.05.91	6h2	Birmingham	18	Feb
6.70	Ronnie Wells	U23		27.03.96	1A2	London (CP)	1	Feb
6.71	David Omoregie	U23		1.11.95	1h1	Cardiff	15	Jan
6.71	Roy Ejiakuekwu	U23		2.02.95	5	Fayetteville, USA	28	Jan
6.73	Tremayne Gilling			27.07.90	2A2	London (CP)	1	Feb

6.73	Ojie Edoburun	U23	2.06.96	3h1	Torun, POL	10	Feb
6.74	Rion Pierre		24.11.87	1s2	London (LV)	14	Jan
6.74	Allan Hamilton		14.07.92	1	Glasgow	28	Jan
6.74	Adam Thomas	U23	15.04.95	1A1	Loughborough	28	Jan
6.74	Leon Reid		26.07.94	1	Athlone, IRL	19	Feb
6.75	Aidan Syers		29.06.83	1A1	Eton	5	Feb
6.75	Ade Adewale		27.08.93	1A1	London (Nh)	15	Feb
6.75	Greg Rutherford		17.11.86	2A1	Eton	5	Mar
6.76	Edmond Amaning		27.10.93	2s2	London (LV)	14	Jan
6.77	Romell Glave	U20	11.11.99	1	London (LV)	14	Jan
(30)							
6.77	Samuel Miller		2.09.93	4s2	Sheffield	11	Feb
6.77	Timothy Duckworth	U23	18.06.96	1H2	College Station, USA	10	Mar
6.78	Reuben Arthur	U23	12.10.96	2A2	London (Nh)	25	Jan
6.78	Deji Tobais		31.10.91	2A1	Eton	5	Feb
6.78	Dom Ashwell	U20	13.06.99	1	Sheffield	25	Feb
6.79	Brandon Murray	U23	20.09.97	3A2	London (Nh)	25	Jan
6.79	Anax DaSilva	U23	27.06.95	2	Cardiff	5	Feb
6.79	Alex Murdock		29.08.91	3A1	London (Nh)	15	Feb
6.80	Confidence Lawson		5.09.90	1h3	London (LV)	14	Jan
6.80	James Williams		1.10.91	4h1	Vienna, AUT	28	Jan
(40)							
6.80	Oliver Bromby	U20	30.03.98	2	Sheffield	25	Feb
6.81	Cameron Tindle	U20	5.06.98	2	Glasgow	28	Jan
6.81	Timothy Fasipe	U23	20.06.97	2A1	Loughborough	28	Jan
6.81	Samuel Landsborough		11.11.92	1A1	Manchester (SC)	29	Jan
6.81A	Ben Shields		17.01.94	2h1	Albuquerque, USA	24	Feb
6.82	Christopher Stone	U23	8.04.95	1	Cardiff	10	Dec
6.83	Judah Simpson		28.07.92	1	Birmingham	12	Feb
6.83	Nick Stewart	U20	22.06.98	2A2	London (Nh)	15	Feb
6.83	Rio Mitcham	U20	30.08.99	3	Sheffield	25	Feb
6.84	Kieran Showler-Davis		14.11.91	1h5	London (LV)	14	Jan
(50)							
6.84	Jack Lawrence	U23	2.07.96	2	Birmingham	12	Feb
6.84	Temitope Adeyeye	U20	12.03.98	1B2	London (Nh)	15	Feb
6.85	Subomi Onanuga		12.06.93	5	London (LV)	14	Jan
6.85	Elliott Hurley	U23	22.09.95	1s4	Sheffield	17	Feb
6.85	Leroy Cain	U23	16.05.95	2	London (LV)	19	Mar
6.86	Scott Bajere		12.05.92	3s2	London (LV)	14	Jan
6.86	David Bolarinwa		20.10.93	1A2	London (CP)	18	Jan
6.86	Marvin Popoola	U23	5.09.95	1	London (LV)	1	Feb
6.86	Omar Grant		6.12.94	4B1	Eton	5	Feb
6.86	Callum Davies	U20	30.11.98	1	Cardiff	11	Feb
(60)							
6.87	Mutara Sheriff		12.10.94	2q2	London (LV)	14	Jan
6.87	Samir Williams	U20	6.01.00	2	London (LV)	14	Jan
6.87	Brandon Mingeli	U20	7.09.00	1	London (LV)	6	Dec
	6.98	U17		1A2	London (LV)	21	Jan
6.87	Dan Putnam		30.12.91	1A1	Loughborough	9	Dec
6.88	Idris Ojuriye		27.12.84	2A2	Sutton	8	Jan
6.88	Omari Barton-Ellington		5.01.90	2q1	London (LV)	14	Jan
6.88	Joshua Olawore	U23	31.07.95	2	London (LV)	1	Feb
6.88	Joshua Brown		27.12.94	3	Cardiff	5	Feb
6.88	Luke Dorrell	U23	23.01.97	5	Sheffield	17	Feb
6.88	Raphael Bouju	U17	15.05.02	1	Sheffield	25	Feb
(70)							
6.88	Ryan Gorman	U20	9.04.98	1	Sheffield	2	Dec
6.89	Daniel Gardiner		25.06.90	1	Sheffield	4	Jan
6.89	Cameron Starr	U23	26.03.96	2A2	London (CP)	18	Jan
6.89	Tommy Ramdhan	U23	28.11.96	6A2	London (Nh)	25	Jan
6.89	Niall Bevan	U20	14.10.98	6	Sheffield	25	Feb
6.90	Thomas Williams	U23	28.01.96	3h1	Cardiff	15	Jan

6.90		Samuel Ige	U23	29.01.96	2s1	Sheffield	17	Feb
6.90		Adam Clayton	U17	26.09.00	2	Sheffield	25	Feb
6.90		Shevhone Lumsden	U17	14.09.00	1	London (LV)	19	Mar
6.91		Damien Powell	U23	29.12.95	3q3	London (LV)	14	Jan
	(80)							
6.91		Lemarl Freckleton		19.03.92	4	Cardiff	5	Feb
6.91		Jordan Gill	U23	18.02.95	3s2	Sheffield	17	Feb
6.91		Michael Olsen	U20	22.03.99	1A2	London (LV)	3	Dec
6.92		Jonathan Grant		26.05.93	5	Kent, USA	14	Jan
6.92		Eden Davis	U20	1.03.99	1s4	London (LV)	14	Jan
6.92		Nicholas Atwell		9.04.86	1	Sutton	19	Feb
6.92		Maxwell Brown	U20	23.11.99	2s1	Sheffield	25	Feb
6.92		Camron Lyttle	U20	28.05.99	1	London (LV)	19	Mar
6.92		Daniel Beadsley	U23	28.02.97	2	Cardiff	10	Dec
6.92		Leon Greenwood	U23	13.06.97	1rB	Cardiff	10	Dec
	(90)							
6.93		Caleb Downes	U23	12.08.97	3A1	Loughborough	28	Jan
6.93		Michael Warner		29.11.90	3A2	Loughborough	28	Jan
6.93		Jack Dearden	U23	24.09.97	6B2	London (LV)	29	Jan
6.93		Jay Raradza	U23	17.06.96	2s1	Birmingham	12	Feb
6.94		Jona Efoloko	U20	23.09.99	1A1	Manchester (SC)	8	Jan
6.94		Isaiah Adekanmbi		7.07.85	1A2	Manchester (SC)	29	Jan
6.94		Kristian Jones	U20	10.03.98	3	London (LV)	1	Feb
6.94		Toby Olubi		24.09.87	3	Sutton	19	Feb
6.94		Nicholas Walsh	U23	27.07.97	1A1	Manchester (SC)	19	Mar
6.94		Shemar Boldizar	U20	24.01.99	1s3	London (LV)	6	Dec
	(100)							
6.95		Grant Plenderleith		15.03.91	2s2	Glasgow	28	Jan
6.95		Chad Miller	U20	31.03.00	1A1	London (LV)	29	Jan
6.95		Zanson Plummer	U23	27.03.97	2B2	London (Nh)	15	Feb
6.95		Kesi Oludoyi	U20	2.09.98	3B2	London (Nh)	15	Feb
6.95		Mark Hanson	V35	13.05.81	4	London (LV)	19	Mar

Additional Under 20 (1-24 above)

6.96		Connor Wood		25.11.98	1	Sheffield	14	Jan
6.96		Regan O'Connell		28.11.98	4s2	Sheffield	25	Feb
6.97		Derrius Greenaway		14.04.99	3	Sheffield	4	Jan
6.97		Andrew Morgan-Harrison		9.03.98	2h4	Sheffield	25	Feb
6.97		Daniel Afolabi	U17	6.09.00	3	Cardiff	5	Mar
6.97		Bailey Wright		14.11.00	2A1	London (LV)	3	Dec
		7.12	U17		2h2	London (LV)	7	Jan
	(30)							
6.98		Zachary Stapleton		1.06.98	3s4	London (LV)	14	Jan
6.98		Marlon Hogg-Williams		27.10.98	1C2	Eton	5	Feb
6.99		Khalil Bruney		13.06.98	2E1	London (LV)	2	Jan
6.99		Bret Okeke		16.02.99	2A2	Birmingham	15	Jan
6.99		Jeremiah Azu	U17	15.05.01	1	Cardiff	11	Feb
6.99		Charles Hilliard		21.09.99	4s1	Sheffield	25	Feb
6.99		Jake Binns		5.11.98	5	London (LV)	6	Dec
7.00		Matthew Treston		20.07.98	4rC	Flagstaff, USA	13	Jan
7.00		Enzo Madden		24.08.98	3h5	Sheffield	25	Feb

Additional Under 17 (1-7 above)

7.02		Kyle Reynolds-Warmington		28.02.02	2	London (LV)	7	Jan
7.02		Dominic Ogbechie		15.05.02	3	London (LV)	7	Jan
7.03		Alex Truscott		8.10.00	1s3	London (LV)	7	Jan
	(10)							
7.05		Ollie Sprio		10.03.01	5	Sheffield	25	Feb
7.07		Joshua Oshunrinde		17.10.01	2s1	London (LV)	7	Jan
7.08		Ben Higgins		14.11.00	1r13A	Manchester (SC)	29	Jan
7.09		Iwan Robinson-Booth		27.09.00	2	Cardiff	11	Feb
7.10		Michael Miller		4.12.00	1B2	London (CP)	1	Feb
7.11		Dylan DaCosta		6.04.01	2	Sutton	18	Feb
7.11		Toby Makoyawo		10.05.02	2h2	London (LV)	19	Mar
7.11		Matthew Elliott		5.09.00	1	London (LV)	19	Mar

7.12		William Adeyeye	4.03.01	1rD2	London (Nh)	25	Jan
7.12		Radix Mulawarman	20.10.00	4	Cardiff	11	Feb
	(20)						
7.13		Jody Smith	17.09.00	1	Birmingham	11	Feb
7.13		Micah Forbes-Agyepong	31.01.02	3	London (LV)	19	Mar
7.13		Kyle Walton	13.11.01	1	Gateshead	16	Nov
7.14		Rami Miller	11.09.00	1s1	Sutton	18	Feb
7.14		Owain Lloyd Hughes	5.12.01	3rB	Cardiff	10	Dec
7.14		Louis Appiah-Kubi	22.09.02	1rB	Manchester (SC)	17	Dec
7.15		Thomas Cooney	10.11.00	1	London (LV)	4	Feb
7.16		Ben Sutton	10.08.01	2B1	London (CP)	18	Jan
7.16		Callum McKay	3.10.00	2	Glasgow	28	Jan
7.16		Rory Kuypers	20.10.00	2	London (LV)	19	Mar

Under 15

7.09		Jaleel Roper	8.02.03	1	Sheffield	25	Feb
7.17		Tyreece Rankin	14.09.02	2	London (LV)	7	Jan
7.18		Louis Appiah-Kubi	22.09.02	2	Sheffield	25	Feb
7.19		Joseph Harding	31.10.02	1G2	London (Nh)	15	Feb
7.19		Jamall Gregory Walters	30.09.02	3	Sheffield	25	Feb
7.24		Tyler Panton	30.04.03	1s2	Sheffield	25	Feb
7.30		Nicholas Shaw	13.10.02	6	Sheffield	25	Feb
7.35		Andrew Nicolaou	13.11.02	3s1	Sheffield	25	Feb
7.36		Graig Anya-Joseph	6.10.03	1h3	London (LV)	4	Feb
7.36		David Adeleye	7.09.02	1	London (LV)	19	Mar
	(10)						
7.36		Zachary Nwogwugwu	10.04.04	1A1	London (LV)	3	Dec
7.40		Nathan Scott	9.08.03	1	Cardiff	11	Feb
7.40		Ben Basten	2.08.03	1	Birmingham	19	Mar
7.41		Benjamin To	7.09.02	7	Sheffield	25	Feb
7.42		Levi Liston	28.06.03	1h2	London (LV)	19	Mar
7.42		Daniel Rajis	26.07.03	2	London (LV)	19	Mar
7.43		Lewis Cant	10.10.02	1s1	Glasgow	12	Feb
7.44		Tariq Wild	22.04.03	2h1	London (LV)	19	Mar
7.45		Samuel Jones	7.09.02	2h4	Sheffield	25	Feb

Under 13

7.87	Ayo Salako	9.11.04	2r13B	Sutton	8	Jan

Foreign

6.56	*Sean Safo-Antwi (GHA)*		31.10.90	1	*Athlone, IRL*	15	Feb
6.71	*Josh Swaray (SEN)*		2.02.86	6	*Athlone, IRL*	15	Feb
6.80	*Adeseye Ogunlewe (NGR)*		30.08.91	1s2	*Sheffield*	17	Feb
6.87	*Dean Adams (IRL)*		14.03.90	3	*Athlone, IRL*	19	Feb
6.88	*Jimmy Thoronka (SLE)*		6.06.94	1rD1	*London (Nh)*	15	Feb
6.91	*Desmond Ojei (NGR)*	U23	11.02.97	2s1	*Glasgow*	28	Jan
6.92	*Antonio Infantino (ITA)*		22.03.91	5A1	*London (Nh)*	25	Jan
6.92	*Christian Robinson (IRL)*	U23	16.08.96	1	*Athlone, IRL*	29	Jan
6.92	*Jonathan Browning (IRL)*		16.12.93	3	*Athlone, IRL*	10	Feb

60 Metres - Outdoors

6.67	0.8	Confidence Lawson	5.09.90	2	Melbourne, AUS	9	Feb
6.76	0.2	Kieran Showler-Davis	14.11.91	3	Melbourne, AUS	4	Feb

100 Metres

9.97	0.0	Chijindu Ujah	5.03.94	1	Zürich, SUI	24	Aug
9.98	-0.3			1	Rabat, MAR	16	Jul
10.02	-0.2			1	Rome, ITA	8	Jun
10.02	0.2			2	Oslo, NOR	15	Jun
10.02	0.3			1	London (O)	9	Jul
10.02	0.7			4	Monaco, MON	21	Jul
10.07	-0.2			2h4	London (O)	4	Aug
10.08	-0.2			1	Birmingham	20	Aug
10.10	0.1			2	Torrance, USA	15	Apr
10.12	0.4			4s3	London (O)	5	Aug

Mark	Wind	Name	Cat	DOB	Pos	Location	Day	Month
9.99	0.6	Nethaneel Mitchell-Blake		2.04.94	2	Columbia, USA	13	May
10.03	1.6				4s3	Eugene, USA	7	Jun
10.07	0.4				1	Columbia, USA	13	May
10.17	0.1				4	Torrance, USA	15	Apr
10.18	-0.3				3	Rabat, MAR	16	Jul
10.03	0.0	Reece Prescod	U23	29.02.96	3h3	London (O)	4	Aug
10.05	-0.2				2s2	London (O)	5	Aug
10.09	1.2				1	London (Nh)	7	May
10.09	0.0				1	Birmingham	1	Jul
10.11	0.5				1	Gavardo, ITA	4	Jun
10.17	-0.8				7	London (O)	5	Aug
10.18	1.5				1h1	London (Nh)	7	May
10.20	0.2				7	Oslo, NOR	15	Jun
10.06	0.3	James Dasaolu		5.09.87	2	London (O)	9	Jul
10.11	0.0				2	Birmingham	1	Jul
10.11	-0.2				2	Birmingham	20	Aug
10.12	0.3				3	Marseille, FRA	3	Jun
10.12	0.2				5	Lausanne, SUI	6	Jul
10.13	0.3				2h6	London (O)	4	Aug
10.16	-0.1				1	Geneva, SUI	10	Jun
10.16	0.8				1s3	Birmingham	1	Jul
10.18	0.4				3r1	Gainesville, USA	28	Apr
10.19	0.9				4	Rovereto, ITA	29	Aug
10.22	-0.5				5s1	London (O)	5	Aug
10.24	0.2				6	Brussels, BEL	1	Sep
10.25	-0.7				1	Manchester	26	May
10.08	1.8	Adam Gemili		6.10.93	1	Azusa, USA	14	Apr
10.10	1.0				3	Berlin, GER	27	Aug
10.13	0.2				4	Oslo, NOR	15	Jun
10.13	0.0				8	Zürich, SUI	24	Aug
10.18	1.1				1	Mannheim, GER	22	Jul
10.21	0.3				4	Zagreb, CRO	29	Aug
10.12	-1.6	Zharnel Hughes	U23	13.07.95	1rB	Kingston, JAM	11	Mar
10.13	-0.2				3	Birmingham	20	Aug
10.12	0.2	Ojie Edoburun	U23	2.06.96	1	Bedford	17	Jun
10.14	0.0				1	Bydgoszcz, POL	14	Jul
10.15	0.7				1A1	London (LV)	24	May
10.20	0.5				4	Gavardo, ITA	4	Jun
10.21	0.0				4	Birmingham	1	Jul
10.22	1.0				1s2	Birmingham	1	Jul
10.22	0.7				1s1	Bedford	29	Jul
10.25	1.4				1s1	Bedford	17	Jun
10.25	-0.2				5	Birmingham	20	Aug
10.13	1.6	Harry Aikines-Aryeetey		29.08.88	1	Loughborough	22	Jul
10.13	1.0				5	Berlin, GER	27	Aug
10.15	1.4				2h1	Prague, CZE	5	Jun
10.16	0.3				4	London (O)	9	Jul
10.18	0.4				5	Prague, CZE	5	Jun
10.19	0.8				2s3	Birmingham	1	Jul
10.19	-0.2				4	Birmingham	20	Aug
10.20	1.5				5	Turku, FIN	13	Jun
10.20	0.0				3	Birmingham	1	Jul
10.21	0.8				2h2	Turku, FIN	13	Jun
10.21	-0.7				1	Villeneuve d'Ascq, FRA	24	Jun
10.25	0.8				1h4	Loughborough	22	Jul
10.18	0.5	Richard Kilty		2.09.89	3	Gavardo, ITA	4	Jun
10.20	1.5				4	Turku, FIN	13	Jun
10.23	0.3				7	London (O)	9	Jul
10.18	0.2	Reuben Arthur	U23	12.10.96	2	Bedford	17	Jun
10.20	1.9				1s3	Bedford	17	Jun

10.21	2.0	Deji Tobais		31.10.91	1rD	Gainesville, USA	28	Apr
10.21	2.0	Kyle de Escofet	U23	4.10.96	1	Aarhus, DEN	2	Jun
10.22	1.0				1rA	Loughborough	21	May
10.22	-0.1				2	Geneva, SUI	10	Jun
10.21	1.6	Samuel Osewa		17.04.91	3	Bydgoszcz, POL	2	Jun
10.24	1.6				4	Loughborough	22	Jul
10.21	1.0	Romell Glave	U20	11.11.99	1	Bedford	17	Jun
10.21	1.6	Joel Fearon		11.10.88	2	Loughborough	22	Jul
10.24	0.4				2rC	Lucerne, SUI	11	Jul
10.25	1.0				3	Bilbao, ESP	24	Jun
10.23	0.5	Andrew Robertson		17.12.90	1h1	Regensburg, GER	11	Jun
10.23	0.0				1	Regensburg, GER	11	Jun
10.24	1.2				2	London (Nh)	7	May
10.23	1.6	Adam Thomas	U23	15.04.95	3	Loughborough	22	Jul
10.25	-0.1	Joseph Dewar	U23	27.01.96	1s2	Bedford	17	Jun
		85 performances to 10.25 by 18 athletes						
10.30	0.7	John Otugade	U23	24.01.95	2A1	London (LV)	24	May
10.31	1.0	Oliver Bromby	U20	30.03.98	2	Bedford	17	Jun
	(20)							
10.31	0.8	Dwain Chambers	V35	5.04.78	3s3	Birmingham	1	Jul
10.32	0.9	Samuel Gordon		5.10.94	1	Cardiff	10	Jun
10.33	1.0	Theo Etienne	U23	3.09.96	4rA	Loughborough	21	May
10.33	1.2	Rechmial Miller	U20	27.06.98	2A2	London (LV)	24	May
10.33	2.0	Leon Reid		26.07.94	2	Aarhus, DEN	2	Jun
10.36	1.0	Dom Ashwell	U20	13.06.99	3	Bedford	17	Jun
10.36	0.4	Omar Grant		6.12.94	1A2	London (LV)	21	Jun
10.37	0.8	Confidence Lawson		5.09.90	1s2	Bedford	29	Jul
10.37	0.3	Danny Talbot		1.05.91	6	Zagreb, CRO	29	Aug
10.38	1.9	Samuel Miller		2.09.93	1	Loughborough	7	Jun
	(30)							
10.39	1.5	Ade Adewale		27.08.93	4h1	London (Nh)	7	May
10.40	1.9	Kieran Showler-Davis		14.11.91	1	London (LV)	16	Aug
10.41	1.9	Rio Mitcham	U20	30.08.99	1	Loughborough	1	Apr
10.41	0.8	Anax DaSilva	U23	27.06.95	1rB	Oordegem, BEL	27	May
10.41	-0.4	Roy Ejiakuekwu	U23	2.02.95	2h6	Birmingham	1	Jul
10.41	1.6	Christopher Stone	U23	8.04.95	2h3	Bedford	29	Jul
10.42	0.8	Cameron Tindle	U20	5.06.98	1	Grangemouth	22	Apr
10.42	-0.6	Emmanuel Stephens		13.03.93	3	London (Nh)	29	May
10.44	0.2	Leroy Cain	U23	16.05.95	5	Bedford	17	Jun
10.45	1.8	Michael Olsen	U20	22.03.99	1A1	Glasgow (S)	9	Aug
	(40)							
10.46	1.0	Eden Davis	U20	1.03.99	4	Bedford	17	Jun
10.46	0.2	David Bolarinwa		20.10.93	5A1	London (LV)	21	Jun
10.46	1.1	Ronnie Wells	U23	27.03.96	1h1	Loughborough	22	Jul
10.47	1.7	Dan Putnam		30.12.91	1	Nuneaton	13	May
10.47	0.9	Imran Rahman		5.07.93	3h3	Birmingham	1	Jul
10.47	1.1	Greg Cackett		14.11.89	2h2	Loughborough	22	Jul
10.51	1.5	Caleb Downes	U23	12.08.97	1rB	Loughborough	22	Apr
10.51	0.7	Timothy Duckworth	U23	18.06.96	1D1	Bydgoszcz, POL	15	Jul
10.51	0.5	Thomas Williams	U23	28.01.96	4s3	Bedford	29	Jul
10.53	1.2	Nick Stewart	U20	22.06.98	6	London (Nh)	7	May
	(50)							
10.53	-0.8	Aidan Syers		29.06.83	1rC	Loughborough	21	May
10.53	1.2	Kristian Jones	U20	10.03.98	1rD	Loughborough	21	May
10.53	1.0	Kesi Oludoyi	U20	2.09.98	6	Bedford	17	Jun
10.54	0.4	Edmond Amaning		27.10.93	6A2	London (LV)	21	Jun
10.55	1.5	Tommy Ramdhan	U23	28.11.96	8h1	London (Nh)	7	May
10.55	0.8	Nicholas Walsh	U23	27.07.97	8s3	Birmingham	1	Jul
10.55	0.9	James Williams		1.10.91	1rC	Loughborough	22	Jul
10.56	1.9	Jacob Fincham-Dukes	U23	12.01.97	1rC	Fort Worth, USA	15	Apr
10.56	1.8	Kaie Chambers-Brown	U20	26.09.99	2s2	Bedford	17	Jun

10.56	1.0	Camron Lyttle	U20	28.05.99	7	Bedford	17	Jun
(60)								
10.56	1.1	Nick Prentice	U23	29.04.97	3h1	Loughborough	22	Jul
10.57	1.3	James Griffiths		30.07.92	1rE	Loughborough	21	May
10.57	1.3	Jona Efoloko	U20	23.09.99	2rE	Loughborough	21	May
10.57	0.5	Omari Barton-Ellington		5.01.90	1B1	London (LV)	21	Jun
10.57	0.8	Dewi Hammond		11.02.94	4s2	Bedford	29	Jul
10.58	0.5	Kieran Daly		28.09.92	2B1	London (LV)	21	Jun
10.58+		Samir Williams	U20	6.01.00	1r1	Gateshead (Q)	8	Sep
	10.61		0.3		1	Birmingham	8	Jul
10.59	1.8	Ben Shields		17.01.94	8	Azusa CA, USA	14	Apr
10.59	1.1	Thomas Somers	U23	28.04.97	2	Loughborough	26	Aug
10.61	0.0	Marvin Popoola	U23	5.09.95	2	Bedford	15	Jul
(70)								
10.62	0.1	Gabriel Odujobi		15.07.87	5rB	Coral Gables, USA	7	Apr
10.62	1.3	Zanson Plummer	U23	27.03.97	3rE	Loughborough	21	May
10.62	1.4	Joshua Brown		27.12.94	2h4	Cardiff	10	Jun
10.62	1.3	Samuel Ige	U23	29.01.96	3h7	Birmingham	1	Jul
10.63	1.8	Daniel Afolabi	U17	6.09.00	1	Birmingham	8	Jul
10.64	0.2	Theo Campbell		14.07.91	3	Munich, GER	3	Jun
10.64	1.8	Shevhone Lumsden	U17	14.09.00	2	Birmingham	8	Jul
10.64	1.7	Samuel Landsborough		11.11.92	3h7	Bedford	29	Jul
10.65	-0.2	Elliott Powell	U23	5.03.96	3rC	Bedford	15	Jul
10.65	0.6	Jeremiah Azu	U17	15.05.01	1	Bedford	26	Aug
(80)								
10.66	1.3	Michael Warner		29.11.90	5h7	Birmingham	1	Jul
10.66	0.3	Maxwell Brown	U20	23.11.99	3	Birmingham	8	Jul
10.68	0.9	Jamal Rhoden-Stevens		27.04.94	2	Frauenfeld, SUI	13	May
10.69	-0.5	Kyle Ennis		9.08.91	1	Bedford	8	Apr
10.69	1.3	Lemarl Freckleton		19.03.92	4rE	Loughborough	21	May
10.69	0.5	Jordan Broome	U23	4.12.96	1rB	Bedford	15	Jul
10.69	1.9	Daniel Obeng		20.05.93	3h2	Bedford	29	Jul
10.69	1.7	Jack Lawrence	U23	2.07.96	4h7	Bedford	29	Jul
10.70	1.6	Nathan Gilbert	U23	2.03.95	4h1	Bedford	17	Jun
10.70	1.8	Kade Thomas	U23	22.11.96	2A1	Glasgow (S)	9	Aug
(90)								
10.71	2.0	Brandon Murray	U23	20.09.97	4h4	Clermont, USA	15	Apr
10.71	-0.4	Grant Plenderleith		15.03.91	1	Grangemouth	13	May
10.71	1.8	Adam Clayton	U17	26.09.00	3s2	Bedford	17	Jun
10.71	1.4	Elijah Skervin		1.04.92	3	Lisbon, POR	17	Jun
10.71	-0.3	Mutara Sheriff		12.10.94	3	Nivelles, BEL	24	Jun
10.71	1.7	Jahde Williams	U23	14.01.97	6h7	Bedford	29	Jul
10.72	0.6	Luke Dorrell	U23	23.01.97	2h1	Bedford	29	Apr
10.72	1.4	Daniel Beadsley	U23	28.02.97	6s1	Bedford	17	Jun
10.73	1.2	John Lane		29.01.89	2D3	Azusa, USA	12	Apr
10.73	0.0	Benjamin Snaith	U23	17.09.95	1	Peterborough	13	May
(100)								
10.73	1.9	Peter Shand		5.12.91	3	Loughborough	7	Jun
10.73	0.0	Byron Robinson		12.09.87	1h1	Bruay La Buissiere, FRA	4	Jul
10.73	1.8	Raphael Bouju	U17	15.05.02	3	Birmingham	8	Jul
10.74	0.6	Brandon Mingeli	U17	7.09.00	3	Bedford	26	Aug
10.75	-0.8	Scott Bajere		12.05.92	5rC	Loughborough	21	May
10.75	0.0	Jordan Kirby-Polidore		26.01.93	3B2	London (LV)	21	Jun
10.75	1.0	Toby Olubi		24.09.87	3h1	Bedford	29	Jul
10.75+		Charlie Dobson	U20	20.10.99	2r1	Gateshead (Q)	8	Sep

Additional Under 20 (1-23 above)

10.77	1.8	Tyler Williams		21.05.98	4s2	Bedford	17	Jun
10.77	0.3	Derrius Greenaway		14.04.99	4	Birmingham	8	Jul
10.78	1.0	Andrew Morgan-Harrison		9.03.98	1	Manchester (SC)	10	Jun
10.79	1.8	Tyrese Johnson-Fisher		9.09.99	5s2	Bedford	17	Jun

10.80	0.8	Callum Davies		30.11.98	1rB	Cardiff	10 Jun
10.80	0.5	Rhys Turner		25.02.99	2	Reading	25 Jun
10.81	1.8	Arron Owen		14.07.98	6s2	Bedford	17 Jun
	(30)						
10.81	-0.5	Enzo Madden		24.08.98	1rD	Manchester (SC)	20 Aug
10.82	1.8	Franklin Fenning		17.05.00	7s2	Bedford	17 Jun
10.82	1.8	Bailey Wright	U17	14.11.00	4	Birmingham	8 Jul
10.84	1.8	Ronan Rawlings	U17	2.03.01	5	Birmingham	8 Jul
10.86	1.7	Robinson Okumu		24.11.99	4s1	Birmingham	7 Jul

Additional Under 17 (1-8 above)

10.89	-0.7	Joshua Oshunrinde		17.10.01	2	London (LV)	8 Apr
10.89	0.6	Jody Smith		17.09.00	7	Bedford	26 Aug
	(10)						
10.93	0.5	Dylan DaCosta		6.04.01	1	Kingston	14 May
10.96		Ben Higgins		14.11.00	1	Stoke-on-Trent	1 Apr
10.96	1.8	Harry Handsaker		12.01.02	7	Birmingham	8 Jul
11.01	-1.1	Adam Cross		12.11.00	1	Peterborough	13 May
11.03		William Andoh		5.09.01	1h3	Lignano, ITA	5 Jul
11.03	0.1	Daniel Brooks		6.12.00	2	Yate	23 Jul
11.04	0.3	Kyle Reynolds-Warmington		28.02.02	2A2	Bromley	12 Jun
11.04	1.8	Niall Price		4.04.01	8	Birmingham	8 Jul
11.04	1.6	Dominique Olaniyi		10.08.01	1rB	London (He)	26 Aug
11.06	0.8	Iwan Robinson-Booth		27.09.00	5rB	Cardiff	10 Jun
	(20)						
11.07	0.0	Cameron Sprague		10.09.00	1	Exeter	17 Jun
11.09	1.9	Thomas Evans		21.09.00	3	Loughborough	1 Apr
11.10	1.0	Dylan Baldock		31.01.01	1	Sutton	15 Apr
11.10	-0.2	Sam Bennett		2.02.01	1h2	Chelmsford	13 May
11.10	-2.0	Alex Truscott		8.10.00	2rB	London (He)	29 Jul
11.11	0.0	Lee Richards		3.09.00	3	Watford	31 May
11.11	0.0	Owain Lloyd Hughes		5.12.01	1	Brecon	26 Aug
11.12	1.5	Micah Forbes-Agyepong		31.01.02	1	Reading	25 Jun
11.12	1.3	Jaiden Aaron		15.11.00	1rB	London (Wil)	15 Aug
11.12	-1.4	Ethan Brown		9.05.01	3	London (CP)	19 Aug

Under 15

10.94	0.5	Graig Anya-Joseph		6.10.03	1s1	Bedford	26 Aug
10.97	0.5	Jaleel Roper		8.02.03	1s2	Bedford	26 Aug
11.05	0.5	Tariq Wild		22.04.03	2s1	Bedford	26 Aug
11.11	0.5	Tyler Panton		30.04.03	2s2	Bedford	26 Aug
11.11	0.5	Louis Appiah-Kubi		22.09.02	3s2	Bedford	26 Aug
11.12		Loreni Jorge		9.01.03	1	Nuneaton	9 Sep
11.18	-0.8	Andrew Nicolaou		13.11.02	1	London (LV)	14 May
11.19	-0.8	Tyreece Rankin		14.09.02	2	London (LV)	14 May
11.22	0.0	Ben Basten		2.08.03	2s2	Birmingham	7 Jul
11.25	0.0	Brandon Rochester		6.10.02	3s2	Birmingham	7 Jul
	(10)						
11.25	0.5	Jacob Nelson		8.09.02	3s1	Bedford	26 Aug
11.28		Jamall Gregory Walters		30.09.02	1	Manchester (Str)	29 May
11.30	1.5	David Adeleye		7.09.02	4s1	Birmingham	7 Jul
11.31	0.5	Ethan Hall		9.02.03	4s1	Bedford	26 Aug
11.32	1.5	Edward Sesay		18.11.02	5s1	Birmingham	7 Jul
11.33	-0.1	Joseph Harding		31.10.02	1	Woodford	2 Jul
11.34		Brody Hinson		26.11.02	2	Nuneaton	9 Sep
11.36		Anthony Douglas		2.07.03	1	Birmingham	17 Jun
11.36		Oluwatobi Oke		10.10.02	3	Nuneaton	9 Sep
11.41		Lewis Cant		10.10.02	1	Gateshead	13 May
	(20)						
11.45	1.5	Nicholas Shaw		13.10.02	6s1	Birmingham	7 Jul
11.46		Emmanuel Fatimehin		20.12.02	1h1	Hemel Hempstead	10 Jun
11.46	-1.0	Remi Jokosenumi		15.02.04	4	London (CP)	20 Aug

11.46	0.0	Julian Priest		24.09.02	1h2	Oxford (H)	9	Sep
11.49		Oliver Preest		2.07.03	1h1	Kingston	10	Jun
11.49	0.7	Matthew Houlden		2.10.02	4h4	Birmingham	7	Jul
11.50	1.5	Josh McKeown		5.03.03	1s1	Glasgow (S)	20	Aug

wind assisted

9.90	4.4	Harry Aikines-Aryeetey		(10.13)	1	Clermont, USA	15	Apr
		9.97	3.3		1rB	Gainesville, USA	28	Apr
		10.16	2.1		3	Loughborough	21	May
		10.17	3.6		1h14	Clermont, USA	15	Apr
9.93	4.4	Ojie Edoburun	U23	(10.12)	2	Clermont, USA	15	Apr
		9.99	4.9		1h11	Clermont, USA	15	Apr
		10.06	2.1		1	Loughborough	21	May
		10.07	3.3		3rB	Gainesville, USA	28	Apr
9.95	2.4	Chijindu Ujah		(9.97)	3	Eugene, USA	27	May
		9.98	2.8		1s1	Birmingham	1	Jul
10.03	2.4	Adam Gemili		(10.08)	7	Eugene, USA	27	May
		10.24	2.4		1h3	Mannheim, GER	22	Jul
10.08	2.3	Zharnel Hughes	U23	(10.12)	1	Kingston, JAM	15	Apr
10.13	2.1	Danny Talbot		(10.37)	2	Loughborough	21	May
10.15	2.2	Prescod	U23	(10.03)	2h3	Gavardo, ITA	4	Jun
10.15	2.5	Andrew Robertson		(10.23)	1	Manchester (SC)	16	Aug
		10.18	3.3		1rB	Manchester (SC)	16	Aug
10.16	4.2	Roy Ejiakuekwu	U23	(10.41)	4h2	Austin, USA	25	May
		10.24	3.7		6q3	Austin, USA	26	May
10.19	5.8	Kieran Showler-Davis		(10.40)	1h15	Clermont, USA	15	Apr
10.20	2.8	Joel Fearon		(10.21)	2s1	Birmingham	1	Jul
		10.23	2.1		4	Loughborough	21	May
10.20	2.8	Samuel Osewa		(10.21)	3s1	Birmingham	1	Jul
10.20	2.8	Arthur	U23	(10.18)	4s1	Birmingham	1	Jul
10.21	2.3	Glave	U20	(10.21)	1s1	Bedford	17	Jun
		25 performances to 10.25 by 14 athletes						
10.26	4.0	Leon Reid		(10.33)	1A2	Waterford, IRL	13	May
10.28	2.2	Rechmial Miller	U20	(10.33)	1h2	Mannheim, GER	1	Jul
10.29	4.8	David Bolarinwa		(10.46)	1	London (LV)	7	Jun
10.30	6.5	Rio Mitcham	U20	(10.41)	1	Nuneaton	11	Jun
10.31	3.0	Dom Ashwell	U20	(10.36)	1s3	Bedford	17	Jun
10.34	2.1	Confidence Lawson		(10.37)	3	Lillebonne, FRA	17	Jun
10.35	6.3	Dan Putnam		(10.47)	1	Nuneaton	11	Jun
10.36	5.8	Emmanuel Stephens		(10.42)	4h15	Clermont, USA	15	Apr
10.36	4.8	Tommy Ramdhan	U23	(10.55)	2	London (LV)	7	Jun
10.36	4.6	Ronnie Wells	U23	(10.46)	1rC	Manchester (SC)	16	Aug
10.37	6.3	Elliott Powell	U23	(10.65)	2	Nuneaton	11	Jun
10.39	3.0	Kristian Jones	U20	(10.53)	2s3	Bedford	17	Jun
10.40	3.6	Nick Stewart	U20	(10.53)	1h2	London (Nh)	7	May
10.43	3.0	Michael Olsen		(10.45)	1	Glasgow (S)	19	Aug
10.44	3.4	Edmond Amaning		(10.54)	3r2	London (LV)	7	Jun
10.45	2.9	Aidan Syers		(10.53)	3h1	Castres, FRA	26	Jul
10.47	6.5	Kaie Chambers-Brown	U20	(10.56)	2	Nuneaton	11	Jun
10.47	2.5	Thomas Williams	U23	(10.51)	2	Belfast	5	Jul
10.50	3.5	Ben Shields		(10.59)	5	El Paso, USA	22	Apr
10.50	2.9	Thomas Somers	U23	(10.59)	1rB	London (LV)	16	Aug
10.53	2.5	Jona Efoloko	U20	(10.57)	1	Manchester (SC)	10	Jun
10.54	6.3	Jack Lawrence	U23	(10.69)	3	Nuneaton	11	Jun
10.54	3.0	Camron Lyttle	U20	(10.56)	4s3	Bedford	17	Jun
10.55	2.2	Joshua Brown		(10.62)	2A2	Cardiff	31	May
10.55	4.8	Daniel Obeng		(10.69)	3	London (LV)	7	Jun
10.55	3.0	Daniel Afolabi	U17	(10.63)	5s3	Bedford	17	Jun
10.55	5.2	Joshua Allaway		24.11.92	2	Visby, SWE	29	Jun
10.56	2.3	Omari Barton-Ellington		(10.57)	1r1	Yate	3	Jun

10.59	2.3	Samir Williams	U20	(10.58)	3s1	Bedford	17	Jun
10.60	2.3	Maxwell Brown	U20	(10.66)	4s1	Bedford	17	Jun
10.60	5.2	Tyler Johnson		24.12.91	3	Visby, SWE	29	Jun
10.61	4.8	Chad Miller	U20	31.03.00	5	London (LV)	7	Jun
10.63	2.6	Kyle Ennis		(10.69)	2	Yeovil	6	May
10.63	2.3	Scott Bajere		(10.75)	2r1	Yate	3	Jun
10.63	2.7	Owen Richardson	U20	5.09.98	1rD	London (LV)	16	Aug
10.64	2.8	Michael Ohioze	U23	6.02.95	1rB	Lisle IL, USA	8	Apr
10.65	3.4	Charlie Dobson	U20	(10.75)	1	Milton Keynes	19	Aug
10.67	3.3	Jamal Rhoden-Stevens		(10.68)	3h12	Clermont FL, USA	15	Apr
10.67	6.5	Bret Okeke	U20	16.02.99	3	Nuneaton	11	Jun
10.68	3.0	Adam Clayton	U17	(10.71)	2	Glasgow (S)	19	Aug
10.68	3.3	Jody Smith	U17	(10.89)	1	Nuneaton	19	Aug
10.69	2.7	Cameron Starr	U23	26.03.96	2rF	Gainesville FL, USA	28	Apr
10.69	4.8	Idris Ojuriye		27.12.84	6	London (LV)	7	Jun
10.69	2.8	Elijah Skervin		(10.71)	5h2	Birmingham	1	Jul
10.69	4.6	Kade Thomas	U23	(10.70)	3rC	Manchester (SC)	16	Aug
10.70	2.1	Grant Plenderleith		(10.71)	8	Loughborough	21	May
10.71	3.0	Joe Lonsdale	U20	4.01.00	6s3	Bedford	17	Jun
10.71	2.1	Joe Ferguson	U20	3.05.00	1h3	Grangemouth	26	Aug
10.72	2.3	Kane Howitt	U23	6.11.96	1	Nuneaton	13	May
10.72	2.3	Shad-Marc Aaron		20.12.94	2	Nuneaton	13	May
10.72	4.8	Niall Bevan	U20	14.10.98	7	London (LV)	7	Jun
10.72	6.3	Jordan Fairclough		8.05.91	4	Nuneaton	11	Jun
10.72	6.3	Rico Ewer	U23	24.09.97	5	Nuneaton	11	Jun
10.72	2.9	Daniel Oderinde	U23	9.09.96	2rB	London (LV)	16	Aug
10.72	2.2	Krishawn Aiken	U23	24.05.95	1rE	London (LV)	16	Aug
10.73	3.4	Joe McGrath	U23	9.09.97	4h3	New Haven CT, USA	6	May
10.74	6.5	Daniel Banks	U20	3.10.99	4	Nuneaton	11	Jun
10.74	3.1	Toby Olubi		(10.75)	1	London (TB)	22	Jul

Additional Under 20 (1-22 above)

10.76	3.0	Rowan Powell		8.12.98	1	Loughborough	25	Jun
10.78	2.4	Robinson Okumu		(10.86)	1	Exeter	17	Jun
10.79	3.0	Enzo Madden		(10.81)	7s3	Bedford	17	Jun
10.79	2.4	Matthew Alvarez		8.01.00	2	Exeter	17	Jun
10.79	2.1	Jacob Berkeley		11.09.98	1	London (He)	26	Aug
10.82	5.3	Jack Sumners	U17	25.10.00	1	Nuneaton	13	May
10.82	3.0	Praise Olatoke		23.06.00	3	Glasgow (S)	19	Aug
10.83	2.3	Greg Kelly		11.04.99	1	Grangemouth	9	Jun
10.85	2.3	Fraser Angus		13.01.00	2	Grangemouth	9	Jun
10.85	6.5	Charles Hilliard		21.09.99	5	Nuneaton	11	Jun
10.86	3.2	Cameron Newton		17.03.99	1	Portsmouth	14	May

Additional Under 17 (1-4 above)

10.89	3.8	Ben Higgins		(10.96)	1	Nuneaton	13	May
10.89	3.3	Ollie Sprio		10.03.01	2	Nuneaton	19	Aug
10.91	5.3	Jaime Nalus		15.10.00	2	Nuneaton	13	May
10.99	3.5	Cameron Sprague		(11.07)	1	Yate	13	May
11.02	3.2	William Adeyeye		4.03.01	6h4	London (Nh)	7	May
11.02	5.3	Oshay Williams		4.02.02	3	Nuneaton	13	May
11.02	2.1	Matthew Buckner		29.12.00	1	Bracknell	14	May
11.04	3.8	Kyle Calhoun		6.11.00	3	Nuneaton	13	May
11.10	3.7	Jack Guthrie		24.01.02	2	Aberdeen	6	May

Under 15

11.40	2.7	Julian Priest		(11.46)	2	Oxford (H)	9	Sep
11.41	2.2	Jacob Fairhurst		25.10.02	1	Nuneaton	13	May
11.41	3.8	Carter Staples		19.09.02	1	Cardiff	10	Jun
11.45	2.2	Jacob Spencer		10.11.02	1	Nuneaton	19	Aug

11.47	4.5	Edward Brown		23.01.03	1	Cambridge	24	Jun
11.48	5.3	Finley Ryves		23.10.02	2	Portsmouth	14	May
11.48	3.8	Thomas Payne		17.05.03	2	Cardiff	10	Jun

Hand timing

10.3	2.0	Rio Mitcham	U20	(10.41)	1r1	Nottingham	30	Apr
10.5		Mutara Sheriff		(10.71)	1	Twickenham	8	Jul
10.5		Samuel Landsborough		(10.64)	1	Blackburn	5	Aug
10.5w		Luke Giblin		15.09.86	1	Crawley	6	May
10.6		Enzo Madden	U20	(10.81)	2	Blackburn	5	Aug
10.7		Luke Dorrell	U23	(10.72)	1	Eton	1	Apr
10.7		Harry Flanagan	U20	24.09.99	1	Litherland	4	Jun
10.7		Regan O'Connell	U20	28.11.98	1	Doncaster	10	Jun
10.7w		Andrew Morgan-Harrison	U20	(10.78)	2	Crawley	6	May
10.7w		Gideon Okoh		5.10.93	3	Crawley	6	May
10.7w		Adam Cross	U17	(11.01)	1	Cambridge	18	Jun

Additional Under 20 (1-7 above)

10.8		Dylan DaCosta	U17	(10.93)	1-17	Dartford	30	Apr
10.8	1.9	Franklin Fenning		(10.82)	2	Nottingham	30	Apr
10.8	2.0	Daniel Banks		(10.74w)	1rB	Nottingham	30	Apr
10.8		Bailey Wright	U17	(10.82)	1-17	London (Cr)	23	Jul
10.8w		William Hughes	U17	28.01.01	1	Boston	7	Jun
10.8w		Ronan Rawlings	U17	(10.84)	2	Cambridge	18	Jun
10.8w		Joshua Oshunrinde	U17	(10.89)	4	Cambridge	18	Jun

Additional Under 17 (1-6 above)

10.9		Oliver Cresswell		17.11.00	1	Abingdon	3	Jun
10.9		Ollie Sprio		(10.89w)	1	Nuneaton	15	Jul
11.0		Thomas Casson		24.01.01	2	Andover	15	Apr
11.0		John Mayingi		18.04.01	h	Uxbridge	10	Jun
11.0		Alex Truscott		(11.10)	1=	Uxbridge	10	Jun
11.0		Joe Martin		27.08.01	1	Brighton	23	Jul
11.0w		Robert Thomas		16.10.01	1	Portsmouth	14	May
		11.1	-0.7		3	St. Clement JER	17	Jun
11.1		Cameron Bailey		10.12.00	1	Ipswich	14	May
11.1		Lee Richards		(11.11)	1	Milton Keynes	10	Jun
11.1		Joseph Eggleton		6.01.02	2	Milton Keynes	10	Jun
11.1		Jack Guthrie		24.01.02	1	Doncaster	25	Jun
11.1		Benjamin Holden		25.02.02	1	Morpeth	25	Jun
11.1		Destiny Ogali		6.09.01	1	London (LV)	13	Aug
11.1w	4.0	Kai Duddfield		14.06.02	2rB	Nottingham	30	Apr
11.1w		Luke Mather		17.09.01	2	Boston	7	Jun
11.1w		Keoghan Taylor		10.08.02	1	Douglas IOM	29	Jul

Under 15

11.0	Andrew Nicolaou		(11.18)	1	Uxbridge	10	Jun
11.1	Joseph Harding		(11.33)	2	Colchester	30	Jul
11.2	Brandon Rochester		(11.25)	2	Uxbridge	10	Jun
11.2	Lewis Cant		(11.41)	1	Morpeth	25	Jun
11.3	Ryan Wilson		1.01.03	1	Barrow	24	Jun
11.3	Julian Priest		(11.46)	1	Cambridge	16	Jul
11.3	Ethan Hall		(11.31)	1	Yate	30	Jul
11.4	George Sudderick		20.11.03	1	Bournemouth	20	May
11.4	Tyler Thomas		31.10.02	2	Morpeth	25	Jun
11.4	Thomas Eccleson		25.01.03	1	Middlesbrough	15	Jul

Under 13

11.99w		Timi Fatona		29.07.05	1	Glasgow (S)	19 Aug
12.08w	2.5	Reece Earle		1.10.04	1rF	London (Wil)	15 Aug
12.3					1	Hemel Hempstead	15 Jul
12.19w	4.3	Christopher Yang		9.12.04	1	Portsmouth	14 May
12.2		Agegnehu Zangrando		16.12.04	1	London (ME)	13 Jun
12.26	1.6	Tye Leo-Stroud		20.11.04	4rD	London (TB)	26 Aug
12.3		Ezekiel Taiwo		17.11.04	2	London (ME)	13 Jun
12.3		Archie Dowds		9.03.05	1	Manchester (SC)	18 Jun
12.3		Alex Nunn		11.12.04	1	Chelmsford	5 Jul
12.3		Arthur Powell		26.09.04	1	Shrewsbury	20 Jul
12.4		Mahki Reid		14.03.05	3	London (ME)	13 Jun
	(10)						
12.4		Aydan Tyrrell		18.09.04	2	London (ME)	18 Jun
12.4		Samuel Ball		18.10.04	1	Reading	6 Aug
12.4w		Thomas Chadwick		22.08.05	1	Douglas IOM	29 Jul

Foreign

10.05	2.0	David Lima (POR)		6.09.90	2h1	Madrid, ESP	14 Jul
10.16w	5.2	Antonio Infantino (ITA)		22.03.91	1h5	Clermont, USA	15 Apr
		10.36	1.2		4	London (Nh)	7 May
10.30	0.7	Adeseye Ogunlewe (NGR)		30.08.91	1	Abuja, NGR	14 Jul
10.31	1.2	Sean Safo-Antwi (GHA)		31.10.90	1A2	London (LV)	24 May
10.43	-1.2	Josh Swaray (SEN)		2.02.86	2	Riga, LAT	25 May
		10.32w	5.1		3	Fort Worth, USA	15 Apr
10.51	-0.6	Eugene Ayanful (GHA)		14.05.90	4	London (Nh)	29 May
10.56	-0.4	Dean Hylton (JAM)		15.09.90	1C2	London (LV)	21 Jun
10.56	1.4	Jason Smyth (IRL)		4.07.87	3	London (Nh)	2 Jul
10.57	0.0	Jimmy Thoronka (SLE)		6.06.94	1B2	London (LV)	21 Jun
10.64	1.7	Christian Robinson (IRL)	U23	16.08.96	3	Dublin (S), IRL	23 Jul
10.67	1.9	Marvin Bheka (ZIM)		29.01.87	1h3	Cardiff	10 Jun
10.68w	2.7	Umar Hameed (PAK)		24.02.89	1h1	Manchester (SC)	10 Jun
10.71	1.0	Adam McMullen (IRL)		5.07.90	2rB	Belfast	5 Jul
10.73	1.7	Dean Adams (IRL)		14.03.90	5	Dublin (S), IRL	23 Jul

With prosthetics

10.64	0.3	Jonathan Peacock	28.05.93	1-T44	London (O)	16 Jul

150 Metres

15.52w	2.8	Dwain Chambers	V35	5.04.78	1	London (Nh)	7 May

150 Metres Straight

15.22	0.4	Harry Aikines-Aryeetey		29.08.88	2	Manchester	26 May
15.26	0.0	Nethaneel Mitchell-Blake		2.04.94	2	Gateshead (Q)	9 Sep
15.43	0.4	Richard Kilty		2.09.89	3	Manchester	26 May
15.54		Romell Glave	U20	11.11.99	1r2	Gateshead (Q)	8 Sep

200 Metres

20.04	-0.4	Nethaneel Mitchell-Blake		2.04.94	1q2	Lexington, USA	27 May
	20.08	0.7			1h7	London (O)	7 Aug
	20.09	0.6			2	Columbia, USA	13 May
	20.15	0.1			1	Baton Rouge, USA	22 Apr
	20.18	0.8			1	Birmingham	2 Jul
	20.24	1.3			1s2	Eugene, USA	7 Jun
	20.24	-0.1			4	London (O)	10 Aug
	20.29	-3.1			2	Eugene, USA	9 Jun
	20.30	0.3			1h3	Lexington, USA	26 May
	20.30	-0.7			4	London (O)	9 Jul
	20.33	0.9			7	Brussels, BEL	1 Sep
	20.46	-0.1			5	Birmingham	20 Aug
	20.82	0.3			1h2	Birmingham	2 Jul

20.16	0.3	Danny Talbot		1.05.91	2h3	London (O)	7	Aug
	20.20	0.8			2	Birmingham	2	Jul
	20.31	1.4			1	Gavardo, ITA	4	Jun
	20.33	-0.7			6	London (O)	9	Jul
	20.36	-1.2			1	Hengelo, NED	11	Jun
	20.38	0.3			5s3	London (O)	9	Aug
	20.43	1.1			1h3	Birmingham	2	Jul
	20.47	-0.1			6	Birmingham	20	Aug
20.22	1.2	Zharnel Hughes	U23	13.07.95	4	Kingston, JAM	10	Jun
	20.22	0.4			3	Rabat, MAR	16	Jul
	20.27	0.9			6	Brussels, BEL	1	Sep
	20.29	1.2			3	Kingston, JAM	20	May
	20.33	-0.7			5	London (O)	9	Jul
	20.42	0.8			4	Birmingham	2	Jul
	20.43	0.6			4h6	London (O)	7	Aug
	20.64	2.0			1h1	Birmingham	2	Jul
	20.85	-0.3			7s2	London (O)	9	Aug
20.35	-0.4	Adam Gemili		6.10.93	3	Shanghai, CHN	13	May
	20.64	-1.2			3	Hengelo, NED	11	Jun
	20.79	1.3			1h4	Birmingham	2	Jul
	20.97	0.8			6	Birmingham	2	Jul
20.38	0.8	Leon Reid		26.07.94	3	Birmingham	2	Jul
	20.57	0.0			5	Lucerne, SUI	11	Jul
	20.59	1.1			2h3	Birmingham	2	Jul
	20.78	-1.5			3	Cork, IRL	18	Jul
	20.79	1.8			1	London (LV)	3	Jun
	20.81	1.8			1h1	Belfast	10	Jun
20.39	1.7	Chijindu Ujah		5.03.94	1	Tempe, USA	8	Apr
20.44	1.7	Miguel Francis	U23	28.03.95	4	Kingston, JAM	15	Apr
	20.46	-1.0			6	Kingston, JAM	13	May
20.51	1.4	Richard Kilty		2.09.89	3	Gavardo, ITA	4	Jun
	20.76	1.5			1	Loughborough	21	May
	20.86	-1.9			1	Gothenburg, SWE	11	Jul
20.65	1.7	Roy Ejiakuekwu	U23	2.02.95	4h6	Austin, USA	26	May
	20.82	1.6			6s3	Eugene, USA	7	Jun
	20.88	1.3			2h4	Birmingham	2	Jul
	20.93	0.2			5	Fayetteville, USA	5	May
20.73	1.7 (10)	James Dasaolu		5.09.87	7	Geneva, SUI	10	Jun
20.79	0.4	Samuel Miller		2.09.93	5	Villeneuve d'Ascq, FRA	25	Jun
	20.80	-0.1			1	Loughborough	22	Jul
	20.83	-0.3			1	Budapest, HUN	3	Jun
	20.85	2.0			2h1	Birmingham	2	Jul
	20.88	1.2			3h1	Villeneuve d'Ascq, FRA	23	Jun
	20.90	0.8			5	Birmingham	2	Jul
20.81	-0.9	Toby Harries	U20	30.09.98	1	Grosseto, ITA	22	Jul
	20.89	0.4			1s3	Grosseto, ITA	22	Jul
	20.90	2.0			3h1	Birmingham	2	Jul
20.86	1.8	Edmond Amaning		27.10.93	2	London (LV)	3	Jun
	20.95	1.8			1s1	Bedford	30	Jul
20.90	2.0	Thomas Somers	U23	28.04.97	1h4	Bedford	18	Jun
	20.92	0.3			2h2	Birmingham	2	Jul
20.92	-0.9	Jona Efoloko	U20	23.09.99	2	Grosseto, ITA	22	Jul
20.94	-0.4	Leroy Cain	U23	16.05.95	1	Bedford	18	Jun
20.94	1.3	Elliott Powell	U23	5.03.96	3h4	Birmingham	2	Jul
20.95	-0.1	Romell Glave	U20	11.11.99	1s1	Bedford	18	Jun
20.96	-0.1	Thomas Williams	U23	28.01.96	3	Ninove, BEL	15	Jul
	20.97	1.0			1	Cardiff	10	Jun
20.98	1.3	Kieran Showler-Davis		14.11.91	3rB	Tallahassee, USA	24	Mar
	20.98	1.8			2	London (LV)	16	Aug

2017 - M - 200

20.98	0.1	Benjamin Snaith	U23	17.09.95	1s2	Bedford	18	Jun

73 performances to 20.99 by 21 athletes

21.00	-1.0	Christopher Stone	U23	8.04.95	1s1	Bedford	18	Jun
21.03	2.0	Deji Tobais		31.10.91	4h1	Birmingham	2	Jul
21.04	1.7	Dwayne Cowan		1.01.85	1rB	Weinheim, GER	27	May
21.04	1.0	Tommy Ramdhan	U23	28.11.96	1	London (Nh)	2	Jul
21.05	0.9	Nick Stewart	U20	22.06.98	3	London (LV)	24	May
21.07	1.2	Rechmial Miller	U20	27.06.98	1rB	Kingston, JAM	6	May
21.09	1.7	James Williams		1.10.91	3	Lier, BEL	5	Aug
21.10	1.5	Cameron Tindle	U20	5.06.98	3	Loughborough	21	May
21.10	0.4	Kyle de Escofet	U23	4.10.96	1	La Roche-sur-Yon, FRA	5	Jul
	(30)							
21.11	0.4	Confidence Lawson		5.09.90	3	Lillebonne, FRA	17	Jun
21.13	0.9	John Otugade	U23	24.01.95	4	London (LV)	24	May
21.14	1.8	Dan Putnam		30.12.91	4	London (LV)	16	Aug
21.15	1.9	Kyle Ennis		9.08.91	1	Yeovil	6	May
21.19	-1.3	Grant Plenderleith		15.03.91	4rB	Oordegem, BEL	27	May
21.19	0.1	Kristian Jones	U20	10.03.98	1	Manchester (SC)	20	Aug
21.20	0.2	Charlie Dobson	U20	20.10.99	2	Birmingham	8	Jul
21.24	0.8	Rio Mitcham	U20	30.08.99	1	Loughborough	1	Apr
21.27	0.1	Marvin Popoola	U23	5.09.95	4s2	Bedford	18	Jun
21.27	1.7	James Gladman		3.06.93	1	Manchester (Str)	20	Jun
	(40)							
21.28		Michael Ohioze	U23	6.02.95	1	Joliet, USA	6	May
21.29	1.1	Jay Raradza	U23	17.06.96	3	Tergnier, FRA	25	May
21.29	0.5	Reuben Arthur	U23	12.10.96	4	London (Nh)	29	May
21.32	0.3	Connor Wood	U20	25.11.98	4h2	Birmingham	2	Jul
21.33	0.1	Max Mondelli	U23	28.10.95	5s2	Bedford	18	Jun
21.33		Michael Warner		29.11.90	1	Wakefield	25	Jun
21.34	-0.4	Chad Miller	U20	31.03.00	2s2	Bedford	18	Jun
21.37	0.9	Zanson Plummer	U23	27.03.97	5	London (LV)	24	May
21.37	2.0	Samuel Landsborough		11.11.92	6h1	Birmingham	2	Jul
21.40		Lee Thompson	U23	5.03.97	1	Preston	5	Aug
	(50)							
21.40	0.1	Jordan Broome	U23	4.12.96	1rB	Manchester (SC)	20	Aug
21.41	-0.1	Samuel Ige	U23	29.01.96	1	London (BP)	8	Jul
21.41	1.3	Allan Hamilton		14.07.92	1rB	Bedford	15	Jul
21.42	-1.2	Omar Grant		6.12.94	2	Swansea	3	Jun
21.42	1.3	David Bolarinwa		20.10.93	2rB	Bedford	15	Jul
21.45	-0.4	Seb Rodger		29.06.91	2	Oordegem, BEL	22	Aug
21.47	1.8	Emmanuel Stephens		13.03.93	4	London (LV)	3	Jun
21.47	1.2	Peter Shand		5.12.91	2	Loughborough	7	Jun
21.48	1.3	Jahde Williams	U23	14.01.97	2rB	Bedford	15	Jul
21.49	0.6	Conrad Williams	V35	20.03.82	2	Zeulenroda, GER	25	May
	(60)							
21.50	1.0	Jordan Kirby-Polidore		26.01.93	3	London (Nh)	2	Jul
21.51	0.7	Gabriel Odujobi		15.07.87	6	Coral Gables, USA	7	Apr
21.51	1.8	Oliver Bromby	U20	30.03.98	5	London (LV)	3	Jun
21.51	0.2	Rhys Turner	U20	25.02.99	3	Birmingham	8	Jul
21.52	1.1	Dominic Ogbechie	U17	15.05.02	1	Bedford	27	Aug
21.54	-0.4	Shayne Dewar	U20	12.11.98	4s2	Bedford	18	Jun
21.56	1.8	Daniel Trueman	U23	5.09.95	1	Yate	9	Apr
21.57	-2.1	Gerald Matthew	U23	10.07.97	1	Sheffield	6	May
21.57	1.2	Alex Beechey		8.06.91	2rC	Loughborough	21	May
21.58		David King		13.06.94	1	Bristol	20	Jun
	(70)							
21.58	-0.1	Andrew Robertson		17.12.90	5	Loughborough	22	Jul
21.59	-0.3	Byron Robinson		12.09.87	2	Budapest, HUN	3	Jun
21.62	1.1	Joel Richardson		30.12.93	1rD	Brussels, BEL	9	Jul
21.63	0.5	Jamal Rhoden-Stevens		27.04.94	1	London (He)	26	Aug
21.65	2.0	Krishawn Aiken	U23	24.05.95	1	Grangemouth	27	Aug

21.66	1.1	Adam Clayton	U17	26.09.00	2	Bedford	27	Aug
21.67	0.5	Joshua Parry	U23	31.10.97	1	Oxford (H)	24	May
21.68	0.0	Eden Davis	U20	1.03.99	1	Jerusalem, ISR	13	Jul
21.70	0.1	Iori Moore	U23	15.04.97	2rB	Manchester (SC)	20	Aug
21.71	1.0	Benjamin Paris	U20	6.10.99	3	Cardiff	10	Jun
	(80)							
21.72	0.7	Cameron Starr	U23	26.03.96	3h1	Bedford	18	Jun
21.73	0.8	Nicholas Pryce		10.11.92	2	Loughborough	24	May
21.73	1.0	Reality Osuoha	U20	7.07.00	2h3	Birmingham	8	Jul
21.73	-1.0	Omololu Abiodun		1.09.92	1	Watford	26	Jul
21.73	1.1	Daniel Afolabi	U17	6.09.00	3	Bedford	27	Aug
21.74	1.5	Ronnie Wells	U23	27.03.96	5	Waterford, IRL	13	May
21.75	0.2	Joe Lonsdale	U20	4.01.00	4	Birmingham	8	Jul
21.75	0.2	Micah Francis-Dwyer	U20	30.06.00	5	Birmingham	8	Jul
21.76	-0.7	Caleb Downes	U23	12.08.97	1rB	Loughborough	22	Apr
21.76	1.2	Alex Knibbs	U20	26.04.99	1	Derby	13	May
	(90)							
21.77	-3.0	Nik Kanonik		24.10.87	4s3	Bedford	1	May
21.77	1.1	Jason Hussain		17.10.86	1rB	Yate	3	Jun
21.77	0.4	Cameron Sprague	U17	10.09.00	1s2	Birmingham	8	Jul
21.77	0.9	Ishmael Smith-John	U23	10.04.95	1	Gillingham	9	Jul
21.77	0.6	Owen Richardson	U20	5.09.98	3	Bedford	15	Jul
21.77	-0.1	Kane Howitt	U23	6.11.96	1	Bromley	14	Aug
21.78	-0.5	Luke Dorrell	U23	23.01.97	1	London (LV)	8	Apr
21.78	1.2	Elliott Rutter	U23	20.08.95	4rC	Loughborough	21	May
21.78	1.1	William Kennedy	U23	21.10.97	2rB	Yate	3	Jun
21.78		Samir Williams	U20	6.01.00	2	London (CP)	10	Jun
	(100)							
21.79	-0.9	Sam Hazel	U23	7.10.96	2rD	London (Nh)	29	May
21.80	0.2	Alec Thomas	U23	22.11.96	2	Grangemouth	22	Apr
21.80	1.2	Freddie Owsley	U23	6.01.97	5rC	Loughborough	21	May
21.80	1.0	Theo Etienne	U23	3.09.96	5	London (Nh)	2	Jul

Additional Under 20 (1-28 above)

21.82	1.6	Andrew Morgan-Harrison		9.03.98	1h1	Manchester (SC)	11	Jun
21.83	-0.3	Michael Olsen		22.03.99	1	Sheffield	23	Jul
	(30)							
21.83	0.1	Alex Haydock-Wilson		28.07.99	3rB	Manchester (SC)	20	Aug
21.84	-0.2	Dylan DaCosta		6.04.01	1	Kingston	13	May
21.84	-0.9	Fraser Angus		13.01.00	4h2	Nassau, BAH	21	Jul
21.86	1.2	Matthew Alvarez		8.01.00	1	Exeter	17	Jun
21.86	2.0	William Hughes	U17	28.01.01	2h3	Bedford	27	Aug
21.86	2.0	Greg Kelly		11.04.99	2	Grangemouth	27	Aug
21.89	1.2	Tyler Williams		21.05.98	3h4	Bedford	18	Jun
21.89	-0.6	Ben Matsuka-Williams		28.03.98	1rC	London (LV)	5	Jul
21.90	-1.3	Ryan Gorman		9.04.98	1h5	Bedford	30	Apr
21.93	-0.4	Regan O'Connell		28.11.98	6s2	Bedford	18	Jun
21.94	-0.2	Shemar Boldizsar		24.01.99	2	Chelmsford	14	May
	(40)							
21.94	1.2	Robinson Okumu		24.11.99	2	Exeter	17	Jun
21.95	-0.5	Camron Lyttle		28.05.99	2	London (LV)	8	Apr
21.95		Keano-Elliott Paris-Samuel		11.05.99	4	London (CP)	10	Jun

Additional Under 17 (1-6 above)

21.96	1.1	Jody Smith		17.09.00	5	Bedford	27	Aug
21.99	1.1	Adam Cross		12.11.00	6	Bedford	27	Aug
22.01	0.4	Dylan Baldock		31.01.01	2s2	Birmingham	8	Jul
22.12	2.0	Cameron Bailey		10.12.00	3h3	Bedford	27	Aug
	(10)							
22.16	2.0	Ben Smith		5.06.01	4h3	Bedford	27	Aug
22.17		Kyle Calhoun		6.11.00	1	Derby	10	Sep
22.18	0.2	Thomas Evans		21.09.00	1	Nottingham	8	Apr

22.19	1.7	Shevhone Lumsden	14.09.00	1rB	London (Nh)	7	May
22.19	1.4	Matthew Buckner	29.12.00	3s1	Birmingham	8	Jul
22.20	0.1	Ethan Brown	9.05.01	1h1	Ashford	14	May
22.21	1.1	Kaya Cairney	19.02.01	4rB	Yate	3	Jun
22.21	0.4	Joseph Eggleton	6.01.02	4s2	Birmingham	8	Jul
22.21	-0.1	Kyle Reynolds-Warmington	28.02.02	2	Bromley	10	Jul
22.22	2.0	Joshua Kumar	11.06.01	5h3	Bedford	27	Aug
	(20)						
22.24	0.6	Craig Strachan	10.09.01	3	Loughborough	1	Sep
22.28	0.2	Owain Lloyd Hughes	5.12.01	1	Brecon	26	Aug
22.28	0.8	Micah Forbes-Agyepong	31.01.02	4h2	Bedford	27	Aug
22.32	0.1	Jaiden Aaron	15.11.00	3h1	Bedford	27	Aug
22.33	0.2	Daniel Cartwright	29.11.01	2	Nottingham	8	Apr
22.34	0.4	Ethan Wiltshire	29.06.02	5s2	Birmingham	8	Jul
22.34	0.6	Alex Truscott	8.10.00	2	London (He)	29	Jul
22.41	1.1	Alexander Wadley	9.05.01	3h1	Birmingham	7	Jul
22.42	0.7	Praise Olalere	28.12.00	2h3	Birmingham	7	Jul
22.43	2.0	Lewis Davey	24.10.00	6h3	Bedford	27	Aug
	(30)						
22.45	0.1	Bailey Wright	14.11.00	1	Crawley	13	May
22.45	0.5	Ronan Rawlings	2.03.01	1rB	Bedford	15	Jul
22.46	0.6	Sam Bennett	2.02.01	1h2	Chelmsford	14	May
22.46		Luke Butler	6.12.00	2	Exeter	17	Jun
22.46	0.6	Jak Mensah	5.09.01	3h2	Birmingham	7	Jul
22.49	1.4	Edward Lake	15.06.01	6s1	Birmingham	8	Jul
22.49	0.1	Iwan Robinson-Booth	27.09.00	5h1	Bedford	27	Aug
22.50	1.1	Harry Grindle	9.04.01	4h1	Birmingham	7	Jul

Under 15

22.13	1.3	Jaleel Roper	8.02.03	1	Bedford	27	Aug
22.44	1.3	Jamall Gregory Walters	30.09.02	2	Bedford	27	Aug
22.47	1.3	Tyler Panton	30.04.03	3	Bedford	27	Aug
22.49	1.1	Julian Priest	24.09.02	2	Birmingham	8	Jul
22.56	1.3	Tariq Wild	22.04.03	4	Bedford	27	Aug
22.61	1.3	Jacob Nelson	8.09.02	5	Bedford	27	Aug
22.84		Jayden Allarnby-John	3.11.02	1	Birmingham	17	Jun
22.84	1.1	Remi Jokosenumi	15.02.04	4	Birmingham	8	Jul
22.88	0.2	Dominic Ariyo-Francis	25.09.02	2h1	Bedford	27	Aug
22.91	2.0	Kristian Samwell-Nash	5.12.02	1h2	Oxford (H)	9	Sep
	(10)						
22.95	0.8	Michael Girdler	29.06.03	1	Grangemouth	9	Jun
22.97	1.1	Brody Hinson	26.11.02	5	Birmingham	8	Jul
23.01	0.8	Josh McKeown	5.03.03	3h3	Bedford	27	Aug
23.05	0.1	Ethan Hall	9.02.03	3h2	Bedford	27	Aug
23.08	1.1	Oliver Preest	2.07.03	7	Birmingham	8	Jul
23.08	0.8	Louis Appiah-Kubi	22.09.02	4h3	Bedford	27	Aug
23.17		Lewis Cant	10.10.02	1	Gateshead	10	Jun
23.19	0.8	Robert Philpott	21.09.02	5h3	Bedford	27	Aug
23.22	0.4	Jayden Smith	8.02.03	2h3	Birmingham	7	Jul
23.24	0.4	Amir Sultan-Edwards	21.02.04	3h3	Birmingham	7	Jul
	(20)						
23.25		Anthony Douglas	2.07.03	2	Manchester (Str)	1	May
23.26	0.8	Finlay Waugh	20.11.02	2	Grangemouth	9	Jun
23.26		Thomas Wood	14.03.03	1	Middlesbrough	3	Sep
23.27	1.9	Samuel Jones	7.09.02	1	Nuneaton	20	Aug
23.31	-0.9	George Sudderick	20.11.03	1	Kingston	14	May
23.31		Charles Fisher	8.11.02	1	Telford	9	Sep
23.33	0.9	Thomas Eccleson	25.01.03	5s1	Birmingham	8	Jul
23.34	1.9	Carter Staples	19.09.02	2rF	Cardiff	21	Jun
23.36	0.2	Prince Chinda	4.04.03	4h1	Bedford	27	Aug
23.38	-0.1	Luke Turner	21.10.02	3	Bromley	15	Jul

23.41	0.6	Benjamin Mattey		4.02.03	1	Hereford	8	Jul
23.43	-0.1	Abraham Fobil		15.11.03	3h1	Birmingham	7	Jul
23.43	0.2	Ben Basten		2.08.03	5h1	Bedford	27	Aug
23.46		Oluwatobi Oke		10.10.02	2	Nuneaton	9	Sep
23.47	-0.1	Luke Fry		3.01.03	4h5	Birmingham	7	Jul
23.50	1.6	Nicholas Shaw		13.10.02	1rB	London (He)	13	Aug
23.50	1.9	Jacob Spencer		10.11.02	2	Nuneaton	20	Aug

wind assisted

19.86	2.9	Danny Talbot		(20.16)	1	Clermont, USA	15	Apr
20.19	2.6	Mitchell-Blake		(20.04)	1h2	Columbia, USA	11	May
20.19	2.1				3s1	London (O)	9	Aug
20.40	2.3	Ojie Edoburun	U23	2.06.96	2rC	Gainesville, USA	28	Apr
20.52	3.3	Edmond Amaning		(20.86)	1	London (LV)	7	Jun
20.78	5.0				2rD	Clermont, USA	15	Apr
20.55	4.2	Roy Ejiakuekwu	U23	(20.65)	5q2	Austin, USA	27	May
20.63	3.3				5h5	Columbia, USA	11	May
20.86	2.6				2	Fayetteville, USA	22	Apr
20.62	3.2	James Dasaolu		(20.73)	2rE	Clermont, USA	15	Apr
20.65	6.0	Dan Putnam		(21.14)	1	Nuneaton	11	Jun
20.68	7.3				1h1	Nuneaton	11	Jun
20.73	5.4	Kieran Showler-Davis		(20.98)	1rH	Clermont, USA	15	Apr
20.73	6.0	Elliott Powell	U23	(20.94)	2	Nuneaton	11	Jun
20.82	3.4				1	Manchester (SC)	16	Aug
20.90	4.3				1h2	Nuneaton	11	Jun
20.91	3.3				1	Nuneaton	14	May
20.74	2.4	Deji Tobais		(21.03)	1rD	Gainesville, USA	28	Apr
20.80	5.6	Rio Mitcham	U20	(21.24)	1	Nuneaton	11	Jun
20.82	2.1	Reid		(20.18)	1rA	Loughborough	21	May
20.85	3.8				1	Bedford	15	Jul
20.83	2.1	Reece Prescod	U23	29.02.96	2rA	Loughborough	21	May
20.84	2.1	Miller		(20.79)	3rA	Loughborough	21	May
20.89	5.9	Niclas Baker		9.09.94	1rJ	Clermont, USA	15	Apr
20.92	4.5	Confidence Lawson		(21.11)	2rF	Clermont, USA	15	Apr
20.98	3.3	Nick Stewart	U20	(21.05)	3	London (LV)	7	Jun

26 performances to 20.99 by 17 athletes

21.00	6.0	Michael Warner		(21.33)	3	Nuneaton	11	Jun
21.01	3.4	James Gladman		(21.27)	1h2	Manchester (SC)	11	Jun
21.03	6.0	Peter Shand		(21.47)	4	Nuneaton	11	Jun
21.09	3.3	Reuben Arthur	U23	(21.29)	5	London (Nh)	7	May
21.10	4.5	Rion Pierre		24.11.87	3rF	Clermont, USA	15	Apr
21.14	2.2	George Caddick		29.07.94	1rC	Lubbock, USA	28	Apr
21.16	3.7	Owen Richardson	U20	(21.77)	1rB	London (LV)	16	Aug
21.17	4.5	Tom Burton		29.10.88	1rL	Clermont, USA	15	Apr
21.19	2.1	Andrew Robertson		(21.58)	5rA	Loughborough	21	May
21.19	3.4	Charlie Dobson	U20	(21.20)	5	Manchester (SC)	16	Aug
21.23	5.6	Kaie Chambers-Brown	U20	26.09.99	2J	Nuneaton	11	Jun
21.26	2.1	Connor Wood	U20	(21.19)	7rA	Loughborough	21	May
21.30	7.3	Kane Howitt	U23	(21.77)	3h1	Nuneaton	11	Jun
21.31	2.3	Oliver Bromby	U20	(21.51)	1	Portsmouth	13	May
21.31	2.7	Omar Grant		(21.42)	1rB	London (LV)	7	Jun
21.33	6.0	Nik Kanonik		(21.77)	6	Nuneaton	11	Jun
21.36	5.6	Charles Hilliard	U20	21.09.99	3J	Nuneaton	11	Jun
21.40	3.5	Krishawn Aiken	U23	(21.65)	1	Kilmarnock	12	May
21.44	4.3	Freddie Owsley	U23	(21.80)	3h2	Nuneaton	11	Jun
21.45	3.9	Niall Flannery		26.04.91	2rM	Clermont, USA	15	Apr
21.46	3.2	Sam Griffin	U23	22.12.97	2	Manchester (SC)	11	Jun
21.47	3.3	Jahde Williams	U23	(21.48)	2h1	Bedford	30	Jul
21.58	2.2	Paul Bennett		11.12.92	1	Cardiff	21	Jun
21.58	3.2	Ben Matsuka-Williams	U20	(21.89)	1	London (LV)	13	Sep

21.60	2.7	Kenneth Shrimpton	U23	10.10.96	3rB	London (LV)	7	Jun
21.60	3.3	Joel Richardson		(21.62)	1	Portsmouth	20	Aug
21.61	3.2	Leon Greenwood	U23	13.06.97	4	Manchester (SC)	11	Jun
21.62	2.8	Jack Lawrence	U23	2.07.96	1rB	Yate	16	Jul
21.62	3.7	Khalil Bruney	U20	13.06.98	3rB	London (LV)	16	Aug
21.66	3.2	Ben Shields		17.01.94	5	Manchester (SC)	11	Jun
21.66	3.4	Jason Hoyle	U23	11.11.96	2h2	Manchester (SC)	11	Jun
21.69	4.4	Cameron Starr	U23	(21.72)	1rN	Clermont, USA	15	Apr
21.69	3.5	Greg Kelly	U20	(21.86)	1	Kilmarnock	12	May
21.72	6.0	Christian Byron		20.12.92	8	Nuneaton	11	Jun
21.73	2.6	Joe Lonsdale	U20	(21.75)	1	Manchester (SC)	11	Jun
21.74	4.4	Daniel Oderinde	U23	9.09.96	1rC	London (LV)	16	Aug
21.75	2.3	Camron Lyttle	U20	(21.95)	2rB	Basingstoke	6	May
21.75	4.4	Matthew Overall	U23	16.02.96	2rC	London (LV)	16	Aug
21.76	8.7	Bret Okeke	U20	16.02.99	1h1	Nuneaton	11	Jun
21.77	3.4	Shad-Marc Aaron		20.12.94	2	Nuneaton	14	May
21.77	5.6	Morgan Amed	U20	2.04.99	4J	Nuneaton	11	Jun
21.77	3.8	Imran Rahman		5.07.93	6	Bedford	15	Jul
21.77	4.4	Kevin Hodgson	U23	24.03.96	3rC	London (LV)	16	Aug
21.79	2.6	Jordan Finch		2.09.91	1	Exeter	14	May
21.79	2.2	Tom Evans		20.05.91	2	Cardiff	21	Jun

Additional Under 20 (1-15 above)

21.89	2.6	Derrius Greenaway		14.04.99	3	Manchester (SC)	11	Jun
21.90	2.7	Niall Bevan		14.10.98	5rB	London (LV)	7	Jun
21.91	2.2	Ceirion Hopkins		11.10.99	4	Cardiff	21	Jun
21.93	3.5	Praise Olatoke		23.06.00	2	Kilmarnock	12	May
21.93	2.6	Jody Smith	U17	(21.96)	1	Nuneaton	20	Aug

Additional Under 17 (1 above)

21.93	2.6	Jody Smith		(21.96)	1	Nuneaton	20	Aug
22.09	2.6	Ben Smith		(22.16)	2	Nuneaton	20	Aug
22.16	2.9	Evan Blackman		22.11.01	1	Nuneaton	14	May
22.19	2.9	Ben Higgins		14.11.00	2	Nuneaton	14	May
22.21	2.6	Ollie Sprio		10.03.01	3	Nuneaton	20	Aug
22.22	3.6	Brandon Mingeli		7.09.00	1rG	London (LV)	7	Jun
22.40	5.8	Ronan Rawlings		(22.45)	2	Cambridge	24	Jun

Under 15

23.26	2.8	Samuel Jones		(23.27)	1h2	Nuneaton	20	Aug
23.37	2.4	Kit Oliver-Stevens		8.10.02	2	Exeter	17	Jun
23.38	2.6	Tyreece Rankin		14.09.02	1rF	London (LV)	26	Apr
23.45	3.2	Luke Fry		(23.47)	1	Nuneaton	14	May

Hand timing

21.3		Samuel Landsborough		(21.37)	1	Bebington	9	Jul
21.5		Mutara Sheriff		(21.83)	1	Twickenham	8	Jul
21.5		Kane Howitt	U23	(21.77)	1	Sutton Coldfield	5	Aug
21.7		Enzo Madden	U20	24.08.98	2	Bebington	9	Jul

Additional Under 20 (1 above)

21.8	1.6	Morgan Amed		(21.77w)	2	Coventry	4	Jun
21.8		Kaie Chambers-Brown		(21.23w)	1	Wolverhampton	25	Jun
21.8w		William Hughes	U17	(21.86)	1	Boston	7	Jun
21.9		Bret Okeke		(21.76w)	1	Sutton Coldfield	28	May
21.9		Shemar Boldizsar		(21.94)	1	London (LV)	17	Jun
21.9		Joe Ferguson		3.05.00	1	Doncaster	25	Jun
21.9		Derrius Greenaway		(21.89w)	1	Hull	5	Aug
21.9w		Lewis Davey	U17	(22.43)	2	Boston	7	Jun
		22.2			2	Bedford	13	Aug
21.9w		Adam Cross	U17	(21.99)	2	Cambridge	18	Jun

161

Additional Under 17 (1-3 above)

22.0w	Praise Olalere		(22.42)	3	Cambridge	18	Jun
22.2	Joseph Eggleton		(22.21)	1	Poole	23	Jul
22.3	Jaiden Aaron		(22.32)	h	Uxbridge	10	Jun
22.3	James Hanson		21.08.01	1	Poole	16	Jul
22.4	Bailey Wright		(22.45)	1	Grays	15	Apr
22.4	Evan Blackman		(22.16w)	1	Corby	23	May

Under 15

22.9	Kristian Samwell-Nash		(22.91)	1	Gillingham	6	Aug
23.0	Ethan Hall		(23.05)	1	Yate	30	Jul
23.1	Joseph Harding		31.10.02	1	Brighton	20	May
23.1	Lewis Cant		(23.17)	1	Morpeth	25	Jun
23.1	Thomas Eccleson		(23.33)	1	Middlesbrough	15	Jul
23.2	Jayden Smith		(23.22)	2	Uxbridge	10	Jun
23.2	Finlay Waugh		(23.26)	1	Barrow	24	Jun
23.4	Andrew Nicolaou		13.11.02	1	London (FP)	20	May
23.4	Abraham Fobil		(23.43)	2	Manchester (Str)	10	Jun
23.4	Loreni Jorge		9.01.03	2	Stoke-on-Trent	18	Jun
23.4	William Calvert		1.09.02	2	Middlesbrough	15	Jul

Under 13

24.94	0.3	Arthur Powell	26.09.04	1	Wrexham	20	Aug
25.1		Aydan Tyrrell	18.09.04	1	Hemel Hempstead	15	Jul
25.22		Timi Fatona	29.07.05	2rD	Aberdeen	23	Jul
25.26	-0.7	Reece Earle	1.10.04	1	London (CP)	20	Aug
25.29		Basil Tuma		1h1	Birmingham	4	Jul
25.4		Samuel Ball	18.10.04	1	Tonbridge	18	Jun
25.4		Rasheed Tijani	14.04.05	1	Gillingham	6	Aug
25.5		Ridwaan Ahmed	10.10.04	1	Hastings	18	Jun
25.5		Brandon Bryan-Waugh		1	Chelmsford	5	Jul
25.5		Jaedon Wilson	7.02.05	1	London (Coul)	9	Jul
	(10)						
25.5		Joseph Ryder	18.10.04	1	Middlesbrough	15	Jul

Indoor performances

20.49	Mitchell-Blake	2.04.94	1rB	Fayetteville, USA	11	Feb
	20.55		1h3	College Station, USA	10	Mar
	20.57		3	Nashville, USA	25	Feb
	20.63		2rB	College Station, USA	11	Mar
	20.89		1h5	Nashville, USA	25	Feb

Indoor where superior to outdoors

21.19	Connor Wood	U20	(21.32)	2	Sheffield	12	Feb
21.33	Ryan Gorman	U20	(21.90)	1h4	Sheffield	12	Feb
21.55	Omololu Abiodun		(21.73)	2	Sheffield	19	Feb
21.60	Fraser Angus	U20	(21.84)	2	Sheffield	26	Feb
21.68	Edmund Ross	U23	1.09.97	2	Birmingham	19	Feb
21.77	Charles Hilliard	U20	(21.36w)	2s2	Sheffield	26	Feb

Under 20

21.81	Andrew Morgan-Harrison	(21.82)	4h3	Sheffield	12	Feb

Under 15

23.41	Andrew Nicolaou	(23.4)	1s2	Sheffield	26	Feb
23.50	Evan Jones	6.10.03	1	Cardiff	3	Dec

Foreign

20.30	*0.6*	*David Lima (POR)*	*6.09.90*	*1*	*La Chaux-de-Fonds, SUI*	*2*	*Jul*
20.45w	*2.9*	*Antonio Infantino (ITA)*	*22.03.91*	*3*	*Clermont, USA*	*15*	*Apr*
	20.59	*1.7*		*2*	*Geneva, SUI*	*10*	*Jun*
20.91w	*3.3*	*Adeseye Ogunlewe (NGR)*	*30.08.91*	*2*	*London (Nh)*	*7*	*May*
21.29	*2.0*	*Dean Hylton (JAM)*	*15.09.90*	*1rB*	*London (Nh)*	*2*	*Jul*
21.33w	*4.5*	*Luke Lennon-Ford (IRL)*	*5.05.89*	*4rF*	*Clermont, USA*	*15*	*Apr*
	21.53	*0.6*		*4*	*La Chaux-de-Fonds, SUI*	*2*	*Jul*
21.40	*0.4*	*Jason Smyth (IRL)*	*4.07.87*	*1-T13*	*London (O)*	*18*	*Jul*
21.43	*-0.8*	*Aaron Sexton (IRL) U20*	*24.08.00*	*1*	*Tullamore, IRL*	*3*	*Jun*
21.52w	*3.2*	*Umar Hameed (PAK)*	*24.02.89*	*3*	*Manchester (SC)*	*11*	*Jun*
21.7		*Alhagie-Salim Drammeh (GAM)*	*27.12.87*	*1*	*Portsmouth (RN)*	*12*	*Jul*
21.71w	*3.6*	*Demetric Nelson (JAM)*	*28.05.94*	*3h1*	*Manchester (SC)*	*11*	*Jun*
21.76w	*2.9*	*Mustafa Mahamuud (NED)U20*	*1.07.98*	*1*	*Nuneaton*	*14*	*May*
21.80	*0.7*	*Frederick Afrifa-Osuwu (ITA)U23*	*5.12.96*	*1rD*	*London (LV)*	*16*	*Aug*

300 Metres

32.95	Rabah Yousif	11.12.86	2	Sopot, POL	16	Aug
	33.59i		1rB	Ostrava, CZE	14	Feb
33.14	James Williams	1.10.91	1	Sint Niklaas, BEL	2	Aug

Under 15

35.79	George Sudderick	20.11.03	1	Bedford	27	Aug
35.96	Kristian Samwell-Nash	5.12.02	2	Bedford	27	Aug
36.20	Samuel Jones	7.09.02	1	Nuneaton	19	Aug
36.2	Kareem Jerome	1.02.03	1	Oxford (H)	1	Jul
36.26	Oliver Briars	17.12.02	3	Birmingham	8	Jul
36.3	Josh McKeown	5.03.03	1	Preston	15	Jul
36.4	Jamall Gregory Walters	30.09.02	1	Manchester (Str)	20	May
36.5	Sam Worthington	7.02.03	2	Preston	15	Jul
	36.82		5	Birmingham	8	Jul
36.61	Jaleel Roper	8.02.03	1	Sutton	9	Apr
36.67	Jack McDonald	29.09.02	2h2	Birmingham	7	Jul
(10)						
36.7	Julian Priest	24.09.02	1	Cambridge	18	Jun
36.75	Tariq Wild	22.04.03	1	London (He)	13	Aug
36.80	Nabil Tezkratt	4.03.03	1h3	Birmingham	7	Jul
36.85	Joseph Reynolds	15.02.03	1	Swansea	9	Jul
36.91	Jacob Spencer	10.11.02	1	Nuneaton	9	Sep
36.93	Oliver Bolland	22.09.02	2h1	Birmingham	7	Jul
36.96	Memphis Ayoade	13.09.02	2	London (CP)	20	Aug
37.01	Joseph Thorne	21.11.02	2	Nuneaton	19	Aug
37.02	Joshua Hale	19.09.02	3h1	Birmingham	7	Jul
37.03	Kyron Morgan	29.11.02	4	London (CP)	20	Aug
(20)						
37.09	Joshua Jolob	2.11.02	1h2	Nuneaton	19	Aug
37.12	David Adeleye	7.09.02	1	Gillingham	9	Jul
37.15	Luke Turner	21.10.02	2h1	London (CP)	19	Aug
37.23	Dale Turner	25.06.03	3h2	Bedford	26	Aug
37.28	Pyers Lockwood	11.10.02	5h1	Birmingham	7	Jul
37.31	Benjamin Mattey	4.02.03	1	Newport	6	Aug
37.4	Tyler Panton	30.04.03	1	Woking	15	Jul
37.41	Daniel Onochie-Williams	7.02.03	1rB	London (He)	13	Aug
37.50	Kit Oliver-Stevens	8.10.02	1	Exeter	25	Jul
37.57	Daniel Joyce	2.01.03	1	Gateshead	13	May
(30)						
37.58	Iwan Glynn	2.12.02	2	Swansea	9	Jul
37.6	Jack Gilland	7.09.02	1	Bebington	10	Jun
	37.61		4h3	Birmingham	7	Jul
37.6	Brandon Morgan	6.03.03	1rB	Manchester (SC)	18	Jun

400 Metres

44.74	Matthew Hudson-Smith		26.10.94	4s2	London (O)	6	Aug
	44.99			1	Birmingham	2	Jul
	45.16			2	Oslo, NOR	15	Jun
	45.31			5h1	London (O)	5	Aug
	45.52			1	Gainesville, USA	28	Apr
	46.08			7	Eugene OR, USA	27	May
	46.09			1h2	Birmingham	1	Jul
45.34	Dwayne Cowan		1.01.85	1	Birmingham	20	Aug
	45.36			3	London (O)	9	Jul
	45.39			3h3	London (O)	5	Aug
	45.46			1	Villeneuve d'Ascq, FRA	24	Jun
	45.63			1	Rovereto, ITA	29	Aug
	45.75			3	Gainesville FL, USA	28	Apr
	45.87			1h1	Birmingham	1	Jul
	45.96			8s1	London (O)	6	Aug
	46.04			1h1	Villeneuve d'Ascq, FRA	23	Jun
	46.12			4	Birmingham	2	Jul
	46.15			3=	Geneva, SUI	10	Jun
	46.22			3	Clermont FL, USA	15	Apr
	46.39			1	Tallahassee, USA	5	May
45.45	George Caddick		29.07.94	3q1	Austin, USA	26	May
	45.76			1h6	Austin, USA	25	May
	45.80			2	Waco, USA	8	Apr
	45.89			7s2	Eugene, USA	7	Jun
	46.10			1h4	Lawrence, USA	12	May
	46.13			4	Waco, USA	22	Apr
	46.13			2	Lawrence, USA	14	May
45.58	Rabah Yousif		11.12.86	3	Birmingham	20	Aug
	45.74			2	Heusden, BEL	22	Jul
	45.76			2	Marseille, FRA	3	Jun
	45.81			1	Turku, FIN	13	Jun
	45.81			1	Gothenburg, SWE	11	Jul
	45.82			2	Birmingham	2	Jul
	45.94			5	London (O)	9	Jul
	45.95			2	Szczecin, POL	10	Jun
	46.04			4	Zagreb, CRO	29	Aug
	46.06			6	Stockholm, SWE	18	Jun
	46.10			2	Brussels, BEL	1	Sep
	46.16			1h3	Birmingham	1	Jul
	46.19			1	Bedford	15	Jul
45.64	Cameron Chalmers	U23	6.02.97	1	Bedford	18	Jun
	45.71			1	Bedford	1	May
	45.93			1	Loughborough	21	May
	46.11			3	Birmingham	2	Jul
	46.29			4	Bydgoszcz, POL	15	Jul
	46.32			3s1	Bydgoszcz, POL	14	Jul
	46.48			2h3	Birmingham	1	Jul
45.65	Martyn Rooney		3.04.87	6rB	Madrid, ESP	14	Jul
	45.75			6h5	London (O)	5	Aug
	45.99			6	London (O)	9	Jul
	46.13			5	Birmingham	2	Jul
	46.18			2h1	Birmingham	1	Jul
	46.28			7	Birmingham	20	Aug
	46.29			3	Brussels, BEL	1	Sep
	46.35			2r1	St. George's, GRN	8	Apr
	46.39			2	Zeulenroda, GER	25	May
	46.41			7	Prague, CZE	5	Jun
45.85	Delano Williams		23.12.93	5	Kingston, JAM	10	Jun
	45.92			1	Kingston, JAM	3	Jun
	46.23			2	Kingston, JAM	6	May

46.21	Benjamin Snaith	U23	17.09.95	2	Bedford	30	Jul
46.48	Miguel Francis	U23	28.03.95	2	Kingston, JAM	25	Mar
46.49	Owen Richardson	U20	5.09.98	5	Grosseto, ITA	22	Jul
(10)							
46.49	Edmond Amaning		27.10.93	3	Bedford	30	Jul
	64 performances to 46.50 by 11 athletes						
46.54	Conrad Williams	V35	20.03.82	6	Geneva, SUI	10	Jun
46.58	Zharnel Hughes	U23	13.07.95	1	Kingston, JAM	11	Feb
46.58	Jarryd Dunn		30.01.92	6	Oordegem, BEL	27	May
46.81	Theo Campbell		14.07.91	1	Lisbon, POR	17	Jun
46.91	Owen Smith		7.11.94	3	Munich, GER	3	Jun
46.92	Thomas Somers	U23	28.04.97	2	Bedford	1	May
46.97	Elliott Rutter	U23	20.08.95	2	Bedford	18	Jun
46.98	Sam Hazel	U23	7.10.96	3	Bedford	18	Jun
46.99	Jamal Rhoden-Stevens		27.04.94	1	Frauenfeld, SUI	13	May
(20)							
47.01	Lee Thompson	U23	5.03.97	4	Bedford	18	Jun
47.05	Niclas Baker		9.09.94	1rD	Gainesville, USA	28	Apr
47.13	Leon Reid		26.07.94	1	Torremolinos, ESP	19	Apr
47.13	James Gladman		3.06.93	1	Loughborough	26	Aug
47.21	Nicholas Atwell		9.04.86	1	London (Nh)	29	May
47.23	Ben Claridge	U23	12.11.97	3	Bedford	1	May
47.26	Michael Ohioze	U23	6.02.95	5	Gulf Shores, USA	27	May
47.29	Robert Shipley	U23	28.09.96	5	Bedford	18	Jun
47.31	Sam Dawkins		18.08.93	1	Kessel-Lo, BEL	19	Aug
47.33	Ben Maze		22.12.91	5	Oordegem, BEL	27	May
(30)							
47.42	Joseph Reid	U23	8.03.96	4	Bedford	1	May
47.43	Christian Byron		20.12.92	1	Nuneaton	11	Jun
47.48	Ellis Greatrex	U20	27.09.99	1rB	Loughborough	22	Jul
47.54	Roy Ejiakuekwu	U23	2.02.95	7	Baton Rouge, USA	28	Apr
47.61	Jack Wightman	U23	30.11.95	1s1	Bedford	30	Apr
47.69	Andrew Osagie		19.02.88	1	Watford	23	Aug
47.82	Tom Druce		18.11.86	3	Hamar, NOR	16	Aug
47.82	Ethan Brown	U17	9.05.01	1	Bedford	27	Aug
47.84	David Hall	U23	25.04.95	1	Watford	19	Apr
47.84	Joseph Brier	U20	16.03.99	2	London (Nh)	29	May
(40)							
47.85	Lewis Brown	U20	2.09.98	3	Bedford	18	Jun
47.85	Matthew Pagan	U20	15.01.98	2	Belfast	5	Jul
47.87	Joel Richardson		30.12.93	1	Manchester (Str)	15	Aug
47.89	Shawn Wright		25.11.94	4s2	Bedford	30	Apr
47.90	Thomas Evans	U17	21.09.00	4	Bedford	18	Jun
47.91	Jason Hoyle	U23	11.11.96	4h3	Bedford	17	Jun
47.92	Jack Lawrie	U23	21.02.96	2rB	London (LV)	3	Jun
47.93	Karl Goodman		7.11.93	3h3	Arlington, USA	13	May
47.98	Matthew Overall	U23	16.02.96	1	Kingston	2	Jul
48.07	Rory Keen	U20	6.04.00	2	Birmingham	8	Jul
(50)							
48.09	Krishawn Aiken	U23	24.05.95	2	London (LV)	20	Aug
48.29	Greg Louden		25.10.92	5h2	Birmingham	1	Jul
48.30	Anthony Young		14.09.92	7rC	Oordegem, BEL	27	May
48.3	Danny Higham		4.11.90	1	Ormskirk	9	Jul
48.31	Alex Knibbs	U20	26.04.99	1	Manchester (SC)	10	Jun
48.33	Iori Moore	U23	15.04.97	2rF	Oordegem, BEL	27	May
48.37	Peter Phillips		12.02.86	2	London (He)	24	Jun
48.4	Rhys Turner	U20	25.02.99	1	Crawley	26	Jul
48.41	Freddie Owsley	U23	6.01.97	2	Yate	3	Jun
48.41	Samuel Adeyemi		15.03.90	1	London (Nh)	2	Jul
(60)							
48.45	Harry Fisher		26.10.91	3rB	Bedford	15	Jul

Time	Name	Cat	DOB	Pos	Venue	Date
48.45	Grant Plenderleith		15.03.91	2	Grangemouth	27 Aug
48.47	Niall Flannery		26.04.91	6	Sheffield	6 May
48.50	Nicholas Pryce		10.11.92	2	Nuneaton	11 Jun
48.5	Psalm Roberts-Nash	U20	7.07.99	1	Tipton	9 Apr
48.5	Gwilym Cooper		17.07.91	1	Crawley	6 May
	48.63			5rB	Loughborough	21 May
48.51	Lynden Olowe	U20	18.06.00	5rB	London (LV)	3 Jun
48.52	Lewis Davey	U17	24.10.00	2	Birmingham	8 Jul
48.53	John Lane		29.01.89	1D3	Azusa, USA	12 Apr
48.57	Mark Cottam	U23	23.09.96	2s4	Bedford	30 Apr
(70)						
48.57	Lennox Thompson		22.10.93	3	London (He)	24 Jun
48.58	Harrison Pocock	U23	8.08.96	1	Manchester (Str)	3 Jun
48.59	Thomas Pitkin	U20	12.01.98	1	Chelmsford	13 May
48.59	Tom Burton		29.10.88	4	London (He)	20 Aug
48.60	William Curtis	U20	27.12.99	3	Birmingham	8 Jul
48.61	Alex Haydock-Wilson	U20	28.07.99	1	London (He)	23 Jul
48.62	Emmanuel Sosanya	U20	29.08.98	2	Chelmsford	13 May
48.63	Richard Strachan		18.11.86	1	London (LV)	15 Apr
48.63	Scott Barker	U23	20.03.97	3s3	Bedford	30 Apr
48.64	Nik Kanonik		24.10.87	1	Birmingham	4 Jun
(80)						
48.66	Connor Wood	U20	25.11.98	1	Swansea	3 Jun
48.69	Christopher McAlister	U23	3.12.95	1	Bromley	14 Aug
48.70	Canaan Solomon	U20	17.09.98	2	London (LV)	8 Apr
48.70	Jordan Layne	U23	17.05.96	2	Swansea	3 Jun
48.70	Rick Beardsell	V35	19.01.79	1	Aarhus, DEN	2 Aug
48.70	Callum Dodds	U17	6.10.00	2	Bedford	27 Aug
48.7	Aidan Leeson	U20	9.11.99	1	Nottingham	30 Apr
	48.85			4	Birmingham	8 Jul
48.7	William Snook	U23	11.10.95	2	Rugby	20 Aug
48.73	Guy Learmonth		20.04.92	3rC	Loughborough	21 May
48.77	Markhim Lonsdale	U20	9.01.99	2	Gateshead	13 May
(90)						
48.8	Tom Harris	U20	6.01.98	1	Carn Brea	13 May
48.81	Sean Adams		1.09.93	1rB	Watford	19 Apr
48.1	Martin Lipton		14.01.89	1h1	Kilmarnock	13 May
48.83	Joseph Rogers	U20	13.04.98	2rB	London (Nh)	29 May
48.85	Reece Ingley		15.02.92	2	Manchester (Str)	3 Jun
48.9	Elliot Dunn	U20	20.10.98	1	Wolverhampton	25 Jun
48.9	Dale Willis		17.06.88	2	Portsmouth	12 Jul
48.93	Mayowa Osunsami	U20	23.10.99	6rB	London (LV)	3 Jun
48.96	Nick Petrou	U23	20.07.96	1	Gateshead	4 Jun
48.97	Kevin Hodgson	U23	24.03.96	2	Merksem, BEL	29 Jul

Additional Under 20 (1-26 above)

Time	Name	Cat	DOB	Pos	Venue	Date
49.0	Alex Botterill		18.01.00	2	Hull	30 Apr
	49.09			1	Preston	5 Aug
49.0	Louis Southwell		6.01.00	1	Uxbridge	17 Jun
49.03	Khalil Bruney		13.06.98	1	London (He)	29 Jul
49.10	Jack Hocking		29.09.98	5	Birmingham	8 Jul
(30)						
49.10	Joshua Hulse	U17	14.03.01	3	Bedford	27 Aug
49.1	Joshua Faulds		7.03.00	1rB	Wolverhampton	25 Jun
49.1	Charles Hilliard		21.09.99	1	Cheltenham	15 Jul
49.1	Thomas Ainsworth		28.03.98	1	Yate	16 Jul
49.14	Nilrem Stewart		8.02.98	1rE	Clermont, USA	15 Apr
49.14	Finley Bigg		2.06.98	2	London (CP)	11 Jun
49.14	Ricky Lutakome		19.11.99	1	Bromley	10 Jul
49.16	Ben Pattison	U17	15.12.01	4	Birmingham	8 Jul
49.20	Blaine Lewis-Shallow		26.04.00	4	Manchester (SC)	20 Aug
49.25	Declan Gall		19.05.99	1h4	Grangemouth	26 Aug

Additional Under 17 (1-6 above)

49.41	Thomas Baines	22.11.00	2h3	Birmingham	7	Jul
49.44	Hakan Dalbal	22.09.00	6	Birmingham	8	Jul
49.46	Jack Higgins	30.01.01	7	Birmingham	8	Jul
49.48	Kyle Calhoun	6.11.00	2h2	Birmingham	7	Jul
(10)						
49.7	Evan Blackman	22.11.01	1	Leicester	10	Jun
50.12			1	Nuneaton	13	May
49.73	Ben Hawkes	5.10.00	5	Bedford	27	Aug
49.78	Billy Doyle	24.10.01	1	Grangemouth	27	Aug
49.87	Michael Fagbenle	22.02.01	1	London (CP)	20	Aug
49.89	Ben Lloyd	13.10.00	1rC	London (LV)	28	Jun
50.10	Matthew Waterfield	20.12.00	1	Hexham	17	Jun
50.1	Oliver Dustin	29.11.00	1	Ashton-under-Lyne	5	Aug
50.1	Seumas MacKay	8.03.01	1	Lerwick	10	Sep
50.14	Max Leslie	13.10.01	2	Grangemouth	27	Aug
50.22	Joshua Pearson	18.05.01	4h1	Birmingham	7	Jul
(20)						
50.24	Adam Clayton	26.09.00	5	Birmingham	3	Sep
50.28	Henry Thorneywork	4.11.00	2h2	Bedford	26	Aug
50.30	Harry Grindle	9.04.01	3h3	Bedford	26	Aug
50.42	Joshua Pearson	6.01.02	1	Bromley	28	May
50.43	Cormac O'Rourke	13.02.01	1	Belfast	1	Jul
50.45	Karl Johnson	15.04.01	2rC	London (LV)	28	Jun

Under 15

51.45	Amir Sultan-Edwards	21.02.04	2rB	Bromley	14	Aug
51.54	Kristian Samwell-Nash	5.12.02	3	Dartford	26	Jul
52.13	Oliver Briars	17.12.02	4	Bromley	22	May
52.6	Tariq Wild	22.04.03	1rB	Bedford	3	Sep

Indoor performance

46.17	Caddick	(45.45)	1	Ames, USA	25	Feb

Indoor where superior to outdoor

46.57	Seb Rodger		29.06.91	1	Athlone, IRL	15	Feb
47.42	Jack Green		6.10.91	1h4	Sheffield	11	Feb
47.43	Jamie Bowie		1.04.89	2	Glasgow	28	Jan
48.17	Luke Smallwood		11.09.88	1	Dublin (B), IRL	5	Feb
48.22	Psalm Roberts-Nash	U20	(48.5)	1s1	Sheffield	25	Feb
48.56	James Forman		12.12.91	2	London (LV)	1	Jan
48.59	Danny Higham		(48.3)	1	Birmingham	19	Feb
48.64	Joe Milton	U20	29.09.98	2s2	Sheffield	25	Feb
48.82	Aidan Leeson	U20	(48.7)	1	Birmingham	12	Feb
48.84	Andrew Smitherman		9.11.90	2	Birmimgham	19	Feb
48.89	Adam McComb		25.07.92	3	Athlone, IRL	10	Feb
48.90	Jack Hocking	U20	(49.10)	3	Sheffield	21	Jan
48.99	Ben Higgins	U17	14.11.00	1	Sheffield	25	Feb

Under 20

49.23	Michael Oku-Ampofo	10.11.98	3s2	Sheffield	25	Feb

Foreign

46.00	*Sadam Koumi (SUD)*		*6.04.94*	*2*	*Clermont, USA*	*15*	*Apr*
47.05i	*Luke Lennon-Ford (IRL)*		*5.05.89*	*2*	*Athlone, IRL*	*19*	*Feb*
	47.18			*2rC*	*Geneva, SUI*	*10*	*Jun*
47.22	*Adrien Coulibaly (FRA)*	*U23*	*13.04.96*	*1*	*London (He)*	*24*	*Jun*
47.31	*Craig Newell (IRL)*	*U23*	*24.09.97*	*1*	*Belfast*	*10*	*Jun*
47.32	*Andrew Mellon (IRL)*	*U23*	*8.11.95*	*1*	*Belfast*	*5*	*Jul*
47.58	*Alhagie-Salim Drammeh (GAM)*		*27.12.87*	*6*	*London (LV)*	*3*	*Jun*
47.71	*Zak Curran (IRL)*		*17.12.93*	*1rB*	*Waco, USA*	*8*	*Apr*
48.13	*Richard Morrissey (IRL)*		*11.01.91*	*1*	*London (LV)*	*8*	*Apr*

48.31	*Peter Moreno (NGR)*			*30.12.90*	*1D6*	*Bedford*	*27 May*
48.54	*Jason Harvey (IRL)*			*9.04.91*	*4rB*	*Bedford*	*15 Jul*
48.80	*Damaine Benjamin (JAM)*			*12.03.88*	*1rB*	*Swansea*	*3 Jun*
48.8	*David Lima (POR)*			*6.09.90*	*1*	*Telford*	*6 May*

600 Metres Indoor

1:16.10	Kyle Langford	U23		2.02.96	1	Athlone, IRL	15 Feb
1:18.90	Jamie Webb			1.06.94	1	Manchester (SC)	17 Dec
1:18.98	Ben Greenwood	U20		24.09.98	1	Glasgow	4 Jan

800 Metres

1:44.99	Elliot Giles			26.05.94	5	London (O)	9 Jul
	1:45.44				5	Birmingham	20 Aug
	1:45.86				3h3	London (O)	5 Aug
	1:46.10				9	Monaco, MON	21 Jul
	1:46.38				7	Hengelo, NED	11 Jun
	1:46.95				6s1	London (O)	6 Aug
	1:47.03				7	Brussels, BEL	1 Sep
	1:47.69				2	Brighton	31 May
1:45.10	Guy Learmonth			20.04.92	4	Rovereto, ITA	29 Aug
	1:45.77				10	London (O)	9 Jul
	1:45.90				3h6	London (O)	5 Aug
	1:46.07				4	Bellinzona, SUI	18 Jul
	1:46.28				8	Birmingham	20 Aug
	1:46.75				5s1	London (O)	6 Aug
	1:47.00i				5	Birmingham	18 Feb
	1:47.04i				3	Karlsruhe, GER	4 Feb
	1:47.20i				1	Vienna, AUT	28 Jan
1:45.25	Kyle Langford	U23		2.02.96	4	London (O)	8 Aug
	1:45.45				8	London (O)	9 Jul
	1:45.69				6	Birmingham	20 Aug
	1:45.81				2s2	London (O)	6 Aug
	1:45.91				3	Hengelo, NED	11 Jun
	1:46.38				5h2	London (O)	5 Aug
	1:46.56				8	Oordegem, BEL	27 May
	1:46.77				2	Los Angeles (ER), USA	18 May
	1:46.79i				3	Birmingham	18 Feb
	1:46.98				1	Dublin (S), IRL	12 Jul
	1:47.57				1	Brighton	31 May
	1:47.63				6	Samorin, SVK	17 Jun
1:45.42	Jake Wightman			11.07.94	7	London (O)	9 Jul
	1:45.82				1	Gothenburg, SWE	10 Jun
	1:46.07				5	Somerville, USA	2 Jun
	1:46.36				1	Solihull	13 May
1:45.54	Andrew Osagie			19.02.88	6	Rovereto, ITA	29 Aug
	1:45.73				2	Huelva, ESP	14 Jun
	1:45.75				3	Andújar, ESP	2 Jun
	1:45.75				9	London (O)	9 Jul
	1:46.05				3	Karlstad, SWE	25 Jul
	1:46.36				6	Bellinzona, SUI	18 Jul
	1:46.93				3	Los Angeles (ER), USA	18 May
	1:47.02i				6	Birmingham	18 Feb
	1:47.30				3	Belfort, FRA	9 Jun
	1:47.55i				4	Madrid, ESP	24 Feb
1:46.40	James Bowness			26.11.91	7	Oordegem, BEL	27 May
	1:47.43				3	Oordegem, BEL	3 Jun
1:46.64	Daniel Rowden	U23		9.09.97	5	Karlstad, SWE	25 Jul
	1:46.86				2	Solihull	13 May
	1:47.51				5	Oordegem, BEL	3 Jun
	1:47.51				1h1	Bydgoszcz, POL	14 Jul
	1:47.79				5	Sopot, POL	16 Aug

1:46.72	Michael Rimmer		3.02.86	9	Hengelo, NED	11	Jun
1:46.89				8	Andújar, ESP	2	Jun
1:47.56				9	Huelva, ESP	14	Jun
1:47.91				5	Lucerne, SUI	11	Jul
1:47.98				4	Cork, IRL	18	Jul
1:46.97	Markhim Lonsdale	U20	9.01.99	1	Manchester (SC)	27	May
1:47.07				1	Loughborough	8	Jul
1:47.63				1	Manchester (Str)	19	Aug
1:47.29	Rory Graham-Watson		3.06.90	1	Manchester (Str)	25	Jul
(10)							
1:47.34	Chris O'Hare		23.11.90	2	Philadelphia, USA	15	Jun
1:47.49	Jamie Webb		1.06.94	4	Oordegem, BEL	3	Jun
1:47.76	Sean Molloy	U23	18.09.95	1	Watford	14	Jun
1:47.79	John Bird		17.05.92	2	Watford	14	Jun
1:47.83	Spencer Thomas	U23	26.08.97	2rC	Oordegem, BEL	27	May
1:47.84				2	Castiglione della Pescaia, ITA	14	May
1:47.84	Neil Gourley	U23	7.02.95	3	Cork, IRL	18	Jul
1:47.98				2	Portland, USA	11	Jun
1:47.92	Matthew Harding	U20	3.04.98	4q1	Lexington, USA	26	May
68 performances to 1:48.0 by 17 athletes including 6 indoors							
1:48.05A	Josh Kerr	U23	8.10.97	1	Logan, USA	13	May
1:48.11	Harry Fisher		26.10.91	4	Watford	14	Jun
1:48.16	Robert Needham		18.04.94	1rB	Watford	24	Jun
(20)							
1:48.44	Alex Coomber		24.07.94	2	Manchester (Str)	25	Jul
1:48.48	Charlie Grice		7.11.93	5	Dublin (S), IRL	12	Jul
1:48.56	Tom Lancashire		2.07.85	3	Manchester (SC)	27	May
1:48.68	Jonathan Monk	U23	27.07.95	1	Bedford	1	May
1:48.68	Ben Waterman		29.09.93	1	Loughborough	21	May
1:48.68	Tom Marshall		12.06.89	1	Watford	24	Jun
1:48.68	Alex Botterill	U20	18.01.00	3	Manchester (Str)	19	Aug
1:48.71	Ben Greenwood	U20	24.09.98	2	Loughborough	8	Jul
1:48.78	Rowan Axe		17.05.91	2	Watford	12	Jul
1:48.92	Canaan Solomon	U20	17.09.98	2rB	Watford	24	Jun
(30)							
1:48.94	Jonathan Davies		28.10.94	3	Manchester (Str)	25	Jul
1:48.99	Oliver Aitchison		13.03.92	1	San Francisco, USA	1	Apr
1:49.03	James West	U23	30.01.96	3rB	Watford	24	Jun
1:49.06	James McMurray	U23	18.01.95	4	Solihull	13	May
1:49.09	James McCarthy	U23	31.10.96	6	Watford	14	Jun
1:49.09	Jack Hallas		7.02.91	4	Manchester (Str)	25	Jul
1:49.13	Nzimah Akpan		25.03.94	7	Watford	14	Jun
1:49.17	David Dempsey		7.02.91	7rC	Oordegem, BEL	27	May
1:49.19	William Snook	U23	11.10.95	5	Manchester (Str)	19	Aug
1:49.24	Finley Bigg	U20	2.06.98	5	Watford	12	Jul
(40)							
1:49.39	Andrew Smith	U23	7.10.95	2	Manchester (Str)	13	Jun
1:49.42	Max Burgin	U17	20.05.02	3rB	Manchester (Str)	27	Jun
1:49.43	Robbie Fitzgibbon	U23	23.03.96	5	Solihull	13	May
1:49.59	Ricky Lutakome	U20	19.11.99	6	Brighton	31	May
1:49.69	Archie Davis	U20	16.10.98	7	Brighton	31	May
1:49.81	Mark Woodley		7.03.88	7	Watford	12	Jul
1:49.86	Anthony Whiteman	V45	13.11.71	8	Manchester (Str)	19	Aug
1:49.99	David Proctor		22.10.85	2rC	Watford	24	Jun
1:50.07	Matthew Wigelsworth	U23	27.09.96	3	Manchester (Str)	13	Jun
1:50.07	Dominic Walton		13.11.93	2	Manchester (Str)	29	Aug
(50)							
1:50.09	Joseph Reid	U23	8.03.96	3	Manchester (Str)	29	Aug
1:50.14	Luke Johnston		16.05.94	4	Madison, USA	5	May
1:50.21	Edward Dodd		10.02.94	7rB	Watford	24	Jun
1:50.33	Jake Heyward	U20	26.04.99	7	Watford	9	Aug
1:50.34	Ashley Sandall	U23	23.09.97	8	Watford	14	Jun

Time	Name	Cat	DOB	Pos	Venue	Date	
1:50.45	Jamie Williamson	U23	3.03.97	9	Loughborough	21	May
1:50.50	Josh Allen	U20	23.01.00	4	Manchester (Str)	13	Jun
1:50.5	Shaun Wyllie	U23	27.02.95	2rB	Solihull	13	May
1:50.56	Ryan Green	U20	19.07.98	2rC	Manchester (SC)	27	May
1:50.59i	Richard Charles		31.05.94	2	London (LV)	1	Feb
(60)							
1:50.6	Thomas Atkinson		22.03.92	4rB	Manchester (Str)	16	May
1:50.71	Alexander Birkett	U20	9.11.99	1rB	Manchester (Str)	25	Jul
1:50.73	John Ashcroft		13.11.92	7	Manchester (Str)	25	Jul
1:50.76	Max Wharton	U23	8.07.96	6	Manchester (SC)	27	May
1:50.80i	Charles Cooper	U23	29.02.96	3	Boston MA, USA	11	Feb
1:51.77				10	Gainesville, USA	31	Mar
1:50.87	Adam Clarke		3.04.91	9	Watford	9	Aug
1:50.88	Sam Petty		7.11.91	5	Auckland, NZL	26	Feb
1:50.9	James Fradley	U20	25.10.98	6rB	Solihull	13	May
1:50.99	Will Crisp	U20	25.11.99	1rD	Watford	24	Jun
1:51.07i	Cameron Steven	U20	5.03.99	2	Glasgow	28	Jan
1:51.13				1	Glasgow (S)	2	Jun
(70)							
1:51.07	Oliver Dustin	U17	29.11.00	1	Birmingham	8	Jul
1:51.1	Robert Umeokafor	U23	22.11.96	9rB	Solihull	13	May
1:51.13	Philip Sesemann		3.10.92	9	Watford	12	Jul
1:51.22	Elliot Slade		5.11.94	3rF	Dublin (S), IRL	12	Jul
1:51.23i	Jordan Donnelly		20.09.87	1rB	Boston, USA	4	Feb
1:51.26i	Dale King-Clutterbuck		1.01.92	1	London (LV)	29	Jan
1:51.29	Lewis Lloyd		29.04.94	2rC	Manchester (Str)	25	Jul
1:51.32	Grant Muir		4.10.93	4	Manchester (Str)	29	Aug
1:51.42	Jeremy Barnes	U23	29.05.97	2rD	Solihull	13	May
1:51.43	Daniel Bebbington	U23	8.06.96	2rB	Manchester (Str)	25	Jul
(80)							
1:51.46	Michael Ward		10.12.94	2	Newport	5	Jul
1:51.47	Kyran Roberts	U23	19.09.95	3rB	Manchester (Str)	25	Jul
1:51.47	Michael Parry	U20	25.11.99	3rC	Manchester (Str)	25	Jul
1:51.48	Cameron Field	U23	16.04.96	4rB	Manchester (Str)	27	Jun
1:51.49	Scott Greeves	U23	30.07.96	10	Watford	14	Jun
1:51.50	Ricky Harvie	U23	17.03.95	1rC	Loughborough	8	Jul
1:51.51	Adam Spilsbury	U20	25.06.99	3rD	Manchester (SC)	27	May
1:51.51	Ian Crowe-Wright	U23	27.03.95	1rB	Brighton	31	May
1:51.58i	Piers Copeland	U20	26.11.98	1	Cardiff	5	Feb
1:51.60	Cameron Bell	U20	2.01.99	1	Manchester (Str)	25	Apr
(90)							
1:51.63	Aaron Bennett		29.01.92	6	London (Elt)	21	Jun
1:51.66	Matthew Williams	U20	20.12.98	3	Newport	5	Jul
1:51.67	Michael Wilson	U23	4.01.96	3	Watford	3	May
1:51.72iA	Thomas Gifford		21.10.93	3	Albuquerque, USA	21	Jan
1:51.83				10rB	Azusa, USA	14	Apr
1:51.73	Will Perkin	U20	16.12.98	2rB	Watford	12	Jul
1:51.76	Alex Goodall	U20	30.09.99	2rH	Oordegem, BEL	27	May
1:51.77	David Banwell-Clode		29.12.92	9	Azusa, USA	14	Apr
1:51.77	Callum Dodds	U17	6.10.00	2rE	Watford	24	Jun
1:51.79	Liam Dee	U23	23.05.96	2	Lowell, USA	20	May
1:51.84	James Downing	U23	12.03.96	3rB	Watford	12	Jul
(100)							
1:51.84	Ciaran Cooper	U23	1.03.97	1rD	Manchester (Str)	19	Aug
1:51.85	Jacob Brown	U23	24.11.97	1rB	Manchester (Str)	13	Jun
1:51.86	Luke Jones	U23	18.10.96	4rC	Manchester (Str)	25	Jul
1:51.87	Andrew Walshe		2.08.94	5	London (LV)	3	Jun
1:51.87	Luke Minns		20.03.89	5rB	Manchester (Str)	27	Jun
1:51.94	Joseph Tuffin	U20	24.06.99	3rC	Solihull	13	May
1:51.97	Dominic Brown		8.10.94	7rB	Manchester (Str)	27	Jun
1:51.97	Simon Coppard	U17	19.02.01	2	Bedford	27	Aug
1:51.98	George Duggan	U23	1.09.96	3rC	Loughborough	8	Jul

Additional Under 20 (1-27 above)

1:52.03	Hamza Kadir		12.09.99	3	London (Elt)	24	May
1:52.21	Daniel Mees		12.09.98	7	London (LV)	3	Jun
1:52.40	Tiarnan Crorken		13.06.99	1	Manchester (Str)	27	Jun
(30)							
1:52.50	Oliver Dane		13.11.98	3rD	Solihull	13	May
1:52.67	Thomas Fulton		16.12.99	5rD	Solihull	13	May
1:52.69	Oliver Carvell	U17	9.04.02	3	Bedford	27	Aug
1:52.7	Joshua Hulse	U17	14.03.01	2	Ipswich	20	May
1:52.83	Joe Wigfield		18.01.00	2rB	Manchester (Str)	29	Aug
1:52.94	Sam Brown		21.03.00	1	Glasgow (S)	20	Aug
1:53.09	Christie Williams		2.12.98	7rD	Solihull	13	May
1:53.32	Seumas MacKay	U17	8.03.01	1	Visby, SWE	27	Jun

Additional Under 17 (1-7 above)

1:53.41	Ben Lee		7.01.01	4	Bedford	27	Aug
1:53.85	Fergus McAuliffe		5.09.00	1	Birmingham	17	Jun
1:54.34	Thomas Eames		4.12.00	8	Watford	14	Jun
(10)							
1:54.45	Callum Abberley		27.10.00	2rE	Manchester (Str)	25	Jul
1:54.61	Jacques Maurice		11.02.01	2rB	Milton Keynes	3	Jun
1:54.71	Thomas Patrick		4.07.01	1rC	Milton Keynes	3	Jun
1:54.81	Hayden Bailey		10.09.00	2	Street	1	May
1:54.93	Luke Duffy		14.11.00	6rB	Watford	3	May
1:54.94	Daniel Howells		28.02.02	1rB	Basingstoke	19	Jul
1:54.95	Angus Harrington		22.06.01	5	Birmingham	8	Jul
1:55.20	Harry Digby		22.10.00	4rB	Milton Keynes	3	Jun
1:55.65	Yusuf Bizimana		16.09.00	6rB	London (Elt)	21	Jun
1:55.73	Oliver Lill		27.06.02	2rC	London (Elt)	24	May
(20)							
1:55.75	Luke Chesters		22.12.00	3	Birmingham	17	Jun
1:55.85	Daniel Preston		25.08.01	2rH	Manchester (SC)	27	May
1:56.14	Cormac O'Rourke		13.02.01	1	Dublin (S), IRL	24	Jun
1:56.19	Archie Richardson		17.09.00	3rF	Manchester (Str)	25	Jul
1:56.3	Joshua Ward		14.10.00	1	Nottingham	5	Aug
1:56.40	Jack Meijer		3.11.00	5	Watford	6	Sep
1:56.4	Adam Saul-Braddock		20.09.01	1	Rugby	28	May
1:56.53	Ben Pattison		15.12.01	7	Street	1	May
1:56.56	Abdifatqh Hasan		14.02.02	1rB	Street	1	May
1:56.58	Joe Smith		20.10.01	2rC	London (Elt)	21	Jun
(30)							
1:56.62	Jed Skilton		6.09.00	1rI	Manchester (SC)	27	May
1:56.62	Christopher McLew		1.09.01	2	Grangemouth	10	Jun
1:56.67	Laurance Edwards		26.11.01	4rC	Watford	12	Jul
1:56.71	Rocco Zaman-Browne		4.12.00	4	Manchester (Str)	27	Jun
1:56.85	Ben Horsfield		26.07.01	1	Gateshead	9	Aug
1:56.91	Harris Pentecost		16.10.00	3	Livingston	23	Aug

Under 15

1:56.04	Daniel Joyce		2.01.03	1	Bedford	27	Aug
1:58.16	Mohamed Sharif Ali		8.08.03	8rB	Watford	6	Sep
1:59.03	Ethan Hussey		5.03.03	2rC	Leeds	26	Jun
1:59.04	Henry Johnson		28.10.02	1	Gateshead	14	May
1:59.40	Liam Blackwell		5.09.02	5rF	Milton Keynes	3	Jun
1:59.47	Oliver Bright		9.04.03	8	London (TB)	22	Jul
1:59.69	Murray Fotheringham		4.06.03	2rD	Glasgow (S)	2	Jun
2:00.07	Gabriel Gisborne		12.10.02	1h2	Birmingham	7	Jul
2:00.15	Adam Ord		21.09.02	2	Bedford	27	Aug
2:00.20	Tom Rickards		18.12.02	6rF	Milton Keynes	3	Jun
(10)							
2:00.47	Jolyon Leavesley		7.12.02	3	Bedford	27	Aug
2:00.70	Joseph Martin		5.09.02	2	Birmingham	17	Jun
2:01.32	Lewis Dow		18.01.03	9	Livingston	23	Aug

2:01.53	Sidnie Ward		9.01.03	5rE	London (Elt)	21	Jun
2:01.78	Harley Norman		14.07.03	1	Basingstoke	17	Jun
2:02.17	Finlay Seeds		30.06.03	1	Inglewood, NZL	7	Apr
2:02.26	Angus Williams		7.12.02	10rC	Watford	6	Sep
2:02.37	Dylan King		27.12.02	5	Bedford	27	Aug
2:02.54	Casey Augustin		6.09.02	3h1	Birmingham	7	Jul
2:02.61	Dylan Bowley		14.05.03	6rD	Watford	17	May
(20)							
2:02.92	Alex Aldred		19.11.02	4h1	Birmingham	7	Jul
2:03.05	Charlie Roberts		25.07.03	3	Leigh	20	Aug
2:03.07	Jamie Rashbrook		10.08.03	5rD	Watford	6	Sep
2:03.10	Daniel Payne		26.12.02	3	Gateshead	14	May
2:03.10	Samuel Heal		5.11.02	5h1	Birmingham	7	Jul
2:03.19	Charlie Holland		14.04.04	1	Newport	6	Aug
2:03.2	Adam Visram Cipolletta		21.02.03	1	Rugby	18	Jun
2:03.25	Ethan Elder		11.10.02	3rB	Livingston	23	Aug
2:03.3	Sam Flaherty		11.10.02	1	Bebington	10	Jun
2:03.37	Jack Dutton		7.01.03	2rC	Exeter	27	Jun
(30)							
2:03.38	Benjamin Reynolds		1.10.02	3rC	Exeter	27	Jun
2:03.50	Liam Dunne		7.12.02	3h3	Birmingham	7	Jul
2:03.50	Ryan Shields		31.01.03	7	Leamington	2	Aug
2:03.77	Fabian Despinoy		9.11.02	4h1	Bedford	26	Aug
2:03.90	Luke Chambers		23.04.03	6h1	Birmingham	7	Jul
2:03.9	Iwan Glynn		2.12.02	5rD	Tipton	20	Jun

Under 13

2:10.75	Harry Ware		26.10.04	3rN	Watford	12	Jul
2:12.65	Roman Hodgson		4.01.05	1	Wrexham	20	Aug
2:14.2	Elliot Savage		16.09.04	1ns	Preston	15	Jul
2:14.88	Elliot Gladwell		7.05.05	1	Birmingham	4	Jul
2:15.2	Evan Savage		16.09.04	2ns	Preston	15	Jul
2:15.22	Jake Minshull		11.10.04	3rR	Watford	12	Jul
2:15.55	Oliver Capps		20.01.05	1	Exeter	20	Aug
2:16.02	Alex Pama			2	Birmingham	4	Jul
2:16.08	Henry Channon		27.05.05	1	Oxford (H)	14	May
2:16.2	Joshua Blevins		15.09.04	1	Gateshead	14	May

Foreign

1:46.88	Christian Von Eitzen (GER)	U23	1.01.97	1	Wiesbaden, GER	30	Aug
1:48.34	Nicholas Landeau (TTO)	U23	30.01.95	5	Watford	14	Jun
1:48.43i	Zak Curran (IRL)		17.12.93	2	Ames, USA	25	Feb
1:48.60				2	Waco, USA	22	Apr
1:50.03	Ossama Meslek (ITA)	U23	8.01.97	6	Manchester (Str)	25	Jul
1:51.80	Mark Hoy (IRL)		21.07.91	9rC	Oordegem, BEL	3	Jun
1:51.94	Louis Rawlings (FRA)	U23	22.03.96	1	Philadelphia, USA	15	Apr

1000 Metres Indoor

2:20.54	Neil Gourley	U23	7.02.95	1	Blacksburg, USA	18	Feb
2:22.06	Andrew Osagie		19.02.88	5	New York (A), USA	11	Feb
2:22.30	Tom Marshall		12.06.89	1	Cardiff	15	Jan

1500 Metres

3:33.61	Chris O'Hare		23.11.90	7	Monaco, MON	21	Jul
3:34.35				3	Los Angeles (ER), USA	18	May
3:34.75				1	London (O)	9	Jul
3:38.14+				2m	Eugene, USA	27	May
3:38.28				12	London (O)	13	Aug
3:38.59				4s2	London (O)	11	Aug
3:39.05				2	Stanford, USA	5	May
3:39.31				1	Somerville, USA	2	Jun
3:40.96+				2m	Birmingham	20	Aug

3:34.17	Jake Wightman		11.07.94	1	Oslo, NOR	15	Jun
3:35.25				7	Zürich, SUI	24	Aug
3:35.93				1	Oordegem, BEL	27	May
3:38.50				4h3	London (O)	10	Aug
3:40.80+				1m	Birmingham	20	Aug
3:41.79				8s1	London (O)	11	Aug
3:34.19	Mo Farah		23.03.83	2	Los Angeles (ER), USA	18	May
3:35.72	Charlie Grice		7.11.93	7	Prague, CZE	5	Jun
3:36.29				5	London (O)	9	Jul
3:37.37+				8m	Eugene, USA	27	May
3:37.78				6	Oslo, NOR	15	Jun
3:39.52				12	Heusden, BEL	22	Jul
3:41.28				4	Bilbao, ESP	24	Jun
3:35.99	Josh Kerr	U23	8.10.97	1	Azusa, USA	14	Apr
3:36.97	Robbie Fitzgibbon	U23	23.03.96	4	Nijmegen, NED	2	Jun
3:37.74				13	London (O)	9	Jul
3:38.00				9	Huelva, ESP	14	Jun
3:40.38				2	Tübingen, GER	20	May
3:40.42				3	Stanford, USA	5	May
3:37.45	Tom Marshall		12.06.89	11	London (O)	9	Jul
3:37.62				1	Watford	14	Jun
3:39.27				9	Oordegem, BEL	27	May
3:37.58i+	Andrew Butchart		14.10.91	1m	New York (A), USA	4	Feb
3:39.61				4	Watford	14	Jun
3:38.12	Rowan Axe		17.05.91	2	Watford	14	Jun
3:42.30				8rB	Heusden, BEL	22	Jul
3:38.35	Adam Clarke		3.04.91	9	Nijmegen, NED	2	Jun
3:39.66				9	Padova, ITA	16	Jul
3:41.63				6rB	Heusden, BEL	22	Jul
3:41.72				8	Brussels, BEL	1	Sep
(10)							
3:38.52i	Tom Lancashire		2.07.85	6	Birmingham	18	Feb
3:38.85				10	Nijmegen, NED	2	Jun
3:39.96i				7	Karlsruhe, GER	4	Feb
3:41.10				8rB	Los Angeles (ER), USA	18	May
3:39.00	Jonathan Davies		28.10.94	3	Watford	14	Jun
3:39.65	James West	U23	30.01.96	5	Watford	14	Jun
3:40.30	Liam Dee	U23	23.05.96	12	Swarthmore, USA	15	May
3:41.58				10	Watford	14	Jun
3:40.52	Neil Gourley	U23	7.02.95	4s1	Eugene, USA	7	Jun
3:40.70	Josh Carr		30.07.94	6	Watford	14	Jun
3:40.78	Scott Snow	U23	29.11.95	4rC	Los Angeles (ER), USA	18	May
3:40.95	James McMurray	U23	18.01.95	7	Watford	14	Jun
3:41.09	Andrew Heyes		22.06.90	8	Watford	14	Jun
3:41.27	Elliot Giles		26.05.94	1	Watford	23	Aug
3:42.50				1	Watford	9	Aug
(20)							
3:41.43	Philip Sesemann		3.10.92	9	Watford	14	Jun
3:41.64	Robbie Farnham-Rose		5.01.94	2rB	Azusa, USA	14	Apr
3:42.12	Jake Heyward	U20	26.04.99	4	Merksem, BEL	29	Jul
3:42.23	William Paulson		17.11.94	1	Princeton, USA	21	Apr
3:42.34	Alex George	U23	6.02.96	12	Azusa, USA	14	Apr
3:42.42	Sam Stabler		17.05.92	1	Loughborough	8	Jul
60 performances to 3:42.5 by 26 athletes including 3 indoors							
3:42.51	James Gormley	U20	3.04.98	2	Watford	24	Jun
3:43.16	Tom Hook	U23	6.06.95	7rB	Oordegem, BEL	27	May
3:43.3i+	Ieuan Thomas		17.07.89	1m	Cardiff	5	Feb
3:48.20				13	Solihull	13	May
3:43.64	John Sanderson		27.02.93	11	Watford	14	Jun
(30)							
3:43.69	Stuart McCallum	U23	15.09.95	12	Watford	14	Jun

3:43.97i	John Ashcroft		13.11.92	5	Vienna, AUT	28	Jan
3:45.36				10	Watford	24	Jun
3:43.98	Archie Davis	U20	16.10.98	8rC	Oordegem, BEL	27	May
3:44.08	Zak Seddon		28.06.94	1	Tallahassee, USA	24	Mar
3:44.34	Ian Crowe-Wright	U23	27.03.95	13	Watford	14	Jun
3:44.36	Patrick Dever	U23	5.09.96	5	Loughborough	21	May
3:44.52	Daniel Wallis	U23	29.01.96	6	Loughborough	21	May
3:44.88	George Duggan	U23	1.09.96	9	Watford	24	Jun
3:44.91	Lewis Moses		9.01.87	2	Loughborough	8	Jul
3:44.96	Guy Smith		11.01.90	2rB	Oordegem, BEL	3	Jun
(40)							
3:45.09	Cameron Boyek		9.10.93	4	Solihull	13	May
3:45.13	Shaun Wyllie	U23	27.02.95	10rB	Oordegem, BEL	27	May
3:45.18	Steve Mitchell		24.05.88	7	Oordegem, BEL	3	Jun
3:45.18	Kyran Roberts	U23	19.09.95	3	Loughborough	8	Jul
3:45.29	Dale King-Clutterbuck		1.01.92	5h1	Birmingham	1	Jul
3:45.39	William Fuller	U23	14.05.97	4	Manchester (Str)	19	Aug
3:45.44	Elliott Dorey		19.04.94	6	Manchester (Str)	19	Aug
3:45.61	Ricky Harvie	U23	17.03.95	3rB	Watford	24	Jun
3:45.62	Kieran Wood	U23	3.11.95	7	Solihull	13	May
3:45.62	Andrew Smith	U23	7.10.95	4	Loughborough	8	Jul
(50)							
3:45.66	Jonathan Tobin	U23	11.04.96	12rC	Oordegem, BEL	27	May
3:45.71	Christopher Olley	U23	26.03.96	8	Manchester (Str)	19	Aug
3:45.74	Max Pickard		4.06.93	1rB	Watford	14	Jun
3:45.76	Tommy Horton		7.11.93	1rB	Manchester (Str)	19	Aug
3:45.78	Jack Crabtree	U23	13.09.96	5	Loughborough	8	Jul
3:45.82	Rob Mullett		31.07.87	1	Atlanta, USA	21	Apr
3:46.17	Matthew Fayers		5.08.94	10	Stanford, USA	22	Apr
3:46.20	Jonathan Cook		31.07.87	9	Ninove, BEL	15	Jul
3:46.25	Matthew Leach		25.09.93	6rB	Watford	24	Jun
3:46.29	Ryan Driscoll		25.01.94	5rB	Stanford, USA	22	Apr
(60)							
3:46.35	Alexander Teuten		3.01.92	13	Watford	24	Jun
3:46.35	Frank Baddick		29.11.85	9	Manchester (Str)	19	Aug
3:46.36	Michael Ward		10.12.94	11rC	Azusa, USA	14	Apr
3:46.47	Luca Russo		7.11.93	1rF	Stanford, USA	31	Mar
3:46.49+	James Bowness		26.11.91	12m	Cork, IRL	18	Jul
3:48.13				1	Glasgow (S)	28	Jul
3:46.62	Dominic Brown		8.10.94	3rB	Watford	14	Jun
3:46.63	Luke Conway		12.01.94	11	Manchester (Str)	19	Aug
3:46.75	Cameron Field	U23	16.04.96	2rB	Manchester (Str)	19	Aug
3:46.82	Mathew Jackson		28.04.91	4rB	Watford	14	Jun
3:46.93	Ellis Cross	U23	22.09.96	3rB	Solihull	13	May
(70)							
3:46.97	Philip Crout	U23	7.04.95	8rB	Watford	24	Jun
3:47.06	Joe Wilkinson	U23	27.06.96	6rB	Watford	14	Jun
3:47.21	Chris Parr		13.11.84	2	Manchester (SC)	27	May
3:47.27	Michael Wilson	U23	4.01.96	4rB	Solihull	13	May
3:47.28	James McCarthy	U23	31.10.96	6	Loughborough	8	Jul
3:47.31	Matthew Wigelsworth	U23	27.09.96	1	Manchester (Str)	25	Jul
3:47.75	Jonathon Roberts		11.05.94	1rC	Watford	24	Jun
3:47.82	Dave Ragan		26.03.83	6	Watford	12	Jul
3:47.85	Lascelles Hussey	U23	1.07.97	7rB	Solihull	13	May
3:47.89	Conor Bradley		6.10.87	2	Belfast	10	Jun
(80)							
3:47.93	Jamie Williamson	U23	3.03.97	3	Manchester (SC)	27	May
3:47.99	Charles Cooper	U23	29.02.96	8	Fairfax, USA	8	Apr
3:48.02	Richard Weir		7.08.84	8rB	Solihull	13	May
3:48.05	Robert Needham		18.04.94	3	Manchester (Str)	25	Jul
3:48.06	Kieran Clements		20.11.93	12rH	Swarthmore, USA	15	May

Time	Name	Cat	DOB	Pos	Venue	Day	Month
3:48.08i	Jamie Webb		1.06.94	1	Sheffield	19	Feb
3:48.12	Alex Brecker		15.12.93	7	Loughborough	8	Jul
3:48.25	Douglas Musson		8.04.94	11	Watford	9	Aug
3:48.26	Archie Rayner	U20	2.06.99	9rB	Solihull	13	May
3:48.31	Jack Gooch	U23	24.04.96	4	Manchester (Str)	25	Jul
(90)							
3:48.37	Jamaine Coleman	U23	22.09.95	1rD	Charlottesville, USA	22	Apr
3:48.47	Tom Dodd	U20	2.10.98	1rC	Loughborough	8	Jul
3:48.59	Hamza Kadir	U20	12.09.99	3rB	Manchester (Str)	19	Aug
3:48.60	Emile Cairess	U23	27.12.97	5	Manchester (Str)	25	Jul
3:48.65	Kyle Langford	U23	2.02.96	2	London (LV)	3	Jun
3:48.72	Anthony Whiteman	V45	13.11.71	2rB	Loughborough	8	Jul
3:48.72	Euan Gilchrist	U20	10.08.98	2rC	Loughborough	8	Jul
3:48.75	Alex Coomber		24.07.94	1	Manchester (SC)	20	Aug
3:48.76	Michael Salter		12.01.90	6	Manchester (Str)	25	Jul
3:48.81	Haran Dunderdale	U23	26.04.96	4	Champaign, USA	22	Apr
(100)							
3:48.82	Daniel Jarvis	U23	21.10.95	4rC	Watford	24	Jun
3:48.86	Dominic Nolan		29.11.94	7rB	Watford	14	Jun
3:48.91i	Andrew Wright	U23	13.09.95	2	Sheffield	19	Feb
3:48.96	Ben Connor		17.10.92	7	Manchester (Str)	25	Jul

Additional Under 20 (1-7 above)

Time	Name	Cat	DOB	Pos	Venue	Day	Month
3:49.35	Joshua Lay		11.04.00	2	Nassau, BAH	20	Jul
3:49.39i	Piers Copeland		26.11.98	2	Cardiff	15	Jan
3:49.70	Luke Duffy	U17	14.11.00	3	Nassau, BAH	20	Jul
(10)							
3:49.88	Jonathan Shields		1.02.98	3	Manchester (Str)	13	Jun
3:49.91	William Richardson		23.02.98	3rC	Loughborough	8	Jul
3:50.43	Jeremy Dempsey		17.12.99	9rB	Watford	14	Jun
3:50.70	Benjamin Davies		12.03.99	1rD	Manchester (Str)	19	Aug
3:50.93	Sol Sweeney		4.12.98	2rB	Manchester (Str)	27	Jun
3:50.93	Archie Walton		14.05.98	1	Exeter	29	Aug
3:51.18	Adam Moore		8.06.98	2rD	Manchester (Str)	19	Aug
3:51.44	Adam Scott		24.01.00	5rB	Manchester (SC)	27	May
3:52.42	Alex Rieley		26.02.98	7rB	Manchester (SC)	27	May
3:52.57	Joseph Tuffin		24.06.99	4rC	Manchester (Str)	19	Aug
(20)							
3:52.61	Scott Beattie		4.12.98	13rB	Solihull	13	May
3:52.87	Samuel Maher		18.01.99	5rD	Merksem, BEL	29	Jul
3:52.90	Fintan Stewart		7.05.99	1rD	Manchester (SC)	27	May
3:53.05	George Grassly		19.07.00	5rE	Watford	24	Jun
3:53.08	Max Burgin	U17	20.05.02	1rB	Manchester (Str)	29	Aug
3:53.11	Alasdair Kinloch		8.02.99	13rC	Solihull	13	May
3:53.11	Oliver Dustin	U17	29.11.00	1rC	Manchester (Str)	25	Jul
3:53.17	Will Perkin		16.12.98	2rB	Watford	3	May
3:53.45	Matthew Harding		3.04.98	1rC	Durham, USA	22	Apr
3:53.46	Ben Greenwood		24.09.98	3	Manchester (Str)	25	Apr
(30)							
3:53.64	Christopher Durney		16.01.98	9rC	Loughborough	8	Jul
3:53.86	Jaymee Domoney		17.04.99	10	London (LV)	3	Jun
3:53.87	Blake Moore		8.06.98	5rD	Manchester (Str)	19	Aug
3:53.89	James Vincent		15.10.99	6rD	Loughborough	8	Jul

Additional Under 17 (1-3 above)

Time	Name	Cat	DOB	Pos	Venue	Day	Month
3:54.86	Thomas Eames		4.12.00	2	Brighton	31	May
3:55.28	Yusuf Bizimana		16.09.00	4	Bedford	27	Aug
3:55.60	Joshua Cowperthwaite		9.04.01	3rC	Manchester (Str)	25	Jul
3:56.25	Thomas Patrick		4.07.01	14rB	Watford	14	Jun
3:57.22	Alex Ediker		14.08.01	5rC	Manchester (Str)	25	Jul
3:57.96	Jacques Maurice		11.02.01	5	Bedford	27	Aug
3:58.19	Joseph Owen		30.04.01	1	Chelmsford	13	May

3:58.24	Thomas Keen	16.06.01	3rB	Watford	28	Jun
3:58.61	Ben Lee	7.01.01	3rB	Manchester (Str)	29	Aug
3:58.96	Kane Elliott	19.01.02	4	Grangemouth	6	Sep
3:59.02	Jack Meijer	3.11.00	6	Bedford	27	Aug
3:59.16	Luke van Oudtshoorn	30.06.02	2	Reading	21	May
3:59.40	Max Heyden	12.09.00	9	Watford	26	Jul
3:59.42	Joshua Ward	14.10.00	7	Bedford	27	Aug
4:00.0	Callum Abberley	27.10.00	1rB	Oxford	29	Jul
4:00.17	Rory Leonard	13.02.01	4rE	Manchester (Str)	19	Aug
4:00.78	Nick Wiltshire	24.10.00	5h2	Bedford	26	Aug
(20)						
4:01.0	Oliver Carvell	9.04.02	4	Tipton	20	Jun
4:01.25	Finn Birnie	26.09.00	9	Milton Keynes	3	Jun
4:01.25	Remi Adebiyi	4.11.00	2	Dublin (S), IRL	5	Aug
4:01.72	Aaron Hunt	3.03.01	6h2	Bedford	26	Aug
4:01.97	Keelan Hopewell	6.02.01	1	Birmingham	17	Jun
4:02.23	Joe Smith	20.10.01	1	Basingstoke	17	Jun
4:02.34	Lachlan Wellington	25.06.01	2	Basingstoke	17	Jun
4:02.76	Jed Skilton	6.09.00	4rl	Watford	24	Jun
4:02.82	Oliver Rouse	12.03.01	6h1	Bedford	26	Aug
4:02.85	Rhys Owen	10.03.01	5	Visby, SWE	30	Jun
(30)						
4:03.49	Connor Bentley	19.01.01	8rB	Manchester (Str)	13	Jun
4:03.60	Harris Mier	7.11.01	2rB	Milton Keynes	3	Jun
4:03.68	Elliot Cordery	6.03.01	1rD	Watford	26	Jul
4:03.69	David Dow	15.10.01	4rB	Milton Keynes	3	Jun
4:03.75	Benjamin Rouse	12.03.01	4h2	Birmingham	7	Jul
4:03.93	Morgan Gallimore	15.04.01	5	Birmingham	8	Jul

Under 15

4:00.20	Ethan Hussey	5.03.03	5rE	Manchester (Str)	19	Aug
4:06.27	Mohamed Sharif Ali	8.08.03	8rC	Watford	28	Jun
4:06.7	Henry Johnson	28.10.02	3	Jarrow	26	Jul
4:08.64	Lewis Dow	18.01.03	10	Glasgow	29	Aug
4:09.03	Daniel Payne	26.12.02	3rC	Chester-Le-Street	5	Jun
4:09.46	Benjamin Reynolds	1.10.02	5rC	Watford	23	Aug
4:10.59	Liam Rawlings	12.01.03	1	Nuneaton	19	Aug
4:10.82	Finlay Seeds	30.06.03	1	Inglewood, NZL	7	Apr
4:10.97	Will Barnicoat	24.03.03	1	Basingstoke	17	Jun
4:11.0	Angus Williams	7.12.02	2rD	Oxford	29	Jul
(10)						
4:11.37	Archie Lowe	16.02.03	4rC	Chester-Le-Street	5	Jun
4:11.69	Fraser Gordon	11.09.02	14rC	Watford	31	May
4:11.86	Aaron Samuel	6.06.03	4h1	Birmingham	7	Jul
4:12.38	OJ Parmenter	18.03.03	3	Bedford	26	Aug
4:12.56	Oliver Bright	9.04.03	1h2	Birmingham	7	Jul
4:12.71	Archie Parkinson	7.04.03	3	Loughborough	9	Aug
4:13.25	Brandon Quinton	22.02.03	6h1	Birmingham	7	Jul
4:14.17	Dylan Bowley	14.05.03	2	Nuneaton	19	Aug
4:14.7	Will Bellamy	31.03.03	1	Jarrow	26	Jul
4:15.2	Liam Dunne	7.12.02	1	Horsham	21	Jul
(20)						
4:15.85	Scott Nutter	19.10.02	8h1	Birmingham	7	Jul
4:15.97	Ryan Shields	31.01.03	7h2	Birmingham	7	Jul
4:16.43	Jaden Kennedy	16.09.03	9h1	Birmingham	7	Jul
4:16.74	Ben Sandilands	7.08.03	10	Grangemouth	6	Sep
4:17.12	Oliver Smart	20.02.03	8h2	Birmingham	7	Jul
4:17.4	Daniel Joyce	2.01.03	1	Jarrow	21	May
4:17.53	Alex Moyse	22.09.02	1	Exeter	17	Jun
4:18.02	Sam Almond	24.11.02	4	Hexham	17	Jun
4:18.11	Jolyon Leavesley	7.12.02	1	Nuneaton	9	Sep

4:18.33 (30)	David Addison		16.10.02	12rD	Glasgow (S)	28	Jul
4:18.69	Isaac Chandler		1.10.02	1rH	Watford	26	Jul
4:18.73	Rhys James		4.12.02	1	Brecon	26	Aug

Under 13

4:29.57	Ethan Scott		20.01.05	11rF	Watford	23	Aug
4:30.75	William Rabjohns		11.02.06	1	Kingston	29	Jul
4:32.11	Matthew Blacklock		3.10.04	1	Bromley	15	Jul
4:32.22	Lewis Sullivan		23.09.04	2	Kingston	29	Jul
4:33.32	Frank Morgan		20.01.05	3rC	Exeter	25	Jul
4:34.8	Daniel Galloway		8.11.04	1	Tamworth	12	Jul
4:35.41	Ben Brown		28.02.05	2	Bromley	15	Jul
4:36.0	Harry Ware		26.10.04	1	Woking	11	Jun
4:36.02	Oliver Capps		20.01.05	5rD	Exeter	29	Aug
4:36.1	Elliot Gladwell		7.05.05	1	Bedford	3	Sep

Foreign

3:42.19	*Ossama Meslek (ITA)*	*U23*	*8.01.97*	*4rB*	*Ninove, BEL*	*15*	*Jul*
3:44.03	*Harvey Dixon (GIB)*		*2.11.93*	*13h3*	*London (O)*	*10*	*Aug*
3:47.70	*Eoin Pierce (IRL)*		*20.05.89*	*1rB*	*Watford*	*12*	*Jul*
3:48.33	*Christian Von Eitzen (GER)*	*U23*	*1.01.97*	*3*	*Watford*	*23*	*Aug*
3:49.34	*Alex Gruen (AUS)*	*U20*	*1.02.98*	*9*	*Manchester (Str)*	*25*	*Jul*

1 Mile

3:53.34	Chris O'Hare		23.11.90	2rB	Eugene, USA	27	May
	3:55.01			2	Birmingham	20	Aug
	3:56.22			1	Huntingdon Station, USA	6	Sep
3:53.62	Charlie Grice		7.11.93	10	Eugene, USA	27	May
3:54.23i	Andrew Butchart		14.10.91	1	New York (A), USA	4	Feb
3:54.92	Jake Wightman		11.07.94	1	Birmingham	20	Aug
	3:57.24i			3	Boston (R), USA	28	Jan
3:58.19i	Liam Dee	U23	23.05.96	6	Boston, USA	26	Feb
	4:04.43			5	Philadelphia, USA	29	Apr
3:58.31	Tom Marshall		12.06.89	8	Dublin (S), IRL	12	Jul
	3:59.84i			3	Athlone, IRL	15	Feb
3:58.53i	Matthew Fayers		5.08.94	6	Seattle, USA	11	Feb
3:59.31i	Ieuan Thomas		17.07.89	1	Cardiff	5	Feb
3:59.90i	Josh Kerr	U23	8.10.97	1h2	College Station, USA	10	Mar
	13 performances to 4:00.0 by 9 athletes including 7 indoors						
4:00.10i (10)	Neil Gourley	U23	7.02.95	4h1	College Station, USA	10	Mar
4:00.58	Jonathan Davies		28.10.94	1	Bedford	30	Jul
4:00.63	Robbie Fitzgibbon	U23	23.03.96	12	Birmingham	20	Aug
4:01.32i	Oliver Aitchison		13.03.92	3rB	Seattle, USA	11	Feb
4:02.99	Adam Visokay		11.03.94	7	Concord, USA	1	Jun
4:03.26	James Bowness		26.11.91	11	Cork, IRL	18	Jul
4:03.92i	Rob Mullett		31.07.87	6	Nashville, USA	14	Jan
4:04.02i	Scott Snow	U23	29.11.95	6	Seattle, USA	25	Feb
4:04.39i	Charles Cooper	U23	29.02.96	5	Boston, USA	4	Feb
4:04.63i	Robbie Farnham-Rose		5.01.94	1	Clemson, USA	27	Jan
4:05.14i (20)	Haran Dunderdale	U23	26.04.96	2rF	Bloomington, USA	20	Jan
4:05.36i	Marc Scott		21.12.93	1	Iowa City, USA	28	Jan
4:05.42	Luca Russo		7.11.93	10	St. Louis, USA	1	Jun
4:05.42	Sam Stabler		17.05.92	2	Bedford	30	Jul
4:05.75i	Dale King-Clutterbuck		1.01.92	1	London (LV)	1	Feb
4:06.10i	Patrick Monaghan		25.10.93	4rD	Seattle, USA	11	Feb
4:06.50i	Stuart Ferguson		10.10.92	3rD	Notre Dame, USA	4	Feb
4:06.56i	Elliot Slade		5.11.94	1	Staten Island, USA	10	Feb
4:06.71	Dominic Brown		8.10.94	3	Bedford	30	Jul
4:06.85i	Jordan Donnelly		20.09.87	11	Boston, USA	10	Feb

2000 Metres

5:10.02+	Andrew Butchart	14.10.91	1m	London (O)	9	Jul
5:10.2+	Mo Farah	23.03.83	2m	London (O)	9	Jul
5:12.28i	Cameron Boyek	9.10.93	1	Sheffield	18	Nov

3000 Metres

7:35.15	Mo Farah	23.03.83	1	London (O)	9	Jul
7:38.64			1	Birmingham	20	Aug
7:41.20			1	Kingston, JAM	10	Jun
7:51.83+			4m	Eugene, USA	27	May
c.7:53+			m	Zürich, SUI	24	Aug
7:56.15i+			4m	Birmingham	18	Feb
7:59.1+			2m	Ostrava, CZE	28	Jun
7:37.56	Andrew Butchart	14.10.91	3	London (O)	9	Jul
7:41.05i+			3m	New York (A), USA	11	Feb
7:42.97i			2	Boston (R), USA	28	Jan
7:44.10			4	Birmingham	20	Aug
7:45.36			8	Doha, QAT	5	May
7:53.83+			18m	Eugene, USA	27	May
7:42.22	Nick Goolab	30.01.90	11	London (O)	9	Jul
7:53.83i+			1m	Birmingham	18	Feb
7:57.64			1	Loughborough	21	May
7:57.71			1	Watford	3	May
7:58.13i			3	Sheffield	12	Feb
7:43.37	Marc Scott	21.12.93	12	London (O)	9	Jul
7:47.57i			1	Ames, USA	11	Feb
7:57.19i			3	College Station, USA	11	Mar
7:58.52			2	Villeneuve d'Ascq, FRA	25	Jun
7:49.29i	Lee Emanuel	24.01.85	2	Winston-Salem, USA	3	Feb
7:55.91i			1	Sheffield	12	Feb
7:54.01	Ben Connor	17.10.92	5	Cork, IRL	18	Jul
7:54.48i	Rob Mullett	31.07.87	10	Boston (R), USA	28	Jan
8:19.24			16	London (O)	9	Jul
7:55.65	Dewi Griffiths	9.08.91	7	Cork, IRL	18	Jul
7:55.76i+	Andrew Heyes	22.06.90	2m	Birmingham	18	Feb
7:57.00i			2	Sheffield	12	Feb
7:59.18i			2	Sheffield	8	Jan
8:04.48			6	Gothenburg, SWE	11	Jul
7:57.20 (10)	Liam Dee	U23 23.05.96	14	Concord, USA	1	Jun
7:58.94i	James West	U23 30.01.96	1	Sheffield	8	Jan
8:00.66			1	Watford	26	Jul
7:58.95i	Zak Seddon	28.06.94	4	Sheffield	12	Feb
7:59.32i	Ieuan Thomas	17.07.89	5	Sheffield	12	Feb
7:59.66	Rowan Axe	17.05.91	2	Watford	3	May

35 performances to 8:00.0 by 14 athletes including 16 indoors

8:00.62	Jake Shelley	16.03.91	3	Watford	3	May
8:00.78i	Philip Sesemann	3.10.92	4	Sheffield	8	Jan
8:03.84			2	Watford	24	Jun
8:01.17	Kieran Clements	20.11.93	2	Watford	26	Jul
8:01.28	Sam Stabler	17.05.92	4	Watford	3	May
8:01.56	Jonathan Taylor	10.10.87	2	Loughborough	21	May
8:01.79 (20)	Robbie Fitzgibbon	U23 23.03.96	4	Watford	26	Jul
8:03.68i	Robbie Farnham-Rose	5.01.94	1	Nashville, USA	14	Jan
8:03.84i	Matthew Leach	25.09.93	4	Seattle, USA	11	Feb
8:04.52	Christopher Olley	U23 26.03.96	5	Watford	26	Jul
8:04.86	Ryan Driscoll	25.01.94	6	Watford	26	Jul
8:04.87i	John Ashcroft	13.11.92	6	Sheffield	8	Jan
8:04.87i	Haran Dunderdale	U23 26.04.96	3	Notre Dame, USA	4	Feb

8:05.24	John Sanderson		27.02.93	7	Watford	26	Jul
8:05.25i	Neil Gourley	U23	7.02.95	1	Nashville, USA	10	Feb
8:06.15i	Michael Ward		10.12.94	3rB	Ames, USA	11	Feb
8:06.38i+	Jonathan Davies		28.10.94	10m	Birmingham	18	Feb
(30)							
8:07.07	Alex Brecker		15.12.93	3	Aarhus, DEN	2	Jun
8:07.39	Paulos Surafel	U23	12.01.97	5	Watford	3	May
8:07.43	Petros Surafel	U23	12.01.97	8	Watford	26	Jul
8:07.58i	William Paulson		17.11.94	4	Boston, USA	11	Feb
8:07.59i	Owen Hind		1.08.90	9	Birmingham, USA	11	Mar
8:07.65i	Kristian Jones		4.03.91	1	Glasgow	4	Jan
	8:10.71			1	Glasgow (S)	2	Jun
8:08.37i	Jac Hopkins	U23	16.05.97	2	Boston, USA	5	Mar
8:08.62	Douglas Musson		8.04.94	3	Watford	24	Jun
8:08.99i	Steve Mitchell		24.05.88	1	Cardiff	10	Dec
8:09.09	Patrick Dever	U23	5.09.96	1	Manchester (Str)	19	Aug
(40)							
8:09.13	Emile Cairess	U23	27.12.97	5	Loughborough	21	May
8:09.30	Graham Rush		8.09.82	4	Watford	24	Jun
8:09.45	Lewis Moses		9.01.87	6	Loughborough	21	May
8:10.39	Alastair Hay		7.09.85	2	Manchester (Str)	19	Aug
8:10.52i	Jonathan Tobin	U23	11.04.96	2	Cardiff	10	Dec
8:10.53	Josh Carr		30.07.94	7	Loughborough	21	May
8:10.83i	Jonathan Hopkins		3.06.92	3	Cardiff	10	Dec
8:10.97i	Edward Shepherd		8.12.93	10rB	Seattle, USA	11	Feb
8:11.23i	Adam Craig	U23	9.05.95	2	Fairfax, USA	26	Feb
8:11.26	Joe Wilkinson	U23	27.06.96	8	Loughborough	21	May
(50)							
8:11.65i	James Bowness		26.11.91	2	Glasgow	4	Jan
8:11.79	Philip Crout	U23	7.04.95	2	Watford	19	Apr
8:11.81i	William Gray		24.01.93	8	Sheffield	8	Jan
8:12.37	Alexander Teuten		3.01.92	1	Bedford	15	Jul
8:12.45	Ben Alcock		19.09.94	6	Watford	24	Jun
8:12.81	Adam Kirk-Smith		30.01.91	2	Bedford	15	Jul
8:13.12	Mohamud Aadan		11.01.90	3	Bedford	15	Jul
8:13.38	Ben Bradley	U23	22.05.95	6	Watford	3	May
8:13.41	Jamie Dee	U23	23.11.97	3	Manchester (Str)	19	Aug
8:13.47	Joshua Trigwell		28.05.93	9	Loughborough	21	May
(60)							
8:13.52	Jack Rowe	U23	30.01.96	8	Watford	24	Jun
8:13.74i	Tom Holden	U23	21.03.97	9	Sheffield	8	Jan
8:13.77i	Tommy Horton		7.11.93	3	Sheffield	19	Feb
8:14.00i	Jamaine Coleman	U23	22.09.95	2	Bloomington, USA	10	Feb
8:14.17i	Adam Visokay		11.03.94	11	Boston, USA	10	Feb
8:14.18+	Ross Millington		19.09.89	m	Stanford, USA	5	May
8:14.57	Jonathan Shields	U20	1.02.98	4	Manchester (Str)	19	Aug
8:14.76	Richard Goodman		4.04.93	4	Bedford	15	Jul
8:14.82	Mathew Jackson		28.04.91	5	Manchester (Str)	19	Aug
8:14.94i	Bradley Goater		13.04.94	6	Sheffield	12	Feb
(70)							
8:14.94	William Richardson	U20	23.02.98	5	Bedford	15	Jul
8:15.29	Guy Smith		11.01.90	6	Manchester (Str)	19	Aug
8:15.83	Archie Rayner	U20	2.06.99	8	Watford	3	May
8:16.50	Adam Clarke		3.04.91	9	Turku, FIN	13	Jun
8:16.53	Lachlan Oates		30.01.92	7	Manchester (Str)	19	Aug
8:17.33i	Michael Wilsmore		8.06.85	4	Cardiff	10	Dec
8:17.69i	Luca Russo		7.11.93	9	Nashville, USA	14	Jan
8:17.71	Andy Maud		28.07.83	1ns	Kingston	6	May
8:17.77i	Nathan Jones		3.10.94	1	Birmingham, USA	23	Feb
8:18.20i	Jonathan Collier	U23	22.08.95	9h2	Staten Island, USA	25	Feb
(80)							

179

8:18.74i	Oliver Lockley			9.11.93	11	Nashville, USA	14 Jan
8:18.86i	Ryan Thomson	U23		21.02.96	4	Glasgow	4 Jan
8:18.93	Jacob Allen			3.10.94	10	Loughborough	21 May
8:19.01	Ian Kimpton			8.11.86	1rB	Watford	26 Jul
8:19.16i	Oliver James			26.03.94	3	Birmingham, USA	23 Feb
8:19.21	William Fuller	U23		14.05.97	1rB	Watford	24 Jun
8:19.31i	Thomas George	U23		6.02.96	13	Nashville, USA	14 Jan
8:19.36	Lucian Allison			11.11.90	2rB	Watford	26 Jul
8:19.37	Michael Coltherd			28.12.82	11	Loughborough	21 May
8:19.39	Jeremy Dempsey	U20		17.12.99	3rB	Watford	26 Jul
(90)							
8:19.69i	Gilbert Grundy			22.06.89	13	Seattle, USA	14 Jan

Additional Under 20 (1-4 above)

8:21.37	Alasdair Kinloch			8.02.99	4	Watford	31 May
8:22.20	Sol Sweeney			4.12.98	3	Glasgow (S)	2 Jun
8:22.86	Tom Mortimer			7.01.99	1	Street	1 May
8:23.34i	Piers Copeland			26.11.98	5	Cardiff	10 Dec
8:23.43	Adam Scott			24.01.00	1	Manchester (Str)	25 Apr
8:23.62	James Gormley			3.04.98	3	Sheffield	6 May
(10)							
8:24.87	Thomas Keen	U17		16.06.01	2	Watford	6 Sep
8:24.93	Luke van Oudtshoorn	U17		30.06.02	7	Watford	31 May
8:25.24	Joshua Cowperthwaite	U17		9.04.01	2	Manchester (Str)	13 Jun
8:27.41	Euan Gilchrist			10.08.98	2	Manchester (Str)	29 Aug
8:27.56	Ben Dijkstra			31.10.98	1	Bedford	17 Jun
8:27.59	Jack Boswell			27.12.98	9	Watford	31 May
8:27.6	Benjamin Davies			12.03.99	4	Cambridge	9 Jun
8:30.28	James Puxty			30.09.99	10	Watford	31 May
8:30.65	Oliver Barbaresi			23.03.00	17	Watford	3 May
8:30.70	Joe Arthur			15.01.99	5	Manchester (Str)	16 May
(20)							
8:30.86	Conor Smith			11.03.99	11	Watford	31 May
8:32.36	Thomas Rogerson			8.11.98	4	Manchester (Str)	25 Apr
8:32.38	Elliot Dee			25.05.00	3rB	Manchester (Str)	19 Aug
8:33.13	Nathan Dunn			1.09.99	4rB	Manchester (Str)	19 Aug
8:33.36i	James Donald			18.11.98	7	Glasgow	4 Jan
	8:33.47				6	Glasgow (S)	2 Jun
8:33.45	Zakariya Mahamed	U17		29.11.00	5	Street	1 May
8:33.51	Angus McMillan			15.03.00	5	Manchester (Str)	25 Jul
8:33.66	Baldvin Magnussen			7.04.99	4	Manchester (Str)	27 Jun

Additional Under 17 (1-4 above)

8:36.49	Christopher McLeod			27.12.00	15	Watford	31 May
8:37.46	Lachlan Wellington			25.06.01	5	Milton Keynes	3 Jun
8:37.91	Jack Meijer			3.11.00	6	Milton Keynes	3 Jun
8:38.63	Max Heyden			12.09.00	3	Basingstoke	19 Jul
8:40.74	Connor Bentley			19.01.01	8	Manchester (Str)	25 Apr
8:40.81	Joshua Dickinson			10.09.01	9rB	Watford	26 Jul
(10)							
8:43.0	Rory Leonard			13.02.01	1	Jarrow	24 May
8:44.64	Thomas Patrick			4.07.01	2rB	Watford	19 Apr
8:45.51	Max Brame			19.07.01	16	Manchester (Str)	16 May
8:46.91	Alex Ediker			14.08.01	10	Manchester (Str)	13 Jun
8:47.11	Jack White			25.10.00	8	Birmingham	8 Jul
8:48.85	Joseph Owen			30.04.01	1	Chelmsford	14 May
8:49.85	David Dow			15.10.01	11rB	Watford	3 May
8:50.29	Milan Campion			21.11.00	1	Nuneaton	20 Aug
8:50.70	Joe Smith			20.10.01	9	Bedford	15 Jul
8:50.75	Sam Hart			6.11.00	10	Street	1 May
(20)							
8:50.78	Fynn Batkin			6.03.01	2	Nuneaton	20 Aug

8:52.31	James Young	28.11.00	13	Watford	5	Apr
8:52.52	Callum Abberley	27.10.00	4	Nuneaton	20	Aug
8:53.16	Fraser Willmore	29.09.01	1rB	Milton Keynes	3	Jun
8:53.47	Morgan James	17.05.01	2rB	Milton Keynes	3	Jun
8:53.50	Thomas Keevil	22.09.00	9	Bedford	15	Jul
8:53.75	Jacob O'Hara	11.02.01	5rB	Street	1	May
8:53.87	William Broom	25.01.01	3rB	Milton Keynes	3	Jun
8:54.85	Max Davis	31.05.01	5rB	Milton Keynes	3	Jun
8:55.1	Oliver Prior	30.01.01	2	Ipswich	20	May

Under 15

8:44.61	Mohamed Sharif Ali	8.08.03	3	London (TB)	22	Jul
8:49.59	Tommy Dawson	2.02.03	4	Leeds	26	Jun
8:53.17	Archie Parkinson	7.04.03	19	Watford	6	Sep
9:01.73	Archie Lowe	16.02.03	2	Bedford	26	Aug
9:05.52	Oliver Bright	9.04.03	12rB	Watford	28	Jun
9:05.82	Isaac Chandler	1.10.02	7	Murcia, ESP	2	Jul
9:08.24	Henry Johnson	28.10.02	1	Leigh	20	Aug
9:09.22	James Jones	20.09.02	1	Cardiff	12	Jul
9:11.20	Will Bellamy	31.03.03	2	Leigh	20	Aug
9:12.28	Angus Williams	7.12.02	1rD	Watford	26	Jul
(10)						
9:12.58	Joseph Reardon	24.10.02	2	Cardiff	12	Jul
9:15.62	Ethan McGlen	26.11.03	3	Leigh	20	Aug
9:18.25	Fraser Gordon	11.09.02	5rD	Watford	26	Jul
9:19.69	Dylan Bowley	14.05.03	8	Watford	23	Aug
9:21.76	Sean Harnett	24.07.03	1rB	Basingstoke	19	Jul
9:21.81	Hanad Ahmed	15.09.02	14rB	Watford	6	Sep
9:22.02	Dylan Spencer	17.06.03	17	Basingstoke	19	Jul
9:23.34	Lewis Hannigan	29.08.03	5	Linwood	18	Apr
9:23.6	Scott Nutter	19.10.02	1	Cudworth	18	Apr
9:24.4	Matthew Ramsden	7.07.03	1	Blackpool	26	Aug
(20)						
9:25.54	Liam Rawlings	12.01.03	2	Nuneaton	20	Aug
9:26.96	Ethan Carolan	28.08.03	2rD	Glasgow (S)	2	Jun
9:27.31	Max McGarvie	18.06.03	16rB	Watford	6	Sep
9:28.42	Johnny Livingstone	11.06.03	1	Exeter	20	Aug
9:28.71	Jaden Kennedy	16.09.03	1	London (CP)	11	Jun
9:29.44	Adam Ireland	28.07.03	13	Watford	23	Aug

Foreign

8:01.58	*Matthew Bergin (IRL)*		*2.03.93*	*3*	*Watford*	*26*	*Jul*
8:12.49	*Abel Tsegay (ETH)*	*U23*	*2.06.96*	*6*	*Aarhus, DEN*	*2*	*Jun*
8:13.10	*Jayme Rossiter (IRL)*		*29.09.90*	*7*	*Watford*	*24*	*Jun*

2 Miles Indoor

8:12.63	Andrew Butchart	14.10.91	3	New York (A), USA	11	Feb

5000 Metres

13:00.70	Mo Farah	23.03.83	1	Eugene, USA	27	May
	13:06.05		1	Zürich, SUI	24	Aug
	13:09.16i		1	Birmingham	18	Feb
	13:25.53+		1m	Ostrava, CZE	28	Jun
	13:30.18		2h1	London (O)	9	Aug
	13:33.22		2	London (O)	12	Aug
	13:36.20+		11m	London (O)	4	Aug
13:11.45	Andrew Butchart	14.10.91	8	Eugene, USA	27	May
	13:12.73		4	Berlin, GER	27	Aug
	13:24.78		7h2	London (O)	9	Aug
	13:38.73		8	London (O)	12	Aug
	13:50.56		1	Birmingham	1	Jul

13:22.37	Marc Scott		21.12.93	4rB	Heusden, BEL	22	Jul
13:37.45				1	Torrance, USA	14	Apr
13:43.83i				2	College Station, USA	10	Mar
13:58.11				18h2	London (O)	9	Aug
13:22.65	Andy Vernon		7.01.86	15	Heusden, BEL	22	Jul
13:54.63				2	Birmingham	1	Jul
13:29.90	Ben Connor		17.10.92	3	Dublin (S), IRL	12	Jul
13:42.89				2	Nijmegen, NED	2	Jun
13:56.71				3	Birmingham	1	Jul
13:33.48	Nick Goolab		30.01.90	13	Oordegem, BEL	27	May
13:59.72				2	Villeneuve d'Ascq, FRA	24	Jun
13:33.60	Dewi Griffiths		9.08.91	5	Dublin (S), IRL	12	Jul
13:50.35				1	Cardiff	10	Jun
13:50.83				1	Swansea	3	Jun
13:57.41				1	Manchester (SC)	20	Aug
13:37.13	Jonathan Davies		28.10.94	11	Carquefou, FRA	23	Jun
13:51.40				25	Oordegem, BEL	27	May
13:58.04i				8	Birmingham	18	Feb
13:37.30	Sam Stabler		17.05.92	10rB	Heusden, BEL	22	Jul
13:38.09				6rB	Oordegem, BEL	27	May
13:59.12				1	Watford	14	Jun
13:37.60	Alexander Yee	U20	18.02.98	2rB	Oordegem, BEL	27	May
(10)							
13:39.21	Adam Clarke		3.04.91	20	Oordegem, BEL	27	May
13:40.66	Alex George	U23	6.02.96	5	Stanford, USA	31	Mar
13:53.83				2	Columbia, USA	13	May
13:47.57i	Alex Short		7.01.94	7	Seattle, USA	11	Feb
14:25.60				2	San Francisco, USA	13	May
13:48.74	Andrew Heyes		22.06.90	3	Nijmegen, NED	2	Jun
13:54.18				10rB	Stanford, USA	5	May
13:51.18	Rob Mullett		31.07.87	7rB	Stanford, USA	5	May
13:55.32	Petros Surafel	U23	12.01.97	3	Ninove, BEL	15	Jul
13:56.87	Alexander Teuten		3.01.92	18rB	Oordegem, BEL	27	May
13:57.80i	Ryan Forsyth	U23	7.07.96	13	Seattle, USA	10	Feb
14:18.90				15	Stanford, USA	21	Apr
13:59.73	Luke Caldwell		2.08.91	2	Watford	14	Jun
13:59.8+e	Callum Hawkins		22.06.92	m	Stanford, USA	5	May
(20)							
13:59.82	Emile Cairess	U23	27.12.97	1	Manchester (SC)	27	May
13:59.94	Richard Goodman		4.04.93	13rC	Heusden, BEL	22	Jul
13:59.99	Patrick Dever	U23	5.09.96	2	Manchester (SC)	27	May

49 performances to 14:00.0 by 23 athletes including 5 indoors

14:00.63	Luke Traynor		6.07.93	1	Glasgow (S)	28	Jul
14:01.30	Lewis Moses		9.01.87	3	Watford	14	Jun
14:01.37	James West	U23	30.01.96	3	Manchester (SC)	27	May
14:01.74	Ellis Cross	U23	22.09.96	1	Watford	24	Jun
14:01.86	Conor Bradley		6.10.87	20	Oordegem, BEL	27	May
14:02.58	Kieran Clements		20.11.93	11	Charlottesville, USA	22	Apr
14:02.92	Douglas Musson		8.04.94	1	Solihull	13	May
(30)							
14:03.29	Christopher Olley	U23	26.03.96	4	Manchester (SC)	27	May
14:03.79	Matthew Leach		25.09.93	14rB	Stanford, USA	5	May
14:03.88	Euan Makepeace	U23	31.05.97	4rB	Torrance, USA	14	Apr
14:04.35	Michael Ward		10.12.94	7	Des Moines, USA	27	Apr
14:05.06	Ben Alcock		19.09.94	11	Los Angeles (ER), USA	6	May
14:05.25	Graham Rush		8.09.82	5	Manchester (SC)	27	May
14:05.79	Mohamud Aadan		11.01.90	16rC	Heusden, BEL	22	Jul
14:05.99	Andy Maud		28.07.83	3	Solihull	13	May
14:06.26	Ben Bradley	U23	22.05.95	4	Watford	24	Jun
c.14:07+	Chris Thompson	V35	17.04.81	1	Manchester (Str)	19	Aug
14:09.61				6	Birmingham	1	Jul

14:07.03	Adam Craig	U23	9.05.95	10	Raleigh, USA	25	Mar
14:07.20	Jack Morris		9.04.93	4	Solihull	13	May
14:09.32	Richard Weir		7.08.84	14	Dublin (S), IRL	12	Jul
14:09.46	Nick Earl		22.09.84	9	Manchester (SC)	27	May
14:10.30	Jack Rowe	U23	30.01.96	4rD	Heusden, BEL	22	Jul
14:10.57	Rhys Park		18.03.94	12	Azusa, USA	14	Apr
14:10.78	Alex Dunbar		24.04.92	6	Watford	24	Jun
14:10.93	William Fuller	U23	14.05.97	10	Ninove, BEL	15	Jul
14:11.10	Henry Pearce		24.01.94	13	Des Moines, USA	28	Apr
14:11.33	Paulos Surafel	U23	12.01.97	10	Manchester (SC)	27	May
(50)							
14:11.60	Ross Skelton		11.05.93	14rC	Oordegem, BEL	27	May
14:11.78	Jamie Dee	U23	23.11.97	11	Manchester (SC)	27	May
14:12.65i	Owen Hind		1.08.90	2	Allendale, USA	10	Feb
14:26.20				11	Watford	24	Jun
14:13.04	Neil Gourley	U23	7.02.95	7	Atlanta, USA	14	May
14:13.61	Peter Huck		10.07.90	6	Solihull	13	May
14:13.94	Lachlan Oates		30.01.92	2	Loughborough	8	Jul
14:14.06	Alex Brecker		15.12.93	11	Ninove, BEL	15	Jul
14:14.62	Matthew Clowes		29.09.89	9	Solihull	13	May
14:14.78	Oliver Lockley		9.11.93	1	Columbia, USA	14	Apr
14:15.96	Joshua Trigwell		28.05.93	8	Watford	24	Jun
(60)							
14:16.64	Tom Mortimer	U20	7.01.99	10	Solihull	13	May
14:16.79	Ben Branagh		11.01.94	11	Solihull	13	May
14:19.63	Joe Wilkinson	U23	27.06.96	12	Manchester (SC)	27	May
14:20.20	Steve Mitchell		24.05.88	3	Loughborough	8	Jul
14:20.73	Jack Gray		10.04.93	13	Solihull	13	May
14:21.23	Jamie Taylor-Caldwell		23.09.91	4	Loughborough	8	Jul
14:21.84i	Nathan Jones		3.10.94	2	Notre Dame, USA	3	Feb
14:21.95	Mathew Jackson		28.04.91	5	Loughborough	8	Jul
14:21.97	James Gormley	U20	3.04.98	1rB	Manchester (SC)	27	May
14:22.12	Philip Crout	U23	7.04.95	4	Bedford	1	May
(70)							
14:22.34	Grant Sheldon		23.08.94	1	Grangemouth	27	Aug
14:22.60	Robbie Fitzgibbon	U23	23.03.96	13	Stanford, USA	31	Mar
14:22.66	Ben Dijkstra	U20	31.10.98	3rB	Manchester (SC)	27	May
14:22.67	Dan Nash		23.03.94	14	Solihull	13	May
14:23.70	Nicholas Torry	V40	19.02.77	1	London (WP)	23	Aug
14:24.14	Jonathan Collier	U23	22.08.95	17rB	Torrance, USA	15	Apr
14:24.78	William Richardson	U20	23.02.98	4rB	Manchester (SC)	27	May
14:24.94i	Jac Hopkins	U23	16.05.97	2	New York, USA	18	Feb
14:25.16	Abdishakur Abdulle		23.06.93	9	Watford	24	Jun
14:25.23	Tom Straw		28.02.91	13rD	Heusden, BEL	22	Jul
(80)							
14:25.53	Stuart McCallum	U23	15.09.95	14	Manchester (SC)	27	May
14:25.80	Michael Christoforou		10.10.92	10	Watford	24	Jun
14:26.25	Robbie Farnham-Rose		5.01.94	4	Auburn, USA	21	Apr
14:26.36	Paul Martelletti	V35	1.08.79	2	London (WP)	23	Aug
14:27.25	Jamie Crowe	U23	9.06.95	3	Glasgow (S)	28	Jul
14:27.31	John Sanderson		27.02.93	3	Swansea	3	Jun
14:27.57i	Adam Visokay		11.03.94	11	Notre Dame, USA	24	Feb
14:27.64	Alastair Hay		7.09.85	3	Grangemouth	27	Aug
14:28.33	Linton Taylor	U23	20.01.95	5rB	Manchester (SC)	27	May
14:28.49	Gus Cockle	U23	7.03.97	7	Bedford	1	May
(90)							
14:28.50	James Straw		1.02.94	6	Loughborough	8	Jul
14:29.00	Dane Blomquist	U23	2.10.96	8	Loughborough	8	Jul
14:29.33	Alexander Goodall		7.11.93	9	Loughborough	8	Jul
14:29.37	Shaun Antell		9.05.87	10	Loughborough	8	Jul
14:30.06	Michael Ferguson	U23	18.03.95	8	Bedford	1	May

Time	Name	Cat	DOB	Pos	Venue	Day	Month
14:31.00	Frank Baddick		29.11.85	9	Watford	14	Jun
14:31.53	Kristian Jones		4.03.91	4	Manchester (SC)	20	Aug
14:32.00	Joshua Grace		11.05.93	17rD	Heusden, BEL	22	Jul
14:32.27	Frankie Conway		29.09.91	9	Melbourne (A), AUS	23	Nov
14:32.50	Cameron Field	U23	16.04.96	17	Solihull	13	May
	(100)						
14:32.89	Jack Bancroft		25.02.88	11	Loughborough	8	Jul
14:33.44	Bradley Goater		13.04.94	10	Bedford	1	May
14:33.79	Harry Earl		10.11.92	2	Chicago, USA	1	Apr
14:34.11	William Ryle-Hodges		20.09.93	11	Bedford	1	May
14:34.44	Zak Tobias		13.09.94	4	Cartagena, ESP	6	May
14:34.78	Jonathan Shields	U20	1.02.98	6rB	Manchester (SC)	27	May
14:34.97	Carwyn Jones	V35	10.10.79	5	Manchester (SC)	20	Aug

Additional Under 20 (1-6 above)

Time	Name	Cat	DOB	Pos	Venue	Day	Month
14:36.31	Sam Stevens	U20	27.03.98	14	Bedford	1	May
14:44.08	Jeremy Dempsey		17.12.99	22	Solihull	13	May
14:44.68	Sol Sweeney		4.12.98	6	Glasgow (S)	28	Jul
14:45.24	James Donald		18.11.98	7	Glasgow (S)	28	Jul
	(10)						
14:52.0	Luke Prior		3.02.98	3	Yate	22	Jul
15:00.50	Alex Brown		2.10.98	1rC	Manchester (SC)	27	May
15:04.7	Ahmed Abdulle		1.05.99	5	London (WF)	30	Jun
15:11.8	Noah Armitage-Hookes		27.10.99	8	London (Cat)	16	Sep
15:12.09	Tristan Rees		3.04.99	12	Glasgow (S)	28	Jul
15:15.63	Harry Halford		22.03.98	10rB	Bedford	1	May
15:15.7	Patrick McNiff		19.08.99	16rB	Loughborough	8	Jul
15:17.67	Thomas Butler		23.02.98	2	Twickenham	18	Mar
15:19.5	Zakariya Mahamed	U17	29.11.00	1	Southampton	19	Aug

Foreign

Time	Name	Cat	DOB	Pos	Venue	Day	Month
14:02.22	*Abel Tsegay (ETH)*	*U23*	*2.06.96*	*5*	*Oslo, NOR*	*6*	*Jul*
14:03.87	*Matthew Bergin (IRL)*		*2.03.93*	*3*	*Watford*	*24*	*Jun*
14:17.58	*James Edgar (IRL)*	*U20*	*12.11.98*	*12*	*Greystones, IRL*	*6*	*May*
14:25.40	*Wondiye Indelbu (ETH)*		*13.02.88*	*15*	*Solihull*	*13*	*May*
14:29.52	*Dejene Gezimu (ETH)*		*29.09.93*	*2*	*London (LV)*	*3*	*Jun*

10000 Metres

Time	Name	Cat	DOB	Pos	Venue	Day	Month
26:49.51	Mo Farah		23.03.83	1	London (O)	4	Aug
27:12.09				1	Ostrava, CZE	28	Jun
27:58.69	Andy Vernon		7.01.86	9	Stanford, USA	5	May
28:21.15				1	London (PH)	20	May
28:33.65				15	Hengelo, NED	11	Jun
28:07.97	Marc Scott		21.12.93	12	Stanford, USA	5	May
29:01.54				1	Eugene, USA	7	Jun
28:16.07	Dewi Griffiths		9.08.91	14	Stanford, USA	5	May
28:24.71				7	Leiden, NED	17	Jun
28:31.88				2	London (PH)	20	May
28:23.58	Ben Connor		17.10.92	6	Leiden, NED	17	Jun
28:46.45				5	London (PH)	20	May
28:40.40	Chris Thompson	V35	17.04.81	1	Manchester (Str)	19	Aug
28:45.48	Matthew Leach		25.09.93	13	Stanford, USA	31	Mar
29:29.79				16	London (PH)	20	May
28:46.83	Alex Short		7.01.94	15	Stanford, USA	31	Mar
29:00.49	Ellis Cross	U23	22.09.96	8	London (PH)	20	May
29:01.76	Luke Caldwell		2.08.91	9	London (PH)	20	May
	(10)						
29:03.64	Sam Stabler		17.05.92	2	Manchester (Str)	19	Aug
29:04.52	Graham Rush		8.09.82	10	London (PH)	20	May
29:05.66	Kristian Jones		4.03.91	11	London (PH)	20	May
29:16.39				1	Glasgow (C)	28	Apr

Time	Name	Cat	DOB	Pos	Location	Day	Month
29:08.52	Luke Traynor		6.07.93	3	Manchester (Str)	19	Aug
29:10.58				8	Eugene, USA	7	Jun
29:15.44				12	Torrance, USA	13	Apr
29:08.94	Mohamud Aadan		11.01.90	12	London (PH)	20	May
29:15.85	Jack Martin		29.04.88	14	Leiden, NED	17	Jun
29:18.38	Matthew Clowes		29.09.89	14	London (PH)	20	May
29:18.50	Ian Kimpton		8.11.86	4	Manchester (Str)	19	Aug
29:24.18	Oliver Lockley		9.11.93	3	San Francisco, USA	31	Mar
29:27.18				5	Manchester (Str)	19	Aug
29:27.04	Owen Hind		1.08.90	5	San Francisco, USA	31	Mar

31 performances to 29:30.0 by 20 athletes

Time	Name	Cat	DOB	Pos	Location	Day	Month
29:32.38	Ryan Forsyth	U23	7.07.96	7	Eugene, USA	13	May
29:33.82	Nathan Jones		3.10.94	7	San Francisco, USA	31	Mar
29:34.26	Joshua Grace		11.05.93	17	London (PH)	20	May
29:37.83	Michael Christoforou		10.10.92	18	London (PH)	20	May
29:38.55	Richard Horton		28.05.93	19	London (PH)	20	May
29:39.72	Adam Craig	U23	9.05.95	1	Williamsburg, USA	30	Mar
29:41.12	Henry Pearce		24.01.94	1rC	Torrance, USA	13	Apr
29:41.88	Jack Morris		9.04.93	19	Leiden, NED	17	Jun
29:45.80	Nick Earl		22.09.84	11	Melbourne (A), AUS	14	Dec
29:48.41	Paul Martelletti	V35	1.08.79	1	London (Cat)	3	Sep
(30)							
29:52.29	Alexander Teuten		3.01.92	24	London (PH)	20	May
29:52.84	Sean Fontana		6.12.90	1	Hillsdale, USA	28	Apr
29:55.01	Philip Crout	U23	7.04.95	25	London (PH)	20	May
29:55.62	Jack Rowe	U23	30.01.96	26	London (PH)	20	May
29:58.39	Nicholas Torry	V40	19.02.77	2	London (Cat)	3	Sep
30:00.16	Alex Dunbar		24.04.92	27	London (PH)	20	May
30:09.36	Lucian Allison		11.11.90	7	Manchester (Str)	19	Aug
30:09.65	Lee Merrien	V35	26.04.79	2rB	London (PH)	20	May
30:09.89	James Straw		1.02.94	8	Manchester (Str)	19	Aug
30:11.69	Nigel Martin		23.03.87	3rB	London (PH)	20	May
(40)							
30:12.24	Phil Beastall		31.08.86	9	Manchester (Str)	19	Aug
30:13.70	Harry Earl		10.11.92	10	Charlottesville, USA	22	Apr
30:14.75	Ben Fish	V35	21.05.82	10	Manchester (Str)	19	Aug
30:15.26	Aaron Scott		11.04.87	11	Manchester (Str)	19	Aug
30:17.3	John Gilbert	V35	24.09.80	1	London (WF)	30	Jun
30:18.91	Tom Straw		28.02.91	4rB	London (PH)	20	May
30:19.30	Kieran Clements		20.11.93	1	Lawrenceville, USA	6	May
30:19.68	Logan Rees	U23	23.02.97	5rB	London (PH)	20	May
30:20.29	Jonathan Collier	U23	22.08.95	2rB	Raleigh, USA	24	Mar
30:23.08	Kojo Kyereme	V40	23.12.74	6rB	London (PH)	20	May
(50)							
30:23.34	Ben Cole		18.06.85	12	Manchester (Str)	19	Aug
30:23.95	James Douglas		18.06.85	7rB	London (PH)	20	May
30:26.18	Steven Bayton		6.08.91	8rB	London (PH)	20	May
30:26.82	Frankie Conway		29.09.91	5	Geelong, AUS	23	Dec
30:26.88	Richard Allen	U23	25.10.95	30	London (PH)	20	May
30:26.95	Paulos Surafel	U23	12.01.97	31	London (PH)	20	May
30:27.67	Ross Skelton		11.05.93	13	Manchester (Str)	19	Aug
30:30.18	Ben Johnson		22.09.88	14	Manchester (Str)	19	Aug
30:30.67	Shane Robinson		19.02.91	15	Manchester (Str)	19	Aug
30:33.03	Dan Nash		23.03.94	10rB	London (PH)	20	May
(60)							
30:33.99	Zak Tobias		13.09.94	11rB	London (PH)	20	May
30:35.35	Jack Bancroft		25.02.88	16	Manchester (Str)	19	Aug
30:35.41	Corey De'Ath	U23	16.02.96	32	London (PH)	20	May
30:40.27	James Donald	U20	18.11.98	17	Manchester (Str)	19	Aug
30:44.46	Oliver Mott		29.11.84	13rB	London (PH)	20	May
30:45.0	Tom Merson		10.02.86	1	Cardiff	12	Aug

30:46.13	Robert Warner			15.06.94	2rC	London (PH)	20 May
30:46.28	Max Nicholls	U23		6.07.96	14rB	London (PH)	20 May
30:47.21	Chris Smith	V40		3.03.77	15rB	London (PH)	20 May
30:48.93	Calum McKenzie			3.05.89	4	Glasgow (C)	28 Apr
(70)							
30:49.27	Jonathan Glen	U23		5.10.96	16rB	London (PH)	20 May
30:51.73	Thomas Bains	U23		3.01.95	8	Williamsburg, USA	30 Mar
30:54.89	William Mackay			3.10.89	1	Grangemouth	13 Aug
30:56.01	Stuart Spencer			11.11.82	19rB	London (PH)	20 May
30:56.25	Paul Navesey			19.04.86	4rC	London (PH)	20 May
30:56.47	Jonathan Poole			16.11.82	4	London (Cat)	3 Sep
30:57.48	Ben Bradley	U23		22.05.95	33	London (PH)	20 May
30:57.66	Stuart Gibson			15.09.83	19	Manchester (Str)	19 Aug
30:58.11	Joe Rainsford			17.06.93	5rC	London (PH)	20 May
30:58.63	Tom Martyn			24.05.89	5	Glasgow (C)	28 Apr

Foreign

28:58.28	*Stephen Scullion (IRL)*		*9.11.88*	*11*	*Portland, USA*	*10 Jun*
28:59.63	*Abel Tsegay (ETH)*	*U23*	*2.06.96*	*7*	*London (PH)*	*20 May*
29:40.92	*Antonio Silva (POR)*		*26.03.87*	*20*	*London (PH)*	*20 May*
30:04.69	*Mohammed Abu-Rezeq (JOR)*		*21.12.83*	*6*	*Manchester (Str)*	*19 Aug*
30:30.65	*John Eves (IRL)*		*17.01.83*	*9rB*	*London (PH)*	*20 May*
30:52.75	*Eoghan Totten (IRL)*		*29.01.93*	*7*	*Dublin (S), IRL*	*22 Jul*

5 Kilometres Road

13:46	Chris O'Hare		23.11.90	8	Boston, USA	15 Apr
13:47	Andrew Heyes		22.06.90	9	Boston, USA	15 Apr
13:53	Andy Vernon		7.01.86	4	Carlsbad, USA	2 Apr
13:55	Ben Connor		17.10.92	1	Armagh	16 Feb
14:00				1	Kingsley	28 Apr
13:56	Sam Atkin		14.03.93	7	San Jose, USA	23 Nov
13:58	Dewi Griffiths		9.08.91	3	Armagh	16 Feb
14:00	Petros Surafel	U23	12.01.97	4	Armagh	16 Feb

8 performances to 14:00 by 7 athletes, further men where faster than track best

14:02	Kristian Jones		4.03.91	5	Armagh	16 Feb
14:08	Ross Millington		19.09.89	14	Boston, USA	15 Apr
14:09	Jake Shelley		16.03.91	9	Armagh	16 Feb
14:09	Philip Sesemann		3.10.92	2	Kingsley	28 Apr
14:14	Charlie Hulson		7.03.93	12	Armagh	16 Feb
14:18	Jake Wightman		11.07.94	14	Armagh	16 Feb
14:18	Joshua Griffiths		3.11.93	15	Armagh	16 Feb
14:20	Mathew Jackson		28.04.91	4	Kingsley	28 Apr
14:20	Jack Gray		10.04.93	5	Kingsley	28 Apr
14:21	Bradley Goater		13.04.94	16	Armagh	16 Feb
14:21	Carl Hardman		20.03.83	7	Kingsley	28 Apr
14:22	George Duggan	U23	1.09.96	17	Armagh	16 Feb
14:23	John Beattie		20.01.86	18	Armagh	16 Feb
14:23	Kyran Roberts	U23	19.09.95	19	Armagh	16 Feb
14:23	Chris Parr		13.11.84	8	Kingsley	28 Apr
14:25	Jamie Crowe	U23	9.06.95	23	Armagh	16 Feb
14:25	William Gray		24.01.93	10	Kingsley	28 Apr
14:26	John Sanderson		27.02.93	26	Armagh	16 Feb
14:26	Shane Robinson		19.02.91	27	Armagh	16 Feb
14:27	Tom Holden	U23	21.03.97	28	Armagh	16 Feb
14:27	Jonathan Mellor		27.12.86	1	Barrowford	16 Jun
14:27	John Ashcroft		13.11.92	1	Barrowford	18 Nov
14:28	Finn McNally		22.09.91	29	Armagh	16 Feb
14:29	Ieuan Thomas		17.07.89	1	Mountain Ash	31 Dec
14:30	Jack Martin		29.04.88	2	Manchester	3 Aug
14:30	Matthew Crehan		10.10.91	2	Barrowford	18 Nov
14:31	Carwyn Jones	V35	10.10.79	32	Armagh	16 Feb

14:31	Tom Lancashire		2.07.85	13	Carlsbad, USA	2	Apr
14:31	David Devine		3.02.92	3	Barrowford	18	Nov
14:32	Gordon Benson		12.05.94	11	Kingsley	28	Apr
14:33	Jack Goodwin		7.06.93	34	Armagh	16	Feb
14:33	Iolo Hughes	U23	22.11.96	35	Armagh	16	Feb
14:34	Jack Douglas	U23	5.06.96	36	Armagh	16	Feb
14:34	Ben Stevenson		26.01.94	37	Armagh	16	Feb
14:34	Cameron Boyek		9.10.93	2	Barrowford	18	Mar
14:35	Tom Marshall		12.06.89	1	Cardiff	30	Apr
14:35	Carl Avery		28.08.86	4	Barrowford	18	Nov

Foreign

14:24	*Dejene Gezimu (ETH)*		*29.09.93*	*9*	*Kingsley*	*28*	*Apr*
14:25	*Weynay Ghebresilasie (ERI)*		*24.03.94*	*22*	*Armagh*	*16*	*Feb*
14:26	*Mohammed Abu-Rezeq (JOR)*		*21.12.83*	*1*	*Manchester*	*3*	*Aug*

5 Miles Road

23:38	Calum McKenzie		3.05.89	1	Greenock	5	Feb
23:44	Jack Martin		29.04.88	1	Alsager	5	Feb
23:57	Jonathan Mellor		27.12.86	2	Alsager	5	Feb
23:58	Matthew Sharp		25.04.89	1	Portsmouth	3	Dec
24:02	Logan Rees	U23	23.02.97	1	Cupar	4	Mar
24:07	Derek Hawkins		29.04.89	2	Cupar	4	Mar
24:12	Mark Mitchell		23.05.88	2	Greenock	5	Feb
24:12	John Millar	U23	18.12.97	1	Great Bentley	7	Jul
24:14	Alastair Hay		7.09.85	3	Cupar	4	Mar
24:16	Ryan Thomson	U23	21.02.96	3	Greenock	5	Feb
(10)							
24:20	Ben Branagh		11.01.94	1	Dublin, IRL	29	Jan

10 Kilometres Road

28:28+	Callum Hawkins		22.06.92	m	Marugame, JPN	5	Feb
	28:46+			1m	New York, USA	19	Mar
	29:14			1	Glasgow	16	Jun
28:28	Dewi Griffiths		9.08.91	2	Swansea	24	Sep
	28:48			1	Cardiff	3	Sep
	28:52+			6m	Cardiff	1	Oct
	29:08			1	Cardiff	2	Apr
	29:20+			m	South Shields	10	Sep
	29:27+			1m	Reading	19	Mar
28:36	Andy Vernon		7.01.86	6	Manchester	28	May
	29:27+			1m	Reading	19	Mar
28:46	Ross Millington		19.09.89	2	Schoorl, NED	12	Feb
28:55	Jonathan Mellor		27.12.86	3	Schoorl, NED	12	Feb
28:55	Chris Thompson	V35	17.04.81	1	Partington	5	Mar
	29:27+			1m	Reading	19	Mar
29:03	Ben Connor		17.10.92	6	Houilles, FRA	31	Dec
	29:20			3	Leeds	5	Nov
29:13	Sam Stabler		17.05.92	1	Leeds	5	Nov
29:18	Andrew Butchart		14.10.91	1	London	29	May
29:19+	Mo Farah		23.03.83	m	South Shields	10	Sep
(10)							
29:22	Andrew Heyes		22.06.90	4	Leeds	5	Nov
29:25	Matthew Leach		25.09.93	5	Leeds	5	Nov
29:27	Richard Horton		28.05.93	2	Partington	5	Mar
29:27	Luke Traynor		6.07.93	2	Glasgow	16	Jun
	29:29			11	Houilles, FRA	31	Dec
29:28	Andy Maud		28.07.83	3	Partington	5	Mar
29:28	Logan Rees	U23	23.02.97	6	Leeds	5	Nov
29:29	Matthew Clowes		29.09.89	1	Arley	26	Mar

28 performances to 29:30 by 17 athletes, further men where faster than track best

29:34+	Tsegai Tewelde		8.12.89	17m	London	23	Apr
29:40	Philip Sesemann		3.10.92	7	Leeds	5	Nov
29:40	Jonathan Hopkins		3.06.92	1	Brighton	19	Nov
29:43	Nick Earl		22.09.84	10	Manchester	28	May
29:46	Carl Hardman		20.03.83	12	Manchester	28	May
29:46	Jack Rowe	U23	30.01.96	4	London	29	May
29:49	Emile Cairess	U23	27.12.97	8	Leeds	5	Nov
29:50	Andrew Davies	V35	30.10.79	9	Leeds	5	Nov
29:54	Jonathan Brownlee		30.04.90	2	Clitheroe	31	Dec
29:55	Adam Hickey		30.05.88	11	Leeds	5	Nov
29:55	Lucian Allison		11.11.90	12	Leeds	5	Nov
29:56	Nigel Martin		23.03.87	13	Leeds	5	Nov
29:56	Alastair Watson	V40	4.08.77	14	Leeds	5	Nov
29:57	John Beattie		20.01.86	6	London	29	May
29:59	Charlie Hulson		7.03.93	2	Cardiff	3	Sep
30:00	Peter Huck		10.07.90	3	Swansea	24	Sep
30:01	Nathan Marsh	U23	8.04.96	15	Leeds	5	Nov
30:02	Patrick Dever	U23	5.09.96	6	Partington	5	Mar
30:02	Dominic Shaw		26.12.88	1	Darlington	13	Aug
30:03	Phil Beastall		31.08.86	16	Leeds	5	Nov
30:04	Shaun Antell		9.05.87	9	Partington	5	Mar
30:04+	Matthew Sharp		25.04.89	3m	Portsmouth	22	Oct
30:06	Daniel Cliffe		23.12.90	10	Partington	5	Mar
30:06	Robbie Fitzgibbon	U23	23.03.96	11	Partington	5	Mar
30:07	Richard Allen	U23	25.10.95	18	Leeds	5	Nov
30:08	Callum Johnson		1.07.94	5	Clitheroe	31	Dec
30:10	Paulos Surafel	U23	12.01.97	15	Partington	5	Mar
30:10	Joshua Griffiths		3.11.93	1	Cwmafan	5	Nov
30:11	Rowan Axe		17.05.91	16	Partington	5	Mar
30:12	Luke Gunn		22.03.85	17	Partington	5	Mar
30:12+	Mahamed Mahamed	U23	18.09.97	6m	Portsmouth	22	Oct
30:12	Lachlan Oates		30.01.92	19	Leeds	5	Nov
30:13	Jonathan Hay		12.02.92	1	London (HP)	1	Jan
30:15	Ben Cole		18.06.85	20	Leeds	5	Nov
30:19	Scott Overall		9.02.83	2	Hamilton, BER	14	Jan
30:19+	Kieran Clements		20.11.93	7m	Portsmouth	22	Oct
30:21	Finn McNally		22.09.91	13	Manchester	28	May
30:22	Peter Newton	V35	24.03.81	19	Partington	5	Mar
30:22	Abraham Tewelde		30.12.91	3	Darlington	13	Aug
30:23	Joe Wilkinson	U23	27.06.96	1	Lincoln	2	Apr
30:24+	Daniel Studley		1.01.92	9m	Portsmouth	22	Oct
30:24	Carwyn Jones	V35	10.10.79	3	Arley	4	Nov
30:25	Shaun Dixon		6.09.82	20	Schoorl, NED	12	Feb
30:25	Kenny Wilson		29.12.89	3	Inverness	24	Sep
30:25	Robert Danson		25.06.90	6	Clitheroe	31	Dec
30:26	Ben Johnson		22.09.88	12	London	29	May
30:27	Chris Farrell		10.10.85	21	Partington	5	Mar
30:28	Richard Goodman		4.04.93	4	Birmingham	30	Apr
30:29	Jake Wightman		11.07.94	22	Partington	5	Mar
30:30	Carl Avery		28.08.86	21	Leeds	5	Nov

Foreign

29:20	*Paul Pollock (IRL)*		*25.06.86*	*2*	*Leeds*	*5*	*Nov*
29:26	*Abel Tsegay (ETH)*	*U23*	*2.06.96*	*2*	*London*	*29*	*May*
29:27	*Dejene Gezimu (ETH)*		*29.09.93*	*8*	*Manchester*	*28*	*May*
30:11	*Weynay Ghebresilasie (ERI)*		*24.03.94*	*1*	*Glasgow*	*28*	*May*
30:27	*Wondiye Indelbu (ETH)*		*13.02.88*	*4*	*Darlington*	*13*	*Aug*

downhill (55m)

28:57	Chris Thompson	V35	(28:55)	9	Madrid, ESP	31	Dec

Foreign

29:12	*Paul Pollock (IRL)*		*(29:20)*	*14*	*Madrid, ESP*	*31*	*Dec*

15 Kilometes Road

42:37+	Callum Hawkins		22.06.92	1m	Marugame, JPN	5	Feb
42:52+				1m	New York, USA	19	Mar
44:45				10	Nijmegen, NED	19	Nov
44:47+				2m	Glasgow	1	Oct
43:19+	Mo Farah		23.03.83	2m	South Shields	10	Sep
43:25+	Dewi Griffiths		9.08.91	5m	Cardiff	1	Oct
44:10+				m	South Shields	10	Sep
43:44	Luke Traynor		6.07.93	5	Montferland, NED	3	Dec
44:21+	Tsegai Tewelde		8.12.89	m	South Shields	10	Sep
44:47+				2m	Glasgow	1	Oct
44:32+	Chris Thompson	V35	17.04.81	1m	Glasgow	1	Oct
44:48+	Ross Millington		19.09.89	m	New York, USA	19	Mar
44:48+	Jonathan Mellor		27.12.86	m	New York, USA	19	Mar
44:53				14	Nijmegen, NED	19	Nov
	13 performances to 45:00 by 8 athletes						
45:07+	Ben Connor		17.10.92	2m	Portsmouth	22	Oct
45:08+	Andy Vernon		7.01.86	2m	Reading	19	Mar
(10)							
45:15+	Matthew Sharp		25.04.89	3m	Portsmouth	22	Oct
45:16+	Alexander Teuten		3.01.92	4m	Portsmouth	22	Oct
45:30+	Mahamed Mahamed	U23	18.09.97	6m	Portsmouth	22	Oct

10 Miles Road

48:32	Chris Thompson	V35	17.04.81	1	Portsmouth	22	Oct
48:35	Matthew Sharp		25.04.89	2	Portsmouth	22	Oct
48:36	Ben Connor		17.10.92	3	Portsmouth	22	Oct
48:38	Alexander Teuten		3.01.92	4	Portsmouth	22	Oct
48:55	Jonathan Hay		12.02.92	1	Bramley	19	Feb
49:05	Mahamed Mahamed	U23	18.09.97	6	Portsmouth	22	Oct
49:08+	Matthew Leach		25.09.93	m	San Jose, USA	8	Oct
49:21	Kieran Clements		20.11.93	7	Portsmouth	22	Oct
49:34	Daniel Studley		1.01.92	1	Melksham	12	Feb
49:36	Peter Huck		10.07.90	8	Portsmouth	22	Oct
(10)							
49:57	Derek Hawkins		29.04.89	2	Motherwell	2	Apr
49:57	Andrew Lemoncello		12.10.82	3	San Diego, USA	2	Apr
49:59	Nicholas Torry	V40	19.02.77	2	Twickenham	15	Oct

Foreign

49:40	*Weynay Ghebresilasie (ERI)*	*24.03.94*	*1*	*Motherwell*	*2*	*Apr*

Half Marathon

60:00	Callum Hawkins		22.06.92	1	Marugame, JPN	5	Feb
60:08				2	New York, USA	19	Mar
63:18				2	Glasgow	1	Oct
60:06	Mo Farah		23.03.83	1	South Shields	10	Sep
61:33	Dewi Griffiths		9.08.91	4	Cardiff	1	Oct
62:53				7	South Shields	10	Sep
63:49+				m	Frankfurt, GER	29	Oct
63:54				3	Reading	19	Mar
64:49				1	Swansea	25	Jun
62:23	Jonathan Mellor		27.12.86	10	New York, USA	19	Mar
64:57				1	Lake Vyrnwy	10	Sep
62:40	Ross Millington		19.09.89	11	New York, USA	19	Mar
62:44	Chris Thompson	V35	17.04.81	1	Glasgow	1	Oct
63:39				2	Reading	19	Mar
64:58				1	Nottingham	24	Sep
63:08	Andy Vernon		7.01.86	1	Reading	19	Mar
63:14	Tsegai Tewelde		8.12.89	9	South Shields	10	Sep
63:18				3	Glasgow	1	Oct

64:10	Luke Traynor		6.07.93	1	Manchester	15	Oct
64:22	Matthew Leach		25.09.93	4	San Jose, USA	8	Oct
(10)							
64:26	Mohamud Aadan		1.01.90	11	South Shields	10	Sep
64:52	Nick Earl		22.09.84	5	Southport, AUS	2	Jul
22 performances to 65:00 by 12 athletes							
65:03	Peter Huck		10.07.90	2	Manchester	15	Oct
65:11	Matthew Clowes		29.09.89	3	Manchester	15	Oct
65:16	Ben Fish		21.05.82	1	Bath	12	Mar
65:18	Joshua Griffiths		3.11.93	1	Llanelli	12	Mar
65:24	Robbie Simpson		14.11.91	4	Manchester	15	Oct
65:33	Charlie Hulson		7.03.93	13	Cardiff	1	Oct
65:37	Richard Horton		28.05.93	4	Reading	19	Mar
65:38	Edward Shepherd		8.12.93	5	Manchester	15	Oct
(20)							
65:48	Toby Spencer		9.06.90	1	Wokingham	12	Feb
65:48	Richard Weir		7.08.84	6	Manchester	15	Oct
65:54	Paul Martelletti	V35	1.08.79	11	Granollers, ESP	5	Feb
65:54	Alexander Teuten		3.01.92	6	Reading	19	Mar
66:01	Ian Kimpton		8.11.86	7	Reading	19	Mar
66:04	Dominic Shaw		26.12.88	16	South Shields	10	Sep
66:11	Kristian Jones		4.03.91	4	Glasgow	1	Oct
66:18	Matthew Gillespie		4.11.90	9	New York, USA	20	May
66:21+	Andrew Lemoncello		12.10.82	26m	London	23	Apr
66:22	Nicholas Torry	V40	19.02.77	17	South Shields	10	Sep
(30)							
66:25	Keith Gerrard		24.03.86	4	Phoenix, USA	15	Jan
66:25	Scott Overall		9.02.83	2	Chertsey	26	Feb
66:27	Daniel Studley		1.01.92	14	Breda, NED	1	Oct
66:29	Peter Newton	V35	24.03.81	2	Wokingham	12	Feb
66:30	Paulos Surafel	U23	12.01.97	7	Manchester	15	Oct
66:31	Matt Bond		17.07.82	2	Wilmslow	19	Mar
66:38+	Matthew Sharp		25.04.89	m	London	23	Apr
66:38	William Richardson	U20	23.02.98	1	Birmingham	15	Oct
66:39	Cameron Milne		6.07.93	3	Lilliebaelt, DEN	6	May
66:40	Luke Gunn		22.03.85	10	Barcelona, ESP	12	Feb
(40)							
66:41+	Jonathan Hay		12.02.92	m	London	23	Apr
66:44	Tom Anderson		12.01.90	37	Houston, USA	15	Jan
66:45	Lee Merrien	V35	26.04.79	1	Visby, SWE	30	Jun
66:51	Dan Nash		23.03.94	1	Budapest, HUN	9	Apr
66:53	Petros Surafel	U23	12.01.97	8	Reading	19	Mar
66:54	Derek Hawkins		29.04.89	4	Lilliebaelt, DEN	6	May
66:55	Paul Whittaker		14.07.89	1	Hackney	30	Apr
67:02	Abraham Tewelde		30.12.91	18	South Shields	10	Sep
67:07+	Aaron Scott		11.04.87	m	London	23	Apr
67:07+	Michael Kallenberg		9.01.91	m	London	23	Apr
(50)							
67:09	Oliver Mott		29.11.84	9	Reading	19	Mar
67:10+	Andrew Davies	V35	30.10.79	m	London	23	Apr
67:12	Tom Wade		14.01.89	6	Lilliebaelt, DEN	6	May
67:14	Philip Matthews	V35	16.05.79	19	Cardiff	1	Oct
67:17	Ben Johnson		22.09.88	5	Glasgow	1	Oct
67:19	Jack Morris		9.04.93	8	Manchester	15	Oct
67:23	James Douglas		18.06.85	11	Reading	19	Mar
67:25	Lachlan Oates		30.01.92	6	Glasgow	1	Oct
67:33	Alex Wall-Clarke		17.03.87	20	South Shields	10	Sep
67:34	Russell Bentley	V35	28.04.81	12	Reading	19	Mar
(60)							
67:37	Andrew Douglas		19.12.86	20	Cardiff	1	Oct
67:37	Kenny Wilson		29.12.89	7	Glasgow	1	Oct

67:42	Michael Hiscott		1.07.83	14	Reading	19	Mar
67:42	Rob Samuel		14.01.86	4	Wilmslow	19	Mar
67:42	Ross Houston	V35	5.12.79	1	Edinburgh	24	Sep
67:44	Thomas Charles		18.02.84	22	South Shields	10	Sep
67:45+	Ben Livesey	V35	20.09.78	m	London	23	Apr
67:45	Lucian Allison		11.11.90	23	South Shields	10	Sep
67:45	Shaun Antell		9.05.87	10	Manchester	15	Oct
67:48	Oliver Lockley		9.11.93	2	Visby, SWE	30	Jun
	(70)						
67:52	Steven Bayton		6.08.91	2	Newark	13	Aug
67:52	Joe Morwood		10.06.91	1	Oxford	8	Oct
67:55	Paul Molyneux	V35	27.01.81	1	Maidenhead	3	Sep
67:56	Patrick Martin		15.05.85	1	Wrexham	19	Feb
67:57	Stuart Spencer		11.11.82	2	Derby	4	Jun
67:57	Alastair Watson	V40	4.08.77	3	Nottingham	24	Sep
67:57	Ben Cole		18.06.85	8	Glasgow	1	Oct
67:58	John Beattie		20.01.86	1	Retford	12	Mar
67:58	Ian Hudspith	V45	23.09.70	24	South Shields	10	Sep
68:00	Dave Webb	V35	17.03.82	1	Shrewsbury	18	Jun
	(80)						
68:02	John Gilbert	V35	24.09.80	1	Bedford	3	Dec
68:06	Jonathan Poole		16.11.82	1	Ealing	24	Sep
68:07	William Mackay		3.10.89	1	Lossiemouth	19	Feb
68:07	Ronnie Richmond	V35	8.09.82	1	Bristol	17	Sep
68:07	Joshua Bull		14.10.92	1	Brussels, BEL	1	Oct
68:08	Alex Milne		11.03.90	2	Oxford	8	Oct
68:11	Mark Mitchell		23.05.88	2	Inverness	12	Mar
68:12	Mark Jenkin	V35	19.09.78	3	Helsby	15	Jan
68:15	Alastair Hay		7.09.85	10	Glasgow	1	Oct
68:16	Jonathan Escalante-Phillips		28.07.92	2	Charleville, IRL	17	Sep
	(90)						
68:17	Tom Aldred	V35	15.03.79	18	Reading	19	Mar
68:22	Ben Gamble		27.01.82	4	Helsby	15	Jan
68:28	Dominic Nolan		29.11.94	3	Bath	12	Mar
68:30	Chris Steele	V35	18.08.81	1	Blackpool	19	Feb

Foreign

64:52	*Kevin Seaward (IRL)*		*3.10.85*	*1*	*Newark*	*13*	*Aug*
65:35	*Iraitz Arrospide (ESP)*		*5.08.88*	*1*	*San Sebastián, ESP*	*26*	*Nov*
65:52	*Dejene Gezimu (ETH)*		*29.09.93*	*1*	*Liverpool*	*2*	*Apr*
65:52	*Stephen Scullion (IRL)*		*9.11.88*	*14*	*South Shields*	*10*	*Sep*
66:27	*Mohammed Abu-Rezeq (JOR)*		*21.12.83*	*1*	*Wilmslow*	*19*	*Mar*
66:27	*Paddy Hamilton (IRL)*	*V35*	*17.03.81*	*1*	*Waterford, IRL*	*2*	*Dec*
66:48	*Weynay Ghebresilasie (ERI)*		*24.03.94*	*1*	*Inverness*	*12*	*Mar*
67:15	*Luuk Metselaar (NED)*		*6.07.92*	*20*	*The Hague, NED*	*12*	*Mar*
67:21	*Eoghan Totten (IRL)*		*29.01.93*	*19*	*South Shields*	*10*	*Sep*

Marathon

2:09:49	Dewi Griffiths		9.08.91	5	Frankfurt, GER	29	Oct
2:10:17	Callum Hawkins		22.06.92	4	London	6	Aug
2:12:57	Jonathan Mellor		27.12.86	10	Berlin, GER	24	Sep
	2:18:48			29	London	23	Apr
2:14:45	Tsegai Tewelde		8.12.89	6	Beirut, LIB	12	Nov
2:14:53	Joshua Griffiths		3.11.93	14	London	23	Apr
	2:20:06			39	London	6	Aug
2:15:04	Robbie Simpson		14.11.91	16	London	23	Apr
2:15:11	Andrew Davies	V35	30.10.79	17	London	23	Apr
	2:17:59			31	London	6	Aug
2:16:02	Matthew Sharp		25.04.89	20	Berlin, GER	24	Sep
	2:17:48			23	London	23	Apr
2:16:54	Scott Overall		9.02.83	21	London	23	Apr

2:17:10	Paul Martelletti	V35	1.08.79	24	Berlin, GER	24	Sep
(10)							
2:17:37	Nicholas Torry	V40	19.02.77	20	Frankfurt, GER	29	Oct
2:17:50	Aaron Scott		11.04.87	24	London	23	Apr
2:18:10	Jonathan Thewlis		7.05.85	26	London	23	Apr
2:19:35	Carl Hardman		20.03.83	41	Berlin, GER	24	Sep
2:19:36	Tom Anderson		12.01.90	31	London	23	Apr
2:19:41	Steven Bayton		6.08.91	45	Berlin, GER	24	Sep
2:19:59	Ben Livesey	V35	20.09.78	32	London	23	Apr
2:20:18	Michael Kallenberg		9.01.91	51	Berlin, GER	24	Sep
2:20:20	Russell Bentley	V35	28.04.81	52	Berlin, GER	24	Sep
2:22:41				42	London	23	Apr
2:20:25	Lee Merrien	V35	26.04.79	28	Frankfurt, GER	29	Oct
(20)							
2:21:13	Matt Bond		17.07.82	34	London	23	Apr
2:21:36	Jonathan Poole		16.11.82	35	London	23	Apr
2:21:47	Rob Samuel		14.01.86	36	London	23	Apr
2:21:49	Lee Grantham		11.02.83	37	London	23	Apr
2:21:52	Ben Johnson		22.09.88	38	London	23	Apr
2:23:24				12	Toronto, CAN	22	Oct
2:22:14	Craig Ruddy		10.04.88	55	Berlin, GER	24	Sep
2:22:26				41	London	23	Apr
2:22:23	Tom Payn	V35	18.10.79	39	London	23	Apr
2:22:25	James Douglas		18.06.85	40	London	23	Apr
2:22:37	Patrick Martin		15.05.85	1	Manchester	2	Apr
2:22:45	Ian Kimpton		8.11.86	27	Amsterdam, NED	15	Oct
2:23:53				48	London	23	Apr
(30)							
2:23:23	Alex Milne		11.03.90	44	London	23	Apr
2:23:30	Rob Keal	V40	6.05.74	46	London	23	Apr
2:23:37	Ronnie Richmond	V35	8.09.82	33	Frankfurt, GER	29	Oct
2:23:42	Ben Gamble	V35	27.01.82	47	London	23	Apr
2:23:55	Thomas Charles		18.02.84	2	Manchester	2	Apr
2:24:02	Jonathan Hay		12.02.92	49	London	23	Apr
2:24:29				14	Houston, USA	15	Jan
2:24:11	Andrew Lemoncello		12.10.82	51	London	23	Apr
2:24:11	Chris Thompson	V35	17.04.81	52	London	23	Apr
2:24:13	Ross Houston	V35	5.12.79	1	York	8	Oct
2:24:24	Andrew Baker		22.07.85	65	Berlin, GER	24	Sep
(40)							
2:24:24	Paul Molyneux	V35	27.01.81	28	Amsterdam, NED	15	Oct
2:24:36	Jarlath McKenna	V35	14.11.81	53	London	23	Apr
2:24:38	Kevin Quinn	V35	24.07.79	67	Berlin, GER	24	Sep
52 performances to 2:25:00 by 43 athletes							
2:25:19	Ben Shearer	V40	27.05.76	55	London	23	Apr
2:25:28	Oliver Lockley		9.11.93	42	Frankfurt, GER	29	Oct
2:26:00	William Mackay		3.10.89	4	Manchester	2	Apr
2:26:07	Tom Evans		3.02.92	48	Frankfurt, GER	29	Oct
2:26:12	Lloyd Biddell	V35	12.08.81	1	Chester	8	Oct
2:26:38	James Westlake		8.08.91	57	London	23	Apr
2:26:46	Christopher Greenwood	V40	29.09.73	59	London	23	Apr
(50)							
2:26:57	Stephen Way	V40	6.07.74	60	London	23	Apr
2:26:59	Iain Trickett		16.08.85	61	London	23	Apr
2:27:07	Paul Piper	V35	25.11.81	41	Chicago, USA	8	Oct
2:27:08	Tom Aldred	V35	15.03.79	5	Manchester	2	Apr
2:27:16	Mark Jenkin	V35	19.09.78	21	Seville, ESP	19	Feb
2:27:20	Martin O'Connell		22.10.85	74	Berlin, GER	24	Sep
2:27:24	Andrew Savery	V35	31.08.82	51	Frankfurt, GER	29	Oct
2:27:26	Gareth Lowe	V40	20.03.73	6	Manchester	2	Apr
2:27:26	Peter Le Grice	V35	10.07.82	20	New York, USA	5	Nov

2:27:29	Peter Lighting	V35	·7.12.80	53	Frankfurt, GER	29	Oct
(60)							
2:27:34	James Bowler	V35	2.09.79	62	London	23	Apr
2:27:35	Zak Tobias		13.09.94	1	Zaragoza, ESP	2	Apr
2:27:36	Stuart Hawkes	V35	22.12.77	1	Brighton	9	Apr
2:27:39	Paul Navesey		19.04.86	15	Stockholm, SWE	3	Jun
2:27:46	Thomas Stevens	V35	7.09.79	7	Malaga, ESP	10	Dec
2:27:48	Andy Greenleaf		21.09.82	64	London	23	Apr
2:27:59	Adam Holland		5.03.87	31	Paris, FRA	9	Apr
2:28:01	James Turner		10.04.90	65	London	23	Apr
2:28:05	Thomas Watkins		21.03.92	66	London	23	Apr
2:28:23	Peter Tucker	V35	17.04.81	82	Berlin, GER	24	Sep
(70)							
2:28:24	Daniel Gaffney		25.02.83	67	London	23	Apr
2:28:24	Adam Stokes		16.02.85	83	Berlin, GER	24	Sep
2:28:27	James Watson	V40	28.04.74	4	Chester	8	Oct
2:28:30	Ian Williams		8.03.85	8	Manchester	2	Apr
2:28:39	Martin Swensson	V40	21.07.75	5	Chester	8	Oct
2:28:47	Robert Danson		25.06.90	89	Berlin, GER	24	Sep
2:28:53	Jonathan Tipper	V35	31.08.80	68	London	23	Apr
2:28:58	Mark Dunham	V35	4.09.80	70	London	23	Apr
2:28:58	Rob McTaggart		14.10.85	71	London	23	Apr
2:28:59	Mark Rushbrook	V35	15.07.81	26	Seville, ESP	19	Feb
(80)							
2:29:02	Christopher Ashford	V35	6.01.81	6	Chester	8	Oct
2:29:04	Richard Marriott	V35	24.01.80	100	Berlin, GER	24	Sep
2:29:08	Mark Newton	V35	15.06.80	72	London	23	Apr
2:29:11	Simon Millett		19.04.87	73	London	23	Apr
2:29:19	Matthew Sharp	V35	2.04.79	53	Chicago, USA	8	Oct
2:29:25	Luke Beevor		4.03.84	55	Chicago, USA	8	Oct
2:29:28	Euan McKenzie		8.08.92	75	London	23	Apr
2:29:35	Chris Jordan	V35	12.05.80	76	London	23	Apr
2:29:37	Alastair Pickburn	V35	5.01.82	77	London	23	Apr
2:29:37	Tristan Steed		27.01.88	79	London	23	Apr
(90)							
2:29:37	Michael Wright		24.03.87	80	London	23	Apr
2:29:44	Ollie Garrod		16.01.93	81	London	23	Apr
2:29:44	Iain Reid	V35	20.07.77	2	Stirling	21	May
2:29:57	Daniel Robinson	V35	18.12.79	8	Chester	8	Oct
2:29:58	Kyle Greig		19.12.85	83	London	23	Apr
2:29:59	James McMullan		16.02.84	84	London	23	Apr

downhill (350m)

2:27:56	Kyle Greig		19.12.85	2	Inverness	24	Sep

Foreign

2:15:30	Paul Pollock (IRL)		25.06.86	18	Oita, JPN	5	Feb
2:15:50	Kevin Seaward (IRL)		3.10.85	19	Berlin, GER	24	Sep
2:18:04	Stephen Scullion (IRL)		9.11.88	25	London	23	Apr
2:18:09	Iraitz Arrospide (ESP)		5.08.88	29	Berlin, GER	24	Sep
2:19:39	Tony Payne (NZL)		13.01.89	44	Berlin, GER	24	Sep
2:22:12	Luuk Metselaar (NED)		6.07.92	26	Amsterdam, NED	15	Oct
2:22:43	Blair McWhirter (NZL)		6.10.82	43	London	23	Apr
2:23:24	Andrius Jaksevicius (LTU)	V35	15.02.81	45	London	23	Apr
2:25:17	Patryk Gierjatowicz (POL)		29.08.89	54	London	23	Apr
2:29:04	Keith Russell (IRL)	V40	28.01.77	61	Valencia, ESP	19	Nov
2:29:49	Richard Hope (AUS)	V45	11.09.70	65	Frankfurt, GER	29	Oct

downhill (350m)

2:22:02	Mohammed Abu-Rezeq (JOR)		21.12.83	1	Inverness	24	Sep

50 Kilometres Road

3:08:25	Lee Grantham		11.02.83	1	Chiang Mai, THA	21	Jan
3:15:58	James Bellward		18.10.84	1	Boddington	25	Jun
3:16:58	Paul Fernandez	V40	24.03.74	2	Boddington	25	Jun
3:18:59	Adam Holland		5.03.87	1	Patrington	21	May
3:18:59	Paul Martelletti	V35	1.08.79	3	Yuxi City, CHN	30	Sep
3:19:04	Robert Weekes	V35	15.03.82	2	Patrington	21	May

100 Kilometres Road

6:42:42	Lee Grantham		11.02.83	1	Patrington	21	May
7:04.30	Anthony Clark	V35	2.08.77	2	Patrington	21	May
7:23:40	David McLure		9.11.83	3	Patrington	21	May
7:25:27	Paul Fernandez	V40	24.03.74	4	Patrington	21	May
7:31:19	Dave Ward	V35	21.11.80	5	Patrington	21	May
7:33:04	Nathan Montague	V35	15.11.80	6	Patrington	21	May
7:33:52	Christopher Ashford	V35	6.01.81	7	Patrington	21	May

24 Hours

245.794km	Craig Holgate	V40	21.09.76	2	Oslo, NOR	26	Nov
245.492km	Steven Holyoak	V50	8.09.64	24	Belfast	2	Jul
242.114km	Patrick Robbins	V45	12.03.72	28	Belfast	2	Jul
241.205km	tDan Lawson		8.05.83	6	Soochow, TPE	3	Dec
234.610km t	Nathan Montague	V35	15.11.80	2	Barcelona, ESP	17	Dec
226.064km	Steve Spiers	V50	18.08.66	2	Cleveland, USA	17	Sep
222.878km	Andy Jordan	V50	5.06.63	5rB	Belfast	2	Jul
222.575km t	Jamie Hauxwell		28.09.84	3	London (TB)	17	Sep
218.557km	Marco Consani	V40	15.11.74	60	Belfast	2	Jul
218.257km t	Matthew Blackburn		14.09.85	4	London (TB)	17	Sep
(10)							
214.703km	Neil Dryland	V45	8.08.71	5	Oslo, NOR	26	Nov
213.031km	Ian McAuley	V45	6.11.70	7rB	Belfast	2	Jul
210.126km	David Bone	V45	14.04.72	8rB	Belfast	2	Jul
203.734km	Dan Masters	V40	11.07.73	10rB	Belfast	2	Jul

1500 Metres Steeplechase - Under 17

4:20.84	Adam Searle		7.11.00	1	Birmingham	8	Jul
4:21.43	Remi Adebiyi		4.11.00	1	Bedford	26	Aug
4:22.51	Ben Thomas		7.07.01	2	Bedford	26	Aug
4:22.61	Shaun Hudson		8.09.00	2	Birmingham	8	Jul
4:24.46	Lewis Pentecost		16.10.00	3	Bedford	26	Aug
4:24.71	Elliot Moran		6.10.00	3	Birmingham	8	Jul
4:27.47	Cameron Wright		25.08.01	1	Grangemouth	26	Aug
4:28.01	James Gillon		10.10.00	1	Grangemouth	3	Jun
4:28.71	Henry-James Cowie		29.03.01	4	Birmingham	8	Jul
4:29.43	Aaron Enser		5.09.00	1	Bromley	28	May
(10)							
4:30.57	Matthew Francis		14.01.02	1	Reading	25	Jun
4:31.05	Archie May		5.12.01	6	Birmingham	8	Jul
4:31.76	Oliver McArthur		24.10.00	4	Milton Keynes	3	Jun
4:32.3	Bill Chesters		23.06.01	2	Wolverhampton	25	Jun
4:32.68	Maxwell Cooper		20.11.00	8	Birmingham	8	Jul
4:33.16	Henry McLuckie		3.05.02	9	Birmingham	8	Jul
4:34.72	Magnus Tait		26.03.01	2	Birmingham	3	Sep
4:34.82	Adam Hay		8.02.01	2	Grangemouth	26	Aug
4:36.64	Brychan Price-Davies		15.07.01	8	Bedford	26	Aug
4:37.62	Lewis Harknett		17.10.00	2	London (CP)	19	Aug
(20)							
4:38.52	Andrew Hagen		9.11.01	1	Antrim	19	May
4:39.3	Benjamin Wills		21.09.00	2	Reading	10	Jun
4:39.98	Robert Sparks		4.01.01	4	Birmingham	3	Sep

4:40.67	Ben Shaw		22.05.01	5	Birmingham	3	Sep
4:40.77	Jonathan Langley		20.11.00	2	York	25	Jun
4:40.98	Owain Edwards		30.07.01	6	Birmingham	3	Sep
4:41.82	Lewis Cotterill		4.03.01	3	Exeter	17	Jun
4:41.9	Ben Marks		27.03.02	2	London (Cr)	23	Jul
4:42.0	Kristian Imroth		19.01.02	1	Hemel Hempstead	17	Sep
4:42.24	Ben McIntyre		27.03.02	4	Exeter	17	Jun
(30)							
4:42.29	Leo Stallard		6.08.01	3	London (CP)	19	Aug

2000 Metres Steeplechase

5:36.19	Zak Seddon		28.06.94	1	Solihull	13	May
5:39.99	Phil Norman		20.10.89	1	London (O)	2	Aug
5:42.87	Luke Gunn		22.03.85	2	Solihull	13	May

Under 20

5:54.43	Alfie Yabsley		12.09.99	1	Birmingham	8	Jul
5:57.2	James Beeks		13.10.98	3	Dartford	15	Apr
5:58.80	Joey Croft		23.05.00	2	Birmingham	8	Jul
6:03.72	William Battershill		25.02.98	1	Houston, USA	16	Mar
6:04.05	Jordan Wood		26.03.99	4	Birmingham	8	Jul
6:04.77	Joss Barber		22.06.99	5	Birmingham	8	Jul
6:05.97	George Groom		20.10.99	1	Bromley	28	May
6:06.36	Ben Davis		13.04.99	6	Birmingham	8	Jul
6:06.48	George Phillips		7.08.99	7	Birmingham	8	Jul
6:07.73	Terence Fawden		19.01.99	2	Bromley	22	May
(10)							
6:10.64	Jack Hope		14.05.98	1	Milton Keynes	19	Aug
6:10.95	Finlay McLear		25.05.00	1	Exeter	10	Jun
6:10.99	Aidan Kent		6.10.99	2	Exeter	2	Jul
6:11.01	Sam Costley		24.02.99	6	Milton Keynes	3	Jun
6:12.70	Bede Pitcairn-Knowles		5.08.00	8	Milton Keynes	3	Jun
6:13.37	Cameron Wright	U17	25.08.01	1	Birmingham	3	Sep
6:13.72	Lewis Mills		1.01.00	2	Birmingham	3	Sep
6:14.01	George Lewis		4.12.98	1	Manchester (Str)	14	May
6:15.0	Edward Mason		9.03.99	1	Portsmouth	14	May
6:16.98	Ben Thomas	U17	7.07.01	2	Dublin (S), IRL	5	Aug
(20)							
6:17.6	Chey Blatchford-Kemp		2.09.99	1	Reading	10	Jun
6:17.75	Lewis Pentecost	U17	16.10.00	2	Glasgow (S)	20	Aug
6:18.41	Magnus Tait	U17	26.03.01	3	Glasgow (S)	20	Aug
6:18.7	Matthew Bradly		27.09.98	2	Reading	10	Jun
6:19.24	Alfie Manthorpe		26.09.99	2	Sheffield (W)	30	Apr

3000 Metres Steeplechase

8:30.06	Rob Mullett		31.07.87	3	Los Angeles (ER), USA	18	May
	8:33.99			4	Villeneuve d'Ascq, FRA	25	Jun
	8:41.43			1	Birmingham	1	Jul
	8:47.99			15h3	London (O)	6	Aug
8:30.17	Zak Seddon		28.06.94	1	Gainesville, USA	31	Mar
	8:32.84			10h1	London (O)	6	Aug
	8:38.00			1	Jacksonville, USA	8	Apr
	8:39.30			6	Taipei, TPE	27	Aug
	8:41.11			2	Copenhagen, DEN	20	Jun
	8:43.14			2	Birmingham	1	Jul
8:33.59	Ieuan Thomas		17.07.89	7	Oordegem, BEL	27	May
	8:33.68			2	Stanford, USA	31	Mar
	8:34.93			2	Leiden, NED	17	Jun
	8:43.77			3	Birmingham	1	Jul
	8:52.96			15h2	London (O)	6	Aug

8:33.68	William Gray		24.01.93	8	Oordegem, BEL	27	May
8:44.57				5	Birmingham	1	Jul
8:46.18				11	Belfort, FRA	9	Jun
8:54.48				12	Letterkenny, IRL	7	Jul
8:34.03	Jonathan Hopkins		3.06.92	9	Oordegem, BEL	27	May
8:36.96				3	Leiden, NED	17	Jun
8:39.42				1	Bedford	1	May
8:42.39				3	Bydgoszcz, POL	2	Jun
8:49.25				1	Manchester (SC)	16	Aug
8:34.19	Jamaine Coleman	U23	22.09.95	2h2	Lexington, USA	26	May
8:40.44				3	Bydgoszcz, POL	16	Jul
8:42.82				1	Charlottesville, USA	21	Apr
8:43.85				6s1	Eugene, USA	7	Jun
8:48.56				1rB	Stanford, USA	31	Mar
8:50.15				1h2	Bydgoszcz, POL	14	Jul
8:37.41	Adam Kirk-Smith		30.01.91	4	Letterkenny, IRL	7	Jul
8:37.62				15	Oordegem, BEL	27	May
8:45.37				6	Birmingham	1	Jul
8:46.26				3	Loughborough	21	May
8:47.06				19	Huelva, ESP	14	Jun
8:51.52				1	Sheffield	6	May
8:38.54	Douglas Musson		8.04.94	5	Letterkenny, IRL	7	Jul
8:41.17				3	Gothenburg, SWE	10	Jun
8:43.34				1	Bedford	29	Jul
8:44.33				4	Birmingham	1	Jul
8:53.56				1	Manchester (SC)	27	May
8:54.74				3	Manchester (SC)	16	Aug
8:38.69	Luke Gunn		22.03.85	16	Oordegem, BEL	27	May
8:54.94				8	Birmingham	1	Jul
8:42.89	Phil Norman		20.10.89	1	Loughborough	21	May
8:46.18				2	Bedford	29	Jul
8:50.53				2	Manchester (SC)	16	Aug
8:53.17				2	Sheffield	6	May
(10)							
8:43.09	Daniel Jarvis	U23	21.10.95	2	Loughborough	21	May
8:52.65				7h1	Bydgoszcz, POL	14	Jul
8:47.34	Adam Visokay		11.03.94	2	Swarthmore, USA	15	May
8:50.51				10	Letterkenny, IRL	7	Jul
8:51.44				2	Charlottesville, USA	22	Apr
8:52.55				11	Nashville, USA	10	Jun
8:48.26	Tommy Horton		7.11.93	3	Bedford	29	Jul
8:49.71				9	Letterkenny, IRL	7	Jul
8:50.43	Haran Dunderdale	U23	26.04.96	3rB	Oordegem, BEL	27	May
8:50.58	Alexander Teuten		3.01.92	2	Bedford	1	May
8:50.87	Ryan Driscoll		25.01.94	4	Los Angeles (ER), USA	6	May
8:53.00				7	Birmingham	1	Jul
8:52.53	Lachlan Oates		30.01.92	4	Loughborough	21	May
	61 performances to 8:55.0 by 17 athletes						
8:55.84	William Battershill	U20	25.02.98	4	Princeton, USA	12	May
8:59.41	Chris Perry		1.03.90	5	Bedford	29	Jul
9:01.07	Harry Lane		1.12.94	1	Bedford	15	Jul
(20)							
9:01.89	William Mycroft		8.01.91	13rB	Oordegem, BEL	27	May
9:06.80	Nick Earl		22.09.84	4	Melbourne (A), AUS	25	Feb
9:06.92	Alex Howard	U23	24.08.95	1	New Haven, USA	8	Apr
9:07.82	Daniel Eckersley		12.11.86	5	Loughborough	21	May
9:08.34	James Senior		4.01.92	6	Bedford	29	Jul
9:08.85	Scott Snow	U23	29.11.95	14	Los Angeles (ER), USA	6	May
9:09.83	Tom Austin		6.04.94	6	Loughborough	21	May
9:10.09	Olivier Heaslip	U23	2.01.96	6	Albi, FRA	9	Jul
9:10.66	Samatar Farah		25.12.85	1	London (LV)	3	Jun

9:12.64	Michael Bartram	U23	6.12.96	6	Bedford	1	May
(30)							
9:14.48	Ciaran Lewis	U23	18.03.97	7	Bedford	1	May
9:15.09	John Millar	U23	18.12.97	8	Bedford	1	May
9:15.66	Joshua Lunn		15.05.92	1	Bedford	15	Jul
9:16.59	Matthew Seddon	U23	26.02.96	10	Belfort, FRA	9	Jun
9:21.74	Jonathan Goringe		22.07.91	3	London (He)	20	Aug
9:22.58	Jermaine Mays		23.12.82	10	Jena, GER	27	May
9:23.00	Glen Watts		9.12.86	3	Bedford	15	Jul
9:23.8	Scott Evans		4.02.91	1	Aldershot	8	Jul
9:25.27	Nyle Clinton	U23	27.03.95	1	Normal, USA	8	Apr
9:26.48	Dave Ragan		26.03.83	2	Manchester (SC)	20	Aug
(40)							
9:26.64	Michael Vennard	U23	19.08.95	10	Azusa, USA	14	Apr
9:26.71	Daniel Owen		5.07.93	6	Manchester (SC)	27	May
9:26.78	Aidan Thompson	U23	19.12.96	4	Bedford	17	Jun
9:28.50	Matthew Arnold	U23	5.08.96	5	Bedford	17	Jun
9:29.40	George Groom	U20	20.10.99	2	Bedford	17	Jun
9:29.80	James Beeks	U20	13.10.98	9	Loughborough	21	May
9:29.92	Bertie Houghton	U23	19.03.95	9	Bedford	1	May
9:30.19	Joseph Turner		3.08.90	2	Perth, AUS	20	Jan
9:32.24	Christopher Greenwood	V40	29.09.73	2	London (LV)	20	Aug
9:32.76	Grant Twist		17.10.90	12	Bedford	29	Jul
(50)							
9:34.44	Edward Banks		30.05.85	6	London (He)	20	Aug
9:34.50	Michael Wright		24.03.87	1	Grangemouth	9	Jul
9:35.09	Sullivan Smith	V40	16.09.76	2V40	Aarhus, DEN	31	Jul
9:35.88	Martin Hayes		16.05.89	2	Swansea	3	Jun
9:36.50	Sam Sommerville	U23	8.12.97	2	Yeovil	6	May
9:36.91	Jack Douglas	U23	5.06.96	6h1	Bedford	29	Apr
9:37.14	Daniel Rothwell		29.04.87	3	Swansea	3	Jun
9:37.14	Robert Warner	V35	30.05.81	13	Bedford	29	Jul
9:37.63	Max Costley		29.08.94	14	Bedford	29	Jul
9:40.70	Alan Corlett		22.12.90	15	Bedford	29	Jul
(60)							
9:41.86	James Wignall		24.11.91	4	Swansea	3	Jun
9:42.33	Terence Fawden	U20	19.01.99	4	Manchester (SC)	20	Aug
9:42.87	Alex Milne		11.03.90	4	Bedford	15	Jul
9:43.53	Edward Mason	U20	9.03.99	2	Visby, SWE	26	Jun
9:44.28	Christoper Hilton		22.05.94	5	London (LV)	3	Jun
9:45.31	Jonathon Roberts		11.05.94	7	Bedford	15	Jul
9:45.56	Jonathan Collier	U23	22.08.95	6	Champaign, USA	22	Apr
9:45.94	Joe Walton	U23	15.09.95	16	Bedford	29	Jul
9:46.28	Michael Cameron	U23	18.11.95	1	Grangemouth	13	Aug
9:46.38	Aidan Kent	U20	6.10.99	5	Bedford	15	Jul
(70)							
9:46.66	Joshua King	U23	3.09.95	1	Yate	3	Jun
9:47.53	Calum Upton	U23	10.12.96	17	Bedford	29	Jul
9:47.9	William Davidson	U23	24.05.96	2	Kingston	6	May

Additional Under 20 (1-6 above)

9:48.08	Sam Costley		24.02.99	7	London (He)	20	Aug
9:52.60	Alfie Manthorpe		26.09.99	8	Sheffield	6	May
9:52.75	George Lewis		4.12.98	10	Manchester (SC)	27	May
9:55.6	Bede Pitcairn-Knowles		5.08.00	1	Hemel Hempstead	21	May
(10)							
9:56.4	Logan Smith		23.01.98	3	Ipswich	20	May
9:58.32	Tristan Rees		3.04.99	1	Grangemouth	13	May
9:58.93	George Phillips		7.08.99	2	Bedford	15	Jul

Foreign

9:08.11	*Jayme Rossiter (IRL)*		*29.09.90*	*2*	*Bedford*	*15*	*Jul*
9:12.60	*Michael Deason (USA)*		*8.01.85*	*3*	*Bedford*	*15*	*Jul*
9:47.2	*Abdi Mahamed (SOM)*	*U23*	*16.09.96*	*1*	*Portsmouth*	*14*	*May*

60 Metres Hurdles - Indoors

7.43	Andy Pozzi		15.05.92	1	Birmingham	18	Feb
7.44				1	Karlsruhe, GER	4	Feb
7.44				1h3	Sheffield	11	Feb
7.49				1h1	Karlsruhe, GER	4	Feb
7.51				1	Sheffield	11	Feb
7.51				1	Belgrade, SRB	3	Mar
7.52				1h1	Belgrade, SRB	3	Mar
7.56				1h1	Cardiff	28	Jan
7.57				1	Cardiff	28	Jan
7.63	David Omoregie	U23	1.11.95	2	Cardiff	28	Jan
7.63				2h2	Karlsruhe, GER	4	Feb
7.64				4	Karlsruhe, GER	4	Feb
7.66				1	Cardiff	15	Jan
7.66				1h2	Cardiff	28	Jan
7.69				1h1	Sheffield	11	Feb
7.71				3h3	Belgrade, SRB	3	Mar
7.63	David King		13.06.94	2	Birmingham	18	Feb
7.65				1	Mondeville, FRA	4	Feb
7.70				1h2	Sheffield	11	Feb
7.70				6h2	Belgrade, SRB	3	Mar
7.73				1h2	Mondeville, FRA	4	Feb
7.74				3	Cardiff	28	Jan
7.74				2h2	Cardiff	28	Jan
7.76				2	Sheffield	11	Feb
7.79	Khai Riley-La Borde	U23	8.11.95	1A1	London (LV)	28	Jan
7.80				1A2	London (LV)	2	Jan
7.81				5	Nantes, FRA	21	Jan
7.82				1A2	London (LV)	28	Jan
7.84				2rB	Mondeville, FRA	4	Feb
7.87				3h3	Mondeville, FRA	4	Feb
7.88				1A2	London (LV)	30	Dec
7.90				4h2	Nantes, FRA	21	Jan
7.90				1A1	London (LV)	30	Dec
7.85	William Sharman		12.09.84	1rC	Mondeville, FRA	4	Feb
7.88				4	Berlin, GER	10	Feb
7.89				2h1	Mondeville, FRA	4	Feb
7.86	Jake Porter		13.11.93	3	Sheffield	11	Feb
7.89				6	Birmingham	18	Feb
7.90				7	Nantes, FRA	21	Jan
7.89	Edirin Okoro		4.04.89	2h3	Sheffield	11	Feb

40 performances to 7.90 by 7 athletes

7.94	David Feeney		17.10.87	6	Sheffield	11	Feb
7.95	James Weaver	U23	25.07.97	1	London (LV)	14	Jan
7.96	Andy Blow		22.09.85	2A2	Eton	5	Feb
(10)							
7.97	Jack Hatton	U23	14.02.96	2A2	London (LV)	2	Jan
7.99	Julian Adeniran		28.09.88	2A1	London (LV)	2	Jan
8.01	Euan Dickson-Earle	U23	9.07.96	4A2	London (LV)	28	Jan
8.03	Timothy Duckworth	U23	18.06.96	3	Bloomington, USA	8	Dec
8.06	Jack Kirby	U23	5.11.96	3A2	Eton	5	Feb
8.06	Miguel Perera	U23	30.09.96	2A2	London (LV)	30	Dec
8.09	Cameron Fillery	U20	2.11.98	4A2	London (LV)	2	Jan
8.09	Ashley Bryant		17.05.91	1A1	Birmingham	15	Jan
8.11	Reece Young	U23	3.10.95	2	London (LV)	1	Feb
8.11	Liam Ramsay		18.11.92	2H1	Belgrade, SRB	5	Mar
(20)							
8.13	Jack Major	U23	23.10.96	4	Sheffield	17	Feb
8.15	Rushane Thomas	U23	27.01.95	3	Kuldigas, LAT	21	Jan
8.18	William Ritchie-Moulin	U23	3.12.96	6h2	Sheffield	11	Feb
8.22	Ben Gregory		21.11.90	2A1	Birmingham	15	Jan

8.22	Glen Elsdon		27.09.92	1	Cardiff	5	Feb
8.23	Matthew Hewitt		27.12.92	3B2	London (LV)	28	Jan
8.25	Calum Innes		17.09.90	4	Edmonton, CAN	10	Mar
8.27	John Lane		29.01.89	1H5	Sheffield	8	Jan
8.30	Jacob Spence	U20	9.01.98	3A1	Birmingham	15	Jan
8.30	Matthew Treston	U20	20.07.98	6h1	New York (A), USA	3	Feb
(30)							
8.33	Kyle Arnold	U23	11.11.96	4h1	Cardiff	28	Jan
8.33	Maranga Mokaya	U23	30.06.96	2h4	Sheffield	17	Feb
8.34	Tony Higbee		21.09.83	4B1	London (LV)	28	Jan
8.36	James Finney	U23	7.04.96	7h1	Sheffield	11	Feb
8.38	George Vaughan	U20	26.06.98	1	London (LV)	18	Mar
8.40	Andrew Murphy		26.12.94	4h4	Sheffield	17	Feb
8.43	Michael Wilson	U23	1.02.97	1	Cardiff	10	Dec
8.44	Aled Price	U23	14.12.95	4	London (LV)	1	Feb
8.46	Curtis Mitchell	U23	29.09.95	2	Sheffield	1	Feb
8.47	Rhys Harris	U20	11.10.98	3	Cardiff	15	Jan
(40)							
8.49	Alex Nwenwu		11.09.91	4B2	London (LV)	28	Jan
8.49A	Harry Maslen	U23	2.09.96	5r2	Alamosa, USA	18	Feb

Foreign

7.77	*Ben Reynolds (IRL)*		*26.09.90*	*1r2*	*Dublin (B), IRL*	*5*	*Feb*
7.92	*Gianni Frankis (ITA)*		*16.04.88*	*1A2*	*Eton*	*5*	*Feb*
8.00	*Alex Al-Ameen (NGR)*		*2.03.89*	*3rB*	*Reims, FRA*	*31*	*Jan*
8.12	*Jared Lane (USA)*		*22.05.93*	*3*	*Sheffield*	*17*	*Feb*
8.23	*Peter Moreno (NGR)*		*30.12.90*	*2A1*	*Eton*	*5*	*Mar*

60 Metres Hurdles - Under 20 (99cm)

7.80	Tre Thomas	26.06.00	1	Sheffield	26	Feb
7.83	Sam Talbot	17.02.99	2	Sheffield	26	Feb
7.86	Jason Nicholson	10.05.99	2	Sheffield	2	Dec
7.87	Cameron Fillery	2.11.98	3	Sheffield	26	Feb
7.94	William Aldred	13.05.99	1	Manchester (SC)	29	Jan
7.97	George Vaughan	26.06.98	2h2	Sheffield	26	Feb
8.08	Jacob Spence	9.01.98	5	Sheffield	26	Feb
8.16	Cameron Meakin	21.10.98	2	Manchester (SC)	29	Jan
8.07	Sam Bennett	2.02.01	1A2	London (LV)	30	Dec
8.28	Rivaldo Brown	7.09.98	3	Manchester (SC)	29	Jan
(10)						
8.32	Tomos Slade	13.04.01	1	Cardiff	10	Dec
8.34	Toby Seal	10.12.99	1	London (LV)	18	Mar
8.35	Joseph Thurgood	11.09.98	4h1	Sheffield	26	Feb
8.36	Joshua Armstrong	23.12.99	2	Athlone, IRL	1	Apr
8.37	Mayowa Osunsami	23.10.99	3A2	London (LV)	28	Jan
8.37	Taylor Roy	25.06.99	1	Glasgow	11	Feb
8.37	Oliver Stacey	5.09.99	2	Birmingham	19	Mar
8.39	Michael Shields	25.04.99	4	London (LV)	14	Jan
8.39	Cameron Amedee	27.09.98	1B1	London (LV)	28	Jan
8.39	Rhys Harris	11.10.98	3	Cardiff	5	Mar
(20)						
8.4	James Greenhalgh	18.02.98	1	Kings Lynn	29	Jan
8.44	Ryan Long	2.09.98	1H4	Sheffield	8	Jan
8.45	Joseph Hobson	29.04.98	2H4	Sheffield	8	Jan
8.46	Caius Joseph	24.07.99	1r2	Eton	3	Dec
8.52	Ben Clarke	30.10.98	2A1	London (LV)	2	Jan
8.55	Howard Bell	2.05.98	4H1	Prague, CZE	29	Jan
8.55	David Aryeetey	25.10.99	3	Sheffield	2	Dec
8.55	Oliver Herring	28.09.00	1	Manchester (SC)	17	Dec
8.56	Dylan Carlsson-Smith	26.07.98	4H4	Sheffield	8	Jan
8.56	Chinua Ebereonwu	14.06.01	2	Cardiff	10	Dec
(30)						
8.57	Joe Fuggle	25.01.99	3h2	London (LV)	14	Jan

Foreign
| 8.06 | Edson Gomes (POR) | 1.11.98 | 3 | London (LV) | 14 | Jan |

60 Metres Hurdles - Under 17 (91.4cm)

7.92	Jack Sumners	25.10.00	1	Cardiff	5	Mar
8.04	Oliver Cresswell	17.11.00	2	Cardiff	5	Mar
8.07	Sam Bennett	2.02.01	2	Sheffield	26	Feb
8.12	Daniel Knight	24.11.01	1A2	London (LV)	30	Dec
8.17	Joshua Zeller	19.10.00	2	London (LV)	7	Jan
8.17	Jordan Ricketts	10.09.01	1	Sheffield	2	Dec
8.29	William Adeyeye	4.03.01	3	London (LV)	4	Feb
8.32	Joshua Watson	15.08.01	2A2	London (LV)	2	Jan
8.32	Ben Higgins	14.11.00	1	Manchester (SC)	29	Jan
8.37	Harri Wheeler-Sexton	25.11.00	1H3	Sheffield	12	Mar
(10)						
8.38	Tomos Slade	13.04.01	4	Cardiff	5	Mar
8.44	Nahom Selemon	20.04.01	2	Manchester (SC)	29	Jan
8.44	Robbie Farquhar	4.01.01	2H3	Sheffield	12	Mar
8.44	Troy McConville	29.04.02	1P	Athlone, IRL	28	Oct
8.46	Rico Cottell	22.11.01	2A1	London (LV)	30	Dec
8.51	Dylan DaCosta	6.04.01	2	Sutton	18	Feb
8.52	Joe Halpin	19.02.01	1	Sheffield	14	Jan
8.52	Oliver Herring	28.09.00	2	Sheffield	14	Jan
8.52	Joel McFarlane	9.10.00	3	Glasgow	2	Feb
8.54	Jonathan Mann	30.04.01	1	London (LV)	18	Mar
(20)						
8.56	Daniel Murathodzic	11.09.01	2	Cardiff	11	Feb
8.56	Zephan Boxall	1.11.01	3h2	Sheffield	26	Feb
8.58	Chinua Ebereonwu	14.06.01	3	Cardiff	11	Feb
8.58	Ethan Williamson	29.09.01	2P	Athlone, IRL	28	Oct
8.60	Ezra Rodriques	8.11.00	3	Sutton	18	Feb
8.61	Matthew Chandler	30.10.00	1h2	Glasgow	2	Feb
8.61	Samuel Tutt	12.03.01	3h1	Sheffield	26	Feb
8.61	Stuart Bladon	13.01.02	3P2	Glasgow	10	Nov

60 Metres Hurdles - Under 15 (84cm)

8.25	Joseph Harding	31.10.02	1P2	Sheffield	12	Mar
8.66	Stephen Simmons	1.07.03	2	Sheffield	26	Feb
8.73	Elliott Harris	13.10.02	2P2	Sheffield	12	Mar
8.78	Oliver Early	26.05.04	1P2	London (LV)	16	Dec
8.83	Michael Adesiyan	11.11.03	1	London (LV)	3	Dec
8.86	Jamie Schleuter	26.10.03	3	Sheffield	26	Feb
8.90	Ben Hillman	16.04.03	1P1	Sheffield	12	Mar
8.96	Reuben Nairne	22.09.02	3h1	Sheffield	26	Feb
8.98	Zak Wall	21.10.03	1P3	Cardiff	7	Oct
9.04	Freddie Fraser	25.01.04	4	Sheffield	26	Feb
(10)						
9.06	Toby Bishop	3.10.03	1P1	London (LV)	16	Dec
9.16	Xander Collins	18.09.03	2	London (LV)	7	Jan
9.18	Louis Clow	22.11.02	2A2	London (LV)	22	Jan
9.21	Callum Gregson	16.11.02	3	London (LV)	7	Jan
9.22	Murray Fotheringham	4.06.03	1	Glasgow	26	Mar
9.23	Iwan Jones	6.05.03	8	Sheffield	26	Feb
9.25	Matthew Register	3.03.03	2	Cardiff	11	Feb
9.25	Kyle McAuley	9.04.03	2P2	Glasgow	4	Mar
9.30	Dale Turner	25.06.03	1P	Gateshead	19	Mar
9.3	Matthew Griffin	29.08.03	1rB	Birmingham	19	Mar
(20)						
9.32	Samuel Ball	18.10.04	2P1	London (LV)	16	Dec
9.34	Cole Williams	12.02.03	6h2	Sheffield	26	Feb
9.37	Alfie Kelway	2.01.03	4h1	Sheffield	26	Feb
9.38	Kai Alland	27.07.03	1	London (LV)	18	Mar

60 Metres Hurdles - Under 13 (76.2cm)

9.87		Zane McQuillan	6.12.04	4h3	Athlone, IRL	1	Apr
9.9		Luke Ball	28.10.04	1	Birmingham	19	Mar

75 Metres Hurdles - Under 13 (76.2cm)

11.48	0.6	Samuel Ball	18.10.04	1r2	Kingston	29	Jul
11.8		Henry Fayehun	4.05.05	1	Chelmsford	5	Jul
11.8		Nathan Wilson		2	Chelmsford	5	Jul
11.88w	2.3	Zane McQuillan	6.12.04	1	Glasgow (S)	19	Aug
11.9		Drew Bradley	13.10.04	1	Leeds	18	Jun
		12.16		1	Manchester (Str)	28	Aug
11.9		Clayton Mytil	21.10.04	2	Bedford	16	Jul
		11.95	0.4	1	London (TB)	26	Aug
12.0		Oliver Robertson	27.09.04	1	Ashford	2	Jul
		12.11	-0.3	1r1	Kingston	29	Jul
12.1		D Mubana		3	Chelmsford	5	Jul
12.1		Jacob Blanc	19.10.04	1	Hornchurch	17	Sep
12.13		Jake Minshull	11.10.04	1	Nuneaton	9	Sep

80 Metres Hurdles - Under 15 (84cm)

10.50	0.7	Joseph Harding	31.10.02	1	Birmingham	8	Jul
11.10	1.6	Stephen Simmons	1.07.03	2P1	Boston	16	Sep
11.13		Elliott Harris	13.10.02	1	Bedford	27	Aug
11.24	0.7	Jami Schlueter	26.10.02	1h2	Birmingham	7	Jul
11.46	1.5	Immanuel Feyi-Waboso	20.12.02	1	Brecon	13	Jul
11.47	-0.4	Freddie Fraser	25.01.04	2h1	Birmingham	7	Jul
11.47		Ben Hillman	16.04.03	2h1	Bedford	27	Aug
11.53	-1.9	Wilfred McKenzie	10.10.02	1	Bromley	15	Jul
11.59	0.7	Cole Williams	12.02.03	2h2	Birmingham	7	Jul
11.61	0.7	Joel Pascall-Menzie	3.11.02	3h2	Birmingham	7	Jul
	(10)						
11.62	1.3	Monty Ogunbanjo	14.01.03	2	Oxford (H)	9	Sep
11.62w	2.1	Gregory Zoppos	10.03.03	1P2	Boston	16	Sep
11.63w	2.1	Seb Wallace	7.09.03	2P2	Boston	16	Sep
		11.64	1.3	3	Oxford (H)	9	Sep
11.64		Jordan Cunningham	22.12.02	2h2	Bedford	27	Aug
11.66	1.3	Joel Evans	13.03.03	4	Oxford (H)	9	Sep
11.73		A Parker		2	Chelmsford	10	Jun
11.73	0.3	Oliver D'Rozario	24.09.03	1	Exeter	25	Jul
11.79		Matthew Griffin	29.08.03	5	Bedford	27	Aug
11.82	0.7	Elliott Evans	3.09.03	4h2	Birmingham	7	Jul
11.82	-0.1	Adam Hoole	25.05.03	1	Glasgow (S)	20	Aug
	(20)						
11.84	1.1	Joseph Fischer	12.03.03	1	Southend	28	Aug
11.84w	2.4	Lewis Swaby	7.06.03	1P3	Boston	16	Sep
11.85	0.7	Xander Collins	18.09.03	5h2	Birmingham	7	Jul
11.85		Joseph Alexander	5.11.02	1	Hereford	8	Jul
11.87w	2.4	George Seery	20.08.03	3P3	Boston	16	Sep
11.87w	2.4	Dale Turner	25.06.03	2P3	Boston	16	Sep
11.88w	2.1	William Scammell	1.12.02	1P4	Boston	16	Sep

hand timing

11.3	Wilfred McKenzie	(11.53)	1	Oxford (H)	2	Jul
11.6	Seb Wallace	(11.64)	1	Horsham	21	Jul
11.7	Joseph Fischer	(11.84)	2P	Brentwood	24	May
11.8	Elliott Evans	(11.82)	1	Bracknell	2	Jul
11.8	Peter Adeosun	15.11.02	2	Swindon	15	Jul
11.8w	Joseph Purbrick	22.04.04	1	Cambridge	18	Jun

100 Metres Hurdles - Under 17 (91.4cm)

12.76	1.9	Sam Bennett		2.02.01	1	Bedford	27	Aug
12.85	1.9	Jack Sumners		25.10.00	1	Nuneaton	13	May
12.93	0.9	Joshua Zeller		19.10.00	1	Birmingham	8	Jul
12.96	0.9	Oliver Cresswell		17.11.00	2	Birmingham	8	Jul
13.03	1.9	Daniel Knight		24.11.01	3	Bedford	27	Aug
13.21	-0.1	Tomos Slade		13.04.01	2h2	Bedford	27	Aug
13.34		Joshua Watson		15.08.01	1	Kingston	10	Jun
13.35	-0.1	Jonathan Mann		30.04.01	3h2	Bedford	27	Aug
13.35	1.9	Jack Turner		11.07.01	5	Bedford	27	Aug
13.47	-0.1	Chinua Ebereonwu		14.06.01	1	Brecon	26	Aug
	(10)							
13.49	-0.4	Rico Cottell		22.11.01	2	Reading	25	Jun
13.53		Jordan Ricketts		10.09.01	2	Birmingham	17	Jun
13.54	1.9	Ben Higgins		14.11.00	1	Nuneaton	13	May
13.57	1.5	William Adeyeye		4.03.01	2	Chelmsford	13	May
13.59	-1.2	Joseph Collins		13.12.00	1	Exeter	17	Jun
13.62	1.6	Joel McFarlane		9.10.00	1D	Grangemouth	2	Jul
13.65		Ezra Rodriques		8.11.00	2	Kingston	10	Jun
13.73	0.0	Robbie Farquhar		4.01.01	3	Loughborough	1	Sep
13.77	1.0	Nahom Selemon		20.04.01	1	Manchester (Str)	25	Jun
13.79	-0.2	Oliver Dakin		1.12.01	1	Derby	13	May
	(20)							
13.81	-0.4	Evan Campbell		17.05.01	3O3	Yeovil	25	Jun
13.91		Matthew Chandler		30.10.00	2P	Grangemouth	3	Jun
13.93	0.3	Samuel Odu		4.04.02	3	Basingstoke	17	Jun
13.95	-1.2	William Westmacott		8.04.01	3	Exeter	17	Jun
13.99	-0.8	Troy McConville		29.04.02	2	Tullamore, IRL	3	Jun
13.99	1.1	Alexander MacKay		13.12.01	2	Grangemouth	26	Aug

wind assisted

13.55w	3.4	Joel McFarlane		(13.62)	1	Grangemouth	9	Jun
13.78w	2.1	Evan Campbell		(13.81)	4O1	Boston	17	Sep
13.91w	2.1	Oliver Herring		28.09.00	5O1	Boston	17	Sep
13.92w	2.2	Adam Coles		22.03.01	1	Leigh	20	Aug

hand timing

12.8		Jack Sumners		(12.85)	1	Abingdon	3	Jun
12.9		Oliver Cresswell		(12.96)	2	Abingdon	3	Jun
13.1		Joseph Harding	U15	31.10.02	1rB	London (LV)	13	Aug
13.3w		Jordan Ricketts		(13.53)	1	Nottingham	30	Apr
13.5		William Adeyeye		(13.57)	1	London (ME)	28	May
13.7		Robert Worman		4.07.01	1	Cheltenham	13	May
13.9		Lewis Davey		24.10.00	1O	Bedford	25	Jun
14.0		Oliver Lambert		18.10.00	1	Rugby	1	Apr
14.0	-0.8	Adam Coles		(13.92w)	1	Hull	30	Apr
14.0		Jack Berwick		3.11.00	3	Worcester	7	May
14.0		Zephan Boxall		1.11.01	3	Stratford on Avon	10	Sep

110 Metres Hurdles - Under 18 (91.4cm)

13.51	2.0	Jack Sumners	U17	25.10.00	1r2	Bedford	27	May
13.54w	2.1	Tre Thomas		26.06.00	1	Loughborough	1	Apr
13.83			-0.2		3	Bedford	18	Jun
13.60	2.0	Sam Bennett	U17	2.02.01	2r2	Bedford	27	May
14.07w	7.0	Oliver Cresswell	U17	17.11.00	3	London (LV)	26	Apr
14.08	0.1				2	Loughborough	10	May
14.41w	7.0	Sam Roberts		17.07.00	4	London (LV)	26	Apr
14.79	-1.7	Shaun Zygadlo		16.06.00	2	Dublin (S), IRL	5	Aug
15.01i		Joel McFarlane	U17	9.10.00	1r1	Motherwell	29	Mar

110 Metres Hurdles - Under 20 (99cm)

13.48	0.0	Robert Sakala	5.03.98	2	Grosseto, ITA	22	Jul
13.64	1.8	Jason Nicholson	10.05.99	1	Loughborough	21	May
13.69	1.8	Cameron Fillery	2.11.98	2	Loughborough	21	May
13.78	-0.1	Onatade Ojora	14.10.99	2h1	Bedford	18	Jun
13.89	0.6	Tre Thomas	26.06.00	3	Birmingham	8	Jul
14.06	-0.2	George Vaughan	26.06.98	4	Bedford	18	Jun
14.11	0.2	Ethan Akanni	5.03.99	1h2	Birmingham	8	Jul
14.14	0.6	Mayowa Osunsami	23.10.99	6	Birmingham	8	Jul
14.36	-2.9	Sam Talbot	17.02.99	1D2	Street	30	Apr
14.46	-0.1	William Aldred	13.05.99	3h1	Bedford	18	Jun
	(10)						
14.53	-0.1	Ryan Long	2.09.98	4h1	Bedford	18	Jun
14.62	0.2	Owen Lawrence	31.10.98	4h2	Birmingham	8	Jul
14.65	-0.1	David Aryeetey	25.10.99	5h1	Bedford	18	Jun
14.70	0.9	Kanya Mtshweni	4.07.00	4h1	Birmingham	8	Jul
14.78	0.2	Cameron Meakin	21.10.98	5h2	Birmingham	8	Jul
14.84	0.2	William Seed	20.10.98	6h2	Birmingham	8	Jul
14.91		Joshua Armstrong	23.12.99	1	Antrim	19	May
14.92	0.9	Joseph Thurgood	11.09.98	2	Gillingham	30	Apr
14.93	-0.1	Toby Seal	10.12.99	1	Stevenage	28	May
14.99	0.9	Oliver Stacey	5.09.99	1	Tonbridge	17	Apr
	(20)						
15.04	-1.1	Taylor Roy	25.06.99	1	Birmingham	3	Sep
15.06	-0.1	Sean Bazanye-Lutu	29.09.98	2	Stevenage	28	May
15.08	-2.4	Thomas Miller	7.10.98	2	Loughborough	22	Apr
15.14	1.6	Howard Bell	2.05.98	1D	Grangemouth	2	Jul
15.19	1.8	Lloyd Ellis	7.07.99	1	Nuneaton	13	May
15.21	0.2	Rivaldo Brown	7.09.98	7h2	Birmingham	8	Jul
15.25		Michael Shields	25.04.99	2	Chelmsford	13	May

wind assisted

13.91	5.0	Ethan Akanni	(14.11)	1	Glasgow (S)	19	Aug
13.95	2.4	George Vaughan	(14.06)	2h2	Bedford	18	Jun
14.10	2.4	Mayowa Osunsami	(14.14)	3h2	Bedford	18	Jun
14.53	4.7	Owen Lawrence	(14.62)	1	Portsmouth	14	May
14.58	4.8	David Aryeetey	(14.65)	1	Nuneaton	11	Jun
14.66	5.0	Taylor Roy	(15.04)	3	Glasgow (S)	19	Aug
14.97	5.0	Daniel McFarlane	10.10.98	2	Grangemouth	9	Jun
15.12	2.1	Michael Shields	(15.25)	1	Cambridge	24	Jun
15.16	2.1	Reni Omotomilola	18.08.00	2D1	Boston	17	Sep
15.18	4.8	Lloyd Ellis	(15.19)	2	Nuneaton	11	Jun

hand timing

14.3		Ryan Long	(14.53)	1	Bournemouth	10	Jun
14.3w	3.3	Jay O'Leary	23.12.99	1	Nottingham	30	Apr
14.5w	3.3	Chris Morgan	31.03.99	2	Nottingham	30	Apr
14.7	-1.2	Taylor Roy	(15.04)	2	Hull	30	Apr
15.0		Rivaldo Brown	(15.21)	1	Wrexham	23	Jul
15.2		Rhys Harris	11.10.98	1	Cheltenham	28	May
15.3		Reni Omotomilola	(15.16w)	1D	Bedford	25	Jun

Foreign

14.37	*-0.2*	*Edson Gomes (POR)*	*1.11.98*	*5*	*Bedford*	*18*	*Jun*
		14.14w 2.4		*4h2*	*Bedford*	*18*	*Jun*

110 Metres Hurdles

13.14	-0.1	Andy Pozzi		15.05.92	2	Paris (C), FRA	1	Jul
	13.19	0.9			5	Eugene, USA	27	May
	13.24	1.8			2	Des Moines, USA	29	Apr
	13.24	-0.3			4	Rome, ITA	8	Jun
	13.24	0.1			2h2	Paris (C), FRA	1	Jul
	13.28	0.7			1h4	London (O)	6	Aug
	13.28	0.6			4s2	London (O)	6	Aug
	13.32	1.4			1	Loughborough	21	May
	13.35	1.4			1r1	Loughborough	21	May
	13.53	-0.6			6	Birmingham	20	Aug
	13.56	0.7			5	Zagreb, CRO	29	Aug
13.34	0.0	David Omoregie	U23	1.11.95	1h1	Villeneuve d'Ascq, FRA	23	Jun
	13.36	0.2			3	Villeneuve d'Ascq, FRA	25	Jun
	13.43	-0.5			1h1	London (O)	9	Jul
	13.47	1.4			2	Loughborough	21	May
	13.51	1.4			2r1	Loughborough	21	May
	13.59	-1.2			6h1	London (O)	6	Aug
	13.64	1.0			1h1	Birmingham	2	Jul
	13.70	0.0			8	London (O)	9	Jul
	13.73	-0.5			5	Madrid, ESP	14	Jul
13.48	1.2	David King		13.06.94	2	Bydgoszcz, POL	2	Jun
	13.49	0.6			1h1	Montgeron, FRA	14	May
	13.51	1.4			3r1	Loughborough	21	May
	13.56	-0.4			6h2	London (O)	9	Jul
	13.57	1.3			2	Montgeron, FRA	14	May
	13.57	-1.4			5	Hengelo, NED	11	Jun
	13.64	1.5			1h2	Birmingham	2	Jul
	13.65	-0.6			7	Birmingham	20	Aug
	13.66	1.0			3	Manchester	26	May
	13.67	1.3			8h2	London (O)	6	Aug
	13.72	1.4			4	Loughborough	21	May
	13.73	0.7			6	Zagreb, CRO	29	Aug
13.59	1.4	Khai Riley-La Borde	U23	8.11.95	3	Loughborough	21	May
	13.65	0.8			2	Bydgoszcz, POL	15	Jul
	13.66	1.1			3	Aarhus, DEN	2	Jun
	13.67	0.2			1	Linz, AUT	25	May
	13.73	1.9			1	London (Nh)	7	May
	13.73	0.0			1h2	Linz, AUT	25	May
	13.73	0.5			1	Bedford	18	Jun
	13.75	0.1			1h3	Birmingham	2	Jul
	13.79	0.4			1h2	Bedford	18	Jun
13.65	1.2	Gabriel Odujobi		15.07.87	1	Clermont, USA	13	May
	13.68	2.0			3h1	Gainesville, USA	28	Apr
	13.71	0.2			2	Linz, AUT	25	May
	13.84	1.7			3	Coral Gables, USA	7	Apr
	13.85	1.2			8	Gainesville, USA	28	Apr
	13.85	0.0			2h2	Linz, AUT	25	May
13.68	1.2	Jake Porter		13.11.93	1	Castres, FRA	26	Jul
	13.79	0.9			2h1	Bedford	29	Jul
	13.81	-0.5			7h1	London (O)	9	Jul
	13.84	-0.1			4	Gateshead (Q)	9	Sep
	13.85	0.1			2h3	Birmingham	2	Jul
13.69	0.9	James Weaver	U23	25.07.97	1h1	Bedford	29	Jul
	13.73	0.0			1	Bedford	29	Jul
	13.75	0.8			4	Bydgoszcz, POL	15	Jul
	13.77	0.5			2	Bedford	18	Jun
	13.85	0.9			1h3	Bydgoszcz, POL	14	Jul
13.72	2.0	William Sharman		12.09.84	4h1	Gainesville, USA	28	Apr
	13.74	-0.7			7	Lahti, FIN	9	Jun
13.77	0.2	Edirin Okoro		4.04.89	3	Loughborough	22	Jul

60 performances to 13.85 by 9 athletes

14.09	1.4	David Feeney		17.10.87	6	Loughborough	21	May
	(10)							
14.09	1.5	Miguel Perera	U23	30.09.96	3rB	Bydgoszcz, POL	2	Jun
14.18	1.7	Jack Hatton	U23	14.02.96	1	Loughborough	7	Jun
14.22	0.9	Cameron Fillery	U20	2.11.98	3h1	Bedford	29	Jul
14.27	1.0	Rushane Thomas	U23	27.01.95	3h1	Aarhus, DEN	2	Jun
14.30	2.0	Timothy Duckworth	U23	18.06.96	1D5	Eugene, USA	8	Jun
14.42	1.4	Euan Dickson-Earle	U23	9.07.96	5rA	Loughborough	21	May
14.49	0.3	Ashley Bryant		17.05.91	3rT	Paris, FRA	1	Jul
14.51	1.4	John Lane		29.01.89	3D2	Götzis, AUT	28	May
14.52	1.7	Jack Major	U23	23.10.96	2rB	Loughborough	21	May
14.52	1.3	Ben Gregory		21.11.90	1D2	Barcelona, ESP	23	Jul
	(20)							
14.54	0.0	Jack Kirby	U23	5.11.96	8	Bedford	29	Jul
14.56	1.4	Glen Elsdon		27.09.92	8	Loughborough	21	May
14.56	-0.5	Jack Lawrie	U23	21.02.96	4	London (LV)	3	Jun
14.60	1.5	William Ritchie-Moulin	U23	3.12.96	5h2	Birmingham	2	Jul
14.67	1.6	Jack Andrew		12.10.91	2	Bedford	15	Jul
14.68	0.5	Maranga Mokaya	U23	30.06.96	5	Bedford	18	Jun
14.72	1.6	James Finney	U23	7.04.96	2D5	Bedford	28	May
14.72	1.5	George Vaughan	U20	26.06.98	6h2	Birmingham	2	Jul
14.74	0.1	Reece Young	U23	3.10.95	4h3	Birmingham	2	Jul
14.78	1.7	Matthew Hewitt		27.12.92	3rB	Loughborough	21	May
	(30)							
14.83	0.1	Onajite Okoro		21.02.92	6h3	Birmingham	2	Jul
14.84	0.0	Jahmal Germain		3.07.92	1rB	London (LV)	3	Jun
14.96	1.7	Alex Nwenwu		11.09.91	5rB	Loughborough	21	May
15.00	0.0	Alexander Wort		18.09.93	4	Basingstoke	6	May
15.05	1.6	Andrew Murphy		26.12.94	4D5	Bedford	28	May
15.05	1.7	William Aldred	U20	13.05.99	1	Portsmouth	20	Aug
15.09	1.5	Calum Innes		17.09.90	1	Grangemouth	27	Aug
15.13	1.9	Deo Milandu		30.10.92	2	Cudworth	14	May
15.13	1.5	Michael Wilson	U23	1.02.97	2	Cardiff	21	Jun
15.15	0.0	Mark Cryer		27.08.93	6	Basingstoke	6	May
	(40)							
15.16	0.0	Peter Glass		1.05.88	2D2	Arona, ESP	4	Jun
15.18	0.4	Ayomide Byron	U23	16.06.97	5h2	Bedford	18	Jun
15.21	-1.3	Niall Flannery		26.04.91	2rB	London (He)	20	Aug
15.23	1.5	Curtis Mathews		22.01.92	3	Cardiff	21	Jun
15.25	0.2	Michael Copeland		2.11.89	2rC	Oordegem, BEL	27	May
15.25	0.0	Bradley Reed		14.01.92	2	London (He)	24	Jun
15.27	1.8	Harry Maslen	U23	2.09.96	2	Waco, USA	22	Apr
15.27	1.8	Ryan Hewitson	U23	4.01.96	3	Grangemouth	13	Aug
15.29	1.4	Tom Nichols		6.04.85	1	London (CP)	3	Jul
15.31	0.0	Glenn Etherington		10.12.86	1	Bedford	15	Jul
	(50)							
15.34	1.4	Lewis Church	U23	27.09.96	2D1	Erith	17	Sep
15.37	-0.3	Adam Hill		9.07.94	1	Belfast	1	Jun
15.38	0.9	Richard Reeks		6.12.85	1	Yate	3	Jun
15.38	1.1	Aled Price	U23	14.12.95	2rB	Bedford	15	Jul
15.43	0.1	Curtis Mitchell	U23	29.09.95	7h2	Bedford	29	Jul
15.48	1.8	Taylor Roy	U20	25.06.99	4	Grangemouth	13	Aug
15.51	0.7	Lee Hamilton		6.12.90	1rB	Bedford	15	Jul
15.54	-0.3	Sean Adams		1.09.93	3rB	Bedford	15	Jul
15.58	-0.8	Sam Plumb		12.04.94	1	Perivale	17	Jun

wind assisted

13.13	5.8	Andy Pozzi		(13.14)	1	Clermont, USA	15	Apr
	13.17	2.2			1h1	Clermont, USA	15	Apr
13.38	5.8	Gabriel Odujobi		(13.65)	2	Clermont, USA	15	Apr
	13.51	2.2			3h1	Clermont, USA	15	Apr

13.55	2.1	King		(13.48)	1	Birmingham	2	Jul
13.71	2.1	Riley-La Borde	U23	(13.59)	2	Birmingham	2	Jul
13.75	2.4				1r2	London (Nh)	7	May
13.78	2.4	Weaver	U23	(13.69)	1h1	Bedford	18	Jun
13.79	2.1	Porter		(13.68)	3	Birmingham	2	Jul
13.79	2.7				1h1	Castres, FRA	26	Jul

10 performances to 13.85 by 6 athletes

14.48	2.4	William Ritchie-Moulin	U23	(14.60)	3h1	Bedford	18	Jun
15.14	3.1	Curtis Mitchell	U23	(15.43)	2	Manchester (SC)	10	Jun
15.34	4.7	Peter Irving		28.01.83	1	Portsmouth	14	May

hand timing

13.8w	3.5	Porter		(13.68)	1	Manchester (SC)	16	Aug
13.8w	3.5	Riley-La Borde	U23	(13.59)	2	Manchester (SC)	16	Aug

2 performances to 13.8 by 2 athletes

14.4w	3.5	Ben Gregory		(14.52)	5	Manchester (SC)	16	Aug
14.9		Sam Plumb		(15.58)	1	Portsmouth	8	Jul
15.0		Ayomide Byron	U23	(15.18)	1	Watford	19	Aug
15.4		Ross Liddle	U20	28.07.99	1	Leigh	6	May
15.5		Michael Dyer		27.09.84	1	Oxford (H)	15	Apr
15.5		Thomas Ashby		5.04.90	1	Sutton	17	Jun

Foreign

13.60	*1.1*	*Ben Reynolds (IRL)*		*26.09.90*	*1*	*Aarhus, DEN*	*2*	*Jun*
13.93	*1.4*	*Alex Al-Ameen (NGR)*		*2.03.89*	*4r1*	*Loughborough*	*21*	*May*
14.09	*1.0*	*Jared Lane (USA)*		*22.05.93*	*2*	*Tourcoing, FRA*	*5*	*Jul*
14.17w	*3.8*	*Gianni Frankis (ITA)*		*16.04.88*	*2*	*Bedford*	*15*	*Jul*
14.31	*0.8*				*3h2*	*Loughborough*	*22*	*Jul*
14.41	*0.9*	*Peter Moreno (NGR)*		*30.12.90*	*4h1*	*Bedford*	*29*	*Jul*
14.93	*1.6*	*Michael Bowler (IRL)*		*28.01.92*	*1rB*	*Cambridge*	*6*	*Aug*
14.79w	*2.1*				*4*	*Dublin (S)*	*23*	*Jul*
15.56	*1.8*	*Christian Hood-Boyce (TTO)*	*U23*	*4.01.95*	*2*	*Loughborough*	*24*	*May*

200 Metres Hurdles Straight

22.89		Seb Rodger		29.06.91	2	Manchester	26	May
22.97		Jack Green		6.10.91	3	Manchester	26	May
23.59		Jacob Paul	U23	6.02.95	4	Manchester	26	May

400 Metres Hurdles

48.77	Jack Green		6.10.91	6	London (O)	9	Jul
49.10				2	Prague, CZE	5	Jun
49.27				1	Loughborough	21	May
49.29				4	Stockholm, SWE	18	Jun
49.34				1	Birmingham	2	Jul
49.41				6	Zürich, SUI	24	Aug
49.47				1	Villeneuve d'Ascq, FRA	24	Jun
49.54				1	Ashford	14	May
49.55				5h5	London (O)	6	Aug
49.75				2	Bydgoszcz, POL	2	Jun
49.78				1	Turku, FIN	13	Jun
49.93				4s2	London (O)	7	Aug
49.96				1h1	Villeneuve d'Ascq, FRA	23	Jun
50.27				1	Kingston	6	May
50.27				5	Zagreb, CRO	29	Aug
49.49	Jacob Paul	U23	6.02.95	8	London (O)	9	Jul
49.60				1rB	Geneva, SUI	10	Jun
49.66				2	Birmingham	2	Jul
49.85				2s1	Bydgoszcz, POL	15	Jul
49.98				5	Bydgoszcz, POL	16	Jul
50.06				3	Loughborough	22	Jul

(Paul)	50.07			1	Bedford	18	Jun
	50.23			2rA	Loughborough	21	May
	50.30			1h1	Birmingham	1	Jul
	50.37			3s3	Taipei, TPE	25	Aug
49.58	Seb Rodger		29.06.91	4	Geneva, SUI	10	Jun
	49.78			2	Loughborough	21	May
	49.82			2	Loughborough	22	Jul
	49.86			3	Bydgoszcz, POL	2	Jun
	49.97			1	Oordegem, BEL	22	Aug
	50.10			3rB	Lucerne, SUI	11	Jul
	50.23			3	Birmingham	2	Jul
	50.29			1	Oordegem, BEL	1	May
	50.32			1	Sheffield	6	May
	50.51			1h4	Birmingham	1	Jul
	50.65			3	Copenhagen, DEN	20	Jun
	50.70			1	Manchester (SC)	16	Aug
49.74	Niall Flannery		26.04.91	1	Loughborough	22	Jul
	50.28			2	Celle Ligure, ITA	5	Jul
	50.35			2rB	Geneva, SUI	10	Jun
	50.48			4	Tarare, FRA	24	Jun
	50.57			2h1	Birmingham	1	Jul
	50.64			4	Cork, IRL	18	Jul
	50.75			6	Birmingham	2	Jul
	50.98			1	Samorin, SVK	17	Jun
49.95	Tom Burton		29.10.88	6	Geneva, SUI	10	Jun
	49.95			1=rB	Madrid, ESP	14	Jul
	50.07			6	Kawasaki, JPN	21	May
	50.36			1	Aarhus, DEN	2	Jun
	50.36			4	Birmingham	2	Jul
	50.84			1h3	Birmingham	1	Jul
50.25	Jack Lawrie	U23	21.02.96	2	Bedford	18	Jun
	50.34			4	Loughborough	22	Jul
	50.40			2h1	Bydgoszcz, POL	14	Jul
	50.46			4s2	Bydgoszcz, POL	15	Jul
	50.55			1	London (LV)	3	Jun
	50.60			7	Bydgoszcz, POL	16	Jul
	50.65			5	Birmingham	2	Jul
	50.70			3	Loughborough	21	May
50.72	James Forman		12.12.91	1	Bedford	30	Jul
	50.73			1	London (He)	24	Jun
	61 performances to 50.99 by 7 athletes						
51.21	Matthew Sumner		17.03.92	2	Bedford	30	Jul
51.33	Martin Lipton		14.01.89	3rA	Loughborough	21	May
51.71	Paul Bennett		11.12.92	1	Swansea	3	Jun
	(10)						
51.82	Christopher McAlister	U23	3.12.95	2h4	Birmingham	1	Jul
52.00	Sam Plumb		12.04.94	3h1	Birmingham	1	Jul
52.06	Alistair Chalmers	U20	31.03.00	1	Bedford	18	Jun
52.09	Alex Knibbs	U20	26.04.99	1	Birmingham	8	Jul
52.21	James Webster	U23	27.02.95	4	Bedford	18	Jun
52.21	Lennox Thompson		22.10.93	5	Bedford	30	Jul
52.58	Sam Wallbridge	U23	6.02.97	2	Visby, SWE	26	Jun
52.81	Tyri Donovan	U20	20.10.98	3	Birmingham	8	Jul
52.84	Sean Adams		1.09.93	2rB	London (LV)	3	Jun
52.92	Niall Carney	U23	8.11.97	2rB	Loughborough	21	May
	(20)						
52.95	Daniel Rees	U23	22.10.96	2	Bedford	1	May
53.04	Joe Fuggle	U20	25.01.99	1	Ashford	14	May
53.12	Gwilym Cooper		17.07.91	4rC	Oordegem, BEL	27	May

53.5	Andrew Faulkner		23.07.86	2	Rugby	20	Aug
	53.55			1	Yeovil	6	May
53.67	Jonny Lodowski		15.07.88	1	London (LV)	20	Aug
53.68	Declan Gall	U20	19.05.99	1	Birmingham	3	Sep
54.13	Oliver Robinson		5.10.87	5	Bedford	1	May
54.15	Max Schopp	U23	5.09.96	5rB	Loughborough	21	May
54.25	Ross Liddle	U20	28.07.99	2h2	Birmingham	7	Jul
54.26	Efekemo Okoro		21.02.92	5	Munich, GER	3	Jun
(30)							
54.29	Maurice Jones		17.12.91	4h2	Birmingham	1	Jul
54.53	James Jackson	U20	12.02.99	2	Portsmouth	13	May
54.56	Adam Walker-Khan	U23	7.03.95	2	Emmitsburg, USA	7	May
54.61	Josiah Filleul	U23	14.10.96	4h2	Bedford	17	Jun
54.66	Ryan Cooper	U23	30.03.96	2rB	Swansea	3	Jun
54.66	Daniel Pearce		11.09.91	1	Yate	3	Jun
54.7	Cameron Amedee	U20	27.09.98	1	London (ME)	28	May
54.74	Joshua Faulds	U20	7.03.00	2	Birmingham	3	Sep
54.88	Ben Lloyd	U17	13.10.00	3	Brno, CZE	16	Sep
54.89	Dale Garland	V35	13.10.80	1	St. Peter Port GUE	6	Aug
(40)							
54.98	Ciaran Barnes	U20	8.08.98	7	Dublin (S), IRL	23	Jul
55.05	Travis Christie	U23	1.05.97	5h1	Bedford	17	Jun
55.13	Thomas Pitkin	U20	12.01.98	1	Loughborough	22	Apr
55.22	Caspar Eliot		29.09.89	4	Kingston	6	May
55.25	Dan Wilde	U20	13.07.99	1	Exeter	17	Jun
55.29	Phil Norman		20.10.89	4rB	London (He)	20	Aug
55.30	Peter Irving		28.01.83	4	Visby, SWE	26	Jun
55.35	Tom Parry		8.06.92	1	Kingston	14	May
55.35	Maranga Mokaya	U23	30.06.96	1	Birmingham	4	Jun
55.39	George Vaughan	U20	26.06.98	1rB	London (LV)	20	Aug
(50)							
55.43	Louis Gardner		1.09.93	6	Philadelphia, USA	15	Apr
55.46	Ben Gregory		21.11.90	5rB	London (He)	20	Aug
55.47	Thomas Miller	U20	7.10.98	2	Loughborough	22	Apr
55.47	Thomas Grantham		12.02.83	2	Cudworth	14	May
55.48	Eddie Betts	V45	18.02.71	4	San Sebastian, ESP	29	Apr
55.69	Alastair Stanley	U23	2.09.95	2	Grangemouth	22	Apr
55.69	Jack McComb	U20	25.06.98	3h1	Bedford	29	Apr
55.80	Owen Lawrence	U20	31.10.98	3	Portsmouth	13	May
55.87	Kane Densley	U23	19.12.96	5h2	Bedford	29	Apr
56.0	Chris Marshall		27.01.91	1	Ipswich	20	May

Additional Under 20 (1-17 above)

56.08	Rhys Harris		11.10.98	4	Cardiff	12	Jul
56.20	Joseph Bacon		17.06.00	1	Oxford (H)	9	Sep
56.43	Connor Aldridge		6.08.98	2	Chelmsford	3	Jun

Foreign

51.19	*Jason Harvey (IRL)*		*9.04.91*	*3*	*Dublin (S), IRL*	*23*	*Jul*
51.61	*Lloyd Hanley-Byron (SKN)*		*15.10.87*	*5*	*Oordegem, BEL*	*3*	*Jun*
52.47	*Connor Henderson (PHI)*		*2.10.92*	*5*	*Loughborough*	*21*	*May*
53.84	*Sam Shore (AUS)*		*6.12.85*	*3*	*London (He)*	*24*	*Jun*
54.30	*Damaine Benjamin (JAM)*		*12.03.88*	*1rB*	*Swansea*	*3*	*Jun*

400 Metres Hurdles - Under 18 (84cm)

51.22	Alistair Chalmers		31.03.00	1	Nassau, BAH	23	Jul
52.00	Seamus Derbyshire		27.01.00	2	Nassau, BAH	23	Jul
52.95	Joshua Faulds		7.03.00	2	Bedford	27	May

400 Metres Hurdles - Under 17 (84cm)

52.98	Ben Lloyd		13.10.00	1	Bedford	27	Aug
53.21	Karl Johnson		15.04.01	2	Bedford	27	Aug

53.25	Ben Higgins		14.11.00	3	Bedford	17	Jun
54.75	Alex O'Callaghan-Brown		30.03.01	3	Birmingham	8	Jul
56.16	Owen Sherriff		25.09.00	1	Birmingham	17	Jun
56.17	Peter Curtis		24.10.00	5	Birmingham	8	Jul
56.44	Coleman Corry		7.04.01	4	Bedford	27	Aug
56.85	Jake Akindutire		15.09.00	3	Loughborough	1	Sep
56.89	Lewis Davey		24.10.00	4	Bedford	27	May
56.89	Daniel Thomas		11.01.01	6	Bedford	27	Aug
	(10)						
57.06	Isaac Milham		17.06.01	3	Basingstoke	17	Jun
57.07	Michael Dunn		15.05.01	4	Loughborough	1	Sep
57.3	Kaya Cairney		19.02.01	1	Cheltenham	28	May
	57.64			1	Yate	23	Jul
57.34	Tyriq Lafeuille		10.05.01	2	London (CP)	19	Aug
57.4	Charlie Price		30.09.01	1	Rugby	28	May
	57.99			1	Derby	13	May
57.42	Oscar Heaney-Brufal		27.09.01	3	London (CP)	19	Aug
57.63	Harvey Reynolds		7.11.01	1	Cardiff	1	Jul
57.71	Rory Howorth		2.07.02	4h1	Birmingham	7	Jul
57.73	William Lloyd		23.12.01	2	Cardiff	1	Jul
58.0	Joseph Collins		13.12.00	1	Gloucester	10	Sep
	58.41			1	Tidworth	14	May
	(20)						
58.13	Joel McFarlane		9.10.00	2	Aberdeen	6	May
58.15	Jack Berwick		3.11.00	1	Derby	13	May
58.31	Guto Tegid		13.03.01	1	Brecon	26	Aug

High Jump

2.31	Robbie Grabarz		3.10.87	2	Doha, QAT	5	May
	2.31			Q	London (O)	11	Aug
	2.30i			2	Belgrade, SRB	5	Mar
	2.28i			2	Birmingham	18	Feb
	2.27			2=	Rabat, MAR	16	Jul
	2.26			1	Birmingham	2	Jul
	2.25i			2	Sheffield	12	Feb
	2.25i			Q	Belgrade, SRB	4	Mar
	2.25			7	Oslo, NOR	15	Jun
	2.25			6=	London (O)	13	Aug
	2.24			6=	Paris (C), FRA	1	Jul
	2.24			4	Zürich, SUI	24	Aug
	2.24			7=	Eberstadt, GER	27	Aug
	2.20			7=	Shanghai, CHN	13	May
	2.20			7=	Birmingham	20	Aug
2.30	Tom Gale	U20	18.12.98	1	Bedford	29	Jul
	2.28			3	Grosseto, ITA	22	Jul
	2.24			3	Birmingham	20	Aug
	2.23			1	Cardiff	12	Jul
	2.22			3=	Loughborough	21	May
	2.22			1	Birmingham	8	Jul
	2.22			1	Klaverblad, NED	10	Sep
	2.20			1	Tidworth	14	May
	2.20			8	Zürich, SUI	24	Aug
2.28	Chris Baker		2.02.91	1	Cork, IRL	18	Jul
	2.27			1	Geneva, SUI	10	Jun
	2.26			7	Doha, QAT	5	May
	2.22			2	Loughborough	22	Jul
	2.21i			6=	Hirson, FRA	21	Jan
	2.21			2	Bedford	29	Jul
	2.20			5	Samorin, SVK	17	Jun
	2.20			2=	Birmingham	2	Jul

Mark	Name	Cat	DOB	Pos	Venue	Date
2.26i	Chris Kandu	U23	10.09.95	3	Hustopeče, CZE	4 Feb
2.25i				3	Sheffield	12 Feb
2.25i				10Q	Belgrade, SRB	4 Mar
2.25				1	Bedford	17 Jun
2.22				1	Bedford	29 May
2.22				3	Loughborough	22 Jul
2.26i	Allan Smith		6.11.92	4=	Hustopeče, CZE	4 Feb
2.25i				2	Hirson, FRA	21 Jan
2.25i				1	Sheffield	12 Feb
2.25i				Q	Belgrade, SRB	4 Mar
2.24				3	Geneva, SUI	10 Jun
2.23i				2	Cologne, GER	25 Jan
2.23				4	Taipei, TPE	25 Aug
2.22				1=	Loughborough	21 May
2.20i				4=	Birmingham	18 Feb
2.20				6	Samorín, SVK	17 Jun
2.20				7	Cologne, GER	19 Jul
2.23	Mike Edwards		11.07.90	1	Columbia, USA	25 Mar
2.22				1=	Loughborough	21 May
2.22				1	Loughborough	22 Jul
2.21				1	Lund, SWE	10 Jun
2.21				2	Cork, IRL	18 Jul
2.20i				1	Birmingham	14 Jan
2.20i				8	Hustopeče, CZE	4 Feb
2.20i				2	Athlone, IRL	15 Feb
2.20				1	Louisville, USA	31 Mar
2.20				1	Jacksonville, USA	8 Apr
2.20				1	Clermont, USA	15 Apr
2.20				2=	Birmingham	2 Jul
2.22	Matt Roberts		22.12.84	3=	Loughborough	21 May
2.20i				9	Hustopeče, CZE	4 Feb
2.21i	David Smith		14.07.91	1	Glasgow	28 Jan
2.21				2	Lund, SWE	10 Jun
2.21				1	Grangemouth	27 Aug
2.20				2=	Birmingham	2 Jul

67 performances to 2.20 by 8 athletes including 19 indoors

Mark	Name	Cat	DOB	Pos	Venue	Date
2.16i	Timothy Duckworth	U23	18.06.96	1H	Lincoln, USA	3 Feb
2.13				2D	Eugene, USA	7 Jun
2.16	Joel Khan	U20	30.09.99	2	Bedford	18 Jun
(10)						
2.16	Lewis McGuire	U23	22.10.97	1	Grangemouth	25 Jun
2.15	Thomas Hewes	U20	15.09.99	3	Birmingham	8 Jul
2.13i	Ryan Webb	U23	19.10.97	9	Sheffield	12 Feb
2.13				4	Loughborough	22 Jul
2.13i	Jonathan Broom-Edwards		27.05.88	2	Birmingham	19 Feb
2.12				8	Birmingham	2 Jul
2.13	Akin Coward	U23	26.07.96	1	London (He)	24 Jun
2.12i	William Grimsey	U23	14.12.96	4	Birmingham	14 Jan
2.09				7=	Bedford	29 May
2.11	Ryan Bonifas		22.09.93	1	London (CP)	10 Jun
2.11	Tom Nichols		6.04.85	3	London (CP)	10 Jun
2.10i	Patrick O'Connor	U23	23.10.95	2	Youngstown, USA	4 Feb
2.10				1	Rock Hill, USA	25 Mar
2.10	William Edwards	U20	5.02.98	1	Carmarthen	14 May
(20)						
2.09	Joshua Hewett	U20	1.10.99	7=	Bedford	29 May
2.08i	Joseph Pearse	U23	21.04.96	1	Cardiff	5 Feb
2.00				7	Bedford	1 May
2.08	Jonathan Bailey	U23	16.07.95	6	Loughborough	22 Jul
2.07i	Dominic Ogbechie	U17	15.05.02	1A	London (LV)	28 Jan
2.02				1	London (LV)	13 May

Mark	Name	Cat	DOB	Pos	Venue	Date	
2.07i	Jake Storey	U23	3.03.97	4	Sheffield	19	Feb
2.06				3	Bedford	1	May
2.06i	Marcus Morton	U23	30.08.96	1	Glasgow	14	Jan
2.05				2	Grangemouth	25	Jun
2.06	Tayo Andrews-Haycocks	U23	31.03.96	4	Bedford	1	May
2.06	Christopher Mann	U23	1.10.95	1	Wakefield	9	Jul
2.05i	Liam Ramsay		18.11.92	1H	Sheffield	7	Jan
2.05i	Matthew Ashley		4.07.89	7=B	Hustopeče, CZE	4	Feb
2.01				9	Bedford	29	May
(30)							
2.05i	Jonathan Heath		12.12.93	10B	Hustopeče, CZE	4	Feb
2.00				1	Doncaster	5	Aug
2.05i	Adam Wall		10.07.93	1	Sheffield	7	Feb
2.05				4	Sheffield	6	May
2.05	Joshuah Hill	U23	23.04.96	1	Leicester	18	Mar
2.05	John Lane		29.01.89	3D	Azusa, USA	12	Apr
2.05	Elior Harris		6.05.88	1	Stevenage	15	Apr
2.05	Harry Baker	U20	18.11.99	1	Kingston	2	Jul
2.05	David Walker		5.01.93	1	Portsmouth	8	Jul
2.04	Jacob Rajkumar	U20	3.06.98	1	Reading	8	Jul
2.04	Kaya Walker	U17	29.03.01	1	Bedford	26	Aug
2.03i	Cameron McCorgray	U20	28.12.98	1	Glasgow	19	Feb
2.00				1	Grangemouth	1	Apr
(40)							
2.03	Adam Jones	U20	8.10.98	9=	London (LV)	3	Jun
2.03	Leon Martin-Evans	U17	23.03.01	1	Birmingham	17	Jun
2.03	Jordan Thompson	U20	22.07.98	6	Bedford	18	Jun
2.03	Toni Ademuwagun	U20	7.08.00	5	Birmingham	8	Jul
2.03	Glen Foster	U20	10.11.98	6	Birmingham	8	Jul
2.03	Kai Finch	U17	24.10.00	1	Litherland	2	Sep
2.03i	Curtis Wood	U23	29.06.97	1	Cardiff	10	Dec
2.00				1	Watford	19	Apr
2.02	Jack Norton	U17	3.10.00	1	Basingstoke	17	Jun
2.02	Luke Okosieme	U17	21.08.01	1	London (CP)	19	Aug
2.02	Lewis Church	U23	27.09.96	1D	Erith	16	Sep
(50)							
2.01	Liam Reveley	U20	24.10.98	1	Hexham	17	Jun
2.01	Martin Lloyd	V35	18.06.80	1	Dartford	19	Jun
2.01	James Finney	U23	7.04.96	3D	Tallinn, EST	1	Jul
2.01	Dean Storry	V35	9.10.79	1	Solihull	2	Jul
2.01	Jamie Horne	U23	7.09.97	1	Peterborough	19	Aug
2.00i	Matthew Watson		27.01.91	5B	London (LV)	28	Jan
2.00				1	Bracknell	21	May
2.00i	James Taylor	U23	11.08.96	13B	Hustopeče, CZE	4	Feb
2.00i	Chris Mackay	U20	3.04.99	2	Glasgow	4	Feb
1.95				2	Sheffield (W)	30	Apr
2.00i	Jordan Charters	U23	14.08.95	4	Glasgow	4	Feb
2.00i	Jamie Anderson	U20	8.03.98	3	Cardiff	5	Feb
1.97				1	Exeter	20	Aug
(60)							
2.00i	Angus Sinclair	U23	22.02.95	6	Birmingham, USA	10	Feb
2.00				6	Lafayette, USA	18	Mar
2.00i	Adam Lubin	U23	9.02.96	4	Birmingham	19	Feb
2.00				1	Rugby	7	May
2.00	Daniel Fitzhenry	U20	12.11.98	1	Nottingham	30	Apr
2.00	Jack Roach	U23	8.01.95	1	Leeds	6	May
2.00	Jason Fox		15.10.88	1	Portsmouth	14	May
2.00	Samuel Brereton	U15	22.09.02	1	Exeter	17	Jun
2.00	Benjamin Saunders	U17	9.12.00	2	Birmingham	17	Jun
2.00	Ieuan Orton	U23	20.05.96	1	Neath	16	Jul
2.00	Jack Turner	U17	11.07.01	1	Braunton	30	Jul

2.00	James Lee	U23	15.11.97	2	Doncaster	5	Aug
(70)							
2.00	Daniel Pearce		11.09.91	1	Par	19	Aug
2.00	Scott Johnson		2.10.90	2	Rugby	20	Aug
2.00	Andrew Murphy		26.12.94	1D	Woerden, NED	26	Aug
1.99i	Ben Gregory		21.11.90	1H	Glasgow	4	Mar
1.96				11D	Azusa, USA	12	Apr
1.99	Curtis Mathews		22.01.92	2D	Erith	16	Sep
1.98i	Ashley Bryant		17.05.91	4H	Prague, CZE	28	Jan
1.97				19D	Götzis, AUT	27	May
1.98i	Emmanuel Sosanya	U20	29.08.98	Q	Sheffield	18	Feb
1.98i	Steven Wheater	U17	21.02.01	3	Sheffield	25	Feb
1.98				1	Middlesbrough	10	Jun
1.98	Iwan Parry	U23	30.06.97	2	Visby, SWE	25	Jun
1.98	Seun Okome	U23	26.03.95	5	Manchester (SC)	20	Aug
(80)							
1.98	Thomas Wright	U17	23.09.00	1	Grays	3	Sep
1.97	Adam Brooks	U20	13.04.99	7	Birmingham	8	Jul
1.96i	David Hall	U23	25.04.95	5H	Sheffield	7	Jan
1.96i	Joseph Hobson	U20	29.04.98	2H	Sheffield	8	Jan
1.96i	Darren Hammond		31.03.89	1	Manchester (SC)	8	Jan
1.96	Sam Talbot	U20	17.02.99	1D	Street	29	Apr
1.96	Owen Dearman	U20	22.11.98	1	Luton	20	May
1.96	Michael Adekunle		12.12.94	2	Basingstoke	8	Jul
1.95i	Joseph Winn	U20	27.09.98	3	London (LV)	15	Jan
1.95i	Tobi Adeniji	U20	2.02.00	1	Manchester (SC)	29	Jan
(90)							
1.95i	Russell Waterson	U23	2.08.95	6	London (LV)	1	Feb
1.95i	Adam Hill		9.07.94	1=	Athlone, IRL	10	Feb
1.95i	Sam Hewitt	U20	1.02.98	13Q	Sheffield	18	Feb
1.95i	Paul Neale	U23	6.01.97	Q	Sheffield	18	Feb
1.95i	Shane Connell	U17	10.03.01	3	Manchester (SC)	5	Mar
1.90				1	Preston	30	Apr
1.95	Ethan Milligan	U20	8.08.00	1	Warrington	2	Apr
1.95	Joshua Watson	U23	25.03.95	1	Bedford	8	Apr
1.95	Jack Moore	U20	19.02.00	2	Rugby	7	May
1.95	Lewis Ely		1.08.89	1	Norwich	13	May
1.95	Lee Johnson	U20	27.05.98	1	Bedford	14	May
(100)							
1.95	Lekan Ogunlana	U20	4.04.99	1	London (Cr)	28	May
1.95	Tyler Mitchell	U20	26.07.00	2	Norwich	17	Jun
1.95	Jake Field	U23	26.11.96	1	Kingston	17	Jun
1.95	Miguel Perera	U23	30.09.96	1	London (BP)	8	Jul
1.95	Alex Cox		13.12.93	1	Bedford	15	Jul
1.95	Harry Rienecker-Found	U17	14.05.02	1-17	Brighton	23	Jul
1.95	Harry Coppell	U23	11.07.96	2	Preston	5	Aug
1.95	Dylan Ferguson	U20	23.09.98	1	Hull	5	Aug
1.95	Harry Kendall	U23	4.10.96	2	Tonbridge	19	Aug

Additional Under 17 (1-13 above)

1.93	Adam Berwick		3.11.00	1	Derby	23	Jul
1.92i	Oliver Thorner		16.03.01	1B	Birmingham	19	Feb
1.90				1	Yeovil	2	Apr
1.92i	Oliver Cresswell		17.11.00	5	Sheffield	25	Feb
1.92	Henry Shields		11.09.00	1	Chelmsford	10	Jun
1.91i	Joel McFarlane		9.10.00	1H	Glasgow	4	Mar
1.91	Harrison Thorne		8.07.02	6	Bedford	26	Aug
1.91	Angus Davren		3.11.01	3	Loughborough	1	Sep
(20)							
1.90	Cameron Darkin-Price		18.11.00	2	Loughborough	1	Apr
1.90	Brandon Sikity		26.09.00	2	London (BP)	10	Jun

1.90	Troy McConville	29.04.02	1-16	Belfast	17	Jun
1.90	Ethan Rigg	3.09.01	2	Middlesbrough	5	Aug
1.90	Samuel Shaw	5.06.01	2	Loughborough	26	Aug
1.90i	Max Thomas	3.10.01	1	Cardiff	3	Dec
1.90i	Jack Ennis	7.06.02	3	Uxbridge	10	Dec

Additional Under 15 (1 above)

1.89	William Bose	6.12.02	1	Chelmsford	10	Jun
1.86	Tom Ridley	7.08.03	2	Bedford	27	Aug
1.85	Jacob Thompson	18.03.03	1	Blackburn	20	May
1.85i	Adam Robinson	6.02.04	3=	Eton	3	Dec
	1.80		1	Basingstoke	19	Jul
1.84	Jamal Thomas	13.11.02	2	Chelmsford	10	Jun
1.84	Callum Gregson	16.11.02	2	Birmingham	7	Jul
1.83	Murray Fotheringham	4.06.03	2	Gothenburg, SWE	2	Jul
1.83	Jerome Henry	11.01.03	3	Bedford	27	Aug
1.81	Tom Foreman	7.11.02	1	Kingston	10	Jun
	(10)					
1.81	Augustas Slavinskas	18.04.03	3	Chelmsford	10	Jun
1.81	Joseph Harding	31.10.02	1	Woodford	2	Jul
1.80	Memphis Ayoade	13.09.02	1	Tonbridge	18	Jun
1.80	Charlie Knott	15.06.03	2	London (CP)	20	Aug
1.78	Ethan Stephenson	10.07.03	1	Gateshead	27	Aug
1.78	Adam Leighton	23.09.02	1	Dunfermline	3	Sep
1.77	Iwan Rees	16.11.02	1	Newport	18	Jun
1.77	Immanuel Feyi-Waboso	20.12.02	1P	Swansea	24	Jun
1.76	Kyle McAuley	9.04.03	2P	Belfast	2	Sep
1.75i	Lionel Owona	23.09.02	1	London (LV)	5	Mar
	1.75		1=	Eton	18	Jun
	(20)					
1.75	Quinn Matthews	22.02.03	1	Portsmouth	10	Jun
1.75	Daniel Stevens	25.10.02	1	Cheltenham	10	Jun
1.75	Patrick Amon	11.02.03	1	London (BP)	10	Jun
1.75	Ethan Robinson	30.12.02	11	Murcia, ESP	2	Jul
1.75	Benjamin King	9.03.03	1	Guildford	15	Jul
1.75	James Margrave	19.05.03	1	Douglas IOM	22	Jul
1.75	Lewis Swaby	7.06.03	1	Gillingham	6	Aug
1.75	Aaron Thomas	25.10.02	2	Birmingham	2	Sep
1.75	Ryan Mansbridge	24.04.03	2	Birmingham	2	Sep
1.75	Aaron Eweka	13.11.03	1	Hornchurch	17	Sep
	(30)					
1.75	Jerome Wilson	5.03.03	1	Hemel Hempstead	17	Sep
1.75	Sam Sanusi	13.11.03	1P	London (LV)	16	Dec

Under 13

1.67	Kehinde Ashaolu		1	Chelmsford	5	Jul
1.65	Luke Ball	28.10.04	1	Bath	10	Jun
1.64	Basil Zola	13.11.04	1	Birmingham	2	Sep
1.62	Jamaal Darlington	9.08.05	1	Kingston	29	Jul
1.61	Connor McNally	8.01.05	1	Kilmarnock	13	May
1.60	George Wallace	5.11.04	1	Woking	2	Jul
1.60	Lexx McConville	9.10.04	3	Bangor, NI	15	Aug
1.60	Kihone Lei-Morton	17.11.04	1	Telford	9	Sep
1.57	Lewis Gurney	13.11.04	1	Kettering	9	Jul
1.57	William Lamprell	12.01.05	1	Bedford	3	Sep

Foreign

2.19	*Montez Blair (USA)*		*23.10.90*	*5*	*Loughborough*	*21 May*
2.05	*Robert Wolski (POL)*		*8.12.82*	*3*	*Sheffield*	*6 May*
2.03	*Damien Chambefort (FRA)*		*22.07.93*	*1*	*Loughborough*	*26 Aug*
2.00i	*Eliot Perez (ESP)*	*U23*	*20.03.97*	*2*	*Cardiff*	*5 Feb*
	1.97			*8*	*Bedford*	*1 May*

1.96	Peter Moreno (NGR)		30.12.90	1D	Bedford	27	May
1.95i	Ethan Sorrell (NZL)	U23	13.09.96	1	London (LV)	4	Mar
1.95	Serg Zotin (EST)		21.05.83	1	Chelmsford	17	Jun
1.95	Pawel Grzaslewicz (POL)		29.10.89	1	Whitley Bay	9	Jul

Pole Vault

5.52i	Jax Thoirs		7.04.93	1	Glasgow	16	Dec
	5.40			2	Birmingham	2	Jul
	5.40			2	Manchester (SC)	16	Aug
	5.33			1	Manchester (SC)	20	Aug
	5.32			1	Grangemouth	26	Aug
	5.31i			2=	Manchester (SC)	21	Jan
5.51	Joel Leon Benitez	U20	31.08.98	1	Cardiff	12	Jul
	5.50			1	Manchester (SC)	16	Aug
	5.40i			1	Sheffield	26	Feb
	5.38			2	Berlin, GER	2	Sep
	5.37			1B	Berlin, GER	2	Sep
	5.33i			2	Cardiff	12	Mar
	5.30			1	Loughborough	21	May
	5.30			3	Mannheim, GER	2	Jul
	5.25i			3	Cardiff	5	Mar
	5.25			1	Bedford	29	Jul
	5.22			1	Yeovil	6	May
	5.21			2	Southampton	5	Aug
5.50i	Adam Hague	U23	29.08.97	1B	Manchester (SC)	8	Jan
	5.50			1	Melbourne, AUS	7	Feb
	5.50i			1	Manchester (SC)	19	Mar
	5.41i			1	Manchester (SC)	21	Jan
	5.40i			1	Gateshead	16	Mar
	5.35i			1=	Cardiff	5	Mar
	5.35			1	Torremolinos, ESP	19	Apr
	5.35			1	Bedford	30	Apr
	5.33i			1	Cardiff	12	Mar
	5.30i			2	Sheffield	19	Feb
	5.30			1	Sheffield	6	May
5.50	Luke Cutts		13.02.88	1	Geneva, SUI	10	Jun
	5.45			1	Birmingham	2	Jul
	5.43i			1	Sheffield	12	Feb
	5.40			1	Innsbruck, AUT	2	Jun
	5.40i			1	Sheffield	18	Nov
	5.35i			1=	Cardiff	5	Mar
	5.31i			2=	Manchester (SC)	21	Jan
	5.30i			1	Birmingham	19	Feb
	5.30			3	Copenhagen, DEN	20	Jun
	5.30			8	Villeneuve d'Ascq, FRA	25	Jun
	5.22i			1	Sheffield	7	Feb
5.45	Charlie Myers	U23	12.06.97	2	Geneva, SUI	10	Jun
	5.40i			1	Sheffield	19	Feb
	5.40			2	Copenhagen, DEN	20	Jun
	5.35			1	Budapest, HUN	3	Jun
	5.35			1	Bedford	18	Jun
	5.32i			4	Sheffield	12	Feb
	5.31			1	Southampton	5	Aug
	5.30i			2	Gateshead	16	Mar
	5.30			2	Loughborough	21	May
	5.30			5	Birmingham	2	Jul
	5.30			1	Gateshead	9	Aug
	5.25			2	Bedford	30	Apr
	5.25			Q	Bydgoszcz, POL	14	Jul
	5.21i			6	Manchester (SC)	21	Jan
	5.21i			1	Glasgow	28	Jan

5.43i	Max Eaves		31.05.88	2	Sheffield	12	Feb
	5.33i			3	Cardiff	12	Mar
	5.31i			2=	Manchester (SC)	21	Jan
	5.31i			2	London (LV)	29	Jan
	5.30			3=	Birmingham	2	Jul
	5.25			1	Cardiff	10	Jun
	5.22i			2	Sheffield	7	Feb
5.40	Harry Coppell	U23	11.07.96	3	Geneva, SUI	10	Jun
	5.40			1	Copenhagen, DEN	20	Jun
	5.32i			3	Sheffield	12	Feb
	5.30			3=	Birmingham	2	Jul
	5.25			2	Bedford	18	Jun
	5.23			1	London (LV)	3	Jun
5.32i	Daniel Gardner		26.03.94	5	Sheffield	12	Feb
	5.31i			5	Manchester (SC)	21	Jan
5.32i	Nick Cruchley		1.01.90	6	Sheffield	12	Feb
	5.30i			3	Sheffield	19	Feb
	5.25i			4	Cardiff	5	Mar
	5.21i			1	Cardiff	28	Jan
	5.20			11	Rehlingen, GER	5	Jun
5.26i	Timothy Duckworth	U23	18.06.96	2H	College Station, USA	11	Mar
	5.07			5	Gainesville, USA	1	Apr
	(10)						
5.26	Scott Huggins		24.07.89	1	Ashford	13	May
5.25i	Jack Phipps		2.04.94	1	Uxbridge	5	Feb
	5.22i			1	Loughborough	28	Jan
	5.10			2	London (CP)	11	Jun
	78 performances to 5.21 by 12 athletes including 38 indoors						
5.20i	Ben Gregory		21.11.90	1H	Prague, CZE	29	Jan
	5.10			1D	Barcelona, ESP	23	Jul
5.16i	Rhys Searles		28.03.91	1	Sutton	5	Feb
	5.00			7	Birmingham	2	Jul
5.15	Euan Bryden		17.05.94	2	Cardiff	10	Jun
5.05	Steve Lewis		20.05.86	2	Mesa, USA	21	Apr
5.05	JJ Lister	U23	6.03.97	2	Cardiff	21	Jun
5.03i	Cameron Walker-Shepherd		28.05.92	8	Cardiff	12	Mar
	5.01			1	Cosford	14	Jun
5.02i	Liam Yarwood		10.09.94	2	Loughborough	28	Jan
5.00i	Gregor MacLean		17.10.91	3	Gateshead	16	Mar
	(20)						
5.00	Rowan May	U23	12.08.95	2=	New Haven, USA	8	Apr
5.00	John Lane		29.01.89	1D	Azusa CA, USA	13	Apr
4.92i	Frankie Johnson	U17	17.01.01	3	Sutton	5	Feb
	4.86			1	Birmingham	7	Jul
4.91i	Nicolas Cole	U23	27.02.95	8=	Manchester (SC)	21	Jan
	4.80			4	Sheffield	6	May
4.88i	Samuel Adams		17.10.94	9=	Geneva, USA	11	Feb
	4.83			4	Manchester (SC)	20	Aug
4.88	George Heppinstall	U23	17.10.97	1	Sheffield	2	Sep
4.85i	Nathan Gardner	U20	9.02.98	1	Cardiff	10	Dec
	4.78			4	London (He)	20	Aug
4.84i	Andrew Murphy		26.12.94	1	Glasgow	25	Feb
	4.65			7	Bedford	30	Apr
4.82i	Tom Farres	U23	4.03.97	4	Uxbridge	5	Mar
	4.82			1	Bedford	15	Jul
4.80	Nikko Hunt	U20	17.02.98	1	Nice, FRA	21	Jun
	(30)						
4.75	Archie McNeillis		7.05.94	1	London (He)	24	Jun
4.73i	Emmanuel Thomas	U20	6.12.99	1	Sutton	24	Sep
	4.63			5	Bedford	15	Jul

4.71	Samuel Bass-Cooper	U23	26.01.96	1	Southampton	31	May
4.71	George Turner	U20	13.07.98	1	London (LV)	20	Aug
4.70	William Gwynne	U20	25.04.98	1	Perivale	17	Jun
4.70	Jack Andrew		12.10.91	1D	Dilbeek, BEL	30	Jul
4.68i	Fraser O'Rourke	U23	28.02.96	2	Glasgow	4	Jan
4.61				1	Grangemouth	22	Apr
4.63	James Finney	U23	7.04.96	2D	Bedford	28	May
4.61	Andrew McFarlane	U20	7.07.00	1	Inverness	23	Jun
4.60	Callum Court		21.10.93	1	Cambridge	6	Aug
(40)							
4.60i	Dylan Thomson	U20	11.05.00	1	Glasgow	22	Dec
4.40				4=	Grangemouth	26	Aug
4.55i	Peter Glass		1.05.88	2	Dublin (B), IRL	5	Feb
4.50				3D	Arona, ESP	4	Jun
4.55	Ethan Walsh	U23	14.06.97	1	Loughborough	22	Apr
4.51	Tom Booth	U23	29.11.96	1	Blackpool	14	May
4.50i	Ashley Bryant		17.05.91	7H	Prague, CZE	29	Jan
4.50				22=D	Götzis, AUT	28	May
4.50	Harry Maslen	U23	2.09.96	5D	Bradenton, USA	26	May
4.50	Thomas Snee		22.07.88	1	Tonbridge	28	Aug
4.43	Adam Carpenter		18.06.93	6	Manchester (SC)	20	Aug
4.43	Thomas Walley	U20	18.03.98	1	Wrexham	20	Aug
4.42i	Christopher Lamb	U20	25.05.00	6	Sheffield	7	Feb
4.30				5	Birmingham	7	Jul
(50)							
4.41i	Liam Ramsay		18.11.92	3H	Sheffield	8	Jan
4.41	Angus Sinclair	U23	22.02.95	6	Lafayette, USA	18	Mar
4.40i	Aiden Davies	U23	26.12.95	9=H	Prague, CZE	29	Jan
4.30				2	Cudworth	13	May
4.40	Shane Martin	U20	10.11.99	1	Antrim	19	May
4.40	Fynley Caudery	U20	9.10.98	2	Birmingham	7	Jul
4.40	Joshua Lindley-Harris	U20	25.10.99	4	Birmingham	7	Jul
4.40	Tom Rottier	U23	15.11.96	1D	Oxford (H)	23	Jul
4.40	Curtis Mathews		22.01.92	1D	Erith	17	Sep
4.37i	Zach Harrop	U20	5.05.98	6	Cardiff	5	Feb
4.15				3B	Bedford	30	Apr
4.36i	Dylan Carlsson-Smith	U20	26.07.98	1H	Sheffield	7	Jan
(60)							
4.35	Charlie Maw	U23	18.11.96	1	London (TB)	1	May
4.35	Greg Conlon	V40	18.12.74	2	Kingston	21	May
4.32i	Egryn Jones	V45	1.11.71	6	Uxbridge	5	Mar
4.32	Tom Chandler	U23	19.09.97	5D	Woerden, NED	27	Aug
4.31i	Maxim Hall		29.12.86	4H	Sheffield	8	Jan
4.20				3D	Oxford (H)	23	Jul
4.30i	Mark Johnson	V50	7.09.64	7	Sheffield	15	Jan
4.30	Elliot Thompson		10.08.92	3D	Dilbeek, BEL	30	Jul
4.30	Tyler Adams	U20	26.11.98	1	Tonbridge	19	Aug
4.30i	Deo Milandu		30.10.92	2	Manchester (SC)	17	Dec
4.30i	Lewis Church	U23	27.09.96	2H	London (LV)	17	Dec
4.20				1	Ashford	6	Sep
(70)							
4.26i	Harry Kendall	U23	4.10.96	1	Sheffield	13	Dec
4.10				3	Torremolinos, ESP	19	Apr
4.25	Jake Watson	U17	19.12.00	1	Nuneaton	19	Aug
4.25	Jools Peters		20.08.90	6	Grangemouth	26	Aug
4.22i	Chris Mills	V40	12.11.75	9	Sutton	5	Feb
4.20				2	Portsmouth	8	Jul
4.21i	David Hall	U23	25.04.95	8H	Sheffield	8	Jan
4.20				2	Dartford	15	Apr
4.21	Glen Quayle	U17	6.03.02	2	Dublin (S), IRL	15	Jul
4.21	Mark Mellor	U17	22.01.02	2	Bedford	27	Aug

4.21	Dylan Baines	U17	3.10.01	4	Bedford	27	Aug
4.20i	Alexander Livingston	U23	25.01.96	2	Jordanstown (NI)	22	Jan
4.20				1	Tallaght, IRL	25	Jun
4.20i	Jacob Clarke	U17	1.06.02	3	Loughborough	9	Dec
4.02				1	Yate	16	Jul
(80)							
4.18	Todd Webster	U20	28.11.99	1	Chelmsford	3	Jun
4.17i	Dougie Graham	V40	1.01.77	2	Glasgow	14	Jan
4.13				1	Dunfermline	3	Sep
4.15	Linton Gardiner	U23	18.07.97	5B	Bedford	30	Apr
4.15	Harry Lord	U20	14.08.98	4D	New Haven, USA	7	May
4.15	Martin Densley	V35	1.05.81	3	Kingston	21	May
4.13i	Conor Kearns	U20	5.02.99	5	Sutton	24	Sep
4.11i	James Allway	U23	25.09.97	2	London (LV)	2	Jan
4.11i	Thomas Grantham		12.02.83	10H	Sheffield	8	Jan
4.11i	David Mann		27.10.94	4	Glasgow	28	Jan
4.11	Callum Woodage	U17	25.10.00	2	Watford	7	May
(90)							
4.11	Matthew Chandler	U17	30.10.00	3	Dublin (S), IRL	15	Jul
4.11	Pedro Gleadall	U17	7.12.01	5	Bedford	27	Aug
4.11	Caius Joseph	U20	24.07.99	1	Crawley	28	Aug
4.11	James Robinson	V40	27.08.76	1	Telford	9	Sep
4.10i	Emyr Jones		5.09.92	4	Cardiff	15	Jan
4.10	Sam Talbot	U20	17.02.99	1D	Street	30	Apr
4.10	Howard Bell	U20	2.05.98	1	Grangemouth	3	May
4.10	Bob Kingman	V40	21.02.73	1	Birmingham	5	Jun
4.10	Jack Harris	U17	6.08.01	1	Lewes	25	Jun
4.10	Ian Parkinson	V35	17.02.79	4	Aarhus, DEN	31	Jul
(100)							
4.10i	George Osbourne	U20	2.04.00	4	Loughborough	9	Dec
4.10i	Samuel Meyler	U23	11.09.95	5	Loughborough	9	Dec
4.10i	Scott Brindley	U17	6.01.02	4	Glasgow	22	Dec
3.90				2	Grangemouth	26	Aug

Additional Under 17 (1-11 above)

4.05	Owen Heard		29.12.01	1	Basingstoke	17	Jun
4.01	Oliver Thorner		16.03.01	6	Bedford	27	Aug
4.00i	Matthew Brining		9.12.01	1	Gateshead	9	Feb
4.00	Robert Worman		4.07.01	1	Exeter	17	Jun
4.00	Joel McFarlane		9.10.00	1D	Grangemouth	2	Jul
3.93i	George Pope		6.12.00	1B	Sutton	24	Sep
3.80				3	Birmingham	3	Sep
3.85	Ieuan Hosgood		6.03.01	1	Newport	23	Jul
3.85	Elliot Breen		2.10.00	1	Ware	30	Jul
3.80	Daniel Hoiles		15.07.01	1	Portsmouth	30	Apr
(20)							
3.80	Tolu Ayo-Ojo		26.08.02	2	Harrow	28	May
3.80	Zamaan Dudhia		4.02.02	3	Hemel Hempstead	10	Jun
3.80	Karran Kapur-Walton		31.01.02	1	Leigh	19	Aug
3.80i	Reuben Nairne		22.09.02	6	Glasgow	22	Dec
3.51		U15		2	Bedford	26	Aug
3.75i	Finlay Walker		28.05.02	1	Glasgow	1	Feb
3.60				1	Kilmarnock	13	Jun
3.70	Thomas Britt		25.12.00	1	Newport	23	Apr
3.70	Alfie Gilby		15.05.02	4	Tonbridge	19	Aug
3.70	Peter Holt		27.10.00	3	Eton	19	Aug
3.70i	Robbie Farquhar		4.01.01	2	Aberdeen	7	Sep
3.68				7D	Manchester (SC)	13	Aug
3.65	Max Young		11.07.02	2	Reading	8	Jul
3.65	Adam Orr		3.06.01	4	Birmingham	3	Sep
(30)							

3.61i		Christopher Thompson	16.01.02	1cD	Manchester (SC)	21	Jan
3.61i		Aran Thomas	6.12.01	4H	Sheffield	12	Mar
3.60		Jack Westley	1.10.01	3	Basingstoke	17	Jun
3.60		Sam Gray	20.03.01	3	Doncaster	25	Jun

Additional Under 15 (1 above)

3.90		Jonathan Rugg	19.09.02	1	Birmingham	8	Jul
3.60		Bryce Breen	22.08.03	1	Ware	30	Jul
3.51		William Snashall	27.09.02	1	Horsham	30	Jun
3.51		George Hopkins	1.06.03	1	Bedford	26	Aug
3.50		Sam Tremelling	1.10.02	1	Woodford	2	Jul
3.36i		William Foot	7.10.03	4	Sheffield	13	Dec
	3.15			6=	Birmingham	8	Jul
3.31		Jack Horne-Smith	17.08.03	4	Bedford	26	Aug
3.30i		Aidan Brindley	9.10.03	8	Glasgow	22	Dec
3.20		Thomas Todd	16.09.03	4	Almuñécar, ESP	11	Jun
(10)							
3.20		Cameron Williams-Stein	29.04.03	1	Nuneaton	18	Jun
3.20i		Benjamin Lazarus	19.01.04	2	Manchester (SC)	17	Dec
3.15		Toby Irving	1.05.03	6=	Birmingham	8	Jul
3.10		Reuben McFarlane	14.10.02	2	Glasgow (S)	20	Aug
3.05		Noah Osborne	5.04.04	1	Birmingham	2	Sep
3.03i		Daniel Dearden	26.09.03	2cD	Sutton	24	Sep
	3.00			2	Guildford	15	Jul
3.02		James May	9.12.02	2B	Sheffield	5	Jul
3.01		Jonathan Cohen	25.09.02	6	Bedford	26	Aug
3.00		Peter Brinton-Quinn	21.10.02	2	Birmingham	2	Sep
2.95		Harley Waller		2	Chelmsford	10	Jun
(20)							
2.93i		Ethan Kitteridge	12.08.03	4cD	Sutton	24	Sep
	2.90			4	Birmingham	2	Sep
2.90		Jami Schlueter	26.10.02	1	Yeovil	13	May
2.90		Oliver Thatcher	11.09.02	1	Bromley	15	Jul
2.90		Dylan Ward	17.11.02	1	Brecon	26	Aug
2.90		Craig Martin	13.09.02	1	Wigan	10	Sep

Under 13

2.80		William Trott	27.02.05	1B	Swansea	26	Apr
2.75		Noah Jones	11.11.04	1	Exeter	26	Sep
2.72		William Lane	20.07.05	3B	Sheffield	5	Jul
2.50		Tony Murray	22.10.06	3	Sheffield	2	Sep
2.30		James Pratt	2.09.04	1	Crawley	28	Aug

Foreign

4.55		*Michael Bowler (IRL)*		*28.01.92*	*2*	*Dublin (S), IRL*	*23*	*Jul*
4.45		*Leigh Walker (IRL)*	*V35*	*17.08.77*	*1*	*Crawley*	*8*	*Jul*
4.45		*Peter Moreno (NGR)*		*30.12.90*	*11*	*Bedford*	*29*	*Jul*
4.40		*Laurenz Kirchmayr (AUT)*	*U20*	*9.02.99*	*3*	*Birmingham*	*7*	*Jul*
	4.15				*4B*	*Bedford*	*30*	*Apr*
4.30		*Tommasco Battisti (ITA)*		*15.05.92*	*6*	*Bedford*	*15*	*Jul*

Long Jump

8.18	0.3	Greg Rutherford	17.11.86	1	Manchester	26	May
	7.95	1.1		1	Gavardo, ITA	4	Jun
8.02	-0.7	Daniel Bramble	14.10.90	1	Birmingham	2	Jul
	8.01	1.7		2	Padova, ITA	16	Jul
	8.00	0.0		2	Marseille, FRA	3	Jun
	8.00	1.2		1	Villeneuve d'Ascq, FRA	24	Jun
	7.95	1.3		1	Manchester (SC)	16	Aug
	7.91w	3.5		1	Clermont, USA	15	Apr
	7.86A	1.9		3	Sestriere, ITA	23	Jul

Mark	Wind	Name	Cat	DOB	Pos	Venue	Date
(Bramble)		7.84 -0.5			5	London (O)	9 Jul
		7.80i			1	Sheffield	11 Feb
		7.72 -0.2			6	Birmingham	20 Aug
		7.71i			1	Uxbridge	5 Feb
		7.70 0.4			1	Loughborough	21 May
8.02w	3.4	Jacob Fincham-Dukes	U23	12.01.97	5	Fort Worth, USA	15 Apr
		7.96 2.0			3Q	Austin, USA	25 May
		7.90 -0.2			3	Birmingham	2 Jul
		7.87w 2.6			1	Lawrence, USA	13 May
		7.86iA			2	Albuquerque, USA	10 Feb
		7.83w 2.5			4	Bydgoszcz, POL	14 Jul
		7.70 0.8			*	Bydgoszcz, POL	14 Jul
7.95w	2.9	Feron Sayers		15.10.94	2	Birmingham	2 Jul
		7.89 -1.0			*	Birmingham	2 Jul
7.87	0.0	Timothy Duckworth	U23	18.06.96	1D	Athens, USA	8 Apr
		7.84w 2.5			4	Birmingham	2 Jul
		7.80i			4	Nashville, USA	24 Feb
		7.77i			2H	College Station, USA	10 Mar
		7.72i			1	Bloomington, USA	8 Dec
7.85w	3.8	Efe Uwaifo	U23	15.05.95	1	New Haven, USA	6 May
		7.15 1.1			*	Cambridge, USA	15 Apr
7.83	1.0	Daniel Gardiner		25.06.90	1	Geneva, SUI	10 Jun
		7.76i			1	Reykjavik, ISL	4 Feb
		7.74i			1	Vienna, AUT	28 Jan
		7.70i			3	Sheffield	11 Feb
7.79i		Ashley Bryant		17.05.91	1H	Prague, CZE	28 Jan
		7.71i			2	Sheffield	11 Feb
		7.70 0.1			3D	Götzis, AUT	27 May
7.77w	4.9	Oliver Newport	U23	7.01.95	1	Louisville, USA	15 Apr
		7.60 0.5			1	Louisville, USA	29 Apr
7.73i		Julian Reid		23.09.88	1	Birmingham	14 Jan
	(10)						
7.71	-0.1	Allan Hamilton		14.07.92	1	Cork, IRL	18 Jul
7.70w	2.7	James Lelliott		11.02.93	1	Bournemouth	6 Aug
		7.65 1.8			1	London (CP)	10 Jun

41 performances to 7.70 by 12 athletes including 12 indoors and 8 wind assisted

Mark	Wind	Name	Cat	DOB	Pos	Venue	Date
7.58	2.0	Jack Roach	U23	8.01.95	2	Bournemouth	6 Aug
7.56i		Patrick Sylla	U20	10.10.98	1U20	London (LV)	29 Jan
		7.32			1	Bournemouth	10 Sep
7.53w	4.0	James McLachlan		12.03.92	1	Sheffield	6 May
		7.27			1	Norwich	13 May
7.53w	2.3	David John Martin		5.05.88	1	Grangemouth	27 Aug
		7.37 0.4			*	Grangemouth	27 Aug
7.52		Michael Causer	U23	27.05.95	1	Halifax	9 Jul
7.52w	3.1	Paul Ogun		3.06.89	4	Manchester (SC)	16 Aug
		7.45 -12.0			2	Belfast	5 Jul
7.51	1.0	Alexander Farquharson	U23	9.06.97	2	Bedford	29 May
7.49w	2.5	Tom French		5.12.91	4	Bournemouth	6 Aug
		7.36 0.5			8	Birmingham	2 Jul
	(20)						
7.48i		Sam Talbot	U20	17.02.99	1	Sheffield	26 Feb
		7.19 1.8			1D	Street	29 Apr
7.46	0.4	Ben Williams		25.01.92	1	Manchester (SC)	20 Aug
7.45w	2.1	Reynold Banigo	U20	13.08.98	1	Manchester (SC)	10 Jun
		7.42i			2	Sheffield	26 Feb
		7.23			1	Cardiff	12 Jul
7.44	0.0	Scott Hall		8.03.94	7	Birmingham	2 Jul
7.43	0.0	John Lane		29.01.89	11D	Götzis, AUT	27 May
7.43	0.1	Bradley Pickup		4.04.89	6	Lyon, FRA	9 Jun
7.41		Darren Morson		16.06.94	1	London (ME)	21 May

Mark	Wind	Name	Cat	DOB	Pos	Venue	Date	
7.40w	3.6	Ben Fisher	U20	21.02.98	1U20	Belfast	10	Jun
7.32	0.0				*	Bedford	17	Jun
7.36		Adam Walker-Khan	U23	7.03.95	2	Princeton, USA	12	May
7.35	1.9	Ben Gregory		21.11.90	7D	Azusa, USA	12	Apr
(30)								
7.34		Stuart Street	U23	18.07.96	1	Nottingham	8	Apr
7.34w	3.6	Ross Jeffs		5.09.91	5	Bournemouth	6	Aug
7.23					1	Bournemouth	10	Sep
7.33i		Craig Jones		28.04.93	1	Manchester (SC)	29	Jan
7.05	1.7				6	Sheffield	6	May
7.33	1.7	Jonathan Ilori		14.08.93	5	London (CP)	10	Jun
7.33wA	3.3	Sam Trigg		1.11.93	4	Logan, USA	12	May
7.00	1.6				8	Stanford, USA	21	Apr
7.33w	5.3	Dominic Ogbechie	U17	15.05.02	1	Dublin (S), IRL	15	Jul
7.22	0.9				1	Loughborough	1	Sep
7.32		Ogo Anochirionye		14.11.92	1	London (WL)	17	Jun
7.31i		Jordan Charters	U23	14.08.95	4	Glasgow	28	Jan
6.91	0.2				10	Loughborough	21	May
7.30w	2.5	Samuel Khogali	U23	15.07.97	6	Bournemouth	6	Aug
7.13i					4	Sheffield	19	Feb
6.92	2.0				8	Sheffield	6	May
7.29i		Joshua Olawore	U23	31.07.95	2	Sheffield	19	Feb
7.14	1.9				6	Bedford	1	May
(40)								
7.27i		Liam Ramsay		18.11.92	5H	Prague, CZE	28	Jan
7.27	0.0	Rowan Powell	U20	8.12.98	1	Birmingham	7	Jul
7.27		JJ Jegede		3.10.85	1	Loughborough	22	Jul
7.26i		Peter Muirhead		6.12.93	2	Glasgow	14	Jan
7.17w					Q	Bedford	30	Apr
7.15	0.1				2	Grangemouth	22	Apr
7.26i		Oliver Clark	U23	9.12.96	1	London (LV)	1	Feb
7.26w		Aled Price	U23	14.12.95	Q	Bedford	30	Apr
6.99					5	Bedford	15	Jul
7.24i		Aiden Davies	U23	26.12.95	6H	Prague, CZE	28	Jan
7.23w	9.4	Harry Maslen	U23	2.09.96	2D	Commerce, USA	4	May
7.14	1.9				6	Commerce, USA	5	May
7.22		Joel Grenfell		31.10.94	1	London (LV)	17	Jun
7.22	2.0	Henry Clarkson	U20	16.06.99	5	Grangemouth	27	Aug
(50)								
7.20	1.8	Anton Dixon		31.05.90	5	London (LV)	3	Jun
7.19	0.8	Montel Nevers	U23	22.05.96	3	Tallahassee, USA	24	Mar
7.18	-0.9	Joseph Ramie		14.12.90	1	Chelmsford	3	Jun
7.18	0.0	Curtis Mathews		22.01.92	1D	Erith	16	Sep
7.16w	3.6	Alessandro Schenini	U20	28.04.00	1	Grangemouth	9	Jun
7.12	1.2				*	Grangemouth	9	Jun
7.15		Myles Durrant-Sutherland	U23	17.07.95	1	Rugby	7	May
7.15		Joe Steele		13.02.88	2	London (WL)	17	Jun
7.15w	3.9	William Adeyeye	U17	4.03.01	2	Dublin (S), IRL	15	Jul
7.13	0.6				2	Birmingham	8	Jul
7.13	0.0	Ade Adefolalu	U23	28.02.97	2	El Dorado, USA	8	Apr
7.13		Michael Ohioze	U23	6.02.95	1	Joliet, USA	5	May
(60)								
7.13	0.0	Nathan Fox		21.10.90	8	London (LV)	3	Jun
7.13	1.8	Andrew Murphy		26.12.94	2D	Woerden, NED	26	Aug
7.12i		Jimi Tele		4.05.94	4	Lynchburg, USA	21	Jan
7.12		Toby Adeniyi	U23	3.09.96	1	Loughborough	24	May
7.11i		Ceirion Hopkins	U20	11.10.99	1	Cardiff	5	Mar
7.08w	3.3				1	Cardiff	1	Jul
7.04					2	Cardiff	12	Jul
7.11	0.8	Shola John-Olojo		5.05.92	3	Oxford, USA	24	Mar
7.11		Robert Woolgar		3.03.93	1	Bournemouth	14	May

Mark	Wind	Name	Cat	DOB	Pos	Venue	Date	
7.11		Chris Mackay	U20	3.04.99	1	Leeds (South)	28	May
7.10		Sebastian Wilson Dyer Gough		2.06.90	1	London (TB)	1	Apr
7.10		Nick Clements		17.06.90	1	Yeovil	15	Apr
	(70)							
7.10w	2.8	Trevor Alexanderson		30.12.89	6	Bedford	30	Jul
	7.09	1.6			*	Bedford	30	Jul
7.09	0.7	Joel McFarlane	U17	9.10.00	1D	Grangemouth	1	Jul
7.08w	2.3	Samuel Challis	U20	15.05.99	1	London (CP)	11	Jun
	7.05	0.0			2	Birmingham	7	Jul
7.08w	2.3	Caius Joseph	U20	24.07.99	1D	Boston	16	Sep
7.06	0.5	Simeon Clarence	U23	4.12.95	1	Cardiff	10	Jun
7.06		Harry Kendall	U23	4.10.96	1	London (Cr)	8	Jul
7.05	0.9	Mark Cryer		27.08.93	2	Basingstoke	6	May
7.05	2.0	Sam Lyon		20.10.92	1	Grangemouth	9	Jul
7.04	0.0	Antony Daffurn		18.10.86	2	Grangemouth	13	Aug
7.04w	2.3	Callum Henderson	U20	3.05.00	1	Grangemouth	13	May
	6.93i				3	Glasgow	1	Feb
	(80)							
7.04w	2.2	Liam Reveley	U20	24.10.98	2D	Boston	16	Sep
7.02i		James Finney	U23	7.04.96	5H	Sheffield	7	Jan
	6.93	1.8			3D	Bedford	27	May
7.01	1.5	Casey Johnson	U23	20.09.97	2	Kingston	2	Jul
7.01		Seb Rodger		29.06.91	1	London (TB)	19	Jul
7.00		Ryan Long	U20	2.09.98	1	Bournemouth	10	Jun
6.98		Sam Richards		9.12.89	3	Cambridge	6	Aug
6.95i		Joseph Hobson	U20	29.04.98	1H	Sheffield	7	Jan
6.95	0.0	Ben McGuire	U23	22.10.97	7	Bedford	18	Jun
6.95		Chris Harris		22.10.92	1P	Par	22	Jul
6.94w	3.4	Robbie Farquhar	U17	4.01.01	4	Dublin (S), IRL	15	Jul
	6.82	2.0			2D	Grangemouth	1	Jul
	(90)							
6.94w	2.8	Thomas Walley	U20	18.03.98	2	Wrexham	19	Aug
6.93		Daniel Hopper	U20	21.08.00	1	Watford	14	May
6.93w	5.3	Charlie Roe		28.04.92	1	Nuneaton	11	Jun
	6.89i				6H	Sheffield	7	Jan
6.92		Jack Sumners	U17	25.10.00	1	Worcester	7	May
6.92w	2.1	Osaze Aghedo	U20	12.02.99	2	Cardiff	1	Jul
6.91i		Theo Adesina	U17	20.05.02	1H	Sheffield	11	Mar
	6.77	0.0			3	Birmingham	8	Jul
6.91w	2.4	Elliott Baines	U23	5.08.97	2	New Haven, USA	8	Apr
6.90	0.8	Shandell Taylor	U20	16.12.99	3	Chelmsford	3	Jun
6.89		Lawrence Harvey	V35	26.08.81	1	Crawley	6	May
6.89		Kevin Feyisetan	U20	24.07.99	1	London (Cr)	28	May
	(100)							
6.89w	4.2	Peter Glass		1.05.88	1D	Street	29	Apr
6.89w	2.1	Callum Orange	U17	1.02.01	1	Bedford	27	Aug
	6.78				2-17	Leeds (South)	28	May
6.89w	2.7	Stephen MacKenzie	U17	28.08.01	2	Grangemouth	27	Aug
	6.85	1.7			*	Grangemouth	27	Aug
6.87		Joel Townley	U17	7.04.01	1	Cheltenham	10	Jun
6.87w	2.2	George Orton	U20	16.10.98	2	Manchester (SC)	10	Jun
6.87w	2.4	Joseph Harding	U15	31.10.02	1P	Boston	16	Sep
	6.77i		U17		1P	Glasgow	10	Nov
	6.76	1.0			1	Chelmsford	13	May
6.86i		Jude Bright-Davies	U20	27.03.99	1	London (LV)	18	Mar
6.85i		Euan Urquhart	U20	25.01.98	1H	Glasgow	4	Mar
6.85		Mark Lawrence	V45	26.01.71	1	Cambridge	29	Apr
6.85		Terry Lucas	U23	5.10.95	1	Basingstoke	21	May

Additional Under 17 (1-10 above)

Perf	Wind	Name	DOB	Pos	Venue	Date	
6.82		Ben Sutton	10.08.01	1	Ashford	10	Jun
6.75	1.9	Joe Halpin	19.02.01	2O	Boston	16	Sep
6.72i		Archie Yeo	8.03.03	1P	Glasgow	10	Nov
	6.58w	2.6	U15 8.03.03	2P	Boston	16	Sep
	6.55	1.8		*	Boston	16	Sep
6.68		Rafe Brooks	29.09.00	1	Oxford (H)	9	Sep
6.65		Sean Gallagher	13.09.00	4	Glasgow (S)	20	Aug
6.62		Luke Southerton	13.09.00	1	Birmingham	17	Jun
6.60w	3.0	Lewis Davey	24.10.00	3O	Boston	16	Sep
	6.58			1O	Bedford	24	Jun
6.58		Joseph Connelly	9.11.00	1	Whitehaven	10	Jun
6.56		Jack Perry	26.04.01	1	Hull	10	Jun
6.55		Josh Woods	5.08.02	1	Watford	14	May
	(20)						
6.55		George Rosam	25.12.00	2	Basingstoke	17	Jun
6.54w	2.3	Oliver Herring	28.09.00	4O	Boston	16	Sep
6.53		Michael Adebakin	22.11.00	1	Hemel Hempstead	10	Jun
6.51w	2.5	Matthew Chandler	30.10.00	3D	Grangemouth	1	Jul
	6.49			3P	Grangemouth	3	Jun
6.50w	3.4	Evan Campbell	17.05.01	5O	Boston	16	Sep
6.49	2.0	Robert Thomas	16.10.01	1	Birmingham	3	Sep
6.48		Charlie Yates	15.02.01	1	Coventry	30	Apr
6.48		Robert Worman	4.07.01	2	Cheltenham	10	Jun
6.48		Matthew Hughes	9.12.01	4	Tonbridge	19	Aug
6.47i		Zachary Elliott	13.09.01	2	Birmingham	14	Jan
	(30)						
6.47		Troy McConville	29.04.02	1P	Antrim	14	Sep
6.47w	2.8	Thomas Britt	25.12.00	1	Cardiff	1	Jul
6.47w	4.1	Tomos Slade	13.04.01	1	Wrexham	19	Aug
6.47i		Murray Fotheringham	4.06.03	3P	Glasgow	10	Nov
	6.23	1.3	U15 4.06.03	2	Bedford	26	Aug
6.45i		Harri Wheeler-Sexton	25.11.00	3H	Sheffield	11	Mar
6.45		Thomas Wright	23.09.00	1	Ipswich	30	Jul
6.45		Brendon Foster	20.10.01	3	Nottingham	5	Aug

Additional Under 15 (1-3 above)

Perf	Wind	Name	DOB	Pos	Venue	Date	
6.35	0.5	Adam Lindo	21.10.02	1	Birmingham	7	Jul
6.34w		Jami Schlueter	26.10.02	1	Exeter	17	Jun
	6.19			*	Exeter	17	Jun
6.28		Callum Hay	6.09.02	1	Nuneaton	9	Sep
6.24		Stephen Simmons	1.07.03	2	London (CP)	20	Aug
6.22		Jordan Cunningham	22.12.02	1	Belfast	17	Aug
6.20i		Daniel Ogutuga	16.09.02	2P	Sheffield	12	Mar
6.20		Theodore Jackson-Clist	16.11.02	1	Exeter	10	Jun
	(10)						
6.19		Morgan Frith	28.12.02	1	Preston	15	Jul
6.17		Elliott Harris	13.10.02	1P	Milton Keynes	24	Jun
6.14		Seb Wallace	7.09.03	2	Basingstoke	17	Jun
6.12	1.3	Ben Hillman	16.04.03	1	Cardiff	1	Jul
6.11i		Kyle Boden	24.09.02	1	Birmingham	14	Jan
	6.06			1	Nuneaton	19	Aug
6.11w		Joseph Fischer	12.03.03	1	Chelmsford	10	Jun
	6.03			2P	Brentwood	24	May
6.10	-1.3	Ransford Ako'nai	18.09.02	3	Birmingham	7	Jul
6.06		David Udeagbara	1.02.03	3	Basingstoke	17	Jun
6.05		Reuben Nairne	22.09.02	1	Grangemouth	29	Jul
6.03		Thomas Payne	17.05.03	1	Swansea	9	Jul
	(20)						
6.03w		Oliver D'Rozario	24.09.03	2	Yeovil	10	Jun

Under 13

5.72		Samuel Ball		18.10.04	1P	Tonbridge	28	Aug
5.22w		Thomas Chadwick		22.08.05	1	Douglas IOM	30	Jul
5.21		Luke Ball		28.10.04	1	Cardiff	15	Jul
5.15		Basil Zola		13.11.04	1	Birmingham	2	Sep
5.12		Sean Emeka-Ugwuadu		14.06.05	1	Grays	3	Sep
5.10		Jake Minshull		11.10.04	1	Grantham	15	Jul
5.09		Fergus MacGilp		17.03.05	1	Grangemouth	18	Jun
5.06		Zane McQuillan		6.12.04	1	Belfast	17	Jun
5.06		Noah Ayivi-Knott		27.11.04	2	Basingstoke	2	Jul
5.03		Rhys Jordan		6.09.04	1	Rugby	18	Jun
	(10)							
5.03		Jack Doodson		18.10.04	1	Manchester (Str)	15	Jul
5.03		Oscar Doran		17.10.04	1	Whitehaven	22	Jul

Foreign

7.94w	*2.4*	*Adam McMullen (IRL)*		*5.07.90*	*2*	*Manchester (SC)*	*16*	*Aug*
7.85	*0.4*				*1*	*Clermont, USA*	*13*	*May*
7.80	*-0.1*	*Che Richards (TTO)*	*U23*	*8.05.97*	*1*	*Port of Spain, TTO*	*24*	*Jun*
7.64w	*3.8*	*Ezekiel Ewulo (NGR)*		*29.01.86*	*4*	*Clermont, USA*	*15*	*Apr*
7.55	*0.2*				*6*	*Argentan, FRA*	*4*	*Jun*
7.10		*Peter Moreno (NGR)*		*30.12.90*	*1*	*Kingston*	*21*	*May*
7.02	*1.0*	*Michael Bowler (IRL)*		*28.01.92*	*1D*	*Bedford*	*27*	*May*

Triple Jump

16.81	-1.4	Nathan Fox		21.10.90	1	Clermont, USA	13	May
		16.53i			1	Sheffield	11	Feb
		16.49	1.4		19Q	London (O)	7	Aug
		16.45i			1	Birmingham	14	Jan
		16.42w	2.4		2	Birmingham	1	Jul
		16.40	-0.2		*	Birmingham	1	Jul
		16.39i			2	Chemnitz, GER	28	Jan
		16.33	0.0		2	Bedford	29	May
		15.99	1.1		1	Tallahassee, USA	5	May
		15.91			4	Loughborough	22	Jul
		15.87	0.7		5	Gothenburg, SWE	11	Jul
16.80	1.7	Nathan Douglas		4.12.82	1	Manchester (SC)	16	Aug
		16.53	1.2		2	Hilversum, NED	9	Jul
		16.40w	2.2		1	Bedford	29	Jul
		16.39	0.0		3	Geneva, SUI	10	Jun
		16.35			2	Loughborough	22	Jul
		16.27	1.1		4	Birmingham	1	Jul
		16.08	1.8		*	Bedford	29	Jul
		16.08w	4.2		3	Clermont, USA	15	Apr
16.73	1.5	Ben Williams		25.01.92	2	Villeneuve d'Ascq, FRA	25	Jun
		16.71	0.5		1	Birmingham	1	Jul
		16.46	1.2		1	Loughborough	21	May
		16.45			1	Loughborough	22	Jul
		16.43	1.0		1	Bedford	29	May
		16.18	0.0		4	Geneva, SUI	10	Jun
16.45	-1.2	Nonso Okolo (GBR/NGR)		7.12.89	5	Clermont, USA	13	May
		16.29	1.6		3	Birmingham	1	Jul
		16.25	0.3		2	Bedford	15	Jul
		16.21	1.2		3	Gothenburg, SWE	11	Jul
		16.07	0.0		1	London (LV)	3	Jun
		15.92	0.9		5	Lisbon, POR	17	Jun
		15.92			3	Loughborough	22	Jul

16.38	1.9	Sam Trigg			1.11.93	Q	Austin, USA	27 May
16.12w	3.3					1	Austin, USA	29 Apr
16.05	2.0					*	Austin, USA	29 Apr
15.97w	2.2					8	Eugene, USA	9 Jun
15.87iA						1	Albuquerque, USA	4 Feb
16.30i		Julian Reid			23.09.88	3	Sheffield	11 Feb
16.01	1.2					2	Loughborough	21 May
16.01	1.1					3	Bedford	29 May
16.18w	2.3	Efe Uwaifo	U23	15.05.95		1	New Haven, USA	7 May
15.91	1.8					1	Bedford	17 Jun
16.06	1.9	Jonathan Ilori			14.08.93	1	London (CP)	11 Jun
15.89	1.9					2	Bedford	29 Jul
16.05w	2.7	Montel Nevers	U23	22.05.96		6	Eugene, USA	9 Jun
15.99	0.4					2	Atlanta, USA	14 May
15.90i						8	College Station, USA	11 Mar
15.88i						3	Notre Dame, USA	25 Feb
15.86w	3.2					3	Tallahassee, USA	5 May
16.01i		Lawrence Davis	U23	31.05.95		1	Sheffield	19 Feb
15.43	1.7					4	Loughborough	21 May
		50 performances to 15.85 by 10 athletes including 8 indoors and 8 wind assisted						
15.74w	2.2	Daniel Lewis			8.11.89	2	London (LV)	3 Jun
15.32	0.7					*	London (LV)	3 Jun
15.71	1.8	Stefan Amokwandoh	U23	11.09.96		3	New Haven, USA	7 May
15.71	0.0	Jude Bright-Davies	U20	27.03.99		3	Loughborough	21 May
15.70i		Kola Adedoyin			8.04.91	4	Sheffield	11 Feb
15.32	-1.1					7	Clermont, USA	13 May
15.66	0.8	James McLachlan			12.03.92	3	London (LV)	3 Jun
15.63	0.3	Daniel Igbokwe	U20	28.06.98		2	Princeton, USA	12 May
15.63	1.9	Chukwudi Onyia			28.02.88	1	Grangemouth	26 Aug
15.57	0.3	Jonathon Sawyers			24.08.92	2	Linz, AUT	25 May
15.50w		Joshua Bones			8.05.93	1	Cambridge	24 Jun
15.21						1	Hull	13 May
15.48w	2.8	Seun Okome	U23	26.03.95		1	Bedford	1 May
15.47	1.5					*	Bedford	1 May
	(20)							
15.45w		Julien Allwood			19.11.92	Q	Bedford	30 Apr
14.49	0.7					8	Bedford	29 May
15.42	1.3	Adam Walker-Khan	U23	7.03.95		4	Princeton, USA	12 May
15.40i		Shola John-Olojo			5.05.92	1	Birmingham, USA	24 Feb
14.70	1.1					5	London (CP)	11 Jun
15.35i		Teepee Princewill	U20	22.08.00		2	Cardiff	5 Mar
15.19	-0.5					1	Bedford	18 Jun
15.33i		Jimi Tele			4.05.94	2	Staten Island, USA	14 Jan
15.33	0.8	Chuko Cribb			30.03.94	3	London (CP)	11 Jun
15.29	1.0	Kevin Metzger	U23	13.11.97		4	Bedford	29 Jul
15.27	0.1	Osaze Aghedo	U20	12.02.99		6	Loughborough	21 May
15.25w	3.2	Emmanuel Odubanjo	U20	7.12.99		1	Basingstoke	6 May
14.88	0.9					*	Basingstoke	6 May
15.24i		Antony Daffurn			18.10.86	1	Glasgow	4 Feb
14.78	0.0					1	Grangemouth	13 Aug
	(30)							
15.06	1.8	Navid Childs	V35	12.05.81		1	Aarhus, DEN	30 Jul
14.93	1.5	Lawrence Harvey	V35	26.08.81		2	Aarhus, DEN	30 Jul
14.90i		Jacob Veerapen	U23	29.09.97		6B	New York, USA	26 Feb
14.40	1.2					5	New Brunswick, USA	14 Apr
14.86		Robert Sutherland	U23	16.10.95		1	London (He)	26 Aug
14.85w		George Drake	U23	3.01.96		Q	Bedford	30 Apr
14.43	1.8					*	Bedford	1 May
14.79	0.0	Peter Kirabo			22.09.92	3	London (LV)	3 Jun
14.76		Jordan Walklett	U20	8.02.98		1	Cardiff	25 Jun

14.73		Joel Townley	U17	7.04.01	1	Exeter	17 Jun
14.73		Ade Adefolalu	U23	28.02.97	2	Cambridge	6 Aug
14.72i		Thomas Walley	U20	18.03.98	2	Cardiff	28 Jan
		14.12 -0.1			1	Brecon	26 Aug
(40)							
14.68i		Wesley Matsuka-Williams	U20	15.06.00	4	Sheffield	25 Feb
14.66	1.6	Alando Alfred	U23	1.12.96	1	London (He)	24 Jun
14.64		Ade Babatunde		21.08.87	1	Middlesbrough	5 Aug
14.60	0.6	Aidan Quinn	U20	10.02.00	1	Kilmarnock	12 May
14.57		Mike McKernan	V35	28.11.78	1	Nuneaton	14 May
14.57		James Lelliott		11.02.93	2	Yate	3 Jun
14.53w	2.1	Sam Lyon		20.10.92	3	Grangemouth	26 Aug
		14.32 0.1			*	Grangemouth	26 Aug
14.50	-1.6	Scott Hall		8.03.94	6	Sheffield	6 May
14.45i		Toby Melville	U23	2.12.96	Q	Sheffield	17 Feb
		14.37w			Q	Bedford	30 Apr
		13.99 1.3			3	London (He)	20 Aug
14.41i		Toby Adeniyi	U23	3.09.96	2B	Birmingham	14 Jan
		14.38 0.1			8	Loughborough	21 May
(50)							
14.32		Patrick Sylla	U20	10.10.98	2	London (He)	26 Aug
14.26i		Jamil Hassan	U20	25.06.99	4	London (LV)	15 Jan
14.25	0.0	Samuel Oduro Antwi	U20	4.06.00	3	Birmingham	8 Jul
14.25w	3.0	Henry Clarkson	U20	16.06.99	2	Glasgow (S)	19 Aug
		14.05 2.0			*	Glasgow (S)	19 Aug
14.24	1.1	Stephen MacKenzie	U17	28.08.01	1	Grangemouth	26 Aug
14.22		Gage Francis	U23	6.10.96	3	Cardiff	12 Jul
14.18		Jean Mozobo	U20	5.05.98	1	Chelmsford	25 Jun
14.16i		Mitchell Kirby		18.04.91	1	Birmingham	12 Feb
		13.72 1.4			5	Bedford	15 Jul
14.15w	2.2	Mahad Ahmed	U23	18.09.95	1	Grangemouth	9 Jul
		14.06 0.4			1	Grangemouth	13 Aug
14.14		Mark Burton	U20	11.06.98	1	Belfast	30 Jul
(60)							
14.12		Jack Joynson	U20	15.12.98	1	Exeter	17 Jun
14.10w	3.3	Emmanuel Gbegli		28.12.92	2	Cambridge	14 May
		13.99 0.0			*	Cambridge	14 May
14.09		Ashley Buckman	U23	15.04.97	1	Gillingham	15 Apr
14.09		Theo Fadayero	U20	29.08.00	1	London (WF)	25 Jun
14.06		Joseph Gilkes	U20	16.08.99	1	Coventry	30 Apr
14.06		Peter Akinhnibosun		23.05.94	1	Bromley	10 Jul
14.04		Ross Jeffs		5.09.91	4	London (LV)	20 Aug
14.03	0.0	Jonathan Ferryman		25.12.88	5	Manchester (SC)	20 Aug
14.02w		Matthew Watson		27.01.91	Q	Bedford	30 Apr
14.01	1.0	Kevin Brown		10.12.90	1	Yeovil	6 May
(70)							
13.99i		Jordan Harry	U23	20.02.97	Q	Sheffield	17 Feb
13.99	1.0	Lewis Guest		28.05.94	2	Yeovil	6 May
13.95		JJ Jegede		3.10.85	6	Loughborough	22 Jul
13.95w	4.8	Robert Graham		12.07.91	1	Aberdeen	6 May
		13.90			1	Glasgow	11 Jun
13.93		Jeff Angila	U23	5.09.97	1	Bath	2 Apr
13.93	2.0	Thomas Atkinson	U17	29.09.00	2	Bedford	26 Aug
13.91		Fraser Kesteven		20.06.92	1	Nottingham	8 Apr
13.91		Tope Fisayo	U20	29.01.98	1	Luton	15 Apr
13.91		Euan Bryden		17.05.94	1	Uxbridge	17 Jun
13.88		Nathan Burke	U20	3.09.98	1	Basingstoke	8 Jul
(80)							
13.87i		Joshua Armstrong	U20	23.12.99	3	Athlone, IRL	1 Apr
13.86		Joseph Ramie		14.12.90	1	Rugby	20 Aug
13.85i		Callum Hunter		20.01.94	2	Jordanstown (NI)	7 Jan

13.85	1.6	Edward Barbour	U20	3.03.98	7	Bedford	1	May
13.83	-1.9	Humphrey Waddington		30.05.87	2	Kingston	6	May
13.83w	2.4	Berachiah Ajala	U17	26.08.02	2	Grangemouth	26	Aug
	13.42	2.0			*	Grangemouth	26	Aug
13.82w	2.5	Miraji Ahmed	U17	5.11.01	4	Dublin (S), IRL	15	Jul
	13.76i				1	Glasgow	28	Jan
	13.71	1.8			*	Glasgow (S)	19	Aug
13.79		Dami Famakin	U23	23.11.97	3	Watford	3	May
13.79		Matthew Madden		17.11.90	1	Derby	14	May
13.78		Rowan Powell	U20	8.12.98	1	Loughborough	25	Jun
	(90)							
13.74		Dominic Blake	U20	21.09.99	1	Manchester (Str)	10	Jun
13.73i		Tobi Adeniji	U20	2.02.00	2	Sheffield	14	Jan
13.73i		James King	U23	28.06.96	5	Cardiff	28	Jan
	13.70	0.3			4	Cardiff	9	Jun
13.72w	2.3	Thomas Hunter	U20	7.12.98	4	Tullamore, IRL	3	Jun

Additional Under 17 (1-5 above)

13.67	0.5	Matthew Bondswell	18.04.02	2	Birmingham	7	Jul
13.62		Denis Assongo Tree	2.02.01	1	Norwich	2	Jul
13.61		Brendon Foster	20.10.01	2	Rugby	7	May
13.58	0.4	Alex Colton	4.12.01	3	Birmingham	7	Jul
13.53	0.0	Josh Woods	5.08.02	4	Birmingham	7	Jul
	(10)						
13.53w	2.7	Louis Sabestini	6.03.01	3	Niort, FRA	21	May
	13.37	0.9		1	Cognac, FRA	10	Jun
13.39		Jean-Peter Tra Bi	25.10.00	1	Uxbridge	10	Jun
13.36		Jonathon Mabonga	4.10.00	2	Norwich	10	Jun
13.34		Daniel Adebayo	22.11.00	2	Uxbridge	10	Jun
13.29	0.3	Benjamin Apps	30.05.01	6	Birmingham	7	Jul
13.26	0.0	Curtis Leembruggen	9.01.01	7	Birmingham	7	Jul
13.20		Kaisan Tulloch	7.09.00	2	Birmingham	17	Jun
13.20	0.0	Olowasubomi Bello	16.11.01	8	Birmingham	7	Jul

Under 15

13.31	-1.6	Oyare Aneju	28.03.03	1	Bedford	27	Aug
13.18	1.5	Josiah Wilson-Kepple	20.06.03	1	Birmingham	7	Jul
13.10		Michael Anderson	28.06.03	1	London (CP)	19	Aug
12.94	-0.5	Deshawn Lascelles	5.02.03	3	Bedford	27	Aug
12.90	-0.4	Archie Yeo	8.03.03	1	Leigh	19	Aug
12.87		Jeff Hagan	14.11.02	2	Uxbridge	10	Jun
12.82	0.0	Daniel Onochie-Williams	7.02.03	2	Birmingham	7	Jul
12.82	-3.4	Jonathan Cochrane	27.09.02	5	Bedford	27	Aug
12.81		Joshua Ogunfolaju	25.05.04	3	London (CP)	19	Aug
12.78	0.0	Nabhi Odeh	17.09.02	3	Birmingham	7	Jul
	(10)						
12.57		Dvontae Augustus	7.09.02	1	Birmingham	17	Jun
12.55		Thomas Clarke		2	Birmingham	17	Jun
12.47	1.2	Louis Clow	22.11.02	5	London (He)	24	Jun
12.34	0.5	Cameron Williams-Stein	29.04.03	8	Birmingham	7	Jul
12.18	-1.1	Niall Maloney	4.03.03	2	Leigh	19	Aug
12.11		Emmanuel Oke	5.05.03	1	Chelmsford	10	Jun
12.07		Jovel Jackson-Davies	21.01.03	1	London (BP)	10	Jun
12.06		Somto Agbugba	15.10.02	1	Ashford	10	Jun
12.04		Brooklyn Cooper	9.10.02	1	Exeter	17	Jun
12.03	-1.4	Ethan Stephenson	10.07.03	3	Leigh	19	Aug
	(20)						
12.00w	3.4	Callum Gregson	16.11.02	1	Portsmouth	14	May

Foreign

16.70	-1.2	Tosin Oke (NGR)	V35	1.10.80	2	Clermont, USA	13	May
15.92Aw	2.2	Thalosang Tshireletso (BOT)		14.05.91	1	Pretoria, RSA	3	Jun
15.68A					1	Gaborone, BOT	29	Apr
15.27i					1	London (LV)	15	Jan
14.88w	4.9	Roberto Oppong (ITA)		18.08.93	2	Swansea	3	Jun
14.68	1.6				*	Swansea	3	Jun
14.64	1.5	Carl Britto (IND)		5.12.90	1	Cambridge	14	May
14.22i		Alan Kennedy (IRL)		19.07.88	1	Jordanstown (NI)	7	Jan
13.86	1.3	Che Richards (TTO)	U23	8.05.97	7	London (LV)	3	Jun

Shot

19.00	Scott Lincoln		7.05.93	5B	Las Palmas de G C, ESP	12	Mar
	18.91			1	Cambridge	6	Aug
	18.87i			1	Sheffield	15	Jan
	18.85			1	Huizingen, BEL	10	Jun
	18.80			1	Grangemouth	27	Aug
	18.79			1	Oordegem, BEL	27	May
	18.76i			1	Sheffield	12	Feb
	18.73			1	Manchester (Str)	25	Jul
	18.71			1	Loughborough	21	May
	18.70i			1	Vienna, AUT	28	Jan
	18.68			1	Jarrow	6	Sep
	18.64			1	Cudworth	14	May
	18.59			3	Cork, IRL	18	Jul
	18.55			7	Halle, GER	20	May
	18.54			2	Bedford	30	Jul
	18.53			1	Letterkenny, IRL	7	Jul
	18.48			1	Preston	5	Aug
	18.41			1	York	2	Sep
	18.40			1	York	2	Jul
	18.38			1	London (LV)	3	Jun
	18.28			1	Liverpool	9	Sep
	18.27			11	Birmingham	20	Aug
	18.25			1	Wigan	9	Jul
	18.01			1	Manchester (SC)	16	Aug
	17.96			10	Villeneuve d'Ascq, FRA	24	Jun
	17.82			1	Birmingham	1	Jul
18.34	Youcef Zatat		13.04.94	2	Loughborough	21	May
	18.22i			2	Sheffield	12	Feb
	17.82			4	Lomza, POL	7	Jun
	17.78			1	Geneva, SUI	10	Jun
	17.63			5	Gothenburg, SWE	11	Jul
	17.58i			1	Sheffield	19	Feb
	32 performances to 17.50 by 2 athletes including 5 indoors						
17.42	Gareth Winter		19.03.92	1	Loughborough	14	Jun
17.16i	Joseph Watson	U23	23.09.95	3	Sheffield	12	Feb
	16.05			2	Bedford	29	Apr
16.56i	Nicholas Percy		5.12.94	4	Lincoln, USA	17	Feb
	14.35			17	Tempe, USA	25	Mar
16.23i	Samuel Heawood		25.09.90	3	Sheffield	19	Feb
	15.54			4	Bedford	29	Apr
16.14	Daniel Cartwright	U20	14.11.98	6	London (LV)	3	Jun
16.04	Kai Jones	U23	24.12.96	3	Bedford	29	Apr
15.87	Craig Sturrock		7.01.85	1	Gateshead	13	May
15.75	Gregory Thompson		5.05.94	1	Kingston	2	Jul
	(10)						
15.73	Michael Wheeler		23.09.91	1	London (TB)	26	Aug
15.72	Matthew Baptiste		28.10.90	1	London (CP)	10	Jun
15.54	Alan Toward		31.10.92	3	London (He)	20	Aug

15.45	Alex Parkinson (also NZL)		8.09.94	2	Hastings, NZL	14	Jan
15.34	Martin Tinkler		9.04.91	1	Stevenage	10	Sep
15.10	Anthony Oshodi		27.09.91	5	London (He)	20	Aug
14.99	Brett Morse		11.02.89	2	Manchester (SC)	20	Aug
14.95i	Aled Davies		24.05.91	1	Cardiff	28	Jan
14.87	Daniel Cork	U23	15.07.97	1	Abingdon	16	Jul
14.86	Louis Mascarenhas	U23	5.01.96	1	Bracknell	21	May
(20)							
14.86	Matthew Blandford	U23	21.10.95	1	Bedford	15	Jul
14.75	Matthew Ridge	U23	12.09.96	4	Loughborough	21	May
14.75	David Dowson	V35	23.11.79	2	York	2	Jul
14.73	Luc Durant	U20	3.10.98	3	Manchester (SC)	20	Aug
14.70	Christopher Dack		28.11.82	2	Kingston	13	May
14.69	Jonathan Edwards		9.10.92	1	Swindon	8	Jul
14.69	Curtis Mathews		22.01.92	1D	Erith	16	Sep
14.66	Archie Leeming	U23	6.10.96	2	Chelmsford	13	May
14.65i	Ashley Bryant		17.05.91	1H	Sheffield	7	Jan
	14.20			15D	Götzis, AUT	27	May
14.56	Jamie Williamson		16.07.87	8	London (LV)	3	Jun
(30)							
14.54	Jacob Gardiner		8.03.94	1	Scunthorpe	25	Mar
14.51	Dan Brunsden		18.04.88	1	Portsmouth	19	Aug
14.51	James Hedger		9.09.84	7	London (He)	20	Aug
14.33	Daniel Brunt	V40	23.04.76	1	Spinkhill	10	Sep
14.26	Patrick Swan	U23	14.09.97	1	Exeter	4	Jun
14.24i	John Nicholls	V50	1.09.65	2	Sheffield	15	Jan
	13.93			1	Leigh	6	May
14.21	Fyn Corcoran	V35	17.03.78	2	Cardiff	10	Jun
14.20	Laurence Goodacre		20.09.92	1	Rugby	20	Aug
14.19	David Dawson		3.02.84	1	Exeter	14	May
14.14	Ed Dunford		15.09.84	10	London (LV)	3	Jun
(40)							
14.14	Craig Charlton		7.03.87	2	Portsmouth (RN)	12	Jul
14.11	William Knight	U23	12.11.97	1	Derby	10	Sep
14.10	Ciaran Wright	U23	17.09.96	1	Grangemouth	1	Apr
13.96	Nick Owen	V35	17.07.80	3	London (LV)	20	Aug
13.92	Stephen McCauley	V40	6.02.74	1-35	Oxford (H)	19	Mar
13.90	Luke Roach-Christie		17.10.94	2	Swansea	3	Jun
13.88i	Leo Rowley	U20	30.07.99	1	Cardiff	15	Nov
	13.23			1	Rotherham	9	Jul
13.84	Angus McInroy		13.02.87	4	Manchester (SC)	16	Aug
13.80	Elliot Thompson		10.08.92	5	Bedford	15	Jul
13.78	Morris Fox	V50	30.04.63	1	Cheltenham	15	Jul
(50)							
13.78	Thomas Bullen		12.10.92	1	London (TB)	23	Sep
13.76	Douglas Stark		25.08.93	1	Nottingham	5	Aug
13.74	Graham Lay	V40	13.11.75	5	Kingston	2	Jul
13.74	Richard Woodhall	V35	9.07.80	1	Loughborough	6	Aug
13.71	Joshua Kelly		25.09.93	1	Portsmouth	14	May
13.70	Peter Maitland	V40	21.01.73	3	Basingstoke	6	May
13.69	Neal Smith		1.07.84	1	Norwich	17	Jun
13.63i	Thomas Dobbs	U20	7.02.98	Q	Sheffield	18	Feb
13.62i	Liam Ramsay		18.11.92	13H	Belgrade, SRB	4	Mar
13.61	Ben Stephens	U20	9.05.98	3	Manchester (SC)	10	Jun
(60)							
13.60	Mark Plowman		26.03.85	2	Rugby	20	Aug
13.56	Erasmus Dwemoh		25.11.90	1	London (TB)	17	Jun
13.55	Jonathan Briggs	U23	12.12.97	2	Nuneaton	11	Jun
13.53	James Taylor	V35	24.04.82	1	Ellesmere Port	4	Jun
13.52i	Aaron Edwards		2.05.86	3	London (LV)	4	Feb
	13.03			1	London (LV)	17	Jun
13.50	Peter Glass		1.05.88	1D	Street	29	Apr

13.48i	John Lane			29.01.89	4H	Sheffield	7	Jan
	13.24				12D	Taipei, TPE	24	Aug
13.48	Kyle Stevens			3.06.85	3	Kingston	13	May
13.47	Nathan Fergus	U23		1.10.97	1	Sutton	15	Apr
13.42	Timothy Duckworth	U23		18.06.96	11D	Eugene, USA	7	Jun
(70)								
13.40	Connor Laverty	U23		14.05.96	5	Basingstoke	6	May
13.38	Jack Paget	U23		30.01.97	2	Cambridge	14	May
13.37i	Jak Carpenter			26.09.90	8	Sheffield	19	Feb
	13.36				1D	Bedford	27	May
13.36	Emmanuel Quarshie			3.03.92	2	Yeovil	6	May
13.34i	Henry Fairclough	U20		22.01.99	3	Sheffield	15	Jan
	13.05				4	Preston	5	Aug
13.32	Lewis Church	U23		27.09.96	1H	London (LV)	16	Dec
13.31	Ben Gregory			21.11.90	6D	Azusa, USA	12	Apr
13.27i	Andrew Murphy			26.12.94	3	Glasgow	28	Jan
	13.24				2D	Bedford	27	May
13.26i	Gary Sweeney			31.01.87	4	Glasgow	28	Jan
13.26i	Aiden Davies	U23		26.12.95	Q	Sheffield	18	Feb
(80)								
13.26i	Thomas Head	U23		15.01.96	1	Uxbridge	5	Mar
13.24	Alistair Prenn			7.11.94	14	Providence, USA	15	Apr
13.18	Michael Martin			15.03.88	1	Warrington	30	Jul
13.15i	Ken Baker	V40		19.02.74	1	London (LV)	12	Mar
13.12	Anthony Norfolk	U23		20.05.95	1	Hull	13	May
13.11	Stephen Birse	V35		8.10.77	2	Leeds	6	May
13.06	Scott Jones			30.12.94	1	Wigan	10	Sep
13.03	Courtney Green			20.08.85	3	London (TB)	17	Jun
13.01	Thomas Ashby			5.04.90	1	London (TB)	7	Jun

Foreign

15.22i	*Gintas Degutis (LTU)*	*V45*		*20.07.70*	*1*	*London (LV)*	*12*	*Feb*
15.04	*Angus Lockhart (AUS)*			*11.01.91*	*1*	*Manchester (SC)*	*20*	*Aug*
14.32	*Vutas Druktenis (LTU)*			*5.02.83*	*1*	*Uxbridge*	*17*	*Jun*
13.51	*Michael McConkey (IRL)*			*5.12.84*	*1*	*Bangor, NI*	*15*	*Aug*
13.10	*Kevin Wilson (POR)*			*6.01.90*	*1*	*Chelmsford*	*8*	*Jul*

Shot - Under 20 - 6kg

17.70i	Daniel Cartwright			14.11.98	1	Sheffield	26	Feb
	17.63				1	Loughborough	21	May
16.89	George Evans			21.01.98	1	Glasgow (S)	19	Aug
15.69	Leo Rowley			30.07.99	2	Birmingham	7	Jul
15.40	Luc Durant			3.10.98	1	London (He)	23	Jul
15.35	Alfie Scopes			12.11.99	4	Bedford	17	Jun
15.14	Henry Fairclough			22.01.99	1	York	25	Jun
15.14	Nicholas Young			17.05.00	1	Cardiff	12	Jul
15.09i	Thomas Dobbs			7.02.98	2	Sheffield	26	Feb
	14.39				1	Bolton	25	Jun
14.99i	Ben Stephens			9.05.98	2	Sheffield	14	Jan
	14.79				3	Manchester (SC)	11	Jun
14.82i	Murdo Masterson			26.09.98	3	Glasgow	12	Feb
	14.76				1	Livingston	19	Apr
(10)								
14.61	Billy Praim-Singh			16.06.99	1	Chelmsford	13	May
14.51	Victor Adebiyi			2.03.00	2	Chelmsford	13	May
14.35	Dominic Barnaby			10.06.99	1	Kingston	10	Jun
14.19	Lewis Byng	U17		29.09.01	1	Cheltenham	26	Jul
14.14	Daniel-James Thomas			26.07.00	1	Crawley	10	Jun
14.10	Beck Phillips			6.10.98	1	Cheltenham	10	Jun
14.05	Alexander Hamling			2.03.99	1	Loughborough	12	Jul
14.01i	Oliver Massingham			17.03.99	1	Kings Lynn	29	Jan
13.82	Joshua Tranmer			5.04.00	2	Hull	30	Apr

Shot - Under 17 - 5kg

17.42	George Hyde		30.03.01	1	Bedford	26	Aug
16.49	Ben Hawkes		8.11.00	1	Portsmouth	17	Sep
15.97	Jay Morse		22.07.01	2	Dublin (S), IRL	5	Aug
	16.05i	U18		1	Cardiff	10	Dec
15.83	Lewis Byng		29.09.01	1	Cheltenham	19	Jul
15.71	Andrew Knight		10.11.01	1	Middlesbrough	3	Sep
14.98i	Thomas Hanson		18.12.00	1	Cardiff	28	Jan
	14.79			1	Carmarthen	14	May
14.93i	Ben Wightman		1.03.01	1	Glasgow	1	Feb
	14.40			1	Inverness	9	Apr
14.81	Chukwuemeka Osamoor		15.06.01	1	Sheffield (W)	30	Apr
14.47i	Sam Mace		20.10.00	1	London (LV)	8	Jan
	14.21			1	Twickenham	3	Sep
14.35	Jack Royden		27.10.00	1	Ashford	10	Jun
	(10)						
14.15	Joseph Connelly		9.11.00	1	Leigh	20	Aug
14.13	Kameron Duxbury		8.10.01	1	Eton	10	Sep
14.04	Evan Campbell		17.05.01	1O	Yeovil	25	Jun
13.98	Emeka Ilione		20.03.02	3	Birmingham	8	Jul
13.95	Scott MacNaughton		7.12.01	1	Uxbridge	10	Jun
13.91	Joshua Douglas		24.12.01	1B	Portsmouth	17	Sep
13.85	Joe Lancaster		16.10.01	2	Hexham	17	Jun
13.77	Josh Tyler		15.01.02	7	Bedford	26	Aug
13.73	Joshua Wise		24.11.01	8	Bedford	26	Aug
13.63	David Koffi		23.04.02	1	Stevenage	13	Aug
	(20)						
13.60	Hosana Kitenge			1	Crawley	10	Jun

Shot - Under 15 - 4kg

14.78i	Jack Halpin		19.03.04	1	Gateshead	14	Dec
	14.47			1	Leigh	19	Aug
14.35	Nathan Wright		24.10.02	1	Loughborough	9	Aug
13.99	Craig Moncur		20.03.03	1	Exeter	26	Sep
13.93	Andre Parker		12.11.02	1	Birmingham	7	Jul
13.90	Kenneth Ikeji		17.09.02	1	Lewes	18	Jun
13.72	James Wordsworth		13.06.03	2	Bedford	27	Aug
13.68	Alfie Williams		8.07.03	1	Peterborough	11	Jun
13.65	Michael Burfoot		1.10.02	2	Birmingham	7	Jul
13.64	Christian Cavalli-Warby		3.10.02	2	Bedford	3	Sep
13.54	James Frith		12.07.03	1	Milton Keynes	24	Sep
	(10)						
13.49	Ricky White		3.02.03	3	Birmingham	7	Jul
13.41	Owen Timms-Shaw		28.12.02	1	Nuneaton	20	Aug
13.40	Nathan Bushnell		29.10.02	1	Chelmsford	10	Jun
13.23	Dylan Phillips		26.10.02	1	Brecon	26	Aug
13.17	Tunde Ajidagba		9.10.02	1	London (BP)	10	Jun
13.16	Senyo Ablorde		7.11.02	3	Oxford (H)	1	Jul
13.12	Yorck Newrick		19.09.02	2	Middlesbrough	3	Sep
13.11	Charlie Finnie		24.12.02	5	Birmingham	7	Jul
13.10	Ben Copley		6.11.02	2	Leigh	19	Aug
13.09	Guy White		6.01.03	5	Bedford	27	Aug
	(20)						
13.06	Christian Archer		30.10.02	1	York	3	Jun
13.03	Isaac Pfaender		15.09.02	1	Cambridge	27	May

Shot - Under 13 - 3.25kg

12.37	Joshua Tutt	30.03.05	1	Kettering	30	Sep
12.02	Donovan Capes	5.04.05	1	Bedford	3	Sep
11.74	William Lamprell	12.01.05	1	Bury St. Edmunds	17	Sep
11.62	William Saltmarsh	18.01.05	1	Exeter	29	Aug
11.53	Joshua Schrijver	4.01.05	1	Yate	13	Aug
10.89	Romeo Osei-Nyarko		1	Chelmsford	5	Jul
10.85	Kieran Isaac	1.09.04	1P	Tonbridge	28	Aug
10.80i	Cameron Unsworth	21.09.04	1	Sheffield	4	Jan
10.76	Tobe Akabogu	31.12.04	1	London (ME)	13	Jun
10.73	Timi Ibinola		2	Chelmsford	5	Jul

Discus

62.91	Nicholas Percy	5.12.94	1	University Park, USA	14	May
62.38			1	Norman, USA	22	Apr
61.27			1	Columbia, USA	15	Apr
61.27			2Q	Austin, USA	26	May
60.78			1	Birmingham	1	Jul
60.61			1	Lubbock, USA	28	Apr
60.33			2	Växjö, SWE	14	Jun
59.82			1	Tempe, USA	25	Mar
59.10			2	Lincoln, USA	8	Apr
57.80			1	Council Bluffs, USA	31	Mar
57.00			4	Helsingborg, SWE	9	Jul
62.68	Zane Duquemin	23.09.91	1	Leiria, POR	15	Apr
62.30			2	Gothenburg, SWE	10	Jun
61.99			1	Loughborough	10	May
61.34			1	Leiria, POR	8	Apr
61.23			5	Villeneuve d'Ascq, FRA	25	Jun
60.80			4B	Halle, GER	20	May
60.36			2	Birmingham	1	Jul
60.26			1	London (LV)	3	Jun
60.14			2	Loughborough	21	May
60.13			5	Leiria, POR	29	Jul
60.02			1	Loughborough	26	Feb
59.98			2	Cheltenham	19	Jul
59.96			1	Leiria, POR	22	Apr
59.56			9	London (O)	9	Jul
59.20			1	Sheffield	6	May
59.14			1	Bedford	29	May
59.09			1	Loughborough	31	May
59.01			6	Leiria, POR	30	Jul
58.83			1	St. Clement JER	4	Feb
58.44			5B	Las Palmas de G C, ESP	11	Mar
57.24			2	St. Peter Port GUE	2	Sep
61.15	Brett Morse	11.02.89	1	Cheltenham	19	Jul
60.97			1	Loughborough	21	May
60.82			2	Leiria, POR	15	Apr
60.12			3	Birmingham	1	Jul
59.76			1	Cardiff	10	Jun
59.63			1	Cardiff	1	Aug
59.56			2	Manchester (SC)	16	Aug
59.33			1	Swansea	3	Jun
59.29			1	Basingstoke	6	May
58.91			1	St. Peter Port GUE	2	Sep
58.84			1	Carmarthen	27	Apr
58.73			1	Swansea	29	Jul
58.26			1	Manchester (SC)	20	Aug
57.91			1	Bedford	15	Jul
57.82			1	Brecon	14	May
57.32			1	Brecon	26	Aug

60.28	Gregory Thompson		5.05.94	1	College Park, USA	5	May
	59.75			1	Manchester (SC)	16	Aug
	59.33			5	Philadelphia, USA	28	Apr
	58.70			1	Jacksonville, USA	24	Mar
	57.94			Q	Taipei, TPE	26	Aug
	57.84			1	Charlottesville, USA	8	Apr
	57.67			4	University Park, USA	14	May
	57.52			8	Taipei, TPE	28	Aug
	57.37			1	London (He)	29	Jul
	57.14			4	Gainesville, USA	1	Apr
59.33	Alan Toward		31.10.92	2	Loughborough	26	Feb
	59.00			1	Gateshead	13	May
	57.87			1	Wigan	9	Jul
	57.59			1	Bedford	30	Jul
	62 performances to 57.00 by 5 athletes						
56.79	Alex Parkinson (also NZL)		8.09.94	1	Hamilton, NZL	11	Feb
56.77	George Armstrong	U23	8.12.97	1	Bedford	17	Jun
56.51	Chris Scott		21.03.88	1	Dartford	15	Apr
55.60	Matthew Blandford	U23	21.10.95	2	Bedford	15	Jul
55.29	Angus McInroy		13.02.87	2	London (He)	20	Aug
(10)							
54.79	Najee Fox		1.12.92	3	Loughborough	26	Feb
54.68	Mark Plowman		26.03.85	1	Bristol	18	Jul
51.24	Louis Mascarenhas	U23	5.01.96	1	Bracknell	21	May
51.21	Emeka Udechuku	V35	10.07.79	6	London (LV)	3	Jun
50.71	Devon Douglas		7.09.89	6	Bedford	15	Jul
50.53	Curtis Mathews		22.01.92	1D	Bedford	28	May
50.52	Matthew Baptiste		28.10.90	8	Bedford	15	Jul
50.43	George Evans	U20	21.01.98	1	Inverness	13	May
50.10	Jonathan Edwards		9.10.92	3	Bedford	15	Jul
49.98	Patrick Swan	U23	14.09.97	5	London (He)	20	Aug
(20)							
49.70	Christopher Linque		26.04.88	1	Bury St. Edmunds	17	Jun
49.10	Youcef Zatat		13.04.94	1	St. Clement JER	19	Sep
48.13	Gareth Winter		19.03.92	1	Cheltenham	14	May
48.12	Matt Brown	V35	10.11.80	1	Sätra, SWE	6	May
47.47	Daniel Fleming	U23	27.10.96	1	Manchester (SC)	11	Jun
47.14	Duane Jibunoh	U23	18.11.95	1	Grays	8	Jul
47.02	Jamie Williamson		16.07.87	3	Preston	5	Aug
46.82	James Hedger		9.09.84	8	London (He)	20	Aug
46.80	Lee Newman	V40	1.05.73	1	Wolverhampton	4	Jun
45.74	Dan Brunsden		18.04.88	1	London (LV)	20	Aug
(30)							
45.55	Christopher Dack		28.11.82	1	Yate	3	Jun
45.55	Niklas Aarre	U23	21.01.96	1	Nottingham	5	Aug
45.33	David Dawson		3.02.84	1	Exeter	15	Apr
45.18	Saoirse Chinery-Edoo		1.11.93	1D	Sutton	10	Sep
45.17	Connor Laverty	U23	14.05.96	2	Visby, SWE	27	Jun
44.98	Joseph Martin	U20	9.03.99	1	York	29	Jul
44.86	James Taylor	V35	24.04.82	1	Sheffield	21	Jun
44.34	William Knight	U23	12.11.97	7	Bedford	17	Jun
44.33	Ashley Bryant		17.05.91	4	Bedford	15	Jul
44.15	Fraser Wright	U23	28.06.96	4B	Vila Nova de Cerveira, POR	23	Apr
(40)							
44.11	Thomas Ashby		5.04.90	1	Bedford	15	Jul
43.97	Craig Sturrock		7.01.85	2	Gateshead	13	May
43.89	Samuel Woodley	U20	17.11.99	1	Stevenage	10	Sep
43.84	Oliver Massingham	U20	17.03.99	1	Ipswich	20	May
43.20	Martin Tinkler		9.04.91	2	Stevenage	10	Sep
43.13	David Coleman		14.02.86	1	Tonbridge	19	Aug
43.12	Roger Bate		16.01.83	2	Manchester (Str)	3	Jun

43.09	Matthew Twigg	V45	18.07.69	1	Corby	13	May
43.06	John Lane		29.01.89	7D	Azusa, USA	13	Apr
43.00	Daniel Brunt	V40	23.04.76	1-40	Derby	14	May
(50)							
42.82	Peter Glass		1.05.88	2D	Arona, ESP	4	Jun
42.81	Andrew Murphy		26.12.94	2	Glasgow (S)	9	Aug
42.51	Rafer Joseph	V45	21.07.68	4	Basingstoke	6	May
42.37	Jonathan Briggs	U23	12.12.97	9	Bedford	17	Jun
42.34	Kevin Brown	V50	10.09.64	1	Abingdon	16	Jul
42.18	Douglas Stark		25.08.93	2	Nottingham	5	Aug
42.08	Ed Dunford		15.09.84	13	London (LV)	3	Jun
42.07	Nathan Fergus	U23	1.10.97	1	Dartford	21	May
42.07	Thomas Dobbs	U20	7.02.98	3	Wigan	9	Jul
42.00	Sam O'Kane		18.12.92	3	Glasgow (S)	9	Aug
(60)							
41.84	Lewis Church	U23	27.09.96	2D	Erith	17	Sep
41.80	Forrest Francis	U23	13.04.95	1	Nuneaton	13	May
41.77	Omar Reid	U23	6.07.96	Q	Bedford	29	Apr
41.67	Robert Russell	V40	5.08.74	1	Leeds	6	May
41.62	Matthew Callaway	U23	19.12.97	3	Exeter	27	Jun
41.60	Michael Painter		9.10.94	3	Stanford, USA	5	May
41.52	Timothy Duckworth	U23	18.06.96	7D	Eugene, USA	8	Jun
41.51	James Lelliott		11.02.93	5	Yate	3	Jun
41.48	David Dowson	V35	23.11.79	2	York	2	Jul
41.43	Dele Aladese	U20	16.05.99	2	Bromley	19	Aug
(70)							
41.40	Jak Carpenter		26.09.90	2	Rugby	7	May
41.24	Andrew Wheble		21.10.86	2	Ewell	19	Jul
41.18	Daniel Cartwright	U20	14.11.98	14	Sheffield	6	May
41.00	Ben Hazell		1.10.84	3	Swansea	3	Jun

Foreign

45.23	*Sergiy Sarayev (UKR)*		*15.01.83*	*1*	*Manchester (Str)*	*3*	*Jun*
43.57	*Kevin Wilson (POR)*		*6.01.90*	*2*	*Chelmsford*	*3*	*Jun*
42.89	*Matthew Harris (AUS)*		*26.04.89*	*2*	*Ashford*	*13*	*May*
42.63	*Raul Rinken (EST)*	*U23*	*20.12.95*	*1*	*Dartford*	*19*	*Aug*

Discus - Under 20 - 1.75kg

60.37	George Evans	21.01.98	1	Leiria, POR	15	Apr
55.40	James Tomlinson	11.01.00	1	Manchester (SC)	16	Aug
49.73	Andrew Peck	20.09.99	1	Doncaster	25	Jun
49.64	Samuel Woodley	17.11.99	1	London (WF)	25	Jun
49.49	Alfie Scopes	12.11.99	2	Bedford	18	Jun
48.82	Thomas Dobbs	7.02.98	1	Manchester (SC)	10	Jun
48.46	Oliver Massingham	17.03.99	2	Norwich	30	Apr
47.31	Joseph Martin	9.03.99	2	Manchester (SC)	10	Jun
47.18	Dele Aladese	16.05.99	1	Kingston	10	Jun
47.09	Charlie Headdock	11.12.98	3	Manchester (SC)	10	Jun
(10)						
46.59	Nicholas Young	17.05.00	1	Wrexham	19	Aug
46.34	Elliot Berryman	2.10.98	1	Exeter	17	Jun
45.02	Oliver Hewitt	27.09.99	1	London (He)	23	Jul
44.52	Nathan Thomas	6.09.98	1	St. Clement JER	10	Jun
43.59	Joshua Tranmer	5.04.00	2	York	25	Jun
43.53	Beck Phillips	6.10.98	1	Cheltenham	10	Jun
43.27	Alexander Hamling	2.03.99	1	Milton Keynes	24	Sep
43.01	Tyler Adams	26.11.98	1D	Boston	17	Sep
42.27	Daniel Cartwright	14.11.98	1	Nottingham	30	Apr

Discus - Under 18 - 1.5kg

63.48	James Tomlinson		11.01.00	1	Loughborough	21	May
55.28	Jay Morse	U17	22.07.01	1	Bedford	26	Aug
53.75	Alfie Scopes		12.11.99	2	Tomblaine, FRA	26	Jun
52.70	Ben Hawkes	U17	8.11.00	2	Bedford	26	Aug
52.66	Oliver Massingham		17.03.99	1	Bury St. Edmunds	22	Apr
52.57	Philip Bartlett	U17	5.09.00	1	Dublin (S), IRL	15	Jul
50.90	Reuben Vaughan	U17	25.10.00	1	Tonbridge	28	Aug

Discus - Under 17 - 1.5kg (1-4 above)

49.87	Joe Worrall	26.04.01	2	Yate	30	Apr
49.81	Joshua Douglas	24.12.01	1	Portsmouth	13	May
49.08	Alfred Mawdsley	13.10.00	1-18	Bedford	17	Jun
48.25	Ruaridh Lang	24.12.00	1	Middlesbrough	3	Sep
47.20	Sam Mace	20.10.00	1	Lewes	25	Jun
45.10	Kai Harrison	21.06.01	1	Peterborough	7	May
(10)						
44.42	Harrison Leach	9.11.00	4	Birmingham	8	Jul
44.31	Anthony Kent	25.09.00	1	Blackburn	24	May
43.98	Ben Wade	6.09.00	5	Birmingham	8	Jul
43.78	Cameron Darkin-Price	18.11.00	1	Nuneaton	20	Aug
43.64	Aran Thomas	6.12.01	1	Cleckheaton	23	Apr
43.31	Michael Furness	4.07.01	2	Hexham	17	Jun
43.22	Ben McLaren-Porter	22.11.00	1	Swindon	16	Jul
42.90	Ryan Whitehead	22.01.01	5	London (CP)	19	Aug
42.74	Finbar Dunne	20.09.01	6	Dublin (S), IRL	15	Jul
42.48	Douglas Noel	1.03.01	2O	Boston	16	Sep
(20)						
42.47	Chukwuemeka Osamoor	15.06.01	1	Sheffield (W)	30	Apr
42.07	Dominic Buckland	5.11.01	1	Sandy	23	Sep
41.79	Andrew Bowsher	10.05.01	1	Aberdeen	10	Sep
41.39	Robert Jedrzejczak	23.03.01	1	Exeter	17	Jun
41.21	Jack Turner	11.07.01	1	Yeovil	10	Sep

Discus - Under 15 - 1.25kg

48.84	Ben Copley	6.11.02	1	Birmingham	8	Jul
46.76	Harry Davies	25.10.02	2	Bedford	27	Aug
44.62	Aaron Worgan	3.10.02	1	Exeter	7	May
42.27	Danny Gracie	30.10.02	1	Glasgow (S)	20	Aug
41.69	Ryan Wilson	1.01.03	2	Leigh	19	Aug
41.54	James Wordsworth	13.06.03	1	Gateshead	10	Jun
40.93	Lukas Bradshaw	18.09.02	2	York	29	Jul
40.90	Craig Moncur	20.03.03	1	Exeter	27	Jun
40.31	Michael Burfoot	1.10.02	1	Bromley	15	Jul
40.04	Lloyd Clarke	6.06.03	1	Brecon	13	Jul
(10)						
39.74	Kyle Thornton	18.02.03	3	Birmingham	8	Jul
39.67	Kenneth Ikeji	17.09.02	1	Colchester	30	Jul
39.34	Harry Booker	9.09.03	1	Sandy	23	Sep
39.23	Owen Timms-Shaw	28.12.02	1	Nuneaton	9	Sep
38.74	George Nixon	31.12.02	1	Blackpool	18	Jun
38.40	Isaac Lecki	24.03.03	1	Manchester (Str)	29	May
38.11	Shay Tarbit	18.06.03	2	Nuneaton	20	Aug
37.85	Dillon Claydon	1.11.03	1	London (CP)	20	Aug
37.80	Senyo Ablorde	7.11.02	1	Bedford	3	Sep
37.78	Ben Cotton	15.08.03	2	Southend	28	Aug
(20)						
37.35	Ben Campion	22.10.02	1	Newport	22	Apr
37.24	Oliver Thatcher	11.09.02	3	Oxford (H)	9	Sep
36.97	Matthew Taylor	17.01.04	1	Liverpool	9	Sep

Discus - Under 13 - 1kg

33.67	Joshua Tutt		30.03.05	1	Kettering	30	Sep
31.97	Donovan Capes		5.04.05	1	Luton	20	Aug
30.84	Joshua Schrijver		4.01.05	1	Yate	13	Aug
29.97	Ben Nolan		22.11.04	1	Erith	16	Sep
28.86	Jay McCarthy		29.11.04	1	Glasgow	29	Aug
27.62	Obinna Nwafor		19.03.05	2	Erith	16	Sep
26.17	Zak Grinsted		9.12.04	1	Stevenage	13	Aug
26.14	Ayomide Johnson		3.11.04	3	Erith	16	Sep
26.12	Nathan Waife			1	Birmingham	10	Jun
26.10	Michael Jenkins		27.10.04	1	Brecon	22	Jul

Hammer

77.51	Nick Miller		1.05.93	1	Salinas, USA	21	Apr
	77.31			6	London (O)	11	Aug
	76.81			3	Halle, GER	20	May
	76.65			3	Villeneuve d'Ascq, FRA	25	Jun
	76.25			5	Székesfehérvár, HUN	4	Jul
	76.18			1	Loughborough	22	Jul
	76.00			3	Szczecin, POL	10	Jun
	75.97			2	Forbach, FRA	28	May
	75.90			6	Ostrava, CZE	27	Jun
	75.59			4	Madrid, ESP	14	Jul
	75.58			1	Stanford, USA	1	Apr
	75.52			Q	London (O)	9	Aug
	75.10			4	Montreuil-sous-Bois, FRA	1	Jun
	74.98			1	Birmingham	2	Jul
	73.74			5	Samorín, SVK	17	Jun
	73.18			1	Huelva, ESP	14	Jun
	72.37			1	Kohila, EST	8	Sep
	71.86			1	Tallinn, EST	2	Sep
	71.69			2	Birmingham	20	Aug
75.72	Chris Bennett		17.12.89	1	Fränkisch-Crumbach, GER	4	Jun
	72.68			2	Loughborough	22	Jul
	72.05			21Q	London (O)	9	Aug
	71.72			2	Loughborough	21	May
	70.65			9	Las Palmas de G C, ESP	12	Mar
	70.50			4	Birmingham	2	Jul
73.40	Taylor Campbell	U23	30.06.96	1	Bedford	30	Apr
	72.89			2	Stanford, USA	1	Apr
	72.87			2	Birmingham	2	Jul
	71.96			1-23	Halle, GER	21	May
	70.59			4	Bydgoszcz, POL	14	Jul
	70.33			1	London (CP)	11	Jun
	69.41			5	Forbach, FRA	28	May
	68.04			5	Loughborough	22	Jul
	67.51			4-23	Vecindario, ESP	11	Mar
	67.43			Q	Bydgoszcz, POL	13	Jul
71.73	Mark Dry		11.10.87	1	Loughborough	21	May
	71.69			2	Nikíti, GRE	11	Jun
	70.81			3	Loughborough	22	Jul
	70.51			3	Birmingham	2	Jul
	70.26			8	Fränkisch-Crumbach, GER	4	Jun
	70.19			1	Bedford	15	Jul
	67.90			1	Manchester (SC)	16	Aug
70.98	Joseph Ellis	U23	10.04.96	1	University Park, USA	12	May
	70.33			8	Eugene, USA	7	Jun
	69.30			1	Austin, USA	28	Apr
	68.05			5	Birmingham	2	Jul
	68.00			1	Austin, USA	14	Apr
	67.07			Q	Lexington, USA	25	May

70.00	Osian Jones		23.06.93	2	Leiria, POR	29	Jul
69.20				1	Belfast	5	Jul
67.89				6	Loughborough	22	Jul
69.80	Chris Shorthouse		23.06.88	1	Loughborough	26	Feb
68.02				1	Loughborough	24	May
67.91				1	Loughborough	10	May
67.77				3	Loughborough	21	May
67.46				7	Loughborough	22	Jul
67.42				1	Loughborough	26	Aug
67.22				6B	Las Palmas de G C, ESP	12	Mar
67.15				3	Bedford	30	Jul
67.03				1	Birmingham	4	Jun
69.15	Michael Bomba		10.10.86	1	Manchester (Str)	25	Apr
67.05				2	Loughborough	26	Feb
69.13	Callum Brown		20.07.94	1	Bedford	30	Jul
68.62				1	Norwich	20	Aug
67.51				2	Manchester (SC)	16	Aug
67.18				2	London (LV)	8	Apr
67.05				1	Grays	15	Apr
68.86	Jake Norris	U20	30.06.99	1	Eton	1	Apr
67.73				1	Basingstoke	6	May
67.65				1	Watford	28	Jun
	(10)						
68.83	Craig Murch		27.06.93	2	Bedford	30	Jul
68.54				1	Cardiff	12	Jul
68.52				1	Bedford	29	May
68.48				1	Chelmsford	3	Jun
68.31				1	Bedford	15	Jul
68.29				4	Loughborough	22	Jul
67.92				6	Birmingham	2	Jul
67.44				1	Nuneaton	13	May
67.44				1	Liverpool	9	Sep
67.42				2	Loughborough	26	Aug
67.32				1	Nuneaton	11	Jun
67.72	Nicholas Percy		5.12.94	1	Columbia, USA	14	Apr
67.16				1	Tempe, USA	24	Mar
	83 performances to 67.00 by 12 athletes						
66.84	Michael Painter		9.10.94	1	Stanford, USA	8	Apr
66.70	James Bedford		29.12.88	1	Hull	9	Apr
66.26	Jonathan Edwards		9.10.92	6	Loughborough	21	May
65.88	Jac Lloyd Palmer	U23	13.03.96	1	Bedford	18	Jun
65.65	Tom Parker		7.10.94	1	London (He)	24	Jun
65.39	Andy Frost	V35	17.04.81	2	Visby, SWE	25	Jun
63.80	Thomas Head	U23	15.01.96	2	Bedford	30	Apr
63.28	Tim Williams		7.07.92	1	Loughborough	14	Jun
	(20)						
62.74	Ciaran Wright	U23	17.09.96	6	Sheffield	6	May
62.39	Mick Jones	V50	23.07.63	1	Crawley	13	May
61.99	Joe Bloomfield		3.11.90	1	Colchester	19	Nov
61.55	Peter Smith		20.07.90	2	Hull	9	Apr
61.35	Richard Martin		8.01.84	1	Sandy	23	Sep
60.80	Alex Smith		6.03.88	2	Bedford	15	Jul
60.15	James Hamblin	U23	1.07.96	1	Nottingham	28	Mar
60.05	Alex Warner		7.11.89	1	Woodford	20	May
59.69	Jacob Lange	U23	5.12.95	4	Bedford	30	Apr
57.85	John Pearson	V50	30.04.66	1	Loughborough	6	Aug
	(30)						
57.25	Mike Floyd	V40	26.09.76	1	Leigh	6	May
57.18	Bayley Campbell	U20	24.06.00	4	Manchester (SC)	20	Aug
57.13	Jamie Potton-Burrell	U23	27.01.96	7	London (LV)	3	Jun

56.85	Edward Jeans	U20	28.09.98	1	Preston	1	Jul
56.77	Jay Hill		27.08.91	1	Kingston	6	May
56.32	Peter Clarke		22.07.91	1	Hemel Hempstead	8	Jul
55.92	Jason Robinson		8.08.89	4	Loughborough	26	Feb
55.59	Jacob Roberts	U20	9.09.99	2	Bebington	4	Jun
54.70	Billy Praim-Singh	U20	16.06.99	1	Colchester	11	Jun
54.05	Graham Holder	V45	16.01.72	2	Grays	15	Apr
(40)							
53.78	Andrew Costello	U20	1.10.99	2	Grangemouth	26	Aug
53.53	Ross Douglas	U23	14.07.96	1	Nottingham	8	Apr
53.44	Gareth Cook	V45	20.02.69	3	Kingston	2	Jul
53.20	Jamie Kuehnel	U23	16.10.97	1	Andover	21	May
52.79	Andrew Elkins		25.05.93	1	Salisbury	8	Jul
52.16	Ben Jones		6.11.82	1	Portsmouth (RN)	12	Jul
52.03	Alex Berrow		10.06.89	2	Nottingham	5	Aug
51.84	Stuart Thurgood	V40	17.05.76	2	Yate	3	Jun
51.81	Jonathan Jones	U20	11.07.98	1	Corby	4	Jun
51.55	Oliver Hewitt	U20	27.09.99	2	Andover	21	May
(50)							
51.26	Matthew Evans		21.06.92	1	Crawley	28	Aug
50.91	Tom Kirk		1.11.94	2	Cudworth	14	May
50.82	Robert Earle	V55	15.09.60	1	Colchester	7	Sep
50.79	Rob Careless	V40	7.09.74	4	Chelmsford	3	Jun
50.74	Steve Whyte	V50	14.03.64	10	London (LV)	3	Jun
50.68	Roger Bate		16.01.83	2	Manchester (Str)	3	Jun
50.64	Patrick Price	U20	1.07.99	3	Birmingham	4	Jun
50.51	Matthew Bell	V35	2.06.78	1	Corby	14	May
50.44	Daniel Nixon	U20	10.12.98	1	Manchester (Str)	20	Aug
50.40	Simon Evans		21.06.92	1	Portsmouth	19	Aug
(60)							
50.33	Peter Cassidy	U20	22.01.98	2	Guildford	19	Aug
50.23	Jack Wuidart	U23	6.09.97	6	Bedford	30	Apr
49.90	Kyle Stevens		3.06.85	2	Ewell	1	Apr
49.76	Christopher Bainbridge	U23	16.06.95	1	Grantham	13	May
49.65	Wayne Powell	V45	27.07.71	1	Bury St. Edmunds	22	Apr
49.52	Richard Bell		17.06.92	3	Visby, SWE	25	Jun
49.28	Robin Walker	V35	8.02.78	3	Woodford	20	May
49.27	Anthony Gillatt	U23	14.09.95	7	Bedford	18	Jun
49.01	Steve Brunsden		17.05.90	4	Kingston	6	May
48.68	Kieran Grimwade	U20	7.12.99	5	Basingstoke	6	May
(70)							
48.58	Nicky Stone		15.12.93	1	Inverness	22	Jul
48.56	George Perkins		17.10.83	2	Rotherham	6	May
48.51	Alexander Reynolds	U20	19.02.99	6	Chelmsford	3	Jun
47.54	James Goss	V40	11.09.73	6	Kingston	2	Jul
47.51	David Little	V35	28.02.81	2	Livingston	8	Apr
47.39	Munroe Ritchie	U20	30.01.98	1	Crawley	25	Mar
47.19	Jake Allen		29.05.94	2	Bury St. Edmunds	17	Jun
47.17	Joseph Watson	U23	23.09.95	1	Lewes	9	Jul
47.06	Sam Mace	U17	20.10.00	3	Kingston	15	Apr
47.01	Wayne Roddis-Clarke	V40	24.12.75	1-40	Grantham	13	May
(80)							
46.93	Joseph Flitcroft		28.01.91	4	Swansea	3	Jun
46.87	Craig Mullins	U20	24.05.98	3	Grangemouth	26	Aug
46.82	Daniel Thirlwell		8.07.83	1	Whitley Bay	6	May
46.70	David McKay	V35	22.09.80	1	Warrington	13	May
46.61	Michael Dawes	U20	24.11.98	1	Nuneaton	15	Jul
46.60	Phil Spivey	V55	15.05.61	1	Horsham	21	May
46.60	Martin Croft	U23	29.04.97	1	Middlesbrough	5	Aug
46.56	Alex Griffiths	U20	6.01.00	1	Stoke-on-Trent	5	Aug
46.44	Shaun Livett	U23	19.11.96	1	Wrexham	24	Sep
46.27	James Taylor	V35	24.04.82	1	Ellesmere Port	4	Jun

46.21	Richard Woodhall	V35	9.07.80	3	Loughborough	6	Aug
45.98	Yasha Bobash		24.12.87	8	Chelmsford	3	Jun
45.96	Mark Elliott	V35	3.04.78	1	Telford	18	May
45.85	Aaron Jeal	U20	30.05.99	1	Gateshead	4	Jun
45.65	Jonathan Briggs	U23	12.12.97	1	Abingdon	16	Jul
45.59	Isaac Huskisson	U23	17.06.97	1	Colchester	17	Jun
45.57	Paul Derrien	V45	5.08.71	1	Kingston	17	Jun
45.40	Matthew Baptiste		28.10.90	4	Woodford	20	May
45.23	Mark Roberson	V40	21.03.75	1	Bedford	21	May
45.20	Kevin Acraman	U23	11.02.96	4	Andover	21	May
(100)							
45.08	Steve Timmins	V40	8.05.75	2	Bromley	12	Jun
45.03	Kieran Thackray		28.09.94	3	Leeds	22	Mar
44.99	Dan Brunsden		18.04.88	3	London (LV)	20	Aug
44.73	Brett Marsh	V40	20.01.76	5	Yate	3	Jun
44.64	Robert Mungham		1.12.84	1	Dartford	19	Aug
44.55	Tom Pearson		17.07.91	1	Loughborough	16	Sep
44.45	Beau Morris	U20	21.11.98	5	Birmingham	4	Jun
44.30	Ryan Winson		21.09.92	8	Rugby	20	Aug
44.24	Jack Lambert	U17	13.06.02	2	Corby	4	Jun

Foreign

70.55	*Dempsey McGuigan (IRL)*		*30.08.93*	*2*	*Torrance, USA*	*13*	*Apr*
64.47	*Fellan McGuigan (IRL)*		*15.03.96*	*1*	*Fort Worth, USA*	*15*	*Apr*
52.98	*Sergiy Sarayev (UKR)*		*15.01.83*	*1*	*Manchester (Str)*	*5*	*Aug*
51.43	*John Osazuwa (NGR)*	*V35*	*4.05.81*	*11*	*Bedford*	*30*	*Jul*
47.85	*Dawid Marchlewicz (POL)*		*1.01.83*	*2*	*Kingston*	*15*	*Apr*
47.85	*Kieran Murphy (IRL)*		*8.05.94*	*1*	*Crawley*	*8*	*Jul*

Hammer - Under 20 - 6kg

78.09	Jake Norris		30.06.99	1	Loughborough	21	May
77.67				1	Bedford	17	Jun
76.97				1	Leiria, POR	15	Apr
76.97				1	Bromley	28	May
76.84				1	Birmingham	8	Jul
76.70				1	Manchester (SC)	16	Aug
76.62				Q	Grosseto, ITA	20	Jul
76.12				1	Bracknell	14	May
69.33	Bayley Campbell		24.06.00	1	London (CP)	10	Jun
68.49	Edward Jeans		28.09.98	1	Blackburn	24	May
65.64	Jacob Roberts		9.09.99	2	Blackburn	21	Jun
63.97	Jonathan Jones		11.07.98	1	Loughborough	9	Apr
63.61	Oliver Hewitt		27.09.99	3	Birmingham	8	Jul
62.81	Billy Praim-Singh		16.06.99	3	Bromley	28	May
61.92	Craig Mullins		24.05.98	1	Hull	30	Apr
61.22	Daniel Nixon		10.12.98	7	Birmingham	8	Jul
59.91	Aaron Jeal		30.05.99	2	Hull	30	Apr
(10)							
59.83	Peter Cassidy		22.01.98	1	Kingston	13	May
59.68	Patrick Price		1.07.99	1	Nuneaton	13	May
59.49	Andrew Costello		1.10.99	1	Linwood	10	Sep
58.47	Kieran Grimwade		7.12.99	1	Cardiff	1	Aug
55.53	Alexander Reynolds		19.02.99	2	Chelmsford	14	May
55.05	Michael Dawes		24.11.98	4	Oxford (H)	9	Sep
54.55	Alex Griffiths		6.01.00	4	Cardiff	12	Jul
54.28	Reiss Senior		30.09.98	1	London (TB)	1	Apr
53.38	Munroe Ritchie		30.01.98	1	Crawley	25	Mar
52.61	Oliver Graham		16.05.01	2	Ipswich	19	Nov
(20)							
51.94	William Schofield		25.03.99	1	Manchester (Str)	25	Apr
51.72	Nathan Thomason		11.02.98	3	Manchester (Str)	28	May
51.35	Ruaridh Gray		28.12.98	2	Grangemouth	12	May

Hammer - Under 18 - 5kg
73.53	Bayley Campbell	24.06.00	1	Loughborough	9	Apr

Hammer - Under 17 - 5kg
71.97	Ben Hawkes	8.11.00	1	Crawley	13	May
64.32	Sam Mace	20.10.00	1	Twickenham	3	Sep
63.93	Harry Ilyk	24.05.01	3	Bedford	27	Aug
60.94	Shaun Kerry	13.12.01	3	Birmingham	8	Jul
60.04	James Lancaster	15.08.01	2	Kingston	13	May
59.79	Jack Lambert	13.06.02	1	Liverpool	9	Sep
59.63	Marcus Jones	11.12.00	2	Crawley	25	Mar
59.22	Jolaoluwa Omotosho	28.12.00	2	London (CP)	20	Aug
59.11	Sam Gaskell	1.11.01	4	Birmingham	8	Jul
58.32	Thomas Milton	21.11.01	1	Tonbridge	23	Jul
	(10)					
57.29	Oliver Graham	16.05.01	1	Stevenage	10	Sep
55.35	James Ericsson-Nicholls	6.11.01	1	Yate	23	Jul
55.25	Samuel Briggs	27.12.00	1	Sheffield	23	Jul
55.01	Sam Illsley	11.04.02	2	Bournemouth	25	Jun
52.38	Joshua Ondoma	26.12.00	1	Ashford	10	Jun
52.29	William Robinson	16.09.00	2	Hull	9	Apr
51.98	Jack Turner	23.08.02	1	Stoke-on-Trent	10	Jun
51.92	James Gardner	27.03.02	1	Bracknell	2	Jul
51.62	Jaquan Moore	18.07.01	1	Cambridge	24	Jun
51.53	Thomas Litchfield	20.04.02	2	Tonbridge	23	Jul
	(20)					
51.13	Jacob Careless	8.10.01	2	Derby	10	Sep
50.45	Michael Knowles	16.01.01	2	Stevenage	10	Sep
50.28	Matt Macfarlane	16.09.01	1	Inverness	3	Aug

Hammer - Under 15 - 4kg
62.08	Kenneth Ikeji	17.09.02	1	Oxford (H)	9	Sep
55.51	Alex Bernstein	13.11.02	1	Leigh	19	Aug
55.22	Danny Gracie	30.10.02	1	Tranent	1	Aug
52.05	Toby Conibear	26.04.03	3	Bedford	26	Aug
51.05	Edward Fileman	19.04.03	1	Yeovil	10	Sep
49.69	Jack Halpin	19.03.04	2	Leigh	19	Aug
49.49	Anton Joseph	14.01.03	4	Bedford	26	Aug
49.26	Alex Ringshall	27.09.02	1	Basingstoke	17	Jun
47.83	Harry Davies	25.10.02	1	Bath	22	Apr
47.24	Jamie Bonella-Duke	20.01.03	3	London (CP)	19	Aug
	(10)					
47.09	Ben Cotton	15.08.03	5	Birmingham	8	Jul
46.55	Joseph Beal	16.11.02	2	Oxford (H)	9	Sep
45.26	Mackenzie Laban	29.10.02	1	Twickenham	3	Sep
44.56	James Shefford	10.02.03	1	Eton	10	Sep
42.39	Daniel McCourt	17.05.03	1	Brighton	1	Sep
41.66	Evan Morgan	1.01.03	2	Yate	20	May
41.57	Bradley Jenvey	23.12.02	2	Birmingham	2	Sep
41.22	Finley Rix-Clancy	14.08.03	3	Chelmsford	10	Jun
40.63	Senyo Ablorde	7.11.02	2	Chelmsford	14	May
40.20	Samuel Clifton	14.03.03	1	Woking	15	Jul

Hammer - Under 13 - 3kg
42.55	Jay McCarthy	29.11.04	1	Livingston	9	Sep
31.68	Luke Finch	1.01.05	1	Woodford	4	Jul

Javelin

77.47	Matti Mortimore		16.05.93	1	Stanford, USA	31	Mar
	77.15			1	Tempe, USA	18	Mar
	77.08			1	Lincoln, USA	8	Apr
	76.82			2	Long Beach, USA	14	Apr
	74.49			1	Fargo, USA	11	May
	74.33			5	Eugene, USA	7	Jun
	73.78			Q	Austin, USA	25	May
	72.42			8	Villeneuve d'Ascq, FRA	24	Jun
	72.19			2	Birmingham	1	Jul
77.03	James Whiteaker	U20	8.10.98	1	Basingstoke	6	May
	74.64			1	Bedford	17	Jun
	73.40			1	Norwich	30	Apr
76.81	Harry Hughes	U23	26.09.97	1	Bedford	1	May
	76.59			4-23	Vecindario, ESP	12	Mar
	74.69			4	Halle, GER	20	May
	72.80			1	Loughborough	26	Feb
	72.03			1	Sheffield	6	May
	71.66			2	Jena, GER	11	Jun
	70.44			2	Loughborough	21	May
	70.21			Q	Bedford	30	Apr
	70.17			1	Bedford	15	Jul
75.71	Joe Harris	U23	23.05.97	1	Bedford	29	Jul
	71.46			1	Loughborough	22	Jul
	70.50			3	Birmingham	1	Jul
74.88	Joe Dunderdale		4.09.92	2	Bedford	29	Jul
	73.58			1	Birmingham	1	Jul
	73.41			1	Letterkenny, IRL	7	Jul
	73.38			1	York	2	Sep
	72.50			1	Sheffield	24	May
	70.63			1	Spinkhill	10	Sep
72.41	Steven Turnock		7.11.92	1B	Leiria, POR	15	Apr
	71.84			1	Loughborough	21	May
	70.82			1	Loughborough	7	Jun
	70.31			4	Birmingham	1	Jul
	70.02			3	Bedford	29	Jul
	70.01			1	Manchester (SC)	16	Aug
71.15	Greg Millar		19.12.92	1	Loughborough	24	May
70.31	Neil Crossley		15.04.88	2	Loughborough	26	Feb
	38 performances to 70.00 by 8 athletes						
69.69	Gavin Johnson-Assoon		19.12.82	1	London (He)	26	Aug
67.97	Ashley Bryant		17.05.91	3D	London (O)	12	Aug
(10)							
67.71	Craig Lacy		17.07.91	1	London (He)	20	Aug
67.70	Neil McLellan	V35	10.09.78	5	Birmingham	1	Jul
67.10	Jack Swain	U23	27.02.95	3	Loughborough	28	May
66.76	Roald Bradstock	V55	24.04.62	1	Clermont, USA	13	May
65.91	Nathan James	U20	5.10.98	1	Brecon	26	Aug
65.58	Sam Dean	U20	23.09.98	1	Swansea	3	Jun
65.12	George Davies	U20	27.01.98	4	Sheffield	6	May
64.77	Jason Copsey		17.02.91	1	Cardiff	9	Jun
63.34	Marshall Childs	U23	18.02.97	1	Cambridge	24	Jun
62.93	Chris Hughff	V35	5.12.81	7	Sheffield	6	May
(20)							
62.81	Gareth Crawford	U20	6.06.99	1	Dublin (S), IRL	28	May
62.79	William Trimble		9.01.92	2	Kingston	14	May
62.46	Daniel Bainbridge	U20	2.06.99	1	Brno, CZE	16	Sep
62.44	Adam Boyle	U20	13.09.99	3	Bedford	17	Jun
62.24	Tom Norton	U23	19.08.97	4	Loughborough	26	Feb
62.10	Don Baker	U20	31.01.00	1	Portsmouth	17	Sep

62.08	James Bongart	U23	30.07.96	1	London (LV)	8	Apr
62.08	Jack Magee	U23	17.12.97	1	Belfast	21	May
61.93	Jonathan Engelking	U23	13.12.97	1	Exeter	27	Jun
61.92	Harry Hollis		2.03.92	1	Loughborough	26	Aug
(30)							
61.45	Aiden Reynolds		5.07.94	1	London (LV)	4	Mar
61.03	Dominic Allen	U23	5.09.97	6	Loughborough	28	May
60.96	Michael Muckelt	U23	3.02.95	1	Portsmouth	20	Aug
60.71	Aaron Morgan		7.04.92	1	Carmarthen	25	May
59.96	Sonny Nash	U20	11.11.98	1	Gillingham	15	Apr
59.90	Richard Dangerfield	U23	17.09.97	4	Bedford	18	Jun
59.68	Scott Staples	U20	1.04.99	1	London (CP)	10	Jun
59.47	Allandre Johnson		8.12.85	4	London (CP)	11	Jun
59.39	Alfie Ingham	U20	10.01.98	4	Bedford	17	Jun
59.38	Chay Pollinger	U20	20.01.98	1	Peterborough	15	Apr
(40)							
59.28	Benji Pearson		23.05.94	2	Loughborough	22	Apr
58.41	James Lelliott		11.02.93	1	Bournemouth	2	Apr
58.36	Alexander Ingham	U23	12.01.96	1	Manchester (Str)	3	Jun
58.21	Joss Foot	U20	22.02.00	1	London (PH)	23	Jul
58.18	Will Marklew	U20	6.07.98	1D	Bedford	28	May
58.07	Ben Gregory		21.11.90	6D	Talence, FRA	17	Sep
57.88	Ben Fisher		25.04.86	6	Bedford	15	Jul
57.83	Luke Johnson		27.11.94	1	Horsham	21	May
57.64	James Bougourd		4.10.89	5	London (CP)	11	Jun
57.29	Simon Bennett	V40	16.10.72	2	Exeter	25	Jul
(50)							
56.91	Henry Rudd		22.01.94	1	Cambridge	14	May
56.82	Leon Bailey		19.07.91	1	Corby	14	May
56.80	Harry Lord	U20	14.08.98	1D	Princeton, USA	20	Apr
56.70	Alistair Prenn		7.11.94	2	Coral Gables, USA	18	Mar
56.67	Daniel Cole	U20	28.11.98	2	Ipswich	14	May
56.67	Jack Moncur	U20	19.12.98	2	Glasgow (S)	20	Aug
56.63	Jim Everard	V35	16.05.81	1	Gillingham	27	May
56.58	William Larkman	U20	28.07.98	1	Exeter	2	Jul
56.08	Connor Martin	U23	29.03.96	1	Plymouth	2	Apr
56.04	Dave Sketchley	V40	25.02.76	1	Birmingham	24	Jun
(60)							
55.98	James Finney	U23	7.04.96	Q	Bedford	30	Apr
55.85	Paddy Dunne	U20	2.12.99	3	Glasgow (S)	20	Aug
55.82	Harry Kendall	U23	4.10.96	1	Eastbourne	17	Jun
55.80	Richard Woodhall	V35	9.07.80	3	Birmingham	24	Jun
55.77	Matthew Stockton	U23	4.05.95	7	Loughborough	26	Feb
55.48	David Hall	U23	25.04.95	4D	Arona, ESP	4	Jun
55.45	Timothy Duckworth	U23	18.06.96	4D	Athens, USA	9	Apr
55.41	Adam Akehurst		13.09.87	2	Portsmouth	20	Aug
55.37	Tom Anstice	U23	27.03.97	1	London (TB)	15	Apr
55.36	Connor Swan	U23	14.07.96	1	Exeter	4	Jun
(70)							
55.19	Logan Didier	U20	5.04.99	1	Kingston	10	Jun
55.06	Luke Miller	U20	10.09.99	5	Birmingham	8	Jul
54.98	Chris Smith	V40	27.11.75	4	Grangemouth	26	Aug
54.80	Stephen Porter		22.09.89	5	Swansea	3	Jun
54.66	Charlie Granville	U23	22.10.95	2	Exeter	4	Jun
54.63	Harry Marshall	U23	10.06.96	3	Leiria, POR	15	Apr
54.61	Joshua Hodge	U20	23.05.00	7	Birmingham	8	Jul
54.58	Richard Woolley		17.08.89	1	Chelmsford	3	Jun
54.58	Bradley Eisnor	U23	24.11.96	1D	Sutton	10	Sep
54.56	Stephen Birse	V35	8.10.77	1	Gateshead	14	May
(80)							
54.49	Michael Tarran	V35	10.12.80	3	Exeter	25	Jul

54.38	Joseph Hardman	U20	4.03.99	1	Worcester	6	May
54.31	Edan Cole	U20	18.02.00	3	Portsmouth	20	Aug
54.29	Paul Dowding		11.08.92	2	Ipswich	20	May
54.29	Maxim Hall		29.12.86	1	Welwyn	17	Jun
54.03	Ivan Tapper	U20	4.04.99	1	Nuneaton	14	May
53.96	Lekan Ogunlana	U20	4.04.99	1	Kingston	14	May
53.86	Peter Glass		1.05.88	5D	Arona, ESP	4	Jun
53.74	David McKay	V35	22.09.80	1	Warrington	14	May
53.64	Aled Price	U23	14.12.95	1D	Oxford (H)	23	Jul
(90)							
53.51	Caspar Whitehead	U23	1.10.96	1	Basingstoke	8	Jul
53.31	David Brice		9.04.91	3B	Loughborough	28	May
53.28	Adam Hobson		4.05.93	Q	Bedford	30	Apr
53.04	Jonathan Harvey		12.09.83	2	Woodford	20	May
53.01	Sean McBride		31.07.90	1	Andover	21	May

Foreign

65.19	*Emmish Prosper (LCA)*		*8.09.92*	*1*	*Vieux-Fort, LCA*	*26*	*Feb*
62.61	*Rory Gunning (IRL)*		*3.05.84*	*1*	*Waterford, IRL*	*13*	*May*
61.39	*Andrea Manfroni (ITA)*		*15.03.89*	*1*	*Bath*	*2*	*Apr*
55.13	*Matthew Harris (AUS)*		*26.04.89*	*1*	*Tonbridge*	*19*	*Aug*
54.25	*Marcio Fernandes (CPV)*		*18.05.83*	*4F44*	*London (O)*	*18*	*Jul*
54.12	*Arran Davis (USA)*		*2.06.89*	*2*	*London (LV)*	*4*	*Mar*
53.87	*Justas Dauparas (LTU)*		*12.02.91*	*2*	*Cambridge*	*14*	*May*
53.70	*Kacper Kalwarski (POL)*	*U23*	*24.09.97*	*2*	*Yate*	*16*	*Jul*

Javelin - Under 18 - 700gm

74.06	Tom Hewson	U17	24.09.00	1	Dublin (S), IRL	5	Aug
66.45	Don Baker		31.01.00	1	Bedford	18	Jun
62.50	Max Law	U17	13.05.02	2	Birmingham	7	Jul
60.73	Joss Foot		22.02.00	1	Kettering	22	Apr
60.68	Finn O'Reilly	U17	2.10.01	3	Birmingham	7	Jul
60.23	Edan Cole		18.02.00	1	Crawley	4	May

Javelin - Under 17 - 700gm (1-3 above)

58.66	Pedro Gleadall		7.12.01	2	London (LV)	8	Apr
58.01	Oliver Wright		21.10.00	1	Hull	2	Jul
57.57	Jess Walker		19.09.01	4	Birmingham	7	Jul
56.98	Harry Ditchfield		3.10.01	3	Bedford	27	Aug
56.55	Kieron Sadler		15.10.00	4B	Loughborough	29	May
56.39	Kameron Duxbury		8.10.01	1	Sandown IOW	9	Jul
55.50	Sam Chance		21.10.00	1	Tipton	18	Jul
(10)							
54.75	Joshua Wise		24.11.01	2	Swindon	4	Jun
54.10	Luke Taylor		5.02.01	5	Bedford	27	Aug
53.24	Oliver McTear		2.01.01	1	Exeter	17	Jun
53.05	Frederick Thornhill		6.03.01	1	Street	22	Jun
52.79	Joel Cable		24.09.01	1O	Kingston	24	Jun
52.68	Ruairidh Scott-Brown		9.10.00	3	Dublin (S), IRL	5	Aug
52.60	Ben Copley	U15	6.11.02	1	Wakefield	13	Aug
52.54	Tom Dollery		20.08.02	1	Yeovil	13	May
52.04	Joe Hirst		26.01.02	1	Stevenage	10	Sep
51.68	Henry Gauntlett		4.09.01	5	Dublin (S), IRL	15	Jul
(20)							
51.23	Daniel Brown		20.03.02	7	Dublin (S), IRL	15	Jul
50.98	Connor Drew		2.02.01	1	Plymouth	2	Apr
50.43	Cameron Darkin-Price		18.11.00	2B	Loughborough	29	May
50.12	Joshua Thomas		13.10.00	8	Dublin (S), IRL	15	Jul

Javelin - Under 15 - 600gm

55.82	Archie Goodliff	26.09.02	1	Oxford (H)	18	Mar
55.74	Ben Copley	6.11.02	1	Bedford	26	Aug
55.66	Thomas Holmes	16.10.02	1	Swindon	23	Sep
55.13	Bradley Jenvey	23.12.02	1	Portsmouth	17	Sep
54.88	Benjamin East	19.11.03	1	Sandy	23	Sep
54.57	Ivo Pitts	16.11.02	2	Bedford	26	Aug
53.19	Charlie Davison	18.10.02	2	Birmingham	7	Jul
51.94	Elliot Odunaiya	23.02.03	3	Birmingham	7	Jul
51.14	Luke Robinson	7.05.03	4	Bedford	26	Aug
50.77 (10)	Lloyd Clarke	6.06.03	1	Newport	6	Aug
50.39	Joshua Miller	20.02.03	5	Birmingham	7	Jul
49.34	Charles McCaig	24.01.03	2	Exeter	17	Jun
49.25	Bradley James	23.09.03	1	Hornchurch	17	Sep
48.09	Thomas D'Souza	24.01.03	2	Wrexham	23	Sep
47.26	Jonah McCafferty	28.01.03	1	Bracknell	14	May
46.38	Sonny Baker	13.03.03	2	Exeter	20	Aug
45.90	Adam Lloyd	11.05.03	11	Birmingham	7	Jul
45.71	Jack Halpin	19.03.04	1	Whitley Bay	9	Apr
45.54	Cameron Harris	29.06.03	12	Birmingham	7	Jul
45.30 (20)	George Hopkins	1.06.03	3	London (CP)	19	Aug
45.21	Michael Graham	12.02.03	13	Birmingham	7	Jul
45.21	Darragh Kirk	16.10.02	3	Dublin (S), IRL	5	Aug
45.00	Marcus Kirby	21.11.02	2	Hull	16	Sep
44.81	Eddie Brown	25.09.02	1	Bromley	7	May

Javelin - Under 13 - 400gm

44.35	Oliver Yexley	29.09.04	1	Cambridge	2	Jul
41.56	Christopher Jones-Parker	4.01.05	1	Swindon	23	Sep
40.88	Aidan Hunt	30.10.04	1B	Portsmouth	17	Sep
40.60	Kian Hockaday	12.06.05	1	Portsmouth	17	Sep
40.38	Edward Enser	3.05.05	1	Portsmouth	6	Aug
38.69	Ben Conrathe	29.03.06	1	Boston	3	Sep
38.57	Toby Hughes	28.09.04	1	Erith	17	Sep
37.84	Lewis Forster	2.08.05	1	Wrexham	24	Sep
37.77	Jolyon Davis	4.11.04	1	Wrexham	23	Sep
37.71	Ben Jones	8.05.05	1	Yeovil	13	May

Decathlon

W = wind assisted under rules until 2009   w = wind assisted under rules since 2010

8163	Ashley Bryant			17.05.91	10	Götzis, AUT		28	May
	10.89w/2.8 7.70/0.1	14.20	1.97	49.69	14.69/0.6	42.52	4.50	67.54	4:31.86
	8049				11	London (OS)		12	Aug
	11.14/-0.8 7.44/-1.0	14.09	1.96	49.24	14.75/1.2	43.95	4.30	67.97	4:27.15
	7635				11	Talence, FRA		17	Sep
	11.37/-1.2 7.26/-0.8	13.41	1.96	50.43	14.70/-0.5	42.34	4.15	63.55	4:40.56
7973	Timothy Duckworth	U23		18.06.96	2	Athens, USA		9	Apr
	10.62/0.3 7.87/0.0	12.25	2.11	49.18	14.64/0.1	40.71	4.97	55.45	5:15.40
	7026				19	Eugene, USA		8	Jun
	10.54/-0.1 nj	13.42	2.13	49.69	14.30/2.0	41.52	5.01	52.19	5:20.56
7965	John Lane			29.01.89	2	Azusa, USA		13	Apr
	10.73/1.2 7.42w/3.3	13.06	2.05	48.53	14.57/1.5	43.06	5.00	48.68	4:50.54
	7362				2	Sydney (OP), AUS		31	Mar
	10.81/1.2 6.74/0.1	12.86	1.89	48.62	15.14/0.0	41.87	4.70	42.71	4:48.73
	7348				11	Tallinn, EST		2	Jul
	11.10/-1.9 7.02w/2.2	12.43	1.92	49.09	14.61/-0.4	42.05	4.60	45.36	5:00.30
	7162				23	Götzis, AUT		28	May
	10.76/0.5 7.43/0.0	12.50	2.00	49.41	14.51/1.4	40.99	4.90	48.85	dnf

7799	Ben Gregory					21.11.90	1	Barcelona (S), ESP		23	Jul
	11.30/0.0	7.11w/3.7	13.17	1.87	49.86	14.52/1.3	40.86	5.10	57.79	4:30.37	
	7669						5	Azusa, USA		13	Apr
	11.39/1.2	7.35/1.9	13.31	1.96	50.77	14.71/1.5	39.74	5.00	52.52	4:39.65	
	7667						9	Talence, FRA		17	Sep
	11.21/0.8	7.04/-0.5	12.43	1.90	50.23	14.66/-0.5	38.23	4.95	58.07	4:28.35	
	7530						10	Tallinn, EST		2	Jul
	11.35/-1.1	7.09/1.2	12.98	1.83	50.31	14.55/0.8	39.72	4.60	55.50	4:26.44	
7500	Curtis Mathews					22.01.92	1	Erith		17	Sep
	11.22/1.6	7.18/0.0	14.69	1.99	52.21	15.30/1.4	43.08	4.40	51.79	4:42.78	
	7170						1	Oxford (H)		23	Jul
	11.51/-0.7	7.12/1.3	12.99	1.89	51.81	15.50/-1.8	45.97	4.20	51.64	4:51.44	
	6736						6	Bedford		28	May
	11.72/-2.3	6.58/0.8	13.02	1.84	53.20	15.65/1.0	50.53	3.83	44.79	4:57.42	
7263	James Finney			U23		7.04.96	1	Bedford		28	May
	11.14/-1.7	6.93/1.8	11.51	1.96	49.16	14.72/1.6	33.92	4.63	54.01	4:59.05	
7248	Andrew Murphy					26.12.94	3	Woerden, NED		27	Aug
	11.27/-1.2	7.13/1.8	12.19	2.00	51.20	15.13/-1.0	40.03	4.42	47.25	4:46.99	
	7170						3	Bedford		28	May
	11.56/-2.3	6.84/0.5	13.24	1.96	51.07	15.05/1.6	39.25	4.63	45.28	4:48.21	
	7084						15	Tallinn, EST		2	Jul
	11.32/-1.1	6.66/1.7	12.82	1.98	51.35	15.16/-1.1	34.88	4.60	44.96	4:41.69	
7120	Peter Glass					1.05.88	7	Arona, ESP		4	Jun
	11.30/0.0	6.80/0.0	13.34	1.91	52.45	15.16/0.0	42.82	4.50	53.86	5:13.57	
7068	Lewis Church			U23		27.09.96	2	Erith		17	Sep
	11.80/1.6	6.70w/2.1	12.71	2.02	52.30	15.34/1.4	41.84	4.20	49.42	4:39.13	
7065	Harry Maslen			U23		2.09.96	4	Bradenton, USA		26	May
	11.25/1.5	6.97w/2.7	11.70	1.84	49.67	15.47/0.6	34.18	4.50	48.18	4:35.28	
	7010W						2	Commerce, USA		5	May
	11.06W/4.6	7.23W/9.4	11.89	1.90	50.72	15.40w/3.1	39.13	4.30	34.35	4:39.11	
(10)											
7048	Jack Andrew					12.10.91	4	Bedford		28	May
	11.60/-2.3	6.48/1.0	12.42	1.87	50.45	14.72/1.6	35.76	4.53	42.93	4:22.75	
	7028						1	Dilbeek, NED		30	Jul
	11.47/0.7	6.24w/3.5	11.93	1.90	49.80	14.87/0.7	33.58	4.70	40.01	4:17.43	
7038	David Hall			U23		25.04.95	9	Arona, ESP		4	Jun
	11.22/1.0	6.74/-1.1	12.91	1.94	49.18	15.76/0.5	32.18	3.80	55.48	4:35.30	
	6601						4	Oxford (H)		23	Jul
	11.42/-1.7	6.39/1.4	12.37	1.86	50.16	16.21/-1.8	35.46	3.70	50.93	4:48.92	
6691	Harry Kendall			U23		4.10.96	2	Oxford (H)		23	Jul
	11.46/-0.7	7.01/1.4	11.49	1.92	50.76	16.25/-0.6	37.04	3.70	50.96	4:56.46	
	6625						7	Bedford		28	May
	11.46/-2.7	6.79/1.0	10.81	1.90	51.33	16.35/1.1	32.77	3.93	54.50	4:47.74	
6538w	Harry Lord			U20		14.08.98	3	New Haven, USA		7	May
	11.86w/3.4	6.71/1.9	12.27	1.87	53.43	17.27w/3.0	35.26	4.15	51.97	4:37.27	
	6504						1	Princeton, USA		20	Apr
	12.02/-0.4	6.61/2.0	12.37	1.88	52.86	17.07/-1.5	33.57	3.98	56.80	4:42.18	
6530	Tom Chandler			U23		19.09.97	6	Woerden, NED		27	Aug
	11.57/-0.6	6.55/0.2	10.93	1.73	51.53	15.91/-0.8	33.01	4.32	48.52	4:39.30	
6523	Charlie Roe					28.04.92	8	Bedford		28	May
	11.53/-1.7	6.69/1.0	10.49	1.93	51.88	15.80/1.0	32.08	3.73	46.86	4:36.15	
34 performances to 6500 points by 16 athletes											
6448	Elliot Thompson					10.08.92	5	Oxford (H)		23	Jul
	11.82/-1.4	6.39/1.2	13.79	1.80	51.72	17.28/-0.6	38.39	4.00	39.45	4:32.04	
6364	Dan Pearce					11.09.91	10	Bedford		28	May
	11.84/-2.7	6.70/0.3	9.54	1.84	49.80	15.69/1.0	28.69	3.43	49.71	4:30.75	
6338	Alastair Prenn					7.11.94	6	Oxford (H)		23	Jul
	11.31/-1.4	6.50/1.5	12.76	1.77	51.13	16.92/0.9	36.26	3.30	51.87	4:59.75	
6317	Deo Milandu					30.10.92	1	Cudworth		27	Aug
	11.61/0.7	6.50/-0.2	12.58	1.84	54.11	15.80/-0.6	33.05	3.80	51.13	5:09.68	

6256	Maxim Hall			29.12.86	7	Oxford (H)		23	Jul
	11.70/-2.1	6.09/1.2	11.51	1.86	53.07	16.05/-1.8	34.27	4.20	51.40	5:20.81
6092	Douglas Stark			25.08.93	11	Bedford		28	May
	12.00/-2.1	5.88/1.3	13.00	1.78	56.15	16.81/1.6	40.05	3.93	48.80	4:57.98
6067	Saoirse Chinery-Edoo			1.11.93	1	Sutton		10	Sep
	11.1/1.4	6.13/1.8	11.49	1.65	52.13	16.05/1.8	45.18	3.70	40.62	5:33.15
6019W	Bradley Eisnor	U23		24.11.96	2	Sutton		10	Sep
	11.5/1.4	6.54W/4.3	10.55	1.80	53.48	16.05/1.8	37.66	3.60	54.58	5:53.37
	5956 with LJ 6.26/0.3								
5973	Tom Rottier	U23		15.11.96	9	Oxford (H)		23	Jul
	11.70/-1.7	6.26w/2.2	10.19	1.68	50.38	17.06/-0.6	27.76	4.40	35.20	4:44.39
5931	Kieran Russ	U23		1.10.95	12	Bedford		28	May
	12.33/-2.7	5.85/1.3	11.47	1.75	54.22	16.77/1.0	33.34	3.23	40.80	4:59.53
5778	Patrick Atkin			15.10.94	13	Bedford		28	May
	11.61/-2.7	5.92/1.0	10.22	1.66	51.34	16.90/1.1	30.63	3.13	47.58	4:43.30
5698	Harry Dalton			26.09.92	14	Bedford		28	May
	11.54/-1.7	5.74/0.4	12.77	1.78	54.34	17.47/1.1	35.02	3.03	52.41	5:28.61
5677	Joe Morris			20.03.93	3	Sutton		10	Sep
	11.4/1.4	5.82/0.2	12.02	1.53	55.63	16.51/1.8	36.32	3.60	48.40	5:15.70
5628	Justin Tarrant	U23		7.10.96	11	Oxford (H)		23	Jul
	12.12/-1.7	5.79/1.6	11.40	1.68	54.81	16.58/-1.8	37.73	3.80	39.42	5:16.20
(30)									
5582	Fionn Wright	U23		25.09.95	16	Bedford		28	May
	11.67/-2.7	6.75/1.0	10.42	1.69	52.60	19.05w/2.5	30.71	3.23	47.00	5:10.50
5517	Ben Hazell (1 hour)			1.10.84	1	Basingstoke		23	Sep
	12.61/-3.1	5.70	12.48	1.80	57.16	18.91	38.50	3.60	50.77	5:11.18
5432	Miguel Perera	U23		30.09.96	4	Sutton		10	Sep
	11.1/1.4	6.31/0.5	9.30	1.86	53.38	15.12/1.8	22.22	2.70	43.87	5:58.49
5432	Jamie Farrell			4.06.91	4	Erith		17	Sep
	11.58/1.1	6.15/1.8	9.98	1.57	51.87	16.79/0.9	30.17	2.30	39.37	4:40.76
5415	Thomas Hughes	U23		9.09.97	12	Oxford (H)		23	Jul
	11.80/-0.7	6.02/1.1	8.27	1.89	52.11	19.37/0.9	27.98	3.60	25.61	4:28.75
5376	Tom Grantham			12.02.83	3	Sheffield		3	Sep
	12.19/0.4	5.57/1.4	11.05	1.67	52.67	19.02/1.8	32.72	3.60	35.33	4:41.99
5365	Jordan Mitchell			23.12.94	2	Cudworth		27	Aug
	11.92/0.7	6.12/0.2	9.63	1.66	55.90	16.69/-0.6	26.31	3.50	42.18	5:03.11
5172	Michael Surman	U23		10.03.97	19	Bedford		28	May
	12.32/-2.1	5.84w/2.3	10.26	1.63	56.55	17.11/1.1	31.95	3.23	37.32	4:57.88
5065	Gordon Belch			7.01.92	2	Grangemouth		2	Jul
	12.16/-0.2	5.87w/2.5	9.68	1.58	55.19	18.58/1.6	29.74	3.60	38.95	5:07.83
4938	Cian O´Donnell			27.09.94	4	Hexham		23	Jul
	11.24/1.0	6.23/2.0	9.79	1.54	53.34	21.93/1.0	29.20	3.00	40.46	5:17.02
(40)									
4920	Thomas Rady			14.12.93	2	Sutton		10	Sep
	12.0/0.9	6.21/1.4	7.01	1.68	57.05	16.19/1.8	22.18	3.80	33.53	5:31.21
4914	Sean Reidy	V35		27.01.81	21	Bedford		28	May
	12.58/-1.6	5.70/0.0	8.53	1.63	52.63	16.24/1.1	22.76	2.63	29.53	4:41.14
4877	Ben Russell	U23		29.02.96	22	Bedford		28	May
	12.15/-2.1	5.68/1.6	8.68	1.81	55.31	16.21/1.1	26.14	2.93	25.76	5:23.99
4793	Alexander Hookway			19.05.91	5	Erith		17	Sep
	12.24/1.1	5.47/0.5	10.35	1.66	53.60	20.97/0.9	27.81	2.40	34.62	4:28.55
4788	Ashley Pritchard	V35		14.07.79	23	Bedford		28	May
	12.76/-1.6	5.38/-0.3	9.57	1.57	59.19	18.14/1.1	36.85	3.63	40.12	5:28.50
4778	Alexander Livingston	U23		25.01.96	2	Belfast		3	Sep
	12.45/-0.4	5.80	8.50	1.75	57.74	18.07/-1.4	28.91	3.80	29.55	5:34.05
4757	David Awde (1 hour)			6.01.84	2	Basingstoke		23	Sep
	12.58/-3.1	5.60	8.79	1.50	56.53	17.75	30.77	3.60	34.29	5:15.01
4755	Ben Morgan	U23		16.10.97	24	Bedford		28	May
	12.64/-1.6	5.83/2.0	8.34	1.60	53.92	17.78w/2.5	24.22	3.13	31.24	4:56.77

4747	Josh Phillipson		U23	5.09.95	4	Sheffield			3 Sep
	12.64/0.4	5.51w/2.4	10.08	1.61	57.60	19.24/1.8	32.12	3.40	39.15	5:16.64
4711	Paul Slater			24.04.89	6	Erith			17 Sep
	11.81/1.6	6.13/0.6	8.93	1.60	55.15	16.86/1.4	24.38	2.50	32.01	5:37.35
(50)									

4631	Mark Andrews			9.01.89	3	Sutton			10 Sep
	12.6/0.9	5.69/0.7	9.21	1.71	56.78	17.75/1.8	28.31	2.40	38.10	5:14.02
4516	Gareth Lewis			16.08.88	5	Sutton			10 Sep
	11.9/1.4	5.87/0.0	8.05	1.47	56.14	18.34/1.8	26.01	3.20	34.13	5:29.92
4503	James Taylor			1.10.93	2	Street			30 Apr
	12.72/-0.5	5.35w/2.7	10.43	1.60	59.43	22.35/-1,6	33.30	3.60	36.50	5:08.98
4475	James Slipper		U23	30.12.97	3	Street			30 Apr
	12.23/-0.5	5.50/0.8	11.09	1.57	56.74	19.74/-1.6	33.36	2.80	34.01	5:51.73
4436	Bilen Ahmet			21.01.85	7	Erith			17 Sep
	12.81/1.1	5.04/1.7	10.18	1.63	61.80	18.89/0.9	27.42	3.80	32.88	5:20.27
4272	Luke Williams			23.02.88	8	Erith			17 Sep
	12.30/1.1	5.31/1.9	6.59	1.45	57.13	19.49/0.9	21.25	3.50	35.29	5:03.03
4261	Tom Beckett		U23	29.05.96	14	Oxford (H)			23 Jul
	11.92/-2.1	6.16/1.2	8.57	1.68	54.91	18.41/0.9	18.83	2.20	28.85	6;04.72
4208	Dan Steel			29.01.93	4	Sutton			10 Sep
	12.4/0.7	5.84/0.6	9.02	1.74	59.09	20.08/1.8	22.30	2.90	32.10	5:39.09

Foreign

7252	*Peter Moreno (NGR)*			*30.12.90*	*2*	*Bedford*			*28 May*
	11.02/-1.7	*6.99/1.5*	*11.96*	*1.96*	*48.31*	*14.42/1.6*	*34.45*	*4.43*	*45.92*	*4:56.87*
7032	*Michael Bowler (IRL)*			*28.01.92*	*5*	*Monzón, ESP*			*2 Jul*
	11.28/-1.7	*6.99/1.1*	*12.06*	*1.92*	*49.95*	*15.22/0.3*	*35.84*	*4.10*	*48.34*	*4:44.69*
5428	*Abdullah Al Dawsari (KSA)U23*			*16.03.95*	*2*	*Sheffield*			*3 Sep*
	11.81/0.4	*5.97/-0.3*	*9.01*	*1.73*	*51.94*	*16.25/1.8*	*26.82*	*2.50*	*42.36*	*4:51.08*
5298	*Daniel Gregory (CAN)*			*11.04.93*	*17*	*Bedford*			*28 May*
	11.50/-2.3	*6.05/-1.1*	*9.21*	*1.78*	*52.32*	*17.83w/2.5*	*23.98*	*2.23*	*46.78*	*4:57.51*
5000	*Kevin Cranmer (MLT)*		*V35*	*14.06.79*	*20*	*Bedford*			*28 May*
	12.75/-1.6	*5.40/1.5*	*10.31*	*1.72*	*56.61*	*16.88/1.1*	*26.72*	*3.33*	*37.51*	*5:02.47*
4878	*Diego Lassini (ITA)*		*U23*	*10.02.96*	*1*	*Basingstoke (1 hour)*			*23 Sep*
	12.58	*5.95*	*11.07*	*1.75*	*57.84*	*18.57*	*25.46*	*3.80*	*35.42*	*5:40.02*

Decathlon - Under 20 with Under 20 implements

7377	Sam Talbot			17.02.99	1	Street			30 Apr
	10.97/1.1	7.19/1.8	12.92	1.96	49.89	14.36/-2.9	35.83	4.10	49.87	4:43.12
6747w	Caius Joseph			24.07.99	1	Boston			17 Sep
	11.02w/2.7	7.08w/2.3	10.94	1.83	50.95	15.49/1.1	38.73	3.90	43.12	4:55.60
	6469				1	Bedford			28 May
	11.45/-0.4	6.42/0.9	12.41	1.84	51.61	15.82w/2.2	37.53	3.93	42.23	5:01.37
6577	Liam Reveley			24.10.98	1	Boston			17 Sep
	11.38w/2.7	7.04w/2.2	11.73	1.92	51.35	15.31/1.1	34.23	3.60	38.80	4:51.71
6424w	Tyler Adams			26.11.98	3	Boston			17 Sep
	11.36w/2.6	6.51w/2.5	12.60	1.86	51.66	17.42/1.8	43.01	4.00	52.20	5:43.59
	5909				2	Kingston			25 Jun
	11.74	6.28/-1.9	12.29	1.92	52.82	18.21/-2.1	38.95	4.10	49.06	6:32.64
6417	Howard Bell			2.05.98	1	Grangemouth			2 Jul
	11.63/-1.1	6.81w/2.2	11.71	1.85	51.70	15.14/1.6	37.65	3.80	42.19	5:21.93
6316	Ryan Long			2.09.98	2	Bedford			28 May
	11.52/-0.4	5.61/0.7	12.49	1.78	51.45	14.78w/2.2	39.64	3.63	40.53	4:58.39
6200w	Charlie Ashdown-Taylor			19.09.99	4	Boston			17 Sep
	11.46w/2.7	6.29w/3.8	12.96	1.80	53.95	16.45/1.5	36.94	3.40	48.31	5:01.97
	5878				5	Bedford			28 May
	11.94/-2.2	6.13/0.8	13.03	1.81	55.62	16.40/1.3	39.86	3.43	40.38	5:18.35
6066	Joss Moffatt			31.01.00	3	Bedford			28 May
	11.73/-2.2	6.41/0.6	10.73	1.84	51.50	15.96w/2.2	32.44	3.03	43.04	4:45.44

```
5996w   Joshua Hodge                    23.05.00  5    Boston           17 Sep
        11.53w/2.6 5.94w/2.2 10.46 1.68 52.06 16.65/1.8 31.33 3.40 52.72 4:40.81
        5552                                      1    Telford          25 Jun
        11.6      5.91      10.23 1.70 52.3  17.4      29.94 2.65 54.39 4:52.7
5994    William Seed                    20.10.98  6    Boston           17 Sep
        11.22w/2.7 6.32/0.7  10.75 1.68 50.34 14.85w/2.1 34.85 2.50 37.94 4:55.84
(10)
5975    Cal McLennan                     1.05.99  1    Cudworth         27 Aug
        11.85/2.0 6.05w/2.1 11.75 1.66 52.16 16.50/-0.9 36.08 3.50 39.78 4:37.96
5969w   Reni Omotomilola                18.08.00  7    Boston           17 Sep
        11.19w/2.7 6.39w/2.2 10.92 1.86 52.93 15.16w/2.1 26.99 3.30 34.74 5:03.66
        5330                                      1    Bedford          25 Jun
        11.5      6.16      11.60 1.80 53.4  15.3      24.89 2.90 21.77 5:16.3
5915    Euan Urquhart                   25.01.98  3    Grangemouth       2 Jul
        11.53/-1.1 6.54/1.8 10.59 1.70 50.60 17.93/1.6 29.69 3.50 36.22 4:28.99
5905    Alexander Clegg                  2.06.98  4    Bedford          28 May
        11.98/-1.6 6.01/1.7 11.23 1.75 53.13 16.86/1.2 32.42 3.23 46.04 4:29.75
5811    Joseph Hobson                   29.04.98  4    Grangemouth       2 Jul
        11.29/-1.1 6.78w/2.1 13.24 1.85 53.49 15.54/1.6 33.05 3.20 45.56 dnf
5799    Cameron Hale                    14.09.99  1    Yeovil           25 Jun
        12.08/0.2 6.25/-0.9 12.20 1.83 56.66 16.43/1.3 40.26 3.30 48.16 5:35.96
5745    Nathan Langley                  18.03.00  7    Bedford          28 May
        12.27/-1.6 5.51/0.9 11.14 1.60 51.76 15.61/1,2 33.97 3.33 42.17 4:40.52
5718    Jamie Worman                    23.12.99  2    Yeovil           25 Jun
        11.94/0.2 6.29/0.0 10.87 1.71 51.44 16.09/1.3 31.41 3.10 34.71 4:52.43
5605    Daniel McFarlane                10.10.98  5    Grangemouth       2 Jul
        11.78/-1.1 6.09w/2.6 12.22 1.67 55.81 15.71/1,6 35.33 3.90 33.30 5:45,88
5509    Rhys Jackson                    14.01.00  8    Bedford          28 May
        12.06/-1.6 5.98/0.8 10.12 1.84 52.19 16.37/1.3 31.53 2.93 29.97 4:52.54
(20)
5501    Joseph Thurgood                 11.09.98  4    Kingston         25 Jun
        11.97     5.79/0.7  11.77 1.80 56.70 15.19/-0.3 31.53 3.20 37.15 5:25.42
5470w   Matthew Smith                   13.09.98 10    Boston           17 Sep
        12.57w/3.7 6.14/1.7 10.98 1.80 55.98 18.07/1.5 35.98 3.30 43.71 5:01.57
5467    Oscar Jopp                      29.09.99 11    Boston           17 Sep
        11.94w/2.2 6.17/1.2  9.97 1.80 59.17 15.52/0.9 27.70 3.80 40.63 5:28.3
5440w   Benjamin Taylor                 27.02.00 12    Boston           17 Sep
        11.75w/3.7 5.74/1.4  9.81 1.77 53.12 17.61w/2.1 28.86 2.60 47.71 4:47.59
        5237                                      6    Kingston         25 Jun
        12.03     5.82w/2.9  9.02 1.71 54.41 17.47/-0.3 30.50 2.50 49.48 4:58.42
5433    Glenn Aspindle                  22.06.98  4    Cudworth         27 Aug
        11.86/2.0 5.90/1.1  10.20 1.69 56.83 16.97/-0.9 30.45 3.60 47.02 5:15.53
5418    James Milburn                   24.09.99 13    Boston           17 Sep
        12.00w/2.2 5.71w/2.5 9.01 1.74 53.62 16.71/0.9 36.87 3.30 32.69 5:00.00
5392w   George Blake                    31.12.99 14    Boston           17 Sep
        11.63w/2.6 5.77w/3.6 10.17 1.50 53.79 17.06/1.8 30.50 3.60 37.36 4:54.55
5386    Kurt Cameron                    13.11.99 15    Boston           17 Sep
        11.60w/2.7 6.39/1.6  9.95 1.74 58.58 16.54/1.5 29.23 3.70 36.98 5:29.52
5383    Kellen Jones                     5.09.99  9    Bedford          28 May
        11.64/-0.4 6.40/0.6 10.57 1.63 54.82 16.87/1.3 29.91 3.33 36.06 5:20.70
5380    Todd Webster                    28.11.99 10    Bedford          28 May
        12.13/-2.2 5.74/0.6  9.59 1.87 55.39 17.78/1.3 26.74 3.93 44.01 5:20.42
(30)
5269    Daniel Carpenter                 7.11.99  4    Yeovil           25 Jun
        11.95/0.2 6.15/-0.4 11.14 1.65 54.51 17.97/1.3 33.26 2.80 33.92 4:54.53
5252    Edward Adams                     1.09.99  1    Oxford (H)       23 Jul
        11.92/0.0 6.17/1.4  10.08 1.56 55.15 15.84/-0.8 25.86 3.20 33.83 5:01.66
5217    Malachi Gair                    21.09.99  7    Kingston         25 Jun
        12.22     5.77/-1.4  9.62 1.89 54.42 16.51/-0.3 25.05 2.80 32.42 4:53.71
5164    Matthew Rushden                 29.03.98  5    Cudworth         27 Aug
        11.55/2.0 5.56/0.0  10.72 1.57 55.14 17.61/-0.9 34.52 3.20 33.90 5:12.60
```

5020	Jack Broadbent				8.07.00	18	Boston			17 Sep
	11.03w/2.7	6.14/1.9	9.54	1.74	52.99	15.44/1.1	25.81	2.90	26.70	7:03.19
5000	Michael Thompson				10.12.99	11	Bedford			28 May
	12.00/-0.4	5.91/1.3	10.95	1.72	59.33	16.38/1.2	32.21	2.93	34.63	5:42.72

Decathlon - Under 17 with Under 17 implements

6781	Joel McFarlane				9.10.00	1	Grangemouth			2 Jul
	11.49/-1.7	7.09/0.7	12.12	1.88	52.14	13.62/1.6	34.06	4.00	46.60	4:50.03
6167	Matthew Chandler				30.10.00	2	Manchester (SC)			13 Aug
	11.95/-1.3	6.35/-0.5	9.94	1.77	52.73	14.03/0.2	36.95	4.08	38.20	4:51.65
6104	Robert Worman				4.07.01	3	Manchester (SC)			13 Aug
	11.72/0.0	6.02/0.0	12.18	1.71	52.55	14.27/0.2	40.22	3.98	36.96	5:13.05
6030	Robert Farquhar				4.01.01	4	Manchester (SC)			13 Aug
	11.41/0.0	6.44/0.5	10.45	1.80	52.73	14.02/0.2	30.90	3.68	34.97	4:59.53
6018	Ollie Thorner				16.03.01	5	Manchester (SC)			13 Aug
	12.21/0.5	5.77/0.0	10.61	1.83	52.22	14.61/0.7	33.49	3.88	41.58	4:42.44
5399	Thomas Britt				25.12.00	7	Manchester (SC)			13 Aug
	12.37/-1.3	5.79/0.3	10.34	1.74	55.50	14.42/0.0	27.34	3.48	39.24	5:03.27
5327	Cameron Darkin-Price				18.11.00	8	Manchester (SC)			13 Aug
	12.20/-0.6	5.73/0.0	12.84	1.83	54.35	14.97/0.2	37.90	3.38	42.85	dnf
5305	Harri Wheeler-Sexton				25.11.00	9	Manchester (SC)			13 Aug
	12.09/0.0	5.82/0.0	11.89	1.71	55.93	14.51/0.2	33.24	3.08	30.47	5:18.98
5231	Scott Brindley				6.01.02	10	Manchester (SC)			13 Aug
	12.20/-1.3	6.12/0.0	9.29	1.77	54.30	14.65/0.7	19.44	3.68	24.79	4:55.53
5166	Pedro Gleadall				7.12.01	11	Manchester (SC)			13 Aug
	12.36/-1.3	6.01/0.0	9.59	1.80	56.60	15.42/-0.1	28.59	3.68	31.37	5:22.31
(10)										
5144	Callum Newby				16.06.02	12	Manchester (SC)			13 Aug
	12.08/-0.6	5.43/0.0	10.76	1.62	54.74	15.27/0.7	27.13	3.38	36.37	5:08.84
5080	Alexander Mackay				13.12.01	13	Manchester (SC)			13 Aug
	11.83/-0.6	5.54/0.0	10.86	1.56	55.83	14.34/0.0	32.94	3.38	30.19	5:44.98
5049	Ben Hughes				12.11.01	14	Manchester (SC)			13 Aug
	12.09/-1.3	5.72/0.0	9.61	1.74	57.21	14.90/0.0	24.78	2.48	42.61	5:00.77

Octathlon - Under 17 (* Octathlon score during Decathlon)

5409*	Joel McFarlane				9.10.00	*	Grangemouth			2 Jul
	7.09/0.7	34.06	46.60	52.14	13.62/1.6	1.88	12.12	4:50.03	(c)	
5207w	Jack Turner				11.07.01	1	Boston			17 Sep
	6.20w/2.3	36.70	45.89	52.67	13.59w/2.1	1.92	11.38	4:51.80	(a)	
	5177					1	Yeovil			25 Jun
	5.61	34.79	48.97	52.55	13.71/-0.4	1.92	11.88	4:40.72	(a)	
5129	Evan Campbell				17.05.01	2	Yeovil			25 Jun
	6.30	38.16	40.18	53.76	13.81/-0.4	1.83	14.04	5:01.80	(a)	
5041w	Lewis Davey				24.10.00	2	Boston			17 Sep
	6.60w/3.0	33.63	34.63	50.17	14.03w/2.1	1.77	10.59	4:38.06	(a)	
	4961					1	Bedford			25 Jun
	6.58	32.21	34.62	49.6	13.9	1.75	10.67	4:45.1	(a)	
5013	Rory Howorth				2.07.02	3	Yeovil			25 Jun
	6.09	31.83	40.27	52.30	15.09/-0.3	1.83	10.97	4:11.72	(a)	
5000w	Cameron Darkin-Price				18.11.00	3	Boston			17 Sep
	6.30w/3.1	40.79	47.66	54.20	14.50/1.2	1.77	13.02	5:16.76	(a)	
	4952					1	Milton Keynes			25 Jun
	6.23	38.53	48.35	54.9	14.1	1.84	12.47	5:18.0	(a)	
4922w	Stuart Bladon				13.01.02	4	Boston			17 Sep
	5.98w/3.5	31.76	49.47	53.44	14.50w/2.6	1.83	9.74	4:32.42	(a)	
	4643					1	Oxford (H)			23 Jul
	5.66/1.9	29.51	37.56	53.27	14.57/-1.9	1.86	9.35	4:31.61	(b)	
4866*	Matthew Chandler				30.10.00	*	Manchester (SC)			13 Aug
	6.35/-0.5	36.95	38.20	52.73	14.03/0.2	1.77	9.94	4:51.65	(c)	

4824*	Ollie Thorner			16.03.01	*	Manchester (SC)	13 Aug
	5.77/0.0	33.49	41.58 52.22	14.61/0.7	1.83	10.61 4:42.44	(c)
4817w	Oliver Herring			28.09.00	6	Boston	17 Sep
	6.54w/2.3	33.38	43.12 55.19	13.91w/2.1	1.77	10.91 5:02.00	(a)

(10)

4813w	Douglas Noel			1.03.01	7	Boston	17 Sep
	5.92w/3.2	42.48	43.81 55.32	15.12w/2.6	1.80	10.73 4:51.46	(a)
	4346				2	Kingston	25 Jun
	5.75/-0.2	29.95	40.26 55.46	15.58/-1.6	1.74	11.43 5:02.82	(a)
4785*	Rob Worman			4.07.01	*	Manchester (SC)	13 Aug
	6.02/0.0	40.22	36.96 52.55	14.27/0.2	1.71	12.18 5:13.05	(c)
	4546				4	Yeovil	25 Jun
	6.02	39.51	33.94 53.96	14.67/-0.4	1.62	11.44 5:05.91	(a)
4729*	Robbie Farquhar			4.01.01	*	Manchester (SC)	13 Aug
	6.44/0.5	30.90	34.97 52.73	14.02/0.2	1.80	10.45 4:59.53	(c)
4704	Dominic Ogbechie			15.05.02	8	Boston	17 Sep
	7.19w/2.7	27.63	48.74 51.14	14.39/1.2	1.95	NDR 4:56.66	(a)
4703w	Theo Adesina			20.05.02	9	Boston	17 Sep
	6.47w/3.3	24.46	35.56 53.67	14.20w/2.1	1.83	12.51 5:00.67	(a)
	(4662 with LJ 6.29/1.5)						
4688w	Kaya Cairney			19.02.01	10	Boston	17 Sep
	6.28w/3.7	27.88	42.35 51.78	14.43w/2.6	1.74	10.65 5:01.39	(a)
	4463				5	Yeovil	25 Jun
	5.90	24.44	38.46 51.15	15.05/-0.3	1.80	10.08 5:00.52	(a)
4643	Henry Thorneywork			4.11.00	11	Boston	17 Sep
	6.25w/2.8	27.18	37.70 51.89	14.39/1.2	1.74	10.90 4:56.47	(a)
4607w	Sam Bennett			2.02.01	12	Boston	17 Sep
	6.38w/2.3	30.08	37.73 54.21	12.92w/2.1	1.62	9.73 5:00.76	(a)
4591	Pedro Gleadall			7.12.01	1	Erith	17 Sep
	6.16	30.70	46.51 55.46	14.95/1.2	1.78	11.28 5:09.61	(d)
4572w	Coleman Corry			7.04.01	13	Boston	17 Sep
	6.06w/2.1	29.24	35.41 53.25	14.71w/2.6	1.65	10.56 4:32.20	(a)
	4481				1	Kingston	25 Jun
	5.77/0.2	27.91	36.20 52.67	14.88/-1.6	1.71	10.33 4:40.56	(a)

(20)

4550w	Jake Akindutire			15.09.00	14	Boston	17 Sep
	5.88w/3.2	34.60	34.83 53.78	14.59/1.2	1.74	11.13 5:01.64	(a)
	(4489 with LJ 5.59w/2.3)						
4539w	Alex Eaglestone			16.11.00	15	Boston	17 Sep
	5.63/1.9	26.91	45.39 52.10	15.12w/2.5	1.56	11.81 4:40.23	(a)
	4352				6	Yeovil	25 Jun
	5.14	25.47	43.45 51.97	15.52/-0.4	1.62	10.82 4:37.29	(a)
4478w	Freddie Reilly			10.02.02	16	Boston	17 Sep
	5.92w/2.6	27.69	32.77 52.42	14.84w/2.5	1.65	11.66 4:45.11	(a)
4468w	David Fullbrook			8.01.01	17	Boston	17 Sep
	6.19w/2.5	33.14	44.76 56.91	15.23w/2.5	1.77	9.67 5:02.93	(a)
	4298				4	Kingston	25 Jun
	5.83/0.6	26.61	44.87 57.20	15.73/0.5	1.83	10.79 5:06.57	(a)
4433	Ben Hughes			12.11.01	18	Boston	17 Sep
	6.06/2.0	29.75	39.80 56.61	14.56/1.2	1.71	10.23 4:51.69	(a)
4388w	Joel Cable			24.09.91	19	Boston	17 Sep
	5.80/2.0	39.20	48.84 57.87	15.29w/2.5	1.65	10.65 5:20.83	(a)
4366	Harri Wheeler-Sexton			25.11.00	2	Oxford (H)	23 Jul
	5.97/1.0	30.07	37.08 55.00	14.63/1.9	1.62	12.69 5:17.65	(b)
4359	Rico Cottell			22.11.01	2	Erith	17 Sep
	6.24	28.77	29.84 55.15	13.96/1.2	1.87	10.87 5:38.08	(d)
4342*	Thomas Britt			25.12.00	*	Manchester (SC)	13 Aug
	5.79/0.3	27.34	39.24 55.50	14.42/0.0	1.74	10.34 5:03.27	(c)
	4329				3	Street	30 Apr
	5.89w/2.5	30.28	37.97 54.97	14.80/-2.7	1.65	10.30 4:59.38	(a)
4337w	Ben Holdsworth			26.12.00	20	Boston	17 Sep
	5.17w/3.8	35.14	45.42 55.41	16.14/1.5	1.62	9.31 4:28.57	(a)

4331 Leon Martin-Evans 23.03.01 3 Bedford 25 Jun
5.62 24.84 44.21 55.3 14.9 1.90 9.93 5:09.6 (a)
4281 Henry Shields 11.09.00 4 Bedford 25 Jun
5.97 27.60 29.35 56.1 15.1 1.87 10.57 4:56.4 (a)
4279 Thomas Mullen 29.09.00 1 Belfast 3 Sep
5.98 28.57 37.76 54.91 16.42/-2.9 1.60 12.33 4:51.27 (e)
4276 Troy McConville 29.04.02 2 Belfast 3 Sep
6.05 20.74 37.90 55.61 14.96/-2.9 1.87 9.74 5:01.03 (e)
4249w Harrison Thorne 8.07.02 21 Boston 17 Sep
6.09w/3.8 25.46 32.93 55.92 14.45w/2.6 1.86 11.71 5:41.25 (a)
4242w Fraser Kilsby 18.01.01 22 Boston 17 Sep
5.69w/2.6 34.01 36.87 55.13 14.74w/2.5 1.59 10.71 5:13.98 (a)

Order of events
    a)   LJ, DT, JT, 400m, 100mh, HJ, SP, 1500m
    b)   LJ, 100mh, JT, 400m, HJ, SP, DT, 1500m
    c)* LJ, SP, HJ, 400m, 100mh, DT, JT, 1500m
    d)   LJ, DT, HJ, 400m, 100mh, SP, JT, 1500m
    e)   HJ, SP, 400m, LJ, 100mh, DT, JT, 1500m

Octathlon - Under 15

4336 Ben Hillman 16.04.03 1 Manchester (SC) 13 Aug
11.96/-0.1 30.79 2.80 55.32 11.78/-2.0 30.62 1.69 2:53.59
4160 Murray Fotheringham 4.06.03 2 Manchester (SC) 13 Aug
12.25/0.1 31.61 2.70 55.04 12.79/-2.0 22.92 1.78 2;47.58
3822 George Asprey 8.01.03 3 Manchester (SC) 13 Aug
12.39/0.1 29.08 2.20 55.03 13.58/-0.6 31.53 1.57 2:56.23
3799 Benjamin Henson 2.09.02 4 Manchester (SC) 13 Aug
12.80/0.1 42.48 2.60 55.74 12.83/-2.0 26.00 1.54 3:10.84
3764 Cameron Williams-Stein 29.04.03 5 Manchester (SC) 13 Aug
12.33/0.1 24.79 3.10 57.60 12.95/-2.0 20.10 1.63 2:56.32
3708 Kyle McAulay 9.04.03 6 Manchester (SC) 13 Aug
12.34/0.0 33.89 2.70 59.54 12.57/-2.0 26.27 1.66 3:17.49

Order of events: 100m, JT, PV, 400m, 80m H, DT, HJ, 1000m

Pentathlon - Under 15

3258 Joseph Harding 31.10.02 1 Boston 16 Sep
10.55/1.6 11.79 6.87w/2.4 1.68 2:17.81
2964w Archie Yeo 8.03.03 2 Boston 16 Sep
11.98w/2.4 10.82 6.58w/2.6 1.68 2:18.27
2646 1 Middlesbrough 24 Jun
12.6 10.58 5.86 1.63 2:19.2
2943w Jami Schlueter 26.10.02 3 Boston 16 Sep
11.31/1.6 11.47 6.20w/3.6 1.59 2:16.65
2889 1 Yeovil 24 Jun
11.56/-1.2 12.00 6.00 1.62 2:19.35
2906w Adam Lindo 21.10.02 4 Boston 16 Sep
12.29/1.1 11.07 6.26w/3.4 1.71 2:17.73
(2866 with LJ 6.08/1.8)
2890 Stephen Simmons 1.07.03 5 Boston 16 Sep
11.10/1.6 10.48 6.11w/2.1 1.62 2:18.09
2847 Murray Fotheringham 4.06.03 1 Oxford (H) 23 Jul
12.59/-0.1 10.03 5.76/0.3 1.77 2:11.35
2828w Craig Moncur 20.03.03 6 Boston 16 Sep
12.46w/2.4 12.97 5.76w/3.7 1.59 2:15.72
2818 2 Yeovil 24 Jun
12.56/-1.2 12.74 5.48 1.68 2:15.57
2822 Jordan Cunningham 22.12.02 1 Belfast 2 Sep
11.81/-0.4 12.50 5.94 1.61 2:22.90
2787 Kyle McAuley 9.04.03 2 Belfast 2 Sep
12.34/-0.4 12.36 5.71 1.76 2:26.07

2777w	Spike Gleave			4.12.02	7	Boston	16 Sep
	12.35w/2.1 10.35	5.65w/3.5 1.74	2:15.75			
	2647			4		Oxford (H)	23 Jul
	12.39/-0.1 9.66	5.62/1.0 1.71	2:19.43			

(10)

2753w	Gregory Zoppos			10.03.03	8	Boston	16 Sep
	11.62w/2.1 10.21	5.83w/2.5 1.56	2:15.02			
	(2726 with LJ 5.70/1.9)					
2709w	Adam Visram Cipolletta			21.02.03	9	Boston	16 Sep
	12.60w/3.0 8.76	5.71w/3.7 1.59	2:05.56			
	2599			2		Milton Keynes	24 Jun
	13.2 8.33	5.66 1.66	2:08.3			
2691	Benjamin Henson			2.09.02	2	Oxford (H)	23 Jul
	12.34/-0.1 11.91	5.41/-0.7 1.59	2:16.59			
2669	Elliott Harris			13.10.02	1	Milton Keynes	24 Jun
	11.5 10.89	6.17 1.60	2:31.3			
2661w	George Seery			20.08.03	10	Boston	16 Sep
	11.87w/2.4 9.83	5.58w/3.8 1.62	2:17.49			
2656	George Asprey			8.01.03	3	Oxford (H)	23 Jul
	13.37/-0.1 11.10	5.53/1.7 1.65	2:13.45			
2619	Elliott Evans			3.09.03	3	Kingston	24 Jun
	12.3/0.6 11.42	5.62/0.2 1.56	2:19.43			
2608	Lewis Swaby			7.06.03	4	Kingston	24 Jun
	12.4/-0.5 8.76	5.73/-0.1 1.71	2:18.16			
2607w	Jude Thorne			14.09.02	12	Boston	16 Sep
	12.41w/2.4 9.14	5.39w/2.7 1.50	2:06.23			
2593	Tom Ridley			7.08.03	13	Boston	16 Sep
	12.84/2.0 9.86	4.80/2.0 1.83	2:16.60			

(20)

2592	Ben Hillman			16.04.03	1	Cardiff	3 May
	11.99w/3.6 10.03	5.77 1.60	2:24.08			
2592w	Callum Gregson			16.11.02	14	Boston	16 Sep
	11.95w/2.1 8.33	5.32w/2.1 1.71	2:16.72			
	2514			5		Kingston	24 Jun
	12.0/-0.5 8.07	5.18/-0.4 1.74	2:18.74			
2564	Immanuel Feyi-Waboso			20.12.02	1	Swansea	24 Jun
	11.93 11.06	5.42 1.77	2:37.95			
2553w	William Scammell			1.12.02	16	Boston	16 Sep
	11.88w/2.1 9.90	5.64w/3.0 1.56	2:23.13			
	2521			3		Yeovil	24 Jun
	12.85/-1.2 11.14	5.49 1.59	2:22.76			
2544	Dale Turner			25.06.03	2	Middlesbrough	24 Jun
	12.4 11.24	5.29 1.57	2:19.0			
2540w	Sebastian Wallace			7.09.03	17	Boston	16 Sep
	11.63w/2.1 9.99	5.98w/2.3 1.59	2:34.62			
2539	Joseph Fischer			12.03.03	2	Brentwood	24 May
	11.7 9.97	6.03 1.59	2:32.6			
2532w	Jamie Russell			11.08.03	1	Leicester	4 Jun
	13.11w/2.9 10.15	5.64 1.56	2:19.41			
2511	Sam Sanusi			13.11.03	3	Bedford	24 Jun
	11.9 11.20	4.87 1.65	2:23.9			

Order of events: 80mh, SP, LJ, HJ, 800m in various orders
Different events – Order: 80mh, LJ, 200m, SP, 800m

2989	Murray Fotheringham			4.06.03	1	Grangemouth	3 Jun
	12.36 5.94	24.40 9.28	2:07.18			
2970	Jordan Cunningham			22.12.02	1	Antrim	14 Sep
	11.94w/2.5 5.76	24.94 12.99	2:20.51			
2829	Kyle McAuley			9.04.03	2	Grangemouth	3 Jun
	12.38 5.95	24.98 12.22	2:26.99			
2537	Adam Hoole			25.05.03	3	Grangemouth	3 Jun
	12.29 5.32	24.66 9.91	2:31.76			

Pentathlon - Under 13

2319	Samuel Ball			18.10.04	1	Tonbridge		28 Aug
	11.75	9.99	1.47	5.72	2:30.81			
2025	Luke Ball			28.10.04	1	Exeter		24 Sep
	12.35/-1.2	9.44	1.61	4.94	2:45.51			
1989	Jake Minshull			11.10.04	2	Tonbridge		28 Aug
	12.33	7.49	1.44	4.74	2:23.30			
1959	Ridwaan Ahmed			10.10.04	3	Tonbridge		28 Aug
	12.55	8.91	1.41	4.99	2:33.04			
1930w	Fergus MacGilip			17.03.05	1	Grangemouth		1 Jul
	12.25w/2.4	7.82	1.39	4.85/1.8	2:29.10			
1895	Finn O'Neill			13.10.05	1	Belfast		2 Sep
	13.72/-0.1	8.09	1.47	4.48	2:21.69			
1837	Oliver Atkinson			16.10.04	1	Stockport		9 Sep
	13.2	7.25	1.53	4.61	2:29.44			
1742	Lexx McConville			9.10.04	2	Belfast		2 Sep
	12.85/0.2	8.90	1.59	4.62	3:05.32			
1726	Isaac Ketterer			9.01.05	2	Exeter		24 Sep
	12.98/-1.2	7.55	1.28	4.44	2:26.76			
1684	Freddie Clemons			21.01.05	2	Leicester		4 Jun
	13.73/0.5	7.19	1.44	4.58	2:33.86			

Order of events: 75mh, SP, HJ, LJ, 800m in various orders.

Heptathlon (Indoors)

6165	Tim Duckworth		U23	18.06.96	2	College Station, USA		11 Mar
	6.77	7.77	13.09	2.16		8.10	5.26	3:04.24
	6006				1	Lincoln, USA		4 Feb
	6.81	7.63	13.02	2.16		8.10	5.12	3:10.75
5975	Ashley Bryant			17.05.91	2	Prague, CZE		29 Jan
	7.08	7.79	14.32	1.98		8.10	4.50	2:40.54
5834	Ben Gregory			21.11.90	1	Glasgow		5 Mar
	7.29	7.30	13.22	1.99		8.22	4.97	2:40.92
5832	Liam Ramsay			18.11.92	1	Sheffield		8 Jan
	7.00	7.21	13.58	2.05		8.28	4.41	2:38.86
5712	John Lane			29.01.89	2	Sheffield		8 Jan
	7.04	7.19	13.48	1.96		8.27	4.91	2:54.14
5512	Aiden Davies		U23	26.12.95	11	Prague, CZE		29 Jan
	7.02	7.24	13.17	1.92		8.84	4.40	2:42.56
5402	Andrew Murphy			26.12.94	2	Glasgow		5 Mar
	7.32	6.85	12.39	1.93	8.40	4.77	2:50.77	
5392	James Finney		U23	7.04.96	4	Sheffield		8 Jan
	7.16	7.02	11.90	1.99		8.41	4.41	2:52.56
5275	Lewis Church		U23	27.09.96	1	London (LV)		17 Dec
	7.50	6.81	13.32	1.99		8.63	4.30	2:48.57
5209	Angus Sinclair		U23	22.02.95	2	Birmingham, USA		21 Feb
	7.25	6.60	12.67	2.00		8.69	4.30	2:53.96
(10)								
5123	Charlie Roe			28.04.92	5	Sheffield		8 Jan
	7.28	6.89	11.86	1.90		8.76	3.81	2:40.00
5100	Maxim Hall			29.12.86	6	Sheffield		8 Jan
	7.25	6.64	12.21	1.87		8.72	4.31	2:51.05
5027	Harry Kendall		U23	4.10.96	2	London (LV)		17 Dec
	7.22	6.77	11.27	1.93		8.91	4.20	2:54.45
5012	Harry Maslen		U23	2.09.96	4	Pittsburg, USA		9 Dec
	7.18	6.46	11.40	1.74		8.61	4.25	2:43.38
5006	Elliot Thompson			10.08.92	4	Glasgow		5 Mar
	7.28	6.53	13.70	1.78		9.07	4.07	2:43.97
4972	Deo Milandu			30.10.92	7	Sheffield		8 Jan
	7.37	6.57	12.41	1.81		8.51	4.21	2:56.11

4880	Tom Rottier			U23	15.11.96	9	Sheffield		8	Jan
	7.38	6.28	10.59	1.81		8.98	4.31	2:40.45		
4726	Timothy Stephens			U23	1.11.97	11	Sheffield		8	Jan
	7.51	6.65	10.15	1.81		9.06	3.61	2:36.85		
4646	Jack Phipps				2.04.94	3	London (LV)		17	Dec
	7.11	6.45	10.06	1.69		9.10	4.60	3:09.19		
4645	Harry Lord			U20	14.08.98	3	Princeton, USA		2	Feb
	7.67	6.41	12.52	1.83		9.41	3.85	2:48.29		

Heptathlon - Under 20 (Indoors)

5109	Joseph Hobson				29.04.98	1	Sheffield		8	Jan
	7.08	6.95	13.14	3.56		8.45	1.96	3:02.51	(PV/HJ)	
5068	Howard Bell				2.05.98	10	Prague, CZE		29	Jan
	7.38	6.68	12.38	1.92		8.55	3.80	2:46.07		
4967	Dylan Carlsson-Smith				26.07.98	3	Sheffield		8	Jan
	7.54	6.33	12.68	4.36		8.56	1.87	2:55.62	(PV/HJ)	
4960	Liam Reveley				24.10.98	1	Glasgow		5	Mar
	7.41	6.40	12.78	2.00		8.71	3.77	2:54.28		
4862	Euan Urquhart				25.01.98	2	Glasgow		5	Mar
	7.36	6.85	10.89	1.76		9.06	3.77	2:37.09		
4782	Ben Clarke				30.10.98	4	Sheffield		8	Jan
	7.47	6.19	10.37	3.46		8.57	1.93	2:40.49	(PV/HJ)	
4700	Caius Joseph				24.07.99	6	Sheffield		8	Jan
	7.30	6.67	11.43	3.56		8.80	1.78	2:55.00	(PV/HJ)	
4676	Ryan Long				2.09.98	7	Sheffield		8.	Jan
	7.36	6.49	10.80	3.76		8.44	1.78	3:01.20	(PV/HJ)	

Heptathlon - Under 17 (Indoors)

4948	Joel McFarlane				9.10.00	1	Sheffield		12	Mar
	7.50	6.90	12.28	1.91		8.66	3.81	2:55.31		
4562	Robbie Farquhar				4.01.01	2	Sheffield		12	Mar
	7.29	6.45	10.17	1.79		8.44	3.41	3:01.87		
4551	Matthew Chandler				30.10.00	3	Sheffield		12	Mar
	7.55	6.18	10.58	1.85		8.66	3.71	2:58.80		
4468	Theo Adesina				20.05.02	4	Sheffield		12	Mar
	7.29	6.91	10.69	1.79		8.78	2.91	3:04.85		
4410	Lewis Davey				24.10.00	5	Sheffield		12	Mar
	7.46	6.44	10.66	1.73		8.63	2.91	2:52.24		
4345	Harri Wheeler-Sexton				25.11.00	6	Sheffield		12	Mar
	7.41	6.45	12.80	1.61		8.37	2.81	3:08.14		
4259	Pedro Gleadall				7.12.01	2	London (LV)		17	Dec
	7.51	5.86	10.73	1.80		9.30	3.80	3:07.41		
4236	Thomas Britt				25.12.00	7	Sheffield		12	Mar
	7.73	5.92	11.35	1.67		8.98	3.61	2:58.62		
4164	Evan Campbell				17.05.01	8	Sheffield		12	Mar
	7.71	6.07	13.45	1.88		8.79	2.11	3:09.90		
4133	Rory Howorth				2.07.02	9	Sheffield		12	Mar
	8.07	5.86	10.97	1.70		9.24	3.01	2:38.00		
4118	Daniel Roffey				6.09.01	3	London (LV)		17	Dec
	7.74	6.20	8.50	1.83		9.18	2.90	2:50.34		
4108	Stuart Bladon				13.01.02	4	London (LV)		17	Dec
	7.60	5.65	10.79	1.83		8.74	2.10	2:49.99		
4104	Douglas Noel				1.03.01	10	Sheffield		12	Mar
	7.87	5.98	11.98	1.79		9.55	3.11	2:57.70		

Pentathlon - Under 15 (Indoors)

3132	Joseph Harding			31.10.02	1	Sheffield		12	Mar
	8.25	6.61	11.00	1.64	2:20.33				
2911	Ben Hillman			16.04.03	2	Sheffield		12	Mar
	8.90	6.02	10.61	1.61	2:12.71				

2831	Murray Fotheringham		4.06.03	1	Glasgow	4	Mar
	9.52	5.88	9.15	1.74	2:08.63		
2612	Oliver Early		26.05.04	1	London (LV)	16	Dec
	8.78	5.50	8.98	1.66	2:23.89		
2558	Kyle McAuley		9.04.03	2	Glasgow	4	Mar
	9.25	5.35	10.33	1.71	2:27.05		
2525	Samuel Ball		18.10.04	2	London (LV)	16	Dec
	9.32	5.63	8.60	1.66	2:21.82		
2491	Elliott Harris		13.10.02	4	Sheffield	12	Mar
	8.73	5.60	9.12	1.61	2:33.81		
2470	Benjamin Henson		2.09.02	6	Sheffield	12	Mar
	9.51	4.98	11.52	1.52	2:18.42		
2463	Archie Yeo		8.03.03	7	Sheffield	12	Mar
	9.53	5.87	9.65	1.55	2:25.30		

Order of events: 60mh, LJ, SP, HJ, 800m

Pentathlon - Under 13 (Indoors)

1945	Jake Minshull		11.10.04	1	London (LV)	26	Mar
	10.10	4.51	8.19	1.45	2:23.69		
1345	Oliver Robertson		27.09.04	2	London (LV)	26	Mar
	10.74	4.35	5.41	1.33	2:42.81		
1330	Etienne Munday		6.11.04	3	London (LV)	26	Mar
	11.23	4.48	5.63	1.36	2:42.10		
1301	Daniel Martin		22.03.06	1	Glasgow	4	Mar
	10.75	4.21	6.62	1.23	2:45.52		
1298	Caleb McLeod		15.05.06	2	Glasgow	4	Mar
	11.24	4.19	4.86	1.20	2:26.95		

Order of events: 60mh, LJ, SP, HJ, 800m

1 Mile Walk

5:31.08	Tom Bosworth		17.01.90	1	London (O)	9	Jul
6:01.93	Callum Wilkinson	U23	14.03.97	1	Leeds	4	Oct
6:02.30	Guy Thomas	U23	1.07.97	5	London (O)	9	Jul
6:09.32	Christopher Snook	U20	14.01.00	6	London (O)	9	Jul

2000 Metres Walk - Track

7:29.19+	Tom Bosworth		17.01.90	1m	Birmingham	2	Jul

Under 13

11:00.19	Christian Hopper		7.09.04	1	Erith	16	Sep
11:30.3	Owen Bradshaw		7.12.04	1	Cudworth	13	May
10:33 Road				1	Sheffield	24	Mar

3000 Metres Walk - Track

11:13.09	Callum Wilkinson	U23	14.03.97	1	Leeds	12	Jun
	11:22.29+			2m	Birmingham	2	Jul
	11:31.43i+			2m	Bratislava, SVK	29	Jan
	11:35.0i			1	Sheffield	8	Jan
	11:57.7+			1m	Bedford	18	Jun
	12:28.72			1	Leeds	22	Mar
11:15.26+	Tom Bosworth		17.01.90	1m	Birmingham	2	Jul
	11:16.43i+			1m	Sheffield	12	Feb
11:19.10	Cameron Corbishley	U23	31.03.97	2	Leeds	4	Oct
12:00.91	Dominic King		30.05.83	1	Chelmsford	14	May
12:03.90B	Guy Thomas	U23	1.07.97	1	Tonbridge	17	Apr
	12:20.49			1	Manchester (SC)	16	Aug
	12:22.4i			2	Sheffield	8	Jan
12:25.73	Christopher Snook	U20	14.01.00	2	Manchester (SC)	16	Aug
12:31.56	Tom Partington	U20	8.07.99	3	Manchester (SC)	16	Aug
12:31.76	Daniel King		30.05.83	2	Chelmsford	14	May

| 12:58.61i | Luc Legon | U23 | 12.09.97 | 1 | London (LV) | 22 | Jan |
| 13:18.8 | Adam Cowin | | 27.06.94 | 1 | Douglas IOM | 23 | Jul |

Under 15

14:48.89	Rory Taylor		6.12.02	1	Pontcharra, FRA	17	Jun
15:27.33	Alex MacHeath		17.02.04	1	Ashford	14	May
	15:15 Road			1	Coventry	29	Apr
15:27.95	Jack Childs		11.06.03	7	Tonbridge	17	Apr

5000 Metres Walk - Track

14:48.89	Rory Taylor		6.12.02	1	Pontcharra, FRA	17	Jun
15:27.33	Alex MacHeath		17.02.04	1	Ashford	14	May
	15:15 Road			1	Coventry	29	Apr
15:27.95	Jack Childs		11.06.03	7	Tonbridge	17	Apr

Under 17

| 26:15.00 | George Wilkinson | | 25.04.02 | 1 | Boston | 16 | Sep |

5 Kilometres Walk - Road

19:54+	Tom Bosworth		17.01.90	3m	London	13	Aug
	19:56+			1m	Coventry	5	Mar
	20:18+			5m	Poděbrady, CZE	21	May
	20:50+			1m	Rio Maior, POR	1	Apr
20:10+	Callum Wilkinson	U23	14.03.97	33m	London	13	Aug
	20:18+			2m	Coventry	5	Mar
	20:22+			10m	Poděbrady, CZE	21	May
20:37+	Cameron Corbishley	U23	31.03.97	3m	Coventry	5	Mar
21:24+	Dominic King		30.05.83	3m	Leeds	25	Jun
21:43+	Guy Thomas	U23	1.07.97	m	La Coruña, ESP	3	Jun
21:51+	Daniel King		30.05.83	m	La Coruña, ESP	3	Jun

where superior to track

| 22:51 | Adam Cowin | | 27.06.94 | 1 | Ronaldsway, IOM | 8 | Jan |
| 22:55 | Gianni Epifani | V45 | 22.02.71 | 1 | Douglas IOM | 12 | Oct |

10000 Metres Walk - Track

41:37.44	Cameron Corbishley	U23	31.03.97	1	Bedford	18	Jun
46:18.98	Christopher Snook	U20	14.01.00	2	Bedford	18	Jun
47:41.10	Tom Partington	U20	8.07.99	3	Bedford	18	Jun
49:47.80	Luc Legon	U23	12.09.97	4	Bedford	18	Jun

10 Kilometres Walk - Road

39:50+	Tom Bosworth		17.01.90	3m	London	13	Aug
	40:14+			5m	Poděbrady, CZE	21	May
	40:20			1	Coventry	5	Mar
	40:39+			1m	Lugano, SUI	19	Mar
	41:15+			1m	Rio Maior, POR	1	Apr
	42:15			22	Mudu, CHN	25	Sep
40:46+	Callum Wilkinson	U23	14.03.97	m	Poděbrady, CZE	21	May
	40:46+			40m	London	13	Aug
	40:59			2	Coventry	5	Mar
	41:03			1	Coventry	29	Apr
	41:51+			10m	Lugano, SUI	19	Mar
41:26	Cameron Corbishley	U23	31.03.97	3	Coventry	5	Mar
	41:55			2	Coventry	29	Apr
42:45+	Dominic King		30.05.83	3m	Leeds	25	Jun
43:24+	Guy Thomas	U23	1.07.97	m	La Coruña, ESP	3	Jun
44:20+	Daniel King		30.05.83	m	La Coruña, ESP	3	Jun
44:23	Christopher Snook	U20	14.01.00	19	Poděbrady, CZE	21	May
45:10	Tom Partington	U20	8.07.99	2	Leeds	25	Jun
46:19	Adam Cowin		27.06.94	1	Douglas IOM	19	Mar

20 Kilometres Walk - Road

1:20:58	Tom Bosworth		17.01.90	2	Rio Maior, POR	1	Apr
1:21:21				4	Poděbrady, CZE	21	May
1:21:53				2	Lugano, SUI	19	Mar
1:24:59				1	Leeds	25	Jun
1:27:48				20	Wuzhong, CHN	24	Sep
1:22:17	Callum Wilkinson	U23	14.03.97	10	Poděbrady, CZE	21	May
1:23:47				8	Lugano, SUI	19	Mar
1:23:54				41	London	13	Aug
1:24:59				2	Leeds	25	Jun
1:26:00	Cameron Corbishley	U23	31.03.97	11	Poděbrady, CZE	8	Apr
1:27:26				36	Poděbrady, CZE	21	May
1:31:20				18	Lugano, SUI	19	Mar
1:26:09	Dominic King		30.05.83	4	Leeds	25	Jun
1:27:20				34	La Coruña, ESP	3	Jun
1:29:28				47	Poděbrady, CZE	21	May
1:29:36				1	Douglas IOM	3	Sep
1:32:57+				36m	London	13	Aug
1:33:19+				15m	Dudince, SVK	25	Mar
1:28:38	Guy Thomas	U23	1.07.97	37	La Coruña, ESP	3	Jun
1:29:10	Daniel King		30.05.83	39	La Coruña, ESP	3	Jun
1:41:27	Tom Partington	U20	8.07.99	3	Douglas IOM	3	Sep

50 Kilometres Walk - Road

4:04:16	Dominic King		30.05.83	13	Dudince, SVK	25	Mar

4 x 100 Metres

37.47	National Team			1	London (O)	12	Aug
	(Chijindu Ujah, Adam Gemili, Danny Talbot, Nethaneel Mitchell-Blake)						
37.76	National Team			2h1	London (O)	12	Aug
	(Chijindu Ujah, Adam Gemili, Danny Talbot, Nethaneel Mitchell-Blake)						
38.08	National Team			1r1	Villeneuve d'Ascq, FRA	24	Jun
	(Chijindu Ujah, Zharnel Hughes, Danny Talbot, Harry Aikines-Aryeetey)						
38.32	National Team			1h3	Nassau, BAH	22	Apr
	(Chijindu Ujah, Zharnel Hughes, Adam Gemili, Danny Talbot)						
38.45	National Team			1	Loughborough	21	May
	(Richard Kilty, Harry Aikines-Aryeetey, Danny Talbot, Joel Fearon)						
39.11	National Under 23 Team	U23		2	Bydgoszcz, POL	16	Jul
	(Theo Etienne, Kyle de Escofet, Reuben Arthur, Oje Edoburun)						
39.35	England			3	London (O)	9	Jul
	(Andrew Robertson, Deji Tobais, Confidence Lawson, Emmanuel Stephens)						
39.40	National Under 23 Team	U23		5	London (O)	9	Jul
	(Theo Etienne, Kyle de Escofet, Reuben Arthur, Christopher Stone)						
39.43	England			2	Loughborough	21	May
	(Theo Etienne, Ojie Edoburun, Reuben Arthur, Reece Prescod)						
39.45	National Under 23 Team	U23		1h1	Bydgoszcz, POL	16	Jul
	(Theo Etienne, Kyle de Escofet, Reuben Arthur, Ojie Edoburun)						
39.50	Wales			6	London (O)	9	Jul
	(James Griffiths, Sam Gordon, Tom Williams, Kristian Jones)						
39.67	National Junior Team	U20		4	Grosseto, ITA	23	Jul
	(Dominic Ashwell, Oliver Bromby, Kristian Jones, Eden Davis)						
39.80	England			1	Manchester (SC)	16	Aug
	(Aidan Syers, Ronnie Wells, Andy Robertson, Christopher Stone)						
39.84	National Junior Team	U20		1h1	Grosseto, ITA	23	Jul
	(Dominic Ashwell, Oliver Bromby, Kristian Jones, Eden Davis)						
39.91	Wales			3	Loughborough	21	May
	(Dewi Hammond, Sam Gordon, Tom Williams, Kristian Jones)						
39.93	National Junior Team	U20		1	Mannheim, GER	1	Jul
	(Dominic Ashwell, Oliver Bromby, Nick Stewart, Rechmial Miller)						

39.94	National Junior Team	U20	4	Loughborough	21	May

(Cameron Tindle, Oliver Bromby, Nick Stewart, Rechmial Miller)

39.98	National Junior Team	U20	3	Mannheim, GER	2	Jul

(Dominic Ashwell, Oliver Bromby, Nick Stewart, Jona Efoloko)

40.02	Wales		1	Oordegem, BEL	17	May

(James Griffiths, Sam Gordon, Tom Williams, Kristian Jones)

40.07	Wales		2	Manchester (SC)	16	Aug

(Kristian Jones, Tom Williams, Dewi Hammond, Sam Gordon)

Additional National Teams

40.35	Northern Ireland		7	London (O)	9	Jul

(Leon Reid, Jason Smyth IRL, Dean Adams IRL, Christian Robinson IRL)

40.68	Scotland		1	Belfast	5	Jul

(Allan Hamilton, Adam Clayton, Fraser Angus, Adam Thomas)

Club Teams

40.47	Loughborough University		5	Loughborough	21	May
40.66	Birchfield Harriers		1	Bedford	15	Jul
40.68	East London University		1	Bedford	1	May
40.85	Sale Harriers Manchester		1	Manchester (SC)	20	Aug
41.11	Croydon Harriers	U20	1	Croydon	28	May
41.19	Newham & Essex Beagles		2	London (LV)	3	Jun
41.23	Blackheath & Bromley H AC		1rB	Bedford	15	Jul
41.25	Shaftesbury Barnet Harriers		2	Bedford	15	Jul
41.44	Harrow AC		1	Swansea	3	Jun
41.44	Swansea Harriers		2	Swansea	3	Jun
41.49	Cardiff Metropolitan University		2	Bedford	1	May
41.63	Enfield & Haringey AC		1	Yate	3	Jun
41.81	Thames Valley Harriers		3	Sheffield	6	May
41.9	Croydon Harriers		1	Gillingham	15	Apr
41.95	Cardiff AAC		3	Manchester (SC)	20	Aug
42.0	Oxford University		1	Cambridge	14	May
42.25	Shaftesbury Barnet Harriers	U20	2	Brno, CZE	16	Sep
42.27	City of Sheffield & Dearne AC		4	Sheffield	6	May
42.30	Blackheath & Bromley H AC	U20	2	London (O)	9	Jul
42.32	Rugby & Northampton AC		1rD	Bedford	15	Jul

Additional Under 20 Teams (1-6 above)

41.30	England South		1	Cardiff	12	Jul
41.60	Surrey Schools		1	Birmingham	8	Jul
41.66	Wales		2	Cardiff	12	Jul

Additional Under 20 Club Teams (1-3 above)

42.8	Harrow School		1	Oxford	4	May
42.8	Birchfield Harriers		1	Rugby	28	May
42.8	Notts AC		1	Wolverhampton	25	Jun
42.90	Windsor SE&H AC		3	London (O)	9	Jul
43.0	Sale Harriers Manchester		1	Preston	30	Apr
43.17	Sutton & District AC	U17	1	London (O)	9	Jul
43.2	Newham & Essex Beagles		1	London (WF)	25	Jun

Under 17 Teams

41.59	England Schools		1	Dublin (S), IRL	15	Jul
42.04	Middlesex Schools		1	Birmingham	8	Jul
42.11	London Schools		2	Birmingham	8	Jul
42.11	Wales Schools		2	Dublin (S), IRL	15	Jul
42.81	Midland Schools		1	Loughborough	1	Sep
42.88	Scotland Schools		2	Loughborough	1	Sep
42.95	Surrey Schools		3	Birmingham	8	Jul
42.96	West Midlands Schools		2h3	Birmingham	8	Jul
43.04	Kent Schools		5	Birmingham	8	Jul
43.06	South of England Schools		3	Loughborough	1	Sep

Additional Under 17 Club Teams (1 above)

43.23	Croydon Harriers	2	London (O)	9	Jul
43.39	Shaftesbury Barnet Harriers	1	Birmingham	3	Sep
43.65	Blackheath & Bromley H AC	2	Birmingham	3	Sep
43.8	Marshall Milton Keynes AC	1	Rugby	28	May
43.93	Giffnock North AAC	1	Grangemouth	22	Apr
43.96	Cardiff AAC	3	Birmingham	3	Sep
44.07	Enfield & Haringey AC	3	London (O)	9	Jul
44.1	Basildon AC	1	London (LV)	13	Aug
44.2	Birchfield Harriers	2	Rugby	28	May

Under 15 Teams

44.01	Surrey Schools	1	Birmingham	8	Jul
44.24	Middlesex Schools	2	Birmingham	8	Jul
44.26	Essex Schools	3	Birmingham	8	Jul
44.33	London Schools	4	Birmingham	8	Jul
44.58	Croydon Harriers	1	London (O)	9	Jul
44.69	Hampshire Schools	1h3	Birmingham	8	Jul
44.90	Shaftesbury Barnet Harriers	1	London (PH)	18	Jun
45.28	Reading AC	2	London (O)	9	Jul

Additional Under 15 Club Teams (1-3 above)

45.64	Harrow AC	3	London (O)	9	Jul
45.8	Basildon AC	1h1	Hornchurch	30	Jun
45.89	Sale Harriers Manchester	1	Birmingham	2	Sep
46.04	Southampton AC	1	Bromley	15	Jul
46.2	Blackheath & Bromley H AC	1	Bromley	10	Sep
46.4	Gateshead Harriers	1	Manchester (SC)	18	Jun
46.4	Newham & Essex Beagles	2	Hornchurch	30	Jun

Under 13 Teams

50.04	Croydon Harriers	1	London (O)	9	Jul
51.24	Sutton & District AC	1	Sutton	10	Sep
51.5	Blackheath & Bromley H AC	1	Bromley	10	Sep
51.59	Reading AC	2	London (O)	9	Jul
51.8	Bexley AC	2	Bromley	10	Sep
51.90	Surrey AA	1r2	Kingston	29	Jul
51.95	Berkshire AA	1	Kingston	29	Jul
52.07	Middlesex AA	2	Kingston	29	Jul
52.10	Ballymena & Antrim AC	1	Belfast	1	Jul
52.23	Coventry Godiva Harriers	1	Birmingham	20	Aug

Additional Under 13 Club Teams (1-7 above)

52.43	Marshall Milton Keynes AC	2	Birmingham	20	Aug
52.45	Bedford & County AC	3	Birmingham	20	Aug
52.47	Harrow AC	3	London (O)	9	Jul

4 x 200 Metres

1:27.57i	Brunel University		1	Sheffield	19	Feb
1:27.98i	Bath University		2	Sheffield	19	Feb
1:28.23i	Loughborough University		1h2	Sheffield	18	Feb
1:28.86i	Cardiff Metropolitan University		3	Sheffield	19	Feb
1:29.22i	Wales	U20	1	Cardiff	5	Mar
1:29.33i	England	U20	2	Cardiff	5	Mar

Under 17 Team

1:31.24i	Giffnock North AAC	1	Glasgow	4	Mar

Under 15 Team

1:38.4	Hercules Wimbledon AC	1	Sutton	30	Apr

Under 13 Team

1:49.3	Blackheath & Bromley H AC	1	Bromley	10	Sep

4 x 300 Metres - Under 15

2:33.4	Sale Harriers Manchester	1	Manchester (SC)	18	Jun
2:33.42	Blackheath & Bromley H AC	1	Bromley	15	Jul
2:34.87	Southampton AC	2	Bromley	15	Jul
2:36.87	Shaftesbury Barnet H	1	London (He)	30	Aug
2:38.3	Ashford AC	2	Bromley	10	Sep
2:39.03	Swansea Harriers	1	Cardiff	12	Jul
2:39.2	Medway & Maidstone AC	2	Ashford	2	Jul
2:40.01	Edinburgh AC	3	Birmingham	2	Sep
2:40.25	Kingston & Poly	1	Sutton	10	Sep
2:40.4	Harrow AC	1	Hemel Hempstead	15	Jul

4 x 400 Metres

2:59.00	National Team	3	London (O)	13	Aug
	(Matthew Hudson-Smith 45.4, Dwayne Cowan 44.3, Rabah Yousif 44.9. Martyn Rooney 44.4)				
3:00.10	National Team	4h2	London (O)	12	Aug
	(Rabah Yousif 45.6, Dwayne Cowan 44.4, Jack Green 45.42, Martyn Rooney 44.66)				
3:03.65	National Under 23 Team	U23 1	Bydgoszcz, POL	16	Jul
	(Lee Thompson 46.6, Benjamin Snaith 45.7, Sam Hazell 46.32, Cameron Chalmers 45.12)				
3:05.19	National Team	2h1	Nassau, BAH	22	Apr
	(Matthew Hudson-Smith 45.96, Delano Williams 45.48, Jarryd Dunn 46.17,Theo Campbell 47.58)				
3:05.63	National Team	6	Nassau, BAH	23	Apr
	(Matthew Hudson-Smith 45.68, Delano Williams 46.35, Jarryd Dunn 46.04,Theo Campbell 47.56)				
3:06.20	National Under 23 Team	U23 2h1	Bydgoszcz, POL	15	Jul
	(Lee Thompson 46.9, Benjamin Snaith 46.4, Sam Hazell 46.60, Thomas Somers 46.36)				
3:07.49	National Team	6r1	Villeneuve d'Ascq, FRA	25 Jun
	(Rabah Yousif 46.0e, Jarryd Dunn 46.0e, Cameron Chalmers 46.19, Sam Miller 49.38)				
3:08.95	England	1	Loughborough	21	May
	(Elliott Rutter 48.1, Benjamin Snaith 46.9, Edmond Amaning 47.8, Sebastian Rodger 46.2)				
3:10.13	National Junior Team	U20 2	Loughborough	21	May
	(Ellis Greatrex 48.5, Owen Richardson 46.9, Joseph Brier 48.1, Connor Wood 46.7)				
3:10.40	Thames Valley Harriers	1	London (LV)	3	Jun
	(Chris McAlister, Luke Lennon-Ford, Victor dos Santos POR, Edmond Amaning)				
3:11.11	Loughborough University	3	Loughborough	21	May
	(Shawn Wright 48.6, Peter De'Ath 48.1, Thomas Somers 48.2, Martyn Rooney 46.2)				
3:11.31	Southampton AC	2	London (LV)	3	Jun
	(Ben Claridge, James Forman, Harry Fisher, Sean Adams)				
3:11.70	Northern Ireland	4	Loughborough	21	May
	(Craig Newell IRL 49.8, Jason Harvey IRL 47.3, Leon Reid 46.9, Ben Maze 47.8)				
3:12.23	Northern Ireland	1	Manchester (SC)	16	Aug
	(Craig Newell, Ben Maze, Leon Reid, Andrew Mellon)				
3:14.02	Thames Valley Harriers	1	Bedford	15	Jul
	(Chris McAlister, Luke Lennon-Ford, Edmond Amaning, Victor Dos Santos Soares, POR)				
3:14.50	City of Sheffield & Dearne AC	1	Sheffield	6	May
	(Lewis Brown, David Dempsey, John Lane, Lee Thompson)				
3:14.70	Bath University	1	Bedford	1	May
	(Sandy Wilson, James Webster, Ben Claridge, Cameron Chalmers)				
3:14.78	Guernsey	1	St Peter Port, GUE	2	Sep
	(Sam Wallbridge 49.8, Alastair Chalmers 48.6, Tom Druce 46.9, Dale Garland 49.5)				
3:14.82	Birchfield Harriers	3	London (LV)	3	Jun
	(Elliott Dunn, Jarryd Dunn, Peter Shand, Sadam Koumi SUD)				
3:14.88	City of Sheffield & Dearne AC	1	London (He)	20	Aug
	(Lewis Brown, David Dempsey, Dominic Walton, Lee Thompson)				

Additional National Teams

3:15.67	Scotland	2	Manchester (SC)	16	Aug
3:18.10	Wales	6	Loughborough	21	May

Additional Club Teams (1-6 above)

3:15.11	Woodford Green with Essex Ladies	2	Sheffield	6	May
3:15.14	Newham & Essex Beagles	2	London (He)	20	Aug
3:15.33	Harrow AC	1	Basingstoke	6	May
3:15.56	Liverpool H & AC	4	Sheffield	6	May
3:15.59	East London University	3	Bedford	1	May
3:15.62	Shaftesbury Barnet Harriers	4	London (LV)	3	Jun
3:16.23	Cardiff AAC	2	Basingstoke	6	May
3:17.83	Crawley AC	1	Yate	3	Jun
3:17.91	Enfield & Haringey AC	2	Yate	3	Jun
3:18.09	Bristol & West AC	1	Bedford	15	Jul
3:18.22	Cardiff Metropolitan University	4	Bedford	1	May
3:19.29	Sale Harriers Manchester	2	Manchester (SC)	20	Aug
3:19.36	Herne Hill Harriers	3	Yate	3	Jun
3:19.80	City of York AC	2	Preston	5	Aug

Under 20 Club Teams

3:20.06	Shaftesbury Barnet Harriers	3	Brno, CZE	16	Sep
3:25.51	Windsor SE&H AC	1	London (He)	23	Jul
3:25.7	Rugby & Northampton AC	1	Rugby	28	May
3:27.5	Birchfield Harriers	1	Wolverhampton	25	Jun
3:27.8	Newquay & Par	1	Carn Brea	13	May
3:27.9	Worcester AC	2	Wolverhampton	4	Jun
3:28.39	Sale Harriers Manchester	1	Stretford	28	May
3:30.33	Blackheath & Bromley H AC	1	Bromley	28	May
3:31.8	Millfield School	1	Oxford	4	May
3:32.1	Orion Harriers	2	London (ME)	28	May
3:32.2	Gateshead Harriers	3	Hull	30	Apr
3:32.51	Charnwood AC	1	Derby	23	Jul

Under 17 Teams

3:19.07	England Schools	1	Dublin (S), IRL	15	Jul
3:19.30	South of England Schools	1	Loughborough	1	Sep
3:21.96	Scotland Schools	2	Loughborough	1	Sep

Under 17 Club Teams

3:25.7	Medway & Maidstone AC	1	Bromley	10	Sep
3:29.4	Blackheath & Bromley H AC	2	Bromley	10	Sep
3:30.25	Shaftesbury Barnet Harriers	1	Reading	25	Jun
3:31.7	Newham & Essex Beagles	1	Hornchurch	30	Jun
3:33.1	Windsor SE&H AC	3	London (He)	23	Jul
3:33.63	Giffnock North AAC	1	Grangemouth	22	Apr
3:34.4	Charnwood AC	1	Coventry	30	Apr
3:34.72	Cardiff AAC	5	Birmingham	3	Sep
3:36.03	Edinburgh AC	2	York	25	Jun
3:36.7	Bromsgrove & Redditch AC	1	Solihull	28	May

2017 LISTS - WOMEN

60 Metres - Indoors

7.06	Asha Philip		25.10.90	1	Belgrade, SRB	5	Mar
	7.18			3	Düsseldorf, GER	1	Feb
	7.19			1	Sheffield	11	Feb
	7.20			1s2	Belgrade, SRB	5	Mar
	7.24			3h1	Birmingham	18	Feb
	7.24			5	Birmingham	18	Feb
	7.25			3h2	Düsseldorf, GER	1	Feb
	7.25			1h5	Belgrade, SRB	4	Mar
	7.28			1A1	London (Nh)	25	Jan
	7.28			1A2	London (Nh)	25	Jan
	7.31			1s3	Sheffield	11	Feb
7.13	Dina Asher-Smith	U23	4.12.95	1h1	Karlsruhe, GER	4	Feb
	7.15			2	Karlsruhe, GER	4	Feb
	7.23			1	Stockholm, SWE	28	Jan
	7.27			1h1	Stockholm, SWE	28	Jan
7.30	Imani Lansiquot	U23	17.12.97	3h1	Torun, POL	10	Feb
	7.34			6	Torun, POL	10	Feb
7.31	Rachel Miller		29.01.90	1	Vienna, AUT	28	Jan
	7.39			1h2	Vienna, AUT	28	Jan
	7.39			6h1	Birmingham	18	Feb
	7.43			1h4	London (LV)	14	Jan
	7.43			1h3	Sheffield	11	Feb
	7.43			1s1	Sheffield	11	Feb
7.31	Hannah Brier	U20	3.02.98	1	Sheffield	17	Feb
	7.32			1s3	Sheffield	17	Feb
	7.36			1s2	Sheffield	25	Feb
	7.36			1	Sheffield	25	Feb
	7.37			1	Cardiff	11	Feb
	7.38			1	London (LV)	1	Feb
	7.38			1h2	Cardiff	11	Feb
	7.42			1	Cardiff	10	Dec
	7.44			1	Cardiff	5	Mar
7.32	Sophie Papps		6.10.94	1h2	London (LV)	14	Jan
	7.32			1s1	London (LV)	14	Jan
7.36	Daryll Neita	U23	29.08.96	5h1	Birmingham	18	Feb
7.37	Shannon Hylton	U23	19.12.96	1s2	Sheffield	11	Feb
	7.38			2	Sheffield	11	Feb
	7.39			1h1	Sheffield	11	Feb
	7.39			7h1	Birmingham	18	Feb
	7.41			1A2	London (LV)	29	Jan
	7.42			1A1	London (LV)	29	Jan
7.38	Amarachi Pipi	U23	26.11.95	2	Norman, USA	28	Jan
	7.41			2	Norman, USA	14	Jan
	7.41			1s1	New York (A), USA	3	Feb
	7.41			2h1	Ames, USA	24	Feb
	7.44			4	New York (A), USA	3	Feb
7.39	Corinne Humphreys		7.11.91	3h2	Mondeville, FRA	4	Feb
	7.41			4	Sheffield	17	Feb
	7.42			5	Mondeville, FRA	4	Feb
	7.45			2h1	Nantes, FRA	21	Jan
	(10)						
7.41	Diani Walker	U23	14.07.95	3	Sheffield	17	Feb
	7.44			1s2	Sheffield	17	Feb
7.42	Laviai Nielsen	U23	13.03.96	2s1	London (LV)	14	Jan
	7.43			1	London (LV)	14	Jan
7.42	Finette Agyapong	U23	1.02.97	3h1	Athlone, IRL	15	Feb
	7.42			4	Athlone, IRL	15	Feb

7.43	Nicola Gilbert		12.03.85	2	Nantes, FRA	21	Jan
	7.44			1h1	Nantes, FRA	21	Jan
7.43	Alisha Rees	U20	16.04.99	1s1	Sheffield	25	Feb
	7.45			3	Sheffield	25	Feb
7.43	Amy Hunt	U17	15.05.02	1	Sheffield	25	Feb
	7.45			2	Cardiff	5	Mar
7.44	Risqat Fabunmi-Alade		25.03.94	3s1	London (LV)	14	Jan
7.45	Marilyn Nwawulor		20.09.92	1	Cardiff	5	Feb
	64 performances to 7.45 by 18 athletes						
7.48	Rebecca Campsall		2.10.90	1h2	Sheffield	14	Jan
7.48	Annie Tagoe		4.06.93	2h1	Cardiff	28	Jan
(20)							
7.49	Olivia Okoli	U20	7.09.99	1	London (LV)	14	Jan
7.49	Shara Proctor		16.09.88	3s1	Sheffield	11	Feb
7.49	Kristal Awuah	U20	7.08.99	2s1	Sheffield	25	Feb
7.50	Vera Chinedu	U20	2.05.00	2	London (LV)	14	Jan
7.50	Rebecca Chapman		27.09.92	1	Cardiff	15	Jan
7.51	Maya Bruney	U20	24.02.98	1A2	London (LV)	29	Jan
7.52	Lukesha Morris	U23	26.11.95	2s1	Sheffield	17	Feb
7.53	Melissa Roberts	U23	6.08.97	2	Cardiff	15	Jan
7.53	Aleasha Kiddle		17.08.92	1	London (LV)	4	Feb
7.53	Yasmin Miller	U23	24.05.95	2	Cardiff	5	Feb
(30)							
7.54mx	Clieo Stephenson	U23	8.04.95	1r14A	Eton	5	Feb
	7.55			3s2	Sheffield	11	Feb
7.55	Annabelle Lewis		20.03.89	1	Sheffield	29	Jan
7.55	Sophie Yorke	U20	7.07.98	1h6	Sheffield	25	Feb
7.58	Jodie Williams		28.09.93	7h2	Birmingham	18	Feb
7.59	Immanuela Aliu	U20	19.04.00	6	Sheffield	25	Feb
7.59mx	Jenna Wrisberg	U20	22.03.98	1	Motherwell	29	Mar
7.60	Beth Dobbin		7.06.94	3A2	London (LV)	29	Jan
7.61	Charmont Webster-Tape	U20	29.11.99	1s2	London (LV)	14	Jan
7.61	Amy Allcock		20.08.93	1	Sheffield	21	Jan
7.61	Eve Wright	U17	8.08.02	1h3	Sheffield	25	Feb
(40)							
7.62	Serita Solomon		1.03.90	1A1	London (LV)	2	Jan
7.62	Amber Anning	U17	18.11.00	3A2	London (LV)	29	Jan
7.62	Joy Ogunleye	U17	27.09.00	2	Sheffield	25	Feb
7.62	Moli Jones	U17	28.10.00	3	Sheffield	25	Feb
7.63	Katy Wyper		17.04.93	1h3	Sheffield	14	Jan
7.63	Charlotte Paterson	U20	26.02.98	1	Sheffield	14	Jan
7.63mx	Stephanie Clitheroe	U23	3.11.95	2r14A	Eton	5	Feb
	7.67			4h4	Sheffield	11	Feb
7.63	Lauren Roy	U17	25.09.00	6	Athlone, IRL	19	Feb
7.63	Hannah Kelly	U17	20.12.00	2s1	Sheffield	25	Feb
7.63	Trinity Powell	U17	29.06.02	1-17	Manchester (SC)	17	Dec
(50)							
7.64	Meghan Beesley		15.11.89	1A1	Loughborough	28	Jan
7.64	Rachel Bell	U23	20.11.96	1h6	Sheffield	17	Feb
7.64	Charlotte Orton	U20	18.07.98	1h8	Sheffield	17	Feb
7.64	Danielle Blake	U20	5.03.98	3s1	Sheffield	17	Feb
7.64mx	Hayley Mills		14.09.88	1	Sheffield	2	Dec
7.65	Yvette Westwood	U20	3.09.98	3	Cardiff	5	Feb
7.66	Laura Clark	U23	17.08.96	3A1	London (Nh)	25	Jan
7.66	Modupe Shokunbi	U20	10.10.98	3s3	Sheffield	25	Feb
7.67	Holly Mills	U20	15.04.00	5	London (LV)	14	Jan
7.67mx	Sophie Money		24.10.93	1F1	Manchester (SC)	29	Jan
	7.75			2h8	Sheffield	17	Feb
(60)							
7.69	Lakeisha Owusu-Junior	U17	6.05.01	4s1	Sheffield	25	Feb
7.69	Ellie Turner	U20	26.05.00	1	London (LV)	19	Mar

7.70	Alicia Barrett	U20	25.03.98	2s2	Sheffield	14	Jan
7.70	Shereen Charles		7.10.84	4s1	London (LV)	14	Jan
7.70	Katie Forbes	U20	19.11.99	2h1	Glasgow	28	Jan
7.70	Madeleine Silcock	U20	13.06.00	1	Glasgow	2	Feb
7.70	Abigail Bishell	U23	11.02.95	5h4	Sheffield	11	Feb
7.70	Anna Short	U23	29.10.96	2h7	Sheffield	17	Feb
7.71	Ebony Carr	U20	21.01.99	2h1	London (LV)	14	Jan
7.71	Cassie-Ann Pemberton	U17	24.07.01	1	Birmingham	11	Feb
(70)							
7.71	Naomi Owolabi	U17	10.10.01	1s1	Sutton	18	Feb
7.73	Mair Edwards	U20	6.09.99	1h2	London (LV)	14	Jan
7.73	Rachel Highfield	U23	2.02.96	3h2	Glasgow	28	Jan
7.73	Katie-Jane Priest	U23	27.09.96	3h1	Cardiff	5	Feb
7.73	Shannon Malone	U23	27.05.97	4h1	Cardiff	5	Feb
7.73	Salome Japal	U20	6.09.98	3A2	London (Nh)	15	Feb
7.73	Catherine Hardy	U20	5.01.98	4s1	Sheffield	25	Feb
7.74	Laura Aregbe	U20	22.03.98	3h1	London (LV)	14	Jan
7.74	Shanice Harrison		30.10.93	3A2	London (CP)	18	Jan
7.74	Caitlin Maguire	U20	2.02.99	5	Athlone, IRL	29	Jan
(80)							
7.74	Jade Hutchison	U17	3.05.02	1	Glasgow	2	Feb
7.74	Leonie Ashmeade	U17	25.01.01	3s3	Sheffield	25	Feb
7.74	Hannah Williams		17.01.89	1rB	Cardiff	5	Mar
7.75	Kayla Bowley	U17	28.12.01	2h1	London (LV)	7	Jan
7.75	Ashleigh Clarke	U23	15.09.97	5s1	London (LV)	14	Jan
7.75	Marcia Sey	U17	7.11.01	4	Cardiff	5	Feb
7.75	Lauren Greig	U17	20.09.00	2s2	Sheffield	25	Feb
7.75mx	Nicola Caygill	U20	30.01.00	1	Gateshead	16	Nov

Additional Under 17 (1-17 above)

7.77	Rachel Bennett	3.07.02	5s1	Sheffield	25	Feb
7.77	Nayanna Dubarry-Gay	15.11.01	1h2	London (LV)	19	Mar
7.78	Akaysha Ellis	16.12.00	1h3	London (LV)	19	Mar
(20)						
7.78	Latifah Harris-Osman	7.05.02	1	London (LV)	19	Mar
7.79mx	Ayoola Babalola	17.12.01	1E2	Eton	8	Jan
7.84			4A1	London (LV)	21	Jan
7.79	Issie Tustin	27.11.01	2	Cardiff	11	Feb
7.79	Angel Asare	10.03.02	2s2	Sutton	18	Feb
7.82	Tia Jackson	5.08.02	3s2	Sheffield	25	Feb
7.83	Shania Umah	17.02.02	2h2	London (LV)	19	Mar
7.84	Ella Wansell	15.01.01	1	London (LV)	19	Mar
7.85	Skye Wicks	20.08.02	1s1	London (LV)	4	Feb
7.86mx	Angela Davis	15.07.02	1r11B	London (LV)	1	Jan
7.89			3A1	London (LV)	21	Jan
7.86	Taiwo Taiwo	23.09.01	4s2	Sheffield	25	Feb
(30)						
7.86mx	Zuriel Owolana	26.10.01	1r12B	Eton	5	Mar
7.87			1B2	London (LV)	21	Jan
7.89	Lauryn Walker	4.05.02	2	Birmingham	19	Mar
7.90	Chinwe Iwunze	6.02.01	5	London (LV)	19	Mar
7.90	Ruka Shonibare	19.06.02	3	Birmingham	19	Mar
7.90mx	Abigail Pawlett	14.01.03	1rE	Sheffield	2	Dec
7.90	Emmanuella Kone	3.04.03	1rB	Cardiff	10	Dec

Under 15

7.76	Leah Duncan	30.10.02	1s1	Sheffield	25	Feb
7.79	Christabel Antwi	18.10.02	1s1	Glasgow	2	Feb
7.81	Toni Bryan	23.12.02	1s2	Sutton	18	Feb
7.82	Monae Winston	31.10.02	1	Sutton	18	Feb
7.85	Precious Adu	3.10.02	1F1	London (Nh)	15	Feb

7.87		Grace Goodsell	4.04.03	2s1	Sheffield	25	Feb
7.88		Rachel Largie-Polean	16.05.03	2s1	Sutton	18	Feb
7.88		Nia Wedderburn-Goodison	9.01.05	3A2	London (Wil)	16	Dec
7.89		Aleeya Sibbons	5.11.02	1s1	London (LV)	4	Feb
7.89		Molly Palmer	27.08.03	1h8	Sheffield	25	Feb
	(10)						
7.90		Macey Morris	12.02.03	1s2	Sheffield	25	Feb
7.90		Zipporah Golding	16.11.03	2s2	Sheffield	25	Feb
7.91		Acacia Williams-Hewitt	8.08.03	2s3	Sheffield	25	Feb
7.96		Cara Russell	19.01.03	3	Sutton	18	Feb
7.96		Alyson Bell	9.11.03	1	Glasgow	22	Dec
7.97		Danai Mugabe	20.10.02	1	Cardiff	11	Feb
7.99		Karen Abiwu	8.10.02	3s1	Sutton	18	Feb
7.99		Kaliyah Young	20.07.03	1	London (LV)	19	Mar
7.99		Ava Jones	21.11.04	1	Manchester (SC)	17	Dec
8.00		Emmanuella Kone	3.04.03	1r9	Cardiff	8	Jan
	(20)						
8.00		Marli Jessop	27.06.03	1h1	London (LV)	19	Mar
8.01		Imaan Denis	27.11.02	2r14B	Eton	5	Feb
8.01		Lottie Jeffrey	3.02.03	3	Glasgow	26	Mar
8.02		Osarumen Odemwengie	23.09.03	2	Manchester (SC)	17	Dec
8.05		Afoma Ofor	7.07.04	1	Sheffield	2	Dec

Under 13

8.05mx	Nia Wedderburn-Goodison	9.01.05	4r19A	Eton	5	Feb
8.11			4r14B	Eton	5	Feb
8.08	India Toasland	1.12.04	1h1	Sutton	18	Feb
8.10	Tyra Khambai-Annan	21.12.04	1A2	London (LV)	5	Mar
8.15	Rayne Tapper	7.04.06	2B2	London (Wil)	16	Dec
8.16mx	Ayomide Cole	27.07.05	2r15B	Eton	5	Mar
8.17			1A2	London (LV)	26	Mar
8.19	Trezeguet Taylor	17.04.05	1	Sheffield	5	Feb

Foreign

7.40		*Adeline Gouenon (CIV)*		*20.10.94*	*2*	*Sheffield*	*17 Feb*
7.44		*Charlotte Wingfield (MLT)*		*30.11.94*	*1*	*Cardiff*	*28 Jan*
7.47		*Gina Akpe-Moses (IRL)*	*U20*	*25.02.99*	*4*	*Sheffield*	*11 Feb*
7.60mx		*Emma Suhonen (FIN)*		*28.01.91*	*1rH2*	*London (LV)*	*1 Jan*
7.65					*1A1*	*Loughborough*	*28 Jan*
7.71		*Sydney Griffin (USA)*		*16.10.93*	*4A2*	*London (Nh)*	*25 Jan*

60 Metres - Outdoors

7.60	0.8	Hannah Williams	23.04.98	5	Melbourne, AUS	4	Feb
7.64	-0.4	Margaret Adeoye	22.04.85	6	Melbourne, AUS	11	Feb

75 Metres - Under 13

9.65		Success Eduan	27.09.04	1	Manchester (Str)	1	May
9.67	1.9	Tyra Khambai-Annan	21.12.04	1	London (BP)	18	Jun
9.70		Trezeguet Taylor	17.04.05	2	Manchester (Str)	29	May
9.7		Emily Kerr	12.01.05	1	Gillingham	6	Aug
9.84	1.8			1h1	Erith	17	Sep
9.8		Ayomide Cole	27.07.05	1	Eton	9	Apr
9.8		Nia Wedderburn-Goodison	9.01.05	1	London (ME)	18	Jun
9.9		Serena Gueye	20.07.05	2	London (ME)	18	Jun
9.99		Ellie Longstaff	25.11.04	1	Middlesbrough	3	Sep
10.0		Isabel Male	17.02.05	1	Sutton Coldfield	8	Apr
10.0		Etienne Maughan	7.12.04	1	Tonbridge	18	Jun
	(10)						
10.0		Lucy Moore	30.03.05	1	Leeds	18	Jun
10.0		Ruby Bowie	2.01.05	1	Middlesbrough	15	Jul
10.0		Rayne Tapper	7.04.06	2	Hemel Hempstead	15	Jul
10.0		Nina Pickavance	22.11.05	1	Warrington	13	Aug

100 Metres

11.09	0.6	Desiree Henry	U23	26.08.95	1rB	Azusa, USA	14	Apr
11.23	1.0				8h2	Birmingham	20	Aug
11.24	-0.2				5s2	London (O)	6	Aug
11.26	-0.2				3rB	Berlin, GER	27	Aug
11.32	0.5				6	Rome, ITA	8	Jun
11.32	-0.3				4h3	London (O)	5	Aug
11.40	1.0				4	Zagreb, CRO	29	Aug
11.41	0.2				3	Boston, USA	4	Jun
11.51	-1.3				6	Hengelo, NED	11	Jun
11.13	0.8	Dina Asher-Smith	U23	4.12.95	2h1	Birmingham	20	Aug
11.21	-1.2				5	Birmingham	20	Aug
11.22+	-0.1				1m	Gateshead (Q)	9	Sep
11.23	1.0				2	Zagreb, CRO	29	Aug
11.41	1.9				2s1	Birmingham	1	Jul
11.41	0.1				5	Lignano, ITA	12	Jul
11.51	-0.8				6h1	London (O)	9	Jul
11.53	-1.3				6	Birmingham	1	Jul
11.14	-0.4	Daryll Neita	U23	29.08.96	4h2	London (O)	9	Jul
11.15	0.6				1h6	London (O)	5	Aug
11.16	0.3				6	Rabat, MAR	16	Jul
11.16	0.8				4s1	London (O)	6	Aug
11.20	1.1				1	Bedford	17	Jun
11.22	-1.4				7	London (O)	9	Jul
11.25	-1.3				2	Birmingham	1	Jul
11.28	1.9				1s1	Birmingham	1	Jul
11.29	1.4				1h2	Bedford	17	Jun
11.38	-0.1				1	London (Nh)	29	May
11.39	-0.2				1	Gavardo, ITA	4	Jun
11.40	1.2				1A1	London (LV)	24	May
11.41	-0.4				1h1	Gavardo, ITA	4	Jun
11.14	1.3	Asha Philip		25.10.90	4h1	London (O)	5	Aug
11.18	-0.8				3h1	London (O)	9	Jul
11.19	-0.9				1s2	Birmingham	1	Jul
11.19	-1.4				6	London (O)	9	Jul
11.19	0.2				7s3	London (O)	6	Aug
11.20	1.0				6h2	Birmingham	20	Aug
11.21	-1.3				1	Birmingham	1	Jul
11.37	-0.7				5	Zürich, SUI	24	Aug
11.43	-0.6				3	Marseille, FRA	3	Jun
11.48	-1.0				1	Manchester	26	May
11.27	-0.9	Ashleigh Nelson		20.02.91	2s2	Birmingham	1	Jul
11.28	-1.3				3	Birmingham	1	Jul
11.30	-0.4				1A1	London (LV)	21	Jun
11.30	1.0	Bianca Williams		18.12.93	1rB	Zürich, SUI	24	Aug
11.40	-0.9				3s2	Birmingham	1	Jul
11.41+	-0.1				2m	Gateshead (Q)	9	Sep
11.47	-1.3				4	Birmingham	1	Jul
11.51	-1.0				2=	Geneva, SUI	10	Jun
11.34	0.5	Imani Lansiquot	U23	17.12.97	2	London (Nh)	2	Jul
11.35	0.7				2h2	Gavardo, ITA	4	Jun
11.39	0.8				1	Loughborough	21	May
11.41	-0.1				2	London (Nh)	29	May
11.43	-1.1				1-23	London (Nh)	29	May
11.47	0.3				2s2	Bydgoszcz, POL	13	Jul
11.48	-0.2				3	Gavardo, ITA	4	Jun
11.53mx	-1.1				1	London (LV)	5	Jul

11.39	1.2	Corinne Humphreys		7.11.91	1h1	Hérouville St.-Clair, FRA	15	Jun
	11.42	0.8			2	Loughborough	21	May
	11.48	1.4			1h1	London (Nh)	7	May
	11.48	1.7			2h7	Taipei, TPE	23	Aug
	11.49	-0.3			4=	Taipei, TPE	24	Aug
	11.50	0.4			3	Villeneuve d'Ascq, FRA	24	Jun
	11.50	-1.3			5	Birmingham	1	Jul
	11.52	-0.9			4s2	Birmingham	1	Jul
	11.52	-0.3			3q4	Taipei, TPE	23	Aug
	11.53	-0.2			2h2	Villeneuve d'Ascq, FRA	23	Jun
	11.54	1.4			1	Argentan, FRA	4	Jun
11.41	-0.6	Lorraine Ugen		22.08.91	1	Bromley	16	Jul
	11.47	0.8			2	Arlington, USA	25	Mar
11.45	1.9	Rachel Miller		29.01.90	3s1	Birmingham	1	Jul
	11.45	1.1			1h2	Bedford	29	Jul
	11.53	1.5			1	Bilbao, ESP	24	Jun
	11.54	1.2			2A1	London (LV)	24	May
	11.54	-0.5			3	Bedford	29	Jul
	(10)							
11.45	-0.5	Diani Walker	U23	14.07.95	1	Bedford	29	Jul
	11.51	1.0			1s2	Bedford	29	Jul
11.47	1.3	Shannon Hylton	U23	19.12.96	1rA	Loughborough	21	May
11.49	1.9	Finette Agyapong	U23	1.02.97	4s1	Birmingham	1	Jul
11.54	-0.6	Zoey Clark		25.10.94	1rB	Bromley	16	Jul
		79 performances to 11.55 by 14 athletes						
11.58	1.4	Montell Douglas		24.01.86	2h1	London (Nh)	7	May
11.60		Rebecca Campsall		2.10.90	1	Eton	3	Jun
11.61	0.8	Hannah Brier	U20	3.02.98	4	Loughborough	21	May
11.61	0.2	Kristal Awuah	U20	7.08.99	1	Bedford	17	Jun
11.62	0.8	Alisha Rees	U20	16.04.99	5	Loughborough	21	May
11.62	1.0	Kimbely Baptiste		27.12.92	2h1	Birmingham	1	Jul
	(20)							
11.62	1.1	Olivia Okoli	U20	7.09.99	2h1	Mannheim, GER	1	Jul
11.63	1.3	Katy Wyper		17.04.93	1	Grangemouth	26	Aug
11.64	0.1	Jodie Williams		28.09.93	3h2	Loughborough	22	Jul
11.64	1.0	Mica Moore		23.11.92	2s2	Bedford	29	Jul
11.65+		Amy Hunt	U17	15.05.02	1r2	Gateshead (Q)	8	Sep
	11.66	1.3			4rA	Loughborough	21	May
11.67	1.4	Cheriece Hylton	U23	19.12.96	3h1	London (Nh)	7	May
11.67	1.3	Louise Bloor		21.09.85	5rA	Loughborough	21	May
11.68	0.5	Chinedu Monye		29.12.89	3	London (Nh)	2	Jul
11.70	1.3	Clieo Stephenson	U23	8.04.95	6rA	Loughborough	21	May
11.70	1.6	Margaret Adeoye		22.04.85	1	Leigh	16	Jul
	(30)							
11.71mx	1.2	Amy Allcock		20.08.93	1	Manchester (Str)	20	Jun
11.71	1.1	Beth Dobbin		7.06.94	3h3	Loughborough	22	Jul
11.72	-0.7	Amarachi Pipi	U23	26.11.95	4rB	Tempe, USA	18	Mar
11.72	0.9	Laura Clark	U23	17.08.96	1A2	London (LV)	24	May
11.72	1.8	Melissa Roberts	U23	6.08.97	2	Cardiff	10	Jun
11.74	1.6	Hannah Williams		17.01.89	2	Leigh	16	Jul
11.76	1.4	Vera Chinedu	U20	2.05.00	2h1	Bedford	17	Jun
11.77		Lukesha Morris	U23	26.11.95	3	Eton	3	Jun
11.77	1.0	Risqat Fabunmi-Alade		25.03.94	3h1	Birmingham	1	Jul
11.77	1.3	Jenna Wrisberg	U20	22.03.98	2	Grangemouth	26	Aug
	(40)							
11.78	1.1	Ebony Carr	U20	21.01.99	2	Birmingham	8	Jul
11.79	0.7	Torema Thompson		15.02.90	2A2	London (LV)	21	Jun
11.79	0.4	Amber Anning	U17	18.11.00	1	Oxford (H)	9	Sep
11.81	-0.5	Aleasha Kiddle		17.08.92	7	Bedford	29	Jul
11.82	1.4	Maya Bruney	U20	24.02.98	4h1	London (Nh)	7	May
11.86	1.4	Charlotte Paterson	U20	26.02.98	4rB	Loughborough	21	May

11.93	1.4	Emily Coope	U20	26.12.99	3h1	Bedford	17	Jun
11.93	0.2	Jazz Crawford	U20	22.01.98	4	Bedford	17	Jun
11.94mx0.7		Georgina Adam	U20	24.03.00	1	Loughborough	31	May
11.94	1.1	Immanuela Aliu	U20	19.04.00	3	Birmingham	8	Jul
(50)								
11.94	0.2	Chloe Lambert		22.05.94	1A1	Glasgow (S)	9	Aug
11.95	1.5	Shereen Charles		7.10.84	4h1	Bedford	29	Jul
11.95	0.4	Dolita Awala-Shaw	U17	7.11.00	2	Oxford (H)	9	Sep
11.96	1.4	Sophie Yorke	U20	7.07.98	2s1	Bedford	17	Jun
11.96	1.3	Yvette Westwood	U20	3.09.98	3s2	Bedford	17	Jun
11.97	1.1	Trinity Powell	U17	29.06.02	2s1	Birmingham	7	Jul
11.98	1.3	Charmont Webster-Tape	U20	29.11.99	4s2	Bedford	17	Jun
11.98	1.0	Leonie Ashmeade	U17	25.01.01	1s2	Bedford	26	Aug
11.99	-0.6	Mair Edwards	U20	6.09.99	1	Bromley	19	Aug
12.01	1.8	Lucy Evans		2.10.82	4	Cardiff	10	Jun
(60)								
12.02	1.3	Salome Japal	U20	6.09.98	5s2	Bedford	17	Jun
12.02	0.5	Marilyn Nwawulor		20.09.92	3h3	Birmingham	1	Jul
12.03	0.4	Anna Short	U23	29.10.96	1h2	Bedford	29	Apr
12.03	0.9	Cassie-Ann Pemberton	U17	24.07.01	2h2	Birmingham	7	Jul
12.04	-0.2	Danielle McGifford	U23	11.04.95	1	Wigan	9	Apr
12.04	1.8	Yasmin Liverpool	U20	15.01.99	1	Haarlem, NED	7	May
12.04	1.9	Madeleine Silcock	U20	13.06.00	2rC	Loughborough	21	May
12.04	1.1	Abigail Bishell	U23	11.02.95	4h2	Bedford	29	Jul
12.04	0.6	Abigail Pawlett	U15	14.01.03	1	Bedford	26	Aug
12.05+		Kiah Dubarry-Gay	U17	15.11.01	2r1	Gateshead (Q)	8	Sep
(70)								
12.06	1.8	Catherine Hardy	U20	5.01.98	5	Cardiff	10	Jun
12.06	1.5	Rebecca Chapman		27.09.92	2rB	Leigh	16	Jul
12.07	1.5	Tia Jackson	U17	5.08.02	1	Exeter	17	Jun
12.07	-1.6	Marcia Sey	U17	7.11.01	1	London (CP)	20	Aug
12.07+		Nicola Caygill	U20	30.01.00	3r1	Gateshead (Q)	8	Sep
	12.12	1.1			5	Birmingham	8	Jul
12.08	1.5	Amy Odunaiya	U23	17.11.96	1ns	Wigan	7	May
12.09	1.3	Darcey Kuypers	U20	27.08.98	6s2	Bedford	17	Jun
12.10	-0.1	Mary Iheke		19.11.90	8	London (Nh)	29	May
12.11		Sarah Malone	U20	15.09.99	1	Edinburgh	7	Jun
12.11	-0.5	Lauren Roy	U17	25.09.00	2	Dublin (S), IRL	24	Jun
(80)								
12.11	1.4	Rebecca Jeggo	U20	12.01.00	1	Cambridge	24	Jun
12.12	1.3	Amelia Reynolds	U20	23.11.98	1	Yate	30	Apr
12.12	0.6	Aleeya Sibbons	U15	5.11.02	1	Birmingham	8	Jul
12.13	1.1	Modupe Shokunbi	U20	10.10.98	1rB	Bromley	28	May
12.13mx1.3		Katie-Jane Priest	U23	27.09.96	1r3	Cardiff	31	May
	12.13				7	Eton	3	Jun
12.13	-0.8	Joy Ogunleye	U17	27.09.00	4	Birmingham	8	Jul
12.14	1.1	Lakeisha Owusu-Junior	U17	6.05.01	4s1	Birmingham	7	Jul
12.14	0.7	Charlotte Orton	U20	18.07.98	4h4	Bedford	29	Jul
12.14	-1.6	Akaysha Ellis	U17	16.12.00	2	London (CP)	20	Aug
12.15	2.0	Rachel Highfield	U23	2.02.96	2h2	Manchester (SC)	10	Jun
(90)								
12.15	-0.6	Vivien Olatunji	U23	6.06.97	2rB	Bromley	16	Jul
12.15	0.3	Eleanor Broome	U20	6.02.99	4h3	Bedford	29	Jul
12.16	-0.7	Hannah Kelly	U17	20.12.00	1	Manchester (Str)	13	May
12.16		Naomi Owolabi	U17	10.10.01	1	Kingston	10	Jun
12.16		Alice McMahon	U23	15.02.95	1	Wakefield	25	Jun
12.17	1.3	Bethan Wakefield		17.10.94	5h4	Birmingham	1	Jul
12.17	0.1	Ellie Turner	U20	26.05.00	1rB	Kingston	2	Jul
12.17	0.5	Ellie Edwards	U23	19.11.96	2	Jerusalem, ISR	13	Jul
12.18	1.0	Codie Burnett	U23	8.05.96	2	Loughborough	7	Jun
12.18	1.4	Ellie McGinty	U23	12.11.97	3h2	Bedford	17	Jun

265

12.18	1.3	Alison McCorry	U23	24.08.96	1ns	Leigh	16	Jul
12.19A	0.0	Amy Teal	U20	8.03.98	1	Ogden, USA	3	May
12.20	1.5	Megan Webber	U17	31.05.01	2	Exeter	17	Jun
12.20	-0.5	Anna McCauley	U17	2.01.01	3	Dublin (S), IRL	24	Jun
12.20	1.3	Rebecca Matheson	U20	7.03.99	4	Grangemouth	26	Aug

Additional Under 17 (1-17 above)

12.22	-0.3	Eve Wright		8.08.02	2	Chelmsford	13	May
12.22	1.6	Ella Wansell		15.01.01	1	Watford	14	May
12.24	0.4	Maisey Snaith		3.04.01	1	Peterborough	13	May
	(20)							
12.24	-1.4	Ayoola Babalola		17.12.01	4s2	Birmingham	7	Jul
12.27	-1.4	Myisha Gordon		14.10.00	5s2	Birmingham	7	Jul
12.28	0.3	Rachel Bennett		3.07.02	5s1	Bedford	26	Aug
12.29		Shania Umah		17.02.02	1	Gillingham	30	Apr
12.29	0.3	Joda Kokovworho		8.05.01	1ns	Dublin (S), IRL	5	Aug
12.32	1.9	Obi Curry		11.04.01	1	Wigan	9	Apr
12.32	-2.5	Nayanna Dubarry-Gay		15.11.01	1	London (LV)	13	May
12.32	1.4	Lauren Greig		20.09.00	5h1	Bedford	17	Jun
12.32	0.9	Hannah Kynman		21.02.01	4h2	Birmingham	7	Jul
12.33	0.8	Isabella Gilkes		23.04.01	1	London (He)	23	Jul
	(30)							
12.34	1.6	Bethany Shaw		16.03.01	2	Watford	14	May
12.34mx	0.0	Zuriel Owolana		26.10.01	1	Watford	31	May
	12.36	1.0			4s2	Bedford	26	Aug
12.34	0.3	Latifah Harris-Osman		7.05.02	6s1	Bedford	26	Aug
12.35	0.3	Kayla Bowley		28.12.01	1	London (Cr)	17	Jun
12.37	1.0	Mary Beetham-Green		26.03.02	5s2	Bedford	26	Aug
12.40	-0.4	Skye Wicks		20.08.02	2h2	Chelmsford	13	May
12.40mx	1.2	Issie Tustin		27.11.01	1r2	Cardiff	31	May

Additional Under 15 (1-2 above)

12.21		Toni Bryan		23.12.02	1	Kingston	10	Jun
12.21	0.6	Leah Duncan		30.10.02	2	Birmingham	8	Jul
12.22	-0.2	Precious Adu		3.10.02	1rC	London (Nh)	29	May
12.22	1.0	Monae Winston		31.10.02	2h1	Birmingham	7	Jul
12.36	0.6	Alyson Bell		9.11.03	1	Glasgow (S)	20	Aug
12.37	0.8	Iona Newbegin		1.09.02	3s3	Bedford	26	Aug
12.41	1.3	Christabel Antwi		18.10.02	1	Grangemouth	13	May
12.45	0.3	Roli Omamuli		3.02.03	1h2	Birmingham	7	Jul
	(10)							
12.45	1.3	Leah Okorhi		17.05.03	2h3	Birmingham	7	Jul
12.47	1.3	Moyin Oduyemi		2.12.03	3h3	Birmingham	7	Jul
12.47	0.4	Lonarra Youngs		2.09.02	1	Oxford (H)	9	Sep
12.48		Zipporah Golding		16.11.03	1	Kingston	14	May
12.49	0.4	Kaliyah Young		20.07.03	1	Dartford	24	Sep
12.50	1.3	Lottie Jeffrey		3.02.03	2	Grangemouth	13	May
12.50		Molly Palmer		27.08.03	1h1	Derby	13	May
12.50	0.7	Serena Grace		6.01.03	2s2	Bedford	26	Aug
12.51		Acacia Williams-Hewitt		8.08.03	1	Wakefield	9	Apr
12.51		Charlotte Richardson		23.02.03	1	Middlesbrough	3	Sep
	(20)							
12.54	-1.0	Imaan Denis		27.11.02	1	London (LV)	14	May
12.54		Alice Rodgers		23.09.02	1-16	Belfast	5	Jul
12.54	-0.2	Afoma Ofor		7.07.04	1	Leigh	20	Aug
12.55	1.3	Matilda Robinson		1.10.02	4h3	Birmingham	7	Jul
12.59	1.0	Philippa Ellis		23.04.03	1	Gateshead	14	May
12.60	-1.0	Macey Morris		12.02.03	1	Cardiff	27	May

wind assisted

11.18	4.6	Bianca Williams		(11.30)	4	Clermont, USA	15	Apr
	11.20	4.4			2h4	Clermont, USA	15	Apr
	11.24	3.1			1rB	Gainesville, USA	28	Apr
11.31	2.5	Lorraine Ugen		(11.41)	3	Fort Worth, USA	15	Apr
11.35	3.9	Montell Douglas		(11.58)	1	London (Nh)	7	May
11.35	3.5	Amarachi Pipi	U23	(11.72)	3h2	Lawrence, USA	13	May
	11.55	3.0			6	Lawrence, USA	14	May
11.39	3.1	Lansiquot	U23	(11.34)	5rB	Gainesville, USA	28	Apr
11.41	2.9	Humphreys		(11.39)	1	Southampton	6	May
11.44	2.2	Diani Walker	U23	(11.45)	1	Manchester (SC)	16	Aug
	11.49	2.8			1h5	Bedford	29	Jul
11.50	2.8	Kimbely Baptiste		(11.62)	2h5	Bedford	29	Jul
	11.51	2.5			1	Leigh	16	Jul
11.53	3.9	Amy Hunt	U17	(11.65)	2	London (Nh)	7	May

14 performances to 11.55 by 9 athletes

11.61	2.2	Katy Wyper		(11.63)	2	Manchester (SC)	16	Aug
11.64	3.9	Maya Bruney	U20	(11.82)	3	London (Nh)	7	May
11.64	3.9	Lukesha Morris	U23	(11.77)	2	London (LV)	7	Jun
11.65	2.5	Louise Bloor		(11.67)	1	Manchester (SC)	10	Jun
11.66		Jenna Wrisberg	U20	(11.77)	1	Glasgow (S)	19	Aug
11.68	3.9	Laura Clark	U23	(11.72)	4	London (Nh)	7	May
11.70	4.9	Yvette Westwood	U20	(11.96)	1	Nuneaton	11	Jun
11.70	2.4	Ebony Carr	U20	(11.78)	1h4	Mannheim, GER	1	Jul
11.70	2.5	Risqat Fabunmi-Alade		(11.77)	1rC	Manchester (SC)	16	Aug
11.71	2.9	Marilyn Nwawulor		(12.02)	2	Southampton	6	May
11.71	2.6	Mair Edwards	U20	(11.99)	1	Portsmouth	13	May
11.72	4.9	Sophie Yorke	U20	(11.96)	2	Nuneaton	11	Jun
11.83	2.6	Abigail Bishell	U23	(12.04)	1	Glasgow (S)	16	Jul
11.86	4.4	Josie Oliarnyk	U20	27.03.00	1h2	Nuneaton	11	Jun
11.87	3.9	Rebecca Chapman		(12.06)	1rB	Southampton	6	May
11.88	5.4	Leah Duncan	U15	(12.21)	1	Cambridge	24	Jun
11.91	3.4	Emily Wright	U20	13.07.98	1	Waco, USA	22	Apr
11.92	3.9	Jazz Crawford	U20	(11.93)	7	London (Nh)	7	May
11.92	3.1	Charmont Webster-Tape	U20	(11.98)	2h4	Bedford	17	Jun
11.92	2.6	Chloe Lambert		(11.94)	2	Glasgow (S)	16	Jul
11.94	4.2	Cassie-Ann Pemberton	U17	(12.03)	1	Nuneaton	14	May
11.94	6.7	Ella Wansell	U17	(12.22)	1rC	London (LV)	7	Jun
11.94	8.6	Dionne Samuels		18.09.92	1	Nuneaton	11	Jun
11.94	2.5	Joey Duck		14.04.89	2	Leigh	16	Jul
11.96	2.2	Rachel Bell	U23	20.11.96	1h7	Bedford	29	Apr
11.97	3.9	Bethan Wakefield		(12.17)	2rB	Southampton	6	May
11.99	2.9	Yasmin Miller	U23	24.05.95	2r2	Cambridge	6	Aug
12.00	2.5	Rachel Highfield	U23	(12.15)	3	Manchester (SC)	10	Jun
12.00	4.0	Charlotte Orton	U20	(12.14)	1h2	Manchester (SC)	10	Jun
12.01	3.9	Salome Japal	U20	(12.02)	3rB	Southampton	6	May
12.01	8.6	Sophie Rowe		20.04.88	2	Nuneaton	11	Jun
12.06	2.6	Holly Mills	U20	15.04.00	2	Portsmouth	13	May
12.06	3.0	Precious Adu	U15	(12.22)	2rB	London (LV)	16	Aug
12.07	3.9	Hephzibah Adeosun	U23	29.08.96	4rB	Southampton	6	May
12.07	2.4	Jade Hutchison	U17	3.05.02	1	Grangemouth	9	Jun
12.08	2.7	Rebecca Jeggo	U20	(12.11)	1	Milton Keynes	19	Aug
12.09	3.1	Katie Forbes	U20	19.11.99	4h4	Bedford	17	Jun
12.10	3.9	Sophie-Ann Haigh	U20	22.10.98	5rB	Southampton	6	May
12.10	2.2	Lauren Roy	U17	(12.11)	8	Manchester (SC)	16	Aug
12.10		Sarah Malone	U20	(12.11)	2	Glasgow (S)	19	Aug
12.11	3.9	Skye Wicks	U17	(12.40)	1	Cambridge	24	Jun
12.11	2.8	Maisey Snaith	U17	(12.24)	3h5	Bedford	29	Jul
12.12	2.9	Lily Beckford	U23	11.08.97	3h7	Clermont, USA	15	Apr
12.12	2.4	Lauren Greig	U17	(12.32)	2	Grangemouth	9	Jun
12.13	2.7	Ellie McGinty	U23	(12.18)	1h2	Grangemouth	22	Apr

12.13	4.4	Harriet Cooper	U20	27.01.99	1	Nuneaton	14	May
12.14	2.5	Lucy Mansfield		10.10.92	4	Manchester (SC)	10	Jun
12.14	4.6	Sophie Money		(12.25)	1rB	Glasgow (S)	16	Jul
12.15	4.8	Gabriella Burton	U23	25.06.96	2h2	Nuneaton	11	Jun
12.16	2.3	Brittany Robinson	U20	9.11.98	3h6	Clermont, USA	15	Apr
12.16	4.8	Amy Bowen	U23	27.06.97	3h2	Nuneaton	11	Jun
12.16	3.5	Holly Turner	U23	15.11.95	1rB	Leigh	16	Jul
12.18	4.1	Paige Fairclough	U23	10.03.97	5	London (LV)	26	Apr
12.19	3.1	Regan Walker	U20	6.02.00	5h4	Bedford	17	Jun
12.19	2.5	Zoe Thompson	U20	10.04.00	3	Leigh	16	Jul
12.20	2.7	Lauren Russell	U20	16.03.98	1h4	London (Nh)	7	May
12.20	2.3	Harriet Jones		30.06.88	3rB	Eton	3	Jun

Additional Under 17 (1-8 above)

12.22	4.1	Victoria Johnson		7.10.01	1	Nuneaton	14	May
12.25	3.6	Angela Davis		15.07.02	2	Woodford	20	May
12.28		Robyn Taylor		21.01.01	3	Glasgow (S)	19	Aug
12.29	4.1	Heidi Norgrove		5.03.01	2	Nuneaton	14	May
12.30	3.9	Bethany Shaw		(12.34)	2	Cambridge	24	Jun
12.30	2.6	Elise Modeste		4.11.00	1rC	London (LV)	16	Aug
12.35	4.3	Issie Tustin		(12.40)	1h2	Brecon	14	May
12.37	4.2	Katie Daniel		30.08.01	2	Nuneaton	14	May

Additional Under 15 (1-2 above)

12.21	5.4	Iona Newbegin		(12.37)	2	Cambridge	24	Jun
12.31	2.8	Alyson Bell		(12.36)	1	Grangemouth	18	Jun
12.33	5.4	Serena Grace		(12.50)	3	Cambridge	24	Jun
12.46	2.2	Molly Palmer		(12.50)	1rB	Loughborough	1	Apr
12.51	2.6	Shona McLay		6.02.03	1	Stornoway	9	Sep
12.55	5.4	Marli Jessop		27.06.03	4	Cambridge	24	Jun

hand timing

11.9		Sophie Yorke	U20	(11.96)	1	Worcester	6	May
11.9		Harriet Jones		30.06.88	1	Eton	19	Aug
11.9w		Maisey Snaith	U17	(12.24w)	1	Cambridge	4	Jun
12.0		Josie Oliarnyk	U20	(11.86w)	2	Worcester	6	May
12.0		Marilyn Nwawulor		(12.02)	1rB	Bedford	3	Jun
12.0		Rachel Highfield	U23	(12.15)	2rB	Bedford	3	Jun
12.0		Akaysha Ellis	U17	(12.14)	1	Uxbridge	10	Jun
12.0		Kate Johnstone	U20	12.04.00	1	Doncaster	25	Jun
12.0		Leah Duncan	U15	(12.21)	1	Cambridge	2	Jul
12.1		Samantha Griffiths		31.05.94	1	Gloucester	11	Mar
12.1		Rebecca Jeggo	U20	(12.11)	2	Luton	30	Apr
12.1		Sophie Rowe		(12.01w)	1	Solihull	6	May
12.1	0.2	Eleanor Broome	U20	(12.15)	2	Rugby	28	May
12.1		Nayanna Dubarry-Gay	U17	(12.32)	1-17	London (WF)	25	Jun
12.1		Angela Davis	U17	15.07.02	2-17	London (WF)	25	Jun
12.1		Eve Wright	U17	(12.22)	1	Cambridge	2	Jul
12.1		Mandy Gault		9.01.84	1	Portsmouth	8	Jul
12.1		Chelsea Walker	U23	29.06.97	2	Wigan	9	Jul

Additional Under 17 (1-5 above)

12.2		Latifah Harris-Osman		(12.34)	h	Uxbridge	10	Jun
12.2		Myisha Gordon		(12.27)	1	Wrexham	23	Jul
12.2		Skye Wicks		(12.40)	1	London (LV)	13	Aug
12.2		Kendrea Nwaelene		7.12.00	2	London (LV)	13	Aug
12.3	1.9	Mary Beetham-Green		(12.37)	2	Rugby	28	May
12.3		Zuriel Owolana		(12.34)	1	Harrow	28	May
12.3		Erin Healy		16.10.01	2	Burton	4	Jun
12.3		Michelle Owusu		5.01.02	2	Cheltenham	15	Jul
12.3		Obi Curry		(12.32)	1	Blackburn	5	Aug

Additional Under 15 (1 above)

12.2	Toni Bryan	(12.21)	1	Tonbridge	18	Jun
12.2	Cara Russell	19.01.03	1rB	Tonbridge	18	Jun
12.3	Kaliyah Young	(12.49)	1	Gillingham	6	Aug
12.4	Lottie Jeffrey	(12.50)	1	Grangemouth	1	Apr
12.4	Lonarra Youngs	(12.47)	1	Ipswich	30	Jul
12.5	Kayleigh Watson	27.04.04	1h1	Whitehaven	15	Apr
12.5	Imaan Denis	(12.54)	1	Harrow	22	Apr
12.5	Ellie Wheeler-Smith	16.01.03	1	Cheltenham	10	Jun
12.5	Afoma Ofor	(12.54)	1	Middlesbrough	10	Jun
12.5	Tia Anderson	19.12.02	1	Morpeth	25	Jun
12.5	Rachel Largie-Polean	16.05.03	2	Guildford	1	Jul
12.5	Sacha Didcote	4.01.03	1	Oldham	15	Jul

Under 13

12.21	0.6	Trezeguet Taylor	17.04.05	2	Bedford	26	Aug
12.54	2.0	Ayomide Cole	27.07.05	1	Portsmouth	13	May
12.54w	6.7	Nia Wedderburn-Goodison	9.01.05	2rC	London (LV)	7	Jun
	12.69	1.5		1	Sutton	9	Apr
12.58w	2.7	Emily Cann	19.02.05	1	Cambridge	24	Jun
	12.8			1	Cambridge	2	Jul
	12.83	0.0		1	Kingston	29	Jul
12.63	2.0	Iona Irvine	22.11.04	2	Portsmouth	13	May
12.7		S Shoyeke-Armstromg		1	Chelmsford	5	Jul
12.7		Lily Thurbon-Smith	1.10.05	1	Bournemouth	10	Sep
12.86	-2.1	Emily Kerr	12.01.05	1	London (CP)	19	Aug
12.87w		Tamsin Fowlie	22.12.04	1	Glasgow (S)	19	Aug
12.90		Mia McIntosh	11.01.05	1h1	Hemel Hempstead	10	Jun

Foreign

11.42	*2.0*	*Amy Foster (IRL)*		*2.10.88*	*3*	*Canberra, AUS*	*19 Feb*
11.54	*1.1*	*Charlotte Wingfield (MLT)*		*30.11.94*	*1*	*Marsa, MLT*	*13 May*
11.56	*0.1*	*Gina Akpe-Moses (IRL)*	*U20*	*25.02.99*	*1rB*	*Oordegem, BEL*	*27 May*
11.86w	*4.0*	*Emma Suhonen (FIN)*		*28.01.91*	*1*	*Cambridge*	*6 Aug*
	12.09	*1.4*			*1*	*Sienajoki, FIN*	*21 Jul*
12.00	*1.0*	*Awa Ndiaye (FRA)*	*U17*	*19.09.01*	*2s2*	*Bedford*	*26 Aug*
12.1		*Marie-Gaelle Foumena (CMR)*	*U23*	*31.07.95*	*1*	*Ashton-under-Lyne*	*7 May*

Under 15

12.46	*1.0*	*Praise Owoeye (IRL)*	*U15*	*13.08.03*	*3h1*	*Birmingham*	*7 Jul*

150 Metres Straight

16.70	-0.1	Dina Asher-Smith	U23	4.12.95	1	Gateshead (Q)	9 Sep
17.00	-0.1	Bianca Williams		18.12.93	2	Gateshead (Q)	9 Sep
17.30		Amy Hunt	U17	15.05.02	1r2	Gateshead (Q)	8 Sep

150 Metres Turn

17.06	0.0	Bianca Williams		18.12.93	1	London (Nh)	29 May
17.61	0.0	Finette Agyapong	U23	1.02.97	2	London (Nh)	29 May
17.53w	2.9	Amy Allcock		20.08.93	1	London (Nh)	7 May

Under 13

18.81		Success Eduan	27.09.04	1	Manchester (Str)	29 May
19.12		Trezeguet Taylor	17.04.05	2	Manchester (Str)	29 May
19.37		Isabel Male	17.02.05	1	Stourbridge	27 Aug
19.4		Etienne Maughan	7.12.04	1	Reading	22 Apr
19.4		Chloe Marrett	6.11.04	1	Yate	30 Jul
19.5		Nia Wedderburn-Goodison	9.01.05	1	London (WL)	20 May
19.5		Ayomide Cole	27.07.05	1	Guildford	4 Jun
19.51	-0.4	Emily Kerr	12.01.05	1	Bromley	15 Jul
19.58		Isabel White	13.09.04	1	Middlesbrough	3 Sep
19.70		Ellie Longstaff	25.11.04	2	Middlesbrough	3 Sep

200 Metres

22.22	0.8	Dina Asher-Smith	U23	4.12.95	4	London (O)	11	Aug
	22.41	0.2			1	Berlin, GER	27	Aug
	22.73	-0.4			1h5	London (O)	8	Aug
	22.73	-0.2			2s3	London (O)	10	Aug
	22.89	-0.2			3	Monaco, MON	21	Jul
	23.15	-1.0			3	Padova, ITA	16	Jul
22.69	1.4	Desiree Henry	U23	26.08.95	2	Azusa, USA	14	Apr
	23.08	1.8			1h3	Birmingham	2	Jul
	23.14	0.0			3	Birmingham	2	Jul
	23.22	-2.3			7	Doha, QAT	5	May
22.81	-2.9	Katarina Johnson-Thompson		9.01.93	1H5	Götzis, AUT	27	May
	22.86	-0.2			1H4	London (O)	5	Aug
	23.43	-1.1			1h2	Marseille, FRA	16	Jul
22.83	-0.3	Bianca Williams		18.12.93	5	Gainesville, USA	28	Apr
	22.89	1.6			1h1	Birmingham	2	Jul
	22.94	-0.5			7	Lausanne, SUI	6	Jul
	23.05	0.0			2	Birmingham	2	Jul
	23.19	0.1			1	Lisbon, POR	17	Jun
	23.30	0.5			4h1	London (O)	8	Aug
	23.35	-1.6			1	Regensburg, GER	11	Jun
	23.38	1.4			5	Oslo, NOR	15	Jun
	23.40	-0.2			6s2	London (O)	10	Aug
22.86	1.3	Finette Agyapong	U23	1.02.97	1s1	Bydgoszcz, POL	15	Jul
	22.87	1.3			1	Bydgoszcz, POL	15	Jul
	23.04	1.1			2h4	Bydgoszcz, POL	14	Jul
	23.22	-0.2			5	Monaco, MON	21	Jul
	23.23	0.4			2	Bedford	18	Jun
	23.24	1.4			1	Tergnier, FRA	25	May
	23.31	0.7			4h1	Villeneuve d'Ascq, FRA	23	Jun
22.94	0.0	Shannon Hylton	U23	19.12.96	1	Birmingham	2	Jul
	23.05	1.4			1h2	Birmingham	2	Jul
	23.09	-0.7			2	Geneva, SUI	10	Jun
	23.20	0.4			1	Bedford	18	Jun
	23.39	0.1			4h3	London (O)	8	Aug
22.95	1.5	Amarachi Pipi	U23	26.11.95	1	Norman, USA	22	Apr
	22.98	1.0			2h1	Austin, USA	26	May
	23.15	1.8			2	Los Angeles (Ww), USA	8	Apr
	23.26	0.7			2s2	Bydgoszcz, POL	15	Jul
	23.37	0.4			2h1	Bydgoszcz, POL	14	Jul
	23.41	1.3			5	Bydgoszcz, POL	15	Jul
	23.53	0.8			2h4	Birmingham	2	Jul
	23.56	0.4			8s1	Eugene, USA	8	Jun
	23.60	0.0			7	Birmingham	2	Jul
23.04	-1.0	Maya Bruney	U20	24.02.98	1	Grosseto, ITA	22	Jul
	23.07	-1.9			1s1	Grosseto, ITA	22	Jul
	23.47	-1.9			1h3	Grosseto, ITA	21	Jul
	23.51	1.4			3	Loughborough	21	May
23.23	-0.7	Cheriece Hylton	U23	19.12.96	4	Geneva, SUI	10	Jun
	23.32	0.4			3	Bedford	18	Jun
	23.44	1.4			1	Loughborough	21	May
23.27	0.0	Jodie Williams		28.09.93	2	Cork, IRL	18	Jul
	23.41	0.0			5	Birmingham	2	Jul
	23.53	1.4			2h2	Birmingham	2	Jul
(10)								
23.28	0.2	Anyika Onuora		28.10.84	3	Madrid, ESP	14	Jul
23.31	0.8	Beth Dobbin		7.06.94	1h4	Birmingham	2	Jul
	23.42	0.0			6	Birmingham	2	Jul
	23.50	1.6			2	Manchester (SC)	16	Aug

23.32	1.6	Alisha Rees	U20	16.04.99	1	Manchester (SC)	16	Aug
		23.52			1	Bedford	18	Jun
		23.54	-1.0		4	Grosseto, ITA	22	Jul
23.34	1.8	Kimbely Baptiste		27.12.92	2h3	Birmingham	2	Jul
		23.36	0.0		4	Birmingham	2	Jul
		23.43	0.0		4	Cork, IRL	18	Jul
		23.54	0.7		1	Bedford	30	Jul
23.36	0.0	Zoey Clark		25.10.94	1	Bromley	16	Jul
23.48	1.4	Amy Allcock		20.08.93	2	Loughborough	21	May
23.60mx	0.0	Margaret Adeoye		22.04.85	1	London (LV)	5	Jul
		23.78	-2.1		1	Dublin (S), IRL	12	Jul
		67 performances to 23.60 by 17 athletes						
23.63	0.8	Asha Philip		25.10.90	2rA	Loughborough	21	May
23.63	1.6	Jessica Taylor-Jemmett		27.06.88	3	Manchester (SC)	16	Aug
23.65	1.6	Louise Bloor		21.09.85	2h1	Birmingham	2	Jul
	(20)							
23.68	1.4	Emily Diamond		11.06.91	4	Loughborough	21	May
23.76	1.0	Amber Anning	U17	18.11.00	1	Bedford	27	Aug
23.79	1.6	Rebecca Campsall		2.10.90	3h1	Birmingham	2	Jul
23.81	0.8	Laviai Nielsen	U23	13.03.96	3rA	Loughborough	21	May
23.87	1.6	Georgina Adam	U20	24.03.00	4	Manchester (SC)	16	Aug
23.89	0.8	Mair Edwards	U20	6.09.99	1	Tomblaine, FRA	26	Jun
23.97	0.7	Diani Walker	U23	14.07.95	4	Bedford	30	Jul
23.99	0.3	Lorraine Ugen		22.08.91	4	Arlington, USA	25	Mar
24.02	1.6	Olivia Okoli	U20	7.09.99	1	Perivale	28	May
24.03	-1.0	Corinne Humphreys		7.11.91	1	London (LV)	8	Apr
	(30)							
24.09	0.0	Stacey Downie		15.04.87	2	Bromley	16	Jul
24.12	1.6	Joey Duck		14.04.89	4h1	Birmingham	2	Jul
24.13	-0.1	Kiah Dubarry-Gay	U17	15.11.01	1	Dublin (S), IRL	15	Jul
24.14	0.1	Rachel Miller		29.01.90	1rB	Cork, IRL	18	Jul
24.15	0.5	Jessica Turner	U23	8.08.95	1ns	Loughborough	10	May
24.18	1.6	Ella Barrett	U20	25.03.98	5h1	Birmingham	2	Jul
24.18	2.0	Katie Stainton	U23	8.01.95	2H3	Woerden, NED	26	Aug
24.21	-0.6	Mary Iheke		19.11.90	3	London (Nh)	29	May
24.25	0.3	Hannah Kelly	U17	20.12.00	2h2	Bedford	18	Jun
24.32	0.6	Ellie Turner	U20	26.05.00	2	Birmingham	8	Jul
	(40)							
24.33	-1.3	Amy Hunt	U17	15.05.02	1rB	London (Nh)	29	May
24.33	1.0	Kelsey Stewart	U23	12.02.97	2	Glasgow (S)	13	Aug
24.34	1.8	Risqat Fabunmi-Alade		25.03.94	3h3	Birmingham	2	Jul
24.35mx	1.4	Caryl Granville		24.09.89	1	Cardiff	21	Jun
		24.50	-0.2		1rB	Bromley	16	Jul
24.35	0.0	Meghan Beesley		15.11.89	3	Bromley	16	Jul
24.36	0.6	Jazmine Moss	U20	16.08.00	3	Birmingham	8	Jul
24.39	1.2	Immanuela Aliu	U20	19.04.00	1	Bromley	15	Apr
24.40	1.3	Katy Wyper		17.04.93	2	Manchester (SC)	11	Jun
24.41mx	1.5	Hannah Thomas		13.02.93	1r7	Cardiff	31	May
		24.47	1.0		1	Belfast	5	Jul
24.42	1.4	Chloe Lambert		22.05.94	6	Loughborough	21	May
	(50)							
24.42	1.0	Ella Wansell	U17	15.01.01	3	Bedford	27	Aug
24.43	1.4	Nicole Kendall	U23	26.01.96	4h2	Birmingham	2	Jul
24.46	-2.0	Hannah Brier	U20	3.02.98	2s3	Bedford	1	May
24.48	-0.2	Ebony Carr	U20	21.01.99	1h4	Bedford	18	Jun
24.49	0.8	Alison McCorry	U23	24.08.96	4h4	Birmingham	2	Jul
24.50	0.6	Mandy Gault		9.01.84	6	Dublin (S), IRL	22	Jul
24.55	1.0	Kirsten McAslan		1.09.93	3rB	Loughborough	21	May
24.55	-0.6	Jessie Knight		15.06.94	4	London (Nh)	29	May
24.56mx	1.0	Melissa Roberts	U23	6.08.97	1r1	Cardiff	31	May
		24.59	0.3		3rB	Eton	3	Jun

24.58	1.7	Skye Wicks	U17	20.08.02	2h1	Bedford	27	Aug
	(60)							
24.58	0.8	Precious Adu	U15	3.10.02	1	Bedford	27	Aug
24.59	0.1	Holly McArthur	U20	20.12.99	2H1	Grosseto, ITA	20	Jul
24.60	0.0	Olivia Caesar	U23	22.07.96	5	Bromley	16	Jul
24.60	0.7	Clieo Stephenson	U23	8.04.95	7	Bedford	30	Jul
24.61	1.0	Kelly Massey		11.01.85	5rB	Loughborough	21	May
24.64	1.6	Lucy Evans		2.10.82	2rB	Oordegem, BEL	27	May
24.64	0.1	Niamh Emerson	U20	22.04.99	3H1	Grosseto, ITA	20	Jul
24.68	0.3	Joanne Ryan		3.10.86	4rB	Eton	3	Jun
24.68	0.4	Yvette Westwood	U20	3.09.98	1h1	Birmingham	8	Jul
24.69	-3.1	Alicia Barrett	U20	25.03.98	1	Cudworth	13	May
	(70)							
24.72	-1.3	Lauren Russell	U20	16.03.98	3rB	London (Nh)	29	May
24.73	1.6	Eleanor Grove	U20	16.10.99	2	Perivale	28	May
24.73	1.8	Jemma Wood	U20	3.03.99	4h3	Birmingham	2	Jul
24.75	1.3	Zoe Pollock	U17	21.12.00	1H1	Boston	16	Sep
24.76	0.0	Aleasha Kiddle		17.08.92	3	London (CP)	11	Jun
24.77	1.6	Jazz Crawford	U20	22.01.98	3rB	Oordegem, BEL	27	May
24.77	2.0	Tia Jackson	U17	5.08.02	3	Loughborough	1	Sep
24.78	1.3	Rachel Highfield	U23	2.02.96	3	Manchester (SC)	11	Jun
24.80mx	-0.4	Laura Clark	U23	17.08.96	1rB	London (LV)	5	Jul
24.83	-1.4	Hannah Foster	U17	15.03.02	1	London (He)	23	Jul
	(80)							
24.85	-0.4	Kayla Bowley	U17	28.12.01	1-17	London (Cr)	28	May
24.85	1.8	Jodie Leslie		1.05.93	6h3	Birmingham	2	Jul
24.85	0.0	Ellie Edwards	U23	19.11.96	1	Jerusalem, ISR	13	Jul
24.85		Eilidh De Klerk	U20	10.04.98	1	Aberdeen	23	Jul
24.86	1.6	Nikita Campbell-Smith	U23	5.09.95	4rB	Oordegem, BEL	27	May
24.86	0.3	Katie-Jane Priest	U23	27.09.96	5rB	Eton	3	Jun
24.87		Ellie Booker	U17	28.03.01	1	Wakefield	9	Apr
24.88	-1.0	Rebecca Jeggo	U20	12.01.00	2	London (LV)	8	Apr
24.88	0.6	Sophie-Ann Haigh	U20	22.10.98	5	Birmingham	8	Jul
24.89	-0.2	Alicia Regis	U17	17.12.01	4h4	Bedford	18	Jun
	(90)							
24.89	0.1	Nardhia Kidd-Walker		1.02.93	3rB	Cork, IRL	18	Jul
24.91	0.4	Amy Odunaiya	U23	17.11.96	6	Bedford	18	Jun
24.91	0.8	Charlotte Orton	U20	18.07.98	6h4	Birmingham	2	Jul
24.92	0.4	Sophie Segun	U20	3.10.98	2h1	Birmingham	8	Jul
24.93	-0.6	Sabrina Bakare	U23	14.05.96	5	London (Nh)	29	May
24.94		Amanda Shaw		28.09.84	1r1	Wakefield	9	Apr
24.94	-0.2	Angie Broadbelt-Blake		12.09.85	3rB	Bromley	16	Jul
24.95	-0.7	Hannah Lesbirel	U23	8.05.96	1	St. Peter Port GUE	25	May
24.95	0.2	Marilyn Nwawulor		20.09.92	1H1	Hexham	22	Jul
24.96	1.7	Emily First	U23	5.07.95	2	Brisbane, AUS	28	Jan
	(100)							
24.96		Joy Ogunleye	U17	27.09.00	2	Chelmsford	14	May
24.98	-0.2	Jahisha Thomas		22.11.94	1rD	Tempe, USA	17	Mar
24.99	0.5	Dolita Awala-Shaw	U17	7.11.00	1	London (CP)	19	Aug
25.00mx	-0.5	Lukesha Morris	U23	26.11.95	1	Watford	19	Apr
25.00	-2.4	Tara Kafke		17.02.89	6	Birmingham	6	May
25.00		Georgia Yearby	U23	19.02.95	1	Leeds	6	May
25.00	1.3	Hannah Williams		17.01.89	3h1	Bedford	30	Jul
25.00	0.0	Rachel Bennett	U17	3.07.02	1	Leigh	20	Aug

Additional Under 17 (1-17 above)

25.04	0.5	Lauren Greig		20.09.00	4h1	Bedford	18	Jun
25.09	-0.8	Sophie Porter		14.03.01	2h3	Bedford	27	Aug
25.12	0.6	Obi Curry		11.04.01	3h3	Birmingham	7	Jul
	(20)							
25.15	-1.0	Jade Hutchison		3.05.02	1	Grangemouth	12	May
25.17		Cassie-Ann Pemberton		24.07.01	1	Birmingham	17	Jun

25.18	-3.6	Isabella Gilkes	23.04.01	1	London (He)	23	Jul
25.28		Leonie Ashmeade	25.01.01	2	Wakefield	9	Apr
25.28	1.1	Abena Oteng	7.09.01	1B	Tomblaine, FRA	26	Jun
25.32	0.5	Chyna Russell	22.12.00	4	London (CP)	19	Aug
25.33	-0.7	Ella Turner	2.06.01	2	Oxford (H)	14	May
25.36		Amelia Bunton	13.06.02	3	Wakefield	9	Apr
25.36	0.2	Moli Jones	28.10.00	2	Dublin (S), IRL	5	Aug
25.37		Taiwo Taiwo	23.09.01	2	Manchester (Str)	14	May
	(30)						
25.37	1.8	Rebecca Watkins	23.08.01	4h2	Birmingham	7	Jul
25.37	1.3	Emily Bee	3.03.02	3H1	Boston	16	Sep
25.38	0.7	Stella Perrett	15.04.01	3h1	Birmingham	7	Jul
25.39		Angela Davis	15.07.02	4	Chelmsford	14	May
25.40	1.7	Lucy Elcock	11.09.01	3h1	Bedford	27	Aug

Additional Under 15 (1 above)

25.01	0.3	Holly Mpassy	12.07.03	2	Birmingham	8	Jul
25.02	0.3	Acacia Williams-Hewitt	8.08.03	3	Birmingham	8	Jul
25.11	0.3	Cara Russell	19.01.03	4	Birmingham	8	Jul
25.20	0.8	Leah Duncan	30.10.02	2h2	Bedford	27	Aug
25.28	-0.1	Macey Morris	12.02.03	5	Dublin (S), IRL	15	Jul
25.38	0.3	Madeleine Whapples	12.04.03	5	Birmingham	8	Jul
25.48	0.0	Alyson Bell	9.11.03	1	Kilmarnock	21	May
25.49	2.0	Lottie Jeffrey	3.02.03	1	Grangemouth	9	Jun
25.49	0.0	Tia Anderson	19.12.02	1	Leigh	20	Aug
	(10)						
25.55	0.8	Imaan Denis	27.11.02	3h2	Bedford	27	Aug
25.58	0.8	Natalie Groves	1.04.04	1h2	Birmingham	8	Jul
25.62	0.0	Alice Rodgers	23.09.02	3	Tullamore, IRL	3	Jun
25.66		Rachel Largie-Polean	16.05.03	1	Kingston	10	Jun
25.67	0.8	Caitlyn Mapps	27.11.02	4h2	Bedford	27	Aug
25.69	1.1	Lucia Gifford Groves	4.08.03	2h4	Birmingham	8	Jul
25.70	0.0	Christabel Antwi	18.10.02	2	Birmingham	2	Sep
25.75	-0.8	Molly Palmer	27.08.03	1	Derby	14	May
25.86	-1.3	Monae Winston	31.10.02	1rD	London (TB)	1	May
25.86	0.8	Jennifer Eduwu	17.04.04	3h2	Birmingham	8	Jul
	(20)						
25.87	1.1	Demi Tuinema	2.01.03	3h4	Birmingham	8	Jul
25.88	2.0	Toni Bryan	23.12.02	1	Sutton	9	Apr
25.89	-0.2	Cedelle Agyei-Kyem	12.09.02	1	London (BP)	18	Jun
25.90	2.0	Eloise Gray	17.09.02	2	Grangemouth	9	Jun
25.91	-1.6	Aleeya Sibbons	5.11.02	6rC	London (Nh)	29	May
25.93	-1.0	Iona Newbegin	1.09.02	1	Peterborough	13	May
25.93	-1.0	Elizabeth Taylor	18.05.04	2	Peterborough	13	May
25.94		Philippa Ellis	23.04.03	1	Middlesbrough	3	Sep
25.96	0.0	Sade Kaka	26.09.02	4h1	Birmingham	8	Jul
25.97	0.0	Osarumen Odemwengie	23.09.03	2	Leigh	20	Aug
	(30)						
25.98		Katie Dinwoodie	27.01.03	1	Inverness	12	May
25.99	0.8	Poppy Glasby-Seddon	24.11.02	4h2	Birmingham	8	Jul

wind assisted

22.83	3.4	Amarachi Pipi	U23	(22.95)	2	Lawrence, USA	14	May
	22.89	4.8			1h2	Lawrence, USA	13	May
	22.99	2.7			5q2	Austin, USA	27	May
23.12	3.2	Alisha Rees	U20	(23.32)	1	Eton	3	Jun
	23.38	2.6			1	Grangemouth	27	Aug
	23.54	3.5			1h2	Grangemouth	27	Aug
23.14	3.2	Zoey Clark		(23.36)	2	Eton	3	Jun
23.25	2.2	Johnson-Thompson		(22.81)	1	Nice, FRA	7	May
23.41	4.8	Jessica Turner	U23	(24.15)	2rE	Clermont, USA	15	Apr

9 performances to 23.60 by 5 athletes

23.81	4.6	Mair Edwards	U20	(23.89)	1	Southampton	6	May
24.16	7.0	Nardhia Kidd-Walker		(24.89)	1h2	Nuneaton	11	Jun
24.16	2.1	Katie Stainton	U23	(24.18)	3H1	Bydgoszcz, POL	13	Jul
24.17	3.2	Olivia Caesar	U23	(24.60)	3	Eton	3	Jun
24.25	4.7	Chloe Lambert		(24.42)	1	Glasgow (S)	16	Jul
24.27	3.1	Montell Douglas		24.01.86	1	Waco TX, USA	22	Apr
24.32	3.2	Meghan Beesley		(24.35)	4	Eton	3	Jun
24.35	4.0	Victoria Ohuruogu		28.02.93	4rF	Clermont, USA	15	Apr
24.35	3.2	Jessie Knight		(24.55)	5	Eton	3	Jun
24.36	5.3	Yvette Westwood	U20	(24.60)	1	Nuneaton	11	Jun
24.52	2.3	Niamh Emerson	U20	(24.64)	4H3	Kladno, CZE	17	Jun
24.56	4.6	Jodie Leslie		(24.85)	2	Southampton	6	May
24.62	2.3	Emily First	U23	(24.96)	1rB	St Lucia, AUS	11	Feb
24.67	3.0	Lily Beckford	U23	11.08.97	1rF	Clermont, USA	15	Apr
24.68	2.3	Amy Odunaiya	U23	(24.91)	1	Wigan	7	May
24.69	4.5	Hannah Lesbirel	U23	(24.95)	1	Visby, SWE	29	Jun
24.74	5.5	Hannah Dunderdale		2.11.94	1H2	Arlington, USA	12	May
24.74	3.4	Amanda Shaw		(24.94)	3h1	Manchester (SC)	11	Jun
24.76	2.2	Tia Jackson	U17	(24.77)	1	Nuneaton	19	Aug
24.77	2.4	Rebecca Jeggo	U20	(24.88)	1	Oxford (H)	9	Sep
24.83	3.2	Tara Kafke		(25.00)	6	Eton	3	Jun
24.84	2.2	Holly Mills	U20	15.04.00	1	Portsmouth	14	May
24.88	4.7	Abigail Bishell	U23	11.02.95	2	Glasgow (S)	16	Jul
24.89	4.4	Holly Pattie-Belleli		9.06.94	5	Columbia, USA	15	Apr
24.89	3.5	Charlotte Orton	U20	(24.79)	2h1	Manchester (SC)	11	Jun
24.89	5.3	Mia Chapman	U20	20.08.99	2	Nuneaton	11	Jun
24.89	4.1	Salome Japal	U20	6.09.98	1rD	London (LV)	16	Aug
24.96		Yasmin Liverpool	U20	15.01.99	2	Haarlem, NED	7	May
24.96	2.4	Zoe Thompson	U20	10.04.00	4h2	Bedford	30	Jul
24.96	2.4	Rebecca Matheson	U20	7.03.99	2h1	Grangemouth	27	Aug
24.99	4.1	Cassie-Ann Pemberton	U17	(25.17)	1	Nuneaton	13	May

Additional Under 17 (1-2 above)

25.15	2.2	Indiana Malik		8.07.02	2	Nuneaton	19	Aug
25.22	3.1	Katie Reville		20.02.02	1	Kilmarnock	12	May
25.24	2.3	Louise Evans		7.10.00	1	Gillingham	23	Apr
25.26	2.1	Megan Webber		31.05.01	1	Exeter	14	May
25.30	2.3	Chyna Russell		(25.32)	1	Sutton	15	Apr
25.38	2.2	Lucy Elcock		(25.40)	3	Nuneaton	19	Aug
25.39	2.2	Erin Healy		16.10.01	4	Nuneaton	19	Aug

Under 15

25.32	4.0	Monae Winston		(25.86)	4rB	London (Nh)	7	May
25.64	2.2	Lucia Gifford Groves		(25.69)	1	Exeter	17	Jun
25.77	3.3	Leah Okorhi		17.05.03	1s1	Nuneaton	19	Aug
25.80	3.1	Iona Newbegin		(25.93)	1h2	Cambridge	24	Jun
25.85	2.6	Shona McLay		6.02.03	2	Grangemouth	29	Jul
25.93	2.1	Ffion Jones		17.11.02	1	Brecon	26	Aug

hand timing

24.0		Rachel Miller		(24.14)	3	Bedford	3	Jun
24.2		Hannah Thomas		(24.41)	4	Bedford	3	Jun
24.6		Rachel Highfield	U23	(24.78)	1rB	Bedford	3	Jun
24.6	0.5	Lucy Jones		20.01.91	1	Loughborough	6	Aug
24.6w	4.4	Megan Davies	U20	31.01.99	2	Nottingham	30	Apr
24.6w	4.3	Jade Hutchison	U17	(25.15)	1-17	Hull	30	Apr
		24.7			1-17	Darlington	28	May
24.7		Josie Oliarnyk	U20	27.03.00	1	Stourport	30	Apr
24.7		Nardhia Kidd-Walker		(24.89)	1	Cheltenham	14	May
24.7		Sophie-Ann Haigh	U20	(24.88)	2rB	Bedford	3	Jun
24.8		Jessica Armah		29.08.83	1	Uxbridge	17	Jun
24.8		Georgia Yearby	U23	(25.00)	1	Morpeth	9	Jul

24.9		Laura Wake		3.05.91	1	London (TB)	15 Apr
24.9		Abigail Bishell	U23	11.02.95	1	Wigan	9 Jul
24.9		Alice McMahon	U23	15.02.95	2	Wigan	9 Jul
24.9mx		Sophie Porter	U17	(25.09)	1	Portsmouth	9 Sep

Additional Under 17 (1-2 above)

25.0	1.1	Cassie-Ann Pemberton		(25.17)	1	Nottingham	30 Apr
25.0		Obi Curry		(25.12)	1	Bebington	4 Jun
25.0		Angela Davis		(25.39)	2	London (WF)	25 Jun
25.1		Ella Turner		(25.33)	1	Bournemouth	23 Apr
25.1		Maisey Snaith		(25.19)	1	Cambridge	4 Jun
25.2		Madeline Wilton		11.04.02	1	Portsmouth	2 Apr
25.3	1.1	Amy Pye		22.11.00	2	Nottingham	30 Apr

Under 15

25.2		Toni Bryan		(25.88)	1rB	Tonbridge	18 Jun
25.3		Tia Anderson		(25.49)	1	Morpeth	25 Jun
25.5		Sacha Didcote		4.01.03	1	Manchester (SC)	20 May
25.5		Imaan Denis		(25.55)	2	Uxbridge	10 Jun
25.5		Esther Jackson		9.08.03	1	Gillingham	6 Aug
25.6		Sade Kaka		(25.96)	1	Middlesbrough	15 Jul
25.7w		Serena Grace		6.01.03	1	Cambridge	18 Jun
25.8		Leah Okorhi		(25.77w)	1	Rugby	18 Jun
25.8		Aleeya Sibbons		(25.91)	1	Hastings	18 Jun
25.9		Maisie Rixon		11.10.02	2	Reading	22 Apr
25.9		Abigail Pawlett		14.01.03	1	Stockport	28 Jun
25.9		Poppy Glasby-Seddon		(25.99)	1	Preston	15 Jul
25.9w	2.2	Katie Dinwoodie		(25.98)	1	Lerwick	3 Jun
25.9w		Samantha Muchina		21.11.02	3	Cambridge	18 Jun

Under 13

25.83	0.8	Ayomide Cole		27.07.05	5	Bedford	27 Aug
26.06	0.0	Success Eduan		27.09.04	1	Leigh	20 Aug
26.5		Trezeguet Taylor		17.04.05	1	Warrington	3 Sep
26.56w	3.5	Nia Wedderburn-Goodison		9.01.05	1rD	London (LV)	7 Jun
26.70w	2.3	Ava Jones		21.11.04	1	Doncaster	1 Apr
		26.72			1	Nuneaton	9 Sep
26.75w	2.5	Tamsin Fowlie		22.12.04	1	Glasgow (S)	19 Aug
26.8		Emily Cann		19.02.05	1	Cambridge	2 Jul
		26.85	-0.3		1r2	Kingston	29 Jul
26.85w	3.5	Isabel Male		17.02.05	1	Nuneaton	13 May
26.88w	3.6	Iona Irvine		22.11.04	2	Portsmouth	14 May
26.89	0.6	Emily Kerr		12.01.05	1rB	Bromley	10 Jul

Indoor where superior to outdoors

23.19		Pipi	U23	(22.95)	1	Ames, USA	25 Feb
		23.21			2h3	College Station, USA	10 Mar
		23.26			4	Fayetteville, USA	11 Feb
		23.44			1	Lincoln, USA	21 Jan
		23.48			1h4	Ames, USA	24 Feb
		23.55			1	New York (A), USA	4 Feb
		6 performances to 23.60 by 1 athlete					
24.04		Amelia Reynolds	U20	23.11.98	2s2	Sheffield	26 Feb
24.16+		Eilidh Doyle		20.02.87	1m	Belgrade, SRB	3 Mar
24.49mx		Abigayle Fitzpatrick		10.06.93	1r3	Manchester (SC)	8 Jan
		24.51			2	Sheffield	21 Jan
24.56		Melissa Roberts	U23	(24.56mx)	1	Cardiff	28 Jan
24.58		Rachel Dickens		28.10.94	1	London (LV)	28 Jan
24.60		Yvette Westwood	U20	(24.68)	1	Birmingham	11 Feb
24.70		Lauren Roy	U17	(25.12)	1	Athlone, IRL	1 Apr
24.72		Alicia Regis	U17	(24.89)	1	Sheffield	26 Feb

24.76	Bethany Close	U23	30.12.95	1s4	Sheffield	19	Feb
24.79	Charlotte Orton	U20	(24.91)	3h3	Sheffield	12	Feb
24.87	Jade Hutchison	U17	(25.15)	2	Glasgow	28	Jan
24.88	Zoe Thompson	U20	(24.96w)	2h4	Sheffield	26	Feb
24.89	Lauren Greig	U17	(25.04)	3	Glasgow	28	Jan
24.94	Josie Oliarnyk	U20	(25.15)	2	Birmingham	11	Feb
24.96	Mhairi Patience	U23	10.09.95	2	Glasgow	4	Feb

Additional Under 17 (1-4 above)

25.16	Abigail Pawlett		(25.9)	2	Manchester	17	Dec
25.19	Maisey Snaith		(25.1)	2s2	Sheffield	26	Feb
25.22	Shania Umah		17.02.02	3s2	Sheffield	26	Feb

Under 15

25.82	Ava Jones		21.11.04	1	Sheffield	3	Dec
25.88	Eloise Gray		(25.90)	1s1	Glasgow	12	Feb

Foreign

23.31w	3.4	Amy Foster (IRL)		2.10.88	2	St Lucia, AUS	11	Feb
	23.63	0.1			3	Rhede, GER	29	Jul
23.78	0.3	Charlotte Wingfield (MLT)		30.11.94	1	Serraville, SMR	4	Jun
24.12i		Gina Akpe-Moses (IRL)	U20	25.02.99	3s2	Sheffield	26	Feb
	24.27	0.4			2s2	Bedford	18	Jun
24.61	-1.3	Sydney Griffin (USA)		16.10.93	2rB	London (Nh)	29	May
24.76	-1.1	Roisin Harrison (IRL)	U23	10.10.96	3	Tullamore, IRL	1	Jul
25.09	0.9	Awa Ndiaye (FRA)	U17	19.09.01	1	London (PH)	18	Jun
25.24	-1.2	Kate O'Connor (IRL)	U17	12.12.00	4H2	Grosseto. ITA	20	Jul

300 Metres

36.86	Finette Agyapong		1.2.97	1	London (Nh)	29	May
37.46	Amy Allcock		20.8.93	1	London (Nh)	7	May
37.72	Margaret Adeoye		22.4.85	2	London (Nh)	29	May
38.36	Lauren Russell	U20	16.3.98	3	London (Nh)	29	May
38.42	Cheriece Hylton	U23	19.12.96	2	London (Nh)	7	May

Indoors

37.6+	Eilidh Doyle		20.2.87	1s1	Belgrade, SRB	3	Mar
37.8+	Laviai Nielsen	U23	13.03.96	1s3	Belgrade, SRB	3	Mar

Under 17

37.79	Amber Anning		18.11.00	1	Loughborough	1	Sep
38.80	Davicia Patterson		15.12.00	1	Tullamore, IRL	3	Jun
38.85	Hannah Foster		15.03.02	1	Dublin (S), IRL	15	Jul
39.34	Chyna Russell		22.12.00	1h1	Birmingham	7	Jul
39.5	Maisey Snaith		3.04.01	1	Cambridge	18	Jun
	39.76			2h1	Birmingham	7	Jul
39.57	Natasha Harrison		17.03.01	2	Birmingham	8	Jul
39.60	Louise Evans		7.10.00	1h2	Birmingham	7	Jul
39.76	Skye Wicks		20.08.02	1	Woodford	2	Jul
39.76	Ella Turner		2.06.01	3	Bedford	27	Aug
39.95	Louisa Saunders		26.12.00	1	Bromley	28	May
	(10)						
39.99i	Sophie Porter		14.03.01	1	Sheffield	26	Feb
40.11	Jemima Copeman		15.06.02	2	Bromley	28	May
40.20	Abigail Dennison		22.01.01	3h2	Birmingham	7	Jul
40.2	Shammah Sowah		21.01.02	1	London (ME)	28	May
	40.63			1	Chelmsford	10	Jun
40.2	Alex Shaw		6.09.00	1	Basingstoke	9	Sep
40.23	Rachel McCann		26.09.01	2	Dublin (S), IRL	24	Jun
40.36	Emily Miller		16.06.02	1	Grangemouth	27	Aug
40.42	Asha Root		15.06.01	3h3	Birmingham	7	Jul
40.44	Armani Williams		29.03.01	1h1	Cardiff	1	Jul
40.46	Emma Rutherford		20.09.01	4	Loughborough	1	Sep

40.48	Mary Takwoingi	13.09.01	1	Nuneaton	20	Aug
40.62	Olivia Vareille	11.12.00	1h4	Grangemouth	9	Jun
40.65i	Amelia Bunton	13.06.02	4	Sheffield	26	Feb
40.88			1	Cudworth	13	May
40.7	Lucy Elcock	11.09.01	1	Solihull	28	May
40.7	Annie Testar	18.04.02	1	Cheltenham	26	Jul
40.72	Emma Mailer	24.02.02	2	Grangemouth	27	Aug
40.73	Megan Webber	31.05.01	1	Exeter	7	May
40.73	Abigail Fitton	10.12.01	3h1	Bedford	26	Aug
40.77	Connie McCafferty	24.02.01	2h2	Bedford	26	Aug
40.79	Lucy Stennett	22.07.02	1h1	Exeter	17	Jun
(30)						
40.84	Iona McDonald	11.11.01	4	Grangemouth	27	Aug

Under 15

40.15	Holly Mpassy	12.07.03	1	Birmingham	2	Sep
40.35	Alyson Bell	9.11.03	1-14	Gothenburg, SWE	2	Jul
40.35	Tia Anderson	19.12.02	1	Bedford	27	Aug
40.50	Macey Morris	12.02.03	2	Bedford	27	Aug
40.58	Madeleine Whapples	12.04.03	1	Leamington	2	Aug
40.89	Elizabeth Taylor	18.05.04	3	Bedford	27	Aug
41.0mx	Hannah Roberts	15.09.02	1rB	Eton	1	Apr
41.21			1	Bracknell	22	Apr
41.16	Emma Morris	20.03.03	1rB	Bromley	15	Jul
41.18i	Acacia Williams-Hewitt	8.08.03	1	Sheffield	19	Mar
41.40			1	Cudworth	13	May
41.38	Imaan Denis	27.11.02	1	London (LV)	8	Apr
(10)						
41.39	Maisie Rixon	11.10.02	3h2	Bedford	26	Aug
41.4	Lisa-Marie Uzokwe	3.03.03	1	Cambridge	2	Jul
41.73			1	London (He)	30	Jul
41.46	Katie Foss	3.06.03	4h2	Bedford	26	Aug
41.5	Angel Gediz	24.04.03	1	Hastings	18	Jun
41.56i	Gemma Bruce	22.09.02	2	Glasgow	2	Feb
41.6	Poppy Glasby-Seddon	24.11.02	1	Blackpool	13	May
41.69	Shakanya Osahon	10.09.03	1rB	Birmingham	2	Sep
41.70	Cedelle Agyei-Kyem	12.09.02	1	London (BP)	18	Jun
41.7	Ashley Nemits	30.03.04	1	Manchester (SC)	20	May
41.7	Lucy-Jane Matthews	17.09.02	2	Southampton	20	May
(20)						
41.7	Sacha Didcote	4.01.03	1	Connah's Quay	18	Jun
41.7	Emily Misantoni	27.09.02	1	Manchester (Str)	15	Jul
41.90			2	Loughborough	9	Aug
41.75	Poppy Oliver	27.02.03	3h1	Bedford	26	Aug
41.8	Poppy Ellis	11.10.02		Oxford (H)	1	Jul
41.8	Darcey Lonsdale	17.10.02	1	Preston	15	Jul
41.8	Layla Zuill	27.09.03	1	Grangemouth	5	Aug
41.8	Serena Grace	6.01.03	2	Norwich	20	Aug
41.89	Poppy Malik	27.11.03	1	Nuneaton	20	Aug
41.93	Amy Kirkpatrick	22.09.03	1rB	Glasgow (S)	9	Aug
41.97	Melissa Coxon	5.12.02	5h2	Bedford	26	Aug

400 Metres

51.67	Emily Diamond	11.06.91	7	London (O)	9	Jul
51.85			2	Gainesville, USA	28	Apr
52.20			5h2	London (O)	6	Aug
52.34			2	Birmingham	2	Jul
52.35			1h1	Birmingham	1	Jul

51.81	Anyika Onuora		28.10.84	3	Madrid, ESP	14	Jul
51.92				3	Gainesville, USA	28	Apr
52.48				3	Sotteville, FRA	7	Jul
52.58				7h6	London (O)	6	Aug
52.82				3	Birmingham	2	Jul
53.10				5	Rovereto, ITA	29	Aug
53.17				2	Leiden, NED	17	Jun
53.30				2h4	Birmingham	1	Jul
51.81	Zoey Clark		25.10.94	7s3	London (O)	7	Aug
51.84				1	Geneva, SUI	10	Jun
51.88				3h5	London (O)	6	Aug
52.30				1	Birmingham	2	Jul
52.33				1	Eton	3	Jun
52.64				1	Loughborough	21	May
52.75				1	Bedford	1	May
52.85				1	Birmingham	6	May
52.87				8	Birmingham	20	Aug
53.04				1h3	Birmingham	1	Jul
52.19	Perri Shakes-Drayton		21.12.88	2	Rovereto, ITA	29	Aug
52.37				2	Sotteville, FRA	7	Jul
52.72				1	Novo Mesto, SLO	19	Jul
53.02				1h4	Birmingham	1	Jul
53.16				2	London (Nh)	29	May
53.49				6	Marseille, FRA	3	Jun
52.32	Margaret Adeoye		22.04.85	1rB	Rovereto, ITA	29	Aug
52.46				1	Brussels, BEL	9	Jul
52.56				1	Kessel-Lo, BEL	19	Aug
52.70				1	Manchester (SC)	16	Aug
53.09				2	Loughborough	22	Jul
53.14				1	Bedford	30	Jul
53.2				1	Treviglio, ITA	9	Sep
53.30				4h1	Birmingham	1	Jul
52.36	Eilidh Doyle		20.02.87	2	Huelva, ESP	14	Jun
52.41	Finette Agyapong	U23	1.02.97	1	London (Wil)	15	Aug
52.55	Hannah Williams	U20	23.04.98	3	Grosseto, ITA	22	Jul
53.08				2h3	Grosseto, ITA	20	Jul
53.39				7	Geneva, SUI	10	Jun
52.60	Laviai Nielsen	U23	13.03.96	4	Oordegem, BEL	27	May
52.80				1h3	Bydgoszcz, POL	14	Jul
52.80				2rB	Rovereto, ITA	29	Aug
53.18				5	Bydgoszcz, POL	15	Jul
53.47				2h3	Birmingham	1	Jul
52.60	Mary Iheke		19.11.90	6	Villeneuve d'Ascq, FRA	24	Jun
52.92				5h2	Villeneuve d'Ascq, FRA	23	Jun
52.99				3	Brussels, BEL	9	Jul
53.47				2h2	Birmingham	1	Jul
(10)							
52.68mx	Cheriece Hylton	U23	19.12.96	1	Gillingham	9	Jul
52.88				3h1	Birmingham	1	Jul
52.98				4	Birmingham	2	Jul
53.16				1	London (Nh)	29	May
52.85	Amy Allcock		20.08.93	2h1	Birmingham	1	Jul
53.40				5	Birmingham	2	Jul
52.90	Kirsten McAslan		1.09.93	1rB	Geneva, SUI	10	Jun
53.10				1rC	Oordegem, BEL	27	May
53.19				6	Bydgoszcz, POL	2	Jun
53.38				1h2	Birmingham	1	Jul
52.9	Ashleigh Nelson		20.02.91	1	Wolverhampton	4	Jun
53.29				1rE	Waco, USA	22	Apr
52.96	Amarachi Pipi	U23	26.11.95	1	Arlington, USA	25	Mar
53.17	Maya Bruney	U20	24.02.98	1h1	Bedford	29	Jul
53.18				2	Bedford	30	Jul

53.25	Christine Ohuruogu		17.05.84	7	Kingston, JAM	20	May
53.33	Desiree Henry	U23	26.08.95	4	Gainesville, USA	30	Mar
53.38	Shelayna Oskan-Clarke		20.01.90	2	Eton	3	Jun
	53.39			3	Ninove, BEL	15	Jul
53.47	Jessie Knight		15.06.94	1	Bromley	16	Jul
	71 performances to 53.50 by 20 athletes						
53.59	Laura Maddox		13.05.90	2	Birmingham	6	May
53.63	Kelsey Stewart	U23	12.02.97	1	Bedford	18	Jun
53.68	Amber Anning	U17	18.11.00	3	Nassau, BAH	21	Jul
53.71	Lauren Russell	U20	16.03.98	3h1	Grosseto, ITA	20	Jul
53.72	Lina Nielsen	U23	13.03.96	5h1	Birmingham	1	Jul
53.91	Stacey Downie		15.04.87	2	Bromley	16	Jul
53.95	Victoria Ohuruogu		28.02.93	2	London (Nh)	7	May
53.95	Kelly Massey		11.01.85	5	Brussels, BEL	9	Jul
54.03	Sabrina Bakare	U23	14.05.96	2	Bedford	18	Jun
54.11	Olivia Caesar	U23	22.07.96	2	Bedford	1	May
(30)							
54.11	Susanna Banjo		28.07.89	2	London (Wil)	15	Aug
54.24mx	Lily Beckford	U23	11.08.97	1	Watford	12	Jul
	54.50			1rB	Bromley	16	Jul
54.34	Catherine Reid	U20	21.04.98	4rB	Columbia, USA	13	May
54.34	Bianca Williams		18.12.93	6rB	Rovereto, ITA	29	Aug
54.35	Ese Okoro		4.07.90	3	Birmingham	6	May
54.37	Jill Cherry	U20	1.03.98	3	Oordegem, BEL	27	May
54.50	Davicia Patterson	U17	15.12.00	2	Belfast	10	Jun
54.54	Seren Bundy-Davies		30.12.94	3	Loughborough	21	May
54.54	Emma Alderson	U20	29.02.00	3	Bedford	18	Jun
54.55	Laura Wake		3.05.91	1	Loughborough	22	Apr
(40)							
54.67	Nicole Kendall	U23	26.01.96	4	Bedford	18	Jun
54.69	Rosie Chamberlain	U23	11.08.95	4h1	Houston, USA	13	May
54.88	Joanne Ryan		3.10.86	5	Bromley	16	Jul
54.89	Jessica Tappin		17.05.90	6	Bromley	16	Jul
54.92	Holly Turner	U23	15.11.95	4h2	Birmingham	1	Jul
54.94	Chloe Lambert		22.05.94	1	Kilmarnock	13	May
54.94	Nikita Campbell-Smith	U23	5.09.95	5rC	Geneva, SUI	10	Jun
54.98	Tara Kafke		17.02.89	2	London (CP)	11	Jun
55.05	Megan Davies	U20	31.01.99	3h1	Bedford	29	Jul
55.09	Mair Edwards	U20	6.09.99	1	London (LV)	8	Apr
(50)							
55.12	Matilda Rainsborough	U23	28.08.96	1rC	Loughborough	21	May
55.16	Amy Gellion	U20	19.02.00	1	Birmingham	8	Jul
55.26	Orla Brothers	U20	27.12.99	1rB	London (Nh)	29	May
55.31	Mandy Gault		9.01.84	1	Crawley	13	May
55.38mx	Leah Barrow		21.01.93	1	Manchester (Str)	20	Jun
55.42	Eleanor Briggs		20.12.92	1	Inverness	13	May
55.44	Hannah Segrave	U23	14.04.95	1	Cullowhee, USA	15	Apr
55.46	Yimika Adewakun		16.06.93	8	Bromley	16	Jul
55.48	Hayley McLean		9.09.94	1	Chelmsford	13	May
55.50mx	Anna Burt	U20	12.07.00	1rC	Yate	9	Apr
(60)							
55.50	Yasmin Liverpool	U20	15.01.99	2	Merksem, BEL	29	Jul
55.54	Georgia Yearby	U23	19.02.95	1	Cudworth	14	May
55.65	Harriet Cooper	U20	27.01.99	1	Cardiff	12	Jul
55.71	Ashton Greenwood	U20	23.01.99	1	Manchester (Str)	25	Jun
55.76	Abigayle Fitzpatrick		10.06.93	1	Wigan	7	May
55.76	Rhiannon Linington-Payne		1.10.91	1	Swansea	29	Jul
55.83	Rebecca Croft	U23	27.05.97	1rB	Sacramento, USA	18	Mar
55.84	Ellie Grove	U20	16.10.99	2	Birmingham	8	Jul
55.86	Lauren Williams	U20	12.02.99	3rB	Bromley	16	Jul
55.87	Rachel Donnison	U23	12.10.96	1	Cardiff	10	Jun

55.9	Kathryn Sutton		23.12.88	1	Dartford	19	Aug
56.28				1	Ashford	14	May
56.00	Alex Shaw	U17	6.09.00	1	London (CP)	20	Aug
56.02	Loren Bleaken	U23	3.09.95	2	Cardiff	10	Jun
56.04	Mhairi Hendry	U23	31.03.96	2	Kilmarnock	13	May
56.06	Avril Jackson		22.10.86	5	Lucerne, SUI	11	Jul
56.08	Nisha Desai		5.08.84	1	Gateshead	14	May
56.10	Rachel Crorken	U20	7.11.99	1	Leeds	10	Jun
56.11	Ellie Baker	U20	3.06.98	1	Reading	25	Jun
56.19	Mhairi Patience	U23	10.09.95	1	Rugby	4	Jun
56.20	Melissa Owusu-Ansah		24.05.94	2	London (Elt)	21	Jun
(80)							
56.20mx	Ella Barrett	U20	25.03.98	1	Loughborough	9	Aug
56.25				2	Manchester (SC)	10	Jun
56.2	Lauren Thompson		12.02.92	1	Welwyn	17	Jun
56.21+	Jennifer Meadows	V35	17.04.81	1m	Zagreb, CRO	29	Aug
56.24	Lauren Rule	U23	24.10.96	3s1	Bedford	30	Apr
56.24	Jodie Leslie		1.05.93	2rC	Loughborough	21	May
56.29	Emily First	U23	5.07.95	3	Brisbane (Nathan), AUS	4	Mar
56.29	Hermione Plumptre		26.11.91	3rC	Loughborough	21	May
56.33	Holly McArthur	U20	20.12.99	1	Grangemouth	16	Apr
56.33	Krystal Galley		13.08.93	4rB	Bromley	16	Jul
56.34	Eleanor Gallagher	U20	20.04.00	4h1	Nassau, BAH	20	Jul
(90)							
56.44	Phoebe Fenwick	U20	6.11.99	1	Bromley	28	May
56.45	Olivia Vareille	U17	11.12.00	2	Grangemouth	13	May
56.45	Natasha Harrison	U17	17.03.01	4rC	Loughborough	21	May
56.47	Mia Spence	U23	27.06.97	2	Birmingham	4	Jun
56.52	Abbey Stanley		4.10.94	3	Manchester (SC)	10	Jun
56.54+mx	Lynsey Sharp		10.11.90	1m	Watford	24	Jun
56.55	Niamh Grahame	U23	3.02.97	2	Dublin (S), IRL	27	May
56.58mx	Roisin Smith	U23	10.11.97	1	Grangemouth	5	Jul
56.6	Ashleigh Lachenicht	U20	10.04.00	1	Douglas IOM	22	Jul
56.67	Emily Strickland	U20	27.12.99	4	Manchester (SC)	10	Jun
(100)							
56.67	Bethany Close	U23	30.12.95	1	Cambridge	6	Aug
56.68	Deborah Willis		24.04.92	1rB	Southampton	6	May
56.69	Sophie Wood		7.05.92	1	Wakefield	9	Apr
56.73	Anna Nelson	U23	14.11.95	5rB	Bromley	16	Jul
56.75mx	Olive Coles	U20	14.09.99	1rB	Watford	12	Jul
56.79				2	Bromley	28	May
56.76	Sophie Porter	U17	14.03.01	5h2	Nassau, BAH	20	Jul
56.8	Jazzmin Kiffin	U20	6.09.99	1	Banbury	28	May

Additional Under 17 (1-6 above)

56.86	Shammah Sowah		21.01.02	2	London (CP)	20	Aug
56.9	Annie Testar		18.04.02	1	Cheltenham	12	Jul
56.91	Havana Allistone-Greaves		6.07.01	1	Salamanca, ESP	11	Jun
56.97	Louise Evans		7.10.00	1	Canterbury	4	Jun
(10)							
57.2	Ella Turner		2.06.01	1	Oxford (H)	15	Apr
57.7	Charlotte Buckley		2.01.02	2	London (WL)	17	Jun
57.77	Louisa Saunders		26.12.00	3	London (CP)	20	Aug
57.83	Tia Anderson	U15	19.12.02	2	Lignano, ITA	7	Jul
57.90mx	Holly Mpassy	U15	12.07.03	1	Bromley	22	May
57.9	Tess McHugh		19.06.02	2	Wrexham	23	Jul
57.93	Asha Root		15.06.01	4	London (CP)	20	Aug
58.0	Olivia Mason		14.10.01	1	Whitehaven	13	Aug
58.01	Rachel McCann		26.09.01	1	Belfast	17	Jun
58.1	Olivia Allbut		17.07.01	1	St. Clement JER	17	Jun
(20)							

58.16	Gabrielle Fakande		1.03.01	4	Cardiff	10	Jun
58.19	Lucy Stennett		22.07.02	1	Exeter	7	May
58.2	Abigail Dennison		22.01.01	1	Portsmouth	30	Apr
58.2	Mary Takwoingi		13.09.01	1	Tipton	16	Jul
58.33	Hannah Roberts	U15	15.09.02	5	London (CP)	20	Aug

Indoor

51.86	Eilidh Doyle		(52.36)	1	Vienna, AUT	28	Jan
			52.33	4	Birmingham	18	Feb
			52.47	1s2	Sheffield	11	Feb
			52.63	1	Sheffield	12	Feb
			52.75	1	London (LV)	15	Jan
			52.81	3s1	Belgrade, SRB	3	Mar
			53.28	1h3	Belgrade, SRB	3	Mar
			53.32	1h4	Sheffield	11	Feb
			53.36	1rB	Mondeville, FRA	4	Feb
51.90	Laviai Nielsen	U23	(52.60)	2	Birmingham	18	Feb
			52.31	2s3	Belgrade, SRB	3	Mar
			52.58	2s2	Sheffield	11	Feb
			52.68	2	Vienna, AUT	28	Jan
			52.79	4	Belgrade, SRB	4	Mar
			52.86	2	Sheffield	12	Feb
52.89	Lina Nielsen	U23	(53.72)	3	Sheffield	12	Feb
			52.94	5	Birmingham	18	Feb
			53.32	1s1	Sheffield	11	Feb
52.99	Phillipa Lowe		7.04.92	4	Sheffield	12	Feb
53.37	Laura Maddox		(53.59)	1rB	Vienna, AUT	28	Jan

20 indoor performances to 53.50 by 5 athletes

where superior to outdoors

54.08	Olivia Caesar	U23	(54.11)	1	Sheffield	19	Feb
54.12	Marilyn Okoro		23.09.84	1rC	Lexington, USA	21	Jan
54.20	Meghan Beesley		15.11.89	3s2	Sheffield	11	Feb
54.91	Holly Turner	U23	(54.92)	3	Sheffield	19	Feb
55.06	Mandy Gault		(55.31)	3	Athlone, IRL	19	Feb
55.06	Mhairi Patience	U23	(56.19)	4	Sheffield	19	Feb
55.47	Rachel Dickens		28.10.94	4	London (LV)	15	Jan
55.76+	Lynsey Sharp		11.07.90	4m	New York (A), USA	4	Feb
55.93	Caryl Granville		24.09.89	1rB	Cardiff	5	Mar
55.96	Mhairi Hendry	U23	(56.04)	1	Glasgow	4	Feb
56.28	Roisin Smith	U23	(56.58mx)	1h1	Glasgow	28	Jan
56.37	Niamh Grahame	U23	(56.55)	2	Glasgow	4	Feb
56.51mx	Abbey Stanley		(56.52)	1	Sheffield	4	Jan
56.59	Anna Nelson	U23	(56.73)	3	Glasgow	4	Feb
56.63	Amelia Reynolds	U20	23.11.98	1	Cardiff	11	Feb
56.73	Amy Hillyard	U23	28.10.95	1	Birmingham	12	Feb

Foreign

55.43mx	Christine McMahon (IRL)		6.07.92	1	Belfast		6 May

600 Metres

1:25.89i	Marilyn Okoro		23.09.84	2	Clemson, USA	28	Jan
1:27.16i	Lynsey Sharp		11.07.90	4	New York (A), USA	4	Feb
1:27.5mx	Kelsey Stewart	U23	12.02.97	1	Oxford	29	Jul
1:27.9mx	Revee Walcott-Nolan	U23	6.03.95	2	Oxford	29	Jul
1:29.57i	Rosie Chamberlain	U23	11.08.95	2	Birmingham, USA	13	Jan
1:29.71i+	Jennifer Meadows	V35	17.04.81	1m	Birmingham	18	Feb
1:29.8i+e	Laura Muir		9.05.93	2m	Birmingham	18	Feb

800 Metres

1:58.01	Lynsey Sharp	11.07.90	6	Monaco, MON	21	Jul
1:58.35			3	Zagreb, CRO	29	Aug
1:58.80			7	Lausanne, SUI	6	Jul
1:58.98			8	London (O)	13	Aug
1:59.33mx			1rl	Watford	24	Jun
1:59.47			4s2	London (O)	11	Aug
1:59.96			4	London (O)	9	Jul
1:59.97			2	Birmingham	20	Aug
2:00.19			8	Stockholm, SWE	18	Jun
2:00.41			8	Oslo, NOR	15	Jun
2:01.04			2h4	London (O)	10	Aug
2:01.13			4	Somerville, USA	2	Jun
2:01.14i			3	New York (A), USA	11	Feb
2:01.23			8	Eugene, USA	27	May
2:01.81			3	Birmingham	2	Jul
2:02.72			1h1	Birmingham	1	Jul
2:02.88i			3	Boston (R), USA	28	Jan
1:58.69	Laura Muir	9.05.93	5	Lausanne, SUI	6	Jul
2:00.56i+			1m	Birmingham	18	Feb
1:59.82	Shelayna Oskan-Clarke	20.01.90	2	London (O)	9	Jul
2:00.17			1	Oordegem, BEL	27	May
2:00.39i			2	Belgrade, SRB	5	Mar
2:00.73			1	Montreuil-sous-Bois, FRA	1	Jun
2:01.30			3h2	London (O)	10	Aug
2:01.54			1	Birmingham	2	Jul
2:01.71i			3	Birmingham	18	Feb
2:02.26			6s3	London (O)	11	Aug
2:00.26	Adelle Tracey	27.05.93	6s1	London (O)	11	Aug
2:00.28			4h6	London (O)	10	Aug
2:00.34			6	London (O)	9	Jul
2:00.35			2	Los Angeles (ER), USA	18	May
2:01.53			1	Dublin (S), IRL	12	Jul
2:01.80			2	Birmingham	2	Jul
2:01.93			6	Oordegem, BEL	27	May
2:00.62	Alexandra Bell	4.11.92	8	London (O)	9	Jul
2:00.69			1	Manchester (Str)	25	Jul
2:01.87mx			1rE	Manchester (Str)	15	Aug
2:02.20			4	Prague, CZE	5	Jun
2:02.30			7	Birmingham	20	Aug
2:02.39			1	Solihull	13	May
2:02.76			1	Loughborough	21	May
2:02.79			4	Birmingham	2	Jul
2:02.88			5	Montreuil-sous-Bois, FRA	1	Jun
2:02.95			5	Dublin (S), IRL	12	Jul
2:00.92mx	Katie Snowden	9.03.94	1	Bromley	14	Aug
2:02.09mx			1rB	Manchester (Str)	16	May
2:01.2	Sarah McDonald	2.08.93	1	Tipton	26	Aug
2:01.25			7	Zagreb, CRO	29	Aug
2:02.47			2	Solihull	13	May
2:02.5			1	Tipton	18	Jul
2:01.23	Hannah England	6.03.87	6	Zagreb, CRO	29	Aug
2:02.15			4	Manchester (Str)	25	Jul
2:01.87	Laura Weightman	1.07.91	2	Manchester (Str)	25	Jul
2:02.67mx			1	Chester-Le-Street	19	Jun
2:02.09	Jacqueline Fairchild	3.05.89	3	Manchester (Str)	25	Jul
(10)						
2:02.14mx	Jessica Judd	U23 7.01.95	2rE	Manchester (Str)	15	Aug
2:02.67mx			1rC	Manchester (Str)	25	Jul
2:02.84mx			1	Watford	6	Sep
2:05.52			1	Bedford	1	May

2:02.50	Marilyn Okoro		23.09.84	1	Gainesville, USA	31	Mar
2:02.79	Hannah Segrave	U23	14.04.95	4	Murfreesboro, USA	10	Jun
60 performances to 2:03.0 by 13 athletes including 3 indoors							
2:03.12	Charlene Thomas	V35	6.05.82	5	Manchester (Str)	25	Jul
2:03.20	Revee Walcott-Nolan	U23	6.03.95	1	Watford	24	Jun
2:03.37	Mhairi Hendry	U23	31.03.96	5	Birmingham	2	Jul
2:03.38	Kaylee Dodd	U23	28.12.95	5	Eugene, USA	10	Jun
2:04.03	Melissa Courtney		30.08.93	3	Watford	9	Aug
2:04.19	Rosie Chamberlain	U23	11.08.95	4	Torrance, USA	14	Apr
2:04.19	Mari Smith	U23	14.11.96	3	Watford	24	Jun
(20)							
2:04.25mx	Jemma Reekie	U20	6.03.98	1	Manchester (Str)	29	Aug
2:05.52i				2	Glasgow	28	Jan
2:07.65				3	Glasgow (S)	2	Jun
2:04.34	Khahisa Mhlanga	U20	26.12.99	4	Watford	9	Aug
2:04.40	Jade MacLaren		1.12.88	5	Watford	24	Jun
2:04.52	Anna Burt	U20	12.07.00	1	Manchester (SC)	27	May
2:04.64	Isabelle Boffey	U20	13.04.00	2	Loughborough	21	May
2:04.67	Ellie Baker	U20	3.06.98	2rC	Oordegem, BEL	27	May
2:04.79	Katy Brown		18.11.93	7	Watford	24	Jun
2:05.48	Katy-Ann McDonald	U20	1.06.00	4	Manchester (Str)	19	Aug
2:05.50	Leah Barrow		21.01.93	9	Watford	24	Jun
2:05.81	Rebecca Croft	U23	27.05.97	3	Stanford, USA	8	Apr
(30)							
2:05.89	Emily Dudgeon		3.03.93	1	Bromley	16	Jul
2:05.97	Ejiro Okoro		4.07.90	1rB	Bromley	16	Jul
2:06.10+	Jennifer Meadows	V35	17.04.81	1m	Lausanne, SUI	6	Jul
2:06.18	Verity Ockenden		31.08.91	2	Bromley	16	Jul
2:06.26	Rhianwedd Price		11.08.94	3h3	Columbia, USA	11	May
2:06.40	Anna Smith	U17	14.09.01	1rD	Watford	24	Jun
2:06.48	Caroline Ford		29.12.92	2rB	Bromley	16	Jul
2:06.55iA	Sophie Connor		21.05.93	2	Albuquerque, USA	25	Feb
2:06.62	Philippa Millage	V35	15.08.80	2	Glasgow (S)	2	Jun
2:06.68mx	Stacey Smith		4.02.90	3	Chester-Le-Street	19	Jun
(40)							
2:06.71	Emily Thompson	U20	19.03.00	2	Birmingham	8	Jul
2:06.83	Emily Williams	U17	25.02.02	1	Birmingham	8	Jul
2:06.84i	Erin Wallace	U20	18.05.00	3	Glasgow	28	Jan
2:08.30				6	Nassau, BAH	22	Jul
2:06.84	Claire Duck		29.08.85	1rB	Manchester (Str)	25	Jul
2:06.85	Keely Hodgkinson	U17	3.03.02	1	Bedford	27	Aug
2:06.91	Ffion Price		11.08.94	2h2	Columbia, USA	11	May
2:06.94	Georgie Hartigan	U23	1.03.96	3	Solihull	13	May
2:07.0	Madeleine Murray		19.10.93	3	Melbourne (BH), AUS	7	Feb
2:07.13	Charlotte Taylor-Green		2.04.85	1rB	Manchester (Str)	19	Aug
2:07.15i	Erin McIlveen		10.03.86	2	Dublin (B), IRL	5	Feb
(50)							
2:07.18	Amy Griffiths	U23	22.03.96	10	Watford	24	Jun
2:07.21	Kelsey Stewart	U23	12.02.97	5	Solihull	13	May
2:07.37	Holly Archer		7.11.93	1rB	Watford	24	Jun
2:07.40i	Sophie Mansfield	U23	3.09.97	3	London (LV)	1	Feb
2:09.50				7	Solihull	13	May
2:07.40	Hollie Parker	U23	20.12.96	3h2	Columbia, USA	11	May
2:07.42	Abbie Hetherington	U23	2.10.95	1	Fayetteville, USA	25	Mar
2:07.44	Lilly Coward	U23	10.09.96	2rB	Watford	24	Jun
2:07.44	Molly Canham	U17	3.11.01	2	Birmingham	8	Jul
2:07.48	Mae Thompson	U23	28.05.96	1	Rock Hill, USA	23	Mar
2:07.50i	Phillipa Lowe		7.04.92	1	London (LV)	1	Jan
(60)							
2:07.51	Ellie Farrow	U17	30.10.01	3	Birmingham	8	Jul
2:07.55	Harriet Knowles-Jones	U20	3.04.98	2rB	Manchester (Str)	19	Aug
2:07.60	Rachel McClay		13.10.92	3rB	Watford	24	Jun

Time	Name	Cat	DOB	Pos	Venue	Date	
2:07.79i	Chelsea Jarvis	U23	23.01.96	4	Fayetteville, USA	28	Jan
2:07.8+	Eilish McColgan		25.11.90	6m	Berlin, GER	27	Aug
2:07.84	Amy-Eloise Neale	U23	5.08.95	2rC	Long Beach, USA	15	Apr
2:07.86	Hannah Nuttall	U23	7.07.97	1rC	Loughborough	8	Jul
2:07.88	Isobel Ives	U20	17.06.98	6	Loughborough	21	May
2:07.93mx	Ella McNiven	U17	4.09.01	1	Manchester (Str)	27	Jun
	2:08.82			8	Manchester (Str)	25	Jul
2:07.93	Bethany Ansell		10.09.94	1rD	Manchester (Str)	19	Aug
(70)							
2:08.07i	Chloe Bradley		27.03.93	5	London (LV)	1	Feb
	2:08.45			4rB	Watford	24	Jun
2:08.07	Rebecca Bullock	U17	6.12.00	2	Bedford	27	Aug
2:08.10mx	Gemma Dawkins		26.06.91	2rE	Watford	17	May
	2:09.50			5rB	Solihull	13	May
2:08.10	Katarina Johnson-Thompson		9.01.93	2H3	London (O)	6	Aug
2:08.11mx	Jenna Hill		16.10.85	1rD	Manchester (Str)	29	Aug
2:08.31	Kimberly Johansen		18.11.94	3	Durham, USA	21	Apr
2:08.31	Mollie O'Sullivan	U20	23.02.00	2	London (Elt)	21	Jun
2:08.31mx	Emma Alderson	U20	29.02.00	2rD	Manchester (Str)	29	Aug
	2:08.57			3rB	Manchester (SC)	27	May
2:08.32	Millie Howard	U20	4.02.98	3	Houston, USA	14	May
2:08.35	Samantha Coleby		4.08.90	2rC	Loughborough	8	Jul
(80)							
2:08.39	Lucy James		18.02.92	4rB	Loughborough	8	Jul
2:08.49	Charlotte Buckley	U17	2.01.02	2rB	Milton Keynes	3	Jun
2:08.49	Beth Barlow	U20	8.04.00	2rB	Manchester (Str)	25	Jul
2:08.69mx	Emma Haley		23.02.88	1rL	Watford	14	Jun
	2:08.89			5h4	Birmingham	1	Jul
2:08.89mx	Olivia Mason	U17	14.10.01	3rC	Manchester (Str)	16	May
	2:09.53			8rB	Loughborough	8	Jul
2:08.96mx	Rosie Johnson	U23	17.09.97	1rF	Manchester (Str)	25	Jul
2:09.02i	Naomi Reid	U20	24.06.00	2	Cardiff	5	Mar
	2:10.24			8rB	Solihull	13	May
2:09.03	Stephanie Pennycook	U23	1.09.95	5	Glasgow (S)	2	Jun
2:09.07	Fiona de Mauny		3.02.83	3rC	Loughborough	8	Jul
2:09.11	Hannah Tarver		22.10.93	3rB	Solihull	13	May
(90)							
2:09.13	Cara Anderson		17.01.92	7rB	Loughborough	8	Jul
2:09.16	Julie Dobbin		8.03.94	4rC	Loughborough	8	Jul
2:09.25	Saskia Huxham	U17	14.11.00	4rD	Watford	24	Jun
2:09.35mx	Francesca Brint	U20	30.08.00	1rH	Manchester (Str)	15	Aug
2:09.51	Olivia Vareille	U17	11.12.00	4	Bedford	27	Aug
2:09.68	Megan Davies	U23	10.05.96	7	Glasgow (S)	2	Jun
2:09.70	Isobel Parry-Jones	U20	17.12.98	1rC	Manchester (Str)	19	Aug
2:09.74	Anna Clark	U23	4.06.97	3rB	Bromley	16	Jul
2:09.83	Lennie Waite		4.02.86	1	Houston, USA	22	Apr
2:09.84	Emily Hosker-Thornhill		27.10.92	6	Watford	14	Jun
(100)							
2:09.86	Amy Hinchly	U20	11.01.98	5rC	Loughborough	8	Jul
2:09.97	Lauren Herrington	U23	28.11.96	4rB	Bromley	16	Jul
2:10.01	Katrina Simpson	U20	4.04.00	7rB	Solihull	13	May
2:10.01mx	Charlotte Crook	U20	14.09.99	1rB	Manchester (Str)	27	Jun
2:10.05	Annie Testar	U17	18.04.02	4	Milton Keynes	3	Jun
2:10.11	Georgia Bell		17.10.93	4h2	Eugene, USA	13	May
2:10.13	Bethany Williams	U20	7.06.99	3rB	Milton Keynes	3	Jun
2:10.18A	Roisin Flanagan	U20	2.05.98	1	Pueblo, USA	2	Apr
2:10.24	Laura Mullin	U20	11.05.99	7	Bedford	18	Jun
2:10.28	Julia Cooke		9.09.88	2rB	Watford	9	Aug
(110)							
2:10.4mx	Jessie Knight		15.06.94	1	Eton	1	Apr
2:10.42	Kirsty Fraser	U23	27.11.95	1rC	Manchester (SC)	27	May
2:10.48mx	Jodie Judd	U20	25.09.98	1rO	Watford	12	Jul

Additional Under 17 (1-12 above)

2:10.76	Shannon Flockhart	5.04.02	1	Peterborough	13	May
2:10.77	Bethan Morley	9.10.01	6	Birmingham	8	Jul
2:11.04	Alex Shaw	6.09.00	2h2	Bedford	26	Aug
2:11.24	Elise Thorner	16.03.01	2	Exeter	17	Jun
2:11.48	Stephanie Moss	24.05.02	3h2	Bedford	26	Aug
2:11.80	Sarah Calvert	29.06.01	1	Dublin (S), IRL	5	Aug
2:12.56	Alexandra Brown	8.04.01	1rD	London (TB)	22	Jul
2:12.95	Kiara Frizelle	10.07.01	2rD	Loughborough	8	Jul
(20)						
2:13.00mx	Olivia Allum	21.06.01	4rM	Watford	14	Jun
2:13.75i	Nuala McCheyne	4.10.01	2	Glasgow	28	Jan
2:14.00			5rB	Glasgow (S)	2	Jun
2:13.79mx	Cyane Robinson	11.06.01	4rl	Manchester (Str)	15	Aug
2:13.97	Anya Pigden	4.05.01	2rC	Milton Keynes	3	Jun
2:14.0	Katie Hopkins	14.08.01	1	Harrow	21	May
2:14.03mx	Hayley Instance	6.05.02	5rM	Watford	14	Jun
2:14.03mx	Meredith Winship	9.12.01	3rO	Watford	14	Jun
2:14.43			3h1	Birmingham	7	Jul
2:14.21mx	Natasha Harrison	17.03.01	3rH	Manchester (Str)	15	Aug
2:14.23mx	Elizabeth Bentham	13.04.02	2rN	Watford	14	Jun
2:14.53i	Maia Hardman	17.10.01	2	London (LV)	8	Jan
(30)						
2:14.63	Murphy Miller	17.01.02	1	Belfast	5	Jul
2:14.8	Mia Roberts	13.07.02	1	Wrexham	23	Jul
2:14.89	Havana Allistone-Greaves	6.07.01	2	Valencia, ESP	3	Jun

Under 15

2:11.35mx	Isla Calvert	28.03.03	1rB	Livingston	23	Aug
2:14.03			1rB	Livingston	24	May
2:11.59	Hannah Roberts	15.09.02	5rB	Milton Keynes	3	Jun
2:12.14	Morgan Squibb	23.06.03	1	London (CP)	20	Aug
2:12.35mx	Saffron Moore	15.09.02	3rM	Watford	14	Jun
2:13.08			1rC	Milton Keynes	3	Jun
2:12.85	Zakia Mossi	15.09.03	2	London (CP)	20	Aug
2:13.1	Ava Taperell	21.12.03	1	Gateshead	24	Jun
2:13.53mx	Amy Kirkpatrick	22.09.03	2	Livingston	24	May
2:14.63			1rC	Glasgow (S)	2	Jun
2:13.90	Emily Misantoni	27.09.02	2	Birmingham	8	Jul
2:14.29mx	Maya Todd-Mcintyre	21.10.02	1	Loughborough	9	Aug
2:15.23			3rB	Street	1	May
2:14.33	Sarah Coutts	9.05.03	2rB	Livingston	24	May
(10)						
2:14.36mx	Daisy Worthington	5.05.03	1	Manchester (Str)	16	May
2:16.39			1h1	Bedford	26	Aug
2:14.80	Darcey Lonsdale	17.10.02	3rC	Milton Keynes	3	Jun
2:15.25	Amy Miller	16.11.02	5rC	Milton Keynes	3	Jun
2:15.37	Aimee Callow	1.01.03	6rC	Milton Keynes	3	Jun
2:15.4	Maisie Collis	2.01.04	1	Tonbridge	18	Jun
2:15.48	Naomi Toft	13.03.04	3	London (TB)	1	May
2:15.5	Abbie Lovering	23.07.03	1	Bournemouth	10	Jun
2:15.53mx	Ava White	20.05.03	2rC	London (TB)	22	Jul
2:15.74			1	London (LV)	14	May
2:15.57	Victoria Lightbody	4.05.04	1-14	Antrim	20	May
2:15.74	Emma Horsey	3.05.03	1	Bedford	27	Aug
(20)						
2:16.27	Femke Rosbergen	23.10.02	2rP	Watford	14	Jun
2:16.3	Kirsten Stilwell	10.07.03	1	Hemel Hempstead	15	Jul
2:16.50	Kate Willis	4.09.02	2	Bedford	27	Aug
2:16.55	Hannah Burn	14.05.04	1-14	Grangemouth	10	Jun
2:16.65	Hannah Anderson	17.09.02	2rC	Glasgow (S)	2	Jun

2:16.76i	Emma Johnson		7.02.04	2rC	Glasgow	14	Jan
2:16.9	Sian Heslop		27.09.02	1	Macclesfield	7	May
2:17.2	Tilia Wood		16.04.03	1	Cudworth	31	May
2:17.27mx	Isabel Pinder		16.11.03	1rJ	Basingstoke	19	Jul
2:17.3	Grace Sullivan		3.07.03	1rB	Hull	3	Jun
(30)							
2:17.38	Nia Clatworthy		2.10.02	2	Exeter	27	Jun
2:17.50	Lucy Broderick		27.09.02	2	Basingstoke	17	Jun
2:17.57	Susannah Lecoutre		5.04.04	1	Kingston	14	May
2:17.8	Annie Bell		17.02.03	1	Litherland	15	Jul
2:17.99mx	Ty Brockley-Langford		8.11.02	3	Manchester (Str)	27	Jun

Under 13

2:13.87	Ruby Simpson		6.07.05	1	Leigh	20	Aug
2:15.93	Emma Shipley		15.02.05	2	Leigh	20	Aug
2:20.0	Ella Greenway		3.01.05	1	Grimsby	30	Sep
2:20.24mx	Katie Johnson		30.04.05	1rC	Grangemouth	7	Jun
2:22.20				5rB	Livingston	24	May
2:21.01	Keira Brady-Jones		25.04.05	3	Leigh	20	Aug
2:21.12	Imogen Blackwell		24.03.05	4	Leigh	20	Aug
2:21.30	Stephanie Okoro		22.04.06	1	Bromley	15	Jul
2:21.46mx	Amy Harland		21.03.05	1	Leamington	2	Aug
2:22.03	Katelyn Howden		2.02.05	2rB	Nuneaton	9	Sep
2:22.2	Amarisa Sibley		27.06.05	1	Gillingham	6	Aug

Foreign

2:02.20	*Ciara Mageean (IRL)*		*12.03.92*	*3*	*Dublin (S), IRL*	*12*	*Jul*
2:05.74	*Joceline Monteiro (POR)*		*10.05.90*	*6*	*Loughborough*	*8*	*Jul*
2:07.47	*Claire Tarplee (IRL)*		*22.09.88*	*6*	*Solihull*	*13*	*May*

1000 Metres

2:31.93i	Laura Muir		9.05.93	1	Birmingham	18	Feb
2:38.49	Sarah McDonald		2.08.93	3	Gothenburg, SWE	11	Jul
2:42.73i	Revee Walcott-Nolan	U23	6.03.95	6	Birmingham	18	Feb
2:46.18i	Abbie Hetherington	U23	2.10.95	1	Ames, USA	25	Feb
2:46.82i	Amy-Eloise Neale	U23	5.08.95	7	Seattle, USA	14	Jan
2:47.13i	Chelsea Jarvis	U23	23.01.96	3	Ames, USA	25	Feb
2:49.22i	Kimberly Johansen		18.11.94	2	Lynchburg, USA	27	Jan

1200 Metres - Under 13

3:43.7	Emma Shipley	15.02.05	1	Rotherham	15	Jul
3:45.8	Ruby Simpson	6.07.05	1	York	20	May
3:49.5	Ella Greenway	3.01.05	1	Cudworth	18	Jun
3:50.21	Holly Weedall	31.12.04	1	Warrington	14	May
3:50.3	Keira Brady-Jones	25.04.05	1	Litherland	2	Sep
3:50.81	Katie Johnson	30.04.05	1	Birmingham	2	Sep
3:52.1	Natalie Simmons	5.06.05	1	Bedford	16	Jul
3:52.22	Grace Roberts	18.11.04	2	Warrington	14	May
3:52.7	Katie Sakaria	1.11.05	1	Guildford	4	Jun
3:53.8	Olivia Breed	28.02.06	1	Chelmsford	20	May

1500 Metres

4:00.35+	Laura Muir	9.05.93	1m	London (O)	9	Jul
	4:00.47		3	Eugene, USA	27	May
	4:02.39i		1	Belgrade, SRB	4	Mar
	4:02.97		4	London (O)	7	Aug
	4:03.64		2s1	London (O)	5	Aug
	4:05.01		1	Padova, ITA	16	Jul
	4:08.97		4h2	London (O)	4	Aug
	4:10.28i		1h1	Belgrade, SRB	3	Mar

4:00.71	Laura Weightman		1.07.91	7	Brussels, BEL	1	Sep
4:01.95				4	Hengelo, NED	11	Jun
4:03.07				4	Rabat, MAR	16	Jul
4:03.23+				6m	London (O)	9	Jul
4:03.50				4h3	London (O)	4	Aug
4:04.11				6	London (O)	7	Aug
4:05.63				4s2	London (O)	5	Aug
4:05.81				8	Birmingham	20	Aug
4:06.49				1	Birmingham	2	Jul
4:10.50				13	Eugene, USA	27	May
4:12.36				1h2	Birmingham	1	Jul
4:01.60	Eilish McColgan		25.11.90	2	Berlin, GER	27	Aug
4:03.73	Jessica Judd	U23	7.01.95	6h1	London (O)	4	Aug
4:05.20				1	Watford	14	Jun
4:07.09				2	Birmingham	2	Jul
4:08.23+				14m	London (O)	9	Jul
4:10.14				10s1	London (O)	5	Aug
4:11.15				1	Solihull	13	May
4:11.96				1h1	Birmingham	1	Jul
4:05.29	Katie Snowden		9.03.94	2	Watford	14	Jun
4:06.39+				11m	London (O)	9	Jul
4:09.32				14	Birmingham	20	Aug
4:09.70				4	Birmingham	2	Jul
4:10.97				1	Gothenburg, SWE	10	Jun
4:12.21				1rB	Stanford, USA	5	May
4:12.25				2rB	Oordegem, BEL	27	May
4:13.61				3h1	Birmingham	1	Jul
4:05.48	Sarah McDonald		2.08.93	9h3	London (O)	4	Aug
4:05.83				8	Hengelo, NED	11	Jun
4:06.73				9s2	London (O)	5	Aug
4:08.14				3	Birmingham	2	Jul
4:08.21				13	Birmingham	20	Aug
4:09.70				2	Tübingen, GER	20	May
4:11.62i				3	Athlone, IRL	15	Feb
4:12.05				5	Stanford, USA	5	May
4:12.50i				2h2	Belgrade, SRB	3	Mar
4:12.73i				1	Cardiff	15	Jan
4:13.36				3h2	Birmingham	1	Jul
4:13.67i				6	Belgrade, SRB	4	Mar
4:05.82+	Melissa Courtney		30.08.93	10m	London (O)	9	Jul
4:06.00				9	Hengelo, NED	11	Jun
4:07.02				2	Dublin (S), IRL	12	Jul
4:08.42				4	Oordegem, BEL	27	May
4:08.42mx				1	Watford	26	Jul
4:10.16				5	Birmingham	2	Jul
4:12.92				2h2	Birmingham	1	Jul
4:06.92+	Stephanie Twell		17.08.89	13m	London (O)	9	Jul
4:07.39mx				1	Watford	31	May
4:09.32	Charlene Thomas	V35	6.05.82	1	Watford	24	Jun
4:11.25				6	Birmingham	2	Jul
4:12.11				5	Dublin (S), IRL	12	Jul
4:13.27				2h1	Birmingham	1	Jul
4:13.35				4	Bydgoszcz, POL	2	Jun
4:09.52	Hannah England		6.03.87	13	Padova, ITA	16	Jul
4:09.84				9	Huelva, ESP	14	Jun
4:13.15				8	Birmingham	2	Jul
(10)							
4:10.30	Adelle Tracey		27.05.93	3	Watford	14	Jun
4:11.00	Amy-Eloise Neale	U23	5.08.95	4s1	Eugene, USA	8	Jun
4:11.02				2	Eugene, USA	5	May
4:13.81				5	Torrance, USA	14	Apr

4:11.72mx	Stacey Smith			4.02.90	1	Chester-le-Street	5 Jun
4:12.07	Rhianwedd Price			11.08.94	6s1	Eugene, USA	8 Jun
	4:13.84				1	Gainesville, USA	31 Mar
4:12.28	Jemma Reekie	U20		6.03.98	7	Birmingham	2 Jul
	4:13.25				1	Grosseto, ITA	23 Jul
4:12.62mx	Alexandra Bell			4.11.92	1	Manchester (Str)	29 Aug
4:12.67	Amy Griffiths	U23		22.03.96	4	Watford	14 Jun
	4:12.69mx				1rB	Manchester (Str)	15 Aug
4:12.99	Sarah Inglis			28.08.91	4	Victoria, CAN	8 Jun
4:13.51mx	Jacqueline Fairchild			3.05.89	1	Manchester (Str)	13 Jun
	4:17.15				2	Manchester (SC)	27 May
4:13.59mx	Harriet Knowles-Jones	U20		3.04.98	2rB	Manchester (Str)	15 Aug
	4:14.95				9	Birmingham	2 Jul
(20)							
4:13.75	Verity Ockenden			31.08.91	5	Watford	14 Jun

80 performances to 4:14.0 by 21 athletes including 5 indoors

4:14.08	Calli Thackery			9.01.93	5	Ninove, BEL	15 Jul
4:14.13	Ffion Price			11.08.94	7rB	Portland, USA	11 Jun
4:14.37	Stephanie Barnes			28.07.88	4	Oordegem, BEL	3 Jun
4:15.02i	Revee Walcott-Nolan	U23		6.03.95	8	Athlone, IRL	15 Feb
	4:20.26				3	Watford	12 Jul
4:15.61	Ella McNiven	U17		4.09.01	3	Watford	24 Jun
4:15.85mx	Amelia Quirk	U20		18.12.99	1rB	Watford	31 May
	4:16.32				10	Birmingham	2 Jul
4:15.94	Stephanie Pennycook	U23		1.09.95	5h2	Birmingham	1 Jul
4:16.17	Lennie Waite			4.02.86	3	Merksem, BEL	29 Jul
4:16.32	Naomi Taschimowitz			19.10.89	3	Manchester (Str)	19 Aug
(30)							
4:16.37mx	Mhairi Hendry	U23		31.03.96	1	Glasgow (S)	28 Jul
	4:20.78				1	Rugby	4 Jun
4:16.49	Hannah Nuttall	U23		7.07.97	4	Manchester (Str)	19 Aug
4:16.61	Erin Wallace	U20		18.05.00	1	Nassau, BAH	20 Jul
4:17.35	Kimberly Johansen			18.11.94	7	Ninove, BEL	15 Jul
4:17.62	Charlotte Taylor-Green			2.04.85	4	Solihull	13 May
4:17.68	Madeleine Murray			19.10.93	2	Melbourne (A), AUS	26 Feb
4:17.99	Anna Smith	U17		14.09.01	4	Nassau, BAH	20 Jul
4:18.01	Emily Hosker-Thornhill			27.10.92	5	Watford	24 Jun
4:18.31i	Elinor Kirk			26.04.89	1	Sheffield	8 Jan
4:18.83mx	Khahisa Mhlanga	U20		26.12.99	1rB	London (Elt)	24 May
	4:22.12				2	Exeter	29 Aug
(40)							
4:18.89	Charlotte Arter			18.06.91	5	Solihull	13 May
4:19.37	Hollie Parker	U23		20.12.96	1	Watford	12 Jul
4:19.41mx	Jenna Hill			16.10.85	1	Watford	23 Aug
4:20.09	Kaylee Dodd	U23		28.12.95	8	Stanford, USA	31 Mar
4:20.22mx	Philippa Millage	V35		15.08.80	2	Glasgow (S)	28 Jul
4:20.28mx	Georgie Hartigan	U23		1.03.96	2	Watford	23 Aug
	4:22.08				5	Manchester (Str)	19 Aug
4:20.29mx	Emily Williams	U17		25.02.02	3rB	Watford	31 May
	4:21.54				10	Watford	24 Jun
4:20.57	Olivia Mason	U17		14.10.01	6	Manchester (SC)	27 May
4:20.64	Bethan Knights	U23		28.09.95	2	Berkeley, USA	29 Apr
4:20.66	Mari Smith	U23		14.11.96	2	Loughborough	21 May
(50)							
4:20.75mx	Caroline Ford			29.12.92	5rB	Watford	31 May
	4:25.74				2rB	Manchester (SC)	27 May
4:20.76mx	Megan Davies	U23		10.05.96	1rC	Manchester (Str)	25 Jul
	4:21.11				4	Loughborough	21 May
4:20.78i	Kate Maltby			26.07.85	3	Sheffield	8 Jan
	4:25.77				1	Leigh	16 Jul
4:20.92	Elizabeth Bird			4.10.94	2	West Point, USA	11 May

4:21.06	Julia Cooke		9.09.88	3	Loughborough	21	May
4:21.16	Anna Tait	U23	5.12.96	5	Loughborough	21	May
4:21.6+	Rosie Clarke		17.11.91	14m	Birmingham	20	Aug
4:21.67	Lilly Coward	U23	10.09.96	1rB	Heusden, BEL	22	Jul
4:21.80	Hannah Segrave	U23	14.04.95	3	Raleigh, USA	24	Mar
4:21.94	Anna Burt	U20	12.07.00	7	Loughborough	21	May
(60)							
4:21.96	Charlotte Taylor		17.01.94	1rB	Stanford, USA	22	Apr
4:22.36	Holly Archer		7.11.93	1	Houston, USA	14	May
4:22.58	Abbie Hetherington	U23	2.10.95	9	Stanford, USA	31	Mar
4:23.24mx	Emelia Gorecka		29.01.94	1rH	Watford	26	Jul
4:23.7	Claire Duck		29.08.85	1	Middlesbrough	5	Aug
4:23.93	Abigail Howarth		8.10.92	1rB	Loughborough	8	Jul
4:24.31	Beth Barlow	U20	8.04.00	1	Birmingham	8	Jul
4:24.36	Jodie Judd	U20	25.09.98	2	Birmingham	8	Jul
4:24.40	Alison Leonard		17.03.90	14	Tübingen, GER	20	May
4:24.45i	Gemma Hillier-Moses		19.06.88	1	Cardiff	28	Jan
(70)							
4:24.57	Hannah Viner	U23	18.07.96	2rB	Loughborough	8	Jul
4:24.62mx	Louise Small		27.03.92	1rl	Watford	26	Jul
	4:24.8			1	Uxbridge	17	Jun
4:24.66mx	Rachael Burns	V35	1.03.80	2rC	Manchester (Str)	25	Jul
	4:26.04			3rB	Loughborough	8	Jul
4:24.86	Cari Hughes	U20	15.03.99	2rB	Watford	24	Jun
4:24.91	Danielle Barnes-Heeney		8.10.85	3	Eton	3	Jun
4:25.0	Catrina Thomas	U23	18.02.97	1	Oxford	29	Jul
4:25.07	Aimee Pratt	U23	3.10.97	9rB	Oordegem, BEL	3	Jun
4:25.10	Roisin Flanagan	U20	2.05.98	4rC	Azusa, USA	14	Apr
4:25.14i	Faye Fullerton		31.05.84	4	Sheffield	8	Jan
4:25.27	Ellie Baker	U20	3.06.98	6	Watford	9	Aug
(80)							
4:25.45	Rachael Franklin		14.12.91	2	Visby, SWE	27	Jun
4:25.49	Kiara Frizelle	U17	10.07.01	3rB	Watford	24	Jun
4:25.52	Lydia Hallam	U23	26.02.97	4rB	Watford	24	Jun
4:25.58	Georgia Bell		17.10.93	12	Stanford, USA	31	Mar
4:25.67mx	Laura-Jane Smith		7.02.91	1	Loughborough	31	May
	4:27.73			11h2	Birmingham	1	Jul
4:25.96	Ashley Gibson		1.03.86	3	London (CP)	11	Jun
4:26.04	Isobel Parry-Jones	U20	17.12.98	2	Belfast	5	Jul
4:26.08	Francesca Brint	U20	30.08.00	1rB	Manchester (Str)	19	Aug
4:26.18mx	Rebecca Burns		19.06.90	1rB	Glasgow (S)	28	Jul
	4:26.24			3	Exeter	29	Aug
4:26.39	Phillipa Stone	U20	1.04.98	5	Bedford	17	Jun
(90)							
4:26.41mx	Hannah Brooks		25.06.88	1	Newport	5	Jul
4:26.45mx	Georgia Malir	U23	20.02.96	3rC	Manchester (Str)	25	Jul
	4:26.48			4rB	Loughborough	8	Jul
4:26.49	Emily Moyes	U20	14.06.98	5rB	Loughborough	8	Jul
4:26.63	Rochelle Harrison		1.02.91	8rB	Watford	24	Jun
4:26.79mx	Kerry MacAngus	U20	31.03.99	1rB	Manchester (Str)	27	Jun
4:26.82mx	Julia Tomczak	U20	28.02.00	1	London (TB)	26	Aug
4:26.91i	Chloe Bradley		27.03.93	7	Sheffield	12	Feb
4:26.95	Rosie Johnson	U23	17.09.97	6rB	Loughborough	8	Jul
4:27.02mx	Rebecca Rigby		17.10.91	1	Sheffield	21	Jun
4:27.17i	Naomi Collier		28.10.94	2	Sheffield	19	Feb
(100)							
4:27.23mx	Carolyn Johnson		22.08.88	1rF	Watford	23	Aug
4:27.36	Hannah Hobbs	U20	4.12.99	2rC	Watford	24	Jun
4:27.41	Sarah Chapman	U20	21.04.98	6rB	Solihull	13	May
4:27.80mx	Amy Hinchly	U20	11.01.98	1rF	Watford	31	May
4:27.82	Almi Nerurkar	U17	9.01.01	9rB	Watford	24	Jun
4:27.85	Emma Clayton		16.07.88	1	Leeds	12	Jun

Additional Under 17 (1-7 above)

4:29.1	Keely Hodgkinson	3.03.02	1	Blackpool	23	Jul
4:30.94mx	Alexandra Brown	8.04.01	2rD	Brighton	31	May
	4:31.87		1	Birmingham	8	Jul
4:32.04	Molly Canham	3.11.01	1	Exeter	30	May
4:32.61mx	Charlotte Alexander	18.01.02	3rl	Watford	26	Jul
	4:33.77		1	London (CP)	20	Aug
(10)						
4:33.17	Faye Ireland	31.08.01	13rB	Solihull	13	May
4:33.19mx	Yasmin Marghini	3.01.02	1rB	London (TB)	1	Apr
	4:38.04		1	London (He)	23	Jul
4:33.34	Lia Radus	1.10.01	2	Bedford	26	Aug
4:34.8mx	Jessica Mitchell	14.05.01	1	Hornchurch	9	Apr
	4:36.21		1	Stevenage	28	May
4:34.95	Mia Roberts	13.07.02	3rC	Manchester (SC)	27	May
4:35.30	Eloise Walker	27.05.01	4	Grangemouth	27	Aug
4:35.43mx	Sarah Calvert	29.06.01	1	Livingston	19	Jul
	4:38.66i		4	Glasgow	1	Feb
	4:39.32		2	Loughborough	1	Sep
4:35.54	Kitty Shepherd-Cross	11.02.02	2	Birmingham	8	Jul
4:36.11	Tilly Simpson	25.10.00	1	Leigh	19	Aug
4:36.68	Olivia Allum	21.06.01	6	Milton Keynes	3	Jun
(20)						
4:37.18	Bethan Morley	9.10.01	1	Sheffield	23	Jul
4:37.56	Ellie Farrow	30.10.01	1rB	Milton Keynes	3	Jun
4:37.92	Molly Hudson	16.08.02	3	Birmingham	8	Jul
4:38.39mx	Hayley Instance	6.05.02	1rG	Watford	31	May
4:38.42	Claudia Lance-Jones	29.09.00	2	Kingston	10	Jun
4:38.68mx	Holly Smith	31.12.01	4rC	Manchester (Str)	16	May
4:38.74	Grace Copeland	11.10.00	9rC	Watford	24	Jun
4:38.93mx	Shannon Flockhart	5.04.02	4rJ	Watford	26	Jul
4:38.96	Molly Sweetman	11.03.02	3	London (CP)	20	Aug
4:39.12mx	Mya Taylor	23.02.01	2rC	Manchester (Str)	27	Jun
(30)						
4:39.18	Jasmine Cooper	25.02.01	2	Leigh	19	Aug
4:39.39	Isobel Mannion	4.04.02	5	Birmingham	8	Jul
4:39.68	Elise Thorner	16.03.01	5	Exeter	30	May

Under 15

4:31.79mx	Sian Heslop	27.09.02	1	Manchester (Str)	25	Jul
	4:32.17		2	Birmingham	8	Jul
4:31.85	Kirsten Stilwell	10.07.03	1	Birmingham	8	Jul
4:32.41	Beatrice Wood	9.10.03	3	Birmingham	8	Jul
4:32.49mx	Lily-Jane Evans-Haggerty	16.06.03	1rC	Glasgow (S)	28	Jul
	4:36.99i		1	Glasgow	12	Feb
	4:38.59		2	Glasgow (S)	20	Aug
4:34.42	Isla Calvert	28.03.03	2	Dublin (S), IRL	5	Aug
4:34.67mx	Morgan Squibb	23.06.03	1rK	Watford	26	Jul
	4:35.67		2	Bedford	26	Aug
4:35.38	Maisie Collis	2.01.04	2h2	Birmingham	7	Jul
4:35.6	Naomi Toft	13.03.04	6	Oxford	29	Jul
4:36.90	Ava White	20.05.03	2	Bromley	15	Jul
4:37.30	Anna Hedley	16.01.04	1	Glasgow (S)	20	Aug
(10)						
4:37.97mx	Sarah Coutts	9.05.03	2	Livingston	19	Jul
	4:39.73		1	Grangemouth	27	Aug
4:39.14mx	Maya Todd-Mcintyre	21.10.02	2	Loughborough	12	Jul
	4:41.7		4rB	Oxford	29	Jul
4:39.44mx	Emma Johnson	7.02.04	1rD	Glasgow (S)	28	Jul
	4:42.38		2	Kilmarnock	21	May
4:39.48mx	Bethany Cook	17.07.04	3rD	Brighton	31	May
	4:44.74		3	Oxford (H)	9	Sep

4:40.20mx	Caitlin Robinson		28.05.03	1rB	Manchester (Str)	25	Jul
4:40.91				9	Birmingham	8	Jul
4:40.25mx	Eva Holland		3.05.04	4rD	Brighton	31	May
4:42.00				1	London (BP)	10	Jun
4:40.63mx	Lara Crawford		20.06.03	2rB	Manchester (Str)	25	Jul
4:44.14				2h3	Birmingham	7	Jul
4:40.88	Grace Sullivan		3.07.03	8	Birmingham	8	Jul
4:40.96	Ella Semple		18.11.02	2	Birmingham	17	Jun
4:41.11	Lily Saxon		28.03.04	3	Birmingham	17	Jun
(20)							
4:41.72mx	Samia Jones		2.09.03	3rB	Manchester (Str)	25	Jul
4:41.79mx	Amy Miller		16.11.02	5rD	Brighton	31	May
4:42.19	Susannah Lecoutre		5.04.04	2	Kingston	10	Jun
4:42.53mx	Saffron Moore		15.09.02	6rD	Brighton	31	May
4:43.45mx	Grace Ingles		7.11.02	2rJ	Watford	31	May
4:43.90	Kiara Valkenburg		21.03.04	3	Kingston	10	Jun
4:44.06mx	Daisy Cumming		17.08.03	1rB	Grangemouth	6	Sep
4:44.19mx	Holly Fisher		2.12.02	4rJ	Watford	31	May
4:44.2	Ines Curran		9.09.03	1	Preston	15	Jul
4:44.49mx	Isabella Hayes		22.04.04	2rE	Brighton	31	May
(30)							
4:44.49	Samantha Mason		2.11.02	6h1	Birmingham	7	Jul
4:44.57mx	Pippa Roessler		8.01.04	2	Bromley	10	Jul
4:44.7	Amy Young		11.02.03	2	Southampton	20	May
4:44.80	Dalis Jones		21.10.03	1	Birmingham	4	Jul

Under 13

4:47.12mx	Katie Johnson		30.04.05	1rE	Glasgow (S)	28	Jul
4:53.2				1	Grangemouth	5	Aug
4:48.2	Maisy Luke		5.05.05	1	Carn Brea	13	May
4:48.2	Amy Harland		21.03.05	1	Tamworth	12	Jul
4:48.2	Beth Rawlinson		17.05.05	2	Tamworth	12	Jul
4:48.4	Ruby Simpson		6.07.05	1	Spinkhill	10	Sep
4:51.9	Holly Weedall		31.12.04	1	Ellesmere Port	3	Jul
4:53.4	Emma Shipley		15.02.05	2	Spinkhill	10	Sep
4:54.7	Sadie Frater-White		30.11.04	1	Watford	7	May
4:56.43mx	Olivia Martin		10.08.05	2rL	Watford	31	May
4:56.8	Keira Brady-Jones		25.04.05	2	Ellesmere Port	3	Jul

Foreign

4:03.57+	*Ciara Mageean (IRL)*		*12.03.92*	*7m*	*London (O)*	*9*	*Jul*
4:04.09				*10*	*Rome, ITA*	*8*	*Jun*
4:14.63i	*Kerry O'Flaherty (IRL)*	*V35*	*15.07.81*	*7*	*Athlone, IRL*	*15*	*Feb*
4:15.32i	*Emma Mitchell (IRL)*		*2.09.93*	*9*	*Athlone, IRL*	*15*	*Feb*
4:19.20				*9*	*Vaasa, FIN*	*25*	*Jun*
4:16.23	*Claire Tarplee (IRL)*		*22.09.88*	*10*	*Tübingen, GER*	*20*	*May*
4:18.25	*Tamara Armoush (JOR)*		*8.05.92*	*6*	*Watford*	*24*	*Jun*
4:18.32	*Chloe Tighe (AUS)*		*28.09.90*	*6*	*Watford*	*14*	*Jun*

1 Mile

4:18.03	Laura Muir		9.05.93	2	London (O)	9	Jul
4:35.0i+e				2m	Karlsruhe, GER	4	Feb
4:20.88	Laura Weightman		1.07.91	6	London (O)	9	Jul
4:23.15	Melissa Courtney		30.08.93	8	London (O)	9	Jul
4:25.39	Stephanie Twell		17.08.89	12	London (O)	9	Jul
4:25.89	Katie Snowden		9.03.94	13	London (O)	9	Jul
4:28.59	Jessica Judd	U23	7.01.95	14	London (O)	9	Jul
4:32.06i	Sarah McDonald		2.08.93	3	New York (A), USA	21	Jan
4:34.15i	Amy-Eloise Neale	U23	5.08.95	2	Seattle, USA	11	Feb
4:36.30mx	Revee Walcott-Nolan	U23	6.03.95	1	London (BP)	21	Jul
4:36.89i	Sophie Connor		21.05.93	2	Notre Dame, USA	18	Feb

4:39.57i	Rhianwedd Price		11.08.94	1	Nashville, USA	11	Feb
4:40.55	Jemma Reekie	U20	6.03.98	1	Manchester (SC)	16	Aug
4:42.77i	Kimberly Johansen		18.11.94	5	Winston-Salem, USA	18	Feb
4:42.84	Charlene Thomas	V35	6.05.82	2	Manchester (SC)	16	Aug
4:43.12	Jacqueline Fairchild		3.05.89	3	Manchester (SC)	16	Aug
4:43.53i	Ffion Price		11.08.94	6	Nashville, USA	25	Feb
4:44.38i	Elizabeth Bird		4.10.94	5	Staten Island, USA	10	Feb
4:45.19i	Roisin Flanagan	U20	2.05.98	5	Birmingham, USA	11	Mar
4:47.1	Madeleine Murray		19.10.93	1	Melbourne, AUS	16	Feb
4:47.43i	Ellie Atkinson	U23	15.10.96	7	Boston, USA	10	Feb
(20)							
4:48.10	Charlotte Taylor-Green		2.04.85	5	Manchester (SC)	16	Aug
4:48.49	Philippa Millage	V35	15.08.80	7	Manchester (SC)	16	Aug

Foreign

4:22.40	*Ciara Mageean (IRL)*		*12.03.92*	*7*	*London (O)*	*9*	*Jul*
4:38.85mx	*Chloe Tighe (AUS)*		*28.09.90*	*2*	*London (BP)*	*21*	*Jul*
4:42.23				*1*	*London (Elt)*	*21*	*Jun*
4:46.23mx	*Tamara Armoush (JOR)*		*8.05.92*	*3*	*London (BP)*	*21*	*Jul*
4:46.82				*2*	*London (Elt)*	*21*	*Jun*

2000 Metres

5:41.5i+	Laura Muir	9.05.93	2m	Karlsruhe, GER	4	Feb
5:43.1+	Eilish McColgan	25.11.90	9m	Birmingham	20	Aug

But Muir must have been faster in Monaco as she went thru 1800m 5:04.3 and 6:14.0 at 2200m and also McColgan who was 5:09.8 and 6:18.7 at those points

3000 Metres

8:26.41i	Laura Muir	9.05.93	1	Karlsruhe, GER	4	Feb
8:30.64			3	Monaco, MON	21	Jul
8:35.67i			1	Belgrade, SRB	5	Mar
8:55.56i			5h2	Belgrade, SRB	3	Mar
8:59.39i+			1m	Glasgow	4	Jan
9:08.46+			10m	London (O)	13	Aug
9:13.82+			7h1	London (O)	10	Aug
8:31.00	Eilish McColgan	25.11.90	5	Birmingham	20	Aug
8:31.39			4	Monaco, MON	21	Jul
8:43.02i			5	Birmingham	18	Feb
8:47.43i			3	Belgrade, SRB	5	Mar
8:49.8+			8m	Brussels, BEL	1	Sep
8:57.85i			2h1	Belgrade, SRB	3	Mar
9:05.07i			1	Sheffield	11	Feb
9:09.15+			12m	London (O)	13	Aug
9:12.31+			12m	Eugene, USA	26	May
9:13.4+			14m	Rome	8	Jun
8:43.24mx	Jessica Judd	U23 7.01.95	1	Watford	6	Sep
8:52.16mx			1	Watford	5	Apr
8:55.76mx			1	Watford	19	Apr
8:59.60			1	Loughborough	21	May
8:43.72mx	Melissa Courtney	30.08.93	2	Watford	6	Sep
9:11.38i			3	Glasgow	4	Jan
9:24.66+			m	Stanford, USA	5	May
8:45.95i	Stephanie Twell	17.08.89	10	Birmingham	18	Feb
8:50.40i			5	Belgrade, SRB	5	Mar
8:55.02i			2h2	Belgrade, SRB	3	Mar
9:00.04mx			1	Watford	31	May
9:01.04			13	Monaco, MON	21	Jul
9:05.30i			2	Sheffield	11	Feb
9:10.60+			1m	Watford	24	Jun
9:12.3+			13m	Rome	8	Jun

8:51.02	Rosie Clarke		17.11.91	12	Birmingham	20	Aug
8:56.08mx	Harriet Knowles-Jones	U20	3.04.98	1	Watford	3	May
9:14.86				9	Villeneuve d'Ascq, FRA	24	Jun
8:58.48	Charlotte Arter		18.06.91	5	Cork, IRL	18	Jul
9:11.79i				4	Sheffield	11	Feb
9:12.47i				2	Manchester (SC)	29	Jan
9:15+e				2m	Watford	24	Jun
9:00.59i	Elinor Kirk		26.04.89	1	Manchester (SC)	29	Jan
9:27.07+				m	Stanford, USA	5	May
9:00.81i	Kate Maltby		26.07.85	7	Boston (R), USA	28	Jan
9:01.97i				2	Glasgow	4	Jan
9:05.6				1	Bedford	3	Jun
(10)							
9:03.85	Emelia Gorecka		29.01.94	8	Rovereto, ITA	29	Aug
9:04.54mx				1rB	Watford	6	Sep
9:07.63				1	Watford	24	Jun
9:07.10mx	Claire Duck		29.08.85	1rB	Manchester (Str)	25	Apr
9:07.64mx	Louise Small		27.03.92	2rB	Watford	6	Sep
9:20+e				3m	Watford	24	Jun
9:09.75+	Laura Weightman		1.07.91	1m	Los Angeles (ER), USA	18	May
9:09.77i	Calli Thackery		9.01.93	1	Cambridge, USA	19	Feb
9:26.40+				m	Stanford, USA	5	May
9:10.70	Verity Ockenden		31.08.91	1	Manchester (SC)	16	Aug
9:11.20mx	Jemma Reekie	U20	6.03.98	2rB	Manchester (Str)	25	Apr
9:24.81				4	Grosseto, ITA	22	Jul
9:11.70mx	Emily Hosker-Thornhill		27.10.92	3rB	Watford	6	Sep
9:12.75	Holly Rees		5.06.93	8	Concord, USA	1	Jun
9:13.70	Naomi Taschimowitz		19.10.89	2	Manchester (SC)	16	Aug
(20)							
9:13.82mx	Jenna Hill		16.10.85	4rB	Watford	6	Sep
9:21.93				1	Manchester (Str)	19	Aug

56 performances to 9:15.0 by 21 athletes including 19 indoors

9:15.12mx	Hannah Nuttall	U23	7.07.97	1rB	Manchester (Str)	29	Aug
9:35.83i				2	Sheffield	19	Feb
9:15.58	Stephanie Barnes		28.07.88	2	Leiria, POR	27	May
9:15.83i	Lauren Howarth		21.04.90	3	Manchester (SC)	29	Jan
9:25.06+				m	Stanford, USA	5	May
9:17.64mx	Phoebe Law	U23	12.01.97	1	Kingston	16	Aug
9:20.45				2	Watford	24	Jun
9:17.94mx	Katrina Wootton		2.09.85	1	Manchester (Str)	25	Apr
9:39.4+e				3m	London (PH)	20	May
9:17.97i	Amy-Eloise Neale	U23	5.08.95	8	Seattle, USA	28	Jan
9:20+e	Jessica Martin		1.10.92	3m	Watford	24	Jun
9:20.72+	Charlotte Taylor		17.01.94	m	Stanford, USA	5	May
9:21.32	Amelia Quirk	U20	18.12.99	3	Manchester (SC)	16	Aug
(30)							
9:21.35i	Bethan Knights	U23	28.09.95	18	Seattle, USA	11	Feb
9:21.83	Stephanie Pennycook	U23	1.09.95	4	Manchester (SC)	16	Aug
9:22.60i	Gemma Hillier-Moses		19.06.88	7	Sheffield	11	Feb
9:23.3	Kate Holt		7.09.92	1	Worcester	6	May
9:24.50mx	Ella McNiven	U17	4.09.01	1	Manchester (Str)	13	Jun
9:29.76				1	Birmingham	8	Jul
9:24.82mx	Ashley Gibson		1.03.86	2	Watford	31	May
9:31.72				3	Manchester (Str)	19	Aug
9:25.18i	Gemma Shepherd	U23	23.11.97	7	Boston, USA	10	Feb
9:25.89	Iona Lake		15.01.93	3	Watford	24	Jun
9:26.35i	Rebecca Murray		26.09.94	1	Sheffield	19	Feb
9:41.03+				1m	Bedford	1	May
9:26.71	Nicole Taylor	U23	18.01.95	4	Watford	24	Jun
(40)							
9:26.92mx	Philippa Bowden	U23	29.03.95	1	Watford	23	Aug
9:39.98i				3	Sheffield	19	Feb

9:27.6	Jenny Nesbitt	U23	24.01.95	2	Worcester	6	May
9:29.01imx	Charlotte Taylor-Green		2.04.85	1	Cardiff	10	Dec
9:29.76mx	Cari Hughes	U20	15.03.99	1rB	Manchester (Str)	16	May
9:29.77i				6	Manchester (SC)	29	Jan
9:43.35				9	Loughborough	21	May
9:30.33	Lauren Deadman		27.03.84	1	Leigh	16	Jul
9:30.74	Julia Paternain	U20	29.09.99	1	Birmingham	8	Jul
9:31.12mx	Charlotte Alexander	U17	18.01.02	3	Watford	31	May
9:34.05				2	Birmingham	8	Jul
9:31.76mx	Anna Tait	U23	5.12.96	1rD	Glasgow (S)	2	Jun
9:36.84				2	Wigan	7	May
9:32.07mx	Laura-Jane Smith		7.02.91	2	Manchester (Str)	13	Jun
9:32.47mx	Bronwen Owen	U23	21.01.97	3rB	Manchester (Str)	25	Apr
(50)							
9:32.49	Julia Tomczak	U20	28.02.00	2	Birmingham	8	Jul
9:33.02i	Erin Wallace	U20	18.05.00	7	Glasgow	4	Jan
9:34.66				5	Loughborough	21	May
9:33.34mx	Faye Fullerton		31.05.84	1rB	Watford	19	Apr
9:40.91				8	Loughborough	21	May
9:33.35mx	Khahisa Mhlanga	U20	26.12.99	2	Watford	5	Apr
9:33.41i	Sarah Mercier		4.11.90	7	Manchester (SC)	29	Jan
9:33.52mx	Katherine Bingle		16.12.93	2	Watford	23	Aug
9:33.89i	Rhianwedd Price		11.08.94	8	Nashville, USA	21	Jan
9:33.96i	Georgina Outten	U23	26.06.96	12	Sheffield	11	Feb
9:34.34mx	Emma Clayton		16.07.88	3	Manchester (Str)	13	Jun
9:34.65mx	Hannah Viner	U23	18.07.96	2	Watford	26	Jul
(60)							
9:34.89i	Elizabeth Bird		4.10.94	1	New Haven, USA	29	Jan
9:36.06	Phoebe Barker	U20	27.11.99	10	Watford	24	Jun
9:36.1	Lucy Crookes		4.05.93	1	Middlesbrough	5	Aug
9:36.21mx	Rebecca Rigby		17.10.91	1	Leeds	26	Jun
9:36.31mx	Annabel Simpson	U23	30.04.97	1	Glasgow	22	Aug
9:36.37	Danielle Hodgkinson		11.10.84	2	Bromley	16	Jul
9:36.99+	Josephine Moultrie		19.11.90	m	Stanford, USA	5	May
9:37.26	Georgia Malir	U23	20.02.96	11	Watford	24	Jun
9:37.34mx	Joanne Hickman-Dunne		4.06.91	6rB	Watford	6	Sep
9:40.47i				4	Sheffield	19	Feb
9:37.37mx	Hannah Hobbs	U20	4.12.99	1	Bristol	18	Jul
(70)							
9:37.47mx	Laura Riches		7.08.93	1rB	Manchester (Str)	25	Jul
9:37.59mx	Mhairi MacLennan	U23	26.03.95	1	Livingston	23	Aug
9:37.74mx	Dani Chattenton	U23	4.07.96	4	Watford	31	May
9:38.42i	Holly Archer		7.11.93	5	Nashville, USA	11	Feb
9:38.54	Sarah Chapman	U20	21.04.98	6	Loughborough	21	May
9:38.78	Zoe Wassell	U20	4.07.99	3	Birmingham	8	Jul
9:38.8	Sophie Harris		12.06.93	1	Southampton	19	Aug
9:39.5+e	Beth Potter		27.12.91	4m	London (PH)	20	May
9:39.51	Claudia Lance-Jones	U17	29.09.00	7	Loughborough	21	May
9:39.65	Naomi Lang	U20	7.02.00	1	Grangemouth	16	Apr
(80)							
9:39.8+e	Jo Pavey	V40	20.09.73	7m	London (PH)	20	May
9:39.88i	Poppy Tank	U23	5.12.97	8	Seattle, USA	25	Feb
9:40.86	Jessica Mitchell	U17	14.05.01	3	Birmingham	8	Jul
9:41.27mx	Chloe Sharp	U20	27.12.99	3	Watford	23	Aug
9:41.80				12	Watford	24	Jun
9:42.26i	Charlotte Murphy	U20	24.08.98	6	Birmingham, USA	25	Feb
9:42.40	Floren Scrafton		24.12.93	12	Bilbao, ESP	24	Jun
9:42.65i	Gemma Kersey		6.02.92	8	Glasgow	4	Jan
9:43.06i	Chloe Richardson		4.12.93	15	Sheffield	11	Feb
9:43.32i	Rachael Burns	V35	1.03.80	16	Sheffield	11	Feb
9:44.1	Almi Nerurkar	U17	9.01.01	1	Crawley	10	Jun
(90)							

9:44.19	Bella Williams	U20	5.10.98	4	Birmingham	8	Jul
9:44.24	Elizabeth Davies	V35	25.12.78	1	Kingston	2	Jul
9:44.34	Katie Ingle	U23	4.03.95	1	Street	1	May
9:44.44	Bryony Gunn	U20	28.02.98	4	Birmingham	6	May
9:44.6	Emily Japp		18.12.90	1	Bury	4	Jun
9:44.97	Jodie Judd	U20	25.09.98	1	Chelmsford	13	May
9:45.32	Caroline Hoyte	V45	30.06.70	2	Kingston	2	Jul
9:46.36	Kiara Frizelle	U17	10.07.01	2	Street	1	May
9:46.46	Hannah Brooks		25.06.88	2	Stevenage	4	Jun
9:46.73i	Caroline Lambert		2.09.93	8	Ypsilanti, USA	25	Feb
(100)							
9:46.80i	Nicole Roberts		30.01.92	8	Manchester (SC)	29	Jan
9:47.20i	Stacie Taylor	U23	12.10.95	1rC	Birmingham, USA	25	Feb
9:47.20mx	Elizabeth Apsley	U23	12.01.97	4rB	Watford	19	Apr
9:47.46i	Samantha Johnson		23.08.90	18	Sheffield	11	Feb
9:47.62	Sophie Cowper		24.12.90	2	Leigh	16	Jul
9:47.8mx	Emma Stepto	V45	4.04.70	1	Par	23	Aug
9:47.95	Rosie Woodhams	U17	24.04.02	4	Birmingham	8	Jul

Additional Under 17 (1-7 above)

9:50.69	Heather Barnes		15.01.02	2	Glasgow (S)	2	Jun
9:52.05	Mya Taylor		23.02.01	5	Birmingham	8	Jul
9:52.48	Elsbeth Grant		8.02.02	6	Birmingham	8	Jul
(10)							
9:52.90	Cera Gemmell		2.07.02	1	Tranent	2	Sep
9:54.05imx	Eloise Walker		27.05.01	1rF	Glasgow	4	Jan
9:54.20mx	Jasmine Cooper		25.02.01	2	Loughborough	26	Apr
	9:59.88			9	Birmingham	8	Jul
9:55.01	Grace Copeland		11.10.00	3	Milton Keynes	3	Jun
9:56.98	Yasmin Marghini		3.01.02	4	Milton Keynes	3	Jun
9:57.6	Holly Smith		31.12.01	1	Warrington	28	May
9:57.73mx	Mia Roberts		13.07.02	1rC	Manchester (Str)	16	May
	9:57.84			1	Wrexham	20	Aug
9:58.01mx	Libby Coleman		3.05.01	3	Loughborough	26	Apr
	10:04.01			11	Birmingham	8	Jul
9:58.40	Esme Davies		26.04.01	4	Glasgow (S)	2	Jun
9:59.33	Alexandra Brown		8.04.01	5	Milton Keynes	3	Jun
(20)							
10:01.30	Olivia Stillman		13.12.00	10	Birmingham	8	Jul
10:03.40	Grace Brock		22.02.01	5	Street	1	May
10:05.53	Tia Wilson		1.06.02	12	Birmingham	8	Jul
10:08.00	Megan Dingle		1.09.02	1	Abu Dhabi, UAE	7	Dec
10:09.13	Emily Andrew		20.08.02	7	Glasgow (S)	2	Jun
10:09.50mx	Faye Ireland		31.08.01	4rC	Manchester (Str)	16	May
10:11.1mx	Molly Canham		3.11.01	1	Exeter	23	Jan
10:13.69	Abigail Fisher		11.11.00	2	Cardiff	1	Jul
10:14.7mx	Jessica Humphreys		30.10.01	1	Tipton	23	May

Under 15

9:49.49	Lily-Jane Evans-Haggerty		16.06.03	1	Glasgow (S)	2	Jun
9:55.14mx	Anna Hedley		16.01.04	1rB	Glasgow	22	Aug
10:05.77mx	Morgan Squibb		23.06.03	3rC	Watford	6	Sep
10:12.75	Pippa Roessler		8.01.04	4rB	Watford	26	Jul
10:14.76	Grace Sullivan		3.07.03	1	Grimsby	29	May
10:15.69	Eva Holland		3.05.04	1	London (CP)	11	Jun
10:18.88mx	Emily Chong		2.11.03	1	Gateshead	9	Aug
	10:29.40			1	Gateshead	13	May
10:19.30mx	Ines Curran		9.09.03	2	Gateshead	9	Aug
	10:34.58			2	Gateshead	13	May
10:20.54mx	Alice Garner		17.01.03	4rC	Basingstoke	19	Jul
	10:35.2			1	Portsmouth	2	Apr
10:24.03mx	Nicole Ainsworth		30.09.02	5rC	Basingstoke	19	Jul

10:25.6	Lara Crawford		20.06.03	1	Warrington	13	Aug
10:28.78mx	Dalis Jones		21.10.03	3	Bristol	18	Jul
10:31.17	Martha Collings		17.11.02	10rB	Watford	26	Jul
10:32.2	Abigail Durand		7.11.02	1	Norwich	14	May
10:32.74mx	Maayan Radus		30.05.04	11rB	Watford	31	May
10:33.0	Samia Jones		2.09.03	1	Litherland	2	Sep
10:33.7	Grace Ingles		7.11.02	1	Hemel Hempstead	16	Jul
10:34.93mx	Aimee Anderson		23.01.03	1rF	Glasgow (S)	2	Jun
10:35.46imx	Kate Richardson		12.09.02	4rH	Glasgow	4	Jan
10:36.84	Emma Hart		23.07.03	3	Gateshead	13	May
(20)							
10:37.06	Rheagan Edwards		8.04.03	1	Wrexham	13	May
10:38.40	Eden Schiller		19.11.02	1	Nuneaton	19	Aug
10:39.85mx	Anya MacLean		15.08.04	5rB	Glasgow	22	Aug

Foreign

9:04.21imx	Emma Mitchell (IRL)		2.09.93	1	Abbotstown, IRL	23	Nov
9:11.89				1	Belfast	6	May
9:08.83i	Ciara Mageean (IRL)		12.03.92	1	Athlone, IRL	18	Feb
9:12.86i	Kerry O'Flaherty (IRL)	V35	15.07.81	4	Glasgow	4	Jan
9:25.64	Tamara Armoush (JOR)		8.05.92	2	Manchester (Str)	19	Aug
9:29.05	Chloe Tighe (AUS)		28.09.90	1	London (CP)	10	Jun
9:46.20mx	Ashley Scott-Wilson (USA)		9.04.91	3	Watford	26	Jul

5000 Metres

14:48.49	Eilish McColgan		25.11.90	8	Brussels, BEL	1	Sep
15:00.38				4h2	London (O)	10	Aug
15:00.43				10	London (O)	13	Aug
15:07.43				6	Eugene, USA	26	May
15:22.12				5	Stanford, USA	5	May
15:38.57				2	Birmingham	2	Jul
14:49.12i	Laura Muir		9.05.93	1	Glasgow	4	Jan
14:52.07				6	London (O)	13	Aug
14:59.34				7h1	London (O)	10	Aug
15:08.24	Laura Weightman		1.07.91	1	Los Angeles (ER), USA	18	May
15:16.65	Stephanie Twell		17.08.89	1	Watford	24	Jun
15:24.05				16	Rome, ITA	8	Jun
15:35.50				1	Birmingham	2	Jul
15:41.29				15h2	London (O)	10	Aug
15:27.6mx	Katrina Wootton		2.09.85	1	Nottingham	25	Aug
15:49.48				2	Solihull	13	May
15:28.95	Melissa Courtney		30.08.93	4rB	Stanford, USA	5	May
15:29.07	Charlotte Taylor		17.01.94	13	Stanford, USA	5	May
15:29.26	Lauren Howarth		21.04.90	5rB	Stanford, USA	5	May
15:34.82	Jessica Judd	U23	7.01.95	1	Manchester (SC)	27	May
15:49.05				5	Birmingham	2	Jul
15:51.19				3	Taipei, TPE	27	Aug
15:55.40				1rB	Bedford	1	May
15:37.90	Calli Thackery		9.01.93	3	Portland, USA	11	Jun
15:39.44				9rB	Stanford, USA	5	May
(10)							
15:39.30	Amy-Eloise Neale	U23	5.08.95	1	Stanford, USA	31	Mar
15:40.15	Charlotte Arter		18.06.91	2	Watford	24	Jun
15:43.46				3	Birmingham	2	Jul
15:56.0mx				1rB	Yate	22	Jul
15:40.5mx	Louise Small		27.03.92	1	London (Cat)	16	Sep
15:42.27				1	Solihull	13	May
15:55.55				4	Taipei, TPE	27	Aug
15:41.29	Sarah Inglis		28.08.91	4	Portland, USA	11	Jun
15:42.47				3	Portland, USA	16	Jun

15:44.34	Emelia Gorecka		29.01.94	10rB	Stanford, USA	5	May
15:51.93				6	Birmingham	2	Jul
15:46.11	Verity Ockenden		31.08.91	4	Birmingham	2	Jul
15:46.85i	Alice Wright		3.11.94	6	Boston (A), USA	2	Dec
15:53.28				3	Azusa, USA	14	Apr
15:56.24i				9	College Station, USA	10	Mar
15:48.56mx	Jessica Martin		1.10.92	1	Lloret de Mar, ESP	16	Jul
15:50.04				3	Watford	24	Jun
15:49.16i	Pippa Woolven		26.07.93	1	Boston (A), USA	27	Jan
15:57.32	Claire Duck		29.08.85	4	Solihull	13	May

44 performances to 16:00.0 by 20 athletes including 4 indoors

16:00.34	Holly Rees		5.06.93	2	Waltham, USA	10	Jun
16:02.62	Bethan Knights	U23	28.09.95	4	Stanford, USA	21	Apr
16:05.55	Stephanie Barnes		28.07.88	3	Karlsruhe, GER	19	May
16:06.87	Elinor Kirk		26.04.89	13rB	Stanford, USA	5	May
16:06.9mx	Kate Maltby		26.07.85	1	Yate	22	Jul
16:14.97				9	Birmingham	2	Jul
16:08.89	Naomi Taschimowitz		19.10.89	1	Philadelphia, USA	15	Apr
16:09.14	Phoebe Law	U23	12.01.97	2	Manchester (SC)	27	May
16:09.35	Rebecca Murray		26.09.94	1	Bedford	1	May
16:11.48	Philippa Bowden	U23	29.03.95	3	Manchester (SC)	27	May
16:12.07+	Beth Potter		27.12.91	17m	London (O)	5	Aug
(30)							
16:12.54	Lennie Waite		4.02.86	1	Nacogdoches, USA	7	Apr
16:12.7mx	Lauren Deadman		27.03.84	2rB	Yate	22	Jul
16:13.56	Rebecca Rigby		17.10.91	2	Bedford	1	May
16:14.5+e	Jo Pavey	V40	20.09.73	5m	London (PH)	20	May
16:14.74	Josephine Moultrie		19.11.90	16rB	Stanford, USA	5	May
16:20.26	Kate Holt		7.09.92	5	Solihull	13	May
16:20.65	Ashley Gibson		1.03.86	6	Solihull	13	May
16:22.95	Jenny Nesbitt	U23	24.01.95	4	Bedford	1	May
16:24.82	Sophie Cowper		24.12.90	5	Watford	24	Jun
16:25.21	Nicole Taylor	U23	18.01.95	5	Bedford	1	May
(40)							
16:29.59mx	Lucy Reid		2.12.92	1	London (WP)	23	Aug
16:31.48	Bronwen Owen	U23	21.01.97	6	Manchester (SC)	27	May
16:32.59	Emily Hosker-Thornhill		27.10.92	7	Manchester (SC)	27	May
16:33.79	Emily Japp		18.12.90	2	Manchester (SC)	11	Jun
16:33.93	Laura-Jane Smith		7.02.91	3	Loughborough	8	Jul
16:33.95	Emma Clayton		16.07.88	8	Solihull	13	May
16:37.48	Poppy Tank	U23	5.12.97	3	San Francisco, USA	31	Mar
16:37.5mx	Hannah Viner	U23	18.07.96	1	London (WF)	30	Jun
16:45.36				11	Manchester (SC)	27	May
16:40.36	Caroline Lambert		2.09.93	9	Charlottesville, USA	22	Apr
16:41.95mx	Annabel Simpson	U23	30.04.97	1	Glasgow	29	Aug
16:47.49				2	Grangemouth	26	Aug
(50)							
16:43.83	Anna Tait	U23	5.12.96	9	Manchester (SC)	27	May
16:44.05	Jenna Hill		16.10.85	3	Bedford	30	Jul
16:44.07	Phoebe Barker	U20	27.11.99	10	Manchester (SC)	27	May
16:45.09	Naomi Lang	U20	7.02.00	1	Grangemouth	26	Aug
16:45.67	Floren Scrafton		24.12.93	5	Loughborough	8	Jul
16:47.89i	Stacie Taylor	U23	12.10.95	1	Birmingham, USA	24	Feb
16:51.93mx				2rB	Glasgow (S)	28	Jul
17:02.30				1rB	Houston, USA	14	May
16:49.06	Elizabeth Bird		4.10.94	3	Princeton, USA	7	Apr
16:49.08	Mhairi MacLennan	U23	26.03.95	7	Loughborough	8	Jul
16:49.88	Beth Kidger		16.03.94	12	Solihull	13	May
16:50.2	Amy Clements	V35	22.05.82	1	Horsham	8	Jul
(60)							
16:51.00	Rebecca Straw	U23	26.04.95	6	Bedford	1	May

16:51.4mx	Sarah Mercier		4.11.90	2rC	Yate	22	Jul
16:58.93				2	Visby, SWE	28	Jun
16:52.53	Rebecca Moore		7.10.91	2	Philadelphia, USA	15	Apr
16:53.3	Iona Lake		15.01.93	1	Norwich	14	May
16:54.29	Charlotte Murphy	U20	24.08.98	4	Houston, USA	14	May
16:54.36	Katherine Bingle		16.12.93	6	Watford	24	Jun
16:55.45	Georgia Malir	U23	20.02.96	7	Bedford	1	May
16:56.6mx	Emily Waugh		6.08.93	1	Kettering	26	Jul
16:57.99	Abigail Howarth		8.10.92	14	Manchester (SC)	27	May
16:58.0mx	Victoria Knight	V40	3.10.76	1	Cambridge	9	Jun
17:11.4				1	Ipswich	20	May
(70)							
16:58.21	Rachael Franklin		14.12.91	4	Manchester (SC)	11	Jun
16:59.45	Charlotte Firth		31.12.84	7	Watford	24	Jun
16:59.74	Jodie Judd	U20	25.09.98	8	Watford	24	Jun
17:01.41mx	Emma Stepto	V45	4.04.70	1	Exeter	20	Aug
17:02.88	Jennifer Elkins		27.01.85	5	Bedford	30	Jul
17:03.04	Sophie Harris		12.06.93	1	London (BP)	8	Jul
17:03.6mx	Fiona Marks		9.03.90	1rD	Yate	22	Jul
17:04.28i	Rachel Felton	V35	27.06.79	8	Boston, USA	10	Feb
17:06.12	Louise Perrio		8.07.82	3	Visby, SWE	28	Jun
17:06.54	Rachael Burns	V35	1.03.80	6	Manchester (SC)	11	Jun
(80)							
17:07.99	Stephanie McCall		27.09.93	9	Watford	24	Jun
17:10.69	Justine Anthony		2.12.93	12rB	San Francisco, USA	31	Mar
17:13.56	Anna MacFadyen	U20	19.06.99	1	Inverness	13	May
17:14.24	Beth Hawling		28.07.94	8rB	Raleigh, USA	24	Mar
17:15.09	Rebecca Evans	U23	2.11.95	21	San Francisco, USA	31	Mar
17:15.35	Bryony Gunn	U20	28.02.98	17	Manchester (SC)	27	May
17:15.45	Kirstin Oakley	U20	25.07.98	15rB	San Francisco, USA	31	Mar
17:15.85mx	Katy Hedgethorne		17.09.88	1rB	London (WP)	23	Aug
17:16.0mx	Molly Browne		8.12.92	3rD	Yate	22	Jul
17:16.02	Abbie Donnelly	U23	2.09.96	9	Bedford	1	May
(90)							
17:16.02	Rebecca Howard	U23	20.01.96	10	Bedford	1	May
17:16.09	Bethanie Murray	U23	16.08.95	11	Bedford	1	May
17:16.32mx	Nicola Gauld	V35	28.03.82	3rB	Glasgow (S)	28	Jul
17:17.7mx	Caroline Hoyte	V45	30.06.70	1	Brighton	17	Aug
17:17.74	Hollie Parker	U23	20.12.96	15	Austin, USA	31	Mar
17:18.79	Sarah Livett		16.11.93	25	San Francisco, USA	31	Mar
17:18.94	Elizabeth Apsley	U23	12.01.97	12	Bedford	1	May
17:19.4mx	Anna Boniface		27.04.91	2	London (WF)	30	Jun

Foreign

15:50.55	*Emma Mitchell (IRL)*		*2.09.93*	*3*	*Solihull*	*13*	*May*
16:32.56	*Kerry O'Flaherty (IRL)*	*V35*	*15.07.81*	*7*	*Solihull*	*13*	*May*
17:01.31	*Danielle Fegan (IRL)*		*3.06.90*	*5*	*Manchester (SC)*	*11*	*Jun*
17:07.42	*Ashley Scott-Wilson (USA)*		*9.04.91*	*16*	*Manchester (SC)*	*27*	*May*

10000 Metres

31:45.63mx	Katrina Wootton		2.09.85	1	London (Cat)	3	Sep
32:27.47				3	London (PH)	20	May
33:49.74				11	Minsk, BLR	10	Jun
32:04.63	Beth Potter		27.12.91	1	London (PH)	20	May
32:15.88				21	London (O)	5	Aug
32:10.59	Eilish McColgan		25.11.90	3	Stanford	31	Mar
32:11.80	Charlotte Taylor		17.01.94	4	Stanford, USA	31	Mar
32:38.57				1	Eugene, USA	8	Jun
32:51.33				27	London (O)	5	Aug
32:16.23	Stephanie Twell		17.08.89	2	London (PH)	20	May

32:29.28	Alice Wright		3.11.94	16	Stanford, USA	5	May
	32:42.64			2	Eugene, USA	8	Jun
32:37.52	Charlotte Arter		18.06.91	1	Manchester (Str)	19	Aug
	32:51.72			6	London (PH)	20	Aug
32:41.19	Sonia Samuels	V35	16.05.79	20	Stanford, USA	5	May
	33:00.74			12	London (PH)	20	May
	33:20.61			6	Huelva, ESP	8	Apr
32:42.93	Jo Pavey	V40	20.09.73	4	London (PH)	20	May
32:51.38	Claire Duck		29.08.85	5	London (PH)	20	May
	(10)						
32:56.11	Louise Small		27.03.92	9	London (PH)	20	May
32:59.52	Jenny Nesbitt	U23	24.01.95	10	London (PH)	20	May
	33:50.37			12	Minsk, BLR	10	Jun
33:00.24	Jessica Martin		1.10.92	11	London (PH)	20	May
	33:55.24			9	Huelva, ESP	8	Apr
33:00.84	Phoebe Law	U23	12.01.97	13	London (PH)	20	May
	33:40.75			4	Bydgoszcz, POL	14	Jul
33:13.33	Gemma Steel		12.11.85	2	Manchester (Str)	19	Aug
33:13.55	Holly Rees		5.06.93	1	Lowell, USA	20	May
33:23.31	Verity Ockenden		31.08.91	3	Manchester (Str)	19	Aug
	33:37.37			16	London (PH)	20	May
33:30.13	Bethan Knights	U23	28.09.95	3	Eugene, USA	13	May
	33:31.25			10	Stanford, USA	31	Mar
33:36.70	Rebecca Rigby		17.10.91	15	London (PH)	20	May
33:44.24	Philippa Bowden	U23	29.03.95	17	London (PH)	20	May
	34 performances to 34:00.0 by 20 athletes						
34:21.50	Caroline Lambert		2.09.93	14	Stanford, USA	31	Mar
34:31.05	Rosie Edwards		20.08.88	4	Manchester (Str)	19	Aug
34:46.25	Nicole Taylor	U23	18.01.95	19	London (PH)	20	May
34:52.30	Isabel Clark		13.03.86	5	Manchester (Str)	19	Aug
34:55.77	Sophie Cowper		24.12.90	21	London (PH)	20	May
35:12.68	Louise Perrio	V35	8.07.82	6	Manchester (Str)	19	Aug
35:15.50	Sarah Mercier		4.11.90	7	Manchester (Str)	19	Aug
35:17.29	Georgina Schwiening		15.12.94	1rB	London (PH)	20	May
35:25.17	Mhairi MacLennan	U23	26.03.95	22	London (PH)	20	May
35:27.76	Rebecca Moore		7.10.91	1	New Haven, USA	8	Apr
	(30)						
35:33.46	Annabel Simpson	U23	30.04.97	1	Glasgow (C)	28	Apr
35:35.46	Sarah Laverty	U23	30.09.96	3	Stanford, USA	22	Apr
35:36.04	Abbie Donnelly	U23	2.09.96	3rB	London (PH)	20	May
35:37.28	Kate Robinson		30.09.94	6	San Francisco, USA	31	Mar
35:39.00	Helen Davies	V35	12.09.79	4rB	London (PH)	20	May
35:44.36	Lucy Reid		2.12.92	5rB	London (PH)	20	May
35:46.5	Emma Stepto	V45	4.04.70	1	Par	26	Jul
35:49.1	Alaw Beynon-Thomas		15.11.89	1	Cardiff	12	Aug

Foreign

32:51.78	*Emma Mitchell (IRL)*		*2.09.93*	*7*	*London (PH)*	*20*	*May*
35:27.66	*Danielle Fegan (IRL)*		*3.06.90*	*2rB*	*London (PH)*	*20*	*Jun*

5 Kilometres Road

15:28	Rosie Edwards	20.08.88	1	Louisville, USA	4	Mar
15:39	Lauren Howarth	21.04.90	5	Boston, USA	15	Apr
15:40	Emelia Gorecka	29.01.94	1	Ipswich	18	Aug
15:45	Rosie Clarke	17.11.91	1	Barrowford	18	Mar
15:58	Melissa Courtney	30.08.93	2	Barrowford	18	Mar
15:59	Elinor Kirk	26.04.89	7	Boston, USA	15	Apr
	6 performances to 16:00 by 6 athletes, further women faster than track best					
16:02	Gemma Steel	12.11.85	1	Ipswich	18	Aug
16:15	Stacey Smith	4.02.90	1	Wallsend	23	Apr
16:18	Amanda Crook	4.04.86	2	Kingsley	24	Aug

16:25	Helen Davies	V35	12.09.79	3	Ipswich	18	Aug
16:25	Rebecca Straw	U23	26.04.95	3	Ipswich	18	Aug
16:28	Sophie Cowper		24.12.90	1	Kingsley	28	Apr
16:28	Jacqueline Fairchild		3.05.89	1	Manchester	3	Aug
16:28	Danielle Hodgkinson		11.10.84	1	Liverpool	2	Sep
16:32+	Rebecca Hilland	V35	11.06.80	3m	Hole, NOR	21	Oct
16:33	Emma Clayton		16.07.88	1	Doncaster	12	Jul
16:34	Rachael Burns	V35	1.03.80	1	Christleton	19	May
16:35	Gemma Hillier-Moses		19.06.88	3	Barrowford	18	Mar
16:37	Holly Archer		7.11.93	4	Ipswich	18	Aug
16:38	Ruth Barnes	V35	7.10.78	1	Bristol	28	Mar
16:39	Rebecca Robinson	V35	28.10.82	1	Barrowford	18	Nov
16:40	Iona Lake		15.01.93	1	Wroxham	14	Jun
16:40	Hannah England		6.03.87	2	Barrowford	18	Nov
16:43	Isabel Clark		13.03.86	1	London (BP)	27	Jul
16:45	Laura Whittle		27.06.85	1	Gayton	22	Jan
16:45	Laura Hesketh		9.04.83	2	Manchester	20	Jul
16:46	Jenny Spink	V35	7.08.81	1	Falesia, POR	14	Mar
16:46	Hannah Nuttall	U23	7.07.97	4	Barrowford	18	Mar
16:46	Juliet Potter	V35	24.10.81	1	Derby	19	Apr
16:48	Sarah Mercier		4.11.90	1	Castel	15	Jan
16:48	Louise Perrio		8.07.82	1	St. Peter Port GUE	14	Apr
16:49	Alaw Beynon-Thomas		15.11.89	1	Mountain Ash	31	Dec
16:50	Stephanie Davis		27.08.90	1	London (BP)	31	Jul
16:50	Charlotte Christensen		27.01.93	5	Ipswich	18	Aug
16:50+	Charlotte Purdue		10.06.91	2m	Glasgow	1	Oct
16:52	India Lee		31.05.88	2	Falesia, POR	14	Mar
16:56	Abigail Howarth		8.10.92	2	Manchester	3	Aug
16:57	Georgia Malir	U23	20.02.96	4	Manchester	20	Jul
16:58	Morag MacLarty		10.02.86	1	Crathie	22	Apr
16:58	Rebecca Burns		19.06.90	2	Edinburgh	5	May
16:58	Lydia Turner	U23	19.11.96	1	Redcar	1	Oct
16:59	Stephanie McCall		27.09.93	2	London (BP)	7	Aug

5 Miles Road

27:24	Lauren Howarth		21.04.90	1	Alsager	5	Feb
27:26	Sonia Samuels	V35	16.05.79	2	Alsager	5	Feb
27:36	Jane Potter	V35	24.10.81	1	Kegworth	2	Jun
27:36	Lucy Reid		2.12.92	1	Portsmouth	3	Dec
27:39	Amanda Crook		4.04.86	1	Preston	13	Aug
27:44	Charlotte Taylor-Green		2.04.85	1	Weston-super-Mare	20	Apr
27:49	Kate Holt		7.09.92	3	Alsager	5	Feb
27:51	Laura Brenton		20.06.86	2	Portsmouth	3	Dec
27:53	Rosie Edwards		20.08.88	9	Indianapolis, USA	18	Feb
27:54	Jennifer Elkins		27.01.85	1	Romsey	29	Jan
	(10)						
27:56	Beth Kidger		16.03.94	3	Portsmouth	3	Dec

10 Kilometres Road

32:01	Eilish McColgan		25.11.90	1	Doha, QAT	13	Jan
32:06				1	Leeds	5	Nov
32:23				1	Sheffield	3	Dec
32:31	Laura Weightman		1.07.91	1	Clitheroe	31	Dec
32:47	Katrina Wootton		2.09.85	1	Brighton	9	Apr
33:18				3	Manchester	28	May
32:57	Jo Pavey	V40	20.09.73	1	London	29	May
32:58	Tish Jones		7.09.85	1	Durban, RSA	11	Jun
33:00	Beth Potter		27.12.91	2	Clitheroe	31	Dec
33:04	Rosie Clarke		17.11.91	3	Houilles, FRA	31	Dec
33:18	Sonia Samuels	V35	16.05.79	2	London	29	May

33:28	Gemma Steel		12.11.85	1	York		6	Aug
33:28	Sarah Inglis		28.08.91	1	Richmond, CAN		24	Sep
33:30	Kate Maltby		26.07.85	1	Bristol		7	May

14 performances to 33:30 by 11 athletes, further women faster than track best

33:32	Charlotte Purdue		10.06.91	3	London		29	May
33:32	Ashley Gibson		1.03.86	3	Leeds		5	Nov
33:33	Elinor Kirk		26.04.89	1	Partington		5	Mar
33:36	Rebecca Hilland	V35	11.06.80	3	Hole, NOR		21	Oct
33:38	Lily Partridge		9.03.91	1	Cardiff		3	Sep
33:40	Josephine Moultrie		19.11.90	4	Leeds		5	Nov
33:43	Alyson Dixon	V35	24.09.78	2	Partington		5	Mar
33:49	Rebecca Robinson	V35	28.10.82	5	Leeds		5	Nov
33:50	Hannah Walker		9.08.91	4	London		29	May
33:51	Emma Clayton		16.07.88	6	Leeds		5	Nov
33:55	Sophie Cowper		24.12.90	7	Leeds		5	Nov
33:58	Mhairi MacLennan	U23	26.03.95	8	Leeds		5	Nov
33:59	Fionnuala Ross		5.11.90	1	Stirling		10	Sep
34:00	Calli Thackery		9.01.93	3	Shelter Island, USA		17	Jun
34:01	Tracy Barlow		18.06.85	5	London		29	May
34:05	Lauren Howarth		21.04.90	3	Partington		5	Mar
34:14+	Jenny Spink	V35	7.08.81	m	Barcelona, ESP		12	Feb
34:17	Jenna Hill		16.10.85	9	Leeds		5	Nov
34:18	Eleanor Davis		21.02.89	10	Leeds		5	Nov
34:19	Rebecca Moore		7.10.91	11	Leeds		5	Nov
34:21	Laura Graham		5.03.86	2	Belfast		25	Nov
34:24	Victoria Knight	V40	3.10.76	7	London		29	May
34:27	Stevie Stockton		23.03.89	3	Clitheroe		31	Dec
34:28	Georgia Malir	U23	20.02.96	12	Leeds		5	Nov
34:29	Ruth Barnes	V35	7.10.78	1	Bromham		3	Dec
34:30	Rebecca Murray		26.09.94	1	Glasgow		1	Oct
34:30	Laura Hesketh		9.04.83	1	Wilmslow		26	Nov
34:34	Laura-Jane Smith		7.02.91	13	Leeds		5	Nov
34:36	Lauren Deadman		27.03.84	1	London (Nh)		2	Jul
34:41	Sophie Harris		12.06.93	3	Cardiff		3	Sep
34:41	Annabel Simpson	U23	30.04.97	2	Stirling		10	Sep
34:41	Lucy Reid		2.12.92	14	Leeds		5	Nov
34:44	Amy Clements	V35	22.05.82	1	London (VP)		12	Aug
34:44	Jessica Coulson		18.04.90	1	Arley		4	Nov
34:46	Katy Hedgethorne		17.09.88	2	Wilmslow		26	Nov
34:47	Sarah Mercier		4.11.90	3	Eastleigh		19	Mar
34:48	Georgina Schwiening		15.12.94	8	London		29	May
34:49	Danielle Hodgkinson		11.10.84	16	Leeds		5	Nov
34:50	Isabel Clark		13.03.86	2	London (Nh)		2	Jul
34:51	Hannah Viner	U23	18.07.96	8	Laredo, ESP		18	Mar
34:52	Jane Potter	V35	24.10.81	5	Brighton		9	Apr
34:52	Julie Briscoe	V40	11.02.76	17	Leeds		5	Nov
34:55	Rachel Felton	V35	27.06.79	2	Bristol		7	May
34:55	Stephanie Davis		27.08.90	1	London (BP)		5	Aug
34:56	Clara Evans		27.11.93	4	Cardiff		3	Sep
34:58+	Susan Partridge	V35	4.01.80	23m	London		23	Apr
34:59	Emma Holt		27.05.85	6	Partington		5	Mar
34:59	Juliet Potter	V35	24.10.81	6	Brighton		9	Apr
34:59	Fiona Brian		27.01.86	19	Leeds		5	Nov

Downhill (55m)

32:57	Alyson Dixon	V35	(33:43)	3	Madrid, ESP		31	Dec
33:26	Sonia Samuels	V35	(33:18)	2	Madrid, ESP		31	Dec

Foreign

32:51	*Emma Mitchell (IRL)*		*2.09.93*	*2*	*Leeds*		*5*	*Nov*
34:28	*Tamara Armoush (JOR)*		*8.05.92*	*6*	*Valencia, ESP*		*19*	*Nov*
34:38	*Kerry O'Flaherty (IRL)*	*V35*	*15.07.81*	*3*	*Dublin, IRL*		*9*	*Apr*

15 Kilometres – Road

50:46+	Gemma Steel		12.11.85	m	South Shields	10	Sep
50:52+	Lily Partridge		9.03.91	m	South Shields	10	Sep
51:00+				3m	Santa Pola, ESP	22	Jan
51:08+	Charlotte Purdue		10.06.91	1m	Reading	19	Mar
51:29+	Alyson Dixon	V35	24.09.78	m	South Shields	10	Sep
51:39+	Jenny Nesbitt	U23	24.01.95	5m	Cardiff	1	Oct
51:43+	Tracy Barlow		18.06.85	m	Barcelona, ESP	12	Feb
51:57+	Jenny Spink	V35	7.08.81	m	Barcelona, ESP	12	Feb
52:21+	Katrina Wootton		2.09.85	3m	Reading	19	Mar
52:22+	Sonia Samuels	V35	16.05.79	m	Berlin, GER	24	Sep
52:28+	Charlotte Arter		18.06.91	19m	London	23	Apr

10 Miles Road

54:53	Emma Pallant		4.06.89	2	Twickenham	15	Oct
55:25	Gemma Steel		12.11.85	1	Portsmouth	22	Oct
55:37	Lily Partridge		9.03.91	2	Portsmouth	22	Oct
55:43	Charlotte Purdue		10.06.91	3	Portsmouth	22	Oct
55:53	Rosie Edwards		20.08.88	1	Louisville, USA	1	Apr
56:24	Sophie Cowper		24.12.90	1	Brampton	19	Nov
56:30	Annabel Simpson	U23	30.04.97	2	Brampton	19	Nov
56:44	Ruth Barnes	V35	7.10.78	1	Melksham	12	Feb
56:54	Sonia Samuels	V35	16.05.79	1	Holme Pierrepont	16	Jun
57:06	Rebecca Murray		26.09.94	4	Portsmouth	22	Oct
	(10)						
57:10	Georgina Schwiening		15.12.94	1	West Walton	29	Oct
57:18	Laura Graham		5.03.86	1	Armagh	8	Oct
57:20	Katrina Wootton		2.09.85	5	Portsmouth	22	Oct
57:21	Isabel Clark		13.03.86	1	Thames Ditton	16	Jul
57:58	Calli Thackery		9.01.93	7	Pittsburgh, USA	5	Nov
58:00	Catherine Whoriskey		15.02.86	1	Londonderry	4	Mar
58:16	Juliet Potter	V35	24.10.81	2	Holme Pierrepont	16	Jun
58:20	Katie White	V35	6.01.81	1	Motherwell	2	Apr
58:21	Jane Potter	V35	24.10.81	1	Leicester	3	Sep
58:31	Laura-Jane Smith		7.02.91	8	Portsmouth	22	Oct
	(20)						
58:36	Georgia Campbell		27.07.88	3	Brampton	19	Nov
58:45	Jennifer Elkins		27.01.85	9	Portsmouth	22	Oct
58:46	Nicola Gauld	V35	28.03.82	2	Motherwell	2	Apr

Foreign

58:26	*Breege Connolly (IRL)*	*V35*	*1.02.78*	*1*	*Trim, IRL*	*5*	*Feb*

Half Marathon

71:29	Charlotte Purdue		10.06.91	13	Okayama, JPN	23	Dec
	72:15			1	Reading	19	Mar
	72:18			2	Glasgow	1	Oct
	72:39			5	Hamburg, GER	25	Jun
	74:01+			21m	London	23	Apr
71:32	Gemma Steel		12.11.85	6	South Shields	10	Sep
	72:47			2	Granollers, ESP	5	Feb
	73:37			2	Reading	19	Mar
	74:27			1	Hamilton, BER	15	Jan
72:10	Lily Partridge		9.03.91	7	South Shields	10	Sep
	72:12			3	Santa Pola, ESP	22	Jan
	74:24+			3m	Seville, ESP	19	Feb
72:29	Alyson Dixon	V35	24.09.78	8	South Shields	10	Sep
	73:21+			17m	London	23	Apr
	74:21+			m	London	6	Aug
72:48	Tracy Barlow		18.06.85	10	Barcelona, ESP	12	Feb
	74:07			1	Paddock Wood	2	Apr
	74:08+			23m	London	23	Apr

73:23	Jenny Nesbitt	U23	24.01.95	5	Cardiff	1	Oct
74:26				4	Reading	19	Mar
73:36	Jenny Spink	V35	7.08.81	12	Barcelona, ESP	12	Feb
73:36	Sarah Inglis		28.08.91	5	Monterey, USA	12	Nov
74:21				1	Victoria, CAN	8	Oct
74:51				16	Lisbon, POR	19	Mar
73:43	Emma Pallant		4.06.89	1	Lanzarote, ESP	9	Dec
73:44	Kate Reed		28.09.82	1	Tallahassee, USA	5	Feb
(10)							
74:00+	Charlotte Arter		18.06.91	18m	London	23	Apr
74:03+	Sonia Samuels	V35	16.05.79	m	Berlin, GER	24	Sep
74:39				9	Olomouc, CZE	24	Jun
74:18	Katrina Wootton		2.09.85	3	Reading	19	Mar
74:22	Caryl Jones		4.04.87	9	South Shields	10	Sep
74:25	Hannah Walker		9.08.91	1	Lilliebaelt, DEN	6	May
74:36				5	Reading	19	Mar
74:26	Fionnuala Ross		5.11.90	3	Glasgow	1	Oct
74:43	Victoria Knight	V40	3.10.76	2	Lillebælt, DEN	6	May
74:49				6	Granollers, ESP	5	Feb
74:45+	Jo Pavey	V40	20.09.73	24m	London	23	Apr
75:00+	Susan Partridge	V35	4.01.80	25m	London	23	Apr
	37 performances to 75:00 by 19 athletes						
75:26	Georgina Schwiening		15.12.94	1	Peterborough	8	Oct
(20)							
75:32	Ruth Barnes	V35	7.10.78	1	Bath	12	Mar
75:34	Clara Evans		27.11.93	6	Reading	19	Mar
75:40	Linda Spencer	V35	16.01.82	1	Sunshine Coast, AUS	20	Aug
75:40	Rebecca Hilland	V35	11.06.80	1	Manchester	15	Oct
75:45+	Tish Jones		7.09.85	29m	London	23	Apr
75:49	Rebecca Murray		26.09.94	10	South Shields	10	Sep
75:50	Georgie Bruinvels		20.10.88	1	Chertsey	26	Feb
75:55	Amy Clements		22.05.82	2	Bath	12	Mar
76:10	Helen Davies	V35	12.09.79	1	Great Bentley	5	Feb
76:10	Rachel Felton	V35	27.06.79	3	Bath	12	Mar
(30)							
76:30	Philippa Bowden	U23	29.03.95	8	Reading	19	Mar
76:35	Lucy Gossage	V35	25.12.79	2	Cambridge	5	Mar
76:35	Anna Boniface		27.04.91	9	Reading	19	Mar
76:37	Gemma Rankin		18.12.84	4	Glasgow	1	Oct
76:41	Emily Waugh		6.08.93	1	Southport	2	Jul
76:50	Rebecca Moore		7.10.91	1	Milton Keynes	1	May
76:52	Catherine Whoriskey		15.02.86	1	Omagh	1	Apr
76:52	Rebecca Rigby		17.10.91	1	Derby	4	Jun
76:54	Katie White	V35	6.01.81	1	Alloa	19	Mar
76:59	Laura Graham		5.03.86	1	Larne (NI)	18	Mar
(40)							
77:06	Julie Briscoe	V40	11.02.76	1	Chester	21	May
77:19	Tracy Millmore		16.07.82	1	York	15	Jan
77:21+	Julia Davis		12.08.86	m	London	23	Apr
77:25	Sophie Kelly		14.01.94	3	Cambridge	5	Mar
77:38	Dani Nimmock		10.05.90	29	New York, USA	19	Mar
77:39	Caroline Lambert		2.09.93	1	Bowling Green, USA	2	Sep
77:42	Emma Stepto	V45	4.04.70	1	Bristol	17	Sep
77:50	Faye Banks	V35	11.08.79	1	Sherburn-in-Elmet	10	Sep
77:56	Isabel Clark		13.03.86	1	Ealing	24	Sep
78:10	Joanne Harvey		27.09.89	1	Wokingham	12	Feb
(50)							
78:10	Elinor Kirk		26.04.89	1	Lancaster	5	Nov
78:16	Fiona Brian		27.01.86	13	South Shields	10	Sep
78:22	Bryher Bowness		10.02.93	1	Gosport	19	Nov
78:23	Hayley Munn		17.09.90	4	Cambridge	5	Mar
78:28	Samantha Amend	V35	25.05.79	2	Wokingham	12	Feb

78:35	Lisa Palmer-Blount	V40	9.02.77	19	Barcelona, ESP	12	Feb
78:36	Heather Timmins		12.02.90	12	Reading	19	Mar
78:38	Diane McVey	V40	22.12.76	1	Wrexham	19	Feb
78:38	Annabel Granger	V40	19.05.73	2	Bristol	17	Sep
78:41	Ruth Senior		16.10.87	4	San Diego, USA	4	Jun
(60)							
78:42	Natasha Cockram		12.11.92	4	Swansea	25	Jun
78:51+	Rosie Edwards		20.08.88	m	London	23	Apr
78:52	Gillian Palmer	V35	30.12.80	2	Annecy, FRA	30	Apr
78:56	Charlotte Firth		31.12.84	3	Bristol	17	Sep

Short Course (146 metres)

74:27	Eleanor Davis		21.02.89	1	Brighton	26	Feb

Foreign

77:07	*Gladys Ganiel-O'Neill (IRL)*	*V40*	*10.03.77*	*1*	*Dublin, IRL*	*13*	*Aug*
77:28	*Fanni Gyurkó (HUN)*		*18.01.87*	*5*	*Glasgow*	*1*	*Oct*
78:22	*Sarah McCormack (IRL)*		*19.08.86*	*11*	*Reading*	*19*	*Mar*
78:32	*Taylor Bickford (USA)*		*27.08.93*	*5*	*Cambridge*	*5*	*Mar*
78:42	*Hayley Kuter (NZL)*	*V35*	*16.01.78*	*1*	*Conwy*	*19*	*Nov*

Marathon

2:29:06	Alyson Dixon	V35	24.09.78	14	London	23	Apr
	2:31:36			18	London	6	Aug
2:29:23	Charlotte Purdue		10.06.91	15	London	23	Apr
	2:29:48			13	London	6	Aug
	2:30:34			4	Saitama, JPN	12	Nov
2:29:34	Sonia Samuels	V35	16.05.79	7	Berlin, GER	24	Sep
2:30:42	Tracy Barlow		18.06.85	16	London	23	Apr
	2:41:03			43	London	6	Aug
2:32:10	Lily Partridge		9.03.91	4	Seville, ESP	19	Feb
2:33:56	Tish Jones		7.09.85	18	London	23	Apr
2:34:16	Caryl Jones		4.04.87	11	Amsterdam, NED	15	Oct
2:36:22	Elinor Kirk		26.04.89	4	Florence, ITA	26	Nov
2:37:03	Georgie Bruinvels		20.10.88	1	Manchester	2	Apr
2:37:05	Laura Graham		5.03.86	14	Berlin, GER	24	Sep
	2:39:07			4	Dublin, IRL	29	Oct
	2:41:46			1	Belfast	1	May
	2:42:38			29	London	23	Apr
(10)							
2:37:17	Anna Boniface		27.04.91	20	London	23	Apr
2:37:51	Susan Partridge	V35	4.01.80	22	London	23	Apr
2:38:11	Jenny Spink	V35	7.08.81	23	London	23	Apr
2:39:20	Amy Clements		22.05.82	24	London	23	Apr
2:39:33	Julia Davis		12.08.86	26	London	23	Apr
2:40:56	Rosie Edwards		20.08.88	27	London	23	Apr
2:42:40	Helen Davies	V35	12.09.79	1	Brighton	9	Apr
2:42:49	Katie White	V35	6.01.81	30	London	23	Apr
2:42:57	Georgina Schwiening		15.12.94	20	Valencia, ESP	19	Nov
2:43:30	Claire Grima	V35	21.07.77	32	London	23	Apr
(20)							
2:44:27	Sarah Lowery	V35	15.04.82	1	Chester	8	Oct
2:44:35	Gemma Rankin		18.12.84	34	London	23	Apr
	2:44:43			7	Dublin, IRL	29	Oct

30 performances to 2:45:00 by 22 athletes

2:45:19	Joasia Zakrzewski	V40	19.01.76	4	Kraków, POL	30	Apr
2:45:29	Charlotte Firth		31.12.84	2	Manchester	2	Apr
2:45:37	Linda Spencer	V35	16.01.82	1	Perth, AUS	18	Jun
2:45:39	Alison Rowatt	V35	16.02.81	3	Los Angeles, USA	19	Mar
2:46:00	Hayley Munn		17.09.90	1	Brighton	9	Apr
2:46:09	Tracy Millmore	V35	16.07.82	1	York	8	Oct
2:46:16	Clara Evans		27.11.93	35	London	23	Apr

2:46:45	Gemma Connolly	V35	18.12.81	3	Manchester	2	Apr
(30)							
2:47:34	Erica Fogg	V35	4.12.78	26	Berlin, GER	24	Sep
2:47:48	Lesley Pirie	V35	11.01.81	1	Stirling	21	May
2:47:57	Jennifer Wetton		28.11.86	4	Manchester	2	Apr
2:47:59	Michelle Nolan	V35	8.12.80	37	London	23	Apr
2:48:08	Shona McIntosh		21.01.83	38	London	23	Apr
2:48:30	Sarah Webster	V35	25.04.79	2	Chester	8	Oct
2:48:41	Catherine Whoriskey		15.02.86	11	Seville, ESP	19	Feb
2:48:47	Fiona Brian		27.01.86	43	Chicago, USA	8	Oct
2:49:00	Fionnuala Ross		5.11.90	25	Frankfurt, GER	29	Oct
2:49:03	Hannah Howard		14.04.85	31	Berlin, GER	24	Sep
(40)							
2:49:09	Christine-Ann Wellington	V40	18.02.77	39	London	23	Apr
2:49:15	Ruth Senior		16.10.87	6	St. Paul, USA	1	Oct
2:49:37	Natasha Cockram		12.11.92	8	Dublin, IRL	29	Oct
2:49:52	Hilary Mott		7.03.88	1	Abingdon	22	Oct
2:49:53	Naomi Mitchell		24.11.93	35	Berlin, GER	24	Sep
2:50:03	Emily Lagomarsino		13.05.92	41	London	23	Apr
2:50:31	Faye Banks	V35	11.08.79	4	Chester	8	Oct
2:50:45	Kath Hardcastle	V35	81	10	Houston, USA	15	Jan
2:50:45	Nicola Squires		8.07.85	42	London	23	Apr
2:50:55	Mary Menon	V35	10.07.79	1	Barnstaple	24	Sep
(50)							
2:50:57	Louise Perrio	V35	8.07.82	35	Frankfurt, GER	29	Oct
2:50:58	Joanne Harvey		27.09.89	43	London	23	Apr
2:51:22	Helen Buller	V35	28.04.78	3	Brighton	9	Apr
2:51:25	Holly Rush	V40	23.09.77	7	Florence, ITA	26	Nov
2:51:37	Zoe McLennan		2.07.83	6	Manchester	2	Apr
2:52:05	Diane Moore	V40	13.12.74	5	Chester	8	Oct
2:52:07	Hannah Jarvis		15.10.84	48	London	23	Apr
2:52:28	Sophie Kelly		14.01.94	1	Birmingham	15	Oct
2:53:16	Nina Griffith		8.07.85	2	Gran Canaria, ESP	22	Jan
2:53:19	Joanne McCandless	V35	19.10.78	49	London	23	Apr
(60)							
2:53:27	Louise Smith	V45	7.07.70	1	Newry	28	May
2:53:35	Laura Trimble		7.07.82	50	London	23	Apr
2:53:38	Rebecca Gallop		10.11.85	44	Frankfurt, GER	29	Oct
2:54:02	Wendy Webber	V35	18.09.78	52	London	23	Apr
2:54:04	Vicky Wright	V35	19.05.77	53	London	23	Apr
2:54:11	Sarah Hill	V40	25.02.73	6	Chester	8	Oct
2:54:11	Hannah Oldroyd		27.05.87	1	Auckland, NZL	29	Oct
2:54:23	Andrea Rowlands	V40	1.06.74	1	Wrexham	12	Mar
2:54:37	Emily Proto		24.11.88	9	Florence, ITA	26	Nov
2:54:43	Helen Waugh	V40	3.12.76	8	Manchester	2	Apr
(70)							
2:54:47	Lucy Ashe		20.10.88	55	London	23	Apr
2:54:48	Dianne Lauder	V40	6.07.76	3	Edinburgh	28	May
2:55:02	Angharad Mair	V55	30.03.61	58	London	23	Apr
2:55:05	Fiona Davies	V40	3.11.73	59	London	23	Apr
2:55:06	Alison Lavender		25.09.88	60	London	23	Apr
2:55:21	Emma Louise Brown		7.02.85	61	London	23	Apr
2:55:34	Sara Bird		28.01.87	3	York	8	Oct
2:55:38	Julie Warner	V50	8.04.67	2	Nottingham	24	Sep
2:55:48	Treena Johnson	V55	29.08.61	62	London	23	Apr
2:55:49	Rose Penfold		11.04.91	63	London	23	Apr
(80)							
2:55:50	Victoria Kenny		3.04.83	64	London	23	Apr
2:55:54	Lesley Locks	V40	22.11.76	65	London	23	Apr
2:56:00	Samantha Amend	V35	25.05.79	32	Valencia, ESP	19	Nov
2:56:03	Julia Belyavin	V35	10.07.79	66	London	23	Apr

2:56:16	Rebecca Gentry			86	56	Berlin, GER	24 Sep
2:56:21	Carla Molinaro		27.07.84		19	Amsterdam, NED	15 Oct
2:56:25	Fiona Maycock	V45	21.08.67		11	Manchester	2 Apr
2:56:31	Emma Prideaux	V40	25.04.73		7	Chester	8 Oct
2:56:39	Hannah Claydon		18.12.93		8	Chester	8 Oct
2:56:40	Hazel Wyness	V35	23.12.77		67	London	23 Apr
(90)							
2:56:45	Sorrell Walsh		19.04.90		55	Boston, USA	17 Apr
2:56:45	Lucy Niemz		11.02.86		49	Frankfurt, GER	29 Oct
2:56:47	Edwina Mcdowall	V45	31.07.70		2	Abingdon	22 Oct
2:56:58	Emma Paull		6.06.85		69	London	23 Apr
2:56:58	Laura Wallace	V35	26.11.79		9	Chester	8 Oct
2:56:59	Alice Whiley		1.07.91		70	London	23 Apr
2:57:01	Vicky Nealon		19.04.83		10	Chester	8 Oct
2:57:05	Caroline Hoskins	V45	29.12.67		3	Abingdon	22 Oct
2:57:06	Jill Smylie	V35	6.04.80		2	Stirling	21 May
2:57:08	Emily Waugh		6.08.93		1	Gloucester	6 Aug
(100)							
2:57:15	Emma Yates	V45	16.01.69		4	York	8 Oct
2:57:21	Emma Ballantyne		20.06.88		5	York	8 Oct
2:57:25	Odette Robson	V45	4.10.71		5	Brighton	9 Apr
2:57:39	Sarah Baxter	V35	15.12.77		72	London	23 Apr
2:57:53	Andrea Banks	V40	27.09.72		20	Rotterdam, NED	9 Apr

downhill

2:56:15	Allison Blackmore	V50		66	110	Sacramento, USA	3 Dec
2:56:39	Chloe Cox		9.04.86		3	Inverness	24 Sep

Foreign

2:37:29	*Breege Connolly (IRL)*	*V35*	*1.02.78*		*13*	*Valencia, ESP*	*19 Nov*
2:37:55	*Gladys Ganiel-O'Neill (IRL)*	*V40*	*10.03.77*		*15*	*Berlin, GER*	*24 Sep*
2:39:48	*Fanni Gyurkó (HUN)*		*18.01.87*		*15*	*Frankfurt, GER*	*29 Oct*
2:43:03	*Taylor Bickford (USA)*		*27.08.93*		*31*	*London*	*23 Apr*
2:53:36	*Marta Bagnati (ITA)*		*11.02.85*		*7*	*Manchester*	*2 Apr*
2:55:05	*Sonka Reimers (GER)*		*1.10.93*		*1*	*Nottingham*	*24 Sep*
2:55:48	*Joanna Zmyslona (POL)*	*V35*			*9*	*Manchester*	*2 Apr*

50 Kilometres - Road

3:36:38	Hannah Oldroyd		27.05.87		1	Christchurch, NZL	7 May
3:43:35	Sophie Carter	V35	10.05.79		1	Gloucester	5 Feb
3:46:25	Gemma Carter		4.01.87		2	Gloucester	5 Feb
3:49:29	Jo Meek	V40	20.05.77		3	Yuxi City, CHN	30 Sep
3:49:35+	Sue Harrison	V45	6.08.71		1m	Patrington	21 May
3:52:12+	Allison Blackmore	V50		66	21	Cape Town, RSA	15 Apr

100 Kilometres - Road

8:01:22	Sue Harrison	V45	6.08.71		1	Patrington	21 May
8:11:38	Sophie Carter	V35	10.05.79		2	Patrington	21 May
8:25:52	Melissa Venables	V40	14.02.75		4	Patrington	21 May
8:50:25	Joasia Zakrzewski	V40	19.01.76		2	Yuxi City, CHN	30 Sep

24 Hours - Road

238.713km	Jessica Baker	V35	6.06.82		7	Belfast	2 Jul
217.875km	Alison Young	V40	26.11.73		26	Belfast	2 Jul
220.509km t	Wendy Shaw	V35	5.10.77		2	Barcelona, ESP	17 Dec
204.118km	Debbie Martin-Consani	V40	4.04.75		39	Belfast	2 Jul
203.414km	tIsobel Wykes	V35	24.04.78		1	London (TB)	17 Sep
182.642km	Sharon Law	V40	9.03.75		67	Belfast	2 Jul

1500 Metres Steeplechase

4:49.30	Aimee Pratt	U23	3.10.97	1	Doncaster	1	Apr
4:54.22	Alexandra Barbour	U20	1.03.99	1	Birmingham	8	Jul
4:55.30	Holly Page	U20	17.08.00	1	Ashford	13	May
4:58.21	Lauren Stoddart		26.06.91	2	Doncaster	1	Apr
4:59.12	Abigail Nolan	U20	16.04.99	1	Milton Keynes	3	Jun
4:59.34	Lucy Davies	U20	17.08.00	1	Exeter	17	Jun
4:59.80	Elise Thorner	U17	16.03.01	1-17	Birmingham	8	Jul
5:00.25	Caitlin Wosika	U20	19.11.99	2	Exeter	17	Jun
5:00.75	Matilda Compton-Stewart	U20	18.03.98	1	London (He)	23	Jul
5:01.31	Lucy Jones	U20	18.09.98	2	Milton Keynes	3	Jun
(10)							
5:01.68	Yasmin Austridge	U20	11.08.00	1	Ashford	10	Jun
5:01.9	Holly Davies	U20	27.11.98	1	Ipswich	14	May
5:04.6	Megan Ormond	U20	21.04.00	1	Bracknell	12	Jul
5:04.75	Elena Carey	U20	14.04.00	6	Birmingham	8	Jul
5:07.93	Maisie Grice	U20	29.06.00	7	Birmingham	8	Jul
5:08.01	Amelia Wills	U17	4.04.02	2-17	Birmingham	8	Jul
5:09.53	Sarah Tait	U17	26.03.01	2	Loughborough	1	Sep
5:09.68	Amelia Lancaster	U20	28.02.00	1	Leeds (South)	28	May
5:10.57	Eevee-May Banbury	U20	19.05.00	1	Exeter	14	May
5:10.74	Rebecca Poole	U17	18.10.00	3-17	Birmingham	8	Jul
(20)							
5:12.16	Elizabeth Stewart	U17	17.04.02	4-17	Birmingham	8	Jul
5:12.46	Emily Bullis	U23	12.12.95	1	Dartford	26	Jul
5:12.49	Amber Owens	U20	27.10.99	10	Birmingham	8	Jul

2000 Metres Steeplechase

6:21.31	Lennie Waite		4.02.86	1	Houston, USA	1	Jun
6:34.12	Charlotte Taylor-Green		2.04.85	1	Southampton	6	May
6:35.07	Emily Moyes	U20	14.06.98	1	Bedford	1	May
6:38.76	Jade Williams		7.09.92	1	Solihull	13	May
6:40.45	Victoria Weir	U20	17.03.98	2	Bedford	1	May
6:44:34	Katie Ingle	U23	4.03.95	2	Solihull	13	May
6:45.41	Laura Riches		7.08.93	3	Bedford	1	May
6:46.0	Iona Lake		15.01.93	1	Norwich	17	Jun
6:50.32	Lauren Stoddart		26.06.91	1	Bromley	16	Jul
6:54.31	Melanie Wilkins		15.07.90	4	Solihull	13	May
(10)							
6:55.76	Dani Chattenton	U23	4.07.96	1	Cambridge	14	May
7:01.53	Rhianwedd Price		11.08.94	2	Leigh	16	Jul
7:01.97	Morag MacLarty		10.02.86	1	Tranent	20	Jun
7:02.06	Sophie Crumly		6.07.90	1	Stevenage	4	Jun
7:03.36	Alexandra Barbour	U20	1.03.99	2	Birmingham	6	May
7:06.55	Matilda Compton-Stewart	U20	18.03.98	2	Bromley	16	Jul
7:07.21	Emily Bullis	U23	12.12.95	1	Leigh	16	Jul
7:07.4	Vicki Cronin		6.12.90	1	Bedford	3	Jun
7:09.69	Emily Brown		8.09.83	4	Bedford	1	May
7:10.06	Priya Crosby		1.01.92	2	Cambridge	14	May
(20)							
7:11.91	Amelia Lancaster	U20	28.02.00	1	Rugby	4	Jun
7:16.28	Victoria Walker		22.10.92	3	Eton	3	Jun
7:16.37	Fiona Marks		9.03.90	3	Leigh	16	Jul
7:17.21	Abigail Nolan	U20	16.04.99	5	Solihull	13	May
7:18.40	Yasmin Austridge	U20	11.08.00	4	Eton	3	Jun

3000 Metres Steeplechase

9:32.10	Rosie Clarke		17.11.91	7	Zagreb, CRO	29	Aug
9:36.75				1	Stanford, USA	5	May
9:38.85				9	Berlin, GER	27	Aug
9:49.36				9h3	London (O)	6	Aug

9:37.94	Lennie Waite		4.02.86	3	Gothenburg, SWE	11	Jul
9:43.33				2	Villeneuve d'Ascq, FRA	24	Jun
9:43.87				2	Letterkenny, IRL	7	Jul
9:48.44				6	Lapinlahti, FIN	16	Jul
9:54.97				10h1	London (O)	9	Aug
10:02.47				7	Portland, USA	11	Jun
10:05.07				1	Los Angeles (ER), USA	6	May
10:06.90				14	Los Angeles (ER), USA	18	May
10:13.81				4	Birmingham	2	Jul
9:39.03	Iona Lake		15.01.93	8	Zagreb, CRO	29	Aug
9:48.87				1	Manchester (SC)	16	Aug
9:50.61				1	Bedford	29	Jul
9:57.53				1	Birmingham	2	Jul
9:58.05				4	Letterkenny, IRL	7	Jul
9:58.85	Charlotte Taylor-Green		2.04.85	8	Huelva, ESP	14	Jun
9:59.58				2	Birmingham	2	Jul
10:01.05				2	Bedford	29	Jul
10:07.86				21	Oordegem, BEL	27	May
10:11.12				5	Stanford, USA	31	May
10:11.61				8	Letterkenny, IRL	7	Jul
9:59.86	Aimee Pratt	U23	3.10.97	9	Huelva, ESP	14	Jun
10:08.64				1	Bedford	18	Jun
10:10.15				2h2	Bydgoszcz, POL	13	Jul
10:02.34	Katie Ingle	U23	4.03.95	3	Birmingham	2	Jul
10:10.73				3	Bedford	29	Jul
10:09.04	Elizabeth Bird		4.10.94	2	Princeton, USA	21	Apr
10:14.34				2	New Haven, USA	7	May
10:14.26	Philippa Bowden	U23	29.03.95	2	Bedford	18	Jun
32 performances to 10:15.0 by 8 athletes							
10:16.07	Stacie Taylor	U23	12.10.95	3	Bedford	18	Jun
10:25:03 (10)	Jade Williams		7.09.92	1	Loughborough	21	May
10:25.23	Emily Moyes	U20	14.06.98	3	Manchester (SC)	16	Aug
10:27.03	Laura Riches		7.08.93	6	Birmingham	2	Jul
10:28.77	Eilish Flanagan	U20	2.05.98	7	Torrance, USA	13	Apr
10:37.50	Melanie Wilkins		15.07.90	7	Birmingham	2	Jul
10:41.79	Lauren Stoddart		26.06.91	5	Manchester (SC)	16	Aug
10:47.16	Holly Page	U20	17.08.00	6	Loughborough	21	May
10:48.05	Kirstin Oakley	U20	25.07.98	4	Wichita, USA	13	May
11:03.55	Halina Rees		6.07.94	2	Grangemouth	27	Aug
11:08.84	Isla Scott-Pearce		11.12.94	2	Dublin (S), IRL	27	May
11:10.52 (20)	Vicki Cronin		6.12.90	6	Bedford	29	Jul
11:18.41	Priya Crosby		1.01.92	2	Philadelphia, USA	15	Apr
11:29.06	Abigail Nolan	U20	16.04.99	9	Loughborough	21	May
11:29.64	Claire Bentley		11.10.94	1	London (CP)	10	Jun

Foreign

9:50.75	Kerry O'Flaherty (IRL)	V35	15.07.81	3	Ninove, BEL	15	Jul

60 Metres Hurdles - Indoors

7.96	Cindy Ofili		5.08.94	5	Karlsruhe, GER	4	Feb
7.98				4h1	Karlsruhe, GER	4	Feb
8.12				3h1	Düsseldorf, GER	1	Feb
8.16				7	Düsseldorf, GER	1	Feb
8.19	Alicia Barrett	U20	25.03.98	1s1	Sheffield	26	Feb
8.20				1h2	Sheffield	26	Feb
8.25				1	Sheffield	26	Feb
8.26				1	Sheffield	17	Feb
8.28				1A2	Bratislava, SVK	29	Jan
8.30				1	Cardiff	5	Mar
8.31				1s1	Sheffield	17	Feb

8.20	Marilyn Nwawulor		20.09.92	1A2	London (LV)	28	Jan
8.22				1	London (LV)	14	Jan
8.28				2h1	London (LV)	14	Jan
8.29				2A1	London (LV)	28	Jan
8.21	Yasmin Miller	U23	24.05.95	2A2	London (LV)	28	Jan
8.22				1s2	Sheffield	17	Feb
8.24				1A1	London (LV)	28	Jan
8.28				1h5	Sheffield	17	Feb
8.29				1	Cardiff	5	Feb
8.30				2	Sheffield	17	Feb
8.23	Serita Solomon		1.03.90	2	London (LV)	14	Jan
8.27				1h1	London (LV)	14	Jan
8.28	Jahisha Thomas		22.11.94	3h2	Geneva, USA	24	Feb
8.35				4h2	Fayetteville, USA	10	Feb
8.30	Sophie Yorke	U20	7.07.98	1s2	Sheffield	26	Feb
8.34				2	Sheffield	26	Feb
8.32	Mollie Courtney	U23	2.07.97	1	Sheffield	12	Feb
8.34	Heather Paton	U23	9.04.96	1	Dublin (B), IRL	5	Feb
8.35	Emma Nwofor	U23	22.08.96	2s1	Sheffield	17	Feb
	30 performances to 8.35 by 10 athletes						
8.38	Gemma Bennett		4.01.84	3A2	London (LV)	28	Jan
8.38	Lucy Hatton		8.11.94	2s2	Sheffield	17	Feb
8.39	Stephanie Clitheroe	U23	3.11.95	3	London (LV)	14	Jan
8.42	Katarina Johnson-Thompson		9.01.93	1h1	Sheffield	12	Feb
8.47	Karla Drew		22.03.89	1	Sheffield	14	Jan
8.52	Danielle McGifford	U23	11.04.95	1P3	Glasgow	5	Mar
8.56	Elise Lovell		9.05.92	3h3	Sheffield	12	Feb
8.57	Meghan Beesley		15.11.89	2r2	Loughborough	14	Jan
8.57	Jessica Taylor-Jemmett		27.06.88	3P4	Prague, CZE	29	Jan
8.57	Niamh Bailey	U23	28.06.95	1r2	Loughborough	9	Dec
(20)							
8.59	Olivia Gauntlett	U20	7.01.98	3	New York, USA	26	Feb
8.60	Holly Pattie-Belleli		9.06.94	1r2	Pittsburg, USA	11	Feb
8.60	Megan Marrs	U23	25.09.97	3h2	Sheffield	17	Feb
8.62	Olivia Montez Brown	U23	22.05.96	1P4	Mankato, USA	12	Feb
8.62	Anastasia Davies	U20	9.04.99	3	Sheffield	26	Feb
8.62	Caryl Granville		24.09.89	2	Cardiff	5	Mar
8.62	Holly Mills	U20	15.04.00	1	Eton	3	Dec
8.66	Jade Simson	U23	9.10.97	1	Cardiff	28	Jan
8.66	Gabriella Burton	U23	25.06.96	4h3	Sheffield	12	Feb
8.67	Isabella Hilditch	U20	15.06.99	2A2	London (LV)	30	Dec
(30)							
8.69	Suzzanne Palmer		11.09.93	3h1	Sheffield	17	Feb
8.69	Zoe Pollock		21.12.00	1P	London (LV)	17	Dec
8.71	Zoe Hughes	U20	1.02.98	1P3	New York, USA	25	Feb
8.72	Hollie Williamson	U20	4.12.98	2A1	Birmingham	15	Jan
8.72	Jessica Tappin		17.05.90	2P3	Glasgow	5	Mar
8.73	Zoe Lucas	U23	7.01.97	3	Sheffield	14	Jan
8.73	Katie Stainton	U23	8.01.95	4h2	Sheffield	12	Feb
8.76	Anya Bates		17.05.00	1h1	Birmingham	11	Feb
8.76	Georgia Hollis-Lawrence	U20	27.06.99	6	Sheffield	26	Feb
8.77	Holly McArthur	U20	20.12.99	1	Glasgow	22	Dec
(40)							
8.79	Jade Nimmo		23.03.91	3P3	Glasgow	5	Mar
8.80	Twinelle Hopeson		23.09.91	4	London (LV)	14	Jan
8.80	Finlay Marriott	U20	21.01.99	3h1	Sheffield	26	Feb
8.81	Isabel Wakefield	U20	5.01.00	1P4	Sheffield	7	Jan
8.83	Emily Russell	U20	12.01.00	3h2	Sheffield	26	Feb
8.84	Emily Dixon	U23	27.11.95	1P1	Lynchburg, USA	10	Feb
8.84	Megan Hildrew	U20	25.06.99	1r1B	Eton	5	Mar
8.84	Olivia Walker	U23	6.07.95	1	Cardiff	10	Dec
8.84	Lucy Turner	U23	14.02.97	1	Manchester (SC)	17	Dec

8.85	Sophie Elliss	U20	2.11.98	3	London (LV)	14	Jan
(50)							
8.85	Catriona Pennet		10.10.83	2	Glasgow	28	Jan
8.89	Lauren Evans	U20	7.08.00	2	Cardiff	28	Jan
8.92	Georgina Sunderland	U23	5.04.97	3h4	Sheffield	17	Feb
8.92	Alice Linaker	U20	6.12.99	4h3	Sheffield	26	Feb
8.93	Georgia Silcox	U20	14.10.98	2	Birmingham	19	Feb
8.93	Lucy Hadaway	U20	11.06.00	5s2	Sheffield	26	Feb
8.93	Jade O'Dowda	U20	9.09.99	4A1	London (LV)	30	Dec
8.95	Katie Garland	U23	27.01.97	3	Loughborough	9	Dec
8.97	Holly Thomas		10.08.94	1	London (LV)	4	Feb
8.97	Jo Rowland		29.12.89	4P3	Glasgow	5	Mar
(60)							
8.98	Olivia Hunter	U20	8.05.99	3h4	Sheffield	26	Feb
8.98	Grace Carter	U20	25.10.99	1	Aberdeen	19	Mar
8.99	Hannah Dunderdale		2.11.94	3h4	Birmingham, USA	20	Feb

Foreign

8.38	Sydney Griffin (USA)		16.10.93	1	d'Coque, LUX	10	Feb
8.52	Mobolaji Adeokun (USA)		14.01.94	3s2	Sheffield	17	Feb
8.61	Tatum Souza (USA)		20.04.92	2h1	Sheffield	17	Feb
8.96	Sarah Connolly (IRL)	U23	3.10.96	2	London (LV)	1	Feb

60 Metres Hurdles - Indoors - Under 17 (76.2cm)

8.41	Pippa Earley		7.09.00	1	Sutton	18	Feb
8.46	Marcia Sey		7.11.01	1A2	London (LV)	30	Dec
8.59	Lucy-Jane Matthews		17.09.02	1A1	London (LV)	3	Dec
8.65	Anna McCauley		2.01.01	1h2	Athlone, IRL	1	Apr
8.74	Amy Pye		22.11.00	3	Sheffield	26	Feb
8.78	Kiera Bainsfair		3.02.02	1s1	London (LV)	7	Jan
8.79	Jade Henry		26.12.00	1	Glasgow	28	Jan
8.79	Amy Carter		24.06.01	2s1	Sheffield	26	Feb
8.80	Jasmine Clark		13.02.01	1h2	Sheffield	26	Feb
8.82	Jasmine Jolly		7.12.01	2h5	Sheffield	26	Feb
(10)							
8.82	Victoria Johnson		7.10.01	4	Sheffield	26	Feb
8.83	Jenna Blundell		12.06.01	1	Birmingham	19	Feb
8.83	Grace Morgan		14.01.02	3P2	Glasgow	10	Nov
8.85	Abigail Pawlett		14.01.03	1	Sheffield	19	Nov
8.85	Katie Bristowe		11.03.02	2A2	London (LV)	30	Dec
8.90	Marissa Sims		18.01.01	2h2	Sheffield	26	Feb
8.90	Eimear Kelly		29.03.02	1P	Athlone, IRL	28	Oct
8.92	Katie Sharkey		19.11.01	1h3	Glasgow	28	Jan
8.92	Venus Morgan		5.06.01	2h1	Sheffield	26	Feb
8.92	Isabel Breeden		26.07.01	3	Cardiff	5	Mar
(20)							
8.93	Emily Race		11.09.00	2	Birmingham	12	Feb
8.96	Chante Williams		21.03.02	3A2	London (LV)	21	Jan
8.96	Marli Jessop		27.06.03	2A2	London (LV)	3	Dec
8.97	Yasmin Uwakwe		14.04.03	3A1	London (LV)	30	Dec
8.99	Talia Morton-Kemsley		20.05.01	3	London (LV)	7	Jan
8.99	Jessica Hopkins		6.01.02	2	London (LV)	4	Feb
9.0	Rebecca Sheffield		19.09.00	3	Birmingham	19	Mar
	9.06			5s2	Sheffield	26	Feb
9.01	Nicole Lannie		24.01.03	3	Sheffield	2	Dec
9.03	Mayi Hughes		5.11.00	3	London (LV)	4	Feb
9.03	Hollie Thurgood		2.07.02	3h2	Sheffield	26	Feb
(30)							
9.05	Jane Davidson		22.07.02	1P3	Glasgow	5	Mar
9.06	Laura Hickey		6.01.02	2	Sheffield	19	Nov
9.07	Mia Lowndes		6.06.02	3	Sheffield	19	Nov
9.07	Kaliyah Young		20.07.03	5A2	London (LV)	3	Dec

60 Metres Hurdles - Indoors - Under 15 (76.2cm)

8.85	Abigail Pawlett	14.01.03	1	Sheffield	26	Feb
8.96	Nicole Lannie	24.01.03	2	Sheffield	26	Feb
8.96	Lucy-Jane Matthews	17.09.02	2P	Sheffield	12	Mar
9.04	Marli Jessop	27.06.03	1h2	Sheffield	26	Feb
9.08	Ruby Bridger	6.05.03	4	Sheffield	26	Feb
9.09	Nicole Hague	18.10.02	1h4	Sheffield	26	Feb
9.14	Kaliyah Young	20.07.03	1	London (LV)	18	Mar
9.15	Alexia Bennett-Cordy	1.02.03	2s2	Sheffield	26	Feb
9.18	Abigail Packham	19.08.03	1A2	Eton	5	Feb
9.23	Milly Gall	20.02.03	1	London (LV)	7	Jan
(10)						
9.25	Elle Hinchliffe	16.10.03	1r2	Sheffield	19	Nov
9.28	Philippa Ellis	23.04.03	1P	Gateshead	19	Mar
9.30	Lily Parris	5.03.03	2h2	Sheffield	26	Feb
9.33	Carys Poole	21.12.03	2P4	Cardiff	7	Oct
9.34	Ruby Mace	5.09.03	1A2	London (LV)	30	Dec
9.36	Briagha Cook	28.10.02	1	Glasgow	12	Feb
9.36	Chloe Eames	19.06.03	1A1	London (LV)	26	Mar
9.37	Emily Knight	5.02.04	2A2	London (LV)	30	Dec
9.38	Sydney Davies	6.09.02	2	Birmingham	12	Feb
9.38	Emily Misantoni	27.09.02	3s3	Sheffield	26	Feb
(20)						
9.40	Coirilidh Cook	13.11.03	2	Glasgow	12	Feb
9.40	Ella Hannyngton	29.11.02	1h2	Sutton	18	Feb
9.40	Abby Masquelier	17.08.04	1	London (LV)	3	Dec
9.4	Danielle Hales	7.11.02	2	Birmingham	19	Mar
9.40	Katie Burr	30.09.03	4P1	Glasgow	10	Nov
9.41	Stephanie Robertson	28.09.02	1	Manchester (SC)	19	Nov
9.42	Lydia Smith	15.03.04	1r7	Cardiff	8	Jan
9.44	Rhiannon Dowinton	7.11.02	4s1	Sheffield	26	Feb

60 Metres Hurdles - Indoors - Under 13 (68.5cm)

9.55	Amber Hughes	3.11.05	1	Sheffield	2	Dec
9.62	Julia Winogrodzka	21.10.04	1P3	Glasgow	4	Mar
9.62	Ayomide Cole	27.07.05	1r2	London (LV)	26	Mar
9.80	Iona Irvine	22.11.04	1A2	Eton	5	Feb
9.86	Mya McMahon	19.09.05	2P3	Glasgow	4	Mar
9.89	Jessica Day	3.09.04	2A1	Birmingham	15	Jan
9.98	Rebecca Grieve	30.01.05	1	Motherwell	29	Mar
9.99	Catriona Scott	1.09.04	1	Glasgow	11	Feb

70 Metres Hurdles - Under 13 (68.5cm)

11.0		Megan Corker	11.10.04	1	Connah's Quay	18	Jun
		11.12		1r4	Manchester (Str)	28	Aug
11.1		Julia Winogrodzka	21.10.04	1	Blackburn	20	May
		11.33		1P	Peterborough	24	Sep
11.12w	3.3	Iona Irvine	22.11.04	1	Portsmouth	13	May
		11.18	-0.9	1	Basingstoke	1	Apr
11.18	0.0	Grace Colmer	13.07.05	1	Birmingham	2	Sep
11.23w	3.3	Ayomide Cole	27.07.05	1h1	Portsmouth	13	May
11.27		Erin Lobley	12.10.04	1	Nuneaton	9	Sep
11.3		Molly White	7.01.05	2	Portsmouth	25	Jun
11.36w	2.8	Catriona Scott	1.09.04	1	Glasgow (S)	19	Aug
11.37	0.6	Amber Hughes	3.11.05	1P2	Jarrow	16	Sep
11.38	0.0	Hermione Mason	1.04.05	2	Birmingham	2	Sep

75 Metres Hurdles - Under 15 (76.2cm)

11.04	2.0	Abigail Pawlett		14.01.03	1P1	Boston	17	Sep
11.05w	2.9	Ruby Bridger		6.05.03	1	Oxford (H)	9	Sep
		11.07	-0.6		1	Bedford	27	Aug
11.16	-0.1	Danielle Hales		7.11.02	1	Birmingham	8	Jul
11.19	1.9	Abigail Packham		19.08.03	1	Crawley	10	Jun
11.26	1.8	Nicole Lannie		24.01.03	2s1	Birmingham	7	Jul
11.27w	2.9	Yasmin Uwakwe		14.04.03	2	Oxford (H)	9	Sep
		11.32	-0.6		3	Bedford	27	Aug
11.28w	2.3	Alexia Bennett-Cordy		1.02.03	1	Nuneaton	20	Aug
		11.46			3	Birmingham	17	Jun
11.29		Milly Gall		20.02.03	1	Hemel Hempstead	10	Jun
11.30	0.5	Briagha Cook		28.10.02	2h4	Bedford	27	Aug
11.30w	2.9	Kaliyah Young		20.07.03	3	Oxford (H)	9	Sep
		11.61	1.4		1	Gillingham	3	Sep
	(10)							
11.32	-0.6	Lily Parris		5.03.03	4	Bedford	27	Aug
11.32		Philippa Ellis		23.04.03	1	Middlesbrough	3	Sep
11.34	-0.1	Marli Jessop		27.06.03	4	Birmingham	8	Jul
11.38	1.6	Ellie Mount		15.08.03	1	Exeter	17	Jun
11.42w	4.6	Rhiannon Dowinton		7.11.02	1h2	Portsmouth	13	May
11.45	2.0	Poppy Oliver		27.02.03	2h3	Bedford	27	Aug
11.49w	2.1	Holly Lawrence		12.02.03	1P2	Boston	17	Sep
11.50	0.4	Lydia Smith		15.03.04	1P4	Yeovil	25	Jun
11.52		Cleo Martin-Evans		8.05.03	4	Birmingham	17	Jun
11.52	1.8	Coirilidh Cook		13.11.03	1rB	Grangemouth	18	Jun
	(20)							
11.54		Stephanie Robertson		28.09.02	1	Manchester (SC)	29	May
11.59	2.0	Tabitha Proudley		27.08.04	2	Basingstoke	17	Jun
11.59	0.8	Elina Dineen		11.09.03	1	Hereford	8	Jul
11.59	0.5	Melissa Coxon		5.12.02	3h4	Bedford	27	Aug
11.61	-0.7	Yasmin Bridet		29.11.02	3h4	Birmingham	7	Jul
11.62		Lucy-Jane Matthews		17.09.02	1	Tidworth	14	May

hand timing

11.2		Nicole Lannie		(11.26)	1	Spinkhill	17	Jun
11.3		Kaliyah Young		(11.30w)	1	Ashford	2	Jul
11.4		Julia Winogrodzka	U13	21.10.04	2	Blackburn	24	May
11.4		Alexia Bennett-Cordy		(11.28w)	1	Stourport	18	Jun
11.4		Poppy Oliver		(11.45)	1rB	Horsham	21	Jul
11.5		Lucy-Jane Matthews		(11.62)	1	Bracknell	22	Apr
11.5		Stephanie Robertson		(11.54)	1	Litherland	15	Jul
11.5		Chloe Eames		19.06.03	2	Bedford	16	Jul
11.5		Rachel Largie-Polean		16.05.03	3	Bedford	16	Jul
11.6		Emily Misantoni		27.09.02	3	Blackburn	24	May
11.6		Yasmin Bridet		(11.61)	1	Bournemouth	10	Jun
11.6		Willa Gibb		11.09.03	1	Cheltenham	18	Jun
11.6		Elle Hinchliffe		16.10.03	1	Leeds	18	Jun
11.6		Myah Booth		20.01.04	1	Blackburn	21	Jun
11.6		Ruby Mace		5.09.03	1	Cambridge	2	Jul

80 Metres Hurdles - Under 17 (76.2cm)

10.94		Pippa Earley		7.09.00	1	Loughborough	1	Sep
11.04		Marcia Sey		7.11.01	2	Loughborough	1	Sep
11.15	0.2	Victoria Johnson		7.10.01	2	Birmingham	8	Jul
11.17	0.2	Samantha Harris		4.11.01	3	Birmingham	8	Jul
11.21	0.1	Emily Bee		3.03.02	3	Bedford	27	Aug
11.33	0.1	Emily Race		11.09.00	4	Bedford	27	Aug
11.34	0.2	Zoe Pollock		21.12.00	4	Birmingham	8	Jul
11.39	0.8	Jade Henry		26.12.00	2h2	Bedford	27	Aug

11.44	0.8	Amy Pye	22.11.00	3h2	Bedford	27	Aug
11.45	0.2	Amy Carter	24.06.01	6	Birmingham	8	Jul
	(10)						
11.65	1.2	Rebecca Johns	9.11.01	4h1	Birmingham	7	Jul
11.70		Grace Morgan	14.01.02	1	Newport	23	Jul
11.73	0.8	Chante Williams	21.03.02	4h3	Birmingham	7	Jul
11.73	-0.2	Venus Morgan	5.06.01	3h4	Bedford	27	Aug
11.75	-0.9	Kiera Bainsfair	3.02.02	1h2	Chelmsford	13	May
11.77	0.2	Hollie Thurgood	2.07.02	8	Birmingham	8	Jul
11.78	0.1	Rachel Broadfoot	6.06.02	1	Grangemouth	13	May
11.81	1.3	Katie Sharkey	19.11.01	2	Grangemouth	9	Jun
11.84	0.6	Katie Bristowe	11.03.02	1	Gillingham	23	Apr
11.85	1.1	Jenna Blundell	12.06.01	1	Yate	23	Jul
	(20)						
11.86	1.7	Holly Mulholland	31.03.02	2	Tullamore, IRL	8	Jul
11.87	-0.5	Sophia Obi	27.05.01	1	London (He)	30	Jul
11.91		Hannah Barnden	8.01.02	1	Derby	23	Jul
11.91		Eimear Kelly	29.03.02	5	Loughborough	1	Sep
11.92		Rebecca Sheffield	19.09.00	4	Birmingham	17	Jun
11.93		Katie Joyce	26.01.01	1	York	7	May
11.93	1.4	Niamh Robertson	31.07.01	2h1	Grangemouth	26	Aug
11.94	-0.6	Emily Tyrrell	4.01.02	3H3	Yeovil	24	Jun
11.97	2.0	Amelia Woodnick	18.02.02	1	Cambridge	24	Jun
11.98	1.7	Mallory Cluley	15.03.02	1	London (BP)	10	Jun
	(30)						
11.99	1.0	Jane Davidson	22.07.02	2	Glasgow (S)	13	Aug
12.00		Orla Brennan	8.02.02	1rB	Reading	25	Jun
12.00	-0.2	Ellie Cleveland	5.08.02	5h4	Bedford	27	Aug

wind assisted

11.17	2.1	Emily Race	(11.33)	1	Nuneaton	20	Aug
11.17	2.4	Emily Bee	(11.21)	2s2	Bedford	27	Aug
11.28	2.1	Amy Pye	(11.44)	2	Nuneaton	20	Aug
11.51	2.5	Kiera Bainsfair	(11.75)	4H1	Boston	16	Sep
11.64	3.5	Hollie Thurgood	(11.77)	1	Portsmouth	13	May
11.75	2.1	Rebecca Sheffield	(11.92)	4	Nuneaton	20	Aug
11.85	4.2	Abigail Williams	11.10.00	1	Yate	13	May
11.85	2.6	Jessica Hopkins	6.01.02	3H2	Boston	16	Sep
11.86	2.8	Ellie Stone	10.02.01	3	Grangemouth	26	Aug

hand timing

11.5		Jasmine Jolly	7.12.01	1	Blackpool	13	May
11.5		Kiera Bainsfair	(11.75)	1H	Bedford	24	Jun
11.6		Temi Ojora	24.01.02	1	Milton Keynes	10	Jun
11.7		Venus Morgan	(11.73)	1P	Hull	7	May
11.7		Hollie Thurgood	(11.77)	1	Brighton	23	Jul
11.8		Katie Sharkey	(11.81)	2	Doncaster	25	Jun
11.9	0.9	Ashleigh West	27.06.01	2H1	Kingston	24	Jun
11.9		Jessica Hopkins	(11.85w)	2H	Bedford	24	Jun
11.9		Mia Chantree	15.11.01	3H	Bedford	24	Jun
11.9		Marcey Winter	17.04.01	1	Guildford	1	Jul
11.9		Mayi Hughes	5.11.00	1	Cambridge	2	Jul
11.9		Amaya Scott	15.02.01	2	Brighton	23	Jul

100 Metres Hurdles - Under 18 (76.2cm)

13.61	-0.5	Pippa Earley	U17	7.09.00	1	Bedford	18	Jun
13.79	0.3	Isabel Wakefield		5.01.00	2r2	London (LV)	24	May
13.87	0.1	Anya Bates		17.05.00	1r2	Bedford	27	May
13.89	-0.5	Holly Mills		15.04.00	2	Bedford	18	Jun
13.95	1.6	Anna McCauley	U17	2.01.01	1r2	Belfast	5	Jul
14.02	0.3	Emily Russell		12.01.00	3r2	London (LV)	24	May
14.11	0.7	Lauren Evans		7.08.00	3	Loughborough	10	May

14.24i		Amy Pye	U17	22.11.00	2	Birmingham	19	Mar
		14.72 -1.6			5	Loughborough	22	Apr
14.45	0.0	Lucy Hadaway		11.06.00	3h2	Tomblaine, FRA	27	Jun
14.53i		Bethany McAndrew		8.01.00	1	Motherwell	25	Jan
		14.58 -2.3			1	Grangemouth	13	May
	(10)							
14.53	-1.6	Amy Carter	U17	24.06.01	4	Loughborough	22	Apr
14.70	-1.1	Isabel Breeden	U17	26.07.01	1rB	Loughborough	22	Apr
14.74i		Jade Henry	U17	26.12.00	5r2	Motherwell	29	Mar
		14.74 -1.1			2rB	Loughborough	22	Apr
14.81	0.1	Imogen Dawe-Lane		30.08.00	3r2	Bedford	27	May

100 Metres Hurdles

12.75	1.6	Tiffany Porter		13.11.87	1	Montverde, USA	10	Jun
		12.87 0.6			5	Boston, USA	4	Jun
		12.89 1.5			1h1	Montverde, USA	10	Jun
		12.93 0.8			5	Oslo, NOR	15	Jun
		12.99 0.5-			2h2	Boston, USA	4	Jun
		13.00 0.0			2	Kawasaki, JPN	21	May
		13.00 -0.2			2h1	Bellinzona, SUI	18	Jul
		13.00 1.2			2	Bellinzona, SUI	18	Jul
		13.03 -0.6			3	Manchester	26	May
		13.07 1.7			2	Greensboro, USA	14	Apr
		13.18 -0.9			6h2	London (O)	11	Aug
		13.20 1.0			8	Des Moines, USA	29	Apr
		13.38 -1.5			1h1	Greensboro, USA	14	Apr
12.92	1.0	Cindy Ofili		5.08.94	6	Des Moines, USA	29	Apr
		13.07 -0.6			4	Manchester	26	May
		13.08 0.0			3	Kawasaki, JPN	21	May
		13.09 1.7			3	Greensboro, USA	14	Apr
		13.42 -2.3			7	Doha, QAT	5	May
13.07	0.5	Alicia Barrett	U20	25.03.98	1h1	Bedford	18	Jun
		13.07 -0.8			1	Bedford	18	Jun
		13.22 -0.2			3	Oordegem, BEL	27	May
		13.23 2.0			1h2	Birmingham	1	Jul
		13.26 -1.4			1	Birmingham	1	Jul
		13.27 0.4			6	Villeneuve d'Ascq, FRA	25	Jun
		13.28 0.1			2	Grosseto, ITA	22	Jul
		13.32 1.0			3h2	Villeneuve d'Ascq, FRA	23	Jun
		13.35 -0.6			4	Geneva, SUI	10	Jun
		13.37 1.2			6h1	Oordegem, BEL	27	May
		13.37 -0.3			1h3	Grosseto, ITA	21	Jul
		13.41 -1.4			1s3	Grosseto, ITA	21	Jul
		13.42 -1.4			8h1	London (O)	11	Aug
13.23	1.2	Yasmin Miller	U23	24.05.95	2h1	Oordegem, BEL	27	May
		13.23 -0.4			1	Bedford	18	Jun
		13.27 -0.2			5	Oordegem, BEL	27	May
		13.29 -1.4			2	Birmingham	1	Jul
		13.32 -0.2			1	Bedford	29	Jul
		13.33 -0.4			1h1	Birmingham	1	Jul
		13.33 1.4			2	Loughborough	22	Jul
		13.34 0.0			6h2	London (O)	9	Jul
		13.40 0.3			3s2	Bydgoszcz, POL	14	Jul
		13.41 0.4			2r2	Loughborough	22	Jul
		13.44 1.6			3	Hérouville St.-Clair, FRA	15	Jun
		13.48 0.5			2h4	Bydgoszcz, POL	14	Jul
		13.52 1.0			1h1	Bedford	29	Jul
13.29	1.2	Katarina Johnson-Thompson		9.01.93	1H4	Götzis, AUT	27	May
		13.33 0.0			5H4	London (O)	5	Aug
		13.45 -0.1			8h1	London (O)	9	Jul

Time	Wind	Name	Cat	DOB	Pos	Venue	Date
13.41	1.8	Lucy Hatton		8.11.94	1	Loughborough	7 Jun
13.51	-0.6				7	Geneva, SUI	10 Jun
13.42	-0.4	Jessica Hunter	U23	4.12.96	2	Bedford	18 Jun
13.43	-0.6				1	Oordegem, BEL	3 Jun
13.45	-1.4				3	Birmingham	1 Jul
13.51	-0.2				2	Bedford	29 Jul
13.52	0.7				1h3	Bedford	29 Jul
13.53	0.5				2h1	Bedford	18 Jun
13.55	0.8				1r2	Oordegem, BEL	3 Jun
13.55	1.8				2h3	Birmingham	1 Jul
13.44	0.5	Mollie Courtney	U23	2.07.97	1h1	Bedford	18 Jun
13.48	2.0				1	Yate	13 May
13.49	1.8				1h3	Birmingham	1 Jul
13.50	1.4				3	Loughborough	22 Jul
13.51	-0.4				3	Bedford	18 Jun
13.51	1.6				1r2	Belfast	5 Jul
13.52	-0.5				1	Bromley	16 Jul
13.53	-0.2				3	Bedford	29 Jul
13.47	1.8	Heather Paton	U23	9.04.96	2	Loughborough	7 Jun
13.55	1.6				2r2	Belfast	5 Jul
13.47	-0.8	Sophie Yorke	U20	7.07.98	2	Bedford	18 Jun
13.51	0.1				5	Grosseto, ITA	22 Jul
		(10)					
13.48	1.0	Caryl Granville		24.09.89	1	Brecon	26 Aug
13.55	-0.3				1rB	Bromley	16 Jul
13.51	0.1	Megan Marrs	U23	25.09.97	5	Warsaw, POL	15 Aug
13.54	1.3				1h1	Belfast	5 Jul

73 performances to 13.55 by 12 athletes

Time	Wind	Name	Cat	DOB	Pos	Venue	Date
13.58	0.4	Angie Broadbelt-Blake		12.09.85	2	Eton	3 Jun
13.60	0.9	Karla Drew		22.03.89	1	Brisbane (Nathan), AUS	4 Mar
13.67	-0.8	Isabella Hilditch	U20	15.06.99	3	Bedford	18 Jun
13.71	0.8	Gemma Bennett		4.01.84	2	Valence, FRA	8 Jul
13.73	-0.7	Serita Solomon		1.03.90	9	Hengelo, NED	11 Jun
13.76	2.0	Holly Pattie-Belleli		9.06.94	1	Lawrence, USA	28 Apr
13.77	-0.4	Stephanie Clitheroe	U23	3.11.95	4	Bedford	18 Jun
13.78	1.4	Zoe Hughes	U20	1.02.98	2H1	Azusa, USA	12 Apr
		(20)					
13.79	1.6	Chelsea Walker	U23	29.06.97	1	Leigh	16 Jul
13.80	2.0	Olivia Gauntlett	U20	7.01.98	6	New Haven, USA	7 May
13.83	1.7	Jahisha Thomas		22.11.94	3	Iowa City, USA	22 Apr
13.84	-0.3	Meghan Beesley		15.11.89	2rB	Bromley	16 Jul
13.89	1.3	Anastasia Davies	U20	9.04.99	1h2	Bedford	18 Jun
13.91	1.2	Marilyn Nwawulor		20.09.92	1H1	Hexham	22 Jul
13.92	-0.4	Emma Nwofor	U23	22.08.96	7	Bedford	18 Jun
13.92	1.2	Lucy Turner	U23	14.02.97	2H1	Hexham	22 Jul
13.93	-1.5	Holly McArthur	U20	20.12.99	1H1	Grosseto, ITA	20 Jul
13.94	1.8	Katie Stainton	U23	8.01.95	4h3	Birmingham	1 Jul
		(30)					
13.95	0.4	Elise Lovell		9.05.92	1	Wigan	7 May
13.98	-0.2	Jessica Taylor-Jemmett		27.06.88	1H1	Talence, FRA	16 Sep
14.01	-1.7	Niamh Emerson	U20	22.04.99	1H2	Grosseto, ITA	20 Jul
14.05	0.5	Sophie Elliss	U20	2.11.98	3h1	Bedford	18 Jun
14.05	-0.2	Niamh Bailey	U23	28.06.95	7	Bedford	29 Jul
14.07	2.0	Holly Thomas		10.08.94	4h2	Birmingham	1 Jul
14.09	1.0	Katie Purves	U23	3.11.96	2	Easton, USA	6 May
14.13	0.1	Olivia Montez Brown	U23	22.05.96	2h2	St. Paul, USA	12 May
14.13	0.5	Emily Russell	U20	12.01.00	4h1	Bedford	18 Jun
14.19	-1.5	Jessica Tappin		17.05.90	1H3	Bedford	27 May
		(40)					
14.19	2.0	Harriet Jones		30.06.88	6h2	Birmingham	1 Jul
14.19	1.8	Twinelle Hopeson		23.09.91	6h3	Birmingham	1 Jul

14.22	0.0	Anya Bates	U20	17.05.00	2h3	Birmingham	7	Jul
14.24	-1.7	Amber-Leigh Hall	U20	10.10.98	1	London (CP)	11	Jun
14.25		Georgia Silcox	U20	14.10.98	1	Braunton	30	Jul
14.30	1.8	Hope Sarti	U20	6.01.98	7	Fresno, USA	29	Apr
14.30	2.0	Georgia Hollis-Lawrence	U20	27.06.99	1	Loughborough	26	Aug
14.33	0.3	Megan Hildrew	U20	25.06.99	5	Birmingham	8	Jul
14.38	-1.9	Gabriella Burton	U23	25.06.96	1	Nottingham	8	Apr
14.38	0.5	Olivia Walker	U23	6.07.95	5h1	Bedford	18	Jun
		(50)						
14.40	1.6	Tayla Benson	U23	20.08.96	1	Basingstoke	8	Jul
14.41	1.4	Katie Garland	U23	27.01.97	4rB	Loughborough	21	May
14.44	-3.7	Danielle McGifford	U23	11.04.95	3H4	Bedford	27	May
14.44	1.2	Jade Nimmo		23.03.91	4H1	Hexham	22	Jul
14.46	-1.5	Suzzanne Palmer		11.09.93	4H3	Bedford	27	May
14.46	-1.7	Holly Mills	U20	15.04.00	2	London (CP)	11	Jun
14.46	0.5	Jade O'Dowda	U20	9.09.99	5h1	Bedford	18	Jun
14.47	0.3	Hollie Williamson	U20	4.12.98	7	Birmingham	8	Jul
14.48	1.2	Anya Turner	U20	8.11.98	1	Exeter	29	Aug
14.49	-0.3	Lauren Evans	U20	7.08.00	3	Cardiff	12	Jul
		(60)						
14.54	1.3	Finlay Marriott	U20	21.01.99	4h2	Bedford	18	Jun
14.63	0.4	Lauren Thompson		12.02.92	5	Wigan	7	May
14.63	0.5	Jade Simson	U23	9.10.97	6h1	Bedford	18	Jun
14.65	1.6	Chloe Williams		10.09.87	3	Leigh	16	Jul
14.67	1.4	Emily Dixon	U23	27.11.95	4h2	Newark, USA	5	May
14.69	0.5	Georgina Sunderland	U23	5.04.97	7h1	Bedford	18	Jun
14.71	1.6	Jo Rowland		29.12.89	4	Leigh	16	Jul
14.71	-1.0	Chloe Vernon-Hamilton		11.10.92	1H2	Oxford (H)	22	Jul
14.75	0.6	Katie Patullo	U20	27.03.98	1	Grangemouth	22	Apr
14.75	-1.4	Sophie Hay	U23	14.08.96	5s1	Bedford	1	May
		(70)						
14.76	-1.1	Gabriella Ade-Onojobi		1.08.93	3h1	London (CP)	11	Jun
14.76	0.8	Chloe Esegbona	U20	23.11.98	1	Manchester (Str)	25	Jun
14.80	0.0	Olivia Galloway	U20	4.07.00	2H2	Yeovil	24	Jun
14.81	2.0	Amy Barclay		14.04.92	8h2	Birmingham	1	Jul
14.82i		Bethany McAndrew	U20	8.01.00	1	Motherwell	25	Jan
		14.91			1	York	25	Jun
14.84	1.3	Catriona Pennet		10.10.83	5rB	Birmingham	6	May
14.84	1.2	Alix Still	U20	15.03.00	5H	Bradenton, USA	20	May
14.85	0.9	Laura Reilly	U23	16.10.95	2	Wigan	7	May
14.85	0.0	Bethan Burley	U20	26.03.00	3H2	Yeovil	24	Jun
14.85	1.2	Lucy Hadaway	U20	11.06.00	1H	Cudworth	26	Aug
		(80)						
14.89		Alice Linaker	U20	6.12.99	2	Preston	5	Aug
14.90	1.0	Mia Evans	U20	24.01.99	2	Brecon	26	Aug
14.92	0.0	Natasha Smith	U20	10.10.99	2	Exeter	17	Jun
14.93	2.0	Hannah Jackson		8.09.91	2	Yate	13	May
14.94		Isabel Breeden	U17	26.07.01	1	Yate	30	Apr
14.97	-2.3	Morgan Lake	U23	12.05.97	5H3	Florence, ITA	28	Apr
14.98	-0.1	Naomi Morgan	U23	23.11.96	1	Belfast	30	Jul
15.01	-0.3	Grace Bower	U20	3.11.99	5	Cardiff	12	Jul
15.07	-0.8	Roxanne Oliver	U23	15.01.97	8s2	Bedford	1	May
15.10	1.0	Leanne Buxton	V35	27.05.78	1H	Aarhus, DEN	27	Jul
		(90)						
15.11	-0.9	Charlotte Robison	U23	13.07.97	7	Amherst, USA	29	Apr
15.11	-0.6	Rebecca Jennings		7.12.90	2	London (He)	24	Jun
15.12		Imogen Dawe-Lane	U20	30.08.00	2	Yate	30	Apr
15.14	-1.0	Lucy Chappell	U23	10.01.97	2	Cudworth	13	May
15.20	0.9	Anna Nicole Rowe	U20	2.09.98	3	Wigan	7	May
15.20	1.7	Anna Nelson	U23	14.11.95	6rB	Eton	3	Jun
15.22	0.5	Sophie Seger	U20	21.09.99	6h1	Bedford	18	Jun

15.23	1.8	Kerry Murch	U23	20.03.95	1	Yate	16	Jul
15.25	0.6	Niamh Guest	U23	16.01.97	3	Grangemouth	22	Apr
15.27	1.8	Kaeshelle Cooke	U23	2.01.96	3	Paris, FRA	16	Jun
	(100)							
15.28	1.4	Emily Madden-Forman	U20	29.09.99	1	Nuneaton	13	May
15.30	-2.9	Jamelia Henson	U20	9.05.00	3h1	Birmingham	7	Jul
15.30	1.7	Avril Jackson		22.10.86	1rB	Glasgow (S)	13	Aug
15.30	-0.2	Ellen Barber	U23	5.12.97	3H1	Woerden, NED	26	Aug

wind assisted

13.16	2.3	Yasmin Miller	U23	(13.23)	1h2	Bedford	18	Jun
		13.23	2.2		3	Loughborough	21	May
		13.23	2.5		5	Bydgoszcz, POL	2	Jun
		13.32	2.4		2h2	Hérouville St.-Clair, FRA	15	Jun
		13.32	2.3		4	Bydgoszcz, POL	15	Jul
13.18	2.2	Barrett	U20	(13.07)	2	Loughborough	21	May
13.31	6.5	Sophie Yorke	U20	(13.47)	1	Nuneaton	11	Jun
		13.55	2.6		1h3	Bedford	18	Jun
13.40	2.4	Mollie Courtney	U23	(13.44)	1	Manchester (SC)	16	Aug
		13.46	2.2		4	Loughborough	21	May
13.42	2.3	Hunter	U23	(13.42)	1rA	Loughborough	21	May
13.45	2.3	Serita Solomon		(13.73)	3	Gavardo, ITA	4	Jun
13.46	2.5	Jahisha Thomas		(13.83)	3	Gainesville, USA	31	Mar
13.46	2.4	Caryl Granville		(13.48)	2	Manchester (SC)	16	Aug
13.52	2.3	Marilyn Nwawulor		(13.91)	2rA	Loughborough	21	May
13.55	5.4	Holly Pattie-Belleli		(13.76)	5	Wichita, USA	14	May
		16 performances to 13.55 by 10 athletes						
13.78	2.1	Chelsea Walker	U23	(13.79)	1rB	Wigan	7	May
13.78	2.3	Elise Lovell		(13.95)	4rA	Loughborough	21	May
13.79	4.9	Holly McArthur	U20	(13.93)	1	Glasgow (S)	19	Aug
13.90	6.5	Gabriella Burton	U23	(14.38)	1	Nuneaton	11	Jun
13.91	2.3	Emma Nwofor	U23	(13.92)	4h2	Bedford	18	Jun
13.92	4.5	Katie Stainton	U23	(13.94)	4	Clermont, USA	15	Apr
14.15	2.6	Amber-Leigh Hall	U20	(14.24)	3h3	Bedford	18	Jun
14.18	3.3	Jade Nimmo		(14.44)	1	Glasgow (S)	13	Aug
14.21	4.9	Finlay Marriott	U20	(14.54)	2	Glasgow (S)	19	Aug
14.22	2.9	Hannah Dunderdale		2.11.94	2H4	Arlington, USA	12	May
14.26	2.3	Jade Simson	U23	(14.63)	7rA	Loughborough	21	May
14.29	2.2	Jade O'Dowda	U20	(14.46)	1H1	Boston	16	Sep
14.34	5.9	Katie Patullo		(14.75)	1h1	Glasgow (S)	19	Aug
14.35	2.3	Tayla Benson	U23	(14.40)	6h2	Bedford	18	Jun
14.39	2.3	Sophie Hay	U23	(14.75)	7h2	Bedford	18	Jun
14.48	2.6	Chloe Esegbona	U20	(14.76)	4h3	Bedford	18	Jun
14.65	4.4	Lucy Chappell	U23	(15.14)	2rB	Southampton	6	May
14.65	2.2	Olivia Galloway	U20	(14.80)	3H1	Boston	16	Sep
14.67	3.1	Caroline Hilley	U23	18.09.96	1	Cambridge	14	May
14.69	2.6	Bethan Burley		(14.85)	1H2	Boston	16	Sep
14.70	6.5	Emily Madden-Forman	U20	(15.28)	2	Nuneaton	11	Jun
14.73	2.6	Alice Linaker	U20	(14.89)	2H2	Boston	16	Sep
14.76	2.3	Rebecca Jennings		(15.11)	2	Southampton	6	May
14.76	3.3	Bethany McAndrew	U20	(14.82)	1	Grangemouth	9	Jun
14.77	2.6	Jamelia Henson	U20	(15.30)	5h3	Bedford	18	Jun
14.81	2.3	Hannah Jackson		(14.93)	3	Southampton	6	May
14.81	2.3	Alix Still	U20	(14.84)	2H	Grangemouth	1	Jul
14.83	6.5	Cliona Perkins	U20	27.02.99	3	Nuneaton	11	Jun
14.92	3.7	Grace Bower	U20	(15.01)	2	Manchester (SC)	10	Jun
15.13	4.4	Nicole Parcell	U20	16.12.99	3rB	Southampton	6	May
15.14		Sophie Ridley	U20	5.10.98	1	Portsmouth	13	May
15.22	6.5	Zoe Mattacks	U20	7.11.98	4	Nuneaton	11	Jun
15.23	2.3	Sara Geary		6.04.91	5	Southampton	6	May

15.24	2.3	Emma Komocki			17.03.92	6	Southampton	6 May
15.28	2.3	Belinda Sergent	U23		19.11.96	7	Southampton	6 May
15.28	6.5	Sophie Domingo	U20		7.01.00	5	Nuneaton	11 Jun
15.29	2.3	Chay Clark	U23		6.12.96	8	Southampton	6 May

hand timing

14.1		Anya Bates	U20	(14.22)	1	Wolverhampton	25 Jun
14.4	-0.4	Danielle McGifford	U23	(14.44)	1	Bebington	13 May
14.5		Lauren Thompson		(14.63)	1	Peterborough	15 Apr
14.6		Jo Rowland		(14.71)	1	Woking	15 Apr
14.6	-0.8	Katie Patullo	U20	(14.75)	2	Hull	30 Apr
14.7		Olivia Galloway	U20	(14.80)	1	Bournemouth	2 Apr
14.7	-0.8	Lucy Hadaway	U20	(14.85)	3	Hull	30 Apr
14.7	-0.3	Chloe Esegbona	U20	(14.76)	1	Preston	30 Apr
14.7		Sophie Domingo	U20	7.01.00	1H	Bedford	24 Jun
14.7		Chloe Vernon-Hamilton		(14.71)	3	Cambridge	19 Aug
14.8	-0.8	Bethany McAndrew	U20	(14.82)	1rB	Hull	30 Apr
14.8		Natasha Smith	U20	(14.92)	1	Cheltenham	13 May
14.8		Lucy Chappell	U23	(15.14)	1rB	Bedford	3 Jun
14.8		Grace Bower	U20	(15.01)	1H	Telford	24 Jun
14.8	0.8	Amy Barclay		(14.81)	1	Crawley	8 Jul
14.9		Olivia Hunter	U20	8.05.99	1	Andover	15 Apr
14.9		Emma Douras	U23	25.02.95	1	Leamington	6 May
14.9		Roxanne Oliver	U23	(15.07)	1	Bebington	9 Jul
14.9		Georgia Whitfield	U23	21.07.95	1	Morpeth	9 Jul
14.9		Cliona Perkins	U20	27.02.99	1	Cheltenham	15 Jul
15.0		Jamelia Henson	U20	(15.30)	2	London (LV)	17 Jun
15.0		Rebecca Jennings		(15.11)	1	London (BP)	8 Jul
15.0w	3.6	Sophie Ridley	U20	(15.14w)	1	Portsmouth	10 Jun
15.1		Ella De Lucis	U23	2.11.96	1	London (ME)	21 May
15.1		Bethan Loveday	U20	9.03.00	1	Solihull	28 May
15.1		Hannah Riley	V35	9.07.82	2	Bebington	9 Jul
15.2		Emma Nanson	U23	6.10.95	1	Cheltenham	19 Jul
15.2		Brittney Wiggan	U20	5.05.00	1	Poole	23 Jul

Additional Under 17 (1 above)

15.55w	3.4	Lily Hulland		1.09.01	2	Monachil, ESP	7 Jul
		15.61	0.8		2	Granada, ESP	4 Jun
15.7		Kia Slade		16.01.01	3	Eton	19 Aug
15.72	1.4	Sophia Obi		27.05.01	4	Bromley	28 May

Foreign

13.51w	*2.2*	*Sydney Griffin (USA)*		*16.10.93*	*2*	*Copenhagen, DEN*	*20 Jun*
		13.63	*1.1*		*1*	*Ried, AUT*	*30 Jun*
13.56	*1.5*	*Mobolaji Adeokun (NGR)*		*14.01.94*	*1*	*Aarhus, DEN*	*2 Jun*
14.1		*Moe Sasegbon (NGR)*		*16.09.91*	*1*	*Cambridge*	*19 Aug*
		14.35	*0.7*		*1H2*	*Woerden, NED*	*26 Aug*
14.50	*-0.8*	*Tatum Souza (USA)*		*20.04.92*	*4s2*	*Bedford*	*1 May*
14.63	*0.7*	*Sarah Connolly (IRL)*	*U23*	*3.10.96*	*2H2*	*Woerden, NED*	*26 Aug*
14.88	*0.0*	*Laura Voss (GER)*		*29.01.94*	*H*	*Cologne, GER*	*22 Jul*
14.90	*-1.5*	*Kate O'Connor (IRL)*	*U17*	*12.12.00*	*2*	*Tullamore, IRL*	*4 Jun*
14.9		*Katy Sealy (BIZ)*		*15.10.90*	*1H*	*Sutton*	*9 Sep*

300 Metres Hurdles

42.67	Avril Jackson		22.10.86	5	Basel, SUI	20 May

Under 17

41.96	Amy Pye		22.11.00	1	Bedford	27 Aug
42.55	Jasmine Jolly		7.12.01	1	Birmingham	8 Jul
43.29	Sophie Porter		14.03.01	1h2	Birmingham	7 Jul
43.51	Hannah Foster		15.03.02	1	London (CP)	20 Aug

43.81	Kiera Bainsfair		3.02.02	2	Loughborough	1	Sep
44.03	Morgan Spink		6.04.02	3	Birmingham	8	Jul
44.09	Lana Culliford		21.09.00	1	Cardiff	1	Jul
44.30	Orla Brennan		8.02.02	2	London (CP)	20	Aug
44.42	Jessica Lambert		31.01.01	4	Birmingham	8	Jul
44.42	Mia Chantree		15.11.01	3	London (CP)	20	Aug
(10)							
44.45	Emma Mailer		24.02.02	1	Grangemouth	10	Jun
44.50	Isabel Breeden		26.07.01	1	Brecon	14	May
44.5	Grace Gentry		7.09.00	1	Stevenage	28	May
45.34				1	Watford	14	May
44.79	Saskia Huxham		14.11.00	1h3	Birmingham	7	Jul
44.92	Grace Vans Agnew		30.12.00	2	Bromley	28	May
45.06	Marcey Winter		17.04.01	3h3	Birmingham	7	Jul
45.06	Elle Wastell		16.02.01	4	Bedford	27	Aug
45.16	Jane Davidson		22.07.02	1	Aberdeen	2	Sep
45.20	Tess McHugh		19.06.02	2	Birmingham	17	Jun
45.23	Stephanie Driscoll		24.10.01	2	Manchester (Str)	28	May
(20)							
45.3	Elise Thorner		16.03.01	1	Yeovil	28	May
45.81	Holly McLachlan		20.04.02	1rB	Birmingham	3	Sep
45.84	Katie Sharkey		19.11.01	2	Grangemouth	10	Jun
45.87	Freya Menzies		12.11.00	3	Grangemouth	10	Jun
45.87	Katie Mackintosh		23.04.01	6h2	Birmingham	7	Jul
45.88	Victoria Johnson		7.10.01	2	Nuneaton	19	Aug
45.89	Maddie Turner		11.11.01	3	Basingstoke	17	Jun
45.9	Ellie Cleveland		5.08.02	2	Uxbridge	4	Jun
46.27				2	Bracknell	14	May
45.9	Olivia Willmore		21.03.02	1	Bournemouth	10	Jun
46.00				7h2	Birmingham	7	Jul
45.99	Sophie Hall		17.01.01	1	Manchester (Str)	14	May
(30)							
46.0	Madeline Wilton		11.04.02	1	Portsmouth	9	Apr
46.01	Louise Robinson		19.11.00	1	Nuneaton	14	May
46.04	Feia Starkey		19.11.01	6	London (CP)	20	Aug
46.21	Katie Hulme		12.08.02	3	Nuneaton	19	Aug
46.24	Dion Ingram		14.03.01	1	Glasgow (S)	13	Aug
46.50	Niamh Robertson		31.07.01	1	Sheffield	23	Jul

400 Metres Hurdles

54.36	Eilidh Doyle		20.02.87	3	Lausanne, SUI	6	Jul
54.60				1	Villeneuve d'Ascq, FRA	24	Jun
54.75				4	Monaco, MON	21	Jul
54.82				4	London (O)	9	Jul
54.89				4	Birmingham	20	Aug
54.92				3	Rabat, MAR	16	Jul
55.04				4	Brussels, BEL	1	Sep
55.09				5	Zürich, SUI	24	Aug
55.33				3s3	London (O)	8	Aug
55.49				3h4	London (O)	7	Aug
55.59				1	Birmingham	2	Jul
55.71				8	London (O)	10	Aug
55.76				1h1	Villeneuve d'Ascq, FRA	23	Jun
55.86				9	Rome, ITA	8	Jun
56.23				1	Lisse, NED	13	May
56.34				1h4	Birmingham	1	Jul
56.08	Jessica Turner	U23	8.08.95	2	Bydgoszcz, POL	16	Jul
56.68				5	Geneva, SUI	10	Jun
56.76				1rB	Oordegem, BEL	27	May
56.79				3	Birmingham	2	Jul
56.98				6h2	London (O)	7	Aug

(Turner)	57.07			2	Aarhus, DEN	2	Jun
	57.32			3s2	Bydgoszcz, POL	15	Jul
	57.45			5	Taipei, TPE	25	Aug
	57.68			1	Bedford	18	Jun
	57.73			2h1	Taipei, TPE	24	Aug
	57.79			1	Loughborough	21	May
	57.99			1	Loughborough	10	May
	58.40			1h3	Birmingham	1	Jul
56.14	Meghan Beesley		15.11.89	2	Loughborough	22	Jul
	56.41			6h5	London (O)	7	Aug
	56.61			6s2	London (O)	8	Aug
	56.63			1	Bromley	16	Jul
	56.68			2	Birmingham	2	Jul
	56.88			6	Geneva, SUI	10	Jun
	57.42			1h1	Birmingham	1	Jul
	58.32			1	Letterkenny, IRL	7	Jul
56.59	Caryl Granville		24.09.89	5	Loughborough	22	Jul
	57.17			2	Bromley	16	Jul
	57.42			1h2	Birmingham	1	Jul
	57.46			4	Birmingham	2	Jul
	57.62			1	Loughborough	22	Apr
	57.62			2	Leiden, NED	17	Jun
	57.67			1	Nivelles, BEL	24	Jun
	57.83			2rC	Oordegem, BEL	27	May
	57.91			1	Manchester (SC)	16	Aug
	58.21			2	Lokeren, BEL	25	Jun
57.31	Kirsten McAslan		1.09.93	1	Bedford	30	Jul
	58.10			1h1	Bedford	29	Jul
57.62	Ese Okoro		4.07.90	5	Birmingham	2	Jul
	57.81			3	Copenhagen, DEN	20	Jun
	57.87			7	Loughborough	22	Jul
	58.03			1rB	Bromley	16	Jul
	58.13			4	Aarhus, DEN	2	Jun
	58.25			2h2	Birmingham	1	Jul
	58.42			2	Loughborough	21	May
57.87	Lina Nielsen	U23	13.03.96	1rB	Loughborough	22	Jul
	57.94			2	Bedford	30	Jul
	58.47			1h1	Bedford	17	Jun
58.00	Jessie Knight		15.06.94	6	Birmingham	2	Jul
	58.43			3h2	Birmingham	1	Jul
	58.50			2h1	Bedford	29	Jul
58.3	Nisha Desai		5.08.84	1	Bedford	3	Jun
	58.38			2h1	Birmingham	1	Jul
58.33	Hayley McLean		9.09.94	6	Oordegem, BEL	27	May
(10)							
58.34	Jessica Tappin		17.05.90	2rB	Bromley	16	Jul
58.38	Bethany Close	U23	30.12.95	3rB	Bromley	16	Jul
67 performances to 58.50 by 12 athletes							
58.52	Abigayle Fitzpatrick		10.06.93	2	Nivelles, BEL	24	Jun
58.62	Lauren Thompson		12.02.92	7	Birmingham	2	Jul
58.66	Avril Jackson		22.10.86	3h1	Bedford	29	Jul
58.69	Mhairi Patience	U23	10.09.95	1	Bedford	1	May
58.79	Laura Wake		3.05.91	2h4	Birmingham	1	Jul
58.91	Chelsea Walker	U23	29.06.97	1	Wigan	7	May
59.38	Shona Richards	U23	1.09.95	8	Oordegem, BEL	27	May
59.46	Orla Brothers	U20	27.12.99	1	Bedford	18	Jun
(20)							
59.88	Lauren Williams	U20	12.02.99	4h1	Birmingham	1	Jul
59.96	Katie Purves	U23	3.11.96	3rB	Philadelphia, USA	27	Apr
60.27	Kerry Dixon		22.10.88	5h3	Birmingham	1	Jul

60.36	Anna Nelson	U23	14.11.95	6h1	Birmingham	1	Jul
60.37	Danel Jansen van Rensberg	U20	28.12.98	2	Birmingham	8	Jul
60.59	Alice Byles	U20	15.11.98	1h1	Bedford	17	Jun
60.87	Alexandra Hill		10.08.93	4rC	Loughborough	22	Jul
60.9	Holly McArthur	U20	20.12.99	1	Hull	30	Apr
61.24	Samantha Brown		24.02.94	2	Southampton	6	May
61.5	Georgina Rogers	U23	1.09.96	1rB	Nottingham	5	Aug
	(30)						
61.53	Chloe Esegbona	U20	23.11.98	1h3	Birmingham	7	Jul
61.55	Caroline Hilley	U23	18.09.96	4	Bedford	1	May
61.90	Olive Coles	U20	14.09.99	3h1	Bedford	17	Jun
62.03	Hermione Plumptre		26.11.91	5h1	Bedford	29	Jul
62.2	Natalie Ainge		12.03.92	1	Nottingham	5	Aug
63.12				1	Loughborough	24	May
62.24	Anna Nicole Rowe	U20	2.09.98	1	Wigan	7	May
62.34	Anna Croft	U20	20.10.99	1	Bromley	28	May
62.43	Stephanie Fisher	U20	17.03.00	1	Reading	25	Jun
62.51	Stephanie Driscoll	U17	24.10.01	1-18	Manchester (SC)	11	Jun
62.59	Bethan Burley	U20	26.03.00	6	Birmingham	8	Jul
	(40)						
62.63	Jenny Gilmour	U23	8.05.97	4	Wigan	7	May
63.01	Amy Hillyard	U23	28.10.95	2h3	Bedford	29	Apr
63.01	Deborah Willis		24.04.92	2	Cardiff	10	Jun
63.03	Emily Craig	U20	5.02.99	1	Glasgow (S)	20	Aug
63.05	Chay Clark	U23	6.12.96	1	London (LV)	8	Apr
63.05	Emma Komocki		17.03.92	4rE	Oordegem, BEL	27	May
63.18	Melanie Grigg	U23	25.11.95	3h3	Bedford	29	Apr
63.22	Holly Pattie-Belleli		9.06.94	2	Norman, USA	22	Apr
63.24	Isabelle Neville	U20	1.09.99	2	Birmingham	4	Jun
63.26	Emma Nanson	U23	6.10.95	3h2	Bedford	29	Apr
	(50)						
63.31	Hannah Dunderdale		2.11.94	4h1	Arlington, USA	13	May
63.32	Megan Gallagher	U20	6.10.99	1	Exeter	17	Jun
63.4	Becky McLinden		2.08.90	1	Chelmsford	17	Jun
63.68				6	London (CP)	11	Jun
63.65	Donna Jones		8.10.90	5	Cardiff	12	Jul
63.71	Jasmine Mitchell	U20	11.05.98	3	London (CP)	11	Jun
63.78	Amy Barclay		14.04.92	1	Gillingham	23	Apr
63.83	Katie Patullo	U20	27.03.98	1	Birmingham	3	Sep
63.9	Charlotte Stamp	U20	20.11.98	1	Wigan	9	Jul
65.03				1	Preston	5	Aug
63.91	Chloe Wilde	U20	24.05.99	2	Nuneaton	11	Jun
64.00	Emma Mailer	U17	24.02.02	2	Glasgow (S)	20	Aug
	(60)						
64.03	Gillian Gordon	U20	14.06.98	3	Glasgow (S)	20	Aug
64.05	Emily Smith	U20	6.06.99	2	London (LV)	9	Apr
64.1	Ellie Ravenscroft	U20	21.07.98	1	Solihull	28	May
64.15	Hannah Knights	U23	14.08.97	7h1	Birmingham	1	Jul
64.2	Nicole Kendall	U23	26.01.96	1	Aldershot	8	Jul
64.3	Mikaela Harrison		5.08.90	1	Ellesmere Port	4	Jun
65.82				1	Cosford	14	Jun
64.41	Amy Taylor	U20	28.01.99	3	Exeter	17	Jun
64.47	Hannah Lloyd		3.03.93	2	Stevenage	1	May
64.48	Catherine Blakeman	U23	19.03.97	5	Monachil, ESP	7	Jul
64.49	Heather Cooke	U20	22.02.98	4h2	Bedford	29	Apr
	(70)						
64.54	Alice Flint	U23	1.04.95	2	London (LV)	8	Apr
64.56	Monique Krefting	V45	13.11.69	1	Bromley	15	Apr
64.56	Julia Machin	V45	26.03.70	1	Ewell	4	Jun
64.64	Lana Culliford	U17	21.09.00	3	Birmingham	3	Sep
64.66	Emma Gilmour	U23	8.05.97	2rB	Wigan	7	May

64.68	Imogen Munday	U20	17.05.99	1	Ashford	13	May
64.78	Seemita Gumbs	V35	27.12.81	2rB	Eton	3	Jun
64.8	Saskia Huxham	U17	14.11.00	1	Doncaster	5	Aug
64.93	Laura Frey		2.06.89	6	Cork, IRL	8	Apr
64.95	Lucy Fligelstone	U23	26.01.97	1	Exeter	4	Jun
	(80)						
65.05	Emily Strickland	U20	27.12.99	1	Hull	9	Apr
65.08	Akesha Smith	U23	11.06.95	4h1	London (CP)	10	Jun
65.11	Holly Talbut-Smith	U23	19.12.96	3rB	Leigh	16	Jul
65.13	Sarah McLellan		4.02.90	5rB	Bromley	16	Jul
65.14	Sarah Kearsey		30.08.94	1	Exeter	20	Aug
65.15	Yasmin Austridge	U20	11.08.00	1rB	Bromley	28	May
65.16	Olivia Allbut	U17	17.07.01	7	Nassau, BAH	23	Jul
65.2	Megan McHugh	U20	25.07.00	2	Wrexham	23	Jul
	65.81			2	Manchester (SC)	11	Jun
65.27	Daisy Irving-Hyman	U23	12.05.96	3	London (LV)	8	Apr
65.28	Lucy Ferguson		23.03.90	4	London (LV)	8	Apr
	(90)						
65.31	Havana Allistone-Greaves	U17	6.07.01	1	Castellon, ESP	13	Jun
65.39	Rebecca Pickard	U20	5.01.98	7h1	Bedford	17	Jun
65.55	Grace Gentry	U17	7.09.00	1	Bedford	27	May
65.66	Nicola Martell-Smith		20.09.85	2	Bromley	15	Apr
65.76	Jessica Lambert	U17	31.01.01	2	Basingstoke	21	May
65.85	Olivia Willmore	U17	21.03.02	1	Oxford (H)	9	Sep
65.86	Shirin Irving	U23	25.09.96	1rB	Torremolinos, ESP	19	Apr

Additional Under 17 (1-9 above)

66.82	Amy Pye		22.11.00	4	Loughborough	22	Apr
	(10)						
66.84	Lily Hulland		1.09.01	4	Torremolinos, ESP	19	Apr
67.34	Eliza Mason		24.09.01	4	Visby, SWE	29	Jun
67.4	Louise Robinson		19.11.00	3	Rugby	7	May
67.77	Maddie Turner		11.11.01	1	Exeter	15	Apr

Foreign

557.86	*Aisha Naibe-Wey (SLE)*		*3.08.93*	*3*	*Saint-Égrève, FRA*	*25*	*Jun*
58.08	*Christine McMahon (IRL)*		*6.07.92*	*6*	*Prague, CZE*	*5*	*Jun*
61.08	*Nessa Millet (IRL)*		*5.12.94*	*3*	*Bedford*	*1*	*May*
63.19	*Kate Kennedy (USA)*	*U23*	*16.02.96*	*2h2*	*Bedford*	*29*	*Apr*
64.75	*Ugne Sauliunaite (LTU)*	*U20*	*17.04.99*	*1*	*Kaunas, LTU*	*19*	*May*

High Jump

1.96	Morgan Lake	U23	12.05.97	1	Birmingham	1	Jul
	1.95			6	London (O)	12	Aug
	1.94			1	Bedford	17	Jun
	1.93			4	Lausanne, SUI	6	Jul
	1.92i			1	Hustopeče, CZE	4	Feb
	1.92			Q	London (O)	10	Aug
	1.91			1H	Bedford	27	May
	1.91			4=	Rome, ITA	8	Jun
	1.91			4	Eberstadt, GER	26	Aug
	1.90i			Q	Belgrade, SRB	3	Mar
	1.90			1H	Florence, ITA	28	Apr
	1.90			7	London (O)	9	Jul
	1.89i			1=	Sheffield	11	Feb
	1.88			5	Zagreb, CRO	29	Aug
	1.87			1	Loughborough	21	May
	1.85i			8	Belgrade, SRB	4	Mar
	1.85			4=	Hengelo, NED	11	Jun
	1.85			7=	Villeneuve d'Ascq, FRA	25	Jun
	1.84			8=	Brussels, BEL	1	Sep
	1.83			1	Eton	3	Jun

Mark	Name	Cat	DOB	Pos	Venue	Date
1.95	Katarina Johnson-Thompson		9.01.93	2H	Götzis, AUT	27 May
1.95				5	London (O)	12 Aug
1.93				1H	Marseille, FRA	14 Jul
1.92				Q	London (O)	10 Aug
1.88				1	Etang Salé, REU	15 Apr
1.89i	Bethan Partridge		11.07.90	1=	Sheffield	11 Feb
1.88i				2	Nantes, FRA	21 Jan
1.86i				1	Birmingham	14 Jan
1.86i				5=	Hustopeče, CZE	4 Feb
1.85				2	Loughborough	21 May
1.84i				1	Birmingham	19 Feb
1.83				2	Carquefou, FRA	23 Jun
1.83				4	Marseille, FRA	15 Jul
1.82				6	Lund, SWE	10 Jun
1.86	Emma Nuttall		23.04.92	5	Lund, SWE	10 Jun
1.86				1	Bedford	30 Jul
1.83				2	Birmingham	1 Jul
1.83				1=	Cork, IRL	18 Jul
1.86	Nikki Manson		15.10.94	2	Bedford	30 Jul
1.85				5	Eugene, USA	10 Jun
1.84i				1	University Park, USA	28 Jan
1.81i				1	Ypsilanti, USA	25 Feb
1.81i				10	College Station, USA	10 Mar
1.81				2	Athens, USA	8 Apr
1.81				5	Karlstad, SWE	25 Jul
1.81				1	Grangemouth	26 Aug
1.83i	Emily Borthwick	U23	2.09.97	1B	Hustopeče, CZE	4 Feb
1.83				1=	Cork, IRL	18 Jul
1.82i				4	Sheffield	11 Feb
1.81				1	Bedford	1 May
1.81				2	Grangemouth	26 Aug
1.83	Niamh Emerson	U20	22.04.99	3	Loughborough	21 May
1.82				2H	Bedford	27 May
1.81				5H	Grosseto, ITA	20 Jul
1.82i	Laura Armorgie	U23	5.12.97	5	Sheffield	11 Feb
1.71				7=	Loughborough	21 May

55 performances to 1.81 by 8 athletes including 15 indoors

Mark	Name	Cat	DOB	Pos	Venue	Date
1.80i	Ada'ora Chigbo	U20	2.01.99	1J	Hustopeče, CZE	4 Feb
1.75				1	Yate	13 May
1.80i	Rebecca Hawkins	U20	27.09.99	1	London (LV)	18 Mar
1.77				2	Bedford	29 May
(10)						
1.80	Kate Anson	U23	14.03.95	1	Bedford	29 May
1.78i	Poppy Lake	U23	26.01.96	2	London (LV)	15 Jan
1.75				4	Bedford	1 May
1.78i	Abby Ward	U20	19.04.99	1	Sheffield	2 Dec
1.70				1	Manchester (SC)	11 Jun
1.77i	Lucy Chappell	U23	10.01.97	1P	Glasgow	5 Mar
1.73				4	Bedford	17 Jun
1.77	Temi Ojora	U17	24.01.02	1	Birmingham	7 Jul
1.76i	Ashleigh West	U17	27.06.01	1	Sheffield	26 Feb
1.71				3	Birmingham	7 Jul
1.76	Katie Garland	U23	27.01.97	3H	Bedford	27 May
1.76	Mollie Courtney	U23	2.07.97	1	Wolverhampton	4 Jun
1.76	Amaya Scott	U17	15.02.01	1	Basingstoke	17 Jun
1.76	Lillie Franks	U20	27.10.99	1	Kingston	2 Jul
(20)						
1.75i	Georgia Nwawulor		30.06.94	3	Sheffield	19 Feb
1.70				1	Bedford	3 Jun
1.75	Katie Stainton	U23	8.01.95	7H	Florence, ITA	28 Apr
1.75	Emily Race	U17	11.09.00	1	Bedford	26 Aug

1.74i	Natasha Smith	U20	10.10.99	1=P	Sheffield	7	Jan
1.71				8=	Birmingham	1	Jul
1.74	Camellia Hayes	U23	6.04.95	3	Bedford	29	May
1.74	Emma Nwofor	U23	22.08.96	1H	Oxford (H)	22	Jul
1.74	Olivia Dobson	U17	27.03.01	1H	Boston	16	Sep
1.73i	Merechi Egbo	U17	29.11.01	2	Sheffield	26	Feb
1.68				1	Hemel Hempstead	4	Jun
1.73	Danielle Hopkins	U17	29.12.01	1-17	Rugby	28	May
1.73	Emma Sherwood	U17	12.09.01	1B	Bedford	29	May
(30)							
1.73	Anna McCauley	U17	2.01.01	1	Loughborough	1	Sep
1.73i	Molly Hole	U17	28.02.03	1	Cardiff	3	Dec
1.71		U15		1	Bournemouth	23	Apr
1.72	Hannah Tapley	U20	1.10.98	1	Worcester	10	Jun
1.72	Isabel Pinder	U15	16.11.03	1	Basingstoke	17	Jun
1.71i	Amelia Jennings McLaughlin	U23	20.04.97	1	Cardiff	28	Jan
1.70				1	Visby, SWE	28	Jun
1.71iA	Isobel Brown		5.12.94	5	Albuquerque, USA	25	Feb
1.70				13	Long Beach, USA	15	Apr
1.71i	Jessica Tappin		17.05.90	2P	Glasgow	5	Mar
1.67				7H	Bedford	27	May
1.71	Molly Hole	U15	28.02.03	1	Bournemouth	23	Apr
1.71	Mia Chantree	U17	15.11.01	1P	Grays	1	May
1.71	Beau Studholme	U17	15.09.01	1-17	Crewe	28	May
1.71	Hannah Moat	U17	2.07.02	2	Birmingham	7	Jul
(40)							
1.70i	Deborah Martin		25.01.94	3	London (LV)	15	Jan
1.70				1	Ashford	13	May
1.70i	Hollie Smith	U20	7.11.98	1	Sheffield	15	Jan
1.70i	Georgia Parris	U23	5.10.97	1	Birmingham	11	Feb
1.69				5B	Bedford	29	May
1.70i	Emma Barbour	U17	17.02.02	1	Glasgow	19	Feb
1.70i	Ellie Fulton	U20	18.06.99	1	Glasgow	26	Mar
1.65				1	Leeds (South)	28	May
1.70	Rachel Gibbens		31.01.86	2=	Wigan	7	May
1.70	Claire McGarvey	U17	15.06.01	1	Perth	7	May
1.70	Rebekah O'Brien	U15	21.10.02	1	Dartford	4	Jun
1.70	Janet Browne		17.10.94	1	Norwich	17	Jun
1.70	Ashleigh Spiliopoulou	U20	2.04.99	6H	Dilbeek, BEL	29	Jul
(50)							
1.70	Bernice Coulson	U20	25.04.98	2	Preston	5	Aug
1.70	Ellen Barber	U23	5.12.97	2H	Woerden, NED	26	Aug
1.70	Lucy Walliker	U20	21.01.99	1	Exeter	29	Aug
1.70	Bethan Siddons		29.09.90	1	Stevenage	10	Sep
1.70i	Holly Mills	U20	15.04.00	1	Eton	3	Dec
1.70i	Molly Newton-O'Brien	U20	5.05.99	1	Cardiff	10	Dec
1.69i	Amelia Hempleman-Adams	U23	1.06.95	Q	Sheffield	18	Feb
1.69	Charlotte Kerr	U17	6.08.01	1	Hull	2	Jul
1.69	Kara Onuiri	U17	18.08.02	2	Bedford	26	Aug
1.69	Sophie Hodgson	U17	25.06.02	3	Bedford	26	Aug
(60)							
1.68i	Becky Owen		8.09.91	2	Cardiff	28	Jan
1.65				4	Leigh	16	Jul
1.68i	Grace Bower	U20	3.11.99	7P	Prague, CZE	28	Jan
1.68				1H	Telford	24	Jun
1.68i	Jo Rowland		29.12.89	4P	Glasgow	5	Mar
1.68				1H	Cudworth	26	Aug
1.68	Elise Thorner	U17	16.03.01	1	Exeter	7	May
1.68	Anna Brophy	U17	14.04.01	1	Exeter	17	Jun
1.68	Katie Hetherington	U20	6.04.00	3	Bedford	18	Jun
1.68	Ndidikama Okoh	U15	3.12.02	1	Tonbridge	18	Jun

1.68	Jessica Gordon	U17	23.04.02	1	Woking	2	Jul
1.68	Isabel Cain-Daley	U20	27.11.98	2	Cardiff	12	Jul
1.68	Jessica Hopkins	U17	6.01.02	1	London (He)	30	Jul
	(70)						
1.68	Evie Grogan		3.04.94	1	Southampton	19	Aug
1.68	Lili Church	U15	30.07.03	1	Brecon	26	Aug
1.68	Amelia Bateman	U17	13.11.00	4H	Boston	16	Sep
1.68i	Jade O'Dowda	U20	9.09.99	1	London (LV)	30	Dec
1.65				1H	Boston	16	Sep
1.67i	Zoe Hughes	U20	1.02.98	3P	Lexington, USA	20	Jan
1.65				3H	New Haven, USA	6	May
1.67i	Daniella Hankins		14.06.93	4B	London (LV)	29	Jan
1.67	Alix Still	U20	15.03.00	1	Tallahassee, USA	24	Mar
1.67	Molly Caudery	U20	17.03.00	1	Carn Brea	13	May
1.67	Lucy Turner	U23	14.02.97	8H	Bedford	27	May
1.67	Leonie Brunning	U15	25.11.02	1	Peterborough	2	Jul
	(80)						
1.67	Carmen Neat	U17	23.10.01	1	Glasgow (S)	13	Aug
1.67	Madeleine Wood	U15	3.09.02	1	Nuneaton	20	Aug
1.66i	Abigail Buxton	U20	3.10.98	1	Swansea	22	Jan
1.66i	Emma Cowell	U23	23.11.95	Q	Sheffield	18	Feb
1.66	Laura Zialor	U20	4.08.98	Q	Bedford	30	Apr
1.66	Ella Widdop-Gray	U23	26.09.96	Q	Bedford	30	Apr
1.66	Olivia Montez Brown	U23	22.05.96	4	St. Paul, USA	12	May
1.66	Kaili Woodward	U17	30.01.02	2-17	Solihull	28	May
1.66	Hollie Williamson	U20	4.12.98	1	Telford	10	Jun
1.66	Megan Porter	U20	4.02.00	1	Peterborough	11	Jun
	(90)						
1.66	Modupe Obideyi	U20	18.02.00	1	Cambridge	18	Jun
1.66	Emily Madden Forman	U20	29.09.99	1H	Milton Keynes	24	Jun
1.66	Anna Forbes	U20	13.10.98	1	Glasgow (S)	20	Aug
1.65i	Ellie Pullin	U23	15.02.97	2	Sheffield	15	Jan
1.65i	Megan McHugh	U20	25.07.00	2J	Sheffield	15	Jan
1.65i	Lauren Evans	U20	7.08.00	1	Cardiff	15	Jan
1.65i	Jessica Taylor-Jemmett		27.06.88	14P	Prague, CZE	29	Jan
1.65i	Danielle McGifford	U23	11.04.95	15P	Prague, CZE	29	Jan
1.65				1H	Hyndburn	15	Apr
1.65i	Elise Lovell		9.05.92	16=P	Prague, CZE	29	Jan
1.65i	Emily Dixon	U23	27.11.95	1P	Lynchburg, USA	10	Feb
1.65				1H	Newark, USA	5	May
	(100)						
1.65i	Phoebe Harland	U17	3.02.01	2	Birmingham	12	Feb
1.65				2	Stourport	2	Apr
1.65i	Kate Davies	U23	27.09.95	2	London (LV)	4	Mar
1.65i	Amy Thurgood	U17	18.11.00	2	London (LV)	18	Mar
1.65				1	St. Albans	7	May
1.65	Ila Burton	U20	2.07.98	1	Yeovil	2	Apr
1.65	Annabelle Bates		12.05.94	5	Philadelphia, USA	15	Apr
1.65	Olivia Jones	U20	20.02.00	2	Nottingham	30	Apr
1.65	Adela Hussain	U23	7.08.95	1	Southampton	6	May
1.65	Georgia Doyle-Lay	U20	27.10.98	1	Exeter	7	May
1.65	Laura Darcey	U20	28.07.98	1H	Naperville, USA	17	May
1.65	Phoebe Tan	U20	18.10.98	2	Antrim	20	May
	(110)						
1.65	Mabel Smith	U15	17.02.04	1	London (BP)	10	Jun
1.65	Rhiana Burrell	U15	14.12.03	1	Birmingham	17	Jun
1.65	Megan Penfold	U17	26.09.01	2H	Bedford	24	Jun
1.65	Bethany Harryman	U17	13.10.00	1	Lignano, ITA	5	Jul
1.65	Renee Jelf	U17	5.02.01	11	Birmingham	7	Jul
1.65	Abigail Packham	U15	19.08.03	1	Guildford	15	Jul
1.65	Funminiyi Olajide	U17	4.06.02	2-17	London (He)	23	Jul
1.65	Jessica Biggerstaff	U17	15.01.01	1	Ware	30	Jul

325

1.65	Jodie Smith	U17	2.11.01	6H	Boston	16	Sep
1.65i	Michelle Blaikie	U17	10.10.02	1	Glasgow	28	Oct
1.62		U15		1	Grangemouth	12	May
(120)							
1.65i	Lucy-Jane Matthews	U17	17.09.02	1	London (LV)	3	Dec
1.61i		U15		1P	Sheffield	12	Mar
1.65i	Bethany Woodhead	U20	1.07.01	1	Manchester (SC)	17	Dec
1.63		U17		1	Preston	30	Apr

Additional Under 17 (1-36 above)

1.64	Mayi Hughes		5.11.00	1	Cambridge	2	Jul
1.63i	Thea Jenkins		14.10.00	1	Swansea	22	Jan
1.63i	Jessica Collins		9.01.02	1	Sutton	19	Feb
1.63	Chloe Allcock		8.02.02	1	Grantham	30	Apr
(40)							
1.63	Alicia Marriott		22.05.02	2	Cudworth	14	May
1.63i	Abigail Pawlett		14.01.03	2=	Sheffield	2	Dec
1.61		U15		1	Macclesfield	7	May

Additional Under 15 (1-13 above)

1.64	Miriam Levy		8.02.03	1	Cudworth	13	May
1.63	Maya Jones		10.02.03	1	Yeovil	10	Jun
1.63	Lara Scott		26.08.04	3=	Birmingham	8	Jul
1.62	Eloise Nowill		2.01.03	2	Birmingham	17	Jun
1.62	Holly Lawrence		12.02.03	1	Oxford (H)	1	Jul
1.62	Ruby Bridger		6.05.03	1P	Peterborough	24	Sep
1.61	Lily Holt		2.10.02	1	Harrow	22	Apr
(20)							
1.61	Abbey Orr		19.11.03	1	Kilmarnock	28	May
1.61	Jilly Lefebvre		1.04.04	2	Kilmarnock	28	May
1.61	Lily Crawley		2.10.02	1P	Exeter	24	Sep
1.60i	Nicole Proudfoot		12.11.02	1	Glasgow	2	Feb
1.60	Katie Chapman		20.09.03	1	Exeter	9	Apr
1.60	Alice Cashin		13.10.02	1	Blackpool	14	May
1.60	Kelsey Sutherland		19.12.02	1	Hastings	20	May
1.60	Katie Burr		30.09.03	1P	Grangemouth	3	Jun
1.60	Charlotte Martin		28.05.03	1	Bristol	20	Jun

Under 13

1.57	Erin Lobley		12.10.04	1	Hull	18	Jun
1.56i	Mya McMahon		19.09.05	1P	Glasgow	4	Mar
1.54				1	Glasgow (S)	19	Aug
1.53	Evie Greig		4.01.05	1	Kilmarnock	28	May
1.53	Iona Irvine		22.11.04	1	Woking	11	Jun
1.53	Saskia Wade		30.05.05	1	Grangemouth	25	Jun
1.53	Halle Ferguson		6.12.04	1	Warrington	3	Sep
1.53	Danielle Olugbile		4.11.04	1P	Sutton	10	Sep
1.51	Gemma Tutton		8.11.04	1	Lewes	18	Jun
1.51	Shanumi Akinfenwa		1.09.04	1	Stevenage	13	Aug
1.51	Ella Isaias		22.11.04	1P	Exeter	24	Sep

Foreign

1.85	Sommer Lecky (IRL)	U20	14.06.00	1	Antrim	20	May
1.82i	Pippa Rogan (IRL)		4.02.94	3	Sheffield	11	Feb
1.78				1	Palafrugell, ESP	27	May
1.78	Teele Palumaa (EST)		31.03.90	2	Bedford	1	May
1.78	Kate O'Connor (IRL)	U17	12.12.00	9H	Grosseto, ITA	20	Jul
1.78	Sarah Connolly (IRL)	U23	3.10.96	1H	Belfast	2	Sep
1.75i	Laura Voss (GER)		29.01.94	1	Gateshead	19	Jan
1.74				1H	Cologne, GER	22	Jul
1.75	Moe Sasegbon (NGR)		16.09.91	2H	Belfast	2	Sep
1.70i	Belen Simarro (ESP)	U23	10.11.95	1	Madrid, ESP	12	Feb
1.68	Katy Sealy (BIZ)		15.10.90	1H	Sutton	9	Sep

Pole Vault

4.81	Holly Bradshaw		2.11.91	1	Rottach-Egern, GER	15	Jul
	4.80			1	Manchester	26	May
	4.70			4	Beckum, GER	27	Aug
	4.65			6	London (O)	6	Aug
	4.62i			4=	Zürich, SUI	23	Aug
	4.61			2	Birmingham	20	Aug
	4.55			4	Doha, QAT	5	May
	4.55			6	London (O)	9	Jul
	4.55			6	Brussels, BEL	1	Sep
	4.50			Q	London (O)	4	Aug
	4.45			1	Birmingham	1	Jul
	4.40			7=	Rome, ITA	8	Jun
4.40i	Lucy Bryan	U23	22.05.95	4	College Station, USA	10	Mar
	4.40			3	Bydgoszcz, POL	15	Jul
	4.35			2	Birmingham	1	Jul
	4.33i			2	Akron, USA	4	Feb
	4.30i			1	Akron, USA	20	Jan
	4.28i			3	University Park, USA	27	Jan
	4.27i			3	Akron, USA	17	Feb
	4.25			1	Cardiff	10	Jun
	4.20			1	Bedford	18	Jun
	4.20			Q	Bydgoszcz, POL	13	Jul
	4.17i			2	Ypsilanti, USA	24	Feb
	4.15			3	Cardiff	21	Jun
	4.10i			1	Lexington, USA	14	Jan
4.36i	Jade Ive		22.01.92	1	Sutton	19	Feb
	4.35i			1	Sheffield	11	Feb
	4.26i			1	Cardiff	5	Mar
	4.20i			1	London (LV)	15	Jan
	4.20			1	Bromley	16	Jul
	4.15			1	Loughborough	21	May
	4.13i			8	Birmingham	18	Feb
	4.13i			1	Sutton	24	Sep
	4.12i			1	Sutton	5	Feb
	4.11i			1	London (LV)	28	Jan
	4.10			1	Sutton	15	Apr
	4.10			1	Kingston	14	May
	4.06			1	Woking	19	Jul
	4.05			2	Bedford	30	Jul
	4.05			2	Manchester (SC)	16	Aug
4.35	Sally Peake		8.02.86	3	Rehlingen, GER	5	Jun
	4.35			6	Villeneuve d'Ascq, FRA	24	Jun
	4.26i			2	Cardiff	5	Mar
	4.25			3	Birmingham	1	Jul
	4.23i			1	Cardiff	12	Mar
	4.16i			2	Sheffield	11	Feb
	4.15i			1	Cardiff	28	Jan
	4.15			2	Loughborough	21	May
	4.13i			7	Birmingham	18	Feb
4.35	Molly Caudery	U20	17.03.00	2	Grosseto, ITA	22	Jul
	4.25			2	Cardiff	21	Jun
	4.20			1	Birmingham	8	Jul
	4.15			1	Manchester (SC)	16	Aug
	4.10i			1	Cardiff	15	Jan
	4.05i			1	Sheffield	25	Feb
	4.05			3	Loughborough	21	May
	4.05			Q	Grosseto, ITA	20	Jul

4.25	Henrietta Paxton		19.09.83	1	Cardiff	21	Jun
	4.15			1	Cardiff	10	Jun
	4.15			4	Birmingham	1	Jul
	4.10i			2	London (LV)	15	Jan
	4.05			1	Loughborough	22	Apr
4.06	Claire Maurer		9.01.94	1	Canterbury	10	Aug
4.05	Abigail Roberts	U23	9.07.97	2	Melbourne (A), AUS	11	Feb
4.05	Rachel Gibbens		31.01.86	1	Chelmsford	17	Jun
	65 performances to 4.05 by 9 athletes including 24 indoors						
4.00	Jessica Swannack	U20	26.09.98	2	Birmingham	8	Jul
(10)							
4.00	Clare Blunt		28.09.87	1	Leigh	16	Jul
4.00	Courtney MacGuire		30.04.90	1	Basingstoke	19	Jul
3.95	Jessica Robinson	U20	26.06.99	4	Loughborough	21	May
3.93	Jessica Abraham		26.01.89	1	Southampton	6	May
3.91i	Sophie Dowson	U20	24.11.98	2B	London (LV)	28	Jan
	3.75			3	Bedford	17	Jun
3.90	Elizabeth Edden		29.06.94	1	Bristol	20	Jun
3.83i	Jade Brewster	U23	20.02.97	1B	Cardiff	12	Mar
	3.65			6	Cardiff	10	Jun
3.83i	Georgia Pickles	U23	19.10.96	2B	Cardiff	12	Mar
	3.30			2	Stevenage	4	Jun
3.83i	Felicia Miloro	U17	5.01.01	3	Sutton	24	Sep
	3.81			1	Bedford	27	Aug
3.82	Natasha Purchas	U17	12.01.01	1	Crawley	28	Aug
(20)							
3.81i	Sophie Cook		12.09.94	6	Sheffield	11	Feb
3.81i	Olivia Curran		10.06.91	7	Sheffield	11	Feb
3.80i	Victoria Barlow	U17	12.02.01	1	Manchester (SC)	29	Jan
	3.71			3	Bedford	27	Aug
3.80i	Fiona Hockey	U20	21.01.98	2	Sheffield	19	Feb
	3.70			1	Wrexham	19	Aug
3.80	Sian Morgan		29.11.88	1	Los Angeles (ER), USA	10	Mar
3.75	Ellen McCartney	U20	8.10.99	1	Tullamore, IRL	1	Jul
3.73i	Jade Spencer-Smith	U17	8.11.01	4B	Cardiff	12	Mar
	3.71			2	Bedford	27	Aug
3.70i	Olivia Connor	U23	6.09.97	5	Sheffield	19	Feb
	3.70			3	Bedford	1	May
3.70	Laura Edwards		1.03.94	2	Basingstoke	19	Jul
3.64	Esther Leong	U20	28.01.00	1	Yate	30	Jul
(30)							
3.63i	Isabel Deacon	U20	11.11.99	5B	Cardiff	12	Mar
	3.35			2	Norwich	30	Apr
3.63i	Jenny Robbins	U23	20.02.96	7B	Cardiff	12	Mar
	3.15			3	Manchester (SC)	26	May
3.61i	Anna Gordon	U23	30.01.97	1	Glasgow	28	Jan
3.60	Chloe Billingham	U20	14.01.98	5	Philadelphia, USA	15	Apr
3.60	Alexa Eichelmann	U20	14.12.99	5	Birmingham	8	Jul
3.56	Sophie Ashurst	U15	26.04.03	1	Bedford	26	Aug
3.55	Rebecca Gray	U20	4.10.98	1	Yate	23	Jul
3.52i	Carys Jones	U20	17.12.98	1B	Cardiff	10	Dec
	3.40			2	Wrexham	19	Aug
3.51i	Holly Brown	U20	21.11.98	1	London (LV)	2	Jan
	3.15			1	Luton	30	Apr
3.51i	Megan Hodgson	U17	16.12.00	7	Cardiff	5	Mar
	3.41			1	Dublin (S), IRL	5	Aug
(40)							
3.50i	Caroline Adams		5.02.91	3	Sheffield	14	Jan
	3.32			2	Sheffield	5	Jul
3.50i	Shaye Emmett	U20	19.08.00	1	London (LV)	15	Jan
	3.50			9	Eton	3	Jun

3.50i	Elise Gauntlett	U23	11.01.95	Q	Sheffield	18	Feb
	3.20			4	Birmingham	4	Jun
3.50i	Lois Warden	U17	26.03.02	5	Sheffield	26	Feb
	3.40			5	Birmingham	8	Jul
3.50	Claudia Lavender	U20	17.06.98	1	Bromley	22	May
3.50	Tamsin Campbell	U20	12.02.99	1	Yeovil	10	Jun
3.50	Daisy Barnes	U20	15.07.00	2	Loughborough	14	Jun
3.50	Imogen Smith	U20	2.09.99	1	Wolverhampton	25	Jun
3.50	Claudia Barkes	U20	1.02.00	9	Birmingham	8	Jul
3.50	Sam Morrison		21.03.94	1	Tonbridge	1	Aug
(50)							
3.50	Megan Bailey	U20	22.01.98	1	Bromley	19	Aug
3.50	Shannon Connolly	U23	19.11.95	1	London (He)	26	Aug
3.46	Gemma Tutton	U13	8.11.04	1	Lewes	12	Jun
3.46	Lucy Allen	U15	1.04.03	2	Bedford	26	Aug
3.46	Jasmine Carey	U15	13.09.02	3	Bedford	26	Aug
3.45	Irie Hill	V45	16.01.69	1	Birmingham	24	Jun
3.43i	Lois Hillman	U20	11.05.00	2C	Cardiff	12	Mar
	3.15			3	Yate	30	Apr
3.42i	Harriet Vaughan	U17	28.09.01	2B	Cardiff	10	Dec
	3.40			6	Birmingham	8	Jul
3.41i	Hannah Lawler	U23	24.10.95	2	Glasgow	28	Jan
	3.30			1	Grangemouth	27	Aug
3.41i	Kirsten Mullen	U23	30.10.96	1	Dublin (S), IRL	27	May
	3.23			1	Dunfermline	3	Sep
(60)							
3.41	Caroline Walder	U17	3.01.01	3	Loughborough	1	Sep
3.40i	Leah Darbyshire	U17	31.10.01	2	Sheffield	14	Jan
	3.20			1-17	Wigan	30	Apr
3.40i	Emily MacDonald	U20	21.12.99	3B	Birmingham	19	Feb
	3.40			1	Bracknell	14	May
3.40	Erin Breen	U20	28.12.98	1	Watford	14	May
3.35i	Megan McInnes	U23	20.10.97	6B	Uxbridge	5	Feb
3.35i	Matilda Waters	U17	20.12.00	1B	Manchester (SC)	5	Mar
	3.10			1	Manchester (Str)	13	May
3.32i	Ffion Llewellyn	U20	11.03.00	9	Cardiff	5	Feb
	3.30			13=	Bedford	17	Jun
3.31	Sasha Birrell	U23	17.05.96	1	London (BP)	19	Aug
3.30i	Jemma Eastwood	V35	15.02.79	1	London (LV)	11	Mar
	3.30			2	Chelmsford	8	Jul
3.30	Kara Bradbeer	U23	28.01.95	1	Grangemouth	13	May
(70)							
3.26i	Caroline Parkinson		31.07.83	4C	London (LV)	28	Jan
	3.24			1	Brighton	17	Jun
3.26i	Jessica Hall	U20	25.01.01	3	Eton	3	Dec
	3.12i	U17		2B	Uxbridge	5	Mar
3.21	Jasmine Presho	U17	18.11.01	1	Oxford (H)	14	May
3.20i	Mercy Gutteridge	U23	8.06.97	11	London (LV)	15	Jan
3.20i	Erin Thomas	U17	12.09.01	2	London (LV)	18	Mar
	3.11			8	Bedford	27	Aug
3.20	Laura-Ann Henderson		1.10.94	1	Ipswich	20	May
3.20	Harriet Dougan	U17	10.06.01	1	Antrim	27	May
3.20	Gillian Cooke		3.10.82	10	Eton	3	Jun
3.20	Cicely Cole	U20	3.02.00	4	London (CP)	11	Jun
3.15	Amelia Shearman	U15	21.01.03	4	Birmingham	7	Jul
(80)							
3.13i	Eleanor Barrett	U17	30.04.02	2C	Sutton	24	Sep
	3.10			2-17	Birmingham	3	Sep
3.12i	Kerry Maguire	U23	8.05.95	1cE	Sutton	5	Feb
3.11i	Bethany Newton	U20	19.02.99	2cD	Manchester (SC)	21	Jan
	3.10			1	Nottingham	8	Apr

3.11	Alana Dunsmore	U20	17.01.00	1	Grangemouth	9	Jun
3.11	Erin Fisher	U17	19.10.01	5	Dublin (S), IRL	15	Jul
3.10i	Amy Haslam	U17	5.01.02	4	Sheffield	14	Jan
3.10i	Georgia Duthie	U17	7.09.00	9	London (LV)	15	Jan
3.10i	Annie Williams	U20	28.09.98	2	Sheffield	15	Jan
3.10	Aisling Begley	U20	27.10.99	1	Reading	8	Apr
3.10	Bronia Greenhalgh	U17	13.03.01	1-17	Crewe	28	May
	(90)						
3.10	Maryanne Eve	U20	1.08.99	1	Harrow	28	May
3.10	Millie Hemsley	U20	31.10.98	2	Crawley	10	Jun
3.10	Katie Sexton	U20	4.12.99	5	London (CP)	11	Jun
3.10	Anousha Wardley	U20	22.10.99	1	London (TB)	17	Jun
3.10	Alison Murray	V50	13.01.67	2	Birmingham	24	Jun
3.10	Sydney Robertson	U23	13.12.96	1	Morpeth	9	Jul
3.10	Georgia West	U17	6.10.00	1	Ware	30	Jul

Additional Under 17 (1-20 above)

3.00	Tamara Kearney		18.08.01	2	Exeter	17	Jun
3.00	Lucie Wolfenden		14.09.01	3	Birmingham	17	Jun
2.95	Naomi Storm		6.03.01	1	Salisbury	8	Jul
2.91i	Tegan Hewitt		22.01.02	2cE	Manchester (SC)	21	Jan
	2.90			1	Hexham	7	May
2.90i	Jessica Smith		5.09.01	1	London (LV)	4	Feb
2.90i	Amelia Birkett		14.09.01	2	Birmingham	18	Mar
2.90	Charlotte Vyvyan		22.10.00	1	Reading	8	Apr
2.90	Kirsty Rushton		13.03.02	1	Wigan	9	Apr

Additional Under 15 (1-4 above)

2.95	Ivy Spencer		23.09.02	5	Birmingham	7	Jul
2.90	Lucy Hughes		16.10.03	2	Exeter	20	Aug
2.90i	Amy Hunt		22.09.04	6	Manchester (SC)	17	Dec
	2.70	U13		1	Wakefield	13	Aug
2.80	Genevieve Haselden		10.10.02	1B	Cheltenham	19	Jul
2.80	Grace Pitman		5.05.03	2	Ashford	5	Aug
2.70	Catherine Davies		13.01.03	1	Reading	22	Apr
	(10)						
2.70	Minnie Rogers		4.08.03	2	Litherland	15	Jul
2.70	Lucy Bayo		16.09.02	1	Crawley	28	Aug
2.67	Lois Green		6.05.03	1B	Sheffield	21	Jun
2.65	Molly Elliott		15.09.02	1	Jarrow	25	Jun
2.63i	Dalila Watson		16.12.02	1cE	Sutton	24	Sep
2.60	Eden Dickens		12.12.03	2	Loughborough	26	Apr
2.60	Sara Barbour		21.01.03	1	Grangemouth	9	Jun
2.60	Evie Lawrence		15.04.03	1	Newport	6	Aug
2.60	Sinead Marshall		21.01.03	1	London (CP)	20	Aug
2.60	Morgan MacDougall		10.03.03	3	Grangemouth	27	Aug
	(20)						
2.60	Emily Scrivener		29.07.03	1	Woking	3	Sep
2.60	Poppy Herbert		21.02.03	3	Woking	3	Sep
2.60i	Emilie Oakden		17.11.04	3	London (LV)	3	Dec
	2.50	U13		3	Lewes	28	Jun

Additional Under 13 (1-3 above)

2.60	Olivia Simon		9.11.04	3	Canterbury	10	Aug
2.44	Chloe Marrett		6.11.04	1	Bristol	18	Jul
2.40	Caitlin Ebbage		14.06.05	8B	Tonbridge	17	Apr
2.30	Erin Hunt		22.09.04	2	Wakefield	13	Aug
2.30	India Barwell		4.03.05	5B	Loughborough	26	Aug

Foreign

4.13i	*Sarah McKeever (IRL)*	*U23*	*11.08.95*	*2*	*Cardiff*	*12*	*Mar*
	3.95			*1*	*Tullamore, IRL*	*1*	*Jul*
3.95	*Emma Andersson (SWE)*		*3.10.91*	*1*	*Helsingborg, SWE*	*25*	*Aug*
3.70	*Silvia Amabilino (LUX)*		*14.10.93*	*3*	*Philadelphia, USA*	*15*	*Apr*
3.55	*Carolin Bauer (GER)*	*U20*	*17.06.00*	*1*	*Grafelking, GER*	*27*	*May*
3.40i	*Claire Wilkinson (IRL)*		*10.02.89*	*2*	*Athlone, IRL*	*19*	*Feb*

Long Jump

6.97i		Lorraine Ugen		22.08.91	2	Belgrade, SRB	5	Mar
		6.80i			Q	Belgrade, SRB	4	Mar
		6.78	0.3		3	Eugene, USA	26	May
		6.76i			1	Birmingham	18	Feb
		6.76	0.4		2	Baie Mahault, FRA	17	May
		6.72i			1	Sheffield	12	Feb
		6.72	0.5		5	London (O)	11	Aug
		6.65	0.1		2	Brussels, BEL	1	Sep
		6.63	0.8		Q	London (O)	9	Aug
		6.61	-0.8		5	Lausanne, SUI	6	Jul
		6.59	0.4		1	Birmingham	2	Jul
		6.59	-0.5		6	London (O)	9	Jul
		6.54i			1	Athlone, IRL	15	Feb
		6.50	0.7		6	Oslo, NOR	15	Jun
		6.49w	3.0		1	Des Moines, USA	29	Apr
		6.48	-0.8		7	Berlin, GER	27	Aug
		6.46	0.2		1	Berlin (BG), GER	2	Sep
		6.46	0.3		1	Gateshead (Q)	9	Sep
		6.45	1.8		*	Des Moines, USA	29	Apr
6.75	-0.8	Katarina Johnson-Thompson		9.01.93	4	London (O)	9	Jul
		6.69i			2	Sheffield	12	Feb
		6.63	0.0		1	Montpellier, FRA	14	May
		6.56	-0.1		2H	London (O)	6	Aug
		6.53	0.7		6H	Götzis, AUT	28	May
6.73	0.4	Shara Proctor		16.09.88	1	Boston, USA	4	Jun
		6.65	1.0		2	Kawasaki, JPN	21	May
		6.63	1.3		5	Eugene, USA	26	May
		6.62	-0.4		3	Berlin, GER	27	Aug
		6.53	1.6		4	Oslo, NOR	15	Jun
		6.50	-0.5		6	Brussels, BEL	1	Sep
		6.45	-0.9		13Q	London (O)	9	Aug
6.71i		Jazmin Sawyers		21.05.94	2	Birmingham	18	Feb
		6.67i			6	Belgrade, SRB	5	Mar
		6.55w	2.8		4	Gothenburg, SWE	11	Jul
		6.54i			3	Sheffield	12	Feb
		6.54i			Q	Belgrade, SRB	4	Mar
		6.53	1.1		1	Bedford	29	May
		6.49	1.7		*	Gothenburg, SWE	11	Jul
		6.48	1.5		2	Montreuil-sous-Bois, FRA	1	Jun
		6.46	-0.4		3	Gateshead (Q)	9	Sep
		6.44	-0.3		9	London (O)	9	Jul
		6.42	-0.9		4	Villeneuve d'Ascq, FRA	25	Jun
		6.34	-0.9		20Q	London (O)	9	Aug
		6.20	0.1		10	Oslo, NOR	15	Jun
6.54	0.7	Rebecca Chapman		27.09.92	2	Birmingham	2	Jul
		6.42w	4.2		1	Southampton	6	May
		6.32			1	Exeter	30	May
		6.31	0.0		1	Cardiff	10	Jun
		6.23	0.2		2	Copenhagen, DEN	20	Jun

6.39i		Jahisha Thomas		22.11.94	3	Fayetteville, USA	10	Feb
	6.35w	2.2			8Q	Austin, USA	25	May
	6.32	1.9			2	University Park, USA	13	May
	6.28	1.3			4	Birmingham	2	Jul
	6.23i				3	Geneva, USA	24	Feb
	6.20i				2	Iowa City, USA	20	Jan
6.31	1.4	Holly Mills	U20	15.04.00	3	Birmingham	2	Jul
	6.22	1.9			1	London (CP)	10	Jun

57 performances to 6.20 by 7 athletes including 13 indoors and 4 wind assisted

6.16	0.0	Danielle McGifford	U23	11.04.95	2	Loughborough	21	May
6.16	1.3	Sarah Warnock		5.06.91	5	Birmingham	2	Jul
6.16	1.4	Eleanor Broome	U20	6.02.99	6	Birmingham	2	Jul
	(10)							
6.16w	2.6	Emily Wright	U20	13.07.98	3	Fort Worth, USA	15	Apr
	6.07	0.4			*	Fort Worth, USA	15	Apr
6.15	0.4	Simi Fajemisin	U23	15.09.97	3	Stanford, USA	21	Apr
6.13	0.9	Jessica Taylor-Jemmett		27.06.88	2H	Tallinn, EST	2	Jul
6.12w	3.5	Olivia Montez Brown	U23	22.05.96	1	Sioux Falls, USA	7	Apr
	5.85i				1	Mankato, USA	7	Jan
	5.84	-0.7			3	St. Paul, USA	12	May
6.12w	2.8	Katie Stainton	U23	8.01.95	1	Manchester (SC)	16	Aug
	6.10	-0.4			6H	Bydgoszcz, POL	14	Jul
6.11w	3.7	Jade Nimmo		23.03.91	1H	Grangemouth	2	Jul
	6.04	1.2			*	Grangemouth	2	Jul
6.09	0.8	Lucy Hadaway	U20	11.06.00	6	Loughborough	21	May
6.09		Angela Barrett		25.12.85	1	London (WL)	17	Jun
6.09w	2.7	Niamh Emerson	U20	22.04.99	4H	Grosseto, ITA	21	Jul
	6.03	-0.8			7	Birmingham	2	Jul
6.08w		Georgia Silcox	U20	14.10.98	1	Yeovil	10	Jun
	5.87	1.2			5	Bedford	29	Jul
	(20)							
6.07i		Zoe Hughes	U20	1.02.98	1P	New York, USA	25	Feb
	5.99	1.6			2H	Azusa, USA	13	Apr
6.02w	5.3	Josie Oliarnyk	U20	27.03.00	1	Nuneaton	11	Jun
	5.98	-0.6			2	Birmingham	8	Jul
6.00	0.9	Jade O'Dowda	U20	9.09.99	1H	Boston	17	Sep
6.00w	2.5	Eavion Richardson	U20	27.06.98	3	Bedford	18	Jun
	5.94				1	Bedford	8	Apr
6.00w	6.8	Ore Adamson	U17	29.10.01	1	Dublin (S), IRL	15	Jul
	5.98	1.6			2	London (CP)	10	Jun
5.97	1.9	Holly McArthur	U20	20.12.99	1	Glasgow (S)	19	Aug
5.96i		Elise Lovell		9.05.92	1P	Sheffield	8	Jan
	5.92	0.0			9	Loughborough	21	May
5.95	0.3	Mary Elcock	U23	3.08.95	8	Loughborough	21	May
5.94		Lucy Turner	U23	14.02.97	1H	Hexham	23	Jul
5.93	1.6	Jo Rowland		29.12.89	8H	Florence, ITA	29	Apr
	(30)							
5.91	1.3	Kitan Eleyae		31.10.91	2	Birmingham	6	May
5.91	0.9	Rachel Alexander	U20	13.02.98	2	Grangemouth	27	Aug
5.90i		Emma Nwofor	U23	22.08.96	1	Uxbridge	10	Dec
	5.71				1	St. Ives	8	Jul
5.88i		Anya Bates	U20	17.05.00	4	Sheffield	25	Feb
	5.76w	3.3			6	Eton	3	Jun
	5.71				4	Bromley	16	Jul
5.88	0.0	Nicole Parcell	U20	16.12.99	1	Watford	14	May
5.88		Pippa Earley	U17	7.09.00	3	Tomblaine, FRA	26	Jun
5.87	0.0	Megan Busby	U17	5.01.01	2	Birmingham	8	Jul
5.86w		Funminiyi Olajide	U17	4.06.02	1	Chelmsford	10	Jun
	5.83	0.0			Q	Birmingham	8	Jul
5.84	-0.3	Morgan Lake	U23	12.05.97	5	Bedford	29	May

5.83i		Diana Adegoke	U23	18.12.97	Q	Sheffield	18	Feb
		5.65			1	Ashford	13	May
	(40)							
5.82w	4.2	Lauren Evans	U20	7.08.00	1H	Street	30	Apr
		5.62			2	Cardiff	1	Jul
5.82w	2.4	Sara Geary		6.04.91	2	Southampton	6	May
		5.75i			2	Cardiff	28	Jan
5.81w	2.5	Joanne Ware	U23	11.08.97	1	Kingston	2	Jul
		5.64i			1	London (LV)	1	Feb
		5.61	1.8		4	London (CP)	11	Jun
5.80	1.3	Ellie McGinty	U23	12.11.97	3	Grangemouth	27	Aug
5.79w	2.5	Alexandra Burns	U20	10.08.99	4	Grangemouth	27	Aug
		5.64i			1	Glasgow	2	Feb
5.77		Eloise Harvey	U17	13.11.00	1	Dartford	15	Apr
5.76i		Anna Short	U23	29.10.96	4	Sheffield	19	Feb
		5.58w	2.2		5	Bedford	30	Apr
		5.55			1	Bromley	15	Apr
5.76		Tia Jackson	U17	5.08.02	1	Birmingham	4	Jun
5.76		Mayong Tabe	U17	23.11.01	1	Ashford	10	Jun
5.75i		Gillian Cooke		3.10.82	1	Glasgow	14	Jan
		5.60	1.9		1	Aberdeen	9	Jul
	(50)							
5.75	1.4	Hannah Dunderdale		2.11.94	9	Memphis, USA	28	Apr
5.75	1.7	Kesari Sacre	U20	4.11.99	1	Cerizay, FRA	13	May
5.75w	2.4	Jessica Hopkins	U17	6.01.02	1H	Boston	17	Sep
		5.72i			1P	Glasgow	10	Nov
		5.71			3	London (CP)	20	Aug
5.74	-1.0	Grace Bower	U20	3.11.99	4	Birmingham	8	Jul
5.74i		Emma Canning	U23	7.03.97	1	Motherwell	11	Nov
5.74w	3.2	Ellen Barber	U23	5.12.97	3H	Grangemouth	2	Jul
		5.66	1.6		8	Bedford	29	Jul
5.73		Lydia Mills	U20	1.02.98	1	Belfast	21	May
5.73w	2.2	Emily Race	U17	11.09.00	2H	Boston	17	Sep
		5.72			1	Grantham	4	Jun
5.72		Heidi Jarosinski		8.03.87	1	Worcester	13	May
5.72		Freya Tarbit	U20	24.08.00	1	Derby	4	Jun
	(60)							
5.71i		Sarah Abrams		11.01.93	1	Sutton	18	Feb
		5.69	-1.0		6	Bedford	29	May
5.70	-1.4	Lauren Thompson		12.02.92	2	Leigh	16	Jul
5.70w	4.7	Mayah Charles	U20	24.07.00	4	Southampton	6	May
		5.55	1.8		*	Southampton	6	May
5.69i		Rachel Robertson	U23	4.06.96	2	Glasgow	28	Jan
5.69		Micaela Brindle		22.02.94	1	Wigan	10	Sep
5.69w	2.9	Lucy Chappell	U23	10.01.97	5	Southampton	6	May
		5.61			2	Bedford	3	Jun
5.68	2.0	Emily Gargan	U20	29.12.98	1	Gateshead	13	May
5.68	1.7	Olivia Galloway	U20	4.07.00	1	Bournemouth	6	Aug
5.67		Alix Still	U20	15.03.00	1	Bradenton, USA	3	Mar
5.67		Izzy Wedderburn	U17	3.01.01	1	Bournemouth	14	May
	(70)							
5.67	0.7	Emily Tyrrell	U17	4.01.02	2	Exeter	17	Jun
5.67	-0.4	Milly Gall	U15	20.02.03	1	Birmingham	7	Jul
5.66w	2.9	Caitlyn Mapps	U15	27.11.02	4	Dublin (S), IRL	15	Jul
		5.52			1	Newport	22	Jul
5.65i		Montana Jackson		2.12.93	Q	Sheffield	18	Feb
5.65i	1.7	Abigail Pawlett	U17	14.01.03	1P	Glasgow	10	Nov
		5.60	1.7	U15	1P	Boston	17	Sep
5.64		Adanna Ekoku	U17	29.08.01	1	Kingston	10	Jul
5.64	0.5	Emma Gayler		4.04.88	2	London (CP)	11	Jun
5.64	1.6	Lia Stephenson	U23	4.03.96	3	London (CP)	11	Jun

5.64		Emily Thomas	U17	21.11.00	1P	Swansea	24	Jun
5.64		Macey Jones	U20	18.07.00	1	Cardiff	1	Jul
	(80)							
5.64w	2.5	Andrea Jesudason		5.12.92	6	Southampton	6	May
		5.60			3	Nottingham	5	Aug
5.64w	2.4	Iris Oliarnyk	U17	6.09.01	3H	Boston	17	Sep
5.63		Molly Palmer	U15	27.08.03	1	Rugby	18	Jun
5.63	2.0	Nikki Manson		15.10.94	5	Grangemouth	27	Aug
5.63		Niamh Bailey	U23	28.06.95	1	Corby	12	Sep
5.62	-1.9	Cleo Martin-Evans	U15	8.05.03	2	Birmingham	7	Jul
5.62		Venus Morgan	U17	5.06.01	1	Rotherham	9	Jul
5.62	0.9	Bethan Murray	U17	18.12.00	1	Leigh	19	Aug
5.62		Shanara Hibbert		22.03.93	1	Bury St. Edmunds	17	Sep
5.62i		Katie Waterworth	U20	17.05.01	1	Manchester (SC)	17	Dec
		5.55 0.0	U17		3	Bedford	26	Aug
	(90)							
5.61i		Lucy Robinson	U17	16.12.01	1	Sheffield	14	Jan
5.61		Temi Ojora	U17	24.01.02	1	Bracknell	25	Mar
5.61		Isabel Wakefield	U20	5.01.00	1	Exeter	14	May
5.61		Suzzanne Palmer		11.09.93	1	Wigan	9	Jul
5.61	1.6	Joanne Frost	V35	23.06.78	1	Aarhus, DEN	31	Jul
5.61i		Katie Garland	U23	27.01.97	1	Loughborough	9	Dec
5.60i		Clara Boothby	U23	18.09.95	8	Sheffield	19	Feb
5.60i		Anna McCauley	U17	2.01.01	2-17	Athlone, IRL	26	Mar
5.60		Libby Wheeler	U17	21.01.01	1	Hull	4	Jun
5.60		Alice Linaker	U20	6.12.99	1	Preston	5	Aug
	(100)							
5.60w	2.9	Laura Darcey	U20	28.07.98	1	Chicago, USA	22	Apr

Additional Under 17 (1-22 above)

5.59		Charlotte Ayton		17.09.00	1	Bournemouth	10	Jun
5.58		Mayi Hughes		5.11.00	1	Cambridge	2	Jul
5.58w	5.2	Lucy Davison		8.11.01	5	Dublin (S), IRL	15	Jul
5.57i		Amy Rolfe		12.12.01	2	Sheffield	17	Dec
5.56		Hannah Barnden		8.01.02	2	Derby	4	Jun
5.55w		Marcia Sey		7.11.01	1	Yeovil	10	Jun
5.54		Jessica Whitbread		12.08.01	1	Cambridge	24	Jun
5.54w	3.2	Katie Joyce		26.01.01	7H	Boston	17	Sep
	(30)							
5.53	-0.8	Devon Weymont		20.04.02	Q	Birmingham	8	Jul
5.53		Sophie Porter		14.03.01	1	Portsmouth	9	Sep
5.52i		Talia Morton-Kemsley		20.05.01	3	Sheffield	25	Feb
5.50	0.0	Lauren Tenn-Mills		16.02.01	1	Grangemouth	27	Aug
5.50i		Grace Goodsell		4.04.03	1	Sheffield	2	Dec
		5.49	U15		2	Birmingham	17	Jun
5.49		Madeline Wilton		11.04.02	1	Kingston	15	Apr
5.49		Mia Chantree		15.11.01	1P	Brentwood	24	May
5.49		Zoe Pollock		21.12.00	2H	Milton Keynes	25	Jun
5.49	0.0	Amelia MacDonald		3.05.01	Q	Birmingham	8	Jul
5.49		Emma Sherwood		12.09.01	1P	Much Wenlock	9	Jul

Additional Under 15 (1-5 above)

5.56w	3.1	Nicole Proudfoot		12.11.02	6	Dublin (S), IRL	15	Jul
		5.52			1P	Grangemouth	3	Jun
5.50		Ruby Bridger		6.05.03	1	London (CP)	19	Aug
5.46i		Lucy-Jane Matthews		17.09.02	1P	Sheffield	12	Mar
5.41		Honour Okoroji		24.01.03	Q	London (CP)	19	Aug
5.41	1.2	Erin Moffatt		12.04.03	1	Leigh	20	Aug
	(10)							
5.37		Eleanor Brown		1.10.02	1	Norwich	10	Jun
5.35i		Ellie O'Hara		4.10.02	1	Glasgow	12	Feb
		5.29			1	Grangemouth	24	Jun

5.35		Marli Jessop		27.06.03	1	Cambridge	24	Jun
5.35		Sophia Bottomley		26.10.02	1	Middlesbrough	15	Jul
5.33w		Lucy Woodward		28.11.02	1	Portsmouth	14	May
5.32	0.0	Lydia Smith		15.03.04	Q	Birmingham	7	Jul
5.30	1.0	Cleo Tomlinson		17.06.04	1	Crawley	14	May
5.30	2.0	Leisha Hunt		5.09.02	1	Chelmsford	14	May
5.28i		Kiikii Brown		20.01.04	2P	Sheffield	12	Mar
	(20)							
5.28		Tilly Smale		31.10.03	1	Bath	10	Jun
5.28		Jessica Lake		25.09.02	1P	Milton Keynes	25	Jun
5.27	0.0	Rachel Okoro		25.07.04	Q	Birmingham	7	Jul
5.26		Jasmyn Allen		14.01.03	1	Southampton	20	May
5.26i		Carys Poole		21.12.03	2P	Cardiff	7	Oct
5.26w	3.0	Demi Tuinema		2.01.03	3P	Boston	17	Sep
5.25		Yasmin Grosvenor		23.02.03	1	Aldershot	22	May
5.25		India Perry		29.06.03	2	Oxford (H)	1	Jul
5.25		Ornella Orfenov		24.10.02	1	Crawley	28	Aug
5.25w	2.9	Emily Misantoni		27.09.02	4P	Boston	17	Sep
	(30)							
5.23i		Holly Aitchison		5.12.02	5	Sheffield	25	Feb
5.23		Lily Parris		5.03.03	1P	Brentwood	24	May
5.23		Briagha Cook		28.10.02	1	Grangemouth	18	Jun

Under 13

5.34i		Julia Winogrodzka		21.10.04	1P	Glasgow	4	Mar
	5.25				1P	Peterborough	24	Sep
5.19	0.8	Erin Lobley		12.10.04	1P	Jarrow	16	Sep
5.10	-0.3	Daphney Adebayo		20.07.05	1	Leigh	20	Aug
5.09w		Iona Irvine		22.11.04	1	Portsmouth	14	May
	5.03				1	Portsmouth	25	Jun
5.02		Florence Matthews		16.11.04	1	Cardiff	15	Jul
4.97		Halle Ferguson		6.12.04	1	Manchester (Str)	29	May
4.97	0.7	Emily Kerr		12.01.05	1B	Kingston	29	Jul
4.96	1.5	Katy Beadle		27.10.04	1	Kingston	14	May
4.93	1.2	Holly Kirkwood		15.12.04	1	Glasgow (S)	19	Aug
4.91w		Grace Colmer		13.07.05	2	Portsmouth	14	May

Foreign

6.10		*Kate O'Connor (IRL)*	*U17*	*12.12.00*	*1*	*Tullamore, IRL*	*18*	*Jun*
6.02w	*3.1*	*Laura Voss (GER)*		*29.01.94*	*H*	*Cologne, GER*	*23*	*Jul*
	5.98	*-0.1*			*1*	*Dormagen, GER*	*29*	*Jun*
5.62		*Sommer Lecky (IRL)*	*U20*	*14.06.00*	*1*	*Antrim*	*20*	*May*

Triple Jump

13.82	1.5	Shara Proctor		16.09.88	1	Azusa, USA	14	Apr
	13.39	0.3			9	Villeneuve d'Ascq, FRA	24	Jun
13.68w	3.0	Naomi Ogbeta	U20	18.04.98	3	Grosseto, ITA	21	Jul
	13.64	0.4			1	Birmingham	1	Jul
	13.50	0.7			*	Grosseto, ITA	21	Jul
	13.47	1.6			2	Manchester (SC)	16	Aug
	13.36w	3.8			1	Bedford	17	Jun
	13.25	0.5			Q	Grosseto, ITA	20	Jul
	13.25w	2.9			1	Bedford	30	Apr
	13.07	1.2			*	Bedford	17	Jun
	12.96i				1	Sheffield	19	Feb
	12.94w	2.2			1	Manchester (SC)	11	Jun
13.60	1.9	Laura Samuel		19.02.91	1	Manchester (SC)	16	Aug
	13.51w	3.7			2	Clermont, USA	15	Apr
	13.36	1.4			*	Clermont, USA	15	Apr
	13.26	0.0			10	Birmingham	20	Aug
	12.97	1.6			2	Lappeenranta, FIN	26	Aug

13.44	-0.3	Sineade Gutzmore		9.10.86	2	Birmingham	1	Jul
13.39w	2.6				2	Copenhagen, DEN	20	Jun
13.32	2.0				*	Copenhagen, DEN	20	Jun
13.16	0.0				2	Loughborough	21	May
13.03	-1.1				1	Bedford	29	May
13.00w	2.9				1	Birmingham	6	May
13.43	1.5	Angela Barrett		25.12.85	3	Manchester (SC)	16	Aug
13.23					1	Cambridge	6	Aug
13.23					1	Dartford	19	Aug
13.15	1.4				1	Bedford	30	Jul
13.05	0.0				4	Birmingham	1	Jul
13.02w	2.6				1	London (He)	24	Jun
12.95	-0.3				1	Bellinzona, SUI	3	Sep
12.90					1	Sandy	23	Sep
13.27i		Alex Russell		27.03.90	1	Sheffield	12	Feb
13.10i					1	Bratislava, SVK	29	Jan
13.07i					1	Sheffield	15	Jan
12.94i					1	Sheffield	4	Jan
13.25	0.4	Jahisha Thomas		22.11.94	3	Birmingham	1	Jul
13.05w	2.2				15Q	Austin TX, USA	27	May
13.00i					1	Iowa City, USA	17	Feb
12.91w	2.8				5	University Park, USA	14	May
13.03	0.0	Emily Gargan	U20	29.12.98	3	Loughborough	21	May
13.00	1.6	Chioma Matthews	V35	12.03.81	1	Eton	3	Jun
13.00	-0.2				5	Birmingham	1	Jul
12.92	0.3				4	Loughborough	21	May
12.96i		Simi Fajemisin	U23	15.09.97	2	New York, USA	26	Feb
12.96	-0.1				13Q	Lexington, USA	27	May

45 performances to 12.90 by 10 athletes including 6 indoors and 10 wind assisted

12.87		Shanara Hibbert		22.03.93	1	Luton	15	Apr
12.66i		Montana Jackson		2.12.93	2	Sheffield	19	Feb
12.44	-0.7				7	Birmingham	1	Jul
12.57	1.7	Zara Asante		7.07.82	1	London (CP)	10	Jun
12.55w	3.4	Allison Wilder		30.10.88	2	Bedford	30	Jul
12.50	0.0				1	East Lansing, USA	31	Mar
12.48	1.6	Ahtollah Rose		6.03.93	3	Bedford	30	Jul
12.48w	3.3	Eavion Richardson	U20	27.06.98	3	Bedford	17	Jun
12.35i					3	Sheffield	19	Feb
12.18	2.0				*	Bedford	17	Jun
12.40	1.2	Laura Zialor	U20	4.08.98	1	London (CP)	11	Jun
12.36		Claudimira Landim	U20	5.07.00	1	London (WF)	25	Jun
12.33w	2.4	Lia Stephenson	U23	4.03.96	1	London (LV)	13	May
12.30	0.6				2	Bedford	18	Jun
12.30		Adelaide Omitowoju	U20	22.10.99	1	Birmingham	7	Jul
	(20)							
12.25	0.0	Jade Oni	U17	29.06.01	1	Bedford	27	Aug
12.24w	2.4	Kerri Davidson	U23	7.09.96	5	New Haven, USA	6	May
11.90i					2	Staten Island, USA	14	Jan
11.81					1	Princeton, USA	8	Apr
12.21	1.3	Jazz Sears	U17	14.12.01	2	Bedford	27	Aug
12.20		Abazz Shayaam-Smith	U20	3.04.00	3	Birmingham	7	Jul
12.19		Eloise Harvey	U17	13.11.00	1	London (CP)	19	Aug
12.18	1.6	Carolyn Harvey	U23	31.05.96	2	Grangemouth	26	Aug
12.10i		Victoria Mould	U23	11.09.95	Q	Sheffield	18	Feb
11.97w	4.2				1	Bournemouth	6	Aug
11.82	0.0				*	Bournemouth	6	Aug
12.09A	0.8	Lily Hulland	U17	1.09.01	3	Monachil, ESP	7	Jul
12.08w	2.4	Sian Swanson		1.03.93	1	Cardiff	10	Jun
11.98	1.7				*	Cardiff	10	Jun

12.07i		Anna Bates		18.05.87	8	Sheffield	12 Feb
12.07w	3.0				1	Southampton	6 May
12.04	1.9				1	Nuneaton	11 Jun
(30)							
12.05i		Yasmin Lakin	U23	8.10.95	4	Sheffield	19 Feb
11.59					1	Twickenham	18 Mar
12.05	1.2	Alexandra Burns	U20	10.08.99	3	Grangemouth	26 Aug
12.04w	3.5	Siobhan Kingham	U20	2.11.98	1	Glasgow (S)	19 Aug
11.82	2.0				*	Glasgow (S)	19 Aug
12.03		Mayi Hughes	U17	5.11.00	1	Chelmsford	10 Jun
12.02i		Gillian Cooke		3.10.82	2	Glasgow	28 Jan
11.81	0.5				1	Aberdeen	9 Jul
11.94w	2.2	Shona Ross	U20	11.08.98	6	Bedford	17 Jun
11.74	1.3				*	Bedford	17 Jun
11.93	2.0	Holly Smith	U20	22.09.99	7	Bedford	17 Jun
11.93w	2.9	Beth Mortiboy	U23	20.03.97	2	Nuneaton	11 Jun
11.76					1	Nottingham	8 Apr
11.92	1.5	Anastasia Davies	U20	9.04.99	4	Brno, CZE	16 Sep
11.90		Macey Jones	U20	18.07.00	1	Neath	16 Jul
(40)							
11.85		Victoria Oshunremi	U23	3.10.96	2	London (ME)	21 May
11.83		Grace Sullivan	U20	4.08.99	2	London (WF)	25 Jun
11.80	1.5	Georgia Green	U23	28.09.96	3	London (CP)	10 Jun
11.76w		Kamela Monks		6.05.87	2	Portsmouth	13 May
11.74i		Charlotte Ogden	U23	22.04.97	2	Birmingham	14 Jan
11.72	-0.8	Michelle Robbins-Hulse		2.06.86	2	Leigh	16 Jul
11.71		Iris Oliarnyk	U17	6.09.01	1	Birmingham	17 Jun
11.70		Hazel Shanley	U20	6.03.99	1	Leeds (South)	28 May
11.68		Georgina Lever	U20	6.12.99	4	Birmingham	7 Jul
11.68	-1.5	Libby Wheeler	U17	21.01.01	4	Birmingham	8 Jul
(50)							
11.62		Emily Maltby	U23	1.03.95	1	King's Lynn	23 Apr
11.60		Emma Pringle		10.01.92	1	Gateshead	4 Jun
11.59	1.2	Kitan Eleyae		31.10.91	5	Eton	3 Jun
11.56		Sonyce Archer	U20	3.02.99	6	Birmingham	7 Jul
11.55	-0.3	Megan Hildrew	U20	25.06.99	1	Kingston	14 May
11.55		Tania Spurling		20.08.87	1	Bury St. Edmunds	17 Jun
11.52		Sophie Worrall		30.01.94	1	Cheltenham	15 Jul
11.50		Grace Plater	U17	20.09.00	1-17	Doncaster	25 Jun
11.48	-1.6	Amber Anning	U17	18.11.00	2	Tomblaine, FRA	27 Jun
11.46		Karina Harris	U17	8.02.01	2	Ashford	10 Jun
(60)							
11.46w	3.7	Emily Thomas	U17	21.11.00	1	Wrexham	19 Aug
11.05					2	Cheltenham	19 Jul
11.44i		Kara Dobbie	U20	3.08.00	5	Glasgow	12 Feb
11.44		Diane Mapamboli	U17	9.03.02	2	Bury St. Edmunds	17 Jun
11.43		Laura Saulters		30.05.88	1	Belfast	21 May
11.41i		Angel Kerin	U20	28.08.98	5	London (LV)	29 Jan
11.15	2.0				4	Bournemouth	6 Aug
11.40i		Chanel Hemmings		21.07.94	6	London (LV)	29 Jan
11.32	1.7				6	Eton	3 Jun
11.40		Hollie Garrathy	U20	18.02.99	1	Bournemouth	25 Jun
11.40w	2.6	Sarah Melbourne	U23	12.09.96	2	Bournemouth	6 Aug
11.22					1	London (TB)	15 Apr
11.39	-1.7	Fiona Davidson	V40	29.01.73	1	Aarhus, DEN	29 Jul
11.37		Mary Adeniji	U20	13.02.99	7	Birmingham	7 Jul
(70)							
11.37		Zoe Hughes	U23	9.12.97	1	Wigan	9 Jul
11.36		Amy Lupton		31.07.94	1	Blackpool	14 May
11.35		Madeleine Smith	U20	5.02.99	2	Bournemouth	25 Jun
11.35		Andrea Jesudason		5.12.92	1	Bournemouth	10 Sep

Mark	Wind	Name	Cat	DOB	Pos	Venue	Date	
11.32		Kierra Grant	U17	17.11.01	1-17	Norwich	30	Apr
11.32		Jessica Fox		28.11.94	2	Stevenage	10	Sep
11.31		Sophie Brown	U17	16.11.01	1	Cheltenham	10	Jun
11.30		Samantha Barrett	U20	22.10.98	2	Cheltenham	26	Jul
11.29i		Hannah Pringle		5.08.94	1	Gateshead	18	Feb
11.29	1.8	Olivia Montez Brown	U23	22.05.96	11	St. Paul, USA	13	May
(80)								
11.29		Nicole Farmer	U20	19.10.99	2	Reading	25	Jun
11.29		Rebecca Johns	U17	9.11.01	1	Nuneaton	15	Jul
11.28		Katie Rowe	U20	12.04.99	1	Derby	13	May
11.28		Iona MacPherson	U17	24.05.01	1-17	Antrim	20	May
11.28	2.0	Letisha Richardson		4.01.93	2	Manchester (SC)	10	Jun
11.27		Laura Keeley		10.10.90	1	Telford	6	May
11.27		Jade Morgan		12.08.89	2	Harrow	21	May
11.26		Katie Waterworth	U17	17.05.01	2	Birmingham	17	Jun
11.26		Kerry Murch	U23	20.03.95	3	Nottingham	5	Aug
11.25		Emily Madden Forman	U20	29.09.99	4	Cardiff	12	Jul
(90)								
11.24	1.3	Ellen Robertson	U23	23.06.96	2	Grangemouth	22	Apr
11.24	0.8	Kayanna Reid	U23	11.06.97	2	Bedford	14	May
11.24		Charlotte Campion	U17	17.09.01	1	Cardiff	1	Jul
11.23i		Holly Aitchison	U17	5.12.02	1	Sheffield	18	Nov
	10.44		U15		1	Stockport	9	Apr
11.21		Donelle Arulanandam	U23	21.04.97	2	Nottingham	8	Apr
11.21i		Ellie O'Hara	U17	4.10.02	1	Glasgow	22	Dec
	11.17	0.0	U15		1	Glasgow (S)	20	Aug
11.19i		Charlotte Jones	U20	6.09.99	3C	Birmingham	14	Jan
11.19w	3.4	Belinda Sergent	U23	19.11.96	7	Southampton	6	May
11.18	-2.7	Rochelle Jones		27.09.90	1	Wigan	7	May
11.18		Rimini Miloro	U20	26.10.98	1	Derby	13	May
(100)								
11.18		Jasmine Lovell	U17	27.06.01	1	Stoke-on-Trent	10	Jun
11.17		Alice Linaker	U20	6.12.99	2	Preston	5	Aug
11.16i		Kendrea Nwaelene	U17	7.12.00	3	London (LV)	8	Jan
11.16	-0.7	Eleanor Brown	U15	1.10.02	1	Bedford	26	Aug
11.16w		Bethany Denial	U20	16.03.99	1	Boston	7	Jun
11.15i		Cara Fairgrieve	U17	13.01.02	5	Sheffield	26	Feb
11.15		Ite Aderoju	U17	9.07.01	1-17	Stevenage	28	May
11.15		Janae Duporte-Clarke	U20	20.01.00	2	Bury St. Edmunds	17	Sep

Additional Under 17 (1-24 above)

Mark		Name		DOB	Pos	Venue	Date	
11.14		Felicia Miloro		5.01.01	1	Nottingham	10	Jun
11.13		Jordan Thrower		12.09.01	1	Middlesbrough	3	Sep
11.11		Danielle Hopkins		29.12.01	2	Nuneaton	20	Aug
11.10i		Madeline Wilton		11.04.02	2	Eton	5	Mar
	11.00				1	Portsmouth	9	Apr
11.10		Nichole Harvey		29.11.00	2	London (WF)	25	Jun
11.08		Ellie Carrow		26.10.01	1	Exeter	6	Jun
(30)								
11.06i		Kate Shingler		23.09.00	7	Sheffield	26	Feb
11.01		Klaudia Walas		17.06.02	1	Reading	10	Jun

Additional Under 15 (1-3 above)

Mark		Name		DOB	Pos	Venue	Date	
11.05		Jasmine Hulland		29.11.02	6	Lorca, ESP	18	Jun
10.78	-1.2	Megan Greenway		20.02.03	3	Bedford	26	Aug
10.68		Sileena Farrell			1	Dartford	24	Sep
10.67	-0.3	Grace Goodsell		4.04.03	4	Bedford	26	Aug
10.57		Kelsey Sutherland		19.12.02	1	London (CP)	20	Aug
10.49		Eloise Longhurst		10.06.03	2	London (CP)	20	Aug
10.46		Sarris Teale		3.05.04	3	London (CP)	20	Aug
(10)								
10.43		Millie Leighton		28.10.03	1	Nuneaton	14	May

10.41	-0.5	Sofia Mella		18.12.02	1	St. Peter Port GUE	1	Aug
10.35		Charlie Yates		30.12.03	1	Loughborough	9	Aug
10.33		Ruth-Ann Otaruoh		9.01.04	4	London (CP)	20	Aug
10.32		Jessica Lake		25.09.02	1	Derby	13	May

Foreign

11.81	1.6	*Teele Palumaa (EST)*		*31.03.90*	*1*	*New Haven, USA*	*8*	*Apr*
11.59		*Judy Ekeh Udochi (ITA)*		*8.08.93*	*1*	*Nottingham*	*5*	*Aug*

Shot

17.47	Rachel Wallader		1.09.89	4	Las Palmas de GC, ESP	11	Mar
17.43i				1	Sheffield	11	Feb
17.35i				10Q	Belgrade, SRB	3	Mar
17.25i				3	Birmingham	18	Feb
17.18i				1	Vienna, AUT	28	Jan
17.08				1	Birmingham	6	May
16.90				1	Bromley	16	Jul
16.87				1	Loughborough	21	May
16.81				23Q	London (O)	8	Aug
16.70				1	Birmingham	2	Jul
15.86				1	Portsmouth	8	Jul
17.13	Amelia Strickler		24.01.94	6	Taipei, TPE	27	Aug
17.12i				1	Notre Dame, USA	4	Feb
17.03i				2	Ypsilanti, USA	24	Feb
16.94				2	Kalamazoo, USA	12	May
16.85				1	Manchester (SC)	16	Aug
16.79				1	Bedford	29	Jul
16.72				2	Bromley	16	Jul
16.65i				1	Allendale, USA	10	Feb
16.61i				10	College Station, USA	10	Mar
16.61				3	Tuscaloosa, USA	7	Apr
16.59				2	Cincinnati, USA	15	Apr
16.59				2	Birmingham	2	Jul
16.47				1	Oxford, USA	29	Apr
16.38				Q	Taipei, TPE	26	Aug
16.37				1	Charlottesville, USA	22	Apr
16.32i				3	Lexington, USA	13	Jan
16.28i				2	Bloomington, USA	27	Jan
16.25i				2	Bloomington, USA	21	Jan
16.00				17Q	Lexington, USA	27	May
17.03	Sophie McKinna		31.08.94	5	Las Palmas de GC, ESP	11	Mar
16.74i				2	Sheffield	11	Feb
16.73i				5	Birmingham	18	Feb
16.62				1	Norwich	13	May
16.61				2	Loughborough	21	May
16.36i				1	Spalding	19	Feb
16.27				1	Bury St. Edmunds	20	Aug
16.23				3	Birmingham	2	Jul
16.18i				1	London (LV)	15	Jan
16.10				2	Manchester (SC)	16	Aug
16.09				2	Eton	3	Jun
15.96				1	London (CP)	11	Jun
15.89i				1	King's Lynn	29	Jan
15.83				1	Bury St. Edmunds	17	Sep
16.64	Divine Oladipo	U20	5.10.98	2	Princeton, USA	22	Apr
16.41i				1	Birmingham, USA	24	Feb
16.03				4	Grosseto, ITA	22	Jul
16.00				18Q	Lexington, USA	27	May
15.92				1	Storrs, USA	15	Apr
15.82				2	Houston, USA	13	May

16.52	Eden Francis		19.10.88	1	Eton	3	Jun
16.29				1	Nuneaton	13	May
16.22				3	Bromley	16	Jul
16.19				2	Birmingham	6	May
16.02				4	Birmingham	2	Jul
15.88				2	Bedford	29	Jul
15.81				1	Bedford	29	May
16.27	Adele Nicoll	U23	28.09.96	3	Loughborough	21	May
16.25				1	Bedford	1	May
16.24				1	Bedford	18	Jun
16.21				3-23	Vecindario, ESP	11	Mar
16.09i				1	Cardiff	5	Mar
15.93i				3	Sheffield	11	Feb
15.90				4	Bromley	16	Jul
15.85				8	Halle, GER	20	May
65 performances to 15.80 by 6 athletes including 19 indoors							
14.59	Sophie Merritt	U20	9.04.98	1	Chelmsford	8	Jul
14.47i	Danielle Opara	U23	22.06.95	2	Sheffield	19	Feb
13.42				3	Bedford	18	Jun
14.12	Sarah Omoregie	U20	2.04.00	6	Birmingham	2	Jul
14.08	Michella Obijiaku	U23	6.11.97	5	Hattiesburg, USA	29	Apr
14.00 (10)	Kirsty Yates		14.05.93	1	Grangemouth	26	Aug
13.64	Jo Rowland		29.12.89	1	London (WL)	17	Jun
13.64	Shaunagh Brown		15.03.90	8	Bromley	16	Jul
13.62	Gaia Osborne	U20	9.08.00	1	London (CP)	10	Jun
13.61	Sophie Littlemore	U23	25.12.95	8	Birmingham	2	Jul
13.45	Toni Buckingham	U20	22.02.98	1	Cleckheaton	9	Jul
13.34	Jessica Taylor-Jemmett		27.06.88	1H	Woerden, NED	26	Aug
13.30	Mhairi Porterfield	V35	19.06.81	7	Manchester (SC)	16	Aug
13.18	Suzzanne Palmer		11.09.93	5	Bedford	29	Jul
13.08i	Emily Ball	U23	31.10.97	4	Sheffield	19	Feb
12.60				6	Bedford	1	May
13.00 (20)	Lucy Underdown		18.05.90	1	Tonbridge	17	Apr
12.99i	Rhea Southcott	U20	30.03.01	1	Sheffield	18	Nov
12.92		U17		1	Leeds	6	May
12.86	Marilyn Nwawulor		20.09.92	8	Bedford	29	Jul
12.85	Katarina Johnson-Thompson		9.01.93	3	Nice, FRA	7	May
12.79	Awen Rosser	U23	28.09.95	1	Carmarthen	14	May
12.79	Morgan Lake	U23	12.05.97	2H	Bedford	27	May
12.76	Lucy Griffiths		3.04.94	2	Carmarthen	14	May
12.73i	Zoe Hughes	U20	1.02.98	3P	College Station, USA	10	Mar
11.93				2H	New Haven, USA	6	May
12.67	Niamh Emerson	U20	22.04.99	7H	Kladno, CZE	17	Jun
12.65	Dara Adebayo	U17	14.06.02	1	Peterborough	15	Apr
12.54 (30)	Phillipa Wingate		12.05.93	1	Eton	19	Aug
12.45i	Chloe Vernon-Hamilton		11.10.92	2P	Sheffield	8	Jan
12.32				2	Leigh	16	Jul
12.45	Rebecca Hall		15.09.88	1	Colchester	17	Jun
12.42	Sabrina Fortune	U23	25.05.97	1	Loughborough	31	May
12.38	Rownita Marston	U20	17.05.98	4	Bedford	3	Jun
12.34	Freya Jones		13.11.93	3	Southampton	19	Aug
12.32	Eleanor Gatrell	V40	5.10.76	3	Southampton	19	Aug
12.28i	Emma Dakin	U20	25.12.99	2	Spalding	19	Feb
12.09				1	Birmingham	7	Jul
12.28i	Ada'ora Chigbo	U20	2.01.99	2	Sheffield	26	Feb
12.17				5	Bedford	17	Jun
12.27i	Ellie Hodgson	U20	26.08.00	1	Uxbridge	10	Dec
11.68				1	Portsmouth	17	Sep

12.23	Hannah Evenden		28.06.91	1	Cleckheaton	2	Apr
12.16	Amelia Cook	U20	31.05.00	2	Portsmouth	13	May
12.11i	Denisha Marshall-Brown	U20	11.08.00	1	Sutton	19	Feb
12.01				2	Wigan	7	May
12.11	Samantha Milner		28.12.92	2	Chelmsford	17	Jun
12.09	Ellen Barber	U23	5.12.97	4H	Woerden, NED	26	Aug
12.02	Sophie Percival	U23	30.07.97	3	Wigan	9	Jul
12.01i	Lucy Holmes		29.12.92	1B	Sheffield	7	Feb
11.88				4	Cudworth	13	May
11.98i	Hannah Dunderdale		2.11.94	1P	Birmingham, USA	21	Feb
11.82				3H	Arlington, USA	12	May
11.94	Catherine Holdsworth		3.01.86	2	Bromley	15	Apr
11.92i	Niamh Bailey	U23	28.06.95	3P	Sheffield	8	Jan
11.85				1	Loughborough	24	May
(50)							
11.90	Katie Stainton	U23	8.01.95	6H	Woerden, NED	26	Aug
11.88i	Sarah Parsons		31.05.94	6	Sheffield	14	Jan
11.65				2	Preston	5	Aug
11.86	Kiona McLennon	U20	11.02.99	4	Wigan	7	May
11.81i	Diana Norman	V40	14.06.74	1	London (LV)	26	Feb
11.49				1	Kingston	17	Jun
11.81i	Holly Bradshaw		2.11.91	2	Cardiff	10	Dec
11.79	Amy Holder	U23	4.08.96	3	Portsmouth	8	Jul
11.75i	Lucy Hadaway	U20	11.06.00	1P	Gateshead	19	Mar
11.13				2	Wakefield	9	Apr
11.72	Sophie Mace	U20	7.10.98	3	Kingston	15	Apr
11.71i	Rachel Hunter		30.08.93	1	Glasgow	28	Jan
11.70	Amy Fleming		5.10.90	1	Portsmouth	19	Aug
11.69	Jade O'Dowda	U20	9.09.99	1H	Boston	16	Sep
(60)							
11.65	Lydia Chamberlin		2.10.87	6	Leigh	16	Jul
11.61i	Emma Nwofor	U23	22.08.96	1	London (LV)	1	Feb
11.28				2	St. Ives	8	Jul
11.60	Nichole Birmingham	U20	9.01.00	1	Tipton	9	Apr
11.60	Abigail Moronkeji		15.11.90	5	London (WL)	17	Jun
11.58i	Jessica Tappin		17.05.90	2P	Glasgow	5	Mar
11.50				6H	Bedford	27	May
11.58	Megan Larkins	U20	2.08.98	1	St. Ives	8	Jul
11.52	Emma Beardmore		6.12.87	3	Leigh	16	Jul
11.47	Luisa Chantler Edmond	U20	7.06.99	1	London (TB)	15	Apr
11.47	Holly McArthur	U20	20.12.99	17H	Grosseto, ITA	20	Jul
(70)							
11.46	Stephanie Hopkinson		27.10.89	1	Whitley Bay	9	Jul
11.44	Emma Seymour	U23	3.10.95	1	Aldershot	24	May
11.41i	Lucy Turner	U23	14.02.97	9	Sheffield	19	Feb
11.17				8H	Bedford	27	May
11.39	Nia Rutter		4.01.86	1	Blackpool	14	May
11.39	Kiarra Francis	U20	18.03.00	1	Wolverhampton	25	Jun
11.34	Carol Parker	V45	22.09.69	1	Abingdon	16	Jul
11.33	Kirsty Law		11.10.86	1	Stevenage	4	Jun
11.33	Priscilla Dadzie	U20	27.11.99	3	Birmingham	7	Jul
11.33	Kiani Pay	U23	12.07.95	10	Bedford	29	Jul
11.32	Shona Crossan	U17	11.12.00	2	Glasgow (S)	19	Aug
(80)							
11.31	Helen Broadbridge		23.07.92	4	Portsmouth	8	Jul
11.29	Bethan Burley	U20	26.03.00	2H	Boston	16	Sep
11.28	Elianne Mahay-Goodrich	U20	13.11.98	6	Southampton	6	May
11.26i	Vikki Adams	U20	23.02.98	2	Sheffield	15	Jan
11.25	Lia Anderson	U17	10.09.00	3	Woking	15	Apr
11.25	Katie Holder		13.01.92	2	Cambridge	14	May

11.25i	Kaitlin Enderwick	U23	31.01.97	2	Gateshead	16	Nov
11.15				3	York	2	Sep
11.24i	Emily Dixon	U23	27.11.95	4P	Boston, USA	3	Mar
11.24i	Amy Herrington	U20	22.05.98	11	North Fargo, USA	9	Dec
11.19i	Leanne Buxton	V35	27.05.78	4P	Sheffield	8	Jan
11.19				2H	Aarhus, DEN	27	Jul
(90)							
11.18	Olivia Montez Brown	U23	22.05.96	9H	Bradenton, USA	25	May
11.17	Lucy Marshall	V35	28.11.81	1	London (TB)	23	Sep
11.16	Anika Olalere	U20	8.04.99	5	Birmingham	7	Jul
11.14i	Megan Nagy	U20	26.02.99	2P	Sheffield	7	Jan
11.13	Leah Hillman	U20	10.06.99	1	Blackpool	29	Apr
11.13	Tara Park	U23	4.04.95	2	Livingston	24	Jun
11.11i	Jade Nimmo		23.03.91	1	Glasgow	4	Feb
11.11	Kerry Murch	U23	20.03.95	1	Rugby	7	May

Additional Under 17 (1-4 above)

11.07	Tara Simpson-Sullivan		2.12.00	5	Wigan	9	Jul
11.05	Anaisa Harney		28.09.00	1	Bracknell	21	May

Foreign

15.31	*Urina Harrell (USA)*		*8.02.94*	*1*	*Loughborough*	*12*	*Jul*
13.75i	*Tatum Souza (USA)*		*20.04.92*	*3*	*Sheffield*	*19*	*Feb*
13.63				*3*	*Bedford*	*1*	*May*
13.73	*Christina Nick (GER)*		*14.11.92*	*1*	*Ellesmere Port*	*4*	*Jun*
13.33	*Moe Sasegbon (NGR)*		*16.09.91*	*1H*	*Belfast*	*2*	*Sep*
13.21	*Mathilde Bilon (FRA)*	*U23*	*13.03.97*	*7*	*Eton*	*3*	*Jun*
13.20	*Jeana Celine Freeman-Gibb (CAN)*		*8.12.91*	*1*	*London (BP)*	*8*	*Jul*
12.90	*Kate O'Connor (IRL)*	*U17*	*12.12.00*	*6H*	*Grosseto, ITA*	*20*	*Jul*
11.95	*Anna Niedbala (GER)*		*11.02.90*	*3*	*New Haven, USA*	*8*	*Apr*
11.44i	*Katy Sealy (BIZ)*		*15.10.90*	*2*	*Uxbridge*	*5*	*Mar*
11.31				*1*	*Ipswich*	*20*	*May*
11.15	*Mia Callenburg (SWE)*		*24.02.89*	*3*	*Bromley*	*15*	*Apr*

Shot - Under 18 - 3kg

16.74	Sarah Omoregie		2.04.00	2	Nassau, BAH	20	Jul
15.71	Gaia Osborne		9.08.00	1	Bedford	18	Jun

Shot - Under 17 - 3kg

15.65	Serena Vincent		5.12.01	1	Swindon	18	Nov
15.64	Rhea Southcott		30.03.01	1H	Cudworth	26	Aug
15.33	Hannah Molyneaux		11.03.01	1	Bedford	26	Aug
14.95	Amaya Scott		15.02.01	2	Tomblaine, FRA	26	Jun
14.14	Olivia Dobson		27.03.01	1H	Boston	16	Sep
14.12i	Dara Adebayo		14.06.02	1	London (LV)	21	Jan
14.06				1	Uxbridge	30	Apr
14.05	Jessica Hopkins		6.01.02	1H	Bedford	24	Jun
13.69	Emma Bakare		20.11.00	1H	Yeovil	24	Jun
13.54	Lia Anderson		10.09.00	2	Uxbridge	30	Apr
13.54	Lily Naylor		14.12.01	2	Leigh	19	Aug
(10)							
13.45	Shona Crossan		11.12.00	1	Grangemouth	9	Jun
13.45	Samantha Callaway		4.03.02	3	London (CP)	20	Aug
13.30	Hannah MacAulay		9.09.01	1	Ashford	10	Jun
13.23	Heather Cubbage		20.01.01	1	Woking	3	Sep
13.19	Zoe Price		14.04.02	1	Liverpool	9	Sep
13.12i	Ashleigh Bailey		19.01.01	6	Sheffield	25	Feb
12.96				2H	Street	29	Apr
13.07	Tara Simpson-Sullivan		2.12.00	1	Wigan	10	Sep
13.02i	Eloise Locke		19.04.01	1	London (LV)	19	Mar
12.40				1	Ashford	13	May

12.89i	Pippa Earley	7.09.00	2P	Sheffield	11	Mar
	12.42		4H	Boston	16	Sep
12.83i	Hannah Barnden	8.01.02	3P	Sheffield	11	Mar
	12.42		3	Hull	2	Jul
(20)						
12.77	Holly Benson	17.08.02	1	York	29	Jul
12.76	Iris Oliarnyk	6.09.01	1	Birmingham	23	Apr
12.71	Charlie Davey James	21.04.01	3	Exeter	17	Jun
12.68i	Charlotte Pickering-Pruvot	10.06.01	1	Gateshead	18	Feb
	12.41		1	Gateshead	9	Aug
12.60	Blessing Joshua	21.05.01	1	Norwich	10	Jun
12.54	Amy-Beth Curtis	6.02.02	4	Exeter	17	Jun
12.48	Maria Schofield	8.09.00	1	York	17	Jun
12.43	Hollie Thurgood	2.07.02	1H	Kingston	24	Jun
12.43	Kiera Canpolat	4.08.01	1	Loughborough	25	Jun
12.39	Caitlin Arnold	24.09.00	1	Bristol	20	Jun
(30)						
12.36	Sarah Hunt	11.10.01	2	Basingstoke	23	Apr
12.31i	Lucy Davison	8.11.01	1	Glasgow	1	Feb
12.30	Britli Francis	18.12.00	1	Sutton	2	Apr
12.30	Kim English	7.07.02	2	Chelmsford	14	May

Foreign

14.63	*Kate O'Connor (IRL)*	*12.12.00*	*1*	*Dublin (S), IRL*	*15*	*Jul*

Shot - Under 15 - 3kg

14.59	Bekki Roche	11.12.02	1	Bebington	10	Jun
14.33	Nana Gyedu	4.11.02	1	Bromley	14	Aug
12.94	Omolola Kuponiyi	5.03.04	1	Birmingham	2	Sep
12.73	Millie Noyce	28.11.02	2B	Portsmouth	17	Sep
12.44	Molly Hole	28.02.03	4	Bedford	27	Aug
12.28	Kenyeh Soyei	26.10.02	1	Bedford	13	Aug
12.18	Kelsey Pearce	11.02.03	3	Birmingham	8	Jul
12.10	Lucy-Jane Matthews	17.09.02	1	Southampton	20	May
12.02i	Vivien Duruh	21.10.03	1	Glasgow	28	Oct
	11.71		1	Kilmarnock	6	Aug
11.78	Zara Obamakinwa	30.03.04	6	Bedford	27	Aug
(10)						
11.69	Hope Dandjinou	19.05.03	1	Woking	3	Sep
11.58	Elizabeth Adamson	6.05.03	1	Portsmouth	2	Apr
11.45i	Amy Battle	31.05.04	1	Sheffield	5	Nov
11.41	Yasmin Grosvenor	23.02.03	8	Bedford	27	Aug
11.38	Jamie Holland	6.01.03	1P	Swansea	24	Jun
11.37	Jasmine de la Touche	4.09.02	1	Kingston	10	Jun
11.29	Teddy Tehoudja	27.03.03	1	Livingston	9	Sep
11.27	Abigail Stewart	15.10.02	6	Birmingham	8	Jul
11.19	Abigail Pawlett	14.01.03	1P	Manchester (SC)	13	Aug
11.17	Hayley Berry	4.07.03	1	Grangemouth	10	Jun
(20)						
11.13	Nicole Lannie	24.01.03	1	Cudworth	14	May
11.08	Holly Adams	30.12.03	1	Hull	10	Jun
11.02i	Erin Lobley	12.10.04	1	Sheffield	18	Nov

Shot - Under 13 - 2.72kg

12.12	Erin Lobley	12.10.04	1	Wakefield	13	Aug
11.91	Meghan Porterfield	2.09.05	1	Glasgow (S)	19	Aug
11.48	Daphney Adebayo	20.07.05	1	Manchester (Str)	28	Aug
11.07	Gabriella Jones	23.09.04	1	Aldershot	30	Jul
10.94	Lily Carlaw	25.11.04	1	St. Ives	21	Jun
10.81	Olivia Austin	31.10.04	1	Basingstoke	30	Aug
10.09	Mae Smith	21.11.04	1	Kirkby-in-Ashfield	20	May

10.05	Samaia Dhir		23.03.05	1	Reading	29	Jun
9.99	Gracie Jenvey		6.02.05	1	Swindon	4	Jun
9.96	Amelia Fettis		22.02.05	1	Bristol	20	Jun
	(10)						
9.96	Caitlin Ebbage		14.06.05	3	Kingston	29	Jul

Discus

62.15	Jade Lally		30.03.87	1	Sydney, AUS	5	Feb
	59.87			2	Canberra, AUS	11	Mar
	58.70			2	Sydney, AUS	25	Feb
	58.24			1	Kingston	13	May
	58.19			1	Dublin (S), IRL	12	Jul
	58.14			1	Birmingham	2	Jul
	57.71			19Q	London (O)	11	Aug
	57.64			1	Loughborough	21	May
	57.56			1	London (CP)	11	Jun
	56.17			1	Bromley	16	Jul
	56.07			1	Eton	3	Jun
	55.75			6	Gothenburg, SWE	11	Jul
	54.01			10	Villeneuve d'Ascq, FRA	24	Jun
	53.76			11	Halle, GER	20	May
	53.65			9	Birmingham	20	Aug
57.53	Eden Francis		19.10.88	1	Nuneaton	11	Jun
	57.44			1	Nuneaton	13	May
	54.88			1	Corby	4	Jun
	54.17			1	Birmingham	6	May
	52.15			1	Stourport	5	Aug
	51.73			1	Loughborough	26	Aug
54.91	Kirsty Law		11.10.86	1	Cheltenham	19	Jul
	54.71			6	Leiria, POR	30	Jul
	54.54			1	Grangemouth	26	Aug
	54.27			1	Stevenage	4	Jun
	54.19			6	Leiria, POR	29	Jul
	53.92			2	Loughborough	21	May
	53.40			1	Loughborough	7	Jun
	53.28			1	Leiria, POR	22	Apr
	52.79			1	Manchester (SC)	16	Aug
	52.78			1	Bebington	9	Jul
	52.73			2	Birmingham	2	Jul
	52.71			1	St. Peter Port GUE	2	Sep
	52.10			1	Leigh	16	Jul
	51.95			1	Leigh	6	May
	51.85			1	Inverness	22	Jul
	51.55			1	London (He)	24	Jun
54.27	Amy Holder	U23	4.08.96	1	Bedford	29	May
	53.05			3	Loughborough	21	May
	52.94			7-23	Vecindario, ESP	12	Mar
	52.84			1	Bedford	17	Jun
	52.47			1	Bracknell	14	May
	52.36			1	London (He)	26	Aug
	51.98			3	Eton	3	Jun
	51.81			9	Bydgoszcz, POL	14	Jul
53.13	Divine Oladipo	U20	5.10.98	13Q	Lexington, USA	26	May
	51.59			2	Philadelphia, USA	27	Apr
51.87	Phoebe Dowson		17.04.94	1	Plymouth	21	May
	51.80			1	Portsmouth	14	May
51.79	Shadine Duquemin		4.11.94	1	Derby	10	Sep
	51.67			8	Leiria, POR	30	Jul

51 performances to 51.50 by 7 athletes

50.64	Kathryn Woodcock	U23	29.04.97	1	Southampton	6	May
48.35	Samantha Milner		28.12.92	2	Derby	10	Sep
47.22A	Tara Park	U23	4.04.95	9	Logan, USA	12	May
	45.45			9	Stanford, USA	22	Apr
(10)							
46.85	Jemma Ibbetson	U23	3.09.97	1	Manchester (SC)	11	Jun
46.48	Luisa Chantler Edmond	U20	7.06.99	6	Loughborough	21	May
46.14	Heather Cubbage	U17	20.01.01	1-17	Portsmouth	17	Sep
45.76	Sophie Mace	U20	7.10.98	1	Kingston	21	May
45.44	Sophie Merritt	U20	9.04.98	4	Bedford	18	Jun
45.11	Jenny Pyatt	U20	13.10.98	1	Preston	30	Apr
45.00	Sarah Parsons		31.05.94	1	Preston	5	Aug
44.99	Sophie Littlemore	U23	25.12.95	2	Manchester (SC)	11	Jun
44.72	Helen Broadbridge		23.07.92	4	London (He)	24	Jun
44.49	Amelia Strickler		24.01.94	3	Terre Haute, USA	5	May
(20)							
44.11	Simone McKen	U20	24.09.98	1	Wrexham	24	Sep
43.72	Shaunagh Brown		15.03.90	7	Birmingham	6	May
43.30	Danielle Broom	U20	28.10.99	2	Bournemouth	15	Apr
43.20	Katie Pattison	U23	9.10.96	1	Rugby	1	Apr
43.16	Awen Rosser	U23	28.09.95	7	Loughborough	21	May
43.03	Isobel Griffin Morris	U20	8.12.99	1	Crawley	26	Jul
42.79	Grace Jenkins		27.08.93	1	London (LV)	17	Jun
42.76	Laurensa Britane		18.05.87	1	Bedford	21	May
42.59	Emma Beales	V45	7.12.71	2	Bedford	8	Apr
42.36	Alice Grosjean		19.09.93	1	Nottingham	5	Aug
(30)							
42.35	Michaela Whitton	U20	11.08.98	1	London (He)	23	Jul
42.32	Dionne Milne	U23	19.10.97	6	Bedford	17	Jun
42.32	Jessica Emery	U17	16.09.00	2	Birmingham	7	Jul
42.26	Charlotte Payne	U17	20.03.02	2	Andover	21	May
42.18	Adele Nicoll	U23	28.09.96	9	Eton	3	Jun
42.04	Samantha Callaway	U17	4.03.02	2	Bedford	26	Aug
41.62	Rachel Forder	U23	3.12.96	7	Amherst, USA	6	May
41.33	Tait Jones	U17	14.02.01	1	Kingston	10	Jun
41.28	Caitlin Emerson	U17	2.05.01	3	Loughborough	7	Jun
41.28	Bronte Jones	U20	17.10.99	1	Doncaster	25	Jun
(40)							
41.25	Georgia Kyle	U20	18.09.99	2	Manchester (SC)	10	Jun
41.22	Emma Botham	U17	28.05.01	1	Derby	10	Jun
40.87	Lucy Underdown		18.05.90	10	Birmingham	6	May
40.66	Phillipa Wingate		12.05.93	1	Kingston	22	Apr
40.42	Isobel Gray	U20	5.11.98	1	Exeter	15	Apr
40.32	Hannah Evenden		28.06.91	2	Wakefield	9	Apr
40.23	Andrea Jenkins	V40	4.10.75	1	Colchester	17	Jun
40.10	Emma Dakin	U20	25.12.99	1	Nuneaton	11	Jun
40.10	Denisa Mihalcea	U20	17.01.00	1	Harrow	25	Jun
40.00	Hayley Rubery		5.09.93	4	Bedford	3	Jun
(50)							
39.82	Emily Robinson	U20	22.06.00	1	Crawley	14	May
39.77	Hannah MacAulay	U17	9.09.01	4	Bedford	26	Aug
39.60	Zara Obamakinwa	U15	30.03.04	1	Oxford (H)	9	Sep
39.48	Emma Sharpe	U17	9.05.01	2	Abingdon	19	Aug
39.45	Kimberley Carter	U23	18.07.95	2	Nuneaton	11	Jun
39.28	Maya Mellor	U20	19.02.00	1	Wakefield	5	Aug
39.21	Lia Anderson	U17	10.09.00	1	Poole	16	Jul
39.12	Amber Simpson	U20	3.01.99	1	Crewe	5	Aug
38.99	Gabrielle Quigley	U20	5.11.99	1	Dartford	16	Aug
38.79	Chloe Jones	U20	1.10.99	2	Cheltenham	19	Jul
(60)							

38.66	Emily Ball	U23	31.10.97	1	Wigan	7	May
38.63	Taia Tunstall	U17	9.01.02	1	Grays	3	Sep
38.56	Eve Hodson	U20	21.01.99	1	Loughborough	25	Jun
38.19	Carla Letheby		10.09.93	3	Kingston	13	May
38.18	Caitlin Stacey	U20	6.12.99	1	Reading	10	Jun
38.09	Sarah Hewitt	V40	31.01.74	1	Crawley	14	May
38.08	Bevhan Trevis	U20	9.01.99	4	Grangemouth	26	Aug
38.02	Melanie Harrison		27.11.85	2	London (LV)	9	Apr
37.98	Melina Irawo	U20	9.07.00	1	Crawley	10	Jun
37.83	Melissa Bird	U20	18.09.98	2	Exeter	17	Jun
	(70)						
37.78	Jemma Bate	V35	13.03.82	4	Leigh	16	Jul
37.73	Sabrina Fortune	U23	25.05.97	2	Wrexham	24	Sep
37.57	Kelse Hutchinson		6.10.94	4	Nuneaton	11	Jun
37.36	Shona Crossan	U17	11.12.00	1	Grangemouth	26	Aug
37.34	Jo Rowland		29.12.89	2	London (WL)	17	Jun
37.32	Megan Larkins	U20	2.08.98	1	Luton	20	Aug
37.13	Sophie O'Hara	U20	3.08.99	3	Hull	30	Apr
37.08	Stephanie Owens		6.09.90	2	York	6	May
37.06	Alice Baxendale	U17	31.10.01	1	Dublin (S), IRL	5	Aug
37.04	Carys Marsden	U20	10.03.00	1	Bromley	22	May
	(80)						
37.02	Anna Peers	U23	28.08.97	1	Preston	1	Jul
36.92	Emma Beardmore		6.12.87	5	Stevenage	4	Jun
36.92	Charlotte Pickering-Pruvot	U17	10.06.01	1	Middlesbrough	5	Aug
36.78	Carol Parker	V45	22.09.69	1	Nuneaton	13	May
36.61	Kirsty-Anne Ebbage	U17	30.08.02	1-17	Luton	30	Apr
36.60	Nina Prells		22.07.94	2	Swansea	29	Jul
36.42	Abigail Thompson	U17	7.12.00	1-17	Bolton	25	Jun
36.30	Danielle Opara	U23	22.06.95	3	London (WL)	17	Jun
36.00	Jessica Hirst	U20	27.05.99	1	Halifax	9	Jul
35.97	Eleanor Gatrell	V40	5.10.76	2	Woking	15	Apr
	(90)						
35.84	Zoe Yule	U20	27.08.98	2	Grangemouth	22	Apr
35.82	Megan Tuck		26.04.92	1	Bournemouth	14	May
35.79	Katie Lyons	U17	8.11.01	1	Harrow	25	Jun
35.78	Jessica Williams	U20	6.07.00	3	Eton	19	Aug
35.67	Toni Buckingham	U20	22.02.98	2	Cleckheaton	9	Jul
35.59	Denisha Marshall-Brown	U20	11.08.00	1	Rugby	4	Jun
35.59	Mia O'Daly	U17	10.11.01	1	Exeter	6	Jun
35.49	Nicola Gregory	U23	2.04.96	1	Cambridge	19	Aug
35.45	Danielle Jones	U17	5.08.01	1-17	Cheltenham	28	May
35.38	Rebecca Hall		15.09.88	2	Crawley	8	Jul
	(100)						
35.01	Stephanie Hopkinson		27.10.89	2	Whitley Bay	9	Apr

Additional Under 17 (1-19 above)

34.66	Grace Thompson		30.11.01	6	Dublin (S), IRL	15	Jul
	(20)						
33.92	Rhian Evans		28.08.01	1	Swansea	9	Apr
33.74	Precious Hamilton		5.03.02	1	Bury St. Edmunds	17	Jun
33.69	Tara Simpson-Sullivan		2.12.00	3	York	6	May
33.07	Rosie Brown		6.09.01	2	Luton	4	Jun
32.63	Emma Hunter		14.02.02	3	Bournemouth	25	Jun
32.36	Megan Lockwood		17.06.02	1	Cleckheaton	7	Jun
32.00	Eleanor Hoyle		24.10.00	2	Norwich	30	Apr

Additional Under 15 (1 above)

34.41	Anna Merritt		3.10.02	1	Portsmouth	17	Sep
33.11	Alice Brown		1.11.03	3	Oxford (H)	9	Sep
32.82	Elizabeth Adamson		6.05.03	1	Basingstoke	17	Jun

32.46	Bekki Roche		11.12.02	1	Litherland	2	Sep
32.11	Elsie Christopher-Soares		12.11.03	2	Birmingham	7	Jul
32.01	Hayley Berry		4.07.03	4	Bedford	27	Aug
31.78	Katie Wright		26.05.03	1	Nuneaton	19	Aug
31.67	Holly Cooper		1.11.02	3-16	Dublin (S), IRL	5	Aug
31.20	Robyn Moody		3.01.03	1	Bedford	3	Sep
(10)							
31.14	Auguste Zakelyte		24.02.03	1	Birmingham	17	Jun
30.67	Ellie Lovett		13.02.03	1	Portsmouth	10	Jun
30.63	Kara Thompson		30.06.03	2	Kilmarnock	12	May
30.12	Alix Fairley		7.08.03	2	Livingston	24	May
30.10	Anjelina Manase		14.10.03	1	Reading	10	Jun
30.00	Sophie Graham		16.05.03	3	Bedford	3	Sep
29.98	Holly Pemberton		8.12.02	1	Ellesmere Port	3	Sep
29.93	Orla Manchester		18.06.03	1	Aldershot	30	Jul
29.91	Cassey Grimwade		27.09.02	1	Cardiff	5	Sep
29.57	Katie Webb		1.12.03	1	Grays	3	Sep
(20)							
29.02	Ellen Madden		28.04.04	2	Bangor, NI	25	Jul

Foreign

45.52	*Christina Nick (GER)*		*14.11.92*	*1*	*Wigan*	*9*	*Jul*
44.62	*Anna Niedbala (GER)*		*11.02.90*	*1*	*Cambridge*	*14*	*May*
41.26	*Eleni Zembashi (CYP)*	*U23*	*8.04.96*	*1*	*Swansea*	*9*	*Apr*
36.46	*Mia Callenburg (SWE)*		*24.02.89*	*1*	*Basingstoke*	*21*	*May*
35.93	*Stephanie Filbay (AUS)*		*29.09.88*	*2*	*London (LV)*	*4*	*Mar*
35.52	*Barbara Norris (SUI)*	*V50*	*20.08.66*	*1*	*Ewell*	*7*	*Oct*
35.41	*Emma O'Hara (IRL)*	*U23*	*3.04.95*	*5*	*College Park, USA*	*5*	*May*

Discus - Under 13 - 0.75kg

33.89	Samaia Dhir	23.03.05	1	Woking	3	Sep
32.78	Lily Carlaw	25.11.04	1	Kettering	30	Sep
32.73	Olivia Austin	31.10.04	1	London (TB)	26	Aug
31.81	Meghan Porterfield	2.09.05	1	Livingston	9	Sep
31.32	Gypsy Nash	29.11.04	1	Erith	17	Sep
30.58	Molly Smith	25.09.04	1	Hereford	9	Sep
30.07	Lucinda White	4.02.05	2	Woking	3	Sep
29.96	Caitlin Ebbage	14.06.05	2	Erith	17	Sep
29.39	Nicole Saunders	18.09.04	1	Blackpool	26	Aug
28.82	Isla Page	1.09.04	1	Basingstoke	9	Sep

Hammer

73.97	Sophie Hitchon	11.07.91	2	Kawasaki, JPN	21	May
	73.68		4	Ostrava, CZE	27	Jun
	73.05		Q	London (O)	5	Aug
	72.32		7	London (O)	7	Aug
	72.02		4	Warsaw, POL	15	Aug
	70.96		2	Birmingham	20	Aug
	70.91		4	Prague, CZE	5	Jun
	69.30		5	Villeneuve d'Ascq, FRA	24	Jun
	68.20		6	Szczecin, POL	10	Jun
	67.58		1	Birmingham	1	Jul
66.46	Rachel Hunter	30.08.93	1	Loughborough	26	Feb
	64.74		1	Loughborough	22	Jul
	64.21		5B	Las Palmas de GC, ESP	11	Mar
	63.67		1	Kilmarnock	12	May
	63.27		2	Birmingham	1	Jul
	61.45		3	Loughborough	21	May

65.32	Carys Parry	V35	24.07.81	1	Cardiff	10	Jun
65.01				1	Cardiff	12	Jul
64.25				2	Loughborough	22	Jul
63.52				1B	Leiria, POR	30	Jul
63.24				2	Leiria, POR	29	Jul
62.72				4	Budapest, HUN	3	Jun
63.41	Sarah Holt		17.04.87	3	Loughborough	22	Jul
63.40				1	Loughborough	21	May
61.53				3	Birmingham	1	Jul
61.31				2	Bedford	29	Jul
63.05	Jessica Mayho		14.06.93	1	Vila Nova de Cerveira, POR	22	Apr
61.62				1	Cudworth	13	May
61.00				3	Birmingham	6	May
60.54				2	Cork, IRL	18	Jul
60.53				5	Loughborough	21	May
60.43				3	Loughborough	9	Apr
62.97	Myra Perkins		21.01.92	1	Bromley	16	Jul
62.54				2	Loughborough	21	May
62.10				1	Loughborough	29	Oct
61.90				4	Loughborough	22	Jul
61.48				1	Grangemouth	27	Aug
61.46				1	Loughborough	9	Apr
61.38				1	Hull	7	Oct
61.33				2	Cardiff	12	Jul
61.31				2	Birmingham	6	May
61.27				4	Birmingham	1	Jul
61.25				1B	Loughborough	29	Oct
61.14				2	Loughborough	24	May
61.10				1	Liverpool	9	Sep
60.41				1	Loughborough	16	Sep
60.34				1	Manchester (SC)	16	Aug
62.96	Christina Jones		5.04.90	1	Yate	13	May
60.91				1	Swansea	26	Apr
60.18				4	Loughborough	9	Apr
60.13				4	Loughborough	26	Feb
62.74	Lucy Marshall	V35	28.11.81	2	Cardiff	10	Jun
62.32				1	Loughborough	24	May
61.35				1	Woodford	20	May
61.32				3	Bromley	16	Jul
61.29				1	Nuneaton	11	Jun
61.11				2	Loughborough	9	Apr
61.03				5	Birmingham	1	Jul
60.76				1	Corby	14	May
60.71				3	Loughborough	26	Feb
60.71				6	Loughborough	22	Jul
60.31				4	Birmingham	6	May
60.14				1	London (FP)	15	Apr
62.07	Susan McKelvie		15.06.85	1	Birmingham	6	May
61.80				1	Bedford	29	Jul
61.75				2	Bromley	16	Jul
61.59				5	Loughborough	22	Jul
61.08				4	Loughborough	21	May
60.36				2	Grangemouth	27	Aug

69 performances to 60.00 by 9 athletes

59.76	Phillipa Wingate		12.05.93	1	Kingston	2	Jul
(10)							
59.57	Hayley Murray		13.09.89	3	Cork, IRL	18	Jul
59.38	Kayleigh Presswell	U23	14.03.95	2	Hull	7	Oct
59.14	Amy Herrington	U20	22.05.98	3	Fargo, USA	21	Apr
58.59	Rebecca Keating	U23	31.08.97	22Q	Austin, USA	25	May

58.27	Annabelle Palmer		21.09.94	1	Derby	14	May
58.27	Katie Lambert	U20	6.11.98	8	Loughborough	21	May
57.96	Olivia Stevenson	U20	9.10.99	1	Hull	10	Jun
57.43	Anna Purchase	U20	15.09.99	1	Nottingham	30	Apr
56.69	Philippa Davenall	U20	26.09.98	1	London (CP)	11	Jun
56.67	Danielle Broom	U20	28.10.99	1	Bournemouth	10	Jun
	(20)						
56.43	Amber Simpson	U20	3.01.99	4	Cardiff	10	Jun
56.03	Alice Barnsdale	U20	23.02.99	1	Leiria, POR	29	Jul
55.25	Katie Head	U20	9.12.99	4	Bedford	17	Jun
54.49	Molly Walsh	U20	23.06.00	3	Loughborough	16	Sep
54.06	Sara Bobash		1.02.94	7	Birmingham	6	May
54.04	Shaunagh Brown		15.03.90	1	Bromley	15	Apr
53.84	Megan Larkins	U20	2.08.98	1	Colchester	19	Aug
53.67	Helen Broadbridge		23.07.92	1	Andover	21	May
53.65	Maggie Okul	U23	1.10.97	2	Rotherham	9	Jul
53.55	Hannah Evenden		28.06.91	1	Cleckheaton	2	Apr
	(30)						
53.15	Mhairi Porterfield	V35	19.06.81	1	Livingston	24	Jun
53.06	Stephanie Fowler	U20	3.08.99	1	Sheffield	23	Jul
52.80	Natalie Robbins	U20	30.11.98	4	Grangemouth	27	Aug
52.27	Charlotte Payne	U17	20.03.02	2	Andover	21	May
52.23	Charlotte Williams	U17	20.09.01	1B	Hull	7	Oct
52.20	Ffion Palmer	U20	20.03.00	1	Bath	28	Jun
51.05	Gemma Vickery	U23	4.04.96	1	London (Cr)	8	Jul
50.67	Jenna Wheatman		6.03.84	1	Wakefield	13	Aug
50.40	Aislinn Baird		4.11.91	1	Abingdon	8	Jul
50.28	Tara Simpson-Sullivan	U17	2.12.00	1	Wigan	9	Jul
	(40)						
50.06	Cathy Coleman	U20	3.07.98	1	Guildford	19	Aug
50.04	Georgina Howe		18.09.93	2	Colchester	19	Nov
49.89	Jenna Winson		7.11.90	1	Derby	4	Jun
49.71	Andrea Jenkins	V40	4.10.75	1	Colchester	17	Jun
49.51	Holly Rodgers	U23	3.02.97	1	Manchester (Str)	27	Jun
49.41	Emma Beardmore		6.12.87	1	London (BP)	8	Jul
49.38	Amelia Strickler		24.01.94	15	Oxford, USA	1	Apr
49.36	Victoria Wiltshire	U20	1.10.99	3	Reading	25	Jun
49.08	Amy Clemens		24.10.92	4	London (CP)	10	Jun
48.81	Ellie Chandler	U20	18.09.98	1	Portsmouth	17	Sep
	(50)						
48.77	Sophie Mace	U20	7.10.98	1	Kingston	14	May
48.76	Amy Clarke		22.04.86	1	Visby, SWE	28	Jun
48.73	Tara Park	U23	4.04.95	6	Davis, USA	11	Mar
48.63	Katie Ord	U23	4.12.96	3	Kilmarnock	12	May
47.93	Stephanie Owens		6.09.90	1	Wrexham	13	May
47.93	Phoebe Baggott	U17	11.11.01	2	Wolverhampton	4	Jun
47.84	Michella Obijiaku	U23	6.11.97	5	Arlington, USA	13	May
47.59	Leah Runnacles	U20	2.10.99	3	Bromley	28	May
47.56	Kelse Hutchinson		6.10.94	1	Derby	10	Sep
47.46	Emma Rae	U20	27.06.00	2	London (He)	23	Jul
	(60)						
47.39	Vicki Pellett	U20	19.10.99	1	Crawley	14	May
47.32	Stephanie Howe	U20	19.01.99	4	Woodford	20	May
46.96	Heather Fawcett	U20	21.01.00	3	Sheffield	23	Jul
46.86	Caitlin Price	U20	25.12.98	2	Manchester (SC)	11	Jun
46.74	Ellen Thrall	U20	8.05.98	2	Bath	2	Apr
46.65	Candy Lockett	U20	13.05.99	8	Birmingham	7	Jul
46.60	Lana Fulcher	U20	27.04.99	Q	Birmingham	7	Jul
46.55	Emma Bowie	U23	22.12.96	1	Inverness	12	May
45.82	Maria Brett	U23	16.10.95	5	Bedford	29	Apr
45.70	Ellie White	U20	10.07.99	2	Bournemouth	2	Apr

45.28	Lauren Hill	U17	19.09.00	3	Hull	4	Jun
45.09	Zoe Price	U17	14.04.02	2	Leigh	6	May
44.98	Shannon Waldron	U17	8.09.01	6	Glasgow (S)	19	Aug
44.96	Chloe Cockell	U23	23.10.95	5	Woodford	20	May
44.80	Carys Smith	U23	15.01.97	1	Bath	28	Jun
44.47	Bekki Roche	U17	11.12.02	1-15	Derby	14	Oct
44.34	Hannah Morgan	U23	3.10.97	6	Bedford	29	Apr
44.31	Lucy Knott	U23	9.01.95	5	Brunswick, USA	21	Apr
44.05	Poppy Bean	U20	18.08.00	1	Derby	14	May
44.01	Hannah Farrell	U23	22.03.95	1	Whitehaven	9	Apr
(80)							
43.97	Kirsty Costello	U15	22.09.02	2	Linwood	10	Sep
43.91	Lauren Aldridge	U20	9.04.99	2	Cambridge	24	Jun
43.84	Leah Weatheritt	V40	18.09.74	1	Gateshead	4	Jun
43.74	Phoebe Dowson		17.04.94	3	Bournemouth	10	Sep
43.66	Paige Barnes	U20	9.01.99	4	Loughborough	26	Aug
43.62	Carla Letheby		10.09.93	2	Kingston	14	May
43.49	Emily Pearce	U20	24.02.99	1	Cheltenham	26	Jul
43.24	Maria Schofield	U17	8.09.00	3	Ellesmere Port	4	Jun
43.23	Lynsey Glover		3.12.87	1	Donegal, IRL	30	Apr
43.17	Jasmine Routledge	U17	4.06.02	3	Loughborough	29	Oct
(90)							
43.11	Kirsty Finlay	U17	2.09.01	1	Corby	4	Jun
43.05	Zoya Styles	U20	26.12.99	1	Perivale	25	Jun
43.03	Laura Duke		12.10.89	4	Milton Keynes	19	Aug
42.72	Mia Shepherd	U23	9.04.97	7	Grangemouth	27	Aug
42.71	Donna Kent		21.01.90	1	Cambridge	19	Aug
42.69	Louise Webster		19.07.85	2	Stoke-on-Trent	5	Aug
42.68	Chrissie Prince	U20	6.10.98	2	Tipton	20	Jun
42.66	Larissa Carter	U20	2.05.00	1	Lewes	9	Jul
42.65	Kathryn Woodcock	U23	29.04.97	3	Abingdon	8	Jul
42.60	Zoe Yule	U20	27.08.98	4	Grangemouth	16	Apr
(100)							
42.56	Megan Tuck		26.04.92	1	Bournemouth	14	May
42.53	Rhianne Moore-Martin	U17	21.09.01	3	Stoke-on-Trent	5	Aug
42.29	Grace Jenkins		27.08.93	2	Wigan	7	May
42.26	Ros Stansbury	V40	27.12.74	2	Portsmouth	13	May
42.24	Nicola McRae	U20	8.09.99	18Q	Birmingham	7	Jul
42.00	Bethany Mitchell		13.11.92	1	Kirkby-in-Ashfield	6	May

Additional Under 17 (1-12 above)

41.81	Cerys Thomas		7.04.01	1	Portsmouth	17	Sep
41.71	Hannah Blood		15.06.01	3	Bebington	4	Jun
41.58	Charlotte Stuchbury		18.10.00	4	Bebington	4	Jun
40.70	Amy Davies		27.04.01	3	Colchester	19	Aug
40.00	Jessica Pelham		19.04.01	3	Bournemouth	15	Apr
39.49	Anastasia Banbury		19.08.01	3	Kingston	15	Apr
39.10	Andreea Golban		30.01.02	7	Woodford	20	May

Foreign

61.76	Alice Delmer (FRA)		30.12.93	1	Marseille, FRA	14	Jul
60.80	Cathrine Beatty (CYP)		12.07.93	2	Loughborough	26	Feb
58.32	Emma O'Hara (IRL)	U23	3.04.95	5	Princeton, USA	21	Apr
57.47	Allessandra Wall (SWE)	U23	11.02.95	7	Loughborough	9	Apr
49.05	Jade Williams (IRL)	U17	22.04.01	1	Athlone, IRL	25	Jun
48.14	Anna Niedbala (GER)		11.02.90	1	Cambridge	14	May
47.35	Debbie McCaw (NZL)	V35	1.01.80	4	Perivale	17	Jun
45.79	Harriet Ahlgren (FIN)		19.05.88	1	Espoo, FIN	2	Aug

Hammer - Under 18 - 3kg

63.52	Molly Walsh		23.06.00	1	Wrexham	24	Sep
62.00	Philippa Davenall		26.09.98	1	Colchester	5	Mar

Hammer - Under 17 - 3kg

63.23	Tara Simpson-Sullivan	2.12.00	1	Wigan	10	Sep
60.53	Charlotte Williams	20.09.01	1-18	Loughborough	9	Apr
59.21	Phoebe Baggott	11.11.01	1	Wolverhampton	25	Jun
59.09	Charlotte Payne	20.03.02	1	London (CP)	19	Aug
56.49	Zoe Price	14.04.02	1	Manchester (Str)	25	Apr
55.83	Laura Runciman	19.05.01	1	Chelmsford	25	Jun
54.77	Lauren Hill	19.09.00	1	Derby	14	May
54.36	Ella Lovibond	26.11.01	3	Loughborough	1	Sep
53.59	Anna Loughlin	25.10.00	1	Bristol	5	Apr
52.90	Shannon Waldron	8.09.01	1	Grangemouth	27	Aug
(10)						
52.37	Jasmine Routledge	4.06.02	1	Loughborough	25	Jun
51.94	Kirsty Finlay	2.09.01	2	Loughborough	25	Jun
51.84	Heather Cubbage	20.01.01	1	Portsmouth	13	May
51.69	Rhianne Moore-Martin	21.09.01	1	Loughborough	14	Jun
51.06	Caitlin Batcheldor	23.04.02	1	Exeter	17	Jun
51.01	Andreea Golban	30.01.02	2	Chelmsford	10	Jun
50.96	Lucy Koenigsberger	4.09.01	1	Norwich	13	May
50.90	Bethan Gammon	10.03.01	1	Wrexham	20	Aug
50.58	Cerys Thomas	7.04.01	8	Birmingham	7	Jul
50.09	Maria Schofield	8.09.00	1	Sheffield	23	Jul
(20)						
50.00	Anastasia Banbury	19.08.01	1	Kingston	14	May
49.55	Alice Steer	9.03.01	2	Reading	25	Jun
49.47	Jessica Pelham	19.04.01	1	Guildford	30	Apr
49.06	Hannah Blood	15.06.01	1	Manchester (Str)	27	Jun
47.89	Amy Wright	3.04.02	1	Peterborough	2	Jul
47.32	Abbie White	20.06.02	1	Exeter	4	Jun
47.17	Lara Spacey	26.08.02	1	Swansea	29	Jul
47.05	Martyna Kolan	23.02.02	3	Birmingham	3	Sep
47.03	Karolinka Bacakova	13.04.02	1	Carmarthen	25	May
46.81	Jasmine Trapnell	15.02.02	3	Rugby	28	May
(30)						
46.75	Charlotte Stuchbury	18.10.00	2	Wrexham	23	Jul
46.58	Kirsty-Anne Ebbage	30.08.02	3	Basingstoke	17	Jun
46.48	Lily Naylor	14.12.01	4-18	Loughborough	9	Apr
46.10	Rachel MacLennan	3.04.02	1	Livingston	8	Apr
46.10	Libby Taylor	16.08.02	1	Stevenage	13	Aug
46.08	Emma Sharpe	9.05.01	1	Plymouth	16	Jul
46.05	Amy Davies	27.04.01	1	Bury St. Edmunds	17	Jun

Foreign

61.09	*Jade Williams (IRL)*	*22.04.01*	*1*	*Dublin, IRL*	*6*	*Aug*

Hammer - Under 15 - 3kg

57.83	Kirsty Costello	22.09.02	2	Dublin (S), IRL	5	Aug
54.26	Bekki Roche	11.12.02	1	Wigan	10	Sep
49.97	Francesca Williams	7.02.03	3	Bedford	26	Aug
49.89	Evie Tipping	13.06.03	4	Liverpool	9	Sep
48.29	Anna Merritt	3.10.02	1	Portsmouth	13	May
46.84	Cassey Grimwade	27.09.02	1	Cardiff	8	Aug
42.92	Elizabeth Finch	6.09.02	2	London (CP)	20	Aug
42.86	Simbiyat Sikiru	5.10.02	1	Stevenage	13	Aug
42.43	Phoebe March	4.12.02	1	Basingstoke	9	Sep
42.23	Stephanie Browne	28.11.02	2	Oxford (H)	9	Sep
(10)						
42.17	Tilly Allsopp	5.06.03	8	Bedford	26	Aug
41.83	Alix Fairley	7.08.03	2	Glasgow (S)	20	Aug
41.70	Lucy Forrest	8.10.02	1	Rotherham	17	Jul
41.58	Emma Hames	30.03.03	1	Swansea	9	Jul

41.37	Stella Coutts		25.09.03	1	Livingston	8	Apr
40.75	Lara Moffat		22.09.03	1	Milton Keynes	10	Jun
40.44	Orla Manchester		18.06.03	2	Basingstoke	9	Sep
39.49	Jessica Bennett		6.02.03	2	Birmingham	2	Sep
39.42	Amy Money		2.08.03	1	Bury St. Edmunds	17	Sep
38.80	Hannah Garrett		9.11.02	4	Glasgow (S)	20	Aug
	(20)						
38.58	Saada Juma		22.05.03	1	Middlesbrough	15	Jul
38.43	Meghan Sharman		4.01.03	5	Birmingham	8	Jul
38.33	Katie Donnelly		29.06.03	4	London (LV)	8	Apr

Hammer - Under 13 - 3kg

47.10	Lily Murray		17.01.05	1	Bromley	12	Jun
40.85	Katie Gibson		8.12.04	1	Kettering	30	Sep
40.03	Gypsy Nash		29.11.04	1	London (TB)	26	Aug
33.09	Dawn Russell		14.12.04	1	Wishaw	27	Sep
31.95	Danielle McNamara		16.11.04	2	Grangemouth	7	Jun

Javelin

55.74	Laura Whittingham		6.06.86	3	Rovereto, ITA	29	Aug
54.88				1	Bedford	30	Jul
53.64				1	Stevenage	4	Jun
53.30				1	Loughborough	21	May
53.01				1	St. Peter Port GUE	2	Sep
52.07				1	Birmingham	2	Jul
51.60				3	Domažlice, CZE	15	Sep
51.56				2	Manchester (SC)	16	Aug
51.52				2	Loughborough	28	May
51.52				1	Bury St. Edmunds	28	Sep
51.33				1	Leigh	16	Jul
51.27				1	Nuneaton	11	Jun
50.37				1	Cardiff	12	Jul
53.52	Jo Blair subject to possible drugs dq		1.03.86	1	Nicosia, CYP	29	Apr
52.63				1	Bedford	14	May
52.47				1	Eton	3	Jun
51.74				1	Loughborough	28	May
51.31				2	Birmingham	2	Jul
50.63				1	London (CP)	10	Jun
50.61				9	Villeneuve d'Ascq, FRA	25	Jun
50.44				6	Melbourne (A), AUS	11	Feb
50.24				6	Melbourne (A), AUS	4	Feb
50.12				1	Bromley	16	Jul
51.57	Hannah Johnson		14.06.94	2	Loughborough	21	May
51.02	Emma Hamplett	U20	27.07.98	3	Birmingham	2	Jul
50.45	Kike Oniwinde		6.10.92	3	Loughborough	21	May
	26 performances to 50.00 by 5 athletes						
49.56	Bethan Rees	U20	27.10.99	4	Birmingham	2	Jul
49.56	Kelly Bramhald		10.06.94	2	Bedford	30	Jul
49.24	Louise Lacy		28.04.89	4	Bedford	30	Jul
49.13	Laurensa Britane		18.05.87	4	Manchester (SC)	16	Aug
47.68	Natasha Wilson	U23	5.11.95	5	Birmingham	2	Jul
	(10)						
47.67	Freya Jones		13.11.93	1	Southampton	19	Aug
46.70	Eloise Meakins		26.01.93	1	Watford	14	May
46.59	Rebekah Walton	U20	20.09.99	3	Bedford	17	Jun
44.76	Rosie Semenytsh		28.05.87	8	Bedford	30	Jul
44.73	Kerry Murch	U23	20.03.95	1	Birmingham	4	Jun
44.18	Leah Hillman	U20	10.06.99	3	Birmingham	8	Jul
44.15	Gemma Thrower	U23	20.01.96	1	London (BP)	19	Aug
43.82	Kate Davies	U23	27.09.95	1	New Haven, USA	8	Apr

43.58	Denisa Mihalcea	U20	17.01.00	4	Bedford	17	Jun
43.54	Aileen Rennie		21.02.94	1	Glasgow (S)	13	Aug
(20)							
43.53	Sophie Percival	U23	30.07.97	1	Warrington	14	May
43.51	Ellen Barber	U23	5.12.97	1H	Grangemouth	2	Jul
43.18	Katie Stainton	U23	8.01.95	6H	Kladno, CZE	18	Jun
43.02	Hollie Arnold		26.06.94	1F46	London (O)	15	Jul
42.86	Sarah Ellis		27.10.83	1	Dartford	15	Apr
42.40	Nicole Davenport	U23	31.03.96	2	Bedford	29	Apr
42.27	Bobbie Griffiths	U17	15.03.01	1	Gateshead	4	Jun
42.21	Georgie Floyd	U23	17.05.95	1	Welwyn	14	Apr
42.17	Maia Dart	U20	2.06.00	3J	Loughborough	29	May
42.00	Elspeth Jamieson	U23	5.09.96	4	Bedford	18	Jun
(30)							
41.93	Morgan Lake	U23	12.05.97	7H	Florence, ITA	29	Apr
41.84	Georgie McTear	U20	20.07.99	1	Yeovil	13	May
41.72	Emily Dibble	U20	17.09.99	2	Yeovil	13	May
41.72	Katarina Johnson-Thompson		9.01.93	20H	London (O)	6	Aug
41.69	Millie Cavanagh	U20	16.07.99	6	Pihtipudas, FIN	29	Jun
41.58	Jo Rowland		29.12.89	8H	Florence, ITA	29	Apr
41.48	Gaia Osborne	U20	9.08.00		Pihtipudas, FIN	29	Jun
41.38	Zoe Fitch	U23	22.09.97	2	Berkeley, USA	4	Mar
41.33	Nikki Manson		15.10.94	3	Athens, USA	8	Apr
41.25	Laura Graham	U20	6.02.99	5J	Loughborough	29	May
(40)							
41.09	Devota Nyakyoma		26.07.94	1	Burnley	4	Jun
40.81	Melissa Arthur	U23	14.01.95	1	Newport	4	Apr
40.81	Emma Christmas		24.06.88	2	Erith	17	Jun
40.58	Francesca Garrott	U20	7.10.98	1	Telford	13	May
40.27	Emily Robinson	U20	22.06.00	1	Crawley	13	May
39.98	Bethan Burley	U20	26.03.00	1H	Boston	17	Sep
39.88	Grace Davies-Redmond	U20	14.06.98	1	Bath	2	Apr
39.82	Emily Cockrill	U20	14.03.98	4	Bedford	29	Apr
39.69	Paula Gass		13.06.94	1	Grangemouth	22	Apr
39.67	Ellie Fulton	U20	18.06.99	2	Glasgow (S)	20	Aug
(50)							
39.51	Leanne Davies	U23	12.05.97	5	Bedford	29	Apr
39.50	Anna Peers	U23	28.08.97	1	Leigh	6	May
39.47	Lucy Smith		16.09.93	1	Exeter	28	Mar
39.47	Isabella Coutts	U23	19.02.97	Q	Bedford	29	Apr
39.47	Evie Harris-Jenkins	U20	22.09.98	2	Rugby	7	May
39.31	Simone Huggins-Ward		7.10.89	2	Telford	6	May
39.28	Sophie Thomas		18.04.89	1	Tidworth	14	May
39.27	Sarah-Anne De Kremer		18.11.90	6	Bedford	29	Apr
38.96	Elise Lovell		9.05.92	1	Hastings	15	Apr
38.90	Vikki Adams	U20	23.02.98	1	Cleckheaton	2	Apr
(60)							
38.89	Jade O'Dowda	U20	9.09.99	2H	Boston	17	Sep
38.82	Paula Holguin	U17	1.10.00	1	Hastings	15	Apr
38.70	Tasia Stephens	U23	8.12.96	1	Brecon	26	Aug
38.41	Lisa O'Neill	U20	20.07.99	1	Dunfermline	8	Apr
38.33	Emma Fossett	U23	19.10.97	2	Kingston	2	Jul
38.27	Paige Ditchfield	U20	22.12.99	2	Leigh	6	May
38.23	Niamh Emerson	U20	22.04.99	14H	Grosseto, ITA	21	Jul
38.21	Demi Bromfield	U23	17.03.96	4	Leigh	16	Jul
37.97	Abi Jones	U20	14.11.99	2	Uxbridge	17	Jun
37.89	Paige MacHeath	U20	21.10.99	2	London (CP)	11	Jun
(70)							
37.46	Suzzanne Palmer		11.09.93	9	Bedford	29	Apr
37.46	Jessica Taylor-Jemmett		27.06.88	4H	Barcelona, ESP	23	Jul
37.38	Maisie Grice	U20	29.06.00	4	Kingston	2	Jul

37.30	Katie Holt	U20	16.06.99	1	Reading	8	Apr
37.25	Holly McArthur	U20	20.12.99	18H	Grosseto, ITA	21	Jul
37.16	Becky Owen		8.09.91	1H	Sutton	10	Sep
37.14	Eloise Locke	U17	19.04.01	2	Bromley	15	Apr
37.13	Isabel Wakefield	U20	5.01.00	2	Exeter	14	May
37.02	Paula Murray		14.07.90	3	Grangemouth	27	Aug
36.88	Neve Palmer	U20	8.08.00	1	Bedford	14	May
(80)							
36.87	Emma Wallis	U17	15.01.02	1	Cambridge	29	Apr
36.81	Trixie Nicholson	U17	1.11.00	1	Exeter	15	Apr
36.78	Annabelle Pask	U23	6.09.97	Q	Bedford	29	Apr
36.78	Jessica Tappin		17.05.90	9	Birmingham	6	May
36.78	Emma Lawrence	U20	18.06.00	1	Dartford	20	Aug
36.77	Paula Williams	V45	18.03.72	2	Nuneaton	14	May
36.74	Lucy Hadaway	U20	11.06.00	1H	Cudworth	27	Aug
36.72	Amy Lupton		31.07.94	2	Blackpool	13	May
36.68	Debbie Castle	U23	14.10.95	1	Braintree	17	Jun
36.64	Holly Hall	U17	22.12.01	2	Twickenham	3	Sep
(90)							
36.63	Keira Waddell	U17	3.10.01	2	Glasgow (S)	13	Aug
36.58	Lauren Hill	U17	19.09.00	1	Hull	5	Aug
36.45	Alice Miell	U20	14.05.00	4	Angouleme, FRA	7	May
36.27	Colette Doran		20.09.83	4	Grangemouth	27	Aug
36.27	Nicola Kellock	U23	13.05.96	1	Livingston	9	Sep
36.20	Caris Morgan	U17	22.09.00	2	Coventry	4	Jun
36.20	Sophie Merritt	U20	9.04.98	3	Leigh	16	Jul

Foreign

45.00	*Kate O'Connor (IRL)*	*U17*	*12.12.00*	*3H*	*Monzón, ESP*	*2*	*Jul*
43.44	*Olga Kotmilloshi (ALB)*		*12.07.83*	*1*	*Kingston*	*2*	*Jul*
42.47	*Nanci Sousa (POR)*		*28.09.90*	*1*	*London (LV)*	*15*	*Apr*
41.23	*Beatrix Turner (ESP)*		*12.01.88*	*1*	*Ciudad Real, ESP*	*3*	*Jun*
40.51	*Tatum Souza (USA)*		*20.04.92*	*4Q*	*Bedford*	*29*	*Apr*
39.20	*Katy Sealy (BIZ)*		*15.10.90*	*1H*	*Managua, NCA*	*10*	*Dec*

Javelin - Under 17 - 500 gm

50.34	Emma Howe		6.04.01	1	Loughborough	1	Sep
46.95	Bethany Moule		21.11.01	1	Bath	2	Apr
46.51	Ellie Vernon		19.01.01	1	Telford	13	May
46.03	Bobbie Griffiths		15.03.01	1	Chester-le-Street	24	Sep
45.66	Paula Holguin		1.10.00	1	Kingston	13	May
44.49	Trixie Nicholson		1.11.00	1	Exeter	10	Jun
43.20	Eloise Locke		19.04.01	1	Reading	25	Jun
42.93	Keira Waddell		3.10.01	2	Loughborough	1	Sep
42.26	Olivia Dobson		27.03.01	2	Exeter	10	Jun
41.99	Phoebe Brown		24.06.01	1	Hereford	30	Apr
(10)							
41.93	Nicola Bell		27.11.00	5	Birmingham	8	Jul
41.85	Gemma Ramsey		27.06.01	1	Peterborough	7	May
41.80	Ottilie Knight		1.02.01	2	Bedford	27	Aug
41.45	Charlotte West		16.10.00	1	Reading	10	Jun
41.34	Evie Barclay		6.10.00	1H	Manchester (SC)	13	Aug
41.30	Serena Vincent		5.12.01	1	Basingstoke	23	Apr
41.01	Annabel Peach		6.04.02	3	Bedford	27	Aug
40.78	Alex Baker		27.12.01	1	Blackpool	10	Jun
40.74	Olivia Steele		22.07.02	1	Hemel Hempstead	10	Jun
40.59	Jodie Smith		2.11.01	1H	Boston	17	Sep
(20)							
40.43	Florence Baulk		10.12.01	2	Kingston	13	May
40.34	Holly Hall		22.12.01	4	Bedford	27	Aug
40.30	Lauren Hill		19.09.00	1	Spinkhill	30	Apr
40.11	Jemima Copeman		15.06.02	2	Reading	25	Jun

39.92	Zoe Kidney		17.10.00	1	Hull	2	Jul
39.57	Rhea Southcott		30.03.01	1	Sheffield (W)	30	Apr
39.43	Megan Hughes		28.11.01	2	Bury St. Edmunds	4	May
39.04	Olivia Willmore		21.03.02	1	Bournemouth	14	May
39.03	Daisy Partridge		12.10.00	1	Ware	30	Jul
39.00	Jessie Brown		26.11.01	1	Derby	10	Jun
(30)							
38.98	Cristina Potter		8.10.01	1	London (He)	30	Jul
38.90	Harriet Cannell		2.02.01	2	Hull	2	Jul
38.90	Daisy Dowling		21.08.02	12	Birmingham	8	Jul
38.86	Martha Taylor		1.03.02	3	Exeter	17	Jun
38.75	Eleanor Butt		21.09.01	1	Cambridge	6	Aug
38.74	Lauren Farley		16.09.01	5	Bedford	27	Aug
38.52	Imogen Onions		15.04.02	1	Nuneaton	20	Aug

Foreign

49.26	*Kate O'Connor (IRL)*		*12.12.00*	*1*	*Dublin (S), IRL*	*15*	*Jul*

Javelin - Under 15 - 500 gm

43.70	Kirsty Costello		22.09.02	1	Bedford	26	Aug
43.62	Elizabeth Korczak		12.04.03	2	Bedford	26	Aug
41.30	Tia Stonehouse		21.11.02	1	Watford	14	May
41.01	Abigail Ward		27.10.02	2	Birmingham	7	Jul
40.47	Millie Quaintance		10.11.02	3	Birmingham	7	Jul
40.44	Megan Galpin		16.11.03	3	Bedford	26	Aug
40.16	Harriette Mortlock		27.11.03	1	Bedford	3	Sep
39.44	Anouska Fairhurst		7.03.04	2	Loughborough	28	May
39.39	Sophie Graham		16.05.03	1	Ipswich	23	Apr
39.22	Katie Mackinson		20.09.02	1	Kingston	14	May
(10)							
39.11	Peanut Meekings		25.03.03	4	Bedford	26	Aug
38.09	Jasmine Walker		30.09.02	1	Nuneaton	20	Aug
37.84	Jamie Holland		6.01.03	1P	Manchester (SC)	12	Aug
37.65	Holly Pemberton		8.12.02	1	Telford	5	Apr
37.28	Lauren Foletti		25.09.02	6	Loughborough	28	May
37.20	Eva Durand		18.07.04	1	Cardiff	15	Jul
36.89	Jessica Thompson	U13	30.11.04	1-14	Hull	13	Jun
36.84	Francesca Sharpe		20.04.03	6	Birmingham	7	Jul
36.41	Megan Howarth		6.09.02	1	Bebington	13	May
35.86	Lucinda White	U13	4.02.05	1	Tonbridge	1	Aug
(20)							
35.30	Imogen Davis		18.05.03	3	Exeter	17	Jun
35.19	Lauren Tunstall		9.09.02	1	Hull	2	Jul
35.16	Eliza Sutton		16.12.03	1	Kingston	2	Sep
35.12	Emma Jennings		28.07.03	10	Loughborough	28	May
34.97	Adelaide Thatcher-Gray		18.09.02	8	Bedford	26	Aug
34.83	Alex Arbon		29.11.03	1	Wrexham	23	Sep
34.35	Caitlin Smith		20.05.03	1	Woking	15	Jul
34.23	Megan Evans		28.09.02	2	Manchester (Str)	1	May

Javelin - Under 13 - 400 gm

38.37	Hannah Lewington		15.03.06	1	Swindon	28	Oct
38.18	Lucinda White		4.02.05	1	Wrexham	23	Sep
35.57	Jasmine Larsen		13.05.05	2	Wrexham	24	Sep
34.25	Caitlin Milborne		15.09.04	2	Birmingham	4	Jul
33.44	Jessica Thompson		30.11.04	1	Leeds	18	Jun
32.50	Erin Lobley		12.10.04	1	Rotherham	15	Jul
32.39	Lily Brand		31.12.04	1	Ware	30	Jul
32.04	Caitlin Jackson		16.07.05	1	St. Peter Port GUE	2	Sep
31.92	Jade Buckley-Ratcliff		15.09.04	2	Wrexham	12	Aug
30.49	Megan Hulbert		29.12.04	2	Portsmouth	13	May

Heptathlon

W = wind assisted according to rules until 2009   w = wind assisted according to rules since 2010

6691	Katarina Johnson-Thompson		9.01.93	4	Götzis, AUT	28	May
	13.29/1.2 1.95	12.72	22.81/-2.9	6.53/0.7	39.98	2:11.12	
	6558			5	London (O)	6	Aug
	13.33/0.0 1.80	12.47	22.86/-0.2	6.56/-0.1	41.72	2:08.10	
6013	Niamh Emerson	U20	22.04.99	4	Grosseto, ITA	21	Jul
	14.01/-1.7 1.81	12.40	24.64/0.1	6.09w/2.7	38.23	2:12.60	
	5801			1	Bedford	28	May
	14.59/-2.5 1.82	11.99	24.97/0.4	6.05w/2.1	34.45	2:12.70	
5873	Katie Stainton	U23	8.01.95	7	Kladno, CZE	18	Jun
	14.12/1.3 1.68	11.80	24.22w/2.6	5.98/1.0	43.18	2:14.27	
	5836			7	Bydgoszcz, POL	14	Jul
	13.96w/2.6 1.66	11.61	24.16w/2.1	6.10/-0.4	38.96	2:13.17	
	5766			5	Florence, ITA	29	Apr
	14.21/0.6 1.75	11.55	24.72/-0.2	6.07/1.2	35.42	2:14.09	
	5664			2	Woerden, NED	27	Aug
	14.34/1.1 1.73	11.90	24.18/2.0	5.97/-0.6	38.12	2:25.22	
5767	Jessica Taylor-Jemmett		27.06.88	7	Talence, FRA	17	Sep
	13.98/-0.2 1.64	12.85	23.72w/3.1	5.81/-0.3	37.26	2:16.58	
	5702			6	Tallinn, EST	2	Jul
	14.44/-3.2 1.60	12.72	23.79/-2.8	6.13/0.9	36.06	2:17.53	
	5674			2	Bedford	28	May
	14.55/-3.7 1.64	13.05	24.39/-0.6	5.94/0.0	36.08	2:15.11	
5687	Holly McArthur	U20	20.12.99	11	Grosseto, ITA	21	Jul
	13.93/-1.5 1.63	11.47	24.59/0.1	5.91/1.0	37.28	2:11.71	
	5478			5	Arona, ESP	4	Jun
	14.06/1.2 1.61	10.97	24.95/0.4	5.78/0.9	35.58	2:13.69	
	5332			1	Bedford	28	May
	14.54/-2.3 1.55	11.14	24.90/0.0	5.75/0.0	35.13	2:14.26	
5614	Jo Rowland		29.12.89	13	Florence, ITA	29	Apr
	14.79/1.6 1.66	12.86	25.76w/2.3	5.93/1.6	41.58	2:16.22	
	5573			3	Arona, ESP	4	Jun
	14.75/1.2 1.64	13.15	25.54/0.0	5.87/0.0	39.22	2:16.02	
	5518			10	Tallinn, EST	2	Jul
	14.94/-0.4 1.68	13.04	25.24/-0.1	5.87/1.6	36.15	2:17.12	
	5512			1	Hexham	23	Jul
	14.81w/2.7 1.63	13.06	25.36/0.2	5.81	38.15	2:16.98	
	5421			1	Cudworth	27	Aug
	14.96/0.9 1.68	13.39	25.72/0.0	5.66/-1.0	39.55	2:24.51	
5444	Zoe Hughes	U20	1.02.98	6	Azusa, USA	13	Apr
	13.79/1.4 1.60	11.77	25.19/1.4	5.99/1.6	32.52	2:20.75	
	5332W			1	New Haven, USA	6	May
	14.05/1.9 1.65	11.93	25.30W/4.3	5.66w/2.2	29.97	2:19.69	
5442	Jade O´Dowda	U20	9.09.99	1	Boston	17	Sep
	14.29w/2.2 1.65	11.69	25.39/0.9	6.00/0.9	38.89	2:27.75	
	5120			1	Milton Keynes	25	Jun
	14.7 1.63	11.13	25.9	5.86	34.54	2:26.3	
	5070			1	Woerden, NED	27	Aug
	14.59/-0.2 1.55	11.31	25.58/1.5	5.60/-0.2	35.51	2:26.76	
5436	Lucy Turner	U23	14.02.97	3	Bedford	28	May
	14.42/-1.5 1.67	11.17	25.27/0.4	5.93w/2.3	35.75	2:20.52	
	5398			2	Hexham	23	Jul
	13.92/1.0 1.63	11.10	25.25/0.2	5.94	31.92	2:19.72	
	5199			18	Tallinn, EST	2	Jul
	14.58/-2.6 1.60	10.51	25.35/-2.2	5.86/0.1	34.44	2:23.35	
5344	Ellen Barber	U23	5.12.97	4	Woerden, NED	27	Aug
	15.30/-0.2 1.70	12.09	25.45/1.5	5.40/-0.8	41.92	2:21.78	
	5088			4	Hexham	23	Jul
	16.00w/2.7 1.60	10.90	25.67/1.9	5.61	43.48	2:24.99	

(Barber)	5082W		1	Grangemouth	2	Jul
	15.91w/2.3 1.66	11.20	26.42W/5.5	5.74w/3.2 43.51	2:31.37	
(10)						
5330	Elise Lovell	9.05.92	4	Bedford	28	May
	14.24/-3.7 1.64	10.18	25.02/-0.6	5.86/0.1 33.18	2:19.36	
5301	Jessica Tappin	17.05.90	5	Bedford	28	May
	14.19/-1.5 1.67	11.50	25.45/-0.6	5.09w/2.7 34.72	2:14.02	
5251	Olivia Montez Brown	U23 22.05.96	4	Bradenton, USA	26	May
	14.19w/2.3 1.63	11.18	26.01/0.3	5.72/0.8 35.41	2:23.20	
	5140		1	Mankota, USA	2	May
	14.61/-1.4 1.64	10.85	25.88/0.0	5.77w/4.0 32.60	2:24.43	
5213W	Hannah Dunderdale	2.11.94	2	Arlington, USA	13	May
	14.22w/2.9 1.51	11.82	24.74W/5.5	5.47/-1.7 32.81	2:17.82	
5111	Emma Nwofor	U23 22.08.96	2	Oxford (H)	23	Jul
	14.10/-0.4 1.74	10.81	26.0/-3.8	5.57/-0.7 32.10	2:33.56	
5076	Katie Garland	U23 27.01.97	7	Bedford	28	May
	15.02/-2.5 1.76	10.23	26.02/-0.6	5.49/1.9 31.25	2:23.88	
5054	Danielle McGifford	U23 11.04.95	1	Hyndburn	16	Apr
	14.7 1.65	10.54	25.1	6.01 29.44	2:31.9	
5015	Bethan Burley	U20 26.03.00	2	Boston	17	Sep
	14.69w/2.6 1.53	11.29	25.28/0.9	5.15/1.6 39.98	2:26.76	
	39 performances to 5000 points by 18 athletes					
4956	Jade Nimmo	23.03.91	5	Hexham	23	Jul
	14.44/1.0 1.60	10.30	25.67/0.2	5.91 27.27	2:30.97	
4928	Alix Still	U20 15.03.00	1	Brandenton, USA	21	May
	14.84/1.2 1.62	9.71	25.75w/2.4	5.61/0.3 29.56	2:23.48	
(20)						
4808	Ashleigh Spiliopoulou	U20 2.04.99	8	Dilbeek, NED	30	Jul
	15.57/0.9 1.70	9.59	26.17/0.0	5.41/0.1 28.45	2:23.32	
4799	Emily Dixon	U23 27.11.95	1	Newark, USA	6	May
	14.80/-0.3 1.65	10.97	26.59w/2.3	5.21/0.7 32.72	2:33.27	
4791	Chloe Vernon-Hamilton	11.10.92	7	Woerden, NED	27	Aug
	14.86/0.7 1.61	11.86	26.34/1.5	5.17/-0.6 29.74	2:30.51	
4776	Grace Bower	U20 3.11.99	1	Telford	25	Jun
	14.8 1.68	9.58	26.4	5.26 32.21	2:28.2	
4776	Georgia Silcox	U20 14.10.98	2	Yeovil	25	Jun
	14.49/0.0 1.59	9.05	25.43/-0.5	5.74/-2.2 18.88	2:22.66	
4686	Natasha Smith	U20 10.10.99	3	Yeovil	25	Jun
	14.96/0.0 1.65	9.59	26.74/-0.5	5.09/-1.0 29.03	2:24.39	
4668w	Anya Turner	U20 8.11.98	3	Boston	17	Sep
	14.74w/2.6 1.56	10.34	26.31w/2.1	5.31w/2.4 35.20	2:41.02	
	4508		3	Bedford	28	May
	15.26/-2.3 1.58	10.17	26.85/0.0	5.04/0.4 33.02	2:36.02	
4658	Olivia Galloway	U20 4.07.00	4	Boston	17	Sep
	14.65w/2.2 1.50	9.97	26.29/0.9	5.19/1.2 33.94	2:30.47	
4634	Lucy Chappell	U23 10.01.97	8	Bedford	28	May
	15.68/-2.5 1.67	9.62	27.25/-1.2	5.48/1.6 26.06	2:24.01	
4590	Becky Owen	8.09.91	1	Sutton	10	Sep
	15.4 1.65	9.96	26.57/1.0	4.91w/2.3 37.16	2:36.55	
(30)						
4589	Alice Linaker	U20 6.12.99	5	Boston	17	Sep
	14.73w/2.6 1.56	9.45	27.11/0.9	5.47/1.3 28.09	2:29.91	
4579	Laura Darcey	U20 28.07.98	2	Naperville, USA	18	May
	15.57/1.2 1.65	8.74	26.59/2.0	5.40/-1.4 28.95	2:29.82	
4531W	Ellie Fulton	U20 18.06.99	2	Grangemouth	2	Jul
	15.54w/2.3 1.63	9.55	27.33W/5.4	5.41w/3.6 36.57	2:44.12	
4514	Leanne Buxton	V35 27.05.78	2	Aarhus, DEN	28	Jul
	15.10/1.0 1.50	11.19	27.35/-1.8	5.16/0.6 29.67	2:29.36	
4484	Georgia Doyle-Lay	U20 27.10.98	5	Bedford	28	May
	16.63/2.0 1.64	10.69	26.67/0.0	5.25/1.5 27.40	2.30.04	

4401	Suzzanne Palmer		11.09.93	9	Bedford		28 May
	14.46/-1.5 1.61	11.51	25.95/-0.6	5.50/1.5	36.98	dnf	
4372W	Anna Forbes	U20	13.10.98	3	Grangemouth		2 Jul
	15.76w/2.3 1.60	7.70	26.44W/5.4	5.42w/3.5	25.96	2:31.38	
	4192			2	Cudworth		27 Aug
	15.96/1.2 1.59	7.89	27.22/0.0	5.22/0.3	24.51	2:31.91	
4336	Naomi Morgan	U23	23.11.96	3	Belfast		3 Sep
	15.06/-1.4 1.60	8.29	26.48w/2.8	5.23W/4.1	20.38	2:31.62	
4301	Olivia Jones	U20	20.02.00	6	Yeovil		25 Jun
	15.67/0.0 1.62	10.15	27.77/-1.1	5.09/0.4	25.89	2:36.29	
4254	Molly Newton-O´Brien	U20	5.05.99	7	Boston		17 Sep
	16.93/2.0 1.59	9.05	26.60/0.9	5.17/0.4	32.47	2:38.98	
(40)							
4198	Sophie Domingo	U20	7.01.00	1	Bedford		25 Jun
	14.7 1.44	7.32	26.9	5.38	30.33	2:38.6	
4187	Lucy Hadaway	U20	11.06.00	3	Cudworth		27 Aug
	14.85/1.2 1.50	10.98	27.09/0.0	5.84/-0.2	36.74	dnf	
4155	Laura Frey		2.06.89	8	Hexham		23 Jul
	16.49w/2.7 1.48	9.75	26.59/1.9	4.89	21.40	2:21.93	
4149	Jessica Dobson	U20	19.01.98	9	Bedford		28 May
	15.78/-2.0 1.49	9.21	26.57/0.0	5.09/1.9	23.49	2:34.79	
4089w	Emily Madden Forman	U20	29.09.99	8	Boston		17 Sep
	15.21w/2.2 1.65	7.29	27.15w/2.1	5.11/1.8	21.65	2:44.90	
`	(4078 with LJ 5.07/1.7)						
4005	Charlotte Robison	U23	13.07.97	12	Amherst, USA		7 May
	15.17/0.6 1.46	7.86	26.79/0.0	5.48/1.5	11.38	2:32.23	
3970	Liberty Hughes	U20	11.01.00	9	Boston		17 Sep
	16.64/1.5 1.50	7.34	27.06w/2.1	5.43/2.0	20.62	2:32.12	
3932	Amy Richards	U23	24.04.97	12	Bedford		28 May
	16.43/-3.4 1.55	8.71	27.75/-1.2	5.09/1.4	19.65	2:35.14	
3927	Megan Nagy	U20	26.02.99	3	Middlesbrough		25 Jun
	18.3 1.47	11.08	26.7	4.64	26.80	2:28.8	
3912	Katie Hetherington	U20	6.04.00	10	Boston		17 Sep
	16.56/2.0 1.65	8.45	28.32/1.3	4.82w/2.2	26.33	2:44.93	
(50)							
3907	Bethan Loveday	U20	9.03.00	2	Telford		25 Jun
	15.3 1.41	6.60	26.6	5.04	28.01	2:40.3	
3892	Nia Rutter		4.01.86	2	Hyndburn		16 Apr
	16.4 1.59	9.95	27.5	4.90	22.26	2:47.5	
3873	Lottie Garratt	U20	13.09.98	8	Yeovil		25 Jun
	17.58/0.1 1.62	8.80	28.20/-1.1	4.88/1.5	27.84	2:41.83	
3835	Bethany Harley	U20	26.08.99	11	Boston		17 Sep
	16.38/2.0 1.50	8.24	27.09/0.9	4.43/1.7	27.35	2:38.63	
3827	Charlotte Skeggs	U20	1.09.98	2	Bedford		25 Jun
	16.6 1.53	8.84	27.8	4.97	28.16	2:48.2	

Foreign

5759	Kate O´Connor (IRL)	U20	12.12.00	8	Grosseto, ITA		21 Jul
	15.06/-0.2 1.78	12.90	25.24/-1.2	5.75/1.3	43.30	2:15.87	
5367	Moe Sasegbon (NGR)		16.09.91	1	Belfast		3 Sep
	14.61/-1.4 1.75	13.33	25.78w/2.8	5.50w/2.4	31.71	2:23.07	
5271	Laura Voss (GER)		29.01.94	1	Cologne, GER		23 Jul
	14.88/0.8 1.74	10.41	25.56/-0.5	6.02w/3.1	30.94	2:24.15	
4837	Sarah Connolly (IRL)	U23	3.10.96	2	Belfast		3 Sep
	14.82/-1.4 1.78	9.32	26.01w/2.8	5.43w/3.4	26.04	2:33.44	
4753w	Katy Sealy (BIZ)		15.10.90	1	Sutton		10 Sep
	14.9 1.68	11.17	27.32/1.0	5.33w/4.0	37.15	2:42.47	
	(4733 with LJ 5.26/1.6)						

Heptathlon - Under 18
IAAF specifications 76.2cms hurdles, 3k Shot, 500gms JT

4699	Anna McCauley			2.01.01	1	Street		30	Apr
	14.59/-3.2	1.66	10.46	26.21/0.7	5.07W/4.3 24.11		2:28.40		
4406	Lauren Evans			7.08.00	2	Street		30	Apr
	14.58/-3.2	1.57	9.73	27.17/0.0	5.82W/4.2 22.41		2:49.59		

Heptathlon - Under 17

5214w	Emily Race			11.09.00	1	Boston		17	Sep
	11.23w/2.6	1.74	11.93	26.35/1.3	5.73w/2.2 33.82		2:32.60		
	(5149 with LJ 5.51/1.8)								
5123w	Pippa Earley			7.09.00	2	Boston		17	Sep
	11.17w/2.5	1.53	12.42	25.68/0.8	5.63w/3.2 27.92		2:17.32		
	(5102 with LJ 5.56/2.0)								
5114W	Olivia Dobson			27.03.01	3	Boston		17	Sep
	12.23W/4.3	1.74	14.14	26.70/1.0	5.37w/4.0 39.15		2:38.67		
	4742				2	Yeovil		25	Jun
	12.58/-0.4	1.65	13.25	27.18/0.9	5.09 39.37		2:42.77		
5050w	Jessica Hopkins			6.01.02	4	Boston		17	Sep
	11.85w/2.6	1.68	13.61	26.55w/2.4	5.75w/2.4 31.84		2:37.90		
	4910				1	Bedford		25	Jun
	11.9	1.66	14.05	26.7	5.29 33.71		2:38.5		
4940w	Zoe Pollock			21.12.00	5	Boston		17	Sep
	11.49w/2.5	1.50	11.45	24.75/1.3	5.36w/3.0 28.74		2:21.73		
	4803				2	Milton Keynes		25	Jun
	11.7	1.45	10.91	25.1	5.49 32.77		2:27.4		
4872	Emily Bee			3.03.02	6	Boston		17	Sep
	11.56w/2.5	1.59	10.54	25.37/1.3	5.46/1.8 26.18		2:23.37		
4833	Rhea Southcott			30.03.01	1	Cudworth		27	Aug
	12.48/-0.2	1.62	15.64	27.60/0.0	5.09/-2.0 31.51		2:30.23		
4743w	Jodie Smith			2.11.01	7	Boston		17	Sep
	12.68w/3.0	1.65	10.88	26.44/1.0	5.25w/2.7 40.59		2:39.15		
	4385			2	Kingston	25		Jun		
	13.2/-0.2	1.62	11.95	27.47/-2.2	5.08/-0.4 35.66		2:48.60		
4731w	Venus Morgan			5.06.01	8	Boston		17	Sep
	11.84w/2.5	1.56	10.75	25.77/1.3	5.61w/2.4 27.40		2:32.16		
	4495				6	Manchester (SC)		13	Aug
	11.91/-0.2	1.49	11.80	26.59/-3.1	5.32/0.0 23.70		2:31.54		
4658w	Hollie Thurgood			2.07.02	9	Boston		17	Sep
	11.73w/2.6	1.50	11.94	26.39w/2.4	5.26/1.8 36.14		2:41.42		
	4623				1	Kingston		25	Jun
	11.9/0.9	1.59	12.43	26.74/-0.7	5.01/0.2 29.37		2:34.72		

(10)

4650	Mia Chantree			15.11.01	2	Bedford		25	Jun
	11.9	1.60	10.75	25.8	5.39 22.42		2:27.4		
4632w	Samantha Harris			4.11.01	10	Boston		17	Sep
	11.36w/2.5	1.56	9.26	26.15/2.0	5.42w/3.3 27.61		2:31.00		
	4234				6	Yeovil		25	Jun
	11.62/-0.6	1.47	9.80	26.85/1.5	5.41 21.49		2:40.89		
4608w	Elise Thorner			16.03.01	12	Boston		17	Sep
	12.48w/2.8	1.65	9.57	26.99/2.0	5.05w/3.9 26.59		2:16.11		
	4484				3	Yeovil		25	Jun
	12.78/-0.4	1.62	8.77	26.93/1.5	5.07 24.38		2:13.86		
4568	Iris Oliarnyk			6.09.01	13	Boston		17	Sep
	12.32w/2.1	1.50	12.22	26.42/0.8	5.64w/2.4 26.07		2:36.80		
4510	Hannah Barnden			8.01.02	5	Manchester (SC)		13	Aug
	12.47/-0.2	1.52	11.47	26.54/0.0	4.92/0.0 33.90		2:32.50		

4447w	Emma Sherwood	12.09.01	14	Boston	17 Sep
	12.98w/2.5 1.62 10.30	26.85w/2.4 5.38w/3.7 25.99 2:31.68			
4383			4	Milton Keynes	25 Jun
	13.7 1.69 9.09	26.6 5.40 27.55 2:33.8			
4418	Bethany Harryman	13.10.00	3	Bedford	25 Jun
	12.5 1.63 11.21	27.5 5.42 26.34 2:40.3			
4410	Ashleigh Bailey	19.01.01	3	Street	30 Apr
	12.38/-2.0 1.48 12.96	27.19/0.0 5.09/1.1 31.72 2:42.16			
4400W	Stephanie Driscoll	24.10.01	15	Boston	17 Sep
	12.67W/4.3 1.56 10.53	27.14/2.0 4.99/1.9 26.61 2:24.55			
4347			1	Telford	25 Jun
	12.5 1.56 10.13	26.8 4.77 25.06 2:22.0			
4379	Morgan Spink	6.04.02	5	Milton Keynes	25 Jun
	12.2 1.57 8.40	25.9 5.18 21.25 2:23.7			

(20)

4378	Anna Brophy	14.04.01	17	Boston	17 Sep
	12.56w/2.8 1.62 9.03	27.77/1.0 4.97w/2.2 30.16 2:25.82			
4363W	Lily Naylor	14.12.01	18	Boston	17 Sep
	12.23w/2.1 1.53 12.02	27.78/1.0 4.93W/4.1 30.62 2:37.61			
	(4289 with LJ 4.65w/2.6)				
4350w	Katie Joyce	26.01.01	19	Boston	17 Sep
	12.00w/2.6 1.56 10.33	26.38/0.8 5.54w/3.2 19.51 2:35.71			
	(4309 with LJ 5.40w/2.2)				
4345	Danielle Hopkins	29.12.01	7	Milton Keynes	25 Jun
	12.8 1.66 10.80	26.7 5.15 26.49 2:43.7			
4332	Lucy Davison	8.11.01	7	Manchester (SC)	13 Aug
	12.58/0.0 1.58 11.18	27.44/-0.8 5.25/0.0 20.47 2:30.51			
4313	Emily Tyrrell	4.01.02	4	Yeovil	25 Jun
	11.94/-0.6 1.53 9.19	26.16/0.9 5.18 22.77 2:34.23			
4298	Rebecca Johns	9.11.01	8	Milton Keynes	25 Jun
	11.7 1.54 8.55	26.9 5.47 22.87 2:35.6			
4258	Ellie Carrow	26.10.01	5	Yeovil	25 Jun
	12.87/-0.4 1.50 10.63	26.77/1.5 5.06 27.84 2:34.86			
4256w	Kiera Bainsfair	3.02.02	22	Boston	17 Sep
	11.51w/2.5 1.56 9.90	25.78w/2.4 5.16w/3.0 nt 2:25.09			
4251	Connie McCafferty	24.02.01	3	Kingston	25 Jun
	13.3/-0.2 1.56 8.92	26.10/-0.7 4.88/-0.2 31.50 2:34.16			

(30)

4221	Lauren Farley	16.09.01	4	Kingston	25 Jun
	12.7/0.9 1.50 11.15	28.23 5.12/-0.2 38.22 2:51.57			
4214	Tia Jackson	5.08.02	7	Yeovil	25 Jun
	12.07/-0.8 1.56 8.37	25.41/1.5 5.58 19.06 2:49.55			
4175	Grace Morgan	14.01.02	9	Manchester (SC)	13 Aug
	11.92/-0.2 1.43 9.95	26.83/0.0 5.01/-0.3 26.02 2:37.14			
4164	Charlotte Ellis	10.10.00	4	Bedford	25 Jun
	12.5 1.51 9.80	27.8 5.29 23.98 2:33.4			
4161	Ashleigh West	27.06.01	5	Kingston	25 Jun
	11.9/0.9 1.65 9.61	27.49/-0.7 5.32/0.2 24.38 3:00.83			
4132	Cerys Lee	4.11.00	8	Yeovil	25 Jun
	12.56/-0.6 1.50 10.41	27.18/0.9 5.15 23.22 2:39.32			
4113	Olivia Willmore	21.03.02	1	Exeter	24 Sep
	13.36/-0.8 1.50 10.05	27.87/0.1 4.71 33.45 2:32.7			
4101	Tia Henry	9.04.01	11	Manchester (SC)	13 Aug
	12.44/-0.8 1.52 10.35	27.71/-0.3 4.89/0.00 27.33 2:41.78			

Hexathlon - Under 15

3750	Abigail Pawlett	14.01.03	1	Manchester (SC)	13 Aug
	11.72/-0.1 5.24/0.0 25.92 11.19 1.59 2:30.71				
3645	Emily Misantoni	27.09.02	2	Manchester (SC)	13 Aug
	11.95/-0.1 4.87/-0.4 24.34 10.29 1.53 2:16.83				

3539	Daisy Worthington				05.05.03	3	Manchester (SC)	13	Aug
	12.61/0.1	5.17/0.2	25.74	9.44	1.47	2:18.24			
3492	Katie Burr				30.09.03	4	Manchester (SC)	13	Aug
	12.13/-0.1	4.63/0.0	27.65	10.20	1.59	2:31.66			
3421	Nicole Proudfoot				12.11.02	5	Manchester (SC)	13	Aug
	12.02/-0.1	5.12/0.0	15.36	9.61	1.59	2:27.39			

Order of events   75m H, LJ, JT, SP, HJ, 800m

Pentathlon - Under 15 (* Pentathlon Score during Hexathlon)

3350*	Abigail Pawlett			14.01.03	*	Manchester (SC)	13	Aug
	11.72/-0.1	11.19	1.59	5.24/0.0	2:30.71			
	3298				1	Boston	17	Sep
	11.04/2.0	10.73	1.56	5.60/1.7	2:45.74			
3275*	Emily Misantoni			27.09.02	*	Manchester (SC)	13	Aug
	11.95/-0.1	10.29	1.53	4.87/-0.4	2:16.83			
	3223w				2	Boston	17	Sep
	11.73/2.0	9.98	1.47	5.25w/2.9	2:23.74	(3143 with LJ 4.96/1.4)		
3223	Nicole Proudfoot			12.11.02	1	Grangemouth	3	Jun
	11.97	9.99	1.48	5.52	2:28.59			
3180w	Ruby Bridger			6.05.03	3	Boston	17	Sep
	11.14/2.0	10.15	1.59	5.40w/2.6	2:49.79			
	3067				1	Bedford	25	Jun
	11.2	10.51	1.58	4.91	2:48.1			
3143*	Daisy Worthington			5.05.03	*	Manchester (SC)	13	Aug
	12.61/0.1	9.44	1.47	5.17/0.2	2:18.24			
	3010				5	Boston	17	Sep
	12.16w/2.5	10.04	1.44	4.97/1.5	2:28.25			
3096	Katie Burr			30.09.03	2	Grangemouth	2	Jul
	11.77w/2.2	10.00	1.57	4.99/1.7	2:37.04			
3086	Rebekah O´Brien			21.10.02	1	Kingston	25	Jun
	12.06/0.4	8.07	1.62	4.81/0.2	2:25.73			
3084	Milly Gall			20.02.03	2	Kingston	25	Jun
	11.41/0.4	10.32	1.56	5.38/-0.3	2:52.91			
3007w	Demi Tuinema			2.01.03	6	Boston	17	Sep
	12.21/1.7	9.65	1.53	5.26w/3.0	2:40.84			
	2959				3	Kingston	25	Jun
	12.37/-2.3	8.98	1.56	4.94/0.3	2:35.01			
2965	Yasmin Grosvenor			23.02.03	2	Oxford (H)	22	Jul
	12.39/-0.4	11.20	1.47	5.22/1.4	2:44.90			
(10)								
2954	Kaliyah Young			20.07.03	1	Erith	17	Sep
	11.96/0.1	9.79	1.59	5.22	2:54.76			
2925	Ella Rush			8.04.04	1	Milton Keynes	25	Jun
	12.4	9.06	1.54	4.90	2:35.2			
2915	Maisie Rixon			11.10.02	4	Kingston	25	Jun
	12.64/0.2	10.98	1.53	4.74/-0.1	2:40.16			
2896	Isabel Pinder			16.11.03	7	Boston	17	Sep
	13.03w/2.3	7.33	1.62	4.94/1.6	2:31.61			
2891	Lucy Woodward			28.11.02	1	Yeovil	25	Jun
	12.20/0.4	8.73	1.50	5.01	2:36.89			
2887	Molly Hole			28.02.03	1	Street	30	Apr
	12.81/-2.9	11.96	1.60	4.54	2:49.56			
2886	Megan Hamilton-Strong			23.09.03	8	Boston	17	Sep
	12.05w/2.8	9.11	1.50	4.77/1.1	2:35.35			
2884w	Holly Lawrence			12.02.03	9	Boston	17	Sep
	11.49w/2.1	8.25	1.59	5.13w/3.5	2:55.02			
	2877				2	Bedford	25	Jun
	11.7	8.05	1.58	4.99	2:47.0			
2870	Leisha Hunt			5.09.02	2	Brentwood	24	May
	12.1	9.23	1.40	5.11	2:35.4			

2850	Sola Taiwo			22.12.02	2	Hemel Hempstead	16	Jul
	12.1	7.60	1.49	4.96	2:33.1			
(20)								
2846	Briagha Cook			28.10.02	2	Grangemouth	3	Jun
	11.77	7.57	1.51	5.21	2:44.45			
2824*	Melissa Coxon			5.12.02	*	Manchester (SC)	13	Aug
	12.09/-0.1	7.76	1.47	4.83/0.0	2:31.52			
	2775				3	Middlesbrough	25	Jun
	12.0	7.94	1.44	4.95	2:37.3			
2819	Philippa Ellis			23.04.03	1	Middlesbrough	25	Jun
	11.9	9.90	1.41	4.60	2:34.9			
2819	Ndidikama Okoh			3.12.02		Bedford	25	Jun
	12.7	7.23	1.61	4.72	2:34.5			
2817	Lydia Smith			15.03.04	2	Yeovil	25	Jun
	11.50/0.4	9.09	1.44	4.96	2:45.62			
2816	Tia Stonehouse			21.11.02	2	Stevenage	4	May
	12.6	10.04	1.50	5.06	2:48.6			
2812	Abbie Lovering			23.07.03	10	Boston	17	Sep
	12.36/1.7	9.23	1.38	4.45/1.0	2:22.42			
2809	Maisie Abel			10.02.03	1	Crawley	31	May
	12.5	8.09	1.53	4.95	2:39.1			
2801	Molly Curran			18.12.03	1	Belfast	3	Sep
	12.75/-2.1	9.32	1.42	4.75	2:29.70			

Order of events: 75mh, SP (3k), HJ, LJ, 800

Pentathlon - Under 13

3114	Erin Lobley			12.10.04	1	Jarrow	16	Sep
	11.36/1.1	5.19/0.8	1.54	11.93	2:42.48			
2718w	Julia Winogrodzka			21.10.04	1	Grangemouth	2	Jul
	11.63w/3.7	5.10w/3.8	1.42	8.26	2:39.77			
	2516				1	Stockport	9	Sep
	11.2	4.80	1.35	8.28	2:48.29			
2553w	Saskia Wade			30.05.05	2	Grangemouth	2	Jul
	12.45w/3.7	4.40/1.6	1.48	8.20	2:36.49			
2519w	Paige Stevens			3.02.05	3	Grangemouth	2	Jul
	12.29w/3.7	4.57/1.0	1.42	8.87	2:42.60			
2481	Mya McMahon			19.09.05	2	Jarrow	16	Sep
	11.80/1.1	4.47/0.2	1.54	7.11	2:49.97			
2432	Grace Colmer			13.07.05	2	Tonbridge	28	Aug
	11.55	4.57	1.38	7.14	2:43.17			
2376	Amber Hughes			3.11.05	3	Jarrow	16	Sep
	11.37/0.6	3.86/1.3	1.39	8.13	2:41.43			
2366w	Rebecca Grieve			30.01.05	5	Grangemouth	2	Jul
	12.18w/3.7	4.70/0.7	1.30	5.53	2:30.61			
2365	Caitlin Kearney			16.10.04	1	Par	22	Jul
	12.7	3.93	1.39	7.39	2:28.7			
2325	Tilly Mycroft			18.11.04	1	Leicester	4	Jun
	13.77/1.1	4.44	1.38	8.89	2:42.59			

Order of events: 70mh, LJ, SP (2.72k), HJ, 800m

Pentathlon - Indoor

4155	Jessica Taylor-Jemmett			27.06.88	3	Prague, CZE	29	Jan
	8.57	1.65	12.32	5.86	2:16.68			
4147	Katie Stainton	U23		8.01.95	5	Prague, CZE	29	Jan
	8.79	1.68	11.88	5.97	2:16.57			
4103	Jo Rowland			29.12.89	1	Glasgow	5	Mar
	8.97	1.68	12.91	5.92	2:20.92			
4093	Zoe Hughes	U20		1.02.98	1	New York, USA	25	Feb
	8.71	1.64	12.07	6.07	2:21.62			
4039	Jessica Tappin			17.05.90	1	Glasgow	5	Mar
	8.72	1.71	11.58	5.36	2:13.77			

3892	Elise Lovell			9.05.92	11	Prague, CZE	29	Jan
	8.58		1.65	9.61	5.83	2:22.15		
3863	Olivia Montez Brown	U23		22.05.96	4	Birmingham, USA	10	Mar
	8.73		1.62	10.87	5.72	2:23.02		
3859	Holly McArthur	U20		20.12.99	4	Prague, CZE	28	Jan
	8.79		1.62	10.03	5.60	2:15.50		
3834	Danielle McGifford	U23		11.04.95	14	Prague, CZE	29	Jan
	8.63		1.65	10.88	5.84	2:32.51		
3780	Lucy Chappell	U23		10.01.97	5	Glasgow	5	Mar
	9.04		1.77	10.39	5.44	2:29.50		
(10)								
3742	Hannah Dunderdale			2.11.94	2	Birmingham, USA	21	Feb
	9.05		1.56	11.98	5.39	2:19.89		
3713	Grace Bower	U20		3.11.99	10	Prague, CZE	28	Jan
	9.18		1.68	9.34	5.66	2:23.46		
3712	Lucy Turner	U23		14.02.97	4	Sheffield	8	Jan
	8.98		1.60	10.46	5.76	2:27.44		
3702	Emily Dixon	U23		27.11.95	1	Lynchburg, USA	10	Feb
	8.84		1.65	11.16	5.22	2:26.56		
3653	Chloe Vernon-Hamilton			11.10.92	5	Sheffield	8	Jan
	9.17		1.63	12.45	5.25	2:30.36		
3637	Zoe Pollock	U20		21.12.00	1	London (LV)	17	Dec
	8.69		1.55	9.71	5.33	2:20.14		
3620	Ada´ora Chigbo	U20		2.01.99	14	Prague, CZE	28	Jan
	9.46		1.71	12.26	5.09	2:31.40		
3599	Katie Garland	U23		27.01.97	6	Sheffield	8	Jan
	9.12		1.69	9.76	5.52	2:33.31		
3560	Emma Nwofor	U23		22.08.96	7	Sheffield	8	Jan
	8.63		1.63	11.06	5.35	2:42.52		
3547	Alix Still	U20		15.03.00	2	New York, USA	11	Mar
	9.28		1.64	9.22	5.35	2:23.53		

Pentathlon - Indoor Under 17

3952	Pippa Earley			7.09.00	1	Sheffield	11	Mar
	8.68	1.55	12.89	5.51		2:18.52		
3788	Jessica Hopkins			6.01.02	4	Glasgow	10	Nov
	9.27	1.68	13.65	5.72		2:40.45		
3582	Amaya Scott			15.02.01	2	Sheffield	11	Mar
	9.36	1.70	13.03	5.28		2:44.28		
3559	Kiera Bainsfair			3.02.02	3	Sheffield	11	Mar
	8.95	1.61	9.94	5.17		2:24.78		
3482	Iris Oliarnyk			6.09.01	5	Sheffield	11	Mar
	9.40	1.55	12.54	5.43		2:37.78		
3434	Lucy Davison			8.11.01	1	Glasgow	5	Mar
	9.31	1.50	12.31	5.38		2:35.94		
3405	Venus Morgan			5.06.01	6	Sheffield	11	Mar
	8.93	1.55	11.10	5.01		2:34.48		
3391	Mia Chantree			15.11.01	7	Sheffield	11	Mar
	9.49	1.67	10.04	5.10		2:34.00		
3375	Emily Race			11.09.00	8	Sheffield	11	Mar
	9.22	1.58	11.78	4.80		2:33.86		
3368	Talia Morton-Kemsley			20.05.01	9	Sheffield	11	Ma
	9.30	1.49	11.74	5.29		2:35.46		
(10)								
3334	Nicole Lannie			24.01.03	1	Sheffield	17	Dec
	9.1	1.53	11.61	5.34		2:42.0		
3323	Stephanie Driscoll			24.10.01	10	Sheffield	11	Mar
	9.76	1.55	10.36	4.83		2:20.25		
3316	Laura Hickey			6.01.02	11	Sheffield	11	Mar
	9.11	1.61	9.80	5.36		2:45.98		

Pentathlon Indoor - Under 15

3649	Lucy-Jane Matthews				17.09.02	1	Sheffield	12	Mar
	8.96	1.61	11.61	5.46	2:32.60				
3341	Abigail Pawlett				14.01.03	2	Sheffield	12	Mar
	8.86	1.52	9.69	5.16	2:33.83				
3328	Milly Gall				20.02.03	3	Sheffield	12	Mar
	9.28	1.55	10.05	5.26	2:34.78				
3236	Katie Burr				30.09.03	6	Glasgow	10	Nov
	9.40	1.56	10.41	4.83	2:33.57				
3192	Nicole Proudfoot				12.11.02	4	Sheffield	12	Mar
	9.58	1.52	9.33	5.22	2:33.48				
3174	Maisie Jeger				24.11.03	1	London (LV)	17	Dec
	9.83	1.44	10.33	4.97	2:23.75				
3156	Carys Poole				21.12.03	1	Cardiff	7	Oct
	9.33	1.41	9.19	5.26	2:30.76				
3098	Rebekah O´Brien				21.10.02	1	London (LV)	26	Mar
	9.86	1.60	8.51	4.55	2:25.44				
3082	Emily Misantoni				27.09.02	5	Sheffield	12	Mar
	9.42	1.52	9.89	4.13	2:25.24				
3061	Daisy Worthington				5.05.03	6	Sheffield	12	Mar
	9.77	1.46	9.00	4.75	2:23.83				
(10)									
3013	Yasmin Grosvenor				23.02.03	7	Sheffield	12	Mar
	9.63	1.46	10.42	4.93	2:41.44				

Pentathlon Indoor - Under 13

2810	Julia Winogrodzka			21.10.04	1	Glasgow	4	Mar
	9.62	1.32	7.87	5.34	2:41.89			
2649	Mya McMahon			19.09.05	2	Glasgow	4	Mar
	9.86	1.56	6.59	4.79	2:55.30			
2412	Rebecca Grieve			30.01.05	4	Glasgow	4	Mar
	10.25	1.32	5.55	4.57	2:35.29			
2332	Grace Colmer			13.07.05	1	London (LV)	26	Mar
	10.14	1.21	7.09	4.29	2:36.99			
2330	Catriona Scott			1.09.04	5	Glasgow	4	Mar
	10 14	1.36	6.82	3.67	2:38.18			
2277	Paige Stevens			3.02.05	6	Glasgow	4	Mar
	10.60	1.38	7.43	4.22	2:50.32			
2257	Scarlett Gammell			9.03.05	2	London (LV)	26	Mar
	10.19	1.30	5.27	4.06	2:35.67			

2000 Metres Walk - Track - U13

11:03.20	Abigail Smith	24.11.04	1	Erith	16	Sep
11:08.6	Katie Stringer	25.06.05	2	Tullamore, IRL	9	Jul
12:05.7	Charlotte Wallis	3.11.04	1	Portsmouth	13	May

Foreign

11:35.9	*Devina Nova (BUL)*	*2.09.05*	*4*	*Tullamore, IRL*	*9*	*Jul*

3000 Metres Walk - Track

12:26.45	Bethan Davies	7.11.90	1	Cardiff	10	Jun
	12:42.26i		1	Cardiff	10	Dec
	12:46.92+		1m	Birmingham	2	Jul
12:59.75	Gemma Bridge	17.05.93	1	Leeds	12	Jun
	13:23.59i		1	Sheffield	12	Feb
	13:25.39i		2	Bratislava, SVK	29	Jan
	13:35.60		1	Leeds	22	Mar
	13:41.33i		1	Sheffield	8	Jan

13:15.52	Heather Lewis		25.10.93	1	Manchester (SC)	16	Aug
	13:25.59i			2	Cardiff	10	Dec
	13:30.05			3	Cardiff	10	Jun
13:15.88	Erika Kelly		6.12.92	2	Manchester (SC)	16	Aug
	13:36.64			2	Leeds	12	Jun
	13:48.54+			4m	Birmingham	1	Jul
	13:50.72			1	Bedford	30	Jul
13:48.83i	Emma Achurch	U23	9.07.97	2	Sheffield	12	Feb
	13:51.23i			2	Sheffield	8	Jan
14:25.11i	Sophie Lewis Ward	U20	7.04.99	5	Sheffield	12	Feb
	14:28.24			1	Ashford	14	May
14:26.43i	Ana Garcia	U17	3.05.01	6	Sheffield	12	Feb
	14:35.57			1	Sheffield	21	Jun
14:35.41i	Hannah Hunter		7.10.82	8	Sheffield	12	Feb

Foreign

13:48.99	*Tatyana Gabellone (ITA)*		*20.10.84*	*4*	*Cardiff*	*10*	*Jun*

5000 Metres Walk

21:21.52	Bethan Davies		7.11.90	1	Birmingham	2	Jul
23:20.19	Erika Kelly		6.12.92	4	Birmingham	2	Jul
24:57.51	Sophie Lewis Ward	U20	7.04.99	4	Birmingham	2	Jul
26:43.59	Ana Garcia	U17	3.05.01	2	Bedford	27	Aug
26:59.87	Emily Ghose	U20	2.06.99	1	Boston	16	Sep
27:02.5	Emma Achurch	U23	9.07.97	1	London (LV)	22	Apr
27:05.6B	Abigail Jennings	U20	10.07.00	1	Tonbridge	18	Nov
27:38.3	Megan Stratton-Thomas	U20	2.07.00	2	London (LV)	22	Apr
27:46.42	Molly Davey	U20	3.09.98	1	Reggio Emilia, ITA	10	Sep
27:51.0	Lucy Lewis Ward	U17	26.02.02	1-17	London (LV)	22	Apr
(10)							
28:03.8B	Penelope Cummings	V40	8.06.76	2	Tonbridge	18	Nov
28:07.6	Isobelle Bridge	U17	24.12.01	2-17	London (LV)	22	Apr

Foreign

23:03.63	*Tatyana Gabellone (ITA)*		*20.10.84*	*1*	*Matera, ITA*	*6*	*May*

5000 Metres Walk - Road

22:36+	Bethan Davies		7.11.90	1m	Coventry	5	Mar
	22:49+			39m	London	13	Aug
	22:52+			m	Poděbrady, CZE	21	May
	22:53+			3m	Leeds	25	Jun
	23:14+			m	Lugano, SUI	19	Mar
22:52+	Gemma Bridge		17.05.93	1m	Leeds	25	Jun
	22:58+			m	Poděbrady, CZE	8	Apr
	23:08+			10m	Poděbrady, CZE	12	Feb
	23:10+			47m	London	13	Aug
	23:31+			3m	Coventry	5	Mar
23:00+e	Heather Lewis		25.10.93	2m	Coventry	5	Mar
24:19	Hannah Hunter		7.10.82	1	Douglas IOM	18	May
24:34	Ana Garcia	U17	3.05.01	1	Poděbrady, CZE	8	Apr

where superior to track

25:48+	Molly Davey	U20	3.09.98	19m	Poděbrady, CZE	8	Apr
27:17	Lisa Kehler	V45	15.03.67	1	Coventry	5	Mar

10000 Metres Walk - Track

47:05.97	Bethan Davies		7.11.90	6	Canberra, AUS	29	Jan
	49:40.95			6	Canberra, AUS	5	Jan

Foreign

47:41.49	*Tatyana Gabellone (ITA)*		*20.10.84*	*1*	*Acquaviva Fonti, ITA*	*23*	*Apr*

10 Kilometres Walk - Road

45:52+	Gemma Bridge		17.05.93	1m	Leeds	25	Jun
	46:42+			m	Poděbrady, CZE	21	May
	47:07			2	Coventry	5	Mar
	47:09+			46m	London	13	Aug
	47:21+			m	Poděbrady, CZE	8	Apr
	47:49+			8m	Lugano, SUI	19	Mar
45:53+	Bethan Davies		7.11.90	3m	Leeds	25	Jun
	46:04+			36m	London	13	Aug
	46:07			1	Coventry	5	Mar
	46:31+			15m	Poděbrady, CZE	21	May
	46:36+			5m	Adelaide, AUS	19	Feb
	47:05+			6m	Lugano, SUI	19	Mar
47:17	Heather Lewis		25.10.93	5	Coventry	29	Apr
	47:51+			10m	Lugano, SUI	19	Mar
	49:17			1	Hayes	1	Oct
48:54	Erika Kelly		6.12.92	1	Coventry	29	Apr
51:45	Hannah Hunter		7.10.82	1	Douglas IOM	19	Mar
51:46	Molly Davey	U20	3.09.98	15	Poděbrady, CZE	8	Apr
51:53	Ana Garcia	U17	3.05.01	3	Leeds	25	Jun
52:45	Sophie Lewis Ward	U20	7.04.99	17	Poděbrady, CZE	8	Apr
53:33B	Lisa Kehler	V45	15.03.67	1	Birmingham	29	Oct

Foreign

47:10	*Tatyana Gabellone (ITA)*		*20.10.84*	*4*	*Coventry*	*5*	*Mar*

20 Kilometres Walk Road

1:32:33	Gemma Bridge		17.05.93	1	Leeds	25	Jun
	1:34:24			14	Poděbrady, CZE	21	May
	1:35:03			10	Poděbrady, CZE	8	Apr
	1:36:04			40	London	13	Aug
	1:37:36			8	Lugano, SUI	19	Mar
1:33:04	Bethan Davies		7.11.90	3	Leeds	25	Jun
	1:33:10			29	London	13	Aug
	1:35:47			6	Adelaide, AUS	19	Feb
	1:36:04			22	Poděbrady, CZE	21	May
1:37:39	Heather Lewis		25.10.93	9	Lugano, SUI	19	Mar
	1:40:06			2	Gleina, GER	14	Oct
	1:42:29			5	Leeds	25	Jun
	1:44:41			39	Poděbrady, CZE	21	May
1:41:27	Erika Kelly		6.12.92	4	Leeds	25	Jun
	1:41:52			2	Douglas IOM	3	Sep
1:47:17	Hannah Hunter		7.10.82	1	Douglas IOM	25	Feb
1:51:39	Molly Davey	U20	3.09.98	7	Cassino, ITA	26	Mar

Foreign

1:39:02	*Tatyana Gabellone (ITA)*		*20.10.84*	*1*	*Cassino, ITA*	*26*	*Mar*

50 Kilometres Walk Road

5:17:31	Karen Chiarello	V50	31.08.63	1	Peel, IOM	23	Apr

4 x 100 Metres

41.86	National Team		2	Zürich, SUI	24	Aug
	(Asha Philip, Desiree Henry, Dina Asher-Smith, Daryll Neita)					
41.93	National Team		2h1	London (O)	12	Aug
	(Asha Philip, Desiree Henry, Dina Asher-Smith, Daryll Neita)					
42.12	National Team		2	London (O)	12	Aug
	(Asha Philip, Desiree Henry, Dina Asher-Smith, Daryll Neita)					
44.17	National Junior Team	U20	3	Grosseto, ITA	23	Jul
	(Ebony Carr, Alisha Rees, Maya Bruney, Olivia Okoli)					
44.20	National Team		2	Geneva, SUI	10	Jun
	(Clieo Stephenson, Shannon Hylton, Jodie Williams, Diani Walker)					
44.45	England		1	Loughborough	21	May
	(Clieo Stephenson, Shannon Hylton, Cheriece Hylton, Imani Lansiquot)					
44.50	National Junior Team	U20	1h2	Grosseto, ITA	23	Jul
	(Ebony Carr, Alisha Rees, Jazz Crawford, Olivia Okoli)					
44.66	National Junior Team	U20	1	Mannheim, GER	1	Jul
	(Ebony Carr, Alisha Rees, Maya Bruney, Olivia Okoli)					
44.74	National Junior Team	U20	2	Mannheim, GER	2	Jul
	(Jazz Crawford, Alisha Rees, Maya Bruney, Olivia Okoli)					
45.23	National Junior Team	U20	2	Loughborough	21	May
	(Hannah Brier, Alisha Rees, Maya Bruney, Charmont Webster-Tape)					
45.59	Wales		3	Loughborough	21	May
	(Hannah Williams, Melissa Roberts, Mica Moore, Amy Odunaiya)					
45.75	Guildford & Godalming AC	U20	2	London (O)	9	Jul
	(Megan Hildrew, Jemma Wood, Ellie Grove, Olivia Okoli)					
45.76	East London University		1	Bedford	1	May
	(Maya Bruney, Sydney Griffin, USA, Mobolaji Adeokun USA, Corrinne Humphreys)					
45.92	Cardiff Metropolitan University		2	Bedford	1	May
	(Catherine Hardy, Amy Odunaiya, Amy Bowen, Charlotte Wingfield, MLT)					
45.98	North of England Schools	U17	1	Loughborough	1	Sep
	(Hannah Kelly, Amy.Carter, Trinity Peruzza-Powell, Amy Hunt)					
46.05	Birchfield Harriers		1	Bromley	16	Jul
	(Heather Paton, Nardhia Kidd-Walker, Mica Moore, Meghan Beesley)					
46.08	Birchfield Harriers		1	Birmingham	6	May
	(Heather Paton, Gina Akpe-Moses, IRL, Mica Moore, Melissa Roberts)					
46.08	Wales		3	Belfast	5	Jul
	(Hannah Williams, Hannah Thomas, Mica Moore, Melissa Roberts)					
46.20	Wales		1	Cardiff	12	Jul
	(Hannah Williams, Melissa Roberts, Mica Moore, Amy Odunaiya)					
46.24	Blackheath & Bromley H AC	U20	2	London (O)	9	Jul
	(Parris Johnson, Maya Bruney, Modupe Shokunobi, Immanuela Aliu)					

Additional Club Teams (1-5 above)

46.77	Swansea Harriers		2	Bromley	16	Jul
46.92	Edinburgh AC		1	Glasgow (S)	13	Aug
46.99	Brunel University		2h2	Bedford	30	Apr
47.21	Bath University		3	Bedford	1	May
47.24	Croydon Harriers	U20	3	London (O)	9	Jul
47.42	Birmingham University		1h1	Bedford	30	Apr
47.47	Windsor SE&H AC		3	Bromley	16	Jul
47.51	Shaftesbury Barnet Harriers	U17	2	London (O)	9	Jul
47.95	Aberdeen AAC		1	Grangemouth	22	Apr
48.01	Thames Valley Harriers		3	Birmingham	6	May
48.06	Crawley AC		1	Wigan	7	May
48.09	Sale Harriers Manchester		1	Leigh	16	Jul
48.10	Woodford Green with Essex Ladies		5	Bromley	16	Jul
48.19	Wigan & District Harriers		2	Wigan	7	May
48.30	Southampton AC		1r2	Leigh	16	Jul

Additional Under 20 Club Teams (1-3 above)

48.51	Windsor SE&H AC	4	London (O)	9	Jul
49.0	Cannock & Stafford AC	1	Rugby	28	May
49.1	Birchfield Harriers	2	Rugby	28	May
49.1	Harrow AC	1	Harrow	25	Jun
49.4	Notts AC	1	Rugby	28	May
49.47	Charnwood AC	1	Loughborough	25	Jun
49.5	Southend High School for Girls	1h3	Oxford	4	May

Additional Under 17 Teams (1 above)

46.54	England Schools	2	Dublin (S), IRL	15	Jul
47.12	London Schools	1	Birmingham	8	Jul
47.21	Greater Manchester Schools	2	Birmingham	8	Jul
47.32	Croydon Harriers	1	London (O)	9	Jul
47.39	South of England Schools	2	Loughborough	1	Sep
47.40	Hertfordshire Schools	3	Birmingham	8	Jul
47.54	Midlands Schools	3	Loughborough	1	Sep
47.62	Surrey Schools	1	Basingstoke	17	Jun

Additional Under 17 Club Teams (1-2 above)

48.9	Enfield & Haringey AC	1	Luton	30	Apr
49.08	Victoria Park & Tower Hamlets	1	London (LV)	15	Apr
49.17	Windsor SE&H AC	3	London (O)	9	Jul
49.55	Orion Harriers	4	London (O)	9	Jul
49.6	Cannock & Stafford AC	1	Rugby	28	May
49.77	Dundee Hawkhill Harriers	1	Grangemouth	22	Apr
49.81	Central AC	2	Grangemouth	22	Apr
49.91	Serpentine RC	1	London (He)	15	Jul

Under 15 Teams

48.09	Middlesex Schools	1	Birmingham	8	Jul
48.12	Croydon Harriers	1	London (O)	9	Jul
48.59	London Schools	2	Birmingham	8	Jul
49.0	Sale Harriers Manchester	1	Preston	15	Jul
49.08	West Midlands Schools	3	Birmingham	8	Jul
49.17	Hampshire Schools	4	Birmingham	8	Jul
49.27	Harrow AC	2	London (O)	9	Jul
49.28	Greater Manchester Schools	1h3	Birmingham	7	Jul
49.37	Essex Schools	2h3	Birmingham	7	Jul
49.41	Kent Schools	1	Basingstoke	17	Jun

Additional Under 15 Club Teams (1- 3 above)

49.88	Herne Hill Harriers	3	London (O)	9	Jul
50.0	Blackheath & Bromley H AC	1	Ashford	2	Jul
50.30	Crawley AC	4	London (O)	9	Jul
50.3	Gateshead Harriers	2	Manchester (SC)	18	Jun
50.3	Cambridge Harriers	1	Bromley	10	Sep
50.4	Stockport Harriers	1	Stretford	20	May
50.4	Newham & Essex Beagles	1	Hornchurch	30	Jun

Under 13 Teams

51.8	Blackheath & Bromley H AC	1	Bromley	10	Sep
52.00	Middlesex AA	1	Kingston	29	Jul
52.26	Croydon Harriers	2	London (O)	9	Jul
52.61	Harrow AC	3	London (O)	9	Jul
52.67	Havering AC	4	London (O)	9	Jul
52.72	Reading AC	5	London (O)	9	Jul
52.86	Sale Harriers Manchester	1	Birmingham	2	Sep
53.56	Hampshire AA	1r2	Kingston	29	Jul
53.78	Surrey AA	3	Kingston	29	Jul
53.86	Andover/Overton	1	Swindon	4	Jun

4 x 200 Metres

1:38.94i	Bath University		1	Sheffield	19	Feb
1:38.96i	Brunel University		2	Sheffield	19	Feb
1:39.53i	Cardiff Metropolitan University		1h1	Sheffield	18	Feb
1:40.84i	Birmingham University		4	Sheffield	19	Feb
1:40.92i	England	U20	1	Cardiff	5	Mar
1:40.95i	Edinburgh AC		1	Glasgow	4	Mar
1:41.24i	Wales	U20	2	Cardiff	5	Mar

Under 17 Team

1:43.92i	Victoria Park City of Glasgow AC	1	Glasgow	4	Mar

Under 15 Team

1:46.62i	Giffnock North AAC	1	Glasgow	4	Mar

Under 13 Team

1:51.1	Blackheath & Bromley H AC	1	Bromley	10	Sep

4 x 300 Metres - Under 17

2:36.77	South of England Schools	1	Loughborough	1	Sep
2:40.45	England Schools	1	Dublin (S), IRL	15	Jul
2:42.43	Scotland Schools	2	Loughborough	1	Sep
2:42.89	North of England Schools	3	Loughborough	1	Sep
2:43.17	Midlands Schools	4	Loughborough	23	Jul
2:43.36	Wales Schools	2	Dublin (S), IRL	15	Jul

Club Teams

2:47.69	Giffnock North AAC	1	Grangemouth	22	Apr
2:47.9	Orion Harriers	1	Hornchurch	30	Jun
2:48.24	Windsor SE&H AC	1	Birmingham	3	Sep
2:48.41	Central AC	2	Grangemouth	22	Apr
2:50.7	Birchfield Harriers	1	Rugby	28	May
2:51.19	Livingston AC	3	Grangemouth	22	Apr
2:51.92	Crawley AC	1	Norwich	30	Apr
2:52.00	Edinburgh AC	4	Grangemouth	22	Apr
2:52.95	Victoria Park City of Glasgow AC	5	Grangemouth	22	Apr
2:53.2	Marshall Milton Keynes AC	2	Rugby	28	May
2:53.2	Cannock & Stafford AC	3	Rugby	28	May

Under 15 Teams

2:49.13	Blackheath & Bromley H AC	1	Bromley	15	Jul
2:51.76	Giffnock North AAC	1	Grangemouth	22	Apr
2:52.6	Sale Harriers Manchester	1	Manchester (SC)	18	Jun
2:54.6	Preston Harriers	2	Preston	15	Jul
2:54.82	Edinburgh AC	3	Birmingham	2	Sep
2:54.85	Bracknell AC	2	Bromley	15	Jul
2:56.3	Eastbourne Rovers AC	1	Brighton	1	Sep
2:56.33	Victoria Park City of Glasgow AC	1	Grangemouth	29	Jul
2:56.77	Southampton AC	4	Birmingham	2	Sep
2:56.8	Tonbridge AC	1	Bedford	16	Jul

4 x 400 Metres

3:24.74	National Team	2h1	London (O)	12	Aug

(Zoey Clark 51.5, Laviai Nielsen 50.4, Perri Shakes-Drayton 52.10, Emily Diamond 50.71)

3:25.00	National Team	2	London (O)	13	Aug

(Zoey Clark 51.5, Laviai Nielsen 51.0, Eilidh Doyle 51.5, Emily Diamond 51.0)

3:28.72	National Team	4	Nassau, BAH	23	Apr

(Emily Diamond 51.55, Laviai Nielsen 51.56, Eilidh Doyle 52.32, Christine Ohuruogu 53.29)

3:28.96	National Team	4r1	Villeneuve d'Ascq, FRA	25	Jun

(Emily Diamond 52.7e, Laviai Nielsen 51.8e, Kirsten McAslan 51.91, Anyika Onuora 52.57)

3:30.74	National Under 23 Team	U23	4	Bydgoszcz, POL	16	Jul

(Lina Nielsen 53.3, Laviai Nielsen 51.8, Jessica Turner 52.99, Cheriece Hylton 52.72)

3:31.05i	National Team		1	Belgrade, SRB	5	Mar

(Eilidh Doyle 53.18, Philippa Lowe 53.27, Mary Iheke 52.85, Laviai Nielsen 51.75)

3:33.00	National Team		2h2	Nassau, BAH	22	Apr

(Eilidh Doyle 52.49, Emily Diamond 52.31, Anyika Onuora 53.22, Kelly Massey 54.98)

3:33.68	National Junior Team	U20	3	Grossetto, ITA	23	Jul

(Mair Edwards 55.4, Maya Bruney 51.7, Ella Barrett 53.73, Hannah Williams 52.98)

3:34.62	Scotland		1	Loughborough	21	May

(Zoey Clark 53.4, Kelsey Stewart 54.3, Beth Dobbin 54.5, Kirsten McAslan 52.5)

3:35.49	England		2	Loughborough	21	May

(Kelly Massey 54.7, Ese Okoro 53.7, Olivia Caesar 54.0, Mary Iheke 53.2)

3:35.82	Loughborough University		3	Loughborough	21	May

(Laura Wake 56.2, Jessie Knight 54.0, Amy Allcock 52.8, Jessica Turner 52.9)

3:38.38	Thames Valley Harriers		1	Bromley	16	Jul

(Jess Tappin, Angela Barrett, Aisha Naibe-Wey, SLE, Zoey Clark)

3:40.13	Scotland		1	Manchester (SC)	16	Aug

(Stacey Downie, Jill Cherry, Beth Dobbin, Kelsey Stewart)

3:40.62	National Junior Team	U20	2h2	Grossetto, ITA	22	Jul

(Jill Cherry 55.9, Mair Edwards 55.2, Ella Barrett 54.70, Holly McArthur 54.92)

3:40.9	Swansea Harriers		2	Bromley	16	Jul

(Caryl Granville, Lauren Williams, Bethany Close, Olivia Caesar)

3:41.91	National Junior Team	U20	4	Loughborough	21	May

(Jill Cherry 55.7, Hannah Williams 55.4, Emma Alderson 55.3, Lauren Russell 55.6)

3:42.04	Sale Harriers Manchester		1	Wigan	7	May

(Chelsea Walker, Kirsten McAslan, Rachael Scott, Jess Taylor-Jemmett)

3:42.8	Birchfield Harriers		3	Bromley	16	Jul

(Ejiro Okoro, Georgina Rogers, Hermione Plumtre, Meghan Beesley)

3:43.21	Wales		5	Loughborough	21	May

(Seren Bundy-Davies 57.1, Caryl Granville 53.6, Rhiannon Linington-Payne 56.5, Laura Maddox 56.1)

3:43.66	Thames Valley Harriers		1	Eton	3	Jun

(Jozae Grant, Sophie Preece, Aisha Naibe-Wey, SLE, Zoey Clark)

Additional Club Teams (1-5 above)

3:44.79	Windsor SE&H AC	2	Eton	3	Jun
3:45.47	Shaftesbury Barnet Harriers	1	London (O)	2	Aug
3:46.90	Bath University	2	Bedford	1	May
3:48.73	Crawley AC	2	Wigan	7	May
3:49.7	Blackheath & Bromley H AC	4	Bromley	16	Jul
3:49.8	Trafford AC	1	Bedford	3	Jun
3:50.70	Cardiff AAC	1	Leigh	16	Jul
3:50.7	Notts AC	2	Bedford	3	Jun
3:50.9	Edinburgh AC	5	Bromley	16	Jul
3:51.22	Victoria Park City of Glasgow AC	1	Glasgow (S)	16	Jul
3:52.19	Achilles Club	2	Philadelphia, USA	15	Apr
3:54.1	Southampton AC	2	Southampton	6	May
3:54.3	Woodford Green with Essex Ladies	6	Bromley	16	Jul
3:54.76i	Oxford University	1	London (LV)	4	Mar
3:55.93	Cambridge University	1	Cambridge	14	May

Additional Under 20 Club Teams

3:50.95	Blackheath & Bromley H AC	2	Brno, CZE	16	Sep
3:56.52	Liverpool H & AC	1	Manchester (Str)	28	May
3:58.0	Tonbridge AC	1	Tonbridge	23	Jul
4:02.6	Bracknell AC	1	Woking	15	Apr
4:03.28	Shaftesbury Barnet Harriers	2	Bromley	28	May
4:03.54	Sale Harriers Manchester	2	Manchester (Str)	28	May
4:03.6	Thames Valley Harriers	1	Perivale	28	May
4:03.87	Trafford AC	3	Manchester (Str)	28	May
4:03.89	Windsor SE&H AC	3	Bromley	28	May
4:04.13	Edinburgh AC	2	Sheffield	23	Jul

ALLARNBY-JOHN Jayden U15 3.11.02, West Midland Sch
200- 22.84
ALLAWAY Joshua 24.11.92, Channel Islands
100- 10.55w (10.78-15)
ALLEN Dominic U23 5.09.97, Southampton/Lough St
JT- 61.03
ALLEN Jacob 3.10.94, Rugby & North/St Marys Un
3k- 8:18.93 (8:05.71-15)
ALLEN Jake 29.05.94, West Suffolk
HT- 47.19
ALLEN Joshua Denis U20 23.01.00, Middlesboro Mandale
800- 1:50.50
ALLEN Richard U23 25.10.95, Aldershot F&D
10k- 30:26.88, 10kR- 30:07 (29:59-16)
ALLISON Lucian 11.11.90, Lincoln Wellington
3k- 8:19.36, 10k- 30:09.36, 10kR- 29:55, HMar- 67:45
ALLWAY James U23 25.09.97, Chelmsford
PV- 4.11i (4.20-16)
ALLWOOD Julien 19.11.92, Herne Hill/London Un
TJ- 15.45w/14.49 (15.51w/15.22-12, 15.37i-13)
ALMOND Sam U15 24.11.02, Eden Runners
1500- 4:18.02
ALVAREZ Matthew U20 8.01.00, Taunton
100- 10.79w, 200- 21.86
AMANING Edmond 27.10.93, Thames Valley
60- 6.76i, 100- 10.44w/10.54 (10.44w-13),
200- 20.52w/20.86, 400- 46.49
AMED Morgan U20 2.04.99, Coventry Godiva
200- 21.77w/21.8
AMEDEE Cameron U20 27.09.98, Ashford
60HJ- 8.39i, 400H- 54.7
AMOKWANDOH Stefan U23 11.09.96, Blackheath & Brom/
Princeton Un   TJ- 15.71
AMON Patrick U15 11.02.03, Herne Hill
HJ- 1.75
ANDERSON Jamie U20 8.03.98, Bristol & West
HJ- 2.00i/1.97 (2.01-16)
ANDERSON Michael U15 28.06.03, Kingston & Poly
TJ- 13.10
ANDERSON Tom 12.01.90, Winchester
HMar- 66:44 (64:03-16), Mar- 2:19.36
ANDOH William U17 5.09.01, VPH &TH
100- 11.03
ANDREW Jack 12.10.91, Sale
110H- 14.67 (14.3-14, 14.54w-13, 14.57-16),
PV- 4.70 (4.86-10), Dec- 7048 (7170-15)
ANDREWS Mark 9.01.89, Holland Sports AC
Dec- 4631
ANDREWS-HAYCOCKS Tayo U23 31.03.96, Herne Hill/
London Un   HJ- 2.06
ANEJU Oyare U15 28.03.03, Radley AC
TJ- 13.31
ANGILA Jeff U23 5.09.97, Exeter/Cardiff Met
TJ- 13.93
ANGUS Fraser John U20 13.01.00, Ayr Seaforth
100- 10.85w, 200- 21.60i/21.84
ANOCHIRIONYE Ogo 14.11.92, TVH/ Birmingham Un
LJ- 7.32 (7.39-16)
ANSTICE Tom U23 27.03.97, Radley AC
JT- 55.37 (64.16-16)
ANTELL Shaun 9.05.87, Bideford
5k- 14:29.37 (14:21.73-16), 10kR- 30:04,
HMar- 67:45 (66:38-16)
ANYA-JOSEPH Graig U15 6.10.03, Colchester H
60- 7.36i, 100- 10.94
APPIAH-KUBI Louis U15 22.09.02, Sale
60- 7.14i/7.18i, 100- 11.11, 200- 23.08
APPS Benjamin U17 30.05.01, Southport
TJ- 13.29
ARCHER Christian U15 30.10.02, Notts
SPB- 13.06
ARIYO-FRANCIS Dominic U15 25.09.02, Woking
200- 22.88
ARMITAGE-HOOKES Noah U20 27.10.99, Cambridge H
5k- 15:11.8
ARMSTRONG George U23 8.12.97, Leeds/Lough St
DT- 56.77

ARMSTRONG Joshua U20 23.12.99, City of Lisburn
60HJ- 8.36i, 110HJ- 14.91, TJ- 13.87i (13.09-16)
ARNOLD Kyle U23 11.11.96, Newport
60H- 8.33i
ARNOLD Matthew U23 5.08.96, Aldershot F&D
3kSt- 9:28.50
ARROSPIDE Iraitz 5.08.88, C of Sheffield/Sheff Un/ESP
HMar- 65:35, Mar- 2:18:09
ARTHUR Joseph U20 15.01.99, Edinburgh AC
3k- 8:30.70
ARTHUR Reuben U23 12.10.96, Enfield & Har/London Un
60- 6.78i (6.71i-16), 100- 10.18, 200- 21.09w/21.29
ARYEETEY David U20 25.10.99, Charnwood
60HJ- 8.55i, 110HJ- 14.58w/14.65
ASHAOLU Kehinde U13, Essex Schools
HJ- 1.67
ASHBY Thomas 5.04.90, Herne Hill
110H- 15.5 (14.66w/14.74-11), SP- 13.01 (14.83-13),
DT- 44.11 (49.98-10)
ASHCROFT John 13.11.92, Liverpool H/Leeds Un
800- 1:50.73, 1500- 3:43.97i/3:45.36 (3:44.93-16),
3k- 8:04.87i, 5kR- 14:27
ASHDOWN-TAYLOR Charlie U20 19.09.99, Bracknell
DECJ- 6200
ASHFORD Christopher V35 6.01.81, BRAT
Mar- 2:29:02, 100kR- 7:33:52
ASHLEY Matthew 4.07.89, City of Sheffield
HJ- 2.05i/2.01 (2.07i-12, 2.05-14)
ASHWELL Dominic U20 13.06.99, Shaftesbury B
60- 6.78i, 100- 10.31w/10.36
ASPINDLE Glenn U20 22.06.98, Spenborough
DECJ- 5433 (5789-16)
ASPREY George U15 8.01.03, Aldershot F&D
PenB- 2656, OctB- 3822
ASSONGO TREE Denis U17 2.02.01, City of Norwich
TJ- 13.62
ATKIN Patrick 15.10.94, Cleethorpes
Dec- 5778
ATKIN Sam 14.03.93, Lincoln Wellington/Lewis Un, USA
5kR- 13:56
ATKINSON Oliver U13 16.10.04, Crewe & Nantwich
PenC- 1837
ATKINSON Thomas Harry U17 29.09.00, Cardiff
TJ- 13.93
ATKINSON Thomas 22.03.92, Sale
800- 1:50.6 (1:49.31-15)
ATWELL Nicholas 9.04.86, Herne Hill
60- 6.92i (6.91i-16), 400- 47.21
AUGUSTIN Casey U15 6.09.02, Harrow
800- 2:02.54
AUGUSTUS Dvontae U15 7.09.02, Rugby & Nor AC
TJ- 12.57
AUSTIN Thomas 6.04.94, Poole
3kSt- 9:09.83 (9:07.92-16)
AVERY Carl 28.08.86, Morpeth
5kR- 14:35, 10kR- 30:30
AWDE David 6.01.84, Andover
Dec- 4757
AXE Rowan 17.05.91, Cardiff
800- 1:48.78, 1500- 3:38.12, 3k- 7:59.66,
10kR- 30:11 (29:55-13)
AYANFUL Eugene 14.05.90, W.Green & Ex L/GHA
100- 10.51 (10.34-12)
AYIVI-KNOTT Noah U13 27.11.04, Camberley
LJ- 5.06
AYOADE Memphis U15 13.09.02, Herne Hill
300- 36.96, HJ- 1.80
AYO-OJO Tolu U17 26.08.02, Camberley
PV- 3.80
AZU Jeremiah U17 15.05.01, Cardiff
60- 6.99i, 100- 10.65

B ABATUNDE Adebayo 21.08.87, Middlesboro Mandale
TJ- 14.64 (15.94-11
BACON Joseph U20 17.06.00, Newquay & Par
400H- 56.20
BADDICK Francis 29.11.85, Newham & Essex B
1500- 3:46.35 (3:42.06-14), 5k- 14:31.00 (14:03.86-16)

BAILEY Cameron U17 10.12.00, Ipswich
100- 11.1, 200- 22.12
BAILEY Hayden U17 10.09.00, Team Bath
800- 1:54.81
BAILEY Jonathan U23 16.07.95, Cardiff/Loughborough St
HJ- 2.08 (2.09-16)
BAILEY Leon 19.07.91, Rugby & Northampton
JT- 56.82
BAINBRIDGE Christopher U23 16.06.95, Grantham
HT- 49.76
BAINBRIDGE Daniel U20 2.06.99, Shaftesbury B
JT- 62.46
BAINES Dylan U17 3.10.01, Stevenage & NH
PV- 4.21
BAINES Elliott U23 5.08.97, Seaton/Cambridge Un
LJ- 6.91w
BAINES Thomas U17 22.11.00, Warrington
400- 49.41
BAINS Thomas Jasbir U23 3.01.95, Hallamshire
10k- 30:51.73
BAJERE Scott 12.05.92, Bristol & West
60- 6.86i (6.80iA-15, 6.84i-13),
100- 10.63w/10.75 (10.5w-11, 10.51-15)
BAKER Andrew 22.07.85, Yeovil Olympiads
Mar- 2:24:24
BAKER Christopher 2.02.91, Sale
HJ- 2.28 (2.36i/2.29-16)
BAKER Donald Edward U20 31.01.00, Ipswich
JT- 62.10, JTY- 66.45
BAKER Harry U20 18.11.99, Horsham BS
HJ- 2.05
BAKER Kenneth V40 19.02.74, Nene Valley H
SP- 13.15i (14.35-11)
BAKER Niclas 9.09.94, Crawley
200- 20.89w (21.63-16), 400- 47.05
BAKER Sonny U15 13.03.03, Torbay
JTB- 46.38
BALDOCK Dylan U17 31.01.01, Sutton & District
100- 11.10, 200- 22.01
BALL Luke U13 28.10.04, Yate
60HC- 9.9i, HJ- 1.65, LJ- 5.21, PenC- 2025
BALL Samuel U13 18.10.04, Reading
100- 12.4, 200- 25.4, 60HB- 9.32i, 75HC- 11.48,
LJ- 5.72, PenC- 2319, PenIB- 2525i
BANCROFT Jack 25.02.88, Bristol & West
5k- 14:32.89, 10k- 30:35.35
BANIGO Reynold U20 13.08.98, Sale
LJ- 7.45w/7.42i/7.23 (7.40-16)
BANKS Daniel U20 3.10.99, Worcester AC
100- 10.74w/10.8
BANKS Edward 30.05.85, Birchfield
3kSt- 9:34.44
BANWELL-CLODE David 29.12.92, Cwmbran/N.Mexico U
800- 1:51.77 (1:50.84-13)
BAPTISTE Matthew 28.10.90, Newham & Essex B
SP- 15.72, DT- 50.52, HT- 45.40 (47.83-15)
BARBARESI Oliver U20 23.03.00, Menai
3k- 8:30.65
BARBER Joss U20 22.06.99, Blackheath & Bromley
2kSt- 6:04.77
BARBOUR Edward U20 3.03.98, Amber Valley/L'pool Un
TJ- 13.85
BARKER Scott U23 20.03.97, Andover/Loughborough St
400- 48.63 (48.38-15)
BARNABY Dominic U20 10.06.99, South London H
SPJ- 14.35
BARNES Ciaran U20 8.08.98, Lisburn
400H- 54.98 (54.86-16)
BARNES Jeremy U23 29.05.97, Coventry Godiva
800- 1:51.42
BARNICOAT Will U15 24.03.03, Aldershot F&D
1500- 4:10.97
BARTLETT Philip U17 5.09.00, South London H
DTY- 52.57
BARTON-ELLINGTON Omari 5.01.90, Enfield & Haringey
60- 6.88i, 100- 10.56w/10.57 (10.40w-16, 10.50-15)

BARTRAM Michael U23 6.12.96, W.Suffolk/Sheffield Un
3kSt- 9:12.64
BASS-COOPER Samuel U23 26.01.96, So'ton/So'ton Un
PV- 4.71 (4.90-16)
BASSUE Mikkel Raquahn U20 15.08.00, Bristol & W/IVB
60- 6.94i
BASTEN Ben U15 2.08.03, Crewe & Nantwich
60- 7.40i, 100- 11.22, 200- 23.43
BATE Roger 16.01.83, Trafford
DT- 43.12 (49.89-04), HT- 50.68 (61.61-09)
BATKIN Fynn U17 6.03.01, Kettering
3k- 8:50.78
BATTERSHILL William U20 25.02.98, Erme Valley/ Harvard
2kSt- 6:03.72 (5:49.44-16), 3kSt- 8:55.84
BATTISTI Tommasco 15.05.92, Cardiff/ITA
PV- 4.30
BAYTON Steven 6.08.91, Hallamshire/Sheffield Un
10k- 30:26.18, HMar- 67:52, Mar- 2:19:41
BAZANYE-LUTU Sean U20 29.09.98, Enfield & Haringey
110Hu- 15.06
BEADSLEY Daniel U23 28.02.97, Swansea/Cardiff Met
60- 6.92i, 100- 10.72 (10.7-16)
BEAL Joseph U15 16.11.02, Worthing
HTB- 46.55
BEARDSELL Richard V35 19.01.79, Trafford
400- 48.70 (47.52-08)
BEASTALL Phil 31.08.86, Cheltenham
10k- 30:12.24, 10kR- 30:03
BEATTIE John 20.01.86, Newham & Essex B
5kR- 14:23 (13:42.03t-10), 10kR- 29:57 (28:32.21t-10),
HMar- 67:58 (64:48-15)
BEATTIE Scott U20 4.12.98, Morpeth
1500- 3:52.61 (3:51.88-16)
BEBBINGTON Daniel U23 8.06.96, Preston/Edge Hill Un
800- 1:51.43
BECKETT Tom U23 29.05.96, Gloucester AC/Exeter Un
Dec- 4261
BEDFORD James 29.12.88, Birchfield
HT- 66.70 (70.82-13)
BEECHEY Alex 8.06.91, Southampton/Southampton Un
200- 21.57 (21.48-16)
BEEKS James U20 13.10.98, Basingstoke & MH
2kSt- 5:57.2, 3kSt- 9:29.80
BEEVOR Luke M. 4.03.84, Luton
Mar- 2:29:25
BELCH Gordon 7.01.92, VP-Glasgow
Dec- 5065
BELL Cameron U20 2.01.99, Hallamshire
800- 1:51.60
BELL Howard U20 2.05.98, Edinburgh AC/Edinburgh Un
60HJ- 8.55i, 110HJ- 15.14 (15.02-16), PV- 4.10,
HepJ- 5068i, DECJ- 6417 (6623-16)
BELL Matthew V35 2.06.78, Kettering
HT- 50.51 (64.22-07)
BELL Richard J 17.06.92, Manx H
HT- 49.52 (50.85-14)
BELLAMY Will U15 31.03.03, Houghton
1500- 4:14.7, 3k- 9:11.20
BELLO Olowasubomi U17 16.11.01, VPH &TH
TJ- 13.20
BELLWARD James 18.10.84, RAF/Bedford & Co
50kR- 3:15:58
BENJAMIN Damaine 12.03.88, Harrow/JAM
400- 48.80, 400H- 54.30
BENJAMIN Lazarus U15 19.01.04, Sale
PV- 3.20i
BENNETT Aaron 29.01.92, Southampton
800- 1:51.63 (1:49.18-14)
BENNETT Christopher 17.12.89, Shaftesbury B
HT- 75.72 (76.45-16)
BENNETT Paul 11.12.92, Cardiff/Cardiff Met
200- 21.58w (21.97-14), 400H- 51.71 (51.55-14)
BENNETT Samuel Morrison U17 2.02.01, Basildon
100- 11.10 (10.97-16), 200- 22.46, 60HJ- 8.23i,
60HY- 8.07i, 100HY- 12.76, 110HY- 13.60, OctY- 4607

BENNETT Simon V40 16.10.72, W.Green & Ex L
JT- 57.29 (66.58-96)
BENSON Gordon 12.05.94, Leeds
5kR- 14:32 (14:17-14)
BENTLEY Connor U17 19.01.01, Wrekin RR
1500- 4:03.49, 3k- 8:40.74
BENTLEY Russell V35 28.04.81, Kent AC
HMar- 67:34, Mar- 2:20:20
BERGIN Matthew 2.03.93, Bedford/New Mexico Un/IRL
3k- 8:01.58 (7:58.63-16), 5k- 14:03.87 (13:54.31-15)
BERKELEY Jacob U20 11.09.98, Shaftesbury B
100- 10.79w
BERNSTEIN Alex U15 13.11.02, Preston
HTB- 55.51
BERROW Alexander 10.06.89, Tamworth
HT- 52.03 (52.09-10)
BERRYMAN Elliot U20 2.10.98, Yeovil Olympiads
DTJ- 46.34
BERWICK Adam U17 3.11.00, Amber Valley
HJ- 1.93
BERWICK Jack U17 3.11.00, Amber Valley
100HY- 14.0, 400HY- 58.15
BETTS Edward George V45 18.02.71, TVH/
Universidad Oviedo ESP   400H- 55.48 (50.49-97)
BEVAN Niall U20 14.10.98, Enfield & Har
60- 6.89i, 100- 10.72w, 200- 21.90w
BHEKA Marvin 29.01.87, Cardiff/Cardiff Met/ZIM
60- 6.94i (6.87i-14), 100- 10.67
BIDDELL Lloyd V35 12.08.81, Mercia Fell Runners
Mar- 2:26:12
BIGG Finley U20 2.06.98, Brighton Phoenix
400- 49.14 (48.66-16), 800- 1:49.24
BINNS Jake U20 5.11.98, Worthing
60- 6.99i
BIRD John 17.05.92, Ipswich
800- 1:47.79
BIRKETT Alexander U20 9.11.99, Kendal
800- 1:50.71
BIRNIE Finn U17 26.09.00, Newquay & Par
1500- 4:01.25
BIRSE Stephen V35 8.10.77, Middlesboro Mandale
SP- 13.11, JT- 54.56 (57.92-95)
BISHOP Toby U15 3.10.03, Havering
60HB- 9.06i
BIZIMANA Yusuf U17 16.09.00, Ilford
800- 1:55.65, 1500- 3:55.28
BLACKBURN Matthew 14.09.85,
24HrT- 218.257kms
BLACKLOCK Matthew U13 3.10.04, Havering
1500- 4:32.11
BLACKMAN Evan U17 22.11.01, Corby
200- 22.16w/22.4, 400- 49.7/50.12
BLACKWELL Liam U15 5.09.02, Preston
800- 1:59.40
BLADON Stuart U17 13.01.02, Team Kennet
60HY- 8.61i, OctY- 4922, HeplY- 4108i
BLAIR Montez 23.10.90, Shaftesbury B/Lough St/USA
HJ- 2.19 (2.27i/2.25-13)
BLAKE Dominic U20 21.09.99, Trafford
TJ- 13.74
BLAKE George U20 31.12.99, Medway & Maidstone
DECJ- 5392
BLANC Jacob U13 19.10.04, Havering
75HC- 12.1
BLANDFORD Matthew U23 21.10.95, Blackheath & Brom/
Exeter Un   SP- 14.86 (15.05i-16), DT- 55.60 (55.68-16)
BLATCHFORD-KEMP Chey U20 2.09.99, Reading
2kSt- 6:17.6 (6:03.70-16)
BLEVINS Joshua James U13 15.09.04, North Shields P
800- 2:16.2
BLOMQUIST Dane U23 2.10.96, Aldershot F&D
5k- 14:29.00
BLOOMFIELD Joseph 3.11.90, Ipswich
HT- 61.99 (64.57-11)
BLOW Andy 22.09.85, Basingstoke & MH
60H- 7.96i

BOBASH Yasha 24.12.87, Chelmsford
HT- 45.98
BODEN Kyle U15 24.09.02, Birchfield
LJ- 6.11i/6.06
BOLARINWA David 20.10.93, Newham & Essex B
60- 6.86i (6.80i-12), 200- 21.42 (20.60-13)
100- 10.29w/10.46 (10.23w/10.29-11)
BOLDIZSAR Shemar U20 24.01.99, Harlow
60- 6.94i, 200- 21.9/21.94
BOLLAND Oliver U15 22.09.02, City of Sheffield
300- 36.93
BOMBA Michael 10.10.86, Liverpool H
HT- 69.15 (70.90-13)
BOND Matthew 17.07.82, Sale
HMar- 66:31 (64:29-12), Mar- 2:21:13 (2:15:32-16)
BONDSWELL Matthew U17 18.04.02, Notts Schools
TJ- 13.67
BONE David V45 14.04.72,
24Hr- 210.126km
BONELLA-DUKE Jamie U15 20.01.03, Reading
HTB- 47.24
BONES Joshua 8.05.93, Scunthorpe
TJ- 15.50w/15.21
BONGART James U23 30.07.96, WG & EL/Notts Trent Un
JT- 62.08
BONIFAS Ryan 22.09.93, Basingstoke & MH
HJ- 2.11 (2.13i-16, 2.11-15)
BOOKER Harry U15 9.09.03, Team Kennet
DTB- 39.34
BOOTH Tom U23 29.11.96, Preston/Salford Un
PV- 4.51 (4.80-15)
BOSE William U15 6.12.02, Essex Schools
HJ- 1.89
BOSWELL Jack U20 27.12.98, Aldershot F&D
3k- 8:27.59
BOSWORTH Thomas 17.01.90, Tonbridge
1MW- 5:31.08, 2kW- 7:29.19+ (7:21.32i+-16), 3kW-
11:15.26+ (10:58.21i-16), 5kW- 18:39.47i/18:43.28,
10kWR- 39:50+ (39:36-15), 20kW- 1:20:58 (1:20:13-16)
BOTTERILL Alex Eric U20 18.01.00, City of York
400- 49.0/49.09, 800- 1:48.68
BOUGOURD James 4.10.89, Southampton
JT- 57.64
BOUJU Raphael U17 15.05.02, Bedford & County
60- 6.88i, 100- 10.73
BOWIE Jamie Kerr 1.04.89, Team East Lothian
400- 47.43i (46.06-13)
BOWLER James V35 2.09.79, Kent AC
Mar- 2:27:34
BOWLER Michael 28.01.92, Birmingham Un/IRL
110H- 14.79w/14.93, PV- 4.55, LJ- 7.02, Dec- 7032
BOWLEY Dylan U15 14.05.03, Kettering
800- 2:02.61, 1500- 4:14.17, 3k- 9:19.69
BOWNESS James Sydney 26.11.91, Trafford/
Glasgow Caledonian Un.   800- 1:46.40 (1:45.96-16),
1500- 3:46.49+/3:48.13 (3:45.74-16), 1M- 4:03.26,
3k- 8:11.65i
BOWSHER Andrew U17 10.05.01, Inverness
DTY- 41.79
BOXALL Zephan U17 1.11.01, Stratford-upon-Avon
60HY- 8.56i, 100HY- 14.0
BOYEK Cameron Ross 9.10.93, Shildon
1500- 3:45.09 (3:39.15-15), 2k- 5:12.28i,
5kR- 14:34 (14:08-15)
BOYLE Adam U20 13.09.99, VP-Glasgow
JT- 62.44
BRADLEY Ben U23 22.05.95, AF&D/St Marys Un
3k- 8:13.38, 5k- 14:06.26, 10k- 30:57.48
BRADLEY Conor 6.10.87, Derry
1500- 3:47.89 (3:43.37i-14, 3:43.39-13), 5k- 14:01.86
BRADLEY Drew U13 13.10.04, Crewe & Nantwich
75HC- 11.9/12.16
BRADLY Matthew U20 27.09.98, WSE&H
2kSt- 6:18.7 (6:14.31-16)
BRADSHAW Lukas U15 18.09.02, City of York
DTB- 40.93

374

BRADSHAW Owen U13 7.12.04, City of Sheffield
2kW- 11:30.3
BRADSTOCK Arne Roald V55 24.04.62,
JT- 66.76 (83.84-87)
BRAMBLE Daniel 14.10.90, Shaftesbury B
LJ- 8.02 (8.21-15)
BRAME Max U17 19.07.01, Liverpool H
3k- 8:45.51
BRANAGH Ben 11.01.94, St Malachy's
5k- 14:16.79, 5MR- 24:20
BRECKER Alex 15.12.93, City of Stoke
1500- 3:48.12 (3:47.62-15), 3k- 8:07.07,
5k- 14:14.06 (14:12.04-16)
BREEN Bryce U15 22.08.03, Herts Phoenix
PV- 3.60
BREEN Elliot U17 2.10.00, Herts Phoenix
PV- 3.85
BRERETON Samuel U15 22.09.02, Newquay & Par
HJ- 2.00
BRIARS Oliver U15 17.12.02, Blackheath & Bromley
300- 36.26, 400- 52.13
BRICE David 9.04.91, Aldershot F&D
JT- 53.31 (61.57-13)
BRIER Joseph U20 16.03.99, Swansea
400- 47.84 (47.62-16)
BRIGGS Jonathan U23 12.12.97, BRAT/Hallam Un
SP- 13.55, DT- 42.37, HT- 45.65
BRIGGS Samuel U17 27.12.00, Falkirk VH
HTY- 55.25
BRIGHT Oliver U15 9.04.03, Kent
800- 1:59.47, 1500- 4:12.56, 3k- 9:05.52
BRIGHT-DAVIES Jude U20 27.03.99, Thames Valley
LJ- 6.86i, TJ- 15.71
BRINDLEY Aidan U15 9.10.03, North Ayrshire
PV- 3.30i
BRINDLEY Scott U17 6.01.02, North Ayrshire
PV- 4.10i/3.90, DecY- 5231
BRINING Matthew U17 9.12.01, New Marske
PV- 4.00i
BRINTON-QUINN Peter U15 21.10.02, Havering
PV- 3.00
BRITT Thomas U17 25.12.00, Cardiff
PV- 3.70, LJ- 6.47w, HepIY- 4236i, DecY- 5399,
OctY- 4342+/4329
BRITTO Carl 5.12.90, Harrow/Oxford Un/IND
TJ- 14.64 (15.26-10)
BROADBENT Jack U20 8.07.00, Basildon
DECJ- 5020
BROMBY Oliver U20 30.03.98, Southampton
60- 6.80i (6.73i-16), 100- 10.31,
200- 21.31w/21.51 (21.32-15)
BROOKS Adam U20 13.04.99, Yate
HJ- 1.97 (1.97-16)
BROOKS Daniel U17 6.12.00, Yate
100- 11.03 (10.8w-16)
BROOKS Rafe U17 29.09.00, Brighton & Hove
LJ- 6.68
BROOM William U17 25.01.01, Chichester R&AC
3k- 8:53.87
BROOME Jordan U23 4.12.96, Coventry Godiva
100- 10.69 (10.68-16), 200- 21.40 (21.15-16)
BROOM-EDWARDS Jonathan 27.05.88, Newham & Ex B
HJ- 2.13i/2.12 (2.15-14)
BROWN Alexander U20 2.10.98, Houghton
5k- 15:00.50
BROWN Ben U13 28.02.05, Southampton
1500- 4:35.41
BROWN Callum 20.07.94, City of Norwich
HT- 69.13
BROWN Daniel U17 20.03.02, Edinburgh AC
JTY- 51.23
BROWN Dominic 8.10.94, Tonbridge/Sheffield Un
800- 1:51.97 (1:51.75-16), 1500- 3:46.62, 1M- 4:06.71
BROWN Eddie U15 25.09.02, Cambridge H
JTB- 44.81

BROWN Edward U15 23.01.03, Braintree
100- 11.47w
BROWN Ethan U17 9.05.01, Blackheath & Bromley
100- 11.12, 200- 22.20, 400- 47.82
BROWN Jacob U23 24.11.97, Vale Royal
800- 1:51.85
BROWN Joshua 27.12.94, Cardiff
60- 6.88i, 100- 10.55w/10.62
BROWN Kevin Dave V50 10.09.64, R Sutton Coldfield
DT- 42.34 (62.10-00)
BROWN Kevin 10.12.90, Southend
TJ- 14.01 (14.55-11)
BROWN Lewis U20 2.09.98, C of Sheffield/Strathclyde Un
400- 47.85
BROWN Matt V35 10.11.80, Enfield & Haringey
DT- 48.12 (56.97-08)
BROWN Maxwell U20 23.11.99, Marshall Milton K
60- 6.92i, 100- 10.60w/10.66
BROWN Rivaldo U20 7.09.98, Trafford
60HJ- 8.28i, 110HJ- 15.0/15.21 (14.68-16)
BROWN Sam U20 21.03.00, Edinburgh AC
800- 1:52.94
BROWNING Jonathan 16.12.93, Ballymena & A/IRL
60- 6.92i (6.80i-16)
BROWNLEE Jonathan 30.04.90, Bingley
10kR- 29:54
BRUNEY Khalil U20 13.06.98, Enfield & Har/Brunel Un
60- 6.99i, 200- 21.62w, 400- 49.03
BRUNSDEN Daniel Peter 18.04.88, Bournemouth
SP- 14.51 (16.78-16), DT- 45.74 (45.75-15),
HT- 44.99 (46.36-10)
BRUNSDEN Steven 17.05.90, Kent AC
HT- 49.01
BRUNT Daniel V40 23.04.76, City of Sheffield
SP- 14.33 (15.72-07), DT- 43.00 (47.94-00)
BRYANT Ashley Ross 17.05.91, WSE&H
60H- 8.09i, 110H- 14.49 (14.1/14.28w-14, 14.31-13),
HJ- 1.98i/1.97 (2.01-16), PV- 4.50i/4.50 (4.70-14),
LJ- 7.79i/7.70, SP- 14.65i/14.20 (14.34-14),
DT- 44.33 (45.38-14), JT- 67.97 (70.44-13), Dec- 8163,
HepIS- 5975i
BRYAN-WAUGH Brandon U13, Essex Schools
200- 25.5
BRYDEN Euan 17.05.94, WSE&H
PV- 5.15, TJ- 13.91
BUCKLAND Dominic U17 5.11.01, Stevenage & NH
DTY- 42.07
BUCKMAN Ashley U23 15.04.97, Ashford/So'ton Un
TJ- 14.09
BUCKNER Matthew U17 29.12.00, Bracknell
100- 11.02w, 200- 22.19
BULL Joshua 14.10.92, Derby AC/Notts Un
HMar- 68:07
BULLEN Thomas 12.10.92, South London H
SP- 13.78
BUNBURY Freddie 9.12.92, Cambridge Un/VIN
PV- 4.10 (4.15-14)
BURFOOT Michael U15 1.10.02, Blackheath & Bromley
SPB- 13.65, DTB- 40.31
BURGIN Max U17 20.05.02, Halifax
800- 1:49.42, 1500- 3:53.08
BURKE Nathan U20 3.09.98, Herts Phoenix
TJ- 13.88
BURTON Mark U20 11.06.98, Lisburn/Queen's Un
TJ- 14.14 (14.30i-15)
BURTON Thomas 29.10.88, Tamworth
200- 21.17w, 400- 48.59 (46.97-14),
400H- 49.95 (49.36-15)
BUSHNELL Nathan U15 29.10.02, Chelmsford
SPB- 13.40
BUTCHART Andrew 14.10.91, Central
1500- 3:37.58i+/3:39.61, 1M- 3:54.23i, 3k- 7:37.56,
2M- 8:12.63i, 5k- 13:11.45 (13:08.61-16),
10kR- 29:18 (28:28-16)
BUTLER Luke U17 6.12.00, Exeter
200- 22.46

BUTLER Thomas U20 23.02.98, Barnet
5k- 15:17.67
BYNG Lewis U17 29.09.01, Stratford-upon-Avon
SPJ- 14.19, SPY- 15.83
BYRON Ayomide David U23 16.06.97, St Albans AC/
Coventry Un 110H- 15.0/15.18
BYRON Christian 20.12.92, Birchfield/Notts Trent Un
200- 21.72w, 400- 47.43 (47.12-16)

CABLE Joel U17 24.09.01, Bracknell
JTY- 52.79, OctY- 4388
CACKETT Greg 14.11.89, Belgrave
100- 10.47 (10.24-13)
CADDICK George 29.07.94, Sale/Baylor Un USA
200- 21.14w, 400- 45.45
CAIN Leroy U23 16.05.95, Thames Valley
60- 6.85i, 100- 10.44, 200- 20.94
CAIRESS Emile U23 27.12.97, Leeds/St Marys Un
1500- 3:48.60, 3k- 8:09.13, 5k- 13:59.82, 10kR- 29:49
CAIRNEY Kaya U17 19.02.01, Newquay & Par
200- 22.21, 400HY- 57.3/57.64, OctY- 4688
CALDWELL Luke Angus 2.08.91, Dorking & MV/ Lond Un
5k- 13:59.73 (13:29.94-13), 10k- 29:01.76 (28:29.61-15)
CALHOUN Kyle U17 6.11.00, Charnwood
100- 11.04w, 200- 22.17, 400- 49.48
CALLAWAY Matthew U23 19.12.97, So'ton/Bath Un
DT- 41.62
CALVERT William U15 1.09.02, Middlesboro Mandale
200- 23.4
CAMERON Kurt U20 13.11.99, Bristol & West
DECJ- 5386
CAMERON Michael U23 18.11.95, Edinburgh AC
3kSt- 9:46.28
CAMPBELL Bayley U20 24.06.00, WSE&H
HT- 57.18, HTJ- 69.33, HTY- 73.53
CAMPBELL Evan U17 17.05.01, Channel Islands
100HY- 13.78w/13.81, LJ- 6.50w, SPY- 14.04,
HepIY- 4164i, OctY- 5129, HepIY- 4164i
CAMPBELL Taylor U23 30.06.96, C of Sheffield/Lough St
HT- 73.40
CAMPBELL Theo 14.07.91, Birchfield
100- 10.64 (10.56-15), 400- 46.81 (46.02-16)
CAMPION Ben U15 22.10.02, Gloucester AC
DTB- 37.35
CAMPION Milan U17 21.11.00, Notts
3k- 8:50.29
CANT Lewis U15 10.10.02, Blaydon
60- 7.43i, 100- 11.2/11.41, 200- 23.1/23.17
CAPES Donovan U13 5.04.05, Nene Valley H
SPC- 12.02, DTC- 31.97
CAPPS Oliver U13 20.01.05, Exeter
800- 2:15.55, 1500- 4:36.02
CARELESS Jacob U17 8.10.01, Notts
HTY- 51.13
CARELESS Robert V40 7.09.74, Notts
HT- 50.79 (60.65-01)
CARLSSON-SMITH Dylan U20 26.07.98, Shaft B/ Brunel U
60HJ- 8.56i, PV- 4.36i (4.40i-15. 4.40-16), HepJ- 4967i
CARNEY Niall U23 8.11.97, Solihull & S H
400H- 52.92
CAROLAN Ethan U15 28.08.03, Giffnock North
3k- 9:26.96
CARPENTER Adam 18.06.93, WSE&H
PV- 4.43 (5.15i-14, 5.00-13)
CARPENTER Daniel U20 7.11.99, Cheltenham
DECJ- 5269
CARPENTER Jak 26.09.90, Cannock & Stafford/Lough St
SP- 13.37i/13.36 (13.72i-16), DT- 41.40
CARR Josh 30.07.94, Thames H & H
1500- 3:40.70, 3k- 8:10.53
CARTWRIGHT Daniel U20 14.11.98, Birchfield
SP- 16.14, SPJ- 17.70i/17.63, DT- 41.18,
DTJ- 42.27 (45.45-16)
CARTWRIGHT Daniel U17 29.11.01, Tamworth
200- 22.33
CARVELL Oliver U17 9.04.02, Bridgnorth
800- 1:52.69, 1500- 4:01.0
CASSIDY Peter U20 22.01.98, Guildford & Godalming
HT- 50.33, HTJ- 59.83 (60.97-16)

CASSON Thomas U17 24.01.01, Poole
100- 11.0
CAUDERY Fynley U20 9.10.98, Cornwall AC
PV- 4.40
CAUSER Michael U23 27.05.95, St Helens Sutton
LJ- 7.52 (7.52i-14)
CAVALLI-WARBY Christian U15 3.10.02, Shaftesbury B
SPB- 13.64
CHADWICK Thomas U13 22.08.05, Manx H
100- 12.4w, LJ- 5.22w
CHALLIS Samuel U20 15.05.99, WSE&H
LJ- 7.08w/7.05
CHALMERS Alistair U20 31.03.00, Channel Islands
400H- 52.06, 400HY- 51.22
CHALMERS Cameron U23 6.02.97, Channel Is/Bath Un
400- 45.64
CHAMBEFORT Damien 22.07.93, Coventry G/FRA
HJ- 2.03 (2.06i/2.04-15)
CHAMBERS Dwain Anthony V35 5.04.78, Belgrave
60- 6.62i (6.41+-99/6.42i-09), 150- 15.52w (15.27st-12)
100- 10.31 (9.97-99, 9.87dq-02),
CHAMBERS Luke U15 23.04.03, Vale Royal
800- 2:03.90
CHAMBERS-BROWN Kaie U20 26.09.99, Birchfield
100- 10.47w/10.56, 200- 21.23w/21.8 (21.72-16)
CHANCE Samuel Thomas U17 21.10.00, Halesowen
JTY- 55.50
CHANDLER Isaac U15 1.10.02, Shaftesbury B
1500- 4:18.69, 3k- 9:05.82
CHANDLER Matthew U17 30.10.00, Central
60HY- 8.61i (8.47i-16), 100HY- 13.91, PV- 4.11,
LJ- 6.51w/6.49, HepIY- 4551i, DecY- 6167, OctY- 4866+
CHANDLER Thomas U23 19.09.97, Central/Brunel Un
PV- 4.32, Dec- 6530
CHANNON Henry U13 27.05.05, Oxford City
800- 2:16.08
CHARLES Richard 31.05.94, Shaftesbury B
800- 1:50.59i (1:47.28-15)
CHARLES Thomas 18.02.84, Trafford
HMar- 67:44, Mar- 2:23:55
CHARLTON Craig 7.03.87, RAF/Morpeth
SP- 14.14 (14.28-16)
CHARTERS Jordan U23 14.08.95, Sale
HJ- 2.00i, LJ- 7.31i/6.91 (7.34i/7.28-16)
CHESTERS Bill U17 23.06.01, Cannock & Stafford
1.5kSt- 4:32.3
CHESTERS Luke U17 22.12.00, Sale
800- 1:55.75
CHILDS Jack U15 11.06.03, Medway & Maidstone
3kW- 15:27.95
CHILDS Marshall U23 18.02.97, Ipswich
JT- 63.34 (67.07-16)
CHILDS Navid V35 12.05.81, RAF/TVH
TJ- 15.06 (15.39-11)
CHINDA Prince U15 4.04.03, Enfield & Haringey
200- 23.36
CHINERY-EDOO Saoirse Jerone 1.11.93, Harrow
DT- 45.18, Dec- 6067 (6136-16)
CHRISTIE Travis U23 1.05.97, Wolves & B/Wolvs Un
400H- 55.05 (54.67-16)
CHRISTOFOROU Michael 10.10.92, Edinburgh AC
5k- 14:25.80, 10k- 29:37.83
CHURCH Lewis U23 27.09.96, Tonbridge
110H- 15.34 (15.23-16), HJ- 2.02, SP- 13.32i, DT- 41.84,
PV- 4.30i/4.20 (4.42-15), Dec- 7068, HepIS- 5275i
CLARENCE Simeon U23 4.12.95, Cardiff/Cardiff Met
LJ- 7.06
CLARIDGE Benjamin U23 12.11.97, White Horse/Bath Un
400- 47.23
CLARK Anthony V35 2.08.77, Bournemouth
100kR- 7:04:30
CLARK Oliver U23 9.12.96, Newquay & Par/Bath Un
LJ- 7.26i (7.45-15)
CLARKE Adam 3.04.91, Aldershot F&D
800- 1:50.87 (1:49.22-15), 1500- 3:38.35,
3k- 8:16.50 (7:55.13-15), 5k- 13:39.21
CLARKE Ben U20 30.10.98, Worcester AC
60HJ- 8.52i, HepJ- 4782i

376

CLARKE Jacob U17 1.06.02, Notts
PV- 4.20i/4.02
CLARKE Lloyd U15 6.06.03, Cardiff
DTB- 40.04, JTB- 50.77
CLARKE Peter 22.07.91, W.Green & Ex L
HT- 56.32 (57.87-11)
CLARKE Thomas U15, Shropshire Schools
TJ- 12.55
CLARKSON Henry U20 16.06.99, Lasswade
LJ- 7.22, TJ- 14.25w/14.05
CLAYDON Dillon U15 1.11.03, Tonbridge
DTB- 37.85
CLAYTON Adam Robert U17 26.09.00, Giffnock N
60- 6.90i, 100- 10.68w/10.71, 200- 21.66, 400- 50.24
CLEGG Alexander U20 2.06.98, BRAT
DECJ- 5905
CLEMENTS Kieran 20.11.93, Ipswich/Iona Coll, USA
1500- 3:48.06 (3:43.55-16), 3k- 8:01.17 (7:57.67i-14),
5k- 14:02.58 (13:53.34i-15), 10kR- 30:19+,
10k- 30:19.30 (28:57.57-15), 10MR- 49:21
CLEMENTS Nick 17.06.90, Yeovil Olympiads
LJ- 7.10 (7.34w-12, 7.29-13)
CLEMONS Freddie U13 21.01.05, Stratford-upon-Avon
PenC- 1684
CLIFFE Daniel John 23.12.90, Liverpool H
10kR- 30:06 (29:46.75t-15)
CLIFTON Samuel U15 14.03.03, Winchester
HTB- 40.20
CLINTON Nyle U23 27.03.95, Swindon/Bradley Un
3kSt- 9:25.27 (9:23.25-15)
CLOW Louis U15 22.11.02, Ealing, S & Mx
60HB- 9.18i, TJ- 12.47
CLOWES Matthew 29.09.89, Staffs Moorlands/Cardiff Met
5k- 14:14.62 (14:05.32i-12, 14:08.01-16), 10k-
29:18.38, HMar- 65:11
COCHRANE Jonathan U15 27.09.02, Ballymena & A
TJ- 12.82
COCKLE Gus U23 7.03.97, AF&D/London Un
5k- 14:28.49 (14:03.26-15)
COHEN Jonathan U15 25.09.02, Shaftesbury B
PV- 3.01
COLE Benedict 18.06.85, Tonbridge
10k- 30:23.34, 10kR- 30:15, HMar- 67:57 (67:53-15)
COLE Daniel U20 28.11.98, Colchester & T
JT- 56.67
COLE Edan U20 18.02.00, Brighton & Hove
JT- 54.31, JTY- 60.23 (65.34-16)
COLE Nicolas Andrew U23 27.02.95, City of Sheffield
PV- 4.91i/4.80 (5.15-16)
COLEMAN David 14.02.86, Tonbridge
DT- 43.13 (56.50-11)
COLEMAN Jamaine U23 22.09.95, Preston/E.Kentucky U
1500- 3:48.37, 3k- 8:14.00i, 3kSt- 8:34.19
COLES Adam U17 22.03.01, Kingston u Hull
100HY- 13.92w/14.0
COLLIER Jonathan U23 22.08.95, Harrow/Butler Un USA
3k- 8:18.20i, 5k- 14:24.14, 10k- 30:20.29, 3kSt- 9:45.56
COLLINS Joseph U17 13.12.00, Team Bath
100HY- 13.59, 400HY- 58.0/58.41 (57.46-16)
COLLINS Liam James O'Neill V35 23.10.78, Gateshead
60H- 8.33i (7.94i-00)
COLLINS Xander U15 18.09.03, Croydon
60HB- 9.16i, 80HB- 11.85
COLTHERD Michael 28.12.82, Barrow Runners
3k- 8:19.37
COLTON Alex U17 4.12.01, City of York
TJ- 13.58
CONIBEAR Toby U15 26.04.03, Yate
HTB- 52.05
CONLON Greg V40 18.12.74, Walton
PV- 4.35 (4.80-05)
CONNELL Shane U17 10.03.01, Sale
HJ- 1.95i/1.90 (1.95i/1.93-16)
CONNELLY Joseph U17 9.11.00, Carlisle Aspatria
LJ- 6.58, SPY- 14.15
CONNOR Benjamin 17.10.92, Derby AC
1500- 3:48.96, 3k- 7:54.01, 5k- 13:29.90, 10k- 28:23.58,
10kR- 29:03, 15kR- 45:07+, 10MR- 48:36

CONRATHE Ben U13 29.03.06, Bourne Town H
JTC- 38.69
CONSANI Marco V40 15.11.74, Garscube
24Hr- 218.557km (250.263km-16)
CONWAY Frankie 29.09.91, Orion/Melbourne Un.
5k- 14:32.27, 10k- 30:26.82
CONWAY Luke 12.01.94, Newham & Essex B
1500- 3:46.63
COOK Austin James Gareth V45 20.02.69, Kingston & P
HT- 53.44 (67.32-91)
COOK Jonathan 31.07.87, W.Green & EL/North'land Un
1500- 3:46.20 (3:38.64-16)
COOMBER Alex 24.07.94, Cardiff
800- 1:48.44, 1500- 3:48.75
COONEY Thomas U17 10.11.00, VPH &TH
60- 7.15i
COOPER Brooklyn U15 9.10.02, Somerset Schools
TJ- 12.04
COOPER Charles U23 29.02.96, Georgetown Un
800- 1:50.80i/1:51.77 (1:49.88-15), 1500- 3:47.99,
1M- 4:04.39i
COOPER Ciaran U23 1.03.97, Swindon
800- 1:51.84
COOPER Gwilym 17.07.91, Brighton & Hove
400- 48.5/48.63 (47.43-16), 400H- 53.12 (51.58-16)
COOPER Maxwell U17 20.11.00, Bracknell
1.5kSt- 4:32.68
COOPER Ryan U23 30.03.96, Cardiff/Cardiff Met
400H- 54.66 (54.08-15)
COPELAND Michael 2.11.89, City of Sheffield
110H- 15.25
COPELAND Piers U20 26.11.98, Wimborne
800- 1:51.58i (1:52.89-16), 1500- 3:49.39i (3:49.68-16),
3k- 8:23.34i (8:10.78i-16)
COPLEY Ben U15 6.11.02, Kingston u Hull
SPB- 13.10, DTB- 48.84, JTY- 52.60, JTB- 55.74
COPPARD Simon U17 19.02.01, Tonbridge
800- 1:51.97
COPPELL Harry U23 11.07.96, Wigan/Liverpool Un
HJ- 1.95, PV- 5.40 (5.42-15)
COPSEY Jason 17.02.91, Cardiff
JT- 64.77 (67.16-14)
CORBISHLEY Cameron U23 31.03.97, Medway & Maid
3kW- 11:19.10, 5kW- 20:10.7, 5kWR- 20:37+,
10kW- 41:37.44, 10kWR- 41:26, 20kW- 1:26:00
CORCORAN Fyn V35 17.03.78, Rhymney Valley
SP- 14.21
CORDERY Elliot U17 6.03.01, Chelmsford
1500- 4:03.68
CORK Daniel U23 15.07.97, Newport
SP- 14.87
CORLETT Alan 22.12.90, Northern (IOM)
3kSt- 9:40.70
CORRY Coleman U17 7.04.01, Blackheath & Bromley
400HY- 56.44, OctY- 4572
COSTELLO Andrew U20 1.10.99, Kilbarchan
HT- 53.78, HTJ- 59.49
COSTLEY Max 29.08.94, Southampton
3kSt- 9:37.63
COSTLEY Sam U20 24.02.99, Southampton
2kSt- 6:11.01, 3kSt- 9:48.08
COTTAM Mark U23 23.09.96, Bristol & W/Birmingham Un
400- 48.57
COTTELL Rico U17 22.11.01, Blackheath & Bromley
60HY- 8.46, 100HY- 13.49, OctY- 4359
COTTERILL Lewis U17 4.03.01, Newquay & Par
1.5kSt- 4:41.82
COTTON Ben U15 15.08.03, Essex Schools
DTB- 37.78, HTB- 47.09
COULIBALY Adrien U23 13.04.96, VPH &TH/FRA
400- 47.22
COURT Callum 21.10.93, Cardiff/Cambridge Un
PV- 4.60
COWAN Dwayne 1.01.85, Hercules Wimbledon
200- 21.04 (20.73-16), 400- 45.34
COWARD Akin U23 26.07.96, Shaftesbury B/B'ham Un
HJ- 2.13
COWIE Henry-James U17 29.03.01, Blackheath & Br
1.5kSt- 4:28.71

COWIN Adam 27.06.94, Manx H
  3kW- 13:18.8, 5kWR- 22:51 (22:46-14), 10kWR- 46:19
COWPERTHWAITE Joshua U17 9.04.01, M'boro Mandale
  1500- 3:55.60, 3k- 8:25.24
COX Alexander 13.12.93, Bournemouth
  HJ- 1.95 (2.08-11)
CRABTREE Jack Alexander U23 13.09.96, Shaftesbury B
  1500- 3:45.78 (3:44.52-14)
CRAIG Adam U23 9.05.95, Edinburgh AC/Un Mount Olive
  3k- 8:11.23i, 5k- 14:07.03, 10k- 29:39.72
CRANMER Kevin V35 14.06.79, Reading/MLT
  Dec- 5000
CRAWFORD Gareth U20 6.06.99, Strabane
  JT- 62.81
CREHAN Matthew 10.10.91, St Helens Sutton
  5kR- 14:30
CRESSWELL Oliver U17 17.11.00, Stratford-upon-Avon
  100- 10.9, 60HY- 8.04i, 100HY- 12.9/12.96,
  110HY- 14.07w/14.08, HJ- 1.92i (1.90-16)
CRIBB Chuko 30.03.94, Marshall Milton Keynes
  TJ- 15.33 (15.48w-16)
CRISP William U20 25.11.99, Swindon
  800- 1:50.99
CROFT Joey U20 23.05.00, Huntingdon
  2kSt- 5:58.80
CROFT Martin U23 29.04.97, M'boro Mandale/Camb Un
  HT- 46.60 (47.87-16)
CRORKEN Tiarnan U20 13.06.99, Preston
  800- 1:52.40
CROSS Adam U17 12.11.00, Cambridge & Coleridge
  100- 10.7w/11.01 (11.0-16), 200- 21.9w/21.99
CROSS Ellis U23 22.09.96, Aldershot F&D/St Marys Un
  1500- 3:46.93, 5k- 14:01.74, 10k- 29:00.49
CROSSLEY Neil 15.04.88, Cheltenham
  JT- 70.31 (73.41-13)
CROUT Philip U23 7.04.95, Shaftesbury B/Cambridge Un
  1500- 3:46.97 (3:46.93-16), 3k- 8:11.79 (8:10.4-16),
  5k- 14:22.12 (14:05.59-16), 10k- 29:55.01
CROWE Jamie U23 9.06.95, Central
  5k- 14:27.25, 5kR- 14:25
CROWE-WRIGHT Ian U23 27.03.95, Brighton & H/ Birm U
  800- 1:51.51, 1500- 3:44.34
CRUCHLEY Nick 1.01.90, Halesowen/Birmingham Un
  PV- 5.32i/5.20 (5.42-11)
CRYER Mark 27.08.93, Blackheath & Bromley/Brunel Un
  110H- 15.15 (15.14-16), LJ- 7.05 (7.17i-16)
CUNNINGHAM Jordan U15 22.12.02, City of Lisburn
  80HB- 11.64, LJ- 6.22, PenB- 2822
CURRAN Zacharias 17.12.93, WSE&H/Baylor Un./IRL
  400- 47.71 (46.96-16), 800- 1:48.43i/1:48.60 (1:46.78-16)
CURTIS Peter U17 24.10.00, Channel Islands
  400HY- 56.17
CURTIS William U20 27.12.99, Gateshead
  400- 48.60
CUTTS Luke Arron 13.02.88, City of Sheffield
  PV- 5.50 (5.83i-14, 5.70-13)

D ACK Christopher 28.11.82, Kingston & Poly
  SP- 14.70 (15.87-15), DT- 45.55 (46.85-15)
DACOSTA Dylan U17 6.04.01, Croydon
  60- 7.11i, 100- 10.8/10.93 (10.8-16), 200- 21.84, 60HY- 8.51i
DAFFURN Antony 18.10.86, Harrow
  LJ- 7.04, TJ- 15.24i/14.78 (15.54w/15.24-14)
DAKIN Oliver U17 1.12.01, Chesterfield
  100HY- 13.79
DALBAL Hakan U17 22.09.00, Longwood
  400- 49.44
DALTON Harry 26.09.92, Marshall Milton Keynes
  Dec- 5698
DALY Kieran 28.09.92, Blackheath & Bromley
  100- 10.58 (10.18-14)
DANE Oliver U20 13.11.98, City of Sheffield
  800- 1:52.50 (1:51.32-16)
DANGERFIELD Richard U23 17.09.97, Cardiff
  JT- 59.90
DANSON Robert 25.06.90, Wesham
  10kR- 30:25, Mar- 2:28:47
DARKIN-PRICE Cameron U17 18.11.00, Charnwood
  HJ- 1.90, DTY- 43.78, JTY- 50.43, DecY- 5327, OctY- 5000

DARLINGTON Jamaal U13 9.08.05, Thames Valley
  HJ- 1.62
DASAOLU Oyeyemi Olatokumbo James 5.09.87, Croydon
  60- 6.57i (6.47i-14), 100- 10.06 (9.91-13),
  200- 20.62w/20.73
DASILVA Anaximandro U23 27.06.95, Cardiff
  60- 6.79i, 100- 10.41
DAUPARAS Justas 12.02.91, Cambridge Un/LTU
  JT- 53.87 (56.12-16)
DAVEY Lewis U17 24.10.00, Peterborough
  200- 21.9w/22.2/22.43, 400- 48.52, 100HY- 13.9,
  400HY- 56.89 (56.36-16), LJ- 6.60w/6.58, HepIY- 4410i,
  OctY- 5041
DAVIDSON Will U23 24.05.96, Bristol & W/Bristol Un
  3kSt- 9:47.9
DAVIES Aiden U23 26.12.95, Doncaster/Leeds Beck Un
  PV- 4.40i/4.30 (4.30-16), LJ- 7.24i, SP- 13.26i,
  HepIS- 5512i
DAVIES Aled 24.05.91, Cardiff
  SP- 14.95i
DAVIES Andrew V35 30.10.79, Stockport
  10kR- 29:50 (29:49-15), HMar- 67:10 (65:20-16),
  Mar- 2:15:11
DAVIES Benjamin U20 12.03.99, Bedford & County
  1500- 3:50.70, 3k- 8:27.6
DAVIES Callum U20 30.11.98, Swansea
  60- 6.66i, 100- 10.80
DAVIES George U20 27.01.98, City of York
  JT- 65.12 (66.12-16)
DAVIES Harry U15 25.10.02, Neath
  DTB- 46.76, HTB- 47.83
DAVIES Jonathan Stuart 28.10.94, Reading/B'ham Un
  800- 1:48.94, 1500- 3:39.00, 1M- 4:00.58, 3k- 8:06.38i+
  (8:00.48i/8:01.38-16), 5k- 13:37.13 (13:23.94-16)
DAVIS Archie U20 16.10.98, Brighton Phoenix
  800- 1:49.69, 1500- 3:43.98 (3:43.81-16)
DAVIS Arran 2.06.89, Oxford Un/USA
  JT- 54.12 (57.91-11)
DAVIS Ben U20 13.04.99, Havering
  2kSt- 6:06.36
DAVIS Eden U20 1.03.99, Herts Phoenix
  60- 6.92i, 100- 10.46, 200- 21.68
DAVIS Jolyon U13 4.11.04, Wolves & Bilston
  JTC- 37.77
DAVIS Lawrence U23 31.05.95, Enfield & Har/B'ham Un
  TJ- 16.01i/15.43 (15.71-15)
DAVIS Max U17 31.05.01, Avon Valley Runners
  3k- 8:54.85
DAVISON Charlie U15 18.10.02, Gloucester Schools
  JTB- 53.19
DAVREN Angus U17 3.11.01, Inverness
  HJ- 1.91
DAWES William U20 24.11.98, Banbury
  HT- 46.61, HTJ- 55.05
DAWKINS Sam 18.08.93, Channel Islands
  400- 47.31
DAWSON David L. 3.02.84, Newquay & Par
  SP- 14.19 (15.22-02), DT- 45.33 (47.71-11)
DAWSON Tommy U15 2.02.03, Leeds
  3k- 8:49.59
DE ESCOFET Kyle U23 4.10.96, Birchfield
  60- 6.59i, 100- 10.21, 200- 21.10
DEAN Sam U20 23.09.98, Sale
  JT- 65.58
DEARDEN Daniel U15 26.09.03, Horsham BS
  PV- 3.03i/3.00
DEARDEN Jack U23 24.09.97, City of Norwich
  60- 6.93i
DEARMAN Owen U20 22.11.98, Watford
  HJ- 1.96
DEASON Michael 8.01.85, Shettleston H/USA
  3kSt- 9:12.60 (9:10.61-15)
DE'ATH Corey U23 16.02.96, Tonbridge/St Marys Un
  10k- 30:35.41
DEE Elliot U20 25.05.00, Bedford & County
  3k- 8:32.38
DEE Jamie U23 23.11.97, Shaftesbury B
  3k- 8:13.41, 5k- 14:11.78

378

DEE Liam U23 23.05.96, Shaftesbury B/Iona Coll, USA
800- 1:51.79 (1:50.66-15), 1500- 3:40.30, 1M-
3:58.19i/4:04.43, 3k- 7:57.20
DEGUTIS Gintas V45 20.07.70, Newham & Ex B/LTU
SP- 15.22i (18.61-02)
DEMPSEY David 7.02.91, City of Sheffield/Sheffield Un
800- 1:49.17 (1:47.96-16)
DEMPSEY Jeremy U20 17.12.99, Shaftesbury B
1500- 3:50.43, 3k- 8:19.39, 5k- 14:44.08
DENSLEY Kane U23 19.12.96, Tamworth/Cardiff Met
400H- 55.87
DENSLEY Martin Richard V35 1.05.81, Ealing, S & Mx
PV- 4.15 (5.10-10)
DERBYSHIRE Seamus U20 27.01.00, City of Stoke
400HY- 52.00
DERRIEN Paul V45 5.08.71, St Mary's Richmond
HT- 45.57 (49.62-08)
DESPINOY Fabian U15 9.11.02, Edinburgh AC
800- 2:03.77
DEVER Patrick U23 5.09.96, Preston/Loughborough St
1500- 3:44.36, 3k- 8:09.09, 5k- 13:59.99, 10kR- 30:02
DEVINE David 3.02.92, Liverpool H
5kR- 14:31
DEWAR Joseph U23 27.01.96, WG & EL/East London Un
60- 6.58i, 100- 10.25 (10.20w-15)
DEWAR Shayne U20 12.11.98, W.Green & Ex L
200- 21.54
DICKINSON Joshua U17 10.09.01, City of York
3k- 8:40.81
DICKSON-EARLE Euan U23 9.07.96, Biggleswade/
Loughborough St   60H- 8.01i, 110H- 14.42
DIDIER Logan U20 5.04.99, Surrey Schools
JT- 55.19
DIGBY Harry U17 22.10.00, Bracknell
800- 1:55.20
DIJKSTRA Ben U20 31.10.98, Leics Coritanian
3k- 8:27.56 (8:21.01-15), 5k- 14:22.66
DITCHFIELD Harry U17 3.10.01, Sale
JTY- 56.98
DIXON Anton 31.05.90, Woodford Green & Ex L
LJ- 7.20 (7.43-16)
DIXON Harvey 2.11.93, Aldershot F&D/GIB
1500- 3:44.03
DIXON Shaun 6.09.82, Highgate H
10kR- 30:25 (30:23+-12)
DOBBS Thomas U20 7.02.98, Wigan/Edge Hill Un
SP- 13.63i (13.16-16), SPJ- 15.09i/14.39, DT- 42.07,
DTJ- 48.82
DOBSON Charlie U20 20.10.99, Colchester H
100- 10.65w/10.75+, 200- 21.19w/21.20
DODD Edward 10.02.94, City of Portsmouth
800- 1:50.21
DODD Thomas U20 2.10.98, Birchfield
1500- 3:48.47
DODDS Callum U17 6.10.00, Enfield & Haringey
400- 48.70, 800- 1:51.77
DOLLERY Tom U17 20.08.02, Taunton
JTY- 52.54
DOMONEY Jaymee U20 17.04.99, Salisbury
1500- 3:53.86
DONALD James U20 18.11.98, Dundee HH
3k- 8:33.36i/8:33.47, 5k- 14:45.24, 10k- 30:40.27
DONNELLY Jordan 20.09.87, W.Green & Ex L
800- 1:51.23i (1:49.67-11), 1M- 4:06.85i
DONOVAN Tyri U20 20.10.98, WSE&H
400H- 52.81
DOODSON Jack U13 18.10.04, Stockport
LJ- 5.03
DORAN Oscar U13 17.10.04, Seaton
LJ- 5.03
DOREY Elliott 19.04.94, Glasgow City
1500- 3:45.44
DORRELL Luke U23 23.01.97, AF&D/Brunel Un
60- 6.88i, 100- 10.7/10.72, 200- 21.78
DOUGLAS Andrew 19.12.86, Inverclyde
HMar- 67:37 (65:38-16)
DOUGLAS Anthony U15 2.07.03, City of Stoke
100- 11.36, 200- 23.25

DOUGLAS Devon 7.09.89, Woodford Green & Ex L
DT- 50.71 (53.21-14)
DOUGLAS Jack U23 5.06.96, Bedford & Co/Coventry Un
5kR- 14:34, 3kSt- 9:36.91 (9:22.07-16)
DOUGLAS James 18.06.85, Border
10k- 30:23.95, HMar- 67:23 (66:48-14), Mar- 2:22:25
DOUGLAS Joshua U17 24.12.01, Southampton
SPY- 13.91, DTY- 49.81
DOUGLAS Nathan James 4.12.82, Oxford City
TJ- 16.80 (17.64-05)
DOUGLAS Ross Alan U23 14.07.96, Charnwood
HT- 53.53 (55.55-16)
DOW David U17 15.10.01, Cambridge & Coleridge
1500- 4:03.69, 3k- 8:49.85
DOW Lewis U15 18.01.03, Central
800- 2:01.32, 1500- 4:08.64
DOWDING Paul 11.08.92, Ipswich
JT- 54.29 (62.90-11)
DOWDS Archie U13 9.03.05, Preston
100- 12.3
DOWNES Caleb U23 12.08.97, Rugby & North/Lough St
60- 6.93i (6.86i-15), 100- 10.51,
200- 21.76 (21.3-15, 21.35-14)
DOWNING James U23 12.03.96, Camb & Col/Brunel Un
800- 1:51.84
DOWSON David V35 23.11.79, Middlesboro Mandale
SP- 14.75 (15.91-10), DT- 41.48 (44.04-14)
DOYLE William U17 24.10.01, Pitreavie
400- 49.78
DRAKE George U23 3.01.96, Leics Cor/Newcastle Un
TJ- 14.85w/14.43 (14.82-14)
DRAMMEH Alhagie-Salem 27.12.87, W.Green & EL/Army/GAM
200- 21.7 (21.64-12), 400- 47.58 (46.37-16)
DREW Connor U17 2.02.01, Cornwall AC
JTY- 50.98
DRISCOLL Ryan 25.01.94, Tonbridge
1500- 3:46.29, 3k- 8:04.86, 3kSt- 8:50.87
D'ROZARIO Oliver U15 24.09.03, Taunton
80HB- 11.73, LJ- 6.03w (5.79)
DRUCE Tom 18.11.86, Channel Islands
400- 47.82 (46.37-11)
DRUKTENIS Vutas 5.02.83, WSE&H/LTU
SP- 14.32 (17.79i-04, 17.40-05)
DRY Mark William 11.10.87, W.Green & Ex L
HT- 71.73 (76.93-15)
DRYLAND Neil V45 8.08.71, SKD BIL (NOR)
24Hr- 214.703km
D'SOUZA Thomas U15 24.01.03, Coventry Godiva
JTB- 48.09
DUCKWORTH Timothy U23 18.06.96, Liverpool H/
Un. Kentucky 60- 6.77i, 100- 10.51, 60H- 8.03i, 110H- 14.30,
HJ- 2.16i/2.13 (2.13-16), PV- 5.26i/5.07 (5.10-16),
LJ- 7.87, SP- 13.42, DT- 41.52, JT- 55.45 (57.22-16),
Dec- 7973, HepIS- 6165i
DUDDFIELD Kai U17 14.06.02, Wolves & Bilston
100- 11.1w (11.3/11.84-16)
DUDHIA Zamaan U17 4.02.02, Barnet
PV- 3.80
DUFFY Luke Gerard U17 14.11.00, Mansfield H
800- 1:54.93 (1:54.87i), 1500- 3:49.70
DUGGAN George U20 1.09.96, Tonbridge/Lough St
800- 1:51.98 (1:51.58-16), 1500- 3:44.88, 5kR- 14:22
DUNBAR Alex 24.04.92, City of Norwich/Lamar Un
5k- 14:10.78, 10k- 30:00.16 (29:34.20-16)
DUNDERDALE Haran U23 26.04.96, Sheffield/ Bradley U
1500- 3:48.81, 1M- 4:05.14i (4:30.4-12),
3k- 8:04.87ios (8:28.18i/8:39.78-14), 3kSt- 8:50.43
DUNDERDALE Joseph 4.09.92, City of Sheffield
JT- 74.88 (76.13-14)
DUNFORD Edward James 15.09.84, Birchfield
SP- 14.14 (15.21-12), DT- 42.08 (45.75-10)
DUNHAM Mark V35 4.09.80, Southport
Mar- 2:28:58
DUNN Elliot U20 20.10.98, Birchfield
400- 48.9 (49.70i/49.87)
DUNN Jarryd 30.01.92, Birchfield
400- 46.58 (45.09-15)
DUNN Michael U17 15.05.01, Clydesdale
400HY- 57.07

DUNN Nathan U20 1.09.99, Preston
3k- 8:33.13
DUNNE Finbar U17 20.09.01, Inverness
DTY- 42.74
DUNNE Liam U15 7.12.02, Chichester R&AC
800- 2:03.50, 1500- 4:15.2
DUNNE Patrick U20 2.12.99, Inverness
JT- 55.85
DUQUEMIN Zane 23.09.91, Shaftesbury B
DT- 62.68 (63.46-12)
DURANT Luc U20 3.10.98, Blackheath & Bromley
SP- 14.73, SPJ- 15.40
DURNEY Christopher U20 16.01.98, Preston/Un C. Lancs
1500- 3:53.64
DURRANT-SUTHERLAND Myles U23 17.07.95, Birchfield/
Birmingham Un   LJ- 7.15
DUSTIN Oliver Luke U17 29.11.00, Border
400- 50.1, 800- 1:51.07, 1500- 3:53.11
DUTTON Jack U15 7.01.03, North Devon
800- 2:03.37
DUXBURY Kameron U17 8.10.01, City of Portsmouth
SPY- 14.73, JTY- 56.39
DWEMOH Erasmus 25.11.90, South London H
SP- 13.56 (13.81-13)
DYER Michael 27.09.84, Reading
110H- 15.5 (14.5/14.55w/14.72-06)

EAGLESTONE Alex U17 16.11.00, Cheltenham
   OctY- 4539
EAMES Thomas U17 4.12.00, Brighton & Hove
800- 1:54.34, 1500- 3:54.86
EARL Harry 10.11.92, Border/East Kentucky Un.
5k- 14:33.79 (14:29.42-15), 10k- 30:13.70
EARL Nicholas 22.09.84, City of Norwich/Melbourne Un.
5k- 14:09.46, 10k- 29:45.80 (29:34.11-16), 10kR- 29:43,
HMar- 64:52, 3kSt- 9:06.80
EARLE Reece U13 1.10.04, Thames Valley
100- 12.08w/12.3, 200- 25.26
EARLE Robert Bernard V55 15.09.60, Colchester H
HT- 50.82 (62.60-95)
EARLY Oliver U15 26.05.04, Chelmsford
60HB- 8.78i, PenIB- 2612i
EAST Benjamin U15 19.11.03, Team Kennet
JTB- 54.88
EAVES Maxwell 31.05.88, Newham & Essex B
PV- 5.43i/5.30 (5.64i-16, 5.62-14)
EBEREONWU Chinua U17 14.06.01, Cardiff Archers
60HJ- 8.56i, 60HY- 8.58i, 100HY- 13.47
ECCLESON Thomas U15 25.01.03, Wirral
100- 11.4, 200- 23.1/23.33
ECKERSLEY Daniel 12.11.86, Kingston & Poly
3kSt- 9:07.82
EDGAR James U20 12.11.98, City of Lisburn/IRL
5k- 14:17.58
EDIKER Alex U17 14.08.01, Chesterfield
1500- 3:57.22, 3k- 8:46.91
EDOBURUN Ojie Dayo U23 2.06.96, Shaftesbury B
60- 6.73i (6.66i-16), 100- 9.93w/10.12,
200- 20.40w (20.87-16)
EDWARDS Aaron 2.05.86, Newham & Essex B
SP- 13.52i/13.03 (13.25-15)
EDWARDS Jonathan 9.10.92, C of Plymouth/Plymouth Un
SP- 14.69 (15.34-13), DT- 50.10 (52.59-16),
HT- 66.26 (66.28-14)
EDWARDS Laurance U17 26.11.01, Harrow
800- 1:56.67
EDWARDS Mike 11.07.90, Birchfield
HJ- 2.23 (2.25-15)
EDWARDS Owain U17 30.07.01, Cardiff
1.5kSt- 4:40.98
EDWARDS William U20 5.02.98, Carmarthen
HJ- 2.10
EFOLOKO Jonathon U20 23.09.99, Sale
60- 6.94i (6.85i-15), 100- 10.53w/10.57, 200- 20.92
EGGLETON Joseph U17 6.01.02, Chiltern H
100- 11.1, 200- 22.2/22.21
EISNOR Bradley U23 24.11.96, Eastbourne RAC
JT- 54.58, Dec- 6019w/5956

EJIAKUEKWU Roy U23 2.02.95, Sale/Arkansas Un.
60- 6.71i, 100- 10.16w/10.41 (10.35-15),
200- 20.55w/20.65, 400- 47.54 (47.21-16)
ELDER Ethan U15 11.10.02, Moorfoot Runners
800- 2:03.25
ELIOT Caspar 29.09.89, Bristol & West
400H- 55.22 (54.68-16)
ELKINS Andrew 25.05.93, Poole
HT- 52.79 (60.16-13)
ELLIOTT Kane U17 19.01.02, Falkirk VH
1500- 3:58.96
ELLIOTT Mark V35 3.04.78, Telford
HT- 45.96
ELLIOTT Matthew U17 5.09.00, Ashford
60- 7.11i
ELLIOTT Zachary Luke U17 13.09.01, Birchfield
LJ- 6.47i (6.26w/6.24-16)
ELLIS Joseph U23 10.04.96, Michigan Univ
HT- 70.98
ELLIS Lloyd Evan U20 7.07.99, Leamington
110HJ- 15.18w/15.19
ELSDON Glen 27.09.92, Carmarthen
60H- 8.22i (8.06i-14), 110H- 14.56 (14.28-15)
ELY Lewis 1.08.89, Blackheath & Bromley
HJ- 1.95 (2.00-12)
EMANUEL Lee 24.01.85, City of Sheffield
3k- 7:49.29i (7:44.48i/7:51.30-15)
EMEKA-UGWUADU Sean U13 14.06.05, Thurrock
LJ- 5.12
ENGELKING Jonathan U23 13.12.97, North Devon
JT- 61.93 (62.48-16)
ENNIS Jack U17 7.06.02, Croydon
HJ- 1.90i (1.87)
ENNIS Kyle 9.08.91, Rugby & Nor AC/East London Un
100- 10.63w/10.69 (10.5-14, 10.53-16),
200- 21.15 (21.01-16)
ENSER Aaron U17 5.09.00, Bracknell
1.5kSt- 4:29.43
ENSER Edward U13 3.05.05, Bracknell
JTC- 40.38
EPIFANI Gianni V45 22.02.71, Manx H
5kWR- 22:55
ERICSSON-NICHOLLS James U17 6.11.01, M.Milton K
HTY- 55.35
ESCALANTE-PHILLIPS Jonathan 28.07.92, Cambr & Col/
Cambridge Un   HMar- 68:16
ETHERINGTON Glen 10.12.86, Yeovil Olympiads
110H- 15.31 (14.34-15)
ETIENNE Theo U23 3.09.96, Hercules Wimbledon
60- 6.59i (6.56i-16), 100- 10.33 (10.14w-10.23-16),
200- 21.80
EVANS Elliott U15 3.09.03, City of Portsmouth
80HB- 11.8/11.82, PenB- 2619
EVANS George Ross U20 21.01.98, Shaftesbury B
SPJ- 16.89 (18.05-16), DT- 50.43, DTJ- 60.37
EVANS Joel U15 13.03.03, Stevenage & NH
80HB- 11.66
EVANS Matthew 31.06.92, Worthing
HT- 51.26 (52.70-16)
EVANS Scott 4.02.91, Kingston & Poly
3kSt- 9:23.8
EVANS Simon 21.06.92, Worthing
HT- 50.40 (50.44-12)
EVANS Thomas U17 21.09.00, Newark AC
100- 11.09, 200- 22.18, 400- 47.90
EVANS Tom 3.02.92, Lewes/Army
Mar- 2:26:07
EVANS Thomas 20.05.91, Newport
200- 21.79w
EVERARD James V35 16.05.81, Basildon
JT- 56.63 (65.34-11)
EVES John 17.01.83, Bedford & County/IRL
10k- 30:30.65 (30:29.60-13)
EWEKA Aaron U15 13.11.03, Havering
HJ- 1.75
EWER Rico U23 24.09.97, Rugby & Nor AC/Middlesex Un
100- 10.72w (10.52w/10.64-16)
EWULO Ezekiel 29.01.86, W.Green & Ex L/NGR
LJ- 7.64w/7.55 (7.90w/7.85-15)

380

FADAYERO Theophilus U20 29.08.00, Newham & Ex B
TJ- 14.09
FAGBENLE Michael U17 22.02.01, Bexley
400- 49.87
FAIRCLOUGH Henry U20 22.01.99, City of York
SP- 13.34i/13.05 (13.22-16), SPJ- 15.14
FAIRCLOUGH Jordan 8.05.91, Liverpool H
100- 10.72w (10.76-15)
FAIRHURST Jacob Benjamin U15 25.10.02, Charnwood
100- 11.41w
FAMAKIN Dami U23 23.11.97, WSE&H
TJ- 13.79 (14.67i-16, 14.47-15)
FARAH Mohamed 23.03.83, Newham & Essex B
1500- 3:34.19 (3:28.81-13), 3k- 7:35.15 (7:32.62-16),
5k- 13:00.70 (12:53.11-11), 10k- 26:49.51 (26:46.57-11),
10kR- 29:19+ (27:44-10), 15kR- 43:19+ (42:03+-16),
HMar- 60:06 (59:22dh/59:32-15)
FARAH Samatar 25.12.85, Newham & Essex B
3kSt- 9:10.66 (8:49.83-12)
FARNHAM-ROSE Robbie 5.01.94, Tonbridge/Un Alabama
1500- 3:41.64, 1M- 4:04.63i (4:00.92i-16),
3k- 8:03.68i (8:18.68-14), 5k- 14:26.25
FARQUHAR Robbie U17 4.01.01, Aberdeen
60HY- 8.44i, 100HY- 13.73, PV- 3.70i/3.68,
LJ- 6.94w/6.82, HepIY- 4562i, DecY- 6030, OctY- 4729+
FARQUHARSON Alexander U23 9.06.97, Coventry God.
LJ- 7.51 (7.70-16)
FARRELL Chris 10.10.85, Horwich
10kR- 30:27 (29:51-16)
FARRELL James 4.06.91, Bexley
Dec- 5432
FARRES Tom U23 4.03.97, C of Portsmouth/St Marys Un
PV- 4.82i/4.82
FASIPE Timothy U23 20.06.97, Enfield & Har/Lough St
60- 6.81i
FATIMEHIN Emmanuel U15 20.12.02, Herts Schools
100- 11.46
FATONA Timi U13 29.07.05, Aberdeen
100- 11.99w, 200- 25.22
FAULDS Joshua Daniel U20 7.03.00, Rugby & Nor AC
400- 49.1, 400H- 54.74, 400HY- 52.95
FAULKNER Andrew 23.07.86, Yeovil Olympiads
400H- 53.5/53.55 (52.51-14)
FAWDEN Terence U20 19.01.99, Highgate H
2kSt- 6:07.73 (6:05.93-16), 3kSt- 9:42.33
FAYEHUN Henry U13 4.05.05, W.Green & Ex L
75HC- 11.8
FAYERS Matthew 5.08.94, Hillingdon/Oklahoma St Un
1500- 3:46.17 (3:43.71-15), 1M- 3:58.53i (4:01.53-12)
FEARON Joel 11.10.88, Birchfield
100- 10.20w/10.21 (9.96-16)
FEENEY David 17.10.87, Amber Valley
60H- 7.94i, 110H- 14.09 (13.89-15)
FENNING Franklin U20 17.05.00, Rugby & Northampton
100- 10.8/10.82
FERGUS Nathan U23 1.10.97, South London H
SP- 13.47, DT- 42.07
FERGUSON Dylan U20 23.09.98, Bingley
HJ- 1.95
FERGUSON Joe U20 3.05.00, Barnsley
100- 10.71w, 200- 21.9
FERGUSON Michael U23 18.03.95, Aberdeen/A'deen Un
5k- 14:30.06
FERGUSON Stuart 10.10.92, Radley AC/Lamar Un
1M- 4:06.50i (4:07.09i-16)
FERNANDES Marcio 18.05.83, Bedford & County/CPV
JT- 54.25
FERNANDEZ Paul M. V40 24.03.74, Abingdon
50kR- 3:16:58 (3:04:07-13), 100kR- 7:25:27
FERRYMAN Jonathan 25.12.88, Sale
TJ- 14.03 (14.05-14)
FEYISETAN Kevin U20 24.07.99, Dartford
LJ- 6.89
FEYI-WABOSO Immanuel U15 20.12.02, Cardiff Archers
80HB- 11.46, HJ- 1.77, PenB- 2564
FIELD Cameron U23 16.04.96, Liverpool H
800- 1:51.48, 1500- 3:46.75, 5k- 14:32.50
FIELD Jake U23 26.11.96, Sutton & District
HJ- 1.95 (2.00i-15, 1.95-16)

FILEMAN Edward U15 19.04.03, Tavistock
HTB- 51.05
FILLERY Cameron U20 2.11.98, Brighton & Hove
60H- 8.09i, 60HJ- 7.87i, 110HJ- 13.69, 110H- 14.22
FILLEUL Josiah U23 14.10.96, City of Sheffield/Bath Un
400H- 54.61 (54.61-15)
FINCH Jordan 2.09.91, Yeovil Olympiads
200- 21.79w
FINCH Kai U17 24.10.00, Liverpool Pembroke Sefton
HJ- 2.03
FINCH Luke U13 1.01.05, Woodford Green & Ex L
HTC- 31.68
FINCHAM-DUKES Jacob U23 12.01.97, Leeds/Okla St U
100- 10.56, LJ- 8.02w/7.96
FINNEY James U23 7.04.96, Leeds/Sunderland Un
60H- 8.36i, 110H- 14.72, HJ- 2.01 (2.01-14), PV- 4.63,
LJ- 7.02i/6.93, JT- 55.98, Dec- 7263, HepIS- 5392i
FINNIE Charlie U15 24.12.02, Crawley
SPB- 13.11
FISAYO Temitope U20 29.01.98, Luton/London Un
TJ- 13.91
FISCHER Joseph U15 12.03.03, Basildon
80HB- 11.7/11.84, LJ- 6.11w/6.03, PenB- 2539
FISH Benjamin 21.05.82, Blackburn
10k- 30:14.75 (29:45.74-12), HMar- 65:16
FISHER Ben U20 21.02.98, City of Lisburn
LJ- 7.40w/7.32
FISHER Benjamin Joseph 25.04.86, Liverpool H
JT- 57.88 (65.99-09)
FISHER Charles U15 8.11.02, Telford
200- 23.31
FISHER Harry 26.10.91, Southampton/Cardiff Met
400- 48.45 (47.58-15), 800- 1:48.11
FITZGIBBON Robbie U23 23.03.96, Brighton Phoenix
800- 1:49.43, 1500- 3:36.97, 1M- 4:00.63 (4:00.18-16),
3k- 8:01.79, 5k- 14:22.60, 10kR- 30:06
FITZHENRY Daniel U20 12.11.98, Cannock & Stafford
HJ- 2.00
FLAHERTY Sam U15 11.10.02, Liverpool H
800- 2:03.3
FLANAGAN Harry U20 24.09.99, Southport
100- 10.7
FLANNERY Niall 26.04.91, Gateshead
200- 21.45w, 400- 48.47 (47.17-15),
110H- 15.21 (14.96w-12, 15.14-16), 400H- 49.74 (48.80-14)
FLEMING Daniel U23 27.10.96, City of York/York Un
DT- 47.47
FLITCROFT Joseph 28.01.91, Basingstoke & MH/Bath Un
HT- 46.93 (47.07-16)
FLOYD Michael Anthony V40 26.09.76, Sale
HT- 57.25 (72.45-11)
FOBIL Abraham U15 15.11.03, Sale
200- 23.4/23.43
FONTANA Sean 6.12.90, VP-Glasgow/Adams State Coll
10k- 29:52.84 (29:16.93-15)
FOOT Joss U20 22.02.00, Orion
JT- 58.21, JTY- 60.73
FOOT William U15 7.10.03, Chesterfield
PV- 3.36i/3.15
FORBES-AGYEPONG Micah U17 31.01.02, Shaftesbury
60- 7.13i, 100- 11.12, 200- 22.28
FOREMAN Tom U15 7.11.02, Guildford & Godalming
HJ- 1.81
FORMAN James 12.12.91, Southampton
400- 48.56i (46.74i-12, 48.08-10), 400H- 50.72 (50.41-11)
FORSTER Lewis U13 2.08.05, Leigh
JTC- 37.84
FORSYTH Ryan U23 7.07.96, Colorado State Un
5k- 13:57.80i/14:18.90 (14:01.27-16), 10k- 29.32.38
FOSTER Brendon U17 20.10.01, Notts
LJ- 6.45, TJ- 13.61
FOSTER Glen U20 10.11.98, Winchester
HJ- 2.03
FOTHERINGHAM Murray U15 4.06.03, Giffnock N
800- 1:59.69, 60HB- 9.22i, HJ- 1.83, LJ- 6.47i/6.23,
PenB- 2847, OctB- 4160, PenIB- 2831i
FOX Jason 15.10.88, Channel Islands
HJ- 2.00 (2.05-08)

FOX Morris V50 30.04.63, City of Stoke
SP- 13.78 (16.14-02)
FOX Najee 1.12.92, Birchfield
DT- 54.79
FOX Nathan 21.10.90, Shaftesbury B
LJ- 7.13, TJ- 16.81
FRADLEY James U20 25.10.98, Newcastle (Staff)
800- 1:50.9
FRANCIS Forrest U23 13.04.95, Leics Cor/Bedford Un
DT- 41.80 (45.23-16)
FRANCIS Gage U23 6.10.96, Cardiff/Cardiff Met
TJ- 14.22
FRANCIS Matthew U17 14.01.02, Blackheath & Bromley
1.5kSt- 4:30.57
FRANCIS Miguel U23 28.03.95, Wolves & Bilston
200- 20.44 (19.88-16 ANT), 400- 46.48
FRANCIS-DWYER Micah U20 30.06.00, Croydon
200- 21.75
FRANKIS Gianni 16.04.88, Newham & Essex B/ITA
60H- 7.92i (7.67i-13),
110H- 14.17w/14.31 (13.53w/13.54-13)
FRASER Freddie U15 25.01.04, Nene Valley H
60HB- 9.04i, 80HB- 11.47
FRECKLETON Lemarl 19.03.92, Swansea
60- 6.91i, 100- 10.69
FRENCH Thomas 5.12.91, Blackheath & Bromley
LJ- 7.49w/7.36 (7.60-16)
FRITH James Alan U15 12.07.03, Marshall Milton K
SPB- 13.54
FRITH Morgan U15 28.12.02, Sale
LJ- 6.19
FROST Andrew Derek V35 17.04.81, W.Green & Ex L
HT- 65.39 (72.79-11)
FRY Luke U15 3.01.03, Corby
200- 23.45w/23.47
FUGGLE Joe U20 25.01.99, Tonbridge
60HJ- 8.57i, 400H- 53.04
FULLBROOK David U17 8.01.01, Tonbridge
OctY- 4468
FULLER William U23 14.05.97, Blackheath & B/Lough St
1500- 3:45.39, 3k- 8:19.21 (8:14.08-16), 5k- 14:10.93
FULTON Thomas U20 16.12.99, Shaftesbury B
800- 1:52.67
FURNESS Michael U17 4.07.01, Blaydon
DTY- 43.31

GAFFNEY Daniel 25.02.83, South London H
    Mar- 2:28:24
GAIR Malachi U20 21.09.99, Basingstoke & MH
DECJ- 5217
GALE Thomas U20 18.12.98, Team Bath
HJ- 2.30
GALL Declan U20 19.05.99, Dundee HH
400- 49.25, 400H- 53.68
GALLAGHER Sean U17 13.09.00, Whitemoss
LJ- 6.65
GALLIMORE Morgan U17 15.04.01, Absolute Tri C (E Mids)
1500- 4:03.93
GALLOWAY Daniel U13 8.11.04, Bridgnorth
1500- 4:34.8
GAMBLE Ben 27.01.82, Tipton
HMar- 68:22 (67:22-10), Mar- 2:23:42
GARDINER Daniel Leslie 25.06.90, City of Sheffield/
Leeds Beckett U   60- 6.89i (6.83i-15), LJ- 7.83 (7.96-16)
GARDINER Jacob 8.03.94, Leeds/RAF
SP- 14.54
GARDINER Linton U23 18.07.97, Cheltenham/Hallam Un
PV- 4.15 (4.30-15)
GARDNER Daniel Colin 26.03.94, Stevenage & NH
PV- 5.32i (5.40i-14, 5.20-13)
GARDNER James U17 27.03.02, Bracknell
HTY- 51.92
GARDNER Louis 1.09.93, City of Sheffield/Oxford Un
400H- 55.43
GARDNER Nathan U20 9.02.98, Stevenage &NH/Card Un
PV- 4.85i/4.78
GARLAND Dale Mark Paul V35 13.10.80, Channel Islands
400H- 54.89 (49.54-09)

GARROD Oliver 16.01.93, Epsom & Ewell
Mar- 2:29:44
GASKELL Sam U17 1.11.01, Blackburn
HTY- 59.11
GAUNTLETT Henry U17 4.09.01, Swansea
JTY- 51.68
GBEGLI Emmanuel 28.12.92, Southend/Cambridge Un
TJ- 14.10w/13.99 (14.24-14)
GEMILI Adam 6.10.93, Blackheath & Bromley
100- 10.03w/10.08 (9.97-15), 200- 20.35 (19.97-16)
GEORGE Alex 6.02.96, Birchfield/Arkansas Un.
1500- 3:42.34, 5k- 13:40.66
GEORGE Thomas U23 6.02.96, Birchfield/Missouri Un.
3k- 8:19.31i
GERMAIN Jahmal 3.07.92, Newham & Essex B
110H- 14.84 (14.53-16)
GERRARD Keith 24.03.86, Newham & Essex B
HMar- 66:25 (63:39-11)
GEZIMU Dejene 29.09.93, Liverpool H/ETH
5k- 14:29.52, 5kR- 14:24, 10kR- 29:27,
HMar- 65:52 (62:25-12)
GHEBRESILASIE Weynay 24.03.94, Birchfield/ERI
5kR- 14:25, 10kR- 30:11 (29:31-13), 10MR- 49:40,
HMar- 66:48
GIBLIN Luke 15.09.86, Kingston upon Hull
100- 10.5w (10.6/10.64-14)
GIBSON Stuart 15.09.83, Cambuslang
10k- 30:57.66 (30:45.44-16)
GIERJATOWICZ Patryk 29.08.89, Hunters Bog Tr/POL
Mar- 2:25:17 (2:24:05-16)
GIFFORD Thomas 21.10.93, Colch & T/Adams State Coll
800- 1:51.72iA/1:51.83
GILBERT John V35 24.09.80, Kent
10k- 30:17.3 (30:06.29-15), HMar- 68:02 (65:42-13)
GILBERT Nathan U23 2.03.95, WSE&H
100- 10.70 (10.41w/10.54-16)
GILBY Alfie U17 15.05.02, Ashford
PV- 3.70
GILCHRIST Euan U20 10.08.98, Sale
1500- 3:48.72, 3k- 8:27.41
GILES Elliot 26.05.94, Birchfield
800- 1:44.99, 1500- 3:41.27
GILKES Joseph U20 16.08.99, Coventry Godiva
TJ- 14.06
GILL Jordan U23 18.02.95, M'boro Mandale/Chich Un
60- 6.91i
GILLAND Jack U15 7.09.02, Liverpool H
300- 37.6/37.61
GILLATT Anthony U23 14.09.95, Scunthorpe
HT- 49.27 (50.90-15)
GILLESPIE Matthew 4.11.90, Shettleston H
HMar- 66:18 (65:39-16)
GILLING Tremayne 27.07.90, Blackheath & Bromley
60- 6.73i (6.68i-12)
GILLON James U17 10.10.00, Law & District
1.5kSt- 4:28.01
GIRDLER Michael U15 29.06.03, Edinburgh AC
200- 22.95
GISBORNE Gabriel U15 12.10.02, Hallamshire
800- 2:00.07
GLADMAN James 3.06.93, Warrington
200- 21.01w/21.27 (20.80w-13), 400- 47.13
GLADWELL Elliot U13 7.05.05, Ipswich
800- 2:14.88, 1500- 4:36.1
GLASS Peter 1.05.88, City of Lisburn
110H- 15.16 (14.76-12), PV- 4.55i/4.50 (4.80-14),
LJ- 6.89w (7.04-11), SP- 13.50 (14.86-16), DT- 42.82 (45.55-14),
JT- 53.86 (56.61-13), Dec- 7120 (7510-13)
GLAVE Romell U20 11.11.99, Croydon
60- 6.77i, 100- 10.21, 150- 15.54st, 200- 20.95
GLEADALL Pedro U17 7.12.01, Blackheath & Bromley
PV- 4.11, JTY- 58.66, HepIY- 4259i, DecY- 5166,
OctY- 4591
GLEAVE Spike U15 4.12.02, Eastbourne RAC
PenB- 2777
GLEN Jonathan U23 5.10.96, Inverclyde/New Mexico Un
10k- 30:49.27 (30:34.28-15)

GLYNN Iwan U15 2.12.02, Carmarthen
300- 37.58, 800- 2:03.9
GOATER Bradley 13.04.94, Shaftesbury B/St Marys Un
3k- 8:14.94i (8:10.09-15), 5k- 14:33.44 (14:06.84-15),
5kR- 14:21
GOMES Edson U20 1.11.98, Shaftesbury B/POR
60HJ- 8.06i, 110HJ- 14.14w/14.37
GOOCH Jack U23 24.04.96, Swansea
1500- 3:48.31
GOODACRE Laurence 20.09.92, Havering/London Un
SP- 14.20 (15.82-15)
GOODALL Alex U20 30.09.99, Elswick
800- 1:51.76
GOODALL Alexander 7.11.93, WSE&H/Loughborough St
5k- 14:29.33
GOODLIFF Archie U15 26.09.02, WSE&H
JTB- 55.82 (56.80-16)
GOODMAN Karl 7.11.93, Vale of Aylesbury/Texas Un
400- 47.93
GOODMAN Richard 4.04.93, Shaftesbury B
3k- 8:14.76 (8:12.94-10), 5k- 13:59.94,
10kR- 30:28 (29:57-16)
GOODWIN Jack 7.06.93, Bedford & County
5kR- 14:33
GOOLAB Nicholas 30.01.90, Belgrave
3k- 7:42.22, 5k- 13:33.48
GORDON Fraser U15 11.09.02, Tonbridge
1500- 4:11.69, 3k- 9:18.25
GORDON Samuel 5.10.94, Cardiff
100- 10.32
GORINGE Jonathan 22.07.91, Kettering
3kSt- 9:21.74 (9:20.57-16)
GORMAN Ryan Lee U20 9.04.98, Notts/York Un
60- 6.98i, 200- 21.33i/21.90 (20.84-16)
GORMLEY James U20 3.04.98, City of Sheffield
1500- 3:42.51, 3k- 8:23.62, 5k- 14:21.97
GOSS James V40 11.09.73, Stevenage & NH
HT- 47.54 (51.32-94)
GOURLEY Neil U23 7.02.95, Giffnock N/Virginia Tech Un
800- 1:47.84, 1k- 2:20.54i, 1500- 3:40.52 (3:39.92-16),
1M- 4:00.10i (3:59.58i-16), 3k- 8:05.25i,
5k- 14:13.04 (14:02.40-16)
GRABARZ Robert 3.10.87, Newham & Essex B
HJ- 2.31 (2.37-12)
GRACE Joshua 11.05.93, Aldershot F&D
5k- 14:32.00 (14:11.49-15), 10k- 29:34.26
GRACIE Danny U15 30.10.02, Annan
DTB- 42.27, HTB- 55.22
GRAHAM Douglas V40 1.01.77, Arbroath
PV- 4.17i/4.13 (4.30i-02, 4.26-96)
GRAHAM Michael U15 12.02.03, Birtley
JTB- 45.21
GRAHAM Oliver U17 16.05.01, Ipswich
HTJ- 52.61, HTY- 59.19/57.29
GRAHAM Robert 12.07.91, Inverclyde
TJ- 13.95w/13.90 (14.11-10)
GRAHAM-WATSON Rory 3.06.90, WSE&H
800- 1:47.29
GRANT Jonathan 26.05.93, Herne Hill/Kent State Un.
60- 6.92i (6.73i-16)
GRANT Omar 6.12.94, Harrow
60- 6.86i, 100- 10.36, 200- 21.31w/21.42
GRANTHAM Lee 11.02.83, East Cheshire
Mar- 2:21:49, 50kR- 3:08:25, 100kR- 6:42:42
GRANTHAM Thomas Richard 12.02.83, City of Sheffield
400H- 55.47 (53.20-11), PV- 4.11i (4.10-16),
Dec- 5376 (6158-14)
GRANVILLE Charles U23 22.10.95, Harrow/Loughboro St
JT- 54.66 (60.62-14)
GRASSLY George U20 19.07.00, Dorking & Mole V
1500- 3:53.05
GRAY Jack 10.04.93, BRAT
5k- 14:20.73 (14:13.59-14), 5kR- 14:20
GRAY Ruaridh U20 28.12.98, Inverness
HTJ- 51.35
GRAY Sam U17 20.03.01, VP-Glasgow
PV- 3.60

GRAY William 24.01.93, Brighton & Hove
3k- 8:11.81i (8:14.81-14), 5kR- 14:25 (14:13.84t-14),
3kSt- 8:33.68
GREATREX Ellis U20 27.09.99, Wolves & Bilston
400- 47.48 (47.47-16)
GREEN Courtney 20.08.85, Kent AC
SP- 13.03 (14.42-13)
GREEN Jack 6.10.91, Kent AC
400- 47.42i (45.99-12), 200H- 22.97st (22.64st-13),
400H- 48.77 (48.60-12)
GREEN Ryan U20 19.07.98, Morpeth
800- 1:50.56
GREENAWAY Derrius U20 14.04.99, Rotherham
60- 6.97i, 100- 10.77, 200- 21.89w/21.9
GREENHALGH James U20 18.02.98, W.Norfolk/Hallam U
60HJ- 8.4i
GREENLEAF Andrew 21.09.82, Serpentine
Mar- 2:27:48 (2:21:46-15)
GREENWOOD Ben U20 24.09.98, Perth Strathtay
600- 1:18.98i, 800- 1:48.71, 1500- 3:53.46 (3:53.26i-16)
GREENWOOD Christopher V40 29.09.73, Kent AC
Mar- 2:26:46 (2:23:38sh-15), 3kSt- 9:32.24 (9:12.36-14)
GREENWOOD Leon U23 13.06.97, Swansea/Cardiff Met
60- 6.92i, 200- 21.61w
GREEVES Scott U23 30.07.96, C of Norwich/Un E Anglia
800- 1:51.49
GREGORY Benjamin Mark Joseph 21.11.90, Birchfield
60H- 8.22i (8.17i-14), 110H- 14.4w/14.52 (14.47-16),
400H- 55.46, HJ- 1.99i/1.96, PV- 5.20i/5.10 (5.20-10),
LJ- 7.35 (7.42-14), SP- 13.31 (13.51-16),
JT- 58.07 (58.73-14), Dec- 7799 (7882-16), HepIS- 5834i
GREGORY Daniel 11.04.93, Oxford Un/CAN
Dec- 5298
GREGORY WALTERS Jamall U15 30.09.02, Trafford
60- 7.19i, 100- 11.28, 200- 22.44, 300- 36.4
GREGSON Callum U15 16.11.02, Southampton
60HB- 9.21i, HJ- 1.84, TJ- 12.00w, PenB- 2592
GREIG Kyle 19.12.85, Forres H
Mar- 2:27:56dh/2:29:58 (2:25:27-16)
GRENFELL Joel 31.10.94, Peterborough/Lough St
LJ- 7.22
GRICE Charles 7.11.93, Brighton Phoenix
800- 1:48.48 (1:45.53-16), 1500- 3:35.72 (3:33.60-16),
1M- 3:53.62 (3:52.64-16)
GRIFFIN Matthew U15 29.08.03, Bromsgrove & R
60HB- 9.3i, 80HB- 11.79
GRIFFIN Sam William U23 22.12.97, Midd M/Teeside Un
200- 21.46w
GRIFFITHS Alex U20 6.01.00, Cheltenham
HT- 46.56, HTJ- 54.55
GRIFFITHS Dewi 9.08.91, Swansea
3k- 7:55.65, 5k- 13:33.60, 5kR- 13:58, 10k- 28:16.07,
10kR- 28:28, 15kR- 43:25+, HMar- 61:33, Mar- 2:09:49
GRIFFITHS James 30.07.92, Cardiff/Cardiff Un
100- 10.57 (10.44-16)
GRIFFITHS Joshua 3.11.93, Swansea
5kR- 14:18, 10kR- 30:10 (29:49-16), HMar- 65:18,
Mar- 2:14:53
GRIMSEY William U23 14.12.96, W.Green & EL/ Lough-
borough St
HJ- 2.12i/2.09 (2.12-15)
GRIMWADE Kieran U20 7.12.99, Cardiff
HT- 48.68, HTJ- 58.47
GRINDLE Harry U17 9.04.01, Belgrave
200- 22.50, 400- 50.30
GRINSTED Zak U13 9.12.04, Luton
DTC- 26.17
GROOM George U20 20.10.99, Shaftesbury B
2kSt- 6:05.97 (5:57.08-16), 3kSt- 9:29.40 (9:29.17-16)
GRUEN Alexander U20 1.02.98, Oxford Un/AUS
1500- 3:49.34
GRUNDY Gilbert 22.06.89, Guildford & Godalming
3k- 8:19.69i
GRZASLEWICZ Pawel 29.10.89, Darlington/POL
HJ- 1.95 (1.95-14)
GUEST Lewis 28.05.94, Yeovil Olympiads
TJ- 13.99 (14.76-15)

GUNN Luke 22.03.85, Derby AC
10kR- 30:12, HMar- 66:40, 2kSt- 5:42.87 (5:35.77-16),
3kSt- 8:38.69 (8:28.48-08)
GUNNING Rory 3.05.84, Kent AC/IRL
JT- 62.61 (62.97-16)
GURNEY Lewis U13 13.11.04, Rugby & Northampton
HJ- 1.57
GUTHRIE Jack U17 24.01.02, Shettleston H
100- 11.10w/11.1
GWYNNE William U20 25.04.98, Kingston & P/Lough St
PV- 4.70

HAGAN Jeff U15 14.11.02, Shaftesbury B
TJ- 12.87
HAGEN Andrew U17 9.11.01, Willowfield
1.5kSt- 4:38.52
HAGUE Adam U23 29.08.97, City of Sheffield/Hallam Un
PV- 5.50i/5.50 (5.60-15)
HALE Cameron U20 14.09.99, Bournemouth
DECJ- 5799
HALE Joshua U15 19.09.02, West Midland Schools
300- 37.02
HALFORD Harry U20 22.03.98, Wolves & Bil./Cov Un
5k- 15:15.63
HALL David U23 25.04.95, Dartford/Brunel Un
400- 47.84 (46.46-15), HJ- 1.96i (2.01-11),
PV- 4.21i/4.20 (4.50-15), JT- 55.48 (55.75-14),
Dec- 7038 (7651-15)
HALL Ethan U15 9.02.03, Team Bath
100- 11.3/11.31, 200- 23.0/23.05
HALL Maxim 29.12.86, Dartford
PV- 4.31i/4.20 (4.40i-14, 4.40-16), JT- 54.29 (63.86-10),
Dec- 6256 (7056-12), HepIS- 5100i (5149i-15)
HALL Scott 8.03.94, Gateshead
LJ- 7.44 (7.56-16), TJ- 14.50 (15.51-14)
HALLAS Jack 7.02.91, Birchfield
800- 1:49.09
HALPIN Jack U15 19.03.04, Gateshead
SPB- 14.78i/14.47, HTB- 49.69, JTB- 45.71
HALPIN Joe U17 19.02.01, Gateshead
60HY- 8.52i, LJ- 6.75
HAMBLIN James U23 1.07.96, Shaftesbury B/Lough St
HT- 60.15
HAMEED Umar 24.02.89, Sale/PAK
100- 10.68w, 200- 21.52w (21.41w/21.58-08)
HAMILTON Allan 14.07.92, Sale/New Mexico Un
60- 6.74i, 200- 21.41 (21.14A/21.20wA/21.33-15),
LJ- 7.71 (7.88-16)
HAMILTON Lee 6.12.90, Newquay & Par
110H- 15.51 (14.5/14.64w-15, 14.86-14)
HAMILTON Patrick V35 17.03.81, Slieve Gullion/IRL
HMar- 66:27
HAMLING Alexander U20 2.03.99, Rugby & Nor AC
SPJ- 14.05, DTJ- 43.27
HAMMOND Darren Raymond James 31.03.89, Sale
HJ- 1.96i (2.11i-10, 2.10-07)
HAMMOND Dewi 11.02.94, Cardiff
100- 10.57 (10.33w-15, 10.35-14)
HANDSAKER Harry U17 12.01.02, Burton
100- 10.96
HANLEY-BYRON Lloyd 15.10.87, Shaftesbury B/SKN
400H- 51.61 (49.62-09) né Gumbs
HANNIGAN Lewis U15 29.08.03, Kilbarchan
3k- 9:23.34
HANSON James U17 21.08.01, Woking
200- 22.3
HANSON Mark V35 13.05.81, Enfield & Har
60- 6.95i (6.68i-03)
HANSON Thomas U17 18.12.00, Cardiff
SPY- 14.98i/14.79 (16.20-16)
HARDING Joseph U15 31.10.02, Basildon
60- 7.19i, 100- 11.1/11.33, 200- 23.1, 60HB- 8.25i,
80HB- 10.50, 100HY- 13.1, HJ- 1.81, PenB- 3258,
LJ- 6.87w/6.77i/6.76, PenIB- 3132i
HARDING Matthew J U20 3.04.98, Colwyn Bay
800- 1:47.92, 1500- 3:53.45
HARDMAN Carl 20.03.83, Salford
5kR- 14:21 (14:17.01t-09), 10kR- 29:46, Mar- 2:19:35

HARDMAN Joseph U20 4.03.99, Worcester AC
JT- 54.38
HARKNETT Lewis U17 17.10.00, Orion
1.5kSt- 4:37.62
HARNETT Sean U15 24.07.03, New Forest Juniors
3k- 9:21.76
HARRIES Toby U20 30.09.98, Brighton Phoenix
200- 20.81 (20.56w-15)
HARRINGTON Angus U17 22.06.01, Blackheath & Br
800- 1:54.95
HARRIS Cameron U15 29.06.03, Blackburn
JTB- 45.54
HARRIS Chris 22.10.92, Newquay & Par
LJ- 6.95
HARRIS Elior 6.05.88, Stevenage & NH
HJ- 2.05 (2.05-11)
HARRIS Elliott U15 13.10.02, Solihull & S H
60HB- 8.73i, 80HB- 11.13, LJ- 6.17, PenB- 2669,
PenIB- 2491i
HARRIS Jack U17 6.08.01, Lewes
PV- 4.10
HARRIS Joe U23 23.05.97, Manx H
JT- 75.71
HARRIS Matthew 26.04.89, Ashford/AUS
PV- 4.10i (4.30-11), DT- 42.89, JT- 55.13 (60.75-13)
HARRIS Rhys U20 11.10.98, Swansea
60H- 8.47i, 60HJ- 8.39i, 110HJ- 15.2 (15.20-16),
400H- 56.08
HARRIS Tom U20 6.01.98, Newquay & Par/Plymouth Un
400- 48.8 (49.13-16)
HARRISON Kai U17 21.06.01, Nene Valley H
DTY- 45.10
HARROP Zach U20 5.05.98, Sale/Cardiff Met
PV- 4.37i/4.15 (4.50i/4.40-16)
HARRY Jordan U23 20.02.97, Bristol & W/Bath Un
TJ- 13.99i (14.16-16)
HART Sam U17 6.11.00, Team Kennet
3k- 8:50.75
HARVEY Jason Marcus 9.04.91, Lagan Valley/IRL
400- 48.54 (47.15-13), 400H- 51.19 (50.13-13)
HARVEY Jonathan 12.09.83, Braintree
JT- 53.04 (58.18-04)
HARVEY Lawrence Edward V35 26.08.81, Trafford
LJ- 6.89 (7.10-11), TJ- 14.93 (15.22-11)
HARVIE Ricky U23 17.03.95, AF&D/St Marys Un
800- 1:51.50, 1500- 3:45.61
HASAN Abdifatqh U17 14.02.02, Yate
800- 1:56.56
HASSAN Jamil U20 25.06.99, Marshall Milton K
TJ- 14.26i (14.46-16)
HATTON Jack U23 14.02.96, Thames Valley/Bath Spa
60H- 7.97i, 110H- 14.18 (14.13w-16)
HAUXWELL Jamie 28.09.84, Redcar
24HrT- 222.575kms
HAWKES Ben U17 5.10.00, Leamington
400- 49.73
HAWKES Ben U17 8.11.00, Worthing
SPY- 16.49, DTY- 52.70, HTY- 71.97
HAWKES Stuart V35 22.12.77, Tipton
Mar- 2:27:36 (2:26:54-16)
HAWKINS Callum 22.06.92, Kilbarchan
5k- 13:59.8+e (14:06.57-15), 10kR- 28:28+/29:14,
15kR- 42:37+, HMar- 60:00, Mar- 2:10:17
HAWKINS Derek John 29.04.89, Kilbarchan
5MR- 24:07 (23:42-15), 10MR- 49:57, HMar- 66:54 (63:53-16)
HAY Adam U17 8.02.01, Inverclyde
1.5kSt- 4:34.82
HAY Alastair Thomas 7.09.85, Central
3k- 8:10.39 (8:07.84i-10), 5k- 14:27.64 (14:12.74-15),
5MR- 24:14 (24:09-09), HMar- 68:15
HAY Callum U15 6.09.02, City of Sheffield
LJ- 6.28
HAY Jonathan 12.02.92, Aldershot F&D
10kR- 30:13, 10MR- 48:55, HMar- 66:41+ (64:09-14),
Mar- 2:24:02 (2:23:52-16)
HAYDOCK-WILSON Alex U20 28.07.99, WSE&H
200- 21.83, 400- 48.61 (47.45-16)

HAYES Martin 16.05.89, VP-Glasgow
3kSt- 9:35.88 (9:19.72-16)
HAZEL Sam U23 7.10.96, Shaftesbury B/Middlesex Un
200- 21.79, 400- 46.98
HAZELL Benjamin Nicholas Rodney 1.10.84, Bstoke & MH
DT- 41.00 (48.01-10), Dec- 5517 (7726-09)
HEAD Thomas U23 15.01.96, Newham & Ex B/Brunel Un
SP- 13.26i (13.85-16), HT- 43.80
HEADDOCK Charlie U20 11.12.98, Sale
DTJ- 47.09 (47.67-16)
HEAL Samuel U15 5.11.02, Avon Schools
800- 2:03.10
HEANEY-BRUFAL Oscar U17 27.09.01, Blackheath & Br
400HY- 57.42
HEARD Owen U17 29.12.01, Camberley
PV- 4.05
HEASLIP Olivier U23 2.01.96, Eaci-S/1 Al Voiron (FRA)
3kSt- 9:10.09
HEATH Jonathan James 12.12.93, Derby AC
HJ- 2.05i/2.00 (2.10-15)
HEAWOOD Samuel Bart 25.09.90, Crawley/Brunel Un
SP- 16.23i/15.54
HEDGER James 9.09.84, Thames Valley/Lough St
SP- 14.51, DT- 46.82
HENDERSON Callum John U20 3.05.00, Edinburgh AC
LJ- 7.04w/6.93i (7.06-16)
HENDERSON Connor Alexande 2.10.92, Kilbarchan/
West Scot Un/PHI   400H- 52.47 (52.22-14)
HENRY Jerome U15 11.01.03, Newham & Essex B
HJ- 1.83
HENSON Benjamin U15 2.09.02, Cardiff
PenB- 2691, OctB- 3799, PenIB- 2470i
HEPPINSTALL George U23 17.10.97, Sheffield/Hall U
PV- 4.88
HERRING Oliver U17 28.09.00, Gateshead
60HJ- 8.55i, 60HY- 8.52i, 100HY- 13.91w, LJ- 6.54w,
OctY- 4817
HEWES Thomas U20 15.09.99, Chelmsford
HJ- 2.15
HEWETT Joshua U20 1.10.99, Liverpool H
HJ- 2.09
HEWITSON Ryan U23 4.01.96, Aberdeen
110H- 15.27
HEWITT Matthew 27.12.92, Southampton
60H- 8.23i, 110H- 14.78 (14.65w-14, 14.66-15)
HEWITT Oliver U20 27.09.99, Newbury
DTJ- 45.02, HT- 51.55, HTJ- 63.61
HEWITT Samuel U20 1.02.98, WSE&H/Sheffield Un
HJ- 1.95i (2.00-14)
HEWSON Thomas U17 24.09.00, Andover
JTY- 74.06
HEYDEN Max U17 12.09.00, Aldershot F&D
1500- 3:59.40, 3k- 8:38.63
HEYES Andrew 22.06.90, Hallamshire/Birmingham Un
1500- 3:41.09, 3k- 7:55.76i+/8:04.48 (8:02.96-15),
5k- 13:48.74, 5kR- 13:47, 10kR- 29:22
HEYWARD Jake U20 26.04.99, Cardiff
800- 1:50.33, 1500- 3:42.12
HICKEY Adam 30.05.88, Southend
10kR- 29:55 (29:04-16)
HIGBEE Anthony 21.09.83, RAF/Basingstoke & MH
60H- 8.34i (8.23i-11)
HIGGINS Benjamin U17 14.11.00, Charnwood
60- 7.08i, 100- 10.89w/10.96, 200- 22.19w, 60HY- 8.32i,
400- 48.99i (50.20-16), 100HY- 13.54, 400HY- 53.25
HIGGINS Jack U17 30.01.01, Southampton
400- 49.46
HIGHAM Daniel 4.11.90, Liverpool Pembroke Sefton
400- 48.3/48.59i (48.36-16)
HILL Adam 9.07.94, City Lisburn/Queen's Un
110H- 15.37, HJ- 1.95i (1.96-14)
HILL Jay 27.08.91, Newquay & Par
HT- 56.77 (58.10-12)
HILL Joshuah U23 23.04.96, Solihull & S H
HJ- 2.05 (2.13i/2.12-14)
HILLIARD Charles U20 21.09.99, Halesowen
60- 6.99i, 100- 10.85w (10.7/10.79-16),
200- 21.36w/21.77i (21.79-15), 400- 49.1

HILLMAN Ben U15 16.04.03, Cardiff
60HB- 8.90i, 80HB- 11.47, LJ- 6.12, PenB- 2592,
OctB- 4336, PenIB- 2911i
HILTON Christoper 22.05.94, Southampton
3kSt- 9:44.28 (9:24.57-15)
HIND Owen 1.08.90, Kent AC/Texas Un
3k- 8:07.59i, 5k- 14:12.65i/14:26.20 (14:06.23-16),
10k- 29:27.04
HINSON Brody U15 26.11.02, Kingston upon Hull
100- 11.34, 200- 22.97
HIRST Joe U17 26.01.02, St Albans AC
JTY- 52.04
HISCOTT Michael 1.07.83, Maidenhead
HMar- 67:42 (67:36-14)
HOBSON Adam 4.05.93, Inverness/Robert Gordon U
JT- 53.28 (54.59-15)
HOBSON Joseph U20 29.04.98, C of Sheffield/Hallam Un
60HJ- 8.45i (8.42i-16), HJ- 1.96i (1.99i-16, 1.98-15),
LJ- 6.95i (7.05i-16, 7.00w-15), HepJ- 5109i,
DECJ- 5811 (6465-15)
HOCKADAY Kian U13 12.06.05, Team Kennet
JTC- 40.60
HOCKING Jack U20 29.09.98, Worcester AC
400- 48.90i/49.10
HODGE Joshua U20 23.05.00, Cumbrian Schools
JT- 54.61, DECJ- 5996
HODGSON Kevin U23 24.03.96, Bournemouth/Lough St
200- 21.77w (21.6/21.74-15), 400- 48.97
HODGSON Roman U13 4.01.05, Deeside
800- 2:12.65
HOGG-WILLIAMS Marlon U20 27.10.98, Newham & Ex B
60- 6.98i
HOILES Daniel U17 15.07.01, Southampton
PV- 3.80
HOLDEN Benjamin U17 25.02.02, New Marske
100- 11.1
HOLDEN Thomas U23 21.03.97, Tonbridge/Lough St
3k- 8:13.74i (8:11.13-16), 5kR- 14:27
HOLDER Graham Paul V45 16.01.72, Bexley
HT- 54.05 (62.01-05)
HOLDSWORTH Ben U17 26.12.00, Isle of Wight
OctY- 4337
HOLGATE Craig V40 21.09.76, Ely
24Hr- 245.794km
HOLLAND Adam 5.03.87, Notfast
Mar- 2:27:59, 50kR- 3:18:59
HOLLAND Charlie U15 14.04.04, Swansea
800- 2:03.19
HOLLIS Harry 2.03.92, Corby
JT- 61.92 (64.03-16)
HOLMES Thomas U15 16.10.02, Marlborough Jnrs
JTB- 55.66
HOLT Peter U17 27.10.00, Reading
PV- 3.70
HOLYOAK Steven V50 8.09.64, RRC
24Hr- 245.492km (252.836km-15)
HOOD-BOYCE Christian U23 4.01.95, City of Portsmouth/
Loughborough St/TTO   110H- 15.56 (15.07-14)
HOOK Tom U23 6.06.95, City of Norwich/St Marys Un
1500- 3:43.16
HOOKWAY Alexander 19.05.91, Tonbridge
Dec- 4793
HOOLE Adam U15 25.05.03, Team East Lothian
80HB- 11.82
HOPE Jack U20 14.05.98, Kettering
2kSt- 6:10.64 (6:04.46-16)
HOPE Richard V45 11.09.70, VPH &TH/AUS
Mar- 2:29:49
HOPEWELL Keelan U17 6.02.01, Solihull & S H
1500- 4:01.97
HOPKINS Ceirion U20 11.10.99, Neath
200- 21.91w, LJ- 7.11i/7.08w/7.04
HOPKINS George U15 1.06.03, Woking
PV- 3.51, JTB- 45.30
HOPKINS Jac U23 16.05.97, Swansea/Iona Coll, USA
3k- 8:08.37i (8:18.72-14), 5k- 14:24.94i (14:29.13-15)
HOPKINS Jonathan 3.06.92, Swansea/Cardiff Met
3k- 8:10.83i, 10kR- 29:40, 3kSt- 8:34.03

385

HOPPER Christian U13 7.09.04, Cambridge H
2kW- 11:00.19
HOPPER Daniel U20 21.08.00, Dacorum & Tring
LJ- 6.93 (7.02-16)
HORNE Jamie U23 7.09.97, Peterborough
HJ- 2.01 (2.01i-15)
HORNE-SMITH Jack U15 17.08.03, Swindon
PV- 3.31
HORSFIELD Benjamin U17 26.07.01, Durham City H
800- 1:56.85
HORTON Richard 28.05.93, Shaftesbury B
10k- 29:38.55, 10kR- 29:27, HMar- 65:37
HORTON Tommy 7.11.93, Hallamshire/Sheffield Un
1500- 3:45.76, 3k- 8:13.77i (8:16.84-16), 3kSt- 8:48.26
HOSGOOD Ieuan U17 6.03.01, Swansea
PV- 3.85
HOUGHTON Bertie U23 19.03.95, Hallamshire/Sheff Un
3kSt- 9:29.92 (8:58.60-16)
HOULDEN Matthew U15 2.10.02, Stockport
100- 11.49
HOUSTON Ross David V35 5.12.79, Central
HMar- 67:42 (65:51-12), Mar- 2:24:13 (2:18:33-13)
HOWARD Alex U23 24.08.95, Tonbridge/Oxford Un
3kSt- 9:06.92 (9:02.48-16)
HOWELLS Daniel U17 28.02.02, Aldershot F&D
800- 1:54.94
HOWITT Kane U23 6.11.96, R Sutton Coldfield
100- 10.72w, 200- 21.30w/21.5/21.77
HOWORTH Rory U17 2.07.02, Team Bath
400HY- 57.71, HepIY- 4133i, OctY- 5013, HepIY- 4133i
HOY Mark 21.07.91, Mid Ulster/IRL
800- 1:51.80 (1:49.68-15)
HOYLE Jason U23 11.11.96, Oldham & Roy/Durham Un
200- 21.66w, 400- 47.91
HUCK Peter 10.07.90, Barrow & Furness
5k- 14:13.61, 10kR- 30:00 (29:56-15), 10MR- 49:36,
HMar- 65:03
HUDSON Shaun U17 8.09.00, WSE&H
1.5kSt- 4:22.61
HUDSON-SMITH Matthew 26.10.94, Birchfield
400- 44.74 (44.48-16)
HUDSPITH Ian V45 23.09.70, Morpeth
HMar- 67:58 (62:53-96)
HUGGINS Scott 24.07.89, Blackheath & Bromley
PV- 5.26
HUGHES Ben U17 12.11.01, Wigan
DecY- 5049, OctY- 4433
HUGHES Harry U23 26.09.97, West Suffolk/Essex Un
JT- 76.81
HUGHES Iolo U23 22.11.96, Sale
5kR- 14:33
HUGHES Matthew U17 9.12.01, Tonbridge
LJ- 6.48
HUGHES Thomas U23 9.09.97, Hallamshire/Sheffield Un
Dec- 5415
HUGHES Toby U13 28.09.04, Medway & Maidstone
JTC- 38.57
HUGHES William U17 28.01.01, Nene Valley H
100- 10.8w, 200- 21.8w/21.86
HUGHES Zharnel U23 13.07.95, Shaftesbury B
100- 10.08w/10.12 (10.10-16), 200- 20.22 (20.02-15),
400- 46.58
HUGHFF Christopher V35 5.12.81, Newham & Essex B
JT- 62.93 (76.92-09)
HULSE Joshua U17 14.03.01, Ipswich
400- 49.10, 800- 1:52.7
HULSON Charlie 7.03.93, Liverpool H
5kR- 14:14 (13:43.35t-16), 10kR- 29:59 (29:30-16),
HMar- 65:33
HUNT Aaron U17 3.03.01, Nene Valley H
1500- 4:01.72
HUNT Aidan U13 30.10.04, City of Portsmouth
JTC- 40.88
HUNT Nikko U20 17.02.98, W.Green & Ex L/Nice(FRA)
PV- 4.80 (5.06i-16)
HUNTER Callum 20.01.94, North Down
TJ- 13.85i (14.23-15)

HUNTER Thomas U20 7.12.98, Ballymena & A
TJ- 13.72w (13.83-15)
HURLEY Elliott U23 22.09.95, City of Sheffield/Leeds Un
60- 6.85i (6.71i-16)
HUSKISSON Isaac U23 17.06.97, Nene Valley H
HT- 45.59 (49.12-15)
HUSSAIN Jason 17.10.86, Crawley
200- 21.77 (21.12-15)
HUSSEY Ethan U15 5.03.03, Leeds
800- 1:59.03, 1500- 4:00.20
HUSSEY Lascelles U23 1.07.97, Herne Hill/B'ham Un
1500- 3:47.85
HYDE George U17 30.03.01, West Cheshire
SPY- 17.42
HYLTON Dean 15.09.90, Blackheath & Bromley/JAM
100- 10.56 (10.56-15), 200- 21.29

IBINOLA Timi U13, Essex Schools
SPC- 10.73
IGBOKWE Daniel U20 28.06.98, WSE&H/Columbia Un
TJ- 15.63
IGE Samuel U23 29.01.96, Belgrave/Un Wales Swansea
60- 6.90i (6.87i-16), 100- 10.62, 200- 21.41
IKEJI Kenneth U15 17.09.02, Basildon
SPB- 13.90, DTB- 39.67, HTB- 62.08
ILIONE Emeka U17 20.03.02, Notts
SPY- 13.98
ILLSLEY Sam U17 11.04.02, Worthing
HTY- 55.01
ILORI Jonathan 14.08.93, Blackheath & Bromley
LJ- 7.33, TJ- 16.06 (16.10w-14)
ILYK Harry U17 24.05.01, Notts
HTY- 63.93
IMROTH Kristian U17 19.01.02, Dacorum & Tring
1.5kSt- 4:42.0
INDELBU Wondiye 13.02.88, Leeds/ETH
5k- 14:25.40, 10kR- 30:27
INFANTINO Antonio 22.03.91, Shaftesbury B/ITA
60- 6.92i (6.87i-08), 100- 10.16w/10.36, 200-
20.45w/20.59 (20.53-16)
INGHAM Alexander U23 12.01.96, Biggleswade/York Un
JT- 58.36 (58.89/54.93-14)
INGHAM Alfie U20 10.01.98, Shaftesbury B
JT- 59.39
INGLEY Reece 15.02.92, Trafford
400- 48.85 (48.69-15)
INNES Calum 17.09.90, VP-Glasgow/Trinity Western Un
60H- 8.25i (7.89i-15), 110H- 15.09 (14.20-14)
IRELAND Adam U15 28.07.03, Hillingdon
3k- 9:29.44
IRVING Peter 28.01.83, Channel Islands
110H- 15.34w (15.02-13), 400H- 55.30 (52.57-13)
IRVING Toby U15 1.05.03, Reading
PV- 3.15
ISAAC Kieran U13 1.09.04, Medway & Maid
SPC- 10.85

JACKSON James U20 12.02.99, Southampton
400H- 54.53
JACKSON Mathew 28.04.91, Liverpool H
1500- 3:46.82, 3k- 8:14.82, 5k- 14:21.95, 5kR- 14:20
JACKSON Rhys U20 14.01.00, Doncaster
DECJ- 5509
JACKSON-CLIST Theodore U15 16.11.02, Exeter
LJ- 6.20
JACKSON-DAVIES Jovel U15 21.01.03, London Schools
TJ- 12.07
JAKSEVICIUS Andrius V35 15.02.81, Belgrave/LTU
Mar- 2:23:24
JAMES Bradley U15 23.09.03, Havering
JTB- 49.25
JAMES Morgan Glyndwr U17 17.05.01, Cardiff
3k- 8:53.47
JAMES Nathan U20 5.10.98, Swansea
JT- 65.91
JAMES Oliver 26.03.94, C of Sheffield/McNeese State Un
3k- 8:19.16i
JAMES Rhys U15 4.12.02, Neath
1500- 4:18.73

JARVIS Daniel U23 21.10.95, Liverpool H/St Marys Un
1500- 3:48.82, 3kSt- 8:43.09
JEAL Aaron U20 30.05.99, Middlesboro Mandale
HT- 45.85 (49.61-16), HTJ- 59.91
JEANS Edward U20 28.09.98, Preston
HT- 56.85, HTJ- 68.49
JEDRZEJCZAK Robert U17 23.03.01, Team Bath
DTY- 41.39
JEFFS Ross 5.09.91, Enfield & Haringey
LJ- 7.34w/7.23, TJ- 14.04 (14.97i/14.50-15)
JEGEDE Olugbayode JJ 3.10.85, Newham & Essex B
LJ- 7.27 (8.11-12), TJ- 13.95
JENKIN Mark V35 19.09.78, Bideford
HMar- 68:12, Mar- 2:27:16 (2:25:26-16)
JENKINS Michael U13 27.10.04, Pembroke
DTC- 26.10
JENVEY Bradley U15 23.12.02, Southampton
HTB- 41.57, JTB- 55.13
JEROME Kareem U15 1.02.03, Havering
300- 36.2
JIBUNOH Duane U23 18.11.95, Havering
DT- 47.14
JOHN-OLOJO Olushola 5.05.92, HHH/Memphis St. Un.
LJ- 7.11 (7.20i-16), TJ- 15.40i/14.70 (15.37-13)
JOHNSON Allandre Toussaint 8.12.85, Herne Hill
JT- 59.47 (62.55-08)
JOHNSON Ayomide U13 3.11.04, Kent Schools
DTC- 26.14
JOHNSON Ben 22.09.88, Southport
10k- 30:30.18, 10kR- 30:26, HMar- 67:17, Mar- 2:21:52
JOHNSON Callum 1.07.94, Gateshead/Leeds Beck Un
10kR- 30:08
JOHNSON Casey U23 20.09.97, Dartford
LJ- 7.01
JOHNSON Frankie U17 17.01.01, Bedford & County
PV- 4.92i/4.86
JOHNSON Henry U15 28.10.02, Houghton
800- 1:59.04, 1500- 4:06.7, 3k- 9:08.24
JOHNSON Karl U17 15.04.01, Newham & Essex B
400- 50.45, 400HY- 53.21
JOHNSON Lee Charles U20 27.05.98, Bedford & County
HJ- 1.95 (2.03-14)
JOHNSON Luke 27.11.94, Horsham BS
JT- 57.83
JOHNSON Mark V50 7.09.64, Leeds
PV- 4.30i (5.26-91)
JOHNSON Scott 2.10.90, Bedford & County
HJ- 2.00 (2.13-13)
JOHNSON Tyler 24.12.91, City of Plymouth
100- 10.60w
JOHNSON-ASSOON Gavin 19.12.82, Thames Valley
JT- 69.69
JOHNSON-FISHER Tyrese U20 9.09.99, Croydon
100- 10.79 (10.72w/10.73-16)
JOHNSTON Luke 16.05.94, Liverpool H/Iowa St Un
800- 1:50.14 (1:49.88-16)
JOKOSENUMI Remi U15 15.02.04, Shaftesbury B
100- 11.46, 200- 22.84
JOLOB Joshua U15 2.11.02, Charnwood
300- 37.09
JONES Adam U20 8.10.98, Southampton
HJ- 2.03 (2.05-15)
JONES Ben 6.11.82, Ipswich/Army
HT- 52.16 (53.00-16)
JONES Ben U13 8.05.05, Taunton
JTC- 37.71
JONES Carwyn V35 10.10.79, Cardiff
5k- 14:34.97, 5kR- 14:31, 10kR- 30:24
JONES Craig 28.04.93, Liverpool H
LJ- 7.33i/7.05 (7.70-14)
JONES Egryn Wyn V45 1.11.71, WSE&H
PV- 4.32i (4.90-95)
JONES Emyr 5.09.92, Cardiff/Bath Un
PV- 4.10i (4.45i-14, 4.40-13)
JONES Evan U15 6.10.03, Bridgend
200- 23.50i
JONES Iwan Pyrs U15 6.05.03, Cardiff
60HB- 9.23i

JONES James U15 20.09.02, Deeside
3k- 9:09.22
JONES Jonathan U20 11.07.98, Gloucester AC
HT- 51.81, HTJ- 63.97
JONES Kai U23 24.12.96, Newham & Essex B/Brunel Un
SP- 16.04 (16.36i-16)
JONES Kellen U20 5.09.99, Newport
DECJ- 5383
JONES Kristian 4.03.91, Swansea
3k- 8:07.65i/8:10.71, 5k- 14:31.53 (14:20.68-16),
5kR- 14:02, 10k- 29:05.66, HMar- 66:11
JONES Kristian U20 10.03.98, Cardiff/Loughborough St
60- 6.94i (6.91i-16), 100- 10.39w/10.53, 200- 21.19
JONES Luke U23 18.10.96, Tamworth
800- 1:51.86
JONES Marcus U17 11.12.00, Crawley
HTY- 59.63
JONES Maurice 17.12.91, Birchfield
400H- 54.29 (50.34-15)
JONES Michael David V50 23.07.63, Crawley
HT- 62.39 (76.43-01)
JONES Nathan 3.10.94, Liverpool H/McNeese State Un
3k- 8:17.77i, 5k- 14:21.84i (14:34.31-16), 10k- 29:33.82
JONES Noah U13 11.11.04, City of Plymouth
PV- 2.75
JONES Osian Dwyfor 23.06.93, Liverpool H
HT- 70.00
JONES Samuel U15 7.09.02, Halesowen
60- 7.45i, 200- 23.26w/23.27, 300- 36.20
JONES Scott 30.12.94, Wigan
SP- 13.06
JONES-PARKER Christopher U13 4.01.05,
City of Portsmouth JTC- 41.56
JOPP Oscar U20 29.09.99, Stevenage & NH
DECJ- 5467
JORDAN Andy V50 5.06.63, Harpenden
24Hr- 222.878km
JORDAN Chris V35 12.05.80, Leics Coritanian
Mar- 2:29:35 (2:27:58-16)
JORDAN Rhys Thomas U13 6.09.04, Marshall Milton K
LJ- 5.03
JORGE Loreni U15 9.01.03, Notts
100- 11.12, 200- 23.4
JOSEPH Anton U15 14.01.03, Guildford & Godalming
HTB- 49.49
JOSEPH Caius U20 24.07.99, Basingstoke & MH
60HJ- 8.46i, PV- 4.11, LJ- 7.08w, HepJ- 4700i,
DECJ- 6747
JOSEPH Rafer Ernest Lewis V45 21.07.68, B'stoke & MH
DT- 42.51 (52.00-96)
JOYCE Daniel U15 2.01.03, Tynedale
300- 37.57, 800- 1:56.04, 1500- 4:17.4
JOYNSON Jack U20 15.12.98, Yate
TJ- 14.12

KADIR Hamza U17 12.09.99, Shaftesbury B
800- 1:52.03, 1500- 3:48.59
KALLENBERG Michael 9.01.91, RAF/Cardiff
HMar- 67:07+ (66:50-16), Mar- 2:20:18 (2:19:00sh-15)
KALWARSKI Kacper U23 24.09.97, Leamington/POL
JT- 53.70
KANDU Chris U23 10.09.95, Enfield & Haringey
HJ- 2.26i/2.25 (2.26i-15)
KANONIK Nicholas Ian 24.10.87, WSE&H/Gloucester U
200- 21.33w/21.77 (21.46-14), 400- 48.64 (47.29-13)
KAPUR-WALTON Karran U17 31.01.02, Leigh
PV- 3.80
KAZEMAKS Kasper 1.06.84, Woking/LAT
HepIS- 4643i
KEAL Rob V40 6.05.74, Notts
Mar- 2:23:30
KEARNS Conor U20 5.02.99, Cheltenham
PV- 4.13i (4.30-16)
KEEN Rory U20 6.04.00, Sale
400- 48.07
KEEN Thomas U17 16.06.01, Cambridge & Col
1500- 3:58.24, 3k- 8:24.87
KEEVIL Thomas U17 22.09.00, Chelmsford
3k- 8:53.50

KELLY Greg U20 11.04.99, East Kilbride
100- 10.83w, 200- 21.69w/21.86
KELLY Joshua 25.09.93, Havant
SP- 13.71
KELWAY Alfie U15 2.01.03, Colchester & Tendring
60HB- 9.37i
KENDALL Harry U23 4.10.96, Tonbridge/Hallam Un
HJ- 1.95 (1.95-15), PV- 4.26i/4.10, LJ- 7.06, JT- 55.82,
Dec- 6691, HepIS- 5027i
KENNEDY Alan 19.07.88, North Down/Ulster Un/IRL
TJ- 14.22i (15.22w-12, 15.19-10)
KENNEDY Jaden U15 16.09.03, Herne Hill
1500- 4:16.43, 3k- 9:28.71
KENNEDY William U23 21.10.97, Bristol & West
200- 21.78
KENT Aidan U20 6.10.99, Newquay & Par
2kSt- 6:10.99, 3kSt- 9:46.38
KENT Anthony U17 25.09.00, Blackburn
DTY- 44.31
KERR Josh U23 8.10.97, Edinburgh AC/New Mexico Un
800- 1:48.05A, 1500- 3:35.99, 1M- 3:59.90i
KERRY Shaun U17 13.12.01, Kingston upon Hull
HTY- 60.94
KESTEVEN Fraser 20.06.92, Notts
TJ- 13.91 (14.00-16)
KETTERER Isaac U13 9.01.05, Newquay & Par
PenC- 1726
KHAN Joel U20 30.09.99, Worcester AC
HJ- 2.16
KHOGALI Samuel U23 15.07.97, Worcester AC/Lough St
LJ- 7.30w/7.13i/6.92 (7.40w/7.26-16)
KILSBY Fraser U17 18.01.01, Wycombe
OctY- 4242
KILTY Richard 2.09.89, Middlesboro Mandale
60- 6.54i (6.49i-14), 100- 10.18 (9.92w/10.01-16),
150st- 15.43 (14.64w-15, 15.07-16), 200- 20.51 (20.34-13)
KIMPTON Ian 8.11.86, Luton
3k- 8:19.01 (8:16.59-15), 10k- 29:18.50,
HMar- 66:01 (64:31-15), Mar- 2:22.45 (2:15:55-15)
KING Benjamin U15 9.03.03, Camberley
HJ- 1.75
KING Daniel 30.05.83, Colchester H
3kW- 12:31.76 (11:34.62-05), 5kW- 21:51+ (19:57.95t-04),
10kW- 44:20+ (42:08-07), 20kW- 1:29:10 (1:26:14-08)
KING David 13.06.94, City of Plymouth
200- 21.58, 60H- 7.63i, 110H- 13.48 (13.4-16)
KING Dominic 30.05.83, Colchester H
3kW- 12:00.91 (11:51.44-06), 5kWR- 21:24+ (19:57.91t-04),
10kWR- 42:45+ (42:17.1t-02), 20kW- 1:26:09,
50kW- 4:04:16 (3:55:48-16)
KING Dylan U15 27.12.02, Birchfield
800- 2:02.37
KING James Elliott U23 28.06.96, Cardiff/Cardiff Met
TJ- 13.73i/13.70
KING Joshua U23 3.09.95, Bournemouth
3kSt- 9:46.66
KING-CLUTTERBUCK Dale 1.01.92, Basildon
800- 1:51.26i (1:48.10-15), 1500- 3:45.29 (3:38.65-15),
1M- 4:05.75i (3:59.23-15)
KINGMAN Robert V40 21.02.73, RAF/Newham & EB
PV- 4.10 (5.02-94)
KINLOCH Alasdair U20 8.02.99, Tonbridge
1500- 3:53.11, 3k- 8:21.37 (8:18.21-16)
KIRABO Peter 22.09.92, Woodford Green & Ex L
TJ- 14.79 (15.01i/14.98-14)
KIRBY Jack U23 5.11.96, Harrow
60H- 8.06i, 110H- 14.54 (14.23w/14.31-16)
KIRBY Marcus U15 21.11.02, Amber Valley
JTB- 45.00
KIRBY Mitchell 18.04.91, Leics Cor
TJ- 14.16i/13.72 (14.43-16)
KIRBY-POLIDORE Jordan 26.01.93, W.Green & Ex L
100- 10.75 (10.55-13), 200- 21.50 (20.77-13)
KIRCHMAYR Laurenz U20 9.02.99, Notts/AUT
PV- 4.40
KIRK Darragh U15 16.10.02, Strabane
JTB- 45.21

KIRK Tom 1.11.94, City of Sheffield
HT- 50.91
KIRK-SMITH Adam 30.01.91, W.Green & Ex L
3k- 8:12.81, 3kSt- 8:37.41
KITENGE Hosana U17, Sussex Schools
SPY- 13.60
KITTERIDGE Ethan U15 12.08.03, Blackheath & Bromley
PV- 2.93i/2.90
KNIBBS Alexander U20 26.04.99, Amber Valley
200- 21.76, 400- 48.31, 400H- 52.09
KNIGHT Andrew U17 10.11.01, Morpeth
SPY- 15.71
KNIGHT Daniel U17 24.11.01, Enfield & Haringey
60HY- 8.12i, 100HY- 13.03
KNIGHT William Joseph U23 12.11.97, Birchfield
SP- 14.11, DT- 44.34
KNOTT Charlie U15 15.06.03, Cambridge & Col
HJ- 1.80
KNOWLES Michael U17 16.01.01, Stevenage & NH
HTY- 50.45
KOFFI David U17 23.04.02, Stevenage & NH
SPY- 13.63
KOUMI Sadam 6.04.94, Birchfield/SUD
400- 46.00 (45.41-15)
KUEHNEL Jamie U23 16.10.97, Newbury
HT- 53.20 (55.09-16)
KUMAR Joshua U17 11.06.01, Shaftesbury B
200- 22.22
KUYPERS Rory U17 20.10.00, Medway & Maidstone
60- 7.16i
KYEREME Kojo V40 23.12.74, Shaftesbury B
10k- 30:23.08 (29:29.55-11)

L ABAN Mackenzie U15 29.10.02, Herne Hill
HTB- 45.26
LACY Craig 17.07.91, Birchfield
JT- 67.71 (68.46-11)
LAFEUILLE Tyriq U17 10.05.01, Shaftesbury B
400HY- 57.34
LAKE Edward U17 15.06.01, City of York
200- 22.49
LAMB Christopher U20 25.05.00, Wigan
PV- 4.42i/4.30 (4.30-16)
LAMBERT Jack U17 13.06.02, Kidd & Stourport
HT- 44.24, HTY- 59.79
LAMBERT Oliver U17 18.10.00, Rugby & Northampton
100HY- 14.0 (13.48-16)
LAMPRELL William U13 12.01.05, Ipswich
HJ- 1.57, SPC- 11.74
LANCASHIRE Thomas 2.07.85, Bolton
800- 1:48.56 (1:45.76-06), 5kR- 14:31 (13:34.44t-09),
1500- 3:38.52i/3:38.85 (3:33.96-10)
LANCASTER James U17 15.08.01, Blackheath & Bromley
HTY- 60.04 (60.14-16)
LANCASTER Joe U17 16.10.01, Barrow & Furness
SPY- 13.85
LANDEAU Nicholas U23 30.01.95, Ealing, S & Mx/TTO
800- 1:48.34
LANDSBOROUGH Samuel 11.11.92, Wirral
60- 6.81i, 100- 10.5/10.64, 200- 21.3/21.37 (21.33-16)
LANE Harry 1.12.94, Bristol & W/Loughborough St
3kSt- 9:01.07 (8:59.90-16)
LANE Jared 22.05.93, N & Ex B/E.London Un/USA
60H- 8.12i (7.94i-15), 110H- 14.09 (13.89-16)
LANE John Ernest 29.01.89, City of Sheffield
100- 10.73 (10.68w/10.71-14), 400- 48.53 (48.01-14),
60H- 8.27i (8.07i-14), 110H- 14.51 (14.32-16), HJ- 2.05,
PV- 5.00 (5.13-13), LJ- 7.43 (7.50-14), DT- 43.06,
SP- 13.48i/13.24 (14.76i-13, 14.12-14), Dec- 7965,
HepIS- 5712i (5982i-14)
LANE William U13 20.07.05, City of Sheffield
PV- 2.72
LANG Ruaridh U17 24.12.00, Morpeth
DTY- 48.25
LANGE Jacob U23 5.12.95, Gloucester AC/Cambridge Un
HT- 59.69
LANGFORD Kyle U23 2.02.96, Shaftesbury B
600- 1:16.10i (1:16.30-14), 800- 1:45.25, 1500- 3:48.65

LANGLEY Jonathan U17 20.11.00, Chester le Street
1.5kSt- 4:40.77
LANGLEY Nathan U20 18.03.00, Worksop
DECJ- 5745
LARKMAN William U20 28.07.98, Taunton/Kent Un
JT- 56.58 (58.68-16)
LASCELLES Deshawn U15 5.02.03, Cambridge & Col
TJ- 12.94
LASSINI Diego U23 10.02.96, Bedford & County/ITA
PV- 4.10, Dec- 4878 (6395-16)
LAVERTY Connor U23 14.05.96, Swansea/Sheffield Un
SP- 13.40 (13.67i-15), DT- 45.17
LAW Max U17 13.05.02, Havering
JTY- 62.50
LAWRENCE Jack U23 2.07.96, Birchfield
60- 6.84i (6.84i-13), 100- 10.54w/10.69, 200- 21.62w
LAWRENCE Mark V45 26.01.71, London Heathside
LJ- 6.85 (7.33-93)
LAWRENCE Owen U20 31.10.98, Southampton
110HJ- 14.53w/14.62, 400H- 55.80
LAWRIE Jack U23 21.02.96, W.Green & Ex L
400- 47.92, 110H- 14.56 (14.50-16), 400H- 50.25
LAWSON Confidence 5.09.90, Shaftesbury B
60- 6.80i (6.76i-15),), 200- 20.92w/21.11 (20.83-16),
100- 10.34w/10.37 (10.25w/10.33-16)
LAWSON Dan Alan 8.05.83, Cambridge Tri
24Hr- 241.205km (261.843km-16)
LAY Graham V40 13.11.75, Southampton
SP- 13.74
LAY Joshua U20 11.04.00, Rugby & Northampton
1500- 3:49.35
LAYNE Jordan Henderson U23 17.05.96, Wycombe
400- 48.70 (47.70-16)
LE GRICE Peter V35 10.07.82, Bristol & West
Mar- 2:27:26 (2:23:23-16)
LEACH Harrison U17 9.11.00, Crawley
DTY- 44.42
LEACH Matthew 25.09.93, Bedford & County
1500- 3:46.25, 3k- 8:03.84i (8:12.65-14), 5k- 14:03.79,
10k- 28:45.48, 10kR- 29:25, 10MR- 49:08+, HMar- 64:22
LEARMONTH Guy 20.04.92, Lasswade
400- 48.73 (48.00-12), 800- 1:45.10
LEAVESLEY Jolyon U15 7.12.02, Corby
800- 2:00.47, 1500- 4:18.11
LECKI Isaac U15 24.03.03, Wrexham
DTB- 38.40
LEE Ben U17 7.01.01, Vale Royal
800- 1:53.41, 1500- 3:58.61
LEE James U23 15.11.97, Hallamshire/Hallam Un
HJ- 2.00
LEEMBRUGGEN Curtis U17 9.01.01, Exeter
TJ- 13.26
LEEMING Archie U23 6.10.96, Basildon/Bath Un
SP- 14.66
LEESON Aidan U20 9.11.99, Rugby & Nor AC
400- 48.7/48.82i/48.85
LEGON Luc Henry Thomas U23 12.09.97, Bexley
3kW- 12:58.61i/13:13.97, 5kW- 22:53.81 (22:28.2-16),
10kW- 49:47.80
LEIGHTON Adam U15 23.09.02, Lasswade
HJ- 1.78
LEI-MORTON Kihone U13 17.11.04, Birchfield
HJ- 1.60
LELLIOTT James 11.02.93, Bournemouth
LJ- 7.70w/7.65, TJ- 14.57 (15.03-16),
DT- 41.51 (41.65-16), JT- 58.41 (59.83-14)
LEMONCELLO Andrew 12.10.82, Fife
10MR- 49:57 (47:08-12), Mar- 2:24:11 (2:13:40-10),
HMar- 66:21+ (63:00-11, 61:52dh-09),
LENNON-FORD Luke 5.05.89, Thames Valley/IRL
200- 21.33w/21.53 (20.91-11), 400- 47.05i/47.18 (45.23-12)
LEON BENITEZ Joel Leon U20 31.08.98, Notts
PV- 5.51
LEONARD Rory U17 13.02.01, Morpeth
1500- 4:00.17, 3k- 8:43.0
LEO-STROUD Tye U13 20.11.04, Swindon
100- 12.26

LESLIE Max U17 13.10.01, Edinburgh AC
400- 50.14
LEWIS Ciaran U23 18.03.97, Cardiff/Cardiff Met
3kSt- 9:14.48
LEWIS Daniel 8.11.89, Shaftesbury B
TJ- 15.74w/15.32 (16.31i/16.26-14)
LEWIS Gareth 16.08.88, Horsham BS
Dec- 4516 (4606-10)
LEWIS George U20 4.12.98, East Cheshire
2kSt- 6:14.01, 3kSt- 9:52.75
LEWIS Steven 20.05.86, Newham & Essex B
PV- 5.05 (5.82-12)
LEWIS-SHALLOW Blaine U20 26.04.00, B'stoke & MH
400- 49.20 (48.33-16)
LIDDLE Ross U20 28.07.99, Blackburn
110H- 15.4, 400H- 54.25
LIGHTING Peter V35 7.12.80, Dulwich Park Runners
Mar- 2:27:29
LILL Oliver U17 27.06.02, Basildon
800- 1:55.73
LIMA David 6.09.90, BRAT/POR
100- 10.05, 200- 20.30, 400- 48.8
LINCOLN Scott 7.05.93, City of York
SP- 19.00 (19.59/19.83dh-16)
LINDLEY-HARRIS Joshua U20 25.10.99, City of Sheffield
PV- 4.40 (4.52i-16)
LINDO Adam U15 21.10.02, Crawley
LJ- 6.35, PenB- 2906
LINQUE Christopher 26.04.88, Woodford Green & Ex L
DT- 49.70 (50.87-16)
LIPTON Martin 14.01.89, Kilbarchan
400- 48.81 (48.22-11), 400H- 51.33
LISTER Joseph U23 6.03.97, Harrow/Brunel Un
PV- 5.05
LISTON Levi U15 28.06.03, Highgate H
60- 7.42i
LITCHFIELD Thomas U17 20.04.02, Bedford & County
HTY- 51.53
LITTLE David Andrew V35 28.02.81, Border
HT- 47.51 (59.15-01)
LIVESEY Ben V35 20.09.78, RAF/Notts
HMar- 67:45+ (64:38-13), Mar- 2:19:59 (2:17:44-14)
LIVETT Shaun T U23 19.11.96, Liverpool H/Liverpool Un
HT- 46.44
LIVINGSTON Alexander U23 25.01.96, Lisburn/Queen's U
PV- 4.20i/4.20 (4.20i/4.20-16), Dec- 4778
LIVINGSTONE Johnny U15 11.06.03, Exeter
3k- 9:28.42
LLOYD Adam U15 11.05.03, Telford
JTB- 45.90
LLOYD Ben U17 13.10.00, Shaftesbury B
400- 49.89, 400H- 54.88, 400HY- 52.98
LLOYD Lewis 29.04.94, Herne Hill/Sussex Un
800- 1:51.29 (1:50.65-13)
LLOYD Martin Andrew V35 18.06.80, Bexley
HJ- 2.01 (2.21i/2.20-07)
LLOYD William U17 23.12.01, Pembroke
400HY- 57.73
LLOYD HUGHES Owain U17 5.12.01, Neath
60- 7.14i, 100- 11.11, 200- 22.28
LOCKHART Angus 11.01.91, Harrow/Camb Un/AUS
SP- 15.04
LOCKLEY Oliver 9.11.93, Manx H/Missouri Un
3k- 8:18.74i, 5k- 14:14.78, 10k- 29:24.18, HMar- 67:48,
Mar- 2:25:28
LOCKWOOD Pyers Jenson U15 11.10.02, Eastbourne
300- 37.28
LODOWSKI Jonathan 15.07.88, Enfield & Har/Army
400H- 53.67 (52.90-11)
LONG Ryan U20 2.09.98, Poole
60HJ- 8.44i, 110HJ- 14.3/14.53, LJ- 7.00, HepJ- 4676i,
DECJ- 6316 (6435-16)
LONSDALE Joe U20 4.01.00, Pendle
100- 10.71w, 200- 21.73w/21.75
LONSDALE Markhim U20 9.01.99, Crook & District
400- 48.77, 800- 1:46.97
LORD Harry U20 14.08.98, Sale/Princeton Un
PV- 4.15, JT- 56.80 (59.36-16), Dec- 6538, HepIS- 4645i

389

LOUDEN Greg 25.10.92, Lasswade
400- 48.29 (46.96-14)
LOWE Archie U15 16.02.03, Middlesboro Mandale
1500- 4:11.37, 3k- 9:01.73
LOWE Gareth V40 20.03.73, Clowne
Mar- 2:27:26 (2:24:20-16)
LUBIN Adam U23 9.02.96, Birchfield
HJ- 2.00i/2.00 (2.05i-16, 2.00-15)
LUCAS Terry Edward U23 5.10.95, Chelmsford
LJ- 6.85 (6.98i/6.93-14)
LUMSDEN Shevhone U17 14.09.00, Enfield & Haringey
60- 6.90i, 100- 10.64, 200- 22.19
LUNN Joshua 15.05.92, Bedford & County
3kSt- 9:15.66
LUTAKOME Ricky U20 19.11.99, Sutton & District
400- 49.14, 800- 1:49.59
LYON Sam 20.10.92, Aberdeen/Robert Gordon U
LJ- 7.05 (7.05-13), TJ- 14.53w/14.32 (14.81-15)
LYTTLE Camron U20 28.05.99, Blackheath & Bromley
60- 6.92i (6.89i-16), 100- 10.54w/10.56,
200- 21.75w/21.95 (21.89-15)

M ABONGA Jonathon U17 4.10.00, Norfolk Schools
TJ- 13.36
MACE Sam U17 20.10.00, Walton
SPY- 14.47i/14.21, DTY- 47.20, HT- 47.06, HTY- 64.32
MACFARLANE Matthew U17 16.09.01, Inverness
HTY- 50.28
MACGILP Fergus U13 17.03.05, Pitreavie
LJ- 5.09, PenC- 1930
MACHEATH Alex U15 17.02.04, Cambridge H
3kW- 15:27.33 (15:15R)
MACKAY Alexander U17 13.12.01, Ross County
100HY- 13.99, DecY- 5080
MACKAY Chris U20 3.04.99, Giffnock North
HJ- 2.00i/1.95 (1.99-16), LJ- 7.11
MACKAY Seumas U17 8.03.01, Shetland
400- 50.1, 800- 1:53.32
MACKAY William 3.10.89, Bedford & County
10k- 30:54.89 (30:30.35-15), HMar- 68:07,
Mar- 2:26:00 (2:25:01-16)
MACKENZIE Stephen U17 28.08.01, Inverness
LJ- 6.89w/6.85, TJ- 14.24
MACLEAN Gregor Kyle 17.10.91, Shaftesbury B
PV- 5.00i (5.45-14)
MACNAUGHTON Scott U17 7.12.01, Middlesex Schools
SPY- 13.95
MADDEN Enzo U20 24.08.98, Sale
60- 7.00i, 100- 10.6/10.79w/10.81, 200- 21.7
MADDEN Matthew 17.11.90, Notts
TJ- 13.79 (14.91w/14.62-14, 14.66i-15)
MAGEE Jack U23 17.12.97, Ballymena & A/Ulster Un
JT- 62.08
MAGNUSSEN Baldvin U20 7.04.99, Kingston upon Hull
3k- 8:33.66
MAHAMED Abdi U23 16.09.96, Southampton/SOM
3kSt- 9:47.2
MAHAMED Mahamed U23 18.09.97, Southampton
10kR- 30:12+, 15kR- 45:30+, 10MR- 49:05
MAHAMED Zakariya U17 29.11.00, Southampton
3k- 8:33.45, 5k- 15:19.5
MAHAMUUD Mustafa U20 1.07.98, Birchfield/NED
200- 21.76w (21.02w/21.33-16)
MAHER Samuel U20 18.01.99, Channel Islands
1500- 3:52.87
MAITLAND Peter V40 V40 21.01.73, Swansea
SP- 13.70 (14.80-09)
MAJOR Jack U23 23.10.96, Southampton/Leeds Beck Un
60H- 8.13i, 110H- 14.52 (14.50-16)
MAKEPEACE Euan U23 31.05.97, Charn/Butler Un USA
5k- 14:03.88
MAKOYAWO Toby U17 10.05.02, Watford
60- 7.11i
MALONEY Niall U15 4.03.03, Horwich
TJ- 12.18
MANFRONI Andrea 15.03.89, Bristol & West/ITA
JT- 61.39
MANN Christopher U23 1.10.95, Bolton/Loughborough St
HJ- 2.06 (2.09-16)

MANN David 27.10.94, VP-Glasgow/Strathclyde Un
PV- 4.11i (4.41i-16, 4.40-15)
MANN Jonathan Leon U17 30.04.01, Bexley
60HY- 8.54i, 100HY- 13.35
MANSBRIDGE Ryan U15 24.04.03, Blackheath & Brom
HJ- 1.75
MANTHORPE Alfie U20 26.09.99, City of Sheffield
2kSt- 6:19.24, 3kSt- 9:52.60
MARCHLEWICZ Dawid 1.01.83, C of Portsmouth/POL
HT- 47.85 (51.93-08)
MARGRAVE James U15 19.05.03, Northern (IOM)
HJ- 1.75
MARKLEW William U20 6.07.98, C of Sheffield/Sheff Un
JT- 58.18 (61.39-15)
MARKS Ben U17 27.03.02, Walton
1.5kSt- 4:41.9
MARRIOTT Richard V35 24.01.80,
Mar- 2:29:04
MARSH Brett V40 20.01.76, Newquay & Par
HT- 44.73 (47.98-99)
MARSH Nathan U23 8.04.96, Tonbridge/Leeds Un
10kR- 30:01
MARSHALL Christopher 27.01.91, C of Norwich/Card Met
400H- 56.0 (54.92-14)
MARSHALL Harry U23 10.06.96, B'field/Derby U
JT- 54.63 (57.46-15)
MARSHALL Thomas 12.06.89, Cardiff
800- 1:48.68, 1k- 2:22.30i, 1500- 3:37.45, 1M- 3:58.31,
5kR- 14:35 (14:19.30t-11)
MARTELLETTI Paul V35 1.08.79, VPH &TH
5k- 14:26.36 (14:19.50-11), 10k- 29:48.41 (29:26.18-16),
HMar- 65:54 (64:18-15), Mar- 2:17:10 (2:16:49-11),
50kR- 3:18:59 (2:50:11-12)
MARTIN Connor U23 29.03.96, Herts Ph/St M & St J Un
JT- 56.08 (57.89-14)
MARTIN Craig U15 13.09.02, Manx H
PV- 2.90
MARTIN Daniel U13 22.03.06, Giffnock North
PenIC- 1301i
MARTIN David John 5.05.88, Channel Islands
LJ- 7.53w/7.37 (7.40-16)
MARTIN Jack 29.04.88, Stockport
5kR- 14:30 (14:11.97t 14), 5MR- 23:44, 10k- 29:15.85
MARTIN Joseph U17 27.08.01, City of Portsmouth
100- 11.0
MARTIN Joseph U15 5.09.02, R Sutton Coldfield
800- 2:00.70
MARTIN Joseph U20 9.03.99, Middlesboro Mandale
DT- 44.98, DTJ- 47.31
MARTIN Michael 15.03.88, Trafford
SP- 13.18
MARTIN Nigel 23.03.87, Sale
10k- 30:11.69, 10kR- 29:56
MARTIN Patrick 15.05.85, Stockport
HMar- 67:56 (65:19-13), Mar- 2:22:37
MARTIN Richard 8.01.84, Bedford & County
HT- 61.35
MARTIN Shane U20 10.11.99, Ballymena & Antrim
PV- 4.40
MARTIN-EVANS Leon U17 23.03.01, Daventry
HJ- 2.03, OctY- 4331
MARTYN Thomas 24.05.89, Hunters Bog Trotters
10k- 30:58.63
MASCARENHAS Louis U23 5.01.96, Blackheath & Brom
SP- 14.86, DT- 51.24
MASLEN Harry U23 2.09.96, Ilkley/Angelo State Un.
60H- 8.49iA, 110H- 15.27, PV- 4.50, LJ- 7.23w/7.14,
Dec- 7065, HepIS- 5012i
MASON Edward U20 9.03.99, Channel Islands
2kSt- 6:15.0 (6:02.96-16), 3kSt- 9:48.53 (9:43.10-16)
MASSINGHAM Oliver U20 17.03.99, City of Norwich
SPJ- 14.01i, DT- 43.84, DTJ- 48.46, DTY- 52.66
MASTERS Dan V40 11.07.73, Albion Runners
24Hr- 203.734km
MASTERSON Murdo U20 26.09.98, Scottish Schools
SPJ- 14.82i/14.76
MATHER Luke U17 17.09.01, Lincoln Wellington
100- 11.1w

MATHEWS Curtis 22.01.92, Cardiff
110H- 15.23 (14.88-14), HJ- 1.99, PV- 4.40, SP- 14.69,
LJ- 7.18 (7.47w/7.21-14), DT- 50.53, Dec- 7500
MATSUKA-WILLIAMS Ben U20 28.03.98, Norwich/Bath U
200- 21.58w/21.89
MATSUKA-WILLIAMS Wesley U20 15.06.00, C of Norwich
TJ- 14.68i (15.43w/15.32-16)
MATTEY Benjamin U15 4.02.03, Rhymney Valley
200- 23.41, 300- 37.31
MATTHEW Gerald U23 10.07.97, Shaftesbury B
200- 21.57 (21.11-16)
MATTHEWS Philip V35 16.05.79, Swansea
HMar- 67:14 (66:24-13)
MATTHEWS Quinn U15 22.02.03, Hampshire Schools
HJ- 1.75
MAUD Andrew 28.07.83, Highgate H
3k- 8:17.71, 5k- 14:05.99 (14:04.67-16),
10k- 29:28 (29:24.43t-16)
MAURICE Jacques U17 11.02.01, Harrogate
800- 1:54.61, 1500- 3:57.96
MAW Charlie U23 18.11.96, Winchester
PV- 4.35 (4.50-14)
MAWDSLEY Alfred U17 13.10.00, Herne Hill
DTY- 49.08
MAY Archie U17 5.12.01, Dartford
1.5kSt- 4:31.05
MAY James U15 9.12.02, City of Sheffield
PV- 3.02
MAY Rowan U23 12.08.95, Birchfield/Oxford Un
PV- 5.00 (5.25-13)
MAYINGI John U17 18.04.01, Enfield & Haringey
100- 11.0
MAYS Jermaine 23.12.82, Basingstoke & MH
3kSt- 9:22.58 (8:30.41-07)
MAZE Ben 22.12.91, Lagan Valley/Queen's Un
400- 47.33
McALISTER Christopher U23 3.12.95, TVH/Birm Un
400- 48.69 (47.57-16), 400H- 51.82 (50.88-16)
McARTHUR Oliver U17 24.10.00, WSE&H
1.5kSt- 4:31.76
McAULEY Ian V45 6.11.70, Antrim
24Hr- 213.031km
McAULEY Kyle U15 9.04.03, Whitemoss
60HB- 9.25i, HJ- 1.76, PenB- 2787, OctB- 3708,
PenIB- 2558i
McAULIFFE Fergus U17 5.09.00, Charnwood
800- 1:53.85
McBRIDE Sean 31.07.90, Strabane
JT- 53.01 (63.21-15)
McCAFFERTY Jonah U15 28.01.03, Bracknell
JTB- 47.26
McCAIG Charles U15 24.01.03, Yeovil Olympiads
JTB- 49.34
McCALLUM Stuart U23 15.09.95, Winchester
1500- 3:43.69, 5k- 14:25.53
McCARTHY James U23 31.10.96, Chiltern H/Warwick Un
800- 1:49.09, 1500- 3:47.28 (3:46.59-16)
McCARTHY Jay U13 29.11.04, Shettleston H
DTC- 28.86, HTC- 42.55
McCAULEY Stephen V40 6.02.74, Oxford City
SP- 13.92 (14.84-05)
McCOMB Adam 25.07.92, Liverpool H/Ulster Un
400- 48.89i (47.61-16)
McCOMB Jack U20 25.06.98, Lisburn/Glasgow Un
400H- 55.69
McCONKEY Michael 5.12.84, North Down/IRL
SP- 13.51 (14.44-11)
McCONVILLE Lexx U13 9.10.04, North Down
HJ- 1.60, PenC- 1742
McCONVILLE Troy U17 29.04.02, North Down
60HY- 8.44i, 100HY- 13.99, HJ- 1.90, LJ- 6.47,
OctY- 5409
McCORGRAY Cameron U20 28.12.98, Central
HJ- 2.03i/2.00 (2.01-16)
McCOURT Daniel U15 17.05.03, Lewes
HTB- 42.39
McDONALD Jack U15 29.09.02, Southampton
300- 36.67

McFARLANE Andrew Joel U20 7.07.00, Ross County
PV- 4.61
McFARLANE Daniel U20 10.10.98, Ross County
110HJ- 14.97w (15.31), DECJ- 5605
McFARLANE Joel U17 9.10.00, Arbroath
60HY- 8.52i (8.50i-16), 100HY- 13.55w/13.62,
110HY- 15.01i, 400HY- 58.13 (56.44-16),
HJ- 1.91i (1.90-16), PV- 4.00, LJ- 7.09, HepIY- 4948i,
DecY- 6781, OctY- 5409+
McFARLANE Reuben U15 14.10.02, Ross County
PV- 3.10
McGARVIE Max U15 18.06.03, Slough Juniors
3k- 9:27.31
McGLEN Ethan U15 26.11.03, Gateshead
3k- 9:15.62
McGRATH Joe U23 9.09.97, Doncaster/Princeton Un
100- 10.73w (10.6-13, 10.67w-16)
McGUIGAN Dempsey 30.08.93, Shaft B/Ole Miss/IRL
HT- 70.55
McGUIGAN Fellan U23 15.03.96, Shaft B/Texas U/IRL
HT- 64.47 (64.47-16)
McGUIRE Ben U23 22.10.97, Shaftesbury B/Glasgow Un
LJ- 6.95 (7.11w/7.10i-16, 6.96-15)
McGUIRE Lewis U23 22.10.97, Shaft B/Strathclyde Un
HJ- 2.16
McINROY Angus 13.02.87, Shaftesbury B
SP- 13.84 (14.87-15), DT- 55.29 (58.77-10)
McINTYRE Ben U17 27.03.02, Swindon
1.5kSt- 4:42.24
McKAY Callum U17 3.10.00, Colchester H
60- 7.16i
McKAY David V35 22.09.80, West Cheshire
HT- 46.70 (49.41-09), JT- 53.74 (70.43-08)
McKENNA Jarlath V35 14.11.81, Bristol & West
Mar- 2:24:36 (2:24:19-16)
McKENZIE Calum 3.05.89, Corstorphine
5MR- 23:38, 10k- 30:48.93
McKENZIE Euan 8.08.92, Shaftesbury B
Mar- 2:29:28
McKENZIE Wilfred U15 10.10.02, Southampton
80HB- 11.3/11.53
McKEOWN Josh U15 5.03.03, Gateshead
100- 11.50, 200- 23.01, 300- 36.3
McKERNAN Michael V35 28.11.78, Birchfield
TJ- 14.57 (16.06-07)
McLACHLAN James 12.03.92, City of Norwich
LJ- 7.53w/7.27 (7.86-13), TJ- 15.66 (15.91i-15,15.78-13)
McLAREN-PORTER Benedict U17 22.11.00, Camberley
DTY- 43.22
McLEAR Finlay U20 25.05.00, Exeter
2kSt- 6:10.95
McLELLAN Neil V35 10.09.78, Stevenage & NH
JT- 67.70 (74.92-07)
McLENNAN Callum U20 1.05.99, Edinburgh AC
DECJ- 5975
McLEOD Caleb U13 15.05.06, Pitreavie
PenIC- 1298i
McLEOD Christopher U17 27.12.00, Solihull & S H
3k- 8:36.49
McLEW Christopher U17 1.09.01, Cambuslang
800- 1:56.62
McLUCKIE Henry U17 3.05.02, Isle of Wight
1.5kSt- 4:33.16
McLURE David 9.11.83, Kilmarnock
100kR- 7:23:40
McMILLAN Angus U20 15.03.00, City of York
3k- 8:33.51
McMULLAN James 16.02.84, Thames H & H
Mar- 2:29:59
McMULLEN Adam 5.07.90, Mid Ulster/IRL
100- 10.71 (10.68w-15), LJ- 7.94w/7.85
McMURRAY James U23 18.01.95, St Albans AC/Lough-
borough St
800- 1:49.06 (1:48.69-15), 1500- 3:40.95
McNALLY Connor U13 8.01.05, VP-Glasgow
HJ- 1.61
McNALLY Finn 22.09.91, Brighton Phoenix
5kR- 14:28, 10kR- 30:21 (29:47-15)

391

McNEILLIS Archie 7.05.94, Halesowen/Oxford Un
PV- 4.75
McNIFF Patrick U20 19.08.99, Newcastle (NI)
5k- 15:15.7
McQUILLAN Zane U13 6.12.04, Ballymena & Antrim
60HC- 9.87i, 75HC- 11.88w, LJ- 5.06
McTAGGART Robert 14.10.85, Bournemouth
Mar- 2:28:58
McTEAR Oliver U17 2.01.01, Swindon
JTY- 53.24
McWHIRTER Blair 6.10.82, Ilford/NZL
Mar- 2:22:43
MEAKIN Cameron U20 21.10.98, Warrington
60HJ- 8.16i, 110HJ- 14.78
MEES Daniel U20 12.09.98, Peterborough
800- 1:52.21 (1:51.87-16)
MEIJER Jack U17 3.11.00, Marshall Milton Keynes
800- 1:56.40, 1500- 3:59.02, 3k- 8:37.91
MELLON Andrew U23 8.11.95, N.Down/Queen's Un/IRL
400- 47.32 (46.80-16)
MELLOR Jonathan 27.12.86, Liverpool H
5kR- 14:27 (13:31.21t-14), 5MR- 23:57 (23:41-07),
10kR- 28:55 (28:42.20t-13), 15kR- 44:48+ (44:06+-12),
HMar- 62:23, Mar- 2:12:57
MELLOR Mark U17 22.01.02, Cardiff Archers
PV- 4.21
MELVILLE Toby U23 2.12.96, Southampton/So'ton Un
TJ- 14.45i/14.37w/13.99 (14.25-16)
MENSAH Jak U17 5.09.01, Team Hounslow
200- 22.46
MERRIEN Lee V35 26.04.79, Newham & Essex B
10k- 30:09.65 (29:23.05-08), HMar- 66:45 (64:07-16),
Mar- 2:20:25 (2:13:41-12)
MERSON Tom 10.02.86, Bristol & West
10k- 30:45.0 (30:41-09)
MESLEK Ossama U23 8.01.97, Leeds/Huddersfield Un/ITA
800- 1:50.03, 1500- 3:42.19
METSELAAR Luuk 6.07.92, Thames H & H/Oxford U/NED
HMar- 67:15, Mar- 2:22:12
METZGER Kevin U23 13.11.97, Sale/MMU
TJ- 15.29
MEYLER Samuel U23 11.09.95, Birchfield
PV- 4.10i
MIER Harris U17 7.11.01, Cornwall AC
1500- 4:03.60
MILANDU Deo 30.10.92, City of Sheffield
110H- 15.13, PV- 4.30i (4.40i-14, 4.20-11), Dec- 6317,
HepIS- 4972i
MILBURN James U20 24.09.99, Kidd & Stourport
DECJ- 5418
MILHAM Isaac U17 17.06.01, Medway & Maidstone
400HY- 57.06
MILLAR Greg 19.12.92, Birchfield/Loughborough St
JT- 71.15
MILLAR John U23 18.12.97, Ipswich/Bath Un
5MR- 24:12, 3kSt- 9:15.09 (9:09.54-16)
MILLER Chad U20 31.03.00, Hercules Wimbledon
60- 6.95i (6.95i-16), 100- 10.61w, 200- 21.34
MILLER Joshua U15 20.02.03, Exeter
JTB- 50.39
MILLER Luke U20 10.09.99, Ealing, S & Mx
JT- 55.06
MILLER Michael U17 4.12.00, Herne Hill
60- 7.10i
MILLER Nicholas 1.05.93, Border/Oklahoma St Un
HT- 77.51 (77.55-15)
MILLER Rami U17 11.09.00, Herne Hill
60- 7.14i
MILLER Rechmial U20 27.06.98, Hercules Wimbledon
100- 10.28w/10.33 (10.23w-16), 200- 21.07
MILLER Samuel 2.09.93, Preston/Loughborough St
60- 6.77i (6.74i-16), 100- 10.38, 200- 20.79
MILLER Thomas U20 7.10.98, City of Portsmouth
110HJ- 15.08 (14.24w/14.37-16), 400H- 55.47 (54.94-16)
MILLETT Simon 19.04.87, WSE&H
Mar- 2:29:11
MILLIGAN Ethan U20 8.08.00, West Cheshire
HJ- 1.95

MILLINGTON Ross 19.09.89, Stockport
3k- 8:14.18+ (7:49.11i-12, 7:52.40-15),
5kR- 14:08 (13:36.39t-11), 10kR- 28:46 (27:55.06t-16),
15kR- 44:48+ (44:39+-15), HMar- 62:40
MILLS Christopher Leslie V40 12.11.75, WSE&H
PV- 4.22i/4.20 (4.90-04)
MILLS Lewis U20 1.01.00, Blackheath & Bromley
2kSt- 6:13.72
MILNE Alexander 11.03.90, Enfield & Har/So'ton Un
HMar- 68:08 (67:41-16), Mar- 2:23:23,
3kSt- 9:42.87 (9:07.70-15)
MILNE Cameron Floyd 6.07.93, Central
HMar- 66:39
MILTON Joseph U20 29.09.98, Liverpool Pemb S
400- 48.64i
MILTON Thomas U17 21.11.01, Southend
HTY- 58.32
MINGELI Brandon U17 7.09.00, Cambridge H
60- 6.87i/6.98i, 100- 10.74, 200- 22.22w
MINNS Luke 20.03.89, Blackpool & Fylde
800- 1:51.87 (1:50.70-14)
MINSHULL Jake U13 11.10.04, Coventry Godiva
800- 2:15.22, 75HC- 12.13, LJ- 5.10, PenC- 1989,
PenIC- 1945i
MITCHAM Rio U20 30.08.99, Birchfield
60- 6.83i, 100- 10.30w/10.3/10.41, 200- 20.80w/21.24
MITCHELL Curtis U23 29.09.95, Preston/Sheffield Un
60H- 8.46i, 110H- 15.14w/15.43
MITCHELL Jordan 23.12.94, Sutton in Ashfield
Dec- 5365
MITCHELL Mark 23.05.88, Birchfield
5MR- 24:12, HMar- 68:11 (66:07-16)
MITCHELL Stephen 24.05.88, Bristol & West
1500- 3:45.18 (3:38.27-14), 5k- 14:20.20 (14:13.01-14),
3k- 8:08.99i (8:04.89i/8:14.44-14)
MITCHELL Tyler U20 26.07.00, Stevenage & NH
HJ- 1.95
MITCHELL-BLAKE Nethaneel 2.04.94, N&ExB/LSU
60- 6.65i (6.65i-16), 100- 9.99, 150- 15.26st,
200- 20.04 (19.95-16)
MOFFATT Joss U20 31.01.00, Rushcliffe
DECJ- 6066
MOKAYA Maranga U23 30.06.96, Notts/Durham Un
60H- 8.33i, 110H- 14.68, 400H- 55.35
MOLLOY Sean U23 18.09.95, Tonbridge
800- 1:47.76
MOLYNEUX Paul V35 27.01.81, Springfield S/Army
HMar- 67:55, Mar- 2:24:24 (2:20:33-15)
MONAGHAN Patrick 25.10.93, Lagan V/Colorado St Un.
1M- 4:06.10i
MONCUR Craig U15 20.03.03, Exeter
SPB- 13.99, DTB- 40.90, PenB- 2828
MONCUR Jack U20 19.12.98, Exeter
JT- 56.67
MONDELLI Max U23 28.10.95, Hercules Wimb/Harvard
200- 21.33 (21.33-16)
MONK Jonathan U23 27.07.95, Leics Cor/Lough St
800- 1:48.68
MONTAGUE Nathan V35 15.11.80, Swindon
100kR- 7:33:04, 24HrT- 234.61km
MOORE Adam U20 8.06.98, WSE&H
1500- 3:51.18
MOORE Blake U20 8.06.98, WSE&H
1500- 3:53.87
MOORE Iori U23 15.04.97, Cardiff
200- 21.70 (21.35-15), 400- 48.33
MOORE Jack David U20 19.02.00, Yate
HJ- 1.95
MOORE Jaquan U17 18.07.01, City of Norwich
HTY- 51.62
MORAN Elliot U17 6.10.00, Exeter
1.5kSt- 4:24.71
MORENO Peter 30.12.90, WSE&H/Army/NGR
400- 48.31, 60H- 8.23i (8.22i-16), 110H- 14.41,
HJ- 1.96 (2.00-15), PV- 4.45 (4.60-15),
LJ- 7.10 (7.34-15), Dec- 7252
MORGAN Aaron 7.04.92, Carmarthen
JT- 60.71 (61.99-15)

392

MORGAN Ben U23 16.10.97, Loughborough St
Dec- 4755
MORGAN Brandon U15 6.03.03, Sale
300- 37.6
MORGAN Chris U20 31.03.99, Rugby & Northampton
110HJ- 14.5w (16.2/16.36-16)
MORGAN Evan U15 1.01.03, Cardiff
HTB- 41.66
MORGAN Frank U13 20.01.05, Carmarthen
1500- 4:33.32
MORGAN Kyron U15 29.11.02, Blackheath & Bromley
300- 37.03
MORGAN-HARRISON Andrew U20 9.03.98, K'ton u Hull
60- 6.97i, 100- 10.7w/10.78, 200- 21.81i/21.82 (21.70-16)
MORRIS Beau U20 21.11.98, Birchfield
HT- 44.45 (45.38-16)
MORRIS Jack 9.04.93, Stockport
5k- 14:07.20, 10k- 29:41.88, HMar- 67:19
MORRIS Joe 20.03.93, Eastbourne
Dec- 5677
MORRISSEY Richard 11.01.91, Shaftesbury B/IRL
400- 48.13 (46.20-14)
MORSE Brett 11.02.89, Cardiff
SP- 14.99 (16.16i-11, 15.92-09), DT- 61.15 (66.84-13)
MORSE Jay U17 22.07.01, Cardiff
SPY- 16.05i/15.97, DTY- 55.28
MORSON Darren 16.06.94, VPH &TH
LJ- 7.41 (7.59-15)
MORTIMER Tom U20 7.01.99, Stroud
3k- 8:22.86, 5k- 14:16.64
MORTIMORE Matti 16.05.93, Ipswich/North Dakota State
JT- 77.47
MORTON Marcus U23 30.08.96, VP-Glasgow/RGordon U
HJ- 2.06i/2.05 (2.05-15)
MORWOOD Joe 10.06.91, Aldershot F&D
HMar- 67:52 (67:26-15)
MOSES Lewis 9.01.87, Gateshead
1500- 3:44.91 (3:41.33i-12, 3:42.6-10),
3k- 8:09.45 (8:08.85-10), 5k- 14:01.30
MOTT Oliver 29.11.84, Cheltenham
10k- 30:44.46, HMar- 67:09
MOYSE Alex U15 22.09.02, Exeter
1500- 4:17.53
MOZOBO Jean U20 5.05.98, Bedford & County
TJ- 14.18 (14.19-16)
MTSHWENI Kanya U20 4.07.00, Winchester
110HJ- 14.70
MUBANA D U13, Essex Schools
75HC- 12.1
MUCKELT Michael U23 3.02.95, City of Portsmouth
JT- 60.96
MUIR Grant 4.10.93, Giffnock North
800- 1:51.32 (1:49.97-14)
MUIRHEAD Peter 6.12.93, City of Sheffield/Stirling Un
LJ- 7.26i/7.17w/7.15 (7.39w/7.25-15, 7.35i-16)
MULAWARMAN Radix U17 20.10.00, Swansea
60- 7.12i
MULLEN Tom U17 29.09.00, Lifford
OctY- 4279
MULLETT Robert 31.07.87, Lewes
1500- 3:45.82 (3:42.01-15), 1M- 4:03.92i (3:59.37i-10,
3:59.47-15), 3k- 7:54.48i/8:19.24 (7:58.65-12), 5k-
13:51.18 (13:41.75i-16), 3kSt- 8:30.06 (8:22.42-16)
MULLINS Craig U20 24.05.98, Edinburgh AC
HT- 46.87 (48.31-16), HTJ- 61.92
MUNDAY Etienne U13 6.11.04, London Heathside
PenIC- 1330i
MUNGHAM Robert 1.12.84, Bracknell
HT- 44.64 (48.04-05)
MURATHODZIC Daniel U17 11.09.01, Cardiff Archers
60HY- 8.56i
MURCH Craig 27.06.93, Rugby & Nor/Loughborough St
HT- 68.83 (69.79-16)
MURDOCK Alex 29.08.91, Harrow
60- 6.79i
MURPHY Andrew 26.12.94, Kilbarchan/West Scot Un
60H- 8.40i, 110H- 15.05, HJ- 2.00, PV- 4.84i/4.65,
LJ- 7.13, SP- 13.27i/13.24 (13.87i-14, 13.38-15),
DT- 42.81, Dec- 7248, HepIS- 5402i

MURPHY Kieran 8.05.94, Blackheath & Bromley/IRL
HT- 47.85
MURRAY Brandon U23 20.09.97, Blackheath & Bromley
60- 6.79i, 100- 10.71
MURRAY Tony U13 22.10.06, City of Sheffield
PV- 2.50
MUSSON Douglas 8.04.94, Notts/Notts Trent Un
1500- 3:48.25 (3:46.14-16), 3k- 8:08.62, 5k- 14:02.92,
3kSt- 8:38.54
MYCROFT William 8.01.91, Enfield & Har/Sheffield Un
3kSt- 9:01.89
MYERS Charlie U23 12.06.97, Middlesboro Mandale/Nor-
thumberland Un PV- 5.45
MYTIL Clayton U13 11.10.04, Herne Hill
75HC- 11.9/11.95

N AGEEYE ABDULLE Abdishakur 23.06.93, Hillingdon
800- 2:13.69
NAIRNE Reuben U15 22.09.02, Giffnock North
60HB- 8.96i, PV- 3.80i/3.51, LJ- 6.05
NALUS Jaime U17 15.10.00, Rugby & Northampton
100- 10.91w (11.2/11.24- 16)
NASH Daniel Tama 23.03.94, Cardiff
5k- 14:22.67, 10k- 30:33.00, HMar- 66:51 (66:49-14)
NASH Sonny U20 11.11.98, Medway & Maidstone
JT- 59.96
NAVESEY Paul 19.04.86, Crawley
10k- 30:56.25, Mar- 2:27:39
NEALE Paul U23 6.01.97, Reading/Bedford Un
HJ- 1.95i (2.03-13)
NEEDHAM Robert 18.04.94, Notts/Notts Trent Un
800- 1:48.16, 1500- 3:48.05
NELSON Demetric 28.05.94, Bingley/JAM
200- 21.71w (21.5-13, 21.54-14)
NELSON Jacob U15 8.09.02, City of Portsmouth
100- 11.25, 200- 22.61
NEVERS Montel U23 22.05.96, Notts/Florida State Un
LJ- 7.19, TJ- 16.05w/15.99 (16.15i/16.14-16)
NEWBY Calum U17 16.06.02, Edinburgh AC
DecY- 5144
NEWELL Craig U23 24.09.97, Ballymena & A/IRL
400- 47.31
NEWMAN Lee Jon V40 1.05.73, Worcester AC
DT- 46.80 (60.48-97)
NEWPORT Oliver U23 7.01.95, Blackheath & Bromley/
Louisville Un   LJ- 7.77w/7.60 (7.78-16)
NEWRICK Yorck U15 19.09.02, Pontefract
SPB- 13.12
NEWTON Cameron U20 17.03.99, Basingstoke & MH
100- 10.86w
NEWTON Mark V35 15.06.80, Springfield Striders
Mar- 2:29:08 (2:28:32-16)
NEWTON Peter V35 24.03.81, Morpeth
10kR- 30:22 (29:54.3t-16), HMar- 66:29 (66:27-12)
NICHOLLS John S. V50 19.09.65, Sale
SP- 14.24i/13.93 (15.98-99)
NICHOLLS Maximillian U23 6.07.96, Tonbridge/Lond Un
10k- 30:46.28
NICHOLS Thomas 6.04.85, Harrow
110H- 15.29 (15.12-15), HJ- 2.11
NICHOLSON Jason U20 10.05.99, Gateshead
60HJ- 7.86i, 110HJ- 13.64
NICOLAOU Andrew U15 13.11.02, Shaftesbury B
60- 7.35i, 100- 11.0/11.18, 200- 23.4/23.41i
NIXON Daniel U20 10.12.98, Middlesboro Mandale
HT- 50.44, HTJ- 61.22
NIXON George U15 31.12.02, Border
DTB- 38.74
NOEL Douglas U17 1.03.01, Invicta
DTY- 42.48, HepIY- 4104i, OctY- 4813
NOLAN Ben U13 22.11.04, Tonbridge
DTC- 29.97
NOLAN Dominic 29.11.94, Croydon/Loughborough St
1500- 3:48.86, HMar- 68:28
NORFOLK Anthony U23 20.05.95, Kingston upon Hull
SP- 13.12 (13.26-12)
NORMAN Harley U15 14.07.03, Epsom & Ewell
800- 2:01.78

NORMAN Phillip 20.10.89, Woodford Green & Ex L
  2kSt- 5:39.99, 3kSt- 8:42.89, 400H- 55.29
NORRIS Jake U20 30.06.99, WSE&H
  HT- 68.86, HTJ- 78.09
NORTON Jack U17 3.10.00, City of Portsmouth
  HJ- 2.02
NORTON Tom U23 19.08.97, C of Sheffield/Lough St
  JT- 62.24
NUNN Alex U13 11.12.04, Southend
  100- 12.3
NUTTER Scott U15 19.10.02, Barnsley
  1500- 4:15.85, 3k- 9:23.6
NWAFOR Obinna U13 19.03.05, Kent Schools
  DTC- 27.62
NWENWU Alexander James 11.09.91, Wolves & Bilston
  60H- 8.49i (8.12i-14), 110H- 14.96 (14.38-12)
NWOGWUGWU Zachary U15 10.04.04, Tonbridge
  60- 7.36i

OATES Lachlan 30.01.92, Shettleston H
  3k- 8:16.53, 5k- 14:13.94, 10kR- 30:12,
  HMar- 67:25, 3kSt- 8:52.53
OBENG Daniel 20.05.93, Queen Mary Coll
  100- 10.55w/10.69 (10.53-16)
O'CALLAGHAN-BROWN Alex U17 30.03.01, Walton
  400HY- 54.75
O'CONNELL Martin 22.10.85, Serpentine
  Mar- 2:27:20
O'CONNELL Regan U20 28.11.98, City of Sheffield
  60- 6.96i, 100- 10.7, 200- 21.93
O'CONNOR Patrick U23 23.10.95, Middlesboro Mandale/
  Seton Hill Un HJ- 2.10i/2.10
ODEH Nabhi U15 17.09.02, Leics Cor
  TJ- 12.78
ODERINDE Daniel U23 9.09.96, M Milton K/Mx Un.
  100- 10.72w (10.72w-16), 200- 21.74w
O'DONNELL Cian 27.09.94, VP-Glasgow
  Dec- 4938
ODU Samuel U17 4.04.02, Sussex Schools
  100HY- 13.93
ODUBANJO Emmanuel U20 7.12.99, Sale
  TJ- 15.25w/14.88
ODUJOBI Gabriel 15.07.87, Sale
  100- 10.62 (10.52w-13), 200- 21.51 (21.02-16),
  110H- 13.38W/13.65 (13.64-16)
ODUNAIYA Elliot U15 23.02.03, Wrexham
  JTB- 51.94
ODURO ANTWI Samuel U20 4.06.00, Enfield & Har
  TJ- 14.25 (14.57-16)
OGALI Destiny U17 6.09.01, Dacorum & Tring
  100- 11.1 (11.38)
OGBECHIE Dominic Chiedu U17 15.05.02, Highgate H
  60- 7.02i, 200- 21.52, HJ- 2.07i/2.02, LJ- 7.33w/7.22,
  OctY- 4704
OGUN Paul 3.06.89, Croydon
  LJ- 7.52w/7.45 (7.79-16)
OGUNBANJO Monty U15 14.01.03, Hillingdon
  80HB- 11.62
OGUNFOLAJU Joshua U15 25.05.04, Chelmsford
  TJ- 12.81
OGUNLANA Olalekan U20 4.04.99, Croydon
  HJ- 1.95 (1.98-16), JT- 53.96
OGUNLEWE Adeseye 30.08.91, Chelmsford/E London Un/NGR
  60- 6.80i (6.68i-13), 100- 10.30 (10.12-16),
  200- 20.91w (20.99-16)
OGUTUGA Daniel U15 16.09.02, Thurrock
  LJ- 6.20i
O'HARA Jacob U17 11.02.01, City of Portsmouth
  3k- 8:53.75
O'HARE Christopher David 23.11.90, Edinburgh AC
  800- 1:47.34, 1500- 3:33.61, 1M- 3:53.34 (3:52.91i-16),
  5kR- 13:46 (13:42.00t-14)
OHIOZE Michael U23 6.02.95, St Ambrose Un USA
  100- 10.64w (10.73-15), 200- 21.28 (21.00-16),
  400- 47.26, LJ- 7.13 (7.16-15)
OJEI Desmond U23 11.02.97, Aberdeen/R Gordon U/NGR
  60- 6.91i

OJORA Onatade U20 14.10.99, WSE&H
  110HJ- 13.78
OJURIYE Idris 27.12.84, Herne Hill
  60- 6.88i (6.81i-11), 100- 10.69w (10.51w-11, 10.61-10)
O'KANE Sam 18.12.92, Kilbarchan/Glasgow Un
  DT- 42.00 (43.05-15)
OKE Emmanuel U15 5.05.03, Thurrock
  TJ- 12.11
OKE Oluwatobi U15 10.10.02, Coventry Godiva
  100- 11.36, 200- 23.46
OKE Tosin V35 1.10.80, W.Green & Ex L/NGR
  TJ- 16.70 (17.23-12)
OKEKE Bret U20 16.02.99, City of Stoke
  60- 6.99i, 100- 10.67w, 200- 21.76w/21.9
OKOH Gideon 5.10.93, Nene Valley H
  100- 10.7w
OKOLO Nonso 7.12.89, Shaftesbury B
  TJ- 16.45
OKOME Oluwaseun U23 26.03.95, Sale/Hallam Un
  HJ- 1.98 (2.12-14), TJ- 15.48w/15.47
OKORO Edirin 4.04.89, Birchfield
  60H- 7.89i (7.81i-14), 110H- 13.77 (13.77-14)
OKORO Efekemo 21.02.92, Birchfield
  400H- 54.26 (51.16-16)
OKORO Onajite 21.02.92, Birchfield
  110H- 14.83 (14.35-13)
OKOSIEME Luke U17 21.08.01, Cambridge H
  HJ- 2.02
OKU-AMPOFO Michael U20 10.11.98, Newham & Ex B
  400- 49.23i (48.31-16)
OKUMU Robinson U20 24.11.99, Dorchester
  100- 10.78w/10.86, 200- 21.94
OLALERE Praise U17 28.12.00, Grantham
  200- 22.0w/22.42
OLANIYI Dominique U17 10.08.01, Harrow
  100- 11.04
OLATOKE Praise U20 23.06.00, Kilbarchan
  100- 10.82w, 200- 21.93w
OLAWORE Joshua U23 31.07.95, Havering/Bath Un
  60- 6.88i, LJ- 7.29i/7.14 (7.49-15)
O'LEARY Jay U20 23.12.99, Rugby & Northampton
  110HJ- 14.3w
OLIVER-STEVENS Kit U15 8.10.02, Exeter
  200- 23.37w, 300- 37.50
OLLEY Christopher U23 26.03.96, Tonbridge/London Un
  1500- 3:45.71 (3:44.22-16), 3k- 8:04.52, 5k- 14:03.29
OLOWE Lynden U20 18.06.00, Southampton
  400- 48.51
OLSEN Michael U20 22.03.99, Edinburgh AC
  60- 6.91i, 100- 10.43w/10.45, 200- 21.83
OLUBI Toby 24.09.87, Blackheath & Bromley
  60- 6.94i (6.82i-13),
  100- 10.74w/10.75 (10.63w-14, 10.69-16)
OLUDOYI Kesi Fisayo U20 2.09.98, Harrow
  60- 6.95i (6.93i-14), 100- 10.53
OMOREGIE David U23 1.11.95, Cardiff/Loughborough St
  60- 6.71i, 60H- 7.63i, 110H- 13.34 (13.24-16)
OMOTOMILOLA Reni U20 18.08.00, Stevenage & NH
  110HJ- 15.16w/15.3, DECJ- 5969
OMOTOSHO Jolaoluwa U17 28.12.00, Dartford
  HTY- 59.22
ONANUGA Olaluwasubomi 12.06.93, Thames Valley
  60- 6.85i
ONDOMA Joshua U17 26.12.00, Bexley
  HTY- 52.38
O'NEILL Finn U13 13.10.05, Derry
  PenC- 1895
ONOCHIE-WILLIAMS Daniel U15 7.02.03, Shaftesbury B
  300- 37.41, TJ- 12.82
ONYIA Chukwudi 28.02.88, Kent AC
  TJ- 15.63
OPPONG Roberto 18.08.93, Swansea/ITA
  TJ- 14.88w/14.68 (15.07-14)
ORANGE Callum U17 1.02.01, Leeds
  LJ- 6.89w/6.78
ORD Adam Craig U15 21.09.02, Durham City H
  800- 2:00.15

O'REILLY Finn U17 2.10.01, Colchester H
JTY- 60.68
O'ROURKE Cormac U17 13.02.01, Lagan Valley
400- 50.43, 800- 1:56.14
O'ROURKE Fraser U23 28.02.96, Glasgow City/
St Andrews Un
PV- 4.68i/4.61 (4.83i-14)
ORR Adam U17 3.06.01, VP-Glasgow
PV- 3.65
ORTON George U20 16.10.98, Holmfirth
LJ- 6.87w (6.71)
ORTON Ieuan U23 20.05.96, Barry & Vale H
HJ- 2.00
OSAGIE Andrew 19.02.88, Harlow
400- 47.69, 800- 1:45.54 (1:43.77-12),
1k- 2:22.06i (2:18.56i-11)
OSAMOOR Chukwuemeka U17 15.06.01, Hallamshire
SPY- 14.81, DTY- 42.47
OSAZUWA Osamudieaken John V35 4.05.81, Belgrave/
Army/NGR   HT- 51.43 (65.66-03)
OSBORNE Noah U15 5.04.04, Swansea
PV- 3.05
OSBOURNE George U20 2.04.00, Notts
PV- 4.10i (4.00)
OSEI-NYARKO Romeo U13, Essex Schools
SPC- 10.89
OSEWA Samuel Ikponmwo 17.04.91, Croydon/Notts Tr U
60- 6.68i, 100- 10.20w/10.21
OSHODI Anthony 27.09.91, Woodford Green & Ex L
SP- 15.10 (17.56-14)
OSHUNRINDE Joshua U17 17.10.01, Medway & M'stone
60- 7.07i, 100- 10.8w/10.89
OSUNSAMI Mayowa U20 23.10.99, Newham & Essex B
400- 48.93, 60HJ- 8.37i, 110HJ- 14.10w/14.14
OSUOHA Reality U20 7.07.00, Oldham & Royton
200- 21.73
OTUGADE John U23 24.01.95, Shaftesbury B/London Un
60- 6.65i, 100- 10.30, 200- 21.13
OVERALL Matthew U23 16.02.96, Crawley/Chich Un
200- 21.75w, 400- 47.98
OVERALL Scott 9.02.83, Blackheath & Bromley
10kR- 30:19 (28:49-11), HMar- 66:25 (61:25-12),
Mar- 2:16:54 (2:10:55-11)
OWEN Arron Ray U20 14.07.98, Cardiff
100- 10.81
OWEN Daniel 5.07.93, Cheltenham
3kSt- 9:26.71 (9:06.40-15)
OWEN Joseph U17 30.04.01, Orion
1500- 3:58.19, 3k- 8:48.85
OWEN Nicolas John Lloyd V35 17.07.80, Kingston & Poly
SP- 13.96 (16.37-03)
OWEN Rhys U17 10.03.01, Western (I.O.M.)
1500- 4:02.85
OWONA Lionel U15 23.09.02, WSE&H
HJ- 1.75i/1.75
OWSLEY Freddie U23 6.01.97, Bristol & West
200- 21.44w/21.80 (21.12-15), 400- 48.41 (47.76-15)

PAGAN Matthew U20 15.01.98, W Cheshire
400- 47.85
PAGET Jack U23 30.01.97, Salisbury/Oxford Un
SP- 13.38
PAINTER Michael 9.10.94, Newham & Ex B/Stanford Un
DT- 41.60 (47.29-15), HT- 66.84
PALMER Jac Lloyd U23 13.03.96, Cardiff/Cardiff Met
HT- 65.88
PAMA Alex U13, London Schools
800- 2:16.02
PANTON Tyler U15 30.04.03, Walton
60- 7.24i, 100- 11.11, 200- 22.47, 300- 37.4
PARIS Benjamin U20 6.10.99, Cardiff Archers
200- 21.71
PARIS-SAMUEL Keano-Elliott U20 11.05.99, TVH
200- 21.95
PARK Rhys 18.03.94, Cheltenham/Boise St Un
5k- 14:10.57
PARKER A U15, Essex Schools
80HB- 11.73

PARKER Andre U15 12.11.02, Herne Hill
SPB- 13.93
PARKER Tom 7.10.94, City of Sheffield/Cambridge Un.
HT- 65.65
PARKINSON Alexander 8.09.94, West Suffolk
SP- 15.45, DT- 56.79
PARKINSON Archie U15 7.04.03, Corby
1500- 4:12.71, 3k- 8:53.17
PARKINSON Ian Philip V35 17.02.79, Wycombe
PV- 4.10 (4.31-14)
PARMENTER Olle-Joseph U15 18.03.03, Camb & Col
1500- 4:12.38
PARR Christopher Daniel 13.11.84, Gateshead
1500- 3:47.21 (3:42.13-06), 5kR- 14:23
PARRY Iwan Sion U23 30.06.97, Menai
HJ- 1.98
PARRY Joshua U23 31.10.97, Wycombe/Chich Un
200- 21.67
PARRY Michael U20 25.11.99, Colwyn Bay
800- 1:51.47
PARRY Thomas 8.06.92, Kingston & Poly
400H- 55.35 (53.37-16)
PARTINGTON Tom U20 8.07.99, Manx H
3kW- 12:31.56, 5kW- 22:04.01, 10kW- 47:41.10,
10kWR- 45:10, 20kW- 1:41:27
PASCALL-MENZIE Joel U15 3.11.02, Newham & Essex B
80HB- 11.61
PATRICK Thomas U17 4.07.01, Shaftesbury B
800- 1:54.71, 1500- 3:56.25, 3k- 8:44.64
PATTISON Ben U17 15.12.01, Basingstoke & MH
400- 49.16, 800- 1:56.53 (1:54.52-16)
PAUL Jacob Arron U23 6.02.95, WSE&H/Bath Un
200H- 23.59st (22.84wSt-16), 400H- 49.49
PAULSON William 17.11.94, Stroud/Princeton Un
1500- 3:42.23, 3k- 8:07.58i
PAYN Thomas V35 18.10.79, Winchester
Mar- 2:22:23 (2:17:29-09)
PAYNE Daniel U15 26.12.02, Middlesboro Mandale
800- 2:03.10, 1500- 4:09.03
PAYNE Thomas U15 17.05.03, Swansea
100- 11.48w, LJ- 6.03
PAYNE Tony 13.01.89, Serpentine/NZL
Mar- 2:19:39
PEARCE Daniel 11.09.91, Newquay & Par
400H- 54.66, HJ- 2.00, Dec- 6364
PEARCE Henry 24.01.94, Tonbridge/Un of Tulsa
5k- 14:11.10, 10k- 29:41.12
PEARSE Joseph U23 21.04.96, Blackburn/Cardiff Met
HJ- 2.08i/2.00 (2.02-16)
PEARSON Benjamin 23.05.94, Wolves & Bilston
JT- 59.28 (74.71-14)
PEARSON John Terry V50 30.04.66, Charnwood
HT- 57.85 (70.33-00)
PEARSON Joshua U17 18.05.01, Bromsgrove & R
400- 50.22
PEARSON Joshua U17 6.01.02, WSE&H
400- 50.42
PEARSON Thomas 17.07.91, Charnwood
HT- 44.55 (47.15-11)
PECK Andrew U20 20.09.99, VP-Glasgow
DTJ- 49.73
PENTECOST Harris U17 16.10.00, Falkirk VH
800- 1:56.91
PENTECOST Lewis U17 16.10.00, Falkirk VH
1.5kSt- 4:24.46, 2kSt- 6:17.75
PERCY Nicholas Christiaan 5.12.94, Shaftesbury B/
Un of Nebraska   SP- 16.56i/14.35 (15.85-16),
DT- 62.91 (63.38-16), HT- 67.72 (67.85-16)
PERERA Shamindra U23 30.09.96, Harrow/Lough St
60H- 8.06i, 110H- 14.09, HJ- 1.95, Dec- 5432
PEREZ Eliot U23 20.03.97, Cardiff/Cardiff Met/ESP
HJ- 2.00i/1.97 (2.00i-16)
PERKIN William U20 16.12.98, Chiltern H
800- 1:51.73, 1500- 3:53.17
PERKINS George Spanton 17.10.83, Rotherham
HT- 48.56
PERRY Christopher 1.03.90, Vale Royal
3kSt- 8:59.41

PERRY Jack U17 26.04.01, Kingston upon Hull
  LJ- 6.56
PETERS Jools 20.08.90, Aberdeen
  PV- 4.25
PETROU Nicholas U23 20.07.96, Leeds
  400- 48.96 (47.15-15)
PETTY Samuel Lewis 7.11.91, North Devon
  800- 1:50.88 (1:49.06-13)
PFAENDER Isaac U15 15.09.02, Cambridge & Col
  SPB- 13.03
PHILLIPS Beck U20 6.10.98, Cheltenham
  SPJ- 14.10, DTJ- 43.53 (43.98-16)
PHILLIPS Dylan U15 26.10.02, Pembroke
  SPB- 13.23
PHILLIPS George U20 7.08.99, Doncaster
  2kSt- 6:06.48, 3kSt- 9:58.93
PHILLIPS Peter 12.02.86, Herne Hill
  400- 48.37 (47.51-15)
PHILLIPSON Josh U23 5.09.95, Blaydon
  Dec- 4747 (5408-15)
PHILPOTT Robert U15 21.09.02, Hercules Wimb
  200- 23.19
PHIPPS Jack 2.04.94, Birchfield/Loughborough St
  PV- 5.25i/5.10 (5.20-15), HepIS- 4646i
PHIRI Eldridge 21.07.83, Tamworth/ZAM
  60- 6.94i (6.85i-13)
PICKARD Max 4.06.93, Brighton Phoenix
  1500- 3:45.74
PICKBURN Alastair V35 5.01.82, Lymington Tri
  Mar- 2:29:37
PICKUP Bradley 4.04.89, Bournemouth
  LJ- 7.43 (8.16-14)
PIERCE Eoin 20.05.89, Newham & Essex B/IRL
  1500- 3:47.70 (3:47.10-15)
PIERRE Rion Joseph 24.11.87, WSE&H
  60- 6.74i (6.60i-14), 200- 21.10w (20.90.20.85St-10)
PIPER Paul V35 25.11.81, West 4
  Mar- 2:27:07
PITCAIRN-KNOWLES Bede U20 5.08.00, Tonbridge
  2kSt- 6:12.70, 3kSt- 9:55.6
PITKIN Thomas U20 12.01.98, Havering/Brunel Un
  400- 48.59, 400H- 55.13
PITTS Ivo U15 16.11.02, Crawley
  JTB- 54.57
PLENDERLEITH Grant 15.03.91, City of Sheffield
  60- 6.95i, 100- 10.70w/10.71 (10.63w-16),
  200- 21.19 (21.11-16), 400- 48.45 (46.65-15)
PLOWMAN Mark 26.03.85, RAF/Yeovil
  SP- 13.60, DT- 54.68 (56.04-14)
PLUMB Samuel 12.04.94, Newbury
  110H- 14.9/15.58 (14.95-16), 400H- 52.00 (51.66-14)
PLUMMER Zanson U23 27.03.97, Shaftesbury B
  60- 6.95i, 100- 10.62 (10.48-16), 200- 21.37 (21.01w-16)
POCOCK Harrison U23 8.08.96, C of Portsmouth/Ports U
  400- 48.58
POLLINGER Chay U20 20.01.98, Chelmsford
  JT- 59.38
POLLOCK Paul 25.06.86, Abbey (NI)/IRL
  10kR- 29:20/29:12dh (28:32.18t-14), Mar- 2:15:30
POOLE Jonathan 16.11.82, Serpentine
  10k- 30:56.47, HMar- 68:06 (67:53-15),
  Mar- 2:21:36 (2:20:38-15)
POPE George U17 6.12.00, Blackheath & Bromley
  PV- 3.93i/3.80
POPOOLA Marvin U23 5.09.95, Herne Hill/Brunel Un
  60- 6.86i (6.72i-15), 100- 10.61 (10.47w/10.51-14),
  200- 21.27 (20.92w-14)
PORTER Jake 13.11.93, Birchfield/Birmingham Un
  60H- 7.86i, 110H- 13.68
PORTER Stephen 22.09.89, Sale
  JT- 54.80 (64.54-09)
POTTON-BURRELL Jamie U23 27.01.96, Luton
  HT- 57.13
POWELL Arthur U13 26.09.04, Maldwyn Harriers
  100- 12.3, 200- 24.94
POWELL Damien U23 29.12.95, Kent/St Marys Un
  60- 6.91i

POWELL Elliott U23 5.03.96, Leics Cor/Loughborough St
  100- 10.37w/10.65 (10.5/10.63-16),
  200- 20.73w/20.94 (20.68-15)
POWELL Rowan U20 8.12.98, Leics Cor
  100- 10.76w, LJ- 7.27, TJ- 13.78
POWELL Wayne V45 27.07.71, Gloucester AC
  HT- 49.65 (58.96-08)
POZZI Andrew 15.05.92, Stratford-upon-Avon
  60H- 7.43i, 110H- 13.13w/13.14
PRAIM-SINGH Billy George U20 16.06.99, Southend
  SPJ- 14.61, HT- 54.70, HTJ- 62.81 (63.01-16)
PRATT James U13 2.09.04, Crawley
  PV- 2.30
PREEST Oliver U15 2.07.03, South London H
  100- 11.49, 200- 23.08
PRENN Alistair 7.11.94, Belgrave/Boston Un
  SP- 13.24, JT- 56.70, Dec- 6338
PRENTICE Nick U23 29.04.97, Birchfield
  100- 10.56
PRESCOD Reece U23 29.02.96, Enfield & Haringey
  60- 6.62i, 100- 10.03, 200- 20.83w (20.38-16)
PRESTON Daniel U17 25.08.01, Liverpool H
  800- 1:55.85
PRICE Aled U23 14.12.95, Carmarthen/Birmingham Un
  60H- 8.44i (8.36i-16), 110H- 15.38 (14.93-16),
  LJ- 7.26w/6.99 (7.23i-16, 7.12-15), JT- 53.64 (61.34-15)
PRICE Charlie U17 30.09.01, Notts
  400HY- 57.4/57.99
PRICE Niall U17 4.04.01, Wolves & Bilston
  100- 11.04
PRICE Patrick U20 1.07.99, Rugby & Northampton
  HT- 50.64, HTJ- 59.68
PRICE-DAVIES Brychan U17 15.07.01, Brecon
  1.5kSt- 4:36.64
PRIEST Julian U15 24.09.02, Huntingdon
  100- 11.3/11.40w/11.46, 200- 22.49, 300- 36.7
PRINCEWILL Teepee U20 22.08.00, WSE&H
  TJ- 15.35i/15.19
PRIOR Luke U20 3.02.98, Wells
  5k- 14:52.0
PRIOR Oliver U17 30.01.01, Ashford
  3k- 8:55.1
PRITCHARD Ashley V35 14.07.79, Macclesfield
  Dec- 4788 (6009-07)
PROCTOR David 22.10.85, Sale
  800- 1:49.99 (1:48.32-12)
PROSPER Emmish 8.09.92, Birchfield/LCA
  JT- 65.19
PRYCE Nicholas 10.11.92, R Sutton Coldfield
  200- 21.73 (21.35-14), 400- 48.50 (48.31-16)
PURBRICK Joseph U15 22.04.04, Huntingdon
  80HB- 11.8w
PUTNAM Daniel 30.12.91, Blackheath & Bromley
  60- 6.87i, 100- 10.35w/10.47,
  200- 20.65w/21.14 (21.05-14)
PUXTY James U20 30.09.99, Tonbridge
  3k- 8:30.28

QUARSHIE Emmanuel 3.03.92, Havering
  SP- 13.36 (14.48-14)
QUAYLE Glen U17 6.03.02, Northern (IOM)
  PV- 4.21
QUINN Aidan U20 10.02.00, Glasgow SOS
  TJ- 14.60
QUINN Kevin V35 24.07.79, South London H
  Mar- 2:24:38
QUINTON Brandon U15 22.02.03, Bury
  1500- 4:13.25

RABJOHNS William U13 11.02.06, Poole
  1500- 4:30.75
RADY Thomas 14.12.93, Southampton
  Dec- 4920
RAGAN David James 26.03.83, Basingstoke & MH
  1500- 3:47.82, 3kSt- 9:26.48 (9:11.46-15)
RAHMAN Imranur 5.07.93, C of Sheffield/Birmingham Un
  60- 6.68i, 100- 10.47 (10.39-15), 200- 21.77w
RAINSFORD Joe 17.06.93, Heanor
  10k- 30:58.11

RAJIS Daniel U15 26.07.03, Cambridge H
  60- 7.42i
RAJKUMAR Jacob U20 3.06.98, Reading
  HJ- 2.04
RAMDHAN Tommy U23 28.11.96, Bexley
  60- 6.89i (6.70i-16), 100- 10.36w/10.55 (10.21w-16, 10.45-15),
  200- 21.04 (20.57w-15, 20.84-16)
RAMIE Joseph 14.12.90, Havering
  LJ- 7.18, TJ- 13.86 (13.98-09)
RAMSAY Liam 18.11.92, City of Sheffield
  60H- 8.11i (8.04i-14), HJ- 2.05i (2.05-15),
  PV- 4.41i (4.75-15), LJ- 7.27i (7.35w/7.28-15),
  SP- 13.62i (13.64i-16, 13.03-14), HepIS- 5832i
RAMSDEN Matthew U15 7.07.03, Blackburn
  3k- 9:24.4
RANKIN Tyreece U15 14.09.02, Highgate H
  60- 7.17i, 100- 11.19, 200- 23.38w
RARADZA Munyaradzi U23 17.06.96, Derby AC/
  Birmingham Un
  60- 6.93i (6.87i-14), 200- 21.29
RASHBROOK Jamie U15 10.08.03, Basildon
  800- 2:03.07
RAWLINGS Liam U15 12.01.03, Oswestry
  1500- 4:10.59, 3k- 9:25.54
RAWLINGS Louis U23 22.03.96, Cambridge & Col/
  Oxford Un/FRA   800- 1:51.94 (1:50.72-14)
RAWLINGS Ronan U17 2.03.01, Nene Valley H
  100- 10.8w/10.84, 200- 22.40w/22.45
RAYNER Archie U20 2.06.99, Mansfield H
  1500- 3:48.26, 3k- 8:15.83
REARDON Joseph U15 24.10.02, Aberdare
  3k- 9:12.58
REED Bradley 14.01.92, Chelmsford
  110H- 15.25 (14.8/14.88w/15.03-15)
REEKS Richard Kenneth 6.12.85, Crawley/R.Navy
  110H- 15.38 (14.00w/14.26-14, 14.2-10)
REES Daniel U23 22.10.96, Aberdeen/Aberdeen Un
  400H- 52.95
REES Iwan U15 16.11.02, Rhymney Valley
  HJ- 1.77
REES Logan U23 23.02.97, Fife
  5MR- 24:02, 10k- 30:19.68, 10kR- 29:28
REES Tristan U20 3.04.99, Fife
  5k- 15:12.09, 3kSt- 9:58.32
REGISTER Matthew U15 3.03.03, Cardiff
  60HB- 9.25i
REID Iain V35 20.07.77, Cambuslang
  Mar- 2:29:44
REID Joseph U23 8.03.96, Cardiff/Cardiff Met
  400- 47.42, 800- 1:50.09
REID Julian 23.09.88, Birchfield
  LJ- 7.73i (8.18w-09, 8.08-11),
  TJ- 16.30i/16.01 (17.10w/16.98 JAM-09, 16.95-15)
REID Leon 26.07.94, Birchfield
  60- 6.74i, 100- 10.26w/10.33, 200- 20.38, 400- 47.13
REID Mahki U13 14.03.05, London Schools
  100- 12.4
REID Omar U23 6.07.96, Croydon/Bath Un
  DT- 41.77 (44.80-16)
REIDY Sean V35 27.01.81, Nene Valley H
  Dec- 4914 (5068-15)
REILLY Freddie U17 10.02.02, Stevenage & NH
  OctY- 4478
REVELEY Liam U20 24.10.98, Blaydon
  HJ- 2.01, LJ- 7.04w, HepJ- 4960i, DECJ- 6577
REYNOLDS Aiden Lewis 5.07.94, Shaft B/Oxford Un
  JT- 61.45 (68.77-13)
REYNOLDS Benjamin Travers 26.09.90, WSE&H/IRL
  60H- 7.77i (7.73i-16), 110H- 13.60 (13.48-15)
REYNOLDS Benjamin U15 1.10.02, Cardiff
  800- 2:03.38, 1500- 4:09.46
REYNOLDS Harvey U17 7.11.01, Cardiff
  400HY- 57.63
REYNOLDS Joseph U15 15.02.03, Pembroke
  300- 36.85

REYNOLDS-WARMINGTON Kyle U17 28.02.02,
  Blackheath & Bromley 60- 7.02i, 100- 11.04 (10.98-16),
  200- 22.21
RHODEN-STEVENS Jamal-Marcus 27.04.94, Shaftesbury
  B/Kingston Un
  100- 10.67w/10.68, 200- 21.63 (21.35-16), 400- 46.99
RICHARDS Che U23 8.05.97, W.Green & Ex L/
  Edinb Un/TTO LJ- 7.80, TJ- 13.86 (14.37w/14.21-13)
RICHARDS Lee U17 3.09.00, Vale of Aylesbury
  100- 11.1/11.11
RICHARDS Samuel 9.12.89, Cambridge & Coleridge
  LJ- 6.98 (7.09-14)
RICHARDSON Archie U17 17.09.00, Lincoln Wellington
  800- 1:56.19
RICHARDSON Joel 30.12.93, Trafford
  200- 21.60w/21.62, 400- 47.87
RICHARDSON Owen U20 5.09.98, Basingstoke & MH
  100- 10.63w (10.59-16), 200- 21.16w/21.77 (21.53-16),
  400- 46.49
RICHARDSON William U20 23.02.98, Birchfield
  1500- 3:49.91, 3k- 8:14.94, 5k- 14:24.78, HMar- 66:38
RICHMOND Aaron V35 8.09.82, Bideford
  HMar- 68:07, Mar- 2:23:37
RICKARDS Tom U15 18.12.02, Reading
  800- 2:00.20
RICKETTS Jordan U17 10.09.01, Birchfield
  60HY- 8.17i, 100HY- 13.3w/13.53
RIDGE Matthew U23 12.09.96, Bournemouth/Lough St
  SP- 14.75
RIDLEY Thomas U15 7.08.03, Worthing
  HJ- 1.86, PenB- 2593
RIELEY Alex U20 26.02.98, Mansfield H
  1500- 3:52.42
RIENECKER-FOUND Harry U17 14.05.02, Brighton & H
  HJ- 1.95
RIGG Ethan U17 3.09.01, Middlesboro Mandale
  HJ- 1.90
RILEY-LA BORDE Khai U23 8.11.95, Enfield & Haringey
  60H- 7.79i (7.74i-16), 110H- 13.59
RIMMER Michael 3.02.86, Liverpool Pembroke Sefton
  800- 1:46.72 (1:43.89-10)
RINGSHALL Alex U15 27.09.02, Dartford
  HTB- 49.26
RINKEN Raul U23 20.12.95, TVH/London Un/EST
  DT- 42.63 (44.65-16)
RITCHIE Munroe U20 30.01.98, Crawley
  HT- 47.39 (50.48-15), HTJ- 53.38 (59.54-15)
RITCHIE-MOULIN William U23 3.12.96, B'field/Durham U
  60H- 8.18i, 110H- 14.48w/14.60
RIX-CLANCY Finley U15 14.08.03, Essex Schools
  HTB- 41.22
ROACH Jack U23 8.01.95, Middlesboro M/North'land Un
  HJ- 2.00 (2.08-14), LJ- 7.58
ROACH-CHRISTIE Luke 17.10.94, Harrow
  SP- 13.90 (15.80-13)
ROBBINS Patrick V45 12.03.72, Bournemouth
  24Hr- 242.114km (256.801km-15)
ROBERSON Mark W. V40 21.03.75, Marshall Milton K
  HT- 45.23 (51.14-05)
ROBERTS Charlie U15 25.07.03, St Helens Sutton
  800- 2:03.05
ROBERTS Jacob U20 9.09.99, Blackburn
  HT- 55.59, HTJ- 65.64
ROBERTS Jonathon 11.05.94, Southampton
  1500- 3:47.75, 3kSt- 9:45.31
ROBERTS Kyran U23 19.09.95, Carmarthen/Lough St
  800- 1:51.47, 1500- 3:45.18, 5kR- 14:23
ROBERTS Matthew 22.12.84, Newham & Essex B
  HJ- 2.22 (2.26-10)
ROBERTS Sam U20 17.07.00, Team Bath
  110HY- 14.41w
ROBERTS-NASH Psalm U20 7.07.99, Wolves & Bilston
  400- 48.22i/48.5 (48.08-16)
ROBERTSON Andrew 17.12.90, Sale
  60- 6.57i (6.54i-16), 100- 10.15w/10.23 (10.10-14),
  200- 21.19w/21.58 (20.76-13)
ROBERTSON Oliver U13 27.09.04, Blackheath & Bromley
  75HC- 12.0/12.11, PenIC- 1345i

ROBINSON Adam U15 6.02.04, Andover
HJ- 1.85i/1.80
ROBINSON Byron 12.09.87, Herne Hill
100- 10.73 (10.69w-14), 200- 21.59 (21.46-14)
ROBINSON Christian U23 16.08.96, Lisburn/IRL
60- 6.92i, 100- 10.64
ROBINSON Daniel V35 18.12.79, BRAT
Mar- 2:29:57
ROBINSON Ethan U15 30.12.02, Arona (ESP)
HJ- 1.75
ROBINSON James V40 27.08.76, Halesowen
PV- 4.11 (4.30i/4.30-94)
ROBINSON Jason 8.08.89, Derby AC
HT- 55.92
ROBINSON Luke U15 7.05.03, City of York
JTB- 51.14
ROBINSON Oliver 5.10.87, Bingley/Leeds Un
400H- 54.13 (52.41-11)
ROBINSON Shane 19.02.91, Lincoln Wellington
5kR- 14:26 (14:20-15), 10k- 30:30.67
ROBINSON William U17 16.09.00, Kingston upon Hull
HTY- 52.29
ROBINSON-BOOTH Iwan U17 27.09.00, Cardiff
60- 7.09i, 100- 11.06, 200- 22.49
ROCHESTER Brandon U15 6.10.02, Ealing, S & Mx
100- 11.2/11.25
RODDIS-CLARKE Wayne A. R. V40 24.12.75, Lincoln W
HT- 47.01 (60.78-01)
RODGER Sebastian William 29.06.91, Shaftesbury B
200- 21.45 (21.34w-16), 400- 46.57i (46.48i/46.68-16),
200H- 22.89st (22.66wst-16), 400H- 49.58 (49.19-13),
LJ- 7.01 (7.27-10)
RODRIQUES Ezra U17 8.11.00, Croydon
60HY- 8.60i (8.60i-16), 100HY- 13.65
ROE Charles 28.04.92, Coventry Godiva/Warwick Un.
LJ- 6.93w/6.89i, Dec- 6523, HepIS- 5123i
ROFFEY Daniel U17 6.09.01, Epsom & Ewell
HepIY- 4118i
ROGERS Joseph U20 13.04.98, Halesowen
400- 48.83
ROGERSON Thomas U20 8.11.98, Liverpool H
3k- 8:32.36
ROONEY Martyn 3.04.87, Croydon
400- 45.65 (44.45-15)
ROPER Jaleel U15 8.02.03, Hercules Wimbledon
60- 7.09i, 100- 10.97, 200- 22.13, 300- 36.61
ROSAM George U17 25.12.00, City of Portsmouth
LJ- 6.55
ROSS Edmund U23 1.09.97, Birchfield
200- 21.68i (21.81-16)
ROSSITER Jayme 29.09.90, Newham & Ex B/
Loughb St/IRL 3k- 8:13.10, 3kSt- 9:08.11 (8:59.82-15)
ROTHWELL Daniel 29.04.87, Swansea
3kSt- 9:37.14
ROTTIER Tom U23 15.11.96, Enfield & Har/Lough St
PV- 4.40 (4.55-16), Dec- 5973 (6381-16), HepIS- 4880i
ROUSE Benjamin U17 12.03.01, Charnwood
1500- 4:03.75
ROUSE Oliver U17 12.03.01, Charnwood
1500- 4:02.82
ROWDEN Daniel U23 9.09.97, W.Green & Ex L
800- 1:46.64
ROWE Jack U23 30.01.96, AF&D/St Marys Un
3k- 8:13.52, 5k- 14:10.30, 10k- 29:55.62, 10kR- 29:46
ROWLEY Leo U20 30.07.99, Rotherham
SP- 13.88i/13.23, SPJ- 15.69
ROY Taylor U20 25.06.99, Pitreavie
60HJ- 8.37i, 110HJ- 14.66w/14.7/15.04 (15.02-16),
110H- 15.48
ROYDEN Jack U17 27.10.00, Medway & Maidstone
SPY- 14.35 (14.38-16)
RUDD Henry 22.01.94, Cambridge Un
JT- 56.91
RUDDY Craig 10.04.88, Inverclyde
Mar- 2:22:14
RUGG Jonathan U15 19.09.02, Enfield & Haringey
PV- 3.90

RUSH Graham 8.09.82, Cheltenham/Gloucester U
3k- 8:09.30, 5k- 14:05.25, 10k- 29:04.52
RUSHBROOK Mark V35 15.07.81, Cardiff
Mar- 2:28:59
RUSHDEN Matthew U20 29.03.98, Dartford
DECJ- 5164
RUSS Kieran U23 1.10.95, Daventry/Winchester Un
Dec- 5931
RUSSELL Ben U23 29.02.96, Bracknell
Dec- 4877 (4928-16)
RUSSELL Jamie U15 11.08.03, Solihull & S H
PenB- 2532
RUSSELL Keith V40 28.01.77, Reading/IRL
Mar- 2:29:04 (2:27:51-13)
RUSSELL Robert V40 5.08.74, Scarborough
DT- 41.67 (53.76-96)
RUSSO Luca 7.11.93, Tonbridge/Missouri Un
1500- 3:46.47, 1M- 4:05.42, 3k- 8:17.69i
RUTHERFORD Greg 17.11.86, Marshall Milton K
60- 6.75i (6.68i-09), LJ- 8.18 (8.51-14)
RUTTER Elliott U23 20.08.95, Birchfield
200- 21.78, 400- 46.97 (46.39-14)
RYDER Joseph U13 18.10.04, Hartlepool
200- 25.5
RYLE-HODGES William 20.09.93, Shaft B/Oxford Un
5k- 14:34.11
RYVES Finley U15 23.10.02, Southampton
100- 11.48w

SABESTINI Louis U17 6.03.01, Sevre Bocage (FRA)
TJ- 13.53w/13.37 (13.64)
SADLER Kieron U17 15.10.00, Ipswich
JTY- 56.55
SAFO-ANTWI Sean 31.10.90, Enfield & Har/GHA
60- 6.56i (6.55i-16), 100- 10.31 (10.07w/10.14-14)
SAKALA Robert U20 5.03.98, Croydon
110HJ- 13.48
SALAKO Ayo U13 9.11.04, Croydon
60- 7.87i
SALTER Michael 12.01.90, Leeds
1500- 3:48.76 (3:44.86-15)
SALTMARSH William U13 18.01.05, Exeter
SPC- 11.62
SAMUEL Aaron U15 6.06.03, Ilford
1500- 4:11.86
SAMUEL Rob 14.01.86, Eryri
HMar- 67:42 (66:08-10), Mar- 2:21:47
SAMWELL-NASH Kristian U15 5.12.02, Ashford
200- 22.9/22.91, 300- 35.96, 400- 51.54
SANDALL Ashley U23 23.09.97, Nene Valley H
800- 1:50.34
SANDERSON John 27.02.93, Guildford & G/York Un
1500- 3:43.64, 3k- 8:05.24, 5k- 14:27.31, 5kR- 14:26
SANDILANDS Ben U15 7.08.03, Fife
1500- 4:16.74
SANUSI Sam U15 13.11.03, Essex Schools
HJ- 1.75i, PenB- 2511
SARAYEV Sergiy 15.01.83, Trafford/UKR
DT- 45.23 (46.42-15), HT- 52.98 (53.50-15)
SAUL-BRADDOCK Adam U17 20.09.01, Wolves & Bilston
800- 1:56.4
SAUNDERS Benjamin U17 9.12.00, Birchfield
HJ- 2.00
SAVAGE Elliot U13 16.09.04, Sale
800- 2:14.2
SAVAGE Evan U13 16.09.04, Sale
800- 2:15.2
SAVERY Andrew V35 31.08.82, Leamington
Mar- 2:27:24 (2:25:43-14)
SAWYERS Jonathon 24.08.92, WSE&H
TJ- 15.57 (15.64-13)
SAYERS Feron 15.10.94, Birchfield
LJ- 7.95w/7.89
SCAMMELL William U15 1.12.02, Team Bath
80HB- 11.88w, PenB- 2553
SCHENINI Alessandro Iain U20 28.04.00, Giffnock N
LJ- 7.16w/7.12

SCHLUETER Jami U15 26.10.02, Yeovil Olympiads
60HB- 8.86i, 80HB- 11.24, PV- 2.90, LJ- 6.34w/6.19,
PenB- 2943
SCHOFIELD William U20 25.03.99, Sale
HTJ- 51.94
SCHOPP Max Rainer U23 5.09.96, Stevenage & NH/
Brunel Un   400H- 54.15 (53.79-15)
SCHRIJVER Joshua U13 4.01.05, Bristol & West
SPC- 11.53, DTC- 30.84
SCOPES Alfie U20 12.11.99, Tonbridge
SPJ- 15.35, DTJ- 49.49, DTY- 53.75 (56.64-16)
SCOTT Aaron 11.04.87, Lincoln Wellington
10k- 30:15.26 (30:06.36-14), HMar- 67:07+ (65:50-16),
Mar- 2:17:50
SCOTT Adam Graham U20 24.01.00, Fife
1500- 3:51.44, 3k- 8:23.43
SCOTT Christopher Mark 21.03.88, Southampton
DT- 56.51 (63.00-11)
SCOTT Ethan U13 20.01.05, East Grinstead
1500- 4:29.57
SCOTT Marc 21.12.93, Richmond & Zet/Un of Tulsa
1M- 4:05.36i, 3k- 7:43.37, 5k- 13:22.37, 10k- 28:07.97
SCOTT Nathan U15 9.08.03, Rhondda
60- 7.40i
SCOTT-BROWN Ruairidh U17 9.10.00, VP-Glasgow
JTY- 52.68
SCULLION Stephen 9.11.88, North Belfast/IRL
10k- 28:58.28, HMar- 65:52 (64:46-13), Mar- 2:18:04
SEAL Toby U20 10.12.99, Tonbridge
60HJ- 8.34i, 110HJ- 14.93
SEARLE Adam U17 7.11.00, Rugby & Nor AC
1.5kSt- 4:20.84
SEARLES Rhys 28.03.91, Enfield & Haringey
PV- 5.16i/5.00 (5.11-11)
SEAWARD Kevin 3.10.85, St Malachy's/IRL
HMar- 64:52, Mar- 2:15:50 (2:14:52-16)
SEDDON Matthew U23 26.02.96, Bracknell/Cardiff Met
3kSt- 9:16.59
SEDDON Zak William 28.06.94, Bracknell/Florida State U
1500- 3:44.08 (3:42.02-15), 3k- 7:58.95i (8:08.61-12),
2kSt- 5:36.19, 3kSt- 8:30.17
SEED William U20 20.10.98, Cleethorpes
110HJ- 14.84, DECJ- 5994
SEEDS Finlay U15 30.06.03, Upper Hutt (NZL)
800- 2:02.17, 1500- 4:10.82
SEERY George U15 20.08.03, Thanet AC
80HB- 11.87w, PenB- 2661
SELEMON Nahom U17 20.04.01, Sale
60HY- 8.44i, 100HY- 13.77
SENIOR James 4.01.92, City of Norwich
3kSt- 9:08.34
SENIOR Reiss U20 30.09.98, Herne Hill
HTJ- 54.28
SESAY Edward U15 18.11.02, Thames Valley
100- 11.32
SESEMANN Philip 3.10.92, Blackheath & Brom/Leeds Un
800- 1:51.13, 1500- 3:41.43, 3k- 8:00.78i/8:03.84,
5kR- 14:09, 10kR- 29:40
SEXTON Aaron U20 24.08.00, North Down/IRL
100- 10.77, 200- 21.43
SHAND Peter 5.12.91, Birchfield
100- 10.73 (10.7-13), 200- 21.03w/21.47 (21.14-16)
SHARIF ALI Mohamed U15 8.08.03, Hillingdon
800- 1:58.16, 1500- 4:06.27, 3k- 8:44.61
SHARMAN William 12.09.84, Belgrave
60H- 7.85i (7.53i-14),
110H- 13.72 (12.9wdt-10, 13.16-14)
SHARP Matthew V35 2.04.79, Hercules Wimbledon
Mar- 2:29:19
SHARP Matthew 25.04.89, Enfield & Haringey
5MR- 23:58 (23:42-16), 10kR- 30:04+ (29:32-16),
15kR- 45:15+ (45:06+-16), 10MR- 48:35 (48:18-16),
HMar- 66:38+ (65:03-14), Mar- 2:16:02
SHAW Ben U17 22.05.01, Giffnock North
1.5kSt- 4:40.67
SHAW Dominic 26.12.88, New Marske
10kR- 30:02 (29:48.35t-16), HMar- 66:04

SHAW Nicholas U15 13.10.02, Shaftesbury B
60- 7.30i, 100- 11.45, 200- 23.50
SHAW Samuel U17 5.06.01, Charnwood
HJ- 1.90
SHEARER Ben V40 27.05.76, Cambridge H
Mar- 2:25:19 (2:25:18-16)
SHEFFORD James U15 10.02.03, Bracknell
HTB- 44.56
SHELDON Grant 23.08.94, Cambuslang
5k- 14:22.34
SHELLEY Jake 16.03.91, Shaftesbury B
3k- 8:00.62 (7:59.57i-15), 5kR- 14:09 (13:46.17t-15)
SHEPHERD Edward 8.12.93, W.Green & Ex L/
San Francisco Un   3k- 8:10.97i (8:17.70-14), HMar- 65:38
SHERIFF Mutara 12.10.94, St Mary's Richmond
60- 6.87i, 100- 10.5/10.71 (10.62w/10.68-16),
200- 21.5 (21.68-16)
SHERRIFF Owen U17 25.09.00, Tamworth
400HY- 56.16
SHIELDS Benjamin Joseph 17.01.94, City of Sheffield/
New Mexico Un   60- 6.81iA (6.85i-14), 200- 21.66w
100- 10.50w/10.59 (10.44w-13, 10.49-16)
SHIELDS Henry U17 11.09.00, East Essex TC
HJ- 1.92, OctY- 4281
SHIELDS Jonathan U20 1.02.98, C of Sheffield/Hallam Un
1500- 3:49.88, 3k- 8:14.57, 5k- 14:34.78
SHIELDS Michael U20 25.04.99, Basildon
60HJ- 8.39i (8.39i-16),
110HJ- 15.12w/15.25 (14.62w/15.11-16)
SHIELDS Ryan U15 31.01.03, Birchfield
800- 2:03.50, 1500- 4:15.97
SHIPLEY Robert U23 28.09.96, City of York/Durham Un
400- 47.29
SHORE Sam 6.12.85, Belgrave/AUS
400H- 53.84
SHORT Alexander 7.01.94, Bedford & Co/ San Francisco Un
5k- 13:47.57i/14:25.60 (14:13.48-16), 10k- 28:46.83
SHORTHOUSE Chris 23.06.88, Birchfield
HT- 69.80 (70.18-15)
SHOWLER-DAVIS Kieran 14.11.91, Basingstoke & MH
60- 6.84i (6.80i-15), 200- 20.73w/20.98 (20.75-10).
100- 10.19w/10.40 (10.03w-16, 10.27-15)
SHRIMPTON Kenneth U23 10.10.96, City of Norwich
200- 21.60w (21.27w/21.40-16)
SIKITY Brandon U17 26.09.00, Cambridge H
HJ- 1.90
SILVA Antonio 26.03.87, Thames Valley/POR
10k- 29:40.92 (29:09.45-15), 10kR- 30:00 (29:40-13)
SIMMONS Stephen U15 1.07.03, Bedford & County
60HB- 8.66i, 80HB- 11.10, LJ- 6.24, PenB- 2890
SIMPSON Judah Howard Eric 28.07.92, Derby AC
60- 6.83i
SIMPSON Robbie 14.11.91, Deeside Runners
HMar- 65:24 (64:41-16), Mar- 2:15:04
SINCLAIR Angus U23 22.02.95, Edinburgh AC/LSU
HJ- 2.00i/2.00 (2.05i/2.02-15), PV- 4.41, HepIS- 5209i
SKELTON Ross 11.05.93, Brighton Phoenix
5k- 14:11.60, 10k- 30:27.67
SKERVIN Elijah Ramone 1.04.92, Notts
100- 10.69w/10.71 (10.29w/10.33-14)
SKETCHLEY David V40 25.02.76, Harrow
JT- 56.04 (67.63-04)
SKILTON Jed U17 6.09.00, Poole
800- 1:56.62, 1500- 4:02.76
SLADE Elliot 5.11.94, Cardiff/Villanova Un
800- 1:51.22 (1:47.70-16), 1M- 4:06.56i
SLADE Tomos U17 13.04.01, Swansea
60HJ- 8.32i, 60HY- 8.38i, 100HY- 13.21, LJ- 6.47w
SLATER Paul 24.04.89, Bexley
Dec- 4711 (5146-09)
SLAVINSKAS Augustas U15 18.04.03, Essex Schools
HJ- 1.81
SLIPPER James U23 30.12.97, Taunton
Dec- 4475
SMALLWOOD Luke Daniel 11.09.88, Blackheath & Brom
400- 48.17i (46.98i-12, 47.60-13)
SMART Oliver U15 20.02.03, Tavistock
1500- 4:17.12

399

SMITH Alexander David 6.03.88, Sale
HT- 60.80 (75.63-12)
SMITH Allan Fraser 6.11.92, Shaftesbury B
HJ- 2.26i/2.24 (2.29i-15, 2.26-13)
SMITH Andrew U23 7.10.95, Pudsey & Bramley/York Un
800- 1:49.39, 1500- 3:45.62
SMITH Ben U17 5.06.01, Notts
200- 22.09w/22.16
SMITH Christopher James V40 27.11.75, Arbroath
JT- 54.98 (66.76-06)
SMITH Chris V40 3.03.77, Thames Valley
10k- 30:47.21
SMITH Conor U20 11.03.99, Bromsgrove & R
3k- 8:30.86
SMITH David Robert Dickie 14.07.91, Shaftesbury B
HJ- 2.21i/2.21 (2.26i-15, 2.25-14)
SMITH Guy 11.01.90, Swansea
1500- 3:44.96 (3:42.55-15), 3k- 8:15.29
SMITH Jayden U15 8.02.03, Middlesex Schools
200- 23.2/23.22
SMITH Jody U17 17.09.00, Charnwood
60- 7.13i, 100- 10.68w/10.89, 200- 21.93w/21.96
SMITH Joe U17 20.10.01, Crawley
800- 1:56.58, 1500- 4:02.23, 3k- 8:50.70
SMITH Logan U20 23.01.98, City of Norwich
3kSt- 9:56.4
SMITH Matthew U20 13.09.98, Brighton & Hove
DECJ- 5470 (5780-16)
SMITH Neal 1.07.84, City of Norwich
SP- 13.69
SMITH Owen 7.11.94, Cardiff
400- 46.91 (46.23-16)
SMITH Peter 20.07.90, Kingston upon Hull
HT- 61.55 (71.75-12)
SMITH Sullivan V40 16.09.76, Cambridge & Coleridge
3kSt- 9:35.09 (9:10.02-07)
SMITHERMAN Andrew 9.11.90, Cheltenham
400- 48.84i (48.6-13, 49.76-16)
SMITH-JOHN Ishmael U23 10.04.95, Blackheath & Br
200- 21.77
SMYTH Jason 4.07.87, Derry/IRL
100- 10.56 (10.17w-12, 10.22-11), 200- 21.40 (20.94-11)
SNAITH Benjamin U23 17.09.95, Enfield & Har/Lough St
100- 10.73 (10.63-14), 200- 20.98 (20.88-14), 400- 46.21
SNASHALL William U15 27.09.02, Crawley
PV- 3.51
SNEE Thomas 22.07.88, Kingston & Poly
PV- 4.50
SNOOK Christopher U20 14.01.00, Aldershot F&D
1MW- 6:09.32, 3kW- 12:25.73, 5kW- 21:31.27,
10kW- 46:18.98, 10kWR- 44:23
SNOOK Timothy U20 18.02.98, Aldershot F&D
5kW- 23:10.1, 10kWR- 50:13 (47:45-16)
SNOOK William U23 11.10.95, Harlow/Leeds Un
400- 48.7/48.93 (48.24-15), 800- 1:49.19
SNOW Scott U23 29.11.95, WSE&H/UCLA
1500- 3:40.78, 1M- 4:04.02i, 3kSt- 9:08.85
SOLOMON Canaan U20 17.09.98, W.Green & Ex L
400- 48.70 (48.52-16), 800- 1:48.92 (1:48.89-16)
SOMERS Thomas U23 28.04.97, City of York/Lough St
100- 10.50w/10.59, 200- 20.90 (20.37-14), 400- 46.92
SOMMERVILLE Sam U23 8.12.97, Yeovil Oly/Sheffield Un
3kSt- 9:36.50
SORRELL Ethan U23 13.09.96, Cambridge Un/NZL
HJ- 1.95i
SOSANYA Emmanuel U20 29.08.98, Newham & Essex B/
East London Un   400- 48.62, HJ- 1.98i
SOUTHERTON Luke U17 13.09.00, Sale
LJ- 6.62
SOUTHWELL Louis U20 6.01.00, Hillingdon
400- 49.0 (49.06-16)
SPARKS Robert U17 4.01.01, Fife
1.5kSt- 4:39.98
SPEIRS Stephen V50 18.08.66, Les Croupiers
24Hr- 226.064km
SPENCE Jacob U20 9.01.98, Yate/Leics Un
60H- 8.30i, 60HJ- 8.08i

SPENCER Dylan U15 17.06.03, AF&D
3k- 9:22.02
SPENCER Jacob U15 10.11.02, Tamworth
100- 11.45w, 200- 23.50, 300- 36.91
SPENCER Stuart 11.11.82, Notts
10k- 30:56.01, HMar- 67:57 (66:06-15)
SPENCER Toby 9.06.90, Coventry Godiva
HMar- 65:48
SPILSBURY Adam U20 25.06.99, Sale
800- 1:51.51
SPIVEY Philip V55 15.05.61, East Grinstead
HT- 46.60 (70.94-86AUS)
SPRAGUE Cameron U17 10.09.00, Team Bath
100- 10.99w/11.07 (10.99w/11.0/11.05-16), 200- 21.77
SPRIO Ollie U17 10.03.01, Banbury
60- 7.05i, 100- 10.89w/10.9, 200- 22.21w (22.4-16)
STABLER Samuel James 17.05.92, OWLS
1500- 3:42.42 (3:42.18-14), 1M- 4:05.42 (4:02.38i-14),
3k- 8:01.28 (7:53.98i-15), 5k- 13:37.30 (13:30.50-15),
10k- 29:03.64, 10kR- 29:13
STACEY Oliver U20 5.09.99, Radley AC
60HJ- 8.37i, 110HJ- 14.99
STALLARD Leo U17 6.08.01, Chichester R&AC
1.5kSt- 4:42.29
STANLEY Alastair John U23 2.09.95, Garscube/
St Andrews Un   400H- 55.69 (55.48-16)
STAPLES Carter U15 19.09.02, Swansea
100- 11.41w, 200- 23.34
STAPLES Scott U20 1.04.99, Lewes
JT- 59.68
STAPLETON Zachary U20 1.06.98, Rugby & Nor AC
60- 6.98i
STARK Douglas 25.08.93, Tamworth/Loughborough St
SP- 13.76 (14.35i-16, 14.20-14), DT- 42.18 (42.74-14),
Dec- 6092 (6824-15)
STARR Cameron Alexander U23 26.03.96, Southampton
60- 6.89i, 100- 10.69w (10.70-16), 200- 21.69w/21.72
STEED Tristan 27.01.88, Army AA
Mar- 2:29:37
STEEL Daniel 29.01.93, Biggleswade
Dec- 4208 (4610-15)
STEELE Chris V35 18.08.81, Borrowdale
HMar- 68:30
STEELE Joseph 13.02.88, Thames Valley
LJ- 7.15 (7.60-10)
STEPHENS Benjamin U20 9.05.98, Nene Valley H
SP- 13.61, SPJ- 14.99i/14.79
STEPHENS Emmanuel 13.03.93, Newham & Essex B
60- 6.67i, 100- 10.36w/10.42, 200- 21.47
STEPHENS Timothy U23 1.11.97, Oxford City/Bath Un
HepIS- 4726i
STEPHENSON Ethan U15 10.07.03, Morpeth
HJ- 1.78, TJ- 12.03
STEVEN Cameron U20 5.03.99, Lasswade
800- 1:51.07i/1:51.13
STEVENS Daniel U15 25.10.02, Stroud
HJ- 1.75
STEVENS Kyle 3.06.85, Kingston & Poly
SP- 13.48 (15.86-07), HT- 49.90 (53.28-05)
STEVENS Samuel U20 27.03.98, Leics Cor/Notts Un
5k- 14:36.31 (14:25.81-16)
STEVENS Thomas V35 7.09.79, Cambridge & Coleridge
Mar- 2:27:46 (2:26:04-14)
STEVENSON Ben 26.01.94, Falkirk VH
5kR- 14:34 (14:13.97t-16)
STEWART Fintan U20 7.05.99, Derry
1500- 3:52.90
STEWART Nick U20 22.06.98, Enfield & Haringey
60- 6.83i, 100- 10.40w/10.53, 200- 20.98w/21.05
STEWART Nilrem U20 8.02.98, Thames Valley
400- 49.14
STOCKTON Matthew U23 4.05.95, North Down/Lough St
JT- 55.77 (58.98-15)
STOKES Adam 16.02.85, Taunton
Mar- 2:28:24
STONE Christopher U23 8.04.95, Bristol & West
60- 6.82i (6.78i-15), 100- 10.41 (10.35w-14),
200- 21.00 (20.92-14)

400

STONE Nicky 15.12.93, Nairn
HT- 48.58
STOREY Jake U23 3.03.97, Harrow/Brunel Un
HJ- 2.07i/2.06 (2.07i-16)
STORRY Dean V35 9.10.79, Notts
HJ- 2.01 (2.03-11)
STRACHAN Craig U17 10.09.01, Banchory
200- 22.24
STRACHAN Richard 18.11.86, Trafford
400- 48.63 (45.48-13)
STRAW James 1.02.94, Lincoln Wellington/Hallam Un
5k- 14:28.50, 10k- 30:09.89
STRAW Tom 28.02.91, Lincoln Wellington
5k- 14:25.23, 10k- 30:18.91
STREET Stuart U23 18.07.96, Notts/Notts Trent Un
LJ- 7.34
STUDLEY Daniel 1.01.92, Bristol & West
10kR- 30:24+ (29:40-16), 10MR- 49:34, HMar- 66:27
STURROCK Craig 7.01.85, Thames Valley
SP- 15.87 (16.87i-13, 16.72-14), DT- 43.97 (46.67-09)
SUDDERICK George U15 20.11.03, Walton
100- 11.4, 200- 23.31, 300- 35.79
SULLIVAN Lewis U13 23.09.04, St Edmunds Pacers
1500- 4:32.22
SULTAN-EDWARDS Amir U15 21.02.04, Blackheath & Br
200- 23.24, 400- 51.45
SUMNER Matthew 17.03.92, City of Plymouth
400H- 51.21
SUMNERS Jack U17 25.10.00, Stratford-upon-Avon
100- 10.82w, 60HY- 7.92i, 100HY- 12.8/12.85,
110HY- 13.51, LJ- 6.92
SURAFEL Paulos U23 12.01.97, Enfield & H/St Marys Un
3k- 8:07.39, 5k- 14:11.33 (14:09.86-16), 10k- 30:26.95,
10kR- 30:10, HMar- 66:30
SURAFEL Petros U23 12.01.97, Enfield & Haringey
3k- 8:07.43, 5k- 13:55.32, HMar- 66:53
SURMAN Michael U23 10.03.97, Derry/Hallam Un
Dec- 5172
SUTHERLAND Robert U23 16.10.95, Wycombe/Lond. Un
TJ- 14.86 (14.99-16)
SUTTON Ben U17 10.08.01, Blackheath & Bromley
60- 7.16i, LJ- 6.82
SWABY Lewis U15 7.06.03, Tonbridge
80HB- 11.84w, HJ- 1.75, PenB- 2608
SWAIN Jack U23 27.02.95, Thames Valley/Coventry Un
JT- 67.10
SWAN Connor U23 14.07.96, Cornwall AC
JT- 55.36 (59.03-14)
SWAN Patrick Anthony U23 14.09.97, Cornwall AC
Plymouth Un
SP- 14.26, DT- 49.98
SWARAY Joshua 2.02.86, Harrow/SEN
60- 6.71i (6.67i-16), 100- 10.32w/10.43 (10.20-13)
SWEENEY Gary 31.01.87, Moray RR
SP- 13.26i (13.88-16)
SWEENEY Sol U20 4.12.98, Perth
1500- 3:50.93, 3k- 8:22.20, 5k- 14:44.68
SWENSSON Martin V40 21.07.75, Penny Lane Striders
Mar- 2:28:39
SYERS Aidan 29.06.83, Newham & Essex B
60- 6.75i (6.72i-14), 100- 10.45w/10.53 (10.31w-01, 10.32-13)
SYLLA Patrick U20 10.10.98, Bournemouth
LJ- 7.56i/7.32 (7.61-16), TJ- 14.32 (14.37-16)

TAIT Magnus U17 26.03.01, Lasswade
1.5kSt- 4:34.72, 2kSt- 6:18.41
TAIWO Ezekiel U13 17.11.04, London Schools
100- 12.3
TALBOT Daniel 1.05.91, Birchfield
60- 6.69i (6.62i-14), 100- 10.13w/10.37 (10.14-14),
200- 19.86w/20.16
TALBOT Samuel J U20 17.02.99, Exeter
60HJ- 7.83i, 110HJ- 14.36, HJ- 1.96, DECJ- 7377,
PV- 4.10 (4.20i/4.20-16), LJ- 7.48i/7.19 (7.51i-16)
TAPPER Ivan U20 4.04.99, Charnwood
JT- 54.03
TARBIT Shay U15 18.06.03, Derby AC
DTB- 38.11

TARRAN Michael V35 10.12.80, Birchfield
JT- 54.49 (71.00-02)
TARRANT Justin U23 7.10.96, Crawley/Cardiff Met
Dec- 5628
TAYLOR Benjamin U20 27.02.00, St Mary's Richmond
DECJ- 5440
TAYLOR James U23 11.08.96, Charnwood/Notts Trent Un
HJ- 2.00i (2.05i-16, 2.04-15)
TAYLOR James 1.10.93, Cheltenham
Dec- 4503
TAYLOR James V35 24.04.82, City of Sheffield
SP- 13.53 (14.11i/13.95-05), DT- 44.86 (45.82-06),
HT- 46.27 (48.81-11)
TAYLOR Jonathan 10.10.87, Morpeth
3k- 8:01.56 (7:55.93-15)
TAYLOR Keoghan U17 10.08.02, Manx H
100- 11.1w
TAYLOR Linton U23 20.01.95, Newark AC/Leeds Un
5k- 14:28.33
TAYLOR Luke U17 5.02.01, Nene Valley H
JTY- 54.10
TAYLOR Matthew U15 17.01.04, Liverpool H
DTB- 36.97
TAYLOR Rory U15 6.12.02, Aix-les-bains FRA
3kW- 14:48.89
TAYLOR Shandell U20 16.12.99, Havering
LJ- 6.90
TAYLOR-CALDWELL Jamie 23.09.91, Ealing S&M/
Texas Un 5k- 14:21.23
TEGID Guto U17 13.03.01, Menai
400HY- 58.31
TELE Jimi 4.05.94, Havering
LJ- 7.12i, TJ- 15.33i (15.33w-13, 15.25-15)
TEUTEN Alexander 3.01.92, Southampton/So'ton Un
1500- 3:46.35, 3k- 8:12.37, 5k- 13:56.87, 10k- 29:52.29,
15kR- 45:16+, 10MR- 48:38, HMar- 65:54, 3kSt- 8:50.58
TEWELDE Abraham 30.12.91, Saltwell
10kR- 30:22, HMar- 67:02
TEWELDE Tsegai 8.12.89, Shettleston H
10kR- 29:34+ (29:07-09), 15kR- 44:21+, HMar- 63:14,
Mar- 2:14:45 (2:12:23-16)
TEZKRATT Nabil U15 4.03.03, Essex Schools
300- 36.80
THACKRAY Kieran 28.09.94, Wakefield
HT- 45.03 (47.02-16)
THATCHER Oliver U15 11.09.02, Southampton
PV- 2.90, DTB- 37.24
THEWLIS Jonathan 7.05.85, Rotherham
Mar- 2:18:10
THIRLWELL Daniel 8.07.83, North Shields Poly
HT- 46.82
THOIRS Jax Donald Will 7.04.93, VP-Glasgow
PV- 5.52i/5.40 (5.65-15)
THOMAS Aaron U15 25.10.02, Sale
HJ- 1.75
THOMAS Adam U23 15.04.95, Bracknell/Loughb St
60- 6.74i, 100- 10.23
THOMAS Alec U23 22.11.96, VP-Glasgow/Glas Cal. Un.
200- 21.80 (21.44w/21.53i/21.67-15)
THOMAS Aran U17 6.12.01, Wakefield
PV- 3.61i (3.40-16), DTY- 43.64
THOMAS Ben U17 7.07.01, Carmarthen
1.5kSt- 4:22.51, 2kSt- 6:16.98
THOMAS Daniel U17 11.01.01, Winchester
400HY- 56.89
THOMAS Daniel-James U20 26.07.00, Sussex Schools
SPJ- 14.14
THOMAS Emmanuel U20 6.12.99, Croydon
PV- 4.73i/4.63
THOMAS Guy Alexander U23 1.07.97, Tonbridge
1MW- 6:02.30, 3kW- 12:03.90 (11:50.34i-16),
5kW- 21:15.4+ (21:14.7+-16), 5kWR- 21:43+,
10kWR- 43:24+ (42:55-16), 20kW- 1:28:38
THOMAS Ieuan 17.07.89, Cardiff
1500- 3:43.3i+/3:48.20 (3:47.14-11), 1M- 3:59.31i,
3k- 7:59.32i (8:18.2-16), 5kR- 14:29 (13:59.89t-13),
3kSt- 8:33.59

401

THOMAS Jamal U15 13.11.02, Havering
HJ- 1.84
THOMAS Joshua U17 13.10.00, Carmarthen
JTY- 50.12
THOMAS Kade U23 22.11.96, VP-Glasgow
100- 10.69w/10.70
THOMAS Max U17 3.10.01, Exeter
HJ- 1.90i
THOMAS Nathan U20 6.09.98, Shaftesbury B
DTJ- 44.52
THOMAS Robert U17 16.10.01, Shaftesbury B
100- 11.0w/11.1, LJ- 6.49
THOMAS Rushane U23 27.01.95, Herne Hill/St Marys Un
60H- 8.15i (8.15i-15), 110H- 14.27 (14.27-16)
THOMAS Spencer U23 26.08.97, Brighton Phoenix
800- 1:47.83
THOMAS Tre U20 26.06.00, Charnwood
60HJ- 7.80i, 110HY- 13.54w/13.83, 110HJ- 13.89
THOMAS Tyler U15 31.10.02, Durham City H
100- 11.4
THOMASON Nathan U20 11.02.98, Colwyn Bay
HTJ- 51.72 (58.43-16)
THOMPSON Aidan U23 19.12.96, Central/Stirling Un
3kSt- 9:26.78 (9:25.72-16)
THOMPSON Christopher V35 17.04.81, AF&D
5k- 14:09.61 (13:11.51-10), 10k- 28:40.40 (27:27.36-11),
10kR- 28:55, 15kR- 44:32+ (43:20+-12),
10MR- 48:32 (47:23-16), HMar- 62:44 (61:00-12),
Mar- 2:24:11 (2:11:19-14)
THOMPSON Christopher U17 16.01.02, Cardiff Archers
PV- 3.61i
THOMPSON Elliot 10.08.92, Enfield & Haringey
PV- 4.30, SP- 13.80, Dec- 6448 (6565-16), HepIS- 5006i
THOMPSON Gregory Leigh 5.05.94, Shaft B/Maryland Un
SP- 15.75, DT- 60.28
THOMPSON Jacob U15 18.03.03, Macclesfield
HJ- 1.85
THOMPSON Jordan U20 22.07.98, Derby AC/Hallam Un
HJ- 2.03
THOMPSON Lee U23 5.03.97, City of Sheffield
200- 21.40, 400- 47.01
THOMPSON Lennox 22.10.93, N&ExB B/East London Un
400- 48.57 (48.19-16), 400H- 52.21
THOMPSON Michael U20 10.12.99, Swansea
DECJ- 5000
THOMSON Dylan U20 11.05.00, Pitreavie
PV- 4.60i/4.40
THOMSON Ryan U23 21.02.96, Cam'lang/Strathclyde Un
3k- 8:18.86i, 5MR- 24:16
THORNE Harrison U17 8.07.02, Slough Juniors
HJ- 1.91, OctY- 4249
THORNE Joseph U15 21.11.02, Charnwood
300- 37.01
THORNE Jude U15 14.09.02, Basildon
PenB- 2607
THORNER Oliver U17 16.03.01, Wells
HJ- 1.92i/1.90 (1.90-16), PV- 4.01, DecY- 6018, OctY- 4824+
THORNEYWORK Henry U17 4.11.00, Solihull & S H
400- 50.28, OctY- 4643
THORNHILL Frederick U17 6.03.01, Taunton
JTY- 53.05
THORNTON Kyle U15 18.02.03, Chelmsford
DTB- 39.74
THORONKA Jimmy 6.06.94, London Heathside/SLE
60- 6.88i, 100- 10.57
THURGOOD Joseph U20 11.09.98, Medway & Maidstone
60HJ- 8.35i, 110HJ- 14.92, DECJ- 5501
THURGOOD Stuart Dennis V40 17.05.76, Herne Hill
HT- 51.84 (59.83-11)
TIJANI Rasheed U13 14.04.05, Bexley
200- 25.4
TIMMINS Stephen V40 8.05.75, Blackheath & Bromley
HT- 45.08 (49.67-13)
TIMMS-SHAW Owen U15 28.12.02, Leics Cor
SPB- 13.41, DTB- 39.23
TINDLE Cameron U20 5.06.98, Edinburgh AC/Stirling Un
60- 6.81i, 100- 10.42 (10.42-15), 200- 21.10 (20.71-16)

TINKLER Martin John 9.04.91, Nene Valley H
SP- 15.34, DT- 43.20
TIPPER Jonathan V35 31.08.80, Kent AC
Mar- 2:28:53
TO Benjamin U15 7.09.02, Bolton
60- 7.41i
TOBAIS Deji-Henry 31.10.91, WSE&H
60- 6.78i (6.75i-10), 100- 10.21 (10.04w/10.18-14),
200- 20.74w/21.03 (20.61-12)
TOBIAS Zak 13.09.94, Bristol & West
5k- 14:34.44, 10k- 30:33.99, Mar- 2:27:35 (2:23:31-16)
TOBIN Jonathan U23 11.04.96, Swansea
1500- 3:45.66 (3:45.04-16), 3k- 8:10.52i
TODD Thomas U15 16.09.03, Cueva de Nerja (ESP)
PV- 3.20
TOMLINSON James Christoph U20 11.01.00, Pembroke
DTJ- 55.40, DTY- 63.48
TORRY Nicholas V40 19.02.77, Serpentine
5k- 14:23.70 (14:18.38-13), 10k- 29:58.39, 10MR- 49:59,
HMar- 66:22 (64:23-13), Mar- 2:17:37 (2:15:08-13)
TOTTEN Eoghan Joseph 29.01.93, Lagan V/Ox Un/IRL
10k- 30:52.75, HMar- 67:21
TOWARD Alan 31.10.92, C of Sheffield/N'berland Un
SP- 15.54, DT- 59.33
TOWNLEY Joel U17 7.04.01, Gloucester AC
LJ- 6.87, TJ- 14.73
TRA Jean-Peter U17 25.10.00, Middlesex Schools
TJ- 13.39
TRANMER Joshua U20 5.04.00, Kingston upon Hull
SPJ- 13.82, DTJ- 43.59
TRAYNOR Luke 6.07.93, Giffnock N/Un of Tulsa
5k- 14:00.63, 10k- 29:08.52, 10kR- 29:27, 15kR- 43:44,
HMar- 64:10
TREMELLING Sam U15 1.10.02, Chelmsford
PV- 3.50
TRESTON Matthew U20 20.07.98, Reading/N Arizona U
60- 7.00i (6.93i-15), 60H- 8.30i
TRICKETT Iain 16.08.85, Dorset Doddlers
Mar- 2:26:59
TRIGG Samuel Alexander 1.11.93, Erme V/ New Mexico U
LJ- 7.33Aw/7.00 (7.45w-15, 7.37-16), TJ- 16.38
TRIGWELL Joshua 28.05.93, Newham & Essex B
3k- 8:13.47, 5k- 14:15.96
TRIMBLE William 9.01.92, Kingston & Poly
JT- 62.79 (67.09-15)
TROTT William U13 27.02.05, Swansea
PV- 2.80
TRUEMAN Daniel U23 5.09.95, Stroud/Cardiff Met
200- 21.56 (21.44-15)
TRUSCOTT Alex U17 8.10.00, Enfield & Haringey
60- 7.03i, 100- 11.0/11.10 (11.02w-16), 200- 22.34
TSEGAY Abel U23 2.06.96, Invicta/ETH
3k- 8:12.49, 5k- 14:02.22, 10k- 28:59.63
TSHIRELETSO Thalosang 14.05.91, W.Green & Ex L/
East London Un/BOT   TJ- 15.92w/15.68
TUCKER Peter Robert V35 17.04.81, Blackheath & Brom
Mar- 2:28:23 (2:23:12-08)
TUFFIN Joseph U20 24.06.99, Rushcliffe
800- 1:51.94, 1500- 3:52.57
TULLOCH Kaisan U17 7.09.00, Here & Worcs Schools
TJ- 13.20
TUMA Basil U13, Oxford Schools
200- 25.29
TURNER Dale U15 25.06.03, Blyth RC
300- 37.23, 60HB- 9.30i, 80HB- 11.87w, PenB- 2544
TURNER George U20 13.07.98, Crawley
PV- 4.71
TURNER Jack U17 23.08.02, Cannock & Stafford
HTY- 51.98
TURNER Jack U17 11.07.01, Exeter
100HY- 13.35, HJ- 2.00, DTY- 41.21, OctY- 5207
TURNER James 10.04.90, Brighton & Hove
Mar- 2:28:01
TURNER Joseph 3.08.90, Cambridge & Coleridge
3kSt- 9:30.19
TURNER Luke U15 21.10.02, Bracknell
200- 23.38, 300- 37.15

402

TURNER Rhys U20 25.02.99, Crawley
100- 10.80, 200- 21.51, 400- 48.4
TURNOCK Steven 7.11.92, Shaftesbury B/Lough St
JT- 72.41
TUTT Joshua U13 30.03.05, Rugby & Northampton
SPC- 12.37, DTC- 33.67
TUTT Samuel U17 12.03.01, Rugby & Northampton
60HY- 8.61i
TWIGG Matthew V45 18.07.69, Rugby & Northampton
DT- 43.09 (54.53-02)
TWIST Grant 17.10.90, Chelmsford
3kSt- 9:32.76
TYLER Josh U17 15.01.02, Exeter
SPY- 13.77
TYRRELL Aydan U13 18.09.04, Harrow
100- 12.4, 200- 25.1

U DEAGBARA David U15 1.02.03, Dartford
LJ- 6.06
UDECHUKU Emeka V35 10.07.79, W.Green & Ex L
DT- 51.21 (64.93-04)
UJAH Chijindu 5.03.94, Enfield & Haringey
60- 6.56i (6.53i-15), 100- 9.95w/9.97 (9.96-14), 200- 20.39
UMEOKAFOR Robert U23 22.11.96, B'field/St Marys Un
800- 1:51.1 (1:50.05-16)
UNSWORTH Cameron U13 21.09.04, Stockport
SPC- 10.80i
UPTON Calum U23 10.12.96, Winchester/Sussex Un
3kSt- 9:47.53
URQUHART Euan U20 25.01.98, VP-Glasgow/Glas Un
LJ- 6.85i (6.85-16), HepJ- 4862i, DECJ- 5915 (6086-16)
UWAIFO Efosa U23 15.05.95, Enfield & Har/Harvard
LJ- 7.85w/7.15 (7.26-12), TJ- 16.18w/15.91 (15.98-16)

V AN OUDTSHOORN Luke U17 30.06.02, Aldershot F&D
1500- 3:59.16, 3k- 8:24.93
VAUGHAN George U20 26.06.98, Enfield & Haringey
60H- 8.38i, 60HJ- 7.97i, 110HJ- 13.95w/14.06,
110H- 14.72 (14.64w-15), 400H- 55.39 (54.54-16)
VAUGHAN Reuben U17 25.10.00, Croydon
DTY- 50.90
VEERAPEN Jacob U23 29.09.97, Sutton & D/
Columbia Un   TJ- 14.90i/14.40 (14.74-16)
VENNARD Michael U23 19.08.95, Vale Royal
3kSt- 9:26.64 (8:56.31-15)
VERNON Andrew James 7.01.86, Aldershot F&D
5k- 13:22.65 (13:11.50-14), 5kR- 13:53 (13:40-12),
10k- 27:58.69 (27:42.62-15), 10kR- 28:36,
15kR- 45:08+ (44:02+-14), HMar- 63:08 (62:46-14)
VINCENT James U20 15.10.99, Cardiff
1500- 3:53.89
VISOKAY Adam 11.03.94, Syracuse Un
1M- 4:02.99, 3k- 8:14.17i, 5k- 14:27.57i (14:27.09-16),
3kSt- 8:47.34
VISRAM CIPOLLETTA Adam U15 21.02.03, Solihull & S H
800- 2:03.2, PenB- 2709
VON EITZEN Christian U23 1.01.97, WSE&H/St Marys U/GER
800- 1:46.88, 1500- 3:48.33 (3:47.48-16)

W ADDINGTON Humphrey 30.05.87, Kingston & Poly
TJ- 13.83 (15.03-09)
WADE Ben U17 6.09.00, Cheltenham
DTY- 43.98
WADE Tom 14.01.89, Aldershot F&D
HMar- 67:12 (65:00-15)
WADLEY Alexander U17 9.05.01, Horsham BS
200- 22.41
WAIFE Nathan U13, West Midland Schools
DTC- 26.12
WALKER David 5.01.93, WSE&H
HJ- 2.05
WALKER Finlay U17 28.05.02, Kilmarnock
PV- 3.75i/3.60 (3.60-16)
WALKER Jess U17 19.09.01, Basildon
JTY- 57.57
WALKER Kaya U17 29.03.01, City of Sheffield
HJ- 2.04
WALKER Leigh V35 17.08.77, Crawley/IRL
PV- 4.45 (5.01-04)

WALKER Robin V35 8.02.78, Orion
HT- 49.28 (49.59-15)
WALKER-KHAN Adam Ali U23 7.03.95, Birch/LIU Brooklyn
400H- 54.56 (53.34-14), LJ- 7.36 (7.42-14), TJ- 15.42
WALKER-SHEPHERD Cameron 28.05.92, Birchfield
PV- 5.03i/5.01 (5.20i-12, 5.15-13)
WALKLETT Jordan U20 8.02.98, Newquay & Par
TJ- 14.76
WALL Adam 10.07.93, City of Sheffield
HJ- 2.05i/2.05 (2.10i-15, 2.09-16)
WALL Zak U15 21.10.03, Cardiff Archers
60HB- 8.98i
WALLACE George U13 5.11.04, Woking
HJ- 1.60
WALLACE Sebastian U15 7.09.03, Horsham BS
80HB- 11.6/11.63w/11.64, LJ- 6.14, PenB- 2540
WALLBRIDGE Samuel U23 6.02.97, Channel Islands/
Loughborough St   400H- 52.58
WALL-CLARKE Alex 17.03.87, Southampton
HMar- 67:33 (66:39-16)
WALLER Harley U15, Essex Schools
PV- 2.95
WALLEY Thomas U20 18.03.98, Wrexham
PV- 4.43, LJ- 6.94w, TJ- 14.72i/14.12
WALLIS Daniel U23 29.01.96, Guildford & G/Lough St
1500- 3:44.52
WALSH Ethan U23 14.06.97, Shaftesbury B
PV- 4.55 (4.90-16)
WALSH Nicholas U23 27.07.97, Sale/Derby Un
60- 6.94i, 100- 10.55 (10.48-16)
WALSHE Andrew 2.08.94, Thames Valley
800- 1:51.87
WALTON Archie U20 14.05.98, Taunton
1500- 3:50.93 (3:50.46-16)
WALTON Dominic 13.11.93, Rossendale/Hallam Un
800- 1:50.07 (1:49.32-16)
WALTON Joe U23 15.09.95, Taunton
3kSt- 9:45.94
WALTON Kyle U17 13.11.01, Shildon
60- 7.13i
WARD Dave V35 21.11.80, Hunters Bog Trotters
100kR- 7:31:19
WARD Dylan U15 17.11.02, Swansea
PV- 2.90
WARD Joshua U17 14.10.00, Cannock & Stafford
800- 1:56.3, 1500- 3:59.42
WARD Michael 10.12.94, Cardiff/Bradley Un
800- 1:51.46,, 3k- 8:06.15i (8:05.66i-16, 8:12.38-14),
1500- 3:46.36 (3:44.33-16), 5k- 14:04.35 (13:54.49-16)
WARD Sidnie U15 9.01.03, Woodford Green & Ex L
800- 2:01.53
WARE Harry U13 26.10.04, Aldershot F&D
800- 2:10.75, 1500- 4:36.0
WARNER Alex 7.11.89, Newham & Essex B
HT- 60.05 (64.43-15)
WARNER Michael 29.11.90, Newham & Essex B
60- 6.93i, 100- 10.66, 200- 21.00w/21.33
WARNER Robert 15.06.94, Blackburn
10k- 30:46.13
WARNER Robert V35 30.05.81, Havering
3kSt- 9:37.14 (9:32.6-08)
WATERFIELD Matthew U17 20.12.00, Morpeth
400- 50.10
WATERMAN Ben 29.09.93, Ealing S&Mx/Birmingham Un
800- 1:48.68 (1:47.57-15)
WATERSON Russell U23 2.08.95, WSE&H/Birmingham U
HJ- 1.95i (1.95-16)
WATKINS Thomas 21.03.92, Newbury
Mar- 2:28:05
WATSON Alastair V40 4.08.77, Notts
10kR- 29:56 (29:32sh-16), HMar- 67:57 (65:41-16)
WATSON Jake U17 19.12.00, Telford
PV- 4.25
WATSON James V40 28.04.74, Taunton
Mar- 2:28:27
WATSON Joseph U23 23.09.95, Birchfield/Brighton Un
SP- 17.16i/16.05 (17.42-16), HT- 47.17 (50.46-16)

WATSON Joshua U23 25.03.95, Biggleswade/Reading Un
HJ- 1.95 (2.00-15)
WATSON Joshua U17 15.08.01, Blackheath & Bromley
60HY- 8.32i, 100HY- 13.34
WATSON Matthew 27.01.91, Southampton/So'ton Un
HJ- 2.00i/2.00 (2.11i-13, 2.10-14), TJ- 14.02w (14.15-11)
WATTS Glen 9.12.86, Shaftesbury B
3kSt- 9:23.00 (8:43.08-11)
WAUGH Finlay U15 20.11.02, Annan
200- 23.2/23.26
WAY Stephen V40 6.07.74, Bournemouth
Mar- 2:26:57 (2:15:16-14)
WEAVER James U23 25.07.97, Enfield & Haringey
60H- 7.95i, 110H- 13.69
WEBB David V35 17.03.82, Telford
HMar- 68:00 (64:45-10)
WEBB Jamie 1.06.94, Liverpool H/Loughborough St
600- 1:18.90i (1:18.78i-16), 800- 1:47.49 (1:46.59-16),
1500- 3:48.08i (3:46.24-15)
WEBB Ryan U23 19.10.97, Birchfield
HJ- 2.13i/2.13 (2.14-16)
WEBSTER James U23 27.02.95, Liverpool H/Bath Un
400H- 52.21
WEBSTER Todd U20 28.11.99, Chesterfield
PV- 4.18, DECJ- 5380
WEEKES Robert V35 15.03.82, East Hull
50kR- 3:19:04
WEIR Richard 7.08.84, Derby AC
1500- 3:48.02 (3:41.93i-15), 5k- 14:09.32 (13:41.83-16),
HMar- 65:48 (65:46-16)
WELLINGTON Lachlan U17 25.06.01, City of Portsmouth
1500- 4:02.34, 3k- 8:37.46
WELLS Ronnie U23 27.03.96, Yeovil Olympiads
60- 6.70i, 100- 10.36w/10.46 (10.46-16),
200- 21.74 (21.58-16)
WEST James U23 30.01.96, Tonbridge/Loughborough St
800- 1:49.03, 1500- 3:39.65,
3k- 7:58.94i/8:00.66 (7:58.47-16), 5k- 14:01.37
WESTLAKE James 8.08.91, Crawley
Mar- 2:26:38
WESTLEY Jack U17 1.10.01, Kingston & Poly
PV- 3.60
WESTMACOTT William U17 8.04.01, Andover
100HY- 13.95
WHARTON Max U23 8.07.96, Liverpool H/St Marys Un
800- 1:50.76 (1:48.81-16)
WHEATER Steven U17 21.02.01, Middlesboro Mandale
HJ- 1.98i/1.98
WHEBLE Andrew 21.10.86, Kingston & Poly
DT- 41.24 (45.37-14)
WHEELER Michael James 23.09.91, Herne Hill
SP- 15.73 (17.08-12)
WHEELER-SEXTON Harri Luca U17 25.11.00, Cardiff
60HY- 8.37i, LJ- 6.45i, HeplY- 4345i, DecY- 5305,
OctY- 4366
WHITE Guy U15 6.01.03, Tonbridge
SPB- 13.09
WHITE Jack U17 25.10.00, City of Norwich
3k- 8:47.11
WHITE Ricky U15 3.02.03, Middlesex Schools
SPB- 13.49
WHITEAKER James U20 8.10.98, Blackheath & Bromley
JT- 77.03
WHITEHEAD Caspar U23 1.10.96, TVH/Oxford Un
JT- 53.51
WHITEHEAD Ryan U17 22.01.01, Enfield & Haringey
DTY- 42.90
WHITEMAN Anthony William V45 13.11.71, Shaftesbury B
800- 1:49.86 (1:45.81-00), 1500- 3:48.72 (3:32.34-97)
WHITTAKER Paul 14.07.89, Southend
HMar- 66:55 (66:01-15)
WHYTE Stephen Anthony V50 14.03.64, Thames Valley
HT- 50.74 (67.82-89)
WIGELSWORTH Matthew U23 27.09.96, Preston/Liv Un
800- 1:50.07, 1500- 3:47.31
WIGFIELD Joseph U20 18.01.00, Wirral
800- 1:52.83

WIGHTMAN Benjamin U17 1.03.01, Perth
SPY- 14.93i/14.40
WIGHTMAN Jack U23 30.11.95, Newquay & Par/Lough St
400- 47.61 (47.32-15)
WIGHTMAN Jake Stanley 11.07.94, Edinburgh AC
800- 1:45.42, 1500- 3:34.17, 1M- 3:54.92 (3:54.20-16),
5kR- 14:18, 10kR- 30:29
WIGNALL James 24.11.91, Sale
3kSt- 9:41.86
WILD Tariq U15 22.04.03, Highgate H
60- 7.44i, 100- 11.05, 200- 22.56, 300- 36.75, 400- 52.6
WILDE Dan U20 13.07.99, Taunton
400H- 55.25
WILKINSON Callum U23 14.03.97, Enfield & Haringey
1MW- 6:01.93, 3kW- 11:13.09, 5kW- 18:56.96,
10kWR- 40:46+ (40:30-16), 20kW- 1:22:17
WILKINSON George U17 25.04.02, Enfield & Haringey
5kW- 26:15.00
WILKINSON Joe U23 27.06.96, Lincoln Wellington
1500- 3:47.06, 3k- 8:11.26, 5k- 14:19.63, 10kR- 30:23
WILLIAMS Alfie U15 8.07.03, West Norfolk
SPB- 13.68
WILLIAMS Angus U15 7.12.02, Chiltern H
800- 2:02.26, 1500- 4:11.0, 3k- 9:12.28
WILLIAMS Benjamin 25.01.92, Sale
LJ- 7.46, TJ- 16.73 (16.74-15)
WILLIAMS Christie U20 2.12.98, West Suffolk
800- 1:53.09
WILLIAMS Cole U15 12.02.03, Stratford-upon-Avon
60HB- 9.34i, 80HB- 11.59
WILLIAMS Conrad V35 20.03.82, Kent
200- 21.49 (20.89w-15, 20.96-11), 400- 46.54 (45.06-15)
WILLIAMS Delano 23.12.93, Enfield & Haringey
400- 45.85 (45.42-15)
WILLIAMS Ian 8.03.85, Tipton
Mar- 2:28:30 (2:24:56-15)
WILLIAMS Jahde U23 14.01.97, Harrow
100- 10.71, 200- 21.47w/21.48
WILLIAMS James 1.10.91, Liverpool H
60- 6.80i, 100- 10.55 (10.37w/10.42-13),
200- 21.90 (21.06w-16), 300- 33.14
WILLIAMS Luke 23.02.88, Ashford
Dec- 4272 (4435-14)
WILLIAMS Matthew U20 20.12.98, Pembroke
800- 1:51.66
WILLIAMS Oshay U17 4.02.02, Birchfield
100- 11.02w
WILLIAMS Samir U20 6.01.00, Croydon
60- 6.87i, 100- 10.58+/10.59w/10.6/10.61, 200- 21.78
WILLIAMS Thomas U23 28.01.96, Barry & Vale/Card Met
60- 6.90i, 100- 10.47w/10.51, 200- 20.96
WILLIAMS Timothy 7.07.92, Gloucester AC
HT- 63.28
WILLIAMS Tyler U20 21.05.98, Swansea/Cardiff Met
100- 10.77, 200- 21.89
WILLIAMSON Ethan U17 29.09.01, Lagan Valley
60HY- 8.58i
WILLIAMSON Jamie 16.07.87, City of Sheffield
SP- 14.56 (18.29i-13, 18.17-12), DT- 47.02 (59.58-12)
WILLIAMSON Jamie U23 3.03.97, Springburn H/Lough St
800- 1:50.45 (1:50.06-15), 1500- 3:47.93 (3:45.45-16)
WILLIAMS-STEIN Cameron U15 29.04.03, Leamington
PV- 3.20, TJ- 12.34, OctB- 3764
WILLIS Dale 17.06.88, Corby/RNAC
400- 48.9 (47.97-15)
WILLMORE Fraser U17 29.09.01, Cheltenham
3k- 8:53.16
WILLS Benjamin U17 21.09.00, Bracknell
1.5kSt- 4:39.3
WILSMORE Michael 8.06.85, Bristol & West
3k- 8:17.33i
WILSON Jaedon U13 7.02.05, Sutton & District
200- 25.5
WILSON Jerome U15 5.03.03, Dacorum & Tring
HJ- 1.75
WILSON Kenneth 29.12.89, Moray RR
10kR- 30:25, HMar- 67:37

WILSON Kevin 6.01.90, Chelmsford/POR
  SP- 13.10 (13.58-16), DT- 43.57 (44.05-16)
WILSON Michael U23 1.02.97, Swansea/Cardiff Met
  60H- 8.43i, 110H- 15.13
WILSON Michael U23 4.01.96, Sunderland/B'ham Un
  800- 1:51.67 (1:49.76-16), 1500- 3:47.27
WILSON Nathan U13, Essex Schools
  75HC- 11.8
WILSON Ryan U15 1.01.03, Barrow & Furness
  100- 11.3, DTB- 41.69
WILSON DYER GOUGH Sebastian 2.06.90, Herne Hill
  LJ- 7.10
WILSON-KEPPLE Josiah U15 20.06.03, Team Hounslow
  TJ- 13.18
WILTSHIRE Ethan U17 29.06.02, Marshall Milton K
  200- 22.34
WILTSHIRE Nick U17 24.10.00, Reading
  1500- 4:00.78
WINN Joseph U20 27.09.98, Thurrock
  HJ- 1.95i (2.00-15)
WINSON Ryan 21.09.92, Derby AC
  HT- 44.30
WINTER Gareth 19.03.92, City of Sheffield
  SP- 17.42 (18.07-15), DT- 48.13 (50.73-16)
WISE Joshua U17 24.11.01, Southampton
  SPY- 13.73, JTY- 54.75
WOLSKI Robert 8.12.82, W.Green & Ex L/POL
  HJ- 2.05 (2.31-06)
WOOD Connor U20 25.11.98, Sale
  60- 6.96i, 200- 21.19i/21.26w/21.32 (21.08-16),
  400- 48.66 (47.45-16)
WOOD Curtis U23 29.06.97, Cambridge & Coleridge
  HJ- 2.03i/2.00
WOOD Jordan U20 26.03.99, Cambridge & Coleridge
  2kSt- 6:04.05
WOOD Kieran U23 3.11.95, Cambridge & Col/Cardiff Met
  1500- 3:45.62
WOOD Thomas U15 14.03.03, Wakefield
  200- 23.26
WOODAGE Callum U17 25.10.00, Watford
  PV- 4.11
WOODHALL Richard V35 9.07.80, Dudley & Stourbridge
  SP- 13.74 (14.08-16), HT- 46.21 (47.69-16),
  JT- 55.80 (60.67-12)
WOODLEY Mark 7.03.88, Chelmsford
  800- 1:49.81
WOODLEY Samuel U20 17.11.99, Herts Phoenix
  DT- 43.89, DTJ- 49.64
WOODS Josh Morgan U17 5.08.02, Dacorum & Tring
  LJ- 6.55, TJ- 13.53
WOOLGAR Robert 3.03.93, Bournemouth
  LJ- 7.11
WOOLLEY Richard 17.08.89, Mansfield H
  JT- 54.58 (62.03-08)
WORDSWORTH James U15 13.06.03, North Shields P
  SPB- 13.72, DTB- 41.54
WORGAN Aaron U15 3.10.02, Cornwall AC
  DTB- 44.62
WORMAN Jamie U20 23.12.99, Cheltenham
  DECJ- 5718
WORMAN Robert U17 4.07.01, Cheltenham
  100HY- 13.7, PV- 4.00, LJ- 6.48, DecY- 6104,
  OctY- 4785+
WORRALL Joseph U17 26.04.01, Carmarthen
  DTY- 49.87
WORT Alexander 18.09.93, Sale/Brunel Un
  110H- 15.00 (14.56w-15, 14.59-16)
WORTHINGTON Sam U15 7.02.03, Sale
  300- 36.5/36.82
WRIGHT Andrew U23 13.09.95, Willowfield/Cardiff Un
  1500- 3:48.91i (3:47.61-16)

WRIGHT Bailey U17 14.11.00, Eastbourne
  60- 6.97i/7.12i, 100- 10.8/10.82, 200- 22.4/22.45
WRIGHT Cameron U17 25.08.01, Kilbarchan
  1.5kSt- 4:27.47, 2kSt- 6:13.37
WRIGHT Ciaran U23 17.09.96, City of Sheffield
  SP- 14.10, HT- 62.74 (63.81-16)
WRIGHT Fionn U23 25.09.95, Exeter/Loughborough St
  Dec- 5582 (5665-16)
WRIGHT Fraser U23 28.06.96, Gateshead/N'land Un
  DT- 44.15 (44.90-15)
WRIGHT Michael 24.03.87, Central
  Mar- 2:29:37 (2:28:34-15), 3kSt- 9:34.50 (9:26.94-13)
WRIGHT Nathan U15 24.10.02, Notts
  SPB- 14.35
WRIGHT Oliver U17 21.10.00, City of York
  JTY- 58.01
WRIGHT Shawn 25.11.94, Livingston/Loughborough St
  400- 47.89
WRIGHT Thomas U17 23.09.00, Dacorum & Tring
  HJ- 1.98, LJ- 6.45
WUIDART Jack U23 6.09.97, Bedford/Leeds Beck Un
  HT- 50.23
WYLLIE Shaun U23 27.02.95, Bracknell/St Marys Un
  800- 1:50.5 (1:49.50-13), 1500- 3:45.13 (3:41.43-14)

Y ABSLEY Alfred U17 12.09.99, Marshall Milton K
  2kSt- 5:54.43
YANG Christopher U13 9.12.04, Hampshire Schools
  100- 12.19w
YARWOOD Liam 10.09.94, Sale
  PV- 5.02i (5.05i-15, 5.01-16)
YATES Charlie U17 15.02.01, Banbury
  LJ- 6.48
YEE Alexander U20 18.02.98, Kent AC
  5k- 13:37.60
YEO Archie U15 8.03.03, Scunthorpe
  LJ- 6.72i/6.58w/6.55, TJ- 12.90, PenB- 2964,
  PenIB- 2463i
YEXLEY Oliver U13 29.09.04, Havering
  JTC- 44.35
YOUNG Anthony 14.09.92, Kilbarchan
  400- 48.30 (47.87-16)
YOUNG James U17 28.11.00, Enfield & Haringey
  3k- 8:52.31
YOUNG Max U17 11.07.02, Reading
  PV- 3.65
YOUNG Nicholas U20 17.05.00, Deeside
  SPJ- 15.14, DTJ- 46.59
YOUNG Reece U23 3.10.95, Blackheath & Br/Brunel Un
  60H- 8.11i, 110H- 14.74
YOUSIF Rabah Mohammed 11.12.86, Newham & Essex B
  300- 32.95 (32.31-14), 400- 45.58 (44.54-15)

Z AMAN-BROWNE Rocco U17 4.12.00, Manchester
  800- 1:56.71
ZANGRANDO Agegnehu U13 16.12.04, Herc Wimbledon
  100- 12.2
ZATAT Youcef 13.04.94, W.Green & Ex L/East London Un
  SP- 18.34, DT- 49.10
ZELLER Joshua U17 19.10.00, Bracknell
  60HY- 8.17i, 100HY- 12.93
ZOLA Basil U13 13.11.04, Sale
  HJ- 1.64, LJ- 5.15
ZOPPOS Gregory U15 10.03.03, Middlesex Schools
  80HB- 11.62w, PenB- 2753
ZOTIN Serg 21.05.83, Chelmsford/EST
  HJ- 1.95 (2.00-07)
ZYGADLO Shaun U20 16.06.00, Pembroke
  110HY- 14.79

WOMEN'S INDEX

ABEL Maisie U15 10.02.03, Guildford & Godalming
PenG- 2809
ABIWU Karen U15 8.10.02, Sutton & District
60- 7.99i
ABRAHAM Jessica Francis 26.01.89, Cardiff
PV- 3.93 (4.02i-11, 4.00-10)
ABRAMS Sarah 11.01.93, Blackheath & Bromley
LJ- 5.71i/5.69 (5.98-11)
ACHURCH Emma U23 9.07.97, Leicester WC
3kW- 13:48.83i (13:29.19i-15, 13:58.73-16),
5kW- 27:02.5 (24:14.96-14)
ADAM Georgina Diana U20 24.03.00, Lincoln Wellington
100- 11.94mx/12.1 (12.0/12.12-16), 200- 23.87
ADAMS Caroline 5.02.91, City of Sheffield/Hallam Un
PV- 3.50i/3.32 (4.05-13)
ADAMS Holly U15 30.12.03, Kingston upon Hull
SPI- 11.08
ADAMS Vikki U20 23.02.98, Leeds/Leeds Beck Un
SP- 11.26i, JT- 38.90 (39.67-15)
ADAMSON Elizabeth U15 6.05.03, Southampton
SPI- 11.58, DT- 32.82
ADAMSON Oreoluwa U17 29.10.01, Herne Hill
LJ- 6.00w/5.98
ADEBAYO Daphney U13 20.07.05, City of Sheffield
LJ- 5.10, SPM- 11.48
ADEBAYO Dara U17 14.06.02, Harrow
SP- 12.65, SPI- 14.12i/14.06
ADEGOKE Diana U23 18.12.97, Thanet AC/Wolvs Un
LJ- 5.83i/5.65 (5.86-16)
ADENIJI Mary U20 13.02.99, Blackheath & Bromley
TJ- 11.37
ADEOKUN Mobolaji 14.01.94, East London Un/NGR
60H- 8.52i (8.27i-15), 100H- 13.56 (13.24w/13.29-15)
ADE-ONOJOBI Gabriella 1.08.93, Cambridge H
100H- 14.76 (13.93w-16, 14.06-12)
ADEOSUN Hephzibah U23 29.08.96, Harrow/Camb Un
100- 12.07w
ADEOYE Margaret Adetutu 22.04.85, Enfield & Haringey
60- 7.64 (7.40i-13), 100- 11.70 (11.28-14),
200- 23.60mx/23.78 (22.88-13), 300- 37.72,
400- 52.32 (51.93-13)
ADEROJU Ite U17 9.07.01, Bedford & County
TJ- 11.15
ADEWAKUN Yimika 16.06.93, Blackheath & Bromley
400- 55.46 (55.29-11)
ADU Precious U15 3.10.02, Enfield & Haringey
60- 7.85i, 100- 12.06w/12.22, 200- 24.58
AGYAPONG Finette U23 1.02.97, N&EB/Brunel Un
60- 7.42i, 100- 11.49, 150- 17.61, 200- 22.86,
300- 36.86, 400- 52.41
AGYEI-KYEM Cedelle U15 12.09.02, Team Hounslow
200- 25.89, 300- 41.70
AHLGREN Harriet 19.05.88, Notts/FIN
HT- 45.79
AINGE Natalie 12.03.92, Cannock & Stafford
400H- 62.2/63.12
AINSWORTH Nicole U15 30.09.02, City of Portsmouth
3k- 10:24.03mx
AITCHISON Holly U15 5.12.02, Stockport
LJ- 5.23i, TJ- 11.23i/10.44
AKINFENWA Shanumi U13 1.09.04, Stevenage & NH
HJ- 1.51
AKPE-MOSES Gina U20 25.02.99, Birchfield/IRL
60- 7.47i, 100- 11.56, 200- 24.12i/24.27
ALDERSON Emma U20 29.02.00, Liverpool H
400- 54.54, 800- 2:08.31mx/2:08.57
ALDRIDGE Lauren U20 9.04.99, Stevenage & NH
HT- 43.91
ALEXANDER Charlotte U17 18.01.02, Herne Hill
1500- 4:32.61mx/4:33.77, 3k- 9:31.12mx/9:34.05
ALEXANDER Rachel U20 13.02.98, Giffnock N/S'clyde U
LJ- 5.91 (6.10-15)
ALIU Immanuela U20 19.04.00, Blackheath & Bromley
60- 7.59i, 100- 11.94, 200- 24.39
ALLBUT Olivia U17 17.07.01, Shaftesbury B
400- 58.1, 400H- 65.16

ALLCOCK Amy 20.08.93, Aldershot F&D
60- 7.61i, 100- 11.71mx (11.90-15), 150- 17.58w,
200- 23.48, 300- 37.46, 400- 52.85 (52.83-14)
ALLCOCK Chloe U17 8.02.02, Mansfield H
HJ- 1.63 (1.65i/1.63-16)
ALLEN Jasmyn U15 14.01.03, Southampton
LJ- 5.26
ALLEN Lucy Emma U15 1.04.03, Newquay & Par
PV- 3.46
ALLISTONE-GREAVES Havana U17 6.07.01, At.Sa-
for-Delikia (ESP)
400- 56.91, 800- 2:14.89, 400H- 65.31
ALLSOPP Tilly U15 5.06.03, Notts
HTI- 42.17
ALLUM Olivia U17 21.06.01, West Suffolk
800- 2:13.00mx, 1500- 4:36.68
AMABILINO Silvia 14.10.93, Bristol & W/Bristol Un/LUX
PV- 3.70
AMEND Samantha V35 25.05.79, Belgrave
HMar- 78:28 (77:10-12), Mar- 2:56:00 (2:42:11-11)
ANDERSON Aimee U15 23.01.03, Airdrie
3k- 10:34.93mx
ANDERSON Cara 17.01.92, Perth/Derby Un
800- 2:09.13
ANDERSON Hannah U15 17.09.02, East Kilbride
800- 2:16.65
ANDERSON Lia U17 10.09.00, Woking
SP- 11.25, SPI- 13.54, DT- 39.21 (39.26-16)
ANDERSON Tia U15 19.12.02, Durham City H
100- 12.5, 200- 25.3/25.49, 300- 40.35, 400- 57.83
ANDERSSON Emma Kiviniemi 3.10.91, Shaft B/SWE
PV- 3.95
ANDREW Emily U17 20.08.02, Inverness
3k- 10:09.13
ANNING Amber Amelia Ka U17 18.11.00, Brighton & Hove
60- 7.62i, 100- 11.79, 200- 23.76, 300- 37.79,
400- 53.68, TJ- 11.48 (11.65-15)
ANSELL Bethany 10.09.94, C of Sheffield/Manchester Un
800- 2:07.93
ANSON Catherine Rose U23 14.03.95, Liverpool/Man Un
HJ- 1.80
ANTHONY Justine 2.12.93, W.Suffolk/South Methodist Un
5k- 17:10.69
ANTWI Christabel U15 18.10.02, Edinburgh AC
60- 7.79i, 100- 12.41, 200- 25.70
APSLEY Elizabeth U23 12.01.97, Stockport/Cambridge U
3k- 9:47.20mx, 5k- 17:18.94
ARBON Alex Emily U15 29.11.03, Sutton in Ashfield
JTI- 34.83
ARCHER Holly 7.11.93, West Suffolk/South Methodist Un
800- 2:07.37 (2:07.27-16), 1500- 4:22.36,
3k- 9:38.42i (9:31.56i-15), 5kR- 16:37
ARCHER Sonyce U20 3.02.99, Croydon
TJ- 11.56
AREGBE Laura U20 22.03.98, Harrow
60- 7.74i
ARMAH Jessica 29.08.83, WSE&H
200- 24.8
ARMORGIE Laura U23 5.12.97, Herts Phoenix
HJ- 1.82i/1.71 (1.78-16)
ARMOUSH Tamara 8.05.92, Birchfield/JOR
1500- 4:18.25, 1M- 4:46.23mx/4:46.82, 3k- 9:25.64,
10kR- 34:28
ARNOLD Caitlin U17 24.09.00, Newport
SPI- 12.39
ARNOLD Hollie 26.06.94, Cleethorpes
JT- 43.02
ARTER Charlotte 18.06.91, Eden Runners
1500- 4:18.89 (4:14.41-15), 3k- 8:58.48, 5k- 15:40.15,
10k- 32:37.52, 15kR- 52:28+ (51:52+-16),
HMar- 74:00+ (73:19-16)
ARTHUR Melissa U23 14.01.95, Newport
JT- 40.81 (42.07-14)
ARULANANDAM Donelle U23 21.04.97, Aylesb/Notts Un
TJ- 11.21

ASANTE Zara 7.07.82, Blackheath & Bromley
TJ- 12.57 (13.00i-15, 12.99-13)
ASARE Angel U17 10.03.02, Herne Hill
60- 7.79i
ASHE Lucy 20.10.88, Harrow
Mar- 2:54:47
ASHER-SMITH Geraldina U23 4.12.95, Blackheath & Br
60- 7.13i (7.08i-15), 100- 11.13 (10.99-15), 150-
16.70st, 200- 22.22 (22.07-15)
ASHMEADE Leonie U17 25.01.01, Wakefield
60- 7.74i, 100- 11.98, 200- 25.28
ASHURST Sophie U15 26.04.03, Sale
PV- 3.56
ATKINSON Ellie U23 15.10.96, Cardiff/Yale Un
1M- 4:47.43i
AUSTIN Olivia U13 31.10.04, Southampton
SPM- 10.81, DTM- 32.73
AUSTRIDGE Yasmin U20 11.08.00, Blackheath & Bromley
1.5kSt- 5:01.68 (4:54.82-15), 2kSt- 7:18.40,
400H- 65.15 (63.98-16)
AWALA-SHAW Dolita U17 7.11.00, Newham & Essex B
100- 11.95, 200- 24.99
AWUAH Kristal U20 7.08.99, Herne Hill
60- 7.49i, 100- 11.61
AYTON Charlotte U17 17.09.00, Wimborne
LJ- 5.59

B ABALOLA Ayoola U17 17.12.01, WSE&H
60- 7.79imx/7.84i, 100- 12.24 (12.17-16)
BACAKOVA Karolinka U17 13.04.02, Neath
HTI- 47.03
BAGGOTT Phoebe U17 11.11.01, Wolves & Bilston
HT- 47.93, HTI- 59.21
BAGNATI Marta 11.02.85, Serpentine/ITA
Mar- 2:53:36
BAILEY Ashleigh U17 19.01.01, Solihull & S H
SPI- 13.12i/12.96, HepI- 4410
BAILEY Megan U20 22.01.98, Harrow
PV- 3.50
BAILEY Niamh U23 28.06.95, Corby/DMU (Beds) Un
60H- 8.57i, 100H- 14.05 (13.95w-16),
LJ- 5.63 (5.92i/5.81-16), SP- 11.92i/11.85
BAINSFAIR Kiera U17 3.02.02, Basildon
60HI- 8.78i, 80HI- 11.5/11.51w/11.75, 300H- 43.81,
HepI- 4256, PenII- 3559i
BAIRD Aislinn 4.11.91, Radley AC
HT- 50.40
BAKARE Emma U17 20.11.00, North Somerset
SPI- 13.69
BAKARE Sabrina U23 14.05.96, Shaftesbury B/Lough St
200- 24.93 (24.49-13), 400- 54.03 (52.77-13)
BAKER Alex U17 27.12.01, Pendle
JTI- 40.78
BAKER Ellie U20 3.06.98, Shaftesbury B
400- 56.11, 800- 2:04.67, 1500- 4:25.27 (4:25.23mx-13)
BAKER Jessica V35 6.06.82, Sydney Striders(AUS)
24Hr- 238.713km
BALL Emily U23 31.10.97, West Cheshire/Sheffield Un
SP- 13.08i/12.60, DT- 38.66 (40.10-15)
BALLANTYNE Emma 20.06.88, City of York
Mar- 2:57:21 (2:55:03-16)
BANBURY Anastasia U17 19.08.01, Walton
HT- 39.49, HTI- 50.00
BANBURY Eevee-May U20 19.05.00, North Devon
1.5kSt- 5:10.57
BANJO Susannah 28.07.89, Newham & Essex B
400- 54.11
BANKS Andrea V40 27.09.72, Jersey Spartan AC
Mar- 2:57:53 (2:54:27-16)
BANKS Faye V35 11.08.79, Pontefract
HMar- 77:50, Mar- 2:50:31
BAPTISTE Kimbely 27.12.92, Crawley/London Un
100- 11.50w/11.62, 200- 23.34
BARBER Ellen U23 5.12.97, Yeovil Olympiads
100H- 15.30, HJ- 1.70 (1.71-16), LJ- 5.74w/5.66,
SP- 12.09, JT- 43.51, Hep- 5344
BARBOUR Alexandra U20 1.03.99, WSE&H
1.5kSt- 4:54.22, 2kSt- 7:03.36

BARBOUR Emma U17 17.02.02, Giffnock N
HJ- 1.70i
BARBOUR Sara U15 21.01.03, Kilmarnock
PV- 2.60
BARCLAY Amy 14.04.92, Crawley
100H- 14.8/14.81 (13.77-14), 400H- 63.78
BARCLAY Evie U17 6.10.00, Wigan
JTI- 41.34
BARKER Phoebe U20 27.11.99, Tonbridge
3k- 9:36.06, 5k- 16:44.07
BARKES Claudia U20 1.02.00, Darlington
PV- 3.50
BARLOW Beth U20 8.04.00, Salford
800- 2:08.49, 1500- 4:24.31
BARLOW Tracy 18.06.85, Thames Valley
10kR- 34:01, 15kR- 51:43+, HMar- 72:48, Mar- 2:30:42
BARLOW Victoria U17 12.02.01, Sale
PV- 3.80i/3.71
BARNDEN Hannah U17 8.01.02, Derby AC
80HI- 11.91, LJ- 5.56, SPI- 12.83i/12.42, HepI- 4510
BARNES Daisy U20 15.07.00, Notts
PV- 3.50
BARNES Heather U17 15.01.02, Giffnock N
3k- 9:50.69
BARNES Paige U20 9.01.99, Marshall Milton K
HT- 43.66
BARNES Ruth V35 7.10.78, Avon Valley R
5kR- 16:38, 10kR- 34:29 (34:18-16), 10MR- 56:44,
HMar- 75:32
BARNES Stephanie 28.07.88, Bristol & West
1500- 4:14.37, 3k- 9:15.58, 5k- 16:05.55 (16:01.78-16)
BARNES-HEENEY Danielle Claire 8.10.85, WSE&H
1500- 4:24.91 (4:15.00-03)
BARNSDALE Alice U20 23.02.99, Lincoln Wellington
HT- 56.03
BARRETT Alicia Helen U20 25.03.98, Chest'fld/Hallam Un
60- 7.70i (7.5imx-14, 7.64i-15), 200- 24.69, 60H- 8.19i,
100H- 13.07
BARRETT Angela 25.12.85, Thames Valley
LJ- 6.09, TJ- 13.43
BARRETT Eleanor U17 30.04.02, Blackheath & Bromley
PV- 3.13i/3.10 (3.10-16)
BARRETT Ella T U20 25.03.98, Chesterfield
200- 24.18 (24.03-15), 400- 56.20mx/56.25 (54.63-16)
BARRETT Samantha U20 22.10.98, Bristol & West
TJ- 11.30
BARROW Leah 21.01.93, WSE&H
400- 55.38mx (54.82mx-15, 54.87-16),
800- 2:05.50 (2:03.18i-16, 2:03.22-15)
BARWELL India U13 4.03.05, Lincoln Wellington
PV- 2.30
BATCHELDOR Caitlin U17 23.04.02, Poole
HTI- 51.06
BATE Jemma V35 13.03.82, Trafford
DT- 37.78 (44.75-06)
BATEMAN Amelia Eve U17 13.11.00, Gateshead
HJ- 1.68 (1.73-15)
BATES Anna 18.05.87, Trafford
TJ- 12.07i/12.07w/12.04 (12.71w/12.58i-07, 12.51-06)
BATES Annabelle 12.05.94, Thames Valley/Cambridge Un
HJ- 1.65 (1.70-16)
BATES Anya U20 17.05.00, Birchfield
60H- 8.76i, 100HI- 13.87, 100H- 14.1/14.22,
LJ- 5.88i/5.76w/5.71 (5.74-16)
BATTLE Amy U15 31.05.04, Stockport
SPI- 11.45i
BAUER Carolin U20 17.06.00, Shaftesbury B/GER
PV- 3.55 (3.65-16)
BAULK Florence U17 10.12.00, Woking
JTI- 40.43
BAXENDALE Alice U17 31.10.01, VP-Glasgow
DT- 37.06
BAXTER Sarah V35 15.12.77, Team Bath
Mar- 2:57:39
BAYO Lucy U15 16.09.02, Crawley
PV- 2.70
BEADLE Katy U13 27.10.04, Slough Juniors
LJ- 4.96

BEALES Emma Jay V45 7.12.71, Marshall Milton K
DT- 42.59 (54.68-95)
BEAN Poppy U20 18.08.00, Notts
HT- 44.05
BEARDMORE Emma 6.12.87, Marshall Milton K
SP- 11.52, DT- 36.92 (37.24-16), HT- 49.41
BEATTY Cathrine 12.07.93, Bristol & W/Lough St/CYP
HT- 60.80
BECKFORD Lily U23 11.08.97, Shaftesbury B/Brunel Un
100- 12.12w, 200- 24.67w (24.91-15),
400- 54.24mx/54.50 (53.50-16)
BEE Emily U17 3.03.02, City of Plymouth
200- 25.37, 80HI- 11.17w/11.21, Hepl- 4872
BEESLEY Meghan Danielle 15.11.89, Birchfield/Lough St
60- 7.64i (7.54i-09), 200- 24.32w/24.35 (23.53-15),
400- 54.20i (52.79-11), 60H- 8.57i (8.54i-14),
100H- 13.84 (13.21-15), 400H- 56.14 (54.52-15)
BEETHAM-GREEN Mary U17 26.03.02, Rugby & North
100- 12.3/12.37
BEGLEY Aisling U20 27.10.99, Reading
PV- 3.10
BELL Alexandra 4.11.92, Pudsey & Bramley
800- 2:00.62 (2:00.53-16), 1500- 4:12.62mx (4:18.83-15)
BELL Alyson U15 9.11.03, Giffnock North
60- 7.96i, 100- 12.31w/12.36, 200- 25.48, 300- 40.35
BELL Annie U15 17.02.03, Border
800- 2:17.8
BELL Georgia 17.10.93, Shaftesbury B/UC Berkeley
800- 2:10.11 (2:03.38-14), 1500- 4:25.58 (4:16.96-15)
BELL Nicola U17 27.11.00, Walton
JTI- 41.93 (42.10-16)
BELL Rachel U23 20.11.96, Cleethorpes/Bath Un
60- 7.64i, 100- 11.96w (12.10-16)
BELYAVIN Julia R. V35 10.07.79, Bristol & West
Mar- 2:56:03 (2:49:51-15)
BENNETT Gemma Samantha 4.01.84, Shaftesbury B
60H- 8.38i (8.06i-09), 100H- 13.71 (13.02-08)
BENNETT Jessica Charlie U15 6.02.03, Southampton
HTI- 39.49
BENNETT Rachel U17 3.07.02, Shildon
60- 7.77i, 100- 12.28 (12.21-16), 200- 25.00
BENNETT-CORDY Alexia U15 1.02.03, Tipton
60HG- 9.15i, 75HG- 11.28w/11.4/11.46
BENSON Holly U17 17.08.02, Stockport
SPI- 12.77
BENSON Tayla U23 20.08.96, Thames Valley/Brunel Un
100H- 14.35w/14.40
BENTHAM Elizabeth U17 13.04.02, Luton
800- 2:14.23mx
BENTLEY Claire 11.10.94, Watford
3kSt- 11:29.64
BERRY Hayley U15 4.07.03, Law & District
SPI- 11.17, DT- 32.01
BEYNON-THOMAS Alaw 15.11.89, Swansea
5kR- 16:49 (16:39.13t-12), 10k- 35:49.1
BICKFORD Taylor 27.08.93, Serpentine/USA
HMar- 78:32
BIGGERSTAFF Jessica U17 15.01.01, Watford
HJ- 1.65
BILLINGHAM Chloe U20 14.01.98, Horsham BS/
Cambridge Un   PV- 3.60
BILON Mathilde U23 13.03.97, WGreen & Ex L/FRA
SP- 13.21
BINGLE Katherine 16.12.93, Aldershot F&D
3k- 9:33.52mx, 5k- 16:54.36
BIRD Elizabeth 4.10.94, Shaftesbury B/Princeton Un
1500- 4:20.92, 1M- 4:44.38i (4:39.32i-16),
3k- 9:34.89i (9:18.42i-16, 9:34.85-13), 5k- 16:49.06,
3kSt- 10:09.04 (9:54.76-15)
BIRD Melissa Anne U20 18.09.98, Cheltenham
DT- 37.83 (38.19-15)
BIRD Sara 28.01.87, Ipswich Jaffa
Mar- 2:55:34 (2:40:00-14)
BIRKETT Amelia U17 14.09.01, Rugby & Northampton
PV- 2.90i
BIRMINGHAM Nichole U20 9.01.00, Birchfield
SP- 11.60
BIRRELL Sasha U23 17.05.96, City of Norwich
PV- 3.31

BISHELL Abigail U23 11.02.95, C of Sheffield/Hallam Un
60- 7.70i, 100- 11.83w/12.04, 200- 24.88w/24.9 (24.72-11)
BLACKMORE Allison V50 66,
Mar- 2:56:15dh, 50kR- 3:52:12+
BLACKWELL Imogen U13 24.03.05, Preston
800- 2:21.12
BLAIKIE Michelle U15 10.10.02, Lasswade
HJ- 1.65i/1.62
BLAIR Joanna Louise 1.03.86, Luton
JT- 53.52 (57.44-16)
BLAKE Danielle U20 5.03.98, Cambridge H/Brunel Un
60- 7.64i
BLAKEMAN Catherine U23 19.03.97, C de Nerja (ESP)
400H- 64.48
BLEAKEN Loren U23 3.09.95, Birchfield/Cardiff Met
400- 56.02 (53.96-14)
BLOOD Hannah U17 15.06.01, Sale
HT- 41.71, HTI- 49.06
BLOOR Louise 21.09.85, Trafford
100- 11.65w/11.67 (11.43-15), 200- 23.65 (23.31-13)
BLUNDELL Jenna U17 12.06.01, Team Bath
60HI- 8.83i, 80HI- 11.85 (11.37w/11.50-16)
BLUNT Clare 28.09.87, Kingston upon Hull
PV- 4.00
BOBASH Sara 1.02.94, Birchfield
HT- 54.06 (56.40-16)
BOFFEY Isabelle Sian U20 13.04.00, Enfield & Haringey
800- 2:04.64
BONIFACE Anna 27.04.91, Reading
5k- 17:19.4mx, HMar- 76:35, Mar- 2:37:17
BOOKER Ellie U17 28.03.01, Rotherham
200- 24.87 (24.67-16)
BOOTH Myah U15 20.01.04, Blackburn
75HG- 11.6
BOOTHBY Clara U23 18.09.95, Liverpool H/Liverpool Un
LJ- 5.60i (5.70i/5.69-16)
BORTHWICK Emily U23 2.09.97, Wigan/Liverpool Un
HJ- 1.83i/1.83
BOTHAM Emma U17 28.05.01, Chesterfield
DT- 41.22
BOTTOMLEY Sophia U15 26.10.02, Harrogate
LJ- 5.35
BOWDEN Philippa U23 29.03.95, AF&D/Brunel Un
3k- 9:26.92mx/9:39.98i, 5k- 16:11.48, 10k- 33:44.24,
HMar- 76:30, 3kSt- 10:14.26
BOWEN Amy U23 27.06.97, Telford/Cardiff Met
100- 12.16w
BOWER Grace U20 3.11.99, Sale
100H- 14.8/14.92w/15.01, HJ- 1.68i/1.68, LJ- 5.74,
Hep- 4776, PentIS- 3713i
BOWIE Emma U23 22.12.96, Moray RR
HT- 46.55 (52.31-13)
BOWIE Ruby U13 2.01.05, Crewe & Nantwich
75- 10.0
BOWLEY Kayla U17 28.12.01, Croydon
60- 7.75i, 100- 12.35 (12.3-16), 200- 24.85 (24.77-16)
BOWNESS Bryher 10.02.93, Southampton
HMar- 78:22
BRADBEER Kara U23 28.01.95, Pitreavie/Heriot Watt
PV- 3.30 (3.57-16)
BRADLEY Chloe 27.03.93, WGreen & Ex L/Lough St
800- 2:08.07i/2:08.45, 1500- 4:26.91i (4:25.59-16)
BRADSHAW Holly Bethan 2.11.91, Blackburn
PV- 4.81 (4.87i-12), SP- 11.81i (11.32-11)
BRADY-JONES Keira U13 25.04.05, Wirral
800- 2:21.01, 1200- 3:50.3, 1500- 4:56.8
BRAMHALD Kelly 10.06.94, Doncaster
JT- 49.56
BRAND Lily U13 31.12.04, Braintree
JTM- 32.39
BREED Olivia U13 28.02.06, Tonbridge
1200- 3:53.8
BREEDEN Isabel Hamilton U17 26.07.01, Cardiff
60HI- 8.92i, 100HI- 14.70, 100H- 14.94, 300H- 44.50
BREEN Erin Rose U20 28.12.98, Herts Phoenix
PV- 3.40
BRENNAN Orla U17 8.02.02, WSE&H
80HI- 12.00, 300H- 44.30

408

BRENTON Laura 20.06.86, Southampton
5MR- 27:51
BRETT Maria U23 16.10.95, Newquay & Par/Oxford Un
HT- 45.82 (47.13-13)
BREWSTER Jade U23 20.02.97, Swansea/Cardiff Met
PV- 3.83i/3.65 (3.70-15)
BRIAN Fiona 27.01.86, Metro Aberdeen
10kR- 34:59, HMar- 78:16, Mar- 2:48:47
BRIDET Yasmin U15 29.11.02, Bournemouth
75HG- 11.6/11.61
BRIDGE Gemma 17.05.93, Oxford City
3kW- 12:59.75, 5kWR- 22:52+, 10kWR- 45:52+, 20kW- 1:32:33
BRIDGE Isobelle U17 24.12.01, Blackheath & Bromley
5kW- 28:07.6
BRIDGER Ruby U15 6.05.03, Thurrock
60HG- 9.08i, 75HG- 11.05w/11.07, HJ- 1.62, LJ- 5.50,
PenG- 3180
BRIER Hannah U20 3.02.98, Swansea/Loughborough St
60- 7.31i, 100- 11.61 (11.37w/11.39-15),
200- 24.46 (23.25w/23.59-15)
BRIGGS Eleanor 20.12.92, Inverness
400- 55.42
BRINDLE Micaela 22.02.94, Wigan
LJ- 5.69 (6.09-13)
BRINT Francesca U20 30.08.00, Sale
800- 2:09.35mx, 1500- 4:26.08
BRISCOE Julie V40 11.02.76, Wakefield
10kR- 34:52 (34:19-14), HMar- 77:06 (73:29-11)
BRISTOWE Katie U17 11.03.02, Crawley
60HI- 8.85, 80HI- 11.84
BRITANE Laurensa 18.05.87, Thames Valley
DT- 42.76 (45.99-14), JT- 49.13
BROADBELT-BLAKE Angelita 12.09.85, Thames Valley
200- 24.94 (24.8-11, 24.88w-15), 100H- 13.58 (13.07w/13.18-11)
BROADBRIDGE Helen Jane 23.07.92, Newbury
SP- 11.31, DT- 44.72, HT- 53.67
BROADFOOT Rachel U17 6.06.02, Dundee HH
80HI- 11.78
BROCK Grace U17 22.02.01, Cornwall AC
3k- 10:03.40 (10:02.0-16)
BROCKLEY-LANGFORD Ty U15 8.11.02, East Cheshire
800- 2:17.99mx
BRODERICK Lucy U15 27.09.02, Reigate
800- 2:17.50
BROMFIELD Demi U23 17.03.96, Newham & Essex B
JT- 38.21 (43.14-12)
BROOKS Hannah 25.06.88, Crawley
1500- 4:26.41mx (4:12.27-12), 3k- 9:46.46 (9:11.86-12)
BROOM Danielle U20 28.10.99, Bournemouth
DT- 43.30, HT- 56.67
BROOME Eleanor U20 6.02.99, Rugby & Northampton
100- 12.1/12.15, LJ- 6.16 (6.26-16)
BROPHY Anna U17 14.04.01, Guildford & Godalming
HJ- 1.68 (1.71-16), Hepl- 4378 (4513-16)
BROTHERS Orla U20 27.12.99, Crawley
400- 55.26, 400H- 59.46
BROWN Alexandra U17 8.04.01, Herne Hill
800- 2:12.56, 1500- 4:30.94mx/4:31.87 (4:29.74-16),
3k- 9:59.33
BROWN Alice U15 1.11.03, Havering
DT- 33.11
BROWN Eleanor U15 1.10.02, City of Norwich
LJ- 5.37, TJ- 11.16
BROWN Emily Jane 8.09.83, Cardiff/Cardiff Met
2kSt- 7:09.69 (6:45.80-13)
BROWN Emma Louise 7.02.85, Barrow Runners
Mar- 2:55:21
BROWN Holly U20 21.11.98, Peterborough
PV- 3.51i/3.15 (3.60-16)
BROWN Isobel 5.12.94, Chichester R /Colorado State Un
HJ- 1.71iA/1.70 (1.78iA/1.75-16, 1.75A-15)
BROWN Jessie U17 26.11.01, Amber Valley
JTI- 39.00
BROWN Katy 18.11.93, Stewartry
800- 2:04.79 (2:02.33-15)
BROWN Kiikii U15 20.01.04, Leeds
LJ- 5.28i
BROWN Phoebe U17 24.06.01, Blaenau Gwent
JTI- 41.99

BROWN Rosie U17 6.09.01, Havering
DT- 33.07
BROWN Samantha 24.02.94, Dartford
400H- 61.24 (60.01-16)
BROWN Shaunagh 15.03.90, Blackheath & Bromley
SP- 13.64 (16.39-13), DT- 43.72 (51.77-14),
HT- 54.04 (66.85-14)
BROWN Sophie U17 16.11.01, Cheltenham
TJ- 11.31
BROWNE Janet 17.10.94, Stevenage & NH/Brunel Un
HJ- 1.70
BROWNE Molly 8.12.92, BRAT
5k- 17:16.0mx
BROWNE Stephanie U15 28.11.02, Cambridge & Col
HTI- 42.23
BRUCE Gemma U15 22.09.02, Ayr Seaforth
300- 41.56i (42.03)
BRUINVELS Georgie 20.10.88, Aldershot F&D
HMar- 75:50 (74:28-15, 73:29sh-16), Mar- 2:37:03
BRUNEY Maya U20 24.02.98, Blackh & Brom/E Lond Un
60- 7.51i, 100- 11.64w/11.82, 200- 23.04, 400- 53.17
BRUNNING Leonie U15 25.11.02, Biggleswade
HJ- 1.67
BRYAN Lucy U23 22.05.95, Bristol & W/Akron Un
PV- 4.40i/4.40 (4.40-13)
BRYAN Toni U15 23.12.02, Croydon
60- 7.81i, 100- 12.2/12.21, 200- 25.2/25.88
BUCKINGHAM Toni U20 22.02.98, Barnsley/MMU
SP- 13.45 (13.63dh-16), DT- 35.67 (35.83-13)
BUCKLEY Charlotte U17 2.01.02, Thames Valley
400- 57.7, 800- 2:08.49
BUCKLEY-RATCLIFF Jade U13 15.09.04, Altrincham
JTM- 31.92
BULLER Helen Jayne V35 28.04.78, Worthing
Mar- 2:51:22
BULLIS Emily U23 12.12.95, Basildon
1.5kSt- 5:12.46 (5:09.0-14), 2kSt- 7:07.21
BULLOCK Rebecca U17 6.12.00, Basingstoke & MH
800- 2:08.07
BUNDY-DAVIES Seren 30.12.94, Trafford
400- 54.54 (51.26-16)
BUNTON Amelia Jane U17 13.06.02, City of York
200- 25.36, 300- 40.65i/40.88
BURLEY Bethan Laura U20 26.03.00, Wimborne
100H- 14.69w/14.85, 400H- 62.59, SP- 11.29,
JT- 39.98, Hep- 5015
BURN Hannah U15 14.05.04, Kilmarnock
800- 2:16.55
BURNETT Codie U23 8.05.96, Newbury/Loughborough St
100- 12.18
BURNS Alexandra U20 10.08.99, Helensburgh
LJ- 5.79w/5.64i (5.55-16), TJ- 12.05
BURNS Rachael V35 1.03.80, Liverpool H
1500- 4:24.66mx/4:26.04 (4:25.47-16), 5k- 17:06.54,
3k- 9:43.32i (9:27.08-16), 5kR- 16:34 (16:29-16)
BURNS Rebecca 19.06.90, Pitreavie
1500- 4:26.18mx/4:26.24, 5kR- 16:58
BURR Katie U15 30.09.03, VP-Glasgow
60HG- 9.40i, HJ- 1.60, SextG- 3492, PenG- 3096,
PenIG- 3236i
BURRELL Rhiana U15 14.12.03, Birchfield
HJ- 1.65
BURT Anna Lily Mabel U20 12.07.00, Team Bath
400- 55.50mx, 800- 2:04.52, 1500- 4:21.94
BURTON Gabriella U23 25.06.96, Cannock & S/Dur Un
100- 12.15w (12.10w-14), 60H- 8.66i, 100H- 13.90w/14.38
BURTON Ila U20 2.07.98, Yeovil Olympiads
HJ- 1.65 (1.66-13)
BUSBY Megan U17 5.01.01, Carlisle Aspatria
LJ- 5.87
BUTT Eleanor U17 21.09.01, Southend
JTI- 38.75
BUXTON Abigail U20 3.10.98, Pembroke
HJ- 1.66i (1.65-16)
BUXTON Leanne V35 27.05.78, Bedford & County
100H- 15.10 (13.96w-00, 13.97-99),
SP- 11.19i/11.19 (12.63-09), Hep- 4514 (5183-07)
BYLES Alice U20 15.11.98, Oxford City
400H- 60.59

CAESAR Olivia U23 22.07.96, Swansea/Bath Un
200- 24.17w/24.60, 400- 54.08i/54.11 (53.45-16)
CAIN-DALEY Isabel U20 27.11.98, Stratford-upon-Avon
HJ- 1.68 (1.76-15)
CALLAWAY Samantha U17 4.03.02, Southampton
SPI- 13.45, DT- 42.04
CALLENBURG Mia 24.02.89, Belgrave/SWE
SP- 11.15 (11.58-15), DT- 36.46
CALLOW Aimee U15 1.01.03, Cardiff Archers
800- 2:15.37
CALVERT Isla U15 28.03.03, Livingston
800- 2:11.35mx/2:14.03, 1500- 4:34.42
CALVERT Sarah U17 29.06.01, Livingston
800- 2:11.80, 1500- 4:35.43mx/4:38.66i/4:39.32
CAMPBELL Georgia 27.07.88, Jarrow & Hebburn
10MR- 58:36
CAMPBELL Tamsin U20 12.02.99, Crawley
PV- 3.50 (3.70-16)
CAMPBELL-SMITH Nikita U23 5.09.95, Birchfield
200- 24.86 (24.31-16), 400- 54.37 (53.60-16)
CAMPION Charlotte U17 17.09.01, Swansea
TJ- 11.24
CAMPSALL Rebecca 2.10.90, City of York
60- 7.48i (7.45i-16), 100- 11.60 (11.46w/11.53-16),
200- 23.79
CANHAM Molly U17 3.11.01, Exeter
800- 2:07.44, 1500- 4:32.04, 3k- 10:11.1mx
CANN Emily U13 19.02.05, West Suffolk
100- 12.58w/12.8/12.83, 200- 26.8/26.85
CANNELL Harriet U17 2.02.01, Kingston upon Hull
JTI- 38.90
CANNING Emma U23 7.03.97, Edinburgh AC/St'clyde Un
LJ- 5.74i (5.88w/5.83-16)
CANPOLAT Kiera U17 4.08.01, Leics Coritanian
SPI- 12.43
CAREY Elena U20 14.04.00, Bracknell
1.5kSt- 5:04.75
CAREY Jasmine U15 13.09.02, Blackpool & Fylde
PV- 3.46
CARLAW Lily U13 25.11.04, Rugby & Northampton
SPM- 10.94, DTM- 32.78
CARR Ebony Alice U20 21.01.99, Marshall Milton K
60- 7.71i (7.67i-15), 100- 11.70w/11.78, 200- 24.48
CARROW Ellie U17 26.10.01, Taunton
TJ- 11.08, HepI- 4258
CARTER Amy Lydia U17 24.06.01, New Marske
60HI- 8.79i, 80HI- 11.45, 100HI- 14.53
CARTER Gemma Diane 4.01.87, Serpentine
50kR- 3:46:25
CARTER Grace U20 25.10.99, Aberdeen
60H- 8.98i
CARTER Kimberley U23 18.07.95, Telford
DT- 39.45
CARTER Larissa U20 2.05.00, Lewes
HT- 42.66
CARTER Sophie V35 10.05.79, Belgrave
50kR- 3:43:35, 100kR- 8:11:38
CASHIN Alice U15 13.10.02, Manx H
HJ- 1.60
CASTLE Debbie U23 14.10.95, Colchester & Tendring
JT- 36.68
CAUDERY Molly U20 17.03.00, Cornwall AC
HJ- 1.67, PV- 4.35
CAVANAGH Melissa U20 16.07.99, City of Portsmouth
JT- 41.69
CAYGILL Nicola U20 30.01.00, Jarrow & Hebburn
60- 7.75imx, 100- 12.07+/12.12
CHAMBERLAIN Rosie U23 11.08.95, Exeter/Florida St Un
400- 54.69, 600- 1:29.57i, 800- 2:04.19
CHAMBERLIN Lydia 2.10.87, Trafford
SP- 11.65 (12.32-12)
CHANDLER Ellie U20 18.09.98, WSE&H
HT- 48.81
CHANTLER EDMOND Luisa U20 7.06.99, Radley AC
SP- 11.47 (11.64i/11.63-16), DT- 46.48
CHANTREE Mia U17 15.11.01, Chelmsford
80HI- 11.9, 300H- 44.42, HJ- 1.71, LJ- 5.49,
HepI- 4650, PenII- 3391i

CHAPMAN Katie U15 20.09.03, Exeter
HJ- 1.60 (1.62-16)
CHAPMAN Mia U20 20.08.99, Bedford & County
200- 24.89w
CHAPMAN Rebecca Charlotte 27.09.92, Cardiff/Card Met
60- 7.50i, 100- 11.87w/12.06, LJ- 6.54
CHAPMAN Sarah U20 21.04.98, WSE&H/Birmingham Un
1500- 4:27.41, 3k- 9:38.54
CHAPPELL Lucy U23 10.01.97, Doncaster/Hallam Un
100H- 14.65w/14.8/15.14 (14.8/15.03-15),
HJ- 1.77i/1.73 (1.73-14), LJ- 5.69w/5.61 (5.69-15),
Hep- 4634, PentIS- 3780i
CHARLES Mayah U20 24.07.00, Notts
LJ- 5.70w
CHARLES Shereen 7.10.84, Shaftesbury B
60- 7.70i (7.62i-11), 100- 11.95 (11.9-11, 11.92mx-15)
CHATTENTON Dani U23 4.07.96, Medway & M/Oxford Un
3k- 9:37.74mx, 2kSt- 6:55.76
CHERRY Jill U20 1.03.98, VP-Glasgow/Glasgow Un
400- 54.37
CHIARELLO Karen V50 31.08.63, Manx H
50kW- 5:17:31
CHIGBO Ada'ora U20 2.01.99, North Somerset
HJ- 1.80i/1.75 (1.83-16), SP- 12.28i/12.17 (12.49i-16),
PentIS- 3620i
CHINEDU Vera U20 2.05.00, Cambridge H
60- 7.50i, 100- 11.76
CHONG Emily U15 2.11.03, Chester le Street
3k- 10:18.88mx/10:29.40
CHRISTENSEN Charlotte 27.01.93, Cambridge & Col
5kR- 16:50
CHRISTMAS Emma 24.06.88, Havering
JT- 40.81 (43.82-09)
CHRISTOPHER-SOARES Elsie U15 12.11.03, Med & M
DT- 32.11
CHURCH Lili U15 30.07.03, Carmarthen
HJ- 1.68
CLARK Anna U23 4.06.97, WGreen & Ex L/Bath Un
800- 2:09.74
CLARK Chay U23 6.12.96, Chelmsford/Southampton Un
100H- 15.29w (15.3-14), 400H- 63.05
CLARK Isabel 13.03.86, Serpentine
5kR- 16:43, 10k- 34:52.30, 10kR- 34:50, 10MR- 57:21,
HMar- 77:56
CLARK Jasmine U17 13.02.01, Middlesboro Mandale
60HI- 8.80i
CLARK Laura U23 17.08.96, Shaftesbury B
60- 7.66i, 100- 11.68w/11.72, 200- 24.80mx
CLARK Zoey 25.10.94, Thames Valley/Aberdeen Un
100- 11.54, 200- 23.14w/23.36, 400- 51.81
CLARKE Amy 22.04.86, Isle of Wight
HT- 48.76 (48.83-06)
CLARKE Ashleigh U23 15.09.97, Croydon
60- 7.75i (7.73i-14)
CLARKE Rosie 17.11.91, Epsom & Ewell
1500- 4:21.6+ (4:12.10-15), 3k- 8:51.02, 5kR- 15:45,
10kR- 33:04, 3kSt- 9:32.10
CLATWORTHY Nia U15 2.10.02, Bridgend
800- 2:17.38
CLAYDON Hannah 18.12.93, Swindon
Mar- 2:56:39
CLAYTON Emma 16.07.88, Leeds
1500- 4:27.85 (4:27.54mx-12), 3k- 9:34.34mx
(9:11.23mx/9:26.7+-16), 5k- 16:33.95 (15:44.38-16),
5kR- 16:33, 10kR- 33:51 (33:28.33t-16)
CLEMENS Amy 24.10.92, Shaftesbury B
HT- 49.08 (49.95-11)
CLEMENTS Amy 22.05.82, Kent AC
5k- 16:50.2 (16:33.8mx/16:47.54-15), 10kR- 34:44,
HMar- 75:55 (75:15-16), Mar- 2:39:20
CLEVELAND Ellie U17 5.08.02, WSE&H
80HI- 12.00, 300H- 45.9/46.27
CLITHEROE Stephanie U23 3.11.95, WSE&H/St Marys U
60- 7.63imx/7.67i (7.64i-16), 60H- 8.39i, 100H- 13.77
(13.71-16)
CLOSE Bethany U23 30.12.95, Swansea/Bath Un
200- 24.76i (24.83-16), 400- 56.67,
400H- 58.38 (57.70-16)

CLULEY Mallory U17 15.03.02, Herne Hill
80HI- 11.98
COCKELL Chloe U23 23.10.95, Braintree/Bedford Un
HT- 44.96
COCKRAM Natasha 12.11.92, Mickey Morris RT
HMar- 78:42, Mar- 2:49:37
COCKRILL Emily Sarah U20 14.03.98, Swansea/UAE
JT- 39.82 (43.46-16)
COLE Ayomide U13 27.07.05, Basingstoke & MH
60- 8.16imx/8.17i, 75- 9.8, 100- 12.54, 150- 19.5,
200- 25.83, 60HM- 9.62i, 70HM- 11.23w
COLE Cicely U20 3.02.00, Crawley
PV- 3.20
COLEBY Samantha 4.08.90, Durham City H
800- 2:08.35 (2:07.84-16)
COLEMAN Cathy U20 3.07.98, Guildford & Godalming
HT- 50.06
COLEMAN Libby Mae U17 3.05.01, Mansfield H
3k- 9:58.01mx/10:04.01
COLES Olive U20 14.09.99, Dacorum & Tring
400- 56.75mx/56.78i/56.79, 400H- 61.90
COLLIER Naomi 28.10.94, Grantham/Birmingham Un
1500- 4:27.17i
COLLINGS Martha U15 17.11.02, Woking
3k- 10:31.17
COLLINS Jessica U17 9.01.02, Herne Hill
HJ- 1.63i (1.63-16)
COLLIS Maisie U15 2.01.04, Herne Hill
800- 2:15.4, 1500- 4:35.38
COLMER Grace U13 13.07.05, Southampton
70HM- 11.18, LJ- 4.91w, PenM- 2432, PenIM- 2332i
COMPTON-STEWART Matilda U20 18.03.98, WSE&H/
Loughb St 1.5kSt- 5:00.75, 2kSt- 7:06.55 (7:03.83-16)
CONNOLLY Breege V. V35 1.02.78, Derry/IRL
10MR- 58:26 (57:40-15), Mar- 2:37:29 (2:37:29-15)
CONNOLLY Gemma Louise V35 18.12.81, St Helens Sut
Mar- 2:46:45
CONNOLLY Sarah U23 3.10.96, N.Down/Brunel Un/IRL
60H- 8.96i, 100H- 14.63 (14.38w-15), HJ- 1.78, Hep- 4837
CONNOLLY Shannon U23 19.11.95, TVH/Bath Un
PV- 3.50 (3.70-15)
CONNOR Olivia U23 6.09.97, Lewes/Birmingham Un
PV- 3.70i/3.70 (3.90-15)
CONNOR Sophie 21.05.93, Shaftesbury B/New Mexico U
800- 2:06.53iA (2:05.95-16), 1M- 4:36.89i
COOK Amelia Daisey U20 31.05.00, Basingstoke & MH
SP- 12.16
COOK Bethany U15 17.07.04, Bodyworks XTC
1500- 4:39.48mx/4:44.74
COOK Briagha U15 28.10.02, Central
60HG- 9.36i, 75HG- 11.30, LJ- 5.23, PenG- 2846
COOK Coirilidh U15 13.11.03, Central
60HG- 9.40i, 75HG- 11.52
COOK Sophie 12.09.94, Birchfield/Coventry Un
PV- 3.81i (4.02-14)
COOKE Gillian Helen 3.10.82, Edinburgh AC
PV- 3.20 (3.90-02), LJ- 5.75i/5.60 (6.43i-08, 6.40w-06,
6.39-07), TJ- 12.02i/11.81 (12.70i-08, 12.56-06)
COOKE Heather U20 22.02.98, Scunthorpe/Brunel Un
400H- 64.49 (64.17-16)
COOKE Julia 9.09.88, Birchfield
800- 2:10.28 (2:05.06-14), 1500- 4:21.06 (4:12.49-15)
COOKE Kaeshelle U23 2.01.96, Enfield & Haringey
100H- 15.27 (14.17-16)
COOPE Emily U20 26.12.99, Amber Valley
100- 11.93
COOPER Harriet U20 27.01.99, Charnwood
100- 12.13w, 400- 55.65
COOPER Holly U15 1.11.02, Swansea
DT- 31.67
COOPER Jasmine U17 25.02.01, Derby AC
1500- 4:39.18, 3k- 9:54.20mx/9:59.88 (9:56.8-16)
COPELAND Grace U17 11.10.00, Wimborne
1500- 4:38.74 (4:35.92-16), 3k- 9:55.01
COPEMAN Jemima U17 15.06.02, WSE&H
300- 40.11, JTI- 40.11
CORKER Megan U13 11.10.04, Warrington
70HM- 11.0/11.12

COSTELLO Kirsty U15 22.09.02, Kilbarchan
HT- 43.97, HTI- 57.83, JTI- 43.70
COULSON Bernice U20 25.04.98, Wigan/Notts Un
HJ- 1.70
COULSON Jessica 18.04.90, Stockport
10kR- 34:44 (32:41.59t-15)
COURTNEY Melissa Jayne 30.08.93, Shaft B/Brunel Un
800- 2:04.03, 1500- 4:05.82+, 1M- 4:23.15, 5k- 15:28.95,
3k- 8:43.72mx/9:11.38i/9:24.66+ (9:13.87-16), 5kR- 15:58
COURTNEY Mollie U23 2.07.97, Cheltenham/Glouc Un
60H- 8.32i, 100H- 13.40w/13.44 (13.28-16), HJ- 1.76
COUTTS Isabella U23 19.02.97, Camb & Col/Oxford Un
JT- 39.47
COUTTS Sarah U15 9.05.03, Pitreavie
800- 2:14.33, 1500- 4:37.97mx/4:39.73
COUTTS Stella U15 25.09.03, Cumbernauld
HTI- 41.37
COWARD Lilly U23 10.09.96, Invicta/St Marys Un
800- 2:07.44, 1500- 4:21.67
COWELL Emma U23 23.11.95, Southampton/St Marys Un
HJ- 1.66i (1.76-13)
COWPER Sophie 24.12.90, Rotherham
3k- 9:47.62 (9:29.71mx/9:42.55-16), 10k- 34:55.77,
5k- 16:24.82 (16:18.84-15), 10kR- 33:55, 10MR- 56:24
COX Chloe 9.04.86, Lothian RC
Mar- 2:56:39dh
COXON Melissa U15 5.12.02, Rotherham
300- 41.97, 75HG- 11.59, PenG- 2824+
CRAIG Emily U20 5.02.99, Whitemoss/Strathclyde Un
400H- 63.03
CRAWFORD Jazz U20 22.01.98, Blackheath & Bromley
100- 11.92w/11.93 (11.90w-12, 11.93-15), 200- 24.77 (24.29-15)
CRAWFORD Lara U15 20.06.03, Sale
1500- 4:40.63mx/4:44.14, 3k- 10:25.6
CRAWLEY Lily U15 2.10.02, Cheltenham
HJ- 1.61
CROFT Anna U20 20.10.99, WSE&H
400H- 62.34
CROFT Rebecca U23 27.05.97, WSE&H/UC Berkeley
400- 55.83, 800- 2:05.81
CRONIN Victoria Ann 6.12.90, Trafford/Manchester Un
2kSt- 7:07.4, 3kSt- 11:10.52 (11:06.52-16)
CROOK Amanda 4.04.86, Southport
5kR- 16:18, 5MR- 27:39
CROOK Charlotte U20 14.09.99, Preston
800- 2:10.01mx
CROOKES Lucy 4.05.93, Leeds
3k- 9:36.1 (9:29.63mx/9:33.73-16)
CRORKEN Rachel U20 7.11.99, Wakefield
400- 56.10
CROSBY Priya 1.01.92, Cambridge Un
2kSt- 7:10.06, 3kSt- 11:18.41
CROSSAN Shona U17 11.12.00, Shettleston H
SP- 11.32, SPI- 13.45 (13.62-16), DT- 37.36
CRUMLY Sophie 6.07.90, Reading
2kSt- 7:02.06
CUBBAGE Heather U17 20.01.01, City of Portsmouth
SPI- 13.23, DT- 46.14, HTI- 51.84
CULLIFORD Lana U17 21.09.00, Cardiff
300H- 44.09, 400H- 64.64
CUMMING Daisy U15 17.08.03, Dunfermline
1500- 4:44.06mx
CURRAN Ines U15 9.09.03, Gateshead
1500- 4:44.2, 3k- 10:19.30mx/10:34.58
CURRAN Molly U15 18.12.03, Carmen Runners
PenG- 2801
CURRAN Olivia 10.06.91, WSE&H
PV- 3.81i (4.05i-14, 3.90-16)
CURRY Obi Elizabeth U17 11.04.01, Wirral
100- 12.3/12.32, 200- 25.0/25.12
CURTIS Amy-Beth U17 6.02.02, Exeter
SPI- 12.54

DADZIE Priscilla U20 27.11.99, Nene Valley H
SP- 11.33
DAKIN Emma U20 25.12.99, Rotherham
SP- 12.28i/12.09, DT- 40.10 (41.24-16)
DANDJINOU Hope U15 19.05.03, Slough Juniors
SPI- 11.69

DANIEL Katie U17 30.08.01, Nuneaton
100- 12.37w (12.2-16)
DARBYSHIRE Leah U17 31.10.01, Wigan
PV- 3.40i/3.20 (3.40i/3.26-16)
DARCEY Laura U20 28.07.98, Kingston & P/Chicago Un
HJ- 1.65 (1.65-14), LJ- 5.60w, Hep- 4579
DART Maia U20 2.06.00, Woodford Green & Ex L
JT- 42.17
DAVENALL Philippa U20 26.09.98, Colchester H
HT- 56.69, HTI- 62.00
DAVENPORT Nicole U23 31.03.96, Swansea/Liverpool U
JT- 42.40 (43.39-16)
DAVEY Molly Jade U20 3.09.98, Montanari Gruzza ITA
5kW- 27:46.42 (25:41.5-15), 5kWR- 25:48+ (25:30-15),
10kWR- 51:46, 20kW- 1:51:39
DAVEY JAMES Charlie U17 21.04.01, North Devon
SPI- 12.71
DAVIDSON Fiona V40 29.01.73, Aberdeen
TJ- 11.39 (12.15i-95, 12.06w/11.91-96)
DAVIDSON Jane U17 22.07.02, Aberdeen
60HI- 9.05i, 80HI- 11.99, 300H- 45.16
DAVIDSON Kerri U23 7.09.96, B'hth & Brom/Princeton Un
TJ- 12.24w/11.90i/11.81 (12.77w-15, 12.48-14)
DAVIES Amy U17 27.04.01, West Suffolk
HT- 40.70, HTI- 46.05
DAVIES Anastasia U20 9.04.99, Blackheath & Bromley
60H- 8.62i, 100H- 13.89, TJ- 11.92 (12.00-16)
DAVIES Bethan 7.11.90, Cardiff
3kW- 12:26.45 (12:24.70-16), 5kW- 21:21.52, 10kW-
47:05.97, 10kWR- 45:53+ (44:59-16), 20kW- 1:33:04
DAVIES Catherine U15 13.01.03, Tonbridge
PV- 2.70
DAVIES Elizabeth V35 25.12.78, Springfield Striders
3k- 9:44.24
DAVIES Esme U17 26.04.01, Eden Runners
3k- 9:58.40
DAVIES Fiona V40 3.11.73, Rotherham
Mar- 2:55:05 (2:51:50-06)
DAVIES Helen J. V35 12.09.79, Ipswich Jaffa
5kR- 16:25, 10k- 35:39.00, HMar- 76:10 (72:35-12),
Mar- 2:42:40 (2:34:11-12)
DAVIES Holly U20 27.11.98, West Suffolk
1.5kSt- 5:01.9
DAVIES Kate U23 27.09.95, Gloucester AC/Oxford Un
HJ- 1.65i (1.67-14), JT- 43.82
DAVIES Leanne U23 12.05.97, AF&D/Brunel Un
JT- 39.51 (43.04-13)
DAVIES Lucy U20 17.08.00, Pembroke
1.5kSt- 4:59.34 (4:58.99-16)
DAVIES Megan U23 10.05.96, Sale/Birmingham Un
800- 2:09.68, 1500- 4:20.76mx/4:21.11
DAVIES Megan U20 31.01.99, Cannock & Stafford
200- 24.6w (24.8/24.97-16), 400- 55.05
DAVIES Sydney U15 6.09.02, Cannock & Stafford
60HG- 9.38i
DAVIES-REDMOND Grace U20 14.06.98, Team Bath
JT- 39.88
DAVIS Angela U17 15.07.02, Orion
60- 7.86imx/7.89i, 100- 12.1/12.25w, 200- 25.0/25.39 (25.03-16)
DAVIS Eleanor 21.02.89, Bristol & West
10kR- 34:18 (33:59-16), HMar- 74:27sh (75:45-15)
DAVIS Imogen U15 18.05.03, Poole
JTI- 35.30
DAVIS Julia 12.08.86, Winchester
HMar- 77:21+, Mar- 2:39:33 (2:39:31-16)
DAVIS Stephanie 27.08.90, Clapham Chasers
5kR- 16:50, 10kR- 34:55
DAVISON Lucy U17 8.11.01, Edinburgh AC
LJ- 5.58w, SPI- 12.31i, Hepl- 4332, PenII- 3434i
DAWE-LANE Imogen U20 30.08.00, Team Bath
100HI- 14.81, 100H- 15.12
DAWKINS Gemma 26.06.91, Channel Islands
800- 2:08.10mx/2:09.50 (2:07.88mx/2:08.49-16)
DAY Jessica U13 3.09.04, Nuneaton
60HM- 9.89i
DE KLERK Eilidh U20 10.04.98, Arbroath/R.Gordon Un
200- 24.85

DE KREMER Sarah-Anne 18.11.90, Corby/Lough St
JT- 39.27 (44.27-06)
DE LA TOUCHE Jasmine U15 4.09.02, Walton
SPI- 11.37
DE LUCIS Ella U23 2.11.96, Peterborough
100H- 15.1 (14.40w/14.42-15)
DE MAUNY Fiona 3.02.83, Walton
800- 2:09.07
DEACON Isabel U20 11.11.99, Bracknell
PV- 3.63i/3.35 (3.56-16)
DEADMAN Lauren 27.03.84, Havering
3k- 9:30.33 (9:04.56mx-15, 9:15.8-16),
5k- 16:12.7mx (15:45.12-15), 10kR- 34:36 (33:05.55t-16)
DELMER Alice 30.12.93, Loughborough St/FRA
HT- 61.76
DENIAL Bethany U20 16.03.99, Nene Valley H
TJ- 11.16w
DENIS Imaan U15 27.11.02, Harrow
60- 8.01i, 100- 12.5/12.54, 300- 41.38mx/41.5 (41.3-16),
200- 25.5/25.55 (25.20w/25.37-16)
DENNISON Abigail U17 22.01.01, Winchester
300- 40.20 (39.96-16), 400- 58.2
DESAI Nisha 5.08.84, Trafford
400- 56.08 (54.86-16), 400H- 58.3/58.38 (58.21-13)
DHIR Samaia U13 23.03.05, WSE&H
SPM- 10.05, DTM- 33.89
DIAMOND Emily Jane 11.06.91, Bristol & West
200- 23.68 (23.30-13, 23.25wSt-16), 400- 51.67 (51.23-16)
DIBBLE Emily U20 17.09.99, Mendip
JT- 41.72
DICKENS Eden U15 12.12.03, Charnwood
PV- 2.60
DICKENS Rachel 28.10.94, Blackheath & Bromley
200- 24.58i (24.27w/24.35-14), 400- 55.47i (54.13-14)
DICKINSON Gabby U15 30.12.03, Cardiff
PenIG- 3002i
DIDCOTE Sacha U15 4.01.03, Colwyn Bay
100- 12.5, 200- 25.5 (25.70-16), 300- 41.7 (41.34-16)
DINEEN Elina U15 11.09.03, Cardiff Archers
75HG- 11.59
DINGLE Megan Haf U17 1.09.02, Desert RR UAE
3k- 10:08.00
DINWOODIE Katie U15 27.01.03, Shetland
200- 25.9w/25.98
DITCHFIELD Paige U20 22.12.99, Sale
JT- 38.27
DIXON Alyson V35 24.09.78, Sunderland Strollers
10kR- 33:43/32:57dh (32:17-15), Mar- 2:29:06
15kR- 51:29+ (49:47+-14), HMar- 72:29 (70:38-14)
DIXON Emily U23 27.11.95, Team Bath/Elon Un
60H- 8.84i (8.79i-14), 100H- 14.67 (14.35-16),
HJ- 1.65i/1.65 (1.70i-11, 1.67-10), Hep- 4799 (5059-16),
SP- 11.24i (11.37-15), PentIS- 3702i
DIXON Kerry 22.10.88, Enfield & Haringey
400H- 60.27 (59.83-14)
DOBBIE Kara U20 3.08.00, Glasgow SOS
TJ- 11.44i (11.52-16)
DOBBIN Beth 7.06.94, Edinburgh AC
60- 7.60i, 100- 11.71, 200- 23.31
DOBBIN Julie 8.03.94, VP-Glasgow/Glasgow Un
800- 2:09.38
DOBSON Jessica U20 19.01.98, Exeter
Hep- 4149 (4269-16)
DOBSON Olivia U17 27.03.01, Exeter
HJ- 1.74, SPI- 14.14, JTI- 42.26, Hepl- 5114w/4742
DODD Kaylee U23 28.12.95, Basildon/Oklahoma St Un
800- 2:03.38, 1500- 4:20.09
DOMINGO Sophie U20 7.01.00, Harborough
100H- 14.7/15.28w, Hep- 4198
DONNELLY Abbie U23 2.09.96, Lincoln W/Lough St
5k- 17:16.02, 10k- 35:36.04
DONNELLY Katherine U15 29.06.03, Medway & Maid
HTI- 38.33
DONNISON Rachel U23 12.10.96, Cardiff/Bath Un
400- 55.87
DORAN Colette 20.09.83, Wigan
JT- 36.27 (39.25-07)

DOUGAN Harriet U17 10.06.01, Lagan Valley
  PV- 3.20
DOUGLAS Montell 24.01.86, Blackheath & Bromley
  100- 11.35w/11.58 (10.95w/11.05-08),
  200- 24.27w (23.34-09)
DOURAS Emma U23 25.02.95, Dudley & Stourbridge
  100H- 14.9 (14.7-16)
DOWINTON Rhiannon U15 7.11.02, Channel Islands
  60HG- 9.44i, 75HG- 11.42w
DOWLING Daisy U17 21.08.02, Blackheath & Bromley
  JTI- 38.90
DOWNIE Stacey 15.04.87, Edinburgh AC
  200- 24.09 (23.80-11), 400- 53.91
DOWSON Phoebe 17.04.94, Bournemouth
  DT- 51.87, HT- 43.74 (49.52-15)
DOWSON Sophie U20 24.11.98, Blackheath & Bromley
  PV- 3.91i/3.75 (3.76-16)
DOYLE Eilidh Shona 20.02.87, Pitreavie
  200- 24.16i+ (24.56-08), 300- 37.6i+ (37.1i+-13),
  400- 51.86i/52.36 (51.45i/51.83-13),
  400H- 54.36 (54.09-16)
DOYLE-LAY Georgia U20 27.10.98, Newquay & Par
  HJ- 1.65, Hep- 4484 (4610-16)
DREW Karla 22.03.89, Southampton/Liverpool Un
  60H- 8.47i (8.33i-13), 100H- 13.60 (13.32w-14,13.36-16)
DRISCOLL Stephanie U17 24.10.01, Liverpool H
  300H- 45.23, 400H- 62.51, Hepl- 4400w/4347,
  PenII- 3323i
DUBARRY-GAY Kiah U17 15.11.01, VPH &TH
  100- 12.05+, 200- 24.13
DUBARRY-GAY Nayanna U17 15.11.01, VPH &TH
  60- 7.77i, 100- 12.1/12.32 (12.17-16)
DUCK Claire 29.08.85, Leeds
  800- 2:06.84, 1500- 4:23.7 (4:18.20-16), 10k- 32:51.38,
  3k- 9:07.10mx (9:11.26-16), 5k- 15:57.32 (15:47.75-16)
DUCK Jacqueline Sarah "Joey" 14.04.89, M. Milton K
  100- 11.94w (11.60-09),
  200- 24.12 (23.38w-15, 23.46-08)
DUDGEON Emily Kathleen 3.03.93, Edinburgh AC
  800- 2:05.89 (2:01.89-14)
DUKE Laura 12.10.89, Crawley
  HT- 43.03 (50.02-11)
DUNCAN Leah U15 30.10.02, Braintree
  60- 7.76i, 100- 11.88w/12.0/12.21, 200- 25.20
DUNDERDALE Hannah 2.11.94, Trafford/Arkansas Un
  200- 24.74w, 60H- 8.99i (8.89i-16), LJ- 5.75,
  100H- 14.22w (14.44-16), 400H- 63.31 (61.10-13),
  SP- 11.98i/11.82, Hep- 5213w (5056-16), PentIS- 3742i
DUNSMORE Alana U20 17.01.00, Pitreavie
  PV- 3.11 (3.21-16)
DUPORTE-CLARKE Janae U20 20.01.00, Ipswich
  TJ- 11.15
DUQUEMIN Shadine 4.11.94, Shaftesbury B
  DT- 51.79 (53.44-14)
DURAND Abigail U15 7.11.02, North Norfolk H
  3k- 10:32.2
DURAND Eva U15 18.07.04, Marshall Milton K
  JTI- 37.20
DURUH Vivien U15 21.10.03, Law & Dist
  SPI- 12.02i/11.71
DUTHIE Georgia U17 7.09.00, Sutton & District
  PV- 3.10i/2.90 (3.00-16)

EAMES Chloe U15 19.06.03, Reading
  60HG- 9.36i, 75HG- 11.5
EARLEY Philippa Karen U17 7.09.00, Kingston & Poly
  60HI- 8.41i, 80HI- 10.94, 100HI- 13.61, LJ- 5.88,
  SPI- 12.89i/12.42, Hepl- 5123, PenII- 3952i
EASTWOOD Jemma V35 15.02.79, Bedford & County
  PV- 3.30i/3.30 (3.80-06)
EBBAGE Caitlin U13 14.06.05, Tonbridge
  PV- 2.40, SPM- 9.96, DTM- 29.96
EBBAGE Kirsty-Anne U17 30.08.02, Tonbridge
  DT- 36.61, HTI- 46.58
EDDEN Elizabeth 29.06.94, Birchfield
  PV- 3.90
EDUAN Success U13 27.09.04, Sale
  75- 9.65, 150- 18.81, 200- 26.06

EDUWU Jennifer U15 17.04.04, Serpentine
  200- 25.86
EDWARDS Eleanor U23 19.11.96, Trafford/B'ham Un
  100- 12.17, 200- 24.85
EDWARDS Laura 1.03.94, Southampton/Southampton Un
  PV- 3.70
EDWARDS Mair U20 6.09.99, Basingstoke & MH
  60- 7.73i (7.73i-16), 100- 11.71w/11.99,
  200- 23.81w/23.89, 400- 55.09
EDWARDS Rheagan U15 8.04.03, Deeside
  3k- 10:37.06
EDWARDS Rosie 20.08.88, Rotherham
  5kR- 15:28, 5MR- 27:53, 10k- 34:31.05, 10MR- 55:53,
  HMar- 78:51+ (76:27-16), Mar- 2:40:56
EGBO Merechi U17 29.11.01, Herts Phoenix
  HJ- 1.73i/1.68 (1.69-16)
EICHELMANN Alexa U20 14.12.99, Shaftesbury B
  PV- 3.60
EKEH UDOCHI Judy 8.08.93, Notts/ITA
  TJ- 11.59
EKOKU Adanna U17 29.08.01, Epsom & Ewell
  LJ- 5.64
ELCOCK Lucy U17 11.09.01, Bridgnorth
  200- 25.38w/25.40, 300- 40.7
ELCOCK Mary U23 3.08.95, Oldham & Royton/Lough
  LJ- 5.95 (6.03-16)
ELEYAE Oghenofego Kitan 31.10.91, WGreen & Ex L
  LJ- 5.91 (6.25-12), TJ- 11.59
ELKINS Jennifer 27.01.85, Southampton
  5k- 17:02.88, 5MR- 27:54, 10MR- 58:45
ELLIOTT Molly U15 19.09.02, Birtley
  PV- 2.65
ELLIS Akaysha U17 16.12.00, Enfield & Haringey
  60- 7.78i, 100- 12.0/12.14
ELLIS Charlotte U17 10.10.00, Nuneaton
  Hepl- 4164
ELLIS Philippa U15 23.04.03, Houghton
  100- 12.59, 200- 25.94, 60HG- 9.28i, 75HG- 11.32,
  PenG- 2819
ELLIS Poppy U15 11.10.02, Havering
  300- 41.8
ELLIS Sarah 27.10.83, Southampton
  JT- 42.86 (45.17-10)
ELLISS Sophie U20 2.11.98, Croydon
  60H- 8.85i (8.75i-16), 100H- 14.05 (13.95-16)
EMERSON Caitlin U17 2.05.01, Amber Valley
  DT- 41.28
EMERSON Niamh U20 22.04.99, Amber Valley
  200- 24.52w/24.64, 100H- 14.01, HJ- 1.83 (1.89-16),
  LJ- 6.09w/6.03 (6.21-16), SP- 12.67, JT- 38.23, Hep- 6013
EMERY Jessica U17 16.09.00, Shaftesbury B
  DT- 42.32
EMMETT Shaye U20 19.08.00, Blackheath & Bromley
  PV- 3.50i/3.50 (3.70-15)
ENDERWICK Kaitlin U23 31.01.97, Middlesboro Mandale
  SP- 11.25i/11.15
ENGLAND Hannah 6.03.87, Oxford City
  800- 2:01.23 (1:59.66-12), 1500- 4:09.52 (4:01.89-11),
  5kR- 16:40
ENGLISH Kim U17 7.07.02, Chelmsford
  SPI- 12.30
ESEGBONA Chloe U20 23.11.98, Trafford
  100H- 14.48w/14.7/14.76 (14.5/14.76-16), 400H- 61.53
EVANS Clara 27.11.93, Hereford
  10kR- 34:56 (34:21-16), HMar- 75:34, Mar- 2:46:16
EVANS Lauren Emilia U20 7.08.00, Cardiff
  60H- 8.89i, 100H- 14.11, 100H- 14.49, LJ- 5.82w/5.62,
  HJ- 1.65i (1.70i-16, 1.68-15), Hep U18- 4406
EVANS Louise U17 7.10.00, Invicta
  200- 25.24w, 300- 39.60 (39.52-16), 400- 56.97
EVANS Lucy Hannah Elizabeth 2.10.82, Sale
  100- 12.01 (11.61-11), 200- 24.64 (23.94-14)
EVANS Megan U15 28.09.02, Vale Royal
  JTI- 34.23
EVANS Mia U20 24.01.99, Swansea
  100H- 14.90
EVANS Rebecca U23 2.11.95, Cardiff/Un Alabama
  5k- 17:15.09

EVANS Rhian U17 28.08.01, Swansea
DT- 33.92 (34.13-16)
EVANS-HAGGERTY Lily Jane U15 16.06.03, VP-Glasgow
1500- 4:32.49mx/4:36.99i/4:38.59, 3k- 9:49.49
EVE Maryanne U20 1.08.99, Woking
PV- 3.10
EVENDEN Hannah Michelle 28.06.91, Edinburgh AC
SP- 12.23 (14.09i-10, 13.63-13), DT- 40.32 (46.06-11),
HT- 53.55 (57.16-12)

FABUNMI-ALADE Risqat 25.03.94, HHH/Bath Un
60- 7.44i, 100- 11.70w/11.77, 200- 24.34 (24.3-11)
FAIRCHILD Jacqueline 3.05.89, Preston
800- 2:02.09, 1500- 4:13.51mx/4:17.15 (4:14.43-13),
1M- 4:43.12, 5kR- 16:28
FAIRCLOUGH Paige U23 10.03.97, Shaftesbury B
100- 12.18w (11.81w-16, 11.90-15)
FAIRGRIEVE Cara U17 13.01.02, Glasgow SOS
TJ- 11.15i
FAIRHURST Anouska U15 7.03.04, Lewes
JTI- 39.44
FAIRLEY Alix U15 7.08.03, Livingston
DT- 30.12, HTI- 41.83
FAJEMISIN Simi U23 15.09.97, Oxford City/Harvard
LJ- 6.15, TJ- 12.96i/12.96
FAKANDE Gabrielle U17 1.03.01, Cwmbran
400- 58.16
FARLEY Lauren U17 16.09.01, Blackheath & Bromley
JTI- 38.74, HepI- 4221
FARMER Nicole U20 19.10.99, Blackheath & Bromley
TJ- 11.29
FARRELL Hannah U23 22.03.95, Border
HT- 44.01 (45.65-12)
FARRELL Sileena U15, Dartford
TJ- 10.68
FARROW Ellie U17 30.10.01, City of Portsmouth
800- 2:07.51, 1500- 4:37.56
FAWCETT Heather U20 21.01.00, Kilbarchan
HT- 46.96
FEGAN Danielle 3.06.90, Armagh/IRL
5k- 17:01.31, 10k- 35:27.66
FELTON Rachel V35 27.06.79, Shaftesbury B
5k- 17:04.28i (16:20.23-14), 10kR- 34:55 (33:27-13),
HMar- 76:10 (73:43-15)
FENWICK Phoebe U20 6.11.99, Bracknell
400- 56.44
FERGUSON Halle U13 6.12.04, Trafford
HJ- 1.53, LJ- 4.97
FERGUSON Lucy 23.03.90, Thames Valley
400H- 65.28 (61.63-16)
FETTIS Amelia U13 22.02.05, Newport
SPM- 9.96
FILBAY Stephanie 29.09.88, Oxford Un/AUS
DT- 35.93
FINCH Elizabeth U15 6.09.02, Chelmsford
HTI- 42.92
FINLAY Kirsty U17 2.09.01, Leicester Coritanian
HT- 43.11, HTI- 51.94
FIRST Emily U23 5.07.95, Queensland Un AUS
200- 24.62w/24.96 (24.32-15), 400- 56.29 (55.08-14)
FIRTH Charlotte 31.12.84, WSE&H
5k- 16:59.45, HMar- 78:56, Mar- 2:45:29 (2:44:52-16)
FISHER Abigail U17 11.11.00, Cardiff
3k- 10:13.69
FISHER Erin U17 19.10.01, City of Lisburn
PV- 3.11
FISHER Holly U15 2.12.02, Ipswich
1500- 4:44.19mx
FISHER Stephanie U20 17.03.00, Holland Sports AC
400H- 62.43
FITCH Zoe U23 22.09.97, Channel Islands/Nevada Un
JT- 41.38
FITTON Abigail U17 10.12.01, Marshall Milton K
300- 40.73
FITZPATRICK Abigayle 10.06.93, Sale
200- 24.49imx/24.51i (24.40imx/24.6/24.72mx-16, 24.47i- 14),
400- 55.76 (54.37i-14, 54.80-13), 400H- 58.52 (57.52-13)
FLANAGAN Eilish U20 2.05.98, Omagh/Adams State Coll
3kSt- 10:28.77

FLANAGAN Roisin U20 2.05.98, Omagh/Adams St Coll
800- 2:10.18A, 1500- 4:25.10, 1M- 4:45.19i
FLEMING Amy 5.10.90, Gateshead/Army
SP- 11.70 (11.90-08)
FLIGELSTONE Lucy Yolande U23 26.01.97, Swansea/
Exeter Un   400H- 64.95 (61.24-14)
FLINT Alice U23 1.04.95, Boston & D/Cambridge Un
400H- 64.54
FLOCKHART Shannon U17 5.04.02, Huntingdon
800- 2:10.76, 1500- 4:38.93mx
FLOYD Georgie U23 17.05.95, Hillingdon/St Marys Un
JT- 42.21 (43.95-16)
FOGG Erica V35 4.12.78, New Forest Runners
Mar- 2:47:34
FOLETTI Lauren U15 25.09.02, Hallamshire
JTI- 37.28
FORBES Anna U20 13.10.98, Whitemoss/Stirling Un
HJ- 1.66, Hep- 4372w/4192
FORBES Katie Frances U20 19.11.99, Edinburgh AC
60- 7.70i, 100- 12.09w
FORD Caroline 29.12.92, Cambridge H/Loughborough St
800- 2:06.48, 1500- 4:20.75mx/4:25.74
FORDER Rachel 3.12.96, Havering/G.Mason Un
DT- 41.62 (46.22-16)
FORREST Lucy U15 8.10.02, Worksop
HTI- 41.70
FORTUNE Sabrina U23 25.05.97, Deeside
SP- 12.42 (12.94-16), DT- 37.73 (40.28-15)
FOSS Katie U15 3.06.03, Law & District
300- 41.46
FOSSETT Emma U23 19.10.97, Croydon/Herts Un
JT- 38.33
FOSTER Amy 2.10.88, City of Lisburn/IRL
100- 11.42 (11.32w-10. 11.40-14),
200- 23.31w/23.63 (23.24w-15, 23.53-11)
FOSTER Hannah U17 15.03.02, Shaftesbury B
200- 24.83, 300- 38.85, 300H- 43.51
FOUMENA GAELLE Marie U23 31.07.95, Manchester/CMR
100- 12.1 (12.1-12)
FOWLER Stephanie U20 3.08.99, Edinburgh AC
HT- 53.06
FOWLIE Tamsin U13 22.12.04, Moray RR
100- 12.87w, 200- 26.75w
FOX Jessica 28.11.94, Cambridge & Col/Un of E Anglia
TJ- 11.32 (11.39-13)
FRANCIS Britli U17 18.12.00, Herne Hill
SPI- 12.30
FRANCIS Eden Cherrelle 19.10.88, Leics Coritanian
SP- 16.52 (17.24-12), DT- 57.53 (59.78-11)
FRANCIS Kiarra U20 18.03.00, Notts
SP- 11.39
FRANKLIN Rachael 14.12.91, Manx H
1500- 4:25.45 (4:22.30-14), 5k- 16:58.21
FRANKS Lillie U20 27.10.99, Crawley
HJ- 1.76
FRASER Kirsty U23 27.11.95, Preston/Leeds Un
800- 2:10.42
FRATER-WHITE Sadie U13 30.11.04, Braintree
1500- 4:54.7
FREEMAN-GIBB Jeana Celine 8.12.91, Harrow/CAN
SP- 13.20 (15.75i/15.37-14)
FREY Laura 2.06.89, Lagan Valley
400H- 64.93 (64.69-16), Hep- 4155
FRIZELLE Kiara U17 10.07.01, Cardiff
800- 2:12.95, 1500- 4:25.49, 3k- 9:46.36
FROST Joanne V35 23.06.78, Bromsgrove & Redditch
LJ- 5.61 (5.91-15)
FULCHER Lana U20 27.04.99, Ipswich
HT- 46.60 (47.58-16)
FULLERTON Faye Alexis 31.05.84, Havering
1500- 4:25.14i (4:10.24-15),
3k- 9:33.34mx/9:40.91 (9:07.52-06)
FULTON Ellie U20 18.06.99, Kilbarchan
HJ- 1.70i/1.65 (1.70i-15,1.70-16), JT- 39.67, Hep- 4531w

GABELLONE Tatyana 20.10.84, Leics WC/ITA
3kW- 13:48.99 (13:01.2-15), 5kW- 23:03.63,
10kW- 47:41.49 (46:43.87-15), 10kWR- 47:10 (46:24-15),
20kW- 1:39:02 (1:34:42-15)

GALL Milly U15 20.02.03, Dacorum & Tring
  60HG- 9.23i (9.23i-16), 75HG- 11.29, LJ- 5.67,
  PenG- 3084, PenIG- 3328i
GALLAGHER Eleanor U20 20.04.00, Channel Islands
  400- 56.34
GALLAGHER Megan U20 6.10.99, North Devon
  400H- 63.32
GALLEY Krystal 13.08.93, Blackheath & Bromley
  400- 56.33 (56.00-11)
GALLOP Rebecca 10.11.85, Newark AC
  Mar- 2:53:38
GALLOWAY Olivia U20 4.07.00, Bournemouth
  100H- 14.65w/14.7/14.80, LJ- 5.68, Hep- 4658
GALPIN Megan U15 16.11.03, Marlborough Jnrs
  JTI- 40.44
GAMMELL Scarlett U13 9.03.05, Watford
  PenIM- 2257i
GAMMON Bethan U17 10.03.01, Cardiff
  HTI- 50.90
GANIEL-O'NEILL Gladys V40 10.03.77, Abbey/IRL
  HMar- 77:07 (75:09-13), Mar- 2:37:55
GARCIA Ana U17 3.05.01, City of Sheffield
  3kW- 14:26.43i/14:35.57 (14:34.2-15), 10kWR- 51:53
  5kW- 26:43.59 (24:58.8-14), 5kWR- 24:34 (24:01-14)
GARGAN Emily U20 29.12.98, Gateshead
  LJ- 5.68, TJ- 13.03
GARLAND Katie U23 27.01.97, Brighton & Hove/Lough St
  60H- 8.95i, 100H- 14.41, HJ- 1.76, Hep- 5076,
  LJ- 5.61i (5.83i/5.78w/5.73-15), PentIS- 3599i
GARNER Alice U15 17.01.03, Aldershot F&D
  3k- 10:20.54mx/10:35.2
GARRATHY Hollie U20 18.02.99, Southampton
  TJ- 11.40
GARRATT Lottie U20 13.09.98, Yeovil Olympiads
  Hep- 3873
GARRETT Hannah U15 9.11.02, Annan
  HTI- 38.80
GARROTT Francesca U20 7.10.98, Telford
  JT- 40.58
GASS Paula 13.06.94, Edinburgh AC/Stirling Un
  JT- 39.69 (44.78-15)
GATRELL Eleanor V40 5.10.76, Woking
  SP- 12.32 (16.17-10), DT- 35.97 (42.93-13)
GAULD Nicola V35 28.03.82, Aberdeen
  5k- 17:16.32mx, 10MR- 58:46
GAULT Mandy 9.01.84, City of Portsmouth
  100- 12.1, 200- 24.50 (24.4w-14), 400- 55.06i/55.31 (54.24-14)
GAUNTLETT Elise U23 11.01.95, Bristol & W/Bath Spa
  PV- 3.50i/3.20 (3.60i-13, 3.50-15)
GAUNTLETT Olivia U20 7.01.98, Team Bath/Harvard
  60H- 8.59i, 100H- 13.80
GAYLER Emma 4.04.88, Harrow
  LJ- 5.64 (5.70w/5.67-14)
GEARY Sara 6.04.91, Yeovil Olympiads
  100H- 15.23w, LJ- 5.82w/5.75i (5.64-12)
GEDIZ Angel U15 24.04.03, Bexley
  300- 41.5
GELLION Amy U20 19.02.00, Rotherham
  400- 55.16
GEMMELL Cera U17 2.07.02, Team East Lothian
  3k- 9:52.90,
GENTRY Grace Nicole U17 7.09.00, Hertford & Ware
  300H- 44.5/45.34 (43.83-16), 400H- 65.55
GENTRY Rebecca .86
  Mar- 2:56:16
GHOSE Emily U20 2.06.99, Tonbridge
  5kW- 26:58.87
GIBB Willa Rose U15 11.09.03, Yate
  75HG- 11.6
GIBBENS Rachel 31.01.86, Marshall Milton K
  HJ- 1.70 (1.73-15), PV- 4.05 (4.13i-16, 4.05-15)
GIBSON Ashley 1.03.86, Tonbridge
  1500- 4:25.96 (4:18.72-12), 5k- 16:20.65,
  3k- 9:24.82mx/9:31.72 (9:23.3-13), 10kR- 33:32
GIBSON Katie U13 8.12.04, Kettering
  HTI- 40.85
GIFFORD GROVES Lucia U15 4.08.03, Thanet AC
  200- 25.64w/25.69

GILBERT Nicola 12.03.85, Enfield & Haringey
  60- 7.43i (7.37i-16)
GILKES Isabella U17 23.04.01, Reading
  100- 12.33 (12.11w-16, 12.3-15)
  200- 25.18 (25.1-16, 25.12w-15)
GILMOUR Emma U23 8.05.97, Gateshead
  400H- 64.66
GILMOUR Jenny U23 8.05.97, Gateshead/Newcastle Un
  400H- 62.63
GLASBY-SEDDON Poppy U15 24.11.02, Sale
  200- 25.9/25.99, 300- 41.6
GLOVER Lynsey 3.12.87, Lagan Valley
  HT- 43.23 (44.08-15)
GOLBAN Andreea U17 30.01.02, Woodford Green & Ex L
  HT- 39.10, HTI- 51.01
GOLDING Zipporah U15 16.11.03, Hercules Wimbledon
  60- 7.90i, 100- 12.48
GOODSELL Grace U15 4.04.03, Bury
  60- 7.87i, LJ- 5.50i/5.49, TJ- 10.67 (10.88i)
GORDON Anna U23 30.01.97, Edinburgh AC/Cardiff Met
  PV- 3.61i (4.00i-16, 3.85-14)
GORDON Gillian U20 14.06.98, Inverness
  400H- 64.03
GORDON Jessica U17 23.04.02, New Forest Juniors
  HJ- 1.68
GORDON Myisha U17 14.10.00, Sale
  100- 12.2/12.27
GORECKA Emelia 29.01.94, Aldershot F&D
  1500- 4:23.24mx (4:14.22mx/4:15.38-12), 5kR- 15:40,
  3k- 9:03.85 (8:55.11-12), 5k- 15:44.34 (15:07.45-14)
GOSSAGE Lucy M V35 25.12.79, TFN Tri
  HMar- 76:35
GOUÉNON Adeline Nanzia 20.10.94, St Marys Un/CIV
  60- 7.40i (7.26i-16), 100- 11.79 (11.49-15)
GRACE Serena U15 6.01.03, City of Norwich
  100- 12.33w/12.50, 200- 25.7w, 300- 41.8
GRAHAM Laura U20 6.02.99, Blackheath & Bromley
  JT- 41.25
GRAHAM Laura 5.03.86, Mourne Runners
  10kR- 34:21, 10MR- 57:18, HMar- 76:59, Mar- 2:37:05
GRAHAM Sophie U15 16.05.03, Ipswich
  DT- 30.00, JTI- 39.39
GRAHAME Niamh U23 3.02.97, Giffnock N/Glasgow Un
  400- 56.37i/56.55
GRANGER Annabel V40 19.05.73, Bristol & West
  HMar- 78:38 (77:50-04)
GRANT Elsbeth U17 8.02.02, Matlock AC
  3k- 9:52.46
GRANT Kierra U17 17.11.01, Shaftesbury B
  TJ- 11.32
GRANVILLE Caryl Sian 24.09.89, Carmarthen
  200- 24.35mx/24.50, 400- 55.93i (55.02i/55.24-12),
  60H- 8.62i (8.56i-16), 100H- 13.46w/13.48, 400H- 56.59
GRAY Eloise U15 17.09.02, Team East Lothian
  200- 25.88i/25.90
GRAY Isobel U20 5.11.98, Winchester
  DT- 40.42
GRAY Rebecca U20 4.10.98, Cornwall AC
  PV- 3.55 (3.75i-15, 3.71-14)
GREEN Georgia U23 28.09.96, Enfield & Har/Aston Un
  TJ- 11.80
GREEN Lois U15 6.05.03, Chesterfield
  PV- 2.67
GREENHALGH Bronia U17 13.03.01, Wigan
  PV- 3.10
GREENWAY Ella U13 3.01.05, Cleethorpes
  800- 2:20.0, 1200- 3:49.5
GREENWAY Megan U15 20.02.03, Sale
  TJ- 10.78
GREENWOOD Ashton U20 23.01.99, Trafford
  400- 55.71
GREGORY Nicola U23 2.04.96, Bexley/Surrey Un
  DT- 35.49 (38.26-12)
GREIG Evie U13 4.01.05, VP-Glasgow
  HJ- 1.53
GREIG Lauren Margaret U17 20.09.00, Kilmarnock
  60- 7.75i, 100- 12.12w/12.22, 200- 24.89i/25.04
GRICE Maisie U20 29.06.00, Aldershot F&D
  1.5kSt- 5:07.93 (4:59.56-16), JT- 37.38

415

GRIEVE Rebecca U13 30.01.05, Edinburgh AC
60HM- 9.98i, PenM- 2366, PenIM- 2412i
GRIFFIN Sydney 16.10.93, N&EB/East London Un/USA
60- 7.71i, 200- 24.61 (24.23-14), 60H- 8.38i,
100H- 13.51w/13.63 (13.53-15)
GRIFFIN MORRIS Isobel U20 8.12.99, Radley AC
DT- 43.03 (46.48-16)
GRIFFITH Nina 8.07.85, Highgate H
Mar- 2:53:16
GRIFFITHS Amy U23 22.03.96, AF&D/St Marys Un
800- 2:07.18 (2:06.17mx-15), 1500- 4:12.67
GRIFFITHS Bobbie U17 15.03.01, Morpeth
JT- 42.27, JTI- 46.03
GRIFFITHS Lucy 3.04.94, Cardiff
SP- 12.76 (13.88i/13.40-16)
GRIFFITHS Samantha 31.05.94, Cheltenham
100- 12.1
GRIGG Melanie U23 25.11.95, Herts Phoenix/Bath Un
400H- 63.18
GRIMA Claire M. V35 21.07.77, Hercules Wimbledon
Mar- 2:43:30 (2:43:01-16)
GRIMWADE Cassey U15 27.09.02, Cardiff
DT- 29.91, HTI- 46.84
GROGAN Evie 3.04.94, Belgrave
HJ- 1.68 (1.74i-15, 1.72-12)
GROSJEAN Alice 19.09.93, Mendip
DT- 42.36
GROSVENOR Yasmin U15 23.02.03, Bracknell
LJ- 5.25, SPI- 11.41, PenG- 2965, PenIG- 3013i
GROVE Eleanor U20 16.10.99, Guildford & Godalming
200- 24.73, 400- 55.84
GROVES Natalie U15 1.04.04, Spenborough
200- 25.58
GUEST Niamh U23 16.01.97, Pitreavie
100H- 15.25
GUEYE Serena U13 20.07.05, Chiltern H
75- 9.9
GUMBS Seemita V35 27.12.81, Birchfield
400H- 64.78 (64.1-07, 64.57-09)
GUNN Bryony U20 28.02.98, Birchfield
3k- 9:44.44 (9:38.03-16), 5k- 17:15.35 (16:39.88-16)
GUTTERIDGE Mercy U23 8.06.97, Shaft B/Brunel Un
PV- 3.20i (3.50i-15, 3.35-16)
GUTZMORE Sineade 9.10.86, Birchfield
TJ- 13.44 (13.70-16)
GYEDU Nana U15 4.11.02, Cambridge H
SPI- 14.33
GYURKO Fanni 18.01.87, Central/Glasgow Un/HUN
HMar- 77:28 (75:45sh-16), Mar- 2:39:48

HADAWAY Lucy Jane U20 11.06.00, City of York
60H- 8.93i, 100HI- 14.45, 100H- 14.7/14.85,
LJ- 6.09, SP- 11.75i/11.13, JT- 36.74, Hep- 4187
HAGUE Nicole U15 18.10.02, Hallamshire
60HG- 9.09i
HAIGH Sophie-Ann U20 22.10.98, Chichester R&AC
100- 12.10w, 200- 24.7/24.88
HALES Danielle U15 7.11.02, Telford
60HG- 9.4i, 75HG- 11.16
HALEY Emma 23.02.88, Radley AC
800- 2:08.69mx/2:08.89
HALL Amber-Leigh U20 10.10.98, WSE&H
100H- 14.15w/14.24 (13.9-15, 14.05-16)
HALL Holly U17 22.12.01, Hillingdon
JT- 36.64, JTI- 40.34
HALL Jessica U17 25.01.01, Guildford & Godalming
PV- 3.26i/3.12i (3.10-16)
HALL Rebecca Ann 15.09.88, Nene Valley H
SP- 12.45 (12.70/12.82dh-16), DT- 35.38 (36.56-16)
HALL Sophie U17 17.01.01, Oldham & Royton
300H- 45.99
HALLAM Lydia U23 26.02.97, Havering/Birmingham Un
1500- 4:25.52
HAMES Emma Dorthea U15 30.03.03, Neath
HTI- 41.58
HAMILTON Precious U17 5.03.02, VPH &TH
DT- 33.74
HAMILTON-STRONG Megan U15 23.09.03, Exeter
PenG- 2886

HAMPLETT Emma U20 27.07.98, Birchfield
JT- 51.02 (52.27-16)
HANKINS Daniella 14.06.93, Bedford & Co/Bedford Un
HJ- 1.67i (1.70i-11, 1.69-10)
HANNYNGTON Ella U15 29.11.02, Horsham BS
60HG- 9.40i
HARDCASTLE Kath V35 81, Fairlands Valley
Mar- 2:50:45 (2:45:42-14)
HARDMAN Maia U17 17.10.01, Brighton Phoenix
800- 2:14.53i (2:14.0mx-16)
HARDY Catherine Jayne Francis U20 5.01.98, Cardiff/
Cardiff Met
60- 7.73i, 100- 12.06 (12.0/12.03w-15)
HARLAND Amy U13 21.03.05, Birchfield
800- 2:21.46mx, 1500- 4:48.2
HARLAND Phoebe U17 3.02.01, Birchfield
HJ- 1.65i/1.65 (1.73-15)
HARLEY Bethany U20 26.08.99, Stevenage & NH
Hep- 3835
HARNEY Anaisa U17 28.09.00, Bracknell
SP- 11.05
HARRELL Urina 8.02.94, Shaftesbury B/Lough St/USA
SP- 15.31 (15.34-16)
HARRIS Karina U17 8.02.01, Blackheath & Bromley
TJ- 11.46
HARRIS Samantha U17 4.11.01, City of Plymouth
80HI- 11.17, HepI- 4632
HARRIS Sophie 12.06.93, Belgrave
3k- 9:38.8, 5k- 17:03.04, 10kR- 34:41
HARRIS-JENKINS Evie U20 22.09.98, Rugby & Nor AC
JT- 39.47 (40.23-16)
HARRISON Melanie 27.11.85, Enfield & Haringey
DT- 38.02 (43.48-11)
HARRISON Mikaela 5.08.90, Wakefield/RAF
400H- 64.3/65.82 (63.13-13)
HARRISON Natasha U17 17.03.01, Stockport
300- 39.57 (39.29-16), 400- 56.45,
800- 2:14.21mx (2:11.57mx-16, 2:11.64-15)
HARRISON Rochelle 1.02.91, Lincoln Wellington
1500- 4:26.63
HARRISON Roisin U23 10.10.96, Aberdeen/Aberd Un/IRL
200- 24.76 (24.12w-15, 24.63-13)
HARRISON Shanice 30.10.93, South London H
60- 7.74i (7.53i-16)
HARRISON Susan V45 6.08.71, Leamington
50kR- 3:49:35+ (3:15:43-10), 100kR- 8:01:22 (7:39:50-15)
HARRIS-OSMAN Latifah U17 7.05.02, Shaftesbury B
60- 7.78i, 100- 12.2/12.34
HARRYMAN Bethany U17 13.10.00, Harlow
HJ- 1.65, HepI- 4418
HART Emma U15 23.07.03, Darlington
3k- 10:36.84
HARTIGAN Georgina U23 1.03.96, Birchfield/Lough St
800- 2:06.94 (2:06.48-16), 1500- 4:20.28mx/4:22.08
HARVEY Carolyn U23 31.05.96, Ayr Seaforth/St'clyde Un
TJ- 12.18
HARVEY Eloise U17 13.11.00, Dartford
LJ- 5.77, TJ- 12.19
HARVEY Joanne Rebecca 27.09.89, Aldershot F&D
HMar- 78:10, Mar- 2:50:58
HARVEY Nichole U17 29.11.00, Basildon
TJ- 11.10
HASELDEN Genevieve U15 10.10.02, Cheltenham
PV- 2.80
HASLAM Amy U17 5.01.02, Sale
PV- 3.10i/2.91 (2.91-16)
HATTON Lucy 8.11.94, Corby/Leics Un
60H- 8.38i (7.90i-15), 100H- 13.41 (12.84-15)
HAWKINS Rebecca 27.09.99, Bexley
HJ- 1.80i/1.77 (1.77-16)
HAWLING Beth 28.07.94, Cheltenham/Virginia Tech Un
5k- 17:14.24
HAY Sophie U23 14.08.96, Cardiff/Cardiff Un
100H- 14.39w/14.75 (14.62-13)
HAYES Camellia U23 6.04.95, WSE&H/London Un
HJ- 1.74 (1.81i-13, 1.80-16)
HAYES Isabella U15 22.04.04, Horsham BS
1500- 4:44.49mx

HEAD Katie U20 9.12.99, Newham & Essex B
  HT- 55.25
HEALY Erin U17 16.10.01, Kettering
  100- 12.3, 200- 25.39w
HEDGETHORNE Katy 17.09.88, Camb & Col/Camb Un
  5k- 17:15.85mx (17:18.75-15), 10kR- 34:46
HEDLEY Anna U15 16.01.04, Fife
  1500- 4:37.30, 3k- 9:55.14mx
HEMMINGS Chanel 21.07.94, Woodford Green & Ex L
  TJ- 11.40i/11.32 (11.60w/11.55-15)
HEMPLEMAN-ADAMS Amelia U23 1.06.95, Bristol & W/
  Birmingham Un   HJ- 1.69i (1.72-11)
HEMSLEY Millie U20 31.10.98, Lewes
  PV- 3.10 (3.20i/3.20-16)
HENDERSON Laura-Ann 1.10.94, Ashford
  PV- 3.20 (3.52i-12, 3.40-11)
HENDRY Mhairi U23 31.03.96, VP-Glasgow/St'clyde Un
  400- 55.96i/56.04 (55.81-16), 800- 2:03.37,
  1500- 4:16.37mx/4:20.78
HENRY Desiree U23 26.08.95, Enfield & Haringey
  100- 11.09 (11.04w-14, 11.06-16),
  200- 22.69 (22.46-16), 400- 53.33 (52.27-16)
HENRY Jade U17 26.12.00, VP-Glasgow
  60HI- 8.79i (8.78i-16), 80HI- 11.39, 100HI- 14.74i/14.74
HENRY Tia U17 9.04.01, Livingston
  Hepl- 4101
HENSON Jamelia U20 9.05.00, Peterborough
  100H- 14.77w/15.0/15.30 (15.29-16)
HERBERT Poppy U15 21.02.03, City of Portsmouth
  PV- 2.60
HERRINGTON Amy U20 22.05.98, WSE&H/N.Dakota St
  SP- 11.24i, HT- 59.14
HERRINGTON Lauren U23 28.11.96, WSE&H/Brunel Un
  800- 2:09.97
HESKETH Laura 9.04.83, Clayton Le Moors
  5kR- 16:45, 10kR- 34:30
HESLOP Sian U15 27.09.02, Macclesfield
  800- 2:16.9, 1500- 4:31.79mx/4:32.17
HETHERINGTON Abbie U23 2.10.95, Border/Okla' St Un
  800- 2:07.42 (2:06.26-16), 1k- 2:46.18i, 1500- 4:22.58
HETHERINGTON Katie U20 6.04.00, Oxford City
  HJ- 1.68 (1.68-16), Hep- 3912
HEWITT Sarah Jayne V40 31.01.74, Brighton & Hove
  DT- 38.09 (40.23-12)
HEWITT Tegan U17 22.01.02, Gateshead
  PV- 2.91i/2.90
HIBBERT Shanara 22.03.93, Luton
  LJ- 5.62 (5.91-14), TJ- 12.87
HICKEY Laura U17 6.01.02, Leigh
  60HI- 9.05i, PenII- 3316i
HICKMAN-DUNNE Joanne 4.06.91, B'hth & Br/Lough St
  3k- 9:37.34mx/9:40.47i (9:33.74mx/9:44.51-16)
HIGHFIELD Rachel U23 2.02.96, Trafford/Durham Un
  60- 7.73i, 200- 24.6/24.78 (24.44-13),
  100- 12.00w/12.0/12.15 (11.91w/12.0/12.06-13)
HILDITCH Isabella U20 15.06.99, Blackheath & Bromley
  60H- 8.67i, 100H- 13.67
HILDREW Megan U20 25.06.99, Guildford & Godalming
  60H- 8.84i (8.77i-16), 100H- 14.33, TJ- 11.55 (11.71-16)
HILL Alexandra 10.08.93, Herts Phoenix
  400H- 60.87
HILL Irie Heidi Alexa V45 16.01.69, WSE&H
  PV- 3.45 (4.20-00)
HILL Jenna 16.10.85, Sale
  800- 2:08.11mx (2:06.50-15), 1500- 4:19.41mx
  (4:13.24-15), 3k- 9:13.82mx/9:21.93 (9:07.17mx-15),
  5k- 16:44.05 (16:07.86-15), 10kR- 34:17 (33:45-15)
HILL Lauren U17 19.09.00, Chesterfield
  HT- 45.28, HTI- 54.77 (55.74-16), JT- 36.58, JTI- 40.30
HILL Sarah V40 25.02.73, Farnham Runners
  Mar- 2:54:11 (2:53:05-13)
HILLAND Rebecca V35 11.06.80, Team Bath
  5kR- 16:32+, 10kR- 33:36, HMar- 75:40 (75:39-16)
HILLEY Caroline U23 18.09.96, Central/Cambridge Un
  100H- 14.67w (14.90-16), 400H- 61.55
HILLIER-MOSES Gemma 19.06.88, Charnwood
  1500- 4:24.45i (4:19.52mx-16, 4.20.28-15),
  3k- 9:22.60i (9:14.63-15), 5kR- 16:35 (16:20-16)

HILLMAN Leah U20 10.06.99, Pendle
  SP- 11.13 (11.46-16), JT- 44.18
HILLMAN Lois U20 11.05.00, Cardiff
  PV- 3.43i/3.15 (3.21-16)
HILLYARD Amy U23 28.10.95, Birchfield/Wolvs Un
  400- 56.73i (54.85-15), 400H- 63.01 (61.48-16)
HINCHLIFFE Elle Grace U15 16.10.03, City of Sheffield
  60HG- 9.25i, 75HG- 11.6
HINCHLY Amy U20 11.01.98, Vale Royal/Hallam Un
  800- 2:09.86, 1500- 4:27.80mx (4:25.76-15)
HIRST Jessica U20 27.05.99, Halifax
  DT- 36.00
HITCHON Sophie 11.07.91, Blackburn
  HT- 73.97 (74.54-16)
HOBBS Hannah U20 4.12.99, Yate
  1500- 4:27.36, 3k- 9:37.37mx
HOCKEY Fiona U20 21.01.98, Blackpool/Cardiff Met
  PV- 3.80i/3.70 (3.70-15)
HODGKINSON Danielle 11.10.84, Birchfield/Army
  3k- 9:36.37 (9:34.24-14), 5kR- 16:28,
  10kR- 34:49 (34:41-12)
HODGKINSON Keely U17 3.03.02, Leigh
  800- 2:06.85, 1500- 4:29.1
HODGSON Ellie U20 26.08.00, Southampton
  SP- 12.27i/11.68
HODGSON Megan U17 16.12.00, Cardiff
  PV- 3.51i/3.41
HODGSON Sophie U17 25.06.02, Notts
  HJ- 1.69
HODSON Eve U20 21.01.99, Coventry Godiva
  DT- 38.56
HOLDER Amy U23 4.08.96, WSE&H/Brunel Un
  SP- 11.79, DT- 54.27
HOLDER Katie 13.01.92, Blackpool/Oxford Un
  SP- 11.25 (11.25-16)
HOLDSWORTH Catherine 3.01.86, Colchester H
  SP- 11.94 (13.10-11)
HOLE Molly U15 28.02.03, Salisbury
  HJ- 1.73i/1.71, SPI- 12.44, PenG- 2887
HOLGUIN Paula U17 1.10.00, Cambridge H
  JT- 38.82, JTI- 45.66 (47.01-16)
HOLLAND Eva U15 3.05.04, Herne Hill
  1500- 4:40.25mx/4:42.00, 3k- 10:15.69
HOLLAND Jamie U15 6.01.03, Swansea
  SPI- 11.38, JTI- 37.84
HOLLIS-LAWRENCE Georgia U20 27.06.99, C of Sheff
  60H- 8.76i, 100H- 14.30
HOLMES Lucy Helen 29.12.92, Wakefield
  SP- 12.01i/11.88 (12.51-11)
HOLT Emma 27.05.85, Morpeth
  10kR- 34:59
HOLT Kate 7.09.92, City of Stoke
  3k- 9:23.3, 5k- 16:20.26, 5MR- 27:49
HOLT Katie U20 16.06.99, Reading
  JT- 37.30 (39.89-16)
HOLT Lily U15 2.10.02, Chiltern H
  HJ- 1.61
HOLT Sarah Joanne 17.04.87, Sale
  HT- 63.41 (68.97-15)
HOPESON Twinelle 23.09.91, Croydon
  60H- 8.80i, 100H- 14.19 (14.04-16)
HOPKINS Danielle U17 29.12.01, Worcester AC
  HJ- 1.73, TJ- 11.11, Hepl- 4345
HOPKINS Jessica U17 6.01.02, Chelmsford
  60HI- 8.99i, 80HI- 11.85w/11.9, HJ- 1.68, SPI- 14.05,
  LJ- 5.75w/5.72i/5.71, Hepl- 5050, PenII- 3788i
HOPKINS Katie U17 14.08.01, Woking
  800- 2:14.0
HOPKINSON Stephanie 27.10.89, Birtley
  SP- 11.46 (12.10-13), DT- 35.01 (38.50-08)
HORSEY Emma U15 3.05.03, Walton
  800- 2:15.74
HOSKER-THORNHILL Emily 27.10.92, Aldershot F&D
  800- 2:09.84, 1500- 4:18.01 (4:17.74-16),
  3k- 9:11.70mx (9:45.81-14), 5k- 16:32.59
HOSKINS Caroline V45 29.12.67, Reading RR
  Mar- 2:57:05

417

HOWARD Hannah 14.04.85, Eastleigh RC
Mar- 2:49:03
HOWARD Millie U20 4.02.98, Harrogate/Temple Un
800- 2:08.32 (2:06.22-16)
HOWARD Rebecca U23 20.01.96, AF&D/St Marys Un C
5k- 17:16.02
HOWARTH Abigail 8.10.92, Leigh/Cardiff Un
1500- 4:23.93, 5k- 16:57.99, 5kR- 16:56
HOWARTH Lauren 21.04.90, Leigh
3k- 9:15.83i/9.25.06+ (8:52.00i-13, 9:04.57mx-16,
9:10.32-12), 5k- 15:29.26, 5kR- 15:39, 5MR- 27:24,
10kR- 34:05 (32:33-11)
HOWARTH Megan U15 6.09.02, Southport
JTI- 36.41
HOWDEN Katelyn U13 2.02.05, Cleethorpes
800- 2:22.03
HOWE Emma U17 6.04.01, West Cheshire
JTI- 50.34
HOWE Georgina 18.09.93, Ipswich
HT- 50.04
HOWE Stephanie U20 19.01.99, Woodford Green & Ex L
HT- 47.32
HOYLE Eleanor U17 24.10.00, Reading
DT- 32.00
HOYTE Caroline V45 30.06.70, Arena 80
3k- 9:45.32 (9:28.9mx-08, 9:32.4-03),
5k- 17:17.7mx (16:17.10-10)
HUDSON Molly U17 16.08.02, Derby AC
1500- 4:37.92
HUGGINS-WARD Simone 7.10.89, Coventry Godiva
JT- 39.31 (45.57-13)
HUGHES Amber U13 3.11.05, Southport
60HM- 9.55i, 70HM- 11.37, PenM- 2376
HUGHES Cari U20 15.03.99, Swansea
1500- 4:24.86, 3k- 9:29.76mx/9:29.77i/9:43.35
HUGHES Liberty U20 11.01.00, Crewe & Nantwich
Hep- 3970
HUGHES Lucy U15 16.10.03, Cornwall AC
PV- 2.90
HUGHES Anandamayi U17 5.11.00, Havering
60HI- 9.03i, 80HI- 11.9 (11.86-16), HJ- 1.64, LJ- 5.58,
TJ- 12.03
HUGHES Megan U17 28.11.01, Ipswich
JTI- 39.43
HUGHES Michelle Zoe U20 1.02.98, Havering/Harvard
60H- 8.71i, 100H- 13.78, HJ- 1.67i/1.65 (1.70-14), LJ-
6.07i/5.99, SP- 12.73i/11.93, Hep- 5444, PentIS- 4093i
HUGHES Zoe U23 9.12.97, Wigan/Edge Hill Un
TJ- 11.37 (11.77-16)
HULBERT Megan U13 29.12.04, Southampton
JTM- 30.49
HULLAND Jasmine U15 29.11.02, Cueva de Nerja ESP
TJ- 11.05
HULLAND Lily Rosa U17 1.09.01, Cueva de Nerja ESP
100H- 15.55w/15.61, 400H- 66.84,
TJ- 12.09A/12.00w/11.99
HULME Katie U17 12.08.02, Shrewsbury AC
300H- 46.21
HUMPHREYS Corinne Dawn 7.11.91, Orion/E.London Un
60- 7.39i (7.38i-16), 100- 11.39, 200- 24.03
HUMPHREYS Jessica U17 30.10.01, Wolves & Bilston
3k- 10:14.7mx
HUNT Amy U17 15.05.02, Charnwood
60- 7.43i, 100- 11.53w/11.65+/11.66, 150- 17.30st,
200- 24.33
HUNT Amy U13 22.09.04, Wakefield
PV- 2.90i/2.70
HUNT Erin U13 22.09.04, Wakefield
PV- 2.30
HUNT Leisha U15 5.09.02, Chelmsford
LJ- 5.30, PenG- 2870
HUNT Sarah U17 11.10.01, City of Portsmouth
SPI- 12.36
HUNTER Emma U17 14.02.02, Southampton
DT- 32.63
HUNTER Hannah 7.10.82, Manx H
3kW- 14:35.41i, 5kWR- 24:19,
10kWR- 51:45 (51:37-16), 20kW- 1:47:17

HUNTER Jessica U23 4.12.96, Vale of Aylesbury
100H- 13.42
HUNTER Olivia U20 8.05.99, Poole
60H- 8.98i, 100H- 14.9 (14.8/14.95w/15.00-16)
HUNTER Rachel Joanne 30.08.93, North Ayrshire
SP- 11.71i (12.65-11), HT- 66.46
HUSSAIN Adela U23 7.08.95, Oxford City/Oxford Brooks
HJ- 1.65 (1.65-15)
HUTCHINSON Kelsie 6.10.94, Derby AC
DT- 37.57 (38.50-11), HT- 47.56
HUTCHISON Jade U17 3.05.02, Pitreavie
60- 7.74i, 100- 12.07w,
200- 24.6w/24.7/24.87i/25.15 (24.64-16)
HUXHAM Saskia U17 14.11.00, Hallamshire
800- 2:09.25, 300H- 44.79, 400H- 64.8
HYLTON Cheriece U23 19.12.96, Blackheath & Bromley
100- 11.67, 200- 23.23 (23.15w-15),
300- 38.42 (37.59-13), 400- 52.68mx/52.88
HYLTON Shannon U23 19.12.96, Blackheath & Bromley
60- 7.37i, 100- 11.47, 200- 22.94 (22.73w/22.94-15)

IBBETSON Jemma U20 3.09.97, Leeds
DT- 46.85
IHEKE Mary Chinwe 19.11.90, Enfield & Haringey
100- 12.10, 200- 24.21 (23.64w-14, 24.01-15), 400- 52.60
INGLE Katie U23 4.03.95, R Sutton Coldfield/B'ham Un
3k- 9:44.34, 2kSt- 6:44.34 (6:43.13-15), 3kSt- 10:02.34
INGLES Grace U15 7.11.02, Shaftesbury B
1500- 4:43.45mx, 3k- 10:33.7
INGLIS Sarah 28.08.91, Lothian RC
1500- 4:12.99 (4:12.58-16), 5k- 15:41.29, 10kR- 33:28,
HMar- 73:36
INGRAM Dion U17 14.03.01, Law & District
300H- 46.24
INSTANCE Hayley U17 6.05.02, Thurrock
800- 2:14.03mx, 1500- 4:38.39mx
IRAWO Melina U20 9.07.00, Enfield & Haringey
DT- 37.98
IRELAND Faye U17 31.08.01, Liverpool H
1500- 4:33.17 (4:29.54-16),
3k- 10:09.50mx (9:49.23mx/9:50.92-16)
IRVINE Iona U13 22.11.04, Basingstoke & MH
100- 12.63, 200- 26.88w, 60HM- 9.80i (9.70i-16),
70HM- 11.12w/11.18, HJ- 1.53, LJ- 5.09w/5.03
IRVING Shirin U23 25.09.96, WSE&H
400H- 65.86
IRVING-HYMAN Daisy U23 12.05.96, Cambridge Un
400H- 65.27
ISAIAS Ella U13 22.11.04, Erme Valley
HJ- 1.51
IVE Jade 22.01.92, Sutton & District
PV- 4.36i/4.20
IVES Isobel U20 17.06.98, Basildon/Bath Un
800- 2:07.88 (2:07.43-13)
IWUNZE Chinwe U17 6.02.01, Barnet
60- 7.90i

JACKSON Avril 22.10.86, Edinburgh AC
400- 56.06 (55.64-16), 100H- 15.30 (15.13w-07),
300H- 42.67 (42.65-16), 400H- 58.66
JACKSON Caitlin U13 16.07.05, Channel Islands
JTM- 32.04
JACKSON Esther U15 9.08.03, Cambridge H
200- 25.5
JACKSON Hannah 8.09.91, Bristol & West
100H- 14.81w/14.93 (14.61-13)
JACKSON Montana 2.12.93, Thames Valley/London Un
LJ- 5.65i (5.53w/5.51-15),
TJ- 12.66i/12.44 (12.72w/12.69-16)
JACKSON Tia U17 5.08.02, Bristol & West
60- 7.82i, 100- 12.07, 200- 24.76w/24.77, LJ- 5.76,
HepI- 4214
JAMES Lucy 18.02.92, Bedford & County
800- 2:08.39 (2:06.42-16)
JAMIESON Elspeth U23 5.09.96, C of Norwich/B'ham Un
JT- 42.00 (43.84-14)
JANSEN VAN RENSBERG Danel U20 28.12.98, Birchfield
400H- 60.37

JAPAL Salome U20 6.09.98, Enfield & Haringey
60- 7.73i, 100- 12.01w/12.02, 200- 24.89w
JAPP Emily 18.12.90, Blackpool & Fylde
3k- 9:44.6, 5k- 16:33.79
JAROSINSKI Heidi 8.03.87, Halesowen
LJ- 5.72 (5.75-16)
JARVIS Chelsea U23 23.01.96, Stockport/Florida State U
800- 2:07.79i (2:04.45i-16, 2:05.89-13), 1k- 2:47.13i
JARVIS Hannah 15.10.84, Dorking & Mole V
Mar- 2:52:07
JEFFREY Lottie U15 3.02.03, Falkirk VH
60- 8.01i, 100- 12.4/12.50, 200- 25.49
JEGER Maisie U15 24.11.03, Southampton
PenIG- 3174i
JEGGO Rebecca U20 12.01.00, Colchester H
100- 12.08w/12.1/12.11, 200- 24.77w/24.88 (24.75w-16)
JELF Renee U17 5.02.01, Team Bath
HJ- 1.65
JENKINS Andrea Louise V40 4.10.75, Nene Valley H
DT- 40.23 (42.68-06), HT- 49.71 (53.25-12)
JENKINS Grace 27.08.93, Newham & Essex B
DT- 42.79 (43.74-14), HT- 42.29
JENKINS Thea U17 14.10.00, Pembroke
HJ- 1.63i
JENNINGS Abigail U20 10.07.00, Aldershot F&D
5kW- 27:05.6
JENNINGS Emma U15 28.07.03, Aldershot F&D
JTI- 35.12
JENNINGS Rebecca 7.12.90, Harrow/London Met Un
100H- 14.76w/15.0/15.11 (14.18-15)
JENNINGS MCLAUGHLIN Amelia U23 20.04.97, Trafford/
Edge Hill Un   HJ- 1.71i/1.70 (1.80i/1.77-15)
JENVEY Gracie U13 6.02.05, Southampton
SPM- 9.99
JESSOP Marli U15 27.06.03, Dacorum & Tring
60- 8.00i, 100- 12.55w, 60HI- 8.96i, 60HG- 9.04i,
75HG- 11.34, LJ- 5.35
JESUDASON Andrea 5.12.92, Bristol & West
LJ- 5.64w/5.60, TJ- 11.35
JOHANSEN Kimberley 18.11.94, Chelmsford/Elon Un
800- 2:08.31, 1k- 2:49.22i, 1500- 4:17.35, 1M- 4:42.77i
JOHNS Rebecca U17 9.11.01, Sutton in Ashfield
80HI- 11.65, TJ- 11.29, HepI- 4298
JOHNSON Carolyn Rose 22.08.88, Blackheath & Bromley
1500- 4:27.23mx (4:20.69mx-14, 4:24.50-15)
JOHNSON Emma U15 7.02.04, Edinburgh AC
800- 2:16.76i (2:17.91mx-16), 1500- 4:39.44mx/4:42.38
JOHNSON Hannah 14.06.94, WSE&H/Cardiff Met
JT- 51.57
JOHNSON Katie U13 30.04.05, Edinburgh AC
800- 2:20.24mx/2:22.20, 1200- 3:50.81, 1500- 4:47.12mx/4:53.2
JOHNSON Rosemary U23 17.09.97, Liv Pemb S/Lough St
800- 2:08.96mx (2:06.94-16),
1500- 4:26.95 (4:15.32mx-14, 4:18.39-15)
JOHNSON Samantha 23.08.90, Rotherham
3k- 9:47.46i (9:27.83mx-16)
JOHNSON Treena V55 29.08.61, Dewsbury
Mar- 2:55:48
JOHNSON Victoria U17 7.10.01, Charnwood
100- 12.22w, 60HI- 8.82i, 80HI- 11.15, 300H- 45.88
JOHNSON-THOMPSON Katarina Mary 9.01.93, L'pool H
200- 22.81 (22.79-16), 800- 2:08.10 (2:07.64-13),
60H- 8.42i (8.18i-15), 100H- 13.29, HJ- 1.95 (1.98-16),
LJ- 6.75 (6.93i-15, 6.92-14), SP- 12.85 (13.14-16),
JT- 41.72 (42.01-15), Hep- 6691
JOHNSTONE Kate U20 12.04.00, Team East Lothian
100- 12.0
JOLLY Jasmine U17 7.12.01, Preston
60HI- 8.82i, 80HI- 11.5, 300H- 42.55
JONES Abigail U20 14.11.99, WSE&H
JT- 37.97
JONES Ava U13 21.11.04, Doncaster
60- 7.99i, 200- 25.82i/26.70w/26.72
JONES Bronte Leigh U20 17.10.99, City of Sheffield
DT- 41.28 (42.53-16)
JONES Caryl Mair 4.04.87, Swansea
HMar- 74:22 (71:18-12), Mar- 2:34:16

JONES Carys U20 17.12.98, Carmarthen
PV- 3.52i/3.40 (3.45-16)
JONES Charlotte U20 6.09.99, Charnwood
TJ- 11.19i (11.49i/11.38-16)
JONES Chloe U20 1.10.99, Gloucester AC
DT- 38.79
JONES Christina 5.04.90, Bristol & West
HT- 62.96 (63.98-15)
JONES Dalis U15 21.10.03, Yate
1500- 4:44.80, 3k- 10:28.78mx
JONES Danielle U17 5.08.01, Carmarthen
DT- 35.45
JONES Donna 8.10.90, Swansea
400H- 63.65
JONES Ffion Louise U15 17.11.02, Cardiff
200- 25.93w
JONES Freya 13.11.93, Southampton
SP- 12.34, JT- 47.67 (55.36-14)
JONES Gabriella U13 23.09.04, City of Portsmouth
SPM- 11.07
JONES Harriet 30.06.88, WSE&H
100- 11.9/12.20w, 100H- 14.19 (13.82w/13.99-13)
JONES Lucy U20.01.91, Dudley & Stourbridge
200- 24.6
JONES Lucy U20 18.09.98, Charnwood
1.5kSt- 5:01.31 (4:59.93-14)
JONES Macey U20 18.07.00, Cwmbran
LJ- 5.64, TJ- 11.90
JONES Maya U15 10.02.03, Taunton
HJ- 1.63
JONES Moli U17 28.10.00, Colwyn Bay
60- 7.62i, 200- 25.36
JONES Olivia U20 20.02.00, Birchfield
HJ- 1.65 (1.68-16), Hep- 4301
JONES Rochelle 27.09.90, Newham & Essex B
TJ- 11.18 (12.11-10)
JONES Samia U15 2.09.03, Menai
1500- 4:41.72mx, 3k- 10:33.0
JONES Tait U17 14.02.01, Walton
DT- 41.33
JONES Latitia 7.09.85, Belgrave
10kR- 32:58, HMar- 75:45+ (72:56-14), Mar- 2:33:56
JOSHUA Blessing U17 21.05.01, Newham & Essex B
SPI- 12.60 (13.00-16)
JOYCE Katie U17 26.01.01, Leeds
80HI- 11.93, LJ- 5.54w, HepI- 4350
JUDD Jessica May U23 7.01.95, Chelmsford/Lough St
800- 2:02.14mx/2:05.52 (1:59.77-14), 1500- 4:03.73,
1M- 4:28.59, 3k- 8:43.24mx/8:59.60, 5k- 15:34.82
JUDD Jodie U20 25.09.98, Chelmsford
800- 2:10.48mx, 1500- 4:24.36, 5k- 16:59.74,
3k- 9:44.97 (9:39.96mx-16)
JUMA Saada U15 22.05.03, Middlesboro Mandale
HTI- 38.58

KAFKE Tara 17.02.89, Radley AC
200- 24.83w/25.00 (24.7-12, 24.96-13),
400- 54.98 (54.51-12)
KAKA Sade U15 26.09.02, City of Sheffield
200- 25.6/25.96
KEANEY Caitlin U13 16.10.04, Cornwall AC
PenM- 2365
KEARNEY Tamara U17 18.08.01, Cornwall AC
PV- 3.00
KEARSEY Sarah 30.08.94, Exeter
400H- 65.14 (64.0-12, 64.22-11)
KEATING Rebecca U23 31.08.97, Shaft B/Missouri Un
HT- 58.59
KEELEY Laura 10.10.90, Coventry Godiva
TJ- 11.27 (11.42-15)
KEHLER Lisa Martine V45 15.03.67, Wolves & Bilston
5kWR- 27:17 (21:42.51t-02), 10kWR- 53:33 (45:03-98)
KELLOCK Nicola U23 13.05.96, Lothian
JT- 36.27
KELLY Eimear U17 29.03.02, Derry
60HI- 8.90i, 80HI- 11.91
KELLY Erika 6.12.92, Northern (IOM)
3kW- 13:15.88, 5kW- 23:20.19, 10kWR- 48:54, 20kW- 1:41:27

419

KELLY Hannah U17 20.12.00, Bolton
60- 7.63i, 100- 12.16, 200- 24.25
KELLY Sophie 14.01.94, Cambridge & Coleridge
HMar- 77:25, Mar- 2:52:28
KENDALL Nicole U23 26.01.96, Kingston & P/Exeter Un
200- 24.43, 400- 54.67 (54.59-16), 400H- 64.2 (64.0-15)
KENNEDY Kate U23 16.02.96, Oxford Un/USA
400H- 63.19 (61.71-15)
KENNY Victoria 3.04.83, Hadleigh Hares
Mar- 2:55:50 (2:53:23-16)
KENT Donna 21.01.90, Bexley
HT- 42.71 (47.87-08)
KERIN Angel U20 28.08.98, Bournemouth
TJ- 11.41i/11.15 (11.45-16)
KERR Charlotte U17 6.08.01, Rotherham
HJ- 1.69
KERR Emily U13 12.01.05, Blackheath & Bromley
75- 9.7/9.84, 100- 12.86, 150- 19.51, 200- 26.89,
LJ- 4.97
KERSEY Gemma 6.02.92, Basildon
3k- 9:42.65i (9:10.48-12)
KHAMBAI-ANNAN Tyra U13 21.12.04, Team Hounslow
60- 8.10i, 75- 9.67
KIDDLE Aleasha 17.08.92, Chelmsford
60- 7.53i, 100- 11.81, 200- 24.76
KIDD-WALKER Nardhia 1.02.93, Birchfield
200- 24.16w/24.7/24.89 (24.89i-13)
KIDGER Beth 16.03.94, Brighton Phoenix
5k- 16:49.88, 5MR- 27:56
KIDNEY Zoe U17 17.10.00, Pendle
JTI- 39.92
KIFFIN Jazzmin U20 6.09.99, Charnwood
400- 56.8
KINGHAM Siobhan U20 2.11.98, Edinburgh AC
TJ- 12.04w/11.82
KIRK Elinor 26.04.89, Swansea
1500- 4:18.31i (4:15.93-14), 5k- 16:06.87 (15:37.65-16),
3k- 9:00.59i/9:27.07+ (9:02.11mx-16, 9:12.50-14),
5kR- 15:59, 10kR- 33:33 (32:17.05t-14),
HMar- 78:10 (74:19-15), Mar- 2:36:22
KIRKPATRICK Amy U15 22.09.03, Central
300- 41.93, 800- 2:13.53mx/2:14.63
KIRKWOOD Holly U13 15.12.04, VP-Glasgow
LJ- 4.93
KNIGHT Emily U15 5.02.04, Enfield & Haringey
60HG- 9.37
KNIGHT Jessie 15.06.94, WSE&H
200- 24.35w/24.55 (24.27-16), 400- 53.47,
800- 2:10.4mx, 400H- 58.00
KNIGHT Ottilie U17 1.02.01, Salisbury
JTI- 41.80
KNIGHT Victoria V40 3.10.76, Cambridge & Coleridge
5k- 16:58.0mx/17:11.4, 10kR- 34:24, HMar- 74:43
KNIGHTS Bethan U23 28.09.95, Bristol & W/UC Berkeley
1500- 4:20.64 (4:19.60-15), 5k- 16:02.62 (15:51.49-15),
3k- 9:21.35i (9:08.77i-16, 9:18.1+-14), 10k- 33:30.13
KNIGHTS Hannah U23 14.08.97, Guildford & G/Lough St
400H- 64.15 (62.68-16)
KNOTT Lucy U23 9.01.95, Thames Valley
HT- 44.31 (45.82-16)
KNOWLES-JONES Harriet U20 3.04.98, Warrington
800- 2:07.55, 1500- 4:13.59mx/4:14.95,
3k- 8:56.08mx/9:14.86
KOENIGSBERGER Lucy U17 4.09.01, West Norfolk
HTI- 50.96 (54.59-16)
KOKOVWORHO Joda U17 8.05.01, Aberdeen
100- 12.29
KOLAN Martyna U17 23.02.02, Edinburgh AC
HTI- 47.05
KOMOCKI Emma 17.03.92, Notts
100H- 15.24w (14.72-14), 400H- 63.05 (60.81-14)
KONE Emmanuela U15 3.04.03, Cardiff
60- 7.90i/8.00i
KORCZAK Elizabeth U15 12.04.03, Brighton & Hove
JTI- 43.62
KOTMILLOSHI Olga 12.07.83, Thames Valley/ALB
JT- 43.44 (47.41-14)
KREFTING Monique V45 13.11.69, Belgrave
400H- 64.56

KUPONIYI Omolola U15 5.03.04, Havering
SPI- 12.94, SPG- 12.19
KURETA Sotiria U17, Enfield & Har/GRE
DT- 33.78
KUTER Hayley V35 16.01.78, Salford/NZL
HMar- 78:42 (78:38-11)
KUYPERS Darcey U20 27.08.98, Medway & M/Brunel Un
100- 12.09
KYLE Georgia U20 18.09.99, Blaydon
DT- 41.25
KYNMAN Hannah U17 21.02.01, Kingston upon Hull
100- 12.32

LACHENICHT Ashleigh U20 10.04.00, Northern (IOM)
400- 56.6
LACY Louise 28.04.89, Havering
JT- 49.24
LAGOMARSINO Emily 13.05.92, San Domenico
Mar- 2:50:03
LAKE Iona 15.01.93, City of Norwich
3k- 9:25.89 (9:22.61mx-14, 9:22.75i- 15), 5kR- 16:40,
5k- 16:53.3 (16:15.93-15), 2kSt- 6:46.0 (6:43.53-14),
3kSt- 9:39.03
LAKE Jessica U15 25.09.02, Mansfield H
LJ- 5.28, TJ- 10.32
LAKE Morgan U23 12.05.97, WSE&H
100H- 14.97 (14.25-14), HJ- 1.96, LJ- 5.84 (6.32-14),
SP- 12.79 (14.85-14), JT- 41.93
LAKE Poppy U23 26.01.96, Chelmsford/Loughborough St
HJ- 1.78i/1.75 (1.81i-14, 1.75-12)
LAKIN Yasmin U23 8.10.95, Shaftesbury B/London Un
TJ- 12.05i/11.59 (12.01-16)
LALLY Jade 30.03.87, Shaftesbury B
DT- 62.15 (65.10-16)
LAMBERT Caroline 2.09.93, Wetherby R/Toledo Un
3k- 9:46.73i, 5k- 16:40.36, 10k- 34:21.50, HMar- 77:39
LAMBERT Chloe 22.05.94, VP-Glasgow/Glasgow Cal. Un
100- 11.92w/11.94, 200- 24.25w/24.42 (24.27-16), 400- 54.94
LAMBERT Jessica U17 31.01.01, Crawley
300H- 44.42, 400H- 65.76
LAMBERT Katie U20 6.11.98, Kidderminster & Stourport
HT- 58.27
LANCASTER Amelia U20 28.02.00, City of Sheffield
1.5kSt- 5:09.68, 2kSt- 7:11.91
LANCE-JONES Claudia Emily U17 29.09.00, Guild & God
1500- 4:38.42 (4:34.68-16), 3k- 9:39.51
LANDIM Claudimira U20 5.07.00, VPH &TH
TJ- 12.36 (12.37-16)
LANG Naomi Helene U20 7.02.00, Aberdeen
3k- 9:39.65, 5k- 16:45.09
LANNIE Nicole U15 24.01.03, Doncaster
60HI- 9.01i, 60HG- 8.96i, 75HG- 11.2/11.26, SPI- 11.13,
PenII- 3334i
LANSIQUOT Imani-Lara U23 17.12.97, Sutton & District
60- 7.30i, 100- 11.34 (11.17-16)
LARGIE-POLEAN Rachel U15 16.05.03, Croydon
60- 7.88i, 100- 12.5, 200- 25.66, 75HG- 11.5
LARKINS Megan U20 2.08.98, Braintree/Loughborough St
SP- 11.58, DT- 37.32, HT- 53.84
LARSEN Jasmine U13 13.05.05, Southampton
JTM- 35.57
LAUDER Dianne Helen V40 6.07.76, Gala
Mar- 2:54:48 (2:49:15-15)
LAVENDER Alison 25.09.88, Oswestry
Mar- 2:55:06
LAVENDER Claudia U20 17.06.98, Bristol & West
PV- 3.50 (3.60-16)
LAVERTY Sarah U23 30.09.96, Edinburgh AC/
New Mexico Un   10k- 35:35.46
LAW Kirsty Marie 11.10.86, Sale
SP- 11.33 (12.63i-08, 11.99-13), DT- 54.91 (57.79-12)
LAW Phoebe U23 12.01.97, Kingston & Poly
3k- 9:17.64mx/9:20.45, 5k- 16:09.14, 10k- 33:00.84
LAW Sharon V40 9.03.75, Gateshead
24Hr- 182.642km (226.107km-13)
LAWLER Hannah U23 24.10.95, Edinburgh AC/GlasUn
PV- 3.41i/3.30 (3.57i-16, 3.50-14)
LAWRENCE Emma U20 18.06.00, Sutton & District
JT- 36.78

LAWRENCE Evie U15 15.04.03, Swansea
PV- 2.60
LAWRENCE Holly U15 12.02.03, Chelmsford
75HG- 11.49w, HJ- 1.62, PenG- 2884
LECKY Sommer U20 14.06.00, Finn Valley/IRL
HJ- 1.85, LJ- 5.62 (5.83-15)
LECOUTRE Susannah U15 5.04.04, Guildford & G
800- 2:17.57, 1500- 4:42.19
LEE Cerys U17 4.11.00, Taunton
Hepl- 4132 (4220-16)
LEE India Alice 31.05.88, Winchester
5kR- 16:52
LEFEBVRE Jilly U15 1.04.04, North Ayrshire
HJ- 1.61
LEIGHTON Amelia U15 28.10.03, Stratford-upon-Avon
TJ- 10.43
LEONARD Alison 17.03.90, Blackburn
1500- 4:24.40 (4:08.96mx/4:09.59-16)
LEONG Esther U20 28.01.00, North Somerset
PV- 3.64
LESBIREL Hannah U23 8.05.96, Channel Islands
200- 24.69w/24.95
LESLIE Jodie 1.05.93, Bedford & County
200- 24.56w/24.85 (24.58-16), 400- 56.24 (54.64-16)
LETHEBY Carla 10.09.93, Thames Valley
DT- 38.19 (41.05-14), HT- 43.62 (45.76-15)
LEVER Georgina U20 6.12.99, Bolton
TJ- 11.68
LEVY Miriam U15 8.02.03, Hallamshire
HJ- 1.64
LEWINGTON Hannah U13 15.03.06, Swindon
JTM- 38.37
LEWIS Annabelle 20.03.89, Kingston upon Hull
60- 7.55i (7.31i-13)
LEWIS Heather 25.10.93, Pembroke
3kW- 13:15.52 (13:07.04-16), 10kWR- 47:17 (46:59-14),
5kWR- 23:00+e (22:09.87t-14), 20kW- 1:37:39
LEWIS WARD Lucy U17 26.02.02, Cambridge H
5kW- 27:51.0
LEWIS WARD Sophie U20 7.04.99, Cambridge H
3kW- 14:25.11i/14:28.24 (13:51.35+-16),
5kW- 24:57.51 (23:37.55-16), 10kWR- 52:45
LIGHTBODY Victoria U15 4.05.04, Lisburn
800- 2:15.57
LINAKER Alice U20 6.12.99, City of York
60H- 8.92i, 100H- 14.73w/14.89, LJ- 5.60, TJ- 11.17,
Hep- 4589
LININGTON-PAYNE Rhiannon 1.10.91, Cardiff
400- 55.76 (55.00-12)
LITTLEMORE Sophie Marie U23 25.12.95, Gateshead
SP- 13.61, DT- 44.99
LIVERPOOL Yasmin U20 15.01.99, Leiden NED
100- 12.04, 200- 24.96w (24.92-16), 400- 55.50
LIVETT Sarah 16.11.93, Menai/Un Alabama
5k- 17:18.79 (16:59.45-14)
LLEWELLYN Ffion Marie U20 11.03.00, Bridgend
PV- 3.32i/3.30 (3.40-16)
LLOYD Hannah 3.03.93, Herts Phoenix
400H- 64.47 (59.38-14)
LOBLEY Erin U13 12.10.04, Hallamshire
70HM- 11.27, HJ- 1.57, LJ- 5.19, SPI- 11.02i,
SPM- 12.12, JTM- 32.50, PenM- 3114
LOCKE Eloise U17 19.04.01, Blackheath & Bromley
SPI- 13.02i/12.40 (13.69-15), JT- 37.14,
JTI- 43.20 (44.08-16)
LOCKETT Candise U20 13.05.99, Birchfield
HT- 46.65
LOCKS Lesley V40 22.11.76, Hart RR
Mar- 2:55:54 (2:50:55-14)
LOCKWOOD Megan U17 17.06.02, Manx H
DT- 32.36
LONGHURST Eloise U15 10.06.03, Worthing
TJ- 10.49
LONGSTAFF Ellie U13 25.11.04, Morpeth
75- 9.99, 150- 19.70
LONSDALE Darcey U15 17.10.02, Preston
300- 41.8, 800- 2:14.80
LOUGHLIN Anna U17 25.10.00, Bristol & West
HTI- 53.59

LOVEDAY Bethan U20 9.03.00, Bridgnorth
100H- 15.1, Hep- 3907
LOVELL Elise 9.05.92, Hastings/Brighton Un
60H- 8.56i, 100H- 13.78w/13.95 (13.86-15), HJ- 1.65i,
LJ- 5.96i/5.92 (6.07w-15, 6.02-16), JT- 38.96,
Hep- 5330, PentIS- 3892i
LOVELL Jasmine U17 27.06.01, Birchfield
TJ- 11.18
LOVERING Abbie U15 23.07.03, Wimborne
800- 2:15.5, PenG- 2812
LOVETT Ellie U15 13.02.03, Isle of Wight
DT- 30.67
LOVIBOND Ella U17 26.11.01, Radley AC
HTI- 54.36
LOWE Phillipa 7.04.92, Dacorum & Tring
400- 52.99i (53.07-16), 800- 2:07.50i (2:12.54-10)
LOWERY Sarah V35 15.04.82, Sheffield RC
Mar- 2:44:27
LOWNDES Mia U17 6.06.02, Sale
60HI- 9.07i
LUCAS Zoe U23 7.01.97, Notts/Notts Trent Un
60H- 8.73i
LUKE Maisy U13 5.05.05, Cornwall AC
1500- 4:48.2
LUPTON Amy 31.07.94, Preston
TJ- 11.36 (11.66-15), JT- 36.72 (44.87-14)
LYONS Katie U17 8.11.01, Kingston & Poly
DT- 35.79

M acANGUS Kerry U20 31.03.99, Kilbarchan
1500- 4:26.79mx
MACAULAY Hannah U17 9.09.01, Blackheath & Bromley
SPI- 13.30, DT- 39.77
MACDONALD Amelia U17 3.05.01, Enfield & Haringey
LJ- 5.49
MACDONALD Emily U20 21.12.99, Bracknell
PV- 3.40i/3.40
MACDOUGALL Morgan U15 10.03.03, East Kilbride
PV- 2.60
MACE Ruby U15 5.09.03, Havering
60HG- 9.34, 75HG- 11.6
MACE Sophie U20 7.10.98, Walton
SP- 11.72 (11.79-15), DT- 45.76 (47.35-15), HT- 48.77
MACFADYEN Anna U20 19.06.99, Forres H
5k- 17:13.56
MACGUIRE Courtney 30.04.90, Edinburgh AC
PV- 4.00 (4.02i-15, 4.00-14)
MACHEATH Paige U20 21.10.99, Cambridge H
JT- 37.89
MACHIN Julia Margaret V45 26.03.70, Brighton & Hove
400H- 64.56 (61.7/61.84-97)
MACKINSON Katie U15 20.09.02, Reigate
JTI- 39.22
MACKINTOSH Katie U17 23.04.01, Newark AC
300H- 45.87
MACLAREN Jade 1.12.88, VP-Glasgow
800- 2:04.40
MACLARTY Morag 10.02.86, Central
5kR- 16:58 (16:14-14), 2kSt- 7:01.97
MACLEAN Anya U15 15.08.04, Garscube
3k- 10:39.85mx
MACLENNAN Mhairi U23 26.03.95, Inverness/Edin Un
3k- 9:37.59mx (9:52.46-15), 5k- 16:49.08 (16:37.31-16),
10k- 35:25.17 (34:39.87-16), 10kR- 33:58
MACLENNAN Rachel U17 3.04.02, Inverness
HTI- 46.10
MACPHERSON Iona U17 24.05.01, City of Lisburn
TJ- 11.28
MADDEN Ellen U15 28.04.04, Ballymena & A
DT- 29.02
MADDEN FORMAN Emily U20 29.09.99, Stratford-u-Avon
100H- 14.70w/15.28, HJ- 1.66 (1.67-14),
TJ- 11.25 (11.57-15), Hep- 4089
MADDOX Laura 13.05.90, Swansea
400- 53.37i/53.59 (52.32i-15, 52.73-14)
MAGEEAN Ciara 12.03.92, City of Lisburn/IRL
800- 2:02.20 (2:00.79-16), 1500- 4:03.57+ (4:01.46-16),
1M- 4:22.40, 3k- 9:08.83i (8:55.09i-15, 9:07.47mx-16)
MAGUIRE Caitlin U20 2.02.99, North Belfast
60- 7.74i

421

MAGUIRE Kerry U23 8.05.95, Gateshead/North'land Un
PV- 3.12i (3.00-13)
MAHAY-GOODRICH Elianne U20 13.11.98, Enfield & Har
SP- 11.28 (11.44-16)
MAILER Emma U17 24.02.02, Central
300- 40.72, 300H- 44.45, 400H- 64.00
MAIR Angharad V55 30.03.61, Newport
Mar- 2:55:02 (2:38:47-96)
MALE Isabel U13 17.02.05, R Sutton Coldfield
75- 10.0, 150- 19.37, 200- 26.85w
MALIK Indiana U17 8.07.02, Notts
200- 25.15w
MALIK Poppy U15 27.11.03, Notts
300- 41.89
MALIR Georgia U23 20.02.96, Leeds/Leeds Un
1500- 4:26.45mx/4:26.48, 3k- 9:37.26, 5k- 16:55.45,
10kR- 34:28
MALONE Sarah U20 15.09.99, Edinburgh AC
100- 12.10w/12.11
MALONE Shannon U23 27.05.97, Deeside
60- 7.73i (7.46i-15)
MALTBY Emily U23 1.03.95, Nene Valley H/Bedford Un
TJ- 11.62
MALTBY Kate 26.07.85, Bristol & West
1500- 4:20.78i/4:25.77 (4:23.97-16), 3k- 9:00.81i/9:05.6,
5k- 16:06.9mx/16:14.97 (16:06.08-16), 10kR- 33:30
MANASE Anjelina U15 14.10.03, Reading
DT- 30.10
MANCHESTER Orla U15 18.06.03, Camberley
DT- 29.93, HTI- 40.44
MANNION Isobel U17 4.04.02, Basingstoke & MH
1500- 4:39.39
MANSFIELD Lucy 10.10.92, Blackpool & Fylde
100- 12.14w (12.0w/12.19-15, 12.11w-14)
MANSFIELD Sophie U23 3.09.97, Brighton Phoenix
800- 2:07.40i/2:09.50 (2:08.94mx-14)
MANSON Nikki 15.10.94, Giffnock N/Akron Un
HJ- 1.86, LJ- 5.63, JT- 41.33
MAPAMBOLI Diane U17 9.03.02, VPH &TH
TJ- 11.44
MAPPS Caitlyn U15 27.11.02, Cardiff Archers
200- 25.67, LJ- 5.66w/5.52
MARCH Phoebe U15 4.12.02, City of Portsmouth
HTI- 42.43
MARGHINI Yasmin U17 3.01.02, Blackheath & Bromley
1500- 4:33.19mx/4:38.04, 3k- 9:56.98
MARKS Fiona 9.03.90, Bristol & W
5k- 17:03.6mx, 2kSt- 7:16.37
MARRETT Chloe U13 6.11.04, Bristol & West
150- 19.4, PV- 2.44
MARRIOTT Alicia U17 22.05.02, Longwood
HJ- 1.63
MARRIOTT Finlay U20 21.01.99, Cambridge & Coleridge
60H- 8.80i, 100H- 14.21w/14.54
MARRS Megan U23 25.09.97, Lisburn/Loughborough St
60H- 8.60i, 100H- 13.51
MARSDEN Carys U20 10.03.00, Blackheath & Bromley
DT- 37.04
MARSHALL Lucy A. V35 28.11.81, WG & Ex L/
Northampton Un   SP- 11.17 (12.00-15), HT- 62.74
MARSHALL Sinead U15 21.01.03, Reading
PV- 2.60
MARSHALL-BROWN Denisha U20 11.08.00, Herne Hill
SP- 12.11i/12.01, DT- 35.59 (36.88-16)
MARSTON Rownita U20 17.05.98, Bristol & West
SP- 12.38 (12.95-16)
MARTELL-SMITH Nicola 20.09.85, Colchester H
400H- 65.66 (60.79-05)
MARTIN Charlotte U15 28.05.03, Bristol & West
HJ- 1.60
MARTIN Deborah 25.01.94, Ashford
HJ- 1.70i/1.70 (1.80-14)
MARTIN Jessica Anne 1.10.92, Aldershot F&D
3k- 9:20+e, 5k- 15:48.56mx/15:50.04 (15:24.02-16),
10k- 33:00.24 (31:35.92-16)
MARTIN Olivia U13 10.08.05, Oxford City
1500- 4:56.43mx
MARTIN-CONSANI Debbie V40 4.04.75, Garscube
24Hr- 204.118km (221.714km-15)

MARTIN-EVANS Cleo U15 8.05.03, Daventry
75HG- 11.52, LJ- 5.62
MASON Eliza U17 24.09.01, Channel Islands
400H- 67.34
MASON Hermione U13 1.04.05, Sale
70HM- 11.38
MASON Olivia Grace U17 14.10.01, Border
400- 58.0, 800- 2:08.89mx/2:09.53, 1500- 4:20.57
MASON Samantha U15 2.11.02, Trafford
1500- 4:44.49
MASQUELIER Abby U15 17.08.04, WSE&H
60HG- 9.40i
MASSEY Kelly Lorraine 11.01.85, Sale
200- 24.61 (23.94-09), 400- 53.95 (51.96-14)
MATHESON Rebecca U20 7.03.99, Aberdeen
100- 12.20 (12.12w-15), 200- 24.96w
MATTACKS Zoe U20 7.11.98, Team Bath
100H- 15.22w
MATTHEWS Chioma V35 12.03.81, Blackheath & Bromley
TJ- 13.00 (13.53-15)
MATTHEWS Florence U13 16.11.04, Rugby & North
LJ- 5.02
MATTHEWS Lucy-Jane U15 17.09.02, Southampton
300- 41.7, 60HI- 8.59i, 60HG- 8.96i, 75HG- 11.5/11.62,
HJ- 1.65i, LJ- 5.46i, SPI- 12.10, PenIG- 3649i
MAUGHAN Etienne U13 7.12.04, Bedford & County
75- 10.0, 150- 19.4
MAURER Claire Louise 9.01.94, Woking/London Un
PV- 4.06
MAYCOCK Fiona J. V45 21.08.67, Cheltenham
Mar- 2:56:25 (2:54:47-12)
MAYHO Jessica 14.06.93, Birchfield
HT- 63.05
McANDREW Bethany Ellen S U20 8.01.00, Pitreavie
60HI- 8.84i, 100HI- 14.53i/14.58,
100H- 14.76w/14.8/14.82i/14.91 (14.83-16)
McARTHUR Holly U20 20.12.99, Whitemoss
200- 24.59, 400- 56.33, 60H- 8.77i, 100H-
13.79w/13.93, 400H- 60.9 (60.23-16), LJ- 5.97,
SP- 11.47, JT- 37.25, Hep- 5687, PentIS- 3859i
McASLAN Kirsten 1.09.93, Sale
200- 24.55 (23.92-13), 400- 52.90 (52.13-15), 400H- 57.31
McCAFFERTY Connie U17 24.02.01, Bracknell
300- 40.77, HepI- 4251
McCALL Stephanie 27.09.93, South London H
5k- 17:07.99 (16:39.30mx/16:52.55-16),
5kR- 16:59 (16:37-16)
McCANDLESS Joanne V35 19.10.78, Stratford
Mar- 2:53:19
McCANN Rachel U17 26.09.01, North Down
300- 40.23, 400- 58.01
McCARTNEY Ellen U20 8.10.99, City of Lisburn
PV- 3.75
McCAULEY Anna U17 2.01.01, City of Lisburn
100- 12.20 (12.20-16), 60HI- 8.65i, 100HI- 13.95,
HJ- 1.73, LJ- 5.60i, Hep U18- 4699
*McCAW Debbie V35 1.01.80, Ealing, S & Mx/NZL
HT- 47.35 (54.58-05)*
McCHEYNE Nuala U17 4.10.01, Inverclyde
800- 2:13.75i/2:14.00
McCLAY Rachel Ella 13.10.92, Bracknell
800- 2:07.60 (2:04.01-15)
McCOLGAN Eilish 25.11.90, Dundee HH
800- 2:07.8+, 1500- 4:01.60, 2k- 5:43.1+, 3k- 8:31.00,
5k- 14:48.49, 10k- 32:10.59, 10kR- 32:01
*McCORMACK Sarah 19.08.86, Ambleside/IRL
HMar- 78:22*
McCORRY Alison U23 24.08.96, Sale/Loughborough St
100- 12.18 (12.1-14, 12.15w-15), 200- 24.49
McDONALD Iona U17 11.11.01, Livingston
300- 40.84
McDONALD Katy-Ann U20 1.06.00, Blackheath & Brom
800- 2:05.48 (2:05.03-16)
McDONALD Sarah 2.08.93, Birchfield/Birmingham Un
800- 2:01.2 (2:01.10-16), 1k- 2:38.49, 1500- 4:05.48,
1M- 4:32.06i (4:46.38-13)
McDOWALL Edwina V45 31.07.70, Headington RR
Mar- 2:56:47

McGARVEY Claire U17 15.06.01, Banchory
HJ- 1.70
McGIFFORD Danielle U23 11.04.95, Wigan
100- 12.04 (11.87-15), 60H- 8.52i, 100H- 14.4/14.44
(13.82w-13, 13.88-14), HJ- 1.65i/1.65 (1.66i-14,1.65-12),
LJ- 6.16, Hep- 5054 (5114-15), PentIS- 3834i (3934i-14)
McGINTY Ellie U23 12.11.97, Edinburgh AC
100- 12.13w/12.18, LJ- 5.80
McHUGH Megan U20 25.07.00, Sale
400H- 65.2/65.81, HJ- 1.65i (1.68-15)
McHUGH Tess U17 19.06.02, Sale
400- 57.9, 300H- 45.20
McILVEEN Erin 10.03.86, City of Lisburn
800- 2:07.15i (2:05.83i-16, 2:05.96-14)
McINNES Megan U23 20.10.97, Shaftesbury B/Bath Un
PV- 3.35i (3.20-16)
McINTOSH Mia Jane U13 11.01.05, St Albans AC
100- 12.90
McINTOSH Shona 21.01.83, Dulwich Runners
Mar- 2:48:08 (2:40:14-15)
McKEEVER Sarah U23 11.08.95, Sale/Cardiff Un/IRL
PV- 4.13i/3.95
McKELVIE Susan Catherine 15.06.85, Edinburgh AC
HT- 62.07 (65.03-11)
McKEN Simone U20 24.09.98, Wolves & Bilston
DT- 44.11
McKINNA Sophie 31.08.94, Great Yarmouth
SP- 17.03 (17.14/18.41dh-16)
McLACHLAN Holly U17 20.04.02, Fife
300H- 45.81
McLAY Shona U15 6.02.03, Central
100- 12.51w, 200- 25.85w
McLEAN Hayley 9.09.94, Chelmsford
400- 55.48 (55.19i-13), 400H- 58.33 (56.43-14)
McLELLAN Sarah 4.02.90, Blackheath & Bromley
400H- 65.13 (64.31-07)
McLENNAN Zoe 2.07.83, City of Chester Tri
Mar- 2:51:37
McLENNON Kiona U20 11.02.99, Rugby & Northampton
SP- 11.86 (12.58-16)
McLINDEN Rebecca 2.08.90, Blackheath & Bromley
400H- 63.4/63.68 (62.89-16)
McMAHON Alice May U23 15.02.95, West Cheshire
100- 12.16 (12.0w-12), 200- 24.9
McMAHON Christine 6.07.92, B'mena & A/Queen's U/IRL
400- 55.43mx (54.77i-13, 55.40-10) 400H- 58.08 (56.06-16)
McMAHON Mya U13 19.09.05, Dunfermline
60HM- 9.86i, HJ- 1.56i/1.54, PenM- 2481, PenIM- 2649i
McNAMARA Danielle U13 16.11.04, Falkirk VH
HTI- 31.95
McNIVEN Ella U17 4.09.01, Liverpool H
800- 2:07.93mx/2:08.82, 1500- 4:15.61,
3k- 9:24.50mx/9:29.76
McRAE Nicola U20 8.09.99, Cleethorpes
HT- 42.24
McTEAR Georgie U20 20.07.99, Swindon
JT- 41.84 (43.82-16)
McVEY Diane V40 22.12.76, Wilmslow
HMar- 78:38
MEADOWS Jennifer V35 17.04.81, Wigan
400- 56.21+ (52.50mx-05, 52.67-03), 800- 2:06.10+ (1:57.93-09)
600- 1:29.71i+ (1:25.81i-07, 1:28.0+-09),
MEAKINS Eloise 26.01.93, Herts Phoenix/Lough St
JT- 46.70 (52.32-12)
MEEK Joanna V40 20.05.77, Winchester
50kR- 3:49:29
MEEKINGS Peanut U15 25.03.03, Horsham BS
JTI- 39.11
MELBOURNE Sarah U23 12.09.96, WSE&H/Brunel Un
TJ- 11.40w/11.22
MELLA Sofia U15 18.12.02, Channel Islands
TJ- 10.41
MELLOR Maya U20 19.02.00, Harrogate
DT- 39.28
MENON Mary V35 10.07.79, Ilfracoombe RC
Mar- 2:50:55
MENZIES Freya U17 12.11.00, Giffnock North
300H- 45.87

MERCIER Sarah 4.11.90, Channel Islands
3k- 9:33.41i (9:35.64-15), 5kR- 16:48 (16:46-15),
5k- 16:51.4mx/16:58.93 (16:31.05-14), 10k- 35:15.50,
10kR- 34:47
MERRITT Anna U15 3.10.02, Southampton
DT- 34.41, HTI- 48.29
MERRITT Sophie U20 9.04.98, So'ton/Jacksonville Un
SP- 14.59, DT- 45.44, JT- 36.20 (42.54-13)
MHLANGA Khahisa U20 26.12.99, Chelmsford
800- 2:04.34, 1500- 4:18.83mx/4:22.12, 3k- 9:33.35mx
MIELL Alice U20 14.05.00, Athletisme Sud 17 FRA
JT- 36.45 (37.81-16)
MIHALCEA Denisa U20 17.01.00, Harrow
DT- 40.10, JT- 43.58
MILBORNE Caitlin U13 15.09.04, Tonbridge
JTM- 34.25
MILLAGE Philippa Claire V35 15.08.80, VP-Glasgow
800- 2:06.62 (2:05.13-16), 1M- 4:48.49,
1500- 4:20.22mx (4:26.27-16)
MILLER Amy U15 16.11.02, Blackheath & Bromley
800- 2:15.25, 1500- 4:41.79mx
MILLER Emily U17 16.06.02, VP-Glasgow
300- 40.36
MILLER Murphy U17 17.01.02, North Down
800- 2:14.63
MILLER Rachel 29.01.90, Harrow
60- 7.31i, 100- 11.45, 200- 24.0/24.14
MILLER Yasmin U23 24.05.95, Derby AC/South Bank Un
60- 7.53i (7.53i-12), 100- 11.99w (11.64w-15, 11.97-14),
60H- 8.21i (8.16i-16), 100H- 13.16w/13.23 (13.13-14)
MILLET Nessa Cooper 5.12.94, Loughborough St/IRL
400H- 61.08 (59.00-13)
MILLMORE Tracy 16.07.82, Birtley
HMar- 77:19, Mar- 2:46:09
MILLS Hayley Victoria (née JONES) 14.09.88, Tamworth/
Notts Un 60- 7.64imx (7.31i-13)
MILLS Holly Erin Keir U20 15.04.00, Andover
60- 7.67i (7.65i-16), 100- 12.06w (12.02w/12.05-16),
200- 24.84w (24.50w-16), 60H- 8.62i, HJ- 1.70i,
100HI- 13.89 (13.79-16), 100H- 14.46 (14.2-16), LJ- 6.31
MILLS Lydia U20 1.02.98, Ballymena & Antrim
LJ- 5.73 (5.80-15)
MILNE Dionne U23 19.10.97, Moray RR/Robert Gordon U
DT- 42.32 (44.09-14)
MILNER Samantha 28.12.92, Blackheath & Brom/Birm U
SP- 12.11 (12.50-11), DT- 48.35 (51.07-13)
MILORO Felicia U17 5.01.01, Sutton in Ashfield
PV- 3.83i/3.81, TJ- 11.14
MILORO Rimini U20 26.10.98, Notts
TJ- 11.18
MISANTONI Emily U15 27.09.02, Stockport
300- 41.7/41.90, 800- 2:13.90, 60HG- 9.38i, 75HG- 11.6,
LJ- 5.25w, SextG- 3645, PenG- 3275+, PenIG- 3082i
MITCHELL Bethany 13.11.92, Sutton in Ashfield
HT- 42.00 (50.47-11)
MITCHELL Emma 2.09.93, Banbridge AC/IRL
1500- 4:15.32i/4:19.20 (4:18.66-16), 5k- 15:50.55,
3k- 9:04.21imx/9:11.89, 10k- 32:51.78, 10kR- 32:51
MITCHELL Jasmine U20 11.05.98, Guildford & Godalming
400H- 63.71
MITCHELL Jessica U17 14.05.01, Havering
1500- 4:34.8mx/4:36.21, 3k- 9:40.86
MITCHELL Naomi 24.11.93, Reading
Mar- 2:49:53
MOAT Hannah U17 2.07.02, Scunthorpe
HJ- 1.71
MODESTE Elise U17 4.11.00, Enfield & Haringey
100- 12.30w
MOFFAT Lara U15 22.09.03, Marshall Milton K
HTI- 40.75
MOFFATT Erin U15 12.04.03, Lancaster & Morecambe
LJ- 5.41
MOLINARO Carla 27.07.84, Clapham Chasers
Mar- 2:56:21 (2:51:50-15)
MOLYNEAUX Hannah U17 11.03.01, Lincoln Wellington
SPI- 15.33
MONEY Amy U15 2.08.03, City of Norwich
HTI- 39.42

423

MONEY Sophie 24.10.93, Liverpool H/Liverpool Un
60- 7.67imx/7.75i, 100- 12.14w (11.98-16)
MONKS Kamela 6.05.87, St Mary's Richmond
TJ- 11.76w (11.59-16)
MONTEIRO Joceline 10.05.90, Chelmsford/POR
800- 2:05.74 (2:03.6mx/2:03.77-16)
MONTEZ BROWN Olivia U23 22.05.96, W Cheshire/
Augustana Un   60H- 8.62i, 100H- 14.13, HJ- 1.66,
LJ- 6.12w/5.85i/5.84 (5.91-16), TJ- 11.29 (11.35-12),
SP- 11.18 (11.24-16), Hep- 5251 (5254-16), PentIS- 3863i
MONYE Chinedu 29.12.89, WSE&H
100- 11.68
MOODY Robyn U15 3.01.03, Havering
DT- 31.20
MOORE Diane V40 13.12.74, Headington RR
Mar- 2:52:05
MOORE Lucy U13 30.03.05, Wirral
75- 10.0
MOORE Mica 23.11.92, Birchfield/Cardiff Met
100- 11.64
MOORE Rebecca 7.10.91, Chichester R/Camb Un
5k- 16:52.53, 10k- 35:27.76 (34:27.85-13),
10kR- 34:19 (34:17-16), HMar- 76:50 (75:25-16)
MOORE Saffron U15 15.09.02, City of Portsmouth
800- 2:12.35mx/2:13.08 (2:12.93-16),
1500- 4:42.53mx (4:40.91-16)
MOORE-MARTIN Rhianne U17 21.09.01, City of Stoke
HT- 42.53, HTI- 51.69
MORGAN Caris U17 22.09.00, Newport
JT- 36.20
MORGAN Grace U17 14.01.02, Cardiff Archers
60HI- 8.83i, 80HI- 11.70, Hep- 4175
MORGAN Hannah Marie U23 3.10.97, Newport/B'm'th Un
HT- 44.34 (49.10-16)
MORGAN Jade 12.08.89, Colchester H
TJ- 11.27 (12.31-11)
MORGAN Naomi U23 23.11.96, Derry
100H- 14.98 (14.7-16, 14.80w/14.98-15), Hep- 4336 (4580-15)
MORGAN Sian 29.11.88, Swansea
PV- 3.80 (4.15-15)
MORGAN Venus U17 5.06.01, Kingston upon Hull
60HI- 8.92i, 80HI- 11.7/11.73 (11.63w-16), LJ- 5.62,
Hepl- 4731, PenII- 3405i
MORLEY Bethan U17 9.10.01, Ilkley
800- 2:10.77, 1500- 4:37.18
MORONKEJI Yetunde Abigail 15.11.90, Thames Valley
SP- 11.60 (12.25-09)
MORRIS Emma U15 20.03.03, Bracknell
300- 41.16
MORRIS Lukesha U23 26.11.95, WSE&H/Brunel Un
60- 7.52i (7.46i-16), 100- 11.64w/11.77 (11.54w/11.56-15)
MORRIS Macey U15 12.02.03, Newport
60- 7.90i, 100- 12.60, 200- 25.28, 300- 40.50
MORRISON Samantha 21.03.94, Woking/Notts Trent Un
PV- 3.50 (3.62-15)
MORTIBOY Beth U23 20.03.97, Notts/Notts Un
TJ- 11.93w/11.76 (11.99-16)
MORTLOCK Harriette U15 27.11.03, Basildon
JTI- 40.16
MORTON-KEMSLEY Talia U17 20.05.01, Dacorum & Tr
60HI- 8.99i, LJ- 5.52i, PenII- 3368i (3375i-16)
MOSS Jazmine U20 16.08.00, Gateshead
200- 24.36
MOSS Stephanie U17 24.05.02, Sale
800- 2:11.48
MOSSI Zakia U15 15.09.03, Blackheath & Bromley
800- 2:12.85
MOTT Hilary 7.03.88, Cheltenham
Mar- 2:49:52
MOULD Victoria U23 11.09.95, Southampton/Lough St
TJ- 12.10i/11.97w/11.82
MOULE Bethany Ellie U17 21.11.01, Neath
JTI- 46.95 (48.84-16)
MOULTRIE Josephine 19.11.90, VP-Glasgow
3k- 9:36.99+ (8:57.14imx-16, 9:17.43-14),
5k- 16:14.74 (15:57.17-13), 10kR- 33:40 (33:35-16)
MOUNT Ellie U15 15.08.03, Team Bath
75HG- 11.38

MOYES Emily U20 14.06.98, West Suffolk/St Marys Un
1500- 4:26.49, 2kSt- 6:35.07, 3kSt- 10:25.23
MPASSY Holly Victoria U15 12.07.03, Blackheath & Br
200- 25.01, 300- 40.15, 400- 57.90mx
MUCHINA Samantha U15 21.11.02, Peterborough
200- 25.9w
MUGABE Danai U15 20.10.02, Swansea
60- 7.97i
MUIR Laura Mary 9.05.93, Dundee HH/Glasgow Un
600- 1:29.8i+e, 800- 1:58.69, 1k- 2:31.93i (2:40.5+e-16),
1500- 4:00.35 (3:55.22-16), 1M- 4:18.03, 2k- 5:41.5i+e,
3k- 8:26.41i/8:30.64, 5k- 14:49.12i/14:52.07
MULHOLLAND Holly U17 31.03.02, City of Lisburn
80HI- 11.86
MULLEN Kirsten Grace U23 30.10.96, Edinb' AC/Edin Un
PV- 3.41i/3.23
MULLIN Laura U20 11.05.99, Charnwood
800- 2:10.24
MUNDAY Imogen U20 17.05.99, Medway & Maidstone
400H- 64.68
MUNN Hayley 17.09.90, Northampton RRC
HMar- 78:23 (75:43-15), Mar- 2:46:00 (2:37:44-14)
MURCH Kerry U23 20.03.95, Rugby & North/Lough St
100H- 15.23, TJ- 11.26, SP- 11.11 (11.14-16),
JT- 44.73 (46.11-13)
MURPHY Charlotte Tara U20 24.08.98, W Suff/ South Meth U
3k- 9:42.26i (9:40.66-16), 5k- 16:54.29
MURRAY Alison V50 13.01.67, Hercules Wimbledon
PV- 3.10 (3.95A-99, 3.60-96)
MURRAY Bethan U17 18.12.00, Stockport
LJ- 5.62
MURRAY Bethanie U23 16.08.95, Oxford Univ
5k- 17:16.09
MURRAY Hayley 13.09.89, Rugby & Northampton
HT- 59.57
MURRAY Lily U13 17.01.05, Thanet AC
HTI- 47.10
MURRAY Madeleine Grace 19.10.93, Edinburgh AC
800- 2:07.0 (2:03.66-15), 1500- 4:17.68 (4:10.17-15),
1M- 4:47.1
MURRAY Paula 14.07.90, Dundee HH/Abertay Un
JT- 37.02 (39.18-14)
MURRAY Rebecca 26.09.94, Bedford & County/Brunel Un
3k- 9:26.35i/9:41.03+ (9:22.92mx/9:34.24-15),
5k- 16:09.35 (16:09.21-16), 10kR- 34:30 (33:19-15),
10MR- 57:06 (56:24-15), HMar- 75:49 (72:59-16)
MYCROFT Tilly U13 18.11.04, City of Sheffield
PenM- 2325

NAGY Megan U20 26.02.99, City of Sheffield
SP- 11.14i, Hep- 3927
NAIBE-WEY Aisha 3.08.93, TVH/Virginia Tech Un/SLE
400H- 57.86 (57.26-15)
NANSON Emma U23 6.10.95, Aldershot F&D/Bath Un
100H- 15.2, 400H- 63.26
NASH Gypsy U13 29.11.04, Medway & Maidstone
DTM- 31.32, HTI- 40.03
NAYLOR Lily-Rose U17 14.12.01, Amber Valley
SPI- 13.54, HTI- 46.48, HepI- 4363w/4289
NDIAYE Awa U17 19.09.01, Serpentine/FRA
60- 7.78i, 100- 12.02, 200- 25.09
NEALE Amy-Eloise U23 5.08.95, Un of Washington
800- 2:07.84, 1k- 2:46.82i, 1500- 4:11.00, 1M- 4:34.15i,
3k- 9:17.97i (9:31.1-14), 5k- 15:39.30
NEALON Victoria 19.04.83, Rugby & Northampton
Mar- 2:57:01
NEAT Carmen U17 23.10.01, Aberdeen
HJ- 1.67
NEITA Daryll U23 29.08.96, Shaftesbury B
60- 7.36i (7.29i-16), 100- 11.14
NELSON Anna U23 14.11.95, WGreen & EL/Edinburgh U
400- 56.59i/56.73, 100H- 15.20, 400H- 60.36
NELSON Ashleigh Louise 20.02.91, City of Stoke
100- 11.27 (11.15w/11.19-14), 400- 52.9/53.29
NEMITS Ashley U15 30.03.04, Warrington
300- 41.7 (43.02)
NERURKAR Almaz U17 9.01.01, Brighton Phoenix
1500- 4:27.82, 3k- 9:44.1

424

NESBITT Jennifer Louise U23 24.01.95, Worc/Bath U
   3k- 9:27.6, 5k- 16:22.95 (15:57.55-16), 10k- 32:59.52,
   15kR- 51:39+ (51:18+-16), HMar- 73:23 (72:54-16)
NEVILLE Isabelle U20 1.09.99, Tamworth
   400H- 63.24
NEWBEGIN Iona U15 1.09.02, Bedford & County
   100- 12.21w/12.37, 200- 25.80w/25.93
NEWTON Bethany U20 19.02.99, Notts
   PV- 3.11i/3.10
NEWTON-O'BRIEN Molly U20 5.05.99, City of York
   HJ- 1.70i (1.70-16), Hep- 4254 (4631-16)
NICHOLSON Trixie U17 1.11.00, Exeter
   JT- 36.81, JTI- 44.49
NICK Christina 14.11.92, City of York/Leeds Un/GER
   SP- 13.73, DT- 45.52
NICOLL Adele Mia U23 28.09.96, Birchfield/Cardiff Met
   SP- 16.27 (16.34-16), DT- 42.18 (46.35-12)
NIEDBALA Anna 11.02.90, Oxford City/Oxford Un/GER
   SP- 11.95, DT- 44.62 (45.83-09), HT- 48.14
NIELSEN Laviai U23 13.03.96, Enfield & Har/London Un
   60- 7.42i, 200- 23.81, 300- 37.8i+,
   400- 51.90i/52.60 (52.25-15)
NIELSEN Lina U23 13.03.96, Enfield & H/Queen Mary C
   400- 52.89i/53.72 (52.97-16), 400H- 57.87
NIEMZ Lucy 11.02.86, Notts
   Mar- 2:56:45
NIMMO Jade Elizabeth 23.03.91, Sale
   60H- 8.79i, 100H- 14.18w/14.44, Hep- 4956
   LJ- 6.11w/6.04 (6.47-12), SP- 11.11i (11.27i/11.25-16)
NIMMOCK Danielle 10.05.90, City of Norwich
   HMar- 77:38
NOLAN Abigail U20 16.04.99, Coventry Godiva
   1.5kSt- 4:59.12, 2kSt- 7:17.21, 3kSt- 11:29.06
NOLAN Michelle V35 8.12.80, Gateshead
   Mar- 2:47:59
NORGROVE Heidi U17 5.03.01, Saffron AC
   100- 12.29w
NORMAN Diana Faye V40 14.06.74, Epsom & Ewell
   SP- 11.81i/11.49 (12.05i-99, 12.00-97)
NORRIS Barbara V50 20.08.66, WSE&H/SUI
   DT- 35.52
NOVA Devina U13 2.09.05, Ashford/BUL
   2kW- 11:35.9
NOWILL Eloise U15 2.01.03, Rugby & Northampton
   HJ- 1.62
NOYCE Millie U15 28.11.02, Crawley
   SPI- 12.73
NUTTALL Emma 23.04.92, Edinburgh AC
   HJ- 1.86 (1.88i-14, 1.87-13)
NUTTALL Hannah U23 7.07.97, Charnwood/Lough St
   800- 2:07.86, 1500- 4:16.49,
   3k- 9:15.12mx/9:35.83i (9:28.62-14), 5kR- 16:46
NWAELENE Kendrea U17 7.12.00, Thurrock
   100- 12.2, TJ- 11.16i (11.49-16)
NWAWULOR Georgia 30.06.94, Harrow/Brunel Un
   HJ- 1.75i/1.70 (1.70-11)
NWAWULOR Marilyn 20.09.92, Harrow
   60- 7.45i, 100- 11.71w/12.0/12.02 (11.59-11),
   200- 24.95 (24.14-12), 60H- 8.20i,
   100H- 13.52w/13.91 (13.55-16), SP- 12.86
NWOFOR Emma U23 22.08.96, N&Ex B/Brunel Un
   60H- 8.35i, 100H- 13.91w/13.92, HJ- 1.74,
   LJ- 5.90i/5.71, SP- 11.61i/11.28 (11.38-16), Hep- 5111,
   PentIS- 3560i
NYAKYOMA Devota 26.07.94, Border
   JT- 41.09 (45.81-14)

OAKDEN Emilie U13 17.11.04, Lewes
   PV- 2.60i/2.50
OAKLEY Kirstin U20 25.07.98, Ayr Seaforth/Bradley Un
   5k- 17:15.45, 3kSt- 10:48.05
OBAMAKINWA Zara U15 30.03.04, Medway & Maidstone
   SPI- 11.78, DT- 39.60
OBI Sophia U17 27.05.01, Shaftesbury B
   80HI- 11.87 (11.8-16), 100H- 15.72
OBIDEYI Modupe U20 18.02.00, Norfolk Schools
   HJ- 1.66
OBIJIAKU Michella Nneoma U23 6.11.97, Herne Hill/
   Un Alabama   SP- 14.08, HT- 47.84

O'BRIEN Rebekah U15 21.10.02, Tonbridge
   HJ- 1.70, PenG- 3086, PenIG- 3098i
OCKENDEN Verity 31.08.91, Swansea
   800- 2:06.18, 1500- 4:13.75, 3k- 9:10.70, 5k- 15:46.11,
   10k- 33:23.31
O'CONNOR Katherine U17 12.12.00, Newry/IRL
   200- 25.24, 100H- 14.90, HJ- 1.78, LJ- 6.10, SP- 12.90,
   SPI- 14.63, JT- 45.00, JTI- 49.09, Hep- 5759
O'DALY Mia U17 10.11.01, City of Plymouth
   DT- 35.59
ODEMWENGIE Fanny Osarumen U15 23.09.03, Sale
   60- 8.02i, 200- 25.97
O'DOWDA Jade U20 9.09.99, Oxford City
   60H- 8.93, 100H- 14.29w/14.46, HJ- 1.68i/1.65 (1.72-15),
   LJ- 6.00, SP- 11.69, JT- 38.89, Hep- 5442
ODUNAIYA Amy Lauren U23 17.11.96, Wrexham/Car Met
   100- 12.08, 200- 24.68w/24.91
ODUYEMI Moyin U15 2.12.03, Marshall Milton K
   100- 12.47
OFILI Cindy 5.08.94, WGreen & Ex L/Michigan Un
   60H- 7.96i (7.89i-16), 100H- 12.92 (12.60-15)
O'FLAHERTY Kerry V35 15.07.81, WSE&H/IRL
   1500- 4:14.63i (4:12.79-15), 3k- 9:12.86i (9:09.50-09),
   5k- 16:32.56 (15:58.67-11), 10kR- 34:38 (34:18-14),
   3kSt- 9:50.75 (9:42.61-15)
OFOR Afomachukwu U15 7.07.04, Middlesboro Mandale
   60- 8.05i, 100- 12.5/12.54
OGBETA Naomi U20 18.04.98, Trafford/Manchester Un
   TJ- 13.68w/13.64
OGDEN Charlotte U23 22.04.97, Stockport/Lough St
   TJ- 11.74i (12.25-15)
OGUNLEYE Joy U17 27.09.00, Colchester & T
   60- 7.62i, 100- 12.13 (12.04-16), 200- 24.96 (24.60w-16)
O'HARA Ellie U15 4.10.02, Edinburgh AC
   LJ- 5.35i/5.29, TJ- 11.21i/11.17
O'HARA Emma U23 3.04.95, Radley/St Francis Un/IRL
   DT- 35.41 (40.27-13), HT- 58.32 (59.79-15)
O'HARA Sophie U20 3.08.99, Kingston upon Hull
   DT- 37.13
OHURUOGU Christine Chika 17.05.84, Newham & Ex B
   400- 53.25 (49.41-13)
OHURUOGU Victoria 28.02.93, Newham & Essex B
   200- 24.35w (24.23-16), 400- 53.95 (52.62-13)
OJORA Temi U17 24.01.02, WSE&H
   80HI- 11.6, HJ- 1.77, LJ- 5.61
OKOH Ndidikama U15 3.12.02, Chelmsford
   HJ- 1.68, PenG- 2819
OKOLI Olivia U20 7.09.99, Guildford & Godalming
   60- 7.49i, 100- 11.62, 200- 24.02
OKORHI Leah U15 17.05.03, Birchfield
   100- 12.45, 200- 25.77w/25.8
OKORO Ejiroghene 4.07.90, Birchfield
   800- 2:05.97 (2:03.37-14)
OKORO Eseniki 4.07.90, Birchfield
   400- 54.35, 400H- 57.62 (56.67-14)
OKORO Marilyn 23.09.84, Shaftesbury B
   400- 54.12i (52.02-06), 600- 1:25.89i (1:24.36-12),
   800- 2:02.50 (1:58.45-08)
OKORO Rachel U15 25.07.04, WSE&H
   LJ- 5.27
OKORO Stephanie U13 22.04.06, Havering
   800- 2:21.30
OKOROJI Honour U15 24.01.03, VPH &TH
   LJ- 5.41
OKUL Maggie U23 1.10.97, Kingston upon Hull
   HT- 53.65 (55.32-16)
OLADIPO Divine Dolapo U20 5.10.98, Blackh & Brom/
   Connecticut Un   SP- 16.64, DT- 53.13
OLAJIDE Funminiyi U17 4.06.02, Thurrock
   HJ- 1.65, LJ- 5.86w/5.83
OLALERE Anika U20 8.04.99, Blackheath & Bromley
   SP- 11.16
OLATUNJI Vivien U23 6.06.97, B'heath & Brom/Middx Un
   100- 12.15 (12.03-15)
OLDROYD Hannah 27.05.87, Saltaire Striders
   Mar- 2:54:11 (2:50:15-15), Mar- 3:36:38 (3:35:57-16)
OLIARNYK Iris U17 6.09.01, Halesowen
   LJ- 5.64w, TJ- 11.71, SPI- 12.76, HepI- 4568, PenII- 3482i

425

OLIARNYK Josie U20 27.03.00, Halesowen
100- 11.86w/12.0 (12.01i/12.12-16), 200- 24.7/24.94i,
LJ- 6.02w/5.98
OLIVER Poppy U15 27.02.03, Crawley
300- 41.75, 75HG- 11.4/11.45
OLIVER Roxanne U23 15.01.97, Bl'burn/Leeds Beck Un
100H- 14.9/15.07 (15.03w-16)
OLUGBILE Danielle U13 4.11.04, Camberley
HJ- 1.53
OMAMULI Roli U15 3.02.03, Harrow
100- 12.45
OMITOWOJU Adelaide U20 22.10.99, Cambridge & Col
TJ- 12.30
OMOREGIE Sarah Victoria U20 2.04.00, Cardiff
SP- 14.12, SPI- 16.74
O'NEILL Lisa U20 20.07.99, Pitreavie
JT- 38.41 (40.11-16)
ONI Jade U17 29.06.01, Medway & Maidstone
TJ- 12.25
ONIONS Imogen U17 15.04.02, Solihull & S H
JTI- 38.52
ONIWINDE Ifeoluwa 6.10.92, Enfield & Haringey
JT- 50.45 (54.71-14)
ONUIRI Kara U17 18.08.02, Shaftesbury B
HJ- 1.69
ONUORA Anyika 28.10.84, Liverpool H
200- 23.28 (22.64-14), 400- 51.81 (50.87-15)
OPARA Danielle U23 22.06.95, Thames Valley/Derby Un
SP- 14.47i/13.42 (14.62-15), DT- 36.30 (41.19-14)
ORD Katie U23 4.12.96, VP-Glasgow/Glasgow Un
HT- 48.63
ORFENOV Ornella U15 24.10.02, Crawley
LJ- 5.25
ORMOND Megan U20 21.04.00, WSE&H
1.5kSt- 5:04.6
ORR Abbey U15 19.11.03, VP-Glasgow
HJ- 1.61
ORTON Charlotte U20 18.07.98, Birchfield/Birmingham U
60- 7.64i, 100- 12.00w/12.14 (12.0/12.01-16),
200- 24.79i/24.89w/24.91 (24.69-16)
OSAHON Shakanya U15 10.09.03, Blackheath & Bromley
300- 41.69
OSBORNE Gaia Elena Paol U20 9.08.00, C of Portsm
SP- 13.62, SPI- 15.71, JT- 41.48
OSHUNREMI Victoria U23 3.10.96, Basildon/Hallam Un
TJ- 11.85
OSKAN-CLARKE Shelayna 20.01.90, WSE&H
400- 53.38 (53.20-11), 800- 1:59.82 (1:58.86-15)
O'SULLIVAN Mollie U20 23.02.00, Herne Hill
800- 2:08.31
OTARUOH Ruth-Ann U15 9.01.04, Thames Valley
TJ- 10.33
OTENG Abena U17 7.09.01, Southend
200- 25.28
OUTTEN Georgina Erin U23 26.06.96, Colwyn Bay
3k- 9:33.96i (9:24.81mx/9:37.16-14)
OWEN Rebecca Louise 8.09.91, Brighton & Hove
HJ- 1.68i/1.65, JT- 37.16, Hep- 4590 (4665-16)
OWEN Bronwen Angharad U23 21.01.97, Scarborough
3k- 9:32.47mx (9:28.24mx-14, 9:30.50+-13),
5k- 16:31.48 (16:21.86-15)
OWENS Amber U20 27.10.99, Newark AC
1.5kSt- 5:12.49
OWENS Stephanie 6.09.90, West Cheshire
DT- 37.08 (38.01-09), HT- 47.93 (50.12-08)
OWOEYE Praise U15 13.08.03, Sale/IRL
100- 12.46
OWOLABI Naomi U17 10.10.01, Croydon
60- 7.71i, 100- 12.16
OWOLANA Zuriel U17 26.10.01, Harrow
60- 7.86imx/7.87i,
100- 12.3/12.34mx/12.36 (12.3/12.33mx/12.34mx-16)
OWUSU Michelle U17 5.01.02, Wolves & Bilston
100- 12.3
OWUSU-ANSAH Melissa 24.05.94, Blackheath & Bromley
400- 56.20 (55.29-16)
OWUSU-JUNIOR Lakeisha U17 6.05.01, Herne Hill
60- 7.69i, 100- 12.14

PACKHAM Abigail U15 19.08.03, Crawley
60HG- 9.18i, 75HG- 11.19, HJ- 1.65
PAGE Holly U20 17.08.00, Dartford
1.5kSt- 4:55.30 (4:53.94-16), 3kSt- 10:47.16
PAGE Isla U13 1.09.04, Maidenhead
DTM- 28.82
PALLANT Emma 4.06.89, Aldershot F&D
10MR- 54:53, HMar- 73:43
PALMER Annabelle 21.09.94, Notts
HT- 58.27 (58.94-16)
PALMER Ffion U20 20.03.00, Cardiff
HT- 52.20
PALMER Gillian V35 30.12.80, Edinburgh AC
HMar- 78:52 (75:49sh-16)
PALMER Molly U15 27.08.03, Charnwood
60- 7.89i, 100- 12.46w/12.50, 200- 25.75, LJ- 5.63
PALMER Neve U20 8.08.00, Cambridge & Coleridge
JT- 36.88
PALMER Suzzanne 11.09.93, City of Sheffield/Hallam Un
60H- 8.69i, 100H- 14.46 (14.17-16), LJ- 5.61 (5.76-13),
SP- 13.18, JT- 37.46, Hep- 4401 (4845-16)
PALMER-BLOUNT Lisa V40 9.02.77, Heanor
HMar- 78:35
PALUMAA Teele 31.03.90, TVH/Oxford Un/EST
HJ- 1.78 (1.79i-15), TJ- 12.20w/11.81 (12.19i/11.98-12)
PAPPS Sophie 6.10.94, WSE&H
60- 7.32i (7.22i-14)
PARCELL Nicole U20 16.12.99, Enfield & Haringey
100H- 15.13w, LJ- 5.88
PARK Tara U23 4.04.95, North Ayr/Nevada Un
SP- 11.13, DT- 47.22A/45.45 (48.09-16), HT- 48.73 (50.30-15)
PARKER Carol Ann V45 22.09.69, Coventry Godiva
SP- 11.34 (14.76i-91, 14.71-90), DT- 36.78 (44.70-89)
PARKER Hollie U23 20.12.96, Enfield & Har/LSU
800- 2:07.40, 1500- 4:19.37, 5k- 17:17.74
PARKINSON Caroline Jane 31.07.83, Wycombe
PV- 3.26i/3.24 (3.53i-16, 3.51-14)
PARRIS Georgia U23 5.10.97, Nuneaton/Coventry Un
HJ- 1.70i/1.69 (1.71-16)
PARRIS Lily U15 5.03.03, Chelmsford
60HG- 9.30i, 75HG- 11.32, LJ- 5.23
PARRY Carys L. V35 24.07.81, Rhondda
HT- 65.32 (66.80-14)
PARRY-JONES Isobel U20 17.12.98, Cwmbran
800- 2:09.70, 1500- 4:26.04
PARSONS Sarah 31.05.94, City of York
SP- 11.88i/11.65 (12.48-16), DT- 45.00 (45.83-16)
PARTRIDGE Bethan 11.07.90, Birchfield
HJ- 1.89i/1.85 (1.87-15)
PARTRIDGE Daisy U17 12.10.00, Braintree
JTI- 39.03
PARTRIDGE Lily 9.03.91, Aldershot F&D
10kR- 33:38 (32:20.77t-15), 15kR- 50:52+ (50:16+-15),
10MR- 55:37 (54:41-16), HMar- 72:10 (70:32-15),
Mar- 2:32:10
PARTRIDGE Susan V35 4.01.80, Leeds City
10kR- 34:58+ (33:13+-13), HMar- 75:00+ (70:32-13),
Mar- 2:37:51 (2:30:46-13)
PASK Annabelle U23 6.09.97, Rugby & Nor/Sheffield Un
JT- 36.78
PATERNAIN Julia U20 29.09.99, Cambridge & Col
3k- 9:30.74
PATERSON Charlotte Lucy U20 26.02.98, Kingston u Hull
60- 7.63i (7.49i-16), 100- 11.86
PATIENCE Mhairi U23 10.09.95, VP-Glasgow/St'clyde Un
200- 24.96i, 400- 55.06i/56.19, 400H- 58.69 (58.67-16)
PATON Heather U23 9.04.96, Birchfield
60H- 8.34i, 100H- 13.47
PATTERSON Davicia U17 15.12.00, Beechmount
300- 38.80, 400- 54.50
PATTIE-BELLELI Holly 9.06.94, WGreen & EL/Missouri U
200- 24.89w (24.08w/24.44-16), 60H- 8.60i (8.59i-16),
100H- 13.55w/13.76 (13.27w/13.36-16),
400H- 63.22 (61.00-16)
PATTISON Katie U23 9.10.96, Kingston u Hull/Warwick U
DT- 43.20

426

PATULLO Katie U20 27.03.98, Dundee HH/Dundee Un
  100H- 14.34w/14.6/14.75 (14.64-16), 400H- 63.83
PAULL Emma 6.06.85, Hayle Runners
  Mar- 2:56:58
PAVEY Joanne Marie V40 20.09.73, Exeter
  3k- 9:39.8+e (8:31.27-02), 5k- 16:14.5+e (14:39.96-06),
  10k- 32:42.93 (30:53.20-12), 10kR- 32:57 (31:47-07),
  HMar- 74:45+ (68:53-08)
PAWLETT Abigail U15 14.01.03, Stockport
  60- 7.90imx, 100- 12.04, 200- 25.16i/25.9, 60HI- 8.85i,
  60DHG- 8.85i, 75HG- 11.04, HJ- 1.63i/1.61,
  LJ- 5.65i/5.60, SPI- 11.19, SextG- 3750,
  PenG- 3350+/3298, PenIG- 3341i
PAXTON Henrietta Margaret 19.09.83, Birchfield
  PV- 4.25 (4.35-10)
PAY Kiani U23 12.07.95, Newquay & Par/RNAC
  SP- 11.33
PAYNE Charlotte U17 20.03.02, Newbury
  DT- 42.26, HT- 52.27, HTI- 59.09
PEACH Annabel U17 6.04.02, Notts
  JTI- 41.01
PEAKE Sally 8.02.86, Birchfield
  PV- 4.35 (4.42i-12, 4.40-14)
PEARCE Emily U20 24.02.99, Rhondda
  HT- 43.49 (46.36-16)
PEARCE Kelsey Nikki U15 11.02.03, Mansfield H
  SPI- 12.18
PEERS Anna U23 28.08.97, Blackburn/Hallam Un
  DT- 37.02 (37.17-16), JT- 39.50 (40.49-16)
PELHAM Jessica U17 19.04.01, Guildford & Godalming
  HT- 40.00, HTI- 49.47
PELLETT Vicki U20 19.10.99, Crawley
  HT- 47.39
PEMBERTON Cassie-Ann U17 24.07.01, Birchfield
  60- 7.71i (7.64i-16), 100- 11.94w/12.03,
  200- 24.99w/25.0/25.17
PEMBERTON Holly U15 8.12.02, Wrexham
  DT- 29.98, JTI- 37.65
PENFOLD Megan U17 26.09.01, Orion
  HJ- 1.65
PENFOLD Rose 11.04.91, Mendip
  Mar- 2:55:49 (2:55:37-16)
PENNET Catriona 10.10.83, Edinburgh AC
  60H- 8.85i (8.79i-04), 100H- 14.84 (13.97w-04,14.04-06)
PENNYCOOK Stephanie U23 1.09.95, Fife/Edinburgh Un
  800- 2:09.03 (2:07.98-16), 1500- 4:15.94, 3k- 9:21.83
PERCIVAL Sophie U23 30.07.97, W.Cheshire/Chester Un
  SP- 12.02, JT- 43.53
PERKINS Cliona Rose U20 27.02.99, Wolves & Bilston
  100H- 14.83w/14.9 (15.27-16)
PERKINS Myra 21.01.92, Falkirk VH
  HT- 62.97 (63.11-14)
PERRETT Stella Rene U17 15.04.01, North Shields P
  200- 25.38
PERRIO Louise 8.07.82, Channel Islands
  5k- 17:06.12 (16:34.68mx/16:39.5-12), 5kR- 16:48,
  10k- 35:12.68, Mar- 2:50:57
PERRY India U15 29.06.03, Basildon
  LJ- 5.25
PHILIP Asha 25.10.90, Newham & Essex B
  60- 7.06i, 100- 11.14 (11.10-15), 200- 23.63 (23.07w/23.45-13)
PICKARD Rebecca U20 5.01.98, Stevenage & NH
  400H- 65.39 (64.7-16)
PICKAVANCE Nina U13 22.11.05, Wirral
  75- 10.0
PICKERING-PRUVOT Charlotte U17 10.06.01, Morpeth
  SPI- 12.68i/12.41 (12.50-16), DT- 36.92
PICKLES Georgia U23 19.10.96, Sale/Cardiff Un
  PV- 3.83i/3.30 (3.65-14)
PIGDEN Anya U17 4.05.01, City of Portsmouth
  800- 2:13.97
PINDER Isabel U15 16.11.03, Basingstoke & MH
  800- 2:17.27mx, HJ- 1.72, PenG- 2896
PIPI Amarachi U23 26.11.95, Enfield & Har/Oklahoma Chr
  60- 7.38i, 100- 11.35mx/11.72 (11.72-14),
  200- 22.83w/22.95, 400- 52.96
PIRIE Lesley V35 11.01.81, VP-Glasgow
  Mar- 2:47:48 (2:41:13-16)

PITMAN Grace U15 5.05.03, Ashford
  PV- 2.80
PLATER Grace U17 20.09.00, Leeds
  TJ- 11.50
PLUMPTRE Hermione 26.11.91, Birchfield
  400- 56.29, 400H- 62.03
POLLOCK Zoe U17 21.12.00, Oxford City
  200- 24.75, 60H- 8.69i, 80HI- 11.34, LJ- 5.49,
  HepI- 4940, PentIS- 3637i
POOLE Carys U15 21.12.03, Swansea
  60HG- 9.33i, LJ- 5.26i, PenIG- 3156i
POOLE Rebecca U17 18.10.00, Basingstoke & MH
  1.5kSt- 5:10.74
PORTER Megan U20 4.02.00, Peterborough
  HJ- 1.66 (1.67-15)
PORTER Sophie U17 14.03.01, Channel Islands
  200- 24.9mx/25.09, 300- 39.99i (40.33-16), 400- 56.76,
  300H- 43.29, LJ- 5.53
PORTER Tiffany Adeaze 13.11.87, WGreen & Ex L
  100H- 12.75 (12.47w-12, 12.51-14)
PORTERFIELD Meghan U13 2.09.05, VP-Glasgow
  SPM- 11.91, DTM- 31.81
PORTERFIELD Mhairi Lee V35 19.06.81, VP-Glasgow
  SP- 13.30 (13.78-15), HT- 53.15 (58.47-02)
POTTER Elizabeth Caven 27.12.91, Shaftesbury B
  3k- 9:39.5+e (8:53.94mx/9:12.41+-16), 10kR- 33:00,
  5k- 16:12.07+ (15:28.32-16), 10k- 32:04.63 (32:03.45-16)
POTTER Cristina U17 8.10.01, Barnet
  JTI- 38.98
POTTER Jane V35 24.10.81, Charnwood
  5MR- 27:36 (27:23-16), 10kR- 34:52 (34:12-08),
  10MR- 58:21 (56:05-11)
POTTER Juliet V35 24.10.81, Charnwood
  5kR- 16:46 (15:57.41-01), 10kR- 34:59 (33:27-08),
  10MR- 58:16 (56:27-12)
POWELL Trinity U17 29.06.02, Manchester
  60- 7.63i, 100- 11.97
PRATT Aimee U23 3.10.97, Sale
  1500- 4:25.07, 1.5kSt- 4:49.30, 3kSt- 9:59.86
PRELLS Nina 22.07.94, Swansea
  DT- 36.60 (37.84-11)
PRESHO Jasmine U17 18.11.01, WSE&H
  PV- 3.21
PRESSWELL Kayleigh U23 14.03.95, M Milton Keynes/
  Un Wales Swansea   HT- 59.38
PRICE Caitlin U20 25.12.98, Liverpool H
  HT- 46.86
PRICE Ffion 11.08.94, Cardiff/Mississippi St
  800- 2:06.91 (2:06.89-16), 1500- 4:14.13,
  1M- 4:43.53 (4:41.49i-16)
PRICE Rhianwedd 11.08.94, Cardiff/Mississippi St
  800- 2:06.26 (2:04.02-15), 1500- 4:12.07 (4:09.56-15),
  1M- 4:39.57i (4:32.74i-15, 4:41.71-14), 3k- 9:33.89i,
  2kSt- 7:01.53 (6:57.08-12)
PRICE Zoe U17 14.04.02, Liverpool H
  SPI- 13.19, HT- 45.09, HTI- 56.49
PRIDEAUX Emma V40 25.04.73, Billericay Striders
  Mar- 2:56:31
PRIEST Katie-Jane U23 27.09.96, Swansea
  60- 7.73i, 100- 12.13mx/12.13 (12.0/12.01-16),
  200- 24.86 (24.77mx-15)
PRINCE Christine U20 6.10.98, R Sutton Coldfield
  HT- 42.68 (44.38-16)
PRINGLE Emma 10.01.92, Gateshead
  TJ- 11.60 (13.01-13)
PRINGLE Hannah 5.08.94, Gateshead
  TJ- 11.29i (11.96-15)
PROCTOR Shara 16.09.88, Birchfield
  60- 7.49i (7.36i-16), LJ- 6.73 (7.07-15), TJ- 13.82 (13.88iAIA-10)
PROTO Emily 24.11.88, Arena 80
  Mar- 2:54:37
PROUDFOOT Nicole U15 12.11.02, Annan
  HJ- 1.60i, LJ- 5.56w/5.52, SextG- 3421, PenG- 3223,
  PenIG- 3192i
PROUDLEY Tabitha U15 27.08.04, Southampton
  75HG- 11.59
PULLIN Ellie U23 15.02.97, Notts/Loughborough St
  HJ- 1.65i (1.63)

PURCHAS Natasha U17 12.01.01, Crawley
 PV- 3.82
PURCHASE Anna U20 15.09.99, Notts
 HT- 57.43
PURDUE Charlotte Lucy 10.06.91, Aldershot F&D
 5kR- 16:50+ (15:23.4t-10), 10kR- 33:32 (32:03.55t-12),
 15kR- 51:08+ (50:00+-11), 10MR- 55:43 (53:45-11),
 HMar- 71:29, Mar- 2:29:23
PURVES Katie U23 3.11.96, Edinburgh AC
 100H- 14.09, 400H- 59.96
PYATT Jenny U20 13.10.98, Liverpool Pembroke Sefton
 DT- 45.11
PYE Amy U17 22.11.00, Cannock & Stafford
 200- 25.3, 60HI- 8.74i (8.74i-16), 80HI- 11.28w/11.44,
 100HI- 14.24i/14.72, 300H- 41.96, 400H- 66.82

QUAINTANCE Millie U15 10.11.02, Newbury
 JTI- 40.47
QUIGLEY Gabrielle U20 5.11.99, Chelmsford
 DT- 38.99
QUIRK Amelia U20 18.12.99, Bracknell
 1500- 4:15.85mx/4:16.32, 3k- 9:21.32

RACE Emily U17 11.09.00, Worksop
 60HI- 8.93i (8.90i-16), 80HI- 11.17w/11.33, HJ- 1.75,
 LJ- 5.73w/5.72, Hepl- 5214, PenII- 3375i
RADUS Lia U17 1.10.01, Shaftesbury B
 1500- 4:33.34
RADUS Maayan U15 30.05.04, Shaftesbury B
 3k- 10:32.74mx
RAE Emma U20 27.06.00, Pitreavie
 HT- 47.46
RAINSBOROUGH Matilda U23 28.08.96, Guildford & G/
 Lough St 400- 55.12
RAMSEY Gemma U17 27.06.01, Ipswich
 JTI- 41.85
RANKIN Gemma 18.12.84, Kilbarchan
 HMar- 76:37 (75:44-13, 75:18sh-16), Mar- 2:44:35 (2:39:33-16)
RAVENSCROFT Eleanor U20 21.07.98, Kidd & Stourport
 400H- 64.1
RAWLINSON Beth U13 17.05.05, Wenlock O
 1500- 4:48.2
REED Kate Amelia 28.09.82, Bristol & West
 HMar- 73:44
REEKIE Jemma U20 6.03.98, Kilbarchan
 800- 2:04.25mx/2:05.52i/2:07.65 (2:07.23-16),
 1500- 4:12.28, 1M- 4:40.55, 3k- 9:11.20mx/9:24.81
REES Alisha U20 16.04.99, Edinburgh AC
 60- 7.43i, 100- 11.62 (11.55w-14), 200- 23.12w/23.32
REES Bethan U20 27.10.99, Cannock & Stafford
 JT- 49.56
REES Halina 6.07.94, Fife/Strathclyde Un
 3kSt- 11:03.55
REES Holly 5.06.93, Cambridge & Coleridge
 3k- 9:12.75, 5k- 16:00.34, 10k- 33:13.55
REGIS Alicia U17 17.12.01, Enfield & Haringey
 200- 24.72i/24.89 (24.36-16)
REID Catherine U20 21.04.98, Manx H/Georgia Un
 400- 54.34 (52.25-15)
REID Kayanna U23 11.06.97, Shaftesbury B
 TJ- 11.24 (11.41-16)
REID Lucy 2.12.92, Tonbridge
 5k- 16:29.59mx, 5MR- 27:36, 10k- 35:44.36,
 10kR- 34:41
REID Naomi Jasmin U20 24.06.00, Cardiff
 800- 2:09.02i/2:10.24
REILLY Laura U23 16.10.95, Belgrave
 100H- 14.85
REIMERS Sonka 1.10.93, Beeston AC/GER
 Mar- 2:55:05
RENNIE Aileen 21.02.94, Edinburgh AC
 JT- 43.54 (45.26-15)
REVILLE Katie U17 20.02.02, Nithsdale
 200- 25.22w
REYNOLDS Amelia U20 23.11.98, Cardiff
 100- 12.12 (12.10-14), 200- 24.04i (24.06-14),
 400- 56.63i (56.35-16)
RICHARDS Amy U23 24.04.97, Orion/Northumberland Un
 Hep- 3932 (4141-14)

RICHARDS Shona U23 1.09.95, WSE&H
 400H- 59.38 (56.05-15)
RICHARDSON Charlotte U15 23.02.03, Gateshead
 100- 12.51
RICHARDSON Chloe 4.12.93, Birchfield
 3k- 9:43.06i (9:34.45-16)
RICHARDSON Eavion U20 27.06.98, Shaftesbury B/
 Birm Coll FTCS LJ- 6.00w/5.94 (6.00w/5.95-16),
 TJ- 12.48w/12.35i/12.18
RICHARDSON Kate U15 12.09.02, Giffnock North
 3k- 10:35.46imx (10:28.82mx-16)
RICHARDSON Letisha 4.01.93, WSE&H/Leeds Un
 TJ- 11.28 (11.42-16)
RICHES Laura 7.08.93, Leigh/Bangor Un
 3k- 9:37.47mx (9:41.73i-15), 2kSt- 6:45.41 (6:38.18-16),
 3kSt- 10:27.03
RIDLEY Sophie U20 5.10.98, Winchester
 100H- 15.0w/15.14w
RIGBY Rebecca 17.10.91, Preston/Sheffield Un
 1500- 4:27.02mx, 3k- 9:36.21mx (9:34.94-16),
 5k- 16:13.56, 10k- 33:36.70, HMar- 76:52
RILEY Hannah V35 9.07.82, Manx H
 100H- 15.1 (14.50-11)
RIXON Maisie Tay U15 11.10.02, Tonbridge
 200- 25.9, 300- 41.39, PenG- 2915
ROBBINS Jenny U23 20.02.96, Notts/Manchester Un
 PV- 3.63i/3.15 (3.75-15)
ROBBINS Natalie U20 30.11.98, Edinburgh AC
 HT- 52.80
ROBBINS-HULSE Michelle 2.06.86, Trafford
 TJ- 11.72 (12.63-14)
ROBERTS Abigail U23 9.07.97, City of Sheffield
 PV- 4.05 (4.08-15)
ROBERTS Grace U13 18.11.04, Vale Royal
 1200- 3:52.22
ROBERTS Hannah U15 15.09.02, Bracknell
 300- 41.0mx/41.21, 400- 58.33, 800- 2:11.59
ROBERTS Melissa U23 6.08.97, Birchfield/Cardiff Met
 60- 7.53i, 100- 11.72,
 200- 24.56i/24.56mx/24.59 (24.38w/24.41i/24.45-15)
ROBERTS Mia U17 13.07.02, Deeside
 800- 2:14.8, 1500- 4:34.95, 3k- 9:57.73mx/9:57.84
ROBERTS Nicole 30.01.92, Birchfield
 3k- 9:46.80i
ROBERTSON Ellen U23 23.06.96, Arbroath/R. Gordon U
 TJ- 11.24 (11.42w-13, 11.27-15)
ROBERTSON Niamh U17 31.07.01, Dundee HH
 80HI- 11.93, 300H- 46.50
ROBERTSON Rachel U23 4.06.96, Edin AC/Napier Un
 LJ- 5.69i (5.86w/5.72-14, 5.75i-15)
ROBERTSON Stephanie U15 28.09.02, Southport
 60HG- 9.41i, 75HG- 11.5/11.54
ROBERTSON Sydney U23 13.12.96, Gateshead
 PV- 3.10
ROBINSON Brittany U20 9.11.98, Thames Valley
 100- 12.16w (11.92w/12.04-16)
ROBINSON Caitlin U15 28.05.03, Liverpool H
 1500- 4:40.20mx/4:40.91
ROBINSON Cyane U17 11.06.01, Rotherham
 800- 2:13.79mx
ROBINSON Emily U20 22.06.00, Brighton & Hove
 DT- 39.82, JT- 40.27
ROBINSON Jessica U20 26.06.99, WSE&H
 PV- 3.95 (4.05-16)
ROBINSON Kate 30.09.94, Salisbury/California Bap Un
 10k- 35:37.28
ROBINSON Louise U17 19.11.00, Birchfield
 300H- 46.01, 400H- 67.4
ROBINSON Lucy U17 16.12.01, Liverpool H
 LJ- 5.61i
ROBINSON Matilda U15 1.10.02, Bracknell
 100- 12.55
ROBINSON Rebecca V35 28.10.82, Kendal
 5kR- 16:39 (15:48-09), 10kR- 33:49 (33:13-12)
ROBISON Charlotte U23 13.07.97, Edinburgh AC/
 UMass Amherst Un 100H- 15.11 (14.99-15), Hep- 4005
ROBSON Odette V45 4.10.71, St Edmunds Pacers
 Mar- 2:57:25

ROCHE Bekki U15 11.12.02, Liverpool H
SPI- 14.59, DT- 32.46, HT- 44.47, HTI- 54.26
RODGERS Alice U15 23.09.02, Ballymena & A
100- 12.54, 200- 25.62
RODGERS Holly U23 3.02.97, Rotherham/Hallam Un
HT- 49.51 (52.57-16)
ROESSLER Pippa U15 8.01.04, Reigate
1500- 4:44.57mx, 3k- 10:12.75
ROGAN Phillipa 4.02.94, Thames Valley/Bath Un/IRL
HJ- 1.82i/1.78 (1.80-16)
ROGERS Georgina U23 1.09.96, Birchfield/Lough St
400H- 61.5 (58.53-16)
ROGERS Minnie U15 4.08.03, Blackpool
PV- 2.70
ROLFE Amy Lauren U17 12.12.01, City of York
LJ- 5.57i (5.51-16)
ROOT Asha U17 15.06.01, Tonbridge
300- 40.42, 400- 57.93
ROSBERGEN Femke U15 23.10.02, City of Norwich
800- 2:16.27
ROSE Ahtollah 6.03.93, Trafford
TJ- 12.48 (12.88-11)
ROSS Fionnuala 5.11.90, Armagh (IRL from Dec 17)
10kR- 33:59, HMar- 74:26, Mar- 2:49:00
ROSS Shona U20 11.08.98, Kilbarchan
TJ- 11.94w/11.74
ROSSER Awen U23 28.09.95, Swansea
SP- 12.79 (12.88i-14, 12.87-16), DT- 43.16 (45.66-14)
ROUTLEDGE Jasmine U17 4.06.02, Charnwood
HT- 43.17, HTI- 52.37
ROWATT Alison V35 16.02.81, Edinburgh TTI
Mar- 2:45:39
ROWE Anna Nicole U20 2.09.98, Liverpool H
100H- 15.20 (14.8/14.90-16), 400H- 62.24 (60.78-16)
ROWE Katie U20 12.04.99, Amber Valley
TJ- 11.28 (11.99-16)
ROWE Sophie 20.04.88, Gloucester AC
100- 12.01w/12.1
ROWLAND Joanne 29.12.89, Crawley
60H- 8.97i (8.91i-13), 100H- 14.6/14.71 (14.46-13),
HJ- 1.68i/1.68 (1.72-12), LJ- 5.93 (6.08-16),
SP- 13.64 (13.71i-14), DT- 37.34, JT- 41.58 (42.81-13),
Hep- 5614 (5702-13), PentIS- 4103i (4115i-15)
ROWLANDS Andrea V40 1.06.74, Eyrri
Mar- 2:54:23
ROY Lauren U17 25.09.00, City of Lisburn
60- 7.63i, 100- 12.10w/12.11 (12.05-16),
200- 24.70i/25.12 (24.46w/24.80-16)
RUBERY Hayley 5.09.93, Telford
DT- 40.00 (41.39-16)
RULE Lauren U23 24.10.96, Stevenage & NH/Kent Un
400- 56.24 (55.64-16)
RUNCIMAN Laura U17 19.05.01, Chelmsford
HTI- 55.83
RUNNACLES Leah U20 2.10.99, Reading
HT- 47.59
RUSH Ella U15 8.04.04, Amber Valley
PenG- 2925
RUSH Holly G. V40 23.09.77, Avon Valley Runners
Mar- 2:51:25 (2:37:35-08)
RUSHTON Kirsty U17 13.03.02, Blackpool & Fylde
PV- 2.90 (2.95-16)
RUSSELL Alexandra 27.03.90, Wigan
TJ- 13.27i (13.40w-16, 13.05-15)
RUSSELL Cara U15 19.01.03, Herne Hill
60- 7.96i, 100- 12.2, 200- 25.11
RUSSELL Chyna U17 22.12.00, Sutton & District
200- 25.30w/25.32, 300- 39.34
RUSSELL Dawn U13 14.12.04, Law & Dist
HTI- 33.09
RUSSELL Emily U20 12.01.00, Harrow
60H- 8.83i, 100HI- 14.02, 100H- 14.13
RUSSELL Lauren U20 16.03.98, Bedford/E London Un
100- 12.20w, 200- 24.72, 300- 38.36, 400- 53.71
RUTHERFORD Emma U17 20.09.01, Perth
300- 40.46
RUTTER NiaBari Zoey 4.01.86, Blackpool & Fylde
SP- 11.39 (11.50-16), Hep- 3892

RYAN Joanne 3.10.86, Loughton
200- 24.68 (24.3/24.32w-07, 24.42-09)
400- 54.88 (54.01-10)

S ACRE Kesari U20 4.11.99, Stade Niortais (FRA)
LJ- 5.75
SAKARIA Katie U13 1.11.05, Guildford & Godalming
1200- 3:52.7
SAMUEL Laura 19.02.91, Birchfield
TJ- 13.60 (14.09-14)
SAMUELS Dionne 18.09.92, Birchfield
100- 11.94w
SAMUELS Sonia V35 16.05.79, Sale
5MR- 27:26, 10k- 32:41.19 (32:39.36-14), 10MR- 56:54,
10kR- 33:18 (32:58sh-14), 15kR- 52:22+ (52:09+-14),
HMar- 74:03+ (72:36-13), Mar- 2:29:34 (2:28:04-15)
SARTI Hope U20 6.01.98, Guildford & G/
Cal St Northridge   100H- 14.30 (13.78-16)
SASEGBON Motunrayo 16.09.91, Steve & NH/NGR
100H- 14.1/14.35 (14.20-14), HJ- 1.75 (1.84-15),
SP- 13.33, Hep- 5367 (5582-16)
SAULIUNAITE Ugne U20 17.04.99, Edinburgh AC/LTU
400H- 64.75 (62.70-15)
SAULTERS Laura 30.05.88, North Down
TJ- 11.43 (11.80-16)
SAUNDERS Louisa U17 26.12.00, Brighton Phoenix
300- 39.95, 400- 57.77
SAUNDERS Nicole U13 18.09.04, Blackburn
DTM- 29.39
SAWYERS Jazmin 21.05.94, City of Stoke
LJ- 6.71i/6.55w/6.53 (6.86w/6.75-16)
SAXON Lily U15 28.03.04, Solihull & S H
1500- 4:41.11
SCHILLER Eden U15 19.11.02, Staffs Moorlands
3k- 10:38.40
SCHOFIELD Maria U17 8.09.00, City of York
SPI- 12.48 (12.67-16), HT- 43.24, HTI- 50.09
SCHWIENING Georgina 15.12.94, Cambridge & Col
10k- 35:17.29, 10kR- 34:48, 10MR- 57:10,
HMar- 75:26 (74:44sh-16), Mar- 2:42:57
SCOTT Amaya U17 15.02.01, Southampton
80HI- 11.9, HJ- 1.76, SPI- 14.95, PenII- 3582i (3667i-16)
SCOTT Catriona U13 1.09.04, VP-Glasgow
60HM- 9.99i, 70HM- 11.36w, PenIM- 2330i
SCOTT Lara U15 26.08.04, Southampton
HJ- 1.63
SCOTT-PEARCE Isla 11.12.94, Corstorphine/Aber Un
3kSt- 11:08.84
SCOTT-WILSON Ashley 9.04.91, Highgate H/USA
3k- 9:46.20mx, 5k- 17:07.42 (16:36.70-13)
SCRAFTON Floren 24.12.93, Bristol & W
3k- 9:42.40, 5k- 16:45.67
SCRIVENER Emily U15 29.07.03, Reading
PV- 2.60
SEALY Katy Louise 15.10.90, Ipswich/Cardiff Met/BIZ
100H- 14.9/15.23, HJ- 1.68 (1.71i/1.70-15),
SP- 11.44i/11.31, JT- 39.20, Hep- 4753 (4817-16)
SEARS Jasmine U17 14.12.01, Shaftesbury B
TJ- 12.21
SEGER Sophie U20 21.09.99, Oxford City
100H- 15.22
SEGRAVE Hannah U23 14.04.95, Middlesboro Mandale/
Milligan Coll   400- 55.44, 800- 2:02.79, 1500- 4:21.80
SEGUN Sophie U20 3.10.98, Herts Phoenix
200- 24.92 (24.86w/24.9-15)
SEMENYTSH Rosanna Marie 28.05.87, Sale
JT- 44.76 (50.43-13)
SEMPLE Ella U15 18.11.02, Wolves & Bilston
1500- 4:40.96
SENIOR Ruth 16.10.87, City of Norwich
HMar- 78:41, Mar- 2:49:15 (2:42:50-12)
SERGENT Belinda U23 19.11.96, Bedford & Co/Bath Un
100H- 15.28w, TJ- 11.19w
SEXTON Katie U20 4.12.99, Crawley
PV- 3.10
SEY Marcia U17 7.11.01, Croydon
60- 7.75i, 100- 12.07, 60HI- 8.46i, 80HI- 11.04,
LJ- 5.55w

SEYMOUR Emma U23 3.10.95, Team Kennet
SP- 11.44
SHAKES-DRAYTON Perresha 21.12.88, VPH &TH
400- 52.19 (50.50-13)
SHANLEY Hazel U20 6.03.99, Livingston
TJ- 11.70
SHARKEY Katie U17 19.11.01, Central
60HI- 8.92i, 80HI- 11.8/11.81, 300H- 45.84
SHARMAN Meghan U15 4.01.03, R Sutton Coldfield
HTI- 38.43
SHARP Chloe U20 27.12.99, Dartford
3k- 9:41.27mx/9:41.80
SHARP Lynsey Gillian 11.07.90, Edinburgh AC
400- 55.76i+/56.54+mx (54.43-16),
600- 1:27.16i (1:27.51+-14), 800- 1:58.01 (1:57.69-16)
SHARPE Emma U17 9.05.01, North Devon
DT- 39.48, HTI- 46.08
SHARPE Francesca U15 20.04.03, Burton
JT- 33.83, JTI- 36.84
SHAW Alexandra U17 6.09.00, Guildford & Godalming
300- 40.2 (39.52-16), 400- 56.00, 800- 2:11.04 (2:09.30-15)
SHAW Amanda 28.09.84, Wakefield
200- 24.74w/24.94 (24.63-16)
SHAW Bethany U17 16.03.01, St Albans AC
100- 12.30w/12.34
SHAW Wendy V40 5.10.77, Reading Joggers
24HrT- 220.509km
SHAYAAM-SMITH Abazz U20 3.04.00, Birchfield
TJ- 12.20
SHEARMAN Amelia U15 21.01.03, Blackpool
PV- 3.15
SHEFFIELD Rebecca U17 19.09.00, Burton
60HI- 9.0i/9.06i, 80HI- 11.75w/11.92
SHEPHERD Gemma U23 23.11.97, Team Bath/Yale Un
3k- 9:25.18i (9:27.58-16)
SHEPHERD Mia U23 9.04.97, Kilbarchan/Strathclyde Un
HT- 42.72
SHEPHERD-CROSS Kitty U17 11.02.02, V of Aylesbury
1500- 4:35.54
SHERWOOD Emma U17 12.09.01, Dudley & Stourbridge
HJ- 1.73 (1.75-16), LJ- 5.49, Hepl- 4447
SHINGLER Kate-Diane U17 23.09.00, Wigan
TJ- 11.06i (11.27-15)
SHIPLEY Emma U13 15.02.05, Hallamshire
800- 2:15.93, 1200- 3:43.7, 1500- 4:53.4
SHOKUNBI Modupe U20 10.10.98, Blackheath & Bromley
60- 7.66i, 100- 12.13 (11.78w/11.97-14)
SHONIBARE Rukayatu U17 19.06.02, Sale
60- 7.90i
SHORT Annalise U23 29.10.96, Blackheath & B/Leeds Un
60- 7.70i, 100- 12.03 (11.81w/11.95-15),
LJ- 5.76i (5.58w/5.55)
SHOYEKE-ARMSTROMG S U13, Essex Schools
100- 12.7
SIBBONS Aleeya U15 5.11.02, Newham & Essex B
60- 7.89i, 100- 12.12, 200- 25.8/25.91 (25.6-16)
SIBLEY Amarisa U13 27.06.05, Blackheath & Bromley
800- 2:22.2
SIDDONS Bethan 29.09.90, Havering
HJ- 1.70 (1.74-15)
SIKIRU Simbiyat U15 5.10.02, Woodford Green & Ex L
HTI- 42.86
SILCOCK Madeleine U20 13.06.00, Banchory
60- 7.70i, 100- 12.04
SILCOX Georgia Kate U20 14.10.98, Yeovil Olympiads
60H- 8.93i, 100H- 14.25, LJ- 6.08w/5.87, Hep- 4776
SIMARRO Belen U23 10.11.95, Cardiff Met/ESP
HJ- 1.70i (1.66-14)
SIMMONS Natalie U13 5.06.05, Bedford & County
1200- 3:52.1
SIMON Olivia U13 9.11.04, Colchester H
PV- 2.60
SIMPSON Amber U20 3.01.99, Deeside
DT- 39.12, HT- 56.43
SIMPSON Annabel U23 30.04.97, Fife/Glasgow Un
3k- 9:36.31mx (9:36.18mx/9:40.07-16), 10k- 35:33.46,
5k- 16:41.95mx/16:47.49 (16:35.81mx-16),
10kR- 34:41, 10MR- 56:30

SIMPSON Katrina U20 4.04.00, Halesowen
800- 2:10.01
SIMPSON Ruby U13 6.07.05, Hallamshire
800- 2:13.87, 1200- 3:45.8, 1500- 4:48.4
SIMPSON Tilly U17 25.10.00, Hallamshire
1500- 4:36.11 (4:21.47-16)
SIMPSON-SULLIVAN Tara U17 2.12.00, Wigan
SP- 13.27, SPI- 13.07 (13.69-16), DT- 33.69 (34.50-16),
HT- 50.28 (50.47-16), HTI- 63.23
SIMS Marissa U17 18.01.01, Enfield & Har
60HI- 8.90i
SIMSON Jade U23 9.10.97, City of Plymouth/Bath Un
60H- 8.66i, 100H- 14.26w/14.63 (14.21-16)
SKEGGS Charlotte U20 1.09.98, Basildon
Hep- 3827
SLADE Kia U17 16.01.01, Reading
100H- 15.7
SMALE Tilly U15 31.10.03, North Somerset
LJ- 5.28
SMALL Louise 27.03.92, Aldershot F&D
1500- 4:24.62mx/4:24.8 (4:20.99mx-16, 4:21.07-09),
3k- 9:07.64mx (9:15.47-09), 10k- 32:56.11,
5k- 15:40.5mx/15:42.27 (15:41.94-16)
SMITH Abigail U13 24.11.04, Blackheath & Bromley
2kW- 11:03.20
SMITH Akesha U23 11.06.95, Enfield & Har/Bedford Un
400H- 65.08 (65.07-13)
SMITH Anna Charlotte U17 14.09.01, Mansfield H
800- 2:06.40, 1500- 4:17.99
SMITH Caitlin U15 20.05.03, New Forest Juniors
JTI- 34.35
SMITH Carys U23 15.01.97, Swansea
HT- 44.80 (44.99-16)
SMITH Emily U20 6.06.99, Wycombe
400H- 64.05 (64.0-16)
SMITH Hollie U20 7.11.98, Trafford
HJ- 1.70i (1.76i/1.75-16)
SMITH Holly U17 31.12.01, Vale Royal
1500- 4:38.68mx, 3k- 9:57.6
SMITH Holly U20 22.09.99, Liverpool H
TJ- 11.93
SMITH Imogen U20 2.09.99, Birchfield
PV- 3.50 (3.50-16)
SMITH Jessica U17 5.09.01, Enfield & Haringey
PV- 2.90i
SMITH Jodie U17 2.11.01, WSE&H
HJ- 1.65, JTI- 40.59, Hepl- 4743
SMITH Laura-Jane 7.02.91, Notts
1500- 4:25.67mx/4:27.73 (4:23.95mx-16, 4:26.37-15),
3k- 9:32.07mx (9:44.32-15), 5k- 16:33.93, 10kR- 34:34,
10MR- 58:31
SMITH Louise V45 7.07.70, North Belfast
Mar- 2:53:27
SMITH Lucy 16.09.93, Exeter
JT- 39.47 (41.34-16)
SMITH Lydia U15 15.03.04, Taunton
60HG- 9.42i, 75HG- 11.50, LJ- 5.32, PenG- 2817
SMITH Mabel U15 17.02.04, Herne Hill
HJ- 1.65
SMITH Madeleine U20 5.02.99, Bournemouth
TJ- 11.35 (11.41w/11.38-16)
SMITH Mae U13 21.11.04, Grantham
SPM- 10.09
SMITH Mari U23 14.11.96, Birchfield/Birmingham Un
800- 2:04.19, 1500- 4:20.66 (4:19.63mx-16)
SMITH Molly U13 25.09.04, Hereford
DTM- 30.58
SMITH Natasha U20 10.10.99, Stroud
100H- 14.8/14.92, HJ- 1.74i/1.71 (1.78i/1.77-16), Hep- 4686
SMITH Roisin Mary U23 10.11.97, Airdrie
400- 56.28i/56.58mx
SMITH Stacey Louise 4.02.90, Gateshead
800- 2:06.68mx (2:01.93-10), 5kR- 16:15,
1500- 4:11.72mx (4:06.81-11)
SMYLIE Jill V35 6.04.80, Giffnock North
Mar- 2:57:06 (2:55:57-13)
SNAITH Maisey U17 3.04.01, Cambridge & Coleridge
100- 11.9/12.11w/12.24 (12.08w-16),
200- 25.1w/25.19i/25.3 (25.08-16), 300- 39.5/39.76

SNOWDEN Katie 9.03.94, Herne Hill
800- 2:00.92mx/2:03.91 (2:01.77-15), 1500- 4:05.29,
1M- 4:25.89
SOLOMON Serita 1.03.90, Blackheath & Bromley
60- 7.62i (7.49i-16), 60H- 8.23i (7.93i-15),
100H- 13.45w/13.73 (12.87-15)
SOUSA Nanci 28.09.90, Enfield & Haringey/POR
JT- 42.47
SOUTHCOTT Rhea U17 30.03.01, Leeds
SP- 12.99i/12.92, SPI- 15.64, JTI- 39.57, Hepl- 4833
SOUZA Tatum 20.04.92, Notts Univ/USA
60H- 8.61i (8.48i-13), 100H- 14.50 (13.72-16),
SP- 13.75i/13.63 (14.40i/14.05-16), JT- 40.51 (44.27-15)
SOWAH Shammah U17 21.01.02, Orion
300- 40.2/40.63, 400- 56.86
SOYEI Kenyeh U15 26.10.02, Bedford & County
SPI- 12.28
SPACEY Lara U17 26.08.02, Swansea
HTI- 47.17
SPENCE Mia Sky U23 27.06.97, Notts/Loughborough St
400- 56.47 (55.77-16)
SPENCER Ivy U15 23.09.02, Lewes
PV- 2.95
SPENCER Linda V35 16.01.82, Chichester R
HMar- 75:40 (74:33-15), Mar- 2:45:37
SPENCER-SMITH Jade U17 8.11.01, Harrow
PV- 3.73i/3.71
SPILIOPOULOU Ashleigh U20 2.04.99, Enfield & Har
HJ- 1.70, Hep- 4808
SPINK Jennifer E. V35 7.08.81, Bristol & West
5kR- 16:46 (16:41-15), 10kR- 34:14+ (33:36-16),
15kR- 51:57+, HMar- 73:36 (73:02-15),
Mar- 2:38:11 (2:36:00-15)
SPINK Morgan U17 6.04.02, Doncaster
300H- 44.03, Hepl- 4379
SPURLING Tania 20.08.87, West Suffolk
TJ- 11.55 (12.61w/12.23-07)
SQUIBB Morgan U15 23.06.03, Blackheath & Bromley
800- 2:12.14, 1500- 4:34.67mx/4:35.67, 3k- 10:05.77mx
SQUIRES Nicola 8.07.85, Hallamshire
Mar- 2:50:45
STACEY Caitlin U20 6.12.99, Reading
DT- 38.18
STAINTON Katie U23 8.01.95, Birchfield/Loughborough St
200- 24.16w/24.18 (24.07-16), 400H- 65.05
100H- 13.92w/13.94, HJ- 1.75 (1.76i-15, 1.75-16),
LJ- 6.12w/6.10 (6.23w/6.18-16), SP- 11.90, JT- 43.18,
Hep- 5873, PentIS- 4147i
STAMP Charlotte U20 20.11.98, City of York
400H- 63.9/65.03
STANLEY Abigail 4.10.94, City of Sheffield/MMU
400- 56.51imx/56.52
STANSBURY Rosalind V40 27.12.74, Crawley
HT- 42.26 (43.96-16)
STARKEY Feia U17 19.11.01, Ealing, S & Mx
300H- 46.04
STEEL Gemma 12.11.85, Charnwood
5kR- 16:02 (15:47.21t-11), 10k- 33:13.33 (32:34.81-12),
10kR- 33:28 (31:27-14), 15kR- 50:46+ (48:15+-14),
10MR- 55:25 (52:00+e-14), HMar- 71:32 (68:13-14)
STEELE Olivia U17 22.07.02, Hertford & Ware
JTI- 40.74
STEER Alice U17 9.03.01, Crawley
HTI- 49.55
STENNETT Lucy U17 22.07.02, Taunton
300- 40.79, 400- 58.19
STEPHENS Tasia U23 8.12.96, Cardiff
JT- 38.70 (43.10-14)
STEPHENSON Clieo U23 8.04.95, TVH/Brunel Un
60- 7.54imx/7.55i (7.53i-16), 100- 11.70, 200- 24.60
STEPHENSON Lia U23 4.03.96, TVH/Southampton Un
LJ- 5.64 (5.80w-14), TJ- 12.33w/12.30 (12.71-14)
STEPTO Emma Louise V45 4.04.70, Cornwall AC
3k- 9:47.8mx (9:32.8-12), 10k- 35:46.5 (34:39.9-14),
5k- 17:01.41mx (16:13.0mx/16:42.16-13),
HMar- 77:42 (72:29-14)
STEVENS Paige U13 3.02.05, Falkirk VH
PenM- 2519, PenIM- 2277i

STEVENSON Olivia U20 9.10.99, Kingston u Hull
HT- 57.96
STEWART Abigail U15 15.10.02, Cambridge H
SPI- 11.27
STEWART Elizabeth U17 17.04.02, Skyrac
1.5kSt- 5:12.16
STEWART Kelsey U23 12.02.97, Aberdeen/Aberdeen Un
200- 24.33, 400- 53.63, 600- 1:27.5mx, 800- 2:07.21
STILL Alix U20 15.03.00, Aberdeen
100H- 14.81w/14.84, HJ- 1.67, LJ- 5.67, Hep- 4928,
PentIS- 3547i
STILLMAN Olivia U17 13.12.00, Herne Hill
3k- 10:01.30
STILWELL Kirsten U15 10.07.03, Wycombe
800- 2:16.3, 1500- 4:31.85
STOCKTON Stevie 23.08.89, Leeds City
10kR- 34:27 (33:12-15)
STODDART Lauren 26.06.91, Edinburgh AC
1.5kSt- 4:58.21, 2kSt- 6:50.32, 3kSt- 10:41.79
STONE Ellie U17 10.02.01, Inverness
80HI- 11.86w
STONE Phillipa U20 1.04.98, M'boro Mandale/Durham Un
1500- 4:26.39
STONEHOUSE Tia U15 21.11.02, Dacorum & Tring
JTI- 41.30, PenG- 2816
STORM Naomi U17 6.03.01, Worthing
PV- 2.95
STRATTON-THOMAS Megan U20 2.07.00, Swansea
5kW- 27:38.3 (27:29.35-16)
STRAW Rebecca U23 26.04.95, Birchfield/Birmingham Un
5k- 16:51.00 (16:03.25-15), 5kR- 16:25
STRICKLAND Emily U20 27.12.99, Scunthorpe
400- 56.67, 400H- 65.05
STRICKLER Amelia Jane 24.01.94, TVH/Miami Un
SP- 17.13, DT- 44.49, HT- 49.38
STRINGER Katie U13 25.06.05, Medway & Maidstone
2kW- 11:08.6
STUCHBURY Charlotte U17 18.10.00, Liverpool H
HT- 41.58 (42.00-16), HTI- 46.75 (48.95-16)
STUDHOLME Beau U17 15.09.01, Carlisle Aspatria
HJ- 1.71
STYLES Zoya U20 26.12.99, Ealing, S & Mx
HT- 43.05
SUHONEN Emma 28.01.91, Charnwood/Lough St/FIN
60- 7.60imx/7.65i, 100- 11.86w/11.99
SULLIVAN Grace U15 3.07.03, Grimsby
800- 2:17.3, 1500- 4:40.88, 3k- 10:14.76
SULLIVAN Grace U20 4.08.99, Ashford
TJ- 11.83
SUNDERLAND Georgina U23 5.04.97, Radley/Cardiff Met
60H- 8.92i, 100H- 14.69
SUTHERLAND Kelsey U15 19.12.02, Worthing
HJ- 1.60, TJ- 10.57
SUTTON Eliza U15 16.12.03, Guildford & Godalming
JTI- 35.16
SUTTON Kathryn 23.12.88, Dartford
400- 55.9/56.28 (55.50-16)
SWANNACK Jessica U20 26.09.98, Preston
PV- 4.00
SWANSON Sian 1.03.93, Swansea/Cardiff Met
TJ- 12.08w/11.98
SWEETMAN Molly U17 11.03.02, Havering
1500- 4:38.96

TABE Mayong U17 23.11.01, Medway & Maidstone
LJ- 5.76
TAGOE Annie 4.06.93, Thames Valley
60- 7.48i (7.41i-11)
TAIT Anna U23 5.12.96, VP-Glasgow/Glasgow Caled. Un
1500- 4:21.16, 3k- 9:31.76mx/9:36.84, 5k- 16:43.83
TAIT Sarah U17 26.03.01, Lasswade
1.5kSt- 5:09.53
TAIWO Sola U15 22.12.02, Thurrock
PenG- 2850
TAIWO Taiwo U17 23.09.01, Bolton
60- 7.86i, 200- 25.37
TAKWOINGI Mary U17 13.09.01, Solihull & S H
300- 40.48, 400- 58.2

TALBUT-SMITH Holly U23 19.12.96, Crawley/
Carson-Talbut Un   400H- 65.11 (65.04-14)
TAN Phoebe U20 18.10.98, City of Lisburn
HJ- 1.65 (1.72-15)
TANK Poppy U23 5.12.97, City of Plymouth/Utah Un
3k- 9:39.88i (9:42.82mx-16), 5k- 16:37.48
TAPERELL Ava U15 21.12.03, Gateshead
800- 2:13.1
TAPLEY Hannah U20 1.10.98, Worcester AC
HJ- 1.72 (1.75i-15, 1.74-14)
TAPPER Rayne U13 7.04.06, Harrow
60- 8.15i, 75- 10.0
TAPPIN Jessica 17.05.90, Thames Valley
400- 54.89, 60H- 8.72i (8.60i-12), PentIS- 4039i,
100H- 14.19 (13.47-14), 400H- 58.34 (58.13-15),
HJ- 1.71i/1.67 (1.75-12), SP- 11.58i/11.50 (12.34-12),
JT- 36.78 (39.12-16), Hep- 5301 (5770-14)
TARBIT Freya U20 24.08.00, Derby AC
LJ- 5.72
TARPLEE Claire 22.09.88, Solihull & S H/IRL
800- 2:07.47 (2:03.29-16), 1500- 4:16.23 (4:10.65-16)
TARVER Hannah 22.10.93, Wirral
800- 2:09.11 (2:01.82-14)
TASCHIMOWITZ Naomi 19.10.89, Shaftesbury B
1500- 4:16.32, 3k- 9:13.70 (9:12.66-11), 5k- 16:08.89
TAYLOR Amy Katherine U20 28.01.99, Tonbridge
400H- 64.41 (63.74-15)
TAYLOR Charlotte 17.01.94, Nene V/San Francisco Un
1500- 4:21.96, 3k- 9:20.72+, 5k- 15:29.07, 10k- 32:11.80
TAYLOR Elizabeth U15 18.05.04, Peterborough
200- 25.93, 300- 40.89
TAYLOR Libby U17 16.08.02, Stevenage & NH
HTI- 46.10
TAYLOR Martha U17 1.03.02, Wimborne
JTI- 38.86
TAYLOR Mya U17 23.02.01, Rotherham
1500- 4:39.12mx, 3k- 9:52.05
TAYLOR Nicole U23 18.01.95, Tonbridge/Brighton Un
3k- 9:26.71, 5k- 16:25.21, 10k- 34:46.25
TAYLOR Robyn U17 21.01.01, VP-Glasgow
100- 12.28w
TAYLOR Stacie U23 12.10.95, Kilmarnock/Un of Tulsa
3k- 9:47.20i (9:36.09mx-16), 3kSt- 10:16.07 (10:13.23-16),
5k- 16:47.89i/16:51.93mx/17:02.30
TAYLOR Trezeguet U13 17.04.05, Trafford
60- 8.19i, 75- 9.70, 100- 12.21, 150- 19.12, 200- 26.5
TAYLOR-GREEN Charlotte 2.04.85, Bristol & West
800- 2:07.13 (2:06.96-16), 1500- 4:17.62, 1M- 4:48.10,
3k- 9:29.01imx, 5MR- 27:44, 2kSt- 6:34.12,
3kSt- 9:58.85
TAYLOR-JEMMETT Jessica R. 27.06.88, Sale
200- 23.63, 60H- 8.57i (8.47i-16), HJ- 1.65i (1.75-14),
100H- 13.98 (13.81-14), LJ- 6.13 (6.18w-16, 6.16-14),
SP- 13.34, JT- 37.46 (38.31-16), Hep- 5767 (5913-16),
PentIS- 4155i (4249i-15)
TEAL Amy U20 8.03.98, Southampton
100- 12.19A (12.1w-15)
TEALE Sarris U15 3.05.04, Ashford
TJ- 10.46
TEHOUDJA Teddy Shalom U15 27.03.03, Shettleston H
SPI- 11.29
TENN-MILLS Lauren U17 16.02.01, Falkirk VH
LJ- 5.50
TESTAR Annie U17 18.04.02, Stroud
300- 40.7, 400- 56.9, 800- 2:10.05
THACKERY Calli 9.01.93, Hallamshire/New Mexico Un
1500- 4:14.08, 5k- 15:37.90 (15:37.44-16),
3k- 9:09.77i/9:26.40+ (9:03.59i/9:13.10+-16)
10kR- 34:00, 10MR- 57:58
THATCHER-GRAY Adelaide U15 18.09.02, Havering
JTI- 34.97
THOMAS Catrina U23 18.02.97, Trafford/Birmingham Un
1500- 4:25.0
THOMAS Cerys Louise U17 7.04.01, City of Portsmouth
HT- 41.81, HTI- 50.58
THOMAS Charlene V35 6.05.82, Wakefield
800- 2:03.12 (2:01.87-09)), 1M- 4:42.84 (4:27.95-07),
1500- 4:09.32 (4:03.74mp-13, 4:05.06-09

THOMAS Emily Sara U17 21.11.00, Cardiff Archers
LJ- 5.64, TJ- 11.46w/11.05
THOMAS Erin U17 12.09.01, Bexley
PV- 3.20i/3.11 (3.25-16)
THOMAS Hannah 13.02.93, Cardiff/Cardiff Un
200- 24.2/24.41mx/24.47 (23.87w/24.02-13)
THOMAS Holly Louise 10.08.94, Newham & Essex B
60H- 8.97i (8.92i-12), 100H- 14.07 (13.90-15)
THOMAS Jahisha 22.11.94, Bl'heath & Brom/Iowa St Un
200- 24.98, 60H- 8.28i, 100H- 13.46w/13.83 (13.67-16),
LJ- 6.39i/6.35w/6.32, TJ- 13.25
THOMAS Sophie Emma 18.04.89, Birchfield
JT- 39.28 (46.98-11)
THOMPSON Abigail U17 7.12.00, Border
DT- 36.42
THOMPSON Emily U20 19.03.00, Banbury
800- 2:06.71
THOMPSON Grace U17 30.11.01, VP-Glasgow
DT- 34.66
THOMPSON Jessica U13 30.11.04, Harrogate
JTM- 33.44
THOMPSON Kara U15 30.06.03, Shettleston H
DT- 30.63
THOMPSON Lauren 12.02.92, Herts Phoenix
400- 56.2, 100H- 14.5/14.63 (13.52w/13.75-15),
400H- 58.62, LJ- 5.70 (5.91-15)
THOMPSON Mae U23 28.05.96, Kingston & Poly
800- 2:07.48
THOMPSON Torema 15.02.90, Enfield & Haringey
100- 11.79 (11.54w/11.58-11)
THOMPSON Zoe U20 10.04.00, Newham & Essex B
100- 12.19w, 200- 24.88i/24.96w
THORNER Elise U17 16.03.01, Yeovil Olympiads
800- 2:11.24, 1500- 4:39.68, 1.5kSt- 4:59.80,
300H- 45.3, HJ- 1.68, HepI- 4608
THRALL Ellen U20 8.05.98, Gloucester AC/Bath Un
HT- 46.74
THROWER Gemma U23 20.01.96, City of Norwich
JT- 44.15
THROWER Jordan U17 12.09.01, New Marske
TJ- 11.13
THURBON-SMITH Lily U13 1.10.05, New Forest Jun
100- 12.7
THURGOOD Amy U17 18.11.00, Dacorum & Tring
HJ- 1.65i/1.65 (1.65-16)
THURGOOD Hollie U17 2.07.02, City of Portsmouth
60HI- 9.03i, 80HI- 11.64w/11.7/11.77, SPI- 12.43,
HepI- 4658
TIGHE Chloe 28.09.90, Herne Hill/AUS
1500- 4:18.32, 1M- 4:38.85mx/4:42.23,
3k- 9:29.05 (9:27.63-08)
TIMMINS Heather 12.02.90, Thames Valley
HMar- 78:36
TIPPING Evie U15 13.06.03, West Cheshire
HTI- 49.89
TOASLAND India U13 1.12.04, Croydon
60- 8.08i
TODD-MCINTYRE Maya U15 21.10.02, Rushcliffe
800- 2:14.29mx/2:15.23, 1500- 4:39.14mx/4:41.7
TOFT Naomi U15 13.03.04, Blackheath & Bromley
800- 2:15.48, 1500- 4:35.6
TOMCZAK Julia U20 28.02.00, South London H
1500- 4:26.82mx, 3k- 9:32.49
TOMLINSON Cleo U15 17.06.04, Horsham BS
LJ- 5.30
TRACEY Adelle Roshumba 27.05.93, Guildford & G
800- 2:00.26 (2:00.04mx-16), 1500- 4:10.30
TRAPNELL Jasmine U17 15.02.02, Marshall Milton K
HTI- 46.81
TREVIS Bevhan U20 9.01.99, Central/Edinburgh Un
DT- 38.08
TRIMBLE Laura 7.07.82, Wimbledon Windmilers
Mar- 2:53:35
TUCK Megan 26.04.92, Southampton
DT- 35.82 (40.58-13), HT- 42.56 (43.14-16)
TUINEMA Demi U15 2.01.03, Dacorum & Tring
200- 25.87, LJ- 5.26w, PenG- 3007
TUNSTALL Lauren U15 9.09.02, Preston
JTI- 35.19

TUNSTALL Taia U17 9.01.02, Watford
DT- 38.63
TURNER Anya U20 8.11.98, Exeter
100H- 14.48, Hep- 4668
TURNER Beatrix 12.01.88, Harrow/ESP
JT- 41.23
TURNER Ella U17 2.06.01, Oxford City
200- 25.1/25.33 (25.13w-16), 300- 39.76, 400- 57.2
TURNER Ellie U20 26.05.00, Medway & Maidstone
60- 7.69i, 100- 12.17, 200- 24.32
TURNER Holly U23 15.11.95, Crawley/Brighton Un
100- 12.16w, 400- 54.91i/54.92
TURNER Jessica Ann U23 8.08.95, Amber Vall/Lough St
200- 23.41w/24.15, 400H- 56.08
TURNER Lucy U23 14.02.97, Gateshead/North'land Un
60H- 8.84i, 100H- 13.92, HJ- 1.67, LJ- 5.94,
SP- 11.41i/11.17, Hep- 5436, PentIS- 3712i
TURNER Lydia U23 19.11.96, Birtley
5kR- 16:58
TURNER Madelaine U17 11.11.01, Winchester
300H- 45.89, 400H- 67.77
TUSTIN Issie U17 27.11.01, Cardiff
60- 7.79i, 100- 12.35w/12.40mx
TUTTON Gemma U13 8.11.04, Lewes
HJ- 1.51, PV- 3.46
TWELL Stephanie 17.08.89, Aldershot F&D
1500- 4:06.92+ (4:02.54-10), 1M- 4:25.39,
3k- 8:45.95i/9:00.04mx/9:01.04 (8:40.98-16),
5k- 15:16.65 (14:54.08-10), 10k- 32:16.23
TYRRELL Emily U17 4.01.02, North Devon
80HI- 11.94, LJ- 5.67, Hepl- 4313

UGEN Lorraine 22.08.91, Thames Valley
100- 11.31w/11.41, 200- 23.99 (23.71w/23.81-15),
LJ- 6.97i/6.78 (6.96w/6.92-15)
UMAH Shania U17 17.02.02, Highgate H
60- 7.83i, 100- 12.29, 200- 25.22i
UNDERDOWN Lucy 18.05.90, Shaftesbury B
SP- 13.00 (13.46-15), DT- 40.87 (49.30-14)
UWAKWE Yasmin U15 14.04.03, Enfield & Haringey
60HI- 8.97i, 75HG- 11.27w/11.32
UZOKWE Lisa-Marie U15 3.03.03, Stevenage & NH
300- 41.4/41.73

VALKENBURG Kiara U15 21.03.04, Epsom & Ewell
1500- 4:43.90
VANS AGNEW Grace U17 30.12.00, Crawley
300H- 44.92
VAREILLE Olivia Marie U17 11.12.00, Falkirk VH
300- 40.62, 400- 56.45, 800- 2:09.51
VAUGHAN Harriet U17 28.09.01, Bury
PV- 3.42i/3.40
VENABLES Melissa V40 14.02.75, Spa Striders
100kR- 8:25:52 (8:15:54-16)
VERNON Eleanor U17 19.01.01, Telford
JTI- 46.51
VERNON-HAMILTON Chloe 11.10.92, Stevenage & NH/
Brunel Un 100H- 14.7/14.71, SP- 12.45i/12.32 (12.64-16),
Hep- 4791 (5121-15), PentIS- 3653i
VICKERY Gemma U23 4.04.96, City of Norwich
HT- 51.05
VINCENT Serena Alexandr U17 5.12.01, C of Portsmouth
SPI- 15.65, JTI- 41.30
VINER Hannah U23 18.07.96, Highgate H
1500- 4:24.57, 3k- 9:34.65mx, 5k- 16:37.5mx/16:45.36,
10kR- 34:51
VOSS Laura 29.01.94, Northumbria Un/GER
100H- 14.88, HJ- 1.75i/1.74 (1.85i-12, 1.83-11),
LJ- 6.02w/5.98, Hep- 5271, PentIS- 3779i
VYVYAN Charlotte U17 22.10.00, Reading
PV- 2.90 (3.01-16)

WADDELL Keira U17 3.10.01, Edinburgh AC
JT- 36.63, JTI- 42.93
WADE Saskia U13 30.05.05, Whitemoss
HJ- 1.53, PenM- 2553
WAITE Eleanor Marguerite 4.02.86, East Kilbride
800- 2:09.83 (2:08.58-09), 1500- 4:16.17 (4:15.33-15),
5k- 16:12.54, 2kSt- 6:21.31, 3kSt- 9:37.94 (9:35.91-16)

WAKE Laura 3.05.91, WSE&H
200- 24.9 (23.98-13), 400- 54.55 (52.98-14),
400H- 58.79 (57.17-14)
WAKEFIELD Bethan 17.10.94, Bristol & West
100- 11.97w/12.17 (11.84w/11.97-11)
WAKEFIELD Isabel U20 5.01.00, North Devon
60H- 8.81i, 100HI- 13.79, LJ- 5.61 (5.80-16), JT- 37.13
WALAS Klaudia U17 17.06.02, WSE&H
TJ- 11.01
WALCOTT-NOLAN Revee U23 6.03.95, Luton
600- 1:27.9mx, 800- 2:03.20 (2:02.32-16), 1k- 2:42.73i,
1500- 4:15.02i/4:20.26 (4:17.05-16), 1M- 4:36.30mx,
WALDER Caroline U17 3.01.01, North Somerset
PV- 3.41
WALDRON Shannon U17 8.09.01, VP-Glasgow
HT- 44.98, HTI- 52.90
WALKER Chelsea U23 29.06.97, City of York
100- 12.1 (12.19-16), 100H- 13.78w/13.79,
400H- 58.91 (58.68-16)
WALKER Diani Akina U23 14.07.95, Birchfield/Middx Un
60- 7.41i, 100- 11.44w/11.45, 200- 23.97
WALKER Eloise U17 27.05.01, Edinburgh AC
1500- 4:35.30, 3k- 9:54.05imx (10:13.90-16)
WALKER Hannah 9.08.91, Run Fast
10kR- 33:50 (32:56.90t-14), HMar- 74:25 (71:50-12)
WALKER Jasmine U15 30.09.02, R Sutton Coldfield
JTI- 38.09
WALKER Lauryn U17 4.05.02, Birchfield
60- 7.89i (7.89i-15)
WALKER Olivia U23 6.07.95, Cannock & Staff/Durham Un
60H- 8.84i (8.45i-14), 100H- 14.38 (14.02-13)
WALKER Regan U20 6.02.00, Sale
100- 12.19w
WALKER Victoria 22.10.92, Shaftesbury B
2kSt- 7:16.28 (7:02.50-12)
WALL Allessandra U23 11.02.95, Cardiff/Lough St/SWE
HT- 57.47 (59.74-14)
WALLACE Erin Heather U20 18.05.00, Giffnock North
800- 2:06.84i/2:08.30 (2:06.59i-16, 2:07.74-15),
1500- 4:16.61, 3k- 9:33.02i/9:34.66
WALLACE Laura V35 26.11.79, Ayr Seaforth
Mar- 2:56:58
WALLADER Rachel 1.09.89, WSE&H
SP- 17.47 (17.53/18.00dh-16)
WALLIKER Lucy U20 21.01.99, Exeter
HJ- 1.70
WALLIS Charlotte U13 3.11.04, Aldershot F&D
2kW- 12:05.7
WALLIS Emma U17 15.01.02, Cambridge & Coleridge
JT- 36.87
WALSH Molly U20 23.06.00, Wolves & Bilston
HT- 54.49, HTI- 63.52
WALSH Sorrell 19.04.90, VPH &TH
Mar- 2:56:45
WALTON Rebekah U20 20.09.99, Blackheath & Bromley
JT- 46.59
WANSELL Ella U17 15.01.01, Enfield & Haringey
60- 7.84i, 100- 11.94w/12.22, 200- 24.42
WARD Abby U20 19.04.99, Wakefield
HJ- 1.78i/1.70 (1.89i/1.86-16)
WARD Abigail U15 27.10.02, Rugby & Northampton
JTI- 41.01
WARDEN Lois U17 26.03.02, Bexley
PV- 3.50/3.40 (3.50i-16)
WARDLEY Anousha U20 22.10.99, Reigate
PV- 3.10
WARE Joanne U23 11.08.97, Tonbridge/Loughborough St
LJ- 5.81w/5.64i/5.61
WARNER Julie V50 8.04.67, Shelton
Mar- 2:55:38
WARNOCK Sarah 5.06.91, Edinburgh AC
LJ- 6.16 (6.42-14)
WASSELL Zoe-Ann U20 4.07.99, Stroud
3k- 9:38.78
WASTELL Eleanor U17 16.02.01, Medway & Maidstone
300H- 45.06
WATERS Matilda U17 20.12.00, Sale
PV- 3.35i/3.10 (3.20-16)

WATERWORTH Katie U17 17.05.01, Stockport
LJ- 5.62i/5.55, TJ- 11.26 (11.30-16)
WATKINS Rebecca U17 23.08.01, Bracknell
200- 25.37
WATSON Dalila U15 16.12.02, Charnwood
PV- 2.63i
WATSON Kayleigh U15 27.04.04, Seaton
100- 12.5
WAUGH Emily 6.08.93, Rugby & Northampton
5k- 16:56.6mx, HMar- 76:41, Mar- 2:57:08
WAUGH Helen V40 3.12.76, Tyne TC
Mar- 2:54:43 (2:54:02-09)
WEATHERITT Leah J. V40 18.09.74, Gateshead
HT- 43.84 (46.72-09)
WEBB Katie U15 1.12.03, Dacorum & Tring
DT- 29.57
WEBBER Megan U17 31.05.01, Torbay
100- 12.20, 200- 25.26w, 300- 40.73
WEBBER Wendy V35 18.09.78, Marshall Milton K
Mar- 2:54:02
WEBSTER Louise 19.07.85, Wolves & Bilston
HT- 42.69 (49.62-14)
WEBSTER Sarah V35 25.04.79, Northern (IOM)
Mar- 2:48:30
WEBSTER-TAPE Charmont U20 29.11.99, Sutton & Dist
60- 7.61i, 100- 11.92w/11.98 (11.84-15)
WEDDERBURN Izzy U17 3.01.01, Bournemouth
LJ- 5.67 (5.67-16)
WEDDERBURN-GOODISON Nia U13 9.01.05, WG & EL
60- 7.88i/8.05imx/8.11i, 75- 9.8, 100- 12.54w/12.69,
150- 19.5, 200- 26.56w
WEEDALL Holly U13 31.12.04, Vale Royal
1200- 3:50.21, 1500- 4:51.9
WEIGHTMAN Laura 1.07.91, Morpeth
800- 2:01.87, 1500- 4:00.71 (4:00.17-14), 1M- 4:20.88,
3k- 9:09.75+ (8:43.46mx-13, 9:02.62-12), 5k- 15:08.24,
10kR- 32:31
WEIR Victoria U20 17.03.98, C of Plymouth/B'ham Un
2kSt- 6:40.45
WELLINGTON Christine-Ann V40 18.02.77, BRAT
Mar- 2:49:09 (2:48:54-10)
WEST Ashleigh U17 27.06.01, Medway & Maidstone
80HI- 11.9, HJ- 1.76i/1.71 (1.71-16), Hepl- 4161
WEST Charlotte U17 16.10.00, Reading
JTI- 41.45
WEST Georgia U17 6.10.00, Watford
PV- 3.10
WESTWOOD Yvette U20 3.09.98, Yate
60- 7.65i, 100- 11.70w/11.96, 200- 24.36w/24.60i/24.68
WETTON Jennifer 28.11.86, Central
Mar- 2:47:57 (2:47:06/2:46:10dh-14)
WEYMONT Devon U17 20.04.02, Sale
LJ- 5.53 (5.56-16)
WHAPPLES Madeleine U15 12.04.03, Solihull & S H
200- 25.38, 300- 40.58
WHEATMAN Jenna 6.03.84, Scarborough
HT- 50.67 (53.39-11)
WHEELER Libby U17 21.01.01, Kingston upon Hull
LJ- 5.60, TJ- 11.68
WHEELER-SMITH Ellie U15 16.01.03, Gloucester AC
100- 12.5
WHILEY Alice 1.07.91, Clapham Chasers
Mar- 2:56:59
WHITBREAD Jessica Mane U17 12.08.01, Thurrock
LJ- 5.54
WHITE Abbie U17 20.06.02, Wimborne
HTI- 47.32
WHITE Ava U15 20.05.03, Blackheath & Bromley
800- 2:15.53mx/2:15.74, 1500- 4:36.90
WHITE Ellie U20 10.07.99, Wimborne
HT- 45.70 (47.28-16)
WHITE Isabel U13 13.09.04, Longwood
150- 19.58
WHITE Katie V35 6.01.81, Sale
10MR- 58:20, HMar- 76:54 (75:41sh-16), Mar- 2:42:49
WHITE Lucinda U13 4.02.05, Tonbridge
DTM- 30.07, JTM- 38.18

WHITE Molly U13 7.01.05, Dorchester
70HM- 11.3
WHITFIELD Georgia U23 21.07.95, Gateshead/Newc Un
100H- 14.9
WHITTINGHAM Laura 6.06.86, Sale/Loughborough St
JT- 55.74 (60.68-10)
WHITTLE Laura Hannah 27.06.85, R Sutton Coldfield
5kR- 16:45 (15:08.58t-16)
WHITTON Michaela U20 11.08.98, Reading
DT- 42.35 (43.72-16)
WHORISKEY Catherine 15.02.86, Derry
10MR- 58:00, HMar- 76:52, Mar- 2:48:41
WICKS Skye U17 20.08.02, Hertford & Ware
60- 7.85i, 100- 12.11w/12.2/12.40, 200- 24.58,
300- 39.76
WIDDOP-GRAY Ella U23 26.09.96, TVH/Manchester Un
HJ- 1.66 (1.72i-13, 1.72-15)
WIGGAN Brittney Anne U20 5.05.00, Harrow
100H- 15.2
WILDE Chloe U20 24.05.99, Cannock & Stafford
400H- 63.91
WILDER Allison 30.10.88, Sutton & District
TJ- 12.55w/12.50 (13.22 USA-11)
WILKINS Melanie Jane 15.07.90, Winchester
2kSt- 6:54.31, 3kSt- 10:37.50
WILKINSON Claire 10.02.89, Ballymena & A/IRL
PV- 3.40i (3.95i-14, 3.90-12)
WILLIAMS Abigail U17 11.10.00, Cheltenham
80HI- 11.85w
WILLIAMS Annie U20 28.09.98, Sale
PV- 3.10i (3.31-16)
WILLIAMS Armani U17 29.03.01, Newport
300- 40.44
WILLIAMS Bella Faye U20 5.10.98, Lincoln Wellington
3k- 9:44.19
WILLIAMS Bethany U20 7.06.99, Mansfield H
800- 2:10.13
WILLIAMS Bianca 18.12.93, Enfield & Haringey
100- 11.18w/11.30 (11.17-14), 150- 17.00st/17.06,
200- 22.83 (22.58-14), 400- 54.34
WILLIAMS Chante U17 21.03.02, Bracknell
60HI- 8.96i, 80HI- 11.73
WILLIAMS Charlotte U17 20.09.01, Blackburn
HT- 52.23, HTI- 60.53
WILLIAMS Chloe 10.09.87, Havering
100H- 14.65 (14.44w/14.5-04, 14.61-15)
WILLIAMS Emily U17 25.02.02, Kettering
800- 2:06.83, 1500- 4:20.29mx/4:21.54
WILLIAMS Francesca U15 7.02.03, WSE&H
HTI- 49.97
WILLIAMS Hannah U20 23.04.98, Herts Phoenix
60- 7.60, 400- 52.55
WILLIAMS Hannah 17.01.89, Bristol & West
60- 7.74i (7.74i-15), 100- 11.74, 200- 25.00 (24.85-15)
WILLIAMS Jade U17 22.04.01, Wrexham/IRL
HT- 49.05, HTI- 61.09
WILLIAMS Jade 7.09.92, Amman V
2kSt- 6:38.76, 3kSt- 10:25.03
WILLIAMS Jessica U20 6.07.00, WSE&H
DT- 35.78
WILLIAMS Jodie 28.09.93, Herts Phoenix
60- 7.58i (7.21i-11), 100- 11.64 (11.13w-14, 11.18-11),
200- 23.27 (22.46-14)
WILLIAMS Lauren U20 12.02.99, Swansea
400- 55.86, 400H- 59.88
WILLIAMS Paula V45 18.03.72, Stratford-upon-Avon
JT- 36.77
WILLIAMS-HEWITT Acacia U15 8.08.03, Hallamshire
60- 7.91i, 100- 12.51, 200- 25.02, 300- 41.18i/41.40
WILLIAMSON Hollie U20 4.12.98, Birchfield
60H- 8.72i, 100H- 14.47 (14.43-16), HJ- 1.66 (1.68-13)
WILLIS Deborah Sarah 24.04.92, Notts
400- 56.68 (55.15-15), 400H- 63.01 (61.6/61.97-15)
WILLIS Kate U15 4.09.02, City of Norwich
800- 2:16.50
WILLMORE Olivia U17 21.03.02, Dorchester
300H- 45.9/46.00, 400H- 65.85, JTI- 39.04, Hepl- 4113

WILLS Amelia U17 4.04.02, Bracknell
1.5kSt- 5:08.01
WILSON Natasha U23 5.11.95, Sale/Hallam Un
JT- 47.68 (48.35-16)
WILSON Tia U17 1.06.02, Bedford & County
3k- 10:05.53
WILTON Madeline U17 11.04.02, City of Portsmouth
200- 25.2, 300H- 46.0, LJ- 5.49, TJ- 11.10i/11.00
WILTSHIRE Victoria U20 1.10.99, Blackheath & Bromley
HT- 49.36
WINGATE Phillipa 12.05.93, Kingston & Poly
SP- 12.54 (12.71-15), DT- 40.66 (44.53-14), HT- 59.76
WINGFIELD Charlotte 30.11.94, Cardiff/Cardiff Met/MLT
60- 7.44i, 100- 11.54, 200- 23.78
WINOGRODZKA Julia U13 21.10.04, Bolton
60HM- 9.62i, 70HM- 11.1/11.33, 75HG- 11.4,
LJ- 5.34i/5.25, PenM- 2718, PenIM- 2810i
WINSHIP Meredith U17 9.12.01, City of Norwich
800- 2:14.03mx/2:14.43
WINSON Jenna 7.11.90, Derby AC
HT- 49.89 (52.95-10)
WINSTON Monae U15 31.10.02, Herne Hill
60- 7.82i, 100- 12.22, 200- 25.32w/25.86
WINTER Marcey U17 17.04.01, Guildford & Godalming
80HI- 11.9 (11.7/11.79-16), 300H- 45.06
WOLFENDEN Lucie U17 14.09.01, Sale
PV- 3.00
WOOD Beatrice U15 9.10.03, Salisbury
1500- 4:32.41
WOOD Jemma U20 3.03.99, Guildford & Godalming
200- 24.73 (24.64-16)
WOOD Madeleine U15 3.09.02, Charnwood
HJ- 1.67
WOOD Sophie 7.05.92, Durham City H
400- 56.69
WOOD Tilia U15 16.04.03, City of Sheffield
800- 2:17.2
WOODCOCK Kathryn U23 29.04.97, Radley/Lough St
DT- 50.64, HT- 42.65 (44.64-16)
WOODHAMS Rosie U17 24.04.02, Dallam RC
3k- 9:47.95
WOODHEAD Bethany U17 1.07.01, Sale
HJ- 1.65i/1.63
WOODNICK Amelia U17 18.02.02, Dacorum & Tring
80HI- 11.97
WOODWARD Kaili U17 30.01.02, Solihull & S H
HJ- 1.66
WOODWARD Lucy U15 28.11.02, Channel Islands
LJ- 5.33w, PenG- 2891
WOOLVEN Pippa 26.07.93, Wycombe/Birmingham Un
5k- 15:49.16i (16:15.69-16)
WOOTTON Katrina 2.09.85, Coventry Godiva
3k- 9:17.94mx (8:50.69i-08, 8:59.68mx/9:03.87-07),
5k- 15:27.64mx/15:49.48 (15:30.82-13), 15kR- 52:21+,
10k- 31:45.63mx/32:27.47, 10kR- 32:47 (31:47-16),
10MR- 57:20 (57:16-09), HMar- 74:18 (73:25-16)
WORRALL Sophie 30.01.94, Wolves & Bilston
TJ- 11.52

WORTHINGTON Daisy U15 5.05.03, Bury
800- 2:14.36mx/2:16.39, SextG- 3539, PenG- 3143+,
PenIG- 3061i
WOSIKA Caitlin U20 19.11.99, Team Bath
1.5kSt- 5:00.25
WRIGHT Alice 3.11.94, Worcester AC/New Mexico Un
5k- 15:46.85i/15:53.28 (15:45.87-15), 10k- 32:29.28
WRIGHT Amy U17 3.04.02, Dacorum & Tring
HTI- 47.89
WRIGHT Emily U20 13.07.98, Bristol & West
100- 11.91w (12.15-12), LJ- 6.16w/6.07 (6.21-15)
WRIGHT Eve U17 8.08.02, Braintree
60- 7.61i, 100- 12.1/12.22
WRIGHT Katie U15 26.05.03, Halesowen
DT- 31.78
WRIGHT Vicky V35 19.05.77, Hyde Village Striders
Mar- 2:54:04
WRISBERG Jenna U20 22.03.98, Giffnock North
60- 7.59imx (7.50i-16), 100- 11.66w/11.77 (11.76-16)
WYKES Isobel V35 24.04.78, Truro RC
24HrT- 203.414km (230.134km-14)
WYNESS Hazel V35 23.12.77, Metro Aberdeen
Mar- 2:56:40
WYPER Katy 17.04.93, Blackpool & Fylde
60- 7.63i (7.61i-16), 100- 11.61w/11.63,
200- 24.40 (24.2-15, 24.22-16)

YATES Charlie U15 30.12.03, Amber Valley
TJ- 10.35
YATES Emma V45 16.01.69, Knavesmire
Mar- 2:57:15
YATES Kirsty Elizabeth 14.05.93, Edinburgh AC
SP- 14.00 (16.42-14)
YEARBY Georgia U23 19.02.95, Leeds/Leeds Beck Un
200- 24.8/25.00, 400- 55.54 (55.40-15)
YORKE Sophie U20 7.07.98, Cheltenham
60- 7.55i, 100- 11.72w/11.9/11.96 (11.61w/11.74-16),
60H- 8.30i, 100H- 13.31w/13.47
YOUNG Alison V40 26.11.73, Clapham Chasers
24Hr- 217.875km
YOUNG Amy U15 11.02.03, WSE&H
1500- 4:44.7
YOUNG Kaliyah U15 20.07.03, Dartford
60- 7.99i, 100- 12.3/12.49, 60HI- 9.07i, 60HG- 9.14i,
75HG- 11.30w/11.3/11.61, PenG- 2954
YOUNGS Lonarra U15 2.09.02, Ipswich
100- 12.4/12.47
YULE Zoe U20 27.08.98, Livingston/Stirling Un
DT- 35.84, HT- 42.60 (42.71-16)

ZAKELYTE Auguste U15 24.02.03, Rugby & North
DT- 31.14
ZAKRZEWSKI Joasia V40 19.01.76, Durham City H
Mar- 2:45:19 (2:39:22-13), 100kR- 8:50:25 (7:31:33-15)
ZEMBASHI Eleni U23 8.04.96, Cardiff/Cardiff Un/CYP
DT- 41.26 (42.55-16)
ZIALOR Laura U20 4.08.98, M Milton K/Brunel Un
HJ- 1.66 (1.75i-16, 1.71-15), TJ- 12.40 (12.96-16)
ZMYSLONA Joanna V35, /POL
Mar- 2:55:48
ZUILL Layla U15 27.09.03, Fife
300- 41.8

John COLLINS (b 25 Nov 1937 Aylesbury) in June. He started athletics with the Vale of Aylesbury, but moved to Pontypool in Wales in 1961 and was a stalwart of Swansea Harriers from 1965. He was secretary of the Welsh Cross Country Association, a member of the AAA General Committee for several years and president of Welsh Athletics 2004-06. He won the Welsh 6 miles CC in 1963 and competed in the International CC in 1965.

Hamish M **DAVIDSON** (b. 25 May 1954 Nairn) on 13 May. He was a larger-than-life character who was Scottish shot champion in 1973, 1975 and 1978, the last with his pb of 17.48, and represented Scotland in seven internationals. He then turned professional, competing at Highland Games, and also competed in the World's Strongest Man competition.

Pamela DAVIES (b. 30 May 1934 Clapham) on 24 January. She was 3rd in the International Cross-country in 1968 (5th 1967, 9th 1969) and had an extraordinary record in the English National CC, winning each year 1965-68, 2nd in 1964 and 1969 and 3rd in 1963 after 6th in 1961-2, and was also twice Southern champion. Pbs: 880y 2:19.7 (1963), 1500m 4:43.6 (1968), 1M 5:02.3 (1963), 3000m 10:19.2 (1968), 2M 11:39.0 (1955).

Anthony G. **'Tony' ELGIE** (b. 17 Apr 1937) died on 2 November. He was club captain of Cardiff AAC when they won the British Athletics League each year 1972-4 and served in the RAF before teaching and coaching (including GB sprint relay teams). In the Welsh Championships he was 2nd at 800m in 1971 and 3rd in the 400m in 1972. Pb 800m 1:51.0 (1970).

Daniel **EVANS** (b. 18 Apr 1998) died in November. A member of Warrington AC, he won the CAU Under 15 boys cross-country and was 3rd in the English School Inters 1500m in 2013 for Cheshire. Pbs: 800m 1:55.32 and 1500m 3:58.18 (both 2014).

Graham Emmerson **EVERETT** (b. 20 Jan 1934) on 30 January. He was Scottish 1 mile champion eight times 1955-61 and 1963 and set native records of 4:07.5 in 1956, 4:06.6 in 1957 and 4:03.9 in 1960. After 3rd place in 1957 he was AAA 1 mile champion in 1958 and had two GB internationals as well as running for Scotland at the 1958 Commonwealth Games (heats 880y and 1M) and four times in the International CC with a best of 18th in 1961. Also Scottish CC champion 1960. Other pbs: 880y 1:51.4 (1960), 1500m 3:45.1 (1960), 1M 4:02.70 (1960), 3000m 8:04.0 (1961), 2M 8:38.2 Scottish record (1961), 3M 13:47.6 (1961).

Trevor FRECKNALL (b. Bathley, Nottinghamshire) on 1 November at the age of 72. He was news editor of Athletics Weekly from 1993 to 2000 and then a media officer for UK Athletics, after being sports editor of the Nottingham Evening Post. He was a hugely enthusiastic supporter of athletics, loved and respected throughout the sport. A full tribute to him by AW editor Jason Henderson is on the athleticsweekly.com website.

Bryan HAWKINS (Gt Britain & NI) (b. 16 Apr 1928 Clapton, London) on 22 December in Sussex. Coached by Harold Whitlock, he was fifth in the 10,000m walk at the 1954 European Champs. In the AAA Champs walks he was 2nd at 2 miles in 1953 and at 7 miles in 1953-54, and was 3rd in the RWA 10 miles in 1953 and 1956. CAU champion at 7 miles 1953, Southern champion 2 miles 1953-4 and 7 miles 1952-6. Walks pbs: 2M 14:05.8 (1953), 10000m 46:16.0 (1954), 7M 52:26.4/52:09R (1954), 10M 1:17:27 (1953. He competed successfully for many years as a veteran, setting a world M60 5000m walk record of 24:48 in 1988. Outside of athletics, he was a professional cartoonist and among other talents he was a stand-up comedian, joke writer (for Tommy Cooper among others) and drummer.

George **Derek IBBOTSON** (b. 17 Jun 1932 Huddersfield) on 23 February in Ossett, West Yorkshire. Running for Longwood Harriers (and for South London Harriers 1957-9), after RAF service he shot into world class in 1955, when he was 2nd to Chris Chataway in the AAA 3 miles. A year later he beat Chataway to win that title and later won the Olympic bronze at 5000m. A great favourite of the British public, 'Ibbo' reached the peak of his fame in 1957. In the midst of a hectic programme of some 70 races that year he set a European record for the mile with 3:58.4, then next month retained his AAA 3 miles title in a British record 13:20.8 and six days later, on 19 Jul 1957, took the world mile record with 3:57.2 at the White City; en route he set a British record for 1500m at 3:41.9. He never quite recaptured such form and was 10th in 1958 and 8th in 1962 at 3 miles in the Commonwealth Games. He ran on the England team that set a world record for 4 x 1 mile in 1958. Indoors he set seven UK records and won AAA titles at 2 miles in 1962 and 1965, when he ran a British indoor record time of 8:42.6. He was also 3rd in the National Cross-country in 1956, followed by 46th in the International CC. 18 UK internationals 1955-65. Other best times: 880y 1:52.2 (1958), 2000m 5:12.8 (1955), 3000m 8:00.0 (1959), 2 miles 8:41.2 (1957), 5000m 13:54.4 (1956), 6 miles 28:52.0 (1955). He was awarded the MBE in the 2008 New Year's Honours. His autobiography was entitled 'Four Minute Smiler'.
His first wife Madeline (née Wooller, b. 31 Dec 1935 Twickenham), who later married squash great Jonah Barrington, was 2nd in the WAAA 1 mile in 1962 and 1963 and won the national cross-country in 1963 and 1964.

Patrick Charles **JONES** (b. 23 Jan 1938) in October. A member of Ilford AC, he won the Welsh title in 1963-66 and the Inter-counties in 1963. Pbs: 200m 21.7, 300y 30.9, 440y 47.8 (all in 1965).

Murray LAMBDEN (b. 14 Oct 1956) on 17 April in Douglas, Isle of Man. He had four internationals for Britain in 1981-2 and was 8th at 30k walk for the Isle of Man at the 1982 Commonwealth Games. Competing for Boundary Harriers, in RWA Championships he was 2nd at 100k in 1981 and 3rd at 50k in 1982, He set a UK record of 2:19:42 for 30k walk in 1981 and his other walks pbs were 20k 1:32:08 (1981), 35k 2:49:37 (1982), 50k 4:20:51 (1982), 50M 7:42:33 (1974) and 100k 9:38:38 (1981). After retiring from race walking due to a back injury he became a distance runner with a marathon best of 2:43:06 at age 48 in 2005. He made a huge contribution to athletics on the Isle of Man.

Ann LEWIS (b. 29 Dec 1947) on 18 June in Camberley. A member of Aldershot, Farnham & District, whom she originally joined as a swimmer/triathlete, she did not take up race walking until into her 40s. She won the CAU 3000m walk in 2000 after 3rd 1998 & 1999 and had considerable success as a Masters competitor. Walks pbs: 3000m 15:52.71i/15:55.0 (1996), 5000m 29:57.98 (2005), 20k 1:56:14 (1996).

Germaine MASON (b. 30 Jan 1983 Kingston, Jamaica) was killed in a motorcycling accident in Kingston on 20 April. He set six Jamaican high jump records from 2002 to 2.34 in 2003 and was 2nd in 2000 and 3rd in 2002 at the World Juniors, Pan-American Games champion in 2003, 5th at the 2002 Commonwealth Games and 2003 World Championships and 4th equal at the 2004 World Indoors as well as being Jamaican champion in 2000, 2002-03 and 2005. He then switched to compete for Britain (his father was born in London) from 8 March 2006, and, after not qualifying for the finals of the 2006 Europeans and 2007 Worlds, matched his best of 2.34 when he took the Olympic silver medal in 2008. UK champion 2009.

Thomas William **'Tom' MISSON** (GBR) (b. 11 May 1930 Hendon, London) on 31 July in Havant, Hampshire. A pharmacist, who competed for Metropolitan Walking Club, he set a UK record for 50k walk with 4:20:31.8 when 4th in the 1958 European Championships in 1958 and was 5th in the 1960 Olympic Games. He had road pbs for 20k 1:35:16, 20M 2:37:30 and 50k 4:14:03, all in 1959. 3 UK internationals 1958-60. He was RWA champion at 20 miles in 1959 and 2nd to Don Thompson at 50k each year 1958-60.

Henry Alexander **'Alec' OLNEY** (b. 4 Jan 1922 Hampstead, London) on 25 April in Harrow, London. Joining Thames Valley Harriers in 1946 after wartime Army service, he achieved immediate cross-country success and was 6th in the 1947 International CC (later 7th in 1950 after 2nd in the National and 1951). On the track he had four internationals for Britain, including 1948 Olympic Games (heats) and 1950 Europeans 8th at 5000m. At 3 miles he was 2nd in the AAAs in 1947-8 and 1950 and 3rd in 1949, winning the CAU title in 1947-48 and 1950 and the Southern in 1948. Pbs: 1M 4:17.4 (1951), 2M 9:20.0u (1949), 3M 14:11.2 (1950), 5000m 14:41.0e (1950), 14:46.4 (1947).

Anthony Frederick **'Tony' PUMFREY** (b. 4 Mar 1932 Bangor) in Bangor on 17 March. Just after he had run (heat 1 mile) in the 1958 Empire Games he ran a Welsh 1 mile record of 4:04.4 when 6th in Dublin behind Herb Elliott's world record 3:54.5, and was Welsh mile champion in 1953, 1955, 1957 and 1959. He was ran for Wales four times in the International Cross-country Championships. He was a member of Coventry Godiva and later Birchfield H. Pb 2M 9:01.0 (1958).

James Arthur Noel **'Jim' RAILTON**(b. 25 Dec 1935 Liverpool) on 16 August in Wallingford, Oxfordshire. Described in his Times obituary as a "Hell-raising rowing coach", he had been a promising young sprinter before a hamstring injury ended his career. He ran 440y in 49.2 at the age of 16 in 1952, twice equalled the British junior record with 9.9 for 100y in 1954 and ran 6.7 for 60y indoors in Germany in 1955 with outdoor pbs of 100y 9.8, 100m 10.8, 220y 21.8 (all in 1959). He graduated with a degree in modern jazz from Loughborough, having won the UAU 220y for them in 1957, and became a PE teacher and a talented rowing coach. He became a perceptive rowing correspondent of the Times and was director of the sports centre at Oxford University.

Philippa Kate **ROLES** (b. 1 Mar 1978 Neath) on 21 May in London. Ranked in the top three in Britain at the discus every year from 1998 to 2010 (no.1 six times), she was the European Junior bronze medallist in 1997 and 4th in the European U23s in 1999 and competed at the Olympic Games in 2004 and 2008 but did not qualify for a final. She also represented Britain in the European Cup six times with a best of 3rd in 2005. She was a member of Swansea H and Sale Harriers Manchester and competed for Wales at four successive Commonwealth Games, placing 6/4/6/4 from 1998 to 2010. She was UK champion 2007 and 2009, AAA champion in 2002 and 2004-05 (with four 2nd places and 3rd) and in the shot was 2nd in the AAA Indoors in 1999 and 2000 (3rd 2001-02) after a great record through the age groups: winning shot and discus at the AAA U15s in 1992 and U17s in 1994, then shot 1995-6 and discus 1997 at the U20s and discus in 1999-2001 at the U23s. She won 14 Welsh discus titles between 1993 and 2001 and the shot in 1995, 1998 and 2001. Pbs: SP 15.95i (1999), 15.62 (2003); DT 62.89 (2003), HT 55.09 (1999). She worked as a train driver in London.
Her sister Rebecca was Welsh discus champion in 2000 and 2003 with a best of 56.25 (2004).

Michael SHERIDAN (b. 1 May 1943) on 13 April. Between 2000 and 2015 the athletics statistician and historian wrote and published eight invaluable books on British athletics during the early post-war period, covering 1946-1949, 1950, 1951, 1952, 1953, 1954 plus "Sunset of the Golden Years" (1951-59) and "Who's Who of British International Athletes" (1945-1960). He was working on a final volume (1955-7) in this pre-NUTS Annual series at the time of his death. Earlier publications were "Good Reasons: 100 years of Olympic marathon races" (1996) and "A Gentle Cyclone", detailing the running career of Sydney Wooderson (1998).

Mike SMITH on 5 March at the age 88. His huge contribution to athletics in Southampton and elsewhere was most notable for his coaching of over 30 British international athletes, particularly 400m runners including Kriss Akabusi, Todd Bennett, Roger Black, Paul Sanders, Iwan Thomas and Donna Murray/Hartley. He was inducted into the English Athletics Hall of Fame in 2011. He worlkd as a school teacher. His daughter Janet was also a 400m international.

(Rev.) **Nicolas** David **STACEY** (b. 25 Nov 1927 Belgravia, London) on 8 May near Canterbury, Kent. He made five international appearances for Britain in 1951-2, including at the 1952 Olympic Games (semis 200m, 5th 4x400m). He won a silver medal at 4x110y at the 1950 Empire Games (ht 100y, sf 220y) and was 2nd in the AAA 220y in 1951 and 3rd in 1950, and had pbs: 100y 9.9 (1949), 100m 10.7 (1950), 220y 21.6 (1951), straight 21.3w (1949), 200m 21.79 auto (1952), 400m 48.4 (1952). He ran on UK record-setting teams at 4x100m and 4x110y in 1951. After Oxford University, he took holy orders in 1952 and was later Dean of Greenwich, but his outspoken views brought his clerical career to an end at the age of 40 and he was the Deputy Director of Oxfam for two years and then a pioneering director of social services for the London Borough of Ealing, moving on to that job for Kent County Council 1974-85.

Gordon SURTEES (GBR) (b. 1932) on 1 September. Based on Teesside, he guided many British distance runners over more than 50 years, including Ikem Billy, Dennis Coates, Ton Hanlon, Steve Kenyon, Tony Morrell and Jonathan Taylor and was a former national marathon and steeplechase coach.

Reg WELLS in August. He was a dedicated worker for race walking: Race Walking Association chairman 1988-9, general secretary 1984-8, treasurer 1983-4 and championship secretary 1976-8. He was honorary secretary of the Essex County Athletic Association 1972-5, also a coach and GB walking team manager on a number of occasions.

OBITUARIES 2018

Hazel Margaret **RIDER** (née Needham) (GBR) (b. 2 Sep 1932) on 6 January. She won the 1951 WAAA mile title when aged 18 (2nd 1950 & 1952). Pbs: 880y 2:16.3 and 1M 5:12.6 (both 1952). A member of Cambridge Harriers, London and later its President. She was WAAA Hon Treasurer 1960-3 and a founder member of the Women's Veterans Association. Her younger sister Sylvia Needham (married name: du Plessis) became in 1950 at 15 one of Britain's youngest ever internationals and was WAAA discus champion in 1957.

Peter WELLS (Gt Britain & NI/New Zealand) (b. 23 May 1929, Barnet) on 5 January in Christchurch, New Zealand. He high jumped at the 1952 (11=) and 1956 (16th) Olympics. Coached in his younger days by Arthur Gold, he placed fifth for England at the 1950 British Empire Games in Auckland. He took such a shine to New Zealand that he did not travel back with the rest of the team but settled instead in Christchurch although he did return briefly to England in 1952 to qualify for the British Olympic team. In 1954 he finished fourth for New Zealand at that year's British Empire & Commonwealth Games in Vancouver. His highest jump of 6ft 7½ in (just short of 2.02) in Papakura in December 1954 was regarded both as a British and New Zealand record. He won seven NZ titles (1951 and 1953-8) and was runner-up in the AAA Champs of 1952 (3rd 1949), winning titles at AAA Juniors 1947, CAU and Southern 1947 and 1952.

OBITUARIES 2016

Michael Coupe **'Mike' ROBINSON** (b. 13 Apr 1936) in May 2016. President of Cambridge University AC in 1960 after winning his Blue in 1958-9, and a member of Rotherham Harriers, he was a GB 'B' international (winning at 110mh against Switzerland in 1961). He ran pbs when just missing qualifying for finals of the 110mh (14.6/14.76) and 400mh ((53.0/53.17) at the World University Games in 1961. He also ran 14.6 for 120yh and 24.2 for 220yh in 1961.

Ian Reeves **SMITH** (b. 6 Aug 1931 Blackburn) in October. Before moving to Perth, Australia he was a leading NUTS compiler of junior rankings in the 1960s and joined the ATFS in 1964. He later produced world rankings for middle distance events, returning to Britain in 1985.

Rex Peter Derryck **VAN ROSSUM** (b. 22 Oct 1933) on 25 Dec 2016. An inspirational leader he was president of Oxford University AC in 1959 when he competed in the Varsity match for the third time. A member of Woodford Green AC, he authored several books on athletics training and coaching in the early 1960s. Pbs: 120yh 14.8 (1959), 220yh 24.6 (1959), 220yh St 24.5 (1958), 24.1w (1959).

John Edward **'Ted' WOODWARD** (b. 17 Apr 1931 Wheeler End, Buckinghamshire) on 16 January. The winner of 15 caps for England as a powerful wing at rugby union 1952-6, he had won the intermediates 100 yards at the English Schools in 1948 while at the Royal Grammar School High Wycombe.

Amendments to BRITISH ATHLETICS 2017

p.107   European Champs: 5000m: 12 Taylor, 15. Davies; 3000mSt: 5 Mullett (& in UK Merits and lists
p.141   Merit Rankings: W JT: 12 Rees b. 27.9.99
p.222   TJ: move to footnote: Drugs dq: 15.68 Nana Owusu-Nyantekyi
p.339   DT: 48.09 Tara Park 4.4.95 9 Fresno, USA 14 May